Critical Theory and Interaction Design

Critical Theory and Interaction Design

edited by Jeffrey Bardzell, Shaowen Bardzell, and Mark Blythe

The MIT Press
Cambridge, Massachusetts
London, England

This book was set in Stone Serif Standard by Westchester Publishing Services. Printed and bound in the United States of America.

Library of Congress Cataloging-in-Publication Data

Names: Bardzell, Jeffrey, editor. | Bardzell, Shaowen, editor. | Blythe, Mark A., editor.
Title: Critical theory and interaction design / edited by Jeffrey Bardzell, Shaowen Bardzell, and Mark Blythe.
Description: Cambridge, MA ; London, England : The MIT Press, [2018] | Includes bibliographical references and index.
Identifiers: LCCN 2017053686 | ISBN 9780262037983 (hardcover : alk. paper)
Subjects: LCSH: Human-computer interaction. | Social psychology.
Classification: LCC QA76.9.H85 C755 2018 | DDC 004.01/9—dc23 LC record available at https://lccn.loc.gov/2017053686

10 9 8 7 6 5 4 3 2

In memory of David Hakken

Contents

Acknowledgments xi

Introduction 1
Jeffrey Bardzell, Shaowen Bardzell, and Mark Blythe

I Fretting in the Shadow of Language: Interpretation and Evaluation 27
Mark Blythe

1 The Seven Veils of Fantasy (1997) 37
Slavoj Žižek

2 Wild Theory, or—Did Somebody Say Žižek? 41
Mark Blythe

3 Rotation of Crops: A Venture in a Theory of Social Prudence (1843) 63
Søren Kierkegaard, edited and translated by Howard V. Hong and Edna H. Hong

4 Against Boredom: The Demonic Pantheism in Design 81
Olav W. Bertelsen

5 Myth Today (1957) 95
Roland Barthes, translated by Annette Lavers

6 Barthes, and Calling the Mundane to Account 131
Jofish Kaye

7 *The Open Work* (1989) 145
Umberto Eco, translated by Anna Cancogni

8 What Does Digital Content Mean? Umberto Eco and *The Open Work* 167
Alan F. Blackwell

9 Encoding/Decoding (1978) 187
Stuart Hall

10 Stuart Hall: Cultural Studies, Human-Computer Interaction, and Encoding/Decoding 199
Elizabeth F. Churchill

11 Grasping a Text (1978) 227
Wolfgang Iser

12 Wolfgang Iser and the Reader as Creator 253
Melanie Feinberg

13 The Intellectual Virtues 271
Aristotle, translated by F. H. Peters

14 Way Back to Some Design Futures: Aristotle's Intellectual Excellences and Their Implications for Designing 287
Gilbert Cockton

II Pugnacious Aesthetes and Barely Closeted Moralists 311
Jeffrey Bardzell

15 The Author as Producer (1934) 319
Walter Benjamin, translated by Edmund Jephcott

16 The (Cultural) Interface Designer as Producer 331
Søren Bro Pold

17 The New Forms of Control (1964) 345
Herbert Marcuse

18 Herbert Marcuse and the "One-Dimensional Man" 357
Erik Stolterman

19 Ideology and Ideological State Apparatuses (Notes towards an Investigation) (1970) 371
Louis Althusser, translated by Ben Brewster

20 Ideology and Interpellation: Althusser's "Ideology and Ideological State Apparatuses" 407
Paul Dourish

21 *Gender Trouble* (1999) 417
Judith Butler

22 Performing Interaction Design with Judith Butler 429
Ann Light

23 Why Has Critique Run Out of Steam? From Matters of Fact to Matters of Concern (2004) 447
Bruno Latour

24 Bruno Latour as Sociologist and Design Theorist? 471
Carl DiSalvo

25 The Politics of Amnesia (2003) 485
Terry Eagleton

26 After Critical Design 499
Mark Blythe

27 The Artworld (1964) 515
Arthur C. Danto

28 Danto's Artworld: Art—and Design—as Inquiry 529
Jeffrey Bardzell

III Lucidly Bewildered: Participatory and Political Design 559
Shaowen Bardzell

29 From Notes Made in 1970–1971 565
Mikhail M. Bakhtin, translated by Vern W. McGee

30 Bakhtin's Dialogics and the "Human" in Human-Centered Design 571
Peter Wright and John McCarthy

31 Nontheatrical Performance (1993) 585
Allan Kaprow

32 Kaprow and HCI: Reflections on "Participation" in Research through Design 599
Kirsten Boehner

33 Panopticism (1975) 625
Michel Foucault, translated by Alan Sheridan

34 Michel Foucault on the Panopticon: A Commentary 651
John Bowers

35 Nature and Space (1998) 679
James C. Scott

36 Seeing Like *Seeing Like a State* 695
Hrönn Brynjarsdóttir Holmer, Phoebe Sengers, and Kaiton Williams

37 Knowing the Oriental (1978) 715
Edward W. Said

38 Representing Others: HCI and Postcolonialism 723
Beki Grinter

39 The Generalized and the Concrete Other (1992) 737
Seyla Benhabib

40 Through the "Cracks and Fissures" in the Smart Home to Ubiquitous Utopia 751
Shaowen Bardzell

List of Contributors 781
Index 785

Acknowledgments

Many people helped to make this book a reality. We thank all our commentators, who not only contributed original chapters to this book, but who also helped with the initial peer reviewing process. We thank Sarah Ng and Austin Toombs for their work in helping us to secure rights to republish the original articles. We also thank the Intel Science and Technology Center for Social Computing for helping to cover the costs of those rights. We also gratefully acknowledge Indiana University and Aarhus University, which helped fund the sabbaticals of co-editors Jeffrey Bardzell and Shaowen Bardzell, during which time we made headway on this book. We also thank Northumbria University and the School of Design for supporting the work of Mark Blythe. We are grateful to MIT Press, including Doug Sery for encouraging us to pursue such an ambitious project and for his forbearance when we promptly missed all our deadlines—as he predicted we would. We also thank Noah Springer at MIT Press for helping to keep everything moving when we got bogged down, as well as all the professionals who contributed via editing and production.

Introduction

Jeffrey Bardzell, Shaowen Bardzell, and Mark Blythe

Why should interaction designers read critical theory?
What exactly is critical theory?
How has interaction design already engaged critical theory, and for what?

We begin with questions, questions that we expect readers bring to this volume. In the three main sections of this introduction we offer preliminary answers; more detailed answers are worked out throughout the book itself. Each of the following three sections has a single author—an editor of this book—writing in her or his own distinctive voice; the Introduction thus resists a monolithic authorial "we." In doing so, we [*sic*] anticipate the book itself, an edited collection of essays, each composed in a distinctive voice.

The critical essay is often rhetorically sui generis, that is, having its own unique structure, contours, and speaking voice. In many academic traditions, scientific writing in particular, individuating stylistic qualities are intentionally played down in the name of clarity, directness, and readability. But in a tradition such as critical theory, built as it is around a love of language and letters, it should not be surprising that academic writing itself is subject to tremendous variation and experimentation. This experimentation is not always felicitous: much writing in the tradition of critical theory is difficult, even obscure. But much of it is literary and engaging in its own right.

Either way, the distinctive verbal pyrotechnics of critical theory reflect, in the words of essayist and film critic Phillip Lopate, each writer's "enacting the struggle for truth in full view" (cited in Bardzell and Bardzell, 2015, 67). As editors of this volume, we faced many struggles—what to include, how to introduce critical theory, how to organize the chapters, how to position the relationship between critical theory and interaction design. We did not always agree with each other in substance or in tone. What would be more engaging to readers—humor and storytelling? thematic clarity and precision? sober storytelling? We chose all three. Our polyvocal introduction thus embodies writerly values dominant in critical theory. It anticipates the variety of writing styles found in this incredibly diverse volume of essays.

Hopefully it prepares you, Dear Reader, for the experiments, provocations, and insights that lie before you.

How and Why (Not) to Read Critical Theory

Mark Blythe

In *Wittgenstein Jr.* (Lars Iyer, 2014), the main character, a Cambridge lecturer, is nicknamed after the eponymous philosopher because he tells his students to give up on their studies and learn something useful instead, like bricklaying. When taking tutorials, he sits for most of the period in stony silence before asking a single question, and then if he gets any answers, he replies, "No, that's no good." Of course such a character would be on their final warning within weeks of being appointed at any sort of university today, but the main character is scathing about contemporary academia: "The dons of Philosophy: academic-output manufacturers! Impact-seekers! Grant-chasers! Citation-trufflers! Self googlers! Web-profile updaters! Facebook posters! Tweedy voids!" (Iyer, 2014, 117).

The novel allows its author, Lars Iyer, a philosophy lecturer at Newcastle University, to ask serious questions in a light form about what universities and knowledge are for. This novel satirizes UK institutions driven by imperatives like the Research Excellence Framework (REF), and yet the book will be eligible for submission to the next REF and, ironically, will constitute evidence of its author's own "output" and "impact." The application form for promotion at one UK university demands that candidates demonstrate that their work is "paradigm shifting" and that it is "considered so internationally." One applicant fumed that he was responsible for at least two paradigm shifts in the last year alone, but he still didn't get the promotion. Increasingly research is judged not only by its contribution to an academic field but also its wider "impact."

What is the place of a book like *Critical Theory and Interaction Design* in such an academic culture?

When the existence of gravitational waves was proven recently, a BBC radio presenter, John Humphrys, asked a physicist how the finding would improve life for "the man on the street." Humphrys, notorious for his confrontational style, pointed out that a new proof of one of Einstein's theories wasn't going to help him find his keys on a morning. He was, in part, joking—but only in part—and the scientist gamely pointed out that it was seemingly arcane discoveries in physics that led to the invention of the medium in which their conversation was being broadcast.

This argument is a familiar and increasingly important one: although the future applications of pure research are unknown, one day something useful could arise from it and retrospectively justify the expense. Of course people working in the field of interaction design can very often make more immediate claims about the relevance or impact of their work. Sometimes, indeed, they are explicitly working on the problem of how to help people find their keys in the morning. The field, since its inception, has taken as its focus the everyday lives of people interacting with computers and now, thanks to its efforts, if you lose your keys in the morning, well, "there's an app for that," or will be soon.

But if Humphrys were interviewing an interaction design researcher who had developed a new key finding system, he would, following his contrarian style, doubtless want to know why the taxpayer's money should be spent on such a trivial concern. Indeed, academic and commercial research is also increasingly criticized for "solutionism." In "To Save Everything Click Here," technology critic Evgeny Morozov defines solutionism as either solving problems that don't really exist or suggesting quick technological fixes for complex social, political, and environmental problems. His favorite example of solutionism is the BinCam, a mobile phone in a rubbish bin that takes a picture of the contents each time the lid is closed and posts it to Facebook, so that the user's friends can see whether they are recycling or not. Morozov is deeply sarcastic about this idea: well done, planet saved. BinCam also annoyed writers of the right-wing tabloid newspaper the *Daily Mail*, who linked it to local councils doing "big brother"–style snooping and asked: have Newcastle dons nothing better to do than waste their time and taxpayers' money on preposterous ideas like this?

Of course the researchers did not make BinCam because they thought it would save the world or because they wanted to further local council surveillance. They made it because they thought it would be quite interesting—and it was, not least because it annoyed so many people. But Morozov has a point, and *To Save Everything, Click Here* (2014) became a bestseller because it highlights a problem familiar not only to academics but also in the wider culture.

Scientific talks have become a branch of popular entertainment and TED talks are now on Netflix, but as design theorist Benjamin Bratton points out, the genre is becoming clichéd. Although TED talks are always very well delivered, thoughtful, and engaging, they follow a set format: the researcher poses a question, describes a very personal journey toward an always surprising revelation, and ultimately gives a solution. Impossible problems become soluble only if they are looked at in the TED way. Morozov borrows the term "solutionism" from Michael Dobbins' book on urban planning. Dobbins argues that city planning is so complex it is always tempting to "dumb down" the problems being addressed. In addition, these problems are usually pressing and immediate so "solution-driven design" becomes almost inevitable. But for philosophers like Slavoj Žižek, we are reaching social, political, and environmental limits or breaking points. We do not face design puzzles to be solved but rather stark political choices based on basic conflicts over finite resources (Bratton 2013).

In the *Structure of Scientific Revolutions*, Thomas Kuhn (1962), who coined the term "paradigm shift," noted that they mostly occur not when a new fact is discovered or when some new consensus is reached, but rather when one generation of academics retires or dies. The baby boomers have begun to retire, and this is already having profound social effects. There are so many boomers that whatever phase of life they have entered has been changed and defined by them. Their departure from the academy will very likely result in a paradigm shift or two. It may be, for example, that the next generation of human-computer interaction (HCI) researchers will not have to be quite as concerned with ethnomethodology as the previous one was. The editors of this volume were educated in the humanities in the 1980s and therefore subjected to then new translations of European critical theory. Samuel Boswell noted that everyone returns to their first subject eventually, so perhaps it is no surprise that those of us exposed to critical theory should find that it resonates years later in unexpected ways.

Critical theory is today seldom taught in literature courses, but as Terry Eagleton points out in *After Theory* (2003), it thrives in fields like media and technology studies, where it is sometimes more obviously applicable and even practical. Vladimir Propp's *Morphology of the Folktale* (which structures narrative into discrete and movable units) might seem like a very dry way to discuss literature, but it is useful when you are trying to construct a story engine in an interactive game (Braun, 2003). Literary theorist Mikhail Bakhtin (1895–1975) described the God's eye view of Tolstoy's novels as "monological" and Dostoevsky's succession of unreliable narrators as "dialogical." Tolstoy's narrator expects a reply no more than would a general giving the order to charge, but Dostoevsky encourages the reader to doubt and suspect the version of events being related. The distinction between monological and dialogical utterances might seem like a somewhat reductive approach to these great Russian novelists, but it allows for interesting ways of thinking about interaction design (McCarthy and Wright, 2004). The choice presented by many software dialogue boxes between "OK" and "Cancel" can be thought of as monological; sometimes we click OK when we really mean "what the hell just happened to my document?"

Similarly, high Marxist theory can be applied to questions of design. For example, in examining how ideology functions in society, Louis Althusser formed the notion of interpellation. Interpellation is exemplified by a situation where a policeman shouts at us on the street: the moment we turn to respond, we are bound up—interpellated—in a power relationship; we are now subjects of state power. This somewhat abstruse theoretical point of political theory raises questions about the ways our interactive devices, like the policeman, frame and address us. For example, the iPhone is configured within a set of fluid power relationships between Apple, the state, and the NSA—any of which might transform it from servant or friend into policeman.

The literary and critical theorists who dissected prose and poetry through these new kinds of structural analysis no more expected their work to be useful than the physicists proving the existence of gravitational waves. Yet these examples show that critical theory's benefits manifest in ways that could not have been anticipated. The notion that research should be of benefit to society (meaning, very often, the business sector) is of course contested. But there is a deeper Enlightenment idea that lies behind the expectation that research should be utilitarian in some respect, and this is that new knowledge and technology will ultimately result in progress, but this is also increasingly contested.

The idea that university research should serve the state, or interests determined by the state, is just one perspective on the value of knowledge, and it is quite a new one. It is entirely at odds with the idea of a university as it was originally conceived. Again, we can approach the difference by way of example. Charles Williams was a writer of fantasy novels now so forgotten that his entire works are available on Kindle for free. He was a member of a group of writers called the Inklings, which included C. S. Lewis and J. R. R. Tolkien. C. S. Lewis attended a lecture given by Williams, on the subject of Milton's *Comus*. For Lewis the lecture was superb as criticism, but also courageous and brave because it flew in the face of the conventions and values of that historical moment. Lewis wrote: "It was 'borne in upon me' that that beautiful carved room had probably not witnessed anything as important since some of the great medieval or Reformation lectures. I have at last, if only for once, seen a university doing what it was founded to do: teaching Wisdom." Wisdom is not necessarily something that is going to boost the economy, stimulate enterprise, or encourage innovation. It might in fact stop such things in their tracks. Lewis believed it was necessary to read at least as many old books as new ones; otherwise, it becomes too easy to accept the doctrines of the age we find ourselves living through. The values of previous ages can seem entirely alien and mad to us (Williams was arguing for the doctrine of virginity), but the degree to which another age's aspirations seem self-evidently wrong, destructive, and crazy is probably a good indication of how our own will appear to our children's children.

Victorians like Matthew Arnold believed that education should be based on "the best that has been thought and said." Much twentieth-century education was based on promoting "the great tradition," a canon of writers and works that it was agreed should be passed from one generation to the next, often within national traditions (e.g., great works that exemplified distinctively British or French artistic and intellectual achievement). This idea was challenged by critical theory: why was so much of the "best" and "most representative" of a nation produced exclusively by white, middle-aged men? One response was to uncover lost, forgotten, or suppressed works by marginalized groups, such as art by women, postcolonial subjects, aboriginals, and so forth. But this kind of endeavor was in turn criticized for continuing to perpetuate the "great books" argument.

A more radical challenge was the notion that we might also learn from the *least* of the culture—from advertisements, political pamphlets, or even haircuts. Engaging cultural works with critical theory does not necessitate a conviction that the writer/artist is one of the greatest thinkers who ever lived. In this view, critical theory is a provocation.

It is not necessary or even desirable to agree with it; it rarely makes truth claims but rather proposes interesting slants and questions. For this reason, writers like Althusser remain interesting despite flaws in their texts and character. Žižek is exasperating and contradictory but all the better for it. Clearly then, as Noam Chomksy remarks, critical theory is not theory in the way that we would normally recognize it in science. But as John Bowers points out in chapter 34, "theoria" means way of seeing. Critical theory is perhaps most useful when it offers us alternative ways of seeing. But what is critical theory exactly?

What Is Critical Theory?

Jeffrey Bardzell

The term "critical theory" is often used in two different (and partially overlapping) senses: as Frankfurt School Critical Theory (as a proper name) and a in a much broader, looser sense of critical theory. As discussed below, the Frankfurt School of Critical Theory refers to a group of mostly prewar social theorists and social scientists who broadly offer a Marxist analysis and emancipatory perspective to social life. However, this book understands "critical theory" in a much broader sense (which, incidentally, also includes the Frankfurt School).

The broader sense of the term critical theory includes the following uses.

- A general *system of concepts intended to support a style of critical analysis* is arguably the most common type of critical theory; it includes critical theories such as New Criticism, Marxism, phenomenological hermeneutics, feminism, reader-response theory, and semiotics, all of which provide a meta-framework that gives readers/critics a "way in" to the analysis of a text, with an output that commonly reflects the framework (e.g., a feminist critical study will commonly feature issues of gender).
- A *poetics* is a theory of a form of artwork or genre. What makes tragic drama distinct from comic drama or tragic narrative? What is the difference between tragedy proper and bad things happening to good people? A poetics typically seeks to identify the form's key features, structures, and major experiential qualities, and to demonstrate how they all cohere or hang together (e.g., how the *form* of a tragic reversal in a tragedy causes *feelings* of pity and fear in the audience).
- A *theory of criticism* is an attempt to define, explicate, and/or justify criticism, or a certain style of criticism, as a practice, to distinguish it from other knowledge practices and to account for it as a way of knowing, as well as to critique its epistemic limitations. The theory of criticism is sometimes referred to as "metacriticism" or even simply "aesthetics."
- A *critical analysis of ideas and/or theory* is a reflexive practice, common in philosophical aesthetics, in which an existing idea or concept is subjected to a skeptical analysis,

sometimes called conceptual analysis. In one form of this analysis, going back to Aristotle, different candidate views are laid out side by side and critiqued, leading to the advancement of the preferred view. In another form of such an analysis, common in analytic aesthetics, a candidate idea is presented sympathetically, and arguments are raised both for and against a candidate idea or concept; hypothetical responses are offered to "save" the idea or concept from the critique; further counters and defenses are offered; and to whatever extent the original idea or concept withstands this attack, it is accepted, rejected, or revised (Nussbaum, 1990, 173–174).

This list is intended to illustrate the diversity of uses of criticality, and of course they often overlap one another and interact with each other. All of the above are reflected in the present volume.

A Historical Survey of Critical Theory

Within and across these broad categories lie several historical and thematic traditions of critical thinking, some of them comparatively recent and others going back millennia. In what follows, I offer a survey of these traditions, which are intended also to reflect how literary theorists, aesthetic philosophers, and social theorists interpretatively understand these traditions.

Criticism from the Ancient World to the Enlightenment

Literary criticism and aesthetic philosophy has been with us since the ancient world, with major statements in Plato and **Aristotle**[1] of ancient Greece, and more from Longinus and Horace in ancient Rome, continuing through the Middle Ages and Renaissance in writers such as Augustine, Thomas Aquinas, Dante, Boccaccio, de Pizan, Sidney, and others. Much of this early work focused on poetics-related concerns of literary forms and experiences (see Russell and Winterbottom, 1989). It offered and developed key aesthetic concepts that we still use today: plot, *in medias res* (beginning a story in the middle of the action), *katharsis* (emotional purgation), *mimesis* (imitation), *ekphrasis* (a narrative description of an important object, such as Achilles' shield), generic classifications (e.g., tragedy vs. epic), poetic meter, and much more. Arguably most significant of these is *mimesis*, which underlies the imitation theory of art—that is, the idea that art imitates reality (e.g., it imitates people, actions, historical events, moral dilemmas) and by doing so helps us understand the world and ourselves better. The imitation theory of art was important because it had profound implications for the role of art in society. On its authority, for example, Plato banishes poets from his Republic, because, he claims, poets offer imitations of imitations of reality. Aristotle and Plotinus responded that poets' imitations are more real than visible reality. In painting, the imitation theory is operative until the mid-nineteenth century, when painters began to experiment with nonimitative forms, such as impressionism.

The Enlightenment saw radical changes in the arts and theories of them. For the first time, the diverse practices of painting, sculpture, architecture, music, and poetry were grouped together under the unifying concept of "art," what is now called the "modern system of the arts" (Kristeller, 2008). Once they were grouped together, it was no longer adequate to theorize tragedy and painting completely independently of each other—a more general theory of these as arts was needed, and so too was a theory of aesthetic response. It was during the eighteenth century that otherwise minor philosopher Alexander Baumgarten coined the term "aesthetics" to name this newly unified theory, understood as "the theory of sensuous knowledge, as a counterpart to logic as a theory of intellectual knowledge" (Kristeller, 2008, 11). In short, "the arts" and "aesthetics"—at least as we understand them today—do not go back to the ancient world but in fact are part of the legacy of the Enlightenment.

The Birth of English as an Academic Discipline and Liberal Humanism

A century later came the final major development that transformed the study of the arts into the modern humanistic disciplines that we have today. The development was the rise of the middle class alongside the secularization of Europe, which placed new demands on public education and meant that study of the Bible was no longer enough to prepare a youth to engage the best, most modern, and most timeless ideas and ways of thinking. Instead, national literatures came to be seen as featuring both enduring ideas that transcend a given age, while reflecting national values (e.g., England, France, or Germany) required to shape the English (etc.) character. Such works needed to be selected, explicated for their transcendent English thoughts, and taught, and this led directly to the emergence of English literature as an academic discipline, including the first English departments in universities in the late nineteenth century (Barry, 2002).

With the professionalization of literature as an academic discipline came an explosion in theory in the twentieth century, peaking around 1980. Early twentieth-century books by Northrop Frye, I. A. Richards, and F. R. Leavis helped define English as a discipline, including the theorization of literary criticism as a cogent and rigorous scholarly practice (Richards, 1929; Leavis, 1948; Frye, 1957). Frye, for example, defines criticism in terms highly consistent with the nineteenth-century view of literature's place in society:

> By criticism I mean the whole work of scholarship and taste concerned with literature which is a part of what is variously called liberal education, culture, or the study of the humanities.... Consequently there is no way of preventing the critic from being, for better or worse, the pioneer of education and the shaper of cultural tradition.... A public that tries to do without criticism, and asserts that it knows what it wants or likes, brutalizes the arts and loses its cultural memory. (3–4)

What is clear from this liberal humanist era of criticism is that the discipline is viewed as the steward and curator of taste and culture. It is unapologetically elitist, and it sees itself as perpetuating the best of its own culture and in so doing ennobling the public. Though today one might justifiably bristle at the elitism, it is clear that this view of criticism is service-oriented, and it remains true today that we continue to turn to cultural experts (from film critics like Roger Ebert to art, music, and literary scholars) for guidance on what cultural works we should be viewing or reading, which ones we should be supporting with public funds, and which ones we should be teaching in public schools.

The Rise of Grand Theory

As we have seen, the liberal humanist take on literature is that literature provides "an intimate and intellectually significant engagement with social and cultural reality ... which we turn to when we want to read the story of our shared form of life [of] our ways of being human" (Gibson, 2007, 2). Most of us agree that this is a legitimate reason to engage literature and the arts, but it is rather general and even vague about that intimate engagement and what it actually gets us. For literary critic Harold Bloom (1994), reading from the great tradition is like eavesdropping on the dialogue of gods, and it is enough. But many readers have other reasons to look to literature and the arts; many turn to the arts because the arts help people understand culture in a way that reveals opportunities for intervention, activism, and emancipation.

Over the course of the twentieth century, a number of major theories developed to support styles of reading targeted at a diverse range of issues focused less on general "appreciation of Great Books" and more on the following issues: reading in support of an emancipatory politics, theorizing texts and textuality, and theorizing the nature and consequences of reading. We call these "grand theories" in part because of their ambition, sophistication, and complexity, often entailing very large systems of interlocking concepts, philosophical commitments, and interpretative techniques. Any of them can take years to master and in the hands of a competent practitioner can yield original and powerful interpretations. At the same time, some of these theories are so powerful that in less competent hands they become deterministic—that is, rather than helping reveal sui generis aspects of the work and its significance, they instead sometimes seem merely to restate themselves using the work as another excuse to do so.

Grand Suspicions

One major grouping of grand theories engages political and emancipatory criticism: Marxism, psychoanalysis, feminism, and postcolonialism. Each of these has been characterized as performing a "hermeneutics of suspicion," of taking as a starting point that things are not as they seem, that hidden forces produce the surface qualities of the work, and that explicating those forces helps reveal how these they operate not just in the work but in life itself. This insight, in turn, opens up opportunities for emancipatory intervention.

A Marxist analysis seeks to expose the hidden machinations of ideology, a value system that quietly reinforces dominant social classes at the expense of working classes, for whom this value system has been presented as natural, inevitable, and unchangeable. In revealing its contingency, a Marxist analysis thereby opens the door to intervention against it. Marx was deeply influential on thinkers associated with the Frankfurt School of Critical Theory, including Max Horkheimer, Theodor Adorno, **Herbert Marcuse**, **Walter Benjamin**, and Jürgen Habermas. For **Stuart Hall**, Raymond Williams, and Richard Hoggart, their Marxist perspective led them to the scholarly analysis of artworks of the working class. Literary theorist **Terry Eagleton** (discussed below) also broadly aligns himself with Marxism.

A psychoanalytic approach seeks to expose the often unconscious conflicts between individuals and their bodily needs/desires and the social world (with its behavioral rules and norms, reflected in language), a conflict that explains many of the anxieties and neuroses that harm us. By bringing these unconscious conflicts to our awareness, psychoanalysis serves a therapeutic function that helps individuals better understand themselves. Key thinkers include Sigmund Freud, Karl Jung, Jacques Lacan, Julia Kristeva, and more recently **Slavoj Žižek**.

A feminist analysis seeks to explicate and intervene on the gender/sex system, as the primary force of gender-based injustice. This system refers to how each society interprets the significance of (biological) *sex* difference and constructs normative theories and rules of (socially constructed) *gender* difference—for example, what it is "proper" for ladies to do, what constitutes "manly" behavior, and so forth—and feminists argue that these systems contribute to the oppression and exploitation of women. Key thinkers include Simone de Beauvoir, Sandra Harding, Helen Longino, **Judith Butler**, Donna Haraway, and **Seyla Benhabib**.

A postcolonial analysis seeks to explicate how the history of colonialism shapes understandings, policies, and actions (e.g., military interventions) in both former colonial European powers and their formerly colonized peoples. Often, this thinking manifests as "Orientalism," that is, the unexamined European habit of treating former colonies as homogenous exotic "Others," often seen as uncivilized and/or trying to "catch up" to Europe culturally, politically, and economically. Key thinkers include **Edward Said**, Gayatri Spivak, and Frantz Fanon.

Some thinkers blend ideas from multiple theoretical and disciplinary perspectives. For example, **Louis Althusser** combined Marxist ideas of ideology with poststructuralist theories of language (see below) and psychoanalytic theories of the subject to develop his conception of the self-propagation of dominant social orders. **James C. Scott** combined anthropology (especially of peasants) and emancipatory political science to develop his analysis of the modern state agenda to render society maximally legible (e.g., by standardizing last names and weights, conducting surveys, designing infrastructure) the better to control that society.

Uniting these theories is the notion of hidden forces that put people in subtle forms of bondage, systems of concepts that support critical interpretations that reveal these forces and/or bondage, and thereby the hope of opening up emancipatory opportunities in the world.

The Grand Text Itself

If grand theories of suspicion seek to use a text to look toward hidden, usually malignant, social forces, another tradition seeks to improve our ability to focus on texts themselves. An early incarnation of this was Russian Formalism, which sought to distinguish poetic language from other forms of language. In the United States, thinkers including William K. Wimsatt, Monroe Beardsley, and Cleanth Brooks proposed the New Criticism; the New Criticism rejected biographical information about the author, authorial intentions, or even readers' emotional responses as criteria for judging works, instead arguing that whatever value was there (often a poetic ambiguity brought about through symbolically dense figurative language) was in "the text itself."

Another thread of text-centric grand theory developed across much of the century, and that was structuralism, based on the semiotic theory of Ferdinand de Saussure. Saussure proposed a radical theory of language that viewed linguistic signs as based on relationality and difference, rather than on reference and correspondence to things. This theory could be applied to all sign systems, from literary texts to ethnographic observations of rituals, from punk fashion to sumo wrestling, from scientific papers to spaghetti advertisements. Key structuralists included Claude Levi-Strauss, **Roland Barthes**, and **Umberto Eco**.

Structuralism originally had scientific aspirations, but these came under fire from within, and structuralism evolved into poststructuralism, characterized by a much more skeptical stance toward knowledge itself, combining structuralism, Marxism, and phenomenological hermeneutics in analyses of social power (e.g., see the work of **Louis Althusser** and **Michel Foucault**) and fusing it with psychoanalysis to propose radical new theories of subjectivity (e.g., the work of Gilles Deleuze). Arguably, poststructuralism reached its apex in the work of Jacques Derrida, whose notion of deconstruction leveraged an analysis of Saussurean theory to offer a radically skeptical critique of the entire Western intellectual tradition.

The Grand Reception

One problem with text-centric theories is that they make it difficult to offer any account of the actual humans involved in making or reading texts. Yet just as the Russian Formalists had asked what distinguishes literary language from other language, many theorists focused on distinguishing aesthetic experience (e.g., Roman Ingarden, in his *The Cognition of the Literary Work of Art*) or on how literary texts are only actualized through the performance of reading (e.g., "reader-response" theorists Jane P. Tomkins and Stanley Fish).

One major strand of this thought is hermeneutics, which has its origins in the nineteenth century as the discipline of developing the correct interpretation of the Bible (often involving philology and other then-emerging textual analysis methods). It was expanded into literary and cultural studies, for example, in the work of Heidegger's student Hans-Georg Gadamer, who viewed the act of reading as an encounter between two "lifeworlds"—the reader's and that expressed in the text—the "fusion" of which "expanded the horizons" of the reader. In this tradition is **Wolfgang Iser**, whose analysis of reading sought to explicate how literary works create conditions that allow actual readers to actualize the meanings in the text. Wrestling with a similar problem in his "The Open Work," **Umberto Eco** distinguishes between closed works, which feature clear and easily accessible meanings, and open works, whose openness demands active and creative interpretative work on the part of the reader.

Rejecting Grand Theories

The heyday of grand theory ran from the 1950s through the end of the 1970s, and by the 1980s a backlash had begun. It is important to recognize that in the history of critical practice and theorizing about criticism, grand theory is anomalous. But because it is recent, and because many of its concepts and promises remain indeed very seductive, many researchers in HCI appear to believe that criticism is coterminous with grand theory, and even more narrowly, with the political variants of grand theory, equating "criticality" with "political resistance." Some contemporary thinkers, **Bruno Latour** in particular, have perpetuated the influence of poststructuralist grand theory through his influence in science and technology studies, which in turn has influenced HCI. Later in his career, Latour himself took a more critical stance toward this version of criticism in his "Has Critique Run Out of Steam?," in which he questions whether grand theory's emancipatory critique actually achieved anything. Similarly, in his *After Theory*, literary and cultural theorist **Terry Eagleton**—who had in earlier writings aligned himself with Marxism—looks back on grand theory a few decades later, castigating its postmodernism for contributing to political quietism, while himself developing his Marxist views in a more Aristotelian and pragmatic direction than had been evident before.

Latour and Eagleton are not alone in questioning the achievements of postmodernism and the theory wars. Literary critic Harold Bloom, in his passionate and often cantankerous defense of the Western canon, writes, "I am not concerned ... with the current debate between the right-wing defenders of the Canon, who wish to defend it for its supposed (and nonexistent) moral values, and the academic-journalistic network I have dubbed the School of Resentment [Bloom's characterization of feminists, Marxists, and multiculturalists], who wish to overthrow the Canon in order to advance their supposed (and nonexistent) programs for social change" (Bloom, 1994, 4). In this, Bloom is in alignment with some "old school" liberal humanists whose careers lasted late into the twentieth century, including M. H. Abrams and F. R. Leavis, both of whom as late as the 1980s rejected grand theory in favor of eclectic and pragmatic uses of concepts and theories in service of lightly updated liberal humanist goals.

In film studies and Anglo-American aesthetics, grand theory has also come under attack. For example, film critic and aesthetic philosopher Noël Carroll argues that psychoanalysis should only be used for films whose characters are literally insane and cannot be explained through modern psychology and/or more commonsense interpretative strategies. Gregory Currie categorically rejects semiotic approaches to film on the grounds that "cinematic language" is categorically different from natural language, and so the whole semiotic project is based on a bad metaphor. In this same eclectic and pragmatic Anglo-American tradition is the work of **Arthur Danto**, who turns to no grand theories at all, and instead argues from art history in general, and certain key works of contemporary art in particular, that theories of art are and should be dependent on works themselves and their position in the art world, that is, the contemporary critical theoretical milieu that grounds the possibility of their having meaning at all.

Summary of the Historical Survey

I have sought in this section to sketch the historical outlines of critical theory. I have done so for several reasons. First, I hope to establish a holistic, big-picture view of critical theory. I seek to establish many of the diverse purposes and methodologies for subjecting cultural phenomena to critical analysis—from works of art and popular culture themselves to the machinations of power and ideology in and through them. My survey shows that such purposes include the cultivation of an educated and informed public, the appreciation of individual works of art, constructive engagement with important ideas, the analysis of human creativity in its fullest capabilities, an analysis of aesthetic experience and sense-making, the analysis of repressive systems, and a mode of activism and political resistance. I also seek to contextualize "grand theory," and in particular to locate it within a particular historical moment—including twentieth-century trends toward professionalizing the humanities and the movement away from elitist goals (e.g., perpetuating the great national traditions of dead white men's greatest works) to more emancipatory goals (i.e., focusing on the cultural achievements of the working class and exposing the regressive ideological effects of popular culture).

Second, I hope to situate the sources included in this volume in that tradition. Philosopher Arthur Danto writes that any given philosophical idea

> is a fragment of a whole. Philosophy ultimately deals only with [holistic systems of thought]. And this means that if philosophers disagree, one must first establish what whole it is to which they are committed.... [Thus,] any given proposition subscribed to by one kind of philosopher will mean something different from that very sentence subscribed to by another kind. (Danto, 1997, xvii)

To read, say, Foucault's analysis of power and not to understand how this is informed by his commitments to a poststructuralist theory of discourse is to risk fundamentally misunderstanding his work. Likewise, to fail to see the deep connections among Marxist, feminist, and postcolonial critics is to miss the analytic power, utility, and variety of the "hermeneutics of suspicion." And to fail to understand the risks of determinism in grand theory removes any possibility of understanding its subsequent rejections in Latour, Eagleton, Bloom, Carroll, and Danto.

Third, I hope that this survey preempts certain common misconceptions of critical theory. One is the notion that critical theory is predominantly negative—negativity, after all, seems to be built into the ordinary language sense of "critical" in the first place. And yet major threads of critical theory are oriented toward the liberal humanistic project of aesthetic appreciation, self-empowerment, and transcendence. Relatedly, it seems that "critical" does not always mean "progressive political critique"; indeed, much of critical theory has arguably been *regressive*, in the sense of indoctrinating the public into an elitist system of thought. Regardless, it is reductive to view critical thinking strictly in terms of politics, however important politics is and remains as an axis of consideration. As philosopher Stanley Cavell observes, any given philosophical system or practice can serve the left or the right: the same skepticism that reveals how scientific practice perpetuates the marginalization of female and minority populations (including female and minority scientists themselves) can also be used to destabilize the scientific consensus on climate change. Finally, I want to contextualize "grand theory," to show that it is somewhat anomalous in the history of critical theory, and to show that by all accounts its heyday is in the past (which is not to say its lessons have been or should be forgotten); most criticism, before and after grand theory, is comparatively eclectic and pragmatic in its stance.

Critical Theory and Interaction Design: The Story So Far

Shaowen Bardzell

I turn now to interaction design and HCI, offering a survey of direct and indirect ways that critical theory has already influenced the field.

The most common narrative—one that we three editors endorse—is that as HCI and interaction design have coevolved with technology, the early focus on enhancing performance, reducing errors, and improving user satisfaction—that is, *usability*—while crucially important, has been too narrow. Interaction designers should also serve individual users' emotional, social, and physical needs and capabilities, and to look beyond white-collar workers to the needs of all people in an increasingly technology-mediated world. We must understand how our work as interaction designers and researchers contributes to sociocultural impacts, including both desirable ones (e.g., those that help loved ones connect with each other, augment individuals' creativity or self-expressiveness, or create jobs) and undesirable ones (e.g., those that compromise user privacy, contribute to the surveillance state, and impose dominant values on marginal cultures and users).

That interaction design and HCI research have expanded in these ways both reflects the use of critical theory in the field and has served as an entry point for much more. Critical theory has been taken up in HCI to

- *Advance the notion of user experience,* which includes a more expansive understanding of experience (Blythe et al., 2004; Höök, 2010), analyzing user experience (Bertelsen and Pold, 2004; McCarthy and Wright, 2004), understanding aesthetics and aesthetic interaction (J. Bardzell, 2011; Boehner, Sengers, and Warner, 2008; Udsen and Jørgensen, 2006), and analyzing interactive technologies as a communicative and expressive medium (Gross, Bardzell, and Bardzell, 2014; Löwgren, 2009).
- *Support emancipatory efforts,* such as feminist takes on gender and computing (S. Bardzell, 2010; S. Bardzell and Churchill 2011; Rode, 2011) and postcolonial analyses of information communication technologies for development (Irani et al., 2010; Taylor, 2011; Kumar and Anderson, 2015).
- *Support our ability to speculate, to think otherwise, and to change perspectives,* especially in critiquing (dominant) assumptions about the relationship between human action and system/machine intelligence (Dreyfus, 1965), countering the shortcomings of scientism (Winograd and Flores, 1986), and critically exploring emerging domains (e.g., embodiment, tangible user interfaces, etc.).

I structure the following survey of the influence of critical theory in HCI and interaction design research and practice into two phases: early developments, which surveys indirect and direct ways that critical theory influenced HCI before it achieved a certain critical mass in the field, and then critical theory in "third wave" HCI, which marks the point where critical theory broke into the field.

Critical Theory and Interaction Design: Early Developments

HCI is a porous interdisciplinary field, with strong links to computer science, cognitive science, sociology, media studies, anthropology, science and technology studies, and more. And as critical theory has influenced (at least some of) these fields, it has also indirectly influenced HCI. As a point of departure, I consider how researchers in these fields apply critical theory in their work.

Media and Internet Studies

Brenda Laurel, a pioneer in designing video games for girls and known for her advocacy of the theory of interactivity, leveraged Aristotle's *Poetics*, the earliest surviving work of dramatic theory, to understand computer interfaces and the human-machine relationship (Laurel, 2013). She did so for two reasons: first, for its "elegance and robustness of the categories and their causal relations," and second because, to Laurel, *Poetics* creates "a disciplined way of thinking about the design of a play in both constructing and debugging activities" (Laurel, 2013, 58). Laurel's work has influenced both interaction design and user research by opening the community to certain dramaturgical and performative characteristics of interaction.

In her landmark study *Life on the Screen*, psychologist Sherry Turkle (1995) evokes postmodernism as a lens to interpret empirical accounts of internet use. To her, postmodernism's challenge to traditional theories of knowledge is a productive way to think about computers, especially when it comes to how technologies of our everyday change the way we view the world—a "world without origins" (Turkle, 1995, 47). Turkle is also drawn to the works of psychoanalytic theorists such as Jacques Lacan and Fredric Jameson to analyze how the self becomes a fragmented subject online. Her emphasis on subjectivity has had significant influence in HCI's conceptualization of the user.

In *The Language of New Media*, Lev Manovich seeks to theorize digital interaction as a communications medium. He analyzes interfaces as manifesting a sort of "language," by which he means "the emergent conventions, recurrent design patterns, and key forms" that collectively provide "strategies for organizing information and structuring the viewer's experience" (Manovich, 2001, 12–13). New media writer Steven Johnson (1997) uses a similar approach, seeking to account for interfaces as cultural objects, explicable using a triangulating methodology centered on technical explanations (i.e., what systems are and can do), historical narratives (how, when, and why a given technology was invented and what happened on its release), and cultural analogies (e.g., how interfaces emerge as cultural objects, in comparison with other communications innovations, such as the novel, the newspaper, and film). Manovich and Johnson have made a strong case for interaction design as a communications medium, comprising its own language and fully analogous to other major cultural forms, including novels and films.

Lisa Nakamura has analyzed the ways that computation and digital culture have perpetuated racial and ethnic signifiers and identities. She characterizes the images of racial identity online that shape these perception "cybertypes" as racial and ethnic stereotypes that are already at work in the offline world (Nakamura, 2002). In a follow-up monograph, *Digitizing Race: Visual Cultures of the Internet* (Nakamura, 2007), Nakamura uses Foucauldian archaeology to systematically reveal the subject positions behind digital images and argues that the internet both supports and disrupts traditional formulations of race and gender. Nakamura's work dispels any notion that computing is somehow "neutral" with regard to race, and has important implications for HCI that emphasizes social justice and/or historically marginal populations.

Although these works do not explicitly position themselves within HCI or interaction design, with the exception of Brenda Laurel, all of them are well cited in HCI and interaction design research. In particular, they have been deployed to motivate research that argues for an expansion of HCI beyond issues of usability and workplace computing; in many ways, all are seminal to what would later be known as "third wave" or "third paradigm" HCI research.

Science and Technology Studies

Perhaps one of the earliest critical theory-informed analyses of computing was the work of philosopher Hubert Dreyfus. In a series of papers beginning in the late 1960s, Dreyfus used the continental philosophy of Heidegger and Merleau-Ponty to attack the field of artificial intelligence (AI) as it was then practiced. He pointed out that the whole field rested on a theory of intelligence—the information processing model—which he claimed was logically incapable of doing the sorts of things that AI researchers were claiming they would do with it. This work was highly controversial at the time of its publication, but twenty years later AI had also changed in ways that appear to vindicate Dreyfus' position. As an important historical side note, Dreyfus was also part of a research group with Winograd, Flores, and Suchman, whose work would have a tremendous influence on the then-emerging field of HCI.

Two other thinkers are also worth mentioning. In *Designing Information Technology in the Postmodern Age* (1995), Richard Coyne shows how the conceptualization, design, and application of computing can be challenged and enhanced by continental theory and postmodernism, especially by the works of Martin Heigegger, Theodor W. Adorno, Walter Benjamin, Hans-Georg Gadamer, Jacques Derrida, Jürgen Habermas, Richard Rorty, and Michel Foucault. In his analyses of logical positivism, analytic philosophy, pragmatism, phenomenology, critical theory, hermeneutics, and deconstruction, among others, Coyne explicates how each shapes (or could shape) the design and development of information and communication technologies. Similarly linking the intellectual traditions of computing and the history of ideas, Philip Agre (1997) coined the term "critical technical practice"—an approach to reconstructing the fundamental ideas and methods of artificial intelligence research, with a focus on the reflexivity of the discursive foundations of computing practice. He observes that the word "critical" here does not call for pessimism and destruction but rather for something more positive: an "expanded understanding of the conditions and goals of technical work" (Agre, 1997, 22–23).

Early HCI

Even in the mid-1980s, when HCI was still just emerging as a field (the first Association of Computing Machinery (ACM) Conference on Human Factors in Computing Systems, or CHI conference, was held in 1983), critical theory was informing seminal work. In their *Understanding Computers and Cognition*, Winograd and Flores (1986) critique the use of rationalism in HCI and computer science, offer an alternative to it based in continental phenomenology, and apply that alternative to several active computing research and practice domains. Notably, they emphasize the importance of philosophy in HCI. They argue that all academic disciplines have theories of the world (ontology, metaphysics), theories of how we learn about it (epistemology), and theories of how it should be and how we can make it better (ethics). Winograd and Flores recognize that such issues are properly philosophical, and thus there is a strong reason to turn to philosophy's mature critical and analytic techniques to test such issues. HCI is specifically philosophical, because practitioners and researchers represent the world via a system, entailing ontological, epistemological, and ethical commitments. As Winograd and Flores write,

> A research programme is more than a set of specific plans for carrying out scientific activities. The observable details of the programme reflect a deeper coherence which is not routinely examined. In the day-to-day business of research, writing, and teaching, scientists operate within a background of belief about how things are. This background invisibly shapes what they choose to do and how they choose to do it. (Winograd and Flores, 1986, 24)

Winograd and Flores use philosophy to articulate the rationalist system underlying early work in HCI, and then critically demonstrate its shortcomings. They propose alternative framings that might address these shortcomings, including phenomenology and speech-act theory. The proposal to turn to phenomenology turned out, in hindsight, to have been extraordinarily generative.

In another seminal work, *Plans and Situated Actions*, Lucy Suchman (1987) leverages speech-act theory, ethnomethodology (especially Mead), and phenomenology (especially Heidegger) in an empirical study of how people use a particular photocopier. Her analysis demonstratively proves the inapplicability of rationalist methods to model the interaction. Suchman builds on this to offer an alternative conceptualization—"situated action"—to account for and support the design of interactions. A situated action is an "action taken in the context of particular, concrete circumstances" (Suchman, 1987, viii), which regards "plans" (e.g., rationalist interaction models) as a "weak resource" for activities that are fundamentally ad hoc. This is so because "plans systematically filter out precisely the particularity of detail that characterizes situated actions" (ix). She goes on to advocate the examination of "how it is that actors use the resources that a particular occasion provides—including, but crucially not reducible to, formulations such as plans—to construct their action's developing purpose and intelligibility" (3). Suchman's work not only fully realizes the promise made in Winograd and Flores with regard to the use of phenomenology and speech-act theory but also serves as a foundational resource for the rise of computer-supported cooperative work (CSCW), which combines the lessons of situated action and similar ideas developed in parallel (e.g., activity theory and distributed cognition) along with a social-collaborative orientation.

Critical Theory in Third-Wave HCI

Scholars of HCI have articulated the field as having three distinct paradigms or waves (Bødker, 2006; Harrison, Tatar, and Sengers, 2007; Rogers, 2012). The first wave is dominated by research on one-user, one-terminal interactions, often employing cognitive modeling to predict interaction-task completion times and error rates in service of usability. The second wave embraces much of first (especially usability) but extends it into CSCW, where research focuses on collaboration and site-specific (or situated) interactions. Common to both is an emphasis on workplace technologies and research methodologies broadly social scientific in nature. The third wave features user experience, embodied interactions, domestic and mobile computing, social media, and entertainment, and it reflects the computer's "reaching out" (Grudin, 1989) of the workplace into the rest of our lives. Again, the third wave embraces much of the earlier waves but adds to them an emphasis on design thinking and critical and philosophical approaches. In this third wave critical theory achieves a critical mass in HCI that, in spite of its influence, it had not achieved in the earlier waves.

Beyond Usability: From Fun to Politics

An early example of third-wave HCI is the 2004 anthology *Funology: From Usability to Enjoyment* (Blythe et al.), which was the culmination of a series of workshops launched by Andrew Monk on computers and fun. The anthology identified various approaches, from psychology, anthropology, and other social sciences, art, literature, and film studies, among others, to unpack the notion of enjoyment and fun, countering the prevailing emphasis on usability. Around this time a series of workshops began exploring critical theory and HCI, including a 2002 workshop led by Peter Wright and Janet Finlay entitled "Understanding User Experience: Literary Analysis Meets HCI" (Wright and Finlay, 2002). This led to "HCI as Image and Text: Using Arts and Humanities Techniques to Further Research Practice" (Wright et al., 2003), and then "Reflective HCI" (Dourish et al., 2004), and finally "Culture, Creativity, and Interaction Design" (Blythe, Light, and Wright, 2006).

During this time, Peter Wright, a key figure in this series of workshops, collaborated with John McCarthy to write the seminal *Technology as Experience* (McCarthy and Wright, 2004), which offers a systematic critical analysis of user experience built on the work of pragmatist philosopher John Dewey and formalist literary critic Mikhail Bakhtin. Pragmatic approaches would continue to influence HCI research, such as somaesthetics research (Bardzell, 2012; Höök et al., 2016; Lee, Lim, and Shusterman, 2014; Schiphorst, 2011) as well as design research (Dalsgaard and Dindler, 2009).

Beyond analyses of user experience, critical theory has been used to develop other HCI research methodologies. One is the critical analysis of individual or small collections of designs. A common activity in design processes is to collect exemplars relevant to the current design project and to critically analyze these designs for insights, inspirations, formal and material considerations, and other forms of problem framing. The research analogue of this is what is called "interface criticism" (Bertelsen and Pold, 2004) or "interaction criticism" (Bardzell, 2009, 2011; Bardzell and Bardzell, 2015). Both advocate for close "readings" of design artifacts, not unlike the way scholars in the traditional humanities offer close readings of literary, painted, musical, or dance works.

Another HCI methodological approach is to introduce concepts from critical theory into social science for perspective-changing and pragmatic results. An example is "Making by Making Strange: Defamiliarization and the Design of Domestic Technologies" (Bell, Blythe, and Sengers, 2005), in which the authors seek to overcome a methodological problem faced by ethnographers investigating domestic settings, in that ethnographers are overly familiar with such environments, which inhibits their perceptive and analytic abilities. As a counter to this, the authors appropriate "defamiliarization," a concept from early twentieth-century literary theory, to develop a methodological tactic to counter the effects of over-familiarization of a research topic.

Critical theory also plays an important role in the growing interest in our field in speculation in design, including critical design (Bardzell and Bardzell, 2013; Dunne and Raby, 2001; Feinberg, Carter, and Bullard, 2014), design fiction (Bleecker, 2009; Blythe 2014b; Tanenbaum, Tanenbaum, and Wakkary, 2012), and science fiction and ubiquitous computing (Bardzell and Bardzell, 2014; Blythe, 2014a; Dourish and Bell, 2014). In each of these, traditions of critical thought are deployed in designs to construct speculative images of preferred futures and to reveal potentially hidden agendas and values—tying together critical theory's strengths in the analysis of medium, human experience, aesthetics, and emancipation.

Third-wave HCI has also seen an upturn in research in support of social justice and broader access to computing, in areas such as gender and computing, HCI for development, sustainability, HCI and poverty, the digital divide and democratization of technology, and so forth. Twentieth-century critical theory includes a heavy emphasis on emancipation, offering plenty of resources to HCI researchers interested in social change, including research on reflective HCI (Sengers et al., 2005), users and nonusers as HCI "subjects" (Cooper and Bowers, 1995; Satchell and Dourish, 2009), feminist HCI (S. Bardzell, 2010; Light, 2011; Rode, 2011), environmental sustainability (Dourish, 2010), and postcolonialism and/in HCI4D (Irani et al., 2010; Kumar and Anderson, 2015; Taylor, 2011).

In Lieu of a Conclusion

Jeffrey Bardzell, Shaowen Bardzell, and Mark Blythe

One would not expect to master bioinformatics or artificial intelligence after a single introductory chapter, and equally we have no such aspirations that this chapter could have done that work for critical theory. We hope instead that we have piqued your intellectual curiosity, answered some questions while prompting others, and encouraged you to try something new, to extend your practice, to take seriously a new perspective.

We believe that interaction design mediates everyday reality, in public and in private, at work and at play, in our social networks and in our bodies. Accordingly, interaction design has the potential to enlighten us or dumb us down; to isolate us or connect us to others; to liberate us or sink us into forms of bondage; to enrich our perceptual, imaginative, and empathic capabilities; to stimulate our creativity and enhance our ability to express ourselves; to help teach us how to experience, to understand others, to be good citizens. The richly diverse yet deeply interwoven 2,000-plus year conversation between the arts—including the so-called high arts as well as popular arts and design—and criticism offers an incredible array of resources, ideas, and examples that interaction designers and HCI researchers can use to take seriously the profound sociocultural implications of our work.

In this book, we take the position that the diverse disciplines that contribute to HCI—engineering, psychology, ethnography, design, critical theory, and more—are complementary and can be used harmoniously. Each offers distinctive resources from its own rich traditions, yet the bounty of historical and practical overlaps among them provides sufficient commonalties to ensure the possibility of meaningful cooperation. In an interdisciplinary field committed to useful designs, good experiences, and the social good, the time has never been riper for critical theory to play its part, alongside of engineering, design, and social science in HCI and interaction design.

We end with questions—questions that readers can take forward from this volume.

How should critical theory and interaction design mutually inform one another?

What roles might interaction design play in ongoing projects of enlightenment and emancipation?

How might interaction design contribute to our deepest needs—for connection to others, competency, self-esteem, physical security and wellbeing?

Note

1. Bolded names are represented in this volume as sources with their own commentaries.

References

Agre, P. (1997) "Toward a Critical Technical Practice: Lessons Learned in Trying to Reform AI." In *Social Science, Technical Systems, and Cooperative Work: Beyond the Great Divide*, edited by G. C. Bowker, S. L. Star, W. Turner, and L. Gasser, 131–158. Mahwah, NJ: Lawrence Erlbaum.

Bardzell, J. (2009) "Interaction Criticism and Aesthetics." In *Proceedings of the SIGCHI Conference on Human Factors in Computing Systems*. New York: ACM, 2357–2366. DOI: 10.1145/1518701.1519063.

Bardzell, J. (2011) "Interaction Criticism: An Introduction to the Practice." *Interacting with Computers* 23 (6): 604–621. DOI: 10.1016/j.intcom.2011.07.001.

Bardzell, J. (2012) "Commentary on: R. Shusterman (2012): Somaesthetics." In *The Encyclopedia of Human-Computer Interaction*, 2nd ed., edited by M. Soegaard and R. F. Dam. Aarhus, Denmark: Interaction Design Foundation. https://www.interaction-design.org/encyclopedia/somaesthetics.html.

Bardzell, J., and S. Bardzell. (2013) "What Is 'Critical' about Critical Design?" In *Proceedings of the SIGCHI Conference on Human Factors in Computing Systems*. New York: ACM, 3297–3306. DOI: 10.1145/2470654.2466451.

Bardzell, J., and S. Bardzell. (2014) "A Great and Troubling Beauty": Cognitive Speculation and Ubiquitous Computing. *Personal and Ubiquitous Computing* 18 (4): 779–794. DOI: 10.1007/s00779-013-0677-8.

Bardzell, J., and S. Bardzell. (2015) *Humanistic HCI*. San Rafael, CA: Morgan and Claypool.

Bardzell, S. (2010) "Feminist HCI: Taking Stock and Outlining an Agenda for Design." In *Proceedings of the SIGCHI Conference on Human Factors in Computing Systems*. New York: ACM, 1301–1310. DOI: 10.1145/1753326.1753521.

Bardzell, S., and E. F. Churchill. (2011) "Feminism and HCI: New Perspectives." *Interacting with Computers* 23 (5): iii—xi.

Barry, P. (2002) *Beginning Theory*. Manchester: Manchester University Press.

Bell, G., M. Blythe, and P. Sengers. (2005) "Making by Making Strange: Defamiliarization and the Design of Domestic Technologies." *Transactions on Computer-Human Interaction (TOCHI)* 12 (2): 149–173.

Bertelsen, O. W., and S. Pold. (2002) "Toward the Aesthetics of Human Computer Interaction." In *Proceedings of the Second Danish Human-Computer Interaction Research Symposium*, 11–12. Copenhagen: University of Copenhagen Technical Report no. 2002/19.

Bleecker, J. (2009) "Design Fiction: A Short Essay on Design, Science, Fact and Fiction." *Near Future Laboratory* (blog). Accessed April 9, 2016, http://blog.nearfuturelaboratory.com/2009/03/17/design-fiction-a-short-essay-on-design-science-fact-and-fiction/.

Bloom, H. (1994) *The Western Canon: The Books and School of the Ages*. New York: Harcourt Brace.

Blythe, M. (2014a) "The Hitchhiker's Guide to Ubicomp: Using Techniques from Literary and Critical Theory to Reframe Scientific Agendas." *Personal and Ubiquitous Computing* 18 (4): 795–808. DOI: 10.1007/s00779-013-0679-6.

Blythe, M. (2014b) "Research through Design Fiction: Narrative in Real and Imaginary Abstracts." In *Proceedings of the SIGCHI Conference on Human Factors in Computing Systems*. New York: ACM, 703–712. DOI: 10.1145/2556288.2557098.

Blythe, M., A. Light, and P. Wright. (2006) *Proceedings of the First International Symposium on Culture, Creativity and Interaction Design*. London: Queen Mary University.

Blythe, M., K. Overbeeke, A. F. Monk, and P. C. Wright, eds. (2004) *Funology: From Usability to Enjoyment*. Springer. DOI: 10.1007/1-4020-2967-5.

Bødker, S. (2006) "When Second Wave HCI Meets Third Wave Challenges." In *Proceedings of the 4th Nordic Conference on Human-Computer Interaction: Changing Roles*. New York: ACM, 1–8. DOI: 10.1145/1182475.1182476.

Boehner, K., P. Sengers, and S. Warner. (2008) "Interfaces with the Ineffable: Meeting Aesthetic Experience on Its Own Terms." *ACM Transactions on Computer-Human Interaction (TOCHI)* 15 (3). DOI: 10.1145/1453152.1453155.

Bratton, B. (2013) "We Need to Talk about TED." *Guardian*, December 30. https://www.theguardian.com/commentisfree/2013/dec/30/we-need-to-talk-about-ted.

Braun, N. (2003) "Storytelling in Collaborative Augmented Reality Environments." In *Journal of the WSCG [World Society for Computer Graphics]* 11 (1–3): 1–8.

Cooper, G., and J. Bowers. (1995) "Representing the User: Notes on the Disciplinary Rhetoric of Human-Computer Interaction." In *The Social and Interactional Dimensions of Human-Computer Interfaces*, edited by P. J. Thomas, 48–66. New York: Cambridge University Press.

Coyne, R. D. (1995) *Designing Information Technology in the Postmodern Age: From Method to Metaphor*. Cambridge, MA: MIT Press.

Dalsgaard, P., and C. Dindler. (2009) "Peepholes as Means of Engagement in Interaction Design." In *Proceedings of Nordic Design Research NORDES'09*. Oslo: The Oslo School of Architecture and Design, 1–10.

Danto, A. (1997) *Connections to the World: The Basic Concepts of Philosophy*. Berkeley: University of California Press.

Dourish, P. (2010) "HCI and Environmental Sustainability: The Politics of Design and the Design of Politics." In *Proceedings of the 8th ACM Conference on Designing Interactive Systems*. New York: ACM, 1–10. DOI: 10.1145/1858171.1858173.

Dourish, P., and G. Bell. (2014) "'Resistance Is Futile': Reading Science Fiction Alongside Ubiquitous Computing." *Personal and Ubiquitous Computing* 18 (4): 769–778. DOI: 10.1007/s00779-013-0678-7.

Dourish, P., J. Finlay, P. Sengers, and P. Wright. (2004) "Reflective HCI: Toward a Critical Technical Practice." *CHI '04 Extended Abstracts on Human Factors in Computing Systems*. New York: AMC, 1727–1728. DOI: 10.1145/985921.986203.

Dreyfus, H. (1965) "Alchemy and Artificial Intelligence." Santa Monica, CA: RAND Corporation. https://www.rand.org/content/dam/rand/pubs/papers/2006/P3244.pdf.

Dunne, A., and F. Raby. (2001) *Design Noir: The Secret Life of Electronic Objects*. Basel, Switzerland: Birkhäuser.

Feinberg, M., D. Carter, and J. Bullard. (2014) "Always Somewhere, Never There: Using Critical Design to Understand Database Interactions." In *Proceedings of the SIGCHI Conference on*

Human Factors in Computing Systems. New York: ACM, 1941–1950. https://ils.unc.edu/~mfeinber/Feinberg,%20Carter,%20Bullard%202014%20preprint.pdf.

Frye, N. (1957) *Anatomy of Criticism: Four Essays*. Princeton, NJ: Princeton University Press.

Gibson, J. (2007) *Fiction and the Weave of Life*. Oxford: Oxford University Press.

Gross, S., J. Bardzell, and S. Bardzell. (2014) "Structures, Forms, and Stuff: The Materiality and Medium of Interaction." *Personal and Ubiquitous Computing* 18 (3): 637–649.

Grudin, J. (1989) *The Computer Reaches Out: The Historical Continuity of Interface Design*. Aarhus, Denmark: Aarhus University Press. DOI: 10.1145/97243.97284.

Harrison, S., D. Tatar, and P. Sengers, P. (2007) "Three Paradigms of HCI." *Proceedings of the Conference on Human Factors in Computing Systems*, alt.chi. New York: ACM, 1–18.

Höök, K. (2010) "Transferring Qualities from Horseback Riding to Design." In *Proceedings of the 6th Nordic Conference on Human-Computer Interaction: Extending Boundaries*. New York: ACM, 226–235. DOI: 10.1145/1868914.1868943.

Höök, K., M. Jonsson, A. Ståhl, and J. Mercurio, J. (2016) "Somaesthetic Appreciation Design." In *Proceedings of the SIGCHI Conference on Human Factors in Computing Systems*. New York: ACM, 3131–3142.

Irani, L., J. Vertesi, P. Dourish, K. Philip, and R. E. Grinter. (2010) "Postcolonial Computing: A Lens on Design and Development." In *Proceedings of the SIGCHI Conference on Human Factors in Computing Systems*. New York: ACM, 1311–1320. DOI: /10.1145/1753326.1753522.

Iyer, L. (2014) *Wittgenstein, Jr*. Brooklyn: Melville House Books.

Johnson, S. (1997) *Interface Culture: How New Technology Transforms the Way We Create and Communicate*. San Francisco: HarperEdge.

Kristeller, P. O. (2008) "Introduction." In *Aesthetics: A Comprehensive Anthology*, edited by S. M. Cahn and A. Meskin, 3–15. Malden, MA: Blackwell.

Kuhn, T. S. (1996) *The Structure of Scientific Revolutions*. 3rd ed. Chicago: University of Chicago Press. DOI: 10.7208/chicago/9780226458106.001.0001.

Kumar, N., and R. Anderson. (2015) "Mobile Phones for Maternal Health in Rural India." In *Proceedings of the 33rd Annual ACM Conference on Human Factors in Computing Systems (CHI '15)*. New York: ACM, 427–436.

Laurel, B. (2013) "The Six Elements and Causal Relations Among Them (from *Computers as Theatre*)." In *The New Media Reader*, edited by N. Wardrip-Fruin and N. Montfort, 564–571. Cambridge, MA: The MIT Press.

Leavis, F. R. (1948) *The Great Tradition: George Eliot, Henry James, Joseph Conrad*. London: Chatto and Windus.

Lee, W., Y.-K Lim, and R. Shusterman. (2014) "Practicing Somaesthetics: Exploring Its Impact on Interactive Product Design Ideation." In *Proceedings of the 2014 conference on Designing Interactive Systems (DIS '14)*. New York: ACM, 1055–1064.

Light, A. (2011) "HCI as Heterodoxy: Technologies of Identity and the Queering of Interaction with Computers." *Interacting with Computers* 23 (5): 430–438. DOI: 10.1016/j.int- com. 20 11.02.002.

Löwgren, J. (2009) "Toward an Articulation of Interaction Esthetics." *New Review of Hypermedia and Multimedia* 15 (2): 129–146. DOI: http://dx.doi.org/10.1080/13614560903117822.

Manovich, L. (2002) *The Language of New Media*. Cambridge, MA: MIT Press.

McCarthy, J., and P. Wright. (2004) *Technology as Experience*. Cambridge, MA: MIT Press. DOI: 10.1145/1015530.1015549.

Morozov, E. (2014) *To Save Everything, Click Here: The Folly of Technological Solutionism*. New York: PublicAffairs.

Nakamura, L. (2002) *Cybertypes: Race, Ethnicity, and Identity on the Internet*. New York: Routledge.

Nakamura, L. (2007) *Digitizing Race: Visual Cultures of the Internet*. Minneapolis: University of Minnesota Press.

Nussbaum, M. (1990) *Love's Knowledge: Essays on Philosophy and Literature*. Oxford: Oxford University Press.

Richards, I. A. (1929) *Practical Criticism: A Study of Literary Judgment*. New York: Harcourt Brace.

Rode, J. A. (2011) "A Theoretical Agenda for Feminist HCI." *Interacting with Computers* 23 (5): 393–400. DOI: 10.1016/j.intcom.2011.04.005.

Rogers, Y. (2012) *HCI Theory: Classical, Modern, and Contemporary: Synthesis Lectures on Human-Centered Informatics*. San Rafael, CA: Morgan and Claypool. DOI: 10.2200/S00418ED1 V01Y201205HCI014.

Russell, D. A., and M. Winterbottom. (1989) Introduction. In *Classical Literary Criticism*. Oxford: Oxford University Press.

Satchell, C., and P. Dourish. (2009) "Beyond the User: Use and Non-Use in HCI." In *Proceedings of the 21st Annual Conference of the Australian Computer-Human Interaction Special Interest Group: Design: Open 24/7*. New York: ACM, 9–16. DOI: 10.1145/1738826.1738829.

Schiphorst, T. (2011) "Self-evidence: Applying Somatic Connoisseurship to Experience Design." In *CHI '11 Extended Abstracts on Human Factors in Computing Systems*. New York: ACM, 145–160.

Sengers, P., K. Boehner, S. David, and J. Kaye. (2005) "Reflective Design." In *Proceedings of the 4th Decennial Conference on Critical Computing: Between Sense and Sensibility*. New York: ACM, 49–58. DOI: 10.1145/1094562.1094569.

Suchman, L. A. (1987) *Plans and Situated Actions: The Problem of Human-Machine Communication*. New York: Cambridge University Press.

Tanenbaum, J., K. Tanenbaum, and R. Wakkary. (2012) "Steampunk as Design Fiction." In *Proceedings of the SIGCHI Conference on Human Factors in Computing Systems*. New York: ACM, 1583–1592. DOI: 10.1145/2207676.2208279.

Taylor, A. S. (2011) "Out There." In *Proceedings of the SIGCHI Conference on Human Factors in Computing Systems*. New York: ACM, 685–694. DOI: 10.1145/1978942.1979042.

Turkle, S. (1995) *Life on the Screen: Identity in the Age of the Internet.* New York: Simon and Schuster.

Udsen, L. E., and A. H. Jørgensen. (2005) "The Aesthetic Turn: Unravelling Recent Aesthetic Approaches to Human-Computer Interaction." *Digital Creativity* 16 (4): 205–216. DOI: 10.1080/14626260500476564.

Winograd, T., and F. Flores. (1986) *Understanding Computers and Cognition: A New Foundation for Design.* Norwood, NJ: Ablex. DOI: 10.1002/bs.3830330107.

Wright, P., and J. Finlay. (2002) "Understanding User Experience: Literary Analysis Meets HCI." In *BCS HCI 2002.* Publisher unknown.

Wright, P., J. Finlay, M. Blythe, and A. Light. (2003) "HCI as Image and Text: Using Arts and Humanities Techniques to Further Research Practice." King's Manor HCI-Lit Workshop, York, UK, July 21.

I

Fretting in the Shadow of Language: Interpretation and Evaluation

Mark Blythe

His language so familiar and so foreign, will always be for me an acquired speech. I have not made or accepted its words. My voice holds them at bay. My soul frets in the shadow of his language.
—James Joyce, *Portrait of the Artist as a Young Man*

In *Portrait of the Artist as a Young Man* the main character, Stephen Dedalus, uses a word his dean of studies has never heard before, calling a part of the lamp they are discussing a "tundish." The dean, who is English, asks if this is an old Irish word. Stephen tells him it is the word used in Lower Drumcondra, where they only speak the best English. Stephen reflects, "The language we are speaking is his before it is mine. How different are the words home, Christ, ale, master on his lips and on mine!" The problem of speaking and writing in English, the language of Ireland's oppressor, is a recurring theme throughout Joyce's work. In *Finnegan's Wake* he set out to destroy the language but promised to return it once he was done. Stephen's consternation before the dean is perhaps resonant for those engaged in interdisciplinary work. In human-computer interaction, computer scientists, engineers, designers, social scientists, psychologists, artists, historians, and even literary scholars must find ways to talk to one another with words that are both familiar and foreign. How different are the words "testing," "evaluation," and "finding" on his lips and on mine. How different are the words "analysis," "interpretation," and "aesthetics" on her lips and yours. The problem of communication across disciplines is not new but it is perhaps more pronounced and obvious now that computing technology has penetrated every area of human life—personal, political, social, sexual, ethical and spiritual.

The first section of this book is broadly concerned with what might have been called "evaluation" ten or fifteen years ago but might be called "interpretation" now. It contains many theories, critical perspectives, or ways of seeing. The aim of this section is not to champion one theory over another but to articulate some of the kinds of theoretical orientations possible. The perspectives in this section span centuries as well as disciplines, running the gamut of philosophy from A to Z, from Aristotle to Žižek. We reverse the order, beginning with Žižek for no better reason than that he is currently the most popular critical theorist alive today and ending with Aristotle because he has spent the longest time dead.

Blythe and Žižek

The Žižek chapter begins with a transcription from a YouTube video. Žižek is a powerfully engaging speaker and his videos are very popular. Though his texts are sometimes difficult, he is perhaps the funniest Hegel scholar currently on the public talk circuit. The YouTube quote is one of Žižek's favorite examples of how any design, even something as purely utilitarian and functional as a toilet, is loaded with cultural and ideological meaning. The commentary offers Žižeckian interpretations of the Prayer Companion, a T-shaped device that delivers news stories to a group of cloistered nuns. Although the nuns were concerned that the device might distract them from their life of prayer, they appreciated it so much that they lived with it for several years. Media responses were also positive and the device was generally described by commentators as elegant or beautiful. The chapter outlines various theories of the beautiful to try to account for this (beauty as something inherent in nature, beauty as a social construct) before turning to some of Žižek's favorite psychoanalytical concepts, in particular the "subject supposed to believe" and "the vanishing mediator." The chapter also considers why so many journalists who declared themselves atheists nevertheless saw the Prayer Companion as an excellent piece of design. It is argued that this is a "fetishistic disavowal" by which atheists take comfort in the religions they do not believe in.

Žižek describes himself as a Christian atheist, someone who does not believe in God yet finds value in the traditions of Christianity. His favorite theologian, G. K. Chesterton, would attribute this to his pessimism. Žižek believes that the universe is fundamentally evil and argues that the reason we are so fond of apocalyptic disaster films is that the end of the world would be a happy ending. Chesterton once proposed a philosophical police force that would route out pessimism and arrest people for writing a sonnet or publishing a pamphlet. Žižek would have been on the "most wanted" list of such a force, but the more famously pessimistic philosopher Søren Kierkegaard would not. Although Kierkegaard is notorious for maxims such as "Marry or don't marry, you will regret it either way," Chesterton would have classified him as fundamentally optimistic because of his faith.

Bertelsen and Kierkegaard

Kierkegaard wrote his philosophical tracts under pseudonyms, and some of his texts resemble novels as much as philosophy. "Either / Or," from which Bertelsen takes his extract, is a dialogue presented within a story involving found manuscripts. The narrator of this text argues that "all people are boring" and claims that only the very boring indeed would disagree. From this premise the amount of boredom in the world increases with the number of people in it, beginning with the first doubling when Adam was bored enough to wish for an Eve. Though boredom itself looks placid and calm, it leads to frantic activity; in this sense it is the root of all evil. Just as farmers rotate their crops to refresh the soil so we must vary our activities to keep ourselves interested in life, by, for example, watching a spider move across the floor while sitting in a boring lecture. Kierkegaard's narrator transforms the experience of listening to a boring man by closely observing the bead of sweat forming on the end of the man's nose. The narrator ends by claiming that the genius of this theory is evident by its ubiquity but refuses to detail where else it might apply. Bertelsen picks up where the narrator leaves off to show how avoiding boredom might stimulate research in HCI. Michel Foucault once suggested that he and his colleagues should stop using the word "structure" for one year as a matter of intellectual housekeeping. Bertelsen makes a similar suggestion based on the idea of crop rotation: cultural probes were once an innovative and stimulating method, and it may be that they would regain some of their power if we refrained from relying on them so much for a while.

With an honesty and bravery seldom seen in academic writing Bertelsen includes some reflections on the way that reading Kierkegaard affected him personally. As a young man he missed the ambiguity of Kierkegaard's writing and the importance of the position of the narrator. Bertelsen's account of the problems resulting from taking Kierkegaard's remarks too seriously shows how much the ethical and aesthetic problems he is discussing matter. Increasingly, HCI research is dealing not just with lists of abstract design principles but also with questions of how to live.

Kaye and Barthes

Much critical theory is concerned with the hidden significance of everyday life and the mundane cultural artifacts that surround us. Roland Barthes found politics in pasta sauce. Barthes had studied literature and used techniques of close and detailed reading to analyze not poems and novels but other "texts" like films and commercials. The same attention to detail that had been applied to the novels of Balzac were given to the interpretation of such cultural products as a soap powder or the sweat on Roman soldiers in Hollywood films.

The advertisement for pasta sauce that Barthes made famous showed an image of a grocery bag spilling tomatoes, onions, and fresh pasta onto a table. The vegetables suggest freshness, even though the pasta is prepackaged. The colors that dominate are red, white, and green, the colors of the Italian flag, suggesting Italy although the product was made in America. Barthes analyzes what is denoted (literally shown) and connoted (what is implied or suggested). Even the kind of bag is of interest—what sort of person would own it? A sophisticated and tasteful one of course, the kind of person the people seeing the poster might want to be. The way in which the bag has been casually thrown on the table is also important, suggesting a carefree sort of manner. This kind of breakdown of the coded messages in advertising is now very well-known, but in the 1960s it was radical and new.

Such approaches to mass culture have been tremendously influential not only in academia but also in advertising, where they are used to make still subtler and more insidious commercials. Writers like Barthes and Umberto Eco performed close readings of everyday contemporary culture. Just as a close reading of a poem would reveal structures of rhythm and rhyme, so a reading of a wrestling match might reveal structures of ritual and catharsis. This approach became known as "semiotics," the study of signs. Jofish Kaye takes this kind of approach to consider massively open online courses (MOOCs) and "Big Data" as a form of myth. He makes a provocative, Barthesian argument, questioning science as the ultimate truth against which all other truths must be measured. Kaye explains and applies key semiotic concepts in a new and perhaps surprising context. Of course it is always possible to object to this kind of analysis and interpretation as "reading too much" into the subject, be it a hairstyle or a MOOC. But for another great figure of semiotics, Umberto Eco, interpretation is a creative act.

Blackwell and Eco

For Umberto Eco interpretation is a performance, as when a musician plays a score. How open and how interpretable a text is depends on the user interface or the instrument. Alan Blackwell applies Eco's arguments around the "open text" to open source code, sampling, and sandbox games like Second Life. For Blackwell the game *Minecraft* crosses conventional boundaries of audience and authorship.

Blackwell provides an entertaining frame for his chapter with an exchange he had with Eric Schmidt, the founder of Google. Schmidt claimed that humanity had created more information in the last ten years than it had in the rest of its history. Blackwell invites us to imagine Schmidt claiming that humanity had created more *meaning* in the last ten years than in the rest of its history. Information can be coded and decoded by machines in multiple ways, and an engineering perspective allows for creative distinctions between noise and signal. But meaning is a matter of poetics. Blackwell points out that interpretation has always been an issue in HCI, though this is seldom acknowledged.

As a novelist Eco read a great many interpretations of his own most famous book, *The Name of the Rose*. Eco's allusions, references, and in-jokes have been successfully interpreted or "decoded" many times. But sometimes interpretations of the work surprised him. A reader might find an allusion or a borrowing of which Eco himself was unaware. Did this mean that the critic was wrong? Eco would say not. Sometimes surprising readings made him aware of the unconscious influences that had percolated into the text without his knowledge. Eco theorized an "ideal reader," one who would pick up on every allusion, get every joke, and appreciate the work as it was intended. But he distinguished this ideal from "empirical readers," real people who bring their own interpretations to the work. Just as the author's interpretation of the work is not final, neither is theirs. Critics of drama and literature have long offered competing interpretations of the same texts, but which interpretations are right and which are wrong?

Churchill and Hall

The rise of social media means that the interpretation of texts is a matter of everyday concern. Twitter and Facebook posts allow anyone to make hasty publications with a potentially global audience. The interpretation of tweets can turn lives. Jon Ronson offers a vivid account of the online shaming of Justine Sacco, who liked to tweet acerbic jokes to her 170 or so followers (Ronson 2015). One of Sacco's tweets referred to a layover at Heathrow: "Chili cucumber sandwiches—bad teeth. Back in London." Just before she got on her plane to South Africa she wrote this now infamous tweet: "Going to Africa. Hope I don't get AIDS. Just kidding. I'm white." While she was in the air, tens of thousands of retweets condemned her as a racist. When she arrived in South Africa eleven hours later, she was the number1 trending topic on Twitter and there was a photographer waiting to capture the moment she realized what had happened. She was fired from her job and so publicly shamed that she left the country. Ronson recognized Sacco's comment as a joke and admits he had made similar (but better) jokes himself. When he met with her, she explained that she thought it was such an insane comment that nobody could possibly take it literally. She elaborated on this point in an email: "Unfortunately, I am not a character on 'South Park' or a comedian, so I had no business commenting on the epidemic in such a politically incorrect manner on a public platform" (Ronson 2015).

The Cartman character in the cartoon *South Park* that Sacco refers to regularly makes offensive and racist jokes in the tradition of characters like Alf Garnett in the UK or Archie Bunker in the United States. The producers encode these characters as racist buffoons that the audience should laugh at. Sacco's tweet was stripped of context, attached to a name, not a character, and so was not recognizable as a joke. Ronson notes that we often think the subjects of public shamings eventually pick their lives up and get themselves back together, though this is not necessarily the case. His haunting account of Sacco's humiliation and lasting disgrace is a stark illustration of the problem of encoding social media.

Stuart Hall, a founding figure in cultural studies, was one of the first writers to theorize about the ways in which media are produced and consumed. The mass media which Hall discussed encoded its content very carefully. Everything on a TV show—the music, titles, set, décor, the looks, tone, and haircuts of the presenters—was meticulously planned and controlled, building on conventions that formed over many decades. Elizabeth Churchill applies Hall's work on encoding and decoding messages to today's technological landscape. Hall was concerned with questions like, Who is saying what to whom? In the age of "fake news," those questions are difficult to answer. Facebook's algorithms present us with clickbait designed to keep us on the site longer and opinions we are predisposed to like. The mass media that Hall described delivered audiences to advertisers based on shows they might like. Cambridge analytica delivers Facebook users to political candidates based on their personality traits. Racist members of TV audiences have long enjoyed racist characters like Cartman, Alf Garnett, and Archie Bunker for the wrong reasons. But now this segment of the audience can be targeted and picked out for advertisers or political campaigners. Fake news or propaganda can go viral before fact checkers have even fired up their laptops. In *The Man and the Echo,* W.B. Yeats wondered, "Did that play of mine send out. Certain men the English shot?" Today we might wonder if that retweet of mine helped to ruin someone's life or sway an election.

Churchill draws on Hall's "Circuit of Culture" to show how design intention is always modified by use through successive iterations. The earliest personal stereos were designed for two sets of earphones because, until then, music was social—who would want to isolate themselves with a set of headphones? The uses of the new technology led to public debate and new forms of social expectations. This focus on cycles of development and reiteration is perhaps a reason to be optimistic: social media is always in flux, this too shall pass. The consumers of social media are also its producers and are therefore in a stronger position to enact change than the audiences of the printed press or television. Hall and Churchill demonstrate that the meanings of media cannot be fixed.

Iser and Feinberg

In *Annie Hall* Woody Allen stands in a queue outside a cinema and becomes increasingly irritated by a man behind him pontificating about Marshall McLuhan. Allen's character asks the camera what you do when you're stuck on a movie line with a person like this. The man in the queue protests: he teaches a course at Columbia and his insights into McLuhan have validity. Allen walks out of the shot and returns with McLuhan himself, who tells the lecturer that he knows nothing of his work and he's amazed that he gets to teach a course of any kind. Allen turns back to the camera and asks—wouldn't be great if life were like this? Of course it is not always possible to ask an author if a given interpretation of their work is correct because they are long dead. But even where there is a live writer capable of answering questions, it is not clear that he or she would necessarily know the answers. Milan Kundera was once asked if a particular interpretation of one his novels was correct; he replied that the meaning might be there but he did not put it there. Designers too are sometimes surprised, if not horrified, by an interpretation of their work.

Books introducing cultural studies are generally arranged by perspective, listed in chronological order, such as formalism, structuralism, poststructuralism, Marxism, psychoanalysis, feminism, phenomenology, postmodernism, and reception theory. The order of perspectives presented in these books varies, but reception theory is often the final destination. Reader response theory is radically different from all of the other interpretive strategies. It argues that there are as many readings of a text as there are readers, that there is no final meaning to be uncovered. Indeed, for reader-response theorists all texts are fundamentally unfinished—they exist only when they are read and have no independent existence at all. Reader reception theory allows for far more diversity than many other interpretive strategies. It also explains how each of these interpretive strategies can coexist so cozily between the pages of cultural studies primers.

In her chapter, Melanie Feinberg draws on Wolfgang Iser's foundational work on reader reception theory to consider a range of responses to hybrid digital knitted products. The mobile phone software Spyn allows knitters to embed digital content in their knitted products as metadata. One Spyn user might hide a message or puzzle in a scarf; another might make a record of an alteration in a hat, leaving some trace of part of a design that is no longer there. Feinberg points out that an Iserian approach to literature accounts for the ways that a book like *Pride and Prejudice* can still surprise us when we reread it. The text has not changed but *we* have, so we find different things in it. Similarly the meanings of embedded Spyn data or a set of tweets may change over time as we revisit them or reflect on them. Feinberg proposes Isers' sense of the imaginary as an alternative to the taxonomies and guidelines of more traditional HCI research.

Cockton and Aristotle

Technology is moving so fast that books on human-computer interaction are outdated as soon as they are published. But researchers in HCI are increasingly called to consider large philosophical questions that do not date so quickly: what is intelligence, what is action, what is time, what is good? Gilbert Cockton examines Aristotle's notion of the "excellences." Aristotle's writing is over two thousand years old and yet it remains so relevant that his classic work on *Poetics* was applied to questions of interaction design almost as soon as they were raised. Brenda Laurel's seminal "Computers as Theatre" draws on Aristotle to make parallels between interacting with computers and engaging with art. Over twenty years ago she explored the ways that computers require us to engage with complex sign systems and metaphors—the desktop for instance, which looks nothing like a desktop.

Cockton draws not on the *Poetics* but rather on the *Nicomachean Ethics*. Cockton has long argued for value-based design and criticized notions of evaluation that continue to draw on classic usability measures like efficiency, time on task, and ease of learning. He claims that we must ask deeper questions of what we consider to be "the good" if we are to have a clear idea of what we mean when we evaluate a design. His commentary explores the ways in which wisdom, the Aristotelian concept of *nous*, and theory can be applied to design.

The chapters in this section draw on radically different theories, traditions of thought, and ways of speaking. When Stephen Dedalus explains the meaning of "tundish," he interrupts the dean in mid flow.

> —To return to the lamp, he said, the feeding of it is also a nice problem. You must choose the pure oil and you must be careful when you pour it in not to overflow it, not to pour in more than the funnel can hold.
> —What funnel? asked Stephen.
> —The funnel through which you pour the oil into your lamp.
> —That? said Stephen. Is that called a funnel? Is it not a tundish?
> —What is a tundish?
> —That. The funnel.

Stephen frets in the shadow of the dean's language but the dean also frets in Stephen's: his monologue is interrupted. The dean is clearly taking pleasure in his didactic account of the technology, the detailed description of pouring and guarding against overflow. He thinks he is teaching Stephen something, but the master becomes pupil when he misnames a part of the device. The dean assumes that he does not know the word "tundish" because it is not an English word, that it must be Irish. Despite Stephen's belief that the language belongs to the dean before it belongs to him, the exchange makes it clear that Stephen is the master. As the title of the novel reminds us, Stephen is a young man, and here, perhaps, he suffers both the arrogance and the insecurity of youth.

HCI is sometimes described as intellectually promiscuous, taking up and discarding theoretical perspectives as and when they seem applicable. Early work in HCI was often a conversation between psychologists and computer scientists as the design space was primarily that of an individual and a machine. As computers entered the workplace it became necessary to broaden the disciplinary scope of the field to consider organizational complexity, and sociologists were brought into the dialogue. Now that computers have moved from our homes to our pockets and impact almost every aspect of our personal, social, and political lives, HCI borrows from writers like the literary and critical theorists in this volume. This magpie tendency might be deplored as superficial, but it can also be lauded as a defense against dogmatism.

Though the words and concepts in *Critical Theory and Interaction Design* are borrowed from critical theory, they are often most interesting when they are an acquired speech.

Terry Eagleton remarks, the masters of English in the twentieth century—Yeats, Joyce, Beckett, Pound, Conrad—were not English. But this would be small comfort to an undergraduate in a dean's office, fretting in the shadow of language.

Reference

Ronson, J. (2015) "How One Stupid Tweet Blew Up Justine Sacco's Life." *New York Times*, February 12. https://www.nytimes.com/2015/02/15/magazine/how-one-stupid-tweet-ruined-justine-saccos-life.html.

1 The Seven Veils of Fantasy (1997)

Slavoj Žižek

"The Truth Is out There"

When, a couple of years ago, the disclosure of Michael Jackson's alleged "immoral" private behaviour (his sexual games with underage boys) dealt a blow to his innocent Peter Pan image, elevated beyond sexual and racial differences (or concerns), some penetrating commentators asked the obvious question: what's all the fuss about? Wasn't this so-called dark side of Michael Jackson always here for all of us to see, in the video spots that accompanied his musical releases, which were saturated with ritualized violence and obscene sexualized gestures (blatantly so in the case of *Thriller* and *Bad*)? The Unconscious is outside, not hidden in any unfathomable depths—or, to quote the *X Files* motto: "The truth is out there."

Such a focusing on material externality proves very fruitful in the analysis of how fantasy relates to the inherent antagonisms of an ideological edifice. Do not the two opposed architectural designs of *Casa del Fascio* (the local headquarters of the Fascist party), Adolfo Coppede's neo-Imperial pastiche (1928) and Giuseppe Teragni's highly modernist transparent glasshouse (1934–36) reveal, in their simple juxtaposition, the inherent contradiction of the Fascist ideological project which simultaneously advocates a return to pre-modern organicist corporatism and the unheard-of mobilization of all social forces in the service of rapid modernization? An even better example is provided by the great projects of public buildings in the Soviet Union of the 1930s, which put on top of a flat multistorey office building a gigantic statue of the idealized New Man, or a couple: in the span of a couple of years, the tendency to flatten the office building (the actual workplace for living people) more and more became clearly discernible, so that it changed increasingly into a mere pedestal for the larger-than-life statue—does not this external, material feature of architectural design reveal the "truth" of the Stalinist ideology in which actual, living people are reduced to instruments, sacrificed as the pedestal for the spectre of the future New Man, an ideological monster which crushes actual living men under his feet? The paradox is that had anyone in the Soviet Union of the 1930s said openly that the vision of the Socialist

New Man was an ideological monster squashing actual people, they would have been arrested immediately. It was, however, allowed—encouraged, even—to make this point via architectural design ... again, "the truth is out there." What we are thus arguing is not simply that ideology also permeates the alleged extra-ideological strata of everyday life, but that this materialization of ideology in external materiality reveals inherent antagonisms which the explicit formulation of ideology cannot afford to acknowledge: it is as if an ideological edifice, if it is to function "normally," must obey a kind of "imp of perversity," and articulate its inherent antagonism in the externality of its material existence.

This externality, which directly embodies ideology, is also occluded as "utility." That is to say: in everyday life, ideology is at work especially in the apparently innocent reference to pure utility—one should never forget that in the symbolic universe, "utility" functions as a reflective notion; that is, it always involves the assertion of utility as meaning (for example, a man who lives in a large city and owns a Land Rover does not simply lead a no-nonsense, "down-to-earth" life; rather, he owns such a car in order to *signal* that he leads his life under the sign of a no-nonsense, "down-to-earth" attitude). The unsurpassed master of such analysis, of course, was Claude Lévi-Strauss, whose semiotic triangle of preparing food (raw, baked, boiled) demonstrated how food also serves as "food for thought." We probably all remember the scene from Buñuel's *Phantom of Liberty*, in which relations between eating and excreting are inverted: people sit on their lavatories around the table, pleasantly talking, and when they want to eat, they silently ask the housekeeper, "Where is that place ... you know?" and sneak away to a small room in the back. So, as a supplement to Lévi-Strauss, one is tempted to propose that shit can also serve as a *matière-à-penser*: do not the three basic types of lavatory form a kind of excremental correlative-counterpoint to the Lévi-Straussian triangle of cooking?

In a traditional German lavatory, the hole in which shit disappears after we flush water is way in front, so that the shit is first laid out for us to sniff at and inspect for traces of some illness; in the typical French lavatory, on the contrary, the hole is in the back—that is, the shit is supposed to disappear as soon as possible; finally, the Anglo-Saxon (English or American) lavatory presents a kind of synthesis, a mediation between these two opposed poles—the basin is full of water, so that the shit floats in it—visible, but not to be inspected. No wonder that Erica Jong, in the famous discussion of different European lavatories at the beginning of her half-forgotten *Fear of Flying*, mockingly claims: "German toilets are really the key to the horrors of the Third Reich. People who can build toilets like this are capable of anything." It is clear that none of these versions can be accounted for in purely utilitarian terms: a certain ideological perception of how the subject should relate to the unpleasant excrement which comes from within our body is clearly discernible—again, for the third time, "the truth is out there."

Hegel was among the first to interpret the geographical triad Germany-France-England as expressing three different existential attitudes: German reflective thoroughness,

French revolutionary hastiness, English moderate utilitarian pragmatism; in terms of political stance, this triad can be read as German conservatism, French revolutionary radicalism and English moderate liberalism; in terms of the predominance of one of the spheres of social life, it is German metaphysics and poetry versus French politics and English economy. The reference to lavatories enables us not only to discern the same triad in the most intimate domain of performing the excremental function, but also to generate the underlying mechanism of this triad in the three different attitudes towards excremental excess: ambiguous contemplative fascination; the hasty attempt to get rid of the unpleasant excess as fast as possible; the pragmatic approach to treat the excess as an ordinary object to be disposed of in an appropriate way. So it is easy for an academic to claim at a round table that we live in a post-ideological universe—the moment he visits the restroom after the heated discussion, he is again knee-deep in ideology. The ideological investment of such references to utility is attested by their *dialogical* character: the Anglo-Saxon lavatory acquires its meaning only through its differential relation to French and German lavatories. We have such a multitude of lavatory types because there is a traumatic excess which each of them tries to accommodate—according to Lacan, one of the features which distinguishes man from the animals is precisely that with humans the disposal of shit becomes a problem.

The same goes for the different ways in which one washes dishes: in Denmark, for example, a detailed set of features opposes the way dishes are washed to the way they do it in Sweden, and a close analysis soon reveals how this opposition is used to index the fundamental perception of Danish national identity, which is defined in opposition to that of Sweden.[1] And—to reach an even more intimate domain—do we not encounter the same semiotic triangle in the three main hairstyles of the female sex organ's public hair? Wildly grown, unkempt public hair indexes the hippie attitude of natural spontaneity; yuppies prefer the disciplinary procedure of a French garden (one shaves the hair on both sides close to the legs, so that all that remains is a narrow band in the middle with a clear-cut shave line); in the punk attitude, the vagina is wholly shaven and furnished with rings (usually attached to a perforated clitoris). Is this not yet another version of the Lévi-Straussian semiotic triangle of "raw" wild hair, well-kept "baked" hair and shaved "boiled" hair? One can see how even the most intimate attitude towards one's body is used to make an ideological statement.[2] So how does this material existence of ideology relate to our conscious convictions? Apropos of Molière's *Tartuffe*, Henri Bergson has emphasized how Tartuffe is funny not on account of his hypocrisy, but because he gets caught in his own mask of hypocrisy:

> He immersed himself so well into the role of a hypocrite that he played it, as it were, sincerely. This way and only this way he becomes funny. Without this purely material sincerity, without the attitude and speech which, through the long practice of hypocrisy, became for him a natural way to act, Tartuffe would be simply repulsive.[3]

Bergson's expression of "purely material sincerity" dovetails perfectly with the Althusserian notion of Ideological State Apparatuses—of the external ritual which materializes ideology: the subject who maintains his distance towards the ritual is unaware of the fact that the ritual already dominates him from within. As Pascal put it, if you do not believe, kneel down, act *as if* you believe, and belief will come by itself. This is also what Marxian "commodity fetishism" is about: in his explicit self-awareness, a capitalist is a commonsense nominalist, but the "purely material sincerity" of his deeds displays the "theological whimsies" of the commodity universe.[4] This "purely material sincerity" of the external ideological ritual, not the depth of the subject's inner convictions and desires, is the true *locus* of the fantasy which sustains an ideological edifice.

Notes

1. See Anders Linde-Laursen, "Small Differences—Large Issues," *South Atlantic Quarterly* 94:4 (Fall 1995), pp. 1123–44.

2. The most obvious case—which, for that very reason, I left out—is, of course, that of the ideological connotation of different positions in the sexual act; that is, of the implicit ideological statements we are making by doing "it" in a certain position.

3. Henri Bergson, *An Essay on Laughter*, London: Smith, 1937, p. 83.

4. For a more detailed elaboration of the paradoxes of fetishism, see Chapter 3 below [not reprinted in this volume].

2 Wild Theory, or—Did Somebody Say Žižek?

Mark Blythe

In France, the hole of the toilet bowl is in the back so that when you produce excrements they quickly disappear in the hole. The German toilets—the old type, now they are disappearing but you still find them—it's the opposite: the hole is in front so that when you produce excrement they are displayed in the back, they don't disappear in water. This is the German ritual, you know, you should every morning—sniff, inspect your shits for traces of illness. It's high hermeneutic—I think the original meaning of hermeneutic [laughter] for German is, maybe, this. Then in [the] Anglo Saxon world, United States you get, you know, the toilet bowl which is full of water so that shit floats in it before it disappears. And then I asked many of my friends, architects, interior designers, why these differences? They gave me two books on the structure of toilets. Nowhere did I get an explanation. And then a wild speculation came to my mind. Do you know that from the late eighteenth century, we had in Europe the idea of European Trinity? It's a racist idea, you are not in it, Italy's not in it; but the idea is that the three crucial European nations are France, Germany, England, each of them standing for a certain level of social life and for a certain politics. France is—politics, is the privileged domain and politically—left, revolution; England—middle of the road, liberal, moderate, and economy; Germany—metaphysics and poetry and conservative. And, my God, it did strike me—isn't this the key? In France: revolutionary approach, hole for the shit in the back, it should quickly be liquidated, like a kind of a guillotine [laugher]. Anglo Saxon—pragmatic, let it float, let's be rational. German—metaphysics and poetry: you observe it, you think and so on [laughter]. OK this may be madness but you see what's my point? It's that something like this had to be at work to account even for such a common thing like the structure of toilets.
—Slavoj Žižek (YouTube)

Critical theory is surprisingly popular on YouTube. If there is a house philosopher for the site, then it is currently Slavoj Žižek. At the time of writing, a search for "Žižek" produced around 113,000 results, with many of the posts viewed hundreds of thousands of times. The most popular Žižek videos include debates about what it means to be a revolutionary today; a short clip from the documentary *Zizek!* in which he discovers that the film crew are all vegetarians and tells them that they are degenerates who will turn into monkeys; a short talk on why the *Sound of Music* is racist; and any of several videos in which he analyses the ideology of toilets. His delivery in the many lectures can be hesitant and at times almost apologetic—"You can correct me if I'm wrong, I

Figure 2.1
Žižek on toilets.

simplify to the utmost." He fidgets constantly, tugging his T-shirt, pulling at his nose, and rubbing his beard, and repeats certain stock phrases—"ideology at its purest," "let me here be very precise," "but wait a minute!" And so on. And all the while he illustrates complex Lacanian and Hegelian theory with examples from film and popular culture. All of this is, perhaps strangely, very entertaining and popular.

The comments on the "Žižek on Toilets" (Žižek, 2010) video indicate more interest in Žižek's mannerisms than anything else. Many of the comments speculate about whether he is using cocaine; one speculates that he tweaked his nose to stop his "melted brains from leaking out." Others deride his fidgeting, sweating, sniffing, and general appearance; one claims the "dude" is the archetype of the "crusty, smelly, bearded college professor." Although the comments are humorous, there is very clear hostility, suspicion, and opposition here, expressed most vehemently as "and the Slovenian toilets turn excrement into academic talks." But many comments also express some kind of enjoyment, agreeing with the analysis, remarking on his brilliance, or simply stating that it is funny. One viewer noted "I don't know why I like listening to him so much." There is also total dismissal, for example "pretentious gibberish" or "he has nothing to say."

Regardless of content, the YouTube viewer comments are very often little more than indications of amusement—"LOL"—bewilderment—"WTF?"—or speculation about whether the person who posted the video is a homosexual. For this reason it is not enough to look for meaning solely, as ethnomethodologists might insist, with reference to members' own accounts. But the reactions to Žižek on YouTube which mix enjoyment, dismissal, and hostility is also a feature of many journalistic and academic accounts of his work.

Although Žižek has garnered plaudits like "intellectual rock star" and "the Elvis of Cultural theory," he himself notes that they are often used as a way to dismiss him. He is just a clown not to be taken too seriously, or conversely it is warned—don't be fooled by his clownish behavior he is really a dangerous ideologue. Alan Johnson, a journalist for the *Telegraph*, calls Žižek a "left fascist" and writes of "the madness of Slavoj Žižek" (Johnson, 2013). But it is not just right-wing British newspapers that consider him dangerous. An introduction to Žižek subtitled "A (Very) Critical Introduction" (Pound, 2008) is so full of criticism that Žižek himself quipped that with supporters like these, who needs enemies? Frederic Jameson, a critic who is largely sympathetic to Žižek, presents the following précis of his work in a book review:

> As every schoolchild knows by now, a new book by Žižek is supposed to include, in no special order, discussions of Hegel, Marx and Kant; various pre- and post-socialist anecdotes and reflections; notes on Kafka as well as on mass-cultural writers like Stephen King or Patricia Highsmith; references to opera (Wagner, Mozart); jokes from the Marx Brothers; outbursts of obscenity, scatological as well as sexual; interventions in the history of philosophy, from Spinoza and Kierkegaard to Kripke and Dennett; analyses of Hitchcock films and other Hollywood products; references to current events; disquisitions on obscure points of Lacanian doctrine; polemics with various contemporary theorists (Derrida, Deleuze); comparative theology; and, most recently, reports on cognitive philosophy and neuroscientific 'advances'. These are lined up in what Eisenstein liked to call 'a montage of attractions', a kind of theoretical variety show, in which a series of 'numbers' succeed each other and hold the audience in rapt fascination. It is a wonderful show; the only drawback is that at the end the reader is perplexed as to the ideas that have been presented, or at least as to the major ones to be retained. (Jameson, 2006)

His critics (and supporters) attack him for various and sometimes inconsistent or contradictory reasons. Critics on the right denounce him as politically correct while those on the left reproach him for sexism and (when he is critical of Israel) anti-Semitism. His philosophy is decried for being too eclectic, drawing on incompatible theories from Hegel, Marx, Freud, Foucault, Derrida, Badiou, and others; at the same time he is condemned for being too dogmatic. It is claimed that he is a slavish follower of Lacan, but also that he doesn't understand Lacan at all. He is derided for being an intellectual and also for sloppy scholarship. He is accused of being politically naïve and irrelevant; at the same time he is charged with being politically dangerous. He is then too worldly and too unworldly; too politically correct and not correct enough; too scholarly and not enough of a scholar. Žižek's favorite theologian, G. K. Chesterton, once pointed out that if the critics of Christianity were right, then it was all the more remarkable: "An historic institution, which never went right, is really quite as much of a miracle as an institution that cannot go wrong" (Chesterton, [1908] 2009). If the most popular living philosopher today is guilty of all of the charges made against him, he is perhaps all the more fascinating.

Despite journalistic and academic caricatures, Žižek remains one of the most consistently witty, provocative, and insightful cultural theorists of our time. Žižek is certainly sometimes bewildering, paradoxical, and challenging, but this is perhaps part of his appeal. It may even be thought of as an intellectual strategy—and not the deficit or weakness it might appear to be. Although his audiences and critics often complain that he repeats himself not only in YouTube talks but also in his books and articles, Žižek insists that examples should do more than one job. Žižek uses the example of French, German, and English toilet designs to illustrate Hegel's geographical interpretation of a European trinity of French radicalism, British empiricism, and German metaphysics, and also Claude Levi-Strauss' triangle of the smoked, roasted, and boiled food. For Levi-Strauss, boiling is the most "cultured" form of cooking because it requires a receptacle, whereas smoking and roasting can be accomplished by placing food on or near a fire. Žižek claims that the toilet that allows excrement to float in water allowing for inspection as well as the removal of odor represents this point in Strauss's triangle (Žižek, 2007b). There are then multiple interpretations to be made even of the most seemingly functional utilitarian designs.

In Žižek's writing and films his examples often serve a double function. The examples are explained by theory, but theory is also explained by the examples. For instance Žižek claims that the three levels of the house in *Psycho* are a precise illustration of Freud's id, ego, and superego: the basement where the dead mother's body is stored is the id, "the reservoir of illicit desire"; the ground floor where Bates meets his victim and appears to be normal is the ego, the self we present to the world; the second floor where Bates hears his taunting mother's voice is the superego yelling its incessant and impossible demands (Žižek, 2006). The film is explained by Freudian theory but Freudian theory is also explained by the film. Žižek's interpretations illuminate not only the examples, the films, the short stories, the jokes, but also the theoretical concepts he is most fond of: "the big other," "object small a," "the real." Not only do we look at Hitchcock anew but we look at Lacan differently also.

Just as there are no neutral artifacts, there are no neutral interpretations. Žižek's own "readings" are shot through with political and ideological purport. This is not to say that we must identify and root out such ideological bias in order to discover some objective and final meaning. The point is rather that all criticism and commentary is ideological and cannot be otherwise. Claims of objectivity and neutrality are themselves profoundly ideological. To claim that a cultural artefact is either one thing or another and that we must decide which, once and for all is, to use one of Žižek's favorite phrases, "ideology at its purest."

Research in HCI increasingly involves the design and evaluation of cultural artefacts. Evaluation has moved far away from lab-based observation of empirical measures such as speed and efficiency. Cultural commentators such as documentary makers and critics have been incorporated into evaluation work (Blythe, Robinson, and Frohlich, 2008; Gaver, 2007). There has also been direct engagement with literary and critical theory (e.g., Bardzell, 2011; Bertelsen and Pold, 2004; Blythe et al., 2006) But traditions of critical enquiry can still appear very alien or, to use another of Žižek's favorite phrases, "slightly crazy" to a traditional HCI audience.

This chapter takes a Žižekian perspective on the design and reception of the Prayer Companion, a device that displays news and current affairs to a group of cloistered nuns. It has long been argued that evaluation techniques measuring ease of use, ease of learning, and efficiency are not appropriate to designs that are not task-focused. The question of how the HCI community should evaluate new designs is still open. Often the strategy is simply to ask participants what they think; this can be useful but it can also result in inconclusive shoulder shrugging, where some people like a thing and others do not. The conference publication on the Prayer Companion (Gaver et al., 2010) makes it clear that the nuns appreciated the device very much. But there was more than one audience for the Prayer Companion. It received, for example, media attention where the response was very different. All of the media accounts were positive and it would be difficult to argue that the device is anything other than a successful design. But the reasons for its appeal are complex and perhaps a Žižekian (willfully eclectic) perspective can help articulate alternative readings.

Alternative Accounts of the Prayer Companion

The Prayer Companion takes RSS feeds from news and other online sources and displays them on a 3D device (Gaver et al., 2010; see figure 2.2). It displays rolling news feeds from RSS sites, including news sources such as online newspapers, Reuters, the Vatican, and We Feel Fine. In 2009 it was installed in a convent of Poor Clares nuns and was used until they moved out of this very large building and into a smaller residence. The nuns' reaction to the device was consistently enthusiastic and they reported that it helped inform their prayer life (Gaver et al., 2010). Although some of the nuns engaged with it more than others, they all agreed that it was beautiful and in keeping with their abbey. That the nuns and most commentators agreed the design was beautiful can be interpreted, like many aspects of the design, from quite different theoretical orientations.

One orientation might be to argue that beauty is something inherent in nature, as exemplified by the "golden ratio" or "the divine proportion." Like pi, this is a number known by its Greek name, phi, and has been known to mathematicians since Pythagoras

Figure 2.2
The Prayer Companion.

and Euclid. Less commonly, it is known as T (tau), the first letter of the Greek alphabet. The ratio is found in nature, in for example, the proportions present in the curves of the nautilus shell; it is also present in the human figure in the proportions of the head to the torso and the torso to the legs, as well as in the dimensions of the face. It is expressed in the Fibonacci series where each number is the sum of the previous two: 0, 1, 1, 2, 3, 5, 8, 13, 21, 34, 55, 89, and so on. The proportion has governed the dimensions of classical buildings such as the Parthenon, the paintings of Renaissance artists such as Leonardo da Vinci, as well as twentieth-century painters like Salvador Dali. It also structured the proportions of the Prayer Companion. Many of the dimensions were defined by the golden ratio, starting with the 350 mm height and dividing by 1.618 over and over (Boucher, personal communication, 2010). This account might be taken to suggest that the nuns found the device beautiful because it exhibited beautiful proportions which are found in nature and emulated in architecture and religious paintings such as the Dali *Crucified Christ*, a reproduction of which hung in the abbey.

The problem with accounts of beauty that posit precedent in nature is that we find many things beautiful that do not conform. The French sociologist and philosopher Pierre Bourdieu would claim that however hideous a painting might be, it could nevertheless be considered "beautiful" if it connected with the "habitus," of the buyer. In the 1960s Bourdieu undertook a large and detailed survey of French taste, finding strong correlations between individual tastes and social background. For Bourdieu our tastes are not dictated solely by individual responses to particular cultural artefacts, and neither are they predicated on universals (e.g., the divine proportion). Our reactions to those artefacts are deeply entwined with our social, occupational, and educational backgrounds, our "habitus"—our set of acquired dispositions. For Bourdieu there could be no response to a cultural artefact that was not shot through with social meanings and values (Bourdieu, 1987). Crucially for HCI, this means that aesthetic categories like "beauty" or "elegance" are not simply properties of artefacts but also the sociocultural contexts in which they are used.

Clearly the Prayer Companion was designed to fit in with the "habitus" of the nuns. Collections of altar artefacts held at the Victoria and Albert museum were consulted during the design process, and the colors of the device were chosen carefully to match those in the abbey (Gaver et al., 2010). When the nuns first saw the device, the mother abbess immediately recognized it as a tau cross, a T-shaped cross particularly associated with Saint Francis. Saint Francis told his friars that if they spread wide their arms, then their cassocks formed the shape of the cross, an emblem of their mission to bear witness to Christ (Chesterton, [1923] 2008). Perhaps, then, the design succeeded because it was so deeply embedded in the habitus of the convent. Or perhaps not.

The device can be interpreted with plausible consistency to support both theories: (1) that beauty is something found in nature and inherent in artifacts and (2) that beauty is a category that is agreed by communities of people. The positions are not mutually exclusive, but the point here is that a case can be made for either side.

The following sections consider a range of still wider interpretations of the significance of the device across different media sources.

Media Reception of the Prayer Companion

A journalist from the Catholic newspaper the *Tablet* was invited to the abbey to see the Prayer Companion and meet the extern nun and mother abbess. Following the publication of the full article in the *Tablet*, an edited version appeared in other newspapers such as the *Guardian*. This was picked up by newspapers like the *Daily Telegraph*, which sent its own journalists and photographers to the abbey. Following this coverage there were a spate of blog entries on the device.

There were a number of inaccuracies in the press coverage. The *Guardian* reported that it took "months to persuade the nuns to try the technology." Actually, the nuns agreed to try out new technologies after my very first visit. I spent the months prior to the development of the device conducting interviews with them. The *Telegraph* reported that the Prayer Companion was a "handheld device" with red letters that scrolled across a black screen; in fact it is a tabletop device and the text is yellow. Inaccuracies multiplied in blogs; for example, the design team at Goldsmiths were mischaracterized as art students. But the accuracy or otherwise of these reports are not of primary interest here. The focus rather is the way in which the newspapers and blogs frame the device.

Two Worlds Collide: The Vanishing Mediator

The Goldsmiths's press release was titled "Prayer Companion Designed at Goldsmiths Helps Keep Nuns' Prayers Pertinent." The newspaper and blog headlines were quite different. Again, the point here is not to offer a correct version but rather to point out the different ways that the work is framed. Clearly newspapers and other media must make a story, a narrative of one kind or another, which will appeal to their readers. The story of the Prayer Companion was most often framed by reporters and bloggers as one of two worlds colliding, as, for example, "Nuns Leading Medieval Lifestyle Log on to the 21st Century" (Pepinster, 2010) and "Secluded Nuns Help with iPrayer" (*Sydney Morning Herald*, 2010). The headlines almost uniformly contrasted the modernity of the technology with the age and traditions of the order (e.g., Fifield, 2010; *Yorkshire Post*, 2010). The blog headlines similarly emphasized the nuns' acceptance of technology and made comparisons to Twitter, such as "The Prayer Companion—Twitter for Nuns?" (*New Humanist*, 2010) and "Poor Clare, Refuge of Tweeters" (Alvarado, 2010).

The newspaper articles began with barriers: "behind six-meter walls" for the *Sydney Morning Herald* and "behind 20ft high walls" for the *Guardian*. The exoticism of the life was stressed—the nuns live in silence and eat strictly vegetarian meals (though neither claim is quite the case). Despite the architectural and historical remoteness (medieval lifestyle, six-meter-high walls) the technology got through. For the *Telegraph* the nuns have tried to "fend off" the technology until now. The *Guardian* quotes Sister Paul, saying "It is not there because we're desperate for news.... We are here for prayer, for channelling people's needs to God" (Pepinster, 2010), and in the *Telegraph*, "I often come here in a quiet moment and just stand for 10 minutes reading what comes up. We do occasionally listen to the radio to catch up with world events, but this is quite a thing of beauty" (*Telegraph*, 2010). The metaphors for the nuns' acceptance of the device are very physical: they "turn" to technology, they "embrace" the twenty-first century (e.g., Fifield, 2010; Ross Parry Agency, 2010). The repetition of the word "embrace" in these headlines is echoed in the images that accompany the articles (see figure 2.3).

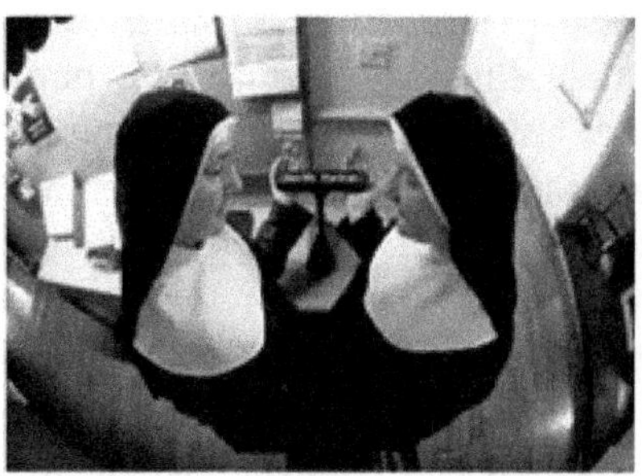

Figure 2.3
Press photography in the *York Press* and *Evening Post*.

The photographer for the *York Press* posed the extern nun almost literally embracing the device, mirrored the imaged, and added a fish-eye effect to suggest two nuns enfolding themselves around it (see figure 2.3). The *Yorkshire Post* photographed the nuns in a different location and then photoshopped an image of the device over their hands in such a way that it looked as if they were holding it (figure 2.3), which, ordinarily, they would not do.

Some of the quotes indicated that not only had the nuns accepted the technology, the designers had accepted the nuns. For example, Gaver is quoted as saying, "It's a very special place and I have come to feel very protective about the nuns." The arc of this story is the "fish out of water" (Booker, 2010)—the unexpected and unlikely intervention of designers into an old and almost lost world. Like most fish-out-of-water stories there is character development in the narrative. There is at first resistance, the physical barriers, the months of negotiation, initial suggestions for "a large screen" are rejected, a digital garden ornament "didn't meet with approval" (*Yorkshire Post*, 2010). The nuns at first are skeptical, flabbergasted, but then won over (*Telegraph*, 2010). The theme is the clash of tradition and technology, the narrative arc shows the new (coming) world meeting the old (inaccessible) world and the ways in which the two get along after all. There is also a secular / sacred juxtaposition best expressed in the *Yorkshire Post*: "The nuns admit their way of life and unshakable faith can seem at odds with a modern world littered with distractions and they understand the strength of their vocation is difficult for many to comprehend" (*Yorkshire Post*, 2010). The focus on the nuns in these stories serves as a link between the alien and the familiar world, perhaps as a "vanishing mediator."

The "vanishing mediator" is a concept developed by Frederic Jameson and later elaborated by Žižek. The vanishing mediator exists to mediate between two opposing ideas as a transition occurs between them. Žižek offers the Protestant work ethic as an example, because it mediated between medieval corporatism and capitalist individualism. The Protestant insistence that religion should be part of everyday life allows for the acquisition of capital without immediate consumption. The form of religious life stays the same but the content changes; once the transition is complete, the religious motivation behind the work ethic vanishes or fades away (Žižek, 1991, 184). With the Prayer Companion, perhaps it is the sensitivity to the values of the nuns that mediates between the technological, secular world and the lost, inaccessible world of faith and belief. There is a long tradition of user-centered design in HCI. It is well established within the community that to achieve successful designs it is essential to understand the needs of intended users and the context of their lives, whether they are air traffic controllers or factory workers. This doctrine also supports the notion that religious beliefs should be taken seriously when one is designing for nuns, but the idea of belief also vanishes after a certain point. The beliefs are taken seriously in the media accounts only to the extent that they are taken seriously by the nuns themselves. The media commentators are very keen to distance themselves from any personal belief, as the next section shows. The starting question is—do the nuns think the Prayer Companion helps them pray to God? If the question becomes—does it *actually* help them pray to God? (not, What do the nuns *think*?)—the mediator vanishes and rationalist materialism asserts itself.

The Subjects Supposed to Believe

Many of the comments in blogs and other media emphasized that praise for the device is independent of any belief. For example: "To those who don't believe: It can't hurt. To those who do believe: It can help a lot. No down sides here" (Cutlack, 2010). A similar sentiment was expressed by the radio broadcaster Bill Thompson: "I mean—I'm an atheist myself. I don't actually believe in prayers of intercession, but I do think that people should have technologies in their lives that serve them." This is an example of what Žižek, following Lacan, calls a fetishistic disavowal *"je sais bien, mais quand même"*—"I know very well but all the same." Žižek frequently employs the notion to illustrate seemingly paradoxical statements or absurd logic. For example, he points out that many of us, including environmental scientists, acknowledge the prospect of ecological catastrophe but fail to act: "I know very well (that global warming is a threat to humanity), but nonetheless … (I cannot really believe it)" (Žižek, 2007a). The structure of disavowed knowledge is also at play in some of the media responses to the device "I know very well (that there is no God so what the nuns think they are doing is delusional), but nonetheless (I see a benefit in making them a device to help them with their delusion)." A later exchange on the same radio show amplifies the secular value of design which accounts for the faith of others:

> And what I liked about it is, it's something of an antithesis of this whole so-called web 2.0 approach, of this two-way flow of information. Nobody's expecting the nuns necessarily to feedback into the process other than spiritually [*laughs*].
>
> I was going to say, they are feeding back. The nuns think they are feeding back because they're changing the way God looks at the people who are unhappy and I think that's a very effective feedback loop for them.
>
> All I mean is they're not just doing it—typing it back into an iPhone—in fact they're doing it on a higher plane, a higher level as it were.
>
> And the technology that's being offered to them makes that possible. (BBC, 2010)

But why this indulgence from the secular technologists? Why the structure of the fetishistic disavowal: "I know very well but all the same…." This indulgence is not always echoed by those that share the nuns' beliefs. There are some Christians who would denounce a life of cloistered enclosure as self-indulgent. If the nuns really want to make a difference they should be out in the world and helping. Why then the approval from the secular and atheistic technologists?

It might be argued that the approval stems from a concern with the well-being of the nuns—it makes them happy to believe their prayer life is meaningful so why not support this? But this argument would not always apply. For example, it may be that the residents of a care home somewhere in the UK were all vehemently racist. A fictional newsfeed might be supplied to them indicating that all immigrants had been repatriated and Britain was now for the British. It is unlikely that critics would adopt the position that they themselves were not racist but approved of the situation because it made the residents happy and took account of their values. There is something more going on in approval of the Prayer Companion than a nonpartisan indulgence of the nuns' beliefs or a simple reframing of the question away from spiritual issues toward merely technological ones.

In a lecture entitled "Why Only an Atheist Can Believe," Žižek (2007c) discusses the Tibetan prayer wheel, where Buddhists hang pieces of paper onto a wheel. Here he claims the person may be thinking about sex or anything else but the prayer wheel prays for them: "Objectively it prays, it prays for you." He makes an analogy to canned laughter in American sitcoms. This he considers an equally mysterious but powerful phenomenon. It is sometimes claimed that the laugh track encourages viewers to laugh, but this is rarely the case: viewers watch silently but feel relieved nonetheless—the show does their laughing for them. "It is as if you've laughed." The most intimate expression, laughter, can be transposed onto others. Žižek argues that this also applies to belief and faith. In families where parents lose their faith they disguise it from their parents or children who do believe. If they discover that these supposed innocents do not believe, it is much more traumatic than the loss of their own faith. Even if we don't believe, we have a need for an innocent "other" to believe for us.

This idea is illustrated very powerfully in the Don DeLillo novel *White Noise* when Jack, a character obsessed by his fear of death, seeks medical help from nuns running an infirmary. Seeing a picture of heaven on the wall he feels "sentimentally refreshed" and enquires about the Church's current teaching on Heaven. A nun replies by asking him if he thinks they are stupid. The dialogue between them is worth quoting at length:

"You don't believe in heaven? A nun?"

"If you don't why should I?"

"If you did, maybe I would."

"If I did, you would not have to."

"All the old muddles and quirks," I said. "Faith, religion, life everlasting. The great old human gullibilities. Are you saying you don't take them seriously? Your dedication is a pretense?"

"Our pretense is a dedication. Someone must appear to believe. Our lives are no less serious than if we professed real faith, real belief. As belief shrinks from the world, people find it more necessary than ever that *someone* believe. Wild eyed men in caves. Nuns in black. Monks who do not speak. We are left to believe. Fools, children. Those who have abandoned belief must still believe in us. They are sure that they are right not to believe but they know belief must not fade completely. Hell is when no one believes. There must always be believers. Fools, idiots, those who hear voices, those who speak in tongues. We are your lunatics. We surrender our lives to make non-belief possible. You are sure that you are right but you don't want everyone to think as you do. There is no truth without fools. We are your fools, your madwomen, rising at dawn to pray, lighting candles, asking statues for good health, long life." (DeLillo, 1986, 319)

This scene appears toward the end of the novel and follows Jack's complete moral and mental breakdown; he comes to the nun, as she says, "bleeding from the street," having just tried to kill a man in order to alleviate his own fear of death. When he shoots the victim he is overwhelmed by guilt and takes the man to the infirmary. Against this backdrop of madness and violence the reader, like Jack, is expecting the infirmary to be some sort of respite or sanctuary from the horror. The shock of the unbelieving nuns then is all the greater. The nun's speech perfectly exemplifies the theoretical construct of "the subject supposed to believe," but, as Žižek points out, theoretical structures are also often to be found in real life where they are sometimes even more shocking.

The late Christopher Hitchens was one of the great polemical writers of the twentieth century. His book *God Is Not Great* is uncompromisingly subtitled "How Religion Poisons Everything." But at the end of a documentary with Douglas Wilson, *Collision*, Hitchens relates this conversation with Richard Dawkins:

I said—"if I could convert everyone in the world—not convert, if I could convince, to be non believers—and I've really done brilliantly and there's only one left, one more, and then it'd be done and there would be no more religion in the world, no more deism, theism, I wouldn't do it." And Dawkins said, "What do you mean you wouldn't do it?!" I said, "I don't quite know why I wouldn't do it." And it's not just because there'd be nothing left to argue with. It's not just that, though it would be that. Somehow, if I could drive it out of the world, I wouldn't. And the incredulity with which he looked at me stays with me still, I've got to say.

The notion of the fetishistic disavowal—"I know very well but nevertheless"—may appear condescending. But it is not an accusation of hypocrisy. For Žižek the relationship between what we explicitly know and our disavowed beliefs is at work in our daily lives in very refined ways. They are perhaps at work in the positive reaction among atheists to the Prayer Companion.

Žižek draws on the Lacanian psychoanalytic theory of the "subject supposed to know." In psychoanalysis the subject supposed to know is the analyst: the patient speaks as if the analyst can see something that he or she cannot and so opens up a space for different kinds of reflection. There must be both distance and belief between the patient and the analyst or the system breaks down. Alain Miller characterized the 2008 financial meltdown as a crisis of the subject supposed to know; from a range of authority figures a voice emerges—for instance Alan Greenspan—as the one supposed to know; although the subject supposed to know is a fiction, belief in that fiction has real effects, and when that faith is shaken or the system tries to do without it altogether the results are equally real—when Greenspan expressed bewilderment at the financial crisis, stock values immediately fell (Žižek, 2009a, 29).

In the Prayer Companion articles and arguably in the design itself, the nuns are the subjects supposed to know. That their faith is "unshakeable" is not only a staple of these news stories but also, in a sense, of the design itself. What if one of the nuns were to go through an intense crisis of faith and lost all of her belief in the power of prayer? The Prayer Companion must be a companion if it is to make any sense at all. The nuns then are, if not the ones supposed to know, then at least the ones supposed to believe.

Competing Interpretations of the Prayer Companion

Some of the media interpretations were directly opposed to one another. The BBC's *Digital Planet* program framed the device as an ingenious solution to a problem:

> It's interesting to see how Bill Gaver and his team have taken on what is a very difficult problem and come up with such an imaginative solution.... It's clear that what the nuns needed was some way of knowing what's happening in the world without it getting in the way, to guide them and by doing it in this way, Gaver and his team have given them a perfect device for their mode of existence. Because it is, it's searching the net on their behalf.... And then it's presenting in a way which is unobtrusive but effective. (BBC, 2010)

The BBC radio presenter was keen to emphasize that the problems are not those of the designers but the nuns. But the blogger Laurance Alvarado rejects this formulation of the problem. After initially wondering about different ways of doing the job, he decides that there was no problem to be solved:

> Now, the practical, iPad loving side of me simply wonders why they didn't just set-up the device with TweetDeck rolling through, but the more I thought about it, the more I loved the stated mission of Goldsmiths and their desire to create an "interdisciplinary approach to interaction." Note, I didn't say an "approach to problem solving." Which brings us back to the Poor Clares. They certainly weren't knocking on the doors of academia or tech firms trying to figure out how to get more news; but, they are here, as Sister Paul says, "for channeling people's needs to God." Not necessarily problem solving, but rather interaction through prayer. Perhaps this is a lesson in taking the right approach—commit it to prayer first, then take the action. And, as technology changes, the need for prayer doesn't. (Alvarado, 2010)

The design can be understood then as a solution to a problem—how to keep prayer pertinent without intruding, or alternatively as a situation—not a problem to be solved at all but rather a context for interaction design.

Just as journalists and bloggers frame the device in different and sometimes opposing ways, so too academic interpretations are multiple. Gaver et al.'s (2010) CHI conference paper frames the device in terms of balancing openness and specificity, materiality and spirituality. But the device can also be framed in relation to other theories, like the psychoanalytical theory above but also in terms of more mainstream psychology. The psychologist Martin Seligman's PERMA theory of well-being can be usefully applied to the design. PERMA stands for: Positive affect (being able to enjoy the present and look forward to the future), Engagement (immersion in an activity, flow), Relationships (the last time you were happy you were probably not alone), Meaning (the sense of belonging to something larger than oneself, a faith tradition, the march toward socialism, the advancement of science), and Achievements (including the development of skill and mastery). Clearly the success of the Prayer Companion for the nuns can be considered in relation to the last two elements of the well-being framework. It supported them in their work in terms of the meaning they attached to their prayer life and possibly also in a sense of achievement. The Prayer Companion can then be framed as a device that supports well-being in terms of meaning, purpose, and accomplishment, though this theory did not inform the actual design process.

Bardzell and Bardzell (2013) offer a further interpretation of the device. They claim that it can be considered as a "critical design," a design that surfaces and critiques certain values and preconceptions. They claim that the work is critical because it addresses not only the nuns in the abbey but also an HCI audience. In this sense, they argue, the device offers an inherent critique in the expression of an alternative approaches to designing for older people. Although these interpretations may be directly at odds with those of the designers this is not to say that they are wrong. This is perhaps most clear in relation to the interpretation of other cultural artefacts such as novels, meaning cannot be confined to what an author or a designer intended.

Parallax Views

There are then a range of possible interpretations and critiques of the Prayer Companion. A particular critique will depend as much on the orientation of the critic as on the artefact. As previously noted, its perceived elegance can be explained with reference to opposing theories: beauty is a property of the device as expressed here in the golden ratio, or beauty is an agreed category in particular communities expressed here in the adherence to traditions of form and size in the shaping of alter artefacts and the connotation of the tau cross. The device can be positioned as an ingenious form of problem solving and its opposite: an instance where the problem solving paradigm is abandoned in favor of a response to a particular design situation. Further, it may be positioned as a design that critiques other approaches to HCI and a design to support well-being in terms of meaning and purpose. How is it then that an artefact can be taken to represent different and sometimes opposing perspectives?

For Žižek there is no contradiction in the act of interpreting an artefact in multiple and even opposing ways. Žižek frequently draws on the notion of the parallax view.

"Parallax" refers to the phenomena where objects appear differently depending on the perspective from which they are viewed. For example, a passenger on a train sees a tree in the distance standing in between a farm house and a hill. As the train passes the view changes and the tree now appears to be standing in front of the farm house. Žižek claims this is not merely a subjective effect that is independent of reality, and his definition of the parallax view is worth quoting in full:

> The standard definition of parallax is the apparent displacement of an object (the shift of its position against a background) caused by a change in observational position that provides a new line of sight. The philosophical twist to be added, of course, is that the observed difference is not simply "subjective," due to the fact that the same object which exists "out there" is seen from two different stances, or points of view. It is rather that, as Hegel would put it, subject and object are inherently "mediated," so that an "epistemological" shift in the subject's point of view always reflects an "ontological" shift in the object itself. Or—to put it in Lacanese—the subject's gaze is always-already inscribed in the perceived object itself, in the guise of its "blind spot," that which is "in the object more than the object itself," the point from which the object itself returns the gaze. "Sure, the picture is in my eye, but I am also in the picture." (Žižek, 2009b, 17)

Although we cannot see ourselves looking, our gaze is an integral part of every observation. Elsewhere Žižek illustrates the point with reference to the Möbius strip and the curved space which bends in on itself: "We do not have two perspectives, we have a perspective and what eludes it, and the other perspective fills in this void of what we could not see from the first perspective" (Žižek, 2009b, 29). The Prayer Companion then, when seen against a backdrop of an illustration of the number phi is not only epistemologically but ontologically different from the Prayer Companion viewed against a backdrop of the tau cross or a Franciscan friar stretching out his arms. It is not merely the case that one is true from a certain perspective but rather that both are true. The reality is not found in the agreement between the two perspectives. Rather, one perspective supplies that which the other cannot. This is not then some form of postmodern relativism where all perspectives are equally valid. It is rather an insistence on the reflexive inclusion of the observer in any observation. The act of observation contains a reflexive twist that includes the observer, albeit as a blind spot. The eye cannot see itself looking. There is no point external to ourselves and the world where we can step outside and make pure observations.

Psychology, Psychoanalysis, and Paradox

HCI has a long history of dialogue with psychology. It has been less inclined to engage with the kind of psychoanalytical theory that Žižek espouses. But psychology itself also has an uneasy relationship with its predecessor, psychoanalysis. The work of Freud and Jung is foundational to the discipline of psychology, but their writing is rarely studied outside of departments of literature. Although psychologists, like the rest of the population, still use terms that Freud and Jung coined—"the unconscious," "the ego," "repression" (Freud), "archetype," "extroverted," "introverted" (Jung)—much of their work has been largely dismissed. Most departments of psychology study cognition and focus on observable behavior. Psychoanalysis as therapy has also been largely discredited with celebrity patients like Woody Allen famously in analysis for forty years to no avail. Cognitive behavioral therapy (CBT) is much more successful in effecting "cures." and it is not interested at all in understanding a behavior but rather in changing it. Psychoanalysis, perhaps like Žižek himself, is clearly intellectually important and yet also desperately unscientific and disreputable. Why then the attraction? Žižek's claims are hyperbolic and wild. The YouTube commenter who didn't know why she liked listening to Žižek so much is probably not alone in finding it difficult to articulate his strange appeal. Žižek's language and traditions are radically different from those of mainstream cognitive psychology. It is perhaps the wildness of his writing that is attractive. His prose is rich in memorable stories, images, and phrases. Like Foucault he writes beautifully and at times poetically. This is very different from the measured and objectified tones of cognitive psychology. Psychology might be considered as prose and psychoanalysis as poetry. And yet there is some surprising overlap between the two approaches.

When Andrew Monk initiated his "computers and fun" series, cognitive psychology had very little to say about pleasure and enjoyment (Blythe et al., 2003). Almost the only measurable and testable concept that the field could offer was Csikszentmihalyi's "flow" (1975, 1991). Psychology had little to say about more mundane forms of enjoyment such as fun, diversion, and amusement, still less about satisfactions and gratifications such as altruism. For Seligman, meaning and purpose is often, but not necessarily, expressed through religion, and like many scientists he is interested in secular forms of spirituality. The Prayer Companion can be understood retrospectively in terms of his PERMA framework, but this framework applies less well to the approval of journalists and other media commentators; for this the wilder Žižekian tropes are helpful supplements.

Further, there may be interesting points of connection between positive psychology and psychoanalysis. For example, Seligman (2011) cites the work of John Gottman and others who have demonstrated empirically that our illusions about our loved ones are important to making our relationships work. One study, for example, asked participants to rate their partners for attractiveness, cleverness, sense of humor, and so on, then asked friends to do the same thing. In this test, if you rate your partner more highly than your partner's friends do, your relationship is probably secure. Seligman suggests that the illusions that our loved ones have about us are useful because we try to live up to them. Similarly Žižek exhorts us to enjoy our symptoms and use our illusions (Žižek, 1992, 2008). Illusions are important whether they are true or not.

Žižek is an emphatic atheist and yet he defends many aspects of the Christian tradition (Žižek, 2000, 2001). For Žižek, Christianity is not just some stupid delusion held by superstitious idiots, as atheists like Richard Dawkins and the late Christopher Hitchens proclaimed. Žižek sometimes refers to himself as a Christian atheist and delights in telling the story of Niels Bohr's horseshoe. Here a friend visiting the famous physicist notices a horseshoe above his door and incredulously asks him if he believes that it brings him good luck. Bohr replies, "No, I'm not an idiot, I am a scientist, of course I don't believe it, but I heard that it works even if you don't believe." Some things are true even when they are not true. This is not a difficult proposition for anyone who has studied literature. The truths contained in fables, novels, and poetry are not verifiable, falsifiable, or repeatable but they are truths nevertheless.

Žižek greatly admires G. K. Chesterton's introduction to the book of Job, in which he claims that Christianity is the only religion where God himself becomes an atheist. Chesterton introduces the text as a philosophical and historical riddle. It begins with the Devil betting God that Job loves him only because he is fortunate. After God accepts the bet and visits upon Job every conceivable misfortune, the suffering man is offered different explanations. One comforter tells him that he must deserve his misfortune for some sin he has committed that he is not aware of. Another tells him—no, it is not a punishment but it is part of some larger plan for the greater good. But God himself tells Job that his comforters are all wrong. It is at this point that Chesterton makes this radical interpretation:

> To startle man, God becomes for an instant a blasphemer; one might almost say that God becomes for an instant an atheist. He unrolls before Job a long panorama of created things, the horse, the eagle, the raven, the wild ass, the peacock, the ostrich, the crocodile. He so describes each of them that it sounds like a monster walking in the sun. The whole is a sort of psalm or rhapsody of the sense of wonder. The maker of all things is astonished at the things he has Himself made.... Instead of proving to Job that it is an explicable world, He insists that it is a much stranger world than Job ever thought it was." (Chesterton, [1916] 2008)

For Žižek, the God who somehow guarantees that everything will end well dies in Christianity. He claims that the lesson of the book of Job and Christ on the cross is that we are alone; the God of intervention dies on the cross and what remains is the community of believers, the holy spirit, us. He reproaches Dawkins and Hitchens for not being materialistic enough, for treating religion solely as an epistemology rather than considering its material effects. In this sense the fictions, the mythologies, the religions matter beyond any truth claim. The Holy Ghost, for Žižek, is the first psychoanalytical society, a revolutionary party "and so on."

Žižek's thinking is dialectical rather than paradoxical (Žižek and Milbank, 2009). In many respects the Prayer Companion is a paradoxical device. Atheist critics praise the design while at the same time believing that the activity it supports is delusional.

But the Prayer Companion is also a paradox for the nuns themselves. Throughout the interviews that took place over several years, the extern nun emphasized the paradox of prayer. Although it was vitally important to bring before God a suffering humanity, God already knew. The nuns might pray for Michael Jackson, mistakenly thinking he was the lead singer for the Rolling Stones, but this does not matter because God knows who he is even if they did not. Why then pray? The paradox of prayer is closely related in Catholic thought to the notion of grace. Grace is given through God's abundance, it is not a just or deserved reward, and yet it must be sought and striven for. Prayer then is at once unnecessary and necessary. Žižek is fond of paradox but usually resolves it into dialectic, and here he parts company with Chesterton who, like the nuns, insist on paradox and on doubting doubt itself.

The Uses of Theory

It is not enough for HCI to simply widen the scope of evaluation—the field must also engage in critical interpretation. Clearly an evaluation of the Prayer Companion which attempted to gauge whether it saved the nuns any time or not would seriously miss the point. But many approaches to evaluation now focus on users' values and take these as the base for considering whether a design is a success or not. Often these approaches explicitly state that the evaluators make no judgments about user values (e.g., Cockton, 2008). Such moves sidestep the central questions of evaluation. As G. K. Chesterton remarked of the modernist project itself, the position can be characterized thus: "Let us not decide what is good, but let it be considered good not to decide it" (Chesterton, [1905] 1928). It is not enough to confirm or deny whether users find a design usable or enjoyable, or even whether it supports their values or not. What is necessary more than ever is critical interpretation.

Alternative forms of evaluation, such as incorporating responses from cultural commentators like filmmakers and journalists, already allow researchers to take more nuanced approaches. And cultural commentary is no longer limited to specialists and professionals. Comment boards and social media are becoming increasingly important sources of data, though these present their own methodological and theoretical challenges. This chapter, and indeed this book, argues that there is a range of interpretive strategies that can be drawn on in critical theory. Critical theory is its own field, replete with methodological and analytical traditions; these are not repeatable scientific procedures but rather systems of analysis and schools of thought. Indeed, the term "theory" in cultural criticism has an entirely different meaning from the word in the natural sciences. "Theory" in cultural studies does not denote a model with either weak or strong predictive power; it is more often a form of analysis which is not in any sense testable or verifiable. Is this therefore an entirely useless form of theory?

Critics like Žižek are often accused of "reading too much into things." It is claimed that his critical interpretations "overtheorize" everything. But Žižekians would claim that the world is always already overtheorized. The challenge is to reveal and challenge these unspoken theoretical accounts. The process of revealing and challenging existing theory is perhaps best illustrated with Žižek's film criticism. Žižek is a startling critic of film who offers interpretations or "readings" of films that are often funny because they are so unexpected. And yet these readings are hard to forget and can often entirely change the way we see a film. For example, his reading of James Cameron's *Titanic* is one which would have occurred to few others. He claims that *Titanic* is not the romantic story of doomed love that it first appears to be, nor is it an allegory of the overreaching hubris of a technologically ambitions humanity pitting itself against nature. For Žižek, the director's superficial Hollywood Marxism (seen in the sympathetic portrayal of the working class having a good time while the vapid, cowardly upper classes carp at one another) is belied by a more reactionary myth. Žižek's interpretive strategy is taken from readings of the horror genre, where it is always crucial to ask, "What is the story of this film if the horror (the monster, the serial killer, or whatever) is subtracted from the story?" Žižek imagines *Titanic* without the iceberg. In this scenario the rich socialite Kate Winslet and her working-class lover arrive safely in New York; their affair continues for a few weeks and then fades away. The love affair is already doomed; the iceberg saves it. This is a stark enough reversal of the usual interpretation, but Žižek adds another twist, reminding us that when we first meet Rose she is about to commit suicide, unable to play her role in the vacuous and vicious world of the super rich. In order to restore her ego she takes some of the working-class vitality that DiCaprio brings; after he saves her he can literally disappear (Žižek, 2013). Is this the intended meaning of the film? Almost certainly not, and anyway, who cares? Is this what most people see? The answer to this question is the same as the previous one. Is this the secret, hidden true meaning of the film? The question is again beside the point. Žižek's interpretation, his wild theory, causes us to look at the film and our own interpretation of it in new ways. This kind of radical shift of perspective is essential to design and particularly important in designing for ageing populations.

The work on the Prayer Companion was funded and situated in the HCI literature as a response to global aging populations. Old age is a particularly good example of the ways in which unspoken theory dictates design practices. When designers consider older people they often end up designing for a set of disabilities. The focus on nuns defamiliarized "older people"; although most of the nuns were over eighty, they were primarily nuns, not older people. But theory can also cause this kind of shift in focus. And theory is not just something that obscure European critical theorists engage in; it is something which is also out there "in the wild." Anyone engaged in making policy or design interventions is engaged in theoretical work whether they know it or not. For example, when older people suffering from dementia are found "wandering," current design responses often focus on ways in which various kinds of monitors might alert caregivers to their movements, or how GPS might be deployed to keep track of them. But when older people are thought of as walking, not wandering, with walking as a basic human right, the design space must be framed in an entirely different way (Marshall and Allan, 2006). Rather than preventing "wandering," the aim shifts toward enabling walking. Design approaches in this space include "dementia dogs," which learn a particular route and guide the older person out and home again (Marshall and Walker, 2006). In this sense, both the activities of problem identification and design response are always already shot through with theoretical and interpretive work. Theory is not an early stage of design or some later adjunct. It is unavoidable and ongoing. So, as Žižek would say, let's do some theory.

References

Alvarado, Laurance. (2010) "Poor Clare, Refuge of Tweeters." *Crisis Magazine*, July 7. https://www.crisismagazine.com/2010/poor-clare-refuge-of-tweeters.

Bardzell, J. (2011) "Interaction Criticism: An Introduction to the Practice." *Interacting with Computers* 23 (6): 604–621.

Bardzell, J., and S. Bardzell. (2013) "What Is 'Critical' about Critical Design?" *Proceedings of the SIGCHI Conference on Human Factors in Computing Systems (Proc. of CHI'2013)*. New York: ACM, 3297–3306.

BBC. (2010) *Digital Planet*. EpisodeTranscript, "The Prayer Companion," aired August 10. http://www.bbc.co.uk/programmes/p008yptc.

Bertelsen, O., and S. Pold. (2004) "Criticism as an Approach to Interface Aesthetics." In *Proceedings of the Third Nordic Conference on Human-Computer Interaction (Proc. of NordiCHI '2004)*. New York: ACM, 23–32.

Blythe, M., J. Reid, P. Wright, and E. Geelhoed. (2006) "Interdisciplinary Criticism: Analysing the Experience of Riot! A Location-Sensitive Digital Narrative." *Behaviour and Information Technology* 25 (2): 127–139.

Blythe M., J. Robinson, and D. Frohlich. (2008) "Interaction Design and the Critics: What to Make of the 'Weegie.'" *Proc. of NordiCHI'2008*, 53–62.

Blythe, M. A., K. Overbeeke, A. F. Monk, and P. C. Wright, eds. (2003) *Funology: From Usability to Enjoyment*. Dordrecht: Kluwer Academic.

Booker, C. J. P. (2010) *The Seven Basic Plots: Why We Tell Stories*. London: Continuum.

Bourdieu, P. (1987) *Distinction: A Social Critique of the Judgement of Taste*. Cambridge, MA: Harvard University Press.

Chesterton, G. K. ([1905] 1928) *Heretics*. New York: John Lane. Citations refer to 1928 edition.

Chesterton, G. K. ([1908] 2009) *Orthodoxy*. Chicago: Moody. Citations refer to 2009 edition.

Chesterton, G. K. ([1916] 2008) "Introduction to the Book of Job." *G. K. Chesterton's Works on the Web*. Accessed September 16, 2017. http://www.cse.dmu.ac.uk/~mward/gkc/books/job.html. Citations refer to online edition.

Chesterton, G. K. ([1923] 2008) *St Francis of Assisi*. Mineola, NY: Dover. Citations refer to 2008 edition.

Csikszentmihalyi, M. (1975) *Beyond Boredom and Anxiety: The Experience of Play in Work and Games*. San Francisco: Jossey-Bass.

Csikszentmihalyi, M. (1991) *Flow: The Psychology of Optimal Experience*. New York: Harper Perennial.

Cutlack, G. (2010) "Selfless Nuns Pray to RSS Feed of Bad News." *Gizmodo*. https://gizmodo.com/5579643/selfless-nuns-pray-to-rss-feed-of-bad-news.

DeLillo, D. (1986) *White Noise*. London: Picador.

Fifield, N. (2010) "Nuns of Poor Clares in York Embrace Technology to Help Them Pray." *New York Press*, July 10. http://www.yorkpress.co.uk/news/8265632.Nuns_of_Poor_Clares_embrace_technology_to_help_them_pray/.

Gaver, W. (2007) "Cultural Commentators: Non-native Interpretations as Resources for Polyphonic Assessment." *International Journal of Human-Computer Studies* 65 (4): 292–305.

Gaver, W., M. Blythe, A. Boucher, N. Jarvis, J. Bowers, and P. Wright. (2010) "The Prayer Companion: Openness and Specificity, Materiality and Spirituality." *Proceedings of the 28th International Conference on Human Factors in Computing Systems (CHI'10)*, New York: AMC, 2055–2064.

Jameson, F. (2006) "First Impressions." Review of *The Parallax View*. *London Review of Books* 28 (17): 7–8. https://www.lrb.co.uk/v28/n17/fredric-jameson/first-impressions.

Johnson, A. (2012) "The Savage Madness of Slavoj Žižek." *Daily Telegraph*, November 27.

Johnson, A. (2013) "Is Slavoj Žižek a Left-Fascist?" *Daily Telegraph*, January 1.

New Humanist Magazine. (2010) "The Prayer Companion—Twitter for Nuns?" July 7. http://blog.newhumanist.org.uk/2010/07/prayer-companion-twitter-for-nuns.html.

Marshall, M., and K. Allan (eds.). (2006) *Dementia: Walking, Not Wandering—Fresh Approaches to Understanding and Practice*. London: Hawker.

Pepinster, C. (2010) "Nuns Leading Medieval Lifestyle Log on to the 21st Century." *Guardian*, July 4. https://www.theguardian.com/uk/2010/jul/04/goldie-electronic-device-for-nuns.

Pound, M. (2008) *Žižek: A (Very) Critical Introduction*. Grand Rapids, MI: William B. Eerdmans.

Schechner, R. (1988) *Performance Theory*. New York: Routledge.

Seligman, M. (2011) *Flourish: A New Understanding of Happiness and Well Being—and How to Achieve Them*. London: Nicholas Brealey.

Sydney Morning Herald. (2010) "Secluded Nuns Help with iPrayer." July 6.

Telegraph. (2010) "Nuns Embrace Technology to Help the Needy." June 13. http://www.telegraph.co.uk/news/7885224/Nuns-embrace-technology-to-help-the-needy.html.

Yorkshire Post. (2010) "News of the World beyond Convent Walls Comes to Nuns Logged on to Modern Life." July 8.

Žižek, S. (1992) *Enjoy Your Symptom! Jacques Lacan in Hollywood and Out.* London: Routledge.

Žižek, S. (2000) *The Fragile Absolute—or Why Is the Christian Legacy Worth Fighting For?* London: Verso.

Žižek, S. (2001) *On Belief.* New York: Routledge.

Žižek, S. (2006) *The Pervert's Guide to Cinema.* DVD. Directed by S. Fiennes. San Francisco: Microcinema International.

Žižek, S. (2007a) "Censorship Today: Violence, or Ecology as a New Opium for the Masses." Accessed September 30, 2012. Lacan.com.

Žižek, S. (2007b) "Slavoj Žižek on Toilets and Ideology." *YouTube* (video). Accessed May 14, 2013. http://www.youtube.com/watch?v=AwTJXHNP0bg.

Žižek, S. (2007c) "Why Only an Atheist Can Believe: Politics on the Edge of Fear and Trembling." *International Journal of Žižek Studies* 1. Accessed April 2013. Site no longer available.

Žižek, S. (2008) "Use Your Illusions." *London Review of Books,* November 14. https://www.lrb.co.uk/2008/11/14/slavoj-zizek/use-your-illusions.

Žižek, S. (2009a) *First as Tragedy Then as Farce.* London: Verso.

Žižek, S. (2009b) *The Parallax View.* Cambridge, MA: MIT Press.

Žižek, S. (2010) "Žižek on Toilets." (video) *YouTube.* Accessed May 14, 2013. http://www.youtube.com/watch?v=rzXPyCY7jbs.

Žižek, S. (2013) *The Pervert's Guide to Ideology.* DVD. Directed by S. Fiennes. New York: Zeitgeist Films.

Žižek, S., and J. Milbank. (2009) *The Monstrosity of Christ: Paradox or Dialectic?,* edited by Creston Davis. Cambridge, MA: MIT Press.

3 Rotation of Crops: A Venture in a Theory of Social Prudence (1843)

Søren Kierkegaard, edited and translated by Howard V. Hong and Edna H. Hong

Χρεμύλος.

189 .... ἐστὶ πάνιων πλησμονί.

190. ἔρωτος.

Καρίων.

ἄρτων.

Χρεμύλος.

μονσικῆς.

Καρίων.

τραγημάτων.

Χρεμύλος.

191. τιμῆξ.

Καρίων.

πλακούντων.

Χρεμύλος.

ἀνδραγαθίας.

Καρίων.

ἰσχάδων.

Χρεμύλος.

192. φιλοτιμίας.

Καρίων.

μάξης.

Χρεμύλος.

στρατηγίας.

Καρίων.

φακῆς.

See *Aristophanis Plutus*, v. 189 ff.[1]

CHREMYLOS.

...... an Allem bekommt man endlich Ueberdruss.
An Liebe [at last one has too much of everything. Of love],

KARION.

Semmel [rolls],

CHREMYLOS.

Musenkunst [the arts],

KARION.

und Zuckerwerk [and sweets].

CHREMYLOS.

An Ehre [Of honor],

KARION.

Kuchen [cakes],

CHREMYLOS.

Tapferkeit [bravery],

KARION.

und Feigenschnitt [and dried figs].

CHREMYLOS.

An Ruhm [Of fame],

KARION.

an Rührei [of scrambled eggs],

CHREMYLOS.

am Kommando [of authority],

KARION.

am Gemüs' [of vegetables].

See Aristophanes, *Plutos*, in Droysen's translation.[2]

People with experience maintain that proceeding from a basic principle is supposed to be very reasonable; I yield to them and proceed from the basic principle that all people are boring. Or is there anyone who would be boring enough to contradict me in this regard? This basic principle has to the highest degree the repelling force always required in the negative, which is actually the principle of motion.[3] It is not merely repelling but infinitely repulsive, and whoever has the basic principle behind him must necessarily have infinite momentum for making discoveries. If, then, my thesis is true, a person needs only to ponder how corrupting boredom is for people, tempering his reflections more or less according to his desire to diminish or increase his *impetus*, and if he wants to press the speed of the motion to the highest point, almost with danger to the locomotive, he needs only to say to himself: Boredom is the root of all evil. It is very curious that boredom, which itself has such a calm and sedate nature, can have such a capacity to initiate motion. The effect that boredom brings about is absolutely magical, but this effect is one not of attraction but of repulsion.

How corrupting boredom is, everyone recognizes also with regard to children. As long as children are having a good time, they are always good. This can be said in the strictest sense, for if they at times become unmanageable even while playing, it is really because they are beginning to be bored; boredom is already coming on, but in a different way. Therefore, when selecting a nursemaid, one always considers essentially not only that she is sober, trustworthy, and good-natured but also takes into esthetic consideration whether she knows how to entertain children. Even if she had all the other excellent virtues, one would not hesitate to give her the sack if she lacked this qualification. Here, indeed, the principle is clearly acknowledged, but things go on so curiously in the world, habit and boredom have gained the upper hand to such a degree, that justice is done to esthetics only in the conduct of the nursemaid. It would be quite impossible to prevail if one wanted to demand a divorce because one's wife is boring, or demand that a king be dethroned because he is boring to behold, or that a clergyman be exiled because he is boring to listen to, or that a cabinet minister be dismissed or a journalist be executed because he is frightfully boring.

Since boredom advances and boredom is the root of all evil, no wonder, then, that the world goes backwards, that evil spreads. This can be traced back to the very beginning of the world. The gods were bored; therefore they created human beings. Adam was bored because he was alone; therefore Eve was created.[4] Since that moment, boredom entered the world and grew in quantity in exact proportion to the growth of population. Adam was bored alone; then Adam and Eve were bored together; then Adam and Eve and Cain and Abel were bored *en famille*. After that, the population of the world increased and the nations were bored *en masse*. To amuse themselves, they hit upon the notion of building a tower so high that it would reach the sky.[5] This notion is just as boring as the tower was high and is a terrible demonstration of how boredom had gained the upper hand. Then they were dispersed around the world, just as people now travel abroad, but they continued to be bored. And what consequences this boredom had: humankind stood tall and fell far, first through Eve, then from the Babylonian tower.

On the other hand, what was it that delayed the fall of Rome? It was *panis* [bread] and *circenses* [games].[6] What is being done in our day? Is consideration being given to any means of amusement? On the contrary, our doom is being expedited. There is the idea of convening a consultative assembly. Can anything more boring be imagined, both for the honorable delegates as well as for one who will read and hear about them? The country's financial situation is to be improved by economizing. Can anything more boring be imagined?[7] Instead of increasing the debt, they want to pay it off in installments. From what I know about the political situation, it would be easy for

Denmark to borrow fifteen million rix-dollars. Why does no one think of this? Now and then we hear that someone is a genius and does not pay his debts; why should a nation not do the same, provided there is agreement? Borrow fifteen million; use it not to pay off our debts but for public entertainment. Let us celebrate the millennium with fun and games. Just as there currently are boxes everywhere for contributions of money, there should be bowls everywhere filled with money. Everything would be free: the theater would be free, prostitutes would be free, rides to Deer Park[8] would be free, funerals would be free, one's funeral eulogy would be free. I say "free," for if money is always available, everything is free in a way.

No one would be allowed to own any property. An exception should be made only for me. I shall set aside for myself one hundred rix-dollars a day deposited in a London bank, partly because I cannot manage on less, partly because I am the one who provided the idea, and finally because no one knows if I will not be able to think up a new idea when the fifteen million is exhausted.[9]

What would be the result of this prosperity? All the great would stream to Copenhagen: the greatest artists, actors, and dancers. Copenhagen would become another Athens. What would be the result? All the wealthy would settle in this city. Among others, the emperor of Persia and the king of England would undoubtedly also come here. Here is my second idea: kidnap the emperor. Someone may say that then there would be a revolution in Persia, a new emperor placed on the throne—it has frequently happened before—and the price of the old emperor would slump. In that case, my idea is that we should sell him to the Turks. They will undoubtedly know how make money out of him.

In addition, there is yet another circumstance that our politicians seem to ignore entirely. Denmark holds the balance of power in Europe. A more propitious position is inconceivable. This I know from my own experience. I once held the balance of power in a family. I could do as I wished. I never suffered, but the others always did.

O may my words penetrate your ears, you who are in high places to counsel and control, you king's men and men of the people, you wise and sensible citizens of all classes! You just watch out! Old Denmark is foundering—it is a matter of life and death; it is foundering on boredom, which is the most fatal of all. In olden days, whoever eulogized the deceased most handsomely became the king.[10] In our age, the king ought to be the one who delivers the best witticism and the crown prince the one who provides the occasion for the best witticism.

But how you do carry me away, beautiful stirring enthusiasm! Should I raise my voice this way in order to address my contemporaries, to initiate them into my wisdom? Not at all, for my wisdom is really not *zum Gebrauch für Jedermann* [for use by everyman], and it is always most prudent to be silent about rules of prudence. Therefore, I want no followers, but if someone were standing beside my deathbed and if I were sure it was all over for me, then in a fit of philanthropic delirium I might whisper my doctrine into his ear, not quite sure whether I would have done him a favor or not.[11] There is so much talk about man's being a social animal,[12] but basically he is a beast of prey, something that can be ascertained not only by looking at his teeth. Therefore, all this chatter about sociality and community is partly inherited hypocrisy and partly studied perfidy.

All human beings, then, are boring. The very word indicates the possibility of a classification. The word "boring" can designate just as well a person who bores others as someone who bores himself. Those who bore others are the plebians, the crowd, the endless train of humanity in general; those who bore themselves are the chosen ones, the nobility. How remarkable it is that those who do not bore themselves generally bore others; those, however, who bore themselves entertain others. Generally, those who do not bore themselves are busy in the world in one way or another, but for that very reason they are, of all people, the most boring of all, the most unbearable.[13] Certainly this class of animals is not the fruit of man's appetite and woman's desire. Like all lower classes of animals, it is distinguished by a high level of fecundity and propagates beyond belief. It is incomprehensible, too, that nature should need nine months to produce such creatures, which presumably could rather be produced by the score. The other class of human beings, the superior ones, are those who bore themselves. As noted above, they generally amuse others—at times in a certain external way the masses, in a deeper sense their co-initiates. The more thoroughly they bore themselves, the more potent the medium of diversion they offer others, also when the boredom reaches its maximum, since they either die of boredom (the passive category) or shoot themselves out of curiosity (the active category).

Idleness, we are accustomed to say, is the root of all evil. To prevent this evil, work is recommended. But it is just as easy to see from the dreaded occasion as from the recommended remedy that this whole view is of very plebian extraction. Idleness as such is by no means a root of evil; on the contrary, it is a truly divine life, if one is not bored. To be sure, idleness may be the occasion of losing one's property etc., but the noble nature does not fear such things but does indeed fear being bored. The Olympian gods were not bored; happy they lived in happy idleness. A female beauty who neither sews nor spins nor irons nor reads nor plays an instrument is happy in idleness, for she is not bored. Idleness, then, is so far from being the root of evil that it is rather the true good. Boredom is the root of evil; it is that which must be held off. Idleness is not the evil; indeed, it may be said that everyone who lacks a sense for it thereby shows that he has not raised himself to the human level. There is an indefatigable activity that shuts a person out of the world of spirit and places him in a class with the animals, which instinctively must always be in motion. There are people who have an extraordinary talent for transforming everything into a business operation, whose whole life is a business operation, who fall in love and are married, hear a joke, and admire a work of art with the same businesslike zeal with which they work at the office. The Latin proverb *otium est pulvinar diaboli* [idleness is the devil's pillow] is quite correct, but the devil does not find time to lay his head on this pillow if one is not bored. But since people believe that it is man's destiny to work, the antithesis idleness/work is correct. I assume that it is man's destiny to amuse himself, and therefore my antithesis is no less correct.

Boredom is the demonic pantheism. It becomes evil itself if one continues in it as such; as soon as it is annulled, however, it is the true pantheism. But it is annulled only by amusing oneself—*ergo*, one ought to amuse oneself. To say that it is annulled by working betrays a lack of clarity, for idleness can certainly be canceled by work, since this is its opposite, but boredom cannot, as is seen in the fact that the busiest workers of all, those whirring insects with their bustling buzzing, are the most boring of all, and if they are not bored, it is because they do not know what boredom is—but then the boredom is not annulled.

Boredom is partly an immediate genius, partly an acquired immediacy.[14] On the whole, the English nation is the model nation. The true genius of indolence is seldom encountered; it is not found in nature; it belongs to the world of spirit. At times one meets an English tourist who is an incarnation of this genius, a heavy, inert woodchuck whose total resource of language consists of a single monosyllable, an interjection[15] with which he indicates his highest admiration and his deepest indifference, for admiration and indifference have become undifferentiated in the unity of boredom. No nation other than the English produces such oddities of nature; every individual belonging to another nation will always be a bit more lively, not so altogether stillborn. The only analogy I know is the apostle of empty enthusiasm, who likewise travels through life on an interjection, people who make a profession of being enthusiastic everywhere, who are present everywhere and, no matter whether what happens is something significant or insignificant, shout: Oh! or Ah! because the difference between what is important and unimportant is undifferentiated in the emptiness of blind, clamorous enthusiasm.

The boredom that comes later[16] is usually a fruit of a misguided diversion. It seems doubtful that a remedy against boredom can give rise to boredom, but it can give rise to boredom only insofar as it is used incorrectly. A mistaken, generally eccentric diversion has boredom within itself, and thus it works its way up and manifests itself as immediacy. Just as a distinction is made between blind staggers and mad staggers in horses, but both kinds are called staggers, so also a distinction can be made between two kinds of boredom that nevertheless are both joined in the category of boredom.

Pantheism ordinarily implies the qualification of fullness; with boredom it is the reverse: it is built upon emptiness, but for this very reason it is a pantheistic qualification.[17] Boredom rests upon the nothing that interlaces existence [*Tilværelsen*]; its dizziness is infinite, like that which comes from looking down into a bottomless abyss. That the eccentric diversion is based upon boredom is seen also in the fact that the diversion sounds without resonance, simply because in nothing there is not even enough to make an echo possible.

Now, if boredom, as discussed above, is the root of all evil, what then is more natural than to seek to conquer it? But here, as everywhere, it is primarily a matter of calm deliberation, lest, demonically possessed by boredom in an attempt to escape it, one works one's way into it. All who are bored cry out for change. In this, I totally agree with them, except that it is a question of acting according to principle.

My deviation from popular opinion is adequately expressed by the phrase "rotation of crops." There might seem to be an ambiguity in this phrase, and if I were to find room in this phrase for a designation of the ordinary method I would have to say that rotation of crops consists in continually changing the soil. But the farmer does not use the expression in this way. For a moment, however, I will use it in this way to discuss the rotation of crops that depends upon the boundless infinity of change, its extensive dimension.

This rotation of crops is the vulgar, inartistic rotation and is based on an illusion.[18] One is weary of living in the country and moves to the city; one is weary of one's native land and goes abroad; one is *europamüde* [weary of Europe] and goes to America etc.; one indulges in the fanatical hope of an endless journey from star to star. Or there is another direction, but still extensive. One is weary of eating on porcelain and eats on silver; wearying of that, one eats on gold; one burns down half of Rome[19] in order to visualize the Trojan conflagration. This method cancels itself and is the spurious infinity.[20] What, after all, did Nero achieve? No, then the emperor Antoninus was wiser; he says: ἀναβιῶναί σοι ἔξεστιν ἴδε πάλιν τὰ πράγματα, ὡς ἑώρας· ἐν τούτῳ γὰρ τὸ ἀναβιῶναι (Βιβλιον Z., β.) [You can begin a new life. Only see things afresh as you used to see them. In this consists the new life (Book VII, 2)].[21]

The method I propose does not consist in changing the soil but, like proper crop rotation, consists in changing the method of cultivation and the kinds of crops. Here at once is the principle of limitation, the sole saving principle in the world. The more a person limits himself, the more resourceful he becomes. A solitary prisoner for life is extremely resourceful; to him a spider can be a source of great amusement. Think of our school days; we were at an age when there was no esthetic consideration in the choosing of our teachers, and therefore they were often very boring—how resourceful we were then![22] What fun we had catching a fly, keeping it prisoner under a nutshell, and watching it run around with it! What delight in cutting a hole in the desk, confining a fly in it, and peeking at it through a piece of paper! How entertaining it can be to listen to the monotonous dripping from the roof![23] What a meticulous observer one becomes, detecting every little sound or movement. Here is the extreme boundary of that principle that seeks relief not through extensity but through intensity.

The more resourceful one can be in changing the method of cultivation, the better, but every particular change still falls under the universal rule of the relation between *recollecting* and *forgetting*. It is in these two currents that all life moves, and therefore it is a matter of having them properly under one's control. Not until hope has been thrown overboard does one begin to live artistically; as long as a person hopes, he cannot limit himself. It is indeed beautiful to see a person put out to sea with the fair wind of hope; one may utilize the chance to let oneself be towed along, but one ought never have it on board one's craft, least of all as pilot, for it is an untrustworthy shipmaster. For this reason, too, hope was one of Prometheus's dubious gifts; instead of giving human beings the foreknowledge of the immortals, he gave them hope.[24]

To forget—this is the desire of all people, and when they encounter something unpleasant, they always say: If only I could forget! But to forget is an art that must be practiced in advance. To be able to forget always depends upon how one remembers, but how one remembers depends upon how one experiences actuality. The person who runs aground with the speed of hope will recollect in such a way that he will be unable to forget. Thus *nil admirari* [marvel at nothing][25] is the proper wisdom of life. No part of life ought to have so much meaning for a person that he cannot forget it any moment he wants to; on the other hand, every single part of life ought to have so much meaning for a person that he can remember it at any moment. The age that remembers best is also the most forgetful: namely, childhood. The more poetically one remembers, the more easily one forgets, for to remember poetically is actually only an expression for forgetting. When I remember poetically, my experience has already undergone the change of having lost everything painful. In order to be able to recollect in this way, one must be very much aware of how one lives, especially of how one enjoys. If one enjoys indiscriminately to the very end, if one continually takes the utmost that enjoyment can give, one will be unable either to recollect or to forget. That is, one has nothing else to recollect than a satiation that one only wishes to forget but that now torments with an involuntary recollection. Therefore, if a person notices that enjoyment or a part of life is carrying him away too forcefully, he stops for a moment and recollects. There is no better way to give a distaste for going on too long. From the beginning, one curbs the enjoyment and does not hoist full sail for any decision; one indulges with a certain mistrust. Only then is it possible to give the lie to the proverb that says that one cannot eat one's cake and have it, too. It is true that the police forbid carrying secret weapons, and yet there is no weapon as dangerous as the art of being able to recollect. It is a singular feeling when in the midst of enjoyment one looks at it in order to recollect it.

When an individual has perfected himself in the art of forgetting and the art of recollecting in this way, he is then able to play shuttlecock with all existence.

A person's resiliency can actually be measured by his power to forget. He who cannot forget will never amount to much. Whether or not a Lethe[26] wells up anywhere, I do not know, but this I do know—that this art can be developed. But it by no means consists in the traceless disappearance of the particular impression, because forgetfulness is not identical with the art of being able to forget. What little understanding people generally have of this art is readily seen, for they usually want to forget only the unpleasant, not the pleasant. This betrays a total one-sidedness. Indeed, forgetting is the right expression for the proper assimilation that reduces experience to a sounding board. The reason nature is so great is that it has forgotten that it was chaos, but this thought can appear at any time. Since forgetting is usually thought of in relation to the unpleasant, it is generally conceived of as a wild force that stifles. But forgetting, on the contrary, is a quiet pursuit, and it ought to be related to the pleasant just as much as to the unpleasant. Furthermore, the pleasant as a bygone, specifically as a bygone, has an intrinsic unpleasantness with which it can awaken a sense of loss; this unpleasantness is canceled by forgetting. The unpleasant has a sting—everyone admits that. This, too, is removed by forgetting. But if one behaves as many do who dabble in the art of forgetting, who brush the unpleasant away entirely, one will soon see what good that is. In an unguarded moment, it often surprises a person with the full force of the sudden. This is completely at odds with the well-ordered pattern in an intelligent head. No misfortune, no adversity is so unfriendly, so deaf that it cannot be flattered a little; even Cerberus[27] accepted honey cakes, and it is not only young maidens one beguiles. One talks around it and thereby deprives it of its sharpness and by no means wishes to forget it—but forgets it in order to recollect it. Indeed, even with reminiscences of such a kind that one would think eternal forgetfulness would be the only means against them, one allows oneself such cunning, and the fakery is successful for the adept. Forgetting is the scissors with which one snips away what cannot be used, but, please note, under the maximal supervision of recollection. In this way, forgetting and recollecting are identical, and the artistically achieved identity is the Archimedean point with which one lifts the whole world.[28] When we speak of writing something in the book of oblivion, we are indeed suggesting that it is forgotten and yet at the same time is preserved.[29]

The art of recollecting and forgetting will also prevent a person from foundering in any particular relationship in life—and assures him complete suspension.[30]

Guard, then, against *friendship*. How is *a friend* defined? A friend is not what philosophy calls the necessary other[31] but the superfluous third. What are the rituals of friendship? One drinks *dus*;[32] one opens an artery, mingles one's blood with the friend's. Just when this moment arrives is difficult to determine, but it proclaims itself in a mysterious way; one feels it and can no longer say *De* to the other. Once this feeling is present, it can never turn out that one has made a mistake such as Gert Westphaler made when he drank *dus* with the executioner.[33]—What are the sure signs of friendship? Antiquity answers: *idem velle, idem nolle, ea demum firma amicitia* [agreement in likes and dislikes, this and this only is what constitutes true friendship][34]—and is also extremely boring. What is the meaning of friendship? Mutual assistance with counsel and action. Two friends form a close alliance in order to be everything to each other, even though no human being can be anything for another human being except to be in his way.[35] Well, we can help each other with money, help each other into and out of our coats, be each other's humble servants, gather for a sincere New Year's congratulation, also for weddings, births, and funerals.[36]

But just because one stays clear of friendship, one will not for that reason live without contact with people. On the contrary, these relationships can take a deeper turn now and then, provided that one always—even though keeping the same pace for a time—has enough reserve speed to run away from them. It may be thought that such conduct leaves unpleasant recollections, that the unpleasantness consists in the diminishing of a relationship from having been something to being nothing. This, however, is a misunderstanding. The unpleasantness is indeed a piquant ingredient in the perverseness of life. Moreover, the same relationship can regain significance in another way. One should be careful never to run aground and to that end always to have forgetting in mind. The experienced farmer lets his land lie fallow now and then; the theory of social prudence recommends the same thing. Everything will surely come again but in a different way; what has once been taken into the rotation process remains there but is varied by the method of cultivation. Therefore, one quite consistently hopes to meet one's old friends and acquaintances in a better world but does not share the crowd's fear that they may have changed so much that one could not recognize them again. One fears, instead, that they may be altogether unchanged. It is unbelievable what even the most insignificant person can gain by such sensible cultivation.[37]

Never become involved in *marriage*. Married people pledge love for each other throughout eternity.[38] Well, now, that is easy enough but does not mean very much, for if one is finished with time one is probably finished with eternity. If, instead of saying "throughout eternity," the couple would say "until Easter, until next May Day," then what they say would make some sense, for then they would be saying something and also something they perhaps could carry out. What happens in marriage? First, one of them detects after a short time that something is wrong, and then the other one complains and screams: Faithlessness! Faithlessness! After a while, the other one comes to the same conclusion and a state of neutrality is inaugurated through a balancing of accounts by mutual faithlessness, to their common satisfaction and gratification. But it is too late now, anyway, because a divorce involves all kinds of huge problems.

Since marriage is like that, it is not strange that attempts are made in many ways to shore it up with moral props. If a man wants to be separated from his wife, the cry goes up: He is a mean fellow, a scoundrel, etc. How ridiculous, and what an indirect assault upon marriage! Either marriage has intrinsic reality [*Realitet*], and then he is adequately punished by losing it, or it has no reality, and then it is unreasonable to vilify him because he is wiser than others. If someone became weary of his money and threw it out the window, no one would say he is a mean fellow, for either money has reality, and then he is adequately punished by not having it anymore, or it has no reality, and then, of course, he is indeed wise.[39]

One must always guard against contracting a life relationship by which one can become many. That is why even friendship is dangerous, marriage even more so. They do say that marriage partners become one, but this is very obscure and mysterious talk. If an individual is many, he has lost his freedom and cannot order his riding boots when he wishes, cannot knock about according to whim. If he has a wife, it is difficult; if he has a wife and perhaps children, it is formidable; if he has a wife and children, it is impossible. Admittedly, there is the example of a gypsy woman who carried her husband on her back[40] throughout life, but for one thing this is a great rarity and, for another, it is very tiring in the long run—for the husband. Moreover, through marriage one falls into a very deadly continuity with custom, and custom is like the wind and weather, something completely indeterminable. To the best of my knowledge, it is the custom in Japan for the husbands also to be confined during childbirth. Perhaps the time is coming when Europe will import the customs of foreign lands.[41]

Even friendship is dangerous; marriage is still more dangerous, for the woman is and will be the man's ruination as soon as he contracts a continuing relationship with her. Take a young man, spirited as an Arabian horse; let him marry and he is lost. At the outset, the woman is proud, then she is weak, then she swoons, then he swoons, then the whole family swoons. A woman's love is only pretense and weakness.

Just because one does not become involved in marriage, one's life need not for that reason be devoid of the erotic. The erotic, too, ought to have infinity—but a poetic infinity that can just as well be limited to one hour as to a month. When two people fall in love with each other and sense that they are destined for each other, it is a question of having the courage to break it off, for by continuing there is only everything to lose, nothing to gain. It seems to be a paradox, and indeed it is, for the feelings, not for the understanding. In this domain it is primarily a matter of being able to use moods; if a person can do that, an inexhaustible variation of combinations can be achieved.

Never take any *official post.* If one does that, one becomes just a plain John Anyman, a tiny little cog in the machine of the body politic. The individual ceases to be himself the manager of the operation, and then theories can be of little help. One acquires a title, and implicit in that are all the consequences of sin and evil. The law under which one slaves is equally boring no matter whether advancement is swift or slow. A title can never be disposed of; it would take a criminal act for that, which would incur a public whipping, and even then one cannot be sure of not being pardoned by royal decree and acquiring the title again.

Even though one stays clear of official posts, one should nevertheless not be inactive but attach great importance to all the pursuits that are compatible with aimlessness; all kinds of unprofitable pursuits may be carried on. Yet in this regard one ought to develop not so much extensively as intensively and, although mature in years, demonstrate the validity of the old saying: It doesn't take much to amuse a child.

Just as one varies the soil somewhat, in accordance with the theory of social prudence (for if one were to live in relation to only one person, rotation of crops would turn out badly, as would be the case if a farmer had only one acre of land and therefore could never let it lie fallow, something that is extremely important), so also must one continually vary oneself, and this is the real secret. To that end, it is essential to have control over one's moods. To have them under control in the sense that one can produce them at will is an impossibility, but, prudence teaches us to utilize the moment. Just as an experienced sailor always scans the sea and detects a squall far in advance, so one should always detect a mood a little in advance. Before entering into a mood, one should know its effect on oneself and its probable effect on others. The first strokes are for the purpose of evoking pure tones and seeing what is inside a person; later come the intermediate tones. The more practice one has, the more one is convinced that there is often much in a person that was never imagined. When sentimental people, who as such are very boring, become peevish, they are often amusing.[42] Teasing in particular is an excellent means of exploration.

Arbitrariness is the whole secret. It is popularly believed that there is no art to being arbitrary, and yet it takes profound study to be arbitrary in such a way that a person does not himself run wild in it but himself has pleasure from it. One does not enjoy the immediate object but something else that one arbitrarily introduces. One sees the middle of a play; one reads the third section of a book. One thereby has enjoyment quite different from what the author so kindly intended. One enjoys something totally accidental; one considers the whole of existence [*Tilværelse*] from this standpoint; one lets its reality run aground on this. I shall give an example. There was a man whose chatter I was obliged to listen to because of the circumstances. On every occasion, he was ready with a little philosophical lecture that was extremely boring. On the verge of despair, I suddenly discovered that the man perspired exceptionally much when he spoke. This perspiration now absorbed my attention. I watched how the pearls of perspiration collected on his forehead, then united in a rivulet, slid down his nose, and ended in a quivering globule that remained suspended at the end of his nose. From that moment on, everything was changed; I could even have the delight of encouraging him to commence his philosophical instruction just in order to watch the perspiration on his brow and on his nose.

Baggesen[43] tells somewhere that a certain man is no doubt a very honest fellow but that he has one thing against him: nothing rhymes with his name. It is very advantageous to let the realities of life be undifferentiated in an arbitrary interest like that. Something accidental is made into the absolute and as such into an object of absolute admiration. This is especially effective when the feelings are in motion. For many people, this method is an excellent means of stimulation. Everything in life is regarded as a wager etc. The more consistently a person knows how to sustain his arbitrariness, the more amusing the combinations become. The degree of consistency always makes manifest whether a person is an artist or a bungler, for up to a point everyone does the same.[44] The eye with which one sees actuality must be changed continually. The Neoplatonists assumed that people who fell short of perfection on earth became after death more or less perfect animals according to their merits; those who, for example, had practiced social virtues on a minor scale (punctilious people) turned into social creatures—for example, bees. Such a view of life, which here in this world sees all human beings transformed into animals or plants (Plotinus also believed this—that some were changed into plants)[45] offers a rich multiplicity of variation. The artist Tischbein[46] has attempted to idealize every human being as an animal. His method has the defect that it is too serious and tries to discover an actual resemblance.

The accidental outside a person corresponds to the arbitrariness within him. Therefore he always ought to have his eyes open for the accidental, always ought to be *expeditus* [ready] if something should come up. The so-called social pleasures for which we prepare ourselves a week or a fortnight in advance are of little significance, whereas even the most insignificant thing can accidentally become a rich material for amusement. To go into detail here is not feasible—no theory can reach that far. Even the most elaborate theory is merely poverty compared with what genius in its ubiquity easily discovers.

Notes

1. See *Aristophanis Comoediae*, I–II, ed. Wilhelm (Guilielm) Dindorf (Leipzig: 1830; *ASKB 1051*), I, pp. 149–150; *Aristophanes*, I–III, tr. Benjamin Bickley Rogers (Loeb, New York: Putnam, 1924), III, pp. 379–381:

CHR. O yes, by Zeus, and many more than these. So that none ever has enough of thee. Of all things else a man may have too much,
Of love,
CA. Of loaves
CHR. Of literature
CA. Of Sweets
CHR. Of honour
CA Cheesecakes
CHR. Manliness
CA. Dried Figs
CHR. Ambition
CA. Barley-meal
CHR. Manliness
CA. Pea Soup

2. *Des Arisophanes Werke*, I–III, tr. Johann Gustav Droysen (Berlin: 1835–1838; *ASKB* 1052–1054), I, pp. 149–150. In the first line of the quoted text, the word *Andern* (else), which appears after *Allem* (everything) is omitted.

3. See, for example, G. W. F. Hegel, *Wissenschaft der Logik*, II, *Georg Wilhelm Friedrich Hegel's Werke. Vollständige Ausgabe*, I–XVIII, ed. Philipp Marheineke et al. (Berlin: 1832–1845; *ASKB* 549–565), V, p. 342; *Sämtliche Werke. Jubiläum-sausgabe* [*J.A.*], I–XXVI, ed. Hermann Glockner (Stuttgart: 1927–1940), V, p. 342; *Hegel's Science of Logic* (tr. Of *W. L.*, Lasson ed., 1923; Kierkegaard had 2 ed., 1833–1834), tr. A. V. Miller (New York: Humanities Press, 1969), p. 835:

Now the negativity just considered constitutes the *turning point* of the movement of the Notion. It is the *simple point of the negative relation* to self, the innermost source of all activity, of all animate and spiritual self-movement, the dialectical soul that everything true possesses and through which alone it is true; for on this subjectivity alone rests the sublating of the opposition between notion and reality, and the unity that is truth.

4. See Genesis 2:20–22.

5. See Genesis 11: 4–0.

6. The only desire of the Roman people, according to Juvenal, *Satires*, X, pp. 80–81; *Die Satiren des Decimus Junius Juvenalis*, tr. F. G. Fineisen (Berlin, Leipzig: 1777; *ASKB* 1250), p. 374; *Juvenal and Persius*, tr. G. G. Ramsay (Loeb, New York: Putnam, 1928), p. 199: "Breat and Games!"

7. With reference to the following sentence, see Supplement, pp. 546–47 (*Pap.* III B 122:1).

8. *Dyrehave*, a large wooded park north of Copenhagen.

9. With reference to the following two paragraphs, see Supplement, p. 547 (*Pap.* III B 122:2).

10. Told of King Hjarne, King Frode's successor, in Scandinavian legendary history. See *Den danske Krønike af Saxo Grammaticus*, tr. Anders Sørensen Vedel (Copenhage: 1851; *ASKB* 2008–2010), VI, 25, p. CXII.

11. See Plato, *Gorgias*, 511 e-512 b; *Platonis quae exstant opera*, I–XI, ed. Fridrich Ast (Leipzig: 1819–1832; *ASKB* 1144–1154), I, pp. 428–431; *Udvalgte Dialoger af Platon*, I–VIII, tr. Carl Johan Heise (Copenhage: 1830–1859; *ASKB* 1164–1167, 1169 [I–VIII]), III, p. 165; *The Collected Dialogues of Plato*, ed. Edith Hamilton and Huntington Cairns (Princeton: Princeton University Press, 1963), pp. 293–294 (Socrates speaking):

For I suppose he [the pilot of a ship] is capable of reflecting that it is uncertain which of his passengers he has benefited and which he has harmed by not suffering them to be drowned, knowing as he does that those he has landed are in no way better than when they embarked, either in body or in soul. He knows that if anyone afflicted in the body with serious and incurable diseases has escaped drowning the man is wretched for not having died and has received no benefit from him; he therefore reckons that if any man suffers many incurable diseases in the soul, which is so much more precious than the body, for such a man life is not worth while and it will be no benefit to him if he, the pilot, saves him from the sea or from the law court or from any other risk. For he knows it is not better for an evil man to live, for he must needs live ill.

See *Irony*, *KW* II (*SV* XIII 268).

12. See, for example, Aristotle, *Politics*, 1253 a; *Aristoteles graece*, ed. Immanuel Bekker, I–II (Berlin: 1831; *ASKB* 1-74-75), II, p. 1253; *The Works of Aristotle*, I–XII, ed. J. A. Smith and W. D. Ross (Oxford: Oxford University Press, 1908–1952), X:

Hence it is evident that the state is a creation of nature, and the man is by nature a political [social] animal. And he who by nature and not by mere accident is without a state, is either a bad man or above humanity; he is like the 'Tribeless, lawless, hearthless one,' whom Homer denounces—the natural outcast is forthwith a lover of war; he may be compared to an isolated piece at draughts.

Now, that man is more of a political animal than bees or any other gregarious animal is evident.

13. With reference to the following sentence, see Supplement, p. 547 (*Pap.* III B 122:3).

14. With reference to the following sentence, see Supplement, p. 547 (*Pap.* III B 122:4).

15. See Supplement, p. 512 (*Pap.* II A 382).

16. See "acquired immediacy" in the first sentence of the preceding paragraph.

17. With reference to the following sentence, see Supplement, p. 547 (*Pap.* III B 122:5).

18. With reference to the remainder of the paragraph, see Supplement, p. 548 (*Pap.* III B 122:6).

19. Nero (37–68), emperor of Rome, burned the city in the year 64. See Suetonius, "Nero," 38; *Caji Suetonii Tranquilli Tolv første Romerske Keiseres Levnetsbeskrivelse*, I–II, tr. Jacob Baden (Copenhagen: 1802–1803; *ASKB* 1281), II, pp. 102–104; *Suetonius*, I–II, tr. J. C. Rolfe (Loeb, New York: Macmillan, 1914), II, pp. 155–157.

20. See, for example, Hegel, *Wissenschaft der Logik*, I, *Werke*, III, pp. 147–148, 154; *J. A.*, IV, pp. 157–158, 164; *Science of Logic*, pp. 137, 142:

The infinite in its simple Notion can, in the first place, be regarded as a fresh definition of the absolute; as indeterminate self-relation it is posited as *being* and *becoming*. The forms of *determinate being* find no place in the series of those determinations which can be regarded as definitions of the absolute, for the individual forms of that sphere are immediately posited only as determinatenesses, as finite in general. The infinite, however, is held to be absolute without qualification for it is determined expressly as negation of the finite, and reference is thus expressly made to the limitedness in the infinite—limitedness of which being and becoming could perhaps be capable, even if not possessing or showing it—and the presence in the infinite of such limitedness is denied.

But even so, the infinite is not yet really free from limitation and finitude; the main point is to distinguish the genuine Notion of infinity from spurious infinity, the infinite of reason from the infinite of the understanding; yet the latter is the *finitized* infinite, and it will be found that in the very act of keeping the infinite pure and aloof from the finite, the infinite is only made finite.

What we have here is an abstract transcending of a limit, a transcending which remains incomplete because *it is not itself transcended.* Before us is the infinite; it is of course transcended, for a new limit is posited, but the result is rather only a return to the finite. This spurious infinity is in itself the same thing as the perennial ought; it is the negation of the finite it is true, but it cannot in truth free itself therefrom. The finite reappears *in the infinite itself* as its other, because it is only in its *connection* with its other, the finite, that the infinite is. The progress to infinity is, consequently, only the perpetual repetition of one and the same content, one of the same tedious *alternation* of this finite and infinite.

21. Marcus Aurelius, *Meditations*, VII, 2; *M. Antoninus Commentarii libri XII*, ed. J. M. Schultz (Leipzig: 1829, *ASKB* 1218), p. 179; *The Communings with Himself of Marcus Aurelius Antoninus*, tr. C. H. Haines (Loeb, Cambridge: Harvard University Press, 1953), p. 165.

22. See Supplement, p. 548 (*Pap. III* B 122:7).

23. With reference to the following sentence, see Supplement, p. 548 (*Pap.* III B 122:8).

24. See, for example, Aeschylus, *Prometheus Bound*, 250–254; *Aeschylos Werke*, tr. Johann Gustav Droysen (Berlin: 1842; *ASKB* 1046), pp. 419–420; *The Complete Greek Tragedies*, I–IV, ed. David Grene and Richmond Lattimore (Chicago: University of Chicago Press, 1958–1960), I, p. 320.

Prometheus
I caused mortals to cease foreseeing doom.
Chorus
What cure did you provide them with against the sickness?
Prometheus
I placed in them blind hopes.
Chorus
That was a great gift you gave to men.
Prometheus
Besides this, I gave them fire.

25. See Horace, *Epistles*, I, 6, 1; *Q. Horatii Flacci Opera* (Leipzig: 1828; *ASKB* 1248), p. 217; *Satires, Epistles and Ars Poetica*, tr. H. Rushton Fairclough (Loeb, New York: Putnam, 1929), p. 287. See also *Eighteen Upbuilding Discourses*, *KWV* (*SV* IV 113); *Fragments*, p. 80 and note 35, *KW* VII (*SV* IV 244).

26. In Greek mythology, the river of forgetfulness or oblivion in the underworld, to be crossed by those entering the realm of the dead.

27. In Greek mythology, the three-headed dog that guarded the gate of Hades. See example, Virgil, *Aeneid*, VI, 417–424; *Virgils AEneide*, I–II, tr. Johan Henrik Schønheyder (Copenhagen: 1812; not listed in *ASKB*), pp. 273–274; *Virgil*, I–II, tr. H. Rushton Fairclough (Loeb, New York: Putnam, 1920), I, p. 535.

28. See Plutarch, "Marcellus," 14, *Lives*; *Plutark's Levnetsbeskrivelser*, I–IV, tr. Stephan Tetens (Copenhagen: 1800–1811; *ASKB* 1197–1200), III, p. 272; *Plutarch's Lives*, I–XI, tr. Bernadotte Perrin (Loeb, New York: Putnam, 1914–1926), V, p. 473: "… Archimedes, who was a kinsman and friend of King Hiero, wrote to him that with any given force it was possible to move any given weight; and emboldened, as we are told, by the strength of his demonstration, he declared that, if there were another world, and he could go to it, he could move this." See Supplement, p. 549 (*Pap.* II B 122.10).

29. With reference to the following sentence, see Supplement, p. 549 (*Pap.* III B 122:11).

30. With reference to the following three sentences, see Supplement, p. 549 (*Pap.* III B 122:12, A 19).

31. See, for example, Hegel, *Wissenschaft der Logik*, I *Werke*, III, pp. 122–124; *J.A.*, IV, pp. 132–134; *Science of Logic*, pp. 117–118:

Something and other are, in the first place, both determinate beings or somethings.

Secondly, each is equally an other. It is immaterial which is first named and solely for that reason called *something*; (in Latin, when they both occur in a sentence, both are called *aliud*, or "the one, the other," *alius alium*; when there is reciprocity the expression *alter alterum* is analogous). If of two things we call one A, and the other B, then in the first instance B is determined as the other. But A is just as much the other of B. Both are, in the same way, *others* ….

Otherness thus appears as a determination alien to the determinate being thus characterized, or as the other *outside* theo one determinate being; partly because a determinate being is determined as other only through being *compared* by a Third, and partly because it is only determined as other on account of the other which is outside it. But is not an other on its own account. At the same time, as has been remarked, every determinate being, even for ordinary thinking, determines itself as an other, so that there is no determinate being which is determined only as such, which is not outside a determinate being and therefore is not itself an other.

Both are determined equally as something and as other, nd are thus the same, and there is so far no distinction between them. But this self-sameness of the determinations likewise arises only from external reflection, from the *comparing* of them; but the other as at first posited, although an other is relation to the something, is nevertheless also an other on its own account, apart from the something.

32. The ritual of pledging friendship (and the use of the familiar second person singular *du* instead of the formal plural *De*). The use of *De* has more or less disappeared in recent years.

33. A scene in Holberg, *Mester Gert Westphaler*, II, 4; *Den Danske Skue-Plads*, I–VII (Copenhagen: 1788; *ASKB* 1566=1567), I, no pagination.

34. See Sallust, *The War with Cataline*, XX; *C. Sallusti Crispi opera quae supersunt*, I–IV, ed. Friedrich Kritzius (Leipzig: 1828; *ASKB* 1269–1272), I, p. 98; *Sallusts Catilinariske Krig*, tr. Rasmus Møller (Copenhage: 1811; *ASKB* 1273), p. 25; *Sallust*, tr. J. C. Rolfe (Loeb, New York: Putnam, 1921), p. 35.

35. With reference to the following sentence, see Supplement, p. 549–550 (*Pap*. III B 122:13).

36. With reference to the following sentence, see Supplement, p. 550 (*Pap*. III B 122:14).

37. With reference to the following sentence, see Supplement, p. 550 (*Pap*. III B 122:15).

38. With reference to the following two sentences, see Supplement, p. 550 (*Pap*. III A 124).

39. With reference to the following paragraph, see Supplement, pp. 550–551 (*Pap*. III B 122:16).

40. See Steen Steensen Blicher, *"Kjeltringliv," Samlede Noveller*, I–V (Copenhagen: 1833–1836; *ASKB* 1521–1523), I, pp. 240–242.

41. With reference to the following paragraph, see Supplement, p. 551 (*Pap*. III B 122:17).

42. With reference to the following sentence, see Supplement, p. 552 (*Pap*. III B 122:18).

43. See Jens Immanual Baggesen, *"Theateradministratoriade," Jens Baggesens danske Voerker*, I–XII (Copenhage: 1827–1832; *ASKB* 1509–1520), I, p. 421. The name was Hassing, for which Baggesen found no suitable rhyme except "two-thirds of Washington—which is as good as nothing" (ed. tr.).

44. With reference to the following sentence, see Supplement, p. 552 (*Pap*. III B 122:19).

45. See Plotinus, *Enneads*, III, 4, 2; *Plotinus*, I–VI, tr. A. H. Armstrong (Loeb, Cambridge: Harvard University Press, 1966–1967), III, pp. 145–147. Cf. Plato, *Phaedo*, 81 c-82 b; Heise, I, pp. 49–52; *Collected Dialogues*, pp. 64–65.

46. Johann Heinrich Wilhelm Tischbein (1751–1829), a friend of Goethe's. See Johann Wolfgang v. Goethe, *"An Denselben," Goethe's Werke. Vollständige Ausgabe letzter Hand*, I–LX (Stuttgart, Tübingen: 1828–1842; *ASKB* 1641–1668 [I–LV]), II, p. 168.

4 Against Boredom: The Demonic Pantheism in Design

Olav W. Bertelsen

The reception of Kierkegaard has been a battlefield in Danish academia. The theology camp has claimed that he is mainly to be understood as a theological thinker and his entire work should be read as building up to a new Christianity, taking the individual and his relation to God as central and seeing clerical institutions as harmful. More or less in parallel, humanistic literary readings of Kierkegaard as an existentialist and aesthetic theorist have been widespread. Kierkegaard has even been read as a "postmodern" thinker. I do not wish to enter into a dispute, and I do not claim this commentary to be a sufficient reading of Kierkegaard's work. I will, however, take the risk and do a reading of one specific text in isolation and apply this reading to human-computer interaction and interaction design. My main personal motivation for this reading is the influence the text has had on my own understanding of the design and use of information technology over the last twenty years, and how well the text reflects the current forefront of human-computer interaction, under labels such as critical design.

The works of Kierkegaard have been read as comprising three interdependent stages, the aesthetic being the fun and erotic, the ethic being boring and responsible. Together they seem to be sublated into the religious stage. This view is supported by the fact that large parts of the works are written pseudonymously.

The text "On Crop Rotation" is part of the two-volume work called *Either/Or* written by Kierkegaard. This work is, like many other works by the author, written pseudonymously. The two volumes are presented as lost writings that the publisher (the first pseudonym we meet here and maybe the closest to Kierkegaard's own voice) has found in a piece of furniture. These papers seem to be written by two distinct authors who the publisher calls "A," the esthete, and "B," the ethicist. The first volume of *Either/Or* is composed of texts, including "On Crop Rotation," written by "A" but ordered by the publisher; the second volume is composed of three letters to "A" written by "B." The publisher speculates that "A" and "B" could be the same person. Thus, Kierkegaard invites the reader to read the two volumes as a continuous argument.

In this commentary, I make an isolated reading of "On Crop Rotation." I do so knowing that I take the piece out of its context, but I think this is justifiable, for two reasons. First, because it is a clear unit of text with a beginning and an end. Second, and maybe more importantly, I argue that the way Kierkegaard stages the assembly of texts in the publisher's introduction indicates that the whole argument of the collection is present in each of the fragments.

The main argument by "A" in the text is to introduce crop rotation as a metaphorical approach to social life.

The basis for the argument is that boredom is a daemonic pantheism. This means that boredom is an evil in everything that all people try to avoid. Therefore, boredom is the basic driving force for all human development, from the book of Genesis onward. According to "A," historically, this has led to an eternal restlessness and a quest for new fields of endeavor. But since boredom is everywhere, there is no point in going to a new place to escape it.

Instead "A" proposes that the agricultural principle of crop rotation should be applied to social life. Crop rotation is an agricultural practice that ensures the soil is not worn out by shifting between different crops. Crop rotation can be understood as opposed to the practice of slash and burn, where the soil is just left when it has been depleted. By rotating crops skillfully, a farmer can produce on the same soil infinitely. "A" transfers this agricultural principle to the domain of social life.

The Text and Its Main Points

"A," the pseudonymous esthete, opens the text by ironically adopting the idea, apparently widespread in philosophy (possibly an ironic reference to the system philosophy of Hegel), of having a basic principle in understanding and governing life. Thus, Kierkegaard encourages the reader to maintain a critical perspective while reading the ambiguous text. The principle "A" puts forward in the first sentence of the text is that all people are boring. This tenet describes a constitutive negative force of movement, because boredom is everywhere and at the same time is what all people try to avoid. Boredom is a negative force in everything that drives development—a demonic pantheism.[1] Thereby, the destination of development is unknown. We only know where we are coming from and why we are leaving it. It is typical for Kierkegaard's writings, and his existentialist position in particular, that important decisions in life, as well as the relation to God, are seen as a personal matter that cannot be reduced to institutional principles. This kind of negatively defined utopianism is, according to Bardzell (2013), found in a number of feminist thinkers.

"A" hints at the lack of wisdom in society by pointing to the area of childcare as the only one where the corruptive power of boredom is acknowledged. Then, the text proceeds to place boredom in historical perspective beginning with Adam. Since Adam the reaction to boredom has been expansion, more people, more places, a taller tower in Babel, more languages, and so on. But boredom just drives a development that produces even more boredom. The history of boredom is concluded by a critique of the emerging democratic assemblies for making boredom even worse. As an alternative, "A" suggests that the nation should not pay its debts but rather borrow a lot of money and give it to the people to have a good time. This idea implies a criticism of that aspect of protestant work ethics that Weber (1920) has described as a precondition for the emerging of capitalism. Wealth and fun can be had without hard work, without endless accumulation. At the same time, this approach is described in a deliberately unrealistic manner, emphasized by the fact that "A" would indeed like to secure himself in the case of a national collapse.

Now, the boringness of human beings is further analyzed. People are divided into two classes: those who are boring others and those who are boring themselves. The first are the common people, the endless crowd. The second group, those who bore themselves, are the noble ones who, the more they are bored, will amuse others. The distinction between being a boring part of the mass, or deteriorating in noble boredom with yourself while contributing in an original manner, may be the ethical distinction for Kierkegaard and "A." This leads to a comparison of boredom to idleness, where "A" argues that idleness is an important part of being human. You become human by differentiating yourself from the indefatigable activity seen in animals, and in some people. You become human through the nobility of inactivity. It is through boredom that idleness becomes problematic. Thus, work is not the antidote. On the contrary, work remains boring and creates more boredom. In the same way, stupid excitement over anything, regardless of quality, is just empty noise. All in all, "A" points out that the common strategies used to avoid boredom through activity just lead to even more and worse boredom.

Crop rotation is then introduced as a principle that can be metaphorically transferred from agriculture to social life. In agriculture, crop rotation means that instead of merely moving to new soil when the old has been depleted, you stay on the same soil, always growing something new so as not to deplete the soil. In the social parallel, proposed by "A," crop rotation comes to mean that you avoid the eternal escape from boredom into new territories, instead staying in the same place while renewing your perspective, the ways you relate, your actions, and so forth. Thus, the core of crop rotation is the principle of limitation. The more you limit yourself the more inventive you get. Instead of leading to eternal flight, "crop rotation" helps you transform boredom into inventiveness and development.

The self-imposed limitation, which is at the core of the principle of this version of crop rotation, is the source of inventiveness and continuous renewal, as it grows in the tension between recollecting, forgetting, and hoping. "A" introduces the idea of poetic recollection, which is the active re-creation of experience. In any moment of life, in particular in moments of significance, what is to be remembered is actively constructed for future enjoyment; it is an enjoyment in itself to engage in this shaping of how the event will be remembered in the future. Poetic recollection is a creative process in which forgetting is an important aspect, not mainly to avoid the unpleasant but more importantly to forget the pleasant, to not become oversaturated with pleasure by administering it carefully through continuous construction of the future memory of the moment. In this argument, the memory of the pleasant and the hope for something defined are seen as hindrances to embracing and co-creating the contingent circumstances of the actual situation. It is the ability to forget that gives a person elasticity, and it is by forgetting that what is useless is left behind.

Poetic recollection is the basis for social crop rotation in the sense that actual events, as a form of soil, are understood as the substrate in which the right variation of recollection-crops is grown. Through poetic recollection, experience is transformed to a resonating basis. "It is a singular feeling when in the midst of enjoyment one looks at it in order to recollect it" (Kierkergaard, [1859] 2009, 293–293). The process of poetic recollection as described by "A" is similar to the six ways of making sense of an experience proposed by McCarthy and Wright (2004), which they based on a reading of Mikhail Bakhtin and John Dewey, and with ideas of perception as being tied to the historical development of action (e.g., Wartofsky, 1973). However, in the "A" concepts, it is in the process of poetic recollection that the direction of future action is constituted.

By using social crop rotation, and poetic recollection, the individual will not be limited by conventions and institutionalized thinking. In particular, "A" explains how the societal institutions of friendship and marriage should be avoided. These institutions are by nature boring and predictable, "A" says, and thereby they become superficial. "A" does not want to avoid social and intimate relations but insists on the deep quality of such relations. By not taking relations for granted, the individual will find they are continuously renewed in the social rotation of crops, and relations will last only as long as they are meaningful and vital. When the erotic relation is at its best, "A" explains, it is time to bring it to an end to avoid turning it into boring habit. Likewise any honorable title or post in society should be avoided, because it will be too hard to get rid of, even if you don't serve it well anymore.

Social crop rotation relies on self-variation, the ability to shift attention. "A" explains that it is a matter of seizing the moment, sensing the mood or atmosphere of the situation. By catching the unintended in a situation, an individual may find a boring lecture wonderfully entertaining. When the eye is constantly changing, arbitrariness can be achieved, corresponding to the accidental in the external world. Contingency is not only a condition of modern life but also an aspect that can be nurtured and used actively in order to overcome the boring expansiveness of bourgeois society and mindset (as also indicated in the more explicit political criticism of the emerging democratic institutions in the text). Practically, this means that a social event that has been planned for weeks can be far less exciting and fruitful than just catching the moment of some random meeting. The social setup is no guarantee.

The key messages of the text are these: first, the introduction of *negativity*, in the shape of boredom, as a driving force for human development; second, that it is a *subjective* responsibility to openly interpret and recollect and not be limited by societal norms; and third, a kind of social *sustainability* in the form of social crop rotation that transforms economic and external expansion into personal or inner expansion. In the view of this sustainability, the renewal of perspective is key.

Crop Rotation in Design and Use of IT

The description of this practical approach to crop rotation seems like a description of modern hypertext. "One sees the middle of a play; one reads the third section of a book" (Kierkergaard, [1859] 2009, 299). However, the whole idea of hypertext since Bush (1945) seems to have been about the consolidation of rational objective knowledge by enabling the recombination of well-established and valid knowledge atoms. Similarly, the kind of hypertext that can be found in hyper fiction and computer games seems mostly to conform to Laurel's (1986) ideas of interactive mimesis, which is actually a closed system based on Aristotle's poetics. Specifically, the central aspect in crop rotation is this: "One thereby has enjoyment quite different from what the author so kindly intended" (Kierkergaard, [1859] 2009, 299). In this way, "A" envisions the experience of the purposeless hypertext of today's internet. Thus, it is the arbitrariness that is the key to crop rotation. "Crop rotation" is not by the work itself, but in the way the work is appropriated.

In "The Point of View for My Work as an Author," Kierkegaard (1859) discusses the relationship between his aesthetic and religious writings. "The religious is present from the very beginning. Conversely, the esthetic is still in the last moment" (30). Thus, we may expect to find the complexity of the whole work in the piece on crop rotation. Look, for example, at the way Kierkegaard lets "A" exaggerate in suggesting that Denmark, instead of paying its debts, should take out a huge loan from the Bank of London to have national fun, and then, to make sure that the reader starts thinking in the direction of the ethical or religious counterpoint, lets "A" aim to secure his own economic well-being by saving money in a foreign bank. The extreme aesthetic playfulness encourages the reader to make up his own mind and sense the antithesis, and he is encouraged to think in terms of balance, or even sublation (*aufhebung*) of the dichotomy between the aesthetic and the religious. In this way, the ambiguity of the very text points to the subject as the instance where truth can be found; not as individualistic subjectivism, but subjectivism that unfolds in relation to the universal (for Kierkegaard the universal is called God).

"A" concludes by indicating that theory is too complicated and that the principle of crop rotation can be better discovered in practice. Kierkegaard returns to this criticism of philosophy and theory several times. In the section "Diapsalmata" of *Either/Or*, one of the aphorisms reads, "What philosophers say about actuality [*virkeligheden*] is often just as disappointing as it is when one reads a sign in a secondhand shop: Pressing Done Here. If a person were to bring his clothes to be pressed, he would be duped, for the sign is just for sale" (35). Philosophy only provides insights and directions in an indirect manner. How you should live your life is something you have to discover in the actuality of life, but philosophy may have something to say that may make sense in the course of life.

This approach to the relationship between theory and actuality ties into what has been emphasized by a lot of different researchers in human-computer interaction with highly different starting points. Thus, Card et al. (1980), in their cognitivist approach to an engineering psychology, point out that "scientific models do not eliminate the design problem [the problem human-computer interaction is to deal with in actuality], but only help the designer control the different aspects" (409). Subsequent generations have, for example with backgrounds in activity theory (Bødker, 1989) or semiotics (Andersen, 1990), pointed out that use qualities of computer artifacts are constituted in the context of use. The meaning of this is that, at the time of design, we cannot know what the product will become in use. With Kierkegaard, and the voice of "A," we may even say that since the connection is so indirect, the purpose of theory may merely be to condition the designer to develop the right sensitivity to the actual world.

The keystroke-level model (Card, Moran, and Newell, 1980), which is a theoretical model for predicting how long time-generalized users will need to perform standardized tasks with a proposed user-interface, may provide sensitivity to, and predictions of, quantitative aspects of interaction, but the model will seriously mislead designers if taken as a general perspective on the use situation. It is up to the subjective judgment of the designer to decide when the model is useful and for what. On the other extreme, the framework of technology-as-experience put forward by McCarthy and Wright (2004) is lacking clear instructions for application in analysis or design. For several years, I have had computer science students read the book and apply the framework in actual analysis of technology in use. While the students have been severely frustrated with the book in general and its lack of practical advice in particular, its influence has shone through their analysis in a very clear manner. In this later case, the theory can, in a much more deliberate way, condition the designer (actually the students) to develop a sensitivity to important aspects of the domain.

As a perspective on IT use and design, "On Crop Rotation" specifically draws attention to contingency and appropriation. Interface designers have long aimed to remove all unnecessary output: low-level status messages that users do not understand, superfluous information in email headers, and so on have been exterminated to reduce the cognitive load on users. But, when "A" focuses on the pearl of perspiration suspended at the end of a boring speaker's nose, it would not help if the only thing left of the speaker is the words coming out of his mouth. Similarly, when we sit in an office and have lost inspiration, looking through the window over the satellite dishes on the rooftops we may see an image reminding us of a jazz band and suddenly realize that participatory design should be understood as a kind of collective improvisation (similar reflections can be found in Bertelsen, 1998, 67). The principle of crop rotation may encourage us to hesitate to produce overspecialized use situations but leave room for the unforeseen. In this way the idea of crop rotation could more banally be related to Keil-Slawik's (1993) idea of reducing enforced sequentiality at the level of the user interfaces, as well as to the general criticism of workflow-based systems in computer supported cooperative work (CSCW) (e.g., Bowers, Button, and Sharrock, 1995).

Similar ideas have been formulated as an aesthetic alternative to "traditional" human-computer interaction by Sengers and Gaver (2006), who advocate for openness of interpretation as an ongoing process in and after design; for example, by blocking expected interpretations and by suggesting evaluation methods that provide no conclusive answers. The latter echoes Card, Moran, and Newell's (1980, 409) statement that scientific models cannot solve the design problem.

While Kierkegaard, through the voice of "A," emphasizes the responsibility of the individual, information technologies increase the possibility of closing interpretation while at the same time providing the means to create opportunities for more open interpretation. The discussion of openness in the interface represents the classical tension between Laurel's seminal formulation of experience-oriented interaction as interactive mimesis (Laurel, 1986) and the Dynabook (Kay and Goldberg, 1977). Laurel proposes carefully planned interactive experience where users can act "freely" as long as they do what their role would do. On the other hand, the Dynabook provided an interactive substrate where users could implement whatever they liked, independently of the designer. In Kierkegaard's terminology, interactive mimesis is a strategy for oversaturated pleasure through catharsis, effectively inhibiting poetic recollection, on top of being closed in the designed space of experience. The Dynabook, however, would, in its complete openness to continuous redesign, encourage users to continuously develop new features, instead of rotating the crops on the existing soil.

The profound design challenge is to provide contingency and to support appropriation through poetic recollection. Crop rotation can inspire interaction design to avoid interfaces, artifacts, and use situations that are staged in closed, inflexible manners, instead striving for the openly interpretable. And we remind ourselves that if we do rigid design we will just have the pearls of perspiration on our noses laughed at.

In understanding, and designing for, the use of IT-based artifacts, understanding the processes of appropriation is central. Appropriation is the process in which users turn artifacts into their own by (re)understanding them in relevant ways and integrating them meaningfully into their practice. Appropriation is basically unforeseeable and often leads to unanticipated or unintended use (Robinson, 1993). One typical manifestation of appropriation is the development of workarounds in which the user finds ways to do important things that the artifact did not support immediately (Gasser, 1986). The process of poetic recollection, discussed by "A," is a key aspect of appropriation. The process of selectively remembering and forgetting, and subsequently turning the constructed memory into a resonant body for future action, conveys a quite precise and condensed image of the process of appropriation.

At the level of physical form, Jones (1988) speaks out against the overspecialization of modern industrial products that makes them useless for purposes other than what they are designed for, such as when a clothes peg is made of plastic so thin that it is useless as a wedge. Overspecialization inhibits crop rotation because it is impossible to see anything other than the designers intended function in it. Thus, boredom will be massive and unavoidable.

In a literal sense, crop rotation, as an agricultural principle, has its obvious relevance in relation to design. The innovative energy of a project group may soon be depleted if it keeps staging the same design activities. Over years, a team, or an entire discipline, may grow with an approach or method, then stagnate and need to explore another way of working. Cultural probes (Gaver and Dunne, 1999) is a good example of a design activity, originally building on situationism and surrealism, that was an attempt to break conventional thinking in design but that has evolved into nothing but a boring habit in mainstream interaction design because the activity has been canonized as obligatory.

Participatory design in general could be another example. However, the way users are systematically involved in design in classical participatory design (e.g., Greenbaum and Kyng, 1991) is indeed reminiscent of an agricultural approach—the innovative powers are bred through a careful combination of resources and crop rotation. This could polemically be opposed to the hunter-and-gatherer approach of user-driven innovation (von Hippel, 2005) in which innovative ideas are not bred but merely collected and exploited. Kierkegaard's principle of crop rotation as the opposite of expansive consumption and depletion of resources could inspire further development of design activities that renew the dynamics of the project group, so that, for example, users in the group continue to have a renewed user perspective despite having been involved with IT design for a longer period. This perspective on crop rotation could be taken further, to include new interpretations of hardware and technological configurations. Thus, crop rotation inspires sustainability in two distinct ways: at the level of social relations and interpretation of situations, and in relation to physical resources.

"A" problematizes the institutions of friendship and marriage. Thus, he inspires a reconsideration of how design projects are organized and he encourages a view where no fixed model for project organization should be taken for granted, not as a repetition of the lazy motto that "systems developers do not follow methods" but rather as a statement of the individual system developer's responsibility to use methods in a sane way and always question whether they still work. In relation to the involvement of users and other stakeholders, or any other participant in design for that matter, there should not be any fixed formula for involvement. As long as users contribute with interesting energy involvement should be maintained, but not any longer. Users in participatory design may turn into boring designers rather than interesting users. At that point it will be time to part with them. Also, a project organization could degenerate into a forum for the execution of organizational power, thereby transforming participatory design into design by committee. In the perspective of "A," this latter situation would be the worst possible, resembling the new parliamentary structures "A" despised so much. The important point in involving users may then be to stay authentic in the engagement with people. However, the very idea of crop rotation may also inspire us to look in new ways at what we have, for example by assigning completely new roles to participants. It is exactly in enabling new views on situations that critical design (Dunne, 1999) may make a practical, valuable contribution.

The importance of "the moment" is pervasive in design. "A" states that social gatherings with formalized rituals may be of little value compared to an accidental meeting. We may complete that argument by reference to Suchmans's (1987) idea of situated actions complementing the planned course of events. Thus, the advice would be to plan design activities that are sufficiently open to enable accidental engagement, and to avoid overly institutionalized activities. Thus, if you are organizing ideation workshops, you may want to plan the day in quite some detail but at the same time prepare yourself, as a workshop leader, to be sensitive to the moments where unpredicted innovation happens, and then be ready to rearrange your plan. This kind of sensitivity to the moment has been approached in some of the classics on the human-computer interaction and interaction design "reading lists." Thus, Schön (1983) talks about how the professional designer reflects in action, and the Dreyfus brothers (1986) talk about levels of expertise, where people at the highest level independent from procedures are able to act intuitively in unknown situations. Where these authors appeal to somewhat mysterious concepts of the humane, Kierkegaard, through the voice of "A," focuses on the evolving mood of a situations and the arbitrariness of action.

It is an open question how Kierkegaard would think about the principle of poetic recollection applied to the collective act of doing design. With the risk of violating the concept, I propose that it makes sense to talk about processes of collective poetic recollection, and that they are central to design. As pointed out elsewhere (Bertelsen 2000, 18), "Users and designers achieve new understanding of the existing world and rooted in this they conceive a new world that transcends the old." This generative process is collective and can be seen as based on poetic recollection. But, in contrast to individual poetic recollection that takes place in the course of experience, the collective process is staged to include the relevant competencies and stakeholders. Through the revisionary process of collective poetic recollection, a new resonating basis is established on which innovative solutions can be built.

Concluding Remarks

For me, personally, reading *Either/Or* as a young man was harmful. In particular, the parts concerned with seduction and love, such as "Seducer's Diary," severely impacted my ability to lead a sound love life. I became convinced that erotic relations were to be temporary and that the breakup was a necessary element to plan for in the act of seduction. To think of love, and particularly seduction, as aesthetics had the effect that I became unable to engage in the banal, unreflected flow of love. Instead, I became an observer, forgetting to be in the moment, not realizing how norms and institutions could be the context for the development of sustainable love. However, Kierkegaard is not to blame for my miseries as a young man. Rather, I must blame myself for not understanding the ambiguity and intended absurdity of the aesthetic position of "A."

To sum up what interaction design and human-computer interaction can learn from "On Crop Rotation," the following points are central.

Most importantly, our discipline should try to be less boring. We should avoid boring design activities and try not to bore people with boring activity through technology that will turn them into even more boring persons.

"A" advocates for the necessity of subjectivity, through a number of illustrative examples, and shows that social norms should not be followed without question. In relation to the design and use of IT, open interpretation and ambiguity are possible approaches to subjective judgment in use and design. Furthermore, the critique of societal institutions such as friendship and marriage as becoming inauthentic can be transferred to a critique of rigid, overly formalized methods, or methods in general in the field of design. Thus, IT research could be encouraged to develop methods that support sensitivity and subjective judgment, such by following Bardzell's (2011) advice and lean toward literary criticism and poetics, instead of psychological models and scientific experimentation.

The essence of crop rotation is social or aesthetic sustainability—not to starve your soil but do something new, not all the time, but when it is appropriate. By renewing relations and roles and by reinterpreting, recombining technologies and artifacts, it is possible to overcome boredom and depletion without constantly introducing new technologies, new domains, new participants, and so on. Traditional approaches to participatory design imply this kind of sustainability with respect to participants. It is through poetic recollection that the subject sets future direction, and that richness is created through self-imposed limitation.

There is an obvious danger in reading the aesthetic texts by Kierkegaard, and that is the complete and well-argued disrespect for societal norms and institutions. The aesthetic playfulness is seductive and may well lead to an inclination to leap into the happy nihilism of random design. When "A" reflects on how one should stay authentic to oneself in relation to other people, it is easy to draw the conclusion that interaction design should not care about commitment, that we should not worry so much about what happens with our users, our informants, and so forth, when we terminate our design projects or our design or action based research activities. But this would be a misreading, most importantly because it is the inflexibility of institutionalized relations that "A" argues against rather than decency, care, and respect in interaction with other people.

Like the young man at the dawn of his sexual career, interaction design and human-computer interaction should read all layers of the text and appreciate the intended ambiguities in order to benefit from the reading.

Note

1. The ordinary meaning of "pantheism" is that God is in everything. The demonic pantheism "A" suggests means that the evil—more specifically boredom—is in everything and that people are fleeing from it.

References

Andersen, P. B. (1990) *A Theory of Computer Semiotics: Semiotic Approaches to Construction and Assessment of Computer Systems.* New York: Cambridge University Press.

Bardzell, J. (2011) "Interaction Criticism: An Introduction to the Practice." *Interacting with Computers* 23 (6): 604–621.

Bardzell, S. (2013) "Utopian Design? Feminism and Critical Design." Presentation at the Barnard Center for Research on Women, 38th Annual Scholar and Feminist Conference. Barnard College, Columbia University, March 1–2.

Bertelsen, O. W. (1998) *Elements of a Theory of Design Artefacts: A Contribution to Critical Systems Development Research.* PhD Thesis. Department of Information Studies, Aarhus University, DAIMI PB 531.

Bertelsen, O. W. (2000) "Design Artefacts: Towards a Design-oriented Epistemology." *Scandinavian Journal of Information Systems* 12 (1): 15–27.

Bowers, J., G. Button, and W. Sharrock. (1995) "Workflow from Within and Without: Technology and Cooperative Work on the Print Industry Shopfloor." *Proceedings of the 4th European Conference on Computer-Supported Cooperative Work (ECSCW'95).* Dordrecht: Kluwer Academic, 51–66.

Bødker, S. (1989) "A Human Activity Approach to User Interfaces." *Human Computer Interaction* 4 (3): 171–195.

Bødker, S. (2006) "When Second Wave HCI Meets Third Wave Challenges." *Proceedings of the 4th Nordic Conference on Human-Computer Interaction: Changing Roles (NordiCHI'06).* New York: AMC, 1–8.

Bush, W. (1945) "As We May Think." *The Atlantic*, July. https://www.theatlantic.com/magazine/archive/1945/07/as-we-may-think/303881/.

Card, S. K., T. P. Moran, and A. Newell. (1980) "The Keystroke-Level Model for User Performance Time with Interactive Systems." *Communications of the ACM* 23 (7): 396–410.

Dreyfus, H. L., and S. E. Dreyfus. (1986) *Mind over Machine: The Power of Human Intuition and Expertise in the Era of the Computer*. New York: Free Press.

Dunne, A. (1999) *Hertzian Tales: Electronic Products, Aesthetic Experience and Critical Design*. London: Royal College of Art.

Gasser, L. (1986) "The Integration of Computing and Routine Work." *ACM Transactions on Information System* 4 (3): 205–225.

Gaver, W., and A. Dunne. (1999) "Projected Realities: Conceptual Design for Cultural Effect." *Proceedings of the SIGCHI Conference on Human Factors in Computing Systems (CHI'99)*. New York: ACM, 600–607.

Greenbaum, J., and M. Kyng. (1991) *Design at Work: Cooperative Design of Computer Systems*. Hillsdale, NJ: Lawrence Erlbaum.

Jones, J. C. (1988) "Softecnica." In *Design after Modernism: Beyond the Object*, edited by J. Thackara, 216–226. London: Thames and Hudson.

Kay, A., and A. Goldberg. (1977) "Personal Dynamic Media." *IEEE Computer*, 10 (3): 31–42.

Keil-Slawik, R. (1993) "Telepresence with Time Delays: Designing the User Interface of a Telemedicine Workstation under Real-Life Constraints." *Proceedings of IMAGINA'93*, Monte Carlo, 6–21. https://pdfs.semanticscholar.org/69e4/960bba35608504b139a4529cfcedd2c93888.pdf.

Kierkegaard, S. Aa. ([1843] 1901) *Samlede Værker* [Collected works], vol. 3, *Enten-Eller*. Copenhagen: Gyldendal.

Kierkegaard, S. ([1859] 2009) *Kierkegaard's Writing*, vol. 22, *The Point of View*, edited and translated by Howard V. Hong and Edna H. Hong. Princeton, NJ: Princeton University Press.

Laurel, B. K. (1986) "Interface as Mimesis." In *User Centered Systems Design: New Perspectives on Human-Computer Interaction*, edited by D. A. Norman and S. W. Draper, 67–86. Hillside, NJ: Erlbaum.

Robinson, M. (1993) "Design for Unanticipated Use." *Proceedings of the Third European Conference on Computer-Supported Cooperative Work (ECSCW'93)*, Norwell, MA: Kluwer Academic, 187–202.

Schön, D. A. (1983) *The Reflective Practitioner: How Professionals Think in Action*. New York: Basic Books.

Sengers, P., and B. Gaver. (2006) "Staying Open to Interpretation: Engaging Multiple Meanings in Design and Evaluation." *Proceedings of the 6th Conference on Designing Interactive Systems (DIS'06)*. New York: ACM, 99–108.

Suchmans, L. A. (1987) *Plans and Situated Actions: The Problem of Human-Machine Communication.* Cambridge: Cambridge University Press.

von Hippel, E. (2005) *Democratizing Innovation.* Cambridge, MA: MIT Press.

Wartofsky, M. W. (1973) "Perception, Representation, and the Forms of Action: Toward an Historical Epistemology." In *Models.* Dordrecht: D. Reidel, 188–210.

Weber, M. (1920) "Die protestantische Ethik und der Geist des Kapitalismus." http://www.zeno.org/Soziologie/M/Weber,+Max/Schriften+zur+Religionssoziologie/Die+protestantische+Ethik+und+der+Geist+des+Kapitalismus.

5 Myth Today (1957)

Roland Barthes, translated by Annette Lavers

What is a myth today? I shall give at the outset a first, very simple answer, which is perfectly consistent with etymology: *myth is a type of speech.*[1]

Myth Is a Type of Speech

Of course, it is not *any* type: language needs special conditions in order to become myth: we shall see them in a minute. But what must be firmly established at the start is that myth is a system of communication, that it is a message. This allows one to perceive that myth cannot possibly be an object, a concept, or an idea; it is a mode of signification, a form. Later, we shall have to assign to this form historical limits, conditions of use, and reintroduce society into it: we must nevertheless first describe it as a form.

It can be seen that to purport to discriminate among mythical objects according to their substance would be entirely illusory: since myth is a type of speech, everything can be a myth, provided it is conveyed by a discourse. Myth is not defined by the object of its message, but by the way in which it utters this message: there are formal limits to myth, there are no "substantial" ones. Everything, then, can be a myth? Yes, I believe this, for the universe is infinitely fertile in suggestions. Every object in the world can pass from a closed, silent existence to an oral state, open to appropriation by society, for there is no law, whether natural or not, which forbids talking about things. A tree is a tree. Yes, of course. But a tree as expressed by Minou Drouet is no longer quite a tree, it is a tree which is decorated, adapted to a certain type of consumption, laden with literary self-indulgence, revolt, images, in short with a type of social *usage* which is added to pure matter.

Naturally, everything is not expressed at the same time: some objects become the prey of mythical speech for a while, then they disappear, others take their place and attain the status of myth. Are there objects which are *inevitably* a source of suggestiveness, as Baudelaire suggested about Woman? Certainly not: one can conceive of very ancient myths, but there are no eternal ones; for it is human history which converts reality into speech, and it alone rules the life and death of mythical language. Ancient or not, mythology can only have a historical foundation, for myth is a type of speech chosen by history: it cannot possibly evolve from the "nature" of things.

Speech of this kind is a message. It is therefore by no means confined to oral speech. It can consist of modes of writing or of representations; not only written discourse but also photography, cinema, reporting, sport, shows, publicity, all of these can serve as a support to mythical speech. Myth can be defined neither by its object nor by its material, for any material can arbitrarily be endowed with meaning: the arrow which is brought in order to signify a challenge is also a kind of speech. True, as far as perception is concerned, writing and pictures, for instance, do not call upon the same types of consciousness; and even with pictures, one can use many kinds of reading: a diagram lends itself to signification more than a drawing, a copy more than an original, and a caricature more than a portrait. But this is the point: we are no longer dealing here with a theoretical mode of representation: we are dealing with *this* particular image, which is given for *this* particular signification. Mythical speech is made of a material which has *already* been worked on so as to make it suitable for communication: it is because all the materials of myth (whether pictorial or written) presuppose a signifying consciousness that one can reason about them while discounting their substance. This substance is not unimportant: pictures, to be sure, are more imperative than writing, they impose meaning at one stroke, without analyzing or diluting it. But this is no longer a constitutive difference. Pictures become like writing as soon as they are meaningful: like writing, they call for a *lexis*.

We shall therefore take *language, discourse, speech*, etc., to mean any significant unit or synthesis, whether verbal or visual; a photograph will be a kind of speech for us in the same way as a newspaper article; even objects will become speech, if they mean something. This generic way of conceiving language is in fact justified by the very history of writing: long before the invention of our alphabet, objects like the Inca *quipu*, or drawings, as in pictographs, have been accepted as speech. This does not mean that one must treat mythical speech like language; myth in fact belongs to the province of a general science, coextensive with linguistics, which is *semiology*.

Myth as a Semiological System

For mythology, since it is the study of a type of speech, is but one fragment of this vast science of signs which Saussure postulated some forty years ago under the name of *semiology*. Semiology has not yet come into being. But since Saussure himself, and sometimes independently of him, a whole section of contemporary research has constantly been referred to the problem of meaning: psychoanalysis, structuralism, eidetic psychology, some new types of literary criticism of which Bachelard has given the first examples, are no longer concerned with facts except inasmuch as they are endowed with significance. Now to postulate a signification is to have recourse to semiology. I do not mean that semiology would account for all these aspects of research equally well: they have different contents. But they have a common status: they all are sciences dealing with values. They are not content with meeting the facts: they define and explore them as tokens for something else.

Semiology is a science of forms, since it studies significations apart from their content. I should like to say one word about the necessity and the limits of such a formal science. The necessity is that which applies in the case of any exact language. Zhdanov made fun of Alexandrov the philosopher, who spoke of *"the spherical structure of our planet." "[I]t was thought until now,"* Zhdanov said, *"that form alone could be spherical."* Zhdanov was right: one cannot speak about structures in terms of forms, and vice versa. It may well be that on the plane of "life" there is but a totality where structures and forms cannot be separated. But science has no use for the ineffable: it must speak about "life" if it wanted to transform it. Against a certain quixotism of synthesis, quite platonic incidentally, all criticism must consent to the *ascesis*, to the artifice of analysis; and in analysis, it must match method and language. Less terrorized by the spectre of "formalism," historical criticism might have been less sterile; it would have understood that the specific study of forms does not in any way contradict the necessary principles of totality and History. On the contrary: the more a system is specifically defined in its forms, the more amenable it is to historical criticism. To parody a well-known saying, I shall say that a little formalism turns one away from History, but that a lot brings one back to it. Is there a better example of total criticism than the description of saintliness, at once formal and historical, semiological and ideological, in Sartre's *Saint Genet?* The danger, on the contrary, is to consider forms as ambiguous objects, half form and half substance, to endow form with a substance of form, as was done, for instance, by Zhdanovian realism. Semiology, once its limits are settled, is not a metaphysical trap: it is a science among others, necessary but not sufficient. The important thing is to see that the unity of an explanation cannot be based on the amputation of one or another of its approaches but, as Engels said, on the dialectical coordination of the particular sciences it makes use of. This is the case with mythology: it is a part both of semiology, inasmuch as it is a formal science, and of ideology, inasmuch as it is a historical science: it studies ideas-in-form.[2]

Let me therefore restate that any semiology postulates a relation between two terms, a *signifier* and a *signified.* This relation concerns objects which belong to different categories, and this is why it is not one of equality but one of equivalence. We must here be on our guard, for despite common parlance, which simply says that the signifier *expresses* the signified, we are dealing, in any semiological system, not with two but with three different terms. For what we grasp is not at all one term after the other, but the correlation which unites them: there are, therefore, the signifier, the signified, and the sign, which is the associative total of the first two terms. Take a bunch of roses: I use it to *signify* my passion. Do we have here, then, only a signifier and a signified, the roses and my passion? Not even that: to put it accurately, there are here only "passionified" roses. But on the plane of analysis, we do have three terms; for these roses weighted with passion perfectly and correctly allow themselves to be decomposed into roses and passion: the former and the latter existed before uniting and forming this third object, which is the sign. It is as true to say that on the plane of experience I cannot dissociate the roses from the message they carry, as to say that on the plane of analysis I cannot confuse the roses as signifier and the roses as sign: the signifier is empty, the sign is full, it is a meaning. Or take a black pebble: I can make it signify in several ways, it is a mere signifier; but if I weight it with a definite signified (a death sentence, for instance, in an anonymous vote), it will become a sign. Naturally, there are among the signifier, the signified, and the sign functional implications (such as that of the part to the whole) which are so close that to analyze them may seem futile; but we shall see in a moment that this distinction has a capital importance for the study of myth as semiological schema.

Naturally, these three terms are purely formal, and different contents can be given to them. Here are a few examples: for Saussure, who worked on a particular but methodologically exemplary semiological system—the language or *langue*—the signified is the concept, the signifier is the acoustic image (which is mental), and the relation between concept and image is the sign (the word, for instance), which is a concrete entity.[3] For Freud, as is well known, the human psyche is a stratification of tokens or representatives. One term (I refrain from giving it any precedence) is constituted by the manifest meaning of behavior, another, by its latent or real meaning (it is, for instance, the substratum of the dream); as for the third term, it is here also a correlation of the first two: it is the dream itself in its totality, the parapraxis (a mistake in speech or behavior) or the neurosis, conceived as compromises, as economies effected thanks to the joining of a form (the first term) and an intentional function (the second term). We can see here how necessary it is to distinguish the sign from the signifier: a dream, to Freud, is no more its manifest datum than its latent content: it is the functional union of these two terms. In Sartrean criticism, finally (I shall keep to these three well-known examples), the signified is constituted by the original crisis in the subject (the separation from his mother for Baudelaire, the naming of the theft for Genet); Literature as discourse forms the signifier, and the relation between crisis and discourse defines the work, which is signification. Of course, this tridimensional pattern, however constant in its form, is actualized in three different ways: one cannot therefore say too often that semiology can have its unity only at the level of forms, not contents; its field is limited, it knows only one operation: reading, or deciphering.

In myth, we find again the tridimensional pattern which I have just described: the signifier, the signified, and the sign. But myth is a peculiar system, in that it is constructed from a semiological chain which existed before it: *it is a second-order semiological system*. That which is a sign (namely the associative total of a concept and an image) in the first system becomes a mere signifier in the second. We must here recall that the materials of mythical speech (the language itself, photography, painting, posters, rituals, objects, etc.), however different at the start, are reduced to a pure signifying function as soon as they are caught by myth. Myth sees in them only the same raw material; their unity is that they all come down to the status of a mere language. Whether it deals with alphabetical or pictorial writing, myth wants to see in them only a sum of signs, a global sign, the final term of a first semiological chain. And it is precisely this final term which will become the first term of the greater system which it builds and of which it is only a part. Everything happens as if myth had shifted the formal system of the first significations sideways. As this lateral shift is essential for the analysis of myth, I shall represent it in the following way, it being understood, of course, that the spatialization of the pattern is here only a metaphor:

It can be seen that in myth there are two semiological systems, one of which is staggered in relation to the other: a linguistic system, the language (or the modes of representation which are assimilated to it), which I shall call the *language object*, because it is the language which myth gets hold of in order to build its own system; and myth itself, which I shall call the *metalanguage*, because it is a second language, *in which* one speaks about the first. When he reflects on a metalanguage, the semiologist no longer needs to ask himself questions about the composition of the language object, he no longer has to take into account the details of the linguistic schema; he will need only to know its total term, or global sign, and only inasmuch as this term lends itself to myth. This is why the semiologist is entitled to treat in the same way writing and pictures: what he retains from them is the fact that they both are *signs*, that they both reach the threshold of myth endowed with the same signifying function, that they constitute, one just as much as the other, a language-object.

It is now time to give one or two examples of mythical speech. I shall borrow the first from an observation by Valéry.[4] I am a pupil in the second form in a French *lycée*. I open my Latin grammar, and I read a sentence, borrowed from Aesop or Phaedrus: *quia ego nominor leo*. I stop and think. There is something ambiguous about this statement: on the one hand, the words in it do have a simple meaning: *because my name is lion*. And on the other hand, the sentence is evidently there in order to signify something else to me. Inasmuch as it is addressed to me, a pupil in the second form, it tells me clearly: I am a grammatical example meant to illustrate the rule about the agreement

Table 5.1

<table>
<tr><td rowspan="3">Language
MYTH</td><td>1. Signifier</td><td>2. Signified</td><td></td></tr>
<tr><td colspan="2">3. Sign
I SIGNIFIER</td><td>II SIGNIFIED</td></tr>
<tr><td colspan="3">III SIGN</td></tr>
</table>

of the predicate. I am even forced to realize that the sentence in no way *signifies* its meaning to me, that it tries very little to tell me something about the lion and what sort of name he has; its true and fundamental signification is to impose itself on me as the presence of a certain agreement of the predicate. I conclude that I am faced with a particular, greater, semiological system, since it is coextensive with the language: there is, indeed, a signifier, but this signifier is itself formed by a sum of signs, it is in itself a first semiological system (*my name is lion*). Thereafter, the formal pattern is correctly unfolded: there is a signified (*I am a grammatical example*), and there is a global signification, which is none other than the correlation of the signifier and the signified; for neither the naming of the lion nor the grammatical example are given separately.

And here is now another example: I am at the barber's, and a copy of *Paris-Match* is offered to me. On the cover, a young Negro in French uniform is saluting, with his eyes uplifted, probably fixed on a fold of the tricolor. All this is the *meaning* of the picture. But, whether naïvely or not, I see very well what it signifies to me: that France is a great Empire, that all her sons, without any color discrimination, faithfully serve under her flag, and that there is no better answer to the detractors of an alleged colonialism than the zeal shown by this Negro in serving his so-called oppressors. I am therefore again faced with a greater semiological system: there is a signifier, itself already formed with a previous system (*a black soldier is giving the French salute*); there is a signified (it is here a purposeful mixture of Frenchness and militariness); finally, there is a presence of the signified through the signifier.

Before tackling the analysis of each term of the mythical system, one must agree on terminology. We now know that the signifier can be looked at, in myth, from two points of view: as the final term of the linguistic system, or as the first term of the mythical system. We therefore need two names. On the plane of language, that is, as the final term of the first system, I shall call the signifier: *meaning* (*my name is lion, a Negro is giving the French salute*); on the plane of myth, I shall call it: *form*. In the case of the signified, no ambiguity is possible: we shall retain the name *concept*. The third term is the correlation of the first two: in the linguistic system, it is the *sign;* but it is not possible to use this word again without ambiguity, since in myth (and this is the chief peculiarity of the latter), the signifier is already formed by the *signs* of the language. I shall call the third term of the myth the *signification*. This word here is all the better justified since myth has in fact a double function: it points out and it notifies, it makes us understand something, and it imposes it on us.

The Form and the Concept

The signifier of myth presents itself in an ambiguous way: it is at the same time meaning and form, full on one side and empty on the other. As meaning, the signifier already postulates a reading, I grasp it through my eyes, it has a sensory reality (unlike the linguistic signifier, which is purely mental), there is a richness in it: the naming of the lion, the Negro's salute are credible wholes, they have at their disposal a sufficient rationality. As a total of linguistic signs, the meaning of the myth has its own value, it belongs to a history, that of the lion or that of the Negro: in the meaning, a signification is already built, and could not very well be self-sufficient if myth did not take hold of it and did not turn it suddenly into an empty, parasitical form. The meaning is *already* complete, it postulates a kind of knowledge, a past, a memory, a comparative order of facts, ideas, decisions.

When it becomes form, the meaning leaves its contingency behind; it empties itself, it becomes impoverished, history evaporates, only the letter remains. There is here a paradoxical permutation in the reading operations, an abnormal regression from meaning to form, from the linguistic sign to the mythical signifier. If one encloses *quia ego nominor leo* in a purely linguistic system, the clause finds again there a fullness, a richness, a history: I am an animal, a lion, I live in a certain country, I have just been hunting, they would have me share my prey with a heifer, a cow, and a goat; but being the stronger, I award myself all the shares for various reasons, the last of which is quite simply that *my name is lion*. But as the form of the myth, the clause hardly retains anything of this long story. The meaning contained a whole system of values: a history, a geography, a morality, a zoology, a Literature. The form has put all this richness at a distance: its newly acquired penury calls for a signification to fill it. The story of the lion must recede a great deal in order to make room for the grammatical example, one must put the biography of the Negro in parentheses if one wants to free the picture, and prepare it to receive its signified.

But the essential point in all this is that the form does not suppress the meaning, it only impoverishes it, it puts it at a distance, it holds it at one's disposal. One believes that the meaning is going to die, but it is a death with reprieve; the meaning loses its value, but keeps its life, from which the form of the myth will draw its nourishment. The meaning will be for the form like an instantaneous reserve of history, a timed richness, which it is possible to call and dismiss in a sort of rapid alternation: the form must constantly be able to be rooted again in the meaning and to get there what nature it needs for its nutriment; above all, it must be able to hide there. It is this constant game of hide-and-seek between the meaning and the form which defines myth. The form of myth is not a symbol: the Negro who salutes is not the symbol of the French Empire: he has too much presence, he appears as a rich, fully experienced, spontaneous, innocent, *indisputable* image. But at the same time this presence is tamed, put at a distance, made almost transparent; it recedes a little, it becomes the accomplice of a concept which comes to it fully armed, French imperiality: once made use of, it becomes artificial.

Let us now look at the signified: this history which drains out of the form will be wholly absorbed by the concept. As for the latter, it is determined, it is at once historical and intentional; it is the motivation which causes the myth to be uttered. Grammatical exemplarity, French imperiality, are the very drives behind the myth. The concept reconstitutes a chain of causes and effects, motives and intentions. Unlike the form, the concept is in no way abstract: it is filled with a situation. Through the concept, it is a whole new history which is implanted in the myth. Into the naming of the lion, first drained of its contingency, the grammatical example will attract my whole existence: Time, which caused me to be born at a certain period when Latin grammar is taught; History, which sets me apart, through a whole mechanism of social segregation, from the children who do not learn Latin; pedagogic tradition, which caused this example to be chosen from Aesop or Phaedrus; my own linguistic habits, which see the agreement of the predicate as a fact worthy of notice and illustration. The same goes for the Negro-giving-the-salute: as form, its meaning is shallow, isolated, impoverished; as the concept of French imperiality, here it is again tied to the totality of the world: to the general History of France, to its colonial adventures, to its present difficulties. Truth to tell, what is invested in the concept is less reality than a certain knowledge of reality; in passing from the meaning to the form, the image loses some knowledge: the better to receive the knowledge in the concept. In actual fact, the knowledge contained in a mythical concept is confused, made of yielding, shapeless associations. One must fully stress this open character of the concept; it is not at all an abstract, purified essence; it is a formless, unstable, nebulous condensation, whose unity and coherence are above all due to its function.

In this sense, we can say that the fundamental character of the mythical concept is to be *appropriated:* grammatical exemplarity very precisely concerns a given form of pupils, French imperiality must appeal to such and such group of readers and not another. The concept closely corresponds to a function, and it is defined as a tendency. This cannot fail to recall the signified in another semiological system, Freudianism. In Freud, the second term of the system is the latent meaning (the content) of the dream, of the parapraxis, of the neurosis. Now Freud does remark that the second-order meaning of behavior is its real meaning, that which is appropriate to a complete situation, including its deeper level; it is, just like the mythical concept, the very intention of behavior.

A signified can also have several signifiers: this is indeed the case in linguistics and psychoanalysis. It is also the case in the mythical concept: it has at its disposal an unlimited mass of signifiers: I can find a thousand Latin sentences to actualize for me the agreement of the predicate, I can find a thousand images which signify to me French imperiality. This means that *quantitively*, the concept is much poorer than the signifier, it often does nothing but re-present itself. Poverty and richness are in reverse proportion in the form and the concept: to the qualitative poverty of the form, which is the repository of a rarefied meaning, there corresponds the richness of the concept which is open to the whole of History; and to the quantitative abundance of the forms there corresponds a small number of concepts. This repetition of the concept through different forms is precious to the mythologist, it allows him to decipher the myth: it is the insistence of a kind of behavior which reveals its intention. This confirms that there is no regular ratio between the volume of the signified and that of the signifier. In language, this ratio is proportionate, it hardly exceeds the word, or at least the concrete unit. In myth, on the contrary, the concept can spread over a very large expanse of signifier. For instance, a whole book may be the signifier of a single concept; and conversely, a minute form (a word, a gesture, even incidental, so long as it is noticed) can serve as signifier to a concept filled with a very rich history. Although unusual in language, this disproportion between signifier and signified is not specific to myth: in Freud, for instance, the parapraxis is a signifier whose thinness is out of proportion to the real meaning which it betrays.

As I said, there is no fixity in mythical concepts: they can come into being, alter, disintegrate, disappear completely. And it is precisely because they are historical that history can very easily suppress them. This instability forces the mythologist to use a terminology adapted to it, and about which I should now like to say a word, because it often is a cause for irony: I mean neologism. The concept is a constituting element of myth: if I want to decipher myths, I must somehow be able to name concepts. The dictionary supplies me with a few: Goodness, Kindness, Wholeness, Humaneness, etc. But by definition, since it is the dictionary which gives them to me, these particular concepts are not historical. Now what I need most often is ephemeral concepts, in connection with limited contingencies: neologism is then inevitable. China is one thing, the idea which a French petit bourgeois could have of it not so long ago is another: for this peculiar mixture of bells, rickshaws, and opium dens, no other word possible but *Sininess*.[5] Unlovely? One should at least get some consolation from the fact that conceptual neologisms are never arbitrary: they are built according to a highly sensible proportional rule.

The Signification

In semiology, the third term is nothing but the association of the first two, as we saw. It is the only one which is allowed to be seen in a full and satisfactory way, the only one which is consumed in actual fact. I have called it: the signification. We can see that the signification is the myth itself, just as the Saussurean sign is the word (or more accurately the concrete unit). But before listing the characters of the signification, one must reflect a little on the way in which it is prepared, that is, on the modes of correlation of the mythical concept and the mythical form.

First we must note that in myth, the first two terms are perfectly manifest (unlike what happens in other semiological systems): one of them is not "hidden" behind the other, they both are given *here* (and not one here and the other there). However paradoxical it may seem, *myth hides nothing:* its function is to distort, not to make disappear. There is no latency of the concept in relation to the form: there is no need of an unconscious in order to explain myth. Of course, one is dealing with two different types of manifestation: form has a literal, immediate presence; moreover, it is extended. This stems—this cannot be repeated too often—from the nature of the mythical signifier, which is already linguistic: since it is constituted by a meaning which is already outlined, it can appear only through a given substance (whereas in language, the signifier remains mental). In the case of oral myth, this extension is linear (*because my name is lion*); in that of visual myth, it is multidimensional (in the center, the Negro's uniform, at the top, the blackness of his face, on the left, the military salute, etc.). The elements of the form therefore are related as to place and proximity: the mode of presence of the form is spatial. The concept, on the contrary, appears in global fashion, it is a kind of nebula, the condensation, more or less hazy, of a certain knowledge. Its elements are linked by associative relations: it is supported not by an extension but by a depth (although this metaphor is perhaps still too spatial): its mode of presence is memorial.

The relation which unites the concept of the myth to its meaning is essentially a relation of *deformation*. We find here again a certain formal analogy with a complex semiological system such as that of the various types of psychoanalysis. Just as for Freud the manifest meaning of behavior is distorted by its latent meaning, so in myth the meaning is distorted by the concept. Of course, this distortion is possible only because the form of the myth is already constituted by a linguistic meaning. In a simple system like language, the signified cannot distort anything at all because the signifier, being empty, arbitrary, offers no resistance to it. But here, everything is different: the signifier has, so to speak, two aspects: one full, which is the meaning (the history of the lion, of the Negro soldier), one empty, which is the form (*because my name is lion; Negro-French-soldier-saluting-the-tricolor*). What the concept distorts is of course what is full, the meaning: the lion and the Negro are deprived of their history, changed into gestures. What Latin exemplarity distorts is the naming of the lion, in all its contingency; and what French imperiality obscures is also a primary language, a factual discourse which was telling me about the salute of a Negro in uniform. But this distortion is not an obliteration: the lion and the Negro remain here, the concept needs them; they are half amputated, they are deprived of memory, not of existence: they are at once stubborn, silently rooted there, and garrulous, a speech wholly at the service of the concept. The concept, literally, deforms, but does not abolish the meaning; a word can perfectly render this contradiction: it alienates it.

What must always be remembered is that myth is a double system; there occurs in it a sort of ubiquity: its point of departure is constituted by the arrival of a meaning. To keep a spatial metaphor, the approximative character of which I have already stressed, I shall say that the signification of the myth is constituted by a sort of constantly moving turnstile which presents alternately the meaning of the signifier and its form, a language object and a metalanguage, a purely signifying and a purely imagining consciousness. This alternation is, so to speak, gathered up in the concept, which uses it like an ambiguous signifier, at once intellective and imaginary, arbitrary and natural.

I do not wish to prejudge the moral implications of such a mechanism, but I shall not exceed the limits of an objective analysis if I point out that the ubiquity of the signifier in myth exactly reproduces the physique of the *alibi* (which is, as one realizes, a spatial term): in the alibi too, there is a place which is full and one which is empty, linked by a relation of negative identity ("I am not where you think I am, I am where you think I am not"). But the ordinary alibi (for the police, for instance) has an end; reality stops the turnstile revolving at a certain point. Myth is a *value*, truth is no guarantee for it; nothing prevents it from being a perpetual alibi: it is enough that its signifier has two sides for it always to have an "elsewhere" at its disposal. The meaning is always there to *present* the form; the form is always there to *outdistance* the meaning. And there never is any contradiction, conflict, or split between the meaning and the form: they are never at the same place. In the same way, if I am in a car and I look at the scenery through the window, I can at will focus on the scenery or on the windowpane. At one moment I grasp the presence of the glass and the distance of the landscape; at another, on the contrary, the transparence of the glass and the depth of the landscape; but the result of this alternation is constant: the glass is at once present and empty to me, and the landscape unreal and full. The same thing occurs in the mythical signifier: its form is empty but present, its meaning absent but full. To wonder at this contradiction I must voluntarily interrupt this turnstile of form and meaning, I must focus on each separately, and apply to myth a static method of deciphering; in short, I must go against its own dynamics: to sum up, I must pass from the state of the reader to that of mythologist.

And it is again in this duplicity of the signifier which determines the characters of the signification. We now know that a myth is a type of speech defined by its intention (*I am a grammatical example*) much more than by its literal sense (*my name is lion*); and that in spite of this, its intention is somehow frozen, purified, eternalized, *made absent* by this literal sense (*The French Empire? It's just a fact: look at this good Negro who salutes like one of our own boys*). This constituent ambiguity of mythical speech has two consequences for the signification, which henceforth appears both like a notification and like a statement of fact.

Myth has an imperative, buttonholing character, stemming from a historical concept, directly springing from contingency (a Latin class, a threatened Empire), it is *I* whom it has come to seek. It is turned towards me, I am subjected to its intentional force, it summons me to receive its expansive ambiguity. If, for instance, I take a walk in Spain, in the Basque country,[6] I may well notice in the houses an architectural unity, a common style, which leads me to acknowledge the Basque house as a definite ethnic product. However, I do not feel personally concerned or, so to speak, attacked by this unitary style: I see only too well that it was here before me, without me. It is a complex product which has its determinations at the level of a very wide history: it does not call out to me, it does not provoke me into naming it, except if I think of inserting it into a vast picture of rural habitat. But if I am in the Paris region and I catch a glimpse, at the end of the rue Gambetta or the rue Jean-Jaurès, of a natty white chalet with red tiles, dark brown half-timbering, an asymmetrical roof, and a wattle-and-daub front, I feel as if I were personally receiving an imperious injunction to name this object a Basque chalet: or even better, to see it as the very essence of "*basquity*." This is because the concept appears to me in all its appropriative nature: it comes and seeks me out in order to oblige me to acknowledge the body of intentions which have motivated it and arranged it there as the signal of an individual history, as a confidence and a complicity: it is a real call, which the owners of the chalet send out to me. And this call, in order to be more imperious, has agreed to all manner of impoverishments: all that justified the Basque house on the plane of technology—the barn, the outside stairs, the dovecote, etc.—has been dropped; there remains only a brief order, not to be disputed. And the adhomination is so frank that I feel this chalet has just been created on the spot, *for me*, like a magical object springing up in my present life without any trace of the history which has caused it.

For this interpellant speech is at the same time a frozen speech: at the moment of reaching me, it suspends itself, turns away, and assumes the look of a generality: it stiffens, it makes itself look neutral and innocent. The appropriation of the concept is suddenly driven away once more by the literalness of the meaning. This is a kind of *arrest*, in both the physical and the legal sense of the term: French imperiality condemns the saluting Negro to be nothing more than an instrumental signifier, the Negro suddenly hails me in the name of French imperiality; but at the same moment the Negro's salute thickens, becomes vitrified, freezes into an eternal reference meant to *establish* French imperiality. On the surface of language something has stopped moving: the use of the signification is here, hiding behind the fact, and conferring on it a notifying look; but at the same time, the face paralyzes the intention, gives it something like a malaise producing immobility: in order to make it innocent, it freezes it. This is because myth is speech *stolen and restored*. Only, speech which is restored is no longer quite that which was stolen: when it was brought back, it was not put exactly in its place. It is this brief act of larceny, this moment taken for a surreptitious faking, which gives mythical speech its benumbed look.

One last element of the signification remains to be examined: its motivation. We know that in a language the sign is arbitrary: nothing compels the acoustic image *tree* "naturally" to mean the concept *tree*: the sign, here, is unmotivated. Yet this arbitrariness has limits, which come from the associative relations of the word: the language can produce a whole fragment of the sign by analogy with other signs (for instance, one says *amiable* in French, and not *amable*, by analogy with *aime*). The mythical signification, on the other hand, is never arbitrary; it is always in part motivated, and unavoidably contains some analogy. For Latin exemplarity to meet the naming of the lion, there must be an analogy, which is the agreement of the predicate; for French imperiality to get hold of the saluting Negro, there must be identity between the Negro's salute and that of the French soldier. Motivation is necessary to the very duplicity of myth: myth plays on the analogy between meaning and form, there is no myth without motivated form.[7] In order to grasp the power of motivation in myth, it is enough to reflect for a moment on an extreme case. I have here before me a collection of objects so lacking in order that I can find no *meaning* in it; it would seem that here, deprived of any previous meaning, the form could not root its analogy in anything, and that myth is impossible. But what the form can always give one to read is disorder itself: it can give a signification to the absurd, make the absurd itself a myth. This is what happens when common sense mythifies surrealism, for instance. Even the absence of motivation does not embarrass myth; for this absence will itself be sufficiently objectified to become legible: and finally, the absence of motivation will become a second-order motivation, and myth will be reestablished.

Motivation is unavoidable. It is nonetheless very fragmentary. To start with, it is not "natural": it is history which supplies its analogies to the form. Then the analogy between the meaning and the concept is never anything but partial: the form drops many analogous features and keeps only a few: it keeps the sloping roof, the visible beams in the Basque chalet, it abandons the stairs, the barn, the weathered look, etc. One must even go further: a *complete* image would exclude myth, or at least would compel it to seize only its very completeness. This is just what happens in the case of bad painting, which is wholly based on the myth of what is "filled out" and "finished" (it is the opposite and symmetrical case of the myth of the absurd: here, the form mythifies an "absence," there a surplus). But in general myth prefers to work with poor, incomplete images, where the meaning is already relieved of its fat, and ready for signification, such as caricatures, pastiches, symbols, etc. Finally, the motivation is chosen among other possible ones: I can very well give to French imperiality many other signifiers besides a Negro's salute: a French general pins a decoration on a one-armed Senegalese, a nun hands a cup of tea to a bedridden Arab, a white schoolmaster teaches attentive pickaninnies: the press undertakes every day to demonstrate that the store of mythical signifiers is inexhaustible. The nature of the mythical signification can in fact be well conveyed by one particular simile: it is neither more nor less arbitrary than an ideograph. Myth is a pure ideographic system, where the forms are still motivated by concepts, which they represent while not yet, by a long way, covering the sum of its possibilities for representation. And just as, historically, ideographs have gradually left the concept and have become associated with the sound, thus growing less and less motivated, so the worn-out state of a myth can be recognized by the arbitrariness of its signification: the whole of Molière is seen in a doctor's ruff.

Reading and Deciphering Myth

How is a myth received? We must here once more come back to the duplicity of its signifier, which is at once meaning and form. It can produce three different types of reading by focusing on the one, or the other, or both at the same time.[8]

1. If I focus on an empty signifier, I let the concept fill the form of the myth without ambiguity, and I find myself before a simple system, where the signification becomes literal again: the Negro who salutes is an *example* of French imperiality, he is a *symbol* for it. This type of focusing is, for instance, that of the producer of myths, of the journalist who starts with a concept and seeks a form for it.[9]
2. If I focus on a full signifier, in which I clearly distinguish the meaning and the form, and consequently the distortion which the one imposes on the other, I undo the signification of the myth, and I receive the latter as an imposture: the saluting Negro becomes the *alibi* of French imperiality. This type of focusing is that of the mythologist: he deciphers the myth, he understands a distortion.
3. Finally, if I focus on the mythical signifier as on an inextricable whole made of meaning and form, I receive an ambiguous signification: I respond to the constituting mechanism of myth, to its own dynamics, I become a reader of myths. The saluting Negro is no longer an example or symbol, still less an alibi: he is the very *presence* of French imperiality.

The first two types of focusing are static, analytical; they destroy the myth, either by making its intention obvious or by unmasking it: the former is cynical, the latter demystifying. The third type of focusing is dynamic, it consumes the myth according to the very ends built into its structure: the reader lives the myth as a story at once true and unreal.

If one wishes to connect a mystical schema to general history, to explain how it corresponds to the interests of a definite society, in short, to pass from semiology to ideology, it is obviously at the level of the third type of focusing that one must place oneself: it is the reader of myths himself who must reveal their essential function. How does he receive this particular myth *today*? If he receives it in an innocent fashion, what is the point of proposing it to him? And if he reads it using his powers of reflection, like the mythologist, does it matter which alibi is presented? If the reader does not see French imperiality in the saluting Negro, it was not worth weighing the latter with it; and if he sees it, the myth is nothing more than a political proposition, honestly expressed. In one word, either the intention of the myth is too obscure to be efficacious or it is too clear to be believed. In either case, where is the ambiguity?

This is but a false dilemma. Myth hides nothing and flaunts nothing: it distorts; myth is neither a lie nor a confession: it is an inflexion. Placed before the dilemma which I mentioned a moment ago, myth finds a third way out. Threatened with disappearance if it yields to either of the first two types of focusing, it gets out of this tight spot thanks to a compromise—it *is* this compromise. Entrusted with "glossing over" an intentional concept, myth encounters nothing but betrayal in language, for language can only obliterate the concept if it hides it or unmask it if it formulates it. The elaboration of a second-order semiological system will enable myth to escape this dilemma: driven to having either to unveil or to liquidate the concept, it will *naturalize* it.

We reach here the very principle of myth: it transforms history into nature. We now understand why, *in the eyes of the myth consumer*, the intention, the adhomination of the concept can remain manifest without, however, appearing to have an interest in the matter: what causes mythical speech to be uttered is perfectly explicit, but it is immediately frozen into something natural; it is not read as a motive but as a reason. If I read the Negro saluting as symbol pure and simple of imperiality, I must renounce the reality of the picture, it discredits itself in my eyes when it becomes an instrument. Conversely, if I decipher the Negro's salute as an alibi of coloniality, I shatter the myth even more surely by the obviousness of its motivation. But for the myth reader, the outcome is quite different: everything happens as if the picture *naturally* conjured up the concept, as if the signifier *gave a foundation* to the signified: the myth exists from the precise moment when French imperiality achieves the natural state: myth is speech justified *in excess*.

Here is a new example which will help with understanding clearly how the myth reader is led to rationalize the signified by means of the signifier. We are in the month of July, I read a big headline in *France-Soir*: THE FALL IN PRICES: FIRST INDICATIONS. VEGETABLES: PRICE DROP BEGINS. Let us quickly sketch the semiological schema: the example being a sentence, the first system is purely linguistic. The signifier of the second system is composed here of a certain number of accidents, some lexical (the words: *first, begins, the* [fall]), some typographical (enormous headlines where the reader usually sees news of world importance). The signified or concept is what must be called by a barbarous but unavoidable neologism: *governmentality*, the Government presented by the national press as the Essence of efficacy. The signification of the myth follows dearly from this: fruit and vegetable prices are falling *because* the government has so decided. Now it so happens in this case (and this is on the whole fairly rare) that the newspaper itself has, two lines below, allowed one to see through the myth which it had just elaborated—whether this is due to self-assurance or honesty. It adds (in small type, it is true): "The fall in prices is helped by the return of seasonal abundance." This example is instructive for two reasons. Firstly, it conspicuously shows that myth essentially aims at causing an immediate impression—it does not matter if one is later allowed to see through the myth, its action is assumed to be stronger than the rational explanations which may later belie it. This means that the reading of a myth is exhausted at one stroke. I cast a quick glance at my neighbor's *France-Soir*: I cull only a *meaning* there, but I read a true signification; I *receive* the presence of governmental action in the fall of fruit and vegetable prices. That is all, and that is enough. A more attentive reading of the myth will in no way increase its power or its ineffectiveness: a myth is at the same time imperfectible and unquestionable; time or knowledge will not make it better or worse.

Secondly, the naturalization of the concept, which I have just identified as the essential function of myth, is here exemplary. In a first (exclusively linguistic) system, causality would be, literally, natural: fruit and vegetable prices fall because they are in season. In the second (mythical) system, causality is artificial, false; but it creeps, so to speak, through the back door of Nature. This is why myth is experienced as innocent speech: not because its intentions are hidden—if they were hidden, they could not be efficacious—but because they are so naturalized.

In fact, what allows the reader to consume myth innocently is that he does not see it as a semiological system but as an inductive one. Where there is only an equivalence, he sees a kind of causal process: the signifier and the signified have, in his eyes, a natural relationship. This confusion can be expressed otherwise: any semiological system is a system of values; now the myth consumer takes the signification for a system of facts: myth is read as a factual system, whereas it is but a semiological system.

Myth as Stolen Language

What is characteristic of myth? To transform a meaning into form. In other words, myth is always a language robbery. I rob the Negro who is saluting, the white and brown chalet, the seasonal fall in fruit prices, not to make them into examples or symbols, but to naturalize through them the Empire, my taste for Basque things, the Government. Are all primary languages a prey for myth? Is there no meaning which can resist this capture with which form threatens it? In fact, nothing can be safe from myth, myth can develop its second-order schema from any meaning and, as we saw, start from the very lack of meaning. But all languages do not resist equally well.

Articulated language, which is most often robbed by myth, offers little resistance. It contains in itself some mythical dispositions, the outline of a sign structure meant to manifest the intention which led to its being used: it is what could be called the *expressiveness* of language. The imperative or the subjunctive mode, for instance, is the form of a particular signified, different from the meaning: the signified is here my will or my request. This is why some linguists have defined the indicative, for instance, as a zero state or degree, compared to the subjunctive or the imperative. Now, in a fully constituted myth, the meaning is never at zero degree, and this is why the concept can distort it, naturalize it. We must remember once again that the privation of meaning is in no way a zero degree: this is why myth can perfectly well get hold of it, give it, for instance, the signification of the absurd, of surrealism, etc. At bottom it would only be the zero degree which could resist myth.

Language lends itself to myth in another way: it is very rare that it imposes at the outset a full meaning which it is impossible to distort. This comes from the abstractness of its concept: the concept of *tree* is vague, it lends itself to multiple contingencies. True, a language always has at its disposal a whole appropriating organization (*this* tree, *the* tree *which*, etc.). But there always remains, around the final meaning, a halo of virtualities where other possible meanings are floating: the meaning can almost always be *interpreted*. One could say that a language offers to myth an openwork meaning. Myth can easily insinuate itself into it, and swell there: it is a robbery by colonization (for instance: *the* fall in prices has started. But what fall? That caused by the season or that caused by the government? The signification becomes here a parasite of the article, in spite of the latter's being definite).

When meaning is too full for myth to be able to invade it, myth goes around it, and carries it away bodily. This is what happens to mathematical language. In itself, it cannot be distorted, it has taken all possible precautions against *interpretation:* no parasitical signification can worm itself into it. And this is why, precisely, myth takes it away en bloc; it takes a certain mathematical formula ($E=mc^2$), and makes of this unalterable meaning the pure signifier of mathematicity. We can see that what is here robbed by myth is something which resists, something pure. Myth can reach everything, corrupt everything, and even the very act of refusing oneself to it. So that the more the language-object resists at first, the greater its final prostitution; whoever here resists completely yields completely: Einstein on one side, *Paris-Match* on the other. One can give a temporal image of this conflict: mathematical language is a *finished* language which derives its very perfection from this acceptance of death. Myth, on the contrary, is a language which does not want to die: it wrests from the meanings which give it its sustenance an insidious, degraded survival, it provokes in them an artificial reprieve in which it settles comfortably, it turns them into speaking corpses.

Here is another language which resists myth as much as it can: our poetic language. Contemporary poetry[10] is *a regressive semiological system.* Whereas myth aims at an ultra-signification, at the amplification of a first system, poetry, on the contrary, attempts to regain an infra-signification, a pre-semiological state of language; in short, it tries to transform the sign back into meaning: its ideal, ultimately, would be to reach not the meaning of words, but the meaning of things themselves.[11] This is why it clouds the language, increases as much as it can the abstractness of the concept and the arbitrariness of the sign and stretches to the limit the link between signifier and signified. The openwork structure of the concept is here maximally exploited: unlike what happens in prose, it is all the potential of the signified that the poetic sign tries to actualize, in the hope of at least reaching something like the transcendent quality of the thing, its natural (not human) meaning. Hence the essentialist ambitions of poetry, the conviction that it alone catches *the thing in itself,* inasmuch, precisely, as it wants to be an anti-language. All told, of all those who use speech, poets are the least formalist, for they are the only ones who believe that the meaning of the words is only a form, with which they, being realists, cannot be content. This is why our modern poetry always asserts itself as a murder of language, a kind of spatial, tangible analogue of silence. Poetry occupies a position which is the reverse of that myth: myth is a semiological system which has the pretension of transcending itself into a factual system; poetry is a semiological system which has the pretension of contracting into an essential system.

But here again, as in the case of mathematical language, the very resistance offered by poetry makes it an ideal prey for myth: the apparent lack of order of signs, which is the poetic facet of an essential order, is captured by myth, and transformed into an empty signifier, which will serve to *signify* poetry. This explains the *improbable* character of modern poetry: by fiercely refusing myth, poetry surrenders to it bound hand and foot. Conversely, the *rules* in classical poetry constituted an accepted myth, the conspicuous arbitrariness of which amounted to perfection of a kind, since the equilibrium of a semiological system comes from the arbitrariness of its signs.

A voluntary acceptance of myth can in fact define the whole of our traditional Literature. According to our norms, this Literature is an undoubted mythical system: there is a meaning, that of the discourse; there is a signifier, which is this same discourse as form or writing; there is a signified, which is the concept of literature; there is signification, which is the literary discourse. I began to discuss this problem in *Writing Degree Zero*, which was, all told, nothing but a mythology of literary language. There I defined writing as the signifier of the literary myth, that is, as a form which is already filled with meaning and which receives from the concept of Literature a new signification.[12] I suggested that history, in modifying the writer's consciousness, had provoked, a hundred years or so ago, a moral crisis of literary language: writing was revealed as a signifier, Literature as signification; rejecting the false nature of traditional literary language, the writer violently shifted his position in the direction of an anti-nature of language. The subversion of writing was the radical act by which a number of writers have attempted to reject Literature as a mythical system. Every revolt of this kind has been a murder of Literature as signification: all have postulated the reduction of literary discourse to a simple semiological system, or even, in the case of poetry, to a pre-semiological system. This is an immense task, which required radical types of behavior: it is well known that some went as far as the pure and simple scuttling of the discourse, silence—whether real or transposed—appearing as the only possible weapon against the major power of myth: its recurrence.

It thus appears that it is very difficult to vanquish myth from the inside: for the very effort one makes in order to escape its stranglehold becomes in its turn the prey of myth: myth can always, as a last resort, signify the resistance which is brought to bear against it. Truth to tell, the best weapon against myth is perhaps to mythify it in its turn, and to produce an *artificial myth:* and this reconstituted myth will in fact be a mythology. Since myth robs language of something, why not rob myth? All that is needed is to use it as the departure point for a third semiological chain, to take its signification as the first term of a second myth. Literature offers some great examples of such artificial mythologies. I shall evoke here only Flaubert's *Bouvard and Pécuchet.* It is what could be called an experimental myth, a second-order myth. Bouvard and his friend Pécuchet represent a certain kind of bourgeoisie (which is incidentally in conflict with other bourgeois strata): their discourse *already* constitutes a mythical type of speech; its language does have a meaning, but this meaning is the empty form of a conceptual signified, which here is a kind of technological unsatedness. The meeting of meaning and concept forms, in this first mythical system, a signification which is the rhetoric of Bouvard and Pécuchet. It is at this point (I am breaking the process into its components for the sake of analysis) that Flaubert intervenes: to this first mythical system, which already is a second semiological system, he superimposes a third chain, in which the first link is the signification, or the final term, of the first myth. The rhetoric of Bouvard and Pécuchet becomes the form of the new system; the concept here is due to Flaubert himself, to Flaubert's gaze on the myth which Bouvard and Pécuchet have built for themselves: it consists of their natively ineffectual inclinations, their inability to feel satisfied, the panic succession of their apprenticeships, in short what I would very much like to call (but I see storm clouds on the horizon): bouvard-and-pécuchet-ity. As for the final signification, it is the book, it is *Bouvard and Pécuchet* for us. The power of the second myth is that it gives the first its basis as a naïveté which is looked at. Flaubert has undertaken a real archaeological restoration of a given mythical speech: he is the Viollet-le-Duc of a certain bourgeois ideology. But less naïve than Viollet-le-Duc, he has strewn his reconstitution with supplementary ornaments which demystify it. These ornaments (which are the form of the second myth) are subjective in kind: there is a semiological equivalence between the subjunctive restitution of the discourse of Bouvard and Pécuchet and their ineffectualness.[13]

Flaubert's great merit (and that of all artificial mythologies: there are remarkable ones in Sartre's work) is that he gave to the problem of realism a frankly semiological solution. True, it is a somewhat incomplete merit, for Flaubert's ideology, since the bourgeois was for him only an aesthetic eyesore, was not at all realistic. But at least he avoided the major sin in literary matters, which is to confuse ideological with semiological reality. As ideology, literary realism does not depend at all on the language spoken by the writer. Language is a form, it cannot possibly be either realistic or unrealistic. All it can do is either to be mythical or not, or perhaps, as in *Bouvard et Pécuchet,* counter-mythical. Now, unfortunately, there is no antipathy between realism and myth. It is well known how often our "realistic" literature is mythical (if only as a crude myth of realism) and how our "literature of the unreal" has at least the merit of being only slightly so. The wise thing would of course be to define the writer's realism as an essentially ideological problem. This certainly does not mean that there is no responsibility of form towards reality. But this responsibility can be measured only in semiological terms. A form can be judged (since forms are on trial) only as signification, not as expression. The writer's language is not expected to *represent* reality, but to signify it. This should impose on critics the duty of using two rigorously distinct methods: one must deal with the writer's realism either as an ideological substance (Marxist themes in Brecht's work, for instance) or as a semiological value (the props, the actors, the music, the colors in Brechtian dramaturgy). The ideal of course would be to combine these two types of criticism; the mistake which is constantly made is to confuse them: ideology has its methods, and so has semiology.

The Bourgeoisie as a Joint-Stock Company

Myth lends itself to history in two ways: by its form, which is only relatively motivated; by its concept, the nature of which is historical. One can therefore imagine a diachronic study of myths, whether one submits them to a retrospection (which means founding a historical mythology) or whether one follows some of yesterday's myths down to their present forms (which means founding prospective history). If I keep here to a synchronic sketch of contemporary myths, it is for an objective reason: our society is the privileged field of mythical signification. We must now say why.

Whatever the accidents, the compromises, the concessions, and the political adventures, whatever the technical, economic, or even social changes which history brings us, our society is still a bourgeois society. I am not forgetting that since 1789, in France, several types of bourgeoisie have succeeded one another in power; but the same status—a certain regime of ownership, a certain order, a certain ideology—remains at a deeper level. Now a remarkable phenomenon occurs in the matter of naming this regime: as an economic fact, the bourgeoisie is *named* without any difficulty; capitalism is openly professed.[14] As a political fact, the bourgeoisie has some difficulty in acknowledging itself: there are no "bourgeois" parties in the Chamber of Deputies. As an ideological fact, it completely disappears: the bourgeoisie has obliterated its name in passing from reality to representation, from economic man to mental man. It comes to an agreement with the facts, but does not compromise about values, it makes its status undergo a real *exnominating* operation: the bourgeoisie is defined as *the social class which does not want to be named.* "Bourgeois," "petit bourgeois," "capitalism,"[15] "proletariat"[16] are the locus of an unceasing hemorrhage: meaning flows out of them until their very name becomes unnecessary.

This ex-nominating phenomenon is important; let us examine it a little more closely. Politically, the hemorrhage of the name "bourgeois" is effected through the idea of *nation*. This was once a progressive idea, which has served to get rid of the aristocracy; today, the bourgeoisie merges into the nation, even if it has, in order to do so, to exclude from it the elements which it decides are allogenous (the Communists).

This planned syncretism allows the bourgeoisie to attract the numerical support of its temporary allies, all the intermediate, therefore "shapeless" classes. A long-continued use of the word *nation* has failed to depoliticize it in depth; the political substratum is there, very near the surface, and some circumstances make it suddenly manifest. There are in the Chamber some "national" parties, and nominal syncretism here makes conspicuous what it had the ambition of hiding: an essential disparity. Thus the political vocabulary of the bourgeoisie already postulates that the universal exists: for it, politics is already a representation, a fragment of ideology.

Politically, in spite of the universalistic effort of its vocabulary, the bourgeoisie eventually strikes against a resisting core which is, by definition, the revolutionary party. But this party can constitute only a political richness: in a bourgeois culture, there is neither proletarian culture nor proletarian morality, there is no proletarian art; ideologically, all that is not bourgeois is obliged to *borrow* from the bourgeoisie. Bourgeois ideology can therefore spread over everything and in so doing lose its name without risk: no one here will throw this name of bourgeois back at it. It can without resistance subsume bourgeois theater, art, and humanity under their eternal analogues; in a word, it can ex-nominate itself without restraint when there is only one single human nature left: the defection from the name "bourgeois" is here complete.

True, there are revolts against bourgeois ideology. This is what one generally calls the avant-garde. But these revolts are socially limited, they remain open to salvage. First, because they come from a small section of the bourgeoisie itself, from a minority group of artists and intellectuals, without public other than the class which they contest, and who remain dependent on its money in order to express themselves. Then, these revolts always get their inspiration from a very strongly made distinction between the ethically and the politically bourgeois: what the avant-garde contests is the bourgeois in art or morals—the shopkeeper, the Philistine, as in the heyday of Romanticism; but as for political contestation, there is none.[17] What the avant-garde does not tolerate about the bourgeoisie is its language, not its status. This does not necessarily mean that it approves of this status; simply, it leaves it aside. Whatever the violence of the provocation, the nature it finally endorses is that of "derelict" man, not alienated man; and derelict man is still Eternal Man.[18]

This anonymity of the bourgeoisie becomes even more marked when one passes from bourgeois culture proper to its derived, vulgarized, and applied forms, to what one could call public philosophy, that which sustains everyday life, civil ceremonials, secular rites, in short the unwritten norms of interrelationships in a bourgeois society. It is an illusion to reduce the dominant culture to its inventive core: there is also a bourgeois culture which consists of consumption alone. The whole of France is steeped in this anonymous ideology: our press, our films, our theater, our pulp literature, our rituals, our Justice, our diplomacy, our conversations, our remarks about the weather, a murder trial, a touching wedding, the cooking we dream of, the garments we wear, everything, in everyday life, is dependent on the representation which the bourgeoisie *has and makes us have* of the relations between the man and the world. These "normalized" forms attract little attention, by the very fact of their extension, in which their origin is easily lost. They enjoy an intermediate position: being neither directly political nor directly ideological, they live peacefully between the action of the militants and the quarrels of the intellectuals; more or less abandoned by the former and the latter, they gravitate towards the enormous mass of the undifferentiated, of the insignificant, in short, of nature. Yet it is through its ethic that the bourgeoisie pervades France: practiced on a national scale, bourgeois norms are experienced as the evident laws of a natural order—the further the bourgeois class propagates its representations, the more naturalized it becomes. The fact of bourgeoisie becomes absorbed into an amorphous universe, whose sole inhabitant is Eternal Man, who is neither proletarian nor bourgeois.

It is therefore by penetrating the intermediate classes that the bourgeois ideology can most surely lose its name. Petit-bourgeois norms are the residue of bourgeois culture, they are bourgeois truths which have become degraded, impoverished, commercialized, slightly archaic, or, shall we say, out of date? The political alliance of the bourgeoisie and the petite bourgeoisie has for more than a century determined the history of France; it has rarely been broken, and each time only temporarily (1848, 1871, 1936). This alliance got closer as time passed, it gradually became a symbiosis; transient awakenings might happen, but the common ideology was never questioned again. The same "natural" varnish covers up all "national" representations: the big wedding of the bourgeoisie, which originates in a class ritual (the display and consumption of wealth), can bear no relation to the economic status of the lower middle class: but through the press, the news, and literature, it slowly becomes the very norm as dreamed, though not actually lived, of the petit-bourgeois couple. The bourgeoisie is constantly absorbing into its ideology a whole section of humanity which does not have its basic status and cannot live up to it except in imagination, that is, at the cost of an immobilization and an impoverishment of consciousness.[19] By spreading its representations over a whole catalog of collective images for petit-bourgeois use, the bourgeoisie countenances the illusory lack of differentiation of the social classes: it is as from the moment when a typist earning twenty pounds a month *recognizes herself* in the big wedding of the bourgeoisie that bourgeois ex-nomination achieves its full effect.

The flight from the name "bourgeois" is not therefore an illusory, accidental, secondary, natural, or insignificant phenomenon: it is the bourgeois ideology itself, the process through which the bourgeoisie transforms the reality of the world into an image of the world, History into Nature. And this image has a remarkable feature: it is upside down.*[20] The status of the bourgeoisie is particular, historical: man as represented by it is universal, eternal. The bourgeois class has precisely built its power on technical, scientific progress, on an unlimited transformation of nature: bourgeois ideology yields in return an unchangeable nature. The first bourgeois philosophers pervaded the world with significations, subjected all things to an idea of the rational, and decreed that they were meant for man: bourgeois ideology is of the scientistic or the intuitive kind, it records facts or perceives values, but refuses explanations; the order of the world can be seen as sufficient or ineffable, it is never seen as significant. Finally, the basic idea of a perfectible mobile world produces the inverted image of an unchanging humanity, characterized by an indefinite repetition of its identity. In a word, in the contemporary bourgeois society, the passage from the real to the ideological is defined as that from an *anti-physis* to a *pseudo-physis*.

Myth Is Depoliticized Speech

And this is where we come back to myth. Semiology has taught us that myth has the task of giving a historical intention a natural justification, and making contingency appear eternal. Now this process is exactly that of bourgeois ideology. If our society is objectively the privileged field of mythical significations, it is because formally myth is the most appropriate instrument for the ideological inversion which defines this society: at all the levels of human communication, myth operates the inversion of *anti-physis* into *pseudo-physis*.

What the world supplies to myth is a historical reality, defined, even if this goes back quite a while, by the way in which men have produced or used it; and what myth gives in return is a *natural* image of this reality. And just as bourgeois ideology is defined by the abandonment of the name "bourgeois," so myth is constituted by the loss of the historical quality of things: in it, things lose the memory that they once were made. The world enters language as a dialectical relation between activities, between human actions; it comes out of myth as a harmonious display of essences. A conjuring trick has taken place; it has turned reality inside out, it has emptied it of history and has filled it with nature, it has removed from things their human meaning so as to make them signify a human insignificance. The function of myth is to empty reality: it is, literally, a ceaseless flowing out, a hemorrhage, or perhaps an evaporation, in short, a perceptible absence.

It is now possible to complete the semiological definition of myth in a bourgeois society: *myth is depoliticized speech.* One must naturally understand *political* in its deeper meaning, as describing the whole of human relations in their real, social structure, in their power of making the world; one must above all give an active value to the prefix *de-*: here it represents an operational movement, it permanently embodies a defaulting. In the case of the soldier Negro, for instance, what is got rid of is certainly not French imperiality (on the contrary, since what must be actualized is its presence); it is the contingent, historical, in one word, *fabricated*, quality of colonialism. Myth does not deny things, on the contrary, its function is to talk about them; simply, it purifies them, it makes them innocent, it gives them a natural and eternal justification, it gives them a clarity which is not that of an explanation but that of a statement of fact. If I *state the fact* of French imperiality without explaining it, I am very near to finding that it is natural and *goes without saying:* I am reassured. In passing from history to nature, myth acts economically: it abolishes the complexity of human acts, it gives them the simplicity of essences, it does away with all dialectics, with any going back beyond what is immediately visible, it organizes a world which is without contradictions because it is without depth, a world wide open and wallowing in the evident, it establishes a blissful clarity: things appear to mean something by themselves.[21]

However, is myth always depoliticized speech? In other words, is reality always political? Is it enough to speak about a thing naturally for it to become mythical? One could answer with Marx that the most natural object contains a political trace, however faint and diluted, the more or less memorable presence of the human act which has produced, fitted up, used, subjected, or rejected it.[22] The language-object, which *"speaks things,"* can easily exhibit this trace; the metalanguage, which *speaks of things*, much less easily. Now myth always comes under the heading of metalanguage: the depolitization which it carries out often supervenes against a background which is already naturalized, depoliticized by a general metalanguage, which is trained to *celebrate* things and no longer *"act them."* It goes without saying that the force needed by myth to distort its object is much less in the case of a tree than in the case of a Sudanese: in the latter case, the political load is very near the surface, a large quantity of artificial nature is needed in order to disperse it; in the former case, it is remote, purified by a whole century-old layer of metalanguage. There are, therefore, strong myths and weak myths; in the former, the political quantum is immediate, the depolitization is abrupt; in the latter, the political quality of the object has *faded* like a color, but the slightest thing can bring back its strength brutally: what is more *natural* than the sea? and what more "political" than the sea celebrated by the makers of the film *The Lost Continent*?[23]

In fact, metalanguage constitutes a kind of preserve for myth. Men do not have with myth a relationship based on truth but on use: they depoliticize according to their needs. Some mythical objects are left dormant for a time; they are then no more than vague mythical schemata whose political load seems almost neutral. But this indicates only that their situation has brought this about, not that their structure is different. This is the case with our Latin-grammar example. We must note that here mythical speech works on a material which has long been transformed: the sentence by Aesop belongs to literature, it is at the very start mythified (therefore made innocent) by its being fiction. But it is enough to replace the initial term of the chain for an instant into its nature as language-object, to gauge the emptying of reality operated by myth: one can imagine the feelings of a *real* society of animals on finding itself transformed into a grammar example, into a predicative nature! In order to gauge the political load of an object and the mythical hollow which espouses it, one must never look at things from the point of view of the signification, but from that of the signifier, of the thing which has been robbed; and within the signifier, from the point of view of the language-object, that is, of the meaning. There is no doubt that if we consulted a *real* lion, he would maintain that the grammar example is a *strongly* depoliticized state, he would qualify as fully *political* the jurisprudence which leads him to claim a prey because he is the strongest, unless we deal with a bourgeois lion who would not fail to mythify his strength by giving it the form of a duty.

One can clearly see that in this case the political insignificance of the myth comes from its situation. Myth, as we know, is a value: it is enough to modify its circumstances, the general (and precarious) system in which it occurs, in order to regulate its scope with great accuracy. The field of the myth is in this case reduced to a seventh-grade class of a French school. But I suppose that a child *enthralled* by the story of the lion, the heifer, and the cow, and recovering through the life of the imagination the actual reality of these animals, would appreciate with much less unconcern than we do that the disappearance of this lion changed into a predicate. In fact, we hold this myth to be politically insignificant only because it is not meant for us.

Myth on the Left

If myth is depoliticized speech, there is at least one type of speech which is the opposite of myth: that which *remains* political. Here we must go back to the distinction between language-object and metalanguage. If I am a woodcutter and I am led to name the tree which I am felling, whatever the form of my sentence, I "speak the tree," I do not speak about it. This means that my language is operational, transitively linked to its object; between the tree and myself, there is nothing but my labor, that is to say, an action. This is a political language: it represents nature for me only inasmuch as I am going to transform it, it is a language thanks to which I *"act the object";* the tree is not an image for me, it is simply the meaning of my action. But if I am not a woodcutter, I can no longer "speak the tree," I can only speak *about* it, *on* it. My language is no longer the instrument of an "acted-upon tree," it is the "tree celebrated" which becomes the instrument of my language. I no longer have anything more than an intransitive relationship with the tree; the tree is no longer the meaning of reality as a human action, it is an *image-at-one's-disposal.* Compared to the real language of the woodcutter, the language I create is a second-order language, a metalanguage in which I shall henceforth not "act the things" but "act their names," and which is to the primary language what the gesture is to the act. This second-order language is not entirely mythical, but it is the very locus where myth settles; for myth can work only on objects which have already received the mediation of a first language.

There is therefore one language which is not mythical, it is the language of man as a producer: wherever man speaks in order to transform reality and no longer to preserve it as an image, wherever he links his language to the making of things, metalanguage is referred to a language-object, and myth is impossible. This is why revolutionary language proper cannot be mythical. Revolution is defined as the cathartic act meant to reveal the political load of the world: it *makes* the world; and its language, all of it, is functionally absorbed in this making. It is because it generates speech which is *fully*—that is to say, initially and finally—political, and not, like myth, speech which is initially political and finally natural, that Revolution excludes myth. Just as bourgeois ex-nomination characterizes at once bourgeois ideology and myth itself, revolutionary denomination identifies revolution and the absence of myth. The bourgeoisie hides the fact that it is the bourgeoisie and thereby produces myth; revolution announces itself openly as revolution and thereby abolishes myth.

I have been asked whether there are myths "on the Left." Of course, inasmuch, precisely, as the Left is not a revolution. Left-wing myth supervenes precisely at the moment when revolution changes itself into "the Left"—that is, when it agrees to wear a mask, to hide its name, to generate an innocent metalanguage, and to distort itself into "Nature." This revolutionary ex-nomination may or may not be tactical, this is no place to discuss it. At any rate, it is sooner or later experienced as a process contrary to revolution, and it is always more or less in relation to myth that revolutionary history defines its "deviations." There came a day, for instance, when it was socialism itself which defined the Stalin myth. Stalin, as a spoken object, has exhibited for years, in their pure state, the constituent characters of mythical speech: a meaning, which was the real Stalin, that of history; a signifier, which was the ritual invocation to Stalin, and the *inevitable* character of the "natural" epithets with which his name was surrounded; a signified, which was the intention to respect orthodoxy, discipline, and unity, *appropriated* by the Communist parties to a definite situation; and a signification, which was a sanctified Stalin, whose historical determinants found themselves grounded in nature, sublimated under the name of *genius*—that is, something irrational and inexpressible: here depoliticization is evident, it fully reveals the presence of a myth.[24]

Yes, myth exists on the Left, but it does not at all have there the same qualities as the bourgeois myth. *Left-wing myth is inessential.* To start with, the objects which it takes hold of are rare—only a few political notions—unless it has itself recourse to the whole repertoire of the bourgeois myths. Left-wing myth never reaches the immense field of human relationships, the very vast surface of "insignificant" ideology. Everyday life is inaccessible to it: in a bourgeois society, there are no "Left-wing" myths concerning marriage, cooking, the home, the theater, the law, morality, etc. Then it is an incidental myth, its use is not part of a strategy, as is the case with the bourgeois myth, but only of a tactic, or, at the worst, of a deviation; if it occurs, it is as a myth suited to a convenience, not a necessity.

Finally, and above all, this myth is, in essence, poverty-stricken. It does not know how to proliferate; being produced on order and for a temporally limited prospect, it is invented with difficulty. It lacks a major faculty, that of fabulizing. Whatever it does, there remains about it something stiff and literal, a suggestion of something done to order. As it is expressively put, it remains barren. In fact, what can be more meager than the Stalin myth? No inventiveness here, and only a clumsy appropriation: the signifier of the myth (this form whose infinite wealth in bourgeois myth we have just seen) is not varied in the least: it is reduced to a litany.

This imperfection, if that is the word for it, comes from the nature of the "Left": whatever the imprecision of the term, the Left always defines itself in relation to the oppressed, whether proletarian or colonized.[25] Now the speech of the oppressed can only be poor, monotonous, immediate: his destitution is the very yardstick of his language: he has only one, always the same, that of his actions; metalanguage is a luxury, he cannot yet have access to it. The speech of the oppressed is real, like that of the woodcutter; it is a transitive type of speech: it is quasi-unable to lie; lying is a richness, a lie presupposes property, truths, and forms to spare. This essential barrenness produces rare, threadbare myths: either transient, or clumsily indiscreet; by their very being, they label themselves as myths, and point to their masks. And this mask is hardly that of a pseudo-physis: for that type of physis is also a richness of a sort, the oppressed can only borrow it; he is unable to throw out the real meaning of things, to give them the luxury of an empty form, open to the innocence of a false Nature. One can say that in a sense, Left-wing myth is always an artificial myth, a reconstituted myth: hence its clumsiness.

Myth on the Right

Statistically, myth is on the right. There, it is essential; well fed, sleek, expansive, garrulous, it invents itself ceaselessly. It takes hold of everything, all aspects of the law, of morality, of aesthetics, of diplomacy, of household equipment, of Literature, of entertainment. Its expansion has the very dimensions of bourgeois ex-nomination. The bourgeoisie wants to keep reality without keeping the appearances: it is therefore the very negativity of bourgeois appearance, infinite like every negativity, which solicits myth infinitely. The oppressed is nothing, he has only one language, that of his emancipation; the oppressor is everything, his language is rich, multiform, supple, with all the possible degrees of dignity at its disposal: he has an exclusive right to metalanguage. The oppressed *makes* the world, he has only an active, transitive (political) language; the oppressor conserves it, his language is plenary, intransitive, gestural, theatrical: it is the Myth. The language of the former aims at transforming, of the latter at eternalizing.

Does this completeness of the myths of Order (this is the name the bourgeoisie gives to itself) include inner differences? Are there, for instance, bourgeois myths and petit-bourgeois myths? There cannot be any fundamental differences, for whatever the public which consumes it, myth always postulates the immobility of Nature. But there can be degrees of fulfillment for expansion: some myths ripen better in some social strata: for myth also, there are microclimates.

The myth of Childhood-as-Poet, for instance, is an *advanced* bourgeois myth: it has hardly come out of inventive culture (Cocteau, for example) and is just reaching consumer culture (*L'Express*). Part of the bourgeoisie can still find it too obviously invented, not mythical enough to feel entitled to countenance it (a whole part of bourgeois criticism works only with duly mythical materials). It is a myth which is not yet well run in, it does not contain enough *nature:* in order to make the Child-Poet part of a cosmogony, one must renounce the prodigy (Mozart, Rimbaud, etc.) and accept new norms, those of psychopedagogy, Freudianism, etc.: as a myth, it is still unripe.

Thus every myth can have its history and its geography; each is in fact the sign of the other: a myth ripens because it spreads. I have not been able to carry out any real study of the social geography of myths. But it is perfectly possible to draw what linguists would call the isoglosses of a myth, the lines which limit the social region where it is spoken. As this region is shifting, it would be better to speak of the waves of implantation of the myth. The Minou Drouet myth has thus had at least three waves of amplification: (1) *L'Express;* (2) *Paris-Match, Elle;* (3) *France-Soir.* Some myths hesitate: Will they pass into tabloids, the home of the suburbanite of private means, the hairdresser's salon, the tube? The social geography of myths will remain difficult to trace as long as we lack an analytical sociology of the press.[26] But we can say that its place already exists.

Since we cannot yet draw up the list of the dialectal forms of bourgeois myth, we can always sketch its rhetorical forms. One must understand here by *rhetoric* a set of fixed, regulated, insistent figures, according to which the varied forms of the mythical signifier arrange themselves. These figures are transparent inasmuch as they do not affect the plasticity of the signifier; but they are already sufficiently conceptualized to adapt to a historical representation of the world (just as classical rhetoric can account for a representation of the Aristotelian type). It is through their rhetoric that bourgeois myths outline the general prospect of the pseudo-physis which defines the dream of the contemporary bourgeois world. Here are its principal figures:

1. *The inoculation.* I have already given examples of this very general figure, which consists in admitting the accidental evil of a class-bound institution the better to conceal its principal evil. One immunizes the contents of the collective imagination by means of a small inoculation of acknowledged evil; one thus protects it against the risk of a generalized subversion. This *liberal* treatment would not have been possible only a hundred years ago. Then the bourgeois Good did not compromise with anything, it was quite stiff. It has become much more supple since: the bourgeoisie no longer hesitates to acknowledge some localized subversions: the avant-garde, the irrational in childhood, etc. It now lives in a balanced economy: as in any sound joint-stock company, the smaller shares—in law but not in fact—compensate the big ones.

2. *The privation of history.* Myth deprives the object of which it speaks of all History.[27] In it, history evaporates. It is a kind of ideal servant: it prepares all things, brings them, lays them out, the master arrives, it silently disappears: all that is left for one to do is enjoy this beautiful object without wondering where it comes from. Or even better: it can only come from eternity: since the beginning of time, it has been made for bourgeois man, the Spain of the *Blue Guide* has been made for the tourist, and "primitives" have prepared their dances with a view to an exotic festivity. We can see all the disturbing things which this felicitous figure removes from sight: both determinism and freedom. Nothing is produced, nothing is chosen: all one has to do is to possess these new objects from which all soiling trace of origin or choice has been removed. This miraculous evaporation of history is another form of a concept common to most bourgeois myths: the irresponsibility of man.

3. *Identification.* The petit bourgeois is a man unable to imagine the Other.[28] If he comes face to face with him, he blinds himself, ignores and denies him, or else transforms him into himself. In the petit-bourgeois universe, all the experiences of confrontation are reverberating, any otherness is reduced to sameness. The spectacle and the tribunal, which are both places where the Other threatens to appear in full view, become mirrors. This is because the Other is a scandal which threatens the petit bourgeois's essence. Dominici cannot have access to social existence unless he is previously reduced to the state of a small simulacrum of the President of the Assizes or the Public Prosecutor: this is the price one must pay in order to condemn him justly, since Justice is a weighing operation and since scales can only weigh like against like. There are, in any petit-bourgeois consciousness, small simulacra of the hooligan, the parricide, the homosexual, etc., which periodically the judiciary extracts from its brain, puts in the dock, admonishes, and condemns: one never tries anybody but analogues *who have gone astray:* it is a question of direction, not of nature, for *that's how men are.* Sometimes—rarely—the Other is revealed as irreducible: not because of a sudden scruple, but because *common sense* rebels: a man does not have white skin, but a black one, another drinks pear juice, not Pernod. How can one assimilate the Negro, the Russian? There is here a figure for emergencies: exoticism. The Other becomes a pure object, a spectacle, a clown. Relegated to the confines of humanity, he no longer threatens the security of the home. This figure is chiefly petit bourgeois. For, even if he is able to experience the Other in himself, the bourgeois can at least imagine the place where he fits in: this is what is known as liberalism, which is a sort of intellectual equilibrium based on recognized places. The petit bourgeois class is not liberal (it produces Fascism, whereas the bourgeoisie uses it): it follows the same route as the bourgeoisie, but lags behind.

4. *Tautology.* Yes, I know, it's an ugly word. But so is the thing. Tautology is this verbal device which consists in defining like by like (*"Drama is drama"*). We can view it as one of those types of magical behavior dealt with by Sartre in his *Emotions: Outline of a Theory*: one takes refuge in tautology as one does in fear, or anger, or sadness, when

one is at a loss for an explanation: the accidental failure of language is magically identified with what one decides is a natural resistance of the object. In tautology, there is a double murder: one kills rationality because it resists one, one kills language because it betrays one. Tautology is a feint at the right moment, a saving aphasia, it is a death, or perhaps a comedy, the indignant "representation" of the *rights* of reality over and above language. Since it is magical, it can of course only take refuge behind the argument of authority: thus do parents at the end of their tether reply to the child who keeps on asking for explanations: *"because that's how it is"* or even better: *"just because, that's all"*—a magical act ashamed of itself, which verbally makes the gesture of rationality, but immediately abandons the latter and believes itself to be even with causality because it has uttered the word which introduces it. Tautology testifies to a profound distrust of language, which is rejected because it has failed. Now any refusal of language is a death. Tautology creates a dead, a motionless world.

5. *Neither/Norism.* By this I mean this mythological figure which consists in stating two opposites and balancing the one by the other so as to reject them both. (I want *neither* this *nor* that.) It is on the whole a bourgeois figure, for it relates to a modern form of liberalism. We find again here the figure of the scales: reality is first reduced to analogues; then it is weighed; finally, equality having been ascertained, it is got rid of. Here also there is magical behavior: both parties are dismissed because it is embarrassing to choose between them; one flees from an intolerable reality, reducing it to two opposites which balance each other only inasmuch as they are purely formal, relieved of all their specific weight. Neither/Norism can have degraded forms: in astrology, for example, ill luck is always followed by equal good luck; they are always predicted in a prudently compensatory perspective: a final equilibrium immobilizes values, life, destiny, etc.: one no longer needs to choose, but only to endorse.

6. *The quantification of quality.* This is a figure which is latent in all the preceding ones. By reducing any quality to quantity, myth economizes intelligence: it understands reality more cheaply. I have given several examples of this mechanism which bourgeois—and especially petit-bourgeois—mythology does not hesitate to apply to aesthetic realities which it deems, on the other hand, to partake of an immaterial essence. Bourgeois theater is a good example of this contradiction: on the one hand, theater is presented as an essence which cannot be reduced to any language and reveals itself only to the heart, to intuition. From this quality it receives an irritable dignity (it is forbidden as a crime of *"lèse-essence"* to speak about the theater *scientifically:* or rather, any intellectual way of viewing the theater is discredited as scientism or pedantic language). On the other hand, bourgeois dramatic art rests on a pure quantification of effects: a whole circuit of computable appearances establishes a quantitative equality between the cost of the ticket and the tears of an actor or the luxuriousness of a set: what is currently meant by the "naturalness" of an actor, for instance, is above all a conspicuous quantity of effects.

7. *The statement of fact.* Myths tend towards proverbs. Bourgeois ideology invests in this figure interests which are bound to its very essence: universalism, the refusal of any explanation, an unalterable hierarchy of the world. But we must again distinguish the language-object from the metalanguage. Popular, ancestral proverbs still partake of an instrumental grasp of the world as object. A rural statement of fact such as "the weather is fine" keeps a real link with the usefulness of fine weather. It is an implicitly technological statement; the word, here, in spite of its general, abstract form, paves the way for actions, it inserts itself into a fabricating order: the farmer does not speak *about* the weather, he "acts it" he draws it into his labor. All our popular proverbs thus represent active speech which has gradually solidified into reflexive speech, but where reflection is curtailed, reduced to a statement of fact, and, so to speak, a timid, prudent, and closely hugging experience. Popular proverbs foresee more than they assert, they remain the speech of a humanity which is making itself, not one which is. Bourgeois aphorisms, on the other hand, belong to metalanguage; they are a second-order language which bears on objects already prepared. Their classical form is the maxim. Here the statement is no longer directed towards a world to be made; it must overlay one which is already made, bury the traces of this production under a self-evident appearance of eternity: it is a counter-explanation, the decorous equivalent of a tautology, of this peremptory *because* which parents in need of knowledge hang above the heads of their children. The foundation of the bourgeois statement of fact is *common sense*, that is, truth when it stops on the arbitrary order of him who speaks it.

I have listed these rhetorical figures without any special order, and there may well be many others: some can become worn out, others can come into being. But it is obvious that those given here, such as they are, fall into two great categories, which are like the Zodiacal signs of the bourgeois universe: the Essences and the Scales. Bourgeois ideology continuously transforms the products of history into essential types. Just as the cuttlefish squirts its ink in order to protect itself, so it cannot rest until it has obscured the ceaseless making of the world, fixed this world into an object which can be forever possessed, catalogued its riches, embalmed it, and injected into reality some purifying essence which will stop its transformation, its flight towards other forms of existence. And these riches, thus fixated and frozen, will at least become computable: bourgeois morality will essentially be a weighing operation, the essences will be placed in scales of which bourgeois man will remain the motionless beam. For the very end of myths is to immobilize the world: they must suggest and mimic a universal order which has fixated once and for all the hierarchy of possessions. Thus, every day and everywhere, man is stopped by myths, referred by them to this motionless prototype which lives in his place, stifles him in the manner of a huge internal parasite, and assigns to his activity the narrow limits within which he is allowed to suffer without upsetting the world: bourgeois pseudo-physis is in the fullest sense a prohibition for man against inventing himself. Myths are nothing but this ceaseless, untiring solicitation, this insidious and inflexible demand that all men recognize themselves in this image, eternal yet bearing a date, which was built of them one day as if for all time. For Nature, in which they are locked up under the pretext of being eternalized, is nothing but a Usage. And it is this Usage, however lofty, that they must take in hand and transform.

Necessity and Limits of Mythology

I must, as a conclusion, say a few words about the mythologist himself. This term is rather grand and self-assured. Yet one can predict for the mythologist, if there ever is one, a few difficulties, in feeling if not in method. True, he will have no trouble in feeling justified: whatever its mistakes, mythology is certain to participate in the making of the world. Holding as a principle that man in a bourgeois society is at every turn plunged into a false Nature, it attempts to find again, under the assumed innocence of the most unsophisticated relationships, the profound alienation which this innocence is meant to make one accept. The unveiling which it carries out is therefore a political act: founded on a responsible idea of language, mythology thereby postulates the freedom of the latter. It is certain that in this sense mythology *harmonizes* with the world, not as it is, but as it wants to create itself (Brecht had for this an efficiently ambiguous word: *Einverstandnis*, at once an understanding of reality and a complicity with it).

This harmony justifies the mythologist but does not fulfill him: his status still remains basically one of being excluded. Justified by the political dimension, the mythologist is still at a distance from it. His speech is a metalanguage, it "acts" nothing; at most, it unveils—or does it? To whom? His task always remains ambiguous, hampered by its ethical origin. He can live revolutionary action only vicariously: hence the self-conscious character of his function, this something a little stiff and painstaking, muddled and excessively simplified which brands any intellectual behavior with an openly political foundation ("uncommitted" types of literature are infinitely more "elegant"; they are in their place in metalanguage).

Also the mythologist cuts himself off from all the myth consumers, and this is no small matter. If this applied to a particular section of the collectivity, well and good.[29] But when a myth reaches the entire community, it is from the latter that the mythologist must become estranged if he wants to liberate the myth. Any myth with some degree of generality is in fact ambiguous, because it represents the very humanity of those who, having nothing, have borrowed it. To decipher the Tour de France and the "good French Wine" is to cut oneself off from those who are entertained or warmed up by them. The mythologist is condemned to live in a theoretical sociality; for him, to be in society is, at best, to be truthful: his utmost sociality dwells in his utmost morality. His connection with the world is of the order of sarcasm.

One must even go further: in a sense, the mythologist is excluded from this history in the name of which he professes to act. The havoc which he wreaks in the language of the community is absolute for him, it fills his assignment to the brim: he must live this assignment without any hope of going back or any assumption of payment. It is forbidden for him to imagine what the rest of the world will concretely be like when the immediate object of his criticism has disappeared. Utopia is an impossible luxury for him: he greatly doubts that tomorrow's truths will be the exact reverse of today's lies. History never ensures the triumph pure and simple of something over its opposite: it unveils, while making itself, unimaginable solutions, unforeseeable syntheses. The mythologist is not even in a Moses-like situation: he cannot see the Promised Land. For him tomorrow's positivity is entirely hidden by today's negativity. All the values of his undertaking appear to him as acts of destruction: the latter accurately cover the former, nothing protrudes. This subjective grasp of history in which the potent seed of the future *is nothing but* the most profound apocalypse of the present has been expressed by Saint-Just in strange saying: *"What constitutes the Republic is the total destruction of what is opposed to it."* This must not, I think, be understood in the trivial sense of: "One has to dear the way before reconstructing." The copula has an exhaustive meaning: there is for some men a subjective dark night of history when the future becomes an essence, the essential destruction of the past.

One last exclusion threatens the mythologist: he constantly runs the risk of causing to disappear the reality which he purports to protect. Quite apart from all speech, the *D.S. 19* is a technologically defined object: it is capable of a certain speed, it meets the wind in a certain way, etc. And this type of reality cannot be spoken of by the mythologist. The mechanic, the engineer, even the user "*speak* the object"; but the mythologist is condemned to metalanguage. This exclusion already has a name: it is what is called ideologism. Zhdanovism has roundly condemned it (without proving, incidentally, that it was, *for the time being,* avoidable) in the early Lukács, in Marr's linguistics, in works like those of Bénichou or Goldmann, opposing to it the reticence of a reality inaccessible to ideology, such as that of language according to Stalin. It is true that ideologism resolves the contradiction of alienated reality by an amputation, not a synthesis (but as for Zhdanovism, it does not even resolve it): wine is objectively good, and *at the same time,* the goodness of wine is a myth: here is the aporia. The mythologist gets out of this as best he can: he deals with the goodness of wine, not with the wine itself, just as the historian deals with Pascal's ideology, not with the *Pensées* in themselves.[30]

It seems that this is a difficulty pertaining to our times: there is as yet only one possible choice, and this choice can bear only on two equally extreme methods: either to posit a reality which is entirely permeable to history, and ideologize; or, conversely, to posit a reality which is *ultimately* impenetrable, irreducible, and, in this case, poetize. In a word, I do not yet see a synthesis between ideology and poetry (by poetry I understand, in a very general way, the search for the inalienable meaning of things).

The fact that we cannot manage to achieve more than an unstable grasp of reality doubtless gives the measure of our present alienation: we constantly drift between the object and its demystification, powerless to render its wholeness. For if we penetrate the object, we liberate it but we destroy it; and if we acknowledge its full weight, we respect it, but we restore it to a state which is still mystified. It would seem that we are condemned for some time yet always to speak *excessively* about reality. This is probably because ideologism and its opposite are types of behavior which are still magical, terrorized, blinded, and fascinated by the split in the social world. And yet, this is what we must seek: a reconciliation between reality and men, between description and explanation, between object and knowledge.

Notes

1. Innumerable other meanings of the word "myth" can be cited against this. But I have tried to define things, not words.

2. The development of publicity, of a national press, of radio, of illustrated news, not to speak of the survival of a myriad rites of communication which rule social appearances, makes the development of a semiological science more urgent than ever. In a single day, how many really non-signifying fields do we cross? Very few, sometimes none. Here I am, before the sea; it is true that it bears no message. But on the beach, what material for semiology! Flags, slogans, signals, sign-boards, clothes, suntan even, which are so many messages to me.

3. The notion of *word* is one of the most controversial in linguistics. I keep it here for the sake of simplicity.

4. *Tel Quel*, II, p. 191.

5. Or perhaps *Sinity*? Just as if Latin/Latinity = Basque/x, x = Basquity.

6. I say "in Spain" because, in France, petit-bourgeois advancement has caused a whole "mythical" architecture of the Basque chalet to flourish.

7. From the point of view of ethics, what is disturbing in myth is precisely that its form is motivated. For if there is a "health" of a language, it is the arbitrariness of the sign which is its grounding. What is sickening in myth is its resort to a false nature, its superabundance of significant forms, as in these objects which decorate their usefulness with a natural appearance. The will to weigh the signification with the full guarantee of nature causes a kind of nausea: myth is too rich, and what is in excess is precisely its motivation. This nausea is like the one I feel before the arts which refuse to choose between *physis* and *anti-physis*, using the first as an ideal and the second as an economy. Ethically, there is a kind of baseness in hedging one's bets.

8. The freedom in choosing what one focuses on is a problem which does not belong to the province of semiology; it depends on the concrete situation of the subject.

9. We receive the naming of the lion as a pure *example* of Latin grammar because we are, *as grown-ups*, in a creative position in relation to it. I shall come back later to the value of the context in this mythical schema.

10. Classical poetry, on the contrary, would be, according to such norms, a strongly mythical system, since it imposes on the meaning one extra signified, which is *regularity*. The alexandrine, for instance, has value both as meaning of a discourse and as signifier of a new whole, which is its poetic signification. Success, when it occurs, comes from the degree of apparent fusion of the two systems. It can be seen that we deal in no way with a harmony between content and form, but with an *elegant* absorption of one form into another. By *elegance* I mean the most economical use of the means employed. It is because of an age-old abuse that critics confuse *meaning* and *content*. The language is never anything but a system of forms, and the meaning is a form.

11. We are again dealing here with the *meaning*, in Sartre's use of the term, as a natural quality of things, situated outside a semiological system (*Saint Genet*, p. 283).

12. *Style*, at least as I defined it then, is not a form, it does not belong to the province of a semiological analysis of Literature. In fact, style is a substance constantly threatened with formalization. To start with, it can perfectly well become degraded into a mode of writing: there is a "Malraux-type" writing, and even in Malraux himself. Then, style can also become a particular language, that used by the writer *for himself and for himself alone*. Style then becomes a sort of solipsistic myth, the language which the writer speaks *to himself*. It is easy to understand that at such a degree of solidification, style calls for a deciphering. The works of J. P. Richard are an example of this necessary critique of styles.

13. A subjunctive form because it is in the subjunctive mode that Latin expressed "indirect style or discourse," which is an admirable instrument for demystification.

14. "The fate of capitalism is to make the worker wealthy," *Paris-Match* tells us.

15. The word *capitalism* is taboo, not economically but ideologically; it cannot possibly enter the vocabulary of bourgeois representations. Only in Farouk's Egypt could a prisoner be condemned by a tribunal for "anti-capitalist plotting" in so many words.

16. The bourgeoisie never uses the word "Proletariat," which is supposed to be a Left-wing myth, except when it is in its interest to imagine the Proletanat being led astray by the Communist Party.

17. It is remarkable that the adversaries of the bourgeoisie on matters of ethics or aesthetics remain for the most part indifferent, or even attached, to its political determinations. Conversely, its political adversaries neglect to issue a basic condemnation of its representations: they often go so far as to share them. This diversity of attacks benefits the bourgeoisie, it allows it to camouflage its name. For the bourgeoisie should be understood only as synthesis of its determinations and its representations.

18. There can be figures of derelict man which lack all order (Ionesco, for example). This does not affect in any way the security of the Essences.

19. To induce a collective content for the imagination is always an inhuman undertaking, not only because dreaming essentializes life into destiny, but also because dreams are impoverished, and the alibi of an absence.

20. "If men and their conditions appear throughout ideology inverted as in a camera obscura, this phenomenon follows from their historical vital progress ..." (Marx, *The German Ideology*).

21. To the pleasure-principle of Freudian man could be added the clarity-principle of mythological humanity. All the ambiguity of myth is there: its clarity is euphoric.

22. cf. Marx and the example of the cherry tree, *The German Ideology*.

23. cf p. 184.

24. It is remarkable that Khrushchevism presented itself not as a political change, but essentially and only as a *linguistic conversion*. An incomplete conversion, incidentally, for Khrushchev devalued Stalin but did not explain him—did not re-politicize him.

25. Today it is the colonized peoples who assume to the full the ethical and political condition described by Marx as being that of the proletariat.

26. The circulation of newspapers is an insufficient datum. Other information comes only by accident. *Paris-Match* has given—significantly, as publicity—the composition of its public in terms of standard of living (*Le Figaro*, July 12th, 1955): out of each 100 readers living in town, 53 have a car, 49 a bathroom, etc., whereas the average standard of living in France is reckoned as follows: car, 22 per cent; bathroom, 13 per cent. That the purchasing power of the *Paris-Match* reader is high could have been predicted from the mythology of this publication.

27. Marx: "... we must pay attention to this history, since ideology boils down to either an erroneous conception of this history, *or to a complete abstraction from it*" (*The German Ideology*).

28. Marx: "... what makes them representative of the petit-bourgeois class, is that their minds, their consciousnesses do not extend beyond the limits which this class has set to its activities" (*The Eighteenth Brumaire*). And Gorki: "the petit-bourgeois is the man who has preferred himself to all else."

29. *It is not only from the public that one becomes estranged; it is sometimes also from the very object of myth. In order to demystify Poetic Childhood, for instance, I have had, so to speak, *to lack confidence* in Mionou Drouet the child. I have had to ignore, in her, under the enormous myth with which she is cumbered, something like a tender, open possibility. It is never a good thing to speak against a little girl.

30. Even here, in these mythologies, I have used trickery: finding it painful constantly to work on the evaporation of reality, I have started to make it excessively dense, and to discover in it surprising compactness which I have savored with delight, and I have given a few examples of "substantial psycho-analysis" about some mythical objects.

6 Barthes, and Calling the Mundane to Account

Jofish Kaye

What impresses me about Barthes is his enormous respect for the mundane and everyday. Barthes writes in a long line of art critics, who treat art with the respect it deserves, as perhaps the supreme and most sublime artifact of our cultures. Yet in his writing about spaghetti, about wrestling, about cars, Barthes, as critic, elevates these topics to the same level of importance and respect, suggesting that humanity's most important cultural ideas (if not its noblest) can also be accessed through its comparatively pedestrian and everyday works.

And in so doing, he performs a neat move.

Allow me an analogy. In the Jewish tradition, when a thirteen-year-old boy stands up and reads from the Torah in front of his community at his bar mitzvah, he becomes a man; when a twelve-year-old girl stands up and reads from the Torah in front of her community at her bat mitzvah, she becomes a woman. These statements do not mean the boy or girl is supposed to be an adult per se, but, rather, it means they are "subject to the commandments"; subject to the *responsibilities* of an adult man or woman. "Bar" means boy (or, literally, son), "bat" means girl, a "mitzvah" is a commandment or law; a boy or girl "subject to mitzvah" is an adult. They are no longer children; they are now responsible for their actions and answerable to laws. They can hold property, they can, under rabbinical law, be married. Before this occurs, they are children and their parents are responsible for their actions; now they have become subject to responsibilities.

This is the move that Barthes performs over and over again in the essays collected in his volume *Mythologies*. The world is full of mundane objects, experiences, texts, and images that normally escape our attention, that can safely be ignored as, well, the mundane details of everyday life. But by treating these mundanities as first-class objects, to be questioned, to be interrogated, to be answerable to the same set of actions and laws and responsibilities to which we hold great works of art, or other important things, Barthes holds them responsible for shaping and changing our lives. And I think this is an awfully important strategy, because the mundane objects we interact with every day have an impact on our lives. Linguists talk about the Sapir-Whorf hypothesis—that the language we use changes how we act—similarly, what we watch on television, what we read and consume, what games we play all impact our assumptions and actions about the world.

The implications of treating these mundane objects as having import is that we can and should and must take them seriously, in the sense that we must hold such objects—and ourselves—to account for the ways that shape our experiences and relationships, and how they reflect and perpetuate our priorities and blind spots. This is where the application to HCI and our sister fields of user experience and interaction design and game design and the like becomes clear. If, for example, a computer game is just a game, then we have no need to take it seriously as a cultural artifact, because, well, it's just a game. But if we perform Barthes's move on the game, of treating it as if it mattered, then all of a sudden we can hold the game accountable—for the way it represents women, for the issues around gun violence it raises, for the statements it makes about which kinds of people it is desirable to kill on sight, for what it says about what games are for, about who owns public space—or for that matter about the details of what a good interface is and should be. This sort of cultural criticism has become almost ordinary and expected: releases of Grand Theft Auto, for example, are accompanied not just with reviews of the gameplay but discussions of the role of women or casual violence inherent in the game. Barthes was a significant player in making such criticism of seemingly mundane objects more commonplace and accepted.

And with this, I want to try to answer the key question which this book addresses, which is why an HCI or design researcher/practitioner should care about critical theory. After all, if you're reading this book, you're most likely trained in computer science or one of its sister fields. Computer science seems to have done reasonably well without a lot of critical theory so far, so what can critical theory bring to that discussion? I suggest that—at least as far as this chapter goes—the great advantage of reading Barthes's work is that it can point to avenues of inquiry that are easily overlooked precisely because they are so mundane, and yet which turn out to be extremely important for our social lives once we do begin to explore them.

Myth Today

In this chapter I concentrate on the essay that comprises the second half of Barthes's book *Mythologies*, "Myth Today." Let's start with some core terms. What we're looking at is "semiotics": the study of signs and symbols, which originated in the late 1nineteenthand early twentieth century in the writings of Charles Sanders Peirce and Ferdinand de Saussure (Saussure used the term "semiology" instead of "semiotics," but semiotics seems to have won that battle). Within semiotics, we talk about a seemingly simple relationship between two terms, a "signifier" and a "signified." The signifier is the word or object; the signified is what it is intended to and understood to mean. If you use a bunch of roses to signify your passion, then the bunch of roses is a signifier, and your passion is a signified. Together, these form a third term, a "sign," meaning these roses-that-signify-passion. In short:

signifier → signified
[signifier → signified] = sign

The aim of semiotics is to be able to rigorously query and interrogate speech and writing so that we can understand and talk about what's happening there. The great advantage of this distinction is that it enables us to talk in a coherent way about the difference between what is said and what is meant.

What is convenient about the sign articulating a relationship between signifier and signified is that it allows us to discuss and characterize multiple different signs. Roses-signifying-passion is one sign. But the same set of roses may signify other things, may represent different signs. If, on checking into a hotel, you see roses in a vase on the reception desk, those might be the sign roses-signifying-luxury, not roses-signifying-passion. A modernist, boutique hotel may deliberately and even explicitly eschew roses-signifying-luxury for, say, a stark-arrangement-of-local-conifer-branches-signifying-modernist-luxury. As we'll see, identifying these as different signs enables us to have this discussion.

So now we have understood the basic notion of signifier, signified, and sign, let's move on to the notion of myth. In his essay *Myth Today*, Barthes discusses the idea of "myth" as a kind of speech that can be analyzed and understood using the same semiotic tools we use to understand other kinds of speech. The word "myth" that as Barthes uses it might be easier to think about nowadays as meaning something close to "meme"; not in the lolcats-bad-photoshop-with-Ariel-Black-writing sense, but in the original Dawkins sense of something that spreads person-to-person within a culture and has a particular meaning within the culture (Dawkins, 1976).

Let's walk through Barthes's analysis. He starts by explaining the cover of the June 25, 1955, issue of *Paris Match*, a French newsmagazine. He starts by describing the cover: a picture of a young black soldier in a French uniform, saluting, eyes fixed on the flag (Barthes, 1972, 116). This is the signifier.

Then there's the signified. Barthes tells us that the signified in this case is that "France is a great empire, that all her sons, without any colour discrimination, faithfully serve under her flag, and that there is not better answer to the detractors of an alleged colonialism than the zeal shown by this Negro in serving his so-called oppressors." For now, we're going to take this statement as given, but we'll come back to it.

And then there's the combination of the two, the sign: this magazine cover suggesting that France is a great empire where all her sons serve under flag, and so on.

Once again, it's important to recognize that there are potentially multiple signifieds and signs for a single signifier. For example, we could look at the same magazine cover in a graphic design class and instead talk about the contrast between the red logo and the soldier's beret, or about the consistent use of sans-serif type. We would be considering the same signifier but a different set of signifieds, resulting in different signs and even a different system of signs (which is close to what Barthes means by "myth"). Or we could look at a different signifier, say the 1952 Bastille Day Parade in Paris, which included the Spahis, cavalry regiments of the French army from Northern Africa, who could be read as having the same signified meaning (France is a great empire, all her sons serve under her flag without discrimination, etc.), but together combining to create a different sign, which fits into the same myth.

The key here is Barthes's meta move: he says that you can take any given sign—the combination of signifier and signified—and treat the whole thing as itself a signifier, which points to another signified, constituting a new sign, which can, once again, be treated as itself a signifier, ad infinitum.

Let's return to the example of roses: "this rose signifies your passion." The rose-signifying-your-passion sign can in turn become a secondary or meta-sign, that is, itself a signifier for a new signified, say, the fact that you are in love, or that you want to apologize to your partner (both are conventional uses of roses of contemporary romantic relationships). Or perhaps the rose-signifying-your-passion in turn signifies bereavement, that you've lost someone you love (again, because flowers are often used to express grief). The color of the roses can also be significant. If someone is making romantic overtures to you, and you want to reciprocate, the rose-signifying-your-passion will be red; if that rose is yellow, the rose signifies mere friendship and an indirect means of communicating your romantic unavailability to that individual. But let's imagine that we're in fifteenth-century England: now the rose-signifying-your-passion more likely indicates your partisan stance in the civil war between the Yorks and the Lancasters, the color of the rose indicating which side you're on. The point of all these examples is to show that signification never stops with a single signifier-signified pairing, or sign, but always goes on, and when it does, cultural practices and conventional meanings very quickly get activated. In this way, semiotics offers an analytic vocabulary to connect the concrete world of individual magazine covers, utterances, flowers, slogans, and so on, with the intangible world of culture, social life, and intersubjective understanding.

Let's try a diagram. What we had before was this:

signifier → signified
[signifier → signified] = sign
Now we have this:
signifier → signified
[signifier → signified] = **sign**
sign becomes a **new signifier** for a **new signified**
rose → your passion
[rose → your passion] = **rose-signifying-your-passion**

rose-signifying-your-passion → **you are indicating** that **you're in love** (or **really sorry that you were a jerk**, or **really sad that so-and-so passed away**, or **a fifteenth-century Yorkist partisan**)

Now, when talking about myths—the cogent (and often unconscious and ideological) sociocultural narratives that comprise these constellations of signs—Barthes uses slightly different vocabulary. The secondary or meta-sign in its new role as signifier he calls the "form" (in the example just above, "rose-signifying-your-passion"). The meaning (i.e., intention and/or understanding) of that form (i.e., "you are symbolizing that you're in love"), the thing we would have called signified, he now calls the "concept" when we're talking about myth, and the combination of the two is the "signification." Why use these extra words to mean the same thing? Barthes points out that we can stack these significations on top of each other again and again and again in one of the key concepts of Barthes's semiotics: an endless chain of signification.

That *Paris Match* cover signifying "France is a great empire" is now the object of study, the form we're looking at here. We can see not only the intended imperial meaning of the original image but also that, today, most of us would read this as a colonial and ultimately racist image. What makes it racist is the subjugation of the person of color to the white nationalist enterprise, which is the myth. Thus, the racism inheres not at the lower level of the signifier but at the higher level of this as a mythic form—and if people can grasp its racism, then they must also be grasping the notion of myth and the mechanism by which it perpetuates itself through signs. Looking at myth, taking it seriously, means that we can recognize and talk about these layers upon layers of signification.

Which then becomes the basis for the analysis of myth, as shown in table 6.1.

This is where Barthes expands on regular notions of semantics: we're moving on from merely looking at signifiers and signifieds to taking seriously the many ways in which these myths perpetuate themselves through the systematic conventions by which we deploy signs every day.

One more note before we go on—and this is going back to Barthes's point about the signified of the cover, about France's empire. Barthes distinguishes between a full versus

Table 6.1

When we talk about *myth* we can do this	form → concept [form → concept] = signification$_1$		
	And we can do this again	signification$_1$ → concept [signification$_1$ → concept] = signification$_2$	
		And again and again ...	signification$_2$ → concept [signification$_2$ → concept] = signification$_3$

an empty signifier, and this matters because it explains in part why "Myth Today" can be difficult to follow. The empty signifier is just the signifier on the page: a picture of a man saluting, say. It's a signifier devoid of context or history. The full signifier is the full history and context of use of that particular signifier—behind the picture on the page is a real man, a person who decided to join the armed forces, maybe because he wanted to leave home, some combination of all those things. At the same time, there's history about French militarization and colonization and civilization, all wrapped up and assumed in that image. But—and here the difficulty comes—readers of this volume probably do not know the same information behind the full signifier that Barthes does *and Barthes assumes that his (contemporary French) reader does*. So the things that Barthes takes for granted will be understood as full signifiers might today be read as empty signifiers, and therein lies the rub.

The reason Barthes thinks myth is worth discussing is all about this relationship between the full history and the empty signifier. Here's his key point in "Myth Today": Evoking the myth lets you skip all the complicated and messy history. Barthes refers to this as "naturalization," and I would like to suggest it's the most important concept to grasp in the whole essay, because it gets at the semiotic mechanisms that underlie the formation and self-perpetuation of ideology. When things seem natural, and are accepted as natural, we don't question them and we accept them as given. Barthes calls attention to this process, to the ways in which myths and stories and assumptions are slipped in under our attention and become accepted as such, become beyond question. But if we have the tools to perceive this hitherto invisible process, we have the tools (and responsibility) to call it out for what it is and to intervene.

Once you recognize this phenomenon, you can see examples of it all over the place. Evoking, say, the all-American values of "Freedom" and "Democracy" and "Capitalism" lets you ignore the subjugation of American Indians, slavery, and exploitation of nonrenewable natural resources that were part of bringing the country to the place it is today. Evoking the world-changing powers of massively open online courses (MOOCs) lets you ignore the necessary skills of discipline, scholarship, self-motivation, and linguistic ability that are so crucial for the very people such courses might most be thought to aid. Evoking the enormous powers of "Big Data" lets you ignore the enormous variety of intentions and desires and needs and situations masked behind actions captured in petabytes and petabytes of database entries and logs. (Yes, I am calling MOOCs and Big Data in contemporary IT discourse myths in the Barthesian sense.) In each case, it is not that one of these readings is the "One True Meaning" and the other is naïve claptrap; it's rather that approaching these myths with Barthes's tools in hand lets you recognize and engage with both sets of meanings.

And this is Barthes's aim in this essay. We could make a good case for dividing his essay into two parts. In the first, Barthes defines his terms and frames his argument. He makes a rigorous and logical case in explaining how language is used to achieve certain sociocultural effects. It's thorough, it's precise, and it's the bedrock on which he rests the rest of the article, where he goes on to apply this system of thought and discourse to a variety of topics. In particular, he starts with looking at poetry, and analyzing what poetry is and how it works, using this system of semiotic analysis. He then goes on to look at some other topics: the changing notion of the bourgeoisie, the politicized speech of the left, the politicized speech of the right. Rather than follow these paths, I think it is more immediately relevant to the world of HCI to think about Barthes's approach and what it would say about not poetry or politics or proverbs, but science.

Science is often presented at the high school (and, unfortunately, often at the collegiate) level as a set of ground truths about the world—things that are true regardless of petty details, like who performs an experiment or where it happened. And for a few basic facts, this is true: for example, objects on Earth start to accelerate downward, when you drop them, at $9.8m/s^2$. But most of the time things are a little more problematic. Questions like who performs an experiment, what they're expecting to discover when they perform that experiment, who paid for an experiment—have all sorts of impacts on the knowledge that is produced by the process of science.

Let's take an example from outside the field of HCI. I did work for a while on computerized smell output, and here's one peer-reviewed paper on smell published in a widely cited journal (impact factor for 2011: 3.968; for comparison, this is roughly equivalent to the impact factor of the journal *HCI*):

Hirsch, A. R. (2000) "Effects of Garlic Bread on Family Interactions." *Psychosomatic Medicine* 62: 103–4.

To summarize the research: after a single-blind, fifty-family study, Dr. Hirsch concludes that serving garlic bread at dinner increases positive family interactions and decreases negative interactions. Very well. Garlic bread for everyone!

So what would Barthes have to say about this exemplar of science? The signifier is this two-page article. And, as noted, we could use this study to signify many things. Let us conjecture that on the plane of a linguistic, nonmythic system, the signified is that garlic bread improves positive family interactions, and thus if you wish to improve your family interactions then you should purchase garlic bread. The combination of these two, the sign, we might state as "Hirsch (2000) says garlic bread improves family interactions."

At the same time, there are many other things going on here. The acknowledgement notes that the research was sponsored by the Campbell Soup Company, which no doubt sponsors significant amounts of research on topics of interest to them. But as the reader of this text probably knows, there is a gap between doing science and getting things published in a peer-reviewed forum. So what additional value is coming from the fact that this paper is published in a peer-reviewed journal? Let's give it the Barthes treatment. We can now treat that sign we discussed in the last paragraph as a form, and then propose that the concept is that the publication of Hirsch (2000) in a peer-reviewed journal means that this research is more scientific, more valid, more validated, more correct, more true, than if it were merely an internal research study. And the signification is that this combination of article and publication venue is a story, a myth about scientific quality and hence reliability. It is a myth that says that because this research is good and valid and scientific, because it's published in a peer-reviewed journal, then you should buy garlic bread if you wish to improve your family interactions, *because science says so.*

Now, one of the myths about science is that is the ultimate truth, that it has the final say on things, regardless of situation or context. You might recall Donna Haraway addressing this myth in her essay *Simians, Cyborgs and Women*, when she describes the omnipotent, omniscient view given by visual scientific instruments:

> Vision in this technological feast becomes unregulated gluttony; all perspective gives way to infinitely mobile vision, which no longer seems just mythically about the god-trick of seeing everything from nowhere, but to have put the myth into ordinary practice. And like the god-trick, this eye fucks the world to make techno-monsters. (Haraway, 1991, 198)

So what does Haraway mean in this glorious, grad-student-delighting paragraph? She is making a point about a new way of knowing which is in contrast to assumptions about the myth of all-knowing science: *situated knowledges*. These are knowledges—or ways of knowing—that are unabashedly unobjective, that recognize that they are from and part of a particular time and place, and that they reflect that particular time and place. In many ways, Haraway is continuing Barthes's project of resisting normalization, of actively resisting, in this case, the myth that science is where all the answers lie.

The myth of science here is that power, that intellectual supremacy over all other ways of knowing—local knowledge, tradition, intuition, and so forth—regardless of situation and context. And that's where Barthes's meta move comes in: it points out that *science doesn't get to have the final say*. Science has to have a conversation like everyone else does; it is answerable to the same questions and conversations and discussions. Science is not "natural"; it is situated and contextual and answerable as much as any other system of knowledge.

I choose science rather than poetry or some other collection of meaning-creation because it is perhaps the most egregious offender in HCI of claiming ultimate knowledge. As such, in treating this myth about science as one that we can and should analyze and hold responsible, we can start to ask questions about how knowledge is produced and legitimated, and how it thereby has influence in how IT actually gets designed and evaluated.

Let's go back to the garlic bread. Do you think this result is valid? More specifically, for the fifty families studied, in Chicago in, say, 1999, do you think there were more positive interactions at the dinners where they ate garlic bread? Do you think that, in general, garlic bread really makes for happier families? Are there families for whom this might not be true? People with celiac disease, perhaps, or with allergies to alliums? This study was performed in Chicago. Do you think the results are valid in Los Angeles? In Jaipur, India? In Jeddah, Saudi Arabia? In Suzhou, China? Did your thoughts on this work change when you notice that it was sponsored by the Campbell Soup Company,[1] makers of Pepperidge Farm® Garlic Bread? How does this make you feel about the value of "peer-reviewed" as a mark of quality or scientific validity?

And that is the power of Barthes's approach to analyzing myth. He's not content to let sleeping myths lie: he picks them up and points them out and shakes them and tries to explain what they're made of, and in so doing enjoins you the reader to do the same. He holds forms, things, objects, and experiences accountable for the myths they engender. His contribution is not his analysis of this or that magazine cover or ad: it is the analytic strategy that he teaches us and exemplifies for us, so that we can do this work ourselves.

Myth in HCI

So let's explore taking Barthes's system of analysis and applying it to HCI. I've picked two subfields of HCI that I think are ripe for such analysis: HCI4D and sustainable HCI. Both are quite aware of the role they play as subfields of the larger field of HCI, but I think both benefit from some thoughtful analysis of the myths on which they rest and which they engender.

First, let's look at ICT4D: information and communication technologies for development. ICT4D is one of the more reflective parts of HCI: it has spent a lot of time thinking about itself and the work that it does. Michael Best's (2010) paper, for example, is a reflective look at ICT4D, thoughtfully examining epistemological differences between computer scientists and social scientists publishing in the same field, and concluding that one of the fundamental problems that the field has failed to become a progressive enterprise, one in which work in the field builds on previous work in the field, learning from their successes and mistakes. We can read Best's analysis as a way to encourage us to further investigate myths in ICT4D—to a greater and lesser degree in different research groups and fields and situations, but myths we can see and identify. This is far from the first attempt scrutinize the mythology inherent in ICT4D. Best's article is reflective from the inside; Irani et al. (2010) draw very similar conclusions in their paper "Postcolonial Computing."

So what do myths of ICT4D look like? Obviously, I cannot in this space conduct a proper analysis, but I can point to some ICT4D myths that have, directly or indirectly, already been called out:

• Technology itself is universal: the assumption that, like a laptop, a technological solution which works and solves a problem in San Francisco will do the same in Tokyo—or

Lima, or in the Kalahari desert. See, for example, Warschauer and Ames's [2010] analysis of One Laptop per Child.

• Technological solutions will solve problems, without any changes in accompanying social structures, infrastructure, support, and assumptions. See, for example, troubles with rolling out a cellphone-based RFID system in Haiti (Kaye et al., 2012. In that case, users complained "You need a depot," meaning a location with spares, replacements, and support for these technological systems.

• Research methods are universal; for example, participatory design, an approach developed in Scandinavian countries, will work as well in South Africa. See, for example, the issues discussed in Toyama (2010).

Barthes gives us a way to analyze these situations in a constructive manner, by pulling forward for our consideration the underlying narratives that shape this research. For example, let's look at the myth that problems can be solved by implementing technological solutions. Michael Best describes the solution to that as "avoid the pitfalls of fetishistic techno-utopianism that, regardless of our rhetoric, is a far-too-common reality" (Best, 2010, 51). Let's look at how we might represent that:

technology → solving problems

[technology in developing country → solving problems in developing country] = ICT4D

Best proposes replacing this myth of technological solutions with a replacement mythology of long-term and constructive intellectual engagement ("Spend time on fundamental innovation and work; this means, in particular, to find patient money supporting multi-year initiatives" [51]) relegating this particular myth to merely a component part of a bigger (and hopefully more powerful) supportive myth of long-term engagement, funding, and innovation.

A note: It's easy to cast stones here, and that's not something particularly useful to do—I enthusiastically apply these criticisms to my own work in ICT4D as much as anyone else's. Indeed, it's easy to point the finger and say "Thou shalt not"—when in fact, it's almost impossible not to as a way to make sense of the situation. Myth making is a powerful part of creating narratives, and consciously doing so—while also noticing and reflecting on existing ones—is arguably part of responsible scholarship.

Let's continue this look at another subfield: sustainable HCI. Sustainable HCI is concerned with bringing HCI's focus and expertise to bear on the problems of environmental sustainability. Once again, I would consider it one of the more reflective subfields of HCI, one that has spent time thinking about its own impact and epistemological approach. But let's try to identify some of the myths of sustainable HCI. For example, they might include:

• There's a technical solution to sustainability problems.

• It is in our power to do something around the problem of climate change by doing HCI as usual, just with a different focus.

- We can solve sustainability problems with individual interventions.
- Sustainability is a problem that can be addressed with HCI; furthermore, it is a problem that can be addressed by changing individual behaviors; even furthermore, individual behaviors will change if only we can bring people's attention to their own practices.

Let's look at this last myth in some detail. For example, I recently received a letter from my local town council asking me to cut back my water consumption by 10 percent.

[Cut personal water use by 10% → saving water] = aggregate personal action resulting in positive change.

This is because in California, where I live, there is a significant water shortage. A Sustainable HCI response to that problem might be, for example, to put a display on my showerhead showing the water usage (e.g., the one reported in Kuznetsov and Paulos, 2010).

But the problem with this myth is that the vast majority of water consumption in California comes from agricultural uses, particularly for high water-consumption crops such as rice or beef: as much as 80 percent, by some estimates, with additional significant usage coming from private lawn (and particularly golf course) sprinklers. There are assumptions inherent in these myths about power and agency that simply aren't true. In a situation like this one, I simply cannot make a significant difference in California's water consumption as an individual householder, but other people, who have more power over the policies that govern that consumption, can indeed have an impact. The latter point seems to let me off the hook. Perhaps the best agency I have to contribute to a solution to the California water shortage is not an ambient display in my bathroom, but a commitment I could make to spend that time contacting appropriate politicians and decision makers to encourage changes in policy. That might be an effective replacement for the existing myth, and one that recognizes the potential danger inherent in such assumptions.

Discussion

Barthes repeatedly describes the construction of myths as a negative criticism: for him, myths are a way of articulating that people are doing something bad or doing something wrong. But I think in HCI, with our emphasis on building and creating as a form of knowledge production, we can be more conciliatory and say it's pretty difficult *not* to create myths, and that the creation of myths is itself productive of a certain kind of thought. It is easy to stand on one side of the fence and point fingers; in HCI, the problem becomes how to build something that does, in one way or another, make positive change in the world. This is perhaps the great challenge of critical HCI approaches: how to recognize the tensions exposed by the myths in a field and yet to build something that contributes anyway.

More than anything else, I think one promising uptake of Barthes and his analysis of myth into HCI is to make us reconsider our notions of failure. A core underlying myth of HCI is that very myth of individual action: the myth, that, for example, someone can build a new app or device, deploy it, and thereby solve a major problem. What an enormous burden to put on ourselves! If you go to an underdeveloped country for a few weeks or months, build a system, and deploy it, and it doesn't solve a major problem, then we consider that to be failure.

But failure itself can generate insights—as shown explicitly in Best (2010), again, or in a carefully argued piece, Gaver et al. (2009). Success, particularly individual success, is perhaps the most pervasive myth in human-computer interaction research, and arguably a larger myth of Silicon Valley, and even of science and capitalism in general. It's a myth that individuals are responsible for their own success or failure; that ultimately unsustainable approaches—a dependence on fossil fuels, on ongoing economic growth—are unremarkable elements of success. There are no easy answers here, and pulling out elements of these myths is itself a disturbing thing to do: where do we draw the line? How can we avoid concluding that it's all a pointless exercise? An analysis of the myths that underlie our research agenda can help us understand those aspects that are unrealistic or downright delusional, so we can try to weed them out of our reasoning. But it can also reveal opportunities for improving our thought, perhaps by reformulating a research question in a more generative way, or by providing peer reviewers (and other gatekeepers charged with maintaining the intellectual quality of our knowledge work) with better standards or criteria.

I would argue that the field, and our own work, benefits from the context and awareness that actively identifying myths brings to a research practice in HCI. What matters is being alert to recognizing and confronting myths, and, in the context of HCI, to hold programs and websites and research studies and research papers accountable and responsible for the myths that they leverage, reference, encourage, and engender and, tacitly, legitimate themselves with. Such a task is much more likely if we have analytic tools to help us do it, and that's what Barthes provides in the excerpt in chapter 5. All of us have been taught to be suspicious about how dominant discourses—be they Hollywood movies or articles in elite science journals—perpetuate assumptions—about the roles for women, the notion of family or citizenship, the "best" ways to make knowledge. But in practice, this is actually a very difficult thing to do—few scientists want to perpetuate bigotry or unexamined assumptions about knowledge-making. What Barthes gives us, then, is a technical vocabulary and methodology that is suited to this task of revealing the mechanisms by which these assumptions enter our language as natural-seeming semiotic structures that—like a magazine ad selling spaghetti sauce—seem unworthy of our attention.

Acknowledgments

I'd like to thank Jeffrey Bardzell for his careful, detailed, and constructive suggestions towards improvement of this chapter, as well as his invitation to contribute in the first place.

Note

1. Full disclosure: I consulted on two occasions for the Campbell Soup Company, in 2003 and 2004, as an expert on kitchens of the future.

References

Barthes, R. (1972) "Myth Today." In *Mythologies*, translated by Annette Lavers, 109–159. London: Hill and Wang.

Best, M. L. (2010) "Understanding Our Knowledge Gaps: Or, Do We Have an ICT4D Field? And Do We Want One?" Special edition, *Information Technologies and International Development* 6: 49–52.

Dawkins, R. (1976) *The Selfish Gene*. New York: Oxford University Press.

Gaver, W., J. Bowers, T. Kerridge, A. Boucher, and N. Jarvis. (2009) "Anatomy of a Failure: How We Knew When Our Design Went Wrong, and What We Learned from It." *Proceedings of the SIGCHI Conference on Human Factors in Computing Systems (CHI'09)*. New York: ACM, 2213–2222.

Haraway, D. J. (1991) "Situated Knowledges: The Science Question in Feminism and the Privilege of Partial Perspective." In *Simians, Cyborgs and Women: The Reinvention of Nature*, 183–202. New York: Routledge.

Hirsch, A, R. (2000) "Effects of Garlic Bread on Family Interactions." *Psychosomatic Medicine* 62 (1): 103–104.

Irani, L., J. Vertesi, P. Dourish, K. Philip, and R. E. Grinter. (2010) "Postcolonial Computing: A Lens on Design and Development." *Proceedings of the SIGCHI Conference on Human Factors in Computing Systems (CHI'10)*. New York: ACM, 1311–1320.

Kaye J., D. Holstius, E. Seto, B. Eddy, and M. Ritter. (2012) "Using NFC Phones to Track Water Purification in Haiti." *Proceedings of the Extended Abstracts on Human Factors in Computing Systems (CHIEA'12)*. New York: ACM, 667–689.

Kuznetsov, S., and E. Paulos. (2010) "UpStream: Motivating Water Conservation with Low-Cost Water Flow Sensing and Persuasive Displays." *Proc. CHI'10*. New York: ACM, 1851–1860.

Toyama, K. (2010) "Human-Computer Interaction and Global Development." *Foundations and Trends in Human-Computer Interaction* 4 (1): 1–79.

Warschauer, M., and M. Ames. (2010) "Can One Laptop per Child Save the World's Poor?" *Journal of International Affairs* 64 (1): 33–51.

7 *The Open Work* (1989)

Umberto Eco, translated by Anna Cancogni

Openness, Information, Communication

In its advocacy of artistic structures that demand a particular involvement on the part of the audience, contemporary poetics merely reflects our culture's attraction for the "indeterminate," for all those processes which, instead of relying on a univocal, necessary sequence of events, prefer to disclose a field of possibilities, to create "ambiguous" situations open to all sorts of operative choices and interpretations.

To describe this singular aesthetic situation and properly define the kind of openness" to which so much of contemporary poetics aspires, we are now going to make a detour into science, and more precisely into information theory, hoping it will provide us with a few indications that might prove useful to our research. There are two main reasons for this detour. In the first place, I believe that poetics in certain cases reflects, in its own way, the same cultural situation that has prompted numerous investigations in the field of information theory. Second, I believe that some of the methodological tools employed in these investigations, duly transposed, might also be profitably used in the field of aesthetics (as we shall see, others have already done this). Some people will object that there can be no effective connections between aesthetics and information theory, and that to draw parallels between the two fields can only be a gratuitous, futile exercise. Possibly so. Before engaging in any kind of transposition, let us therefore examine the general principles of information theory with no reference to aesthetics, and only then decide whether there are any connections between the two fields and, if so, of what sort, and whether it might be profitable to apply to one the methodological instruments used in the other.

Information Theory

Information theory tries to calculate the quantity of information contained in a particular message. If, for instance, on August 4 the weather forecaster says, "Tomorrow, no snow," the amount of information I get is very limited; my own experience would have easily allowed me to reach that conclusion. On the other hand, if on August 4 the forecaster says, "Tomorrow, snow," then the amount of information I get is considerable, given the improbability of the event. The quantity of information contained in a particular message is also generally conditioned by the confidence I have in my sources. If I ask a real estate broker whether the apartment he has just shown me is damp or not and he tells me that it is not, he gives me very little information, and I remain as uncertain as I was before I asked him the question. On the other hand, if he tells me that the apartment *is* damp, against my own expectation and his own interest, then he gives me a great deal of information and I feel I have learned something relevant about a subject that matters to me.

Information is, therefore, an *additive* quantity, something that is added to what one already knows as if it were an original acquisition. All the examples I have just given, however, involved a vast and complex amount of information whose novelty greatly depended on the expectations of the receiver. In fact, information should be first defined with the help of much simpler situations that would allow it to be quantified mathematically and expressed in numbers, without any reference to the knowledge of a possible receiver. This is the task of information theory. Its calculations can suit messages of all sorts: numerical symbols, linguistic symbols, sound sequences, and so on.

To calculate the amount of information contained in a particular message, one must keep in mind that the highest probability an event will take place is 1, and the lowest is 0. The mathematical probability of an event therefore varies between 1 and 0. A coin thrown into the air has an equal chance of landing on either heads or tails; thus, the probability of getting heads is 1/2. In contrast, the chance of getting a 3 when rolling a die is 1/6. And the probability that two independent events will occur at the same time is the product of their individual probabilities; thus, when rolling a pair of dice, the probability of getting a 1 and a 6 is 1/36.

The relationship between the number of possible events in a series and the series of probabilities connected to each of them is the same as that between an arithmetic progression and a geometric progression, and can be expressed by a logarithm, since the second series is the logarithm of the first. The simplest expression for a given quantity of information is the following:

$$\text{Information} = \log \frac{\text{odds that addressee will know content of message after receiving it}}{\text{odds that addressee will know content of message before receiving it}}$$

In the case of the coin, if I am told that the coin will show heads, the expression will read:

$$\log_2 1/\tfrac{1}{2} = 1.$$

Information theory proceeds by binary choices, uses base 2 logarithms, and calls the unit of information a "bit," a contraction of "binary" and "digit." The use of a base 2 logarithm has one advantage: since $\log_2 2 = 1$, one bit of information is enough to tell us which of two probabilities has been realized. For a more concrete example, let's take a common 64-square chessboard with a single pawn on it. If somebody tells me that the pawn is on square number 48, the information I receive can be measured as follows: since, initially, my chances to guess the right square were 1/64, I can translate this into the expression $-\log_2 (1/64) = \log_2 64 = 6$. The information I have received is therefore 6 bits.[1]

To conclude, we can say that *the quantity of information conveyed by a given message is equal to the binary logarithm of the number of possibilities necessary to define the message without ambiguity.*[2]

To measure an increase or a decrease in information, theoreticians have borrowed a concept from thermodynamics that by now has become an integral part of the lexicon of information theory: the concept of entropy. The term has been bandied about long enough for everyone to have heard of it and, in most cases, to have used it somewhat loosely. We should therefore take a fresh look at it, so as to divest it of all the more or less legitimate echoes it has carried over from thermodynamics. According to the second law of thermodynamics, formulated by Rudolf Clausius, although a certain amount of work can be transformed into heat (as stated by the first law), every time heat is transformed into work certain limitations arise to prevent the process from ever being fully completed. To obtain an optimum transformation of heat into work, a machine must provoke exchanges of heat between two bodies with different temperatures: a heater and a cooler. The machine draws a certain amount of heat from the heater but, instead of transforming it all into work, passes part of it on to the cooler. The amount of heat, Q, is then partly transformed into work, Q_1, and partly funneled into the cooler, $Q - Q_1$. Thus, the amount of work that is *transformed into* heat will be greater than the amount of work *derived from* a subsequent transformation of heat into work. In the process, there has been a degradation, more commonly known as a consumption, of energy that is absolutely irreversible. This is often the case with natural processes: "Certain processes have only *one direction:* each of them is like a step forward whose trace can never be erased."[3] To obtain a general measure of irreversibility, we have to consider the possibility that nature favors certain states over others (the ones at the receiving end of an irreversible process), and we must find a physical measure that could quantify nature's preference for a certain state and that would increase whenever a process is irreversible. This measure is entropy.

The second law of thermodynamics, concerning the consumption of energy, has therefore become the law of entropy, so much so that the concept of entropy has often been associated with that of consumption, and with the theory stating that the evolution of all natural processes toward an increasing consumption and progressive degradation of energy will eventually result in the "thermic death" of the universe. And here it is important to stress, once and for all, that although in thermodynamics entropy is used to define consumption (thereby acquiring pessimistic connotations—whether or not it is reasonable to react emotionally to a scientific concept), in fact it is merely a *statistical measure* and, as such, a mathematically neutral instrument. In other words, entropy is the measure of that state of maximal *equiprobability* toward which natural processes tend. This is why one can say that nature shows certain preferences: nature prefers greater uniformity to lesser uniformity, and heat moves from a warmer body to a cooler body because a state in which heat is equally distributed is more probable than a state in which heat is unequally distributed. In other words, the reciprocal speed of molecules tends toward a state of uniformity rather than toward a state of differentiation, in which certain molecules move faster than others and the temperature is constantly changing. Ludwig Boltzmann's research on the kinetic theory of gases demonstrated that nature tends toward an elemental disorder of which entropy is the measure.[4]

It is, therefore, important to insist on the *purely statistical* character of entropy—no less purely statistical than the principle of irreversibility, whereby, as proved by Boltzmann, the process of reversion within a closed system is not impossible, only improbable. The collisions of the molecules of a gas are governed by statistical laws which lead to an average equalization of differences in speed. When a fast molecule hits a slow one, it may occasionally happen that the slow molecule loses most of its speed and imparts it to the fast one, which then travels away even faster; but such occurrences are exceptions. In the overwhelming number of collisions, the faster molecule will lose speed and the slower one will gain it, thus bringing about a more uniform state and an increase in elemental disorder.

As Hans Reichenbach has written, "The law of the increase of entropy is guaranteed by the law of large numbers, familiar from statistics of all kinds, but it is not of the type of the strict laws of physics, such as the laws of mechanics, which are regarded as exempt from possible exceptions."[5]

Reichenbach has provided us with the clearest and simplest explanation of how the concept of entropy has passed from the theory of energy consumption to that of information. The increase in entropy that generally occurs during physical processes does not exclude the possibility of other physical processes (such as those we experience every day, since most organic processes seem to belong to this category) that entail an organization of events running counter to all probability—in other words, involving a decrease in entropy. Starting with the entropy curve of the universe, Reichenbach calls these decreasing phases, characterized by an interaction of events that leads to a new organization of elements, *branch systems*, to indicate their deviation from the curve.

Consider, for example, the chaotic effect (resulting from a sudden imposition of uniformity) of a strong wind on the innumerable grains of sand that compose a beach:

amid this confusion, the action of a human foot on the surface of the beach constitutes a complex interaction of events that leads to the statistically very improbable configuration of a footprint. The organization of events that has produced this configuration, this form, is only temporary: the footprint will soon be swept away by the wind. In other words, a deviation from the general entropy curve (consisting of a decrease in entropy and the establishment of *improbable order*) will generally tend to be reabsorbed into the universal curve of increasing entropy. And yet, for a moment, the elemental chaos of this system has made room for the appearance of an order, based on the relationship of cause and effect: the cause being the series of events interacting with the grains of sand (in this case, the human foot), and the effect being the organization resulting from it (in this case, the footprint).

The existence of these relationships of cause and effect in systems organized according to decreasing entropy is at the basis of memory. Physically speaking, memory is a record (an imprint, a print), an "ordered macroarrangement, the order of which is preserved: a frozen order, so to speak."[6] Memory helps us reestablish causal links, reconstruct facts. "Since the second law of thermodynamics leads to the existence of records of the past, and records store information, it is to be expected that *there is a close relationship between entropy and information.*"[7]

We shouldn't, therefore, be too surprised by the frequent use of the term "entropy" in information theories, since to measure a quantity of information means nothing more than to measure the levels of order and disorder in the organization of a given message.

The Concept of Information in the Work of Norbert Wiener

For Norbert Wiener—who has relied extensively on information theory for his research in cybernetics, that is, in his investigation of the possibilities of control and communication in human beings and machines—the informative content of a message is given by the degree of its organization. Since information is a measure of order, the measure of disorder, that is to say, entropy, must be its opposite. Which means that the information of a message depends on its ability to elude, however temporarily, the equiprobability, the uniformity, the elemental disorder toward which all natural events seem destined, and to organize according to a particular order. For instance, if I throw in the air a bunch of cubes with different letters printed on their faces, once they hit the ground they will probably spell out something utterly meaningless—say, AAASQMFLLNSUHOI. This sequence of letters does not tell me anything in particular. In order to tell me something, it would have to be organized according to the orthographic and grammatical laws of a particular language—in other words, it would have to be organized according to a particular linguistic *code*. A language is a human event, a typical *branch system* in which several factors have intervened to produce a state of order and to establish precise connections. In relation to the entropy curve, language—an organization that has escaped the equiprobability of disorder—is another *improbable* event, a naturally improbable configuration that can now establish its own *chain of probability* (the probabilities on which the organization of a language depends) within the system that governs it. This kind of organization is what allows me to predict, with a fair amount of certainty, that in an English word containing three consonants in a row the next letter will be a vowel. The tonal system, in music, is another language, another code, another *branch system.* Though extremely improbable when compared to other natural acoustic events, the tonal system also introduces, within its own organization, certain criteria of probability that allow one to predict, with moderate certainty, the melodic curve of a particular sequence of notes, as well as the specific place in the sequence where the tonic accent will fall.

In its analysis of communication, information theory considers messages as organized systems governed by fixed laws of probability, and likely to be disturbed either from without or from within (from the attenuation of the text itself, for instance) by a certain amount of disorder, of communication consumption—that is to say, by a certain increase in entropy commonly known as "noise." If the meaning of the message depends on its organization according to certain laws of probability (that is, laws pertaining to the linguistic system), then "dis-order" is a constant threat to the message itself, and entropy is its measure. In other words, *the information carried by a message is the negative of its entropy.*[8]

To protect the message against consumption so that no matter how much noise interferes with its reception the gist of its meaning (of its order) will not be altered, it is necessary to "wrap" it in a number of conventional reiterations that will increase the probability of its survival. This surplus of reiterations is what we commonly call "redundancy." Let's say I want to transmit the message "Mets won" to another fan who lives on the other side of the Hudson. Either I shout it at him with the help of a loudspeaker, or I have it wired to him by a possibly inexperienced telex operator, or I phone it to him over a static-filled line, or I put a note in the classic bottle and abandon it to the whims of the current. One way or another, my message will have to overcome a certain number of obstacles before it reaches its destination; in information theory, all these obstacles fall under the rubric "noise." To make sure that neither the hapless telex operator nor a water leak is going to turn my victorious cry into the rather baffling "Met swan," or the more allusive "Met Swann," I can add "Red Sox lost," at which point, whether the message reaches my friend or not, its meaning will probably not be lost.

According to a more rigorous definition, "redundancy," within a linguistic system, results from a set of syntactic, orthographic, and grammatical laws. As a system of preestablished probabilities, language is a *code of communication.* Pronouns, particles, inflections—all these linguistic elements tend to enrich the organization of a message and make its communication more probable. It might be said that even vowels can contribute to the redundancy of a message, because they facilitate (and make more probable) one's ability to distinguish and to comprehend the consonants in a word. The sequence of consonants *bldg* suggests the word "building" more clearly than the vowels *uii*; on the other hand, the insertion of these three vowels between the consonants makes the word easier to utter and to understand, thus increasing its comprehensibility. When information theorists say that 50 percent of the English language consists of redundancy, what they mean is that only 50 percent of what is said concerns the message to be communicated, while the other 50 percent is determined by the statistical structure of the language and functions as a supplementary means of clarification. When we speak of a "telegraphic style," we generally refer to a message that has been stripped of most of its redundancy (pronouns, articles, adverbs)—that is, of all that is not strictly necessary to its communication. On the other hand, in a telegram the lost redundancy of the message is replaced by another set of conventions also aiming at facilitating its communication by constituting a new form of probability and order. Indeed, linguistic redundancy is so dependent on a particular system of probability that a statistical study of the morphological structure of words from any language would yield an *x* number of frequently recurring letters which, when arranged in random sequences, would reveal some traits of the language from which they have been taken.[9]

Yet this also means that the very order which allows a message to be understood is also what makes it absolutely predictable—that is, extremely banal. The more ordered and comprehensible a message, the more predictable it is. The messages written on Christmas cards or birthday cards, determined by a very limited system of probability, are generally quite clear but seldom tell us anything we don't already know.

The Difference between Meaning and Information

All of the above seems to invalidate the assumption, supported by Wiener's book, that the *meaning* of a message and the *information* it carries are synonymous, strictly related to the notions of *order* and *probability* and opposed to those of entropy and disorder.

But, as I have pointed out, the quantity of information conveyed by a message also depends on its source. A Christmas card sent by a Soviet official would, by virtue of its improbability, have a much higher information value than the same card sent by a favorite aunt. Which again confirms the fact that information, being essentially additive, depends for its value on both originality and improbability. How can this be reconciled with the fact that, on the contrary, the more meaningful a message, the more probable and the more predictable its structure? A sentence such as "Flowers bloom in the spring" has a very clear, direct meaning and a maximal power of communication, but it doesn't add anything to what we already know. In other words, it does not carry much information. Isn't this proof enough that *meaning and information are not one and the same thing?*

Not so, according to Wiener, who maintains that information means *order* and that entropy is its opposite. Wiener, however, is using information theory to explore the power of communication of an electronic brain, in order to determine what makes a message comprehensible. He is not concerned with the differences between information and meaning. And yet, at a particular point in his work, he makes an interesting declaration: "A piece of information, in order to contribute to the general information of a community, must say something substantially different from the community's previous common stock of information." To illustrate this point, he cites the example of great artists, whose chief merit is that they introduce new ways of saying or doing into their community. He explains the public consumption of their work as the consequence of the work's inclusion within a collective background—the inevitable process of popularization and banalization that occurs to any novelty, any original work, the moment people get used to it.[10]

On reflection, one sees that this is precisely the case with everyday speech, whose very power of communication and information seems to be directly proportional to the grammatical and syntactic rules it constantly eludes—the very same rules deemed necessary to the transmission of meaning. It often happens that in a language (here taken to mean a system of probability), certain elements of disorder may in fact increase the level of information conveyed by a message.

Meaning and Information in the Poetic Message

This phenomenon, the direct relationship between disorder and information, is of course the norm in art. It is commonly believed that the poetic word is characterized by its capacity to create unusual meanings and emotions by establishing new relationships between sounds and sense, words and sounds, one phrase and the next—to the point that an emotion can often emerge even in the absence of any clear meaning. Let's imagine a lover who wants to express his feelings according to all the rules of probability imposed on him by his language. This is how he might speak: "When I try to remember events that occurred a long time ago, I sometimes think I see a stream, a stream of smoothly flowing, cool, clear water. The memory of this stream affects me in a particular way, since the woman I then loved, and still love, used to sit on its banks. In fact, I am still so much in love with this woman that I have a tendency, common among lovers, to consider her the only female individual existing in the world. I should add, if I may, that the memory of this stream, being so closely connected to the memory of the woman I love (I should probably mention that this woman is very beautiful), has the power to fill my soul with sweetness. As a result, following a procedure that is also fairly common among lovers, I like to transfer this feeling of sweetness to the stream that indirectly causes me to feel it, and attribute the emotion to it as if the sweetness were really a quality of the stream. This is what I wanted to tell you. I hope I have explained myself clearly." This is how the lover's sentence would sound if, afraid of not being able to communicate exactly what he wants to say, he were to rely on all the rules of redundancy. Although we would certainly understand what he says, we would probably forget it shortly thereafter.

But if the lover were Petrarch, he would do away with all the conventional rules of construction, shun all logical transitions, disdain all but the most daring metaphors, and, refusing to tell us that he is describing a memory but using the past tense to suggest it, he would say: "Chiare, fresche e dolci acque—dove le belle membra—pose colei che sola a me par donna" ("Clear, fresh and sweet waters where she who alone to me seems woman rested her lovely limbs").[11] In fewer than twenty words, he would also succeed in telling us that he still loves the woman he remembers, and would manage to convey the intensity of his love through a rhythm whose liveliness imbues the memory with the immediacy of a cry or a vision. Nowhere else have we thus savored the sweetness and violence of love and the languor of memory. This communication allows us to accumulate a large capital of information about both Petrarch's love and the essence of love in general. Yet from the point of view of *meaning,* the two texts are absolutely identical. It is the second one's originality of organization—that is, its deliberate disorganization, *its improbability in relation to a precise system of probability*—which makes it so much more informative.

At this point, of course, one could easily object that it is not just the amount of unpredictability that charms us in a poetic discourse. If that were the case, a nursery rhyme such as "Hey diddle diddle / The cat and the fiddle / The cow jumped over the moon" would be considered supremely poetic. All I am trying to prove here is that *certain unorthodox uses* of language can often result in poetry, whereas this seldom, if ever, happens with more conventional, probable uses of the linguistic system. That is, it will not happen unless the novelty resides in what is said rather than in how it is said, in which case a radio broadcast that announces, according to all the rules of redundancy, that an atomic bomb has just been dropped on Rome will be as charged with news as one could wish. But this sort of information does not really have much to do with a study of linguistic structures (and even less with their aesthetic value—further evidence that aesthetics cares more about *how* things are said than about *what* is said). Besides, whereas Petrarch's lines can convey a certain amount of information to any reader, including Petrarch, the radio broadcast concerning the bombing of Rome would certainly carry no information to the pilot who has dropped the bomb or to all those listeners who heard the announcement during a previous broadcast. What I want to examine here is the possibility of conveying a piece of information that is not a common "meaning" by *using conventional linguistic structures to violate the laws of probability that govern the language from within.* This sort of information would, of course, be connected not to a state of order but to a state of disorder, or, at least, to some *unusual and unpredictable non-order.* It has been said that the positive measure of such a kind of information is entropy; on the other hand, if entropy is disorder to the highest degree, containing within itself *all* probabilities and *none*, then the information carried by a message (whether poetic or not) that has been intentionally organized will appear only as a very particular form of disorder, a "dis-order" that is such only in relation to a pre-existing order. But can one still speak of entropy in such a context?

The Transmission of Information

Let us now briefly turn to the classic example of the kinetic theory of gas, and imagine a container full of molecules all moving at a uniform speed. Since the movement of these molecules is determined by purely statistical laws, the entropy of the system is very high, so that although *we* can predict the general behavior of the entire system, it is very difficult to predict the trajectory of any particular molecule. In other words, the molecule can behave in a variety of ways, since it is full of possibilities, and we know that it can occupy a large number of positions, but we do not know which ones. To have a clearer idea of the behavior of each molecule, it would be necessary to differentiate their speeds—that is, to introduce an order into the system so as to decrease its entropy. In this way we would increase the probability that a molecule might behave in a particular manner, but we would also limit its initial possibilities by submitting them to a *code*.

If I want to know something about the behavior of a single molecule, I am seeking the kind of information that *goes against* the laws of entropy. But if I want tô know all the possible behaviors of any given molecule, then *the information I am seeking will be directly proportional to the entropy of the system.* By organizing the system and decreasing its entropy, I will simultaneously learn a great deal and not much at all.

The same thing happens with the transmission of a piece of information. I shall try to clarify this point by referring to the formula that generally expresses the value of a piece of information: $I = N \log h$, in which h stands for the number of elements among which we can choose, and N for the number of choices possible (in the case of a pair of dice, $h = 6$ and $N = 2$; in the case of a chessboard, $H = 64$ and $N =$all the moves allowed by the rules of chess).

Now, in a system of high entropy, in which all the combinations can occur, the values of N and h are very high; also very high is the value of the information that could be transmitted concerning the behavior of one or more elements of the system. But it is quite difficult to communicate as many binary choices as are necessary to distinguish the chosen element and define its combinations with other elements.

How can one facilitate the communication of a certain bit of information? By reducing the number of the elements and possible choices in question: by introducing a code, a system of rules that would involve a fixed number of elements and that would exclude some combinations while allowing others. In such a case, it would be possible to convey information by means of a reasonable number of binary choices. But in the meantime, the values of N and h would have decreased, and, as a result, so would the value of the information received.

Thus, the larger the amount of information, the more difficult its communication; the clearer the message, the smaller the amount of information.

For this reason Shannon and Weaver, in their book on information theory, consider information as directly proportional to entropy.[12] The role played by Shannon—one of the founders of the theory—in the research on this particular question has been particularly acknowledged by other scholars in the field.[13] On the other hand, they all seem to insist on the distinction between information (here taken in its strictest statistical sense as the measure of a possibility) and the actual validity of a message (here taken as meaning). Warren Weaver makes this particularly clear in an essay aiming at a wider diffusion of the mathematics of information: "The word *information*, in this theory, is used in a special sense that must not be confused with its ordinary usage. In particular, *information* must not be confused with meaning.... To be sure, this word information in communication theory relates not so much to what you do say, as to what you could say. That is, information is a measure of one's freedom of choice when one selects a message.... Note that it is misleading (although often convenient) to say that one or the other message conveys unit information. The concept of information applies not to the individual messages (as the concept of meaning would), but rather to the situation as a whole.... [A mathematical theory of communication] deals with a concept of information which characterizes the whole statistical nature of the information source, and is not concerned with the individual messages.... The concept of information developed in this theory at first seems disappointing and bizarre—disappointing because it has nothing to do with meaning, and bizarre because it deals not with a single message but rather with the statistical character of a whole ensemble of messages, bizarre also because in these statistical terms the two words *information* and *uncertainty* find themselves to be partners."[14]

Thus, this long digression concerning information theory finally leads back to the issue at the heart of our study. But before going back to it, we should again wonder whether in fact certain concepts borrowed from information theory as tools of investigation can legitimately be applied to questions of aesthetics—if only because it is now clear that "information" has a far wider meaning in *statistics* than in *communication*. Statistically speaking, I have information when I am made to confront all the probabilities at once, before the establishment of any order. From the point of view of communication, I have information when (1) I have been able to establish an order (that is, a code) as a system of probability within an original disorder; and when (2) within this new system, I introduce—through the elaboration of a message that violates the rules of the code—elements of disorder in dialectical tension with the order that supports them (the message challenges the code).

As we proceed with our study of poetic language and examine the use of a disorder aiming at communication, we will have to remember that this particular disorder can no longer be identified with the statistical concept of entropy except in a roundabout way: the disorder that aims at communication is a disorder only in relation to a previous order.

The Open Work in the Visual Arts

Openness and Information

In its mathematical formulations (but not necessarily in its application to cybernetics), information theory makes a radical distinction between "meaning" and "information." The meaning of a message (and by "message" here I also mean a pictorial configuration, even though the way such a configuration communicates is not by means of semantic references but rather by means of formal connections) is a function of the order, the conventions, and the redundancy of its structure. The more one respects the laws of probability (the preestablished principles that guide the organization of a message and are reiterated via the repetition of foreseeable elements), the clearer and less ambiguous its meaning will be. Conversely, the more improbable, ambiguous, unpredictable, and disordered the structure, the greater the information—here understood as potential, as the inception of possible orders.

Certain forms of communication demand meaning, order, obviousness—namely, all those forms which, having a practical function (such as a letter or a road sign), need to be understood univocally, with no possibility for misunderstanding or individual interpretation. Others, instead, seek to convey to their readers sheer information, an unchecked abundance of possible meanings. This is the case with all sorts of artistic communications and aesthetic effects.

As I have already mentioned, the value of every form of art, no matter how conventional or traditional its tools, depends on the degree of novelty present in the organization of its elements—novelty that inevitably entails an increase of information. But whereas "classical" art avails itself of sudden deviations and temporary ruptures only so as to eventually reconfirm the structures accepted by the common sensibility it addresses, thereby opposing certain laws of redundancy only to reendorse them again later, albeit in a different fashion, contemporary art draws its main value from a deliberate rupture with the laws of probability that govern common language—laws which it calls into question even as it uses them for its subversive ends.

When Dante writes, "Fede è sustanzia di cose sperate" ("Faith is the substance of hope"), he adopts the grammatical and syntactic laws of the language of his time to communicate a concept that has already been accepted by the theology of that time. However, to give greater meaning to the communication, he organizes his carefully selected terms according to unusual laws and uncommon connections. By indissolubly fusing the semantic content of the expression with its overall rhythm, he turns what could have been a very common sentence into something completely new, untranslatable, lively, and persuasive (and, as such, capable of giving its reader a great deal of information—not the kind of information that enriches one's knowledge of the concepts to which it refers, but rather a kind of aesthetic information that rests on formal value, on the value of the message as an essentially reflexive act of communication.

When Eluard writes, "Ciel don't j'ai dépassé la nuit" ("Sky whose night I've left behind"), he basically repeats the operation of his predecessor (that is, he organizes sense and sound into a particular form), but his intentions are quite different. He does not want to reassert received ideas and conventional language by lending them a more beautiful or pleasant form; rather, he wants to break with the conventions of accepted language and the usual ways of linking thoughts together, so as to offer his reader a range of possible interpretations and a web of suggestions that are quite different from the kind of meaning conveyed by the communication of a univocal message.

My argument hinges precisely on this plural aspect of the artistic communication, over and above the aesthetic connotations of a message. In the first place, I would like to determine to what extent this desire to join novelty and information in a given message can be reconciled with the possibilities of communication between author and reader. Let's take a few examples from music.

In this short phrase from a Bach minuet (found in the *Notenbüchlein für Anna Magdalena Bach*), we can immediately perceive how adhesion to a system of probability and a certain redundancy combine to clarify and univocalize the meaning of the musical message. In this case, the system of probability is that of tonal grammar, the most familiar to a Western post-medieval listener. Here each interval is more than a change in frequency, since it also involves the activation of organic relations within the context. An ear will always opt for the easiest way to seize these relations, following an "index of rationality" based not only on so-called "objective" perceptual data but also, and above all, on the premises of assimilated linguistic conventions. The first two notes of the first measure make up a perfect F major chord. The next two notes in the same measure (G and E) imply the dominant harmony, whose obvious purpose is to reinforce the tonic by means of the most elementary cadences; in fact, the second measure faithfully returns to the tonic. If this particular minuet began differently, we would have to suspect a misprint. Everything is so clear and linguistically logical that even an amateur could infer, simply by looking at this line, what the eventual harmonic relations (that is to say, the "bass") of this phrase will be. This would certainly not be the case with one

Figure 7.1

of Webern's compositions. In his work, any sequence of sounds is a constellation with no privileged direction and no univocality. What is missing is a rule, a tonal center, that would allow the listener to predict the development of the composition in a particular direction. The progressions are ambiguous: a sequence of notes may be followed by another, unpredictable one that can be accepted by the listener only after he has heard it. "Harmonically speaking, it would appear that every sound in Webern's music is closely followed by either one or both of the sounds that, along with it, constitute a chromatic interval. More often than not, however, this interval is not a halftone, a minor second (still essentially melodic and connective, in its role as leader of the same melodic field); rather, it assumes the form, somewhat stretched, of a major seventh or a minor ninth. Considered as the most elementary links of a relational network, these intervals impede the automatic valorization of the octaves (a process which, given its simplicity, is always within the ear's reach), cause the meaning of frequential relationships to deviate, and prohibit the imagining of a rectilinear auditive space."

If a message of this kind is more ambiguous—and therefore more informative—than the previous type, electronic music goes even further in the same direction. Here sounds are fused into "groups" within which it is impossible to hear any relationship among the frequencies (nor does the composer expect as much, preferring, as a rule, that we seize them in a knot, with all its ambiguity and pregnancy). The sounds themselves will consist of unusual frequencies that bear no resemblance to the more familiar musical note and which, therefore, yank the listener away from the auditive world he has previously been accustomed to. Here, the field of meanings becomes denser, the message opens up to all sorts of possible solutions, and the amount of information increases enormously. But let us now try to take this imprecision—and this information—beyond its outermost limit, to complicate the coexistence of the sounds, to thicken the plot. If we do so, we will obtain "white noise," the undifferentiated sum of all frequencies—a noise which, logically speaking, should give us the greatest possible amount of information, but which in fact gives us none at all. Deprived of all indication, all direction, the listener's ear is no longer capable even of choosing; all it can do is remain passive and impotent in the face of the original chaos. For there is a limit beyond which wealth of information becomes mere noise.

But, of course, even noise can be a signal. Concrete music and, in some cases, electronic music are nothing more than organizations of noise whose order has elevated them to the status of signal. But the transmission of this kind of message poses a problem: "If the sonic material of white noise is formless, what is the minimum 'personality' it must have to assume an identity? What is the minimum of spectral form it must have to attain individuality? This is the problem of 'coloring white noise.'"[15]

Something similar also happens with figurative signals. Let us take the example of a Byzantine mosaic, a classic form of redundant communication that lends itself particularly well to this kind of analysis. Every piece of the mosaic can be considered as a unit of information: a bit. The sum of all the pieces will constitute the entire message. But in a traditional mosaic (such as *Queen Theodora's Cortege* in the church of San Vitale, in Ravenna), the relationship between one piece and the next is far from casual; it obeys very precise laws of probability. First is the figurative convention whereby the work must represent a human body and a surrounding reality. Based on a precise model of perception, this convention prompts our eye to connect each piece according to the outlines of the bodies and the chromatic differences that define them. But the pieces do not limit themselves to suggesting the outline of a body; they insist on it by means of a highly redundant distribution and a series of repetitions. If a black sign represents the pupil of an eye, a series of other appropriately placed signals, representing eyebrows and lids, will reiterate the message till the entire eye will unambiguously offer itself to our view. The fact that there are two eyes constitutes yet another element of redundancy—let's not forget that modern painting seldom needs more than one eye to suggest the entire face. But in the Ravenna mosaic there are two eyes because that is what the figurative convention demands—a figurative convention which, in information theory, would correspond to the law of probability of a given system. As a result, most traditional mosaics are figurative messages that have a univocal meaning and convey a limited amount of information.

Suppose we take a white sheet of paper and spill some ink on it. The result will be a random image with absolutely no order. Let's now fold the paper in two so that the ink blot will spread evenly on both sides of the sheet. When we unfold the paper we will find before us an image that has a certain order—i.e., symmetrical repetition, one of the most elementary forms of redundancy as well as the simplest avatar of probability. Now, even though the drawing remains fundamentally ambiguous, the eye has a few obvious points of reference: indications of a particular direction, suggestions of possible connections. The eye is still free, much freer than it was with the traditional mosaic, and yet it is directed toward the recognition of some forms rather than others, varied and variable forms whose very identification involves the unconscious tendencies of the viewer, while the variety of possible solutions they invite reconfirms the freedom, the ambiguity, and the suggestive power of the figure. And yet, as I have already mentioned, the figure contains a number of interpretive directions, enough so that the psychologist who proposes the test feels quite disoriented if his patient's answer falls outside the province of his predictions.

Let's now transform both the ink blot and the pieces of the mosaic into the gravel which, crushed and pressed by a steamroller, becomes pavement. Whoever looks at the surface of a road can detect in it the presence of innumerable elements disposed in a nearly random fashion. There is no recognizable order in their disposition. Their configuration is extremely open and, as such, contains a maximum amount of information. We are free to connect the dots with as many lines as we please without feeling compelled to follow any particular direction. This situation is very similar to that of white noise: an excess of equiprobability does not increase the potential for information but completely denies it. Or rather, this potential remains at a mathematical level and does not exist at the level of communication. The eye no longer receives any direction.

This is again evidence that the richest form of communication—richest because most open—requires a delicate balance permitting the merest order within the maximum disorder. This balance marks the limit between the undifferentiated realm of utter potential and a field of possibilities.

This problematic, liminal situation is characteristic of the kind of painting that thrives on ambiguity, indeterminacy, the full fecundity of the informal, the kind of painting that wants to offer the eye the most liberating adventure while remaining a form of communication—albeit the communication of extreme noise endowed with barely enough intention to deserve the status of signal. Otherwise, the eye might as well contemplate the surface of a road or a stained wall: there is no need to frame these unlimited sources of information that nature and chance have so kindly put at its disposal. Again, it must be emphasized that intention alone is enough to give noise the value of *a* signal: a frame suffices to turn a piece of sackcloth into an artifact. This intention can, of course, assume all sorts of different forms: our present task is to consider how persuasive they must be in order to give a direction to the freedom of the viewer.

If I draw a square around a crack in a wall with a piece of chalk, I automatically imply that I have chosen that crack over others and now propose it as a particularly suggestive form—in other words, I have turned it into an artifact, a form of communication, simply by isolating it, by calling attention to it in a rather mechanical fashion not unlike the use of quotation marks in literature. But at times this intention may assume a much more complex form, intrinsic to the configuration itself. The direction I insert into the figure may retain a high degree of indeterminacy and yet steer the viewer toward a particular field of possibilities, automatically excluding other ones. This is what a painter does even in his most casual creation, even when he limits himself to scattering his signals across a canvas in a rather random fashion. If, after looking at Dubuffet's *Materiologies*—which are much like a road surface or other bare terrain in their attempt to reproduce the absolute freedom and unlimited suggestiveness of brute matter—somebody had told him that they bore a strong resemblance to Henri IV or Joan of Arc, the artist would probably have been so shocked that he would have questioned the sanity of the speaker.

In a perplexed essay on *tachisme* entitled "A Seismographic Art,"[16] Herbert Read wonders whether the numerous ways in which we can interpret blot of ink on a piece of paper have anything to do with an aesthetic response. According to him, there is a fundamental distinction between objects that are imaginative and objects that merely evoke images. In the second instance, the artist is the person who views the image, not the person who creates it. A blot lacks the element of control, the intentional form that organizes the vision. By refusing to use any form of control, *tachisme* rejects beauty in favor of *vitality*.

If contemporary art merely upheld the values of vitality (as the negation of form) over those of beauty, there would be no problem: at this particular stage in the evolution of taste, we all could easily make do without the latter. What concerns us here is not the aesthetic value of an act of vitality but rather its power to communicate. Our civilization is still far from accepting the unconditional abandonment to vital forces advocated by the Zen sage. He can sit and blissfully contemplate the unchecked potential of the surrounding world: the drifting of clouds, the shimmer of water, cracks in the ground, sunlight on a drop of dew. And to him everything is a confirmation of the endless, polymorphous triumph of the All. But we still live in a culture in which our desire to abandon ourselves to the free pursuit of visual and imaginative associations must be artificially induced by means of an intentionally suggestive construct. As if that were not enough, not only do we have to be pushed to enjoy our freedom to enjoy, but we are also asked to evaluate our enjoyment, and its object, at the very moment of its occurrence. In other words, we still live in a culture dominated by dialectics: I am supposed to judge both the work in relation to my experience of it, and my experience of it in relation to the work. I might even have to try to locate the reasons for my reaction to the work in the particular ways the work has been realized—if nothing else, in order to judge it as a means to an end, at once process and result, the fulfillment or the frustration of certain expectations and certain goals. For the only criterion I can use in my evaluation of the work derives from the degree of coincidence between my capacity for aesthetic pleasure and the intentions to which the artist has implicitly given form in his work.

Thus, even an art that upholds the values of vitality, action, movement, brute matter, and chance rests on the dialectics between the work itself and the "openness" of the "readings" it invites. A work of art can be open only insofar as it remains a work; beyond a certain boundary, it becomes mere noise.

To define this threshold is not a function of aesthetics, for only a critical act can determine whether and to what extent the "openness" of a particular work to various readings is the result of an intentional organization of its field of possibilities. Only then can the message be considered an act of communication and not just an absurd dialogue between a signal that is, in fact, mere noise, and a reception that is nothing more than solipsistic ranting.

Form and Openness

The lures of vitality are clearly denounced in an essay on Dubuffet by André Pieyre de Mandiargues. He notes that in *Mirobolus, Macadam and Co.* Dubuffet has pushed his art to its extreme limit, showing his audience perpendicular views of the most basic ground formations. All abstraction is gone, and what's left is the immediate presence of matter in all its concreteness. We contemplate the infinite in a layer of dust: "Just before the exhibition, Dubuffet had written to me that he was afraid his 'texturologies' brought art to a very dangerous point where all difference between the object—supposed to provoke thought and act as a screen for the viewer's visions and meditations—and the basest and least interesting material formation had become very subtle and uncertain. It is hence not surprising that art lovers get scared whenever they see art pushed to an extreme where it is nearly impossible to distinguish what is art from what is not."[17]

On the other hand, if the painter is aware of a distinction, then the viewer can either work toward the recognition of an intentional message or abandon himself to the vital and unchecked flux of his most unpredictable reactions. The latter is the attitude Mandiargues assumes when he compares what he feels while contemplating Dubuffet's texturologies to the emotions evoked in him by the powerful. muddy flow of the Nile, or to the real happiness one feels at plunging one's hands into the sand of a beach and then watching it coolly and quickly flow through the fingers while the palms are still soothed by the deep warmth of matter. But if this is indeed the case, why bother with the painting, which is so much more limited in possibilities than the real sand or the immensity of natural matter at our disposal? Obviously because the painting organizes crude matter, underlining its crudeness while at the same time defining it as a field of possibilities; the painting, even before becoming a field of actualizable choices, is already a field of actualized choices. This is why, before launching into a hymn to vitality, the critic celebrates the painter and what he proposes. Only after his sensibility has been thus directed does he feel ready to move on to unchecked associations prompted by the presence of signs which, however free and casual, are nevertheless the products of an intention and, therefore, the marks of a work of art.

The critical analysis that seems to be closest to the Western conception of artistic communication is the one that tries to recognize, at the heart of the "accidental" and the "fortuitous" that are the substance of a work, the signs of a "craft" or "discipline" by virtue of which, at the right moment, the artist is able to activate the forces of chance that will turn his work into a *chance domestiquée*, "a sort of torque, whose poles, when they come into contact, far from nullifying each other, retain their potential difference." Geometry is what finally provides Dubuffet's "texturology" with a check and a direction, so that, in the end, the painter will still be the one "who plays on the keyboard of evocation and reference."[18] Similarly, drawing is what finally controls the freedom of Fautrier's colors by providing them with a dialectics between the presence of a limit and its absence, in which "the sign shores up the overflow of matter."[19]

Even in the most spontaneous expressions of action painting, the multitude of forms that assail the viewer and allow him extreme freedom of interpretation is not like the record of an unexpected telluric event: it is the record of a series of gestures, each of which has left a trace with both a spatial and a temporal direction of which the painting is the only witness. Of course, we can retrace the sign back and forth in every sense, without changing the fact that the sign is a field of reversible directions which an irreversible gesture has imposed on the canvas—a field that invites us to explore all possible directions in search of the original (and now lost) gesture till we finally find it and, with it, the communicative intention of the work. This sort of painting tries to retain the freedom of nature, but of a nature whose signs still reveal the hand of a creator, a pictorial nature that, like the nature of medieval metaphysics, is a constant reminder of the original act of Creation. This sort of painting is, therefore, still a form of communication, a passage from an intention to a reception. And even if the reception is left open—because the intention itself was open, aiming at a plural communication—it is nevertheless the end of an act of communication which, like every act of information, depends on the disposition and the organization of a certain form. Understood in this sense, the "informal" is a rejection of classical forms with univocal directions but not a rejection of that form which is the fundamental condition of communication. The example of the informal, like that of any open work, does not proclaim the death of form; rather, it proposes a new, more flexible version of it—form *as a field of possibilities.*

Here we realize not only that this art of chance and vitality is still dependent on the most basic categories of communication (since it bases its informativeness on its formativity) but that it also offers us, along with all the connotations of formal organization, the conditions for aesthetic appreciation. Let us take Jackson Pollock's art as an example. The disorder of the signs, the disintegration of the outlines, the explosion of the figures incite the viewer to create his own network of connections. But the original gesture, fixed by and in the sign, is in itself a direction that will eventually lead us to the discovery of the author's intention. Of course, this is possible only because the gesture, unlike a conventional referent, is not extraneous and exterior to the sign (in other words, it is not a hieroglyph of vitality that can be serially reproduced, and which will forever evoke the notion of "free explosion"). Gesture and sign coexist in a particular balance, impossible to reproduce, resulting from the fusion of inert materials and formative energy, and from a series of connections among the various signs that allow our eyes to discern, beyond these, the interrelationship of the original gestures (and the accompanying intentions). Here again we confront a fusion of elements similar to the one that, in the best moments of traditional poetry, weds sound and sense, the conventional value of the sound and the emotion it evokes. Western culture considers this particular fusion as an aesthetic event characteristic of art. The "reader" who, at the very moment in which he abandons himself to the free play of reactions that the work provokes in him, goes back to the work to seek in it the origin of the suggestion and the virtuosity behind the stimulus, is not only enjoying his own personal experience but is also appreciating the value of the work itself, its aesthetic quality. Similarly, the free play of associations, once it is recognized as originating from the disposition of the signs, becomes an integral part of the work, one of the components that the work has fused into its own unity and, with them, a source of the creative dynamism that it exudes. At this point, the viewer can savor (and describe, for that's what every reader of informal art does) the very quality of the form, the value of a work that is open precisely because it is a work.

It becomes clear that quantitative information has led us to something much richer: aesthetic information.[20]

The former type of information consists in drawing as many suggestions as possible out of a totality of signs—that is, in charging these signs with all the personal reactions that might be compatible with the intentions of the author. This is the value all open works deliberately pursue. Classical art forms, in contrast, imply it as a condition necessary to interpretation but, rather than giving it a privileged status, prefer to keep it in the background, within certain limits.

The latter type of information consists in referring the results drawn from the former type back to their original organic qualities, in seizing, behind the suggestive wealth we exploit, a conscious organization, a formative intention, and in enjoying this new awareness. This awareness of the project that underlies the work will, in turn, be another inexhaustible source of pleasure and surprise, since it will lead us to an ever-growing knowledge of the personal world and cultural background of the artist.

Thus, in the dialectics between work and openness, the very persistence of the work is itself a guarantee of both communication and aesthetic pleasure. Not only are the two values intimately connected, but each implies the other—which is certainly not the case with a conventional message such as a road sign, where the act of communication exists without any aesthetic effect and exhausts itself in the apprehension of the referent, without ever inducing us to return to the sign to enjoy the effectiveness of its message in the way it is formally expressed. "Openness," on the other hand, is the guarantee of a particularly rich kind of pleasure that our civilization pursues as one of its most precious values, since every aspect of our culture invites us to conceive, feel, and thus see the world as possibility.

Notes

The source for this chapter is an Eco compilation volume, translated by Anna Cancogni and with an introduction by David Robey, which was published by Harvard University Press (1989) under the title *The Open Work*. We are reproducing parts of Chapter 3, "Openness, Information, Communication," and Chapter 4, "The Open Work in the Visual Arts," the Italian versions of which originally appeared in Eco's *Opera Aperta* (1962).

1. Sec Stanford Goldman's exhaustive study, *Information Theory* (New York: Prentice-Hall, 1953), as well as A. A. Moles, *Information Theory and Esthetic Perception*, tr. Joel E. Cohen (Urbana: University of Illinois Press, 1966).

2. This definition can be traced back to a principle adopted by linguists, namely that, in phonology, every distinctive feature implies a choice between the two terms of an opposition. See N. S.

Troubetskoy, *Principes de phonologic* (Paris: Klincksieck, 1949), esp. pp. 15, 33; Roman Jakobson, *Essais de linguistique, générale* (Paris: Editions de Minuit, 1959), p. 104; and G. T. Guilbaud, *La Cybernétique* (Paris: Presses Universitaires de France, 1954), p. 103. As F. Boas has very clearly shown, the choice of a grammatical form by the speaker presents the listener with a definite number of bits of information. To give a precise meaning to a message such as "The man killed the bull," the addressee must choose among a number of possible alternatives. In information theory, linguists have found a privileged tool for their investigation. Thus, the dialectics between *redundancy* and *improbability* in information theory (of which more later) has been measured against the dialectics between *basis of comparison* and *variants*, between *distinctive features* and *redundant features*. Jakobson speaks of a *granulary structure* of language that lends itself to quantification.

3. Max Planck, *Wege zur physikalischen Erkenntnis* (Leipzig: S. Hirzel Verlag), ch. 1.

4. Ibid.

5. Hans Reichenbach, *The Direction of Time* (Berkeley: University of California Press, 1956), pp. 54–55. Unlike Reichenbach, Planck considers entropy a natural reality that excludes a priori all those facts that would seem empirically impossible.

6. Ibid., p. 151.

7. Ibid., p. 167.

8. Norbert Wiener, *The Human Use of Human Beings* (Boston: Houghton Mifflin. 1950; New York: Avon Books, 1967), p. 31. In short, there is an equiprobability of disorder in relation to which order is an improbable event because it is the choice of only one chain of probability. Once a particular is realized, it becomes a system of probabilities in relation to which all deviation appears improbable.

9. For instance, a sequence of letters randomly drawn from the most probable trigrams in Livy's language will yield a certain number of pseudo-words with an unmistakable Latin sound: *ibus, cent, ipitia, vetis, ipse, cum, vivius, se, acetiti, dedentur*. See Guilbaud, *La Cybernétique*, p. 82.

10. Wiener, *The Human Use of Human Beings*, p. 163.

11. *Penguin Book of Italian Verse*, ed. George Kay (Harmondsworth: Penguin, 1958).

12. R. Shannon and W. Weaver, *The Mathematical Theory of Communication* (Urbana: Illinois University Press, 1949).

13. See Goldman, *Information Theory*, pp. 330–331; and Guilbaud, *La Cybernétique*, p. 65.

14. Shannon and Weaver, *The Mathematical Theory of Communication*, pp. 99–100, 104, 106.

15. See Abraham Moles, *Information Theory and Esthetic Perception* (New York: Prentice-Hall, 1953), p. 82, as well as the section "Information, Order, and Disorder" in Chapter 3 above.

16. In Herbert Read, *The Tenth Muse* (London: Routledge and Kegan Paul, 1957), pp. 297–303.

17. "Jean Dubuffet ou le point extrême," *Cahiers du musée de poche* 2: 52.

18. See Renato Barilli, "La pittura di Dubuffet," in Il Verri (October 1959), in which he also refers to Dubuffet's *Prospectus aux amateurs de tout genre* (Paris, 1946)—in particular, to the section titled "Notes pour les fins-lettrés."

19. See Palma Bucarelli, "Jean Fautrier: Pittura e materia," *Il Saggiatore* (Milan, 1960), for an analysis (p. 67) of the constant opposition between the effervescence of matter and the limits of the outline, as well as for the distinction between the suggested freedom of the infinite and the anguish caused by the absence of a limit, considered as negative to the work. P. 97: "In these *Objects*, the outline is quite independent from the blotch of color, which nonetheless exists: it is something that goes beyond matter, that indicates a space and a time-in other words, something that frames matter in the dimension of consciousness." These critical readings are limited to the works in question, and they do not provide a categorial system valid for every kind of "informal" experiment. In cases where there is no dialectics between outline and color (I am thinking of Matta, Imai, or Tobey), our investigation would have to follow a different course. In Dubuffet's later work, the geometric subdivisions of the texturologies no longer exist, but we can still search the canvas for the suggestion of a direction and a choice.

20. An example of this relationship between *iconographic* meaning and aesthetic meaning already exists in classical figurative art. The iconographic convention is an element of redundancy: an old bearded man flanked by a ram and a child is—according to medieval iconography—Abraham. The convention *insists* on both the character and his personality. Erwin Panofsky cites the example of Maffei's *Judith and Holofernes*; see Panofsky, "Zum Problem der Beschreibung und Inhaltsdeutung von Werken der bildenden Kunst," *Logos* 21 (1932). The woman represented in this painting is holding a tray on which rest, side by side, a head and a sword. The first item could lead the viewer to think she is Salomé, but according to Baroque iconography Salomé is never represented with a sword. On the other hand, Judith is often represented carrying Holofernes's head on a tray. Another iconographic element will further facilitate the identification: the expression of the beheaded is more like that of a wretch than like that of a saint. The redundancy of the elements casts more light on the meaning of the message and conveys some quantitative information, however limited. But this quantitative information, in turn, contributes to the aesthetic information of the canvas, to one's appreciation of the composition, and to one's judgment of the artistic realization. As Panofsky notes, "Even simply from an aesthetic point of view, the painting will be judged in a completely different way depending on whether it is seen as the representation of a courtesan who is carrying the head of a saint or as that of a heroine, protected by God, who is holding the head of a sinner."

8 What Does Digital Content Mean? Umberto Eco and *The Open Work*

Alan F. Blackwell

Shortly before writing this chapter, I was asked to contribute to a discussion with Eric Schmidt, the chairman of Google,[1] in front of an audience of humanities professors. Schmidt had made the reasonably commonplace claim that the human race had created more information in recent decades than in the whole of its previous history. I took him to task, saying that as a trained engineer, he should take care over the difference between "bits"—states of computer memory—and "information" as it is understood in everyday language.

After the expansion of memory capacity described by Moore's law, there are certainly a lot of bits about. And the simple mathematics of that law means most of these have been created in recent decades (indeed there were no computers at all, and hence no bits, for millennia of human history). But my point was that mass-produced text is not always valued by readers. The acceleration of cheap paper and printing presses through the nineteenth and twentieth centuries created many books that nobody reads today. And the huge ratio of bits over ink has now "published" millions of banal and trivial observations of no interest even to their authors. Schmidt's response? First, that my argument was "elitist." Second, that he himself never reads anything remotely near the median quality of public commentary. Third, that "PageRank will take care of it."[2]

This chapter addresses these themes, establishing a critical apparatus that can be used to engage with those like Schmidt who determine public policy from an engineering perspective. Unfortunately, few humanities professors are familiar with information theory, or the way it posits the relationship among bits, readers, and meaning. But the seminal work discussed in this chapter comes from another humanities professor—Umberto Eco—who not only read information theory decades ago, but also provides us with a basis for understanding readership in an age of information engineering.

For readers who are already familiar with information theory, I should observe that, as Schmidt did, this chapter plays around with potential ambiguity in use of the word "information." Luciano Floridi (2010) suggests that confusion could be avoided simply by renaming "information theory" as the "mathematical theory of communication." Readers familiar with this theory may also wish to skip the section on "signal and noise," which is intended to provide a brief, nontechnical introduction to the main issues. However, you should be aware that Eco also offers a couple of twists on the way that this topic would be taught in an engineering text. Although confusion might be avoided by adopting a simpler definition, I hope the reader will forgive me if I prefer not to do so.

Semiotics and the Engineering of Language

Umberto Eco was an Italian media theorist and philosopher who gained broader fame as a popular novelist. Novels such as *The Name of the Rose* and *Foucault's Pendulum* not only attracted a wide readership and major movie productions but drew on Eco's academic work exploring the relationship between philosophy, literature, and popular culture. His early career included both literary editorship and work in television production, and he was a central figure in the introduction of semiotics as a fundamental concern of European critical theory.

The English collection of Eco's writings translated by Anna Cancogni under the title *The Open Work* (Eco, 1989) spans the period during which these threads in his thinking were being drawn together. Eco's early academic career had been concerned with the political and philosophical context of medieval scholasticism, in the work of the philosopher-monk Thomas Aquinas. But as a young leader of the Italian literary scene, Eco had also become particularly engaged with the complexly layered novels of twentieth-century Irish author James Joyce (who himself engaged with an immense range of classical philosophy in his work). These strands of enquiry are interwoven, in the essays collected in *The Open Work*, with communication theory and media practice, resulting in a new conception of the relationship between the creators and interpreters of works of art.

The contrast that Eco had experienced between the rigorous but rigid intellectual systems of medieval scholastic philosophy on one hand, and the ambiguity, earthiness, and reflexivity of James Joyce on the other, suggested to him the potential for works of art to be owned and appropriated by many kinds of reader. At the time he was writing these essays, much European philosophy was still pursuing a structuralist agenda, systematizing the study of science, literature, and society. As a basis for technological progress, economic management, and operational policy, structuralism suggests the potential to categorize, order, and even regulate life well beyond the bounds of the academy. However, rather than accepting mass communications technology as a further source of Big Brother-like control over mass culture, Eco argued that this revival of the scholastic impulse was being countered by the implications of new media and art forms.

Although these essays were written before digital media became widespread, the response of contemporary art and popular culture to recording and communications technologies was already displaying many of the dynamics that remain relevant to digital content today. In particular, Eco's work draws attention to the ways in which communication technologies encourage a culture that persistently democratizes both the production and consumption of art works. Low-cost recording devices and broadcast media increase both the size of the audience and the variety of responses that might result. These "open works" are therefore open in the sense that they are openly accessible but also in the sense that they are open to alternative reading.

The essays in *The Open Work* were originally written in the 1960s, before Eco published the first of his major texts on semiotic theory. As David Robey (1989) says in his introduction to the translated collection, they are thus "pre-semiotic" in terms of Eco's most influential work, although they were already popular in Italy as a manifesto of the avant-garde. (The term "avant-garde," French for "advance guard," was popular for its implication that experimental arts and new forms of criticism will be the forerunners of new trends in society.) The translation of this early work into English was in part a response to increasing interest in the whole body of Eco's writing after the popular success in English of *The Name of the Rose*. But these essays also happen to be of particular interest to students of HCI. Eco has undoubtedly been a major figure in the contemporary theory of semiotics, and that body of theory has been influential in HCI—especially in the ongoing work of Clarisse Sieckenius de Souza. De Souza's sophisticated conception of "semiotic engineering" (De Souza, 2005) is a valuable analytic perspective and design resource for interaction designers.[3] However, my goal in this chapter is not to reiterate the ways in which Eco and other semiotic theorists are essential to understanding the user interface, but rather to return to some of the other themes that stirred up Eco's encounter between structuralism and the twentieth-century avant-garde.

The parallels that Eco drew between twentieth-century structuralism and medieval scholasticism seem to continue in the core concerns of computer science. In Eco's view, structuralist thought is concerned with the articulation of laws, not simply the relations between objects of study. From this perspective, the "Semantic Web," with its proliferating ontologies and markup languages, is a full-blown scholastic/structuralist endeavor—a complete philosophical system that extends across science, art, morality, and belief. Umberto Eco, in fact, offered an entertaining critique of these tendencies in his later book, *The Search for the Perfect Language* (1995). The knowledge representation languages of the "Fifth Generation" artificial intelligence projects in the 1980s had already attempted much the same program of universal formalization. By comparing these formalizing projects to medieval theology, as well as to a large cast of other well-meaning systematizers throughout human history, Eco demonstrates the ways in which overarching dynamics of meaning are likely to resist even digital technologies, which seem to recapitulate the ambitions and errors of earlier idealists over the centuries.

But to return to *The Open Work*, Eco's main concern when he wrote the essays was with poetics—the ancient branch of philosophy that explores the relationship between the play and its viewer (as in Aristotle's *Poetics*), or more recently between an author and a reader. In our multi- and digital-media setting, an author can of course be any producer of "content," and a reader can be any consumer. From the perspective of semiotics and media theory, all content acquires the status and generic character of a text. This piece of critical-theoretic jargon is relevant throughout the current volume, where its universality might be compared to the generic software engineering concepts of the "document," "file," or "application." But whereas engineering is concerned with encoding, transmitting, and rendering these buckets of digital content, poetics is concerned with reading them—as texts. To return to my conversation with Eric Schmidt with which this chapter opens, counting the bits might be a question of engineering, but reading them, in a human engagement with meaning, is a question of poetics.

Eco's analysis cuts to the core of challenges that face HCI, as a discipline concerned both with engineering and interpretation. Engineering, according to some views, is only concerned with measurement, calculation, and optimization, and therefore it adopts a scope that excludes considerations of interpretation or judgment. As phrased by satirist Tom Lehrer, "'Once the rockets are up, who cares where they come down? That's not my department,' says Wernher von Braun" (Lehrer and Searle, 1999).

Measuring Information—Signal and Noise

At the heart of the collection *The Open Work* is the essay "Openness, Information, Communication," in which Eco explains the implications for critical philosophy of Shannon's information theory. The engineering definition of information that Eco acquires from Shannon indeed lends itself to measurement, calculation, and optimization—in ways that may seem mysteriously independent of meaning—to those who have not previously encountered this technical perspective. This section therefore attempts to provide a brief introduction to the mathematical theory of communication commonly known as information theory (and may be skipped by those already familiar with the issues).

Consider the two illustrations in figure 8.1. Figure 8.1b contains more information, in an information theory sense. It includes all the information shown in figure 8.1a, but with many additional pixels. This can be tested by compressing the two figures—that is, by using information theory to remove those bits that are redundant.[4] A compressed GIF file producing figure 8.1a measures only 4 kilobytes, while figure 8.1b is many times larger, at 199 kilobytes. Indeed, the minimum description length of figure 8.1a could be even smaller: simply "letter a" (or the single byte 01100001). The relatively small content is an opportunity for engineering optimization, because we needn't store or transmit all those predictable and redundant bits. Transmission and storage

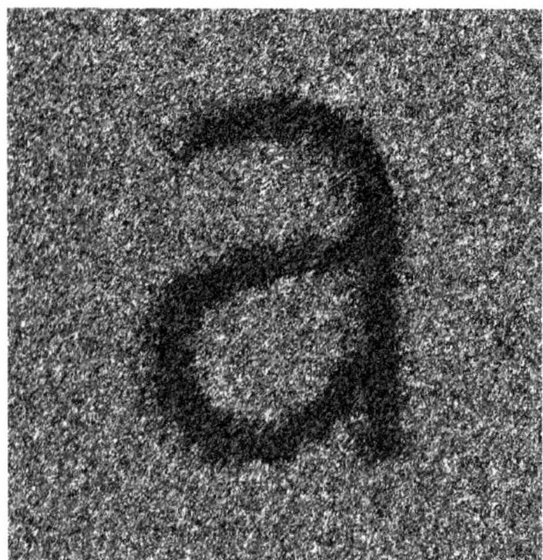

Figure 8.1a and Figure 8.1b
A small amount of information (left) versus a large amount (right).

is expensive, so figure 8.1b costs more than figure 8.1a. Of course to a nontechnical reader, figure 8.1a probably has less value because it has poor legibility, and valuing it according to the number of bits is irrelevant to this judgment. But wait—what if the bits were actually a code, spelling out the first paragraph of Eco's article? In that case, I've tricked you, and the figure should have a high price (like all smuggled goods).

The apparently counterintuitive expense of the noisy figure 8.1b arises because Shannon's work is not mainly focused on optimum quantity of information, but rather on quality—the ratio between signal and noise. We see figure 8.1b as having poorer quality because it includes a lot of noise. Whenever we transmit or store information, entropy intervenes—bursts of static on the wires or leaking current from memory chips. The essential distinction, for an engineer applying Shannon, is to answer the question "What is the signal, and what is the noise?" In figure 8.1b, the additional bits might be either dirty noise or a sophisticated code.

To be clear, the core of information theory is judgment—who determines the difference between signal and noise, and how? For example, in judging the information on the World Wide Web, we might answer these two questions with "Google determines the difference," and "they do it with PageRank."

The core abstraction of information theory, apart from the bit, is the communication channel along which signals might be faithfully transmitted or become adulterated with noise. Eco's question is to ask more carefully what goes in and out of a communication channel. If the people at each end are considered as an author and reader, then we see that the otherwise abstract channel is itself a text—a device used to carry meaning from one person to another. It is poetics, and the interpretation of meaning, that determines the distinction between signal and noise.

As already explained, the central concern of HCI as a discipline is to integrate engineering and interpretation in order to create and carry meaning. This is where it becomes clear that although the chairman of Google may be an information engineer, he is no semiotician. Imagine he had said that the human race has created more meaning in the past ten years than in all its previous history! At this point, the assembled humanities professors in his audience would certainly have realized that a contentious claim was being advanced.

Language as a Code: The Meaning behind the Meaning

Eco emphasizes the fact that the distinction between signal and noise depends on whether you know the code. In fact, as with my trivial example of the smuggled code in an image, the same message might have many meanings, decoded in different ways by different readers. Eco quotes Shannon and Weaver's popular explanation of information theory (1949) as follows: "In particular, information must not be confused with meaning ... [it] relates not so much to what you do say, as to what you could say.... [It is] a measure of one's freedom of choice when one selects a message" (Shannon and Weaver, quoted in Eco, 1989, 57—my emphasis). The notion that all communication depends on a code shared between the writer and reader is a fundamental principle of semiotics, whether or not that communication involves technological channels. But the additional emphasis on freedom of choice is particularly relevant in Eco's thinking. The contemporary artists of the avant-garde at the time Eco was writing were intentionally reversing figure and ground, or signal and noise, as in the famous example of *4′33″*—a piece of music in which the performer makes no sound at all, thereby turning the ambient noises and sounds of the concert hall into the music itself. Imagine if a well-meaning sound engineer cleaned up a recording of this piece, so that the coughs and rustles of the audience (or hiss of a recording tape?) were removed, and only absolute silence remained. In terms of Shannon's ideal communication channel, she may have improved the ratio of signal to noise. But an essential feature of Cage's piece is that the removal of information from the score (it contains no notes) results in an opportunity to hear many other things. The engineer's concern for technical efficiency is not always consistent with such freedom.

Artistic strategies such as those of John Cage promise new kinds of freedom to the listener—a kind of democracy that might be opposed to the authoritarianism of strictly defined interpretations—but even more than this, they draw attention to the mechanism of the code itself. In the case of Google, the mechanism by which signal is extracted from the noise of the internet is a particular convergence of commercial interests and Californian libertarianism. Although publicly neutral in its even-handedness to advertisers and governments, Google's corporate slogan "Don't Be Evil" clearly represents a political commitment. But from Eco's perspective, Google itself is a coded message, in the way that it determines which parts of the internet are signal and which are noise. Just as Eco explains this in regard to media as diverse as medieval theology and comic book characters, the ways in which Google defines (meaningful) signal in relation to (unwanted) noise also reveals particular sets of commercial and power relations (see, for example, Pasquinelli, 2009).

Code and Power: Openness as a Political Commitment

To someone in the software industry, the term "open" in Eco's *Open Work* is immediately suggestive of open-source code—the principle that the source code of an application or operating system should be published or made available to everyone in some form. There is certainly a relationship between that idea and the title of Eco's collection, but the principles involved are complementary, rather than necessarily dependent. The phrase "open source" has become associated with a set of legal and commercial arrangements, related to the same industry standardization processes that increase the overall size of a market through shared voltages and plug connections.[5]

Most technology industries have been subject to such dynamics in their early phases, including railways, telegraphy, motion pictures, electrical appliances, and digital computers. In all cases, companies have initially attempted to capture monopolies over a whole technical field by manufacturing consumption devices (whether receivers, appliances, or projectors) that work only with their own infrastructure and standards. But such strategies usually fail. Ultimately, both consumers and producers benefit from open standards that promote creativity and increase total market size.

Open source software is escaping these monopolistic dynamics, albeit just as slowly as occurred in previous generations of technology infrastructure. Open standards such as the World Wide Web have massively increased market size over previous proprietary hypertext architectures, while operating system platforms such as Android, Windows, and Mac OS have published source code and interfaces to varying degrees. However, there is continued tension between those who recognize the straightforward commercial benefits accruing from some degree of openness, and those who were the early campaigners for all software source code to be published and unconstrained. Richard Stallman of the Free Software Foundation has advocated for many years that software should be "free as in speech, not free as in beer," meaning that it was not immoral to make money from free software, only to restrict users from doing whatever they liked with it.

At the time Eco was writing, the European avant-garde was just as powerfully associated with political activism, democratization, and freedom from institutional control, as, for example, expressed during the Paris events of 1968, in which student protests were accompanied by demands for new philosophical and aesthetic freedom. Subsequent international youth movements, including Californian "flower power," similarly emphasized individual freedom of expression and creativity in contrast to the institutional control associated with the military-industrial complex. The assertion that the reader of an artistic text might have the freedom to construct any meaning he or she likes is therefore a commitment to a mode of poetics that embodies a certain kind of political order.

While some people might regard open source software as simply an efficient business strategy, the activist community that operates under the title of FLOSS—"Free/Libre Open Source Software"—is both aesthetic and political. We might contrast two views of liberty and free speech in digital media, one that is represented by much of the Silicon Valley-led technology establishment, desiring a fluid business environment that removes constraints on engineering innovation, and the other (often using the term FLOSS) that is composed notably of artists and radical politicians, rather than engineers or businessmen, which desires freedom of expression. Although it would be a crude oversimplification of my argument, one might say that Google is a prominent exemplar of the first, while Eco's *Open Work* is fundamentally aligned with the second.

The structures of engineering, law, and business are inherently conservative, aiming for and relying on stability. The artistic avant-garde, as with political revolutionaries, questions, reinterprets and subverts established orders. But as seen by Eco, structuralism, like medieval scholasticism, becomes a mechanism for the maintenance of established order, in which intellectual authority must be preserved as a bastion against the decay of civilization (Bondanella, 1997).

The Poetics of Interaction

Eco defines a first and second degree of openness (Eco, 1989, 74). I will return to the second, but the first is a kind of aesthetic pleasure evoked by cognitive mechanisms of integration—the work that the reader does to interpret the text as it is literally given and relate it to everything that he or she already knows in order to render it meaningful.

For example, when Johnny Rotten of the Sex Pistols sings "God Save the Queen," we might be surprised, because we know that as a 1970s punk rocker he represents a confrontational anarchist youth movement,[6] and so is unlikely to express a royalist sentiment. When listening to the song, we must therefore integrate the surprising words we have just heard to arrive at an understanding of what they might mean. In this case, we recognize the rhetorical device as one of simple irony, immediately apparent in the lines that follow: "The Fascist regime / that calls you a moron" (and the ironic tone is further enhanced in Rotten's barbed reference to liberal hippy idiom in his next verse—the deliciously sneering sarcasm of "God save the Queen ... we mean it, maaan").

To phrase this experience in information-theoretic terms, we as the listeners have gained information from a message we did not expect to hear. If the British prime minister says "God save the Queen," we have gained no information, because this is exactly what we might expect the prime minister to say. When Johnny Rotten says it, we are going to learn something. However, in order to learn, we must stop to think about why we have heard these surprising words, given what we already know about the performer and his cultural context. Integrating unexpected information with our prior expectations involves more cognitive effort, but the effort often yields the satisfaction or aesthetic pleasure of learning or making new connections.

For the technically oriented, this can be regarded as an application of Bayes theorem to aesthetic experience. And Eco anticipates that analysis, referring to pioneering research in the quantitative aesthetics of music by Abraham Moles, who calculated the rate at which a listener is expected to absorb unexpected information (Moles, 1969). More frequent changes in rhythm or harmony, or larger pitch jumps within a melody, are less probable (in terms of Bayes theorem), less expected, and carry more information. If the changes are too frequent and unexpected (to an extreme of random noise), listening becomes less pleasurable, but if there is too little change (to an extreme of a constant tone), it is unstimulating and boring. Skilled composers often explore the further extents of this phenomenon. At one extreme, the serialism of Arnold Schönberg and the complexity of Harrison Birtwistle, respectively, prevent the listener from forming expectations by avoiding modal tonality or bombarding the listener with huge quantities of notes and rhythmic structure. At the other extreme, the sparse palette of Brian Eno's *Music for Airports* is so successfully soporific because each phrase seems to be the inevitably expected successor to the one preceding it.

The pleasures of cognitive integration—interpreting the information contained in a rich work of art—are increased where the work carries multiple meanings, either through layered reference to other works and experiences, or ambiguities within the work itself. This kind of layering and ambiguity is evident everywhere in Eco's poetics, but is also fundamental to the texts that we describe as "poetry," as explained in a classic book by William Empson (1947), which analyses the multiple ways in which poetry is pleasurable to read because of the fact that each line can be read in multiple ways.

However, works that are ambiguous require more effort from the reader. According to Eco's analysis, they contain more information because the ambiguity makes them less predictable. In contrast, when carrying out routine user interface design, we often aim for simplicity, transparency, and ease of learning rather than richness. Just as Eco observes of the ambiguous open work, user interface designers must ask "Are such works legible? If so, what are the conditions of their communicability and what are the guarantees that they will not suddenly lapse into silence or chaos? ... And is there a possible agreement between the intention of the author and the viewer's response?"

(Eco, 1989, 86). Of course, these issues became central concerns for many of the semioticians building on Eco's work—but this chapter cannot do justice to the whole field of study, so I will leave those connections for others to make.

Nevertheless, the tension implicit in any work of art, between accessibility and novelty, between learnability and open interpretation, has been a constant but little acknowledged source of conflict in HCI (as reviewed in Blackwell [2006]). A key focus of debate has been the role of metaphor in the construction and interpretation of user interfaces. In poetry, metaphor introduces ambiguity and the potential for misinterpretation. The tension between literal and intended meanings in any metaphor requires Eco's cognitive integration during reading, but also risks loss of legibility. But HCI has for many years had a relatively unsophisticated view of these issues.

Poetic metaphor involves literal contradiction. If I say "my daughter is a girl," there is no contradiction, but neither is there metaphor or poetry. If I say "my daughter is a peach," the literal contradiction in that phrase invites you, the reader, to resolve it by constructing mental images. Every metaphor is an open work in this sense—aesthetic pleasure is evoked by cognitive mechanisms of integration.

However, an unfortunate turn in HCI led us to treat the word "metaphor" not as an opportunity for interpretation but as a mechanism of instruction. The "desktop metaphor" is a rather lumpen analogy, prosaically illustrating the ways in which conceptual elements of computing such as the "file" were named by analogy to the trappings of office bureaucracy (as in a filing cabinet or paper file folder). Rather than letting these new coinages float free of their physical origins,[7] the little mnemonic pictures of desktop icons constrained the words to refer literally to the original analogy. As noted by Alan Kay, Ted Nelson, and others, this bureaucratic analogy removed the magic from computing (Blackwell, 2006).

The poetic role of metaphor, as argued by Eco, should be a starting point for creative interpretation of an open work rather than a mechanical process of analogical correspondence. To take a rather mundane example, many people argued, at the introduction of the desktop metaphor, that the "trash can" (or waste basket) icon for file deletion was misleading, because in many ways it did not correspond to the real world behavior of trash cans. However, attempts to modify those behaviors to be more precise, involving "recycling" or indeed any other direct analogy, misses the point that the icon is only there as a starting point, to lead the user into imagining a new domain of experience.

It is also useful to make a distinction, in the case of user interfaces, between opportunities for creative interpretation that might be offered to the reader, and the creative work that is done by the designers of new systems. It has been observed in the past that user interface designers often use metaphor as a starting point for design, perhaps inspiring new interface features or interaction modes such as the "shopping basket" of online commerce. Indeed, HCI researchers have more recently drawn attention to the ways that designers and design researchers, as well as users, might take advantage of ambiguity of interpretation as a creative resource for new kinds of user experience (Gaver, Beaver, and Benford, 2003; Sengers and Gaver, 2006).

The creative practices advocated by these authors can be distinguished from more literalistic approaches to system design, in which user requirements are supposed to be systematically identified, organized, and implemented through a predictable process. Those structured design methodologies might remind us of the structuralism that Eco was responding to in his work. More interestingly, the relationship between authorship of "texts" (by the designer(s)) and readership (by the users) can become reconfigured in a variety of ways through programmable and customizable technologies. Both designers and users can become interpreters and performers. This question is explored further below.

Processing and Performance

Earlier, I observed that Eco identified two degrees of openness, and defined the first as the degree to which the text, in its nonobviousness, places demands on the reader to access other knowledge—for example of history, conventions, and so forth—to render it meaningful. The second degree of openness described by Eco moves beyond simple reading and interpretation to a reflexive appreciation of these processes. The introduction to *The Open Work* states that "every reception of a work of art is both an *interpretation* and a *performance* of it" (Eco, 1989, 4). To understand this point, we might think of the work of art as if it were a musical score. When musicians or orchestra conductors reads a score, they take the literal notes—the composer's instructions—as a starting point for their own creative work. Notes may be played more or less quickly, louder and softer, with many kinds of inflection and tone. Crowds flock to hear a great cellist play (or "interpret") a Bach sonata, while a competent amateur could play precisely the same notes in the same order, to no great effect. Indeed, every performance of a given musical work is unique, offering infinite variety.[8]

Now consider other works of art—novels or paintings for example. Every viewer of a painting allows her gaze to wander over its surface, lingering here and there, perhaps constructing a story to explain the arrangement of figures, imagining a fantasy world into which this is a window, or invoking memories of an emotional occasion. Just like a musical score, the painting is a starting point for an infinite variety of private performances. Similarly, the reader of a novel may pause at any point, turn back a few pages to reinterpret a plot development, or simply stop and daydream. Each of these can be regarded as a performance of the work. When a painting is more abstract, or a novel omits details of scene and character, it introduces bigger gaps for the reader to fill in, and so the variety of possible interpretive performances often becomes further and further extended—the work becomes more open.

In understanding such kinds of artwork, Eco observes that "contemporary aesthetics situates aesthetic pleasure less in final recognition of a form than apprehension of the continuously open process" (1989, 74). Eco draws attention to avant-garde musical scores that extended the freedom of the performer, far beyond the established conventions of choosing dynamics, tempo, and phrasing, to allow use of alternative notes or completely new improvised structures. These works that are "open" to acts of conscious freedom on the part of the performer draw the attention of the audience to the creative process itself, as it takes place on stage before them.

However, my own view is that digital technologies have profoundly reconfigured the processes of musical performance in recent times. A MIDI score can be "performed" by computer—but this is technically a rendering, simply following a set of mechanical rules as defined in the MIDI standard, to turn the score into sound. A conventional orchestral performance could also be described as a "mechanical rendering" (if the notes are played accurately and in the correct order) but this description would be understood as a harsh aesthetic critique rather than praise of accuracy.

But these distinctions between rendering and interpretive performance are rapidly mutating into new forms. The live sample remixer (for example Girl Talk) or house DJ (for example Fatboy Slim) "simply" cues and filters the recorded performances of other artists. We should certainly question whether these performers are engaged in "mechanical reproduction." It is true that these artists are employing a computer to mechanically render predetermined digital specifications. However, they are also interpreting this digital material, in their selections, edits, and effects, and indeed are themselves performers in the commonly understood sense—they are on stage, in front of an audience who have traveled to see them.

To some extent, the reception of a DJ's work is determined by the ability of the audience to interpret the technical interventions he is making. In the slightly more established case of the turntablist, the technical demands of performance have become understood within an interpretive culture of virtuosity, critique, and conservatoire education. In fact, all musical sound sources are to some degree mechanical (vibrating strings, wood, hammers, keys, and so on). It is the user interface to the instrument that determines freedom of choice, and thus the parameters of virtuosic performance and critical appreciation. Recall that Shannon and Weaver characterize information content in terms of the freedom to choose an interpretation of a signal. Where software technologies such as Google's PageRank exist partly in order to make choices for us (based on the choices already made by others), the artistic open work is experienced in terms of the freedoms that both authors and readers of texts have to interpret and perform. Perhaps we will see a future genre of search engine performance, in which an audience admires the "Google-fu" of a virtuoso.

The case of live coding offers a particular challenge for the critical analysis of digital music. Here, the performer works with the user interface of a program editor, often using domain-specific programming languages for audio synthesis and temporal sequencing such as Max/MSP, SuperCollider, or Overtone. The stage set for a live coding performance typically includes a projection of the performer's screen, allowing the audience to read the program code as it is being typed. In conventional musicological terms, the program might be considered to correspond to a musical score. It specifies the sounds to be made and the sequence in which they will appear. Of course, this programming language "score" does not resemble common music notation, but it still falls comfortably within the range of notational techniques that have been explored in previous generations of experimental and avant-garde music.

The execution of this program (or "performance" of the notation) is a mechanical rendering, in the sense that I have already discussed. The programming language semantics are predetermined, and the computer will always create music that follows those semantics. In information theory terms, no information is added by the machine, so witnessing the execution of an audio program might seem like a rather dry musical experience. However, just as with a turntablist or concert pianist, the live coding audience is also observing technical proficiency with a user interface—here, the interface of the programming language and development environment. Improvised programming is a virtuosic achievement. It can be admired in the same manner as live piano, saxophone, or organ improvisation. But in a programming language, the interface itself can also be reconfigured while playing—defining new functions, declaring variables, and so on. Whereas the minimum description length of a live coded score may seem small by comparison to a Beethoven symphony, the freedom of the performer is very large, and the audience is able to explore, not only the sonic experience, but the interpretation of its score in the second sense of openness described by Eco.

Reconfiguring Performance and Creation through Customization

In the case study that opened this chapter, I address the ways in which Eco asserts that meaning is associated with freedom—freedom for readers or an audience to establish their own boundaries between signal and noise, and hence derive their own meanings. I have observed that PageRank, in some ways, reduces this freedom by offering a single filtering algorithm that is driven by consensus rather than authorship. Of course, anyone is free to create a web page (and Google offers many tools with which a user might do so), but no one is free to modify the algorithm by which others will encounter this page—as a signal among the noise of other possible search results. In principle, a searcher could find the new page by specifying it with sufficiently precise search terms—but such a specification presumes that she knows what she is looking for. Like many giants of the internet economy at the time I write, Google acts as a broker, delivering texts ("content") from authors to readers while defining the terms on which this delivery can be achieved—and of course profiting from the middleman role, via advertising revenue. There is a constant underlying tension between faithful delivery of the advertiser's message, and the freedom for readers and writers to transform that message into a new one.

As an example of the way in which online platforms might offer different configurations of reading and writing, interpretation and performance, an interesting example is provided by the popular multiplayer sandbox game from Sweden, *Minecraft*. As with all sandbox video games, players are able to modify and construct their shared world—in *Minecraft*, by collecting construction materials and digging for ores that can be used to craft tools and buildings. However, whereas earlier sandbox games such as Second Life emphasized the virtual-realistic appearances of fantastic characters and products, the *Minecraft* world is almost absurdly low-resolution, built from individual blocks that are nominally a meter on each side. In contrast to the technical virtuosity of expert control just discussed in the live coding of electro-acoustic contemporary music, the apparent lack of technical refinement in *Minecraft* seems primitive and childlike with its blocky textures and behaviors. But this simplicity is also democratic, because its less detailed rendering offers a larger space of interpretive possibility, like that of an abstract artwork.

The game play in *Minecraft* is simple, although at first sight, this does not appear to be a special example of "open work." All "open world" video games[9] offer similar opportunities for the individual player to "perform" the work (in Eco's sense) by exploring and acting in the game world—at first sight, in a far more dramatic way than simply looking at a painting or reading a book. Sandbox games offer a further layer of performance, in which the player performs a repertoire of construction actions to modify the world. To some extent, this kind of sandbox experience shifts the boundary between author and reader, in that players may collaborate or compete within a shared performance. Eco did not anticipate openness of this kind, although some other chapters in this volume (e.g., Kirsten Boehner's commentary on Kaprow, chapter 32) describe artistic genres that draw members of the audience more intimately into the creation of the work.

But *Minecraft* is especially interesting as a case study because of the way in which it extends this open culture outside the frame of the game itself. During the early development of *Minecraft*, a technically sophisticated audience was nurtured by means of regular beta releases, giving players the impression that they were participating in the development process. The game documentation is delivered in the form of wikis that can be edited to include contributions from the player community. More distinctively, the wiki text documentation is supplemented with extended video tutorials that have been recorded as screen captures from live game play with audio narration by an expert player/instructor. These recorded performances of live construction might be compared to the live coding of software in front of a music audience—prominent live coders such as Sam Aaron also gain large audiences for their recorded demonstrations of tool use.[10]

The architect and lead developer of *Minecraft*, known to fans as "Notch," supports this culture of openness as an outspoken commentator on intellectual property issues, campaigning against software patents, and in favor of open source software. If we compare Notch's stated political views to the earlier case of Johnny Rotten and the Sex Pistols, it is clear that Notch also belongs to a very particular global subculture, and that his work should be interpreted in this light, just as the Sex Pistols should be interpreted in relation to the English Punk Rock scene. In the case of Notch, Sweden is popularly associated with European leadership in Open Source software,[11] for example through Andrew Tanenbaum's pioneering educational operating system Minix, and most prominently, through Linus Torvalds, who appropriated those ideas, together with those of Richard Stallman, to create Linux. In the free software world, authority is associated with technical skill. And like Tanenbaum and Torvalds, Notch is celebrated as a virtuoso programmer. Famously, Notch was not only the lead architect of *Minecraft* but also promotes and participates in online hacking contests and demonstrations, coding live in front of a global audience.[12]

A distinctive feature of this open development culture in the context of a sandbox game is that many *Minecraft* players, as creators of their own sandbox worlds within *Minecraft*, are thus able to identify with Notch, the creator of the *Minecraft* platform itself. Furthermore, these fans have the opportunity to modify the platform—not just the worlds created within it. The relatively low-resolution of the blocks that constitute the *Minecraft* world make it easy for players to change the appearance of those blocks by directly editing the texture maps. By replacing the standard collection of block types (trees, grass, gravel, etc.) with new textures, players can change the appearance of a whole world. Even more radically, the *Minecraft* software distributions preserve the ability, usually disabled in commercial software releases, to decompile the Java code of the application, substituting alternative implementations for any one of its components. *Minecraft* enthusiasts spend a great deal of time "modding"—modifying the software of their clients and servers to create new kinds of capability and game extensions.

In this case study, I would argue that we see something beyond simply another open source project. *Minecraft* has been interesting because its layers of interpretation and performance cross many conventional boundaries of authorship and readership. Of course, the audience of *Minecraft* (at the time I wrote this, my eleven-year-old daughter seemed to be in one core demographic) may become bored with the technical hurdles of modding, or the restrictions of a digital block world, especially as the excitement of *Minecraft*'s beta release era becomes more remote. Nevertheless, increased understanding of code as a media form seems likely to prevail in coming decades, such that the reading (and writing) of code is itself recognized as a semiotic and aesthetic pursuit.

By this stage of my argument, there may seem to be few remaining similarities to the media and cultural forms of the 1960s that prevailed when Eco was writing *The*

Open Work. Nevertheless, the cultural forms of live coding and video games, as with software user interfaces and HCI, clearly offer space for critical reading. Their openness as artworks is embedded in political and cultural contexts, just as John Cage's work was embedded in the 1950s, or the Sex Pistols in the 1970s. And as with those earlier creative pioneers, new media technologies continue to offer the opportunity for reconfigured constructions and understandings of semiotic texts. Computer programs, as texts, must be highly structured in order for the machine to interpret them. Yet human readings, modifications, and virtuoso constructions resist that structure through human interpretation and performance of software infrastructure (Cox and McLean, 2013). Despite the provocative example of *Minecraft*, it is not yet clear how the algorithmic corporate structures of Google and Facebook might be appropriated into freer readings and new open forms. Nevertheless, I believe we can be reasonably confident that this will occur.

Conclusions

Interactive digital media offer dramatic exemplars of the open work described by Umberto Eco. Although he could not have anticipated this at the time he wrote those essays, the democratizing tendencies already apparent at that time in art, music, literature, and film have become extended and universalized through the internet and ubiquitous computing.

This chapter has discussed three respects in which digital media offer new experiences of the open work.

The first of these lies in the distinction between "raw" information carried over networks or stored on servers, and the meaning that derives from interpretation by human readers. No pure algorithm offers freedom of this kind—meaning is obtained through interaction between readers and authors, and rooted in moral commitment.

The second is the ways in which the dynamics of the software industry—standardization and usability—have always been in tension with the open interpretation recognized by Eco. Even where we speak of open source software, or employ metaphor in user interface design, the poetics of the open work bring political commitments beyond those comfortably adopted in a business context.

The last of these is the many ways in which digital performance reconfigures the relation between the score and the audience. Digital media encode structural relations via notational formalism (including source code, scripting languages, design diagrams, and user interfaces). These can be shared directly with audiences, as well as offering potential for unbounded reflexivity and reconfiguration in the performance. Fluid communication between designers and users allows reading to become a process of exploration and challenge, rather than simple reception of a single message.

It is important to recognize the ways in which openness in digital media challenges purely engineering conceptions of information transfer between content producers and consumers, especially those at the core of companies like Google. Optimization of data rates, protocol standardization, and above all financial returns, result in media applications that are restricted along all these dimensions of openness. As noted by Zittrain (2009), the business imperatives of the digital economy are creating walled gardens, in which the bounds of potential interpretation and usage are strictly constrained by the most controllable and profitable readings.

Nevertheless, case studies such as live coding and open game platforms demonstrate the ways in which more subversive digital languages continue to realize the implications of Eco's open work. These media worlds are in part structured and performed by their own audiences. Although such configurations might once have been associated with the esoteric and experimental avant-garde, *Minecraft* is a popular mass-market success, and recent experiments in my own research group are exploiting live coding for early school education that crosses the boundary between arts and sciences, via music and computing (Aaron and Blackwell, 2013). The reflexive implications of modding and meta-narratives, although sophisticated, have not proven incompatible with popular acceptance. Eco's identification of the open work and its transformational potential seems likely to prove increasingly prophetic in the digital age.

Notes

1. Schmidt was the visiting humanitas professor, hosted by the Cambridge Centre for Research in the Arts, Social Science and Humanities (CRASSH), and convened by John Naughton. Google is a large technology company, established in the "search engine" market during the early 2000s. During Schmidt's tenure, Google had a high stock market valuation based on income from a contemporary cultural practice called "advertising."

2. PageRank is the key invention underlying the foundation of Google. PageRank is an algorithm—a (secret) statistical calculation used to judge the likely quality or relevance of a particular web page. Maintaining PageRank is a continual battle between web page authors who wish to promote their own views, and the judgment criteria encoded by Google engineers as a mathematical reputation market. It is essential to Google's business that those criteria are perceived as neutral—either a statistically objective "view from nowhere" or a morally superior policy expressed in the company motto, "Don't Be Evil."

3. We should also note the pioneering work of Peter Bøgh Andersen, the first extensive exploration of computer systems from a semiotic perspective (1990).

4. All file compression algorithms, as well as media formats such as MP3, JPEG, and digital broadcasting, are based on information theory.

5. As opposed (in the popular rhetoric of the open source movement) to attempting to "lock in" customers to the products of a single manufacturer through proprietary infrastructure protected by copyright, patents, or commercial secrets. At the hardware level, the USB connector is an

example of a market-expanding standard, while the original iPhone dock connector locked customers in to accessories that would only work with other Apple products.

6. Another Rotten lyric—"I am an anarchist, I am an Anti-Christ"—is perhaps slightly more overt.

7. This floating free has happened to the word "metaphor" itself, whose original Greek meaning is literally "to carry across."

8. Note that in this chapter, I am addressing performance as framed by the discourse of the performing arts. In chapter 22, Ann Light addresses the question of "performativity"—the construction of identity through the performance of semiotic acts—as explored in the writings of Judith Butler. The concepts of artistic performance and Butler's analysis of self-making via performativity are of course related and intertwined in various ways. For example, any analysis of poetics could also be elaborated in the light of gender identity. However, in this chapter I focus more closely on the experience of digital media as an art form, through the lens of literary criticism as developed by Eco.

9. "Open world" is a genre classification distinguishing video games in which the player is free to move around and act in the virtual world, rather than simply following a predefined narrative path.

10. See Aaron's *Quick Intro to Live Programming with Overtone,* http://vimeo.com/22798433.

11. And with other forms of democratic digital activism, such as hosting the WikiLeaks site.

12. The popular celebration of Notch as an artist-hero was somewhat diminished, after this chapter was first drafted, by the sale of *Minecraft* to Microsoft. Nevertheless, he appears to have maintained a degree of independence from the new corporate owner of his work.

References

Aaron, S., and A. F. Blackwell. (2013) "From Sonic Pi to Overtone: Creative Musical Experiences with Domain-Specific and Functional Languages." *Proceedings of the First ACM SIGPLAN Workshop on Functional Art, Music, Modeling & Design.* New York: AMC, 35–46.

Andersen, P. B. (1990) *A Theory of Computer Semiotics: Semiotic Approaches to Construction and Assessment of Computer Systems.* Cambridge: Cambridge University Press.

Blackwell, A. F. (2006) "The Reification of Metaphor as a Design Tool." *ACM Transactions on Computer-Human Interaction (TOCHI)* 13 (4): 490–530.

Bondanella, P. (1997) *Umberto Eco and the Open Text.* Cambridge: Cambridge University Press.

Cox, G., and A. McLean. (2013) *Speaking Code: Coding as Aesthetic and Political Expression.* Cambridge, MA: MIT Press.

De Souza, C. S. (2005) *The Semiotic Engineering of Human-Computer Interaction.* Cambridge, MA: MIT Press.

Eco, U. (1989) *The Open Work*, translated by A. Cancogni. Cambridge, MA: Harvard University Press.

Eco, U. (1995) *The Search for the Perfect Language*. Cambridge, MA: Blackwell.

Empson, W. (1947) *Seven Types of Ambiguity*. London: Chatto and Windus.

Floridi, L. (2010) *Information: A Very Short Introduction*. Oxford: Oxford University Press.

Gaver, W., J. Beaver, and S. Benford. (2003) "Ambiguity as a Resource for Design." *Proceedings of the SIGCHI Conference on Human Factors in Computing Systems*. New York: ACM, 233–240.

Lehrer, T., and R. Searle. (1999) *Too Many Songs*. London: Methuen.

Moles, A. A. (1969) *Information Theory and Esthetic Perception*, translated by J. E. Cohen. Urbana: University of Illinois Press.

Pasquinelli, M. (2009) "Google's PageRank Algorithm: A Diagram of Cognitive Capitalism and the Rentier of the Common Intellect." In *Deep Search: The Politics of Search beyond Google*, edited by K. Becker and F. Stalder, 152–162. London: Transaction.

Robey, D. (1989) Introduction to *The Open Work*, by U. Eco, vii–xxxii. Translated by A. Cancogni. Cambridge, MA: Harvard University Press.

Sengers, P., and W. Gaver. (2006) "Staying Open to Interpretation: Engaging Multiple Meanings in Design and Evaluation." *Proceedings of the 6th Conference on Designing Interactive Systems (DIS'06)*. New York: ACM, 99–108.

Zittrain, J. (2009) *The Future of the Internet: And How to Stop It*. London: Penguin.

9 Encoding/Decoding (1978)

Stuart Hall

Traditionally, mass-communications research has conceptualized the process of communication in terms of a circulation circuit or loop. This model has been criticized for its linearity—sender/message/receiver—for its concentration on the level of message exchange and for the absence of a structured conception of the different moments as a complex structure of relations. But it is also possible (and useful) to think of this process in terms of a structure produced and sustained through the articulation of linked but distinctive moments—production, circulation, distribution/consumption, reproduction. This would be to think of the process as a "complex structure in dominance," sustained through the articulation of connected practices, each of which, however, retains its distinctiveness and has its own specific modality, its own forms and conditions of existence. This second approach, homologous to that which forms the skeleton of commodity production offered in Marx's *Grundrisse* and in *Capital,* has the added advantage of bringing out more sharply how a continuous circuit—production–distribution–production—can be sustained through a "passage of forms."[1] It also highlights the specificity of the forms in which the product of the process "appears" in each moment, and thus what distinguishes discursive "production" from other types of production in our society and in modern media systems.

The "object" of these practices is meanings and messages in the form of sign-vehicles of a specific kind organized, like any form of communication or language, through the operation of codes within the syntagmatic chain of a discourse. The apparatuses, relations and practices of production thus issue, at a certain moment (the moment of "production/circulation") in the form of symbolic vehicles constituted within the rules of "language." It is in this discursive form that the circulation of the "product" takes place. The process thus requires, at the production end, its material instruments—its "means"—as well as its own sets of social (production) relations—the organization and combination of practices within media apparatuses. But it is in the *discursive* form that the circulation of the product takes place, as well as its distribution to different audiences. Once accomplished, the discourse must then be translated—transformed, again—into social practices if the circuit is to be both completed and effective. If no "meaning" is taken, there can be no "consumption." If the meaning is not articulated in practice, it has no effect. The value of this approach is that while each of the moments, in articulation, is necessary to the circuit as a whole, no one moment can fully guarantee the next moment with which it is articulated. Since each has its specific modality and conditions of existence, each can constitute its own break or interruption of the "passage of forms" on whose continuity the flow of effective production (that is, "reproduction") depends.

Thus while in no way wanting to limit research to "following only those leads which emerge from content analysis,"[2] we must recognize that the discursive form of the message has a privileged position in the communicative exchange (from the viewpoint of circulation), and that the moments of "encoding" and "decoding," though only "relatively autonomous" in relation to the communicative process as a whole, are *determinate* moments. A "raw" historical event cannot, *in that form*, be transmitted by, say, a television newscast. Events can only be signified within the aural-visual forms of the televisual discourse. In the moment when a historical event passes under the sign of discourse, it is subject to all the complex formal "rules" by which language signifies. To put it paradoxically, the event must become a "story" before it can become a *communicative event*. In that moment the formal sub-rules of discourse are "in dominance," without, of course, subordinating out of existence the historical event so signified, the social relations in which the rules are set to work or the social and political consequences of the event having been signified in this way. The "message form" is the necessary "form of appearance" of the event in its passage from source to receiver. Thus the transposition into and out of the "message form" (or the mode of symbolic exchange) is not a random "moment," which we can take up or ignore at our convenience. The "message form" is a determinate moment; though, at another level, it comprises the surface movements of the communications system only and requires, at another stage, to be integrated into the social relations of the communication process as a whole, of which it forms only a part.

From this general perspective, we may crudely characterize the television communicative process as follows. The institutional structures of broadcasting, with their practices and networks of production, their organized relations and technical infrastructures, are required to produce a programme. Using the analogy of *Capital*, this is the "labour process" in the discursive mode. Production, here, constructs the message. In one sense, then, the circuit begins here. Of course, the production process is not without its "discursive" aspect: it, too, is framed throughout by meanings and ideas: knowledge-in-use concerning the routines of production, historically defined technical skills, professional ideologies, institutional knowledge, definitions and assumptions, assumptions about the audience and so on frame the constitution of the programme through this production structure. Further, though the production structures of television originate the television discourse, they do not constitute a closed system. They draw topics, treatments, agendas, events, personnel, images of the audience, "definitions of the situation" from other sources and other discursive formations within the wider socio-cultural and political structure of which they are a differentiated part. Philip Elliott has expressed this point succinctly, within a more traditional framework, in his discussion of the way in which the audience is both the "source" and the "receiver" of the television message. Thus—to borrow Marx's terms—circulation and reception are, indeed, "moments" of the production process in television and are reincorporated, via a number of skewed and structured "feedbacks," into the production process itself. The consumption or reception of the television message is thus also itself a "moment" of the production process in its larger sense, though the latter is "predominant" because it is the "point of departure for the realization" of the message. Production and reception of the television message are not, therefore, identical, but they are related: they are differentiated moments within the totality formed by the social relations of the communicative process as a whole.

At a certain point, however, the broadcasting structures must yield encoded messages in the form of a meaningful discourse. The institution-societal relations of production must pass under the discursive rules of language for its product to be "realized." This initiates a further differentiated moment, in which the formal rules of discourse and language are in dominance. Before this message can have an "effect" (however defined), satisfy a "need" or be put to a "use," it must first be appropriated as a meaningful discourse and be meaningfully decoded. It is this set of decoded meanings which "have an effect," influence, entertain, instruct or persuade, with very complex perceptual, cognitive, emotional, ideological or behavioural consequences. In a "determinate" moment the structure employs a code and yields a "message": at another determinate moment the "message," via its decodings, issues into the structure of social practices. We are now fully aware that this re-entry into the practices of audience reception and "use" cannot be understood in simple behavioural terms. The typical processes identified in positivistic research on isolated elements—effects, uses, "gratifications"—are themselves framed by structures of understanding, as well as being produced by social and economic relations, which shape their "realization" at the reception end of the chain and which permit the meanings signified in the discourse to be transposed into practice or consciousness (to acquire social use value or political effectivity).

Clearly, what we have labelled in the diagram "meaning structures 1" and "meaning structures 2" may not be the same. They do not constitute an "immediate identity." The codes of encoding and decoding may not be perfectly symmetrical. The degrees of symmetry—that is, the degrees of "understanding" and "misunderstanding" in the communicative exchange—depend on the degrees of symmetry/asymmetry (relations of equivalence) established between the positions of the "personifications," encoder-producer and decoder-receiver. But this in turn depends on the degrees of identity/non-identity between the codes which perfectly or imperfectly transmit, interrupt or systematically distort what has been transmitted. The lack of fit between the codes has a great deal to do with the structural differences of relation and position between broadcasters and audiences, but it also has something to do with the asymmetry between the codes of "source" and "receiver" at the moment of transformation into and out of the discursive form. What are called "distortions" or "misunderstandings" arise precisely from the *lack of equivalence* between the two sides in the communicative exchange. Once again, this defines the "relative autonomy," but "determinateness," of the entry and exit of the message in its discursive moments.

The application of this rudimentary paradigm has already begun to transform our understanding of the older term, television "content." We are just beginning to see how it might also transform our understanding of audience reception, "reading" and response as well. Beginnings and endings have been announced in communications research before, so we must be cautious. But there seems some ground for thinking that a new and exciting phase in so-called audience research, of a quite new kind, may be opening up. At either end of the communicative chain the use of the semiotic paradigm promises to dispel the lingering behaviourism which has dogged mass-media research for so long, especially in its approach to content. Though we know the television programme is not a behavioural input, like a tap on the knee cap, it seems to have been almost impossible for traditional researchers to conceptualize the communicative process without lapsing into one or other variant of low-flying behaviourism. We know, as Gerbner has remarked, that representations of violence on the TV screen "are not violence but messages about violence":[3] but we have continued to research the question of violence, for example, as if we were unable to comprehend this epistemological distinction.

The televisual sign is a complex one. It is itself constituted by the combination of two types of discourse, visual and aural. Moreover, it is an iconic sign, in Peirce's terminology, because "it possesses some of the properties of the thing represented."[4] This is a point which has led to a great deal of confusion and has provided the site of intense controversy in the study of visual language. Since the visual discourse translates a three-dimensional world into two-dimensional planes, it cannot, of course, *be* the referent or concept it signifies. The dog in the film can bark but it cannot bite! Reality exists outside language, but it is constantly mediated by and through language: and what we can know and say has to be produced in and through discourse. Discursive "knowledge" is the product not of the transparent representation of the "real" in language but of the articulation of language on real relations and conditions. Thus there is no intelligible discourse without the operation of a code. Iconic signs are therefore coded signs too—even if the codes here work differently from those of other signs. There is no degree zero in language. Naturalism and "realism"—the apparent fidelity of the representation to the thing or concept represented—is the result, the effect, of a certain specific articulation of language on the "real." It is the result of a discursive practice.

Certain codes may, of course, be so widely distributed in a specific language community or culture, and be learned at so early an age, that they appear not to be constructed—the effect of an articulation between sign and referent—but to be "naturally" given. Simple visual signs appear to have achieved a "near-universality" in this sense: though evidence remains that even apparently "natural" visual codes are culture-specific. However, this does not mean that no codes have intervened; rather, that the codes have been profoundly *naturalized.* The operation of naturalized codes reveals not the transparency and "naturalness" of language but the depth, the habituation and the near-universality of the codes in use. They produce apparently "natural" recognitions. This has the (ideological) effect of concealing the practices of coding which are present. But we must not be fooled by appearances. Actually, what naturalized codes demonstrate is the degree of habituation produced when there is a fundamental alignment and reciprocity—an achieved equivalence—between the encoding and decoding sides of an exchange of meanings. The functioning of the codes on the decoding side will frequently assume the status of naturalized perceptions. This leads us to think that the visual sign for "cow" actually *is* (rather than *represents*) the animal, cow. But if we think of the visual representation of a cow in a manual on animal husbandry—and, even more, of the linguistic sign "cow"—we can see that both, in different degrees, are *arbitrary* with respect to the concept of the animal they represent. The articulation of an arbitrary sign—whether visual or verbal—with the concept of a referent is the product not of nature but of convention, and the conventionalism of discourses requires the intervention, the support, of codes. Thus Eco has argued that iconic signs "look like objects in the real world because they reproduce the conditions (that is, the codes) of perception in the viewer."[5] These "conditions of perception" are, however, the result of a highly coded, even if virtually unconscious, set of operations—decodings. This is as true of the photographic or televisual image as it is of any other sign. Iconic signs are, however, particularly vulnerable to being "read" as natural because visual codes of perception are very widely distributed and because this type of sign is less arbitrary than a linguistic sign: the linguistic sign, "cow" possesses *none* of the properties of the thing represented, whereas the visual sign appears to possess *some* of those properties.

This may help us to clarify a confusion in current linguistic theory and to define precisely how some key terms are being used in this article. Linguistic theory frequently employs the distinction "denotation" and "connotation." The term "denotation" is widely equated with the literal meaning of a sign: because this literal meaning is almost universally recognized, especially when visual discourse is being employed, "denotation" has often been confused with a literal transcription of "reality" in language—and thus with a "natural sign," one produced without the intervention of a code. "Connotation," on the other hand, is employed simply to refer to less fixed and therefore more conventionalized and changeable, associative meanings, which clearly vary from instance to instance and therefore must depend on the intervention of codes.

We do *not* use the distinction—denotation/connotation—in this way. From our point of view, the distinction is an *analytic* one only. It is useful, in analysis, to be able to apply a rough rule of thumb which distinguishes those aspects of a sign which appear to be taken, in any language community at any point in time, as its "literal" meaning (denotation) from the more associative meanings for the sign which it is possible to generate (connotation). But analytic distinctions must not be confused with distinctions in the real world. There will be very few instances in which signs organized in a discourse signify *only* their "literal" (that is, near-universally consensualized) meaning. In actual discourse most signs will combine both the denotative and the connotative *aspects* (as redefined above). It may, then, be asked why we retain the distinction at all. It is largely a matter of analytic value. It is because signs appear to acquire their full ideological value—appear to be open to articulation with wider ideological discourses and meanings—at the level of their "associative" meanings (that is, at the connotative level)—for here "meanings" are *not* apparently fixed in natural perception (that is, they are not fully naturalized), and their fluidity of meaning and association can be more fully exploited and transformed.[6] So it is at the connotative *level* of the sign that situational ideologies alter and transform signification. At this level we can see more clearly the active intervention of ideologies in and on discourse: here, the sign is open to new accentuations and, in Vološinov's terms, enters fully into the struggle over meanings—the class struggle in language.[7] This does not mean that the denotative or "literal" meaning is outside ideology. Indeed, we could say that its ideological value is strongly *fixed*—because it has become so fully universal and "natural." The terms "denotation" and "connotation," then, are merely useful analytic tools for distinguishing, in particular contexts, between not the presence/absence of ideology in language but the different levels at which ideologies and discourses intersect.[8]

The level of connotation of the visual sign, of its contextual reference and positioning in different discursive fields of meaning and association, is the point where *already coded* signs intersect with the deep semantic codes of a culture and take on additional, more active ideological dimensions. We might take an example from advertising discourse. Here, too, there is no "purely denotative," and certainly no "natural," representation. Every visual sign in advertising connotes a quality, situation, value or inference, which is present as an implication or implied meaning, depending on the connotational positioning. In Barthes's example, the sweater always signifies a "warm garment" (denotation) and thus the activity/value of "keeping warm." But it is also possible, at its more connotative levels, to signify "the coming of winter" or "a cold day." And, in the specialized sub-codes of fashion, sweater may also connote a fashionable style of *haute couture* or, alternatively, an informal style of dress. But set against the right visual background and positioned by the romantic sub-code, it may connote "long autumn walk in the woods."[9] Codes of this order clearly contract relations for the sign with the wider universe of ideologies in a society. These codes are the means by which power and ideology are made to signify in particular discourses. They refer signs to the "maps of meaning" into which any culture is classified; and those "maps of social reality" have the whole range of social meanings, practices, and usages, power and interest "written in" to them. The connotative levels of signifiers, Barthes remarked, "have a close communication with culture, knowledge, history, and it is through them, so to speak, that the environmental world invades the linguistic and semantic system. They are, if you like, the fragments of ideology."[10]

The so-called denotative *level* of the televisual sign is fixed by certain, very complex (but limited or "closed") codes. But its connotative *level*, though also bounded, is more open, subject to more active *transformations*, which exploit its polysemic values. Any such already constituted sign is potentially transformable into more than one connotative configuration. Polysemy must not, however, be confused with pluralism. Connotative codes are *not* equal among themselves. Any society/culture tends, with varying degrees of closure, to impose its classifications of the social and cultural and political world. These constitute a *dominant cultural order*, though it is neither univocal nor uncontested. This question of the "structure of discourses in dominance" is a crucial point. The different areas of social life appear to be mapped out into discursive domains, hierarchically organized into *dominant or preferred meanings*. New, problematic or troubling events, which breach our expectancies and run counter to our "common-sense constructs," to our "taken-for-granted" knowledge of social structures, must be assigned to their discursive domains before they can be said to "make sense." The most common way of "mapping" them is to assign the new to some domain or other of the existing "maps of problematic social reality." We say *dominant*, not "determined," because it is always possible to order, classify, assign and decode an event within more than one "mapping." But we say "dominant" because there exists a pattern of "preferred readings"; and these both have the institutional/political/ideological order imprinted in them and have themselves become institutionalized.[11] The domains of "preferred meanings" have the whole social order embedded in them as a set of meanings, practices and beliefs: the everyday knowledge of social structures, of "how things work for all practical purposes in this culture," the rank order of power and interest and the structure of legitimations, limits and sanctions. Thus to clarify a "misunderstanding" at the connotative level, we must refer, *through* the codes, to the orders of social life, of economic and political power and of ideology. Further, since these mappings are "structured in dominance" but not closed, the communicative process consists not in the unproblematic assignment of every visual item to its given position within a set of prearranged codes, but of *performative rules*—rules of competence and use, of logics-in-use—which seek actively to *enforce* or *pre-fer* one semantic domain over another and rule items into and out of their appropriate meaning-sets. Formal semiology has too often neglected this practice of *interpretative work*, though this constitutes, in fact, the real relations of broadcast practices in television.

In speaking of *dominant meanings*, then, we are not talking about a one-sided process which governs how all events will be signified. It consists of the "work" required to enforce, win plausibility for and command as legitimate a *decoding* of the event within the limit of dominant definitions in which it has been connotatively signified. Terni has remarked:

> By the word *reading* we mean not only the capacity to identify and decode a certain number of signs, but also the subjective capacity to put them into a creative relation between themselves and with other signs: a capacity which is, by itself, the condition for a complete awareness of one's total environment.[12]

Our quarrel here is with the notion of "subjective capacity," as if the referent of a televisional discourse were an objective fact but the interpretative level were an individualized and private matter. Quite the opposite seems to be the case. The televisual practice takes "objective" (that is, systemic) responsibility precisely for the relations which disparate signs contract with one another in any discursive instance, and thus continually rearranges, delimits and prescribes into what "awareness of one's total environment" these items are arranged.

This brings us to the question of misunderstandings. Television producers who find their message "failing to get across" are frequently concerned to straighten out the kinks in the communication chain, thus facilitating the "effectiveness" of their communication. Much research which claims the objectivity of "policy-oriented analysis" reproduces this administrative goal by attempting to discover how much of a message the audience recalls and to improve the extent of understanding. No doubt misunderstandings of a literal kind do exist. The viewer does not know the terms employed, cannot follow the complex logic of argument or exposition, is unfamiliar with the language, finds the concepts too alien or difficult or is foxed by the expository narrative. But more often broadcasters are concerned that the audience has failed to take the meaning as they—the broadcasters—intended. What they really mean to say is that viewers are not operating within the "dominant" or "preferred" code. Their ideal is "perfectly transparent communication." Instead, what they have to confront is "systematically distorted communication."[13]

In recent years discrepancies of this kind have usually been explained by reference to "selective perception." This is the door via which a residual pluralism evades the compulsions of a highly structured, asymmetrical and non-equivalent process. Of course, there will always be private, individual, variant readings. But "selective perception" is almost never as selective, random or privatized as the concept suggests. The patterns exhibit, across individual variants, significant clusterings. Any new approach to audience studies will therefore have to begin with a critique of "selective perception" theory.

It was argued earlier that since there is no necessary correspondence between encoding and decoding, the former can attempt to "pre-fer" but cannot prescribe or guarantee the latter, which has its own conditions of existence. Unless they are wildly aberrant, encoding will have the effect of constructing some of the limits and parameters within which decodings will operate. If there were no limits, audiences could simply read whatever they liked into any message. No doubt some total misunderstandings of this kind do exist. But the vast range must contain *some* degree of reciprocity between encoding and decoding moments, otherwise we could not speak of an effective communicative exchange at all. Nevertheless, this "correspondence" is not given but constructed. It is not "natural" but the product of an articulation between two distinct moments. And the former cannot determine or guarantee, in a simple sense, which decoding codes will be employed. Otherwise communication would be a perfectly equivalent circuit, and every message would be an instance of "perfectly transparent communication." We must think, then, of the variant articulations in which encoding/decoding can be combined. To elaborate on this, we offer a hypothetical analysis of some possible decoding positions, in order to reinforce the point of "no necessary correspondence."[14]

We identify *three* hypothetical positions from which decodings of a televisual discourse may be constructed. These need to be empirically tested and refined. But the argument that decodings do not follow inevitably from encodings, that they are not identical, reinforces the argument of "no necessary correspondence." It also helps to deconstruct the common-sense meaning of "misunderstanding" in terms of a theory of "systematically distorted communication."

The first hypothetical position is that of the *dominant-hegemonic position.* When the viewer takes the connoted meaning from, say, a television newscast or current affairs programme full and straight, and decodes the message in terms of the reference code in which it has been encoded, we might say that the viewer *is operating inside the dominant code.* This is the ideal-typical case of "perfectly transparent communication"—or as close as we are likely to come to it "for all practical purposes." Within this we can distinguish the positions produced by the *professional code.* This is the position (produced by what we perhaps ought to identify as the operation of a "metacode") which the professional broadcasters assume when encoding a message which has *already* been signified in a hegemonic manner. The professional code is "relatively independent" of the dominant code, in that it applies criteria and transformational operations of its own, especially those of a technico-practical nature. The professional code, however, operates *within* the "hegemony" of the dominant code. Indeed, it serves to reproduce the dominant definitions precisely by bracketing their hegemonic quality and operating instead with displaced professional codings which foreground such apparently neutral-technical questions as visual quality, news and presentational values, televisual quality, "professionalism" and so on. The hegemonic interpretations of, say, the politics of Northern Ireland, or the Chilean *coup* or the Industrial Relations Bill are principally generated by political and military elites: the particular choice of presentational occasions and formats, the selection of personnel, the choice of images, the staging of debates are selected and combined through the operation of the professional code. How the broadcasting professionals are able *both* to operate with "relatively autonomous" codes of their own *and* to act in such a way as to reproduce (not without contradiction) the hegemonic signification of events is a complex matter which cannot be further spelled out here. It must suffice to say that the professionals are linked with the defining elites not only by the institutional position of broadcasting itself as an "ideological apparatus,"[15] but also by the structure of *access* (that is, the systematic "over-accessing" of selective elite personnel and their "definition of the situation" in television). It may even be said that the professional codes serve to reproduce hegemonic definitions specifically by *not overtly* biasing their operations in a dominant direction: ideological reproduction therefore takes place here inadvertently, unconsciously, "behind men's backs."[16] Of course, conflicts, contradictions and even misunderstandings regularly arise between the dominant and the professional significations and their signifying agencies.

The second position we would identify is that of the *negotiated code* or position. Majority audiences probably understand quite adequately what has been dominantly defined and professionally signified. The dominant definitions, however, are hegemonic precisely because they represent definitions of situations and events which are "in dominance," (*global*). Dominant definitions connect events, implicitly or explicitly, to grand totalizations, to the great syntagmatic views-of-the-world: they take "large views" of issues: they relate events to the "national interest" or to the level of geo-politics, even if they make these connections in truncated, inverted or mystified ways. The definition of a hegemonic viewpoint is (a) that it defines within its terms the mental horizon, the universe, of possible meanings, of a whole sector of relations in a society or culture; and (b) that it carries with it the stamp of legitimacy—it appears coterminous with what is "natural," "inevitable," "taken for granted" about the social order. Decoding within the *negotiated version* contains a mixture of adaptive and oppositional elements: it acknowledges the legitimacy of the hegemonic definitions to make the grand significations (abstract), while, at a more restricted, situational (situated) level, it makes its own ground rules—it operates with exceptions to the rule. It accords the privileged position to the dominant definitions of events while reserving the right to make a more negotiated application to "local conditions," to its own more *corporate* positions. This negotiated version of the dominant ideology is thus shot through with contradictions, though these are only on certain occasions brought to full visibility. Negotiated codes operate through what we might call particular or situated logics; and these logics are sustained by their differential and unequal relation to the discourses and logics of power. The simplest example of a negotiated code is that which governs the response of a worker to the notion of an Industrial Relations Bill limiting the right to strike or to arguments for a wages freeze. At the level of the "national interest" economic debate the decoder may adopt the hegemonic definition, agreeing that "we must all pay ourselves less in order to combat inflation." This, however, may have little or no relation to his/her willingness to go on strike for better pay and conditions or to oppose the Industrial Relations Bill at the level of shop-floor or union organization. We suspect that the great majority of so-called "misunderstandings" arise from the contradictions and disjunctures between hegemonic-dominant encodings and negotiated-corporate decodings. It is just these mismatches in the levels which most provoke defining elites and professionals to identify a "failure in communications."

Finally, it is possible for a viewer perfectly to understand both the literal and the connotative inflection given by a discourse but to decode the message in a *globally* contrary way. He/she detotalizes the message in the preferred code in order to retotalize the message within some alternative framework of reference. This is the case of the viewer who listens to a debate on the need to limit wages but "reads" every mention of the "national interest" as "class interest." He/she is operating with what we must call an *oppositional code*. One of the most significant political moments (they also coincide with crisis points within the broadcasting organizations themselves, for obvious reasons) is the point when events which are normally signified and decoded in a negotiated way begin to be given an oppositional reading. Here the "politics of signification"—the struggle in discourse—is joined.

Notes

This article is an edited extract from "Encoding and Decoding in Television Discourse," CCCS Stencilled Paper no. 7.

1. For an explication and commentary on the methodological implications of Marx's argument, see S. Hall, "A reading of Marx's 1857 *Introduction to the Grundrisse*," in *WPCS* 6 (1974).

2. J. D. Halloran, "Understanding television," Paper for the Council of Europe Colloquy on "Understanding Television" (University of Leicester 1973).

3. G. Gerbner et al., *Violence in TV Drama: A Study of Trends and Symbolic Functions* (The Annenberg School, University of Pennsylvania 1970).

4. Charles Peirce, *Speculative Grammar*, in *Collected Papers* (Cambridge, Mass.: Harvard University Press 1931–58).

5. Umberto Eco, "Articulations of the cinematic code," in *Cinemantics*, no. 1.

6. See the argument in S. Hall, "Determinations of news photographs," in *WPCS* 3 (1972).

7. Vološinov, *Marxism and the Philosophy of Language* (The Seminar Press 1973).

8. For a similar clarification, see Marina Camargo Heck, "Ideological dimensions of media messages," pages 122–7 above.

9. Roland Barthes, "Rhetoric of the image," in *WPCS* 1 (1971).

10. Roland Barthes, *Elements of Semiology* (Cape 1967).

11. For an extended critique of "preferred reading," see Alan O'Shea, "Preferred reading" (unpublished paper, CCCS, University of Birmingham).

12. P. Terni, "Memorandum," Council of Europe Colloquy on "Understanding Television" (University of Leicester 1973).

13. The phrase is Habermas's, in "Systematically distorted communications," in P. Dretzel (ed.), *Recent Sociology 2* (Collier-Macmillan 1970). It is used here, however, in a different way.

14. For a sociological formulation which is close, in some ways, to the positions outlined here but which does not parallel the argument about the theory of discourse, see Frank Parkin, *Class Inequality and Political Order* (Macgibbon and Kee 1971).

15. See Louis Althusser, "Ideology and ideological state apparatuses," in *Lenin and Philosophy and Other Essays* (New Left Books 1971).

16. For an expansion of this argument, see Stuart Hall, "The external/internal dialectic in broadcasting," *4th Symposium on Broadcasting* (University of Manchester 1972), and "Broadcasting and the state: the independence/impartiality couplet," AMCR Symposium, University of Leicester 1976 (CCCS unpublished paper).

10 Stuart Hall: Cultural Studies, Human-Computer Interaction, and Encoding/Decoding

Elizabeth F. Churchill

Cultures consist of the maps of meaning, the frameworks of intelligibility, the things which allow us to make sense of a world which exists, but is ambiguous as to its meaning until we've made sense of it. So, meaning arises because of the shared conceptual maps which groups or members of a culture or society share together.

—Hall, quoted in Jhally, 2005, 9

Stuart Hall (1932–2014) was a founding member of the Birmingham Centre for Cultural Studies. With Richard Hoggart, Raymond Williams, and E. P. Thompson, he launched and shaped cultural studies as an academic enterprise. His pioneering work during the late 1960s and the 1970s introduced the theorizing of continental European philosophers to scholars interested in understanding social structures, formations, and experiences, and thus shaped discourse in the humanities in the UK for the ensuing decades.

Not satisfied with containing his insights within academia, Stuart Hall was an activist scholar and a "public intellectual." In the mold of intellectuals like Antonio Gramsci, Hall always moved between work in academia and active political involvement. He was a key figure in the emergence of the New Left in England and Scotland between 1956 and 1961, was the first editor of the *New Left Review*, was active in political events during the 1980s—coining the term "Thatcherism"—and wrote a number of highly influential articles for the magazine *Marxism Today* (Coates, 2013). Until his death in 2014, he remained an active commentator on the political landscape. His work was foundational for putting the topics of race and gender on the map as legitimate spheres of academic investigation and intellectual enquiry.

Stuart Hall's work and legacy is timely for several reasons. First, the notion of culture is increasingly mobilized in our narrations of technologies that are globally available yet locally experienced. At the same time, some have claimed that the word "culture" has been so overused that it has lost its explanatory power (e.g., Sewell, 1999). Thus, in order to better address the role of culture in explaining the ways in which individuals and groups take up, adopt, and adapt designed artifacts and styled experiences, it may be time for us to reconnect with a more active and activist use of the word "culture."

Such an engagement with the concept of culture, with cultural theory, and with cultural studies fits most closely with what has been called the "third wave" in the field of human-computer interaction (HCI), and with the "critical turn" that HCI has taken in the last decade. This notion of the "third wave" is articulated in Suzanne Bødker's article, "When Second Wave HCI Meets Third Wave Challenges" (2006). Drawing on Liam Bannon's work (Bannon, 1991), Bødker describes how HCI as an area of enquiry moved from its first wave—with a focus on "human factors," drawing on psychology and ergonomics and concerns with measuring cognitive dimensions of the "man-machine fit" to produce "rigid guidelines, formal methods, and systematic testing"—to its second wave and a focus on "actors" (Bødker, 2006, 1).

This second wave of HCI focused on groups working with collections of applications, laying the foundation for the research area of "computer-supported cooperative work" (CSCW) and explicitly acknowledging the social nature of engagement with technologies. In this second wave, theory focused on work settings and interaction within well-established communities of practice. Ideas such as situated action, distributed cognition, and activity theory were developed and used as "sources of theoretical reflection" (Bødker, 2006, 1). Theorists and practitioners wrangled conceptualizations of "context" in creating scenarios of imagined use for interactive technologies. The methods of the earlier wave of HCI were "mostly abandoned for proactive methods such as a variety of participatory design workshops, prototyping and contextual inquiries" (1).

Following this, the third wave turned from work settings and acknowledged that things were changing at such a fast pace that earlier perspectives, theories, and models were simply inadequate for the emerging technosphere: computers were moving into nonwork settings, into private and public spheres, and being used for "nonwork, non-purpose, and nonrational" uses (Bødker, 2006, 1–2). The third wave of HCI required the "expansion of the cognitive" to include emotional and aesthetic aspects of experience, which were needed to bring in concepts such as identity and personal/shared meaning, and turned toward cultural-historical interpretations of technology design, development, adoption, and appropriation. It is within this emergence of the third wave that cultural studies is most relevant, and in particular the perspective on cultural studies that derives from the pioneering work of Stuart Hall, his colleagues, and the scholars who have continued the trajectory of his work.

What Is Cultural Studies and How Was It Shaped by Stuart Hall?

Cultural studies is a field of endeavor, a set of foci, and a collection of methods drawn from many disciplines, and it is concerned with the ways in which societal structures impact everyday life. Scholars address the acceptances, adoptions, adaptations, and/

or resistances that people enact, and the structures that enable or constrain them—that limit, align with, enable, or amplify their agency. Cultural studies engages with the discourse(s) between external governance and self-governance. It follows, therefore, that cultural theorists study the ways in which dominant groups in society assert power, and how these assertions are accepted, adopted, adapted, and/or resisted and reformulated by individuals through their actions and their (dis)engagements with popular cultural artifacts. One can imagine many examples where these acceptances, adoptions, adaptations, and resistances are played out—think about who creates, who consumes, who critiques, and who resists the following: advertising in magazines and media channels; broadcast programming on radio, television, and the internet; entertainment events such as the Olympics, the Super Bowl, or the World Cup; approved and mandated educational curricula; high and low fashion, in the form of "haute couture" versus "high street" fashion; tourist destinations and experiences as "high" or "low" culture; and computer technologies, internet services, and applications—the last being the most relevant for us as HCI scholars, researchers, and practitioners.

Cultural studies scholars often focus on the margins of power where dominant forms are taken up, resisted, and/or transformed, considering how culture is used and transformed by ordinary and marginal social groups. Central to this is a focus on how human "subjects" are formed, how they experience cultural and social space, and how they do or do not resist and/or contest their place in those cultural and social spaces. Individuals are seen as the producers of new social values and cultural languages. In representing the margins and the marginalized, many cultural studies scholars have taken the stance of advocates, embodying a commitment to progressive change and focusing on social movements and actionable policy.

These concerns and the approach to addressing them—textual analysis of popular culture with a strong social theory lens—stem from Hall's work, which reflects a continual engagement with a desire to understand the essence of culture, of personal and cultural identity, and how ideologies are crafted and, in their turn, craft and coerce us as people, as individuals. While his work shifted somewhat over the decades that he contributed to scholarly discourse, Hall focused predominantly on the places where conflicts exist in cultural formations, aiming to show how those conflicts are rendered invisible by dominant groups, and to show us how individuals and groups who are not part of the dominant social order—those at the margins—resist what is taken for granted and create new ways of understanding social life. He thus addressed the social nature of culture, but not from an abstract perspective. He looked closely at how people experience life, at their projected and experienced "identities," and at the dissonances between "official" culture and people's everyday, practical consciousness. He addressed how people absorb, resist, and transform messages about who they can—or feel they *should*—be. Throughout his work, Hall invites us to resist the notion that any cultural formation is "natural." Building on these foundations, key work in cultural studies has focused on subcultures, with many studies addressing issues such as gender, race, class, and sexuality in everyday life (e.g., Butsch, 1992; D'Emilio and Freedman, 1988; Doty, 1993; Hall and Jefferson, 1993; Hebdige, 1979; Howes, 1996; McKay, 1996; Nanda, 2000; Schwartz and Rutter, 1998; Thornton, 1995).

Hall's work interweaves concepts from many continental philosophers, including Karl Marx, Claude Levi-Strauss, Louis Althusser, Antonio Gramsci, Ferdinand de Saussure, and Michel Foucault. From Gramsci, he draws a notion of the hegemonic, the influence or authority over others manifested by those in power—for example, the ways in which consent is secured to maintain existing and dominant social order(s), and the idea that the dominant culture appears normal and natural to us and is, therefore, not available for question. From Marx, Hall takes the idea that structures of society and class are managed. Following Althusser, he calls for a focus on how dominance is maintained and structured through language; it is in this arena that we see other influences from semiotics on Hall's work, including Ferdinand de Saussure, Claude Levi Strauss, and Roland Barthes. And from Michel Foucault (see Bowers, this volume), Hall draws the notion that uncovering how power is made and felt in everyday action is a critical endeavor.

One of the best illustrations of how these influences come together is the essay "Encoding/decoding," written in 1980. The essay focuses on media consumption and on broadcast television in particular. It is to this essay that I turn in the next section of this chapter.

Stuart Hall: "Encoding/decoding" (1980)

Stuart Hall's essay "Encoding/decoding" signals the beginnings of structuralism and semiotics as central approaches for analysis in cultural studies. The essay deals with how "messages" are produced and disseminated through media channels, and how they are "read" or understood by audience members. Hall invites us to question what messages seem "natural," and to see ourselves as active producers of the cultural formations within which we sit.

Backdrop to the Work

Hall's work offers us a critical and interpretive purchase on media communication, but it also embodies an explicit critique of the communication models that were predominant when he wrote the essay. Hall's point in that regard was that models of message sending and receiving are too simplistic. At the time mass communication research had conceptualized the process of communication in terms of a linear model of messages encoded by a sender, delivered, and then decoded by a receiver.

The best example of this "transmission" conception of communication is the Shannon-Weaver model, which has been dubbed the "mother of all models" (Hollnagel

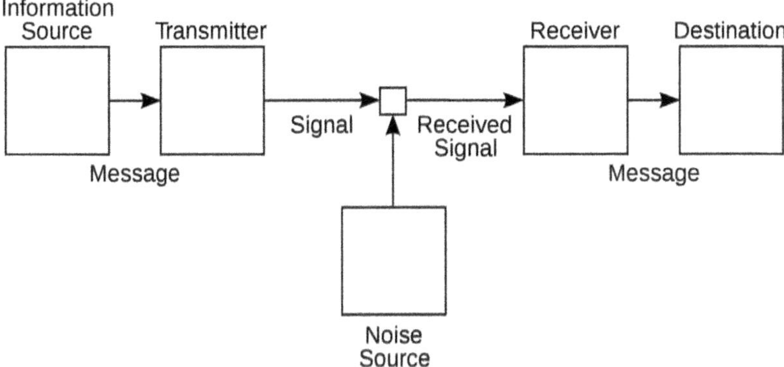

Figure 10.1
The Shannon-Weaver model of communication.
Source: Creative Commons license, https://upload.wikimedia.org/wikipedia/commons/thumb/f/f3/Shannon_communication_system.svg/2000px-Shannon_communication_system.svg.png.

and Woods, 2005, 11) (see figure 10.1). This model has its roots in mathematical modeling and cybernetics, and gained popularity in the 1950s. Based on work done regarding signal viability in telecommunications, this model includes concepts such as information source, message, transmitter, signal, channel, noise, receiver, information destination, probability of error, encoding, decoding, information rate, and channel capacity (Weaver and Shannon, 1963).

Shannon and Weaver were clear that this model had utility for its original focus, telephony. They also cautioned that it was too simplistic for more complex scenarios than transmission quality of service assessments in telephony. Ignoring this caution, information theoretic communications scholars took up the model, positing that in human-to-human communication we can also frame information exchange as the sender's message is encoded, transmitted, and received and decoded by a recipient (see figures 10.2a and 10.2b). These scholars formulated human communication across all contexts to be akin to this message-passing model, including consumption of messages through and from media channels such as television.

Hall was extremely critical of this approach, particularly its linearity—sender/message/receiver. He was not alone. Reflecting back in 1972 on his own early work in stimulus–response (or behaviorist) psychology in the 1950s (Schramm, 1955), Wilbur Schramm notes that in the formulation of communication that he calls the "bullet theory of communication," "the audience was considered relatively passive and defenceless, and communication could *shoot something into them*, just as an electric circuit could deliver electrons to a light bulb" (Schramm and Roberts, 1971, quoted in Babe, 2015, 110; italics in original). Continuing, Schramm notes that over time "the Bullet

sign in subscribe search jobs US edition

theguardian

Winner of the Pulitzer prize 2014

US world opinion sports soccer tech arts lifestyle fashion business travel environment science browse all sections

home

General election 2015

Cameron prepares to form Conservative government after election victory

Unexpected results deliver Tories overall Commons majority and claim scalps of Ed Miliband, Nick Clegg and Nigel Farage

Patrick Wintour Political editor

Friday 8 May 2015 09.29 EDT

Shares 50

David Cameron, with his wife Samantha, outside 10 Downing Street from where he is set to serve a second term as prime minister. Photograph: Andy Rain/EPA

A triumphant David Cameron is preparing to form his first government comprised solely of Conservative cabinet members after a tumultuous election unexpectedly delivered him an overall Commons majority.

The result claimed the scalps of an unprecedented three party leaders in one day as Labour's Ed Miliband, the Liberal Democrats' Nick Clegg and Nigel Farage of Ukip announced their resignations.

Cameron and his wife, Samantha, travelled to Buckingham Palace where he accepted the invitation of the Queen to form a government.

Advertisement

Olive Garden

Most popular in US

General election live: Cameron to announce top four cabinet posts this afternoon

Live UK election results - in full

British PM David Cameron confounds polls to win second term

Figure 10.2a

The Guardian, a centrist-left newspaper, reports the UK election result.

Theory, if you will pardon the expression, was shot full of holes. If anything really passed from sender to receiver, it certainly appeared in very different form to different receivers.... We had been concerned with 'getting the message through,' getting it accepted, getting it decoded in approximately the same form as the sender intended—and we had undervalued the activity of the receiver in the process" (Babe, 2015, 110).

Hall took up the challenge not only to critique but also to offer an alternative approach to understanding media communication. Drawing on semiotics and centralizing the importance of meaning, Hall says meanings are created "through the operation of codes within the syntagmatic chain of a discourse" and that codes may "be so widely distributed in a specific community or culture, and be learned at so early an age, that they appear not to be constructed—the effect of an articulation between sign and referent—but to be 'naturally given'" (Hall, 1980, 95). Hall's invocation of the concepts sign, signification, code, and meaning help him unpack the ways in which

Feedback Like 2.6m Follow @MailOnline DailyMail

Friday, May 8th 2015 8AM 54°F 11AM 66°F 5-Day Forecast

Daily Mail .com News

Home | U.K. | News | Sports | U.S. Showbiz | Australia | Femail | Health | Science | Money | Video | Travel | Columnists

Latest Headlines | News | Arts | Headlines | Pictures | Most read | News Board | Wires Login

Underwater graveyard of

American doctor cured of Ebola is

Vermont Republican senator,

Former American Apparel CEO Dov

Senior Al-Qaeda figure who claimed

Why Joni Mitchell fears she's being

TOGETHER WE'LL MAKE GREAT BRITAIN GREATER STILL: Cameron hails shock Tory outright majority as Miliband, Clegg and Farage all QUIT. SNP wins near clean-sweep of seats in Scotland

- David Cameron has returned from an audience with the Queen after winning a shock Conservative majority
- The Tory leader is on course for a five-seat majority in the best Conservative result for more than 20 years
- Ed Miliband resigned with immediate effect after suffering a crushing defeat, losing seats in Scotland and England
- Nigel Farage resigned as Ukip leader just minutes after losing his seventh bid to become an MP in Thanet South
- Nick Clegg also stood down admitting the 'cruel and punishing' defeat was the worst in his party's history
- Lib Dems suffered almost total wipeout, with Vince Cable, Ed Davey, Jo Swinson and Simon Hughes all out
- Nicola Sturgeon's SNP swept to victory across Scotland, winning all but three of Scotland's 59 seats

By MATT CHORLEY, POLITICAL EDITOR and TOM MCTAGUE, DEPUTY POLITICAL EDITOR FOR MAILONLINE

PUBLISHED: 16:01 EST, 7 May 2015 | UPDATED: 06:47 EST, 8 May 2015

Share 4.1k shares 9.7k View comments

David Cameron today vowed to make Great Britain 'greater still' as he set out how he will use his shock outright Tory majority to ensure the 'good life is in reach for everyone who's willing to work and do the right thing'.

The Prime Minister used a statement outside Number 10 to pay tribute to both Labour's Ed Miliband and his former Lib Dem deputy Nick Clegg who have both resigned after suffering heavy losses in one of the most unpredictable election results for a generation.

Mr Cameron returned to Number 10 with his wife Samantha after making the short trip to Buckingham Palace for a meeting with the Queen to confirm what he described as the 'sweetest victory of all'.

Big political names including Ed Balls, Vince Cable, Ed Davey, Doulgas Alexander, David Laws, Jim Murphy and Esther McVey all lost their seats as the political map of Britain was dramatically redrawn with vast swathes of Tory blue and SNP yellow.

In an incredible night of political drama, Labour suffered a bloodbath in Scotland and failed to make any gains in England. Mr Miliband said he accepted 'absolute and total responsibility' for the electoral disaster, and resigned with immediate effect. His deputy Harriet Harman also announced she will stand aside.

Figure 10.2b

The *Daily Mail*, a right-leaning UK newspaper, responds to the 2015 UK election results.

a concept, whether represented as a textual or a visual/image sign, is communicated, as well as how those signs and codes are interpreted and understood. Denoted meanings are what the sign refers to; connoted meanings are what that reference implies. To offer a simple example, an image of a sweater denotes an article of clothing that keeps us warm, but it also has connotations—for example, the advance of winter. Meanings derive, he says, "from the wider universe of ideologies in a society.… Codes are the means by which power and ideology are made.… Any society/culture tends, with varying degrees of closure, to impose its classifications of the social and cultural and political world. These constitute a *dominant cultural order*" (Hall, 1980, 97). While this dominant order may be imposed, it can be resisted. The "receiver" is an active participant in meaning-making, able to resist the sent meanings and create personally meaningful interpretations. This richer conception of communication recognizes the agency of the receivers, casting them as active readers of messages rather than passive, dumb receptacles of information. This directly confronts the notion embedded within transmission models of communication that messages received will correspond to the messages that were originally sent. This perspective is further codified in Hall's essay and the four-stage model it describes.

A Four-Stage Model

Hall proposes a four-stage theory of communication: *production, circulation, consumption (or use), and reproduction.* These four stages are "linked but distinctive moments" (Hall, 1980, 91) and understanding them as such invites us to break down and analyze the different moments as involving different kinds of active engagement and management of meaning on the part of the people involved. Each of the four stages has its own "imprinting"—that is, the institutional power relations that shape the message, that cumulatively reflect a "complex structure of dominance" (91). And, the power relations at the point of production will only loosely fit, if they fit at all, those at the point of consumption.

On Encoding

To give an example, Hall starts with where message(s) become encoded, addressing the production of a television news broadcast. It is easy to imagine that production of a television news broadcast involves many opinions and ideas that are negotiated, as particular message(s) with particular spins arise, to accommodate and reflect the dominant perspective of the production company and/or their sponsors. Beyond this, though, are routines of production that are shaped by the roles and technical skills of those involved. These roles and skills give scope to the level of influence and kind of influence that those involved in the production can have. Roles include director, producer, camera technician, stagehand, scriptwriter, makeup artist, and so on. Each of these has its own professional ideologies, institutional knowledge, definitions and assumptions about scope and purview, and possibly consonant or perhaps dissonant assumptions about the key messages and about the intended audience.

Hall argues that the perspective produced by the professional broadcasters is likely to already be part of the dominant-hegemonic code; he suggests that any professional code typically operates within the hegemony of the dominant code. However, within that are many points where message-shaping occurs. For example, even the selection of specific personnel from these areas of expertise is a factor: do you engage an execution-oriented person who follows requirements and specifications, or do you engage a strategically minded contrarian to invoke internal questioning and creative rethinking? All these factors frame the emerging program through formal and informal production processes and structures. These influences manifest in what topics are covered, treatment of those topics, sequencing of topics, time allotted to particular foci and agendas, narration of events, the ways in which the audience is (or is not) explicitly defined, addressed, or called on, the inclusion of other perspectives, and sources that may derive from the broader sociocultural infrastructure within which the production is situated.

Thus, encoding a message is already a profoundly complex process; the messages offered in a television program are shaped by negotiated institutional knowledge, by the available resources including the technical possibilities and constraints, by the dovetailed practices of the core production team, and by the input of those with influence and/or power around them. A plethora of viewpoints or perspective positions exist within and shape the produced artifact itself. What constitutes news in a news program, the specific presentational values, the televisual quality, projections of "professionalism," the choice of representational formats, the selection of personnel for different roles, the choice of images, the staging of debates, and other features are all combined through the operation of the professional code. These features may appear to be neutral, even natural, but they are not. In Hall's analysis, they are linked to defining elites not only by the institutional position of broadcasting itself as an ideological apparatus (invoking the work of Althusser), but also by the structure of access, and the hierarchies of privilege and authority within the group that has access. Notably, ideological reproduction of the dominant-hegemonic codes can take place here inadvertently, unconsciously, and without intention.

To offer a contemporary example, we can look at a news media story that was widely reported through traditional televisual media channels, as well as online—the 2015 UK parliamentary elections. Figures 11.3a and 11.3b show three media sites' reports of the news of the elections. Each of these has its own production processes, and each has within it a set of encoded messages. From layout, idea/word/concept prioritization, and wording to what surrounds the story itself—including advertising, site and page navigational elements, images—all of these are part of the framing of the story, part of the encoding of the messages. Some are intentional framings, such as the reporter and editorial content and the story-specific images; some derive from the institutional structures that are inscribed in the technologies that produce the pages, represented in the page layout and the spaces that exist for algorithmic placement of content, such as advertising and recommended related stories. It is worth remembering that the specific site production, management, and rendering technologies are themselves chosen, including design and engineering choices—design and engineering are contemporary arenas of professionalization akin to those in Hall's analysis. Each has its own professional codes, its own dominant ideologies and strategies for negotiating meaning-making. Therefore, as in Hall's example, many roles and a great deal of expertise were involved in this encoding, and there are many "structures of dominance" at play here

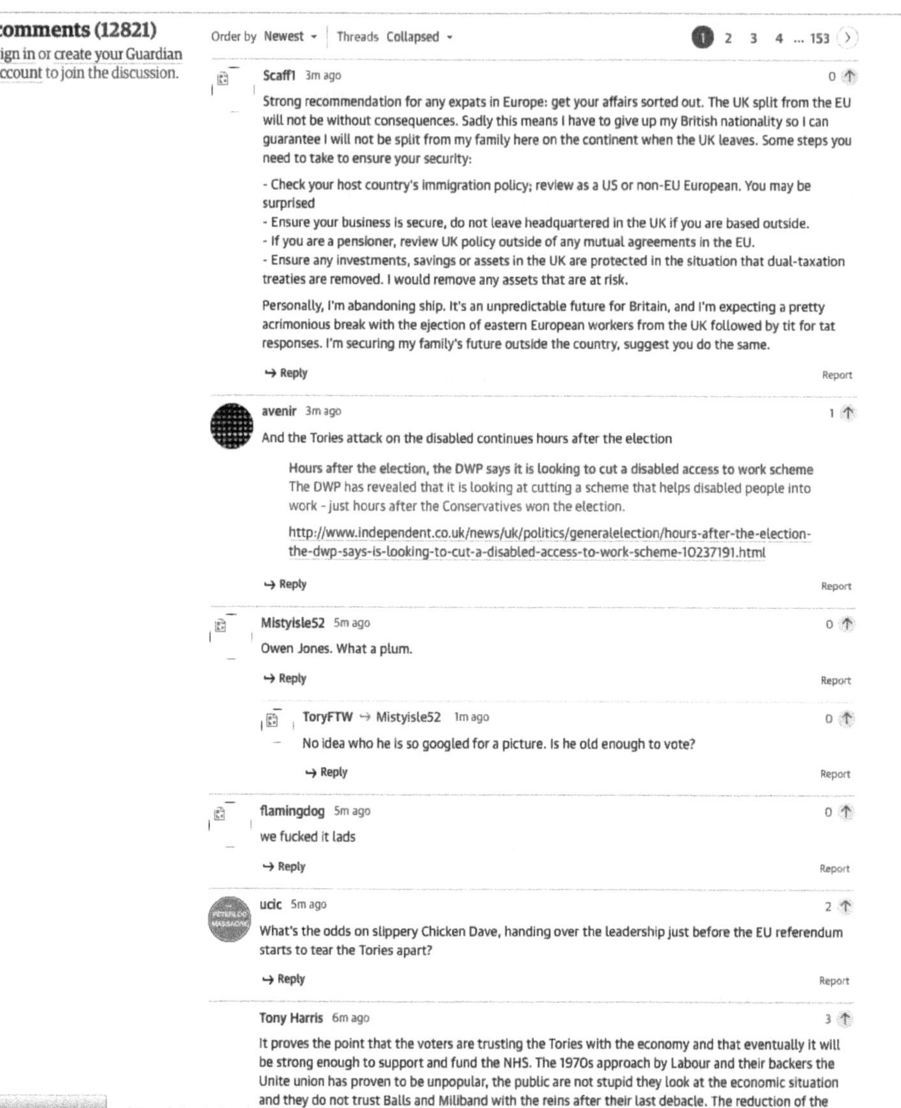
comments (12821)
Sign in or create your Guardian account to join the discussion.
Order by Newest | Threads Collapsed
1 2 3 4 ... 153

Scaffl 3m ago 0
Strong recommendation for any expats in Europe: get your affairs sorted out. The UK split from the EU will not be without consequences. Sadly this means I have to give up my British nationality so I can guarantee I will not be split from my family here on the continent when the UK leaves. Some steps you need to take to ensure your security:

- Check your host country's immigration policy; review as a US or non-EU European. You may be surprised
- Ensure your business is secure, do not leave headquartered in the UK if you are based outside.
- If you are a pensioner, review UK policy outside of any mutual agreements in the EU.
- Ensure any investments, savings or assets in the UK are protected in the situation that dual-taxation treaties are removed. I would remove any assets that are at risk.

Personally, I'm abandoning ship. It's an unpredictable future for Britain, and I'm expecting a pretty acrimonious break with the ejection of eastern European workers from the UK followed by tit for tat responses. I'm securing my family's future outside the country, suggest you do the same.

Reply Report

avenir 3m ago 1
And the Tories attack on the disabled continues hours after the election

Hours after the election, the DWP says it is looking to cut a disabled access to work scheme
The DWP has revealed that it is looking at cutting a scheme that helps disabled people into work - just hours after the Conservatives won the election.

http://www.independent.co.uk/news/uk/politics/generalelection/hours-after-the-election-the-dwp-says-is-looking-to-cut-a-disabled-access-to-work-scheme-10237191.html

Reply Report

Mistyisle52 5m ago 0
Owen Jones. What a plum.

Reply Report

ToryFTW → Mistyisle52 1m ago 0
No idea who he is so googled for a picture. Is he old enough to vote?

Reply Report

flamingdog 5m ago 0
we fucked it lads

Reply Report

ucic 5m ago 2
What's the odds on slippery Chicken Dave, handing over the leadership just before the EU referendum starts to tear the Tories apart?

Reply Report

Tony Harris 6m ago 3
It proves the point that the voters are trusting the Tories with the economy and that eventually it will be strong enough to support and fund the NHS. The 1970s approach by Labour and their backers the Unite union has proven to be unpopular, the public are not stupid they look at the economic situation and they do not trust Balls and Miliband with the reins after their last debacle. The reduction of the

Figure 10.3a and Figure 10.3b
Online comments concerning the 2015 election.

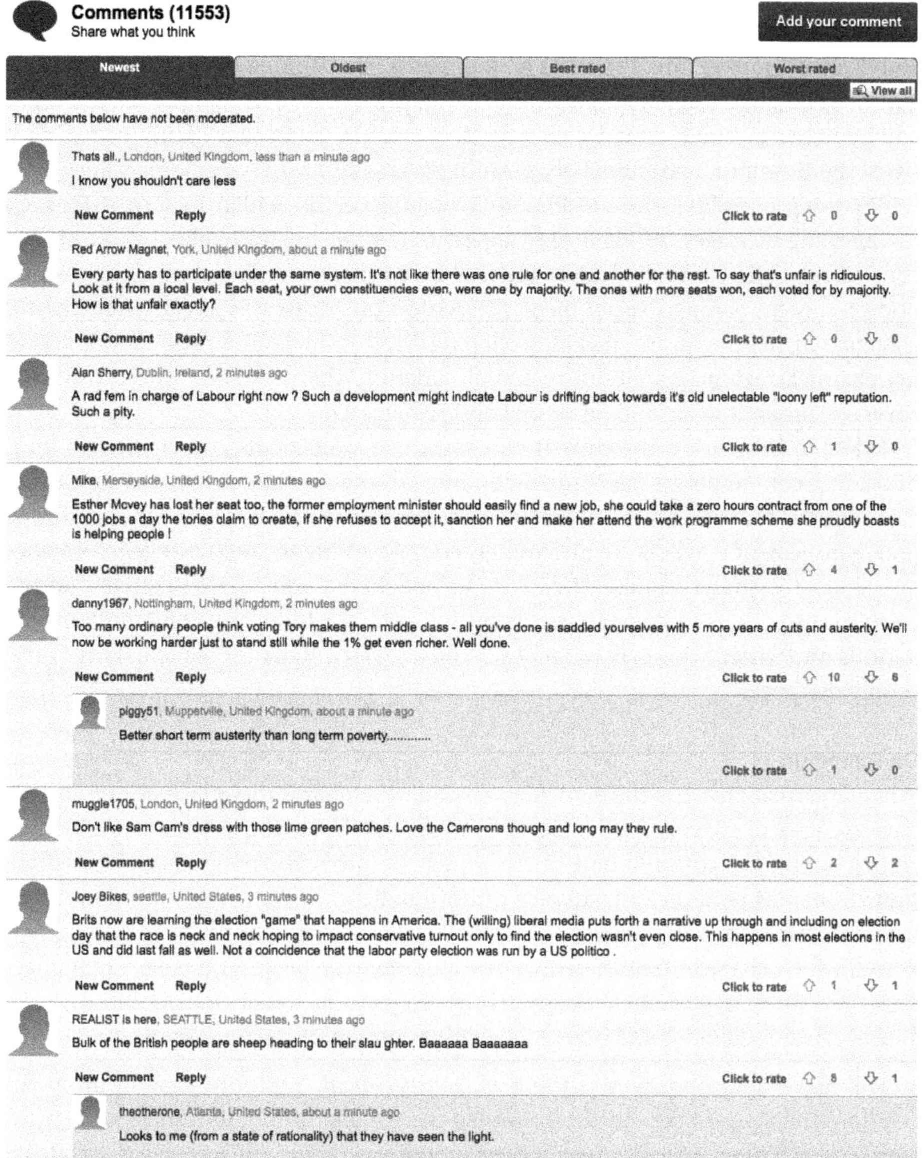

Comments (11553)
Share what you think
Add your comment
Newest
Oldest
Best rated
Worst rated
View all
The comments below have not been moderated.
Thats all., London, United Kingdom, less than a minute ago
I know you shouldn't care less
New Comment Reply Click to rate 0 0
Red Arrow Magnet, York, United Kingdom, about a minute ago
Every party has to participate under the same system. It's not like there was one rule for one and another for the rest. To say that's unfair is ridiculous. Look at it from a local level. Each seat, your own constituencies even, were one by majority. The ones with more seats won, each voted for by majority. How is that unfair exactly?
New Comment Reply Click to rate 0 0
Alan Sherry, Dublin, Ireland, 2 minutes ago
A rad fem in charge of Labour right now ? Such a development might indicate Labour is drifting back towards it's old unelectable "loony left" reputation. Such a pity.
New Comment Reply Click to rate 1 0
Mike, Merseyside, United Kingdom, 2 minutes ago
Esther Mcvey has lost her seat too, the former employment minister should easily find a new job, she could take a zero hours contract from one of the 1000 jobs a day the tories claim to create, if she refuses to accept it, sanction her and make her attend the work programme scheme she proudly boasts is helping people !
New Comment Reply Click to rate 4 1
danny1967, Nottingham, United Kingdom, 2 minutes ago
Too many ordinary people think voting Tory makes them middle class - all you've done is saddled yourselves with 5 more years of cuts and austerity. We'll now be working harder just to stand still while the 1% get even richer. Well done.
New Comment Reply Click to rate 10 6
piggy51, Muppetville, United Kingdom, about a minute ago
Better short term austerity than long term poverty............
Click to rate 1 0
muggle1705, London, United Kingdom, 2 minutes ago
Don't like Sam Cam's dress with those lime green patches. Love the Camerons though and long may they rule.
New Comment Reply Click to rate 2 2
Joey Bikes, seattle, United States, 3 minutes ago
Brits now are learning the election "game" that happens in America. The (willing) liberal media puts forth a narrative up through and including on election day that the race is neck and neck hoping to impact conservative turnout only to find the election wasn't even close. This happens in most elections in the US and did last fall as well. Not a coincidence that the labor party election was run by a US politico .
New Comment Reply Click to rate 1 1
REALIST is here, SEATTLE, United States, 3 minutes ago
Bulk of the British people are sheep heading to their slau ghter. Baaaaaa Baaaaaaa
New Comment Reply Click to rate 8 1
theotherone, Atlanta, United States, about a minute ago
Looks to me (from a state of rationality) that they have seen the light.

including the ideologies of the hosting organizations (I have selected one news organization that leans left politically and one that leans right, one that is identified with "intellectual" storytelling, the other with populist reporting) to the shaping of the content through algorithmic personalization using collaborative filtering of related stories and advertising. These design elements all coexist to produce a highly coded set of signs, significations, and ultimately meanings that align with hegemonic values.

Following encoding, the process of circulation begins, which in turn shapes and reshapes the messages. While it may appear that a televisual broadcast was a simpler context than the current world of internet-based media content, including distribution of content through social media, television broadcast was already fraught with audience management and meaning-shaping choices, including negotiations regarding channel, regional variation, temporal variation, the possibility of reruns, media coverage, promotion, and so on (Fisher and Fisher, 1996).

Again, to bring us to the current context, there are benefits and challenges for us in reading contemporary news media online. On the one hand it would appear that circulation is broader; on the other hand we live in a world of "glut," where information management practices are increasingly complex (Wright, 2007), where information overload necessitates the use of careful, personal seek-and-curate practices, and we often turn to others to be our curators by, for example, following commentators and pundits on Twitter, who may in fact be using uneven criteria for recirculation or may simply disappear.

On Decoding

When an artifact reaches the audience, we enter the phases that make up the complementary area of concern: decoding the message(s). Following production and circulation, during the consumption phase, when the produced program is released and shown, there is latitude and variance in how audience members are positioned with regard to "receiving" the presented material. Hall suggests a number of "reading positions," which characterize different stances that may be taken in the decoding phase. There are three hypothetical positions he discusses in detail that mobilize several concepts from semiotics and draw on Gramsci's notion of the hegemonic:

1. The first reading position is the *dominant-hegemonic* position. Reading from this position, the viewer takes on the connoted meaning(s) from a television newscast or current affairs program as intended by the producers. That is, the message is decoded in terms of the "reference code" in which it has been encoded; thus we might say that the viewer is operating *inside* the dominant code. This is the case where "perfectly transparent communication" occurs—or as close as we are likely to come to it for all practical purposes (looking at figures 10.3a and 10.3b, one may say "the election outcome was fair, represents the majority vote, and is good for the country").

Hall reminds us that dominant definitions are hegemonic precisely because they represent definitions of situations and events that are "in dominance." Dominant definitions are intended to connect events, implicitly or explicitly, to grand "totalization," that is, to an unquestioned larger picture.

2. The second reading position is that of the *negotiated-code* position. Most audiences probably have a sense, if not a sophisticated perspective, on what is being positioned from a dominant-hegemonic position, and what is thus being professionally signified. They have an inkling of the positions of the producers, what point of view the producers are trying to get across, and possibly even why the producers are promoting a particular point of view because of the larger ideological frame(s) with which they align. Hall asserts that the majority of so-called misunderstandings derive from the contradictions and disjunctions between hegemonic dominance encodings and negotiated decoding.

Decoding within a negotiated reading position involves a mixture of adaptive and oppositional elements. People acknowledge—or at least recognize the legitimacy of—the hegemonic definitions to make the grand significations ("the election resulted in a winning political party"), while, at the more restricted, situational (situated) and local level, may engage exceptions and disagreements ("I am unhappy about this outcome for me personally as it may mean a split with the EU, and I have family there"). This second reading position thus acknowledges the privileged position of the dominant definitions of events while reserving the right to make more negotiated application to "local conditions," to explore more personally relevant positions. The negotiated version of the dominant ideologies are likely to be full of contradictions, which may not be visible to others and may not even be clear to the individuals experiencing those contradictions.

One of the ways we can see such negotiations today is through question-asking and online commenting spaces. Figure 10.4 offers some examples of those engaged in dialogue associated with the media sites shown in figures 10.3a and 10.3b. In some of the commentary one can see the kinds of negotiated positions Hall refers to being played out in debate where personal issues clash with the resulting political and inferred social and cultural formations that result from the elections.

Indeed, Hall suggests that this second position, the negotiated code position, can really be best understood by thinking about the difference between global interest ("the outcome of the election is good for the country on the world stage"), national interest ("the outcome reflects the majority view and may mean continuity in certain policies"), and personal interest ("the outcome of the election is bad for me personally as it may affect my family situation in the EU"). It is also possible that all these levels can be sustained simultaneously.

3. Finally, the third reading position is the *global-contrary*. This is the oppositional code. Here the viewer/audience member rejects the message completely. That is to say, the message is explicitly resisted and is likely met with proposals for alternative

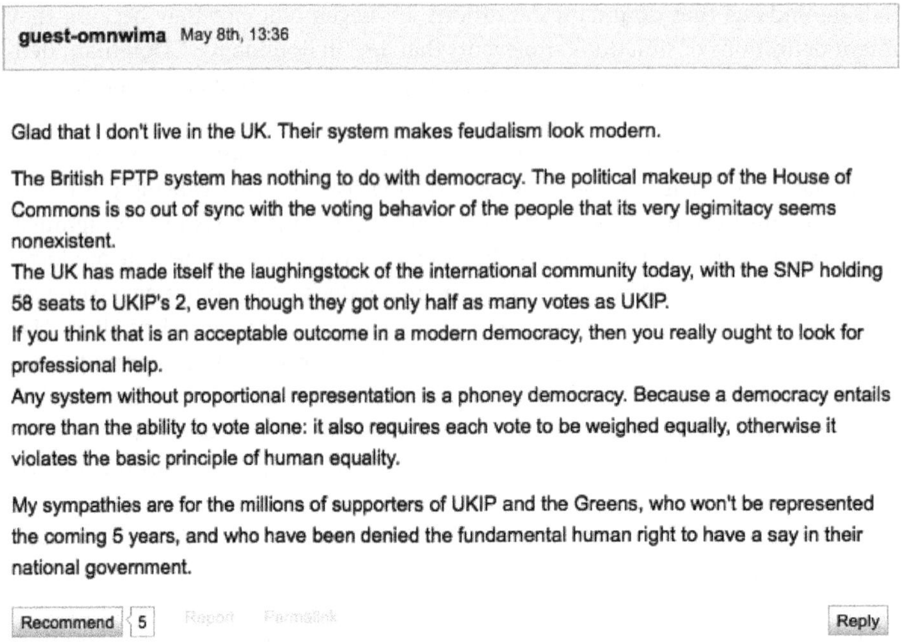

guest-omnwima May 8th, 13:36

Glad that I don't live in the UK. Their system makes feudalism look modern.

The British FPTP system has nothing to do with democracy. The political makeup of the House of Commons is so out of sync with the voting behavior of the people that its very legimitacy seems nonexistent.
The UK has made itself the laughingstock of the international community today, with the SNP holding 58 seats to UKIP's 2, even though they got only half as many votes as UKIP.
If you think that is an acceptable outcome in a modern democracy, then you really ought to look for professional help.
Any system without proportional representation is a phoney democracy. Because a democracy entails more than the ability to vote alone: it also requires each vote to be weighed equally, otherwise it violates the basic principle of human equality.

My sympathies are for the millions of supporters of UKIP and the Greens, who won't be represented the coming 5 years, and who have been denied the fundamental human right to have a say in their national government.

Recommend 5 Report Permalink Reply

Figure 10.4
In opposition to the proportional representation electoral model of the UK political system, a comment on an article by the *Economist* suggests the outcome of the election is not representative of the opinion of the populace.

frameworks. One of the most significant political moments is the point when events that are normally signified and decoded in negotiated ways begin to be given oppositional readings.

Examples of the global-contrary position can be seen in the comments in figure 10.4. Two examples of this positioning are also shown in figure 10.5; staying with the UK 2015 election as an example, some in their comments on this site blame the UK's electoral system of proportional representation and the resulting "first past-the-post" system for an untenable and contested election outcome (see *Economist*, 2015).

These three positions correspond to acceptance, conscious or unconscious skeptical engagement, and resistance to the meanings in messages that are transmitted through the codes in the messages. By seeing the differences in these positions, we can reframe how we understand audience reception and message-reading, and recognize all audience processes as active. We can also see that readings are never "natural" but reflect the "maps of meaning" we consciously or unconsciously share, and actively or passively accept, question, or resist.

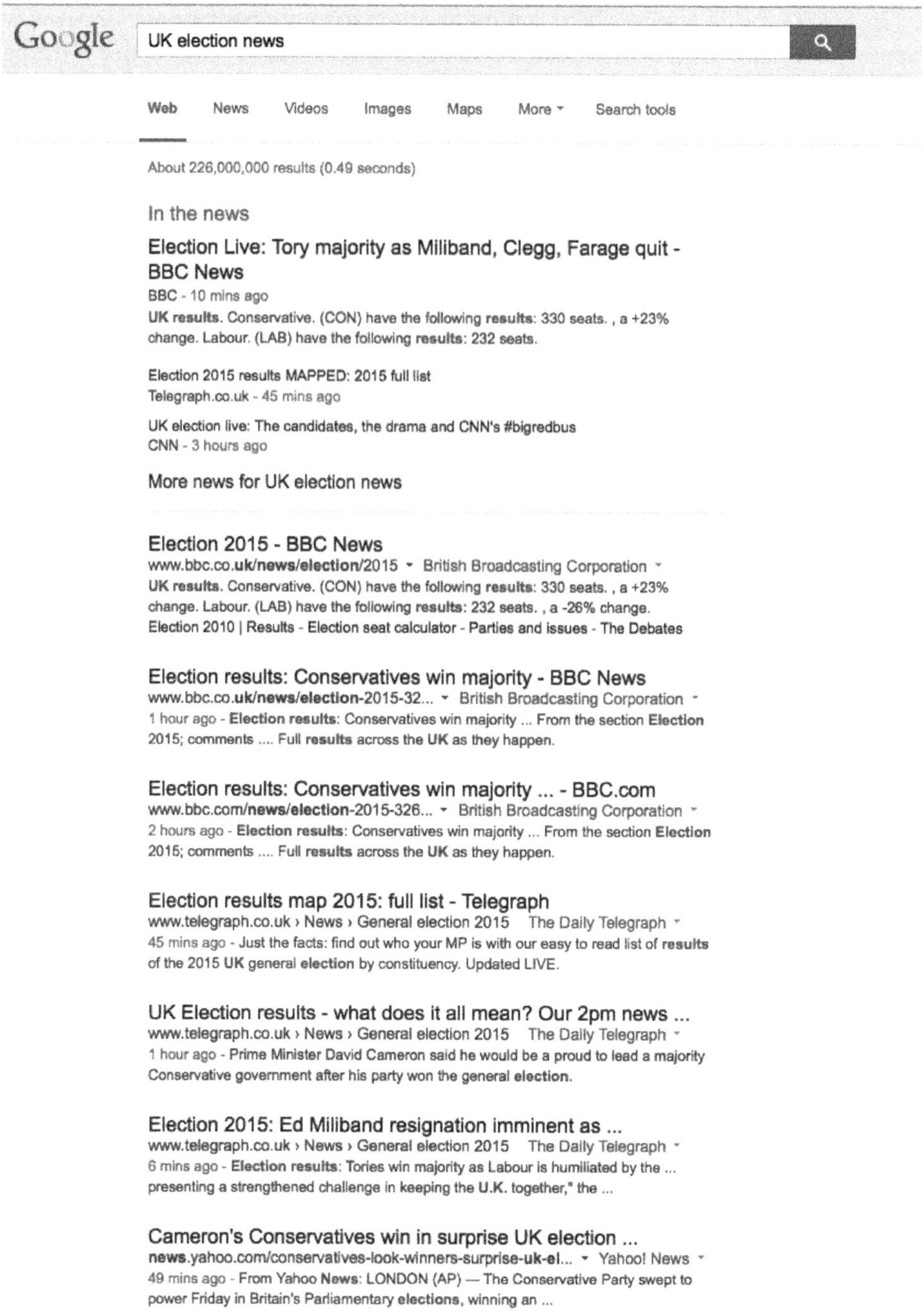

Google UK election news

Web News Videos Images Maps More Search tools

About 226,000,000 results (0.49 seconds)

In the news

Election Live: Tory majority as Miliband, Clegg, Farage quit - BBC News
BBC - 10 mins ago
UK results. Conservative. (CON) have the following results: 330 seats. , a +23% change. Labour. (LAB) have the following results: 232 seats.

Election 2015 results MAPPED: 2015 full list
Telegraph.co.uk - 45 mins ago

UK election live: The candidates, the drama and CNN's #bigredbus
CNN - 3 hours ago

More news for UK election news

Election 2015 - BBC News
www.bbc.co.uk/news/election/2015 British Broadcasting Corporation
UK results. Conservative. (CON) have the following results: 330 seats. , a +23% change. Labour. (LAB) have the following results: 232 seats. , a -26% change.
Election 2010 | Results - Election seat calculator - Parties and issues - The Debates

Election results: Conservatives win majority - BBC News
www.bbc.co.uk/news/election-2015-32... British Broadcasting Corporation
1 hour ago - Election results: Conservatives win majority ... From the section Election 2015; comments .... Full results across the UK as they happen.

Election results: Conservatives win majority ... - BBC.com
www.bbc.com/news/election-2015-326... British Broadcasting Corporation
2 hours ago - Election results: Conservatives win majority ... From the section Election 2015; comments .... Full results across the UK as they happen.

Election results map 2015: full list - Telegraph
www.telegraph.co.uk › News › General election 2015 The Daily Telegraph
45 mins ago - Just the facts: find out who your MP is with our easy to read list of results of the 2015 UK general election by constituency. Updated LIVE.

UK Election results - what does it all mean? Our 2pm news ...
www.telegraph.co.uk › News › General election 2015 The Daily Telegraph
1 hour ago - Prime Minister David Cameron said he would be a proud to lead a majority Conservative government after his party won the general election.

Election 2015: Ed Miliband resignation imminent as ...
www.telegraph.co.uk › News › General election 2015 The Daily Telegraph
6 mins ago - Election results: Tories win majority as Labour is humiliated by the ... presenting a strengthened challenge in keeping the U.K. together," the ...

Cameron's Conservatives win in surprise UK election ...
news.yahoo.com/conservatives-look-winners-surprise-uk-el... Yahoo! News
49 mins ago - From Yahoo News: LONDON (AP) — The Conservative Party swept to power Friday in Britain's Parliamentary elections, winning an ...

Figure 10.5
Search results from a major search engine to the query "UK election news."

In today's media world, where communication and commentary are key, it may appear that Hall's analysis is outdated and outmoded. However, in keeping with the filter bubble around media content (Pariser, 2011), those of us involved in the online media world who try to enact everyday practices that align most with negotiated positions may not be aware that we ourselves are operating within our own complex "structures of dominance," our own personal, filtered worlds that reflect only the dominant-hegemonic messages. Apparently unbiased search queries are often "personalized" according to past interests, and search results are thus skewed, offering a view of the world that corresponds to an ever-narrowing view of our interests (see figure 10.5) (Churchill, 2013). Images from search queries provide results that are in keeping with dominant-hegemonic forms—for example, occupation-related image search queries offer gender-biased results, reinforcing dominant cultural stereotypes (Kay, Matuszek, and Munson, 2015). In reality, we may not see that which would make us question broadly enough or deeply enough. We, too, may believe we are experiencing "perfectly transparent communication" in our search results and reading recommendations, but what we are actually being offered are the results of what Hall calls "systematically distorted communication" (Hall, 1980, 100).

This happens both on a personal level and on an analytic level. To illustrate and to return to the UK 2015 election as an example, Nate Silver, the American statistician, was not able to predict the UK elections although his ability to analyze data and derive predictive analytics has been applauded worldwide. Why? Because his data derived from a bubble. Reporting for *Fortune* online, Geoffrey Smith says "The noise from Twitter, Facebook and the like was far more skewed to the Left than the actual result. Hardly surprising, says Roger Mortimore, director of political analysis at polling firm IPSOS Mori: 'The stereotypical Tory voter is over 50 and probably isn't on Twitter or Facebook and doesn't use his mobile phone'" (Smith, 2015).

Summary

To summarize Hall's contribution and resituate ourselves in his 1980 essay, there are three key points to take away. Hall offered a framework that highlighted the limitations of simple information theoretic models and offered an alternative—an alternative that gives members of an audience agency. His analysis introduces us to the use of semiotic and discursive analysis of the creation, circulation, consumption, and reproduction of messages, and reminds us that each of these stages has its own logic of power—its own set of acceptances and resistances to the hegemonic order. Further, Hall offers us variants in the reading positions of consumers: dominant-hegemonic, negotiated-code, and global-contrary. By articulating a four-stage process and these reading positions, he is attempting to move away from behaviorist models of human psychology and simplistic transmission models of communication toward an analysis that acknowledges not only individual agency but also participation in collective cultural meaning-making. The coding of a message by a producer may, to some extent, influence its reception by the receiver, but the process of transmission between sender and receiver is not necessarily linear, nor is it transparent or obvious, nor is it guaranteed; clearly, the meaning that the receiver derives from the message may not be the same meaning the sender intended by its production. This lack of "fit" or alignment between the codes has, Hall states, "a great deal to do with the structural differences of relation and position between broadcasters and audiences, but it also has something to do with the asymmetry between the codes of 'source' and 'receiver' at the moment of transformation into and out of the discursive form. What are called 'distortions' or 'misunderstandings' arise precisely from the *lack of equivalence* between the two sides in the communicative exchange" (Hall, 1980, 94). From this, Hall argues that there is space for messages to be used or understood at least somewhat "against the grain"—that is, in ways that are explicitly or tacitly, knowingly or unknowingly, resistant to the original producer's intent. In this way, official channels may reproduce a pattern of domination, but they can also be sites of resistance and reformulation.

While Hall's 1980 examples and my own beginnings of an analysis of the UK 2015 parliamentary elections focus more on institutional and professional production and consumption (Hall's by focusing on television production and mine by focusing on known and established online media sites), we can turn this kind of analysis to our own identity self-production on social media and the participation of others in that identity production. Indeed, as identity was central to Hall's theorizing and analysis, his perspective would be well applied here. To illustrate, we hear a lot about the pressure to produce a professionalized personal persona, profile, and identity online (see, for example, Marwick, 2013), and the need to create and maintain partitioned identities (Farnham and Churchill, 2011; Haimson et al., 2015) lest other aspects of our lives be included, misinterpreted, or misrepresented and thus challenge our desire to have others read us within or contrary to some hegemonic ideology within which we wish to fit. Who has not managed or thought of managing who can see or not see (or comment on) our posts on social media? Who has not worried that an image deemed out of line with our personal or professional identity may surface, be taken out of context, or damage our public identity and what we now refer to as our "reputation?" There are questions as to who does and who does not worry about such concerns. We are told that the founder of Facebook, Mark Zuckerberg, has no great concerns in this regard. From Hall, we can read Zuckerberg's comfort as deriving from his cultural fit within and control of the meaning-making of the dominant-hegemonic; he is in no sense at the cultural margins and he has the ability to define and manage the institutions of meaning-making. Others arguably can also do this, using the apparatus of the dominant communication structures; see, for example, UK comedian and political

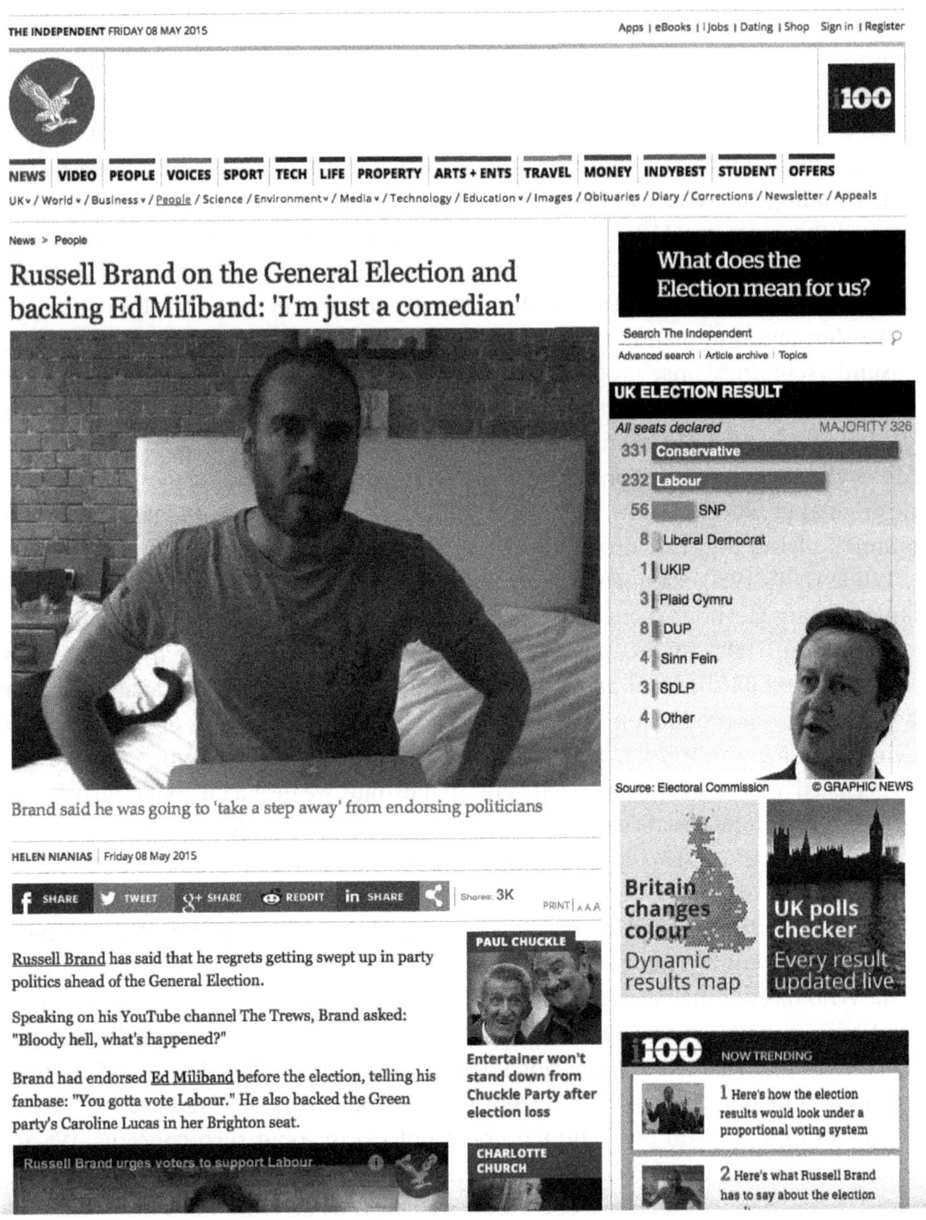

THE INDEPENDENT FRIDAY 08 MAY 2015

Apps | eBooks | Jobs | Dating | Shop Sign in | Register

i100

NEWS VIDEO PEOPLE VOICES SPORT TECH LIFE PROPERTY ARTS + ENTS TRAVEL MONEY INDYBEST STUDENT OFFERS

UK / World / Business / People / Science / Environment / Media / Technology / Education / Images / Obituaries / Diary / Corrections / Newsletter / Appeals

News > People

Russell Brand on the General Election and backing Ed Miliband: 'I'm just a comedian'

Brand said he was going to 'take a step away' from endorsing politicians

HELEN NIANIAS | Friday 08 May 2015

SHARE TWEET SHARE REDDIT SHARE Shares: 3K PRINT | A A A

Russell Brand has said that he regrets getting swept up in party politics ahead of the General Election.

Speaking on his YouTube channel The Trews, Brand asked: "Bloody hell, what's happened?"

Brand had endorsed Ed Miliband before the election, telling his fanbase: "You gotta vote Labour." He also backed the Green party's Caroline Lucas in her Brighton seat.

Russell Brand urges voters to support Labour

PAUL CHUCKLE

Entertainer won't stand down from Chuckle Party after election loss

CHARLOTTE CHURCH

What does the Election mean for us?

Search The Independent

Advanced search | Article archive | Topics

UK ELECTION RESULT

All seats declared MAJORITY 326

Seats	Party
331	Conservative
232	Labour
56	SNP
8	Liberal Democrat
1	UKIP
3	Plaid Cymru
8	DUP
4	Sinn Fein
3	SDLP
4	Other

Source: Electoral Commission © GRAPHIC NEWS

Britain changes colour Dynamic results map

UK polls checker Every result updated live

i100 NOW TRENDING

1 Here's how the election results would look under a proportional voting system

2 Here's what Russell Brand has to say about the election

Figure 10.6

Russell Brand, an outspoken UK comedian and political commentator, responds to 2015 UK election results, commenting "Bloody Hell, What Happened?"

commentator Russell Brand's attempts to do this in his response to the results of the UK election, "Bloody hell, what happened?" (figure 10.6) as he distances himself from his own (unofficial but nevertheless powerful) role in the election campaign.

But others are less privileged. It is not possible to manage ways in which our media are interpreted and understood by others, nor how they move through social networks and become repositioned, as in the production of remixed viral video copies that underlie successes and failures (Yew, Shamma, and Churchill, 2011). The most egregious form of this loss of ability to manage our identities, and the best example, is the public shaming of individuals in social media, where professional and personal lives are disrupted, endangered, and/or destroyed, as was the case with Justine Sacco (Ronson, 2015) and the harassment of feminist game developers in the online controversy known as "gamergate" (Hathaway, 2014). There are consequences when others contradict our representation of self, read us against the grain, challenge our sense of identity, and then recruit others to do the same. These are the kinds of vulnerabilities that invite regulation, as in the calls in Europe for the "right to be forgotten," itself a highly contested topic (Bennett, 2012; Hoboken, 2013).

Following on from "Encoding/decoding"

The early cultural analysis of communication, focused on media studies, in "Enoding/decoding" laid the groundwork for much future work. Of particular interest, having raised the issue of regulation is a framework proposed by Hall and his colleagues called the "circuit of culture." With an illustration focused on a device, the Sony Walkman, the circuit of culture is worth considering in brief as a continuation of Hall's work from this early essay.

The Circuit of Culture and Technology

The circuit of culture framework—or "circuit"—was most articulately presented in a 1997 text by Paul du Gay, Stuart Hall, Linda Janes, Hugh MacKay, and Keith Negus, entitled *Doing Cultural Studies: The Story of the Sony Walkman.* As the title suggests, the authors chart the envisioning, iterative design and development, marketing, uptake, and regulation of the Sony Walkman, a technology that changed personal and public auditory and physical space in the 1980s.

The circuit of culture extended Hall's earlier concepts to artifacts, suggesting that understanding a cultural text or artifact should include analysis of its *representation,* its *identity,* its *production,* its *consumption,* and its *regulation* (figure 10.7). Addressing not just the artifact itself but also its marketing through advertising, nuances of design, and its role in conferring and/or maintaining a lifestyle helps us see how different discourses encode meanings about desired or desirable lifestyles into objects. Du Gay and Hall

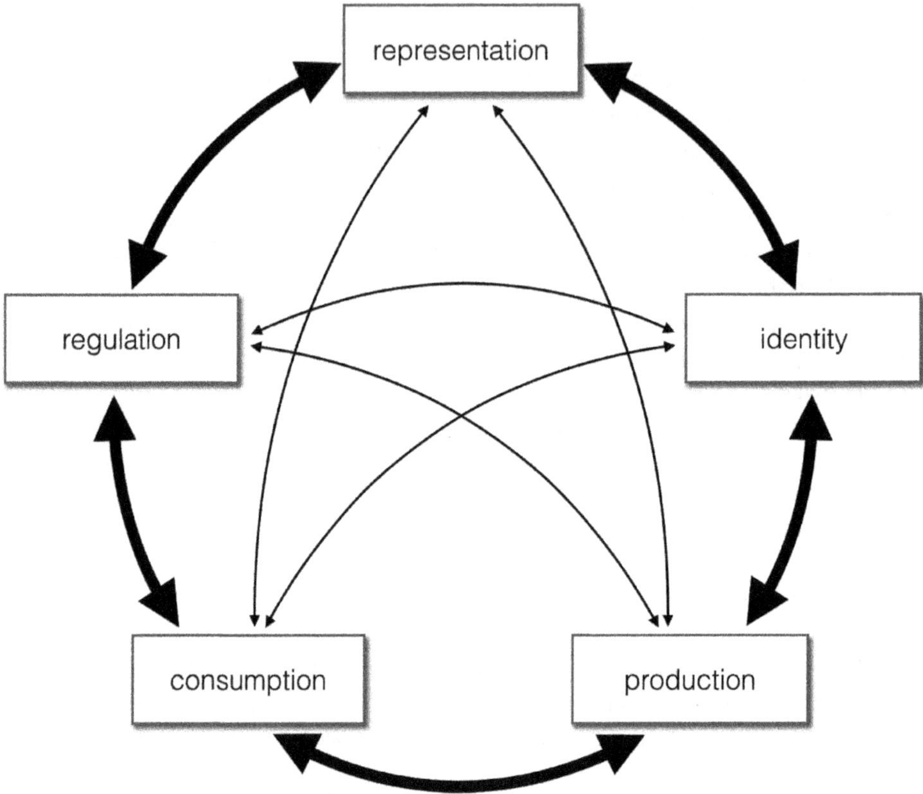

Figure 10.7
Redrawn by Jeffrey Bardzell.

traced the development of the Walkman in terms of its physical design, marketing, and consumption. The name had to be "cool" and early ideas included "soundabout," "stowaway," and "freestyle." Ironically, the original design for the Sony Walkman included two headphone ports: the idea was to share music with someone intimate, to create a shared soundtrack for life. User testing revealed this use case to be somewhat less than compelling—people wanted their own, personal soundtrack, and the consequences of a personal and isolated experience in public became a topic of public debate. The analysis of the Walkman stressed the ways in which use and consumption fed back and shaped the process of production in a circuit of culture.

The circuit is a useful metaphor for understanding the multiple values and meanings of any object, and how those are produced, consumed, recirculated, and refashioned, potentially to spawn new productions and updated versions through the modifications and suggestions of people's everyday activities and practices. Addressing each of these in turn, it is easy to see how Hall's early work plays out in this updated model, but also how relevant these concepts are for understanding the technological design, development, and dissemination landscape today.

Representation and identity: Representation is the practice of constructing meanings through the use of signs and language, principally through the language of advertising, which "must engage with the meaning the product has accumulated and it must try to construct an identification between us the consumers and those meanings" (du Gay et al., 1997, 25). Here, cultural meanings are generated and given shape, and as with Hall's points in "Encoding/decoding," meaning is neither inherent in the representations that result nor static. As with the active processes of the meaning-maker and of those who read the artifacts, meaning is constructed through signs, codes, and the things they are believed to refer to based on the existing cultural "maps of meaning."

Production and consumption: Marketing and public relations professionals engage in initial and ongoing evaluations of feedback on advertising and design. Design is, of course, a key role in articulating the meanings of new objects. In this sense, designers are cultural intermediaries (to use Pierre Bourdieu's terminology; Bourdieu, 1984) who attempt to encode objects with meanings that are emblematic of lifestyles, meanings that may be understood or received by individuals. To make artifacts that sell, designers have to embody culture in the things that are designed. In their symbolic work—making products meaningful—designers are a key link in the cultural circuit. Among many other things they do, they build bridges between the world of engineers and that of the market and consumers. The designer acts as the cultural mediator identifying and, if possible, producing something that is resonant with the imagined lifestyle that the product is intended to connote for the customer/consumer. Put simply, designers imagine and produce artifacts for customers, including their imagined aspirations. Production processes are constrained and shaped by a number of factors at a number of levels, including individual talents, the organizational culture, what resources are available, and various circumstantial happenstance issues within any current production process. Arguably, it is the organizational culture that probably plays the largest role, because production is most often dictated by corporate constraints and cultural norms.

Consumption: As objects are designed, they are imbued with meaning(s). Every design choice has a message as well as an interaction consequence. However, the design process, the production of the artifact or experience, is not complete and not realized until the artifact is consumed, until there is someone engaging with it who was not part of the design and development process in its broadest sense. As du Gay and his coauthors say, "The processes of production only provide a series of possibilities that have to be realized in the true consumption" (du Gay et al., 1997). In "Encoding/decoding," Hall points out that messages in a television news broadcast may be produced/encoded and then circulated with one intent, but the meaning that was encoded may not be that which is decoded. So it is in product and service design: meaning does not reside in the designed object, it resides in how that object is consumed and used. The meanings that are encoded during production are just one set that may be articulated through consumption and reproduced (see also Curtin and Gaither, 2005).

Returning to earlier comments regarding the dissemination of comments online, the internet is possibly the best example where consumption transforms the artifact either explicitly through remix practices or tacitly through adoption and framing—a video posted as "spiritual" may be taken up and reposted as "comedy" and operate/disseminate very differently in its newly framed incarnation (Yew, Shamma, and Churchill, 2011). Du Gay and his coauthors remind us that consumption practices can highlight social differentiation and can reveal subcultural themes that can be classified as reading more or less against the grain of the dominant cultural formations. But as Hebdige points out, in his analysis of subcultures, things that are resistant may be absorbed and neutralized or domesticated (Hebdige, 1979). Observational and ethnographic methods are needed to explore how subcultures appropriate objects as part of their own identity formulations.

Regulation: As seen from the examples above, regulation reflects some explicit or tacit control of the cultural. This control can be in the form of formal or legal controls of technological infrastructures, recommendations and requirements from regulatory bodies, or inscriptions and assertions from institutionalized education systems. It can also be formulated as "soft" controls that are socially instilled as cultural norms and expectations and enforced through more or less subtle social cues. Internet engagement in public spaces through personal devices remains a topic of debate (Snow, Morrill, and White, 2005; Turkle, 2011).

Applying the Circuit Analysis to Technology

A number of technology researchers have applied both Hall's "Encoding/decoding" model and the circuit of culture to the technological design sphere, covering the design, development, marketing, and uptake of mobile technologies (Churchill and Wakeford, 2001), the development of cell phone culture (Goggin, 2006), and peer-to-peer media sharing platforms, specifically Napster (Taylor et al., 2002). What all of these works show is that technologies are not stable, designed artifacts with uses and utilities that are predictable, mandated, and always enacted as envisioned in the initial design. Technologies have a shape that comes into being through use (consumption). And use is managed to a greater or lesser extent through regulation, which may be explicit (it is a finable offense to use a cell phone to make calls on certain train carriages), through social sanction (it is rude to use a cell phone in a movie theater when the film is showing), or through the availability of, or regulations over, substrate or dependent infrastructures (services are not available in certain parts of the world due to bandwidth availability or prohibitive pricing).

In sum, the circuit of culture offers us a framework for addressing the design, development, and dissemination of any cultural artifact. Although it has been critiqued for being simplistic and for having little strong prescriptive or predictive capability (Fine, 2002), it is a useful model for battling techno-deterministic or overly libertarian interpretations of the production of cultural artifacts and the meaning, which can be simultaneously multiple and varied but which can also change over time. The framework also calls into play the arenas of responsibility for production and narration of not just the artifact but also the identifications and identities of those who consume it. The circuit invites a degree of systems thinking and blurs the boundaries of our personal and ethical responsibility and agency in the production of a cultural artifact. The framework is an interpretive one: it does not claim to offer pragmatic purchase for those looking for design solutions and design certainties, but rather offers us a way of asking questions about the production and adoption process, agency, and power.

Stuart Hall and Human-Computer Interaction

Engaging with Hall's work invites us to understand the purview of HCI to be broad, even if our personal, individual, interests and practiced skill sets may be narrow and focused (front-end development, interface design, experimental methods, prototyping, user modeling, field studies, mobility, conversation analysis, and so on). Hall's work points out that we engage head-on with the fact that deterministic design is a fanciful pipe dream: we *cannot* control the message such that it is received as we intended. Hall's work invites us to take an expansive approach to methods and requires that we question received requirements, illuminate the underlying tacit assumptions of any project, and lay bare motivations for designs and designing. The work requires that we engage in the enterprise of designing ethically while understanding that we may not be able to grasp how our intentions and our designs will be received, reproduced, or rejected. What makes Hall's work most remarkable is that it invites us to engage with multiple levels of analysis and multiple perspectives on what we create, reminding us that the abstracted concept of culture is deeply connected to the concrete decisions in our analyses as HCI scholars, researchers, and practitioners, and as interaction designers and developers.

Designers, design engineers, and developers are increasingly called on to make decisions about interaction with and through "globally relevant" technologies and are in many ways acting as reflectors and intermediaries of culture, but they are also actively participating in creating cultures. It is not easy to distance oneself from everyday experiences and the practical consciousness of everyday people, to understand what forms of struggle, resistance, and marginalization occurs as a result of design decisions. It is often easier to engage with aggregate numbers of "active users," of transactions, of views and likes and comments, and to fail to understand ourselves as participating in cultural formations and creations. Hall's work entreats us to avoid this trap.

As a first step toward thinking critically, in the vein of Stuart Hall, here are some questions to consider when taking up a project, reviewing a technology, consuming a media artifact, or engaging in a designed experience like a visit to a theme park or an event:

- Who designed/created it?
- Who makes it?
- Who profits from its sale? How?
- Who profits from its use/engagement? How?
- What is its intended purpose?
- Does it create or fill a need?
- Has its appearance, function, usage, popularity changed over time?
- Who uses it? How? When? Where? Why?
- How does its use spread? How was/is adoption promoted?
- How does someone learn to use it?
- Do different people use it differently?
- What is the interface? Is that also an object? Or a practice? Or is it both?
- Does it have a "fan base?" Who are they? How do they communicate their appreciation, their love, their engagement?
- Is it a status symbol? How?
- Does it have associated social identities? How is its use signaled to others?
- Does its use differ among different subgroups? If so how is that difference signaled/shared? Is the difference important to the subgroup?
- Is it modifiable? Can people change or hack it? How?
- How does the technology change the user? How does it become part of a person's sense of self (identity)?
- Who doesn't use it? Why not?
- Does it have active detractors?
- Is it legally regulated? If so how?
- Is it informally regulated? If so how?
- Should it be regulated? Why? How? By whom?
- Has it been appropriated and reinterpreted, reproduced? If so, what is being created, by whom, and for what purpose? How is the appropriated product being circulated, communicated, decoded?

As HCI scholars we often invite some of these questions but not others. What Hall's work asks of us—demands of us—is that we do not see these questions as standing alone, as separable research questions and projects that are not held within a broader framework of mutually influencing causes and effects. Our research projects and questions might seem local to the issue at hand, but they can also be seen as relevant for and able to contribute to a bigger question of culture. In our actions we are designing culture, and we are responsible therefore for the culture we participate in producing.

It's worth ending this chapter with a quote from Stuart Hall that invites us to consider how the practices, procedures, and passions we engage in are influenced by the structures within which we work, and in turn how those "maps of meaning" and "structures of dominance" are influenced by us and our actions.

The products of signifying practices, practices with a carrying meaning ... in our world happen to be widely circulated by the media, the media being one of the most powerful and extensive systems for the circulation of meaning, although one ought to always remind oneself, especially in media studies, that the media are, by no means, the only means by which meaning is circulated in our society.... The most obvious way is in actual talk and conversation with other people in personal communication. That is the medium in which the exchange of meaning absolutely saturates the world. But, of course, we are right noticing that to see what happens when systems—complicated, institutional systems with complicated technologies—then intervene and take the place of face-to-face, person-to-person communication and exchange. And the means of circulating those meanings become very widespread because, of course, the question of the circulation of meaning almost immediately involves the question of power. *Who has the power, in what channels, to circulate which meanings to whom?* (Stuart Hall, 2005, quoted in Jhally, 2005, 15; italics mine)

References

Babe, R. E. (2015) *Wilbur Schramm and Noam Chomsky Meet Harold Innis: Media, Power, and Democracy*. Lanham, MD: Lexington Books.

Bannon, L. J. (1991) "From Human Factors to Human Actors: The Role of Psychology and Human-Computer Interaction Studies in System Design." In *Design at Work: Cooperative Design of Computer Systems*, edited by J. Greenbaum, 25–44. Hillsdale, NJ: Lawrence Erlbaum.

Bennett, S. C. (2012) "The 'Right to be Forgotten': Reconciling EU and US Perspectives." *Berkeley Journal of International Law* 30 (1): http://scholarship.law.berkeley.edu/cgi/viewcontent.cgi?article=1429&context=bjil.

Bødker, S. (2006) "When Second Wave HCI Meets Third Wave Challenges." *Proceedings of the Fourth Nordic Conference on Human-Computer Interaction (NordiCHI'06)*. New York: ACM, 1–8.

Bourdieu, P. (1984) *Distinction: A Social Critique of the Judgement of Taste*. Cambridge, MA: Harvard University Press.

Butsch, R. (1992) "Class and Gender in Four Decades of Television Situation Comedy: Plus ça change ...." *Critical Studies in Mass Communication* 9 (4): 387–399.

Churchill, E. F. (2013) "Putting the *Person* Back into Personalization." *Interactions* 20 (5): 12–15.

Churchill, E. F., and N. Wakeford. (2001) "Framing Mobile Collaborations and Mobile Technologies." In *Wireless World*, edited by B. Brown and N. Green, 154–179. New York: Springer.

Coates, A. (2013) "Stuart Hall, Thatcherism, and Marxism Today." *North Star* http://www.thenorthstar.info/?p=9079.

Curtin, P. A., and T. K. Gaither. (2005) "Privileging Identity, Difference, and Power: The Circuit of Culture as a Basis for Public Relations Theory." *Journal of Public Relations Research* 17 (2): 91–115.

D'Emilio, J., and E. B. Freedman. (1988) *Intimate Matters: A History of Sexuality in America.* Chicago: University of Chicago Press.

Doty, A. (1993) *Making Things Perfectly Queer: Interpreting Mass Culture.* Minneapolis: University of Minnesota Press.

Economist. (2015) "Square Pegs, Round Hole: Britain's Election 2015; Seats-to-votes Calculator." May 8. http://www.economist.com/blogs/graphicdetail/2015/05/britain-s-election-2015-seats-votes-calculator.

Farnham, S., and E. F. Churchill. (2011) "Faceted Identity, Faceted Lives: Social and Technical Issues with Being Yourself Online." *Proceedings of the ACM 2011 Conference on Computer Supported Cooperative Work (CSCW'11).* New York: ACM, 359–368.

Fine, B. (2002) *World of Consumption: The Material and Cultural Revisited,* 2nd ed. London: Routledge.

Fisher, D. E., and M. J. Fisher. (1996) *Tube: The Invention of Television.* Washington, DC: Counterpoint.

du Gay, P., S. Hall, L. Janes, H. MacKay, and K. Negus. (1997) *Doing Cultural Studies: The Story of the Sony Walkman.* Thousand Oaks, CA: Sage.

Goggin, G. (2006) *Cell Phone Culture: Mobile Technology in Everyday Life.* New York: Routledge.

Haimson, O. L., A. E. Bowser, E. F. Melcer, and E. F. Churchill. (2015) "Online Inspiration and Exploration for Identity Reinvention." *Proceedings of the 33rd Annual ACM Conference on Human Factors in Computing Systems (CHI'15).* New York: AMC, 3809–3818.

Hall, S. (1980) "Encoding/decoding." In *Culture, Media, Language,* edited by S. Hall, D. Hobson, A. Love, and P. Willis, 128–138. London: Hutchinson.

Hall, S. (1981a) "Notes on Deconstructing 'the Popular.'" In *People's History and Socialist Theory,* edited by R. Samuel, 227–240. London: Routledge.

Hall, S. (1981b) "The Whites of Their Eyes: Racist Ideologies and the Media." In *Silver Linings: Some Strategies for the Eighties,* edited by G. Bridges and R. Brunt, 18–22. London: Lawrence and Wishart.

Hall, S., and T. Jefferson, eds. (1993) *Resistance through Rituals: Youth Subcultures in Post-War Britain.* London: Routledge.

Hathaway, J. (2014) "What Is Gamergate, and Why? An Explainer for Non-Geeks." *Gawker,* October 10, http://gawker.com/what-is-gamergate-and-why-an-explainer-for-non-geeks-1642909080.

Hebdige, D. (1979) *Subculture: The Meaning of Style*. London: Routledge.

Hoboken, J. (2013) *The Proposed Right to be Forgotten Seen from the Perspective of Our Right to Remember: Freedom of Expression Safeguards in a Converging Information Environment*. Amsterdam: European Commission. http://www.law.nyu.edu/sites/default/files/upload_documents/VanHoboken_RightTo%20Be%20Forgotten_Manuscript_2013.pdf.

Hollnagel, E., and D. D. Woods. (2005) *Joint Cognitive Systems: Foundations of Cognitive Systems Engineering*. Boca Raton, FL: Taylor & Francis.

Howes, D. (1996) *Cross-Cultural Consumption: Global Markets, Local Realities*. New York: Routledge.

Jhally, S. (2005) *Stuart Hall: Representation and the Media*. Media Education Foundation Collection. Accessed July 21, 2013. http://www.mediaed.org/assets/products/409/transcript_409.pdf.

Kay, M., C. Matuszek, and S. A. Munson. (2015) "Unequal Representation and Gender Stereotypes in Image Search Results for Occupations." *Proceedings of the 33rd Annual ACM Conference on Human Factors in Computing Systems (CHI'15)*. New York: AMC, 3819–3828. DOI=10.1145/2702123.2702520.

Marwick, A. E. (2013) *Status Update: Celebrity, Publicity, and Branding in the Social Media Age*. New Haven, CT: Yale University Press.

McKay, G. (1996) *Senseless Acts of Beauty: Cultures of Resistance since the Sixties*. London: Verso.

Nanda, S. (2000) *Gender Diversity: Crosscultural Variations*. Prospect Heights, IL: Waveland.

Pariser, E. (2011) *The Filter Bubble: What the Internet Is Hiding from You*. London: Penguin.

Ronson, J. (2015) *So You've Been Publicly Shamed*. New York: Riverhead Books.

Schramm, W., ed. (1955) *The Process and Effects of Mass Communication*. Urbana: University of Illinois Press.

Schramm, W., and D. F. Roberts, eds. (1971) *The Process and Effects of Mass Communication*, rev. ed. Urbana: University of Illinois Press.

Schwartz, P., and V. Rutter. (1998) *The Gender of Sexuality*. Thousand Oaks, CA: Pine Forge.

Sewell, W. H. (1999) "The Concept(s) of Culture." In *Beyond the Cultural Turn*, edited by V. E. Bonnell and L. Hunt, 35–61. Berkeley: University of California Press.

Smith, G. (2015) "Even Nate Silver Got It Totally Wrong—5 Takeaways from the U.K. Election." *Fortune*, May 8, http://fortune.com/2015/05/08/even-nate-silver-got-it-totally-wrong-5-takeaways-from-the-u-k-election/.

Snow, D. A., C. Morrill, and C. H. White, eds. (2005) *Together Alone: Personal Relationships in Public Places*. Berkeley: University of California Press.

Taylor, B. C., C. Demont-Heinrich, K. J. Broadfoot, J. Dodge, and C. Jian. (2002) "New Media and the Circuit of Cyber-Culture: Conceptualizing Napster." *Journal of Broadcasting and Electronic Media* 46 (4): 607–629.

Thornton, S. (1995) *Club Cultures: Music, Media, and Subcultural Capital.* Cambridge: Polity.

Turkle, S. (2011) *Alone Together: Why We Expect More from Technology and Less from Each Other.* New York: Basic Books.

Weaver, W., and C. E. Shannon. (1963) *The Mathematical Theory of Communication.* Urbana: University of Illinois Press.

Wright, A. (2007) *Glut: Mastering Information through the Ages.* Washington, DC: Joseph Henry.

Yew, J., D. A. Shamma, and E. F. Churchill. (2011) "Knowing Funny: Genre Perception and Categorization in Social Video Sharing." *Proceedings of the SIGCHI Conference on Human Factors in Computing Systems (CHI'11).* New York: ACM, 297–306.

11 Grasping a Text (1978)

Wolfgang Iser

Interplay Between Text and Reader

Textual models designate only one aspect of the communicatory process. Hence textual repertoires and strategies simply offer a frame within which the reader must construct for himself the aesthetic object. Textual structures and structured acts of comprehension are therefore the two poles in the act of communication, whose success will depend on the degree in which the text establishes itself as a correlative in the reader's consciousness. This "transfer" of text to reader is often regarded as being brought about solely by the text. Any successful transfer however—though initiated by the text—depends on the extent to which this text can activate the individual reader's faculties of perceiving and processing. Although the text may well incorporate the social norms and values of its possible readers, its function is not merely to *present* such data, but, in fact, to use them in order to secure its uptake. In other words, it offers guidance as to what is to be produced, and therefore cannot itself be the product. This fact is worth emphasizing, because there are many current theories which give the impression that texts automatically imprint themselves on the reader's mind of their own accord. This applies not only to linguistic theories but also to Marxist theories, as evinced by the term *"Rezeptionsvorgabe"*[1] (structured prefigurement) recently coined by East German critics. Of course, the text is a "structured prefigurement," but that which is given has to be received, and the *way* in which it is received depends as much on the reader as on the text. Reading is not a direct "internalization," because it is not a one-way process, and our concern will be to find means of describing the reading process as a dynamic *interaction* between text and reader. We may take as a starting-point the fact that the linguistic signs and structures of the text exhaust their function in triggering developing acts of comprehension. This is tantamount to saying that these acts, though set in motion by the text, defy total control by the text itself, and, indeed, it is the very lack of control that forms the basis of the creative side of reading.

This concept of reading is by no means new. In the eighteenth century, Laurence Sterne was already writing in *Tristram Shandy*: "... no author, who understands the just boundaries of decorum and good-breeding, would presume to think all: The truest respect which you can pay to the reader's understanding, is to halve this matter amicably, and leave him something to imagine, in his turn, as well as yourself. For my own part, I am eternally paying him compliments of this kind, and do all that lies in my power to keep his imagination as busy as my own."[2] Thus author and reader are to share the game of the imagination, and, indeed, the game will not work if the text sets out to be anything more than a set of governing rules. The reader's enjoyment begins when he himself becomes productive, i.e., when the text allows him to bring his own faculties into play. There are, of course, limits to the reader's willingness to participate, and these will be exceeded if the text makes things too clear or, on the other hand, too obscure: boredom and overstrain represent the two poles of tolerance, and in either case the reader is likely to opt out of the game.

Sterne's thoughts on reader participation are echoed some two hundred years later by Sartre—whom one would otherwise scarcely consider to be a kindred spirit of the eighteenth-century English humorist. He calls the relationship a "pact"[3] and goes on: "When a work is produced, the creative act is only an incomplete, abstract impulse; if the author existed all on his own, he could write as much as he liked, but his work would never see the light of day as an object, and he would have to lay down his pen or despair. The process of writing, however, includes as a dialectic correlative the process of reading, and these two interdependent acts require two differently active people. The combined efforts of author and reader bring into being the concrete and imaginary object which is the work of the mind. Art exists only for and through other people."[4]

The Wandering Viewpoint

In our attempts to describe the intersubjective structure of the process through which a text is transferred and translated, our first problem is the fact that the whole text can never be perceived at any one time. In this respect it differs from given objects, which can generally be viewed or at least conceived as a whole. The "object" of the text can only be imagined by way of different consecutive phases of reading. We always stand outside the given object, whereas we are situated inside the literary text. The relation between text and reader is therefore quite different from that between object and observer: instead of a subject-object relationship, there is a moving viewpoint which travels along *inside* that which it has to apprehend. This mode of grasping an object is unique to literature.

A further complication consists in the fact that literary texts do not serve merely to denote empirically existing objects. Even though they may select objects from the empirical world—as we have seen in our discussion of the repertoire—they depragmatize them, for these objects are not to be denoted, but are to be transformed. Denotation presupposes some form of reference that will indicate the specific meaning of the thing denoted. The literary text, however, takes its selected objects out of their pragmatic context and so shatters their original frame of reference; the result is to reveal aspects (e.g., of social norms) which had remained hidden as long as the frame of reference remained intact. In this way, the reader is given no chance to detach himself, as he would have if the text were purely denotative. Instead of finding out whether the text gives an accurate or inaccurate description of the object, he has to build up the object for himself—often in a manner running counter to the familiar world evoked by the text.

The reader's wandering viewpoint is, at one and the same time, caught up in and transcended by the object it is to apprehend. Apperception can only take place in phases, each of which contains aspects of the object to be constituted, but none of which can claim to be representative of it. Thus the aesthetic object cannot be identified with any of its manifestations during the time-flow of the reading. The incompleteness of each manifestation necessitates syntheses, which in turn bring about the transfer of the text to the reader's consciousness. The synthetizing process, however, is not sporadic—it continues throughout every phase of the journey of the wandering viewpoint.

It may help us to understand the nature of this synthetizing activity if we examine in detail one paradigmatic moment in the process of reading. We shall, for the present, restrict our analysis to the sentence perspective of the text, and here we may turn for support to the empirical findings of psycholinguistics. What is known as the "eye-voice span,"[5] when applied to the literary text will designate that span of the text which can be encompassed during each phase of reading and from which we anticipate the next phase: "... decoding proceeds in 'chunks' rather than in units of single words, and ... these 'chunks' correspond to the syntactic units of a sentence."[6] The syntactic units of sentences are residual "chunks" for perception within the literary text, although here they cannot be identified merely as perceptual objects, because the denotation of a given object is not the prime function of such sentences. The main interest here lies in the sentence correlate, for the world of the literary object is built up by these intentional correlates.

> Sentences join in diverse ways to form semantic units of a higher order which exhibit quite varied structures; from these structures arise such entities as a story, a novel, a conversation, a drama, a scientific theory. By the same token, finite verbs constitute not only states of affairs which correspond to the individual sentences, but also whole systems of very diverse types of states of affairs, such as concrete situations, complex processes involving several objects, conflicts and agreements among them, etc. Finally, a whole world is created with variously determined elements and the changes taking place in them, all as the purely intentional correlate of a sentence complex. If this sentence complex finally constitutes a literary work, then I call the whole stock of interconnected intentional sentence correlates the "portrayed world" of the work.[7]

How is one to describe the connections between these correlates—especially as they do not have that degree of determinacy pertaining to a declarative sentence? When Ingarden speaks of intentional sentence correlates, the statement and information are already qualified in a certain sense, because each sentence can achieve its end only by aiming at something beyond itself. As this is true of all the sentences in a literary text, the correlates constantly intersect, giving rise ultimately to the semantic fulfillment at which they had aimed. The fulfillment, however, takes place not in the text, but in the reader, who must "activate" the interplay of the correlates prestructured by the sequence of sentences. The sentences themselves, as statements and assertions, serve to point the way toward what is to come, and this in turn is prestructured by the actual content of the sentences. In brief, the sentences set in motion a process which will lead to the formation of the aesthetic object as a correlative in the mind of the reader.

In describing the inner consciousness of time, Husserl once wrote: "Every originally constituent process is inspired by protensions, which construct and collect the seed of what is to come, as such, and bring it to fruition."[8] This remark draws attention to an elementary factor which plays a central part in the reading process. The semantic pointers of individual sentences always imply an expectation of some kind—Husserl calls these expectations "protensions." As this structure is inherent in *all* intentional sentence correlates, it follows that their interplay will lead not so much to the fulfillment of expectations as to their continual modification. Now herein lies a basic structure of the wandering viewpoint. The reader's position in the text is at the point of intersection between retention and protension. Each individual sentence correlate prefigures a particular horizon, but this is immediately transformed into the background for the next correlate and must therefore necessarily be modified. Since each sentence correlate aims at things to come, the prefigured horizon will offer a view which—however concrete it may be—must contain indeterminacies, and so arouse expectations as to the manner in which these are to be resolved. Each new correlate, then, will answer expectations (either positively or negatively) and, at the same time, will arouse new expectations. As far as the sequence of sentences is concerned, there are two fundamentally different possibilities. If the new correlate begins to confirm the expectations aroused by its predecessor, the range of possible semantic horizons will be correspondingly narrowed. This is normally the case with texts that are to describe a particular object, for their concern is to narrow the range in order to bring out the individuality of that object. In most literary texts, however, the sequence of sentences is so structured that the correlates serve to modify and even frustrate the expectations they have aroused. In so doing, they automatically have a retroactive effect on what has already been read, which now appears quite different. Furthermore, what has been read shrinks in the memory to a foreshortened background, but it is being constantly evoked in a new context and so modified by new correlates that instigate a restructuring of past syntheses. This does not mean that the past returns in full to the present, for then memory and perception would become indistinguishable, but it does mean that memory undergoes a transformation. That which is remembered becomes open to new connections and these in turn influence the expectations aroused by the individual correlates in the sequence of sentences.

It is clear, then, that throughout the reading process there is a continual interplay between modified expectations and transformed memories. However, the text itself does not formulate expectations or their modification; nor does it specify how the connectability of memories is to be implemented. This is the province of the reader himself, and so here we have a first insight into how the synthetizing activity of the reader enables the text to be translated and transferred to his own mind. This process of translation also shows up the basic hermeneutic structure of reading. Each sentence correlate contains what one might call a hollow section, which looks forward to the next correlate, and a retrospective section, which answers the expectations of the preceding sentence (now part of the remembered background). Thus every moment of reading is a dialectic of protension and retention, conveying a future horizon yet to be occupied, along with a past (and continually fading) horizon already filled; the wandering viewpoint carves its passage through both at the same time and leaves them to merge together in its wake. There is no escaping this process, for—as has already been pointed out—the text cannot at any one moment be grasped as a whole. But what may at first sight have seemed like a disadvantage, in comparison with our normal modes of perception, may now be seen to offer distinct advantages, in so far as it permits a process through which the aesthetic object is constantly being structured and restructured. As there is no definite frame of reference to regulate this process, successful communication must ultimately depend on the reader's creative activity.

We must now take a closer look at the basic structures that regulate this process. Even on the level of the sentences themselves, it is clear that their sequence does not by any means bring about a smooth interaction of protension and retention. This fact has been pointed out by Ingarden, though his interpretation of it is debatable:

> Once we are transposed into the flow of thinking the sentence, we are prepared, after having completed the thought of one sentence, to think its "continuation" in the form of another sentence, specifically, a sentence which has a connection with the first sentence. In this way the process of reading a text advances effortlessly. But when it happens that the second sentence has no perceptible connection whatever with the first, the flow of thought is checked. A more or less vivid surprise or vexation is associated with the resulting hiatus. The block must be overcome if we are to renew the flow of our reading.[9]

Ingarden regards this interruption to the flow as a defect, and this shows the extent to which he applies even to the reading process his classical concept of the work of art as polyphonic harmony. If the sequence of sentences is to be regarded as an uninterrupted *flow*, each sentence will obviously have to fulfill the expectations aroused by its predecessor, and a failure to do so will arouse "vexation." But in literary texts, not only is the sequence full of surprising twists and turns, but indeed we *expect* it to be so—even to the extent that if there *is* a continuous *flow*, we will look for an ulterior motive. There is no need for us now to go into Ingarden's reasons for demanding a *"flow* of sentence thinking"; what concerns us here is the fact that there *is* such a hiatus, and that it has a very important function. The "obstacle" condemned by Ingarden enables the sentence correlates to be set off against one another. On the level of sentences themselves, the interruption of expected connections may not be of any great significance; however it is paradigmatic of the many processes of focusing and refocusing that take place during the reading of the literary text. This need for readjustment arises primarily from the fact that the aesthetic object has no existence of its own, and can consequently only come into being by way of such processes.

It is difficult for individual sentences to be distinguished from one another as regards the textual perspectives they establish, because as a rule the repertoire of signals in the literary text is extremely restricted. Quotation marks are perhaps the most striking of these, to denote that a sentence is in fact the utterance of a character. Indirect speech is less clearly indicated, and there are no specific markers to indicate the intervention of the author, the development of the plot, or the position ascribed to the reader. A sequence of sentences may contain something about a character, the plot, the author's evaluation, or the reader's perspective, without any explicit signals to distinguish these very different points of orientation from one another. But the importance of such differentiation can be gauged from the manner in which some authors insist on different lettering (e.g., italics) to draw distinctions which would not otherwise have emerged from the sequence of sentences.

In James Joyce, Virginia Woolf, and William Faulkner (particularly *The Sound and the Fury*), such signals are most frequently to be found where different depths of consciousness are to be plumbed; these cannot be explicitly formulated, and so the use of differentiated signals enables the various layers of consciousness to be offset from one another without recourse to extraneous codes. In most novels, however, as has already been observed, there are no signals to distinguish between the various textual perspectives through which the narrator, the characters, the plot, and the reader's position are represented. Although we have a syntactically ordered sequence of sentences, each sentence is only part of the textual perspective in which it is situated, and such segments will alternate with segments of other perspectives, with the result that the perspectives are continually throwing one another into relief. This alternation can be accelerated to the point at which each new sentence switches the viewpoint in a positive kaleidoscope of perspectives, as occasionally in *Ulysses* for instance. The term perspective here implies a channeled view (from the standpoint of narrator, characters, etc.), and it also sets out the specific mode of access to the object intended.[10] In a nondenotative text, both characteristics are of equal importance; standpoint and accessibility are two basic conditions under which the aesthetic object is to be produced.

As the sentences of a text are always situated within the perspective that they constitute, the wandering viewpoint is also situated in a particular perspective during every moment of reading, but—and herein lies the special nature of the wandering viewpoint—it is not confined to that perspective. On the contrary, it constantly switches between the textual perspectives, each of the switches representing an articulate reading moment; it simultaneously offsets and relates the perspectives. What Ingarden rejected as "hiatus" in a sequence of sentences, is in fact an indispensable condition for the process of reciprocal spotlighting, and without it the process of reading would remain nothing but an inarticulate time-flow. But if the wandering viewpoint defines itself by way of the changing perspectives, it follows that throughout the reading past perspective segments must be retained in each present moment. The new moment is not isolated, but stands out against the old, and so the past will remain as a background to the present, exerting influence on it and, at the same time, itself being modified by the present. This two-way influence is a basic structure in the time-flow of the reading process, for this is what brings about the reader's position within the text. As the wandering viewpoint is not situated exclusively in any one of the perspectives, the reader's position can only be established through a combination of these perspectives. But the act of combining is only possible by way of the retained modifications in the many reading moments made articulate by the spotlighting process.

For the sake of analysis we might halt the time-flow of reading and take as an example of one paradigmatic reading moment an incident in Thackeray's *Vanity Fair.* During one particular phase of reading, the viewpoint of the reader is situated within Becky Sharp's perspective, as she writes a letter to her friend Amelia to tell her what she is hoping to gain from her new position at the Crawley's country seat; here the narrator's perspective is present as a background. It is evoked by a signal from the author, who has called this chapter "Arcadian Simplicity."[11] This pointer ensures that the reader will never lose sight of the narrator's views on the social ambitions and, especially, the flexibility with which the "little Becky puppet" performs her social high-wire act. This evocation of the narrator's perspective throws the new segments into sharp relief. But at this particular moment, *both* perspectives undergo a degree of modification. On the one hand, Becky's naive desire to do all she can to please her new masters no longer seems to express the amiability she intended, but instead denotes her habitual opportunism. On the other hand, the narrator's general metaphor for Becky—a puppet on a tightrope—begins to take on the more specific significance of a form of opportunism characteristic in nineteenth-century society: the opportunist could only succeed through moral conduct, though this was not motivated by the selflessness normally inherent in morality. At this reading moment, the ability to manipulate morality—and with it, the central code of conduct of the nineteenth-century middle class—emerges as the developing individualization of the narrator's perspective as against the characters' perspective.

In the same way, every reading moment sends out stimuli into the memory, and what is recalled can activate the perspectives in such a way that they continually modify and so individualize one another. Our example shows clearly that reading does not merely flow forward, but that recalled segments also have a retroactive effect, with the present transforming the past. As the evocation of the narrator's perspective undermines what is stated explicitly in the characters' perspective, there emerges a configurative meaning, which shows the character to be an opportunist and the narrator's comments to have a hitherto unsuspected individual connotation.

It is clear, then, that the present retention of a past perspective qualifies both past and present. It also qualifies the future, because whatever modifications it has brought about will immediately affect the nature of our expectations. These may radiate in several different directions at once. The expectations arising from our Thackeray example will in the first place relate to the future success or failure of Becky's opportunism. If she succeeds, we shall then expect to learn something about society, and if she fails, it will be something about the fate of opportunism in that society. However, it may be that at this particular reading moment, the character perspectives are already so clearly individualized that such general expectations serve only as a frame, and instead of waiting for success or failure, we wait for a detailed picture of this particular type of conduct. Indeed, the multiplicity of character perspectives tends to lead us in this direction, for the perspective of the simple-minded and sentimental Amelia, to whom Becky addresses her letter, is liable to yield a different view of opportunism from that of the upper-class society in which Becky now finds herself. Consequently, the reader will expect an individualization of that form of opportunism which the author wishes to convey as typical of that society.

This example clearly illustrates what we might call the basic fabric of the wandering viewpoint. The switch of viewpoints brings about a spotlighting of textual perspectives,[12] and these in turn become reciprocally influenced backgrounds which endow each new foreground with a specific shape and form. As the viewpoint changes again, this foreground merges into the background, which it has modified and which is now to exert its influence on yet another new foreground. Every articulate reading moment entails a switch of perspective, and this constitutes an inseparable combination of differentiated perspectives, foreshortened memories, present modifications, and future expectations. Thus, in the time-flow of the reading process, past and future continually converge in the present moment, and the synthetizing operations of the wandering viewpoint enable the text to pass through the reader's mind as an ever-expanding network of connections. This also adds the dimension of space to that of time, for the accumulation of views and combinations gives us the illusion of depth and breadth, so that we have the impression that we are actually present in a real world.

One further aspect of the wandering viewpoint needs to be discussed if we are to pinpoint the way in which the written text is grasped by the reader. The reciprocal evocation of perspectives does not normally follow a strict time sequence. If it did, what had been read earlier would gradually disappear from view, as it would become increasingly irrelevant. The pointers and stimuli therefore evoke not just their immediate predecessors, but often aspects of other perspectives that have already sunk deep into the past. This constitutes an important feature of the wandering viewpoint. If the reader is prodded into recalling something already sunk into memory, he will bring it back, not in isolation but embedded in a particular context. The fact of recall marks the limit to which the linguistic sign can be effective, for the words in the text can only denote a reference, and not its context; the connection with context is established by the retentive mind of the reader. The extent and the nature of this recalled context are beyond the control of the linguistic sign. Now if the reference invoked is embedded in a context (however variable), clearly, it can be viewed from a point outside itself, and so it is possible that aspects may now become visible that had not been so when the fact had settled in the memory. It follows that whatever is evoked from the reading past will appear against the background of its own observability, and it is at this point that the textual sign and the reader's conscious mind merge in a productive act that cannot be reduced to either of its component parts. As the past fact is recalled against the background of its own observability, this constitutes an apperception, for the invoked fact cannot be separated from its past context as far as the reader is concerned, but represents part of a synthetic unit, through which the fact can be present as something already apprehended. In other words, the fact itself is present, the past context and synthesis are present, and at the same time the potential for reassessment is also present.

This feature of the reading process is of great significance for the compilation of the aesthetic object. As the reader's conscious mind is activated by the textual stimulus and the remembered apperception returns as a background, so the unit of meaning is linked to the new reading moment in which the wandering viewpoint is now situated. But as the perspective invoked already possessed a configurative meaning and does not return in isolation, it must inevitably provide a differentiated spectrum of observation for the new perspective which has recalled it and which thereby undergoes an increasing degree of individualization.

We can illustrate this process with the Thackeray example. The textual sign "Arcadian Simplicity" invokes the narrator's perspective just when the reader is more or less immersed in the perspective of the character, because Becky at the time is writing a letter. Our position is that described by Butor: "If the reader is placed in the position of the hero, he must also be placed in the hero's time and situation: he cannot know what the hero does not know, and things must appear to him precisely as they appear to the hero."[13] The textual sign "Arcadian Simplicity" is explicitly ironic and invokes the attitude characteristic of the narrator's perspective. The term "Arcadian Simplicity" is in itself a comparatively mild form of irony, but it bears with it the whole panoply of past ironies. Against this background of ironic variations, the term is open to observation and judgment as regards its appropriateness. It is, in fact, present against two backgrounds—that of the narrator's perspective and that of the character's perspective. As each of these influences and modifies the other, Becky's desire to please everyone is not to be viewed solely in relation to the background of irony; it also calls forth a judgment as to whether the irony is appropriate or inappropriate, and the extent to which it is inappropriate endows Becky's intentions with a dimension which—although it remains unformulated—possesses a high degree of semantic individuality.

In this way the two perspectives throw each other into distinct relief. The narrator's irony demands an evaluation of what the character is after, while the ambitions of the character subject the narrator's perspective to an evaluation of its appropriateness. Once again, then, the backgrounds and their connections are differentiated, and it is this constant reshuffling of viewpoints and relations that spurs the reader on to build up the syntheses which eventually individualize the aesthetic object.

As we have seen, the perspectives invoked are present in the articulate reading moment as configurative meanings and not as isolated elements, and this intersubjective structure always conditions the way in which it will be subjectively realized. The degree to which the retaining mind will implement the perspective connections inherent in the text depends on a large number of subjective factors: memory, interest, attention, and mental capacity all affect the extent to which past contexts become present. There is no doubt that this extent will vary considerably from reader to reader, but this is what first conditions the apperceptions that arise out of the interaction between the fact invoked and its context. The resultant retroactive link-up in turn helps to individualize the stimulant perspective, and the nuances of this individualization will depend precisely on these subjective factors. This is why the same intersubjective structure of the literary text may give rise to so many different subjective realizations, and without this structure there could be no basis for comparing and assessing interpretations.

To sum up, then, we have observed that the wandering viewpoint permits the reader to travel through the text, thus unfolding the multiplicity of interconnecting perspectives which are offset whenever there is a switch from one to another. This gives rise to a network of possible connections, which are characterized by the fact that they do not join together isolated data from the different perspectives, but actually establish a relationship of reciprocal observation between stimulant and stimulated perspectives. This network of connections potentially encompasses the whole text, but the potential can never be fully realized; instead it forms the basis for the many selections which have to be made during the reading process and which, though intersubjectively not identical—as is shown by the many different interpretations of a single text—nevertheless remain intersubjectively comprehensible in so far as they are all attempts to optimize the same structure.

Correlatives Produced by the Wandering Viewpoint

Consistency-Building as a Basis for Involvement in the Text as an Event

The wandering viewpoint is a means of describing the way in which the reader is present in the text. This presence is at a point where memory and expectation converge, and the resultant dialectic movement brings about a continual modification of memory and an increasing complexity of expectation. These processes depend on the reciprocal spotlighting of the perspectives, which provide interrelated backgrounds for one another. The interaction between these backgrounds provokes the reader into a synthetizing activity. It "is the prerogative of the perceiver, not a characteristic of the stimuli, to decide which differences shall be significant—which sets of features shall be criterial—in the establishment of equivalences."[14] These syntheses, then, are primarily groupings that bring the interrelated perspectives together in an equivalence that has the character of a configurative meaning. Here we have one of the basic elements of the reading process: the wandering viewpoint divides the text up into interacting structures, and these give rise to a grouping activity that is fundamental to the grasping of a text.

The nature of this process is shown clearly by a remark of Gombrich's: "In the reading of images, as in the hearing of speech, it is always hard to distinguish what is given to us from what we supplement in the process of projection which is triggered off by recognition.... It is the guess of the beholder that tests the medley of forms and colours for coherent meaning, crystallizing it into shape when a consistent interpretation has been found."[15] Inherent in this process—which Gombrich originally derived from decoding distorted messages and then applied to the observation of pictures—is a problem which is highly relevant to the consistency-building that takes place during the reading process. The "consistent interpretation" or gestalt, is a product of the interaction between text and reader, and so cannot be exclusively traced back either to the written text or to the disposition of the reader. Now psycholinguistic experiments have shown that meanings cannot be grasped merely by the direct or indirect decoding of letters or words, but can only be compiled by means of grouping.

When we read a printed page, our attention is not focused on the little flaws in the paper, even though they are in the middle of our field of vision, and in fact we get nothing but a blurred and latent idea of the form of the letters used. On a still higher plane of observation, we know from the extensive work done by perception psychologists in connection with the reading of the printed page (e. g., Richaudeau, Zeitler, Shen) that during continuous reading, the number of focal points for the eye does not exceed two or three per line, and it is physically impossible for the eye to grasp the form of each individual letter. There are innumerable examples of "typographical illusions," and all the findings lead psychologists to accept the gestalt theory, as opposed to the one-sided concepts of scanning.[16]

For if the reader were really to scan letters and words like a computer, the reading process would simply entail registering these units which, however, are not yet units of meaning. "Meaning is at a level of language where words do not belong.... Meaning is part of the deep structure, the semantic, cognitive level. And you may recall that between the surface level and the deep level of language there is no one-to-one correspondence. Meaning may always resist mere words."[17]

As meaning is not manifested in words, and the reading process therefore cannot be mere identification of individual linguistic signs, it follows that apprehension of the text is dependent on gestalt groupings. If we may borrow a term from Moles, we can define these gestalten elementally as the "autocorrelation" of textual signs.[18] The term is apposite, because it relates to the interconnection between the textual signs prior to the stimulation of the individual reader's disposition. A gestalt would not be possible if there were not originally some potential correlation between the signs. The reader's task is then to make these signs consistent, and as he does so, it is quite possible that the connections he establishes will themselves become signs for further correlations. By "autocorrelation," then, we mean that connections constitute the gestalt, but the gestalt is not the connection itself—it is an equivalent, in other words, the projection of which Gombrich speaks. The reader's part in the gestalt consists in identifying the connection between the signs; the "autocorrelation" will prevent him from projecting an arbitrary meaning on the text, but at the same time the gestalt can only be formed as an identified equivalence through the hermeneutic schema of anticipation and fulfillment in relation to the connections perceived between the signs.

To illustrate this process and its consequences, we might refer to an example already adduced in another context.[19] In Fielding's *Tom Jones*, Allworthy is introduced as the *homo perfectus*. He lives in Paradise Hall "and ... might well be called the favourite of both nature and fortune."[20] In a new chapter, Dr. Blifil enters the Allworthy family circle, and of him we learn: "the doctor had one positive recommendation—this was a great appearance of religion. Whether his religion was real, or consisted only in appearance, I shall not presume to say, as I am not possessed of any touchstone which can distinguish the true from the false."[21] However, it is said that the doctor seems like a saint. And so at this point in the text, we are given a certain number of signs which set in motion a specific interplay of correlations. The signs denote first that Blifil gives an appearance of deep piety and that Allworthy is a perfect man. At the same time, however, the narrator lets out a warning signal that one must differentiate between true and false appearances. Next Blifil meets Allworthy, and so the Allworthy perspective—retained in the reader's memory—now becomes present again. Because of the narrator's explicit signal, two different segments of the characters' perspective now confront one another with reciprocal effect. The linguistic signs are correlated by the reader, who thus forms a gestalt of the two complexes of signs. In the one case, these signs denoted Blifil's apparent piety, and in the other Allworthy's perfection, and so now the narrator's sign makes it necessary for the reader to apply criteria for differentiation. The equivalence of the signs is established at the moment when we anticipate Blifil's hypocrisy and Allworthy's naiveté, and this, too, is the point at which we fulfill the narrator's demand for differentiation. Blifil's appearance of piety is put on in order that he may impress Allworthy, with a view to worming his way into the family and perhaps gaining control of their estate: Allworthy trusts him, because perfection is simply incapable of conceiving a mere pretence of ideality. The realization that the one is hypocritical and the other naive involves building an equivalence, with a consistent gestalt, out of no less than three different segments of perspectives—two segments of character and one of narrator perspective. The forming of the gestalt resolves the tensions that had resulted from the various complexes of signs. But this gestalt is not explicit in the text—it emerges from a projection of the reader, which is guided in so far as it arises out of the identification of the connections between the signs. In this particular example, it actually brings out something which is not stated by the linguistic signs, and, indeed, it shows that what is *meant* is the opposite of what is said.

Thus the consistent gestalt endows the linguistic signs with their significance, and this grows out of the reciprocal modifications to which the individual positions are subjected, as a result of the need for establishing equivalences. The gestalt coherency might be described in terms used by Gurwitsch, as the perceptual *noema* of the text.[22] This means that as each linguistic sign conveys more than just itself to the mind of the reader, it must be joined together in a single unit with all its referential contexts. The unit of the perceptual *noema* comes about by way of the reader's acts of apprehension: he identifies the connections between the linguistic signs and thus concretizes the references not explicitly manifested in those signs. The perceptual *noema* therefore links up the signs, their implications, their reciprocal influences, and the reader's acts of identification, and through it the text begins to exist as a gestalt in the reader's consciousness.

The perceptual *noema* is quite straightforward in our Fielding example, as far as it goes, and the gestalt coherency will, for the most part, be regarded as intersubjectively valid. However, this gestalt does not stand in isolation. The different Allworthy/Blifil sign complexes brought about a tension which was quite easily resolved by an equivalence, but now the question arises as to whether this gestalt—with Allworthy naive and Blifil hypocritical—is self-sufficient. Open gestalten naturally bring about further tensions, which can only be resolved by way of a wider range of integration. Now if the naive Allworthy/hypocritical Blifil gestalt is regarded as self-sufficient, the conclusion must be simply that Allworthy is deceived by a Tartuffe. But generally readers will tend to be dissatisfied with such a conclusion. There arise such questions as "how"? and "why"?, and these are stimulated not least by the sign of the narrator himself, who has pointed out to us how difficult it is to find a touchstone that can distinguish the true from the false. The reader's attention is thus drawn to the problem of criteria; but if these criteria were confined to this one single case, the narrator's perspective would automatically be deprived of its original function, namely, to establish the overall pattern. The resultant gestalt (i.e., that Allworthy is taken in by a Tartuffe) takes on considerably more significance when viewed (as it must be) in the light of all its ramifications. This "extra" significance is, of course, not arbitrary; it is moulded by the weight of the narrator's sign and by the now obvious paradox that something is missing from Allworthy's "perfection." However, the manner in which the latent openness of the gestalt may be closed is by no means defined. There are various possibilities. (1) The reader may, for instance, ask why it is that he can see through Blifil, whereas Allworthy, who is supposed to be perfect, cannot. He must conclude that perfection lacks one vital attribute: discernment. And then the reader will recall a previous misjudgment of Allworthy's, when as justice of the peace he convicted Jenny Jones, an irreproachable maid-servant, simply because she had seemed to be guilty. (2) The reader may also ask why lack of discernment should be illustrated through a perfect man. He may conclude that this paradox helps lay stress on the importance of discernment—a gestalt which the narrator supports with his own comments. (3) If we should feel superior to the perfect man, because we can see things he cannot, we may now begin to wonder what qualities he possesses that we ourselves are lacking.

Clearly, then, the initial open gestalt can lead in several different directions toward another, closed gestalt, and this fact automatically brings into play a process of selection. The perceptual *noema* therefore involves subjective preferences in relation to the intersubjective acts of consistency-building. All the possibilities outlined above are legitimate, though they all point in different directions. The first instance illustrates the major theme of the novel: discernment is a basic factor in human nature. The second instance illustrates the significance of that theme: discernment can only be acquired through negative experiences and is not a faculty dependent on fortune or nature; this is why Fielding allows discernment and perfection to clash—in order to underline the vital importance of experience. Our third possibility fulfills the didactic purpose. The reader should see himself reflected in the characters, and so should come to a better understanding of himself; a sense of discernment is useless without a moral foundation, for it would then only lead to the cunning deceit of a Blifil.

These are only some of the possibilities of selection, but from this one example we can already draw a general conclusion as regards the process of consistency-building. We have seen that there are two distinct stages in this process: first, the formation of an initial, open gestalt (Allworthy is deceived by a Tartuffe); second, the selection of a gestalt to close the first. These two operations are closely linked, and together they make up the product of the consistency-building process. Now the primary gestalt emerges out of the interacting characters and the plot development, and it is clear from our example that both components depend on gestalt-forming and are not given by the printed text. This Allworthy-Blifil gestalt emerged from the reader's retention of past gestalten and subsequent modification of present linguistic signs; the denoted perfection of Allworthy and the denoted piety of Blifil were both equally transformed in the equivalence of the gestalt. Thus even the plot level of a text develops through gestalt-forming. However, the plot is not an end in itself—it always serves a meaning, for stories are not told for their own sake but for the demonstration of something that extends beyond themselves. And so a gestalt that represents the plot development is still not completely closed. The closing can only come about when the *significance* of the action can be represented by a further gestalt. And here, as we have seen, there are many different possibilities which can only be fulfilled selectively.

On the level of plot, then, there is a high degree of intersubjective consensus, but on the level of significance selective decisions have to be taken which are subjective not because they are arbitrary, but because a gestalt can only be closed if one possibility is selected and the rest excluded. The selection will depend on the reader's individual disposition and experience, but the interdependence of the two types of gestalten (plot-level and significance) remains an intersubjectively valid structure. This relation between subjective selection and intersubjective structure has been described by Sartre as follows:

> The reader is left with everything to do, and yet everything has already been done, the work only exists precisely on the level of his abilities; while he reads and creates, he knows that he could always go further in his reading, and that he could always create more profoundly; and this is why the work appears to him as inexhaustible and as impenetrable as an object. This productiveness, whatever its quality may be, which before our very eyes transforms itself into impenetrable objectivity in accordance with the subject that produces it, is something I should like to compare to the "rational intuition" KANT reserved for divine reason.[23]

This more profound creating, with its resultant impenetrable objectivity, can be seen from the developments of our Fielding example, where the plot-level gestalt broadened out into a range of different significances. Each individual selection retains the character of "impenetrable objectivity" in so far as the resultant gestalt remains intersubjectively accessible, even though its restrictive determinacy excludes other possibilities, thereby revealing the impenetrability of the reader's subjectivity.

This brings us to an important aspect of the gestalt, which the literary text exploits in order to build up its correlatives in the reader's consciousness. A gestalt closes itself in proportion to the degree in which it resolves the tensions between the signs that are to be grouped. This is also true of gestalt sequences dependent on the *good continuation* principle of coherence. The equivalence of the signs comes about through their reciprocal modification, and this in turn depends on the extent to which expectations are fulfilled. Expectations, however, may lead to the production of illusion, in the sense that our attention is confined to details which we imbue with an overall representative validity. Gombrich is right when he says: Whenever "consistent reading suggests itself ... illusion takes over."[24] Consistency-building itself is not an illusion-making process, but consistency comes about through gestalt groupings, and these contain traces of illusion in so far as their closure—since it is based on selection—is not a characteristic of the text itself, but only represents a configurative meaning.

The importance of illusion to acts of comprehension has been highlighted by Eco, in his description of television viewers' reactions to live transmissions. Here we have a "narrative type which, however coherent and consistent it may seem, always uses for its original material the raw sequence of natural events; here the narrative, even if it has a continual plot-line, is always going off at a tangent in order simply to take note of inessentials."[25] And so in a live transmission—as in the deliberate contingency of some modern films—there is a "frustration of the viewer's 'fictional' instinct."[26]

The course of the live transmission is determined by the specific expectations and demands of the public—a public which, in its demand for a report on events, thinks of these events in terms of the traditional novel, and only recognizes life as real if its contingent elements are removed and it seems to have been selected and united in a plot.... It is only natural that life should be more like *Ulysses* than like *The Three Musketeers*; and yet we are all more inclined to think of it in terms of *The Three Musketeers* than in terms of *Ulysses*—or, rather, I can only remember and judge life if I think of it as a traditional novel.[27]

One might continue the argument by saying that only in memory do we have the degree of freedom necessary, if we are to bring the disordered multiplicity of everyday life into the harmonious form of a coherent gestalt—perhaps because this is the only way we can retain meanings of life. Thus the gestalten of memory extract meaning from and impose order on the natural heterogeneity of life. If this is so, then the traditional realistic novel can no longer be regarded as a mirror-reflection of reality, but is, rather, a paradigm of the structure of memory, since reality can only be retained as reality if it is represented in terms of meaning. This is why the modern novel presents reality as contingent and "meaningless," and in so doing it shows a reaction to conventional habits of perception by releasing reality from the illusion-making structure of memory. This very unmasking of a traditional way of grasping reality must also be represented, however, and so the need for illusion in consistency-building—the precondition for securing uptake—is not even obviated by those texts that resist illusion-making in order to direct our attention to the causes of this resistance.

The illusion element in gestalt-forming is one vital condition for grasping the literary text. "The reader is interested in gaining the necessary information with the least trouble to himself.... And so if the author sets out to increase the number of code systems and the complexity of their structure, the reader will tend to reduce them to what he regards as an acceptable minimum. The tendency to complicate the characters is the author's; the contrastive black-white structure is the reader's."[28]

The Text as an Event

Consistency-building is the indispensable basis for all acts of comprehension, and this in its turn is dependent upon processes of selection. This basic structure is exploited by literary texts in such a way that the reader's imagination can be manipulated and even reoriented. We must now take a closer look at the modes of influence that guide the reader. Walter Pater once wrote, apropos of the experience of reading, "For to the grave reader words too are grave; and the ornamental word, the figure, the accessory form or colour or reference, is rarely content to die to thought precisely at the right moment, but will inevitably linger awhile, stirring a long 'brainwave' behind it of perhaps quite alien associations."[29] Thus consistency-building brings in its wake all those elements that cannot be integrated into the gestalt of the moment. Even in the background-foreground dialectic of the wandering viewpoint, we saw that the interaction and interrelation of textual perspectives leads inevitably to selections in favor of specific connections, for this is the only way in which gestalten can be formed. But selection automatically involves exclusion, and that which has been excluded remains on the fringes as a potential range of connections. It is the reader who unfolds the network of possible connections, and it is the reader who then makes a selection from that network. One of the factors conditioning this selection is that in reading we think the thoughts of another person. Whatever these thoughts may be, they must to a greater or lesser degree represent an unfamiliar experience, containing elements which at any one moment must be partially inaccessible to us. For this reason, our selections tend first to be guided by those parts of the experience that still seem to be familiar. They will influence the gestalt we form, and so we will tend to leave out of account a number of other possibilities which our selective decisions have helped to formulate but have left on the fringes. But these possibilities do not disappear; in principle they always remain present to cast their shadow over the gestalt that has relegated them.

It might be said, then, that the selections we make in reading produce an overflow of possibilities that remain virtual as opposed to actual. These incorporate that section of the unfamiliar experience which is outlined without being brought into focus. From their virtual presence arise the "alien associations" which begin to accumulate and so to bombard the formulated gestalten, which in turn become undermined and thus bring about a reorientation of our acts of apprehension. This is why readers often have the impression that characters and events have undergone a change in significance; we see them "in another light." This means, in fact, that the direction of our selection has changed, because the "alien associations"—i.e., those possibilities that had hitherto remained virtual—have now so modified our earlier gestalten that our attitude has begun to shift.

It is this process that also lends itself to being manipulated by textual strategies. They can be devised in such a way that the range of virtual possibilities—bound to arise out of each selective decision—will be eclipsed during the processing of the text. In such cases, the text takes on a didactic tone. But if the strategies are so organized that they increase the pressure exerted by the "alien associations"—i.e., the equivalence of the signs represented in a gestalt no longer corresponds to the apparent intention—then we have a text in which the original implications of the signs themselves become the objects of critical attention. This is what normally happens with literary texts where gestalten are so formulated as to bring with them the seeds of their own modification or even destruction. This process has a vital bearing on the role of the reader. Through gestalt-forming, we actually participate in the text, and this means that we are caught up in the very thing we are producing. This is why we often have the impression, as we read, that we are living another life. For Henry James, this "illusion of having lived another life"[30] was the most striking quality of narrative prose. It is an illusion because our involvement makes us leave behind that which we are. An "event in which we participate is not knowable apart from our knowledge of our participation in it."[31] Gombrich comes to a similar conclusion in relation to experiments in Gestalt psychology: "... though we may be intellectually aware of the fact that any given experience *must* be an illusion, we cannot, strictly speaking, watch ourselves having an illusion."[32] This entanglement brings out another quality of illusion, different from that which we considered in our discussion of consistency-building. There the illusory factor was that gestalten represented totalities in which possible connections between signs had been sufficiently reduced for the gestalt to be closed. Here illusion means our own projections, which are our share in gestalten which we produce and in which we are entangled. This entanglement, however, is never total, because the gestalten remain at least potentially under attack from those possibilities which they have excluded but dragged along in their wake. Indeed, the latent disturbance of the reader's involvement produces a specific form of tension that leaves him suspended, as it were, between total entanglement and latent detachment. The result is a dialectic—brought about by the reader himself—between illusion-forming and illusion-breaking. It provokes balancing operations, if only because a gestalt that has been undermined by "alien associations" will not immediately fade out of the reckoning; it will continue to have after-effects, and these are necessary if the "alien associations" are to attain their ends. The "conflict" can only be resolved by the emergence of a third dimension, which comes into being through the reader's continual oscillation between involvement and observation. It is in this way that the reader experiences the text as a living event. The event links together all the contrary strands of the gestalten, and it takes on its essential openness by making manifest those possibilities which had been excluded by the selection process and which now exert their influence on these closed gestalten. The experience of the text as an event is an essential correlative of the text; it arises out of the manner in which the strategies disrupt consistency-building, and by thus opening the potential range and interaction of gestalten, it enables the reader to dwell in the living world into which he has transmuted the text.

These balancing operations have been described by B. Ritchie, with reference to the nature of expectations. From the very beginning, each text arouses particular expectations, proceeds then to change these, or sometimes fulfills them at a time when we have long since ceased to envisage their fulfillment and have already lost sight of them altogether.

> Furthermore, to say merely that our "expectations are satisfied" is to be guilty of another serious ambiguity. At first sight such a statement seems to deny the obvious fact that much of our enjoyment is derived from surprises, from betrayals of our expectations. The solution of this paradox is to find some ground for a distinction between "surprise" and "frustration." Roughly, the distinction can be made in terms of the effects which the two kinds of experiences have upon us. Frustration blocks or checks activity. It necessitates new orientation for our activity, if we are to escape the *cul de sac*. Consequently, we abandon the frustrating object and return to blind impulsive activity. On the other hand, surprise merely causes a temporary cessation of the exploratory phase of the experience, and a recourse to intense contemplation and scrutiny. In the latter phase the surprising elements are seen in their connection with what has gone before, with the whole drift of the experience, and the enjoyment of these values is then extremely intense. Finally, it appears that there must always be some degree of novelty or surprise in all these values if there is a progressive specification of the direction of the total act … and any aesthetic experience tends to exhibit a continuous interplay between "deductive" and "inductive" operation.[33]

It follows that the meaning of the text does not reside in the expectations, surprises, disappointments or frustrations that we experience during the process of gestalt-forming. These are simply the reactions that take place when the gestalten are disturbed. What this really means, though, is that as we read, we react to what we ourselves have produced, and it is this mode of reaction that, in fact, enables us to experience the text as an actual event. We do not grasp it like an empirical object; nor do we comprehend it like a predicative fact; it owes its presence in our minds to our own reactions, and it is these that make us animate the meaning of the text as a reality.

Involvement as a Condition of Experience

The event-correlative of the text arises out of a gestalt-forming process in which the individual gestalt is both a unit and a transition. A basic element of this process is the fact that each gestalt bears with it those possibilities which it has excluded but which may eventually invalidate it. This is the way in which the literary text exploits the consistency-building habit which underlies all comprehension. But as the excluded possibilities become more and more obtrusive, so they may come more and more to take on the status of alternatives rather than fringe influences. In everyday language we call these alternatives ambiguities, by which we mean not just the disturbance but also the hindrance of the consistency-building process. This hindrance is particularly noticeable when the ambiguity is brought about by our own gestalt-forming, for then it is not merely the product of the printed text but that of our own activity. Obvious textual ambiguities are like a puzzle which we have to solve ourselves; ambiguities arising from our own gestalt-forming, however, stimulate us into trying to balance all the more intensively the contradictions that we have produced. Just as the reciprocal disturbance of the gestalten brings about the dimension of the event, in which illusion-building and illusion-breaking are integrated, here too we have a need for integration. What, though, is the effect of this intensified struggle for balance?

This question might best be answered by taking a relatively straight-forward example from Joyce's *Ulysses*. There is a passage which induces the reader to compare Bloom's cigar to Ulysses's spear. The spear is evoked as a specific part of the Homeric repertoire, but is equated with the cigar as if they were two things of a kind. The very fact that we equate them causes us to be aware of their differences, and so to wonder why they should have been linked together. Our answer may be that the equation is ironic—at least that is how many reputable Joyce critics have interpreted the passage.[34] Irony would then be the gestalt through which the reader would identify the connection between the signs. But what exactly is the recipient of this ironic treatment—Ulysses's spear, or Bloom's cigar? The lack of clarity already poses a threat to the gestalt of irony. But even if irony does appear to endow the equation with the necessary consistency, this irony is of a peculiar nature. After all, irony normally leads us to the conclusion that the meaning is precisely the opposite of what is formulated in the text, but such an intention is not evident here. At best we might say that here the formulated text means something that has not been formulated, but perhaps it may even mean something that lies beyond a "formulated" irony, though this irony may be, as it were, a stepping-stone to such an interpretation. Whatever may be the significance of the equation, it is clear that the consistency vital for comprehension will bear with it a discrepancy. This will be more than just an excluded or nonselected possibility, because in this case the discrepancy has the effect, not just of disturbing a formulated gestalt but of showing up its inadequacy. Instead of being modified or replaced, it becomes itself an object of scrutiny, because it seems to lack the motivation necessary for an equivalence of signs to be found.

This, of course, does not mean that it is pointless to formulate such inadequate gestalten. On the contrary, their very inadequacy will stimulate the reader into searching for another gestalt to represent the connection between the signs—and, indeed, he may do so precisely because he has been unable to stick to the original, most obvious gestalt. Again we may illustrate this with reference to the Joyce example. Many readers have tried to smooth out the discrepancy of the irony gestalt by taking the phallus as the connection between the signs. As far as the spear is concerned the equation seems to work, both in terms of tradition and mythological dignity; but we must also incorporate the cigar into our gestalt. The cigar, however, jerks the imagination onto so many different planes that it not only shatters the mythological paradigm but also explodes the gestalt. The apparent consistency now fragments itself into the various associations of the individual reader's imagination. But as he indulges in these associations he will become more and more subjected to the influence of the discarded irony gestalt, which now returns to belittle every product of the gestalt-forming imagination. In such cases, the vital process of consistency-building is used to make the reader himself produce discrepancies, and as he becomes aware of both the discrepancies and the processes that have produced them, so he becomes more and more entangled in the text.

Such processes certainly occur more frequently in modern than in older literature. However, throughout the history of narrative prose, certain literary devices have been built into the structure of the work in order to stimulate the production of discrepancies. From Cervantes to Fielding, we find the interpolated story that functions as a reversal of the main action, so that gestalten are formed by way of an undermining interaction between plot and subplot. This brings to the fore hitherto concealed possibilities, which in turn produce a configurative meaning. In the nineteenth century, the traditional narrator frequently assumes the character of an *unreliable narrator* who either openly or indirectly disputes the judgments of the *implied author*.[35] Conrad's *Lord Jim* (1900) introduced divergent textual perspectives which resist integration and so devalue their own individual authenticity. Joyce then split up the textual perspectives and intermingled them in such a way as to prevent the reader from ever gaining a single reliable vantage point. And, finally, Beckett has devised a sentence structure in which each statement is followed by a negation, which itself is a statement eliciting further negations in a unending process that leads the reader to search for the key, which becomes more and more elusive.

What all these techniques of inversion have in common is the fact that the discrepancies produced by the reader make him dispute his own gestalten. He tries to balance out these discrepancies, but the questionable gestalt which was the starting-point for this operation remains as a challenge in the face of which the newly attempted integration has to prove itself. This whole process takes place within the reader's imagination, so that he cannot escape from it. This involvement, or entanglement, is what places us in the "presentness" of the text and what makes the text into a presence for us. "In so far as there is entanglement, there is also presence."[36]

This entanglement entails several effects at the same time. While we are caught up in a text, we do not at first know what is happening to us. This is why we often feel the need to talk about books we have read—not in order to gain some distance from them so much as to find out just what it is that we were entangled in. Even literary critics frequently do no more than seek to translate their entanglement into referential language. As our presence in the text depends upon this involvement, it represents a correlative of the text in the mind, which is a necessary complement to the event-correlative. But when we are present in an event, something must happen to us. The more "present" the text is to us, the more our habitual selves—at least for the duration of the reading—recede into the "past." The literary text relegates our own prevailing views into the past by itself becoming a present experience, for what is now happening or may happen was not possible so long as our characteristic views formed our present.

Now experiences do not come about merely through the recognition of the familiar. "It is true that we should never talk about anything if we were limited to talking about those experiences with which we coincide."[37] Experiences arise only when the familiar is transcended or undermined; they grow out of the alteration or falsification of that which is already ours. Shaw once wrote: "You have learnt something. That always feels at first as if you had lost something."[38] Reading has the same structure as experience, to the extent that our entanglement has the effect of pushing our various criteria of orientation back into the past, thus suspending their validity for the new present. This does not mean, however, that these criteria or our previous experiences disappear altogether. On the contrary, our past still remains our experience, but what happens now is that it begins to interact with the as yet unfamiliar presence of the text. This remains unfamiliar so long as our previous experiences are precisely as they had been before we began our reading. But in the course of the reading, these experiences will also change, for the acquisition of experience is not a matter of adding on—it is a restructuring of what we already possess. This can be seen even on an everyday level; we say, for instance, that we have benefited from an experience when we mean that we have lost an illusion.

Through the experience of the text, then, something happens to our own store of experience. This cannot remain unaffected, because our presence in the text does not come about merely through recognition of what we already know. Of course, the text does contain a good deal of familiar material, but this usually serves not as a confirmation, but as a basis out of which the new experience is to be forged. The familiar is only momentarily so, and its significance is to change in the course of our reading. The more frequent these "moments" are, the clearer will be the interaction between the present text and our past experience. What is the nature of this interaction? "The junction of the new and old is not a mere composition of forces, but a re-creation in which the present impulsion gets form and solidity while the old, the 'stored,' material is literally revived, given new life and soul through having to meet a new situation."[39] For our purposes, Dewey's description is revealing in two respects: first, as an account of the interaction itself, and second as showing the actual effects of this interaction. The new experience emerges from the restructuring of the one we have stored, and this restructuring is what gives the new experience its form. But what actually happens during this process can again only be experienced when past feelings, views, and values have been evoked and then made to merge with the new experience. The old conditions the form of the new, and the new selectively restructures the old. The reader's reception of the text is not based on identifying two different experiences (old versus new), but on the interaction between the two.

This interrelationship applies to the structure of experience in general, but it does not in itself manifest any aesthetic qualities. Dewey tries to bring out the aesthetic element of the structure with two different arguments: "That which distinguishes an experience as esthetic is conversion of resistance and tensions, of excitations that in themselves are temptations to diversion, into a movement toward an inclusive and fulfilling close.... An object is peculiarly and predominantly esthetic, yielding the enjoyment characteristic of esthetic perception, when the factors that determine anything which can be called an experience are lifted high above the threshold of perception and are made manifest for their own sake."[40]

The first argument accords with the views of the Russian formalists, who regarded the prolongation of perception as a central criterion for aesthetic experience. Dewey's other argument is that aesthetic experience differs from ordinary experience because the interacting factors become a theme in themselves. In other words, aesthetic experience makes us conscious of the acquisition of experience and is accompanied by continual insight into the conditions that give rise to it. This endows the aesthetic experience with a transcendental character. While the structure of everyday experience leads to pragmatic action, that of aesthetic experience serves to reveal the workings of this process. Its totality lies not so much in the new experience brought about by interaction, as in the insight gained into the formation of such a totality. Why this is so is explained by Dewey as being due to the nonpragmatic nature of art.

Now Dewey's observations may be developed along a different line. Apprehension of a literary work comes about through the interaction between the reader's presence in the text and his habitual experiences, which are now a past orientation. As such it is not a passive process of acceptance, but a productive response. This reaction generally transcends the reader's previous range of orientation, and so the question arises as to what actually controls his reaction. It cannot be any prevailing code and it cannot be his past experience, for both are transcended by the aesthetic experience. It is at this point that the discrepancies produced by the reader during the gestalt-forming process take on their true significance. They have the effect of enabling the reader actually to become aware of the inadequacy of the gestalten he has produced, so that he may detach himself from his own participation in the text and see himself being guided from without. The ability to perceive oneself during the process of participation is an essential quality of the aesthetic experience; the observer finds himself in a strange, halfway position: he is involved, and he watches himself being involved. However, this position is not entirely nonpragmatic, for it can only come about when existing codes are transcended or invalidated. The resultant restructuring of stored experiences makes the reader aware not only of the experience but also of the means whereby it develops. Only the controlled observation of that which is instigated by the text makes it possible for the reader to formulate a reference for what he is restructuring. Herein lies the practical relevance of aesthetic experience: it induces this observation, which takes the place of codes that otherwise would be essential for the success of communication.

Notes

1. See Manfred Naumann et al., *Gesellschaft—Literatur—Lesen. Literaturrezeption in theoretischer Sicht* (Berlin and Weimar, 1973), p. 35.

2. Laurence Sterne, *Tristram Shandy II*, 11 (Everyman's Library; London, 1956), p. 79.

3. J. P. Sartre, *Was ist Literatur?* (rde 65), transl. by Hans Georg Brenner (Hamburg, 1958), p. 35.

4. Ibid., pp. 27f.

5. See I. M. Schlesinger, *Sentence Structure and the Reading Process* (The Hague, 1968), pp. 27ff. The similarity between and indeed congruence of the "eye-voice span" and the span of short-term memory has been demonstrated with psycholinguistic experiments by Frank Smith, *Understanding Reading. A Psycholinguistic Analysis of Reading and Learning to Read* (New York, 1971), pp. 196–200. His book also contains important observations on the part played by the "eye-voice span" in "identification of meaning."

6. Schlesinger, *Sentence Structure*, p. 42; see also Ronald Wardhaugh, *Reading: A Linguistic Perspective* (New York, 1969), p. 54.

7. Roman Ingarden, *The Cognition of the Literary Work of Art*, transl. by Ruth Ann Crowley and Kenneth R. Olson (Evanston, 1973), p. 31.

8. Edmund Husserl, *Zur Phänomenologie des inneren Zeitbewußtseins*, Gesammelte werke X (The Hague, 1966), p. 52.

9. Ingarden, *Cognition*, p. 34.

10. For a closer description of this function, see C. F. Graumann, *Motivation. Einführung in die Psychologie I* (Berne and Stuttgart, 1971), p. 118.

11. For further details, and also for the premises underlying the following argument, see my book *The Implied Reader: Patterns of Communication in Prose Fiction from Bunyan to Beckett* (Baltimore and London, 2 1975), pp. 108ff.

12. Smith, *Understanding Reading*, pp. 185ff., uses psycholinguistic experiments to show the extent to which differences and contrasts in the reading process itself have to be discovered and stabilized.

13. Michel Butor, *Répertoire II*, transl. by H. Scheffel (Munich, 1965), p. 98.

14. Smith, *Understanding Reading*, p. 113.

15. E. H. Gombrich, *Art and Illusion* (London, 2 1962), p. 204.

16. Abraham A. Moles, *Informationstheorie und ästhetische Wahrnehmung*, transl. by H. Ronge et al. (Cologne, 1971), p. 59.

17. Smith *Understanding Reading*, p. 185.

18. See Moles, *Informationstheorie*, pp. 140ff.

19. See Part II, Chap. 3, pp. 65–67.

20. Henry Fielding, *Tom Jones* I, 2 (Everyman's Library; London, 1962), p. 3.

21. Ibid., I, 10, p. 26.

22. See Aron Gurwitsch, *The Field of Consciousness* (Pittsburgh, 1963), pp. 175ff.; he develops this concept in conjunction with Husserl's concept of the *sense of perception*.

23. Sartre, *Was ist Literatur?*, p. 29; see also Pierre Bourdieu, *Zur Soziologie der Symbolischen Formen* (stw 107), transl. by Wolfgang Fietkau (Frankfort, 1974), pp. 165, 169.

24. Gombrich, *Art and Illusion*, p. 278.

25. Umberto Eco, *Das offene Kunstwerk*, transl. by G. Memmert (Frankfort, 1973), p. 202.

26. Ibid., p. 203.

27. Ibid., p. 206.

28. Ju. M. Lotman, *Die Struktur literarischer Texte* (UTB 103), transl. by Rolf Dietrich Keil (Munich, 1972), pp. 418f.

29. Walter Pater, *Appreciations* (London, 1920), p. 18.

30. Henry James, *Theory of Fiction*, James E. Miller, Jr., ed. (Lincoln, Nebraska, 1972), p. 93. The exact quotation reads: "The success of a work of art … may be measured by the degree to which it produces a certain illusion; that illusion makes it appear to us for the time that we have lived another life—that we have had a miraculous enlargement of experience." The statement was made in 1883.

31. Stanley Cavell, *The World Viewed* (New York, 1971), p. 128.

32. Gombrich, *Art and Illusion*, p. 5.

33. Benbow Ritchie, "The Formal Structure of the Aesthetic Object," in *The Problems of Aesthetics*, Eliseo Vivas and Murray Krieger, eds. (New York, 1965), pp. 230f.

34. Richard Ellmann, "Ulysses. The Divine Nobody," in *Twelve Original Essays on Great English Novels*, Charles Shapiro, ed. (Detroit, 1960), p. 247, calls this allusion "mock-heroic."

35. See Wayne C. Booth, *The Rhetoric of Fiction* (Chicago, 4 1963), pp. 2llff., 339ff.

36. Wilhelm Schapp, *In Geschichten verstrickt* (Hamburg, 1953), p. 143.

37. Maunce Merleau-Ponty, *Phenomenology of Perception*, transl. by Colin Smith (New York, 1962), p. 337.

38. G. B. Shaw, *Major Barbara* (London, 1964), p. 316.

39. John Dewey, *Art as Experience* (New York, 12 1958), p. 60.

40. Ibid., pp. 56f.; see also p. 272. Eliseo Vivas, *Creation and Discovery* (Chicago, 1955), p. 146, describes the aesthetic experience as follows: "Grounded on this assumption the aesthetic experience can be defined, I submit, in terms of attention. The advantages of such a definition are manifold, and the only difficulty it presents is the rather easy task of distinguishing *aesthetic* attention from that involved in other modes of experience. A brief statement of such definition would read as follows: *An aesthetic experience is an experience of rapt attention which involves the intransitive apprehension of an object's immanent meanings and values in their full presentational immediacy.*"

12 Wolfgang Iser and the Reader as Creator

Melanie Feinberg

When a work of fiction resonates, many of us will read that book again, perhaps many times over the course of our lives. Although we know full well that, for example, Elizabeth and Mr. Darcy will end up together in perfect happiness, we don't find it dull to read *Pride and Prejudice* for the twenty-eighth time. How can we read a work over and over and still be delighted by it, and even find fresh aspects to engage with, or come to reconsider other elements? (When I first read Austen's novel, I scorned Elizabeth's heedless younger sister Lydia and her scandalous, selfish actions, but now I find Lydia tragic.) In contrast, there's no fun in redoing a puzzle once you've figured it out. After I finish today's *New York Times* crossword, I'll toss it away and not think about it again, but I'll never be "done" with *Pride and Prejudice* like that, no matter how many times I "finish" reading it. There must be more to one's engagement with a beloved novel—with reading fiction—than merely finding an answer, or pulling an ultimate meaning out of a set of symbols.

Literary theorist Wolfgang Iser is associated with the reader-response school of interpretation, which rejects the notion that the reader is a passive consumer who merely decodes content that was already there "in" the text. Instead, reader-response focuses on the active and creative meaning-making demanded of the reader. Iser attempts to understand literature as a structure through which a particular sort of active reading is generated on each encounter with the text. A novel, for Iser, is a set of governing rules against which each reader, for every reading, weaves a tapestry of meanings, and, ultimately, significance. The structure provided by the text supports, guides, and constrains the reader's process, but ultimately, Iser asserts, "the reader's enjoyment begins … when the text allows him to bring his own faculties into play," connecting and internally commenting on the novel's elements (Iser, 1978, chapter 11). The quality of this interaction, for Iser, is distinctive. Certainly a puzzle demands interaction as well, but its scope is more clearly bounded. A crossword has a single correct answer for each clue, and the puzzle doesn't encourage its solver to find some larger significance beyond that answer, as *Pride and Prejudice* might encourage us to think beyond the details of how Elizabeth acts and thinks about the various events of her life to ask about how class and wealth figure into our own determinations of a person's worth. In contrast, a work of fiction sketches part of the world of the story and requires the reader to fill in the rest, spurring a creative response. More, the text supports multiple avenues of attention from the reader and diverse conclusions. (With equal consideration of the textual evidence, one might scorn or sympathize with Lydia, and take from that appraisal further ideas about personal and social responsibility.)

This chapter introduces Iser's work and provides a sense of how his ideas about literature can be productively applied in the HCI context. First, I illustrate Iser's approach to textual interpretation and its potential application to HCI through an extended example taken from Daniela Rosner and Kimiko Ryokai's discussion of their Spyn project (2008; 2010). I apply Iser's conceptual apparatus to the parody Twitter account @ElBloombito as a complementary example to Spyn. Next, I explicate the Iser chapter "Grasping a Text" (chapter 11, this book), from his book the *The Act of Reading* (1978), continuing to use Spyn as an example to demonstrate the extension of Iser's work to HCI. I conclude by suggesting how HCI might design systems that orient themselves toward an Iserian idea of "active reading."

Textual Interpretation and Spyn

To understand how Iser's perspective on literature can illuminate qualities of human-computer interaction from a user's, or reader's, point of view, I begin with Rosner and Ryokai's Spyn project (2008; 2010). The hybrid knitted/digital products that users create with Spyn demonstrate the potential for interactive artifacts to embody the rich interpretive environment of fiction, and so illustrate the utility of Iser's approach in understanding the work of HCI. Spyn provides a means to augment knitted artifacts with various forms of automatically generated and explicitly crafted metadata, as a contrasting example to literary references such as *Pride and Prejudice*. With Spyn, captured images of knitting projects, along with computer vision techniques, enable knitters to embed a variety of annotations into their knitted products. In several prototype deployments, knitters used Spyn to attach annotations, including images, text, video, and audio, with particular locations in the knitted fabric, as represented through captured images of the knit. These memory points were also associated with data automatically captured by Spyn, such as the location on the knit fabric, the GPS location where knitting occurred, and the time of annotation. The knitted artifact could be used as any knitted item might be used (that is, worn, if it were a sweater or a scarf), and also read, through its visual representation and associated annotations via Spyn. In the prototype deployments, Spyn users integrated many types of information with their knits. Annotation content was associated with the intended recipient of the item (such as an accompanying video of baking cookies, another item that the knitter meant for the recipient to associate with the warmth of home), with the knitter and the knitting process (such as details of the knitter's life occasioned by images of the locations where the knitting took place or reflections spurred by mistakes such as skipped stitches), and with the knitted artifact itself (rationale behind decisions such as choice of yarn, or cultural associations behind the selection of particular patterns and decorative motifs).

Jane's Text

In the third deployment of Spyn, knitters completed gift projects that were then presented to recipients, and Rosner and Ryokai (2010) describe the reactions of the recipients to the knits augmented by Spyn, as well as the reflections of the creators as they developed their Spyn gifts. These examples lend themselves well to interpretation in the mode of Iser and reader response. In one case, the creator, "Jane," used Spyn to overlay a puzzle with a hidden message onto the knit artifact. Unlike my *Times* crossword, however, this puzzle served as the framework for an encompassing story. The unraveling of the puzzle was a mechanism that led not only to the text of the "secret message," but also a deeper story about Jane, her craft process, and her inventiveness, and the anticipated appreciation of her craft by the recipient, "Victor," himself a knitter. Victor described the experience of reading the Spyn artifact as a "4D" project, where another dimension has been added to the typical knit artifact. In this use of Spyn, Victor's delight in the knit presented to him arises when his background knowledge of Jane, of knitting, and of his relationship with Jane is actively put to work in making sense of and appreciating—or reading—the augmented artifact as a form of experiential text, in which the puzzle works as both content and interface, or the means through which the story is generated. An Iserian analysis of this Spyn knit extends the basic premise of constructivism—that Victor can make sense of Jane's gift because both are members of the community of knitters—to focus on the ways that the artifact itself structures Victor's interaction with it and his subsequent interpretation. Just as, when reading a novel, we might at the same time consider not only the substance of a story but also the means by which that story was produced, causing us to reflect on potential alternate possibilities for the story, Victor's interpretation of the Spyn artifact is instigated not only through Jane's story itself, but also through the means by which Jane produced it. It is through this concurrent examination of the designer's choices with the design experience that Victor is able to understand not just what the Spyn artifact "says" (the literal message that Jane embedded for him) but to contemplate what the activity of knitting, as well as the knit product, might be.

This active reading process is highlighted even further when we contemplate how someone other than the intended recipient might comprehend Jane's annotated knit. If we see Jane and Victor as two characters whose partial story is expressed through the Spyn project, then elements of Iser's view of reading become even more salient. In attempting to read and understand the significance of Jane and Victor's story, the reader may engage with broader issues of friendship, memory, gift-giving, and craft, via Iser's notion of the imaginary—the space of interpretive possibility and alternate reality that opens up when readers are drawn to actively consider not only the story itself, but the means through which the author conveys the story world's various elements.

In the Spyn context, the additional character of the automatically generated metadata contributes to the story world, too, functioning as a kind of omniscient, limited narrator, and adding an additional perspective to the tale.

Irene's Text

The Spyn project that creator "Irene" began for her new boyfriend "Uri" further illustrates how a memory-oriented system like Spyn can attain qualities more often associated with fictional worlds. Irene and Uri broke up during the Spyn deployment period, and Irene initially stops work on the project, as she will no longer give it to Uri. However, Irene finds herself going back to both the scarf and its annotations, unable to detach the scarf from Spyn and give it to another friend, without its previously associated metadata focused on Uri. As reported by Rosner and Ryokai, Irene's abandoned project, with its final Spyn message, "can't seem to figure out what to do," becomes a complex, multilayered tale of romantic loss, with various entwined characters: Irene, the absent Uri, the potential substitute recipient, a narrator represented by automatically generated metadata, and ultimately the Spyn system itself as the focus of Irene's final lament. Moreover, this is the kind of story that supports, even in skeletal form, multiple interpretations and embellishments in the reader's imagination, and ultimately multiple pathways to significance. Via such a story as this, one might ponder on what basis we assign value to objects, or reconsider the role of authorial intention in understanding texts, or the nature of romantic attachment and its progress: how distressed can one really be about the demise of a relationship that only lasted a few weeks? That doesn't seem realistic. Wait, this is real! Or is it? What does "real" mean here?

If we as HCI practitioners, researchers, and designers can "read" the artifacts that we create in this sort of way, then we can better understand the expressive and cultural aspects of human-computer interaction, in addition to the functional aspects. We don't read literature merely to extract a basic plot summary; we read literature for its entire immersive experience. Iser's approach provides a set of insightful concepts to describe that reading experience and the interpretive process through which this experience unfolds. Similarly, the experience of interactive artifacts comprises more than basic functions. An Iser-inspired approach to understanding interactive artifacts makes use of Iser's literary concepts to describe additional levels of user experience, and the interpretive process through which this experience unfolds.

Iser's Imaginary: Where Readers (and Users) Experiment with Interpretive Possibilities

As briefly referenced earlier, in Iser's terminology the portion of the literary experience that transpires in the reader's imagination is called "the imaginary" (Iser, 1993). Literature invokes the imaginary by calling attention to itself as a fiction, becoming an object to be observed, contemplated, and imagined as one is experiencing (reading) it. (Iser uses the term "bracketed" here, referring to the philosophical tradition of phenomenology, a school of thought that has also found currency within HCI.) A work of fiction proposes itself as an alternate world (an "as-if condition," in Iser's words) by selecting particular elements from reality, combining those elements in particular ways, and calling attention to these choices as a creative act. This alignment with reality and concurrent embrace of make-believe places the reader both "inside" and "outside" the text at the same time, making the reader an observer of his or her own involvement with the story. One way of establishing this alternate reality state in literature is to juxtapose multiple perspectives on the action, such as those of different characters, of a narrator, and of an implied author. The implied author may be different from the narrator; one might say, for example, that the narrator of *Pride and Prejudice,* in describing Elizabeth's dutiful older sister Jane, finds her the epitome of virtue, but that the implied author, through the selection of Jane's statements and actions, sees Jane's passivity in a less admirable light. The reader merges and assesses these perspectives in the imaginary, creating an interpretation of the text in this process. Moreover, the imaginary is a space of experiment, where the reader can consider the actions of fictional people and events with a freedom that is often thwarted by the constraints of real-word situations. Meaning is enacted as the reader "pragmatizes" the imaginary, or turns it into something practical, something to be taken away from the reading experience.

The creators and recipients in the Spyn prototype deployments are indeed real people, and they inhabit the real world, not a fictional one. But any representation of reality, however true it might be, is nonetheless selective; any memoir, no matter how closely it aligns with real events, is nonetheless an interpretive account that is given shape by the narrative form. Some Spyn creators were conscious of constructing authorial personas, or characters, through the conjunction of annotation and knit artifact; one creator noted that while she could have described life difficulties and challenges via her added metadata, she chose instead to create a more positive and uplifting story for the recipient. As with actual fiction, personal accounts have a sort of acknowledged artificiality about them, enabling their "bracketing" in much the same way that Iser describes for literature, even if we know the author and are the intended audience—but more so if we do not, as when we as outside readers perceive the as-if condition instantiated by Jane's or Irene's Spyn projects. By using Iser's approach to examine and describe the ways that interactive artifacts like Spyn can provoke and structure such interpretive processes for users, we as HCI practitioners and researchers, can better comprehend—and design for—the fullness of potential user experience.

Invoking the Imaginary via Social Media Streams

Social media streams, such as Twitter feeds and Facebook updates, are another example where the line between fictive persona and edited "real" persona becomes blurred, and where a reader—or user—might find herself (or himself) "inside" and "outside" the text at the same time. The popularity of parody social media profiles, which are explicitly fictional, mixed in with "real" ones, contributes to this sense of social media overall as an alternate reality—perhaps not entirely fictional, but not entirely "true," either. One of my favorite such parody profiles was @ElBloombito, the Twitter satire of Michael Bloomberg, mayor of New York City 2002–2014 and poor Spanish speaker. (A sample tweet, making reference to the New York Police Department's controversial "stop and frisk" program, which targeted young men of color for random searches: "If yo could stop y frisko todos los everyone, yo wouldo. Pero yo can't. So soy just stoppingo y frisko los browño personas.") While clearly fake, @ElBloombito was accurate enough to be hilarious, in part because Bloombito, like all good satires, amplified characteristics noted in the real person: in this case, brusqueness, autocratic tendencies, and immense personal wealth. In contrast, the "real" profile of Michael Bloomberg, @MikeBloomberg, sounded like it was written by a public relations staff and had no personality whatsoever. (A sample tweet: "Immigrants make up 37% of NYC's population and are key to growing our economy and flourishing communities.") On Twitter, the line between a "fictional" profile like @ElBloombito and a "real" profile, like @MikeBloomberg, becomes indistinct. The parody profile—the fictional one—"sounds real" from a certain perspective; the actual profile, on the other hand, seems fake.

Where a system like Spyn might invoke Iser's imaginary in an even stronger and more interesting way than a social media environment like Twitter is through the conjunction of multiple data sources, including not only the knit artifact but the automatically generated data about it. The commentary on the "action" of the knit artifact and creator-authored annotations provided by the automatic metadata provides a form of narration outside the characters, a form of implied author that provokes the merging of perspectives and potential experiment that Iser describes for the imaginary. Too, a system like Spyn implicates multiple readers in its ecology, and these readers are also characters of a sort: there is the creator, who is also "reading" the system in using it to create the knit artifact; the recipient for whom the artifact is explicitly prepared; and other readers, who are outside the creator-recipient relationship but can nonetheless experience the knit artifact through Spyn. When any of these readers interacts with the artifact through Spyn, the absent other readers may be called to mind in the imaginary.

The Dynamic, Emergent Interaction Experience

Not every Spyn user will engage the same set of characters. Likewise, Iser emphasizes that a literary text will support many decision paths toward potential meanings. An array of contextual factors might suggest certain paths instead of others, such as theories of literary interpretation, expectations from reading similar texts, knowledge of a text's placement within literary traditions, personal values and beliefs, and so on. This is why a text can produce many readings; interpretation is a process carried out at a specific time, making it historical and ephemeral. The interpretation of literature is an event that each reader participates in. It is not a fact to be discovered for once and for all, like the answer to a riddle. More, the indeterminate nature of this process is enjoyable. While I don't expect to reevaluate my ideas about Lydia when I reread *Pride and Prejudice*, doing so causes pleasure at finding something new, not dismay that my previous readings were "wrong." Iser isn't saying that literature should be confusingly dense, or that good literature is difficult to understand. He's saying that different people will find different meanings in it at different times. (These ideas align with work in HCI that endorses goals of ambiguity and open interpretation in design, such as Gaver et al., 2003, and Sengers and Gaver, 2006.)

Similarly, Spyn seems quite simple to use and understand, for both creators and recipients; at the same time, the system is plastic enough that it can be used in many unanticipated ways, and any user's understanding might change over time. For example, one of the Spyn creators decided to unravel a partially finished hat project and start again using a new color, as inspired by a recent conversation with the hat's recipient. This creator realized that she could document the decision to rip and rework with Spyn, using the Spyn features to create a story of what was no longer there, as well as what was actually knitted. This creator (here, as a user of Spyn, in the "reader" role) came to understand Spyn as a system differently—that it could tell stories of nonexistent items as well as existing ones.

Social media, as well, is quite simple to use, and yet it too can support complex interpretation over time. When I first discovered the tweets of the parody @ElBloombito, I merely laughed at them. But over time, especially as the tweets piled up and became cited by many others, I began to reconsider @ElBloombito: Was I laughing at the wealthy mayor of New York and his white privilege, or was my laughter indulging my own white privilege? Indeed, it was probably both. I began to think more closely about myself and even about the parody tweet as a form of commentary, with its reliance on a very particular online audience. I still laugh at @ElBloombito, but I notice what drives my laughter, and I see the parody's significance differently: it is a parody of me, the reader, as well as of the New York mayor.

A Dialogic Approach to Meaning-making

It is in this way that, although Iser directs his work specifically toward literature as a unique form of expression, I find his characterization of the reader-text dialogue to productively inform my sense of meaning-making through interactive artifacts. Iser's depiction of reading identifies the work of fiction as the site where multiple actants encounter each other: author, reader, literary tradition, historical situation. (Criticism often takes on one or more of these perspectives; see Bardzell, 2011, and Bertelsen and Pold, 2004, for work that explores interaction criticism in relation to more established critical traditions from other disciplines.) The literary text nurtures what is ultimately a collaborative, creative act of meaning production and new understanding. Certainly this is an idealized view: an author may, consciously or no, write a piece that manipulates a reader toward certain ends, perhaps directly oppressive ones. Austen's delightful character of Elizabeth, for example, can be seen as encouraging the reader to believe that only slight modifications to a hierarchical social order are enough for the worthy to prevail and happiness ensue, upholding what is essentially an entrenched system of inequality. However, while the author, in Iser's characterization, sets the stage, the reader controls the final action, and the literary text supports this through its quality of being both immersive and the object of reflection at the same time. Correspondingly, I feel that embracing my agency as a reader facilitates my concurrent acceptance of accountability as an author (or designer). I don't "consume" a novel like *Pride and Prejudice;* I creatively produce its meaning as an active reader, and that's why I continue to read and enjoy it. As a designer, when I think of my audience as a reader, and not as a user or consumer, I feel empowered to acknowledge and pursue my own interests in design. Similarly to how an author can seem to endorse or condemn a character's actions, I can endorse or condemn a particular practice enabled through an interactive artifact; the reader may come to a different conclusion in either case. But just as the literary work calls attention to itself as a work of fiction, and so enables its contemplation within the reader's imagination, so might the interactive artifact call attention to itself as a type of fiction, as a contingent transformation of practice, so that it too can be contemplated in the reader's imagination.

Grasping HCI

In the selection included here, "Grasping a Text," a chapter from his book *The Act of Reading*, Iser describes the interaction between reader and literary work. *The Act of Reading* outlines Iser's response theory as a mode of literary interpretation. Iser's notion of response proceeds from consideration of the ideal reader implied by the structure of a literary text, and the actions that the text makes available to the reader. Accordingly, the reader's experience, for Iser, is best understood through a particular approach toward the text itself—that is, through a mode of reading the text that surfaces the potential reader experience, and not through the reported particular experiences of actual readers, which are inevitably only partial. "Grasping a Text" provides the core concepts that inform Iser's reading method: the idea of the wandering viewpoint, where elements of the story build over time; the notion of intersubjective comprehensibility, or acceptance of the rationale for particular interpretations; and the ways that reader agency interacts with the structure of a text over time to produce a range of potential, equally valid, interpretations.

HCI researchers and practitioners can also use these concepts to examine the interpretive potential of interactive artifacts, and so to more fully describe the interpretive component of user experience. The following paragraphs outline Iser's argument in

"Grasping a Text" and show how its approach can help us to "read" interactive artifacts and understand how they work a form of expressive text, using Spyn as a continuing example.

The Wandering Viewpoint

In framing the chapter, Iser notes that the text must supply enough, but not too much, guidance: in achieving this delicate balance, a successful work of fiction encourages the reader to participate in the creative process. Time is a key element here. Iser uses the term "wandering viewpoint" to emphasize that a literary text, unlike a painting or a statue, cannot be perceived all at once, but only in parts over time. (Of course, we do not understand a painting all at once, but we can see the whole expanse in one look, whereas we cannot do this with a novel. A novel may take days or weeks to merely "get through," just in terms of the physical process of reading the words.) Each sentence, as it is read, "set[s] in motion a process which will lead to the formation of the aesthetic object as a correlative in the mind of the reader" (Iser, 1978, 110). A sentence can confirm expectations set by previous sentences (or expectations from other sources, such as genre conventions) or it can modify or upend those expectations. In literature, the "correlates" tend toward such modification, perhaps causing the reader to reexamine what has come before. (Does Elizabeth really hate Mr. Darcy, as she claims, or does she actually like him?) The realm of expectations and potentially refigured memories is in the mind of the reader, not the text itself, although the text suggests certain perspectives through which it might be perceived. The use of the term "horizon" throughout the chapter refers to both the reader's perspective through which the text is filtered and the potential perspectives offered through the text. The philosopher Hans-Georg Gadamer ([1960] 2004) describes interpretation as a fusing of horizons, an integration of the author's perspective (as perceived through the text) with the reader's horizon, as formed against an evolving background of what we understand literature to be. (There is no understanding of art, according to Gadamer, without a previous sense of what art might be; while our current interpretations might react against this tradition, we cannot begin outside our existing understandings.)

Iser asserts that although each reader may notice different elements of meaning in the text and recall different past elements when synthesizing material at a particular point in the reading process, the suppositions and connections that the reader makes are "intersubjectively comprehensible" if they are not "intersubjectively identical"; a text can be interpreted many ways, but all interpretations are "attempts to optimize the same structure" (Iser, 1973, 118). A valid reading, in other words, must be comprehensible on explanation; it must align with the text, even as it is not limited to the text. I can't base my interpretation of *Pride and Prejudice* on a misunderstanding of its events; for example, I cannot claim that the character of Elizabeth finds her mother, Mrs. Bennet, to be wise, when Elizabeth finds her mother to be silly. That interpretation would not be intersubjectively comprehensible. But I might use other elements of the text to suggest that Mrs. Bennet is wiser than Elizabeth gives her credit for. Although this interpretation might be uncommon, it is still valid if I can show how it emanates from the "same structure" that we are all reading.

Intersubjective Comprehensibility in HCI

While digital artifacts are typically experienced gradually over time, similarly to literature, there are also significant differences in the basic interaction experience. Except in certain experimental forms, such as hypertext, literature has a linear flow, and all readers follow the same path through a work, even as they might interpret the text differently. This linearity is rare for digital artifacts, and elements cannot build on each other in the same way as sentences in a novel can. Indeed, for many digital artifacts, a user may never experience all possible content, or all possible actions that can be performed. Even with the simple Spyn system, some creators in the prototype deployment, as documented by Rosner and Ryokai, didn't use features associated with managing multiple projects, for example, and most social media users will only interact with a tiny portion of the potential environment—no person could read all possible tweets. This fragmentation leads the new media scholar Lev Manovich to argue that the linear form of a narrative and the random-access form of the database are as enemies (Manovich, 2001). However, I would nonetheless propose that, although progress through the "texts" of digital artifacts is unpredictable, users do form expectations in a manner similar to that described by Iser as they interact with digital systems. Instead of one sentence building on another, it is perhaps more apt in the HCI context to think of one action building on another, leading to the construction of an experiential world, analogous to the story world, in the mind of the active user, or reader. Some of these actions confirm expectations set by previous actions. The process of adding a new memory annotation in Spyn is always the same. This confirmation of the program's behavior may lead to a confirmation of the user's relationship with the program, and, accordingly, a consistent sense of the program's creative possibilities, in a way that is similar to finding continued evidence for one's interpretation of a literary character in an ongoing text (that Mr. Darcy is such an arrogant jerk!). In the Spyn deployment, some creators used these annotations consistently throughout their making process, for example to mark their progress through sections of the knit. Some actions modify expectations, perhaps as the result of reflection. Rosner and Ryokai describe how some creators began thinking of their recipients much more actively during the knitting process, as a result of marking memory pins with Spyn. They began to feel as if they were in conversation with the recipients throughout the process, and that the Spyn annotations were a means to explore and extend this imagined conversation. These Spyn users began to think somewhat differently about their relationships with Spyn, with the knitted artifact, and with the recipient, which opened up an extended sense of the program's capabilities, and even with the activity of knitting itself. This has similarities to the way that one might come to reevaluate a literary character as one proceeds through a novel. (Mr. Darcy *is* an arrogant jerk, but he also has integrity and tries to behave morally.) Some actions upend expectations, perhaps when users are beguiled into trying something new. In the Spyn deployment, one creator, "Laura," a writer, surprised herself by using primarily audio in her Spyn annotations, which she had not envisioned. But the audio seemed appropriate for the conversational mode that Laura had entered through the process of interacting with Spyn. Via Spyn, Laura was prompted to reconsider her relationship with audio itself as a means of expression. This is like the experience, in literature, of altering one's impression of previous events based on a new understanding of a character. (Maybe Mr. Darcy isn't quite as arrogant as I had thought; and in fact, maybe when he and Elizabeth first meet, she is kind of an arrogant jerk, too.) I suggest that a form of wandering viewpoint is achieved through the interplay of user actions with different kinds of data in different situations, where the action acts like a kind of sentence—albeit a variable sort of sentence, where the specific values of the words can change, as when we might add different types of annotations to different projects. Even with this variability, though, the actions performed with an interactive system build on each other, in a way that has similarities to the way that sentences in a novel build on each other. Over time, as more actions are completed, users may reevaluate their relationships with an interactive system, with the objects being manipulated with that system, and with the activities being mediated through the system. The idea of the wandering viewpoint may, in this fashion, be a means to extend and refine ideas of productive ambiguity in HCI (as proposed by authors such as Gaver, Beaver, and Benford, 2003; Aoki and Woodruff, 2005; and Sengers and Gaver, 2006).

As a means of thinking about the extent of ambiguity in interaction, Iser's reference to intersubjective comprehensibility also seems salient in the HCI context. For interactive artifacts, as with literature, not all readings are valid, particularly if they don't credibly align with the text. But what does "align with the text" mean for HCI? For literature, this is relatively straightforward. Although we might not agree about the *Pride and Prejudice* character Lydia's ultimately tragic nature, we must all acknowledge that Lydia elopes to Scotland with Mr. Wickham; those elements of the plot are not in question, and a reading that misrepresents those textual elements has some problems. But these sorts of determinations aren't easily made for interactive artifacts. As we have already discussed, readers of a novel will all perceive the same sentences in the same order, while users of interactive systems may each experience a digital artifact differently, and may never encounter some of its "sentences," or potential actions, at all. The reader of a novel can't skip every other page and be said to have adequately "read" it, in terms of constructing an interpretation that "aligns with the text." But the user of an interactive artifact can employ only some of its features and still be said to have adequately "used" it. So how can "align with the text" be a useful mechanism for invoking intersubjective comprehensibility in the HCI context?

For HCI, I propose that intersubjective comprehensibility can be understood via user actions that might be possible, but not supported, through a coherent interpretation of the overall system. For example, using Spyn to document a decision to rip out half of a hat and rework it in a different color is an interpretively creative move, in associating a memory with a version of the knit artifact that no longer exists. This action nonetheless seems to align with the spirit of the system as a means to digitally augment handicrafts, and in particular on the aspect of Spyn that focuses on the annotation as a means of more strongly associating the knit item with the recipient. (In this case, the decision to use a different color was based on the creator's learning of the recipient's new preference for yellow.) In contrast, while it might be possible to use Spyn to annotate a knitted item with images algorithmically plucked at random from the social photo database Flickr, placed at random spots on the fabric, I would argue that this is not a supported action; using Spyn to enact random relationships between digital and handmade artifacts does not (at least without further explanation) seem to align with "plotlike" actions of the system. A user who employed Spyn in this manner could be said to misrepresent the text, similar to a reader who claimed that Lydia did not elope to Scotland.

Reader Agency and the Process of Interpretation

In "Grasping a Text," Iser further elaborates on these ideas by contending that meaning emerges through the reader's internal process of connecting textual elements to preserve a consistent account of events. An author can shape this process by leaving characters or actions open to multiple interpretations for some duration of the narrative. In making this point, Iser uses an example from the eighteenth-century British novel *Tom Jones*, by Henry Fielding (although Iser is German, his field is British literature, and that's where his examples come from). One character, Squire Allworthy, is described as a perfect man. Another, Dr. Blifil, is described ambiguously: he has the appearance of a saint, but this appearance may be deceptive. Eventually, it becomes clear that Blifil is a hypocrite—he means to deceive Allworthy for his own ends—and that Allworthy is naive, because he is taken in by Blifil's manipulations. The novel's depiction provides a frame through which the reader compares the two characters, but the ultimate comparison emerges through the reader's own synthesis of various elements, and not according to some authorial mandate. A reader may wonder how a perfect person like Allworthy can be so easily deceived by Blifil, and the reader may reconsider other actions that Allworthy has taken. Perhaps Allworthy lacks discernment because he doesn't need to be skeptical—Allworthy is rich, a member of the landed gentry. The reader may accordingly think critically about the nature of privilege. But this is only one potential judgment that the reader may make about Allworthy, given the portrayal in the novel. Moreover, implications leading from such an appraisal can vary: one might feel sorry for Allworthy or contemptuous of him. While a novel's plot may achieve intersubjective consensus (e.g., we must eventually agree that Allworthy gets taken in by a deceiver), the perceived significance of plot elements varies depending on the reader's choices. Iser suggests that a reader's decisions about what to notice in the text will build on each other in a quest for consistency; if one initially reads Allworthy as an innocent fool, then one will continue to do so. A reader disposed to be critical of Allworthy, on the other hand, will focus on textual clues that lead to that conclusion, paying less attention to others that hint at his ultimate decency and moral worth. However, even if initially ignored, textual evidence for either interpretation of Allworthy don't go away; they remain "on the fringes" to be called up if necessary. An author can work with this, suggesting "gestalten" or connections that have within them "the seeds of their own modification or even destruction" (Iser, 1978, 127).

According to Iser, this can lead to a satisfying experience, as the reader is compelled to reevaluate an interpretation and its accompanying evidence (an "aha!" moment). Iser says, "We react to what we ourselves have produced"; what we react to is our evolving understanding of what we have read, not an object or a "fact" (i.e., the text itself) (Iser, 1973, 128). Our progress of interactions with the text contributes to both our continuing experience and the ultimate product of that experience. That we might change our minds regarding Allworthy and his import is a feature of the way that literature is able to spur the development of the imaginary. As readers, when we find ourselves needing to construct a coherent account of a messy situation like that of assessing Allworthy, we may also reevaluate our previous beliefs based on our interaction with the text. (Perhaps no one is blameless for ignorance that comes from a privileged position.) This interaction between "old" experience and the "new" experience of reading the text is the center of a reader's reception.

As this extended example about Allworthy illustrates, Iser contends that much of the power and pleasure of literature emerges from the reader's agency. The literary text nurtures and encourages that creative activity, often through provoking the reevaluation of initial expectations. But this doesn't mean that characters in novels should behave unpredictably, or that genre conventions must be flouted. In fact, the opposite is necessary: in order for readers to be able to creatively manipulate the story world in the imaginary, they have to be able to consider the characters and events independently, in effect to continue writing the story themselves, internally. To do that, readers need to feel like they know the characters and how they would behave in different situations.

User Agency and the Process of Interpretation in HCI

Similarly, when thinking about Iser's work in the HCI context, the potential for a digital artifact to spark creative interrogation in a form of the imaginary does not mean that a digital artifact should behave unpredictably or that it must violate usability standards.

The examples from Rosner and Ryokai's Spyn deployments demonstrate this. Laura, the writer, found certain expectations upended as she began using audio in her annotations. Laura's reevaluation of audio was prompted through her own, internally consistent account of Spyn as enabling a conversation with her knitting project's recipient. Spyn did not trick Laura into using audio by disabling other input modes, or by making it confusing to switch modes. Indeed, another user, who had not begun to interpret the recipient relationship in the same way as Laura, would read the textual clues provided by Spyn differently, perhaps keeping another potential interpretation consistent. Laura's mode of using Spyn was not at all universal; Rosner and Ryokai note that only 20 percent of the annotations used audio, and they mention two users who avoided it entirely. Spyn encouraged Laura to use audio by supporting, through its features, Laura's own nascent interpretation of how the annotations mediated a relationship between knitter and recipient, and by enabling Laura herself to elaborate on this relationship, its characteristics, and its means of expression. In extending this "story" of Spyn herself, Laura came to reinterpret her beliefs about recorded audio.

The Reader's Awareness of Fictionality

At the end of "Grasping a Text," Iser emphasizes the fictional element of literature as central to his perspective on reading. Iser expands Dewey's description of aesthetic experience to propose that a reader's awareness of how literary texts work is a key element of active reading. As an example of how this awareness is invoked, when I read a novel like *Tom Jones*, I know that Allworthy is just a character in a novel that was written over two hundred and fifty years ago, and I also know that selecting the name "Allworthy" is not an accident, just as I know that a novel selects certain events from the fictional world to depict, and not others. The success of the aesthetic experience is due partly to the reader's awareness of such communicative devices, which primes the substance of fiction for reflection. For Iser, the imaginary is the product of mechanisms that are specific to literature, and much of his discussion focuses on how literary elements combine to open up this third space between fiction and reality. Literature presents an incomplete fictional world that nonetheless aligns with reality in a way that makes our own experience relevant to the fiction and enables us to supply elements not specified by the author. (Even in science fiction, historical fiction, or other genres that presents settings superficially different from our own, characters express themselves in language, have thoughts and emotions, interact with others, and so on. Try to imagine a novel focused around a virus, where the virus is not endowed with sentience or any "human" characteristics. One could write the life experiences of such a hypothetical virus, but it would not be recognizable as literature, I think.) Moreover, the devices of fiction, such as a narrative voice, call attention to the status of literature as fictive, enabling the reading process itself to be bracketed, or made a focus of perception by the reader. One might notice, for example, that a text is showing a human side to the putative villain, and think about this choice as one proceeds with reading. Through this specific form of bracketing, the reader is drawn to engage with the story at the same time as noticing how the story is produced; via these means, literature encourages a particular form of attentive reading that stimulates the imaginative faculties, spurring contemplation of alternate, or transformed, realities: how might Allworthy have avoided his episodes of poor judgment? How might anyone do so?

"Fictionality" in HCI

In this chapter, various examples from Rosner and Ryokai's Spyn project, as well as Twitter's @ElBloombito, provide a preliminary sense of how a similar type of bracketing can invoke the imaginary, or a form of the imaginary, in the experience of digital artifacts. I would also propose that thinking about how these and other concepts, aligned with Iser's discussion of literary reading, do (or do not) align with various modes of human-computer interaction can help us not only to understand the interactive potential of particular systems with more precision and acuity (in the vein of interaction criticism, see J. Bardzell, 2011; Bertelsen and Pold, 2004) but also to design systems oriented toward such "active reading." Like Spyn, many interactive artifacts provide a structure through which potential future states can be constructed, compared, and appraised through activities of making. These making processes may involve outright authoring (of documents and other outputs) or the manipulation of stored information, such as the generation of queries in a database or the selection of dimensions in a visualization. The intense malleability of these possibilities and the indeterminacy of potential actions on them can lend these making activities some aspect of "fictionality" that goes beyond the mere hypothetical, which is more securely tied to the existing world. When I contrast the fictional and hypothetical, I am pointing out the difference between asking oneself a question like "How would my life change if I quit my job and sold pickles at the farmer's market instead?" as opposed to asking oneself a question like "In what world would Allworthy act differently?" The second option, where I construct an alternate world to explore potential changes in a fictional character, enacts the imaginary: it is easier for me to transform an alternate fictional world than it is for me to perform similar operations on the "real" one, where I can't escape considerations like my monthly mortgage payment, considerations that constrain my thinking.

I have suggested here that situations like that of the Spyn user Laura, who began using audio annotations despite her general preferences for written text, approaches the transformative potential of the second option, the intersection of the fictional and real. The alternate world here, created through Laura's interaction with Spyn, was a space to examine the nature of the relationship between a knitter, the recipient of the knit, and the knitted artifact, as mediated through an environment like Spyn. In a world where the knitted artifact represents an extended conversation between knitter and recipient, audio annotations are especially appropriate, in Laura's interpretation.

The activity of making a new kind of thing, a digitally augmented knit, enabled this mode of creative experimentation and critical interrogation. While not equal to the imaginary enabled through literature, this liminal space of making is, I suggest, a form of the imaginary.

Conclusion: Enacting the Imaginary in HCI

One means of both further investigating the imaginary within an HCI context, and enacting it in design, might be to identify particular structural elements that heighten the sense of software itself as material, as an ingredient being shaped in the process of making something else, as opposed to a tool or environment that is separate from the product, extending the notion of design as material suggested by Redström (2008). One might think about how, for example, "software as material" in turn highlights certain characteristics of the material it is manipulating. For example, regular notifications of auto-saving an application emphasize the fluidity and instability of the object being made. How might this experience, perhaps, be heightened? Would an application that enabled a constellation of versions for an output, rather than a linear sequence, illuminate more of a "fictional" quality to the making process? This is one example of the potential research directions that might arise in HCI from applying a perspective like Iser's to the domain of interactive artifacts.

In contemplating such endeavors, I think it is helpful to note as well the basic question Iser asks and his means of approaching it, and the contrast with more typical forms of inquiry in HCI. In HCI, for example, the default starting place for investigating "the act of reading" (or using) would likely be some form of user studies, either with usability tests or with field observations of "actual" use, although alternative modes of understanding have been proposed, including interaction criticism (Bardzell and Bardzell, 2008; Bardzell, 2011; Bertelsen and Pold, 2004) and creative responses via cultural commentators (Gaver, 2007). However, as Brook Thomas (2000) explains, Iser is interested in what literature can do, and not what literature does; Iser wants to illuminate the possible, not document the actual. Iser uses examples, like Fielding's *Tom Jones*, to describe an ideal reading situation, or how the text might be read, and not to predict how it will be read. An advantage with this approach is in its quite general level of abstraction and scope. Iser's conclusions are not limited to his examples, and he can be broadly suggestive.

In contrast, HCI research, even speculative work, tends to involve implementation tactics, as when Gaver, Beaver, and Benford suggest how to achieve various forms of ambiguity in design, in addition to describing ambiguity and its potential effects on the interaction experience. While such practical focus is often a strength of HCI as a discipline, systemic emphasis on easily digestible taxonomies and guidelines can dampen the range and depth of potentially transformative ideas. In thinking about how constructs like Iser's imaginary can extend HCI, we might include the form of the work, as well as its substance.

References

Aoki, P., and A. Woodruff. (2005) "Making Space for Stories: Ambiguity in the Design of Personal Communication Systems." *Proceedings of the SIGCHI Conference on Human Factors in Computing Systems (CHI'05)*. New York: ACM, 181–190.

Bardzell, J. (2011) "Interaction Criticism: An Introduction to the Practice." *Interacting with Computers* 23 (6): 604–621.

Bardzell, J., and S. Bardzell. (2008) "Interaction Criticism: A Proposal and Framework for a New Discipline of HCI." *Extended Abstracts on Human Factors in Computing System (CHI EA'08)*. New York: ACM, 2463–2472.

Bertelsen, O., and S. Pold. (2004) "Criticism as an Approach to Interface Aesthetics." *Proceedings of the 3rd Nordic Conference on Human-Computer Interaction (NordiCHI'04)*. New York: ACM, 23–32.

Gadamer, H. G. (2004) *Truth and Method*, translated by J. Weinsheimer and D. Marshall. 2nd rev. ed. London: Continuum. First published 1960 in Tübingen, Germany, by Mohr.

Gaver, W. (2007) "Cultural Commentators: Non-native Interpretations as Resources for Polyphonic Assessment." *International Journal of Human-Computer Studies* 65 (4): 292–305.

Gaver, W., J. Beaver, and S. Benford. (2003) "Ambiguity as a Resource for Design." *Proceedings of the SIGCH Conference on Human Factors in Computing Systems (CHI'03)*. New York: AMC, 233–240.

Iser, W. (1978) *The Act of Reading: A Theory of Aesthetic Response*. Baltimore, MD: Johns Hopkins University Press.

Iser, W. (1993) *The Fictive and the Imaginary: Charting Literary Anthropology*. Baltimore, MD: Johns Hopkins University Press.

Manovich, L. (2001) *The Language of New Media*. Cambridge, MA: MIT Press.

Redström, J. (2008) "RE: Definitions of Use." *Design Studies* 29 (4): 410–423.

Rosner, D. K., and K. Ryokai. (2008) "Spyn: Augmenting Knitting to Support Storytelling and Reflection." *Proceedings of the 10th International Conference on Ubiquitous Computing (UbiComp'08)*. New York: ACM, 340–349.

Rosner, D. K., and K. Ryokai. (2010) "Spyn: Augmenting the Creative and Communicative Potential of Craft." *Proceedings of the SIGCHI Conference on Human Factors in Computing Systems (CHI'10)*. New York: AMC, 2407–2416.

Sengers, P., and W. Gaver. (2006) "Staying Open to Interpretation: Engaging Multiple Meanings in Design and Evaluation." *Proceedings of the 6th Conference on Designing Interactive Systems (DIS'06)*. New York: AMC, 99–108.

Thomas, B. (2000) "Restaging the Reception of Iser's Early Work, or Sides Not Taken in Discussions of the Aesthetic." *New Literary History* 31 (1): 13–43.

13 The Intellectual Virtues

Aristotle, translated by F. H. Peters

1

We said above that what we should choose is neither too much nor too little, but "the mean," and that "the mean" is what "right reason" prescribes. This we now have to explain.

Each of the virtues we have discussed implies (as every mental habit implies) some aim which the rational man keeps in view when he is regulating his efforts; in other words, there must be some standard for determining the several modes of moderation, which we say lie between excess and deficiency, and are in accordance with "right reason." But though this is quite true, it is not sufficiently precise. In any kind of occupation which can be reduced to rational principles, it is quite true to say that we must brace ourselves up and relax ourselves neither too much nor too little, but "in moderation," "as right reason orders"; but this alone would not tell one much; *e.g.* a man would hardly learn how to treat a case by being told to treat it as the art of medicine prescribes, and as one versed in that art would treat it.

So in the case of mental habits or types of character also it is not enough that the rule we have laid down is correct; we need further to know precisely what this right reason is, and what the standard is which it affords.[1]

The virtues or excellences of the mind or soul, it will be remembered, we divided[2] into two classes, and called the one moral and the other intellectual. The moral excellences or virtues we have already discussed in detail; let us now examine the other class, the intellectual excellences, after some preliminary remarks about the soul.

We said before that the soul consists of two parts, the rational and the irrational part. We will now make a similar division of the former, and will assume that there are two rational faculties: (1) that by which we know those things that depend on invariable principles, (2) that by which we know those things that are variable. For to generically different objects must correspond generically different faculties, if, as we hold, it is in virtue of some kind of likeness or kinship with their objects that our faculties are able to know them.

Let us call the former the scientific or demonstrative, the latter the calculative or deliberative faculty. For to deliberate is the same as to calculate, and no one deliberates about things that are invariable. One division then of the rational faculty may be fairly called the calculative faculty.

Our problem, then, is to find what each of these faculties becomes in its full development, or in its best state; for that will be its excellence or virtue.

But its excellence will bear direct reference to its proper function.

The function of the intellect, both in practice and speculation, is to attain truth.

2

Now, the faculties which guide us in action and in the apprehension of truth are three: sense, reason,[3] and desire.

The first of these cannot originate action, as we see from the fact that brutes have sense but are incapable of action.

If we take the other two we find two modes of reasoning, viz. affirmation and negation [or assent and denial], and two corresponding modes of desire, viz. pursuit and avoidance [or attraction and repulsion].

Now, moral virtue is a habit or formed faculty of choice or purpose, and purpose is desire following upon deliberation.

It follows, then, that if the purpose is to be all it should be, both the calculation or reasoning must be true and the desire right, and that the very same things must be assented to by the former and pursued by the latter.

This kind of reasoning, then, and this sort of truth has to do with action.

But speculative reasoning that has to do neither with action nor production is good or bad according as it is true or false simply: for the function of the intellect is always the apprehension of truth; but the function of the practical intellect is the apprehension of truth in agreement with right desire.

Purpose, then, is the cause—not the final but the efficient cause or origin—of action, and the origin of purpose is desire and calculation of means; so that purpose necessarily implies on the one hand the faculty of reason and its exercise, and on the other hand a certain moral character or state of the desires; for right action and the contrary kind of action are alike impossible without both reasoning and moral character.

Mere reasoning, however, can never set anything going, but only reasoning about means to an end—what may be called practical reasoning (which practical reasoning also regulates production; for in making anything you always have an ulterior object in view—what you make is desired not as an end in itself, but only as a means to, or a condition of, something else; but what you do is an end in itself, for well-doing or right action is the end, and this is the object of desire).

Purpose, then, may be called either a reason that desires, or a desire that reasons; and this faculty of originating action constitutes a man.

No past event can be purposed; *e.g.* no one purposes to have sacked Troy; for no one deliberates about that which is past, but about that which is to come, and which is variable: but the past cannot be undone; so that Agathon is right when he says—

"This thing alone not God himself can do—
To make undone that which hath once been done."

We have thus found that both divisions of the reason, or both the intellectual faculties, have the attainment of truth for their function; that developed state of each, then, in which it best attains truth will be its excellence or virtue.

3[4]

Let us describe these virtues then, starting afresh from the beginning.

Let us assume that the modes in which the mind arrives at truth, either in the way of affirmation or negation, are five in number, viz. art, science, prudence, wisdom, reason;[5] for conception and opinion may be erroneous.

What science is we may learn from the following considerations (for we want a precise account, and must not content ourselves with metaphors). We all suppose that what we know with scientific knowledge is invariable; but of that which is variable we cannot say, so soon as it is out of sight, whether it is in existence or not. The object of science, then, is necessary. Therefore it is eternal: for whatever is of its own nature necessary is eternal: and what is eternal neither begins nor ceases to be.

Further, it is held that all science can be taught, and that what can be known in the way of science can be learnt. But all teaching starts from something already known, as we have explained in the Analytics; for it proceeds either by induction or by syllogism. Now, it is induction that leads the learner up to universal principles, while syllogism starts from these. There are principles, then, from which syllogism starts, which are not arrived at by syllogism, and which, therefore, must be arrived at by induction.[6]

Science, then, may be defined as a habit or formed faculty of demonstration, with all the further qualifications which are enumerated in the Analytics. It is necessary to add this, because it is only when the principles of our knowledge are accepted and known to us in a particular way, that we can properly be said to have scientific knowledge; for unless these principles are better known to us than the conclusions based upon them, our knowledge will be merely accidental.[7]

This, then, may be taken as our account of science.

4[8]

That which is variable includes that which man makes and that which man does; but making or production is different from doing or action (here we adopt the popular distinctions). The habit or formed faculty of acting with reason or calculation, then, is different from the formed faculty of producing with reason or calculation. And so the one cannot include the other; for action is not production, nor is production action.

Now, the builder's faculty is one of the arts, and may be described as a certain formed faculty of producing with calculation; and there is no art which is not a faculty of this kind, nor is there any faculty of this kind which is not an art: an art, then, is the same thing as a formed faculty of producing with correct calculation.

And every art is concerned with bringing something into being, *i.e.* with contriving or calculating how to bring into being some one of those things that can either be or not be, and the cause of whose production lies in the producer, not in the thing itself which is produced. For art has not to do with that which is or comes into being of necessity, nor with the products of nature; for these have the cause of their production in themselves.

Production and action being different, art of course has to do with production, and not with action. And, in a certain sense, its domain is the same as that of chance or fortune, as Agathon says—

"Art waits on fortune, fortune waits on art."

Art, then, as we said, is a certain formed faculty or habit of production with correct reasoning or calculation, and the contrary of this (*ἀτεχνία*) is a habit of production with incorrect calculation, the field of both being that which is variable.

5[9]

In order to ascertain what prudence is, we will first ask who they are whom we call prudent.

It seems to be characteristic of a prudent man that he is able to deliberate well about what is good or expedient for himself, not with a view to some particular end, such as health or strength, but with a view to well-being or living well.

This is confirmed by the fact that we apply the name sometimes to those who deliberate well in some particular field, when they calculate well the means to some particular good end, in matters that do not fall within the sphere of art. So we may say, generally, that a man who can deliberate well is prudent.

But no one deliberates about that which cannot be altered, nor about that which it is not in his power to do.

Now science, we saw, implies demonstration; but things whose principles or causes are variable do not admit of demonstration; for everything that depends upon these principles or causes is also variable; and, on the other hand, things that are necessarily determined do not admit of deliberation. It follows, therefore, that prudence cannot be either a science or an art: it cannot be a science, because the sphere of action is that which is alterable; it cannot be an art, because production is generically different from action.

It follows from all this that prudence is a formed faculty that apprehends truth by reasoning or calculation, and issues in action, in the domain of human good and ill;

for while production has another end than itself, this is not so with action, since good action or well doing is itself the end.

For this reason Pericles and men who resemble him are considered prudent, because they are able to see what is good for themselves and for men; and this we take to be the character of those who are able to manage a household or a state.

This, too, is the reason why we call temperance *σωφροσύνη*, signifying thereby that it is the virtue which preserves prudence. But what temperance preserves is this particular kind of judgment. For it is not *any* kind of judgment that is destroyed or perverted by the presentation of pleasant or painful objects (not such a judgment, for instance, as that the angles of a triangle are equal to two right angles), but only judgments about matters of practice. For the principles of practice [or the causes which originate action][10] are the ends for the sake of which acts are done; but when a man is corrupted by pleasure or pain, he straightway loses sight of the principle, and no longer sees that this is the end for the sake of which, and as a means to which, each particular act should be chosen and done; for vice is apt to obliterate the principle.

Our conclusion then is that prudence is a formed faculty which apprehends truth by reasoning or calculation, and issues in action, in the field of human good.

Moreover, art [or the artistic faculty] has its excellence [or perfect development] in something other than itself, but this is not so with prudence. Again, in the domain of art voluntary error is not so bad as involuntary, but it is worse in the case of prudence, as it is in the case of all the virtues or excellences. It is plain, then, that prudence is a virtue or excellence, and not an art.

And the rational parts of the soul or the intellectual faculties being two in number, prudence will be the virtue of the second, [the calculative part or] the faculty of opinion; for opinion deals with that which is variable, and so does prudence.

But it is something more than "a formed faculty of apprehending truth by reasoning or calculation"; as we see from the fact that such a faculty may be lost, but prudence, once acquired, can never be lost.[11]

6[12]

Science is a mode of judging that deals with universal and necessary truths; but truths that can be demonstrated depend upon principles, and (since science proceeds by demonstrative reasoning) every science has its principles. The principles, then, on which the truths of science depend cannot fall within the province of science, nor yet of art or prudence; for a scientific truth is one that can be demonstrated, but art and prudence have to do with that which is variable.

Nor can they fall within the province of wisdom; for it is characteristic of the wise man to have a demonstrative knowledge of certain things.

But the habits of mind or formed faculties by which we apprehend truth without any mixture of error, whether in the domain of things invariable or in the domain of things variable, are science, prudence, wisdom, and reason.[13] If then no one of the first three (prudence, science, wisdom) can be the faculty which apprehends these principles, the only possible conclusion is that they are apprehended by reason.

7[14]

The term *σοφία* (wisdom[15]) is sometimes applied in the domain of the arts to those who are consummate masters of their art; *e.g.* it is applied to Phidias as a master of sculpture, and to Polyclitus for his skill in portrait-statues; and in this application it means nothing else than excellence of art or perfect development of the artistic faculty.

But there are also men who are considered wise, not in part nor in any particular thing (as Homer says in the Margites—

"Him the gods gave no skill with spade or plough,
Nor made him wise in aught"),

but generally wise. In this general sense, then, wisdom plainly will be the most perfect of the sciences.

The wise man, then, must not only know what follows from the principles of knowledge, but also know the truth about those principles. Wisdom, therefore, will be the union of [intuitive] reason with [demonstrative] scientific knowledge, or scientific knowledge of the noblest objects with its crowning perfection, so to speak, added to it. For it would be absurd to suppose that the political faculty or prudence is the highest of our faculties, unless indeed man is the best of all things in the universe.

Now, as the terms wholesome and good mean one thing in the case of men and another in the case of fishes, while white and straight always have the same meaning, we must all allow that wise means one thing always, while prudent means different things; for we should all say that those who are clear-sighted in their own affairs are prudent, and deem them fit to be entrusted with those affairs. (And for this reason we sometimes apply the term prudent even to animals, when they show a faculty of foresight in what concerns their own life.)

Moreover, it is plain that wisdom cannot be the same as statesmanship. If we apply the term wisdom to knowledge of what is advantageous to ourselves, there will be many kinds of wisdom; for the knowledge of what is good will not be one and the same for all animals, but different for each species. It can no more be one than the art of healing can be one and the same for all kinds of living things.

Man may be superior to all other animals, but that will not make any difference here; for there are other things of a far diviner nature than man, as—to take the most conspicuous instance—the heavenly bodies.

It is plain, then, after what we have said, that wisdom is the union of scientific [or demonstrative] knowledge and [intuitive] reason about objects of the noblest nature.

And on this account people call Anaxagoras and Thales and men of that sort wise, but not prudent, seeing them to be ignorant of their own advantage; and say that their knowledge is something out of the common, wonderful, hard of attainment, nay superhuman, but useless, since it is no human good that they seek.

Prudence, on the other hand, deals with human affairs, and with matters that admit of deliberation: for the prudent man's special function, as we conceive it, is to deliberate well; but no one deliberates about what is invariable, or about matters in which there is not some end, in the sense of some realizable good. But a man is said to deliberate well (without any qualifying epithet) when he is able, by a process of reasoning or calculation, to arrive at what is best for man in matters of practice.

Prudence, moreover, does not deal in general propositions only, but implies knowledge of particular facts also; for it issues in action, and the field of action is the field of particulars.

This is the reason why some men that lack [scientific] knowledge are more efficient in practice than others that have it, especially men of wide experience; for if you know that light meat is digestible and wholesome, but do not know what meats are light, you will not be able to cure people so well as a man who only knows that chicken is light and wholesome.

But prudence is concerned with practice; so that it needs knowledge both of general truths and of particular facts, but more especially the latter.

But here also [*i.e.* in the domain of practice] there must be a supreme form of the faculty [which we will now proceed to consider].

8[16]

And in fact statesmanship and prudence are the same faculty, though they are differently manifested.

Of this faculty in its application to the state the supreme form is the legislative faculty, but the special form which deals with particular cases is called by the generic name statesmanship. The field of the latter is action and deliberation; for a decree directly concerns action, as the last link in the chain.[17] And on this account those engaged in this field are alone said to be statesmen, for they alone act like handicraftsmen.

But it is when applied to the individual and to one's own affairs that this faculty is especially regarded as prudence, and this is the form which receives the generic name prudence or practical wisdom (the other forms being (1) the faculty of managing a household, (2) the legislative faculty, (3) statesmanship [in the narrower sense], which is subdivided into (*a*) the deliberative, (*b*) the judicial faculty).

Knowing one's own good, then, would seem to be a kind of knowledge (though it admits of great variety),[18] and, according to the general opinion, he who knows and attends to his own affairs is prudent, while statesmen are busybodies, as Euripides says—

"What? was I wise, who might without a care
Have lived a unit in the multitude
Like any other unit?...
For those who would excel and do great things—"

For men generally seek their own good, and fancy that is what they should do; and from this opinion comes the notion that these men are prudent.

And yet, perhaps, it is not possible for a man to manage his own affairs well without managing a household and taking part in the management of a state.

Moreover, how a man is to manage his own affairs is not plain and requires consideration. And this is attested by the fact that a young man may become proficient in geometry or mathematics and wise[19] in these matters, but cannot possibly, it is thought, become prudent. The reason of this is that prudence deals with particular facts, with which experience alone can familiarize us; but a young man must be inexperienced, for experience is the fruit of years.

Why again, we may ask, can a lad be a mathematician but not wise, nor proficient in the knowledge of nature? And the answer surely is that mathematics is an abstract science, while the principles of wisdom and of natural science are only to be derived from a large experience;[20] and that thus, though a young man may repeat propositions of the latter kind, he does not really believe them, while he can easily apprehend the meaning of mathematical terms.

Error in deliberation, again, may lie either in the universal or in the particular judgment; for instance, you may be wrong in judging that all water that weighs heavy is unwholesome, or in judging that this water weighs heavy. But prudence [in spite of its universal judgments] plainly is not science; for, as we said,[21] it deals with the ultimate or particular fact [the last link in the chain], for anything that can be done must be of this nature.

And thus it is in a manner opposed to the intuitive reason also: the intuitive reason deals with primary principles which cannot be demonstrated, while prudence deals with ultimate [particular] facts which cannot be scientifically proved, but are perceived by sense—not one of the special senses, but a sense analogous to that by which we perceive in mathematics that this ultimate [particular] figure is a triangle;[22] for here too our reasoning must come to a stand. But this faculty [by which we apprehend particular facts in the domain of practice] should, after all, be called sense rather than prudence; for prudence cannot be defined thus.[23]

9[24]

Inquiry and deliberation are not the same; for deliberation is a particular kind of inquiry. But we must ascertain what good deliberation is—whether it is a kind of science or opinion, or happy guessing, or something quite different.

It is not science; for we do not inquire about that which we know: but good deliberation is a kind of deliberation, and when we deliberate we inquire and calculate.

Nor is it happy guessing; for we make happy guesses without calculating and in a moment, but we take time to deliberate, and it is a common saying that execution should be swift, but deliberation slow.

Good deliberation, again, is different from sagacity, which is a kind of happy guessing.

Nor is it any kind of opinion.

But since in deliberating ill we go wrong, and in deliberating well we go right, it is plain that good deliberation is a kind of rightness, but a rightness or correctness neither of science nor opinion; for science does not admit of correctness (since it does not admit of error), and correctness of opinion is simply truth; and, further, that concerning which we have an opinion is always something already settled.

Good deliberation, however, is impossible without calculation.

We have no choice left, then, but to say that it is correctness of reasoning (*διάνοια*); for reasoning is not yet assertion: and whereas opinion is not an inquiry, but already a definite assertion, when we are deliberating, whether well or ill, we are inquiring and calculating.

But as good deliberation is a kind of correctness in deliberation, we must first inquire what deliberation means, and what its field is.[25]

Now, there are various kinds of correctness, and it is plain that not every kind of correctness in deliberation is good deliberation; for the incontinent man or the vicious man may duly arrive, by a process of calculation, at the end which he has in view,[26] so that he will have deliberated correctly, though what be gains is a great evil. But to have deliberated well is thought to be a good thing; for it is only a particular kind of correctness in deliberation that is called good deliberation—that, namely, which arrives at what is good.

But, further, what is good may be arrived at by a false syllogism; I mean that a right conclusion as to what is to be done may be arrived at in a wrong way or upon wrong grounds—the middle term being wrong;[27] so that what leads to a right conclusion as to what should be done is not good deliberation, unless the grounds also be right.

A further difference is that one may arrive at the right conclusion slowly, another rapidly. So we must add yet another condition to the above, and say that good deliberation means coming to a right conclusion as to what is expedient or ought to be done, and coming to it in the right manner and at the right time.

Again, we speak of deliberating well simply, and of deliberating well with a view to a particular kind of end. So good deliberation simply [or without any qualifying epithet] is that which leads to right conclusions as to the means to the end simply; a particular kind of good deliberation is that which leads to right conclusions as to the means to a particular kind of end. And so, when we say that prudent men must deliberate well, good deliberation in this case will be correctness in judging what is expedient to that end of which prudence has a true conception.

10[28]

The faculty of intelligence or sound intelligence, in respect of which we say a man is intelligent or of sound intelligence, is not the same as science generally, nor as opinion (for then all men would be intelligent), nor is it identical with any particular science, such as medicine, which deals with matters of health, and geometry, which deals with magnitudes; for intelligence has not to do with what is eternal and unchangeable, nor has it to do with events of every kind, but only with those that one may doubt and deliberate about. And so it has to do with the same matters as prudence; but they are not identical: prudence issues orders, for its scope is that which is to be done or not to be done; while intelligence discerns merely (intelligence being equivalent to sound intelligence, and an intelligent man to a man of sound intelligence).

Intelligence, in fact, is equivalent neither to the possession nor to the acquisition of prudence; but just as the learner in science is said to show intelligence when he makes use of the scientific knowledge which he hears from his teacher, so in the domain of prudence a man is said to show intelligence when he makes use of the opinions which he hears from others in judging, and judging fitly—for soundly [when we speak of sound intelligence] means fitly.

And from this use of the term with regard to learning comes its employment to denote that faculty which we imply when we call a man intelligent; for we often speak of the intelligence of a learner.

11[29]

Judgment (what we mean when we speak of a man of kindly judgment, or say a man has judgment) is a correct discernment of that which is equitable. For the equitable man is thought to be particularly kindly in his judgments, and to pass kindly judgments on some things is considered equitable. But kindly judgment (*συγγνώμη*) is judgment (*γνώμη*) which correctly discerns that which is equitable—correctly meaning truly.

Now, all these four formed faculties which we have enumerated not unnaturally tend in the same direction. We apply all these terms—judgment, intelligence, prudence, and reason—to the same persons, and talk of people as having, at a certain age, already acquired judgment and reason, and as being prudent and intelligent. For all these four faculties deal with ultimate and particular[30] facts, and it is in virtue of a power of discrimination in the matters with which prudence deals that we call a person intelligent, or a man of sound judgment, or kindly judgment; for equitable is a common term that is applicable to all that is good in our dealings with others.

But that which is to be done is always some particular thing, something ultimate. As we have seen, it is the business of the prudent man to know it, and intelligence and judgment also have to do with that which is to be done, which is something ultimate.

And the intuitive reason [the last of the four faculties above enumerated] also deals with ultimate truths, in both senses of the word;[31] for both primary principles and ultimate facts [in the narrower sense of the word ultimate = particular] are apprehended by the intuitive reason, and not by demonstration: on the one hand, in connection with deductions [of general truths in morals and politics],[32] reason apprehends the unalterable first principles; on the other hand, in connection with practical calculations, reason apprehends the ultimate [particular] alterable fact (which forms the minor premise [in the practical syllogism]). These particular judgments, we may say, are given by reason, as they are the source of our conception of the final cause or end of man; the universal principle is elicited from the particular facts: these particular facts, therefore, must be apprehended by a sense or intuitive perception; and this is reason.[33]

And so it is thought that these faculties are natural, and that while nature never makes a man wise, she does endow men with judgment and intelligence and reason. This is shown by the fact that these powers are believed to accompany certain periods of life, and that a certain age is said to bring reason and judgment, implying that they come by nature.

(The intuitive reason, then, is both beginning and end; for demonstration both starts from and terminates in these ultimate truths.)

And on this account we ought to pay the same respect to the undemonstrated assertions and opinions of men of age and experience and prudence as to their demonstrations. For experience has given them a faculty of vision which enables them to see correctly.[34]

We have said, then, what prudence is, and what wisdom is, and what each deals with, and that each is the virtue of a different part of the soul.

12[35]

But here an objection may be raised. "What is the use of them?" it may be asked. "Wisdom does not consider what tends to make man happy (for it does not ask how anything is brought about). Prudence indeed does this, but why do we need it? Prudence is the faculty which deals with what is just and noble and good for man, *i.e.* with those things which it is the part of the good man to do; but the knowledge of them no more makes us apter to do them, if (as has been said) the [moral] virtues are habits, than it does in the case of what is healthy and wholesome—healthy and wholesome, that is, not in the sense of conducing to, but in the sense of issuing from, a healthy habit; for a knowledge of medicine and gymnastics does not make us more able to do these things.

"But if it be meant that a man should be prudent, not in order that he may do these acts, but in order that he may become able to do them, then prudence will be no use to those who *are* good, nor even to those who are not. For it will not matter whether they have prudence themselves, or take the advice of others who have it. It will be enough to do in these matters as we do in regard to health; for if we wish to be in health, we do not go and learn medicine.

"Again, it seems to be a strange thing that prudence, though inferior to wisdom, must yet govern it, since in every field the practical faculty bears sway and issues orders."

We must now discuss these points; for hitherto we have been only stating objections.

First, then, we may say that both prudence and wisdom must be desirable in themselves, since each is the virtue of one of the parts of the soul, even if neither of them produces anything.

Next, they *do* produce something.

On the one hand, wisdom produces happiness, not in the sense in which medicine produces health, but in the sense in which health produces health;[36] that is to say, wisdom being a part of complete virtue, its possession and exercise make a man happy.

On the other hand [in the sphere of action], man performs his function perfectly when he acts in accordance with both prudence and moral virtue; for while the latter ensures the rightness of the end aimed at, the former ensures the rightness of the means thereto.

The fourth[37] part of the soul, the vegetative part, or the faculty of nutrition, has no analogous excellence; for it has no power to act or not to act.

But as to the objection that prudence makes us no more apt to do what is noble and just, let us take the matter a little deeper, beginning thus:—

We allow, on the one hand, that some who do just acts are not yet just; *e.g.* those who do what the laws enjoin either unwillingly or unwittingly, or for some external motive and not for the sake of the acts themselves (though they do that which they ought and all that a good man should do). And, on the other hand, it seems that when a man does the several acts with a certain disposition he is good; *i.e.* when he does them of deliberate purpose, and for the sake of the acts themselves.

Now, the rightness of the purpose is secured by [moral] virtue, but to decide what is proper to be done in order to carry out the purpose belongs not to [moral] virtue, but to another faculty. But we must dwell a little on this point and try to make it quite clear.

There is a faculty which we call cleverness (*δεινότης*)—the power of carrying out the means to any proposed end, and so achieving it. If then the end be noble, the power merits praise; but if the end be base, the power is the power of the villain. So we apply the term clever both to the prudent man and the villain.[38]

Now, this power is not identical with prudence, but is its necessary condition. But this power, the "eye of the soul" as we may call it, does not attain its perfect development[39] without moral virtue, as we said before, and as may be shown thus:—

All syllogisms or deductive reasonings about what is to be done have for their starting point [principle or major premise] "the end or the supreme good is so and so" (whatever it be; any definition of the good will do for the argument). But it is only to the good man that this presents itself as the good; for vice perverts us and causes us to err about the principles of action. So it is plain, as we said, that it is impossible to be prudent without being morally good.

13[40]

This suggests a further consideration of moral virtue; for the case is closely analogous to this—I mean that just as prudence is related to cleverness, being not identical with it, but closely akin to it, so is fully developed moral virtue related to natural virtue.

All admit that in a certain sense the several kinds of character are bestowed by nature. Justice, a tendency to temperance, courage, and the other types of character are exhibited from the moment of birth. Nevertheless, we look for developed goodness as something different from this, and expect to find these same qualities in another form. For even in children and brutes these natural virtues are present, but without the guidance of reason they are plainly hurtful. So much at least seems to be plain—that just as a strong-bodied creature devoid of sight stumbles heavily when it tries to move, because it cannot see, so is it with this natural virtue; but when it is enlightened by reason it acts surpassingly well; and the natural virtue (which before was only like virtue) will then be fully developed virtue.

We find, then, that just as there are two forms of the calculative faculty, viz. cleverness and prudence, so there are two forms of the moral qualities, viz. natural virtue and fully developed virtue, and that the latter is impossible without prudence.

On this account some people say that all the virtues are forms of prudence, and in particular Socrates held this view, being partly right in his inquiry and partly wrong—wrong in thinking that all the virtues are actually forms of prudence, but right in saying that they are impossible without prudence.

This is corroborated by the fact that nowadays every one in defining virtue would, after specifying its field, add that it is a formed faculty or habit in accordance with right reason, "right" meaning "in accordance with prudence."

Thus it seems that every one has a sort of inkling that a formed habit or character of this kind (*i.e.* in accordance with prudence) is virtue.

Only a slight change is needed in this expression. Virtue is not simply a formed habit *in accordance with* right reason, but a formed habit *implying* right reason.[41] But right reason in these matters is prudence.

So whereas Socrates held that the [moral] virtues are forms of reason (for he held that these are all modes of knowledge), we hold that they imply reason.

It is evident, then, from what has been said that it is impossible to be good in the full sense without prudence, or to be prudent without moral virtue. And in this way we can meet an objection which may be urged. "The virtues," it may be said, "are found apart from each other; a man who is strongly predisposed to one virtue has not an equal tendency towards all the others, so that he will have acquired this virtue while he still lacks that." We may answer that though this may be the case with the natural virtues, yet it cannot be the case with those virtues for which we call a man good without any qualifying epithet. The presence of the single virtue of prudence implies the presence of all the moral virtues.

And thus it is plain, in the first place, that, even if it did not help practice, we should yet need prudence as the virtue or excellence of a part of our nature; and, in the second place, that purpose cannot be right without both prudence and moral virtue; for the latter makes us desire the end, while the former makes us adopt the right means to the end.

Nevertheless, prudence is not the mistress of wisdom and of the better part of our nature [the reason], any more than medicine is the mistress of health. Prudence does not employ wisdom in her service, but provides means for the attainment of wisdom—does not rule it, but rules in its interests. To assert the contrary would be like asserting that statesmanship rules the gods, because it issues orders about all public concerns [including the worship of the gods.]

Notes

1. This really forms quite a fresh opening, independent of §§ 1–3; and it is one among many signs of the incomplete state in which this part of the treatise was left, that these two openings of Book VI. were never fused together. The scheme of the treatise, as unfolded in Book I. (*cf.* especially I. **7**, 13; **13**, 20), gives the intellectual virtues an independent place alongside of, or rather above, the moral virtues; now that the latter have been disposed of it naturally remains to consider the former: this is the natural transition which we have in § 4. But besides this the dependence of the moral virtues upon the intellectual virtues makes an examination of the latter absolutely necessary to the completion of the theory of the former; thus we get the transition of §§ 1–3.

2. *Supra*, I. 13, 20.

3. *νοῦς*: the word is used here in its widest sense.

4. *Of the five modes of attaining truth:* (1) *of demonstrative science of things invariable.*

5. *νοῦς*—used now in a narrower special sense which will presently be explained.

6. Though, as we see later, induction can elicit them from experience only because they are already latent in that experience.

7. We may know truths of science, but unless we know these in their necessary connection, we have not scientific knowledge.

8. *Of knowledge of things variable, viz.* (2) *of art in what we make;*

9. *and* (3) *of prudence in what we do, the virtue of the calculative intellect.*

10. The conception of the end is at once a cause or source of action and a principle of knowledge; *ἀρχή* covers both.

11. For it implies a determination of the will which is more permanent in its nature than a merely intellectual habit. And further, when once acquired it must be constantly strengthened by exercise, as occasions for action can never be wanting.

12. (4) *Of intuitive reason as the basis of demonstrative science.*

13. Art, which is one of the five enumerated above, is here omitted, either in sheer carelessness, or perhaps because it is subordinate to prudence: *cf. supra* 5, 7.

14. (5) *of wisdom as the union of science and intuitive reason. Comparison of the two intellectual virtues, wisdom and prudence.*

15. Of course we do not use "wisdom" in this sense.

16. *Prudence compared with statesmanship and other forms of knowledge.*

17. *πρακτὸν ὡς τὸ ἔσχατον*, *i.e.* as the last link in the chain of causes leading to the proposed end—last in the order of deliberation, but first in the order of events: *cf.* III. **3**, 12.

18. Varying as the good varies; *cf. supra*, **7**, 4, and I. 3, **2**.

19. Here in the looser sense, below (§ 6) in the stricter sense, which is the technical meaning of the term in Aristotle: *cf. supra*, 7, 12.

20. He does not mean that the principles of mathematics are not derived from experience, but only that they are derived from the primitive experience which every boy has, being in fact (as we should say) the framework on which the simplest knowledge of an external world is built.

21. *Cf. supra*, § 2.

22. The perception "that the ultimate fact is a triangle" (which is the more obvious translation of these words), whether this means "that three lines is the least number that will enclose a space," or "that the possibility of a triangle is a fact that cannot be demonstrated," is in either case not the perception of a *particular* fact; but it is the perception of a particular fact that is needed if the illustration is to be relevant.

23. The intuitive reason (*νοῦς*) is here opposed to prudence (*φρόνησις*), but presently (cap. 11) is found to be included in it: reason (*νοῦς*) was similarly in cap. 6 opposed to wisdom (*σοφία*), but in cap. 7 found to be included in it.

24. *Of deliberation.*

25. This, however, is not done here, perhaps because it has been already done at length in III. 3.

26. Omitting *ἰδεῖν*.

27. *e.g.* this act should be done simply because it is just; I may decide to do it for reputation, or for pleasure's sake, or thinking it to be an act of generosity.

28. *Of intelligence*

29. *Of judgment; Of reason on intuitive perception as the basis of the practice intelligence.*

30. All particular facts (τὰ καθ' ἕκαστον) are ultimate (ἔσχατα), i.e. undemonstrable; but not all ultimate facts (ἔσχατα) are particular facts—as presently appears.

31. Lit. in both directions, *i.e.* not the last only, but the first also.

32. *Cf. supra*, **8**, 1, 2.

33. This αἴσθησις may be called νοῦς, which is the faculty of universals, because the universal (the general conception of human good) is elicited from these particular judgments.

34. Throughout this chapter we are concerned with the practical intellect alone. He has already stated in cap. 6 that the intuitive reason is the basis of the speculative intellect; here he says that it is also the basis of the practical intellect. We have to distinguish here three different employments of the practical faculty:

(1) (if we invert the order), undemonstrated assertion, viz. that under the circumstances this is the right thing to do (§ 6): here the judgment is altogether intuitive; *i.e.* no grounds are given.
(2) demonstration (improperly so called, more properly calculation) that this is the right thing to do; *e.g.* this act is to be done because it is just: here the intuitive reason supplies the minor premise of the practical syllogism (this act is just), and also (indirectly) the major (whatever is just is good), *i.e.* it supplies the data—the several particular intuitions from which the general proposition is elicited: ἐν ταῖς πρακτικαῖς, *sc.* ἀποδείξεσι (practical calculations), § 4; *cf.* τῶν ἀποδείξεων, § 6, and οἱ συλλογισμοὶ τῶν πρακῶν, 12, 10.
(3) deduction or demonstration (also improperly so called) of general truths in morals and politics: κατὰ τὰς ἀποδείξεις, § 4: here also the data from which deduction starts can only be apprehended by intuitive perception or reason: *cf.* I. 4, 7, 7, 20. The difference between (2) and (3) is plainly shown *supra* **8**, 2, where πολιτυιή in the wider sense (=νομοθετική) which deals with laws, is distinguished from πολιτυιή in the narrower sense which has to do with decrees: *cf.* also I. **2**, 7, and X. 9, 14.

35. *Of the use of wisdom and prudence. How prudence is related to cleverness.*

36. *i.e.* in the sense in which a healthy state of the body (ὑγίεια as a ἕξις in Aristotle's language) produces healthy performance of the bodily functions (ὑγίεια as an ἐνέργεια).

37. The other three are sense, reason, desire (αἴσθησις,νοῦς, ὄρεξις): *cf. supra*, cap. **2**. The excellences or best states of the desires have already been described as the moral virtues. Wisdom and prudence are the excellences of the reason or intellect (νοῦς in its widest meaning). Sense (αἴσθησις) does not need separate treatment, as it is here regarded as merely subsidiary to reason and desire; for human life is (1) speculative, (2) practical, and no independent place ill allowed to the artistic life, The fourth part therefore alone remains.

38. Reading τοὺς πανούργονς.

39. As φρόνησις, prudence.

40. *How prudence is related to moral virtue*

41. *μετὰ λόγου:* the agent must not only be guided by reason, but by his own reason, not another's.

14 Way Back to Some Design Futures: Aristotle's Intellectual Excellences and Their Implications for Designing

Gilbert Cockton

Looking Back a Few Millennia

Science has long been regarded as producing the best form of knowledge. As a philosopher, Aristotle rejected the possibility of any other form of knowledge being put in authority over science. He founded biological sciences: 25 percent of his extant corpus addresses zoology. His systematic method for the comprehensive study of animals was unmatched until the sixteenth century (Lennox, 2014). His preference for scientific knowledge was not just an argument but something that he lived by. With medieval (Aristotelian) scholasticism's fall from favor during the Scientific Revolution, trends in scientific values and practice demoted argument and promoted evidence in ways that were not systematically challenged until the mid-twentieth century (e.g., Quine, 1951). These challenges developed over the next four decades as the weight of historical and contemporary evidence indicated that many scientists' understandings of science were not scientific. There were significant gaps between ideals and realities. However, many scientists were not willing to accept the evidence of historical and contemporary studies, resulting in a backlash that became known as the "science wars" (Ashman and Baringer, 2001).

Aristotle may have found it difficult to take sides in the science wars. On the one hand, he placed *sophia* (scientific or philosophical wisdom) above all other intellectual excellences. On the other hand, he required more than *episteme* (scientific knowledge) for *sophia*, which also required *nous* (intuition). He may well have seen the sociological and historical critiques of idealized scientific values as being a necessary rebalancing back to the position he held—that intuition has to be brought to bear on knowledge to produce true scientific wisdom, and that neither objectivity nor evidence are enough. Regardless of what Aristotle would actually think if he could return to tell us, the science wars are evidence of turbulent intellectual times where very substantial gaps can open up between leading and trailing edges of intellectual thinking.

More recently in design, as the science wars calmed down, advocacy of "design thinking" led to a similar cycle of excessive confidence, backlash, and more measured confidence (Ford, 2012). Design thinking involves the application of design practices and values beyond established craft areas such as fashion, automotive, or graphic design. For its most enthusiastic advocates, there is no area that design thinking cannot transform, pushing aside established disciplines and practices such as strategic management, product and service innovation, social action research, and even scientific research itself. However, beyond the relatively small group of design-thinking faithful, traditional scientific norms continue to prevail in national funding agencies, major conference and journal reviewing practices, and other forms of intellectual gatekeeping. While there has been over half a century of growing doubts over the superiority of scientific values and practices, design research and practice have not yet established themselves as rivals to science. Thus, although for an increasing band of design thinkers this will be design's century, the articulation of the intellectual values here remains underdeveloped, as do well-grounded contrasts between design and science, whatever the latter is (and the former too!).

Design work, and its innovative impact on both practice and research, may well be able to reach the parts of the world that scientific work does not, because science values the universally true over the specifically worthwhile, where the opposite is true for design. Value differences here result in different ways of knowing. This presents us with a narrow problem (i.e., how to legitimate design knowledge) and a broader problem (i.e., how to rebalance ways of knowing to support the best and most impactful research). I will argue that Aristotle's conceptualization of intellectual excellences offers a "way in" to the broader problem, which in turn helps explicate the forms of rigor and social contributions of design knowledge.

This chapter focuses primarily on the narrow problem—the nature of design knowledge and the resulting implications for design practice and research. Aristotle's relevance here is that he engaged with this problem in a wider context of productive practical reasoning, using a network of concepts that can frame and guide critical reflection on design research and practice. More specifically, this chapter focuses on Book 6 of the *Nicomachean Ethics*, in which Aristotle introduces intellectual excellences that support being practical, productive, and theoretical. Aristotle's separation of theoretical from practical and productive knowledge has largely survived two and a half millennia of human intellectual development. While his writing mostly concerns theoretical knowledge, his forays into practical (*praxis*) and productive (*poesis*) action have remained very influential, largely because (unlike science) they have not been comprehensively superseded by modern developments.

The *Nicomachean Ethics* is among the most influential ethical treatises ever written. It takes its name from Aristotle's son, *Nicomachus*, its assumed editor; Kenny (1978) estimated that one commentary per decade has appeared on Aristotle's *Nicomachean Ethics* since the Middle Ages. Key twentieth-century philosophers such as Heidegger, Derrida, and Nussbaum have engaged with Aristotle's thinking. Within the last few decades, philosophers such as Alasdair MacIntyre (2007) have revisited Aristotle's thinking on ethical behavior. As such, Aristotle's *Nicomachean Ethics* is relevant to design as an ethical practice. In it, Aristotle develops a conceptual system to guide practical reasoning in context, moving beyond the axiomatic deduction favored by his teacher, Plato. Formed long before the Scientific Revolution and Enlightenment rationality, his system avoids many assumptions that constrain contemporary academic research and thinking in scientific disciplines.

Book 6 of the *Nicomachean Ethics* provides a compact concept set for critical analysis of design as both practice and research. Design theory has long drawn on Aristotle's ethical concepts (e.g., Nelson and Stolterman, 2003; Kuutti, 2003), both directly and indirectly, especially Aristotle's analyses of *phronesis* (practical wisdom). This chapter contributes to a discourse on design as both a practical and intellectual activity. The research discourse here is barely fifty years old. Before this, it was primarily an educational discourse (e.g., Potter, [1969] 2002), a professional discourse (e.g., Dreyfuss, 1955), or a mix of both (e.g., Read, 1934). The key distinctions between research into, for, and through design are the start of an ongoing research discourse (Frayling, 1994) that actually has educational origins (Read, 1934). The influence of educators on design thinking has been extensive, with key contributions from the Bauhaus, HfG Ulm, and more recently Ivrea (e.g., Smith, 2007).

The project addressed here is thus the nature and worth of design as both practice and research, which often seeks to legitimate itself through reference to science (e.g., Cross, 2001). This can lead to reification of both science and design, with the risk of reducing centuries and continents of situated human activities to caricatures that bear only a passing resemblance to actual practices. The value of looking through a critical lens from Aristotle is that we can gain fresh insight into the issues away from distractions of contemporary science wars or credulous fawning over design thinking.

What follows is a selective overview of Book 6 of the *Nicomachean Ethics* that focuses on concepts and relations that have implications for design research and practice. The full Ross translation (Aristotle, 2009) is available online and readers are encouraged to consult this to see the selected excerpts below in context.

Intellectual Excellences in the Nicomachean Ethics

The first five books of the *Nicomachean Ethics* discuss the following: the nature of the human good (Book 1); moral virtue (Book 2); responsibility and choice, plus courage and temperance as specific moral virtues (Book 3); ten further moral virtues including magnificence, pride, and truthfulness (Book 4); and justice (Book 5). Books 7–10 discuss four further moral virtues: continence, pleasure, friendship, and happiness. Each book of the *Nicomachean Ethics* is divided into chapters. Book and chapter (section) numbers are given as, for example, 2.6 (Book 2, chapter 6). Quotations below are from the 1925 translation by David Ross (Aristotle, 2009), which remains the basis for many published translations. Numbers [in square brackets] refer by convention to Bekker's 1831–1870 Prussian Academy of Sciences edition of Aristotle and are used as a near-universal standard to help scholars point specifically to passages independent of translation, pagination, and other contingencies. Thus [1139a28] refers to page 1139, first column (a), line 28 in Bekker's edition; most modern translations of Aristotle include this numbering in addition to their own pagination.

All moral virtues require choice of a *meson*, or (golden) mean (2.6). For example, "courage" avoids the extreme vices of both recklessness and cowardice, (3.6). However, knowing that moral virtues exist in combination with avoidance of extremes is not an adequate basis for virtuous conduct. Thus in Book 6, Aristotle introduces "intellectual excellences" (*aretai dianoetikai*)[1] to underpin all moral virtues. Whereas moral excellences are witnessed externally by others, intellectual excellences are witnessed internally within our *psyche*, understood in a broad sense. The breadth and subtleties of *psyche* in Aristotle rules out any sole adequate translation term, so it can be left untranslated (Nussbaum and Rorty, 1995). It is translated as "Self" below, and not "soul" or "spirit" (to avoid religious connotations now, but appropriate for Aristotle's culture), nor "mind" (too narrow a cognitive meaning). For Aristotle, *zoe* (life) is a near equivalent to *psyche*, which is thus neither disembodied (it has a nutritive part [1144a10]), nor without emotions.

Intellectual excellences belong to the rational part of our Self with scientific and calculative subparts (6.1). For the scientific subpart (6.2), "the good and the bad state are truth and falsity respectively" for an "intellect which is contemplative, not practical nor productive" [1139a28]. For the calculative part, "which is practical and intellectual the good state is truth in agreement with right desire" [1139a30], as "reasoning must be true and the desire right" [1139a24]. Only the calculative subpart can initiate choice (6.2), which is reasoning with a view to an end, rather than pure intellect (valued for its own sake).

Both the scientific and calculative subparts of the rational Self are involved in intellectual excellences: scientific knowledge (6.3); art (6.4); practical wisdom (6.5); intuition (6.6); and (philosophical) or scientific wisdom (6.7). These result in three major forms of knowledge: practical (things done), productive (things made), and theoretical (the universally true). A compact but comprehensive conceptual system results from contrasts between each form of knowledge.

Scientific knowledge (*episteme*, 6.3) is that which "is not even capable of being otherwise" [1139b20]; is eternally and universally necessarily so; and can be taught and learned. *Episteme* must be complemented by intuition (*nous*, 6.6), which provides first principles (6.8) "for which no reason can be given" [1142a27]), and which must not be confused with opinion (*doxa*: 6.9–10). *Sophia* (6.7) "must be intuitive reason combined with scientific knowledge" [1141a19]. The three theoretical excellences thus have a fixed relation to each other. The productive and practical excellences relate dynamically to each other and the three theoretical ones.

Art (*techne*, 6.4) is the first form of variable truth (i.e., contingent or particular). The second is *phronesis* (6.5). Each involves different reasoned capacities: "making and acting are different" [1140a2]. Art addresses how things come into being through their maker, and not through essence, necessity, or nature (as with *sophia*). Aristotle adds little to "discussions outside our school," which he treats as "reliable" [1140a3]. This leaves gaps in his coverage of an intellectual excellence of major relevance to creative design.

Practical wisdom (*phronesis*, often translated as "prudence," 6.5), requires a person to deliberate on what conduces to the good life in general, rather than to specifics such as health, strength, or art objects. Excellence in practical wisdom arises from the calculative subpart of the rational Self, where it is refined through a reasoned "capacity to act with regard to the things that are good" [1140b20]. While *sophia* can have a single universal goal (truth), *phronesis* must be rooted in the complexities of human existence.

Aristotle builds a conceptual system by contrasting each additional intellectual excellence with previous ones. Art thus involves nothing beyond excellence in its completed forms (6.7), but scientific wisdom is "the most finished of the forms of knowledge" [1141a16], "the best knowledge," and "remarkable, admirable, difficult, and divine, but useless" [1141b8]. Practical wisdom (*phronesis*) is "concerned with things human and things about which it is possible to deliberate" [1141b9], and with "good that can be brought about by action" [1141b13], but must be of "a controlling kind" [1141b23]. It must "also recognize the particulars; for it is practical, and practice is concerned with particulars" [1141b16–17]. *Phronesis* is contrasted with *political wisdom* (6.8), where Aristotle quickly moves out to several important observations and conceptual extensions. He argues that age and experience are needed to develop *phronesis*. He then contrasts *phronesis* with *episteme* and then *nous*. In the first contrast, Aristotle asserts the need for an end (*eschaton*) for *phronesis*, that is, a mark at which to aim, because practical wisdom, in contrast to scientific knowledge, is "concerned with the ultimate particular fact, since the thing to be done is of this nature" [1142a26]. *Eschaton*, and several synonyms, refer to the *final cause* of phronesis. One of Aristotle's four causes (the others being material, formal and efficient; *Physics* 2.3, *Metaphysics* 5.2), the final cause for anything is the end toward which it directs. Aristotle devotes little attention in the *Nicomachean Ethics* to the final cause for *sophia* (truth) and *techne* (bringing something into being), but he subjects the final cause for *phronesis* to extensive analysis.

Reasons for practical reasoning result from *aisthesis*, which does not involve our physical senses (6.8) but is instead a practical perception through which (6.11) one must grasp "the last and variable fact" [1143b3], that is, a specific endpoint of practical reasoning. This is not something that can be proven, but results from *aisthesis* drawing on experience, which gives older people "an eye they see aright" [1143b14].

The intensity of 6.8 eases with subsequent consideration of minor subordinate intellectual excellences: deliberation (6.9), understanding (6.10), and judgment (6.11). Deliberation concerns reasoning about one's own action, whereas understanding concerns the positions of others. Judgment from years of reason develops practical wisdom and understanding that "deal with ultimates, i.e. with particulars" [1143a29], "for not only must the man of practical wisdom know particular facts, but understanding and judgement are also concerned with things to be done, and these are ultimate" [1143a34–35].

Having built a conceptual system through contrasts, oppositions, and interrelations between major and minor intellectual excellences, Aristotle introduces a puzzle (*aporia*, 6.12): if practical wisdom concerns "things just and noble and good for man ... which it is the mark of a good man to do" [1143b23], then "practical wisdom will be of no use to those who are good ... [or] to those who have not virtue" [1143b30–31]. Aristotle moves toward eliminating the need for *phronesis* because it is "inferior to philosophic wisdom" [1143b33] and should not "be put in authority over it" [1143b46]. However, Aristotle retains *phronesis* for the following reasons: all excellences and related states of the Self are worthy; moral virtue requires phronesis because "virtue makes us aim at the right mark, and practical wisdom makes us take the right means" [1144a8–10], which will be exhibited in cleverness "to do the things that tend towards the mark we have set before ourselves and to hit it" [1144a24–26], but only "if the mark be noble" [1144b27] (otherwise we are smart, not clever).

Having retained *phronesis* as an intellectual excellence, Aristotle closes Book 6 by stating the need to nurture it (6.13). Aristotle's intertwined contrasts and comparisons lead him to conclude that intellectual excellences do not "exist in separation from each other" [1144b33], "for with the presence of the one quality, practical wisdom, will be given all the virtues" [1145a1–2], but even so "it is not supreme over philosophic wisdom ... for its coming into being; it issues orders, then, for its sake, but not to it" [1145a8–9], that is to say, for the sake of, but not to, philosophic wisdom. Aristotle maintains the ultimate supremacy of scientific wisdom (repeated in Book 10). However, this must not obscure what Aristotle's system requires for intellectual excellence: not acts alone, but acts with motives; not intention alone, but intention with understanding; not character alone, but character with understanding (Urmson, 1988).

Implications for Design Research and Practice

This brief contextual review of Book 6 supports four implications for designing:

1. All intellectual virtues are involved in design, but these must be coordinated under the direction of *phronesis* (practical wisdom, oriented toward everyday, situated ends), and not of *sophia* (scientific or philosophical wisdom, oriented to truth). Similar implications

have been expressed in recent literature on design research (e.g., Gaver 2012; Höök and Löwgren, 2012).

2. Since all intellectual virtues are involved in design, then the distinctive end goals of each (final causes) are involved in design. None will always dominate. The ultimate particular (*eschaton*) is neither just the artefact of *techne* nor just the purpose of *phronesis* nor just the truth of *sophia*. It is all of them. Each takes precedence in separate design arenas.

3. Since all intellectual virtues are involved across all design arenas, then only designers are ethically capable of the holistic deliberation, understanding, and judgment required by *phronesis*. *Sophia* and *techne* are necessary, but not sufficient.

4. Because intellectual virtues were not fully described and analyzed to closure by Aristotle, we must resolve some, but not all, of his puzzles (*aporiai*) for progress in design research and practice.

The *Nicomachean Ethics* has already influenced theory development in design, but Book 6 has broader value by demonstrating that tensions between design and science are not products of postmodern science wars (and must not be marginalized as such) but reflect how different forms of knowledge have long been constructed and valued. Aristotle's intellectual excellences provide a useful complement to far more recent critical perspectives in this volume, but like them, must be subjected to criticism to expose limitations, as well as its constructive implications.

I first researched Aristotle in 2007 within a UK National Endowment for Science Technology and the Arts (NESTA) fellowship on value-centered design. I applied the concepts of virtues and golden means to some meta-principles for designing (Cockton, 2009). After my UK NESTA fellowship, I moved from computing to design research, and have since been interested in how Aristotle's concepts of *sophia*, *theoria*, *nous*, *episteme*, *phronesis*, *praxis*, *techne*, and *poesis* could be relevant to constructive design research (Koskinen, et al., 2011). The relevance of these concepts is shown through three positions (corresponding to implications 1–3 above), where *phronesis*

1. provides an initial integrative holistic basis for design research that takes precedence over scientific reasoning;
2. must always be directed in *praxis* (action) toward *eschata* (ultimate ends), which must extend beyond the overly narrow confines of *sophia* (scientific wisdom), *episteme* (scientific knowledge), and *techne* (art); and
3. requires mature and experienced designers who can choose and deliver on *eschata* through deliberation before, during, and after action.

With "during" and "after" in the third point, we move beyond the unbending rationalism of Aristotle and contemporary axiologists who still require deliberative understanding and judgment to rationally precede action, and not follow it (e.g., Rescher, 2014).

An important gap in Aristotle is his lack of attention to reasoning in creative practice, with *techne* something that even people outside of his Lyceum ("our school") understood so reliably (6.4) that it needs only the most limited analysis. This gap needs to be filled to value subjective creative practices in design research. Schön's (1983) concept of *reflection in and on action* provides a starting point for this, in that reflection on something must follow, not precede: what precedes future actions is *nous* or even *episteme* (the *eschaton* of research for design; Frayling, 1994). Such gap filling (or gap acceptance, along with some *aporia*) is the focus of this chapter's fourth and last implication for designing.

Sophia Is Not the Queen of Design: Phronesis Rules

The current standard model of research practice grounds applied research, including practice-based design research, in fundamental theoretical research. The model here is that universal truths (as we know them) underpin, support, and guide specific practices (truths as we do them): all applied research is thus an application of theoretical research in this model. However, in the *Nicomachean Ethics*, *sophia* and *phronesis* often contend for superiority. The superiority of the universal over the particular is not clear cut, and Aristotle has to work hard to keep *phronesis* in what he sees as its place, a place still regarded as proper in contemporary ideologies of science. However, unlike Aristotle, designers must put *phronesis* in authority over *sophia*. Scientific truths are provisional and potentially useless [1141b8] inputs to complex interactions in design between understanding, deliberation, and judgment. In no context can science be of (6.7) "a controlling kind" [1141b23], only practical wisdom can.

Aristotle himself may have agreed that *phronesis* takes precedence over *sophia* in creative contexts. Design work can bring judgment to the integration of *praxis*, *poetics*, and *episteme*. *Episteme* (scientific knowledge) alone is insufficient. Episteme requires *nous* to create *sophia*, and thus scientific knowledge alone cannot have implications for design. Facts never have and never will speak for themselves. They can only speak through an explicit systematic network of interrelated concepts ("perspectivism," as Hahn [2015] puts it) that focuses rigorous critical analysis. Aristotle's system of intellectual excellences challenges the preference for theoretical knowledge that, however universally true, can never have mechanistic implications for the practical wisdom of design.

Given the relative shelf space dedicated to scientific wisdom in Aristotle's writing (i.e., the vast majority), it is a tribute to the worth of the epistemic David of *phronesis* that it could contest the Goliath of *sophia* and its universal eternal theoretical knowledge. The latter is half praised (6.7) as "remarkable, admirable, difficult, and divine, but useless" [1141b7–8], but (6.12) "it would be thought strange if practical wisdom, being inferior to philosophic wisdom, is to be put in authority over it" [1143b33]. For Aristotle, the truth as we know it must always trump any truth as we do it.

In 6.12, Aristotle arguably anticipated Dourish's (2006) critique of requirements for implications for design by almost two and a half millennia. Theoretical knowledge can only have implications for a design, for this design, through deliberation (6.9) "in respect both of the [particular] end, the manner, and the time" [1142b28–29], where "excellence in deliberation will be correctness with regard to what conduces to the end of which practical wisdom is the true apprehension" [1142b30]. There are no universal truths here, no inevitable consequences of scientific knowledge. It is not *episteme*, but *phronesis* that provides implications for a project through judgment (6.11) that must find (golden) means (*mesa*, 2.6) within the evolving balance of design choices.

It is impossible to proceed logically, by implication, from information about stakeholders or evaluations to full detailed design decisions (Simon, 1981). Design provides limited opportunities for the rational thought of scientific wisdom. Options within one design arena are rarely logical consequences of another. Instead the balance and integration of separate arenas within design (e.g., artefacts, purpose, beneficiaries, and evaluations; Cockton, 2013) coevolve continuously as the result not of *sophia*, but *phronesis*, through which they become related, refined, and rationalized. It is only in this process of holistic synthesis across separate arenas that research knowledge can have any implications for design.

The question of primary user research having any implications for design results from the current standard model of research practice that grounds applied research in prior scientific theory and knowledge. The irony here is that expectations of implications for design result directly from the human-centered dogma (Cockton, 2012) that we must avoid any thoughts about design until usage contexts are fully understood. If instead we follow standard creative practice to let problem and solution spaces coevolve (Cockton, 2014; Cross, 2011), rather than insist on closure of the former before considering the latter, then *episteme* can support *phronesis*. This avoids current human-centered extremes, which are vices rather than virtues. A golden mean here needs design inputs and ideas to be balanced and integrated simultaneously. No design arena can dominate. Design isn't a shape and has no dominant center. It is a complex activity in which all design arenas can be involved. While *sophia* can be the primary intellectual excellence for the user-centered arenas of beneficiaries and evaluations, *techne* is the primary intellectual excellence for artefacts and *phronesis* for purpose. *Phronesis*, however, remains the primary intellectual excellence overall for design, since the balance and integration of design arenas can only be achieved through understanding, deliberation, and judgment.

Aristotle's requirement for a balanced combination of intellectual excellences thus challenges the fetish for empirical knowledge (*episteme*) of users and their activities as the center of design, whether this is knowledge of beneficiaries, from evaluations, or about design options for artefacts. Design purpose is always a matter of judgment (6.11), not scientific knowledge (6.3). Practical wisdom depends on all intellectual excellences, and it is not possible for scientific research alone to have direct implications for design. Science's universals are unsuited to design's situated particulars. This differs from the well-established position in human-computer interaction (HCI) research that users' practical knowledge is situated and contextual (e.g., Winograd and Flores, 1986; Suchman, 1987). The position here relates to universals within *sophia.* It is not a position on *phronesis.* It is not the particular nature of contexts of usage that calls for *phronesis,* but the nature of appropriate understandings in support of design, and the role of deliberation and judgment in design processes.

The relationship between science and design is indirect, with theoretical knowledge contributing to understanding (6.9) as a relevant input to deliberation (6.10), which in turn provides the inputs to judgment (6.11). The human-centered design paradigm has privileged *episteme* as empirical data about usage and contexts (Cockton, 2008), independently of whether this enables universal knowledge.

All intellectual excellences are thus involved in design and only *phronesis* can coordinate them through the minor excellences of deliberation, understanding, and judgment, which primarily support *phronesis,* since they are not involved in *sophia* via *nous* or *episteme.* For example, deliberation (6.9) is not "scientific knowledge ... for men do not inquire about the things they know about" [1141b35]. Similarly (6.10), "understanding is neither about things that are always and are unchangeable" [1143a5] and (6.11) "being a man of understanding and of good or sympathetic judgement consists in being able judge about the things with which practical wisdom is concerned" [1143a30-31]. Deliberation, understanding and judgment are all essential within design, and neither are within the scope of *sophia,* the end of which is universal eternal truth and not "truth in agreement with right desire" (6.2). The latter is within the scope of both *phronesis* and *techne* as calculative subparts of the rational Self. *Techne* (6.4) "is a state concerned with making, involving a true course of reasoning" [1140a20], but Aristotle never explores what such a "true course of reasoning" may be in Book 6.

The requirement for all intellectual excellences under the direction of *phronesis* can extend to requirements for research through design, where the writing and curation of design-led research remains a focus for much debate. Research through design must balance and integrate the scientific truths of *sophia* with the aesthetic truths of *techne* via the practical truths of *phronesis.* In research through design, *sophia* cannot dominate, despite Aristotle's preferences. Given Aristotle's exertions to maintain the superiority of *sophia* over *phronesis,* it is reasonable to invert the rankings here, especially within a domain where *sophia* cannot dominate. In some ways, Aristotle's attempts to maintain the superiority of *sophia* only make sense when we accept the possibility of universal truths, which are the basis for the superiority of *sophia.* Within the practical domains, asserting the superiority of *phronesis* does not entail making an argument for its universal superiority. Indeed, such an argument cannot make sense within a universal domain, but only in a practical one where all is always relative to specific ends, marks, or targets.

For all intellectual excellences to be present in accounts of design research, design researchers need to record and report

- *nous:* all significant insights and ideas;
- *episteme:* all primary and secondary sources of information that strongly influenced the exploration and choice of design options;
- *sophia:* all associations between *nous* and *episteme* above that integrate and coordinate design moves;
- *techne:* all craft knowledge, expertise and production values that were vital to the design research outcomes; and
- *phronesis:* how deliberation, understanding, and judgment were used to holistically integrate the separate intellectual excellences.

The above provides a framework for reflection on action (Schön, 1983) in research through design, during which design researchers become objective by presenting themselves as others, i.e., they re-present their design research practice as if they were critics. However, even though design (research) requires *sophia* to yield to *phronesis*, *phronesis* alone is not enough. Kuutti (2003) notes that "the phronesis-component of design knowledge is growing in importance, and that we do not have suitable approaches to deal with it and to integrate different types [of knowledge] for design purposes" (29). However, this view overlooks *sophia* and *nous*, with only *episteme* alongside *techne* and *phronesis*. Phronesis thus does have a key role in design (research), which is "heavily dependent on the existence and production of phronesis-type of knowledge" (Kuutti, 2003). Kuutti's use of *phronesis* is secondhand, and draws on Toulmin (2001), either repeating or adding misunderstandings that only a close reading of the original can avoid. Kuutti thus refers to "tacit" *phronesis* knowledge, which runs the risk of too closely associating Polanyi's (1958) positions on tacit knowledge with Aristotle's positions from almost two and a half millennia earlier. Aristotle's grounding of *phronesis* in deliberation, understanding, and judgment clearly indicates that few aspects of *phronesis* are tacit, and thus phronesis should not be presented as if it is always tacit: only some aspects are.

Good judgments will never be solely the result of the understandings of people, processes, and things that feed understandings into design deliberations. Instead, they have three additional vital sources that are explored in turn. First, good judgments partially result from immersion in complex, worthwhile, diverse design practices. Second, good judgments partially result from the character of designers, which unlike empirical knowledge, can aim design work at (6.12) a "noble mark" [1144b27] in a way that "conduces to the end" [1142b30]. Third, good judgments partially result from designers' intuitive wisdom in response to rationally irresolvable puzzles and empirically unfillable gaps in design work. This has long been understood in design education, where "personal judgment [of] what is good design ... has always been one of [its] goals" (Kuutti, 2009, 45).

The Ultimate Particular: It's Complicated

The implications of Book 6 of the *Nicomachean Ethics* for design research must start with explicit positions and arguments in it that can be argued to remain true today. Only then can its implications for design research be fairly argued. Secondhand, thirdhand, or even more distant readings can readily wander away from what was actually written, especially when Aristotelian concepts are used with limited apparent understanding of their context and origins. For example, Stolterman (2008) draws on Nelson and Stolterman (2003) to assert that the "*ultimate particular* is a design concept of the same dignity and importance as truth in science." Although no link to Aristotle is acknowledged in either Stolterman (2008) or Nelson and Stolterman (2003), "ultimate particular" is a fairly rare translation for *eschaton*, which supports some positions in the *Nicomachean Ethics* but occurs more in other work, especially Aristotle's *Metaphysics*.

"Ultimate particular" is Ross's translation of the first occurrence of *eschaton* (6.8). Ross uses the phrase only once more for *toiouton* (the thing before), which refers back to the previous *eschaton*. Ross never translates *eschaton* as "ultimate particular" again. He next translates it as "limit" ("in that direction ... there will be a limit" [1142a29]), for which Urmson (1988) and Rackham (Aristotle, 1934) prefer "stop." *Eschaton* is difficult to translate consistently (Cooper, 1975). Ross translates the next four occurrences of *eschaton* as "ultimates," the two after that as "last," and the last as "individual facts." Such reasonable inconsistencies are poor foundations for characterizing design, especially given the tutorial function of "ultimate particular": *eschaton* is "ultimate" in sense of a "last" thing, that is, an end of or goal for practical wisdom. Ross adds "particular" to contrast *phronesis* with universal *sophia* (to foreground a key conceptual relation by opposing the particular to the universal). *Eschaton* is a very minor concept, with only nine uses relative to extensive alternatives in the *Nicomachean Ethics* that express ends for *phronesis* (e.g., ultimate, aim, mark, end, particular, right desire). For example, *phronesis* must have a reason for reasoning, a right desire, in contrast to intuitive reason (*nous*), for which no reasons can be given (6.8). It is such a reason, a right desire (*te orexei te orthe*), that *eschaton* refers to. It is thus a goal, or purpose for *phronesis*. It is not an artefact, which would be a purpose for *techne*, nor, in a more contemporary understanding, is it an artefact in use or the outcomes of this use. Stolterman (2008), however, does not appear to be aware of how *phronesis* relates to *eschaton*, and what this means for a correct understanding of the latter.

Stolterman (2008) defines the "ultimate particular" as the "actual final manifested outcome, ... a result of an intentional design process ... digital artefact or an information system implemented in a specific organization is an ultimate particular [that] ...

may be similar to a specific type or class of systems .... in its specific use context." It is important to read through here from the initial association of "ultimate particular" with a specific intentionally designed artefact to "in its specific use context," since the latter links to important concerns such as "*qualities-in-use* and [user] *experience.*" Even so, neither artefacts nor their contextualization through use correspond to *eschaton* in the *Nicomachean Ethics.* Nor does Aristotle give *eschaton* "the same dignity and importance as truth in science." Had Stolterman (with Nelson) not used "ultimate particular" as a central concept in their approaches to design, there would be no issue here. Had they simply referred to "design outcomes" (as actually finally manifested), the issue of a proper reading of Aristotle would not arise.

The issues that do arise, however, are useful in that they open up a helpful discussion about appropriate forms and standards for knowledge in design. First, for Aristotle "truth in science" corresponds to the good state for the scientific subpart of the rational Self, responsible for *sophia* (6.2). In contrast, the good state for the calculative subpart, responsible for *techne* and *phronesis,* is "truth in agreement with right desire" (6.2). *Eschaton* is only the latter part, that is, the right desire. *Eschaton* is not something that Aristotle compares directly to truth. What he does compare is *phronesis* and *sophia,* which he does come close to giving equal status, but *phronesis* is never explicitly given the "same dignity and importance as" (truth in) *sophia.* Stolterman overextends the scope of *eschaton* here in ways that conflate different aspects of Aristotle's thought and cut off lines of thought as a result.

Second, since *eschaton* is only the right desire, Stolterman also overextends it to the "actual final manifested outcome, ... a result of an intentional design process ... artifact ... in its specific use context" (Stolterman 2008, 59). *Eschaton* can only refer to the intention driving a design process, i.e., design purpose, a single design arena, and not the complex integration referred to by Stolterman (beneficiary usage of artefacts to achieve purpose). Where Stolterman does align himself with Aristotle is the rationalist association of design outcomes with design intentions. However, we know that the outcomes of design are rarely wholly what were intended, and that intentions are rarely wholly achieved.

If the ultimate particular is to be associated with only one design arena (Cockton, 2013), then this should be design purposes, and not artefacts, beneficiaries, or evaluations, since purpose is what Aristotle means through *eschaton.* However, just as Kuutti (2003) and others diverge from Aristotle's position when *phronesis* is emphasized to the exclusion of *nous, episteme, sophia,* and *techne* (which must all be present in design research), so too should no one design arena be emphasized over another. Creative design has tended to emphasize the artefact, especially once Darke (1979) had exposed how a single unifying concept can drive through a design's structure at all levels of abstraction. Darke called such a concept or idea a "primary generator." At times, Stolterman comes close to equating the ultimate particular with Darke's primary generator.

Interestingly, before he focuses on the ultimate particular, Stolterman first characterizes design practice with its goal to create "something in the world with a *specific* purpose, for a *specific* situation, for a *specific* client and user, with *specific* functions and characteristics" that must satisfy "the demands and needs of the organization" (11, emphases in original). Here we see the integration of all four design arenas: the artefact ("something in the world ... with *specific* functions and characteristics"), its purpose, its beneficiaries ("*specific* client and user ... the organization"), and evaluations (testing the satisfaction of "demands and needs"). However, the latter arena apart, all of this is in place before any mention of the ultimate particular, which when mentioned overly reduces the scope of design work by being insufficiently composite in relation to the goals of design practice.

The sensible position is thus that the ultimate particular in design research should not be the artefact in any narrow sense, as in Darke (1979), nor design purpose, as in Cockton (2006), nor *episteme* in relation to beneficiaries and evaluations as in Gould and Lewis (1985), but any composite of these. Just as we elevated *phronesis* above *sophia,* so a composite ultimate particular can have "the same dignity and importance as truth in science." None of this of course is a direct implication of Book 6 of the *Nicomachean Ethics* for design. However, it is through attempting to align Stolterman's ambiguous characterization of the ultimate particular with Aristotle's position on *eschaton* that we realize that associating the ultimate particular exclusively with one single design arena would result in a distorted understanding of design. There is no design arena in particular that can provide a simple ultimate particular for design. Instead, the ultimate particular has to be a balanced composite integration across design arenas. To put this much more simply, in a quote from Charles Eames: "Eventually everything connects—people, ideas, objects ... the quality of the connections is the key to quality per se" (Eames Foundation, 2015). Design truths are ones of substance and relation, but ontologies that combine both are recent philosophical innovations (Cockton, 2010).

It may well be that we can give "the same dignity and importance as truth in science" to a composite ultimate particular. Such a composite is consistent with the position that all of Aristotle's five intellectual excellences are essential in design research. Similarly, all design arenas have evolving associated ends or goals as design research progresses. Zimmerman, Forlizzi, and Evenson (2007) come close to this position when outlining the nature and benefits of research through design, as does Buchanan (2001) when characterizing the broadening scope of design. A composite ultimate particular has the advantage of removing ambiguities through an explicitly broad scope of purpose for design research, that we demonstrate (through evaluation) achievement of design purpose for chosen beneficiaries (who are understood in a chosen way) via a designed artefact. Each design arena relies on different intellectual excellences: *sophia* is the appropriate excellence for beneficiaries and evaluation, and *techne* for artefacts, but purpose is the domain of *phronesis* (which must also guide choices of evaluations).

Praxis as the manifestation of *phronesis* aims at ends in an "unqualified sense," while *poesis* deliver the means (6.2): "that which is made is not an end in the unqualified sense" [1139b2]. *Praxis* acts for reasons other than making: "good action is an end, and desire aims at this" [1139b4]. This requires *phronesis* with its "controlling kind" [1141b23], since this alone can aim at "good that can be brought about by action" [1141b13].

A composite ultimate particular can merge the three major design paradigms to enable design that is balanced, integrated, and generous (BIG; see Cockton, 2013). Here, the generosity of applied arts design (if aimed at noble marks via a worth focus) is reasoned through to success with relevant understandings from engineering and human sciences.

We need to align "truth in agreement with right desire" with a broad view of design practice. "Right desire" can be grounded in worth (Cockton, 2006) or similar as design purpose, but "truth" has to be understood as the truth of *techne* for artefact quality and the truth of *sophia* for the relationship of the artefact in use to research data on beneficiaries and from evaluations. The associated requirement for a complex primary generator can extend to requirements for research through design, where design researchers need to identify and report the

- major phases of a design research project, and how complex ultimate particulars for each design arena evolve to direct design moves; and
- the role of *phronesis* as supported by deliberation, understanding, and judgment, in balancing the effort devoted to, and influence of each design arena.

This adds to a framework for reflection on action (Schön, 1983) that provides a basis for grounding research *through* design in research *into* design by making designers' own research practice an object of their research. Indeed, since the design arena for the artefact is not solely or sufficiently where research can result in knowledge, it is not clear how research through design can result in new knowledge except in combination with reflective, reflexible research into design.

One Thousand Swallows Can Make a Designer

The *Nicomachean Ethics* prepares the young for the lifetime of development required to achieve excellences through accumulated instructive experiences: "human good turns out to be activity of soul in accordance with virtue ... in a complete life. For one swallow does not make a summer, nor does one day; and so too one day, or a short time, does not make a man blessed and happy" (1.7 [1098a.18–19]).

Design in its simplest form as decorative arts falls within *techne*, which "is concerned with coming into being, i.e. contriving and considering how something may come into being which is capable of either being or not being, and whose origin is in the maker " [1140a11–13]. Success for design in all its forms requires individual excellences of character and capabilities that develop and coalesce with age. Where design fields are dominated by the relatively young, this will limit potential achievements unless the scale, complexity, and challenge of practical wisdom frames young expectations, and encourages acceptance that design excellence cannot be achieved through a short period of education and practice (in contrast to mathematics, 6.8).

By placing character at the heart of all intellectual excellences, Aristotle places designers center stage, with their character, intellect, judgment, and "an eye they see aright" [1143b14]. He is offering a view of the "expert subject," who stands in contrast to the objective scientist, in mastering her or his subjectivity (unique capabilities of perception, experience, and judgment; Bardzell, 2011). "Seeing aright" here is required for the many judgment calls that are constantly required in design. First, no contextual research in support of a design is possible until that design has been scoped in some way. No project starts with a zero scope. There are almost always commitments to a form of artefact (e.g., garment, flatware, mobile app, motorcycle, web site, taxi service), and often parallel commitments to specific user groups and other stakeholders or beneficiaries. Further commitments to forms of evaluation and to design purpose are possible during a project. The resulting scope must draw on *nous* "for which no reason can be given" (6.8 [1142a26]), since there can be no *episteme* in place until *nous* directs attention to potential interactions between a slice of life and new design opportunities. Such *nous* can only come from a design team. Design needs designers. Without designers' *nous*, *episteme* will remain useless and will never add to *sophia*.

Second, design practices move actively toward the achievement of quality through conscious deliberation ("reflection" in Schön, 1983) prior to forming judgments about current design options and choices. Judgments are after the fact here, with design not being fully planned in advance but instead being analyzed as it progresses. Broad sources of understandings are important, but not as important as knowledge of how understandings are used in design work: "for not only must the man of practical wisdom know particular facts, but understanding and judgement are also concerned with things to be done, and these are ultimate" [1143a34–35].

Even when we understand "designer" to mean "design team," this team cannot rise above all circumstances, however much designers love a challenge (and they do). Aristotle briefly touches on working contexts, noting that practical wisdom for individuals' benefit needs to be underpinned by well-managed households and government (6.8). This reminds us that no human activity exists in isolation, and that excellent designers need excellent work settings, both physical and cultural. Also, working contexts extend beyond the studio and related workplaces. Public understanding of design is vital to professional and academic well-being. Designers design better in supportive cultures. No one should expect rules for design work, but all should respect the complexities of design settings.

Support beyond designers' existing excellences is thus needed for the demands of BIG design, but once necessary resources are in place, it is designers with their coalesced expertise who must bring designs to fruition, not just through passion or capacity (competences), but through repeated choices of appropriate golden means in the face of competing demands. Universal knowledge can only be tainted by such subjective particularities. Rigorous design research must thus acknowledge, fully incorporate, and respect subjective factors that render universals useless. The acceptance of the subjective nature of design is growing within interaction design research (e.g., Greenberg and Buxton, 2008), but preferences for impossible dogmatic forms of objectivity still dominate. Just as initial design scopes rely on *nous*, so too do the cumulative design moves that add detail to each design arena. While *episteme* can support design moves up to a point, many choices, especially with regard to design purpose, can only be based in intuitive reason (*nous*), but only *phronesis* can then lift designers away from *nous* toward sound judgment.

The requirement for designers to be fully present in research through design (and related research into or for design) adds to a framework for reflection on action (Schön, 1983). Also, research for design must leave room for designers. It must not attempt to bypass character and judgment with simplistic methods and rules. Effective research for design must develop resources that can be exploited and adapted via *phronesis* with respect to "the [particular] end, the manner, and the time" [1142b28–29]. In such open situations, it may well take a thousand swallows to bring about a designer's summer.

Aristotle's Aporiai and Gaps for Design: Solving, Filling, and Accepting

Like Socrates, Aristotle used puzzles (*aporiai*) to open up issues. *Analytika* (as in the titles of his *Prior* and *Posterior Analytics*) means "unraveling," which Aristotle often does well, but he only ties up the separate strands some of the time. At other times, a pile of loose ends is left for readers to tie together. Sometimes this may result from how Aristotle's works have been edited and handed down to us. The extracts here from the *Nicomachean Ethics* are one translation from one edition of secondhand writing. However, transcription and translation losses cannot explain every lack of resolution. Opposing and often inconsistent positions are presented equivocally, forcing readers to take a position or suspend judgment until a conclusion is hopefully drawn, but within Aristotle's reordered writings such conclusions may not arrive. For example, he regularly elevates *sophia* over *phronesis*, but never overcomes the critiques of *sophia* in 6.12–13. However, the unresolved puzzles here are valuable for design research and practice because of their challenges to naïve (but strongly and extensively held) contemporary positions on scientific knowledge and practice.

As well as leaving some *aporiai* unresolved, Aristotle left others to common sense or prevailing wisdom. This leaves gaps in his reasoning that are not the result of manuscript problems (i.e., lost text). Some of the most important gaps are deliberate. For example, a designer's ethics, and the resulting purposes that they choose for their design projects, are evidenced in context through action. Aristotle's ethics thus have little specific content and no rules. His analyses of justice, friendship, courage, happiness, and other moral excellences do not establish what these are but instead focus on how they are achieved, to what extent, in what manner, and at what time. Designers looking for rules or targets will not find what they are looking for in the *Nicomachean Ethics*. Instead, it will be clear that choosing the right target is their contextual responsibility. Designers must act ethically, but their ethics must already be present. They cannot look elsewhere for them. Every design project has its own noble mark as a specific set of goals for design purpose. There can be no single ultimate particular for *phronesis* in design or anywhere else, and it is thus impossible to have a simple a priori view on any single universal "new good" after the relegation of usability as the "good" of interaction design (Fallman, 2011). Design is necessarily an ethical activity, but it cannot have a single ethics.

Some of Aristotle's gaps can now be regarded as conceptual oversights. He said relatively little about art and still less about design. His specialist writings on the arts focused on the spoken word of tragedy (*Poetics*) and oratory (*Rhetoric*). Specialist works apart, Aristotle tended to assume that everyone knew what art was: "making and acting are different (for their nature we treat even the discussions outside our school as reliable)" (6.4) [1140a2–3]. Aristotle had little to say beyond this prevailing wisdom. Such intellectual neglect of the fine and decorative arts persisted until the eighteenth century, but even the interest in aesthetics developed here did little to move beyond Aristotle's separation of art (the result of *poesis:* making) and practical wisdom (which should guide *praxis:* doing). Art has remained valued for what it creates, and practical wisdom for what it achieves.

A rigid separation of *praxis* and *poetics*, due to Aristotle's asserted differences between *phronesis* and *techne*, is rarely if ever questioned: *poetics* focuses on forms; *praxis* focuses on considered actions (i.e., not creative crafting of artefacts). This unreasonable gulf has persisted for millennia, and thus there is little in the best of what has been thought to guide our development of design theory.

Today we need to consider the possibility of a theory of design that systematically relates the *poetics* of artefacts to creative design *praxis*. We will have to think for ourselves, but Aristotle may have given us somewhere to start. His qualification and circumscription of *aisthesis* as a practical *aesthesis* drew Heidegger's attention. Heidegger (re)framed this as a "circumspective looking" ("*umsichtiges Hinsehen,*" McNeill, 1999). It is not enough to look at the objects of the arts within the safe confines of formal systems of perceptual aesthetics. Instead, we must look around them to the practical contexts of their making and use. Such critical circumspection could significantly deepen Schön's (1983) "reflection on action" and may hold a key to integrating *praxis* and *poetics*.

After two and a half millennia, we should be able to move beyond Aristotle's separation of scientific wisdom, practical wisdom, and art, which far from unraveling from a tangled ball he entwines through his contrasts and comparisons. Design research and practice need to occupy a central space between *techne*, *phronesis*, and *sophia*, exploiting their overlaps and intersections as well as their distinctive qualities. In an intellectual space of *both ... and* that can transition temporarily into *either ... or*, we may never achieve the absolute clarity sought for idealized scientific values (1.3): "We must be content, then, in speaking of such subjects and with such premises to indicate the truth roughly and in outline, and in speaking about things which are only for the most part true and with premises of the same kind to reach conclusions that are no better [1094b19–20]." However, as Aristotle was clear in his valuing of *phronesis* and *techne*, there will be more than adequate rewards to compensate for gaps in his writings. We can now solve some of Aristotle's puzzles (*aporiai*) and fill some of his gaps, but accepting what remains unsolved and unfilled is better for design than dogmatic denial of their existence.

The requirement to accept *aporiai* and gaps sets requirements for reviewers and funders rather than design researchers. The tacit nature of *techne* and judgment means that a full recovery of the deliberations and understandings involved in every design move is not possible.

Summary

Aristotle's contrasts and conclusions are made possible by his systematic construction of a conceptual system, often based on intuition and evidenced only through post hoc examples. Two millennia after Aristotle, the Scientific Revolution consigned such scholastic gymnastics to the epistemic dustbin, safe within a new dogma that *episteme* needed no *nous* to create *sophia*. The result has been to demand evidence, preferably quantitative, so that all argument can proceed via calculation and not the slippery rhetoric of words. While Enlightenment philosophers, especially Kant, demonstrated the logical limits of empiricism as the Scientific Revolution settled down into the scientific establishment, the latter's institutions had achieved a hold similar to that which the Catholic Church once exercised over medieval scholasticism. While denial of Aristotle's conceptual truths lead to the execution of Giordano Bruno and the forced recantation of Galileo Galilei, today denial of the completeness or adequacy of empiricism within scientific cultures can result in academic marginalization and even exclusion.

The truths of design do not lie out there. They lie within us all, to different extents, and with different levels of understanding. They emerge in practice and through practice. Design research practices must embrace a wide range of subjective phenomena, cope with the presence of bias, and replace experimental controls with phronesis "of a controlling kind" [1141b23]. *Phronesis* is not *sophia*, and it cannot be bound or judged by the same truth criteria. The truths of practical wisdom lie not in what is and what will always be, but within what has been achieved somewhere, sometime, by someone in specific circumstances. These truths reside in both the process and the product, within both *praxis* and *poetics*. The resulting excellences can be shared and appreciated, and incorporated into others' practices only if they are understood as a result of deliberations and applied as a result of judgment. These are the foundational implications of design for research.

Research can have no implications for design until it has been deliberated on, understood, and cleverly applied through the exercise of wise judgment. There has to be "correctness of thinking" and excellence (6.12) "in respect both of the end, the manner, and the time" [1142b29]. "Practical wisdom is the true apprehension" [1142b35] "with regard to what conduces to the end" [1142b30]. Whenever the end of design research is to have useful implications for design, researchers must understand and respect the essential role of practical wisdom within design. Theoretical wisdom will never be enough. Designers must be fully present in design research and must design excellently to ensure that their practice base reflects the best of *techne* in the context of the wisest *phronesis* underpinned by demonstrably relevant *sophia*. The demands of scientific truth seem so much more attainable in comparison, which is why this will be design's century. The new will be created, not discovered, but rigorously so.

Returning to Aristotle for the basis for twenty-first century design research may come initially as a surprise to many readers. However, much of what is being attempted in research through design is new. There is little precedent, and we need to be open to a wide range of influences and direction—Aristotle's intellectual excellences can provide some useful direction here.

Note

1. This phrase is often translated as "intellectual virtues," but "virtues" implies "morals" in English in a way that *aretai* does not in Greek, and so "excellences" is preferred (Urmson, 1988).

References

Aristotle. (1934) *The Nicomachean Ethics*, translated by H. Rackham. Loeb Classical Library 73, Aristotle, 19. Cambridge, MA: Harvard University Press.

Aristotle. (2009) *The Nicomachean Ethics*, translated by W. D. Ross, with introduction and notes by L. Brown. Oxford: Oxford University Press. 1925 Ross translation available at http://classics.mit.edu/Aristotle/nicomachaen.mb.txt.

Ashman, K. M., and P. S. Baringer, eds. (2001) *After the Science Wars*. New York: Routledge.

Bardzell, J. (2011) "Interaction Criticism: An Introduction to the Practice." *Interacting with Computers* 23 (6): 604–621.

Buchanan, R. (2001) "Design Research and the New Learning." *Design Issues* 17(4): 3–23.

Cockton, G. (2006) "Designing Worth Is Worth Designing." *Proceedings of the 4th Nordic Conference on Human-computer Interaction: Changing Roles (NordiCHI'06)*. New York: ACM, 165–174.

Cockton, G. (2008) "Revisiting Usability's Three Key Principles." *Extended Abstracts on Human Factors in Computing Systems (CHI EA'08)*. New York: ACM, 2473–2484.

Cockton, G. (2009) "Getting There: Six Meta-Principles and Interaction Design." *Proceedings of the SIGCHI Conference on Human Factors in Computing Systems (CHI'09)*. New York: ACM, 2223–2232.

Cockton, G. (2010) "Design Situations and Methodological Innovation in Interaction Design," *Extended Abstracts on Human Factors in Computing Systems (CHI EA'10)*. New York: ACM, 2745–2754.

Cockton, G. (2012) "UCD: Critique via Parody and a Sequel." *Extended Abstracts on Human Factors in Computing Systems (CHI EA'12)*. New York: ACM, 1–10.

Cockton, G. (2013) "Design Isn't a Shape and It Hasn't Got a Centre: Thinking BIG about Post-centric Interaction Design." *Proceedings of the International Conference on Multimedia, Interaction, Design, and Innovation (MIMI'13)*. New York: ACM, Article 2.

Cockton, G. (2014) "A Critical, Creative UX Community: CLUF." *Journal of Usability Studies* 10 (1): 1–16. http://uxpajournal.org/a-critical-creative-ux-community-cluf/.

Cooper, J. M. (1975) *Reason and Human Good in Aristotle*. Cambridge, MA: Harvard University Press.

Cross, N. (2001) "Designerly Ways of Knowing: Design Discipline versus Design Science." *Design Issues* 17 (3): 49–55.

Cross, N. (2011) *Design Thinking: Understanding How Designers Think and Work*. Oxford: Berg.

Darke, J. (1979) "The Primary Generator and the Design Process." *Design Studies* 1 (1): 36–44.

Dourish, P. (2006) "Implications for Design." *Proceedings of the SIGCHI Conference on Human Factors in Computing Systems (CHI'06)*. New York: ACM, 541–550.

Dreyfuss, H. (1955) *Designing for People*. New York: Simon and Schuster.

Eames Foundation. (2015) *Welcome to the Eames Foundation*. http://www.eamesfoundation.org/.

Fallman, D. (2011) "The New Good: Exploring the Potential of Philosophy of Technology to Contribute to Human-Computer Interaction." *Proceedings of the SIGCHI Conference on Human Factors in Computing Systems (CHI'11)*. New York: ACM, 1051–1060.

Ford, S. (2012) "Reports of Design Thinking's Death Were an Exaggeration." *Fast Company*, January 27. http://www.fastcompany.com/1811688/reports-design-thinkings-death-were-exaggeration.

Frayling, C. (1994) "Research in Art and Design." Monograph. *Royal College of Art Research Papers* 1 (1).

Gaver, W. (2012) "What Should We Expect from Research Through Design?" *Proceedings of the SIGCHI Conference on Human Factors in Computing Systems (CHI'12)*. New York: ACM, 937–946.

Greenberg, S., and B. Buxton. (2008) "Usability Evaluation Considered Harmful (Some of the Time)." *Proceedings of the SIGCHI Conference on Human Factors in Computing Systems (CHI'08)*. New York: ACM, 111–120.

Hahn, S. H. (2015) "Perspectivism." In *The Oxford Handbook of German Philosophy in the Nineteenth Century*, edited by M. Forster and K. Gjesdal, 622–650. Oxford: Oxford University Press.

Höök, K., and J. Löwgren. (2012) "Strong Concepts: Intermediate-Level Knowledge in Interaction Design Research." *AMC Transactions on Computer-Human Interaction (TOCHI)* 19 (3): Article 23.

Kenny, A. (1978) *The Aristotelian Ethics: A Study of the Relationship between the Eudemian and Nicomachean Ethics of Aristotle*. Oxford: Claredon.

Koskinen, I. K., J. Zimmerman, T. Binder, J. Redström, and S. Wensveen. (2011) *Design Research through Practice: From the Lab, Field, and Showroom*. Waltham, MA: Morgan Kaufmann.

Kuutti, K. (2003) "Searching Knowledge for Design—Nurminen's 'Humanistic Perspective' Revisited." In *People and Computers: Twenty-One Ways of Looking at Information Systems*, edited by T. Järvi and P. Reijonen, 29–40. TUCS General Publication No 26. Turku, Finland: Turku Centre for Computer Science. http://tucs.fi/publications/attachment.php?fname=G26.pdf.

Kuutti, K. (2009) "HCI and Design—Uncomfortable Bedfellows?" In *(Re)searching the Digital Bauhaus*, edited by T. Binder, J. Löwgren, and L. Malmborg, L., 43–59. London: Springer.

Lennox, J. (2014) "Aristotle's Biology." *Stanford Encyclopedia of Philosophy*, edited by E. N. Zalta. http://plato.stanford.edu/archives/spr2014/entries/aristotle-biology/.

MacIntyre, A. (2007) *After Virtue: A Study in Moral Theory*, 3rd ed. Notre Dame, IN: University of Notre Dame Press.

McNeill, W. (1999) *The Glance of the Eye: Heidegger, Aristotle, and the Ends of Theory*. Albany, NY: State University of New York Press.

Nelson, H. G., and E. Stolterman. (2003) *The Design Way: Intentional Change in an Unpredictable World*. Englewood Cliffs, NH: Educational Technology.

Nussbaum, M.C., and Rorty, A.O. 1995. *Essays on Aristotle's De Anima*. Oxford.

Polanyi, M. (1958) *Personal Knowledge: Towards a Post-Critical Philosophy*. Chicago: University of Chicago Press.

Potter, N. ([1969] 2002) *What Is a Designer: Things, Places, Messages*, 4th ed. London: Hyphen. Citations refer to 2002 edition.

Quine, W. V. O. (1951) "Two Dogmas of Empiricism." *Philosophical Review* 60 (1): 20–43.

Read, H. E. (1934) *Art and Industry: The Principles of Industrial Design*. London: Faber and Faber.

Rescher, N. (2014) *Vagaries of Value: Basic Issues in Value Theory*. New Brunswick, NJ: Transaction.

Schön, D. (1983) *The Reflective Practitioner: How Professionals Think in Action*. New York: Basic Books.

Simon, H. A. (1981) *The Sciences of the Artificial*, 2nd ed. Cambridge, MA: MIT Press.

Smith, G. C. (2007) Foreword to *Designing Interactions*, by B. Moggridge. Cambridge, MA: MIT Press.

Stolterman, E. (2008) "The Nature of Design Practice and Implications for Interaction Design Research." *International Journal of Design* 2 (1): 55–65.

Suchman, L. (1987) *Plans and Situated Actions: The Problem of Human-Machine Communication.* Cambridge: Cambridge University Press.

Toulmin, S. E. (2001) *Return to Reason.* Cambridge, MA: Harvard University Press.

Urmson, J. O. (1988) *Aristotle's Ethics.* Oxford: Blackwell.

Winograd, T., and Flores, F. (1986) *Understanding Computers and Cognition.* Reading, MA: Addison-Wesley.

Zimmerman, J., J. Forlizzi, and S. Evenson. (2007) "Research through Design as a Method for Interaction Design Research in HCI." *Proceedings of the SIGCHI Conference on Human Factors in Computing Systems (CHI '07).* New York: ACM. https://doi.org/10.1145/1240624.1240704.

II

Pugnacious Aesthetes and Barely Closeted Moralists

Jeffrey Bardzell

I was a pugnacious aesthete and barely closeted moralist.
—Susan Sontag, "Thirty Years Later ..."

"The history of art," writes art critic and philosopher Arthur Danto, "is the history of the suppression of art" (1986, 4). Beginning with Plato's famous exile of poetry from his *Republic* and continuing through twentieth-century obscenity trials over the novels of James Joyce and D. H. Lawrence, to today's "Great Firewall" of China and Molleindustria's App Store-banned iPhone game about the dark side of the iPhone, the suppression of art crosses time, genres, cultures, and technologies. According to Danto, this suppression is political, a reaction to the power of art to shape people's minds, to give them ideas, and to challenge ideas coming from the status quo—traditional morality, governments, sages, global multinationals like Apple, and so on.

The essays and commentaries in this section of the book focus on the power of art and design to help us think beyond conventional wisdom or received ideas (whatever their provenance). Such works can be understood to serve a critical purpose: to change our perspectives, imagine alternative forms of life, cultivate our intellectual virtues, and help us reflect. Such purposes can stimulate political action, or it can contribute to individual enlightenment or aesthetic contemplation. Perspectives along these lines are developed in this section of the book, in particular in the essay-commentary pairings by and on Walter Benjamin, Herbert Marcuse, and Judith Butler.

But accompanying this sense of power is also a fear that it might be exaggerated. Plato's dismissal of art amounted to a criticism that it was merely the copy of a copy (i.e., a picture or representation of a thing in the world that itself is merely an instance of a Form)—that its power was, in fact, illusory. After the Holocaust, the poet W. H. Auden would write, "I know that all the verse I wrote, all the positions I took in the [nineteen] thirties, did not save a single Jew" (Auden, quoted in Danto, 1986, 2). Designers Anthony Dunne and Fiona Raby have sought to distinguish their critical and speculative designs from art in part because of their belief that art is "bracketed" off from real life—that like Auden's poetry, art is too neutered to effect change. These issues extend beyond art to theorizing about art for political change: literary critic Harold Bloom writes that multiculturalist critical theorists are destroying literary studies "in order to advance their supposed (and non-existent) programs for social change" (Bloom, 1994, 4). In this section, relatively recent essays by Bruno Latour and Terry Eagleton fret that critical theory—for all of its progressive rhetoric and political aspirations—has achieved very little, while a much earlier essay by Louis Althusser offers a rather pessimistic view of why such change is so difficult to begin with.

The essays and commentaries in this section thus reflect different positions on a spectrum from optimism to pessimism concerning art and theory's ability to get beyond conventional wisdom or meaningfully challenge the status quo. The optimistic view is that art has the potential to denaturalize the status quo and present the public with real alternatives, all of which can be used to mobilize and support social activism. The pessimistic view is that the systemic and self-reinforcing power of our present status quo is so great that what it can't suppress, it can absorb (e.g., the way haute couture absorbed punk, rendering a threatening working class social movement into consumer fashion). "[I]t is easier to imagine the end of the world than to imagine the end of capitalism," writes Frederic Jameson (2003).

Within this section, a few key ideas surface across the readings, so they are worth pointing out here. One is the Marxist distinction between "base" and "superstructure," which separately accounts for the material systems of production, labor arrangements, property, and so on, which constitute the base; and cultural values, ideologies, rituals, the state, and so forth, which constitute the superstructure. In Marxist analysis, base causes superstructure, and it is difficult to enact change at the level of superstructure (e.g., ideological change) without enacting change at the level of the base. Further, mainstream media and other cultural forms are seen to present the present status quo as if it were natural, rather than contingent, with the effect of discouraging thinking about or acts toward challenging the status quo. Yet works of art and theory have at least the potential to do more than merely serve the status quo, because they can also do disruptive ideological work (e.g., by presenting alternative cultural images and/or by offering social realist accounts that interrogate the causes and consequences of human misery), while themselves circulating within and through the base and thereby potentially intervening at that all-important level.

Another key idea throughout the essays and commentaries in this section is the role of nonhuman agency—cultural forces that contribute to and/or suppress change that are, in a sense, outside of any individual's or groups' hands. Social structures and norms, language and conventions of communication, and technology are such forces: all give shape to human actions, selfhood, and our relations with others. More specifically, they have the capability to frame or position humans into specific structures, such as how a novel casts humans as "readers," how a digital interface casts humans as "users," how prisons (or schools or hospitals) cast humans as "prisoners" (or students or patients) versus "guards" (or teachers or doctors).

Works of art have the capability to reinforce or to disrupt social norms, in part based on the ways that they cast humans as certain types of subjects. For example, feminist literary critic Janice Radway (1984) argues that romance novels encourage (especially working class) women's complacency against patriarchal norms by offering reassuring fantasies in which the male protagonist finally figures out how to be a good partner—so long as the female protagonist waits for this epiphany. In contrast, the feminist films of Laura Mulvey and the feminist video games of Brenda Laurel take an emancipatory stance as the core of their creative practice, seeking new subject roles for female viewers and players as active meaning-makers.

At any rate, the essays throughout this part of the book agree that one role of critique—whether it is embodied as textual theory and criticism or embodied in art or design objects—is to expose relations between nonhumans and humans in ways that reveal the contingency of these relationships and illuminate alternative ways of doing and being that would better serve human needs and desires.

In HCI and design, art-based and humanistic practices of critique have been taken up in a number of ways. A burgeoning literature on design theory and design thinking has risen across the past several decades, a key strand of which is the problem of constructing images of preferred futures and the processes, attitudes, and skills needed to pursue them, as seen in the work of Herbert Simon, Donald Schön, Victor Papanek, and more recently Dunne and Raby. Contemporary discourses on research through design, critical design, speculative design, and constructive design all tap into art-based ways of knowing and doing, a topic that comes up in the commentaries on Terry Eagleton and Arthur Danto in this section of the book. One hope of research through design, critical design, and so on is that design processes and outcomes can contribute to social change by offering disruptive yet plausible visions of better futures, cultivating consumers' ability to distinguish between false pleasures and deeper needs, and by extending design as a discipline, resource, or cultural actor. We have also in recent years seen an accompanying rise in design criticism, broadly modeled on the humanities while seeking to contribute toward the distinctive qualities and capabilities of design (as opposed to, for example, literary texts or paintings). Collectively, the readings in this section offer both cautionary tales of art's and theory's failures to enact social change as well as, more positively, some tools, concepts, and practices that might support design's ability to disclose preferred futures.

The first two essay-commentary pairings in this section are connected to the Frankfurt School of Critical Theory: Walter Benjamin and Herbert Marcuse. The Frankfurt School was active in Weimar Germany; its core thinkers, who also included Max Horkheimer and Theodor Adorno, were suspicious of the "culture industry" and used a Marxist framework to analyze how this industry served the status quo. In his "The

Author as Producer" (chapter 15), Walter Benjamin contributes to this analysis with the suggestion that authors should not operate only in the superstructure (i.e., by constructing narratives and disseminating ideas), but that they should directly engage the base as well, for example, by seeking to change reader-writer relations, the production and distribution of texts, and so on.

Commentator Søren Pold (chapter 16) then applies this argument to contemporary issues in digital media and design, reflecting on the ways (for example) that Apple's App Store policies, censorship tactics, use of a proprietary product ecology, and so on assert extraordinary control over the material base of digital interaction that in turn allows them also to control flows of ideas (i.e., superstructure). Aiming closer to home for many readers of this book, Pold also observes how researchers publishing in for-profit journals and similar venues, where the research is hidden behind paywalls, closes out participation from scholars who can't pay for that access (e.g., in the Global South), thus reinforcing the inequality of research access and prestige in different regions of the world.

In "The New Forms of Control" (chapter 17) from his *One Dimensional Man*, Frankfurt theorist Herbert Marcuse argues that modern industrial society has been so effective at serving citizens' needs that we have become complacent. In doing so we have become "one dimensional," that is, unquestioning of social structures and norms.

In Erik Stolterman's commentary (chapter 18), the implications of such a perspective for designing become clear: when our designs please consumers, do we not contribute to their complacency and the construction of easy desires and easy gratifications? Where might designers turn for inspiration to create more challenging or disruptive designs? Following Marcuse, Stolterman argues that both art and theorizing have the power to offer alternative visions, visions with the potential to challenge our one dimensionality. In making this point, Stolterman taps into a fascinating idea that runs throughout these essays, that art and theorizing might in certain important ways do the same work—to move thought beyond the conventional—just in different communications media.

Louis Althusser's "Ideology and Ideological State Apparatuses" (chapter 19) combines Marxism, psychoanalysis, and structuralism to offer a theory of how ideology "interpellates" us as its "subjects." The basic idea is that ideological structures initiate contact with us and, in doing so, structure the range of responses, such that by the time we respond, we are already operating from within; that is, we are already subjected to the ideology. Althusser's classic example is of the policeman who calls out, "Hey you!" When you turn to look at the policeman, you've already been constituted as a subject of his police power and the ideological apparatus that stands behind it. In other words, ideology inscribes us within it by its mode of address, and this happens prior to and independent of acts of consent on our part.

For commentator Paul Dourish (chapter 20), user-centered design has similar effects: it positions people as (and only as) users. In doing so, it suppresses all the other ways that people might relate to technology (e.g., as citizens who must cope with e-waste) and preempts relevant questions from even coming up; this is, of course, ideological. Dourish's hope is to find an alternative to this ideological subjection, and he turns to Althusser as a resource for resistance—beginning by revealing how HCI and technology have already ideologically circumscribed us.

In "Gender Trouble" (chapter 21), Judith Butler also deploys the concepts of ideology and subjecthood, specifically considering the ways that gender structures our identity and personhood. Similar to the Marxist claim that the base determines the superstructure, Butler argues that the ways that we perform and deploy our bodies—always already circumscribed by gender—(re-)produces gender norms. Butler then asks how we might "trouble" gender, and her response is that we can "queer" it—that is, we can deploy our bodies in queer ways to disrupt the power of gender norms and reveal/explore alternative ways of being and doing.

Commentator Ann Light (chapter 22) wonders how we might queer interaction to open up different ways of interacting with each other and how we might support people's ability to relate to and transform themselves. Whereas Dourish uses Althusser to put his finger on a key way that HCI as a field and technological systems ideologically circumscribe us, Light uses Butler to offer several design tactics to resist and break that ideological circumscription.

Common to the these essays is their participation in what is sometimes referred to as "grand theory," which includes Marxism, feminism, poststructuralism, semiotics, psychoanalysis, and so forth. These theories are sometimes called "grand" descriptively, and sometimes pejoratively. The descriptive sense refers to the scale, sophistication, and complexity of these theories: to use one is to master a philosophical stance comprising metaphysical, ontological, and epistemological commitments as well as an interlocking technical vocabulary (e.g., Marxism's base and superstructure, ideology, false consciousness, alienation, class, dialectic materialism, etc.) as a way to take on a complex hermeneutic problem (e.g., how to read popular culture in a way that is emancipatory). Grand theories can take years to master. The pejorative sense is the belief that they are so grand they overwhelm whatever phenomenon one uses them to analyze, ultimately telling the same story over and over again: for example, every text involves ideology, false consciousness, exploitative systems of production, and class struggle. In Western academic humanities, grand theory peaked in the 1970s and 1980s, and since then something of a backlash has been underway.

The backlash has two motivations. One is the pejorative objection just cited: that grand theories obfuscate the particularity and significance of important works, like looking through a telescope backward. The other is what we might call the futility objection, which is that grand theory never actually brought about the social changes it promised it would. Bruno Latour's "Why Has Critique Run Out of Steam?" (chapter 23) is a retrospective essay that takes the futility objection seriously, even observing that the postmodernist skepticism deployed so brilliantly by Foucault and Derrida to question institutional structures and dominating practices are now being deployed by conservatives to deny climate change, racism, and sexism.

In his commentary (chapter 24), Carl DiSalvo similarly observes disturbing trends in HCI and design: where, for example, instead of pursuing the serious and deeper issue of sustainability, researchers and designers are pursuing the much easier problem of behavior change. In short, HCI and design are, in Marcuse's language, "one-dimensional" and thereby ideologically circumscribed. For those interested in critical and/or reflective design, DiSalvo argues that Latour's essay offers a useful warning.

At the height of grand theory in the 1980s, Marxist literary theorist Terry Eagleton published the most popular book on theory ever written, *Literary Theory* (as evidence of its reach, we three editors—who went to university in the United States, Taiwan, and the United Kingdom—all had to read this book as undergraduates). In it, Eagleton surveys major critical theories and offers his own political take on them. Some decades later, he wrote *After Theory*, a selection of which ("The Politics of Amnesia," chapter 25) is included here. In it, Eagleton reflects on literary theory after its fall from fashion, including its legacy—successes and failures—and what remains to be done. Invoking the Marxist notion of base and superstructure, he argues that literary readings must be grounded in the materiality of their production and consumption—not merely the superstructural realm of ideas and cultural signifiers.

Commentator Mark Blythe (chapter 26) proposes to extend this thinking to critical design. Critical design clearly seeks to operate in the superstructure—disrupting the status quo, proposing alternative ideological stances, and the like—and yet Blythe observes that critical designs participate in the base, even somewhat embarrassingly: they are shown in elite cultural institutions and are sold for significant sums of actual money as desirable consumer objects in the very marketplace they ostensibly seek to undermine. Like much of grand theory itself, critical design's actual political impacts appear to be quite limited. Where Terry Eagleton claims that grand theory is born of political defeat—for example, the rise of National Socialism and Stalinism for the Frankfurt School and the "gentrified" Marxism that subsequently became so fashionable (but politically futile) in academic circle—Blythe somewhat pessimistically wonders whether critical design should be read the same way.

The vast majority of the theories in this book are associated with twentieth-century theorizing on the European continent, in France and Germany in particular. This tradition, broadly speaking, applied many of the concepts developed by the philosophers Marx, Husserl, Heidegger, Gadamer, de Beauvoir, Foucault, Derrida, and Butler to the analysis of cultural works (from literature to pop culture) and the elaboration of complex theories. But another intellectual tradition was also active throughout the twentieth century and into the present, one that largely ignored (or outright disparaged) continental philosophers: the tradition of Anglo-American so-called analytic philosophy. Its leading thinkers included Gottlob Frege, Ludwig Wittgenstein, George Edward Moore, Bertrand Russell, Gilbert Ryle, J. L. Austin, and Willard van Orman Quine. Key features of this tradition are a sympathy (even fetish) for science, an analytic and even "deflationary" stance toward philosophical theory (including a fierce distaste for metaphysics), and an emphasis on pragmatism and "garden-variety common sense," to borrow a phrase of analytic philosopher Noël Carroll.

The sole author in this book representing this tradition is philosopher and art critic for *The Nation*, Arthur Danto (with whom we began this introduction). Philosophers of art in the Anglo-American tradition had, in the 1950s and 1960s, been seeking to justify critical statements about art, for example, claims that distinguish art from nonart, evaluate art, that account for art's effects (e.g., aesthetic experience), and that theorize the distinctive qualities of individual art forms (e.g., painting vs. dance). Such questions were pragmatic, aiming to support artistic development, curatorial decisions, art education in public schools, public funding for the arts, and the advancement of art criticism. In the decades from Marcel Duchamp to Andy Warhol, these questions had taken on additional urgency. Aesthetic philosophers at the time sought answers to these questions in features or qualities intrinsic in artworks and art forms as well as in the aesthetic experience. Danto's contribution to these debates was to argue that what makes something art is not intrinsic to the object or any experience it causes but rather a theory of art that could account for an object *as art*, which in his influential 1964 essay of the same name Danto referred to as the "artworld" (chapter 27).

In his commentary (chapter 28), Jeffrey Bardzell uses Danto to take on a similar challenge, that of research through design (RtD), which claims to be both design and research, and which is often denied to be one, the other, or both—rather like the way modernist artworks are frequently denied to be art at all. Bardzell argues that if Danto is right, that it is a certain theory that allows Duchamp's and Warhol's works to be art—then perhaps there remains a gap in theory that is inhibiting the HCI and design communities' uptake of research through design. Here again the intimate relationship between theory and art objects is emphasized, undercutting the intuitive but problematic notion that text-based theory and art/design inhabit different discursive universes. Art objects and research through design are able to do theory, but certain theories have to be in place for this work to occur.

References

Bloom, H. (1994) *The Western Canon: The Books and School of the Ages*. New York: Riverhead Books.

Danto, A. (1986) *The Philosophical Disenfranchisement of Art*. New York: Columbia University Press.

Jameson, F. (2003) "Future City." *New Left Review* 21 (May–June), https://newleftreview.org/II/21/fredric-jameson-future-city.

Radway, J. (1984) *Reading the Romance: Women, Patriarchy, and Popular Literature*. Chapel Hill: University of North Carolina Press.

15 The Author as Producer (1934)

Walter Benjamin, translated by Edmund Jephcott

The task is to win over the intellectuals to the working class by making them aware of the identity of their spiritual enterprises and of their conditions as producers.
—Ramón Fernandez

You will remember how Plato, in his model state, deals with poets. He banishes them from it in the public interest. He had a high conception of the power of poetry. But he believed it harmful, superfluous—in a *perfect* community, of course. The question of the poet's right to exist has not often, since then, been posed with the same emphasis; but today it poses itself. Probably it is only seldom posed in this *form*. But it is more or less familiar to you all as the question of the autonomy of the poet: of his freedom to write whatever he pleases. You are not disposed to grant him this autonomy. You believe that the present social situation compels him to decide in whose service he is to place his activity. The bourgeois writer of entertainment literature does not acknowledge this choice. You prove to him that, without admitting it, he is working in the service of certain class interests. A more advanced type of writer does recognize this choice. His decision, taken on the basis of a class struggle, is to side with the proletariat. That puts an end to his autonomy. His activity is now decided by what is useful to the proletariat in the class struggle. Such writing is commonly called *tendentious*.

There you have the catchword around which has long circled a debate familiar to you. Its familiarity tells you how unfruitful it has been. For it has not advanced beyond the monotonous reiteration of arguments for and against: *on one hand*, the correct political line is demanded of the poet; *on the other*, it is justifiable to expect his work to have quality. Such a formulation is of course unsatisfactory as long as the connection between the two factors, political line and quality, has not been *perceived*. Of course, the connection can be asserted dogmatically. You can declare: a work that shows the correct political tendency need show no other quality. You can also declare: a work that exhibits the correct tendency must of necessity have every other quality.

This second formulation is not uninteresting, and, further: it is correct. I make it my own. But in doing so I abstain from asserting it dogmatically. It must be *proved*. And it is in order to attempt to prove it that I now claim your attention. This is, you will perhaps object, a very specialized, out-of-the-way theme. And how do I intend to promote the study of fascism with such a proof? That is indeed my intention. For I hope to be able to show you that the concept of political tendency, in the summary form in which it usually occurs in the debate just mentioned, is a perfectly useless instrument of political literary criticism. I should like to show you that the tendency of a literary work can only be politically correct if it is also literarily correct. That is to say that the politically correct tendency includes a literary tendency. And I would add straight away: this literary tendency, which is implicitly or explicitly contained in every *correct* political tendency, alone constitutes the quality of the work. The correct political tendency of a work includes its literary quality *because* it includes its literary *tendency.*

This assertion—I hope I can promise you—will soon become clearer. For the moment I should like to interject that I might have chosen a different starting point for my reflections. I started from the unfruitful debate on the relationship between tendency and quality in literature. I could have started from an even older and no less unfruitful debate: what is the relationship between form and content, particularly in political poetry? This kind of question has a bad name: rightly so. It is the textbook case of the attempt to explain literary connections with undialectical clichés. Very well. But what, then, is the dialectical approach to the same question?

The dialectical approach to this question—and here I come to my central point—has absolutely no use for such rigid, isolated things as: work, novel, book. It has to insert them into the living social context. You rightly declare that this has been done time and again among our friends. Certainly. Only it has often been done by launching at once into large, and therefore necessarily often vague, questions. Social conditions are, as we know, determined by conditions of production. And when materialist criticism approach a work, it was accustomed to ask how this work stood in relation to the social relations of production of its time. This is an important question. But also a very difficult one. Its answer is not always unambiguous. And I should like now to propose to you a more immediate question. A question that is somewhat more modest, somewhat less far-reaching, but which has, it seems to me, more chance of receiving an answer. Instead of asking: what is the attitude of a work to the relations of production of its time? Does it accept them, is it reactionary—or does it aim at overthrowing them? Is it revolutionary?" Instead of this question, or at any rate before this question, I should like to propose another. Rather than asking: what is the *attitude* of a work to the relations of production of its time? I should like to ask: what is its *position* in them? This question directly concerns the function the work has within the literary relations of production of its time. It is concerned, in other words, directly with the literary *technique* of works.

In the concept of technique, I have named that concept which makes literary products directly accessible to a social and therefore a materialist analysis. At the same time, the concept of technique provides the dialectical starting point from which the unfruitful antithesis of form and content can be surpassed. And furthermore, this concept of technique contains an indication of the correct determination of the relation between tendency and quality, the question raised at the outset. If, therefore, we stated earlier that the correct political tendency of a work includes its literary quality, because it includes its literary tendency, we can now formulate this more precisely by saying that this literary tendency can consist either in progress or of regression in literary technique.

You will certainly approve if I now pass on, with only an appearance of arbitrariness, to very concrete literary conditions. Russian conditions. I should like to direct your attention to Sergei Tretiakov and to the type, defined and embodied by him, of the "operating" writer. This operating writer provides the most tangible example of the functional interdependency which always and under all conditions exists between the correct political tendency and progressive literary technique. I admit only one example: I hold others in reserve. Tretiakov distinguishes the operating from the informing writer. His mission is not to report but to struggle; not to play the spectator but to intervene actively. He defines this mission by the account he gives of his own activity. When, in 1928, at the time of the total collectivization of agriculture, the slogan "Writers to the *kolkhoz!*" was proclaimed, Tretiakov went to the commune "Communist Lighthouse" and there, during two lengthy stays, set about the following tasks: calling mass meetings; collecting funds to pay for tractors; persuading independent peasants to enter the *kolkhoz* [collective farm]; inspecting the reading rooms; creating wall newspapers and editing the *kolhhoz* newspaper; reporting for Moscow newspapers; introducing radio and mobile cinemas, etc. It is not surprising that the book *Commanders of the Field,* which Tretiakov wrote following these stays, is said to have had considerable influence on the further development of collective agriculture.

You may have a high regard for Tretiakov, and yet still be of the opinion that his example does not prove a great deal in this context. The tasks he performed, you will perhaps object, are those of a journalist or a propagandist; all this has little to do with literature. However, I did intentionally quote the example of Tretiakov in order to point out to you how comprehensive is the horizon within which we have to rethink our conceptions of literary forms or *genres,* in view of the technical factors affecting our present situation, if we are to identify the forms of expression that channel the literary energies of the present. There were not always novels in the past, and there will not always have to be; not always tragedies, not always great epics; not always were the forms of commentary, translation, indeed, even so-called plagiarism, playthings in the margins of literature; they had a place not only in the philosophical but also in the literary writings of Arabia and China. Rhetoric has not always been a minor form, but set its stamp in antiquity on large provinces of literature. All this is to accustom you to the thought that we are in the midst of a mighty recasting of literary forms, a melting-down in which many of the opposites in which we have been accustomed to think may lose their force. Let me give an example of the unfruitfulness of such opposites and of the process of their dialectical transcendence. And we shall remain with Tretiakov. For this example is the newspaper. "In our writing," a left-wing author writes,[1]

> opposites which in happier periods fertilized one another, have become insoluble antinomies. Thus science and *belles lettres*, criticism and production, education and politics, fall apart in disorder. The theatre of this literary confusion is the newspaper, its content 'subject matter,' which denies itself any other form of organization than that imposed on it by the readers' impatience. And this impatience is not only that of the politician expecting information or of the speculator on the lookout for a tip; behind it smolders that of the man on the sidelines who believes he has the right to see his own interests expressed. The fact that nothing binds the reader more tightly to his paper than this impatient longing for daily nourishment, the publishers have long exploited by constantly opening new columns to his questions, opinions, protests. Hand in hand, therefore, with the indiscriminate assimilation of facts goes the equally indiscriminate assimilation of readers who are instantly elevated to collaborators. In this, however, a dialectic moment is concealed: the decline of writing in the bourgeois press proves to be the formula for its revival in that of Soviet Russia. For as writing gains in breadth what it loses in depth, the conventional distinction between author and public, which is upheld by the bourgeois press, begins in the Soviet press to disappear. For the reader is at all times ready to become a writer, that is, a describer, but also a prescriber. As an expert—even if not on a subject but only on the post he occupies—he gains access to authorship. Work itself has its turn to speak. And the account it gives of itself is a part of the competence needed to perform it. Literary qualification is no longer founded on specialized but rather on polytechnic education, and is thus public property. It is, in a word, the literarization of the conditions of living that masters the otherwise insoluble antinomies, and it is in the theatre of the unbridled debasement of the word—the newspaper—that its salvation is being prepared.

I hope to have shown by this quotation that the description of the author as a producer must extend as far as the press. For by the press, at any rate by the Soviet Russian press, one recognizes that the mighty process of recasting which I spoke of earlier not only affects the conventional distinction between *genres*, between writer and poet, between scholar and popularizer, but also revises even the distinction between author and reader. Of this process the press is the decisive example, and therefore any consideration of the author as producer must include it.

It cannot, however, stop at this point. For the newspaper in Western Europe does not constitute a serviceable instrument of production in the hands of the writer. It still belongs to capital. Since on one hand the newspaper, technically speaking, represents the most important literary position, but, on the other, this position is in the hands of the opposition, it is no wonder that the insight of the writer into his social conditionality, his technical means and his political task, has to grapple with the most immense difficulties. It has been one of the decisive processes of the last ten years in Germany that a considerable proportion of its productive minds, under the pressure of economic conditions, have passed through a revolutionary development in their attitudes, without being able simultaneously to rethink their own work, their relation to the means of production, their technique, in a really revolutionary way. I am speaking, as you see, of the so-called left-wing intellectuals, and will limit myself to the bourgeois Left. In Germany the leading politico-literary movements of the last decade have emanated from this left-wing intelligentsia. I shall mention two of them, Activism and New Matter-of-Factness, to show by these examples that a political tendency, however revolutionary it may seem, has a counterrevolutionary function as long as the writer feels his solidarity with the proletariat only in his attitudes, not as a producer.

The catchword in which the demands of Activism are summed up is "logocracy," in plain language, rule of the mind. This is apt to be translated as rule of the intellectuals. In fact, the concept of the intellectual, with its attendant spiritual values, has established itself in the camp of the left-wing intelligentsia, and dominates its political manifestoes from Heinrich Mann to Döblin. It can readily be seen that this concept has been coined without any regard for the position of the intellectuals in the process of production. Hiller, the theoretician of Activism, himself means intellectuals to be understood not as "members of certain professions" but as "representatives of a certain characterological type." This characterological type naturally stands as such between the classes. It encompasses any number of private individuals without offering the slightest basis for organizing them. When Hiller formulates his denunciation of the party leaders, he concedes them a good deal; they may be "in important matters better informed ... have more popular appeal ... fight more courageously" than he, but of one thing he is sure: that they "think more defectively." Probably, but what does this matter, since politically it is not private thinking but, as Brecht once expressed it, the art of thinking in other people's heads that is decisive. Activism attempted to replace materialistic dialectics by the notion—in class terms unquantifiable—of common sense.[2] Its intellectuals represent at best a social group. In other words: the very principle itself on which this collective is formed is reactionary; no wonder that its effect could never be revolutionary.

However, this pernicious principle of collectivization continues to operate. This could be seen three years ago, when Döblin's *Wissen und Verändern* [*Know and Change*] came out. As is known, this pamphlet was written in reply to a young man—Döblin calls him Herr Hocke—who had put to the famous author the question "What is to be done?" Döblin invites him to join the cause of socialism, but with reservations. Socialism, according to Döblin, is: "freedom, a spontaneous union of men, the rejection of all compulsion, indignation at injustice and coercion, humanity, tolerance, a peaceful disposition." However this may be, on the basis of this socialism, he sets his face against the theory and practice of the radical workers' movement. "Nothing," Döblin declares, "can come out of anything that was not already in it—and from a murderously exacerbated class war justice can come, but not socialism." "You, my dear sir," thus Döblin formulates the recommendation which, for these and other reasons, he gives Herr Hocke, "cannot put into effect your agreement in principle with the struggle (of the proletariat) by joining the proletarian front. You must be content with an agitated and bitter approval of this struggle, but you also know that if you do more, an immensely important post will remain unmanned ... the original communistic position of human individual freedom, of the spontaneous solidarity and union of men.... It is this position, my dear sir, that alone falls to you." Here it is quite palpable where the conception of the "intellectual," as a type defined by his opinions, attitudes or dispositions, but not by his position in the process of production, leads. He must, as Döblin puts it, find his place *beside* the proletariat. But what kind of place is that? That of a benefactor, of an ideological patron. An impossible place. And so we return to the thesis stated at the outset: the place of the intellectual in the class struggle can be identified, or, better, chosen, only on the basis of his position in the process of production.

For the transformation of the forms and instruments of production in the way desired by a progressive intelligentsia—that is, one interested in freeing the means of production and serving the class struggle—Brecht coined the term *Umfunktionierung* [functional transformation]. He was the first to make of intellectuals the far-reaching demand: not to supply the apparatus of production without, to the utmost extent possible, changing it in accordance with socialism. "The publication of the *Versuche*," the author writes in introducing the series of writings bearing this title, "occurred at a time when certain works ought no longer to be individual experiences (have the character of works), but should rather concern the use (transformation) of certain institutes and institutions." It is not spiritual renewal, as fascists proclaim, that is desirable: technical innovations are suggested. I shall come back to these innovations. I should like to content myself here with a reference to the decisive difference between the mere supplying of a productive apparatus and its transformation. And I should like to preface my discussion of the "New Matter-of-Factness" with the proposition that to supply a productive apparatus without—to the utmost extent possible—changing it would still be a highly censurable course even if the material with which it is supplied seemed to be of a revolutionary nature. For we are faced with the fact—of which the past decade in Germany has furnished an abundance of examples—that the bourgeois apparatus of production and publication can assimilate astonishing quantities of revolutionary themes, indeed, can propagate them without calling its own existence, and the existence of the class which owns it, seriously into question. This remains true at least as long as it is supplied by hack writers, even though they be revolutionary hacks. I define the hack writer as the man who abstains in principle from alienating the productive apparatus from the ruling class by improving it in ways serving the interests of socialism. And I further maintain that a considerable proportion of so-called left-wing literature possessed no other social function than to wring from the political situation a continuous stream of novel effects for the entertainment of the public. This brings me to the New Matter-of-Factness. Its stock-in-trade was reportage. Let us ask ourselves to whom this technique was useful.

For the sake of clarity I shall place its photographic form in the foreground. What is true of this can also be applied to the literary form. Both owe the extraordinary increase in their popularity to the technology of publication: the radio and the illustrated press. Let us think back to Dadaism. The revolutionary strength of Dadaism consisted in testing art for its authenticity. Still lifes put together from tickets, spools of thread, cigarette butts, that were linked with artistic elements. They put the whole thing in a frame. And they thereby show the public: look, your picture frame ruptures the age; the tiniest authentic fragment of daily life says more than paintings. Just as the bloody finger print of a murderer on the page of a book says more than the text. Much of this revolutionary content has sought survival in photomontage. You need only think of the work of John Heartfield, whose technique made the book cover into a political instrument. But now follow the path of photography further. What do you see? It becomes ever more *nuancé*, ever more modern, and the result is that it can no longer photograph a tenement block or a refuse heap without transfiguring it. It goes without saying that it is unable to say anything of a power station or a cable factory other than this: what a beautiful world! "A Beautiful World"—that is the title of the well-known picture anthology by Renger-Patsch, in which we see New Matter-of-Fact photography at its peak. For it has succeeded in making even abject poverty, by recording it in a fashionably perfected manner, into an object of enjoyment. For if it is an economic function of photography to restore to mass consumption, by fashionable adaptation, subjects that had earlier withdrawn themselves from it—springtime, famous people, foreign countries—it is one of its political functions to renew from within—in other words: fashionably—the world as it is.

Here we have a flagrant example of what it means to supply a productive apparatus without changing it. To change it would have meant to overthrow another of the barriers, to transcend another of the antitheses, which fetter the production of intellectuals. In this case, the barrier between writing and image. What we require of the photographer is the ability to give his picture that caption which wrenches it from modish commerce and gives it a revolutionary use-value. But we shall make this demand most emphatically when we—the writers—take up photography. Here, too, therefore, technical progress is for the author as producer the foundation of his political progress. In other words: only by transcending the specialization in the process of production that, in the bourgeois view, constitutes its order can one make this production politically useful; and the barriers imposed by specialization must be breached jointly by the productive forces that they were set up to divide. The author as producer discovers—in discovering his solidarity with the proletariat—simultaneously his solidarity with certain other producers who earlier seemed scarcely to concern him. I have spoken of the photographer; I shall very briefly insert a word of Eisler's on the musician: "In the development of music, too, both in production and in reproduction, we must learn to perceive an ever-increasing process of rationalization.... The phonograph record, the sound film, jukeboxes can purvey top-quality music ... canned as a commodity. The consequence of this process of rationalization is that musical reproduction is consigned to ever-diminishing, but also ever more highly qualified groups of specialists. The crisis of the commercial concert is the crisis of an antiquated form of production made obsolete by new technical inventions." The task therefore consisted of an *Umfunktionierung* of the form of the concert that had to fulfill two conditions: to eliminate the antithesis first between performers and listeners and second between technique and content. On this Eisler makes the following illuminating observation: "One must beware of overestimating orchestral music and considering it the only high art. Music without words gained its great importance and its full extent only under capitalism." This means that the task of changing the concert is impossible without the collaboration of the word. It alone can effect the transformation, as Eisler formulates it, of a concert into a political meeting. But that such a transformation does indeed represent a peak of musical and literary technique, Brecht and Eisler prove with the didactic play *The Measures Taken.*

If you look back from this vantage point on the recasting of literary forms that I spoke of earlier, you can see how photography and music, and whatever else occurs to you, are entering the growing molten mass from which the new forms are cast. You find it confirmed that only the literarization of all the conditions of life provides a correct understanding of the extent of this melting-down process, just as the state of the class struggle determines the temperature at which—more or less perfectly—it is accomplished.

I spoke of the procedure of a certain modish photography whereby poverty is made an object of consumption. In turning to New Matter-of-Factness as a literary movement, I must take a step further and say that it has made the *struggle against poverty* an object of consumption. The political importance of the movement was indeed exhausted in many cases by the conversion of revolutionary reflexes, insofar as they occurred in the bourgeoisie, into objects of amusement which found their way without difficulty into the big-city cabaret business. The transformation of the political struggle from a compulsion to decide into an object of contemplative enjoyment, from a means of production into a consumer article, is the defining characteristic of this literature. A perceptive critic has explained this, using the example of Erich Kästner, as follows:

> With the workers' movement this left-wing radical intelligentsia has nothing in common. It is, rather, as a phenomenon of bourgeois decomposition, a counterpart of the feudalistic disguise that the Second Empire admired in the reserve officer. The radical-life publicists of the stamp of Kästner, Mehring or Tucholsky are the proletarian camouflage of decayed bourgeois strata. Their function is to produce, from the political standpoint, not parties but cliques; from the literary standpoint, not schools but fashions; from the economic standpoint, not producers but agents. Agents or hacks who make a great display of their poverty, and a banquet out of yawning emptiness. One could not be more totally accommodated in an uncozy situation.

This school, I said, made a great display of its poverty. It thereby shirked the most urgent task of the present-day writer: to recognize how poor he is and how poor he has to be in order to begin again from the beginning. For that is what is involved. The

Soviet state will not, it is true, banish the poet like Plato, but it will—and this is why I recalled the Platonic state at the outset—assign him tasks which do not permit him to display in new masterpieces the long-since counterfeit wealth of creative personality. To expect a renewal in terms of such personalities and such works is a privilege of fascism, which gives rise to such scatterbrained formulations as that with which Günter Gründel in his *Mission of the Young Generation* rounds off the section on literature: "We cannot better conclude this ... survey and prognosis than with the observation that the *Wilhelm Meister* and the *Green Henry* of our generation have not yet been written." Nothing will be farther from the author who has reflected deeply on the conditions of present-day production than to expect, or desire, such works. His work will never be merely work on products but always, at the same time, on the means of production. In other words, his products must have, over and above their character as works, an organizing function, and in no way must their organizational usefulness be confined to their value as propaganda. Their political tendency alone is not enough. The excellent Lichtenberg has said: "A man's opinions are not what matters, but the kind of man these opinions make of him." Now it is true that opinions matter greatly, but the best are of no use if they make nothing useful out of those who have them. The best political tendency is wrong if it does not demonstrate the attitude with which it is to be followed. And this attitude the writer can only demonstrate in his particular activity: that is in writing. A political tendency is the necessary, never the sufficient condition of the organizing function of a work. This further requires a directing, instructing stance on the part of the writer. And today this is to be demanded more than ever before. *An author who teaches writers nothing, teaches no one.* What matters, therefore, is the exemplary character of production, which is able first to induce other producers to produce, and second to put an improved apparatus at their disposal. And this apparatus is better the more consumers it is able to turn into producers, that is, readers or spectators into collaborators. We already possess such an example, to which, however, I can only allude here. It is the epic theater of Brecht.

Tragedies and operas are constantly being written that apparently have a well-tried theatrical apparatus at their disposal, while in reality they do nothing but supply one that is derelict. "The lack of clarity about their situation that prevails among musicians, writers and critics," says Brecht, "has immense consequences that are far too little considered. For, thinking that they are in possession of an apparatus which in reality possesses them, they defend an apparatus over which they no longer have any control and which is no longer, as they still believe, a means for the producers, but has become a means against the producers." This theater, with its complicated machinery, its gigantic supporting staff, its sophisticated effects, has become a means against the producers not least in seeking to enlist the producers in the hopeless competitive struggle in which film and radio have enmeshed it. This theater—whether in its educating or its entertaining role; both are complementary—is that of a sated class for which everything it touches becomes a stimulant. Its position is lost. Not so that of a theater which, instead of competing with newer instruments of publication, seeks to use and learn from them, in short, to enter into debate with them. This debate the epic theater has made its own affair. It is, measured by the present state of development of film and radio, the contemporary form.

In the interest of this debate Brecht fell back on the most primitive elements of the theater. He contented himself, broadly, with a podium. He dispensed with wide-ranging plots. He thus succeeded in changing the functional connection between stage and public, text and performance, director and actor. Epic theater, he declared, had to portray situations rather than develop plots. It obtains such situations, as we shall see presently, by interrupting the plot. I remind you here of the songs, which have their chief function in interrupting the action. Here—in the principle of interruption—epic theater, as you see, takes up a procedure that has become familiar to you in recent years from film and radio, press and photography. I am speaking of the procedure of montage: the superimposed element disrupts the context in which it is inserted. But that this procedure has here a special, perhaps even a perfect right, allow me briefly to indicate. The interruption of action, on account of which Brecht described his theater as *epic*, constantly counteracts an illusion in the audience. For such illusion is a hindrance to a theater that proposes to make use of elements of reality in experimental rearrangements. But it is at the end, not the beginning, of the experiment that the situation appears. A situation that, in this or that form, is always ours. It is not brought home to the spectator but distanced from him. He recognizes it as the real situation, not with satisfaction, as in the theater of naturalism, but with astonishment. Epic theater, therefore, does not reproduce situations, rather, it discovers them. This discovery is accomplished by means of the interruption of sequences. Only interruption does not have here the character of a stimulant but of an organizing function. It arrests the action in its course, and thereby compels the listener to adopt an attitude vis-à-vis the process, the actor vis-à-vis his role. I should like to show you by an example how Brecht's discovery and use of the *gestus* is nothing other than the restoration of the method of montage decisive in radio and film, from an often merely modish procedure to a human event. Imagine a family scene: the wife is just about to grab a bronze sculpture to throw it at her daughter; the father is opening the window to call for help. At this moment a stranger enters. The process is interrupted; what appears in its place is the situation on which the stranger's eyes now fall: agitated faces, open window, disordered furniture. There are eyes, however, before which the more usual scenes of present-day existence do not look very different. The eyes of the epic dramatist.

To the total dramatic art work he opposes the dramatic laboratory. He makes use in a new way of the great ancient opportunity of the theater—to expose what is present. At the center of his experiment is man. Present-day man; a reduced man, therefore, chilled in a chilly environment. Since, however, this is the only one we have, it is in our interest to know him. He is subjected to tests, examinations. What emerges is this:

events are alterable not at their climaxes, not by virtue and resolution, but only in their strictly habitual course, by reason and practice. To construct from the smallest elements of behavior what in Aristotelian dramaturgy is called "action," is the purpose of epic theater. Its means are therefore more modest than those of traditional theater; its aims likewise. It is less concerned with filling the public with feelings, even seditious ones, than with alienating it in an enduring manner, through thinking, from the conditions in which it lives. It may be noted by the way that there is no better start for thinking than laughter. And, in particular, convulsion of the diaphragm usually provides better opportunities for thought than convulsion of the soul. Epic theater is lavish only in occasions for laughter.

It has perhaps struck you that the train of thought that is about to be concluded presents to the writer only one demand, the demand *to think*, to reflect on his position in the process of production. We may depend on it: this reflection leads, sooner or later, for the writers *who matter*, that is, for the best technicians in their subject, to observations which provide the most factual foundation for their solidarity with the proletariat. I should like to conclude by adducing a topical illustration in the form of a small extract from a journal published here, *Commune*. *Commune* circulated a questionnaire: "For whom do you write?" I quote from the reply of Réne Maublanc and from the comment added by Aragon. "Unquestionably," says Maublanc,

> I write almost exclusively for a bourgeois public. First, because I am obliged to [here Maublanc refers to his professional duties as a grammar school teacher] and second, because I have bourgeois origins and a bourgeois education and come from a bourgeois *milieu*, and so am naturally inclined to address myself to the class to which I belong, that I know and understand best. This does not mean, however, that I write in order to please or support it. On one hand I am convinced that the proletarian revolution is necessary and desirable, on the other that it will be the more rapid, easy, successful, and the less bloody, the weaker the opposition of the bourgeoisie.... The proletariat today needs allies from the camp of the bourgeoisie, exactly as in the eighteenth century the bourgeoisie needed allies from the feudal camp. I wish to be among those allies.

On this Aragon comments:

> Our comrade here touches on a state of affairs that affects a large number of present-day writers. Not all have the courage to look it in the face.... Those who see their own situation as clearly as René Maublanc are few. But precisely from them more must be required.... It is not enough to weaken the bourgeoisie from within, it is necessary to fight them *with* the proletariat.... René Maublanc and many of our friends among the writers who are still hesitating, are faced with the example of the Soviet Russian writers who came from the Russian bourgeoisie and nevertheless became pioneers of the building of socialism.

Thus Aragon. But how did they become pioneers? Certainly not without very bitter struggles, extremely difficult debates. The considerations I have put before you are an attempt to draw some conclusions from these struggles. They are based on the concept to which the debate on the attitude of the Russian intellectuals owes its decisive clarification: the concept of the specialist. The solidarity of the specialist with the proletariat—herein lies the beginning of this clarification—can only be a mediated one. The Activists and the representatives of New Matter-of-Factness could gesticulate as they pleased: they could not do away with the fact that even the proletarianization of an intellectual hardly ever makes a proletarian. Why? Because the bourgeois class gave him, in the form of education, a means of production which, owing to educational privilege, makes him feel solidarity with it, and still more it with him. It was thereby entirely correct when Aragon, in another connection, declared: "The revolutionary intellectual appears first and foremost as the betrayer of his class of origin." This betrayal consists, in the case of the writer, in conduct which turns him, from a supplier of the productive apparatus, into an engineer who sees it as his task to adapt this apparatus to the purposes of the proletarian revolution. This is a mediating activity, yet it frees the intellectual from that purely destructive task to which Maublanc and many of his comrades believe it necessary to confine him. Does he succeed in promoting the socialization of the intellectual means of production? Does he see ways of himself organizing the intellectual workers in the production process? Has he proposals for the *Umfunktionierung* of the novel, the drama, the poem? The more completely he can orient his activity towards this task, the more correct will be the political tendency, and necessarily also the higher the technical quality, of his work. And on the other hand: the more exactly he is thus informed on his position in the process of production, the less it will occur to him to lay claim to "spiritual" qualities. The spirit that holds forth in the name of fascism *must* disappear. The spirit which, in opposing it, trusts in its own miraculous powers, *will* disappear. For the revolutionary struggle is not between capitalism and spirit but between capitalism and the proletariat.

Notes

1. Benjamin himself; see *Schriften*, Frankfurt/M., 1955, vol. I, p. 384.—ED.

2. In place of this sentence there was in the manuscript originally a different one that was deleted: "Or, to speak with Trotsky: 'If the enlightened pacifists attempt to abolish war by means of rationalistic argument, they simply make fools of themselves, but if the armed masses begin to use the arguments of reason against war, that means the end of war.'"—ED.

16 The (Cultural) Interface Designer as Producer

Søren Bro Pold

Software is mind control—get some.
I/O/D, http://bak.spc.org/iod/

I

When participatory design (PD) was developed as a way of designing with the workers and not only for the workers (or for their boss), it was a new way of dealing with the politics of IT design. However, at that time it was still fairly clear that IT design was seen as producing a functional tool for the workplace (Ehn and Kyng, [1991] 2003). Today, with the widespread adaptation of IT in settings where specific purposes or production processes are more difficult to define, it becomes clear that IT can no more be specified as just a tool and primarily related to the "base" of production. Instead, it becomes increasingly evident that IT design influences and is part of the "superstructure." The notions of "base" and "superstructure" are central concepts from Marxist theory used to distinguish between the primary, economical, societal forces and relations of production (the base) and the ideological, cultural, and religious superstructure. In classical Marxist thinking, the base determines the superstructure; however, in the current postindustrial or postmodern society a sharp distinction is becoming increasingly difficult and technology takes part in this blurring by engaging both in the base and superstructure, thus creating relations and blurring the borders (Jameson, 1984). Examples of IT in superstructure areas are diverse and increasing, from the importance of IT in art and cultural consumption and production, in communication, and as a social platform (e.g., through smartphones and social networking software), to the importance of IT in urban space (in media architecture, smart city development), to the implementation of IT in structures that implement power, law, and politics such as management and governmental systems, and to the role of IT in the market as a way of providing the backbone for financial capitalism and for a (neoliberal) expansion of capitalist strategies.

However, when IT design becomes part of the superstructure as part of designing for public spaces, commons, communication, social settings, culture, and identity—then discussing the political role of IT design becomes not only more important but also more complicated than in the original PD attempts, where it was a question of bringing the workers into the design process. If PD researchers discovered that software design is political, this discovery now has implications beyond the workplace and the way workers relate to the production process. Today software contains ideological values and directions, including ways of distributing what can be seen, what can be acted on, and what remains hidden (Rancière, 2004), distributing access, rights, and power, allocating money and framing economies through technological business models, or enabling new ways of capturing, monitoring, and thereby reorganizing activities and organizations (Agre, [1994] 2003). Examples of this are smartphones, tablets, and social media, including the ways companies like Apple and Facebook control access to their platforms and networks, exclude nudity, and suppress some political activism and criticism—especially if it targets their own platforms, as was the case with the Molleindustria game Phone Story, a smartphone game criticizing the manufacturing of smartphones, which was banned from Apple's App Store (http://phonestory.org/). In this sense Apple and others control what Rancière (2004) terms the "distribution of the sensible"—a concept that describes how sense perception in culture discloses aspects of the common by defining specific perspectives in relation to classes and groups in society—in very literal ways. With an iPhone and social software you have a particular access to the social environment; with a streaming music service and headphones, a pervasive game, or a GPS-based map you have other kinds of access. All of these interfaces are integrated in smartphones, and just by carrying a smartphone you are potentially always connected to the augmented reality space. All these accesses are of course heavily mediated by software and hardware, and developed as business models and power relations. Furthermore, the distribution of the sensible happens not only in front of the interfaces but also behind them through the ways they extensively monitor the behavior of their users, collect and capitalize this behavioral data, and even deliver it to intelligence agencies like the National Security Agency, as has become evident with the Snowden case (Andersen and Pold, 2014).

Today, Marxist thinking has, through materialist dialectics, to a large extent become a foundation for theories around (new) media and aesthetics that can be labeled material or media aesthetics, including important theorists like Walter Benjamin, Marshall McLuhan, Raymond Williams, and, later, J. D. Bolter, Richard Grusin, and Lev Manovich. Of course not all of the later positions would count as Marxist; McLuhan especially would not fit the political scheme, though one can find many common notions in McLuhan and Benjamin concerning their materialist thinking about media and the role of art in relation to media. Furthermore, there have been many discussions on how to understand the dialectical relationship between base and superstructure, such as whether it should be understood as technological determinism where the "medium is the message," or whether the dialectics open up for more nuanced ways of analyzing relations between technological media and the superstructure of aesthetics and culture (see, for example, Bolz, 1990).

A good reason for turning to materialist aesthetics, however, is that it is well suited to discussion about the computer and its interface, which can even be understood as a mechanism for coupling base and superstructure. As the pioneer of computer graphics and semiotics Frieder Nake has argued, the computer is an "instrumental medium," combining the instrumental machine with the representational medium (Nake, 2000). One could say that we use it as a tool while communicating with it as a medium, but in most cases the machine and the medium are even more intertwined, as when we play a computer game, use social media, or browse the web, where it is almost meaningless to distinguish the machine from the medium. The interface connects the functional machine—its tool character and possibilities for execution, automation, and transactions—with the representational medium—its signs, metaphors and cultural traditions.

In this way, it seems obvious that we can learn from discussions within materialistic aesthetics about relations between the material basis and the ideological superstructure in order to find a way to discuss the political role of the cultural designer. With this in mind, let us turn to one of the founding theoreticians, Walter Benjamin, and one of the first texts in which he develops his materialist aesthetics.

II

Walter Benjamin (1892–1940) was a German Jewish literary theorist who, during the 1930s, was engaged in opposing and criticizing the Nazi use of art and media until his death by suicide, when he failed to escape the Nazi military advances at the border of Spain in France in 1940. Broadly speaking, Benjamin sought alternatives to Nazism in Marxism combined with some Jewish messianic thinking and carried out through a re-reading of the history of phantasmagoric, mediated forms of society from the sixteenth century through the early twentieth century.[1] "The Author as Producer," an address that Benjamin intended to read at the Communist Institute for the Study of Fascism in Paris (which was probably never held), is probably as Marxist as Benjamin gets, including as it does references to the Soviet Union (Benjamin [1934] 1996, 781n1). In this manuscript Benjamin develops his thoughts on the relations between art and politics. He returns to this subject in a later seminal essay, "The Work of Art in the Age of Mechanical Reproduction," which is about relations between art and media and which is probably the single most cited reference in new media theory.

The title of the essay, "The Author as Producer" ("Der Autor als Produzent"), relates directly to the dialectics between base and superstructure. In it, Benjamin argues that authors, normally placed within the superstructure, should consider how writing and publishing is production and thus also directly related to the base. The essay discusses what it could mean to see the author as producer of his own text, including the apparatus it is produced and published through, as well as a producer of writing, understood as an ideological construct that rests on the apparatus of production and distribution. Furthermore, the author should consider writing in ways that break down professional hierarchies between writers and readers and instead write for a new kind of audience, a writerly reader—a reader on the brink of becoming a writer, a collaborative, participatory reader-writer. Referring to the socialist playwright Bertolt Brecht, Benjamin demands authors partake in an "Umfunktionierung" (functional transformation) of the production system in order "not to supply the apparatus of production without, to the utmost extent possible, changing it in accordance with socialism" (Benjamin, [1934] 1996, 774). If an author does not acknowledge this challenge, Benjamin contents, he is working in the service of the established powers. Instead, the challenge for the author "consists in conduct that transforms him from a supplier of the productive apparatus into an engineer who sees it as his task to adapt this apparatus to the purposes of the proletarian revolution" (Benjamin, [1934] 1996, 780).

Whether or not one believes that a proletarian revolution is something imminently to wish for, one point is clear: that even as a producer in the superstructure, one has to think about how one's work feeds the production apparatus and which kinds of power it supports. As quoted above, Benjamin is rather forward speaking in demanding the author transform from "a supplier of the productive apparatus into an engineer" who is able to adapt the production apparatus, including the institutions, and technology—today including hardware and software—that his work is part of. It is not just the writing that is important, but how it fits into, modifies, or even revolutionizes the productive apparatus.

Benjamin insists on changing the relations between writers and readers that he sees exemplified in newspapers, as, for example, in worker correspondence and reportage. This might sound fitting to the gospel of Web 2.0 (e.g., O'Reilly, 2005), but only if we forget about the capitalistic business model behind Web 2.0, which the artist and activist Dmitry Kleiner characterizes as "private capture of community-created value" (Kleiner, 2010, 17). If contemporary authors write for Web 2.0 they are only suppliers, not engineers engaging with the power structures of the publication apparatus. They are like traditional authors producing the expected and recognized masterpieces that fit the capitalist production system Benjamin criticizes. Instead, he asks for work written for a new, writerly reader, a reader who "is at all times ready to become a writer" (Benjamin, [1934] 1996, 771). Benjamin asks the author to extend his role to become a teacher, an organizer, an engineer, and a producer:

> *An author who teaches writers nothing, teaches no one*. What matters, therefore, is the exemplary character of production, which is able first to induce other producers to produce, and second to put an improved apparatus at their disposal. And this apparatus is better the more consumers it is able to turn into producers, that is, readers or spectators into collaborators. (Benjamin, [1934] 1996, 777)

In all these ways the author must become a producer: he must write in ways that relate to the conditions of production, to the material base; he must do so in order to prepare his readers to become writers and even to make this possible for them by engineering an "improved apparatus"; and finally, he must work toward turning consumers into producers and collaborators.

III

Seen from today, this transformation is both straightforward and very demanding. On the one hand, it has become a leading business model within Web 2.0 services like Facebook and Twitter, and with multinational IT and culture industries like Amazon, Apple, and Google, to transform readers, spectators, consumers, or users into collaborators and (co-)producers through platforms such as Facebook, YouTube, and Amazon's CreateSpace Kindle Direct Publishing print-on-demand, e-book, and publishing platforms. However, the way this transformation happens is tightly controlled and monitored by combinations of software and hardware from these global-market monopolies, and it has become increasingly difficult to get insight into, if not change, how your writing and collaboration is used, captured, and capitalized as a user of, for example, Facebook or Google. And if it is difficult to manage your privacy in Facebook or figure out and control what Google knows about you, this is just the beginning of a development of new IT appliances with limited access for users. As the writer, editor, and journalist Cory Doctorow argues, current trends in IT development are concerned with making limited IT appliances instead of universal computers, and in this sense the apparatus becomes increasingly opaque and inaccessible for ordinary users. Examples of this include smartphones, tablets (e.g., Apple's iOS platform), e-readers (like Amazon Kindle), and game consoles (e.g., PlayStation and X Box), which are protected and controlled by "a combination of rootkits, spyware and code-signing to prevent the user from knowing which processes are running, from installing her own software, and from terminating processes that she doesn't want" (Doctorow, 2012).

Consequently it has become easier to collaborate—in fact many contemporary Web 2.0 business models build on capitalizing user-driven collaboration—but increasingly difficult to adapt and modify or even understand the platform one is collaborating with.

In line with this, Geoff Cox and Joasia Krysa also take their starting point in "The Author as Producer" in their introduction to an anthology of critical perspectives on *Engineering Culture*. They argue that we find "contradictory tendencies" when we look at modern "user-friendly" interfaces and operating systems: "Despite surface appearances, however, the underlying processes are decidedly complex and there is a vast amount of expertise invested in the operating system. The operating system "masks" the "real" operation of the computer by interposing itself between the user and the Central Processing Unit" (Cox and Krysa, 2005, 12). Cox and Krysa's argument points to a condition for all interfaces that to some extend hide "complex underlying processes" and mask "real" operations behind a user-friendly surface, even though one could ask whether the coded layers (e.g., assembly language, higher-level languages) behind the graphical user interface are more real than the icons on its surface. In any case, there is a balance between deliberately masking functioning behind an interface and more enlightening interface design, which might aim to reduce complexity while educating the user about what goes on behind the screen.

Cox and Krysa also argue that something new is at stake in the digital economy where networks promote a post-industrial factory, which is not defined by a fixed place and time but by the free labor taking place on, for example, collaborative Web 2.0 platforms. To critically explore this and "engineer change," they argue with a quotation from Benjamin that "it remains necessary to transform the cultural producer 'from a supplier of the production apparatus, into an engineer who sees his task in adapting the apparatus'" (Cox and Krysa, 2005, 26). Whereas earlier much interface design aimed at enlightening and emancipating the user toward the possibility of adapting the apparatus—such as through the personal computer revolution spearheaded by Kay and Goldberg at Xerox PARC (Kay and Goldberg, [1977] 2003) and followed up by free software (Stallman, [1985] 2003)—currently there seems to be a countertrend toward more closed and manipulative interface design as described above in relation to Doctorow's IT appliances. A particularly malicious example is the Brightest Flashlight Free Android app, which secretly collects and sends data to advertisers while the user thinks he or she just got a free flashlight (Arthur, 2013).

IV

Benjamin's version of materialist dialectics lays the foundation for a way of thinking about media that he would further elaborate in a later essay, "The Work of Art." Already in "The Author as Producer," Benjamin links this thinking to Brecht and his attempt at dismantling the phantasmagorical forms on stage in his Epic theater in order to teach the audience to see through the staging.

In relation to Brecht's Epic theater, Benjamin argues that instead of competing with newer means of publication, including media such as film and radio, it should "enter into debate with them" (Benjamin, [1934] 1996, 776). He quotes Brecht's criticism of cultural producers who do not understand the apparatus of which they are a part:

> The lack of clarity about their situation that prevails among musicians, writers, and critics [says Brecht] has immense consequences that are far too little considered. For, thinking that they are in possession of an apparatus which in reality possesses them, they defend an apparatus over which they no longer have any control and that is no longer, as they still believe, a means for the producers, but has become a means against the producers." (Brecht, quoted in Benjamin, [1934] 1996, 777)

Benjamin describes how Brecht goes against a form of theater that is competing with radio and cinema through the use of complicated machinery, gigantic supporting staff, and sophisticated effects with the result that "everything it touches becomes a stimulant." Instead Brecht falls back on "the most primitive elements of the theater" and explores the effects of interruption and montage in order to change the "functional connection between stage and public, text and performance, director and actor" (778). In other words, instead of relying on phantasmagorical forms and competing with the media spectacle, Brecht aimed to educate his audience through entering into debate with media, demonstrating and deconstructing its phantasmagorical forms.

This criticism could very well be considered by digital producers or even by the mass of collaborators in contemporary social networking software. How does software and design incorporate users and their collaboration? Are they truly empowered, are they put in a position where they are able to understand—if not control—the apparatus and how their collaboration is part of it? Or has the apparatus become a means against the producers—a criticism which could be raised in relation to how consumption and production are controlled by contemporary smartphone platforms and "IT appliances" due to their way of restricting access to the file system, file distribution, operating system, and hardware (Doctorow, 2012; Andersen and Pold, 2014). What does it mean to be a producer in such a standardized system? As many cultural producers have realized, it means being prone to Apple's deliberately vague guidelines, their constant updates of software and hardware, and generally serving their platform and business model. The creator Molleindustria of the above-mentioned critical game, Phone Story, was told that they were banned from Apple's App Store because they violated four guidelines. None of these four guidelines states that a game should not criticize the iPhone, but it is, for example, forbidden to "depict violence or abuse of children." As a consequence the game got rejected for describing and criticizing how the production of iPhones entails abuse and violence. Furthermore it was banned from not following Apple's specific prescribed models of generating revenue for charitable games but aiming to raise money in other ways (http://www.phonestory.org/banned.html). Numerous other cases have also demonstrated that companies like Apple deliberately have extensive but unclear policies in order to enforce self-censorship from producers. Finally, Apple keeps out apps that can function as alternatives to their own business: for example, they banned an Android magazine from the Newsstand app store (Andersen and Pold, 2014).

As a user it is difficult to control—or even know about—which kinds of behavior these platforms monitor and what they use this data for because of the ways the platforms and services are locked down or hidden in the cloud. The current unrolling NSA leaks by Edward Snowden document how much these platforms are used for monitoring behind our backs, which risks making them impossible to use for sensitive communication. An editorial in *The Guardian* commented on the NSA scandal and on the future use of digital networks and platforms for sensitive journalists like the main reporter on the case, Glenn Greenwald: "That work is immensely complicated by the certainty that it would be highly unadvisable for Greenwald (or any other journalist) to regard any electronic means of communication as safe.... Soon we will be back to pen and paper" (Rusbridger, 2013). In this way, being able to "enter into debate" and understand the media apparatus one is taking part of has become both more difficult and urgent because of such recent developments.

V

As stated earlier, "The Author as Producer" is probably as Marxist as Benjamin gets; however, he develops a dialectic tension between "the correct political line" and (literary, artistic) quality in stating that "the tendency of a literary work can be politically correct only if it is also literarily correct" (Benjamin, [1934] 1996, 769). Consequently, it is not just a question of the "correct' political content, but of a deep investigation of form and technique, which Benjamin sums up with a rephrasing of how to question the political tendency of a work: "Rather than asking: what is the *attitude* of a work to the relations of production of its time? I should like to ask: what is its *position* in them? This question directly concerns the function the work has within the literary relations of production of its time. It is concerned, in other words, directly with the literary *technique* of works" (Benjamin, [1934] 1996, 770). Consequently, Benjamin's version of materialist dialectics calls for a deep consideration of the dialectical relation between content and technique, between what one wants to achieve and the technique applied—for example, the kinds of technology, mediation, representation, semiotics, and aesthetics that are used. Furthermore, he argues for an introspective way of exploring this, questioning how the work critically explores, reflects on, and develops its own technique, including how this internal technique is part of contemporary relations of production. In this way, the tendency of a work is both an internal question between form and content and a question about how these internal dialectics—how the relations of production is positioned *in* the work—are related to the contemporary relations of production of which it is part.

If we want to follow this, discussing media and IT design, we will have to analyze and critically discuss the materials—technologies, designs, interfaces, aesthetics, rhetoric—we use in order to figure out the tendency of our work. We should develop a critical analysis of materials and materiality, and this analysis should be simultaneously introspective and dialectic. Only in this way can we discover how the current design is part of and "enter[s] into a debate" with its technological context.

This is of course also relevant to reflect on when we publish our research in academic systems consisting of commercial publishers or academic associations with software-based systems and business models that might serve, for example, to exclude readers from outside the academy or from the Global South—in fact, Bodó Balázs argues that if academics want a readership outside of the first world, the best we can do is to upload our publications to pirate shadow libraries (Renzenbrink, 2015). While serving to uphold disciplines and create academic communities, sometimes our academic professional environment, with its peer review systems and established methods, might not be the best way to "enter into debate" with others than addressing our immediate peers. In these cases we are as academics also part of a production system that is difficult to negotiate or break away from without losing our professional positions. We are certainly under a pressure to publish (and to get grants) that would have thwarted many great researchers if they had been under the same pressure. As an anecdote, I remember one of the key developers of Scandinavian participatory design saying that when he was working with unions and typographers for years to better their working conditions and developing new design methods, they almost ceased to publish academic papers and only published manuals and articles for workers. His conclusion was that this would never have been possible in the highly competitive university of today. It is probably also worth mentioning here that Walter Benjamin himself never had an academic career—was his dissertation rejected by Frankfurt University. While it is difficult to break completely away from today's academic publishing system, we might still think of negotiating it, for example, by choosing publishers without steep pay walls, opting for open access whenever possible and perhaps even overlooking a bit of everyday piracy.

In order to understand how IT reconfigures relations between base and superstructure, we need critical theory. I have argued that dialectic materialistic theory is relevant and that Benjamin might be a good starting point and an important addition to the growing awareness of criticism and critical theory in HCI, interaction design and interface criticism (see, e.g., Bardzell, 2009; Bardzell and Bardzell, 2008; Bardzell, Bolter, and Löwgren, 2010; Bertelsen and Pold, 2004; Blythe, Robinson, and Frohlich, 2008; Andersen and Pold, 2011).

Dialectic materialistic theories are especially relevant in situations where it is difficult, with current PD methods, to identify users, purposes, and stakeholders or where the design will be used by people who cannot be meaningfully defined as stakeholders or users but are just passersby, perhaps unconsciously being captured by the system or taking part in a transaction they cannot escape or understand. In such cases, dialectical materialism can help us discuss and engage with political issues such as power relations of and in the interface.

A particular aspect could be issues of transparency that goes beyond usability toward a more political understanding of transparency, allowing for transparent technologies, where users and prodUsers (i.e., users as content creators) are given a chance to see, understand, and influence how their data, interactions, and productions are treated (Arns, 2011). And of course this critical engagement is not only analytic and theoretic but also interventionist, designerly, and construction oriented. We also need (more) critical design that entails critical understandings of its interfaces and technologies, design that realizes software is ideological, design that explores conflicts and struggles and their techno-culture political dimensions instead of always aiming to mediate opposition through technical fixes and attempts at solutionism.

VI

"The Author as Producer" does not provide easy answers on how to evaluate work politically despite its Marxist language. Benjamin probably realized that. Toward the end of the piece, he rhetorically addresses possible objections by stating that the purpose is a call for reflection:

> It has perhaps struck you that the train of thought that is about to be concluded presents the writer only one demand, the demand *to think*, to reflect on his position in the process of production. We may depend on it: this reflection leads, sooner or later, for the writers *who matter*, that is, for the best technicians in their subject, to observations which provide the most factual foundation for their solidarity with the proletariat. (Benjamin, [1934] 1996, 779)

Who is this proletariat? Maybe we all belong to it now and then—proletarians without ownership to the means of production—when using corporate systems like Google and Facebook, iPhone and Kindle without any control over the means of production, which is closed off by opaque interfaces and licenses that limit our rights of use and ownership. For example, the iPhone and the Kindle are designed to limit sharing and make secondhand selling virtually impossible—how many secondhand iPhone games or Kindle e-books have you seen at garage sales lately? Such systems combine a specific use of technology to distribute the relations between the "authors" (transmitters, companies, software producers) and the "prodUsers" in ways that secure their monopolistic business models by limiting the potential of the technology. As the German poet and essayist Hans Magnus Enzensberger eloquently put it in 1970, arguing for bringing the lessons of Benjamin into late 1960s leftist theory in a critical engagement with the media instead of simple rejection:

> Monopoly capitalism develops the consciousness-shaping industry more quickly and more extensively than other sectors of production; it must at the same time fetter it. A socialist media theory has to work at this contradiction, demonstrate that it cannot be solved within the given productive relationships—rapidly increasing discrepancies, potential destructive forces. (Enzensberger, [1970] 2003, 261)

A bit further down Enzensberger also writes about how the "technical distinction between receivers and transmitters [which is constructed and upheld for political and economic reasons] reflects the social division of labor into producers and consumers" (Enzensberger [1970] 2003, 262). Enzensberger writes mainly about radio and the way it is enclosed in a broadcast model, but his starting point is the many new "electronic media" of the late 1960s, including video, satellite technologies, and computers, which he, with great foresight, observed were "constantly forming new connections both with each other and with older media ... [and were] clearly coming together to form a universal system" (261). In this sense his argument for truly emancipatory, mobilizing, collective, and reciprocal media is even more relevant today. However, if you wonder whether this is just leftist utopianism, then looking at the development of "free software" might provide a concrete example of the potential of critical software development. As software freedom activist Richard Stallman puts it, he started producing free software because he refused to "break solidarity with other users" and instead argued for building software as a "social contribution" (Stallman, [1985] 2003, 546, 548). Furthermore, in his ethnographic study of the free software movement, technology anthropologist Christopher Kelty points to how software design and political significance are intertwined in his concept of a recursive public, which is

> a public that is vitally concerned with the material and practical maintenance and modification of the technical, legal, practical, and conceptual means of its own existence as a public; it is a collective independent of other forms of constituted power and is capable of speaking to existing forms of power through the production of actually existing alternatives. (Kelty, 2008, 3)

Free software is definitely not an automatic guarantee for open and fair IT design, as can be seen be with, for example, Google's appropriation of free software for its Android smartphone platform, which in many ways work like Apple's IOS platform—perhaps with a slightly more open architecture but probably with even more behavioral monitoring in order to generate data and traffic for Google. However, if we follow Kelty's analysis of how criticism is a vital part of the construction of a recursive public, we might have a contemporary example of what Benjamin asks for and what we need in order to design technology for a better future. If we want a future where we will not have to go "back to pen and paper" (Rusbridger, 2013) to be able to trust and "enter into debate" (Benjamin, [1934] 1996, 776) with our technologies, we will need more critical approaches to and in IT design. Luckily, there are germs for a different way of looking at IT design and HCI that allow designers to think about their material and their role in superstructure contexts—as producers of values, ideology, power relations, and culture.

Note

1. The concept of phantasmagoria was made famous by Karl Marx, who used it in his analysis of the fetish character of the commodity and how the commodity conceals its production process and instead is staged in spectacular ways through advertising, and so forth, in order to identify the commodity with bourgeois desire instead of the exploitation of labor. (See Buck-Morss, 1992; Marx, [1867] 1974.) "Phantasmagoria" was originally a name for a laterna magica projection-based ghost show invented by Etienne Gaspard Robertson in Paris in 1798, which was staged in a way that it concealed its mechanism and way of working. Phantasmagoria became an

important concept for Benjamin, who, during the 1930s, worked consistently with tracing the phantasmagorical forms in the early-modern urban Paris in order to find the roots—and possible alternatives—to Fascist and Nazi use of art, media, and propaganda in an anesthetization of politics and society.

References

Agre, P. E. ([1994] 2003) "Surveillance and Capture: Two Models of Privacy." In Montfort and Wardrip-Fruin 2003, 737–760.

Andersen, C. U., and S. Pold, eds. (2011) *Interface Criticism: Aesthetics beyond Buttons.* Aarhus, Denmark: Aarhus University Press.

Andersen, C. U., and S. Pold. (2014) "Controlled Consumption Culture: When Digital Culture Becomes Software Business." In *The Imaginary App,* edited by S. Matviyenko and P. D. Miller, 17–33. Cambridge, MA: MIT Press.

Arns, I. (2011) "Transparent World: Minoritarian Tactics in the Age of Transparency." In Andersen and Pold 2011, 253–276.

Arthur, C. (2013) "Android Torch App with over 50m Downloads Silently Sent User Location and Device Data to Advertisers." *Guardian,* December 6. https://www.theguardian.com/technology/2013/dec/06/android-app-50m-downloads-sent-data-advertisers.

Bardzell, J. (2009) "Interaction Criticism and Aesthetics." *Proceedings of the SIGCHI Conference on Human Factors in Computing Systems (CHI'09).* New York: ACM, 2357–2366.

Bardzell, J., and S. Bardzell. (2008) "Interaction Criticism: A Proposal and Framework for a New Discipline of HCI." *Extended Abstracts on Human Factors in Computing Systems (CHI EA'08).* New York: ACM, 2463–2472.

Bardzell, J., J. Bolter, and J. Löwgren. (2010) "Interaction Criticism: Three Readings of an Interaction Design, and What They Get Us." *interactions* 17 (2): 32–37.

Benjamin, W. ([1934] 1996) "The Author as Producer." In *Walter Benjamin: Selected Writings,* vol. 2, edited by M. W. Jennings, H. Eiland, and G. Smith, 768–782. Cambridge, MA: Belknap Press of Harvard University Press.

Bertelsen, O. W., and S. Pold. (2004) "Criticism as an Approach to Interface Aesthetics." *Proceedings of the Third Nordic Conference on Human-Computer Interaction (NordiCHI'04).* New York: ACM, 23–32.

Blythe, M., J. Robinson, and D. Frohlich. (2008) "Interaction Design and the Critics: What to Make of the 'Weegie.'" *Proceedings of the 5th Nordic Conference on Human-Computer Interaction: Building Bridges (NordiCHI'08).* New York: ACM, 53–62.

Bolz, N. (1990) "Abschied von der Gutenberg-Galaxis: Medienästhetik nach Nietzsche, Benjamin, und McLuhan." In *Armaturen der Sinne: Literarische und technische Medien 1870 bis 1920,* edited by J. Hörisch and M. Wetzel, 139–156. Munich: Fink.

Buck-Morss, S. (1992) "Aesthetics and Anaesthetics: Walter Benjamin's Artwork Essay Reconsidered," *October* 62: 3–41.

Cox, G., and J. Krysa. Introduction to *Engineering Culture: On the Author as (Digital) Producer.* Brooklyn, NY: Autonomedia, 7–30.

Doctorow, C. (2012) "Lockdown: The Coming War on General-Purpose Computing." *BoingBoing* (blog). http://boingboing.net/2012/01/10/lockdown.html.

Ehn, P., and M. Kyng. ([1991] 2003) "Cardboard Computers: Mocking-It-Up or Hands-On the Future." In Montfort and Wardrip-Fruin 2003, 651–662.

Enzensberger, H. M. ([1970] 2003) "Constituents of a Theory of the Media." In Montfort and Wardrip-Fruin 2003, 261–275.

Jameson, F. (1984) "Postmodernism, or the Cultural Logic of Late Capitalism." *New Left Review* 1 (146): 53–93.

Kay, A., and A. Goldberg. ([1977] 2003) "Personal Dynamic Media." In Montfort and Wardrip-Fruin 2003, 391–404.

Kelty, C. M. (2008) *Two Bits: The Cultural Significance of Free Software.* Durham, NC: Duke University Press.

Kleiner, D. (2010) *The Telekommunist Manifesto.* Amsterdam: Institute of Network Cultures.

Marx, K. ([1867] 1974) *Das Kapital.* Vol. 1, *Der Produktionsprozeß des Kapitals.* Berlin: Dietz.

Montfort, N., and N. Wardrip-Fruin, eds. (2003) *The New Media Reader.* Cambridge, MA: MIT Press.

Nake, F. (2000) "Der Computer als Automat, Werkzeug und Medium und unser Verhältnis zu ihm." In *Menschenbild und Computer. Selbstverständnis und Selbstbehauptung des Menschen im Zeitalter der Rechner*, edited by H. Buddemeier, 73–90. Bremen, German: University of Bremen.

O'Reilly, T. (2005) "What Is Web 2.0: Design Patterns and Business Models for the Next Generation of Software." *O'Reilly* (blog). http://www.oreillynet.com/pub/a/oreilly/tim/news/2005/09/30/what-is-web-20.html.

Rancière, J. (2004) *The Politics of Aesthetics: The Distribution of the Sensible.* London: Continuum.

Renzenbrink, T. (2015) "Pirate Libraries and the Future of Access." *Elektor*, February 27. https://www.elektormagazine.com/articles/pirate-libraries-and-the-future-of-access.

Rusbridger, A. (2013) "David Miranda, Schedule 7 and the Danger That All Reporters Now Face." *Guardian*, August 19.

Stallman, R. ([1985] 2003) "The GNU Manifesto." In Montfort and Wardrip-Fruin 2003, 545–550.

17 The New Forms of Control (1964)

Herbert Marcuse

A comfortable, smooth, reasonable, democratic unfreedom prevails in advanced industrial civilization, a token of technical progress. Indeed, what could be more rational than the suppression of individuality in the mechanization of socially necessary but painful performances; the concentration of individual enterprises in more effective, more productive corporations; the regulation of free competition among unequally equipped economic subjects; the curtailment of prerogatives and national sovereignties which impede the international organization of resources. That this technological order also involves a political and intellectual coordination may be a regrettable and yet promising development.

The rights and liberties which were such vital factors in the origins and earlier stages of industrial society yield to a higher stage of this society: they are losing their traditional rationale and content. Freedom of thought, speech, and conscience were—just as free enterprise, which they served to promote and protect—essentially *critical* ideas, designed to replace an obsolescent material and intellectual culture by a more productive and rational one. Once institutionalized, these rights and liberties shared the fate of the society of which they had become an integral part. The achievement cancels the premises.

To the degree to which freedom from want, the concrete substance of all freedom, is becoming a real possibility, the liberties which pertain to a state of lower productivity are losing their former content. Independence of thought, autonomy, and the right to political opposition are being deprived of their basic critical function in a society which seems increasingly capable of satisfying the needs of the Individuals through the way in which it is organized. Such a society may justly demand acceptance of its principles and institutions, and reduce the opposition to the discussion and promotion of alternative policies *within* the status quo. In this respect, it seems to make little difference whether the increasing satisfaction of needs is accomplished by an authoritarian or a non-authoritarian system. Under the conditions of a rising standard of living, non-conformity with the system itself appears to be socially useless, and the more so when it entails tangible economic and political disadvantages and threatens the smooth operation of the whole. Indeed, at least in so far as the necessities of life are involved, there seems to be no reason why the production and distribution of goods and services should proceed through the competitive concurrence of individual liberties.

Freedom of enterprise was from the beginning not altogether a blessing. As the liberty to work or to starve, it spelled toil, insecurity, and fear for the vast majority of the population. If the individual were no longer compelled to prove himself on the market, as a free economic subject, the disappearance of this kind of freedom would be one of the greatest achievements of civilization. The technological processes of mechanization and standardization might release individual energy into a yet uncharted realm of freedom beyond necessity. The very structure of human existence would be altered; the individual would be liberated from the work world's imposing upon him alien needs and alien possibilities. The individual would be free to exert autonomy over a life that would be his own. If the productive apparatus could be organized and directed toward the satisfaction of the vital needs, its control might well be centralized; such control would not prevent individual autonomy, but render it possible.

This is a goal within the capabilities of advanced industrial civilization, the "end" of technological rationality. In actual fact, however, the contrary trend operates: the apparatus imposes its economic and political requirements for defense and expansion on labor time and free time, on the material and intellectual culture. By virtue of the way it has organized its technological base, contemporary industrial society tends to be totalitarian. For "totalitarian" is not only a terroristic political coordination of society, but also a non-terroristic economic-technical coordination which operates through the manipulation of needs by vested interests. It thus precludes the emergence of an effective opposition against the whole. Not only a specific form of government or party rule makes for totalitarianism, but also a specific system of production and distribution which may well be compatible with a "pluralism" of parties, newspapers, "countervailing powers," etc.

Today political power asserts itself through its power over the machine process and over the technical organization of the apparatus. The government of advanced and advancing industrial societies can maintain and secure itself only when it succeeds in mobilizing, organizing, and exploiting the technical, scientific, and mechanical productivity available to industrial civilization. And this productivity mobilizes society as a whole, above and beyond any particular individual or group interests. The brute fact that the machine's physical (only physical?) power surpasses that of the individual, and of any particular group of individuals, makes the machine the most effective political instrument in any society whose basic organization is that of the machine process. But the political trend may be reversed; essentially the power of the machine is only the stored-up and projected power of man. To the extent to which the work world is conceived of as a machine and mechanized accordingly, it becomes the *potential* basis of a new freedom for man.

Contemporary industrial civilization demonstrates that it has reached the stage at which "the free society" can no longer be adequately defined in the traditional terms of economic, political, and intellectual liberties, not because these liberties have become insignificant, but because they are too significant to be confined within the traditional forms. New modes of realization are needed, corresponding to the new capabilities of society.

Such new modes can be indicated only in negative terms because they would amount to the negation of the prevailing modes. Thus economic freedom would mean freedom *from* the economy—from being controlled by economic forces and relationships; freedom from the daily struggle for existence, from earning a living. Political freedom would mean liberation of the individuals *from* politics over which they have no effective control. Similarly, intellectual freedom would mean the restoration of individual thought now absorbed by mass communication and indoctrination, abolition of "public opinion" together with its makers. The unrealistic sound of these propositions is indicative, not of their utopian character, but of the strength of the forces which prevent their realization. The most effective and enduring form of warfare against liberation is the implanting of material and intellectual needs that perpetuate obsolete forms of the struggle for existence.

The intensity, the satisfaction and even the character of human needs, beyond the biological level, have always been preconditioned. Whether or not the possibility of doing or leaving, enjoying or destroying, possessing or rejecting something is seized as a *need* depends on whether or not it can be seen as desirable and necessary for the prevailing societal institutions and interests. In this sense, human needs are historical needs and, to the extent to which the society demands the repressive development of the individual, his needs themselves and their claim for satisfaction are subject to overriding critical standards.

We may distinguish both true and false needs. "False" are those which are superimposed upon the individual by particular social interests in his repression: the needs which perpetuate toil, aggressiveness, misery, and injustice. Their satisfaction might be most gratifying to the individual, but this happiness is not a condition which has to be maintained and protected if it serves to arrest the development of the ability (his own and others) to recognize the disease of the whole and grasp the chances of curing the disease. The result then is euphoria in unhappiness. Most of the prevailing needs to relax, to have fun, to behave and consume in accordance with the advertisements, to love and hate what others love and hate, belong to this category of false needs.

Such needs have a societal content and function which are determined by external powers over which the individual has no control; the development and satisfaction of these needs is heteronomous. No matter how much such needs may have become the individual's own, reproduced and fortified by the conditions of his existence; no matter how much he identifies himself with them and finds himself in their satisfaction, they continue to be what they were from the beginning—products of a society whose dominant interest demands repression.

The prevalence of repressive needs is an accomplished fact, accepted in ignorance and defeat, but a fact that must be undone in the interest of the happy individual as well as all those whose misery is the price of his satisfaction. The only needs that have an unqualified claim for satisfaction are the vital ones—nourishment, clothing, lodging at the attainable level of culture. The satisfaction of these needs is the prerequisite for the realization of *all* needs, of the unsublimated as well as the sublimated ones.

For any consciousness and conscience, for any experience which does not accept the prevailing societal interest as the supreme law of thought and behavior, the established universe of needs and satisfactions is a fact to be questioned—questioned in terms of truth and falsehood. These terms are historical throughout, and their objectivity is historical. The judgment of needs and their satisfaction, under the given conditions, involves standards of *priority*—standards which refer to the optimal development of the individual, of all individuals, under the optimal utilization of the material and intellectual resources available to man. The resources are calculable. "Truth" and "falsehood" of needs designate objective conditions to the extent to which the universal satisfaction of vital needs and, beyond it, the progressive alleviation of toil and poverty, are universally valid standards. But as historical standards, they do not only vary according to area and stage of development, they also can be defined only in (greater or lesser) *contradiction* to the prevailing ones. What tribunal can possibly claim the authority of decision?

In the last analysis, the question of what are true and false needs must be answered by the individuals themselves, but only in the last analysis; that is, if and when they are free to give their own answer. As long as they are kept incapable of being autonomous, as long as they are indoctrinated and manipulated (down to their very instincts), their answer to this question cannot be taken as their own. By the same token, however, no tribunal can justly arrogate to itself the right to decide which needs should be developed and satisfied. Any such tribunal is reprehensible, although our revulsion does not do away with the question: how can the people who have been the object of effective and productive domination by themselves create the conditions of freedom?

The more rational, productive, technical, and total the repressive administration of society becomes, the more unimaginable the means and ways by which the administered individuals might break their servitude and seize their own liberation. To be sure, to impose Reason upon an entire society is a paradoxical and scandalous idea—although one might dispute the righteousness of a society which ridicules this idea while making its own population into objects of total administration. All liberation depends on the consciousness of servitude, and the emergence of this consciousness is always hampered by the predominance of needs and satisfactions which, to a great extent, have become the individual's own. The process always replaces one system of preconditioning by another; the optimal goal is the replacement of false needs by true ones, the abandonment of repressive satisfaction.

The distinguishing feature of advanced industrial society is its effective suffocation of those needs which demand liberation—liberation also from that which is tolerable and rewarding and comfortable—while it sustains and absolves the destructive power and repressive function of the affluent society. Here, the social controls exact the overwhelming need for the production and consumption of waste; the need for stupefying work where it is no longer a real necessity; the need for modes of relaxation which soothe and prolong this stupefication; the need for maintaining such deceptive liberties as free competition at administered prices, a free press which censors itself, free choice between brands and gadgets.

Under the rule of a repressive whole, liberty can be made into a powerful instrument of domination. The range of choice open to the individual is not the decisive factor in determining the degree of human freedom, but *what* can be chosen and what *is* chosen by the individual. The criterion for free choice can never be an absolute one, but neither is it entirely relative. Free election of masters does not abolish the masters or the slaves. Free choice among a wide variety of goods and services does not signify freedom if these goods and services sustain social controls over a life of toil and fear—that is, if they sustain alienation. And the spontaneous reproduction of superimposed needs by the individual does not establish autonomy; it only testifies to the efficacy of the controls.

Our insistence on the depth and efficacy of these controls is open to the objection that we overrate greatly the indoctrinating power of the "media," and that by themselves the people would feel and satisfy the needs which are now imposed upon them. The objection misses the point. The preconditioning does not start with the mass production of radio and television and with the centralization of their control. The people enter this stage as preconditioned receptacles of long standing; the decisive difference is in the flattening out of the contrast (or conflict) between the given and the possible, between the satisfied and the unsatisfied needs. Here, the so-called equalization of class distinctions reveals its ideological function. If the worker and his boss enjoy the same television program and visit the same resort places, if the typist is as attractively made up as the daughter of her employer, if the Negro owns a Cadillac, if they all read the same newspaper, then this assimilation indicates not the disappearance of classes, but the extent to which the needs and satisfactions that serve the preservation of the Establishment are shared by the underlying population.

Indeed, in the most highly developed areas of contemporary society, the transplantation of social into individual needs is so effective that the difference between them seems to be purely theoretical. Can one really distinguish between the mass media as instruments of information and entertainment, and as agents of manipulation and indoctrination? Between the automobile as nuisance and as convenience? Between the horrors and the comforts of functional architecture? Between the work for national defense and the work for corporate gain? Between the private pleasure and the commercial and political utility involved in increasing the birth rate?

We are again confronted with one of the most vexing aspects of advanced industrial civilization: the rational character of its irrationality. Its productivity and efficiency, its capacity to increase and spread comforts, to turn waste into need, and destruction into construction, the extent to which this civilization transforms the object world into an extension of man's mind and body makes the very notion of alienation questionable. The people recognize themselves in their commodities; they find their soul in their automobile, hi-fi set, split-level home, kitchen equipment. The very mechanism which ties the individual to his society has changed, and social control is anchored in the new needs which it has produced.

The prevailing forms of social control are technological in a new sense. To be sure, the technical structure and efficacy of the productive and destructive apparatus has been a major instrumentality for subjecting the population to the established social division of labor throughout the modem period. Moreover, such integration has always been accompanied by more obvious forms of compulsion: loss of livelihood, the administration of justice, the police, the armed forces. It still is. But in the contemporary period, the technological controls appear to be the very embodiment of Reason for the benefit of all social groups and interests—to such an extent that all contradiction seems irrational and all counteraction impossible.

No wonder then that, in the most advanced areas of this civilization, the social controls have been introjected to the point where even individual protest is affected at its roots. The intellectual and emotional refusal "to go along" appears neurotic and impotent. This is the socio-psychological aspect of the political event that marks the contemporary period: the passing of the historical forces which, at the preceding stage of industrial society, seemed to represent the possibility of new forms of existence.

But the term "introjection" perhaps no longer describes the way in which the individual by himself reproduces and perpetuates the external controls exercised by his society. Introjection suggests a variety of relatively spontaneous processes by which a Self (Ego) transposes the "outer" into the "inner." Thus introjection implies the existence of an inner dimension distinguished from and even antagonistic to the external exigencies—an individual consciousness and an individual unconscious *apart from* public opinion and behavior.[1] The idea of "inner freedom" here has its reality: it designates the private space in which man may become and remain "himself."

Today this private space has been invaded and whittled down by technological reality. Mass production and mass distribution claim the *entire* individual, and industrial psychology has long since ceased to be confined to the factory. The manifold processes of introjection seem to be ossified in almost mechanical reactions. The result is, not adjustment but *mimesis:* an immediate identification of the individual with *his* society and, through it, with the society as a whole.

This immediate, automatic identification (which may have been characteristic of primitive forms of association) reappears in high industrial civilization; its new "immediacy," however, is the product of a sophisticated, scientific management and organization. In this process, the "inner" dimension of the mind in which opposition to the status quo can take root is whittled down. The loss of this dimension, in which the power of negative thinking—the critical power of Reason—is at home, is the ideological counterpart to the very material process in which advanced industrial society silences and reconciles the opposition. The impact of progress turns Reason into submission to the facts of life, and to the dynamic capability of producing more and bigger facts of the same sort of life. The efficiency of the system blunts the individuals' recognition that it contains no facts which do not communicate the repressive power of the whole. If the individuals find themselves in the things which shape their life, they do so, not by giving, but by accepting the law of things—not the law of physics but the law of their society.

I have just suggested that the concept of alienation seems to become questionable when the individuals identify themselves with the existence which is imposed upon them and have in it their own development and satisfaction. This identification is not illusion but reality. However, the reality constitutes a more progressive stage of alienation. The latter has become entirely objective; the subject which is alienated is swallowed up by its alienated existence. There is only one dimension, and it is everywhere and in all forms. The achievements of progress defy ideological indictment as well as justification; before their tribunal, the "false consciousness" of their rationality becomes the true consciousness.

This absorption of ideology into reality does not, however, signify the "end of ideology." On the contrary, in a specific sense advanced industrial culture is *more* ideological than its predecessor, inasmuch as today the ideology is in the process of production itself.[2] In a provocative form, this proposition reveals the political aspects of the prevailing technological rationality. The productive apparatus and the goods and services which it produces "sell" or impose the social system as a whole. The means of mass transportation and communication, the commodities of lodging, food, and clothing, the irresistible output of the entertainment and information industry carry with them prescribed attitudes and habits, certain intellectual and emotional reactions which bind the consumers more or less pleasantly to the producers and, through the latter, to the whole. The products indoctrinate and manipulate; they promote a false consciousness which is immune against its falsehood. And as these beneficial products become available to more individuals in more social classes, the indoctrination they carry ceases to be publicity; it becomes a way of life. It is a good way of life—much better than before—and as a good way of life, it militates against qualitative change. Thus emerges a pattern of *one-dimensional thought and behavior* in which ideas, aspirations, and objectives that, by their content, transcend the established universe of discourse and action are either repelled or reduced to terms of this universe. They are redefined by the rationality of the given system and of its quantitative extension.

The trend may be related to a development in scientific method: operationalism in the physical, behaviorism in the social sciences. The common feature is a total empiricism in the treatment of concepts; their meaning is restricted to the representation of particular operations and behavior. The operational point of view is well illustrated by P. W. Bridgman's analysis of the concept of length:[3]

> We evidently know what we mean by length if we can tell what the length of any and every object is, and for the physicist nothing more is required. To find the length of an object, we have to perform certain physical operations. The concept of length is therefore fixed when the operations by which length is measured are fixed: that is, the concept of length involves as much and nothing more than the set of operations by which length is determined. In general, we mean by any concept nothing more than a set of operations; *the concept is synonymous with the corresponding set of operations.*

Bridgman has seen the wide implications of this mode of thought for the society at large:[4]

> To adopt the operational point of view involves much more a mere restriction of the sense in which we understand "concept," but means a far-reaching change in all our habits of thought, in that we shall no longer permit ourselves to use as tools in our thinking concepts of which we cannot give an adequate account in terms of operations.

Bridgman's prediction has come true. The new mode of thought is today the predominant tendency in philosophy, psychology, sociology, and other fields: Many of the most seriously troublesome concepts are being "eliminated" by showing that no adequate account of them in terms of operations or behavior can be given. The radical empiricist onslaught (I shall subsequently, in chapters VII and VIII, examine its claim to be empiricist) thus provides the methodological justification for the debunking of the mind by the intellectuals—a positivism which, in its denial of the transcending elements of Reason, forms the academic counterpart of the socially required behavior.

Outside the academic establishment, the "far-reaching change in all our habits of thought" is more serious. It serves to coordinate ideas and goals with those exacted by the prevailing system, to enclose them in the system, and to repel those which are irreconcilable with the system. The reign of such a one-dimensional reality does not mean that materialism rules, and that the spiritual, metaphysical, and bohemian occupations are petering out. On the contrary, there is a great deal of "Worship together this week," "Why not try God," Zen, existentialism, and beat ways of life, etc. But such modes of protest and transcendence are no longer contradictory to the status quo and no longer negative. They are rather the ceremonial part of practical behaviorism, its harmless negation, and are quickly digested by the status quo as part of its healthy diet.

One-dimensional thought is systematically promoted by the makers of politics and their purveyors of mass information. Their universe of discourse is populated by self-validating hypotheses which, incessantly and monopolistically repeated, become hypnotic definitions or dictations. For example, "free" are the institutions which operate (and are operated on) in the countries of the Free World; other transcending modes of freedom are by definition either anarchism, communism, or propaganda. "Socialistic" are all encroachments on private enterprises not undertaken by private enterprise itself (or by government contracts), such as universal and comprehensive health insurance, or the protection of nature from all too sweeping commercialization, or the establishment of public services which may hurt private profit. This totalitarian logic of accomplished facts has its Eastern counterpart. There, freedom is the way of life instituted by a communist regime, and all other transcending modes of freedom are either capitalistic, or revisionist, or leftist sectarianism. In both camps, non-operational ideas are non-behavioral and subversive. The movement of thought is stopped at barriers which appear as the limits of Reason itself.

Such limitation of thought is certainly not new. Ascending modern rationalism, in its speculative as well as empirical form, shows a striking contrast between extreme critical radicalism in scientific and philosophic method on the one hand, and an uncritical quietism in the attitude toward established and functioning social institutions. Thus Descartes' *ego cogitans* was to leave the "great public bodies" untouched, and Hobbes held that "the present ought always to be preferred, maintained, and accounted best." Kant agreed with Locke in justifying revolution *if and when* it has succeeded in organizing the whole and in preventing subversion.

However, these accommodating concepts of Reason were always contradicted by the evident misery and injustice of the "great public bodies" and the effective, more or less conscious rebellion against them. Societal conditions existed which provoked and permitted real dissociation from the established state of affairs; a private as well as political dimension was present in which dissociation could develop into effective opposition, testing its strength and the validity of its objectives.

With the gradual closing of this dimension by the society, the self-limitation of thought assumes a larger significance. The interrelation between scientific-philosophical and societal processes, between theoretical and practical Reason, asserts itself "behind the back" of the scientists and philosophers. The society bars a whole type of oppositional operations and behavior; consequently, the concepts pertaining to them are rendered illusory or meaningless. Historical transcendence appears as metaphysical transcendence, not acceptable to science and scientific thought. The operational and behavioral point of view, practiced as a "habit of thought" at large, becomes the view of the established universe of discourse and action, needs and aspirations. The "cunning of Reason" works, as it so often did, in the interest of the powers that be. The insistence on operational and behavioral concepts turns against the efforts to free thought and behavior *from* the given reality and *for* the suppressed alternatives. Theoretical and practical Reason, academic and social behaviorism meet on common ground: that of an advanced society which makes scientific and technical progress into an instrument of domination.

"Progress" is not a neutral term; it moves toward specific ends, and these ends are defined by the possibilities of ameliorating the human condition. Advanced industrial society is approaching the stage where continued progress would demand the radical subversion of the prevailing direction and organization of progress. This stage would be reached when material production (including the necessary services) becomes automated to the extent that all vital needs can be satisfied while necessary labor time is reduced to marginal time. From this point on, technical progress would transcend the realm of necessity, where it served as the instrument of domination and exploitation which thereby limited its rationality; technology would become subject to the free play of faculties in the struggle for the pacification of nature and of society.

Such a state is envisioned in Marx's notion of the "abolition of labor." The term "pacification of existence" seems better suited to designate the historical alternative of a world which—through an international conflict which transforms and suspends the contradictions within the established societies—advances on the brink of a global war. "Pacification of existence" means the development of man's struggle with man and with nature, under conditions where the competing needs, desires, and aspirations are no longer organized by vested interests in domination and scarcity—an organization which perpetuates the destructive forms of this struggle.

Today's fight against this historical alternative finds a firm mass basis in the underlying population, and finds its ideology in the rigid orientation of thought and behavior to the given universe of facts. Validated by the accomplishments of science and technology, justified by its growing productivity, the status quo defies all transcendence. Faced with the possibility of pacification on the grounds of its technical and intellectual achievements, the mature industrial society closes itself against this alternative. Operationalism, in theory and practice, becomes the theory and practice of *containment.* Underneath its obvious dynamics, this society is a thoroughly static system of life: self-propelling in its oppressive productivity and in its beneficial coordination. Containment of technical progress goes hand in hand with its growth in the established direction. In spite of the political fetters imposed by the status quo, the more technology appears capable of creating the conditions for pacification, the more are the minds and bodies of man organized against this alternative.

The most advanced areas of industrial society exhibit throughout these two features: a trend toward consummation of technological rationality, and intensive efforts to contain this trend within the established institutions. Here is the internal contradiction of this civilization: the irrational element in its rationality. It is the token of its achievements. The industrial society which makes technology and science its own is organized for the ever-more-effective domination of man and nature, for the ever-more-effective utilization of its resources. It becomes irrational when the success of these efforts opens new dimensions of human realization. Organization for peace is different from organization for war; the institutions which served the struggle for existence cannot serve the pacification of existence. Life as an end is qualitatively different from life as a means.

Such a qualitatively new mode of existence can never be envisaged as the mere by-product of economic and political changes, as the more or less spontaneous effect of the new institutions which constitute the necessary prerequisite. Qualitative change also involves a change in the *technical* basis on which this society rests—one which sustains the economic and political institutions through which the "second nature" of man as an aggressive object of administration is stabilized. The techniques of industrialization are political techniques; as such, they prejudge the possibilities of Reason and Freedom.

To be sure, labor must precede the reduction of labor, and industrialization must precede the development of human needs and satisfactions. But as all freedom depends on the conquest of alien necessity, the realization of freedom depends on the *techniques* of this conquest. The highest productivity of labor can be used for the perpetuation of labor, and the most efficient industrialization can serve the restriction and manipulation of needs.

When this point is reached, domination—in the guise of affluence and liberty—extends to all spheres of private and public existence, integrates all authentic opposition, absorbs all alternatives. Technological rationality reveals its political character as it becomes the great vehicle of better domination, creating a truly totalitarian universe in which society and nature, mind and body are kept in a state of permanent mobilization for the defense of this universe.

Notes

1. The change in the function of the family here plays a decisive role: its "socializing" functions are increasingly taken over by outside groups and media. See my *Eros and Civilization* (Boston: Beacon Press, 1955), p. 96ff.

2. Theodor W. Adorno, *Prismen. Kulturkritik und Gesellschaft.* (Frankfurt: Suhrkamp, 1955), p. 24f.

3. P. W. Bridgman, *The Logic of Modern Physics* (New York: Macmillan, 1928), p. 5. The operational doctrine has since been refined and qualified. Bridgman himself has extended the concept of "operation" to include the "paper-and-pencil" operations of the theorist (in Philipp J. Frank, *The Validation of Scientific Theories* [Boston: Beacon Press, 1954], Chap. II). The main impetus remains the same: it is "desirable" that the paper-and-pencil operations "be capable of eventual contact, although perhaps indirectly, with instrumental operations."

4. P. W. Bridgman, *The Logic of Modern Physics*, loc. cit., p. 31.

18 Herbert Marcuse and the "One-Dimensional Man"

Erik Stolterman

A comfortable, smooth, reasonable, democratic unfreedom prevails in advanced industrial civilization, a token of technical progress.
—Herbert Marcuse, *One-Dimensional Man*

The purpose and motives behind research in HCI and interaction design are many and highly diverse. Some researchers are interested in examining and revealing the true nature about technology and its use. Some are driven by the idea of challenging and critiquing the existing role and influence of technology. Others are interested in promoting progress that would satisfy industrial and commercial considerations. Of course, a lot of research is also driven by policy and funding considerations; still, there is among many researchers a will to change and improve the human condition with reference to some personal or societal ideal. This motivation to examine, critique, or improve is either based on some form of discontent with the existing state of things or on a sense that more can be achieved. The aspects of our society that most trigger improvement ambitions in HCI research seem to be related to issues of individual health and well-being, learning and education, and of course topics such as management, planning, and collaboration.

One of the questions that regularly emerge when enhancement of social or individual human conditions is attempted is whether a chosen design really engages with root causes or only deals with symptoms. It is, for instance, possible to imagine technology that could improve the experience of having family time even when family members are in different locations with a technological "solution" that makes the problem of being apart tolerable (for instance, through some form of simple and efficient communication). At the same time, the same solution may become an argument or even a reason for more families living apart, and by that the technological solution has led to an increased number of dislocated families. A design can make existing conditions bearable by reducing the need to address the root cause of a problem. In other words, a design can lead to a reinforcement of underlying structural issues while offering enjoyable experiences.

To any researcher engaged with the development of new technological solutions and with an ambition to make a difference, it is important to know if your contribution to society is in line with your beliefs and ideals or if you are only patching symptoms or even making things worse. There is hopefully a widespread suspicion among researchers about the "correctness" of their own understanding of the complex reality they are investigating and manipulating. According to Herbert Marcuse, we should all be suspicious.

Marcuse argues that the modern industrial society has been extraordinary successful in establishing systems and mechanisms that provide citizens with all they need in a way that drastically lowers their ambition to critically investigate their own society. Marcuse argues that it is not only the case that we, as citizens, don't have the ambition to challenge the existing order, we don't even have the ability. According to Marcuse, we are all "shaped" or molded by society in a way that makes us all "one-dimensional."

Marcuse introduced the concept of the "one-dimensional man." He used it to label what he saw as a fundamental and unquestioning acceptance of structures, norms, and behaviors. He further argued that this conformist understanding of society has led to a human inability to see and appreciate society in diverse ways. Serious critique becomes almost impossible. One-dimensionality transforms all our efforts to improve our conditions into a reinforcement of the existing and established structures that then intensifies and strengthens the one-dimensionality. Marcuse makes a strong argument that we need to be more careful and critical in our ambitions and efforts to understand and improve society.

Since many interaction design researchers are engaged in critically examining existing society with a desire to improve existing human conditions, the skeptical perspective of Marcuse poses some difficult but highly needed questions about the approaches used in those aspirations. Marcuse argues that we are all "prisoners" of a system that makes it extremely challenging for us to critically assess its structures and processes. Even if there are disagreements about what is the way forward and what constitute "good" designs, in most cases the disagreements are only about surface issues or symptoms and not about the underlying causes. As a field we have to ask ourselves if we are "prisoners" and if we are only scratching the surface of the reality that we eagerly want to engage with. Reading Marcuse raises serious questions but also offers some possible ways forward.

Herbert Marcuse

Herbert Marcuse was a philosopher who devoted his life to the idea that our lives are controlled by underlying structures and processes manifested by modern society. Marcuse argued that it is extremely difficult for individuals to fully grasp the way in which society controls our lives and how our own actions contribute to the existing order even if we do not want to. We all contribute, as designers or users, to the development of technology that "serves to institute new, more effective, and more pleasant forms of social control and cohesion" (Marcuse, 1964, xlvii). The notion of "pleasant" in the previous sentence is an essential aspect of Marcuse's work. It is not that technology forces us to believe or do certain things. Instead we find it pleasurable and satisfying to conform to and accept the existing order.

Herbert Marcuse was born in Berlin, Germany, in 1898. As a philosophy student he had the famous philosophers, Husserl and Heidegger, as his teachers. For some time Marcuse functioned as Heidegger's assistant. He was also highly influenced by thinkers such as Marx and Hegel. Marcuse wrote a doctoral dissertation in which he discussed why and how artists are often in conflict with society—a theme that came to follow his writings over the years (Feenberg and Leiss, 2007; Farr, 2014). The teachings of Husserl and Heidegger, and particularly the "phenomenological" approach of Husserl, stayed with Marcuse even though over the years he found many aspects of the approach to be inadequate for his own purposes. But it was the introduction to the philosophy of these thinkers that made it possible for Marcuse to formulate his own critique of science and its practice. He labeled what he saw as a dominating scientific approach as "technical rationality," a notion that appears in many of his books and essays, and a notion that he constantly analyzed and critiqued.

After having developed his own critical thinking, Marcuse got involved in the Institute for Social Research in Frankfurt and became one of the core members of what today is known as the Frankfurt School of critical theory. Marcuse and the institute had to leave Germany for Switzerland in 1933; shortly after that Marcuse moved to the United States, where he stayed for the rest of his career. Today Marcuse is primarily known for a philosophy related to issues with industrialism and technology in modern society and for the influence he achieved during the 1960s when he was considered to be a main intellectual force of the New Left.

Marcuse is known for being highly opinionated in his analysis and argumentation. Sometimes, especially in his later writings, his philosophical language reads more like an ideological pamphlet than a philosophical treatise. Marcuse wrote around a dozen books. Several of them were philosophical examinations of others' writings and thinking, particularly Hegel and Marx, while many were expressions of his own views and thoughts.

It is obvious that Marcuse's ideas were highly influenced by the society he lived in and the overall belief in "progress" in the industrial world. There are those who argue that we are not living in the same environment today and that the overall pessimism of the Frankfurt School and of Marcuse is not relevant any more or at least has to be adjusted in relation to our present times. The opposite argument can be made that many of the observations about societal development that Marcuse examined are still around and are even stronger, but more subtle and difficult to distill, today. There has in recent years been "a new surge of interest in Marcuse" (Farr, 2014).

As an introduction to Herbert Marcuse and his thoughts about the modern society the first chapter of his most famous book, *One-Dimensional Man*, serves well (Marcuse, 1964). The chapter examines how modern society embraces and integrates criticism and alternative societal solutions into a totalitarian repressive system that makes citizens content and satisfied and unable to see any other possible way of organizing society. This is also the piece of Marcuse's work that seems most relevant to anyone today working with the design and development of technology, in particular technology for everyday use. It is relevant to ask whether HCI and interaction design are unknowingly instrumental in reinforcing one-dimensionality. And if so, what that means and why we as a field should care.

One-Dimensionality

Marcuse makes the argument that "one-dimensionality" is in place when we all think and understand the fundamental "given" nature, structure, and mechanisms of our society in similar ways. Marcuse makes the case that technology produced by a highly successful technical rationality offers people not only what they need but also what they desire, at least on the surface. The established order provides people with the basics, such as shelter and food, but also with entertainment and pleasure. Marcuse argues that because society provides its citizens with all that they need and desire, it becomes difficult to "see through" the existing order or even to wish to do so. He writes, "Independence of thought, autonomy, and the right to political opposition are being deprived of their basic critical function in a society which seems increasingly capable of satisfying the needs of the individuals through the way in which it is organized" (Marcuse, 1964, 1). Marcuse makes the case that "by virtue of the way it has organized its technological base, contemporary industrial society tends to be totalitarian" (3). The argument is that in a society that gives its citizens all they need, the ability to distinguish between "true and false needs" is lost. The societal one-dimensionality makes us all believe that we need and want those things that society offers, even though they might be false needs. He writes, "Most of the prevailing needs to relax, to have fun, to behave and consume in accordance with advertisements, to love and hate what others love and hate, belong to this category of false needs" (5). However, one-dimensionality is not unbreakable. There are possible ways to see through one-dimensionality and to discover and expand cracks in the dominating understanding. Marcuse's approach to real change includes concepts like negative thinking, imaginative fantasy, aesthetics, and art. He sees all these concepts as having the potential power to break "one-dimensionality." The Marcuse text included in chapter 17, however, does not include much of Marcuse's solution to the problem, but it does include his initial outlining of what the existing problem is.[1]

The task for the thinker, researcher, and all of us then becomes, according to Marcuse "the abandonment of repressive satisfaction" (7), that is, to critically examine our needs and desires and to reveal what our true needs are. This is not only a philosophical or individual challenge, it is a question of economics and ideology as manifested in societal structures and processes.

The relation between philosophy, reason, and critical theory is something that Marcuse constantly returns to in his writings. He discusses this relationship in detail in "Philosophy and Critical Theory" (Marcuse, 1968). He makes an argument that philosophy is basically empty and worthless if not connected to the economic conditions of society. He writes, "Once critical theory had recognized the responsibility of economic conditions for the totality of the established world and comprehended the social framework in which reality was organized, philosophy became superfluous as an independent scientific discipline dealing with the structure of reality" (99). Since philosophy has lost its critical ambition and edge, at least in relation to everyday life, Marcuse argues that critical theory is the only way to reveal the "economic conditions" in a way that makes us able to see the real underlying structures shaping our reality. For Marcuse, this task of revealing the true nature of reality became his major goal.

Marcuse presents an understanding of the industrial society as repressive in a way that almost makes his own ambition of liberation impossible. It is noteworthy that the almost overwhelmingly negative interpretation of our modern society that Marcuse delivers is balanced with a strong ambition, desire, and conviction that it is possible to liberate and support what he labels "human happiness." So, improvement of the human condition is possible!

Technology has a special place in Marcuse's thinking. It is the tool by which the mechanisms of societal repression and influence are manifested. Marcuse's definition of technology is broad and encompasses more than most would assume. He writes about the "technical apparatus of production and distribution" and he comments that we cannot see technology as "the sum-total of mere instruments which can be isolated from the social and political effects, but rather as a system which determines a priori the product of the apparatus as well as the operations of servicing and extending it" (xlvii). So, technology can and should be understood as a big machine that makes our society function.

Technology leads to a "flattening out of the contrast or (conflict) between the given and the possible." That is, technology makes it difficult if not impossible for people to see that things could be any other way than what they are, the "given" and the "possible" become the same. It is not only that technology preserves one-dimensionality, people "recognize themselves in their commodities, they find their soul in the automobile, hi-fi set, split-level home, kitchen equipment" (9). And they cannot see any other way of life. Technology removes their freedom to imagine alternatives. It is not only that we can no longer imagine alternatives; the attempts become futile. Marcuse writes, "The intellectual and emotional refusal 'to go along' appears neurotic and impotent" (9). This means that anyone who challenges the existing order becomes an outsider who does not appreciate what today's technology is able to provide us with, someone who provokes and is to some degree even seen as dangerous. For instance, today some see those who refuse to use modern social media in this way. Their refusal seems provoking and suspicious because it questions the fundamental belief that faster and simpler social communication is inherently good.

To Marcuse this means that technology design is political. Ideology is made into reality when technology is designed. The underlying structure of society is strengthened as soon as new designs add to the existing structure and make it even more pleasant to be part of society and more difficult to imagine alternatives. Each and every designer is, on a daily basis, part of this process because he or she adds new or "improved" designs to the existing "apparatus." Marcuse makes the case that technology development is guided by a belief that every aspect of everyday life can be supported by new technology, and, not only that, it can also be made pleasant. This line of argument has been developed further in modern times by prominent philosophers of technology, such as Albert Borgmann and his now-famous notion of the device paradigm (Borgmann, 1984) and Andrew Feenberg, who was a student of Marcuse's and who has devoted a lot of writing to Marcuse (Feenberg, 1999; Feenberg, 2005).

It could be argued that the focus in HCI and interaction design on user experiences and "pleasant" uses of technology directly contributes to this development. It seems as if every function and aspect of life is on the interaction design agenda and that the intention is to make all these functions not just efficient but also pleasurable, enjoyable user experiences. It seems as if the ambition is to design for people's every shortcoming when it comes to knowledge, skill, or character, and to provide them with a reality where they have a feeling of being in control, of feeling satisfied, of not really wanting or needing anything else. This is the process that creates and produces the technological apparatus that is the precondition for one-dimensionality.

Reflective designers try to base their designs on true needs and not false needs. Therefore they engage in user research and studies aimed at revealing the "true" need of people. But it is not that easy. Marcuse's philosophy also leads to the recognition that empiricism is not necessarily a way to expose the true needs of people. Close examination of people's behavior and desires will only reflect the existing order and will lead to propositions of improvements that are already inscribed in the existing one-dimensionality. He writes, "The insistence on operational and behavioral concepts turns against the efforts to free thought and behavior *from* the given reality and *for* the suppressed alternatives" (16).

Marcuse makes the case that on a fundamental level taking a critical stance is not about "fixing" problems with food, entertainment, or consumption, it is about freedom. The fundamental problem we face as humans is that in a society where technology has reached the success that we experience today, it is extremely difficult to examine and reveal the underlying causes of our problems when every aspect of reality is seen as contributing to a desired way of living.

Industrial society has reached a point at which everything that potentially can be seen as disruptive to the existing structure becomes embraced by the established structures. For instance, the power that the fashion industry exerts on all of us is astonishing. The industry produce styles and aesthetics preferences that affect us all, whether we like it or not. Now and then there are groups of people who, in creative and defiant ways, deviate from the norm and develop their own style, often in direct conflict with the existing aesthetics of the fashion industry. However, the fashion industry, as a well-functioning apparatus, is quick to recognize and absorb new styles. For the industry this is a way of using the creativity of people who are able to see alternatives and the courage to explore them. It also means that it is practically impossible to be an outsider, to challenge the existing order and to not be part of it. Any possible alternative becomes embraced by the apparatus, absorbed and normalized. Marcuse comments that society "swallows up or repulses all alternatives." One-dimensionality is the consequence—it is not established by force or persuasion but by giving people what they want.

However, there is hope. Marcuse sees art and imaginative fantasy as potential tools, with the ability to break the repressive one-dimensional image and understanding of society. When the one-dimensional society advances, the relation between the rational and the irrational changes. The irrational, in the form of art, fantasy, and aesthetics qualities, "becomes the home of the really rational—of the ideas which may promote the art of life" (Marcuse, 1964, 247). He continues, "The aesthetic dimension still retains a freedom of expressions" that can "name the otherwise unnamable." There is hope in artistic expressions because they can name what it is not possible to see or reveal within the existing one-dimensionality. Marcuse refers to aesthetics as a "fundamental category of social experience and not confined to the realm of art" (Feenberg, 2005, 137).

Using Marcuse

Marcuse presents views of a repressive society that might not immediately and easily resonate with contemporary readers. For those who see themselves as independent thinkers and consider themselves not to be trapped by societal structures and norms, the notion of one-dimensionality may seem to apply only to the broad masses.

It is possible, of course, to read, analyze, and position Marcuse as an advocate for a particular philosophical perspective that both builds on traditional philosophy and expands it into critical theory and political action. Such a reading is valid and of interest if the purpose is to expose his philosophical contributions and shortcomings.

However, that is not why we engage with Marcuse in this context. Instead, we read Marcuse as someone who can help us ask big questions, someone who can challenge our ambitions and ourselves.

It is possible to narrow down our use of Marcuse by relating his ideas to some fundamental beliefs or assumptions that are common in our field as a way of examining their validity and usefulness. In that spirit, we engage here in two reflections concerning the state of interaction design research in relation to some fairly free interpretations of Marcuse.

Interaction Design as an Individualistic Enterprise

The first reflection has to do with the fact that interaction design research seems to be mostly attentive to individuals and less so to societal conditions. The analysis that Marcuse offers is a societal analysis; that is, his major concern and his objects of study are the structures, processes, and mechanisms that shape our overall human experience of society and reality. Such an analysis is less common in our field. At the most, researchers sometimes leave the level of the individual to engage with the group or the community, and in some cases the organization. Even though interaction design can be seen as dealing with societal issues, the tendency is to reduce these issues to individual choices and actions. For instance, one of the most active research areas today, the area of health and well-being, is primarily seen as something that has to be dealt with by the individual. The flood of interactive systems developed by industry and academia is primarily aimed at an individual user with the purpose to support his or her struggle with dieting, exercising, and so on. From Marcuse's perspective, it is possible to argue that since the issues addressed are symptoms of societal structures and mechanisms they cannot be solved on the level of the individual.

Marcuse argues that any addition to or repair of the existing structure, based on one-dimensional thinking, will instead likely lead to a strengthening of the established order. This would mean that any attempt to solve societal issues by making them a problem for the individual only increases one-dimensionality. For instance, one popular approach today is to develop technological tools to help people with stress related to work-life balance. These time-management tools are meant to be used by the individual to solve their work-life balance by being better at planning and more efficient. As with the health example above, attempts like this only support the underlying structures and reinforces existing societal structures and mechanisms that constitute the underlying cause of the problem. They do not address the underlying structural causes of stress, instead making it a problem for the individual. Instead of repairing, this leads to reinforcement of the existing structure.

In our field, we may ask to what extent our technological designs complement and strengthen what is already in place. Are our research and the designs we develop only reflecting and strengthening the existing structure? And if so, are there alternative approaches that would make it possible to engage with real change based on true needs? To be able to answer such questions, the field of interaction design research has to engage in ambitious investigations of how each technological design adds, contributes, disrupts, and shapes the overall societal structure. This is not only an ambitious undertaking, it is also complex and difficult, but according to Marcuse necessary.

Interaction Design as Empirically Trapped

The second reflection relates to the strong conviction in HCI regarding the importance of user research, context analysis, ethnography, user participation, user experience, and so on. These are all concepts that relate to the idea that any design for change should be based on a deep understanding of the existing situation. Many of these approaches, methods, and techniques promote careful and intimate investigations of an existing situation as a way to reveal "true" problems, needs, and opportunities.

To Marcuse, such a reliance on empirical reality is a mistake. He argues that inspecting existing reality, guided by what he labels "operationalism," is a one-dimensionality trap. Marcuse writes that "a rising standard of living" is an almost unavoidable byproduct of the industrial society and because it produces the "good life" it "is the rational and material ground for the unification of opposites" (Marcuse, 1964, 49). This means that forces that could potentially lead to change are "arrested, and qualitative change appear possible only as a change from without."

The ambition to operationalize all aspects of our lives, that is, to make them empirically distinguishable, means that "many of the most seriously troublesome concepts are being 'eliminated' by showing that no adequate account of them in terms of operations or behavior can be given" (13). We cannot escape what is empirically in front of us. Of course, Marcuse does not mean that understanding existing conditions is unnecessary, but he argues that it is not enough. Examinations of existing conditions have to be complemented with theoretical creativity and critical inspections that can help us to "see through" and disturb the image of reality that is provided empirically.

For interaction design this means that being too close to the rational and material ground through the use of methodological approaches devoted to careful investigation of existing reality does not necessarily result in truly critical investigations of existing conditions. Instead it may only lead to changes that turn out to be refinements of already established mechanisms and structures. From Marcuse's perspective one can argue that interaction design commonly engages in technological designs aimed at changing human behavior and experiences in concert or resonance with an existing repressive one-dimensionality.

Moving Forward

Marcuse discusses some possible ways for achieving change that could challenge one-dimensionality. Because one-dimensionality is such a strong force, shaping our thoughts and the way we can interpret reality, Marcuse proposes we need to tap other, equally strong forces that can break the trap. He argues for leaving the safe confines of rationality as defined by society. He writes, "The realm of the irrational becomes the home of the really rational—of the ideas which may 'promote the art of life'" (Marcuse, 1964, 247).

Marcuse argues that there are at least two types of activities that potentially can break one-dimensionality. Simplified, these two can be labeled as "imagination" and "theorizing." Marcuse makes the case that artistic creativity has the power of imagining not just existing but potential realities and conditions that can break out us out of one-dimensionality and the empirical trap. Artistic creativity is not bound by rationality of the given and by considerations of what is possible. The same goes for theorizing. Marcuse believes that engaging in critical theoretical investigations can force our thinking to develop ideas and perspectives that in turn make it possible to see and realize aspects of our reality that we otherwise are blind to.

Marcuse also sees the hope for real change in ambitions and attempts that many might see as offensive and maybe even dangerous. He often mentions how the outsider, the outcast, even the criminal may be the person who can break out of the conceptual prison that one-dimensionality presents.

If we take Marcuse seriously, our field should engage in two forms of investigation, one guided by imaginative and artistic creativity with the ambition to critically create and design new solutions or realities, and another guided by serious theorizing.

It is important to note that our field does not lack attempts at developing critical alternatives to the existing order and at taking a critical position in relation to established societal structures and processes. Work has been done that, to different degrees, sides with Marcuse without necessarily using his ideas and language.

The two forms of investigation mentioned above also already exist to some extent in contemporary HCI research. For instance, it is possible to find frequent attempts to engage in artistic and creative activities without the explicit purpose of developing solutions to well-defined problems. There is a growing field of artistically expressive designs situated slightly outside mainstream HCI. In many cases the people making these attempts are not aware of or building on the ideas of Marcuse, but they can still, unintentionally, create cracks in the dominating understanding of technology. This is exactly how Marcuse believed the power of art could work. He writes, "It seems that art as art expresses a truth, an experience, a necessity which, although not in the domain of radical praxis, are nevertheless essential components of revolution" (Marcuse, 1978, 1).

There are also examples of researchers intentionally trying to challenge existing conditions, such as in the expanding use of labels such as "speculative design" (Dunne and Raby, 2013; Lukens and DiSalvo, 2011), "adversarial design" (DiSalvo, 2012), and "critical design" (Bardzell and Bardzell, 2013; Dunne and Raby, 2001). These attempts are based on a belief that radical creativity and artistic expressions can lead to new designs that, without necessarily answering to explicit contextually defined problems, can help us understand our existing reality and conditions in new ways. Some of the values and ideas underlying these attempts and approaches resonate with the ideas of Marcuse even though they may not be explicit.

It is also possible to find examples in our field engaged with the theorizing form of investigation that Marcuse advocates. There are, for instance, some attempts to broaden and enrich the understanding of critical theory in a way that can inform our field (Bardzell et al., 2012; Bardzell and Bardzell, 2013; Bell, Blythe, and Sengers, 2005; DiSalvo, 2012; Light, 2011; Mazé and Redström, 2009; McCarthy and Wright, 2004). There are also theoretical attempts that engage with other theoretical traditions such as feminism (Bardzell, 2010; Bardzell and Bardzell, 2011; Bardzell and Churchill, 2011) and postcolonial theory (Irani et al., 2010; Merritt and Bardzell, 2011). In Marcuse's own search for new theoretical perspectives that could possibly challenge one-dimensionality, feminism emerged as a central and key theory at the end of his career. However, even though all these examples are today quite well-known in the research field, they have so far had very little impact when it comes to professional practice or education.

The lack of impact does not mean that there is no interest in Marcuse-like ideas. One of the most obvious examples of the growing interest in Marcuse's theories is the present book. It is possible to see all these fairly recent attempts as associated with Marcuse's idea of developing theoretical perspectives and societal critiques based on the assumption that research does not have to have simplistic improvement of existing conditions as its primary agenda. Instead they are explicitly aiming at developing new theoretical positions that can support a more radical examination and revealing of the existing order.

It is also important to see attempts that are clearly outside the theoretical sphere as potentially disrupting the existing order. For instance, the invention of new technologies that opens up new design spaces can function as forces that challenge one-dimensionality, even though they may be developed without any attempt or ambition to engage in societal change. This is sometimes difficult to accept by those who subscribe to more human-oriented approaches.

All through his life Marcuse was intrigued by grass-root movements, in particular the student movement in the 1960s. These movements emerge as responses to local and particular situations or events and, at least in the beginning, without any intention of reaching or influencing the larger system. These often emotionally driven movements may be so strong that they lead to increasing awareness of cracks in the one-dimensionality. It seems as if contemporary technology, specifically social media, is suited to support such grass-root initiatives. So, even though a specific technology is developed for other purposes, it may lead to unintended consequences that in turn could support a societal development in line with Marcuse's ideas, such as the way social media has played a role in revolutionary movements and activities around the world.

However, even though these attempts in many ways are promising there is a need for more. It is important to remember that these attempts still only represent a small fraction of all the research activity in our field.

Overall Reflections

So, what is the overall value of reading this text by Marcuse? The strength of his chapter is that it challenges us to ask questions that are uncomfortable, difficult, and complex. Even if some might find the text somewhat dated and claim that contemporary society is not comparable with what Marcuse experienced, Marcuse's perspective forces us to reflect on our research and to ask ourselves what our designs and research is contributing to. Are we contributing to an overall societal development that is in line with our values and beliefs? Are we by our well-meaning designs contributing and strengthening an existing one-dimensionality that, in the long term, goes against what we believe in?

Marcuse shows us that there is a possibility or risk that we are trapped in the way we think about our research and our role. He also shows us that maybe some of our accepted research approaches do not have the power to help us break out of the trap.

There is no simple solution to the questions that Marcuse asks, and maybe that is fine. Marcuse does not provide simple guidelines or any recipe on how to go about creating the good society. He does not provide us with the right way or best research approach. Instead, the value of reading Marcuse is that he pushes us to inspect our own ambitions and actions. He forces us to question what to do as researchers. He makes it clear that even with the best intentions and with values and beliefs we hold to be true and indisputable, we may in our everyday activities and actions support a societal structure that, on a deeper level, goes against our values and that may be counterproductive, perhaps even destructive. However, as we have seen above, there is hope and there are ways to move forward. As a field we are slowly engaging with new and potentially rewarding approaches. Hopefully we will see more of these in the years to come, and in relation to that we may also see more theoretical development inspired by the writings of Marcuse.

Note

1. Excellent introductions to Marcuse's ideas and writings can be found in the first chapter of Feenberg and Leiss (2007) and in Farr (2014).

References

Bardzell, J., and S. Bardzell. (2013) "What Is 'Critical' about Critical Design?" *Proceedings of the SIGCHI Conference on Human Factors in Computing Systems (CHI'13)*. New York: ACM, 3297–3306.

Bardzell, S. (2010) "Feminist HCI: Taking Stock and Outlining an Agenda for Design." *Proceedings of the SIGCHI Conference on Human Factors in Computing Systems (CHI'10)*. New York: ACM, 1301–1310.

Bardzell, S., J. Bardzell, J. Forlizzi, J. Zimmerman, and J. Antanitis. (2012) "Critical Design and Critical Theory: The Challenge of Designing for Provocation." *Proceedings of the Designing Interactive Systems Conference (DIS'12)*. New York: ACM, 288–297.

Bardzell, S., and E. Churchill, eds. (2011) "Feminism and HCI: New Perspectives." Special Issue, *Interacting with Computers* 23 (5).

Bell, G., M. Blythe, and P. Sengers. (2005) "Making by Making Strange: Defamiliarization and the Design of Domestic Technologies." *ACM Transactions on Computer-Human Interaction (TOCGI)* 12 (2): 149–173.

Borgmann, A. (1984) *Technology and the Character of Contemporary Life: A Philosophical Inquiry*. Chicago: The University of Chicago Press.

DiSalvo, C. (2012) *Adversarial Design*. Cambridge, MA: MIT Press.

Dunne, A., and F. Raby. (2013) *Speculative Everything: Design, Fiction, and Social Dreaming*. Cambridge, MA: MIT Press.

Farr, A. (2014) "Herbert Marcuse." *The Stanford Encyclopedia of Philosophy*, edited by Edward N. Zalta. Stanford, CA: Stanford University. http://plato.stanford.edu/archives/fall2014/entries/marcuse/.

Feenberg, A. (1999) *Questioning Technology*. London: Routledge.

Feenberg, A. (2005) *Heidegger and Marcuse: The Catastrophe and Redemption of History*. New York: Routledge.

Feenberg, A., and W. Leiss, eds. (2007) *The Essential Marcuse: Selected Writings of Philosopher and Social Critique Herbert Marcuse*. Boston: Beacon Press.

Irani, L., J. Vertesi, P. Dourish, K. Philip, and R. Grinter. (2010) "Postcolonial Computing: A Lens on Design and Development." *Proceedings of the SIGCHI Conference on Human Factors in Computing Systems (CHI'10)*. New York: ACM, 1311–1320.

Light, A. (2011) "HCI as Heterodoxy: Technologies of Identity and the Queering of Interaction with Computers." *Interacting with Computers* 23 (5): 430–438.

Lukens, J., and C. DiSalvo. (2011) "Speculative Design and Technological Fluency." *International Journal of Learning and Media* 3 (4): 23–40.

Marcuse, H. (1964) *One-Dimensional Man: Studies in the Ideology of Advanced Industrial Society*. Boston: Beacon Press.

Marcuse, H. (1968) *Negations: Essays in Critical Theory*. Boston: Beacon Press.

Marcuse, H. (1978) *The Aesthetic Dimension: Toward a Critique of Marxist Aesthetics*. Boston: Beacon Press.

Mazé, R., and J. Redström. (2009) "Difficult Forms: Critical Practices of Design and Research." *Research Design Journal* 1 (12): 28–39.

McCarthy, J., and P. Wright. (2004) *Technology as Experience*. Cambridge, MA: MIT Press.

Merritt, S., and S. Bardzell. (2011) "Postcolonial Language and Culture Theory for HCI4D." *Extended Abstracts on Human Factors in Computing Systems*. New York: ACM, 1675–1680.

19 Ideology and Ideological State Apparatuses (Notes towards an Investigation) (1970)

Louis Althusser, translated by Ben Brewster

On the Reproduction of the Conditions of Production[1]

I must now expose more fully something which was briefly glimpsed in my analysis when I spoke of the necessity to renew the means of production if production is to be possible. That was a passing hint. Now I shall consider it for itself.

As Marx said, every child knows that a social formation which did not reproduce the conditions of production at the same time as it produced would not last a year.[2] The ultimate condition of production is therefore the reproduction of the conditions of production. This may be "simple" (reproducing exactly the previous conditions of production) or "on an extended scale" (expanding them). Let us ignore this last distinction for the moment.

What, then, is *the reproduction of the conditions of production?*

Here we are entering a domain which is both very familiar (since *Capital* Volume Two) and uniquely ignored. The tenacious obviousnesses (ideological obviousnesses of an empiricist type) of the point of view of production alone, or even of that of mere productive practice (itself abstract in relation to the process of production) are so integrated into our everyday "consciousness" that it is extremely hard, not to say almost impossible, to raise oneself to the *point of view of reproduction.* Nevertheless, everything outside this point of view remains abstract (worse than one-sided: distorted)—even at the level of production, and, *a fortiori*, at that of mere practice.

Let us try and examine the matter methodically.

To simplify my exposition, and assuming that every social formation arises from a dominant mode of production, I can say that the process of production sets to work the existing productive forces in and under definite relations of production.

It follows that, in order to exist, every social formation must reproduce the conditions of its production at the same time as it produces, and in order to be able to produce. It must therefore reproduce:

1. the productive forces,
2. the existing relations of production.

Reproduction of the Means of Production

Everyone (including the bourgeois economists whose work is national accounting, or the modern "macro-economic" "theoreticians") now recognizes, because Marx compellingly proved it in *Capital* Volume Two, that no production is possible which does not allow for the reproduction of the material conditions of production: the reproduction of the means of production.

The average economist, who is no different in this than the average capitalist, knows that each year it is essential to foresee what is needed to replace what has been used up or worn out in production: raw material, fixed installations (buildings), instruments of production (machines), etc. I say the average economist=the average capitalist, for they both express the point of view of the firm, regarding it as sufficient simply to give a commentary on the terms of the firm's financial accounting practice.

But thanks to the genius of Quesnay who first posed this "glaring" problem, and to the genius of Marx who resolved it, we know that the reproduction of the material conditions of production cannot be thought at the level of the firm, because it does not exist at that level in its real conditions. What happens at the level of the firm is an effect, which only gives an idea of the necessity of reproduction, but absolutely fails to allow its conditions and mechanisms to be thought.

A moment's reflection is enough to be convinced of this: Mr X, a capitalist who produces woollen yarn in his spinning-mill, has to "reproduce" his raw material, his machines, etc. But *he* does not produce them for his own production—other capitalists do: an Australian sheep-farmer, Mr Y, a heavy engineer producing machine-tools, Mr Z, etc., etc. And Mr Y and Mr Z, in order to produce those products which are the condition of the reproduction of Mr X's conditions of production, also have to reproduce the conditions of their own production, and so on to infinity—the whole in proportions such that, on the national and even the world market, the demand for means of production (for reproduction) can be satisfied by the supply.

In order to think this mechanism, which leads to a kind of "endless chain," it is necessary to follow Marx's "global" procedure, and to study in particular the relations of the circulation of capital between Department I (production of means of production) and Department II (production of means of consumption), and the realization of surplus-value, in *Capital*, Volumes Two and Three.

We shall not go into the analysis of this question. It is enough to have mentioned the existence of the necessity of the reproduction of the material conditions of production.

Reproduction of Labour-Power

However, the reader will not have failed to note one thing. We have discussed the reproduction of the means of production—but not the reproduction of the productive forces. We have therefore ignored the reproduction of what distinguishes the productive forces from the means of production, i.e., the reproduction of labour power.

From the observation of what takes place in the firm, in particular from the examination of the financial accounting practice which predicts amortization and investment, we have been able to obtain an approximate idea of the existence of the material process of reproduction, but we are now entering a domain in which the observation of what happens in the firm is, if not totally blind, at least almost entirely so, and for good reason: the reproduction of labour power takes place essentially outside the firm.

How is the reproduction of labour power ensured?

It is ensured by giving labour power the material means with which to reproduce itself: by wages. Wages feature in the accounting of each enterprise, but as "wage capitals,"[3] not at all as a condition of the material reproduction of labour power.

However, that is in fact how it "works," since wages represents only that part of the value produced by the expenditure of labour power which is indispensable for its reproduction: sc. indispensable to the reconstitution of the labour power of the wage-earner (the wherewithal to pay for housing, food and clothing, in short to enable the wage-earner to present himself again at the factory gate the next day—and every further day God grants him); and we should add: indispensable for raising and educating the children in whom the proletarian reproduces himself (in n models where $n=0$, 1, 2, etc.…) as labour power.

Remember that this quantity of value (wages) necessary for the reproduction of labour power is determined not by the needs of a "biological" Guaranteed Minimum Wage (*Salaire Minimum Interprofessionnel Garanti*) alone, but by the needs of a historical minimum (Marx noted that English workers need beer while French proletarians need wine)—i.e., a historically variable minimum.

I should also like to point out that this minimum is doubly historical in that it is not defined by the historical needs of the working class "recognized" by the capitalist class, but by the historical needs imposed by the proletarian class struggle (a double class struggle: against the lengthening of the working day and against the reduction of wages).

However, it is not enough to ensure for labour power the material conditions of its reproduction if it is to be reproduced as labour power. I have said that the available labour power must be "competent," i.e., suitable to be set to work in the complex system of the process of production. The development of the productive forces and the type of unity historically constitutive of the productive forces at a given moment produce the result that the labour power has to be (diversely) skilled and therefore reproduced as such. Diversely: according to the requirements of the socio-technical division of labour, its different "jobs" and "posts."

How is this reproduction of the (diversified) skills of labour power provided for in a capitalist regime? Here, unlike social formations characterized by slavery or serfdom, this reproduction of the skills of labour power tends (this is a tendential law) decreasingly to be provided for "on the spot" (apprenticeship within production itself), but is achieved more and more outside production: by the capitalist education system, and by other instances and institutions.

What do children learn at school? They go varying distances in their studies, but at any rate they learn to read, to write and to add—i.e., a number of techniques, and a number of other things as well, including elements (which may be rudimentary or on the contrary thoroughgoing) of "scientific" or "literary culture," which are directly useful in the different jobs in production (one instruction for manual workers, another for technicians, a third for engineers, a final one for higher management, etc.). Thus they learn "know-how."

But besides these techniques and knowledges, and in learning them, children at school also learn the "rules" of good behaviour, i.e., the attitude that should be observed by every agent in the division of labour, according to the job he is "destined" for: rules of morality, civic and professional conscience, which actually means rules of respect for the socio-technical division of labour and ultimately the rules of the order established by class domination. They also learn to "speak proper French," to "handle" the workers correctly, i.e., actually (for the future capitalists and their servants) to "order them about" properly, i.e., (ideally) to "speak to them" in the right way, etc.

To put this more scientifically, I shall say that the reproduction of labour power requires not only a reproduction of its skills, but also, at the same time, a reproduction of its submission to the rules of the established order, i.e., a reproduction of submission to the ruling ideology for the workers, and a reproduction of the ability to manipulate the ruling ideology correctly for the agents of exploitation and repression, so that they, too, will provide for the domination of the ruling class "in words."

In other words, the school (but also other State institutions like the Church, or other apparatuses like the Army) teaches "know-how," but in forms which ensure *subjection to the ruling ideology* or the mastery of its "practice." All the agents of production, exploitation and repression, not to speak of the "professionals of ideology" (Marx), must in one way or another be "steeped" in this ideology in order to perform their tasks "conscientiously"—the tasks of the exploited (the proletarians), of the exploiters (the capitalists), of the exploiters' auxiliaries (the managers), or of the high priests of the ruling ideology (its "functionaries"), etc.

The reproduction of labour power thus reveals as its *sine qua non* not only the reproduction of its "skills" but also the reproduction of its subjection to the ruling ideology or of the "practice" of that ideology, with the proviso that it is not enough to say "not only but also," for it is clear that *it is in the forms and under the forms of ideological subjection that provision is made for the reproduction of the skills of labour power.*

But this is to recognize the effective presence of a new reality: *ideology.*

Here I shall make two comments.

The first is to round off my analysis of reproduction.

I have just given a rapid survey of the forms of the reproduction of the productive forces, i.e., of the means of production on the one hand, and of labour power on the other.

But I have not yet approached the question of the *reproduction of the relations production*. This is a *crucial question* for the Marxist theory of the mode of production. To let it pass would be a theoretical omission—worse, a serious political error.

I shall therefore discuss it. But in order to obtain the means to discuss it, I shall have to make another long detour.

The second comment is that in order to make this detour, I am obliged to re-raise my old question: what is a society?

Infrastructure and Superstructure

On a number of occasions[4] I have insisted on the revolutionary character of the Marxist conception of the "social whole" insofar as it is distinct from the Hegelian "totality." I said (and this thesis only repeats famous propositions of historical materialism) that Marx conceived the structure of every society as constituted by "levels" or "instances" articulated by a specific determination: the *infrastructure*, or economic base (the "unity" of the productive forces and the relations of production) and the *superstructure*, which itself contains two "levels" or "instances": the politico-legal (law and the State) and ideology (the different ideologies, religious, ethical, legal, political, etc.).

Besides its theoretico-didactic interest (it reveals the difference between Marx and Hegel), this representation has the following crucial theoretical advantage: it makes it possible to inscribe in the theoretical apparatus of its essential concepts what I have called their *respective indices of effectivity*. What does this mean?

It is easy to see that this representation of the structure of every society as an edifice containing a base (infrastructure) on which are erected the two "floors" of the superstructure, is a metaphor, to be quite precise, a spatial metaphor: the metaphor of a topography (*topique*).[5] Like every metaphor, this metaphor suggests something, makes some thing visible. What? Precisely this: that the upper floors could not "stay up," (in the air) alone, if they did not rest precisely on their base.

Thus the object of the metaphor of the edifice is to represent above all the "determination in the last instance," by the economic base. The effect of this spatial metaphor is to endow the base with an index of effectivity known by the famous terms: the determination in the last instance of what happens in the upper "floors" (of the superstructure) by what happens in the economic base.

Given this index of effectivity "in the last instance," the "floors" of the superstructure are clearly endowed with different indices of effectivity. What kind of indices?

It is possible to say that the floors of the superstructure are not determinant in the last instance, but that they are determined by the effectivity of the base; that if they are determinant in their own (as yet undefined) ways, this is true only insofar as they are determined by the base.

Their index of effectivity (or determination), as determined by the determination in the last instance of the base, is thought by the Marxist tradition in two ways: (1) there is a "relative autonomy" of the superstructure with respect to the base; (2) there is a "reciprocal action" of the superstructure on the base.

We can therefore say that the great theoretical advantage of the Marxist topography, i.e., of the spatial metaphor of the edifice (base and superstructure) is simultaneously that it reveals that questions of determination (or of index of effectivity) are crucial; that it reveals that it is the base which in the last instance determines the whole edifice; and that, as a consequence, it obliges us to pose the theoretical problem of the types of "derivatory" effectivity peculiar to the superstructure, i.e., it obliges us to think what the Marxist tradition calls conjointly the relative autonomy of the superstructure and the reciprocal action of the superstructure on the base.

The greatest disadvantage of this representation of the structure of every society by the spatial metaphor of an edifice, is obviously the fact that it is metaphorical: i.e., it remains *descriptive*.

It now seems to me that it is possible and desirable to represent things differently. NB, I do not mean by this that I want to reject the classical metaphor, for that metaphor itself requires that we go beyond it. And I am not going beyond it in order to reject it as outworn. I simply want to attempt to think what it gives us in the form of a description.

I believe that it is possible and necessary to think what characterizes the essential of the existence and nature of the superstructure *on the basis of reproduction.* Once one takes the point of view of reproduction, many of the questions whose existence was indicated by the spatial metaphor of the edifice, but to which it could not give a conceptual answer, are immediately illuminated.

My basic thesis is that it is not possible to pose these questions (and therefore to answer them) *except from the point of view of reproduction.*

I shall give a short analysis of Law, the State and Ideology *from this point of view.* And I shall reveal what happens both from the point of view of practice and production on the one hand, and from that of reproduction on the other.

The State

The Marxist tradition is strict, here: in the *Communist Manifesto* and the *Eighteenth Brumaire* (and in all the later classical texts, above all in Marx's writings on the Paris Commune and Lenin's on *State and Revolution*), the State is explicitly conceived as a repressive apparatus. The State is a "machine" of repression, which enables the ruling classes (in the nineteenth century the bourgeois class and the "class" of big landowners) to ensure their domination over the working class, thus enabling the former to subject the latter to the process of surplus-value extortion (i.e., to capitalist exploitation).

The State is thus first of all what the Marxist classics have called *the State Apparatus*. This term means: not only the specialized apparatus (in the narrow sense) whose existence and necessity I have recognized in relation to the requirements of legal practice, i.e., the police, the courts, the prisons; but also the army, which (the proletariat has paid for this experience with its blood) intervenes directly as a supplementary repressive force in the last instance, when the police and its specialized auxiliary corps are "outrun by events"; and above this ensemble, the head of State, the government and the administration.

Presented in this form, the Marxist-Leninist "theory" of the State has its finger on the essential point, and not for one moment can there be any question of rejecting the fact that this really is the essential point. The State Apparatus, which defines the State as a force of repressive execution and intervention "in the interests of the ruling classes" in the class struggle conducted by the bourgeoisie and its allies against the proletariat, is quite certainly the State, and quite certainly defines its basic "function."

From Descriptive Theory to Theory as Such

Nevertheless, here too, as I pointed out with respect to the metaphor of the edifice (infrastructure and superstructure), this presentation of the nature of the State is still partly descriptive.

As I shall often have occasion to use this adjective (descriptive), a word of explanation is necessary in order to remove any ambiguity.

Whenever, in speaking of the metaphor of the edifice or of the Marxist "theory" of the State, I have said that these are descriptive conceptions or representations of their objects, I had no ulterior critical motives. On the contrary, I have every grounds to think that great scientific discoveries cannot help but pass through the phase of what I shall call *descriptive "theory."* This is the first phase of every theory, at least in the domain which concerns us (that of the science of social formations). As such, one might—and in my opinion one must—envisage this phase as a transitional one, necessary to the development of the theory. That it is transitional is inscribed in my expression: "descriptive theory," which reveals in its conjunction of terms the equivalent of a kind of "contradiction." In fact, the term theory "clashes" to some extent with the adjective "descriptive" which I have attached to it. This means quite precisely: (1) that the "descriptive theory" really is, without a shadow of a doubt, the irreversible beginning of the theory; but (2) that the "descriptive" form in which the theory is presented requires, precisely as an effect of this "contradiction," a development of the theory which goes beyond the form of "description."

Let me make this idea clearer by returning to our present object: the State.

When I say that the Marxist "theory" of the State available to us is still partly "descriptive," that means first and foremost that this descriptive "theory" is without the shadow of a doubt precisely the beginning of the Marxist theory of the State, and that this beginning gives us the essential point i.e., the decisive principle of every later development of the theory.

Indeed, I shall call the descriptive theory of the State correct, since it is perfectly possible to make the vast majority of the facts in the domain with which it is concerned correspond to the definition it gives of its object. Thus, the definition of the State as a class State, existing in the Repressive State Apparatus, casts a brilliant light on all the facts observable in the various orders of repression whatever their domains: from the massacres of June 1848 and of the Paris Commune, of Bloody Sunday, May 1905 in Petrograd, of the Resistance, of Charonne, etc., to the mere (and relatively anodyne) interventions of a "censorship." which has banned Diderot's *La Réligieuse* or a play by Gatti on Franco; it casts light on all the direct or indirect forms of exploitation and extermination of the masses of the people (imperialist wars); it casts light on that subtle everyday domination beneath which can be glimpsed, in the forms of political democracy, for example, what Lenin, following Marx, called the dictatorship of the bourgeoisie.

And yet the descriptive theory of the State represents a phase in the constitution of the theory which itself demands the "supersession" of this phase. For it is clear that if the definition in question really does give us the means to identify and recognize the facts of oppression by relating them to the State, conceived as the Repressive State Apparatus, this "interrelationship" gives rise to a very special kind of obviousness, about which I shall have something to say in a moment: "Yes, that's how it is, that's really true!"[6] And the accumulation of facts within the definition of the State may multiply examples, but it does not really advance the definition of the State, i.e., the scientific theory of the State. Every descriptive theory thus runs the risk of "blocking" the development of the theory, and yet that development is essential.

That is why I think that, in order to develop this descriptive theory into theory as such, i.e., in order to understand further the mechanisms of the State in its functioning, I think that it is indispensable to *add* something to the classical definition of the State as a State Apparatus.

The Essentials of the Marxist Theory of the State

Let me first clarify one important point: the State (and its existence in its apparatus) has no meaning except as a function of *State power.* The whole of the political class struggle revolves around the State. By which I mean around the possession, i.e., the seizure and conservation of State power by a certain class or by an alliance between classes or class fractions. This first clarification obliges me to distinguish between State power (conservation of State power or seizure of State power), the objective of the political class struggle on the one hand, and the State Apparatus on the other.

We know that the State Apparatus may survive, as is proved by bourgeois "revolutions" in nineteenth-century France (1830, 1848), by *coups d'état* (2 December, May 1958), by collapses of the State (the fall of the Empire in 1870, of the Third Republic in 1940), or by the political rise of the petty bourgeoisie (1890–95 in France), etc., without the State Apparatus being affected or modified: it may survive political events which affect the possession of State power.

Even after a social revolution like that of 1917, a large part of the State Apparatus survived after the seizure of State power by the alliance of the proletariat and the small peasantry: Lenin repeated the fact again and again.

It is possible to describe the distinction between state power and state apparatus as part of the "Marxist theory" of the state, explicitly present since Marx's *Eighteenth Brumaire* and *Class Struggles in France.*

To summarize the "Marxist theory of the State" on this point, it can be said that the Marxist classics have always claimed that (1) the state is the repressive state apparatus, (2) state power and state apparatus must be distinguished, (3) the objective of the class struggle concerns state power, and in consequence the use of the state apparatus by the classes (or alliance of classes or of fractions of classes) holding state power as a function of their class objectives, and (4) the proletariat must seize state power in order to destroy the existing bourgeois state apparatus and, in a first phase, replace it with a quite different, proletarian, state apparatus, then in later phases set in motion a radical process, that of the destruction of the state (the end of state power, the end of every state apparatus).

In this perspective, therefore, what I would propose to add to the "Marxist theory" of the state is already there in so many words. But it seems to me that even with this supplement, this theory is still in part descriptive, although it does now contain complex and differential elements whose functioning and action cannot be understood without recourse to further supplementary theoretical development.

The State Ideological Apparatuses

Thus, what has to be added to the "Marxist theory," of the state is something else.

Here we must advance cautiously in a terrain which, in fact, the Marxist classics entered long before us, but without having systematized in theoretical form the decisive advances implied by their experiences and procedures. Their experiences and procedures were indeed restricted in the main to the terrain of political practice.

In fact, i.e., in their political practice, the Marxist classics treated the State as a more complex reality than the definition of it given in the "Marxist theory of the state," even when it has been supplemented as I have just suggested. They recognized this complexity in their practice, but they did not express it in a corresponding theory.[7]

I should like to attempt a very schematic outline of this corresponding theory. To that end, I propose the following thesis.

In order to advance the theory of the State it is indispensable to take into account not only the distinction between *state power* and *state apparatus*, but also another reality which is clearly on the side of the (repressive) State apparatus, but must not be confused with it. I shall call this reality by its concept: *the Ideological State Apparatuses.*

What are the Ideological State Apparatuses (ISAs)?

They must not be confused with the (repressive) State apparatus. Remember that in Marxist theory, the State Apparatus (SA) contains: the Government, the Administration, the Army, the Police, the Courts, the Prisons, etc., which constitute what I shall in future call the Repressive State Apparatus. Repressive suggests that the State Apparatus in question "functions by violence"—at least ultimately (since repression, e.g., administrative repression, may take non-physical forms).

I shall call Ideological State Apparatuses a certain number of realities which present themselves to the immediate observer in the form of distinct and specialized institutions. I propose an empirical list of these which will obviously have to be examined in detail, tested, corrected and re-organized. With all the reservations implied by this requirement, we can for the moment regard the following institutions as Ideological State Apparatuses (the order in which I have listed them has no particular significance):

- the religious ISA (the system of the different churches),
- the educational ISA (the system of the different public and private "schools"),
- the family ISA,[8]
- the legal ISA,[9]
- the political ISA (the political system, including the different parties),
- the trade-union ISA,
- the communications ISA (press, radio and television, etc.),
- the cultural ISA (literature, the arts, sports, etc.).

I have said that the ISAs must not be confused with the (Repressive) State Apparatus. What constitutes the difference?

As a first moment, it is clear that while there is *one* (Repressive) State Apparatus, there is a *plurality* of Ideological State Apparatuses. Even presupposing that it exists, the unity that constitutes this plurality of ISAs as a body is not immediately visible.

As a second moment, it is clear that whereas the—unified—(Repressive) State Apparatus belongs entirely to the *public* domain, much the larger part of the Ideological State Apparatuses (in their apparent dispersion) are part, on the contrary, of the *private* domain. Churches, Parties, Trade Unions, families, some schools, most newspapers, cultural ventures, etc., etc., are private.

We can ignore the first observation for the moment. But someone is bound to question the second, asking me by what right I regard as Ideological *State* Apparatuses, institutions which for the most part do not possess public status, but are quite simply *private* institutions. As a conscious Marxist, Gramsci already forestalled this objection in one sentence. The distinction between the public and the private is a distinction internal to bourgeois law, and valid in the (subordinate) domains in which bourgeois law exercises its "authority." The domain of the State escapes it because the latter is "above the law": the State, which is the State *of* the ruling class, is neither public nor private; on the contrary, it is the precondition for any distinction between public and private. The same thing can be said from the starting-point of our State Ideological Apparatuses. It is unimportant whether the institutions in which they are realized are "public" or "private." What matters is how they function. Private institutions can perfectly well "function" as Ideological State Apparatuses. A reasonably thorough analysis of any one of the ISAs proves it.

But now for what is essential. What distinguishes the ISAs from the (Repressive) State Apparatus is the following basic difference: the Repressive State Apparatus functions "by violence," whereas the Ideological State Apparatuses *function "by ideology."*

I can clarify matters by correcting this distinction. I shall say rather that every State Apparatus, whether Repressive or Ideological, "functions" both by violence and by ideology, but with one very important distinction which makes it imperative not to confuse the Ideological State Apparatuses with the (Repressive) State Apparatus.

This is the fact that the (Repressive) State Apparatus functions massively and predominantly *by repression* (including physical repression), while functioning secondarily by ideology. (There is no such thing as a purely repressive apparatus.) For example, the Army and the Police also function by ideology both to ensure their own cohesion and reproduction, and in the "values" they propound externally.

In the same way, but inversely, it is essential to say that for their part the Ideological State Apparatuses function massively and predominantly *by ideology*, but they also function secondarily by repression, even if ultimately, but only ultimately, this is very attenuated and concealed, even symbolic. (There is no such thing as a purely ideological apparatus.) Thus Schools and Churches use suitable methods of punishment, expulsion, selection, etc., to "discipline" not only their shepherds, but also their flocks. The same is true of the Family.... The same is true of the cultural IS Apparatus (censorship, among other things), etc.

Is it necessary to add that this determination of the double "functioning" (predominantly, secondarily) by repression and by ideology, according to whether it is a matter of the (Repressive) State Apparatus or the Ideological State Apparatuses, makes it clear that very subtle explicit or tacit combinations may be woven from the interplay of the (Repressive) State Apparatus and the Ideological State Apparatuses? Everyday life provides us with innumerable examples of this, but they must be studied in detail if we are to go further than this mere observation.

Nevertheless, this remark leads us towards an understanding of what constitutes the unity of the apparently disparate body of the ISAs. If the ISAs "function" massively and predominantly by ideology, what unifies their diversity is precisely this functioning, insofar as the ideology by which they function is always in fact unified, despite its diversity and its contradictions, *beneath the ruling ideology*, which is the ideology of "the ruling class." Given the fact that the "ruling class" in principle holds State power (openly or more often by means of alliances between classes or class fractions), and therefore has at its disposal the (Repressive) State Apparatus, we can accept the fact that this same ruling class is active in the Ideological State Apparatuses insofar as it is ultimately the ruling ideology which is realized in the Ideological State Apparatuses, precisely in its contradictions. Of course, it is a quite different thing to act by laws and decrees in the (Repressive) State Apparatus and to "act" through the intermediary of the ruling ideology in the Ideological State Apparatuses. We must go into the details of this difference—but it cannot mask the reality of a profound identity. To my knowledge, *no class can hold State power over a long period without at the same time exercising its hegemony over and in the State Ideological Apparatuses.* I only need one example and proof of this: Lenin's anguished concern to revolutionize the educational Ideological State Apparatus (among others), simply to make it possible for the Soviet proletariat, who had seized State power, to secure the future of the dictatorship of the proletariat and the transition to socialism.[10]

This last comment puts us in a position to understand that the Ideological State Apparatuses may be not only the *stake*, but also the *site* of class struggle, and often of bitter forms of class struggle. The class (or class alliance) in power cannot lay down the law in the ISAs as easily as it can in the (repressive) State apparatus, not only because the former ruling classes are able to retain strong positions there for a long time, but also because the resistance of the exploited classes is able to find means and occasions to express itself there, either by the utilization of their contradictions, or by conquering combat positions in them in struggle.[11]

Let me run through my comments.

If the thesis I have proposed is well-founded it leads me back to the classical Marxist theory of the State, while making it more precise in one point. I argue that it is necessary to distinguish between State power (and its possession by …) on the one hand, and the State Apparatus on the other. But I add that the State Apparatus contains two bodies: the body of institutions which represent the Repressive State Apparatus on the one hand, and the body of institutions which represent the body of Ideological State Apparatuses on the other.

But if this is the case, the following question is bound to be asked, even in the very summary state of my suggestions: what exactly is the extent of the role of the Ideological State Apparatuses? What is their importance based on? In other words: to what does the "function" of these Ideological State Apparatuses, which do not function by repression but by ideology, correspond?

On the Reproduction of the Relations of Production

I can now answer the central question which I have left in suspense for many long pages: *how is the reproduction of the relations of production secured?*

In the topographical language (Infrastructure, Superstructure), I can say: for the most part,[12] it is secured by the legal-political and ideological superstructure.

But as I have argued that it is essential to go beyond this still descriptive language, I shall say: for the most part,[12] it is secured by the exercise of State power in the State Apparatuses, on the one hand the (Repressive) State Apparatus, on the other the Ideological State Apparatuses.

What I have just said must also be taken into account, and it can be assembled in the form of the following three features:

1. All the State Apparatuses function both by repression and by ideology, with the difference that the (Repressive) State Apparatus functions massively and predominantly by repression, whereas the Ideological State Apparatuses function massively and predominantly by ideology.
2. Whereas the (Repressive) State Apparatus constitutes an organized whole whose different parts are centralized beneath a commanding unity, that of the politics of class struggle applied by the political representatives of the ruling classes in possession of State power, the Ideological State Apparatuses are multiple, distinct, "relatively autonomous" and capable of providing an objective field to contradictions which express, in forms which may be limited or extreme, the effects of the clashes between the capitalist class struggle and the proletarian class struggle, as well as their subordinate forms.
3. Whereas the unity of the (Repressive) State Apparatus is secured by its unified and centralized organization under the leadership of the representatives of the classes in power executing the politics of the class struggle of the classes in power, the unity of the different Ideological State Apparatuses is secured, usually in contradictory forms, by the ruling ideology, the ideology of the ruling class.

Taking these features into account, it is possible to represent the reproduction of the relations of production[13] in the following way, according to a kind of "division of labour."

The role of the repressive State apparatus, insofar as it is a repressive apparatus, consists essentially in securing by force (physical or otherwise) the political conditions of the reproduction of relations of production which are in the last resort *relations of exploitation*. Not only does the State apparatus contribute generously to its own reproduction (the capitalist State contains political dynasties, military dynasties, etc.), but also and above all, the State apparatus secures by repression (from the most brutal physical force, via mere administrative commands and interdictions, to open and tacit censorship) the political conditions for the action of the Ideological State Apparatuses.

In fact, it is the latter which largely secure the reproduction specifically of the relations of production, behind a "shield" provided by the repressive State apparatus. It is here that the role of the ruling ideology is heavily concentrated, the ideology of the ruling class, which holds State power. It is the intermediation of the ruling ideology that ensures a (sometimes teeth-gritting) "harmony" between the repressive State apparatus and the Ideological State Apparatuses, and between the different State Ideological Apparatuses.

We are thus led to envisage the following hypothesis, as a function precisely of the diversity of ideological State Apparatuses in their single, because shared, role of the reproduction of the relations of production.

Indeed we have listed a relatively large number of Ideological State Apparatuses in contemporary capitalist social formations: the educational apparatus, the religious apparatus, the family apparatus, the political apparatus, the trade-union apparatus, the communications apparatus, the "cultural" apparatus, etc.

But in the social formations of that mode of production characterized by "serfdom" (usually called the feudal mode of production), we observe that although there is a single repressive State apparatus which, since the earliest known Ancient States, let alone the Absolute Monarchies, has been formally very similar to the one we know today, the number of Ideological State Apparatuses is smaller and their individual types are different. For example, we observe that during the Middle Ages, the Church (the religious Ideological State Apparatus) accumulated a number of functions which have today devolved on to several distinct Ideological State Apparatuses, new ones in relation to the past I am invoking, in particular educational and cultural functions. Alongside the Church there was the family Ideological State Apparatus, which played a considerable part, incommensurable with its role in capitalist social formations. Despite appearances, the Church and the Family were not the only Ideological State Apparatuses. There was also a political Ideological State Apparatus (the Estates General the *Parlement*, the different political factions and Leagues: the ancestors of the modern political parties, and the whole political system of the free Communes and then of the *Villes*). There was also a powerful "proto-trade-union" Ideological State Apparatus, if I may venture such an anachronistic term (the powerful merchants' and bankers' guilds and the journeymen's associations, etc.). Publishing and Communications even, saw an indisputable development as did the theatre; initially both were integral parts of the Church, then they became more and more independent of it.

In the pre-capitalist historical period which I have examined extremely broadly, it is absolutely clear that *there was one dominant Ideological State Apparatus, the Church*, which concentrated within it not only religious functions, but also educational ones, and a large proportion of the functions of communications and "culture." It is no accident that all ideological struggle, from the sixteenth to the eighteenth century, starting with the first shocks of the Reformation, was *concentrated* in an anti-clerical and anti-religious struggle; rather this is a function precisely of the dominant position of the religious Ideological State Apparatus.

The foremost objective and achievement of the French Revolution was not just to transfer State power from the feudal aristocracy to the merchant-capitalist bourgeoisie, to break part of the former repressive State apparatus and replace it with a new one (e.g., the national popular Army)—but also to attack the number-one Ideological State Apparatus: the Church. Hence the civil constitution of the clergy, the confiscation of ecclesiastical wealth, and the creation of new Ideological State Apparatuses to replace the religious Ideological State Apparatus in its dominant role.

Naturally, these things did not happen automatically: witness the Concordat, the Restoration and the long class struggle between the landed aristocracy and the industrial bourgeoisie throughout the nineteenth century for the establishment of bourgeois hegemony over the functions formerly fulfilled by the Church: above all by the Schools. It can be said that the bourgeoisie relied on the new political, parliamentary-democratic, Ideological State Apparatus, installed in the earliest years of the Revolution, then restored after long and violent struggles, for a few months in 1848 and for decades after the fall of the Second Empire, in order to conduct its struggle against the Church and wrest its ideological functions away from it, in other words, to ensure not only its own political hegemony, but also the ideological hegemony indispensable to the reproduction of capitalist relations of production.

That is why I believe that I am justified in advancing the following Thesis, however precarious it is. I believe that the Ideological State Apparatus which has been installed in the *dominant* position in mature capitalist social formations as a result of a violent political and ideological class struggle against the old dominant Ideological State Apparatus, is the *educational ideological apparatus.*

This thesis may seem paradoxical, given that for everyone, i.e., in the ideological representation that the bourgeoisie has tried to give itself and the classes it exploits, it really seems that the dominant Ideological State Apparatus in capitalist social formations is not the Schools, but the political ideological State apparatus, i.e., the regime of parliamentary democracy combining universal suffrage and party struggle.

However, history, even recent history, shows that the bourgeoisie has been and still is able to accommodate itself to political Ideological State Apparatuses other than parliamentary democracy: the First and Second Empires, Constitutional Monarchy (Louis XVIII and Charles X), Parliamentary Monarchy (Louis-Philippe), Presidential Democracy (de Gaulle), to mention only France. In England this is even clearer. The Revolution was particularly "successful" there from the bourgeois point of view, since unlike France, where the bourgeoisie, partly because of the stupidity of the petty aristocracy, had to agree to being carried to power by peasant and plebeian *"journées révolutionnaires,"* something for which it had to pay a high price, the English bourgeoisie was able to "compromise" with the aristocracy and "share" State power and the use of the State apparatus with it for a long time (peace among all men of good will in the ruling classes!). In Germany it is even more striking, since it was behind a political Ideological State Apparatus in which the imperial Junkers (epitomized by Bismarck), their army and their police provided it with a shield and leading personnel, that the imperialist bourgeoisie made its shattering entry into history, before "traversing" the Weimar Republic and entrusting itself to Nazism.

Hence I believe I have good reasons for thinking that behind the scenes of its political Ideological State Apparatus, which occupies the front of the stage, what the bourgeoisie has installed as its number-one, i.e., as its dominant Ideological State Apparatus, is the educational apparatus, which has in fact replaced in its functions the previously dominant Ideological State Apparatus, the Church. One might even add: the School-Family couple has replaced the Church-Family couple.

Why is the educational apparatus in fact the dominant Ideological State Apparatus in capitalist social formations, and how does it function?

For the moment it must suffice to say:

1. All Ideological State Apparatuses, whatever they are, contribute to the same result: the reproduction of the relations of production, i.e., of capitalist relations of exploitation.
2. Each of them contributes towards this single result in the way proper to it. The political apparatus by subjecting individuals to the political State ideology, the "indirect" (parliamentary) or "direct" (plebiscitary or fascist) "democratic" ideology. The communications apparatus by cramming every "citizen" with daily doses of nationalism, chauvinism, liberalism, moralism, etc., by means of the press, the radio and television. The same goes for the cultural apparatus (the role of sport in chauvinism is of the first importance), etc. The religious apparatus by recalling in sermons and the other great ceremonies of Birth, Marriage and Death, that man is only ashes, unless he loves his neighbour to the extent of turning the other cheek to whoever strikes first. The family apparatus ... but there is no need to go on.
3. This concert is dominated by a single score, occasionally disturbed by contradictions (those of the remnants of former ruling classes, those of the proletarians and their organizations): the score of the Ideology of the current ruling class which integrates into its music the great themes of the Humanism of the Great Forefathers, who produced the Greek Miracle even before Christianity, and afterwards the Glory of Rome, the Eternal City, and the themes of Interest, particular and general, etc. nationalism, moralism and economism.
4. Nevertheless, in this concert, one Ideological State Apparatus certainly has the dominant role, although hardly anyone lends an ear to its music: it is so silent! This is the School.

It takes children from every class at infant-school age, and then for years, the years in which the child is most "vulnerable," squeezed between the Family State Apparatus and the Educational State Apparatus, it drums into them, whether it uses new or old methods, a certain amount of "know-how" wrapped in the ruling ideology (French, arithmetic, natural history, the sciences, literature) or simply the ruling ideology in its pure state (ethics, civic instruction, philosophy). Somewhere around the age of sixteen, a huge mass of children are ejected "into production": these are the workers or small peasants. Another portion of scholastically adapted youth carries on: and, for better or worse, it goes somewhat further, until it falls by the wayside and fills the posts of small and middle technicians, white-collar workers, small and middle executives, petty bourgeois of all kinds. A last portion reaches the summit, either to fall into intellectual semi-employment, or to provide, as well as the "intellectuals of the collective labourer," the agents of exploitation (capitalists, managers), the agents of repression (soldiers, policemen, politicians, administrators, etc.) and the professional ideologists (priests of all sorts, most of whom are convinced "laymen").

Each mass ejected *en route* is practically provided with the ideology which suits the role it has to fulfil in class society: the role of the exploited (with a "highly-developed" "professional," "ethical," "civic," "national" and a-political consciousness); the role of the agent of exploitation (ability to give the workers orders and speak to them: "human relations"), of the agent of repression (ability to give orders and enforce obedience "without discussion," or ability to manipulate the demagogy of a political leader's rhetoric), or of the professional ideologist (ability to treat consciousnesses with the respect, i.e., with the contempt, blackmail, and demagogy they deserve, adapted to the accents of Morality, of Virtue, of "Transcendence," of the Nation, of France's World Role, etc.).

Of course, many of these contrasting Virtues (modesty, resignation, submissiveness on the one hand, cynicism, contempt, arrogance, confidence, self-importance, even smooth talk and cunning on the other) are also taught in the Family, in the Church, in the Army, in Good Books, in films and even in the football stadium. But no other Ideological State Apparatus has the obligatory (and not least, free) audience of the totality of the children in the capitalist social formation, eight hours a day for five or six days out of seven.

But it is by an apprenticeship in a variety of know-how wrapped up in the massive inculcation of the ideology of the ruling class that the *relations of production* in a capitalist social formation, i.e., the relations of exploited to exploiters and exploiters to exploited, are largely reproduced. The mechanisms which produce this vital result for the capitalist regime are naturally covered up and concealed by a universally reigning ideology of the School, universally reigning because it is one of the essential forms of the ruling bourgeois ideology: an ideology which represents the School as a neutral environment purged of ideology (because it is ... lay), where teachers respectful of the "conscience" and "freedom" of the children who are entrusted to them (in complete confidence) by their "parents" (who are free, too, i.e., the owners of their children) open up for them the path to the freedom, morality and responsibility of adults by their own example, by knowledge, literature and their "liberating" virtues.

I ask the pardon of those teachers who, in dreadful conditions, attempt to turn the few weapons they can find in the history and learning they "teach" against the ideology, the system and the practices in which they are trapped. They are a kind of hero. But they are rare and how many (the majority) do not even begin to suspect the "work" the system (which is bigger than they are and crushes them) forces them to do, or worse, put all their heart and ingenuity into performing it with the most advanced awareness (the famous new methods!). So little do they suspect it that their own devotion contributes to the maintenance and nourishment of this ideological representation of the School, which makes the School today as "natural," indispensable-useful and even beneficial for our contemporaries as the Church was "natural," indispensable and generous for our ancestors a few centuries ago.

In fact, the Church has been replaced today *in its role as the dominant Ideological State Apparatus* by the School. It is coupled with the Family just as the Church was once coupled with the Family. We can now claim that the unprecedentedly deep crisis which is now shaking the education system of so many States across the globe, often in conjunction with a crisis (already proclaimed in the *Communist Manifesto*) shaking the family system, takes on a political meaning, given that the School (and the School-Family couple) constitutes the dominant Ideological State Apparatus, the Apparatus playing a determinant part in the reproduction of the relations of production of a mode of production threatened in its existence by the world class struggle.

On Ideology

When I put forward the concept of an Ideological State Apparatus, when I said that the ISAs "function by ideology," I invoked a reality which needs a little discussion: ideology.

It is well known that the expression "ideology" was invented by Cabanis, Destutt de Tracy and their friends, who assigned to it as an object the (genetic) theory of ideas. When Marx took up the term fifty years later, he gave it a quite different meaning, even in his Early Works. Here, ideology is the system of the ideas and representations which dominate the mind of a man or a social group. The ideologico-political struggle conducted by Marx as early as his articles in the *Rheinische Zeitung* inevitably and quickly brought him face to face with this reality and forced him to take his earliest intuitions further.

However, here we come upon a rather astonishing paradox. Everything seems to lead Marx to formulate a theory of ideology. In fact, *The German Ideology* does offer us, after the *1844 Manuscripts*, an explicit theory of ideology, but ... it is not Marxist (we shall see why in a moment). As for *Capital*, although it does contain many hints towards a theory of ideologies (most visibly, the ideology of the vulgar economists), it does not contain that theory itself, which depends for the most part on a theory of ideology in general.

I should like to venture a first and very schematic outline of such a theory. The theses I am about to put forward are certainly not off the cuff, but they cannot be sustained and tested, i.e., confirmed or rejected, except by much thorough study and analysis.

Ideology Has No History

One word first of all to expound the reason in principle which seems to me to found, or at least to justify, the project of a theory of ideology *in general*, and not a theory of particular ideologies, which, whatever their form (religious, ethical, legal, political), always express *class positions*.

It is quite obvious that it is necessary to proceed towards a theory of ideologies in the two respects I have just suggested. It will then be clear that a theory of ideologies depends in the last resort on the history of social formations, and thus of the modes of production combined in social formations, and of the class struggles which develop in them. In this sense it is clear that there can be no question of a theory of ideologies *in general*, since *ideologies* (defined in the double respect suggested above: regional and class) have a history, whose determination in the last instance is clearly situated outside ideologies alone, although it involves them.

On the contrary, if I am able to put forward the project of a theory of ideology *in general*, and if this theory really is one of the elements on which theories of ideologies depend, that entails an apparently paradoxical proposition which I shall express in the following terms: *ideology has no history*.

As we know, this formulation appears in so many words in a passage from *The German Ideology*. Marx utters it with respect to metaphysics, which, he says, has no more history than ethics (meaning also the other forms of ideology).

In *The German Ideology*, this formulation appears in a plainly positivist context. Ideology is conceived as a pure illusion, a pure dream, i.e., as nothingness. All its reality is external to it. Ideology is thus thought as an imaginary construction whose status is exactly like the theoretical status of the dream among writers before Freud. For these writers, the dream was the purely imaginary, i.e., null, result of "day's residues," presented in an arbitrary arrangement and order, sometimes even "inverted," in other words, in "disorder." For them, the dream was the imaginary, it was empty, null and arbitrarily "stuck together" (*bricolé*), once the eyes had closed, from the residues of the only full and positive reality, the reality of the day. This is exactly the status of philosophy and ideology (since in this book philosophy is ideology *par excellence*) in *The German Ideology*.

Ideology, then, is for Marx an imaginary assemblage (*bricolage*), a pure dream, empty and vain, constituted by the "day's residues" from the only full and positive reality, that of the concrete history of concrete material individuals materially producing their existence. It is on this basis that ideology has no history in *The German Ideology*, since its history is outside it, where the only existing history is, the history of concrete individuals, etc. In *The German Ideology*, the thesis that ideology has no history is therefore a purely negative thesis, since it means both:

1. ideology is nothing insofar as it is a pure dream (manufactured by who knows what power: if not by the alienation of the division of labour, but that, too, is a *negative* determination);
2. ideology has no history, which emphatically does not mean that there is no history in it (on the contrary, for it is merely the pale, empty and inverted reflection of real history) but that it has no history *of its own*.

Now, while the thesis I wish to defend formally speaking adopts the terms of *The German Ideology* ("ideology has no history"), it is radically different from the positivist and historicist thesis of *The German Ideology*.

For on the one hand, I think it is possible to hold that ideologies *have a history of their own* (although it is determined in the last instance by the class struggle); and on the other, I think it is possible to hold that ideology *in general has no history*, not in a negative sense (its history is external to it), but in an absolutely positive sense.

This sense is a positive one if it is true that the peculiarity of ideology is that it is endowed with a structure and a functioning such as to make it a non-historical reality, i.e., an *omni-historical* reality, in the sense in which that structure and functioning are immutable, present in the same form throughout what we can call history, in the sense in which the *Communist Manifesto* defines history as the history of class struggles, i.e., the history of class societies.

To give a theoretical reference-point here, I might say that, to return to our example of the dream, in its Freudian conception this time, our proposition: ideology has no history, can and must (and in a way which has absolutely nothing arbitrary about it, but, quite the reverse, is theoretically necessary, for there is an organic link between the two propositions) be related directly to Freud's proposition that the *unconscious is eternal*, i.e., that it has no history.

If eternal means, not transcendent to all (temporal) history, but omnipresent, trans-historical and therefore immutable in form throughout the extent of history, I shall adopt Freud's expression word for word, and write *ideology is eternal*, exactly like the unconscious. And I add that I find this comparison theoretically justified by the fact that the eternity of the unconscious is not unrelated to the eternity of ideology in general.

That is why I believe I am justified, hypothetically at least, in proposing a theory of ideology *in general*, in the sense that Freud presented a theory of the unconscious *in general*.

To simplify the phrase, it is convenient, taking into account what has been said about ideologies, to use the plain term ideology to designate ideology in general, which I have just said has no history, or, what comes to the same thing, is eternal, i.e., omnipresent in its immutable form throughout history (= the history of social formations containing social classes). For the moment I shall restrict myself to "class societies" and their history.

Ideology Is a "Representation" of the Imaginary Relationship of Individuals to Their Real Conditions of Existence

In order to approach my central thesis on the structure and functioning of ideology, I shall first present two theses, one negative, the other positive. The first concerns the object which is "represented" in the imaginary form of ideology, the second concerns the materiality of ideology.

Thesis I: Ideology represents the imaginary relationship of individuals to their real conditions of existence.

We commonly call religious ideology, ethical ideology, legal ideology, political ideology, etc., so many "world outlooks." Of course, assuming that we do not live one of these ideologies as the truth (e.g., "believe" in God, Duty, Justice, etc.…), we admit that the ideology we are discussing from a critical point of view, examining it as the ethnologist examines the myths of a "primitive society," that these "world outlooks" are largely imaginary, i.e., do not "correspond to reality."

However, while admitting that they do not correspond to reality, i.e., that they constitute an illusion, we admit that they do make allusion to reality, and that they need only be "interpreted" to discover the reality of the world behind their imaginary representation of that world (ideology = *illusion/allusion*).

There are different types of interpretation, the most famous of which are the *mechanistic* type, current in the eighteenth century (God is the imaginary representation of the real King), and the "*hermeneutic*" interpretation, inaugurated by the earliest Church Fathers, and revived by Feuerbach and the theologico-philosophical school which descends from him, e.g., the theologian Barth (to Feuerbach, for example, God is the essence of real Man). The essential point is that on condition that we interpret the imaginary transposition (and inversion) of ideology we arrive at the conclusion that in ideology "men represent their real conditions of existence to themselves in an imaginary form."

Unfortunately, this interpretation leaves one small problem unsettled: why do men "need" this imaginary transposition of their real conditions of existence in order to "represent to themselves" their real conditions of existence?

The first answer (that of the eighteenth century) proposes a simple solution: Priests or Despots are responsible. They "forged" the Beautiful Lies so that, in the belief that they were obeying God, men would in fact obey the Priests and Despots, who are usually in alliance in their imposture, the Priests acting in the interests of the Despots or *vice versa*, according to the political positions of the "theoreticians" concerned. There is therefore a cause for the imaginary transposition of the real conditions of existence: that cause is the existence of a small number of cynical men who base their domination and exploitation of the "people" on a falsified representation of the world which they have imagined in order to enslave other minds by dominating their imaginations.

The second answer (that of Feuerbach, taken over word for word by Marx in his Early Works) is more "profound," i.e., just as false. It, too, seeks and finds a cause for the imaginary transposition and distortion of men's real conditions of existence, in short, for the alienation in the imaginary of the representation of men's conditions of existence. This cause is no longer Priests or Despots, nor their active imagination and the passive imagination of their victims. This cause is the material alienation which reigns in the conditions of existence of men themselves. This is how, in *The Jewish Question* and elsewhere, Marx defends the Feuerbachian idea that men make themselves an alienated (=imaginary) representation of their conditions of existence because these conditions of existence are themselves alienating (in the *1844 Manuscripts:* because these conditions are dominated by the essence of alienated society—*"alienated labour"*).

All these interpretations thus take literally the thesis which they presuppose, and on which they depend, i.e., that what is reflected in the imaginary representation of the world found in an ideology is the conditions of existence of men, i.e., their real world.

Now I can return to a thesis which I have already advanced: it is not their real conditions of existence, their real world, that "men" "represent to themselves" in ideology, but above all it is their relation to those conditions of existence which is represented to them there. It is this relation which is at the centre of every ideological, i.e., imaginary, representation of the real world. It is this relation that contains the "cause" which has to explain the imaginary distortion of the ideological representation of the real world. Or rather, to leave aside the language of causality it is necessary to advance the thesis that it is the *imaginary nature of this relation* which underlies all the imaginary distortion that we can observe (if we do not live in its truth) in all ideology.

To speak in a Marxist language, if it is true that the representation of the real conditions of existence of the individuals occupying the posts of agents of production, exploitation, repression, ideologization and scientific practice, does in the last analysis arise from the relations of production, and from relations deriving from the relations of production, we can say the following: all ideology represents in its necessarily imaginary distortion not the existing relations of production (and the other relations that derive from them), but above all the (imaginary) relationship of individuals to the relations of production and the relations that derive from them. What is represented in ideology is therefore not the system of the real relations which govern the existence of individuals, but the imaginary relation of those individuals to the real relations in which they live.

If this is the case, the question of the "cause" of the imaginary distortion of the real relations in ideology disappears and must be replaced by a different question: why is the representation given to individuals of their (individual) relation to the social relations which govern their conditions of existence and their collective and individual life necessarily an imaginary relation? And what is the nature of this imaginariness? Posed in this way, the question explodes the solution by a "clique,"[14] by a group of individuals (Priests or Despots) who are the authors of the great ideological mystification, just as it explodes the solution by the alienated character of the real world. We shall see why later in my exposition. For the moment I shall go no further.

Thesis II: Ideology has a material existence.

I have already touched on this thesis by saying that the "ideas" or "representations," etc., which seem to make up ideology do not have an ideal (*idéale* or *idéelle*) or spiritual existence, but a material existence. I even suggested that the ideal (*idéale*, *idéelle*) and spiritual existence of "ideas" arises exclusively in an ideology of the "idea" and of ideology, and let me add, in an ideology of what seems to have "founded" this conception since the emergence of the sciences, i.e., what the practicians of the sciences represent to themselves in their spontaneous ideology as "ideas," true or false. Of course, presented in affirmative form, this thesis is unproven. I simply ask that the reader be favourably disposed towards it, say, in the name of materialism. A long series of arguments would be necessary to prove it.

This hypothetical thesis of the not spiritual but material existence of "ideas" or other "representations" is indeed necessary if we are to advance in our analysis of the nature of ideology. Or rather, it is merely useful to us in order the better to reveal what every at all serious analysis of any ideology will immediately and empirically show to every observer, however critical.

While discussing the Ideological State Apparatuses and their practices, I said that each of them was the realization of an ideology (the unity of these different regional ideologies—religious, ethical, legal, political, aesthetic, etc.—being assured by their subjection to the ruling ideology). I now return to this thesis: an ideology always exists in an apparatus, and its practice, or practices. This existence is material.

Of course, the material existence of the ideology in an apparatus and its practices does not have the same modality as the material existence of a paving-stone or a rifle. But, at the risk of being taken for a Neo-Aristotelian (NB Marx had a very high regard for Aristotle), I shall say that "matter is discussed in many senses," or rather that it exists in different modalities, all rooted in the last instance in "physical" matter.

Having said this, let me move straight on and see what happens to the "individuals" who live in ideology, i.e., in a determinate (religious, ethical, etc.) representation of the world whose imaginary distortion depends on their imaginary relation to their conditions of existence, in other words, in the last instance, to the relations of production and to class relations (ideology = an imaginary relation to real relations). I shall say that this imaginary relation is itself endowed with a material existence.

Now I observe the following.

An individual believes in God, or Duty, or Justice etc. This belief derives (for everyone, i.e., for all those who live in an ideological representation of ideology, which reduces ideology to ideas endowed by definition with a spiritual existence) from the ideas of the individual concerned, i.e., from him as a subject with a consciousness which contains the ideas of his belief. In this way, i.e., by means of the absolutely ideological "conceptual" device (*dispositif*) thus set up (a subject endowed with a consciousness in which he freely forms or freely recognizes ideas in which he believes), the (material) attitude of the subject concerned naturally follows.

The individual in question behaves in such and such a way, adopts such and such a practical attitude, and, what is more, participates in certain regular practices which are those of the ideological apparatus on which "depend" the ideas which he has in all consciousness freely chosen as a subject. If he believes in God, he goes to Church to attend Mass, kneels, prays, confesses, does penance (once it was material in the ordinary sense of the term) and naturally repents and so on. If he believes *in* Duty, he will have the corresponding attitudes, inscribed in ritual practices "according to the correct principles." If he believes in Justice, he will submit unconditionally to the rules of the Law, and may even protest when they are violated, sign petitions, take part in a demonstration, etc.

Throughout this schema we observe that the ideological representation of ideology is itself forced to recognize that every "subject" endowed with a "consciousness" and believing in the "ideas" that his "consciousness" inspires in him and freely accepts, must "*act* according to his ideas," must therefore inscribe his own ideas as a free subject in the actions of his material practice. If he does not do so, "that is wicked."

Indeed, if he does not do what he ought to do as a function of what he believes, it is because he does something else, which, still as a function of the same idealist scheme, implies that he has other ideas in his head as well as those he proclaims, and that he acts according to these other ideas, as a man who is either "inconsistent" ("no one is willingly evil") or cynical, or perverse.

In every case, the ideology of ideology thus recognizes, despite its imaginary distortion, that the "ideas" of a human subject exist in his actions, or ought to exist in his actions, and if that is not the case, it lends him other ideas corresponding to the actions (however perverse) that he does perform. This ideology talks of actions: I shall talk of actions inserted into *practices*. *And* I shall point out that these practices are governed by the *rituals* in which these practices are inscribed, within the *material existence of an ideological apparatus*, be it only a small part of that apparatus: a small mass in a small church, a funeral, a minor match at a sports club, a school day, a political party meeting, etc.

Besides, we are indebted to Pascal's defensive "dialectic" for the wonderful formula which will enable us to invert the order of the notional schema of ideology. Pascal says more or less: "Kneel down, move your lips in prayer, and you will believe." He thus scandalously inverts the order of things, bringing, like Christ, not peace but strife, and in addition something hardly Christian (for woe to him who brings scandal into the world!)—scandal itself. A fortunate scandal which makes him stick with Jansenist defiance to a language that directly names the reality.

I will be allowed to leave Pascal to the arguments of his ideological struggle with the religious Ideological State Apparatus of his day. And I shall be expected to use a more directly Marxist vocabulary, if that is possible, for we are advancing in still poorly explored domains.

I shall therefore say that, where only a single subject (such and such an individual) is concerned, the existence of the ideas of his belief is material in that *his ideas are his material actions inserted into material practices governed by material rituals which are themselves defined by the material ideological apparatus from which derive the ideas of that subject.* Naturally, the four inscriptions of the adjective "material" in my proposition must be affected by different modalities: the materialities of a displacement for going to mass, of kneeling down, of the gesture of the sign of the cross, or of the *mea culpa,* of a sentence, of a prayer, of an act of contrition, of a penitence, of a gaze, of a hand-shake, of an external verbal discourse or an "internal" verbal discourse (consciousness), are not one and the same materiality. I shall leave on one side the problem of a theory of the differences between the modalities of materiality.

It remains that in this inverted presentation of things, we are not dealing with an "inversion" at all, since it is clear that certain notions have purely and simply disappeared from our presentation, whereas others, on the contrary, survive, and new terms appear.

Disappeared: the term *ideas.*

Survive: the terms *subject, consciousness, belief, actions.*

Appear: the terms *practices, rituals, ideological apparatus.*

It is therefore not an inversion or overturning (except in the sense in which one might say a government or a glass is overturned), but a reshuffle (of a non-ministerial type), a rather strange reshuffle, since we obtain the following result.

Ideas have disappeared as such (insofar as they are endowed with an ideal or spiritual existence), to the precise extent that it has emerged that their existence is inscribed in the actions of practices governed by rituals defined in the last instance by an ideological apparatus. It therefore appears that the subject acts insofar as he is acted by the following system (set out in the order of its real determination): ideology existing in a material ideological apparatus, prescribing material practices governed by a material ritual, which practices exist in the material actions of a subject acting in all consciousness according to his belief.

But this very presentation reveals that we have retained the following notions: subject, consciousness, belief, actions. From this series I shall immediately extract the decisive central term on which everything else depends: the notion of the *subject.*

And I shall immediately set down two conjoint theses:

1. there is no practice except by and in an ideology;
2. there is no ideology except by the subject and for subjects.

I can now come to my central thesis.

Ideology Interpellates Individuals as Subjects

This thesis is simply a matter of making my last proposition explicit: there is no ideology except by the subject and for subjects. Meaning, there is no ideology except for concrete subjects, and this destination for ideology is only made possible by the subject: meaning, *by the category of the subject* and its functioning.

By this I mean that, even if it only appears under this name (the subject) with the rise of bourgeois ideology, above all with the rise of legal ideology,[15] the category of the subject (which may function under other names: e.g., as the soul in Plato, as God, etc.) is the constitutive category of all ideology, whatever its determination (regional or class) and whatever its historical date—since ideology has no history.

I say: the category of the subject is constitutive of all ideology, but at the same time and immediately I add that *the category of the subject is only constitutive of all ideology insofar as all ideology has the function (which defines it) of "constituting" concrete individuals as subjects.* In the interaction of this double constitution exists the functioning of all ideology, ideology being nothing but its functioning in the material forms of existence of that functioning.

In order to grasp what follows, it is essential to realize that both he who is writing these lines and the reader who reads them are themselves subjects, and therefore ideological subjects (a tautological proposition), i.e., that the author and the reader of these lines both live "spontaneously" or "naturally" in ideology in the sense in which I have said that "man is an ideological animal by nature."

That the author, insofar as he writes the lines of a discourse which claims to be scientific, is completely absent as a "subject" from "his" scientific discourse (for all scientific discourse is by definition a subject-less discourse, there is no "Subject of science" except in an ideology of science) is a different question which I shall leave on one side for the moment.

As St Paul admirably put it, it is in the "Logos," meaning in ideology, that we "live, move and have our being." It follows that, for you and for me, the category of the subject is a primary "obviousness" (obviousnesses are always primary): it is clear that you and I are subjects (free, ethical, etc....). Like all obviousnesses, including those that make a word "name a thing" or "have a meaning" (therefore including the obviousness of the "transparency" of language), the "obviousness" that you and I are subjects—and that that does not cause any problems—is an ideological effect, the elementary ideological effect.[16] It is indeed a peculiarity of ideology that it imposes (without appearing to do so, since these are "obviousnesses") obviousnesses as obviousnesses, which we cannot *fail to recognize* and before which we have the inevitable and natural reaction of crying out (aloud or in the "still, small voice of conscience"): "That's obvious! That's right! That's true!"

At work in this reaction is the ideological *recognition* function which is one of the two functions of ideology as such (its inverse being the function of *misrecognition—méconnaissance*).

To take a highly "concrete" example, we all have friends who, when they knock on our door and we ask, through the door, the question "Who's there?," answer (since "it's obvious") "It's me." And we recognize that "it is him," or "her." We open the door, and "it's true, it really was she who was there." To take another example, when we recognize somebody of our (previous) acquaintance ((*re*)-*connaissance*) in the street, we show him that we have recognized him (and have recognized that he has recognized us) by saying to him "Hello, my friend," and shaking his hand (a material ritual practice of ideological recognition in everyday life—in France, at least; elsewhere, there are other rituals).

In this preliminary remark and these concrete illustrations, I only wish to point out that you and I are *always already* subjects, and as such constantly practice the rituals of ideological recognition, which guarantee for us that we are indeed concrete, individual, distinguishable and (naturally) irreplaceable subjects. The writing I am currently executing and the reading you are currently[17] performing are also in this respect rituals of ideological recognition, including the "obviousness" with which the "truth" or "error" of my reflections may impose itself on you.

But to recognize that we are subjects and that we function in the practical rituals of the most elementary everyday life (the hand-shake, the fact of calling you by your name, the fact of knowing, even if I do not know what it is, that you "have" a name of your own, which means that you are recognized as a unique subject, etc.)—this recognition only gives us the "consciousness" of our incessant (eternal) practice of ideological recognition—its consciousness, i.e., its *recognition*—but in no sense does it give us the (scientific) *knowledge* of the mechanism of this recognition. Now it is this knowledge that we have to reach, if you will, while speaking in ideology, and from within ideology we have to outline a discourse which tries to break with ideology, in order to dare to be the beginning of a scientific (i.e., subject-less) discourse on ideology.

Thus in order to represent why the category of the "subject" is constitutive of ideology, which only exists by constituting concrete subjects as subjects, I shall employ a special mode of exposition: "concrete" enough to be recognized, but abstract enough to be thinkable and thought giving rise to a knowledge.

As a first formulation I shall say: *all ideology hails or interpellates concrete individuals as concrete subjects*, by the functioning of the category of the subject.

This is a proposition which entails that we distinguish for the moment between concrete individuals on the one hand and concrete subjects on the other, although at this level concrete subjects only exist insofar as they are supported by a concrete individual.

I shall then suggest that ideology "acts" or "functions" in such a way that it "recruits" subjects among the individuals (it recruits them all), or "transforms" the individuals into subjects (it transforms them all) by that very precise operation which I have called *interpellation* or hailing, and which can be imagined along the lines of the most commonplace everyday police (or other) hailing: "Hey, you there!"[18]

Assuming that the theoretical scene I have imagined takes place in the street, the hailed individual will turn round. By this mere one-hundred-and-eighty-degree physical conversion, he becomes a *subject.* Why? Because he has recognized that the hail was "really" addressed to him, and that "it was *really him* who was hailed" (and not someone else). Experience shows that the practical telecommunication of hailings is such that they hardly ever miss their man: verbal call or whistle, the one hailed always recognizes that it is really him who is being hailed. And yet it is a strange phenomenon, and one which cannot be explained solely by "guilt feelings," despite the large numbers who "have something on their consciences."

Naturally for the convenience and clarity of my little theoretical theatre I have had to present things in the form of a sequence, with a before and an after, and thus in the form of a temporal succession. There are individuals walking along. Somewhere (usually behind them) the hail rings out: "Hey, you there!" One individual (nine times out of ten it is the right one) turns round, believing/suspecting/knowing that it is for him, i.e., recognizing that "it really is he" who is meant by the hailing. But in reality these things happen without any succession. The existence of ideology and the hailing or interpellation of individuals as subjects are one and the same thing.

I might add: what thus seems to take place outside ideology (to be precise, in the street), in reality takes place in ideology. What really takes place in ideology seems therefore to take place outside it. That is why those who are in ideology believe themselves by definition outside ideology: one of the effects of ideology is the practical *denegation* of the ideological character of ideology by ideology: ideology never says, "I am ideological." It is necessary to be outside ideology, i.e., in scientific knowledge, to be able to say: I am in ideology (a quite exceptional case) or (the general case): I was in ideology. As is well known, the accusation of being in ideology only applies to others, never to oneself (unless one is really a Spinozist or a Marxist, which in this matter, is to be exactly the same thing). Which amounts to saying that ideology *has no outside* (for itself), but at the same time *that it is nothing but outside* (for science and reality).

Spinoza explained this completely two centuries before Marx, who practised it but without explaining it in detail. But let us leave this point, although it is heavy with consequences, consequences which are not just theoretical, but also directly political, since, for example, the whole theory of criticism and self-criticism, the golden rule of the Marxist-Leninist practice of the class struggle, depends on it.

Thus ideology hails or interpellates individuals as subjects. As ideology is eternal, I must now suppress the temporal form in which I have presented the functioning of ideology, and say: ideology has always-already interpellated individuals as subjects, which amounts to making it clear that individuals are always-already interpellated by ideology as subjects, which necessarily leads us to one last proposition: *individuals are always-already subjects*. Hence individuals are "abstract" with respect to the subjects which they always-already are. This proposition might seem paradoxical.

That an individual is always-already a subject, even before he is born, is nevertheless the plain reality, accessible to everyone and not a paradox at all. Freud shows that individuals are always "abstract" with respect to the subjects they always-already are, simply by noting the ideological ritual that surrounds the expectation of a "birth," that "happy event." Everyone knows how much and in what way an unborn child is expected. Which amounts to saying, very prosaically, if we agree to drop the "sentiments," i.e., the forms of family ideology (paternal/maternal, conjugal/fraternal) in which the unborn child is expected: it is certain in advance that it will bear its Father's Name, and will therefore have an identity and be irreplaceable. Before its birth, the child is therefore always-already a subject, appointed as a subject in and by the specific familial ideological configuration in which it is "expected" once it has been conceived. I hardly need add that this familial ideological configuration is, in its uniqueness, highly structured, and that it is in this implacable and more or less "pathological" (presupposing that any meaning can be assigned to that term) structure that the former subject-to-be will have to "find" "its" place, i.e., "become" the sexual subject (boy or girl) which it already is in advance. It is clear that this ideological constraint and pre-appointment, and all the rituals of rearing and then education in the family, have some relationship with what Freud studied in the forms of the pre-genital and genital "stages" of sexuality, i.e., in the "grip" of what Freud registered by its effects as being the unconscious. But let us leave this point, too, on one side.

Let me go one step further. What I shall now turn my attention to is the way the "actors," in this *mise en scène* of interpellation, and their respective roles, are reflected in the very structure of all ideology.

An Example: The Christian Religious Ideology

As the formal structure of all ideology is always the same, I shall restrict my analysis to a single example, one accessible to everyone, that of religious ideology, with the proviso that the same demonstration can be produced for ethical, legal, political, aesthetic ideology, etc.

Let us therefore consider the Christian religious ideology. I shall use a rhetorical figure and "make it speak," i.e., collect into a fictional discourse what it "says" not only in its two Testaments, its Theologians, Sermons, but also in its practices, its rituals, its ceremonies and its sacraments. The Christian religious ideology says something like this:

It says: I address myself to you, a human individual called Peter (every individual is called by his name, in the passive sense, it is never he who provides his own name), in order to tell you that God exists and that you are answerable to Him. It adds: God addresses himself to you through my voice (Scripture having collected the Word of

God, Tradition having transmitted it, Papal Infallibility fixing it for ever on "nice" points). It says: this is who you are: you are Peter! This is your origin, you were created by God for all eternity, although you were born in the 1920th year of Our Lord! This is your place in the world! This is what you must do! By these means, if you observe the "law of love" you will be saved, you, Peter, and will become part of the Glorious Body of Christ! Etc....

Now this is quite a familiar and banal discourse, but at the same time quite a surprising one.

Surprising because if we consider that religious ideology is indeed addressed to individuals,[19] in order to "transform them into subjects," by interpellating the individual, Peter, in order to make him a subject, free to obey or disobey the appeal, i.e., God's commandments; if it calls these individuals by their names, thus recognizing that they are always-already interpellated as subjects with a personal identity (to the extent that Pascal's Christ says: "It is for you that I have shed this drop of my blood!"); if it interpellates them in such a way that the subject responds: *"Yes, it really is me!"* if it obtains from them the *recognition* that they really do occupy the place it designates for them as theirs in the world, a fixed residence: "It really is me, I am here, a worker, a boss or a soldier!" in this vale of tears; if it obtains from them the recognition of a destination (eternal life or damnation) according to the respect or contempt they show to "God's Commandments," Law become Love;—if everything does happen in this way (in the practices of the well-known rituals of baptism, confirmation, communion, confession and extreme unction, etc....), we should note that all this "procedure" to set up Christian religious subjects is dominated by a strange phenomenon: the fact that there can only be such a multitude of possible religious subjects on the absolute condition that there is a Unique, Absolute, *Other Subject,* i.e., God.

It is convenient to designate this new and remarkable Subject by writing Subject with a capital S to distinguish it from ordinary subjects, with a small s.

It then emerges that the interpellation of individuals as subjects presupposes the "existence" of a Unique and central Other Subject, in whose Name the religious ideology interpellates all individuals as subjects. All this is clearly[20] written in what is rightly called the Scriptures. "And it came to pass at that time that God the Lord (Yahweh) spoke to Moses in the cloud. And the Lord cried to Moses, 'Moses!' And Moses replied 'It is (really) I! I am Moses thy servant, speak and I shall listen!' And the Lord spoke to Moses and said to him, *'I am that I am.'*"

God thus defines himself as the Subject *par excellence,* he who is through himself and for himself ("I am that I am"), and he who interpellates his subject, the individual subjected to him by his very interpellation, i.e., the individual named Moses. And Moses, interpellated—called by his Name, having recognized that it "really" was he who was called by God, recognizes that he is a subject, a subject *of* God, a subject subjected to God, *a subject through the Subject and subjected to the Subject.* The proof: he obeys him, and makes his people obey God's Commandments.

God is thus the Subject, and Moses and the innumerable subjects of God's people, the Subject's interlocutors-interpellates: his *mirrors*, his *reflections*. Were not men made *in the image* of God? As all theological reflection proves, whereas He "could perfectly well have done without men" God needs them, the Subject needs the subjects, just men need God, the subjects need the Subject. Better: God needs men, the great Subject needs subjects, even in the terrible inversion of his image in them (when the subjects wallow in debauchery, i.e., sin).

Better: God duplicates himself and sends his Son to the Earth, as a mere subject "forsaken" by him (the long complaint of the Garden of Olives which ends in the Crucifixion), subject but Subject, man but God, to do what prepares the way for the final Redemption, the Resurrection of Christ. God thus needs to "make himself" a man, the Subject needs to become a subject, as if to show empirically, visibly to the eye, tangibly to the hands (see St Thomas) of the subjects, that, if they are subjects, subjected to the Subject, that is solely in order that finally, on Judgement Day, they will re-enter the Lord's Bosom, like Christ, i.e., re-enter the Subject.[21]

Let us decipher into theoretical language this wonderful necessity for the duplication of *the Subject into subjects* and of *the Subject itself into a subject-Subject.*

We observe that the structure of all ideology, interpellating individuals as subjects in the name of a Unique and Absolute Subject is *speculary*, i.e., a mirror-structure, and *doubly* speculary: this mirror duplication is constitutive of ideology and ensures its functioning. Which means that all ideology is *centred*, that the Absolute Subject occupies the unique place of the Centre, and interpellates around it the infinity of individuals into subjects in a double mirror-connexion such that it *subjects* the subjects to the Subject, while giving them in the Subject in which each subject can contemplate its own image (present and future) the *guarantee* that this really concerns them and Him, and that since everything takes place in the Family (the Holy Family: the Family is in essence Holy), "God will *recognize* his own in it," i.e., those who have recognized God, and have recognized themselves in Him, will be saved.

Let me summarize what we have discovered about ideology in general.

The duplicate mirror-structure of ideology ensures simultaneously:

1. the interpellation of "individuals" as subjects;
2. their subjection to the Subject;
3. the mutual recognition of subjects and Subject, the subjects' recognition of each other, and finally the subject's recognition of himself;[22]
4. the absolute guarantee that everything really is so, and that on condition that the subjects recognize what they are and behave accordingly, everything will be all right: Amen—*"So be it."*

Result: caught in this quadruple system of interpellation as subjects, of subjection to the Subject, of universal recognition and of absolute guarantee, the subjects "work," they "work by themselves" in the vast majority of cases, with the exception of the "bad subjects" who on occasion provoke the intervention of one of the detachments of the (Repressive) State Apparatus. But the vast majority of (good) subjects work all right "all by themselves," i.e., by ideology (whose concrete forms are realized in the Ideological State Apparatuses). They are inserted into practices governed by the rituals of the ISAs. They "recognize" the existing state of affairs (*das Bestehende*), that "it really is true that it is so and not otherwise," and that they must be obedient to God, to their conscience, to the priest, to de Gaulle, to the boss, to the engineer, that thou shalt "love thy neighbour as thyself," etc. Their concrete, material behaviour is simply the inscription in life of the admirable words of the prayer: *"Amen—So be it."*

Yes, the subjects "work by themselves." The whole mystery of this effect lies in the first two moments of the quadruple system I have just discussed, or, if you prefer, in the ambiguity of the term *subject.* In the ordinary use of the term, subject in fact means: (1) a free subjectivity, a centre of initiatives, author of and responsible for its actions; (2) a subjected being, who submits to a higher authority, and is therefore stripped of all freedom except that of freely accepting his submission. This last note gives us the meaning of this ambiguity, which is merely a reflection of the effect which produces it: the individual *is interpellated as a (free) subject in order that he shall submit freely to the commandments of the Subject, i.e., in order that he shall (freely) accept his subjection,* i.e., in order that he shall make the gestures and actions of his subjection "all by himself." *There are no subjects except by and for their subjection.* That is why they "work all by themselves."

"So be it! ..." This phrase which registers the effect to be obtained proves that it is not "naturally" so ("naturally": outside the prayer, i.e., outside the ideological intervention). This phrase proves that it *has* to be so if things are to be what they must be, and let us let the words slip: if the reproduction of the relations of production is to be assured, even in the processes of production and circulation, every day, in the "consciousness," i.e., in the attitudes of the individual-subjects occupying the posts which the socio-technical division of labour assigns to them in production, exploitation, repression, ideologization, scientific practice, etc. Indeed, what is really in question in this mechanism of the mirror recognition of the Subject and of the individuals interpellated as subjects, and of the guarantee given by the Subject to the subjects if they freely accept their subjection to the Subject's "commandments"? The reality in question in this mechanism, the reality which is necessarily *ignored* (*méconnue*) in the very forms of recognition (ideology = misrecognition/ignorance) is indeed, in the last resort, the reproduction of the relations of production and of the relations deriving from them.

January–April 1969

P.S. If these few schematic theses allow me to illuminate certain aspects of the functioning of the Superstructure and its mode of intervention in the Infrastructure, they are obviously *abstract* and necessarily leave several important problems unanswered, which should be mentioned:

1. The problem of the *total process* of the realization of the reproduction of the relations of production.

As an element of this process, the ISAs *contribute* to this reproduction. But the point of view of their contribution alone is still an abstract one.

It is only within the processes of production and circulation that this reproduction is *realized*. It is realized by the mechanisms of those processes, in which the training of the workers is "completed," their posts assigned them, etc. It is in the internal mechanisms of these processes that the effect of the different ideologies is felt (above all the effect of legal-ethical ideology).

But this point of view is still an abstract one. For in a class society the relations of production are relations of exploitation, and therefore relations between antagonistic classes. The reproduction of the relations of production, the ultimate aim of the ruling class, cannot therefore be a merely technical operation training and distributing individuals for the different posts in the "technical division" of labour. In fact there is no "technical division" of labour except in the ideology of the ruling class: every "technical" division, every "technical" organization of labour is the form and mask of a *social* (=class) division and organization of labour. The reproduction of the relations of production can therefore only be a class undertaking. It is realized through a class struggle which counterposes the ruling class and the exploited class.

The *total process* of the realization of the reproduction of the relations of production is therefore still abstract, insofar as it has not adopted the point of view of this class struggle. To adopt the point of view of reproduction is therefore, in the last instance, to adopt the point of view of the class struggle.

2. The problem of the class nature of the ideologies existing in a social formation.

The "mechanism" of ideology *in general* is one thing. We have seen that it can be reduced to a few principles expressed in a few words (as "poor" as those which, according to Marx, define production *in general*, or in Freud, define *the* unconscious *in general*). If there is any truth in it, this mechanism must be *abstract* with respect to every real ideological formation.

I have suggested that the ideologies were *realized* in institutions, in their rituals and their practices, in the ISAs. We have seen that on this basis they contribute to that form of class struggle, vital for the ruling class, the reproduction of the relations of production. But the point of view itself, however real, is still an abstract one.

In fact, the State and its Apparatuses only have meaning from the point of view of the class struggle, as an apparatus of class struggle ensuring class oppression and guaranteeing the conditions of exploitation and its reproduction. But there is no class struggle without antagonistic classes. Whoever says class struggle of the ruling class says resistance, revolt and class struggle of the ruled class.

That is why the ISAs are not the realization of ideology *in general,* nor even the conflict-free realization of the ideology of the ruling class. The ideology of the ruling class does not become the ruling ideology by the grace of God, nor even by virtue of the seizure of State power alone. It is by the installation of the ISAs in which this ideology is realized and realizes itself that it becomes the ruling ideology. But this installation is not achieved all by itself; on the contrary, it is the stake in a very bitter and continuous class struggle: first against the former ruling classes and their positions in the old and new ISAs, then against the exploited class.

But this point of view of the class struggle in the ISAs is still an abstract one. In fact, the class struggle in the ISAs is indeed an aspect of the class struggle, sometimes an important and symptomatic one: e.g., the anti-religious struggle in the eighteenth century, or the "crisis" of the educational ISA in every capitalist country today. But the class struggles in the ISAs is only one aspect of a class struggle which goes beyond the ISAs. The ideology that a class in power makes the ruling ideology in its ISAs is indeed "realized" in those ISAs, but it goes beyond them, for it comes from elsewhere. Similarly, the ideology that a ruled class manages to defend in and against such ISAs goes beyond them, for it comes from elsewhere.

It is only from the point of view of the classes, i.e., of the class struggle, that it is possible to explain the ideologies existing in a social formation. Not only is it from this starting-point that it is possible to explain the realization of the ruling ideology in the ISAs and of the forms of class struggle for which the ISAs are the seat and the stake. But it is also and above all from this starting-point that it is possible to understand the provenance of the ideologies which are realized in the ISAs and confront one another there. For if it is true that the ISAs represent the *form* in which the ideology of the ruling class must *necessarily* be realized, and the form in which the ideology of the ruled class must *necessarily* be measured and confronted, ideologies are not "born" in the ISAs but from the social classes at grips in the class struggle: from their conditions of existence, their practices, their experience of the struggle, etc.

April 1970

Notes

All text in this chapter is from *Lenin and Philosophy and Other Essays* by Louis Althusser, translated by Ben Brewster, © 1971. By permission of Monthly Review Press.

1. This text is made up of two extracts from an ongoing study. The sub-title "Notes towards an Investigation" is the author's own. The ideas expounded should not be regarded as more than the introduction to a discussion.

2. Marx to Kugelmann, 11 July 1868, *Selected Correspondence,* Moscow, 1955, p. 209.

3. Marx gave it its scientific concept: *variable capital.*

4. In *For Marx* and *Reading Capital,* 1965 (English editions 1969 and 1970 respectively).

5. *Topography* from the Greek *topos:* place. A topography represents in a definite space the respective *sites* occupied by several realities: thus the economic is *at the bottom* (the base), the superstructure *above it.*

6. See p. 158 below, *On Ideology* [not printed in this volume].

7. To my knowledge, Gramsci is the only one who went any distance in the road I am taking. He had the "remarkable" idea that the State could not be reduced to the (Repressive) State Apparatus, but included, as he put it, a certain number of institutions from *"civil society":* the Church, the Schools, the trade unions, etc. Unfortunately, Gramsci did not systematize his institutions, which remained in the state of acute but fragmentary notes (cf. Gramsci, *Selections from the Prison Notebooks,* International Publishers, 1971, pp. 12, 259, 260–3; see also the letter to Tatiana Schucht, 7 September 1931, in *Lettre del Carcere,* Einaudi, 1968, p. 479. English-language translation in preparation.

8. The family obviously has other "functions" than that of an ISA. It intervenes in the reproduction of labour power. In different modes of production it is the unit of production and/or the unit of consumption.

9. The "Law" belongs both to the (Repressive) State Apparatus and to the system of the ISAs.

10. In a pathetic text written in 1937, Krupskaya relates the history of Lenin's desperate efforts and what she regards as his failure.

11. What I have said in these few brief words about the class struggle in the ISAs is obviously far from exhausting the question of the class struggle.

To approach this question, two principles must be borne in mind:

The first principle was formulated by Marx in the Preface to *A Contribution to the Critique of Political Economy:* "In considering such transformations [a social revolution] a distinction should always be made between the material transformation of the economic conditions of production, which can be determined with the precision of natural science, and the legal, political, religious, aesthetic or philosophic—in short, ideological forms in which men become conscious of this conflict and fight it out." The class struggle is thus expressed and exercised in ideological forms, thus also in the ideological forms of the ISAs. But the class struggle *extends far beyond* these forms, and it is because it extends beyond them that the struggle of the exploited classes may also be exercised in the forms of the ISAs, and thus turn the weapon of ideology against the classes in power.

This by virtue of the *second principle:* the class struggle extends beyond the ISAs because it is rooted elsewhere than in ideology, in the Infrastructure, in the relations of production, which are relations of exploitation and constitute the base for class relations.

12. For the most part. For the relations of production are first reproduced by the materiality of the processes of production and circulation. But it should not be forgotten that ideological relations are immediately present in these same processes.

13. *For that part* of reproduction to which the Repressive State Apparatus and the Ideological State Apparatus *contribute.*

14. I use this very modem term deliberately. For even in Communist circles, unfortunately, it is a commonplace to "explain" some political deviation (left or right opportunism) by the action of a "clique."

15. Which borrowed the legal category of "subject in law" to make an ideological notion: man is by nature a subject.

16. Linguists and those who appeal to linguistics for various purposes often run up against difficulties which arise because they ignore the action of the ideological effects in all discourses—including even scientific discourses.

17. NB: this double "currently" is one more proof of the fact that ideology is "eternal," since these two "currentlys" are separated by an indefinite interval; I am writing these lines 6 April 1969, you may read them at any subsequent time.

18. Hailing as an everyday practice subject to a precise ritual takes a quite "special" form in the policeman's practice of "hailing" which concerns the hailing of "suspects."

19. Although we know that the individual is always already a subject, we go on using this term, convenient because of the contrasting effect it produces.

20. I am quoting in a combined way, not to the letter but "in spirit and truth."

21. The dogma of the Trinity is precisely the theory of the duplication of the Subject (the Father) into a subject (the Son) and of their mirror-connexion (the Holy Spirit).

22. Hegel is (unknowingly) an admirable "theoretician" of ideology insofar as he is a "theoretician" of Universal Recognition who unfortunately ends up in the ideology of Absolute Knowledge. Feuerbach is an astonishing "theoretician" of the mirror connexion, who unfortunately ends up in the ideology of the Human Essence. To find the material with which to construct a theory of the guarantee, we must turn to Spinoza.

20 Ideology and Interpellation: Althusser's "Ideology and Ideological State Apparatuses"

Paul Dourish

It is the proudest and most characteristic achievement of human-computer interaction (HCI), as both a discipline and a movement, that "user-centered" has become an essential characteristic of computer system design. At different moments, different disciplinary contributors to HCI have claimed to be best positioned to take up the role of advocates for the users of interactive digital systems (Cooper and Bowers, 1995) but they have largely shared the fundamental idea that HCI's primary concern is user advocacy that creates a space for and gives voice to the user within processes of engineering design from which users might otherwise be excluded.

While this is laudable enough (and as I sit here typing on my computer, I am, as usual, simultaneously grateful for the efforts made by HCI researchers and practitioners, and hopeful that their efforts might bear more fruit), it has resulted in a somewhat unfortunate problem that some in HCI have lately been addressing. The problem is that the centrality of user-centered design in HCI's efforts have left us with little to say about how people might be positioned with respect to information technology and digital media *except* as users. In consequence, what we can say about them is largely limited to questions of usability, efficiency, and effectiveness. This is perhaps unsurprising given the field's origins at a time when the primary context of computer application was the workplace. The goal of user-centered design, after all, was not to liberate users from drudgery or serfdom, but rather to beat a new (user-centered) path toward the primary goal of organizational and hence economic productivity with these newfangled and expensive machines; usability problems were bad because they produced inefficiency. Consequently, the user-relation was always narrowly defined. However, the contemporary contexts of encounters with digital media make it ever more pressing to find alternative and more encompassing ways to understand how people relate to information technology.

Althusser's article, "Ideology and Ideological State Apparatuses," begins to offer us a way to do so. It is not, of course, itself directed toward digital or interactive technologies, but the analysis that it provides is a powerful one. In particular, it offers us intellectual resources for opening up three questions that we might want to ask in HCI. The first is how particular kinds of conditions have been bound up within the user-relation as traditionally conceived and carried over from the domain of traditional industrial labor into digital media contexts. The second is how specific subject positions are produced in this context, a process that Althusser calls "interpellation." The third is how digital media function as mechanisms (or "apparatuses" in Althusser's terminology) that reproduce social relations and in doing so reproduce too the system of attitudes and values that those relations depend on.

Born in Algeria in 1918, Louis Althusser lived and worked in France throughout his professional career. Although sometimes labeled as a part of the French structuralist movement of the 1960s, along with figures such as Barthes, Lévi-Strauss, and Lacan, Althusser was critical of many elements of structuralism and is not so easily classified. (That said, the structuralist movement is perhaps particularly marked by those who distanced themselves from the term—including others listed above.) He came to prominence for his interpretations of Marx's work, most especially in his books *For Marx* and *Reading Capital.* Althusser put forward an argument that Marx's work exhibits an "epistemological break" that separates his early writing from his more mature work, and suggested that these two bodies of work have different philosophical foundations. This reading was not without controversy within the context of contemporary Marxist thinking, although today Althusser is widely recognized as one of the founders of neo-Marxist thought, not least for the treatment of ideology that concerns us here. Althusser is controversial too for some of the elements of his personal life; he struggled with depression all of his life, and during one particularly tragic depressive episode, strangled his wife to death. He wrote and published relatively little following his psychiatric hospitalization, and died in 1990.

The treatment of ideology is one of the areas in which Althusser's writings have been particularly influential, and it is the primary topic of this particular essay. What precisely does the term "ideology" mean for Althusser? Let's leave to one side the notion of ideology that suggests flag-waving, man-the-barricades, political-with-a-capital-P accounts of society and its needs. Ideology in the sense that Althusser wants to explore refers to a comprehensive set of ideas about society and everyday life that play a defining role in society. Ideology has three particular functions. First, it makes particular social arrangements appear as natural objects; that is, things that are the products of social forces appear instead to be the natural order (with the effect, of course, of obscuring their origins). Second, ideology makes the needs of some into the needs of all; that is, it turns those things that are to the advantage of particular groups into natural, and so universal, goods. Third, in and through these functions, it justifies particular arrangements and their perpetuation and enrolls people in them. In doing so, it mediates between social arrangements and our understanding of them as being in our own interest and genuinely the way things are ("Amen—So be it!" [Althusser, chapter 19, this volume]). As Althusser clarifies in this essay, "Ideology is a representation of the imaginary relationship of individuals to their real conditions of existence." As he somewhat more pithily observes later, ideology "imposes ... obviousnesses as obviousnesses."

Our starting point for encountering this article in the context of interactive systems and digital media is the way that media and communication infrastructures are brought into the frame. Critical theories of media play a bridging role here, so we need to begin with some background.

Althusser's thought is a key component of the reevaluation of the traditional separation between base and superstructure that characterizes the Frankfurt School and post-Frankfurt School work in critical theory. The terms "base" and "superstructure" here come from Marx, where they refer to different elements of society. In his writings, Marx separates the economic base—the forces and relations of capitalist production, including labor arrangements, production and consumption, and economic power—from what he calls the "superstructure," which comprises the institutions of contemporary life—a society's culture, systems of governance, law, art, religion, ritual practice, and so on (Marx, [1859] 1979). Further, Marx argues that the base determines the superstructure; that is, the structure and organization of society (superstructure) are a consequence of the economic arrangements (base). Much work in critical theory, and especially in the critical theory of media and culture, has questioned this arrangement (Williams, 1973), arguing that the flow is not one directional in the way that Marx suggests. In doing so, it has examined the way in which the superstructure is not simply produced by the base but also reinforces and supports the base by reproducing and naturalizing it. So, for example, to return to the question of media from this perspective, popular media (superstructure) provide images of social organization and function that reinforce the separation of labor and capital, the pleasures of consumption, the alienation of labor in exchange for wages, and so on, which supports and furthers the economic status quo (base). This reappraisal of the base-superstructure relation takes many forms, and different positions are expressed by different theorists. For Frankfurt School critical theorists Theodor Adorno and Max Horkheimer, for example, popular media are a means of manipulation on the part of capital in the form of "official culture" (Adorno and Horkheimer, [1947] 1972), while for cultural theorist Stuart Hall (see chapters 9 and 10 in this volume) and others, popular media are less of a one-way street and the audience played a more active part in creating their own, potentially quite subversive, interpretation of and meaning for the media that they consumed (e.g., Hall, 1981).

If media have the effect of reinforcing and reproducing the conditions of the economic base, how do they do that? This is the question that Althusser's paper addresses. He supplements traditional views of the repressive state, which he formulates in terms of the Repressive State Apparatus (such as for instance the police and military), which operates primarily through violence, with Ideological State Apparatuses, which operate primarily through ideology. Among the latter he numbers such things as the church, the family, the political system, media, and the legal system. Although these are labeled here as "state" apparatuses, in the sense that they support the ongoing reproduction of the state, they may themselves be private in their constitution and their domains of action; however, Hall argues, they are apparatuses through which the state operates and that reinforce the constitution of the state. (A school, for instance, may be a private institution but is still in the business of training people in the models of achievement, examination, certification, and discipline on which capitalist production relies.) What Althusser provides for us, then, is a mechanism by which we can understand how communication media (among other arrangements) fit into the broader operation of ideology and serve particular kinds of ideological functions.

For Althusser, this is not simply about media or authority or institutions but about the dynamics of our encounters with them. In his classic example, Althusser discusses a person who hears a policeman call, "Hey, you there!" What we hear in this, Althusser suggests, is the possibility that we are the "you" in question—and in our turning toward the policeman, responding to the hail, we make ourselves into the subject of the hail (and of the policeman's authority). "Ideology interpellates the individual as a subject," Althusser explains; that is, ideology calls out to us in a way that provokes a recognition of its structures, and that very recognition is part of a response that makes it so. The "ideological state apparatuses" that Althusser discusses operate in just this way.

Digital means are now among the primary channels through which entertainment and media communication are transmitted, whether that be digital versions of formerly analogue media (digital TV transmissions, online movie rentals, internet radio, or magazines on e-readers), so digital technologies and areas such as HCI are clearly brought into the scope of Althusser's argument about communication media as Ideological State Apparatuses. To the extent, at least, that the phrase "digital media" has entered our lexicon, and that computer technologies are often understood from a media perspective, this link to Althusser's argument seems uncontroversial, and, by the same token, rather uninteresting. We can, however, take the argument a little further and examine those areas where the particular considerations of digital technologies or the techniques of human-computer interaction might have relevance for Althusser's argument. Three are of note here—practices of digital representation, the user as subject, and the rhetoric of innovation and creative practice.

The first concern—that of the practices of digital representation—is inescapable in the domain of software production and HCI. Software is a representational medium. The process of building software systems is, in essence, a process whereby designers construct both representational analogues of elements of the real world (people, cars, spaces, books, etc.) and representational analogues of the actions to be created on these, such that a digital domain of human action is crafted (think of the computer "desktop" for example). Perhaps more importantly, these objects are supplemented by digital representational analogues of intrinsically digital objects, through the operation of abstraction. So, alongside database records of cars, accounts that represent people, and so on, we find encodings of internet routes, representations of database files, metadata about interface actions, and other digital representations of inward-directed digital phenomena. This representational practice, then, maintains an ontic parity between these different kinds of objects. People, cars, spaces, and books become "real" in the interactive experience through the process of their representational availability in just the same way as do "virtual objects" such as internet routes, database records, and interface actions.

The point here is that the objects of the human world have to be distilled down to essences in order to be represented for the computer system, and that the range of human actions must also be narrowed to define the actions that can be taken within a system. Interactive systems must provide particular ways of working that make a certain sense, but the ways that they make sense invoke particular logics that embody ideological assumptions. One regular assumption, for example, is that one wants to do things efficiently—so that a map, for example, should show you the fastest or shortest route between two points (rather than, say, the most historically interesting route, or the route that will most likely lead to casual window-shopping, or that will offer the most distractions).[1] Another regular assumption is that multiplicities should be handled by distilling objects down to their essences and then dealing with those uniformly—that all my books, for example, would be understood as being otherwise featureless objects distinguished by their different titles, dimensions, topics, and page counts. These kinds of assumptions turn us all into object-processors to be understood in terms of our efficiencies; digital technologies become yet another way in which the cultural logics of efficiency and regularity (indeed, efficiency through regularity) operate in the world.

The figuring of objects of the social world as those that are naturally and straightforwardly subject to processes of representation, encoding, and digital manipulation, and the casual elision of representation as an active human process in the construction of digital objects both play a key role in the way that computationalism operates as a mode of technological management and expert governance. One might take as an example the rhetoric of "big data" which, at the time of writing, can be found everywhere as a narrative of the triumph of raw empiricism over theoretical analysis in domains as diverse as electing politicians and marketing breakfast foods (Mayer-Schönberger and Cukier, 2013). The very positioning of data processing as empiricism serves to undercut and hide from scrutiny the processes by which data are produced (Gitelman, 2013).

What Althusser's analysis draws our attention to is the system of statistical reasoning as a foundation for governance (Desrosières, 1998). This system simultaneously naturalizes numerical representations, statistical artifacts (such as mean and standard deviation), and the enterprise of managing through representations. We are interpellated, in his term, within statistical distributions—called into positions of subjection to specific forms of disciplinary reasoning and accounting. For instance, he suggests that "all ideology represents in its necessarily imaginary distortions not the existing relations of production (and the other relations that derive from them) but above all the (imaginary) relationship of individuals to the relations of production and the relations that derive from them" (Althusser, chapter 19, this volume). Our enrollment into systems of statistical and numerical reasoning, in part through the ontic equivalence between representations of physical and virtual objects in our encounters with digital media and information systems, are part of just this imaginary relationship.

Turning to the second consideration—that is, how subject positions are created in digital media contexts—reading Althusser's work might bring into sharper relief long-held concerns about the notion of the "user" as a focus of attention within HCI (Bannon, 1991; Cooper and Bowers, 1995; Satchell and Dourish, 2009). Althusser's discussion of interpellation identifies the way in which people recognize (or rather, via Lacan, *mis*recognize) themselves as subjects of domination through ideology. In other words, ideology supports the operation of state power by providing a channel whereby we become complicit in our own subjection. One question that this raises, then, is what forms of subjection, and what subject positions, are made available through the operation of specific Ideological State Apparatuses. We might bring this into the conversation then about the forms of subject position available for people within the frame of HCI analysis, and in particular the forms of design-use relations at the heart of that process. That is, in what ways HCI might deal with people other than as users (and, hence, as potential users, lagging users, "power users," etc.).

The concern here is not simply that the processes of "user-centered design" leave us with a fairly impoverished vocabulary for talking about (or therefore for attending to or engaging with) forms of subjectivity experienced in or enacted through the encounter with digital media. Other positions are clearly produced (Satchell and Dourish, 2009; Warner 2002) even if they are not made visible within the operation of HCI as an analytic or design practice. The concern is more, perhaps, with the logic that naturalizes the position of "user," as this manifests itself most particularly with respect to the speculative or anticipatory nature of design processes. Elsewhere, Christine Satchell and I (Satchell and Dourish, 2009) have explored some of the consequences of this perspective, and discussed different ways that people might have of being something-other-than-users. Our point has been that in conventional HCI approaches, other ways of relating to technology (or of relating to each other through technology)—that is, the human ends to which technology is placed in service—disappear from the picture. I frame this here not so much as concerning a particular position for the user but rather as a manifestation of design-use relations, since it operates in both directions—producing a particular imagination of design and its logics as it produces a logic of use (Dourish, 2006).

The user, of course, becomes visible in the practice of design long before a specific occasion of use; the user, as an imaginary projection of design, is manifest first in the notion of "requirements," the formulae that capture "what users want" and, consequently, the particular conditions of use that will mark a design as successful. We can see bound up in here a host of issues, including the various accountabilities of professional design practice, the nature of relations between a "designer" and a "user," the concept of these domains as separate spheres mediated by accounts of "user needs," and so on. More broadly, we see that design-use relations have ideological foundations. In *The Consumer Society*, Baudrillard ([1970] 1998) rejects the idea that consumer desire is inherently inauthentic, and hence that consumer needs are simply the product of productive forces, saying instead that "the system of needs is the product of the system of production" (45). He is arguing, in other words, that we shouldn't simply decry someone's eagerness to purchase an iPhone as a case of a person manipulated by cynical marketing machinery into a set of desires that are somehow inauthentic; the desire, he argues, is quite authentic and should be treated so. Rather, what we want to focus on critically is the nature of productive cycles, of the ways in which market competition systematically produces arrangements within which these authentic needs arise. So, in engaging with the topic of design-use relations and the position of the user, Althusser's analysis directs us toward a recognition of the entwining of the system of needs within the system of production, in just how ideology mediates the relationship between the individual and the capitalist state—that is, in the way that the goal of HCI is to find ever more irresistible things to make that people will want to buy and use.

This discussion brings us to the third point at which we can see a consequential tie between Althusser's argument and the disciplinary logic of HCI, that of our conception of innovation and creative practice. To the extent that HCI is a design-centered discipline (which is different from saying that it is "a design discipline"), a persistent question asks what the role or roles of design might be there. In particular, this manifests itself around two considerations, each of which is symptomatically useful here. The first is whether specific instances of design practice can be imagined or valued that do not orient themselves toward industrial innovation as typically construed; that is, which do not present themselves as prototype products (Gaver, 2012). The second concerns what role might be found for research that takes human-computer interaction as its topic but refuses to commit itself to design interventions. For instance, the disciplinary demand for "implications for design" systematically robs much ethnographic research in HCI of its force by requiring essentially that it translate its subjects into users or potential users of digital technologies (Dourish, 2006). Simultaneously, in doing so, it frames the topic of HCI as being only and entirely the production of new, more compelling, more irresistible interactive technologies. Carl DiSalvo and Ann Light, among others, have illustrated ways of using design engagements not in service of the production of new products but as part of processes of participation and deliberation (DiSalvo, 2012; Light, 2011).

The question of the role of design practice as a form of cultural critique or critical practice as well as a form of industrial production is a concern that a number of researchers have taken up, and they are well represented in the pages of this volume.

To the extent that the book itself represents (and presents) an argument for the significance of critical humanities in HCI research and practice, and to the extent too that this is an argument that engages with and takes up the mantle of HCI theorist Phil Agre's "critical technical practice" (1997) to a greater or lesser extent, then it is scarcely breaking new ground to suggest that the conception of technological investigation that has been traditional within HCI over the past several decades has largely yoked design, innovation, and industrial production together. That said, Althusser provides us with a framework for drawing this issue of the constitution of HCI as a discipline reflexively into focus as a research topic in its own right.

At this writing, tertiary education and academic research are increasingly measured by their impact on regional and national economies, in which the *sine qua non* of engineering-oriented research impact is the startup. Althusser, of course, points to education as the dominant contemporary Ideological State Apparatus. So, the framing of innovation as the core contribution of HCI or digital technology research—the idea that what scholarly work in HCI needs to do is to answer industry's questions and provide a platform for new forms of industrial production—is a particularly critical one to identify and examine.

That said, it is important to place Althusser's work in the context of more recent scholarship on ideology, culture, and media. Although Althusser's work does not specifically address questions of media and culture, and although it was not institutionally a part of the Frankfurt School, it shares a common intellectual heritage with that school's writings, including those analyses that directly concern themselves with media and culture. In particular, Althusser subscribes to a model of ideological domination that similarly pervades Adorno's critiques of the corrosive power of "the culture industry," one that frames people as passive and powerless recipients of media messages. As was briefly noted earlier, subsequent work in media and cultural studies—perhaps most visibly in the British cultural studies tradition pioneered at the Centre for Contemporary Cultural Studies at the University of Birmingham in the 1970s and 1980s—argues for a revision of this model that recognizes the interpretive agency media "consumers" bring to table—that is, the way in which they creatively appropriate, interpret, revise, play with, disrupt, and evaluate the messages encoded in media of all sorts. In the HCI context, we might similarly observe that, while different interactive technologies do indeed interpellate people as users to different degrees and in different ways, the mix of technologies, services, media, and applications that constitute any given person's "mediascape" (to misuse slightly Arjun Appadurai's [1996] useful concept) provide a framework in which individuals have a good deal more freedom and flexibility than Althusser's writings might suggest. For example, while Microsoft Word might try to fit me into a particular box, the fact that I use Microsoft Word along with, say, Apple's Keynote presentation software, an open-source text editor, Facebook, git, iOS, and Linux means that my experience of Word is contextualized by many different elements which, to some extent, I get to assemble for myself. However, despite the force of these later critiques and developments, Althusser's essay provides a framework within which we can begin to understand both the power of interpellation and the ideological functions of interactive technology.

The three points of connection between Althusser's argument and HCI practice—representation, users, and innovation—show that digital media are relevant to Althusser's analysis as more than simply a new channel through which ideological messages can be conveyed. Certainly, when we look at movies delivered online, sitcoms reframed as "web series," and advertising on Facebook, we could be forgiven for seeing digital media simply as a shift in technological arrangements. As McLuhan (1964) famously noted, new media tend to act as containers for old media, and by that token, (some) digital media certainly act simply as new sites for old practices. However, turning our attention to the specificity and materiality of digital technologies reveals distinctly new ways in which they operate ideologically. Such attention is warranted. New media scholars have argued for a more profound shift than McLuhan's analysis would suggest; Manovich (2002), for example, suggests that the database plays the role of cultural form in the twenty-first century that the movie played in the twentieth century or the novel in the nineteenth. Althusser provides us with tools for examining the consequences of the specific materialities and design practices that arise in the domain of interactive digital systems, and to see in them their roles in and relationships to broader historical and social processes.

Acknowledgments

Thanks to Julie Barmazel, Mark Blythe, and Ann Light for careful reading, thoughtful critique, and valuable suggestions. This work is supported in part by the Intel Science and Technology Center for Social Computing.

Note

1. Asked to provide a user interface critique of an online map interface by a recruiter for a high-tech company, a friend of mine suggested, "This seems to be a tool for people who want to get to where they are going." The interviewer was nonplussed.

References

Adorno, T., and M. Horkheimer. (1972) *Dialectic of Enlightenment*, translated by J. Cumming. New York: Continuum. Originally published as *Dialektik der Aufklärung* by Querido Verlag in Amsterdam in 1947.

Agre, P. 1997. "Toward a Critical Technical Practice: Lessons Learned in Trying to Reform AI." In *Social Science, Technical Systems, and Cooperative Work: Beyond the Great Divide*, edited by G. Bowker, S. L. Star, W. Turner, and L. Gasser, 131–157. Mahwah, NJ: Erlbaum.

Appadurai, A. (1996) *Modernity at Large: Cultural Dimensions of Globalization.* Minneapolis: University of Minnesota Press.

Bannon, L. (1991) "From Human Factors to Human Actors: The Role of Psychology and Human-Computer Interaction Studies in Systems Design." In *Design at Work: Cooperative Design of Computer Systems*, edited by J. Greenbaum and M. Kyng, 25–44. Hillsdale, NJ: Erlbaum.

Baudrillard, J. (1998) *The Consumer Society: Myths and Structures*, translated by Chris Turner. London: Sage. Originally published as *La société de consommation* by Editions Denoël in 1970.

Cooper, G., and J. Bowers. (1995) "Representing the User: Notes on the Disciplinary Rhetoric of HCI." In *The Social and Interactional Dimensions of Human-Computer Interfaces*, edited by P. Thomas, 48–66. Cambridge: Cambridge University Press.

Desrosières, A. (1998) *The Politics of Large Numbers: A History of Statistical Reasoning.* Cambridge, MA: Harvard University Press.

DiSalvo, C. (2012) *Adversarial Design.* Cambridge, MA: MIT Press.

Dourish, P. (2006) "Implications for Design." *Proceedings of the SIGCHI Conference on Human Factors in Computing Systems (CHI'06)* New York: ACM, 541–550.

Gaver, W. (2012) "What Should We Expect from Research through Design?" *Proceedings of the SIGCHI Conference on Human Factors in Computing Systems (CHI'12)* New York: ACM, 937–946.

Gitelman, L., ed. (2013) *"Raw Data" Is an Oxymoron.* Cambridge, MA: MIT Press.

Hall, S. (1981) "Notes on Deconstructing 'The Popular.'" In *People's History and Socialist Theory*, edited by R. Samuel, 227–239. London: Routledge.

Light, A. (2011) "Democratising Technology: Inspiring Transformation with Design, Performance and Props." *Proceedings of the SIGCHI Conference on Human Factors in Computing Systems (CHI'11).* New York: ACM, 2239–2242.

Manovich, L. (2002) *The Language of New Media.* Cambridge, MA: MIT Press.

Marx, K. ([1859] 1979) *A Contribution to the Critique of Political Economy.* Translated by M. Dobb. New York: Intl.

Mayer-Schönberger, V., and K. Cukier. (2013) *Big Data: A Revolution That Will Transform How We Live, Work, and Think.* Boston: Houghton Mifflin Harcourt.

McLuhan, M. (1964) *Understanding Media: The Extensions of Man.* New York: McGraw-Hill.

Satchell, C., and Dourish, P. (2009) "Beyond the User: Use and Non-Use in HCI." *Proceedings of the 21st Annual Conference of the Australian Computer-Human Interaction Special Interest Group: Design: Open 24/7 (OZCHI'09).* New York: ACM, 9–16.

Warner, M. (2002) *Publics and Counterpublics.* New York: Zone Books.

Williams, R. (1973) "Base and Superstructure in Marxist Cultural Theory." *New Left Review* 82: 3–16.

21 *Gender Trouble* (1999)

Judith Butler

It was and remains my view that any feminist theory that restricts the meaning of gender in the presuppositions of its own practice sets up exclusionary gender norms within feminism, often with homophobic consequences. It seemed to me, and continues to seem, that feminism ought to be careful not to idealize certain expressions of gender that, in turn, produce new forms of hierarchy and exclusion. In particular, I opposed those regimes of truth that stipulated that certain kinds of gendered expressions were found to be false or derivative, and others, true and original. The point was not to prescribe a new gendered way of life that might then serve as a model for readers of the text. Rather, the aim of the text was to open up the field of possibility for gender without dictating which kinds of possibilities ought to be realized. One might wonder what use "opening up possibilities" finally is, but no one who has understood what it is to live in the social world as what is "impossible," illegible, unrealizable, unreal, and illegitimate is likely to pose that question.

Gender Trouble sought to uncover the ways in which the very thinking of what is possible in gendered life is foreclosed by certain habitual and violent presumptions.[1] The text also sought to undermine any and all efforts to wield a discourse of truth to delegitimate minority gendered and sexual practices. This doesn't mean that all minority practices are to be condoned or celebrated, but it does mean that we ought to be able to think them before we come to any kinds of conclusions about them. What worried me most were the ways that the panic in the face of such practices rendered them unthinkable. Is the breakdown of gender binaries, for instance, so monstrous, so frightening, that it must be held to be definitionally impossible and heuristically precluded from any effort to think gender?

Some of these kinds of presumptions were found in what was called "French Feminism" at the time, and they enjoyed great popularity among literary scholars and some social theorists.

Even as I opposed what I took to be the heterosexism at the core of sexual difference fundamentalism, I also drew from French poststructuralism to make my points. My work in *Gender Trouble* turned out to be one of cultural translation. Poststructuralist theory was brought to bear on U.S. theories of gender and the political predicaments of feminism. If in some of its guises, poststructuralism appears as a formalism, aloof from questions of social context and political aim, that has not been the case with its more recent American appropriations. Indeed, my point was not to "apply" poststructuralism to feminism, but to subject those theories to a specifically feminist reformulation. Whereas some defenders of poststructuralist formalism express dismay at the avowedly "thematic" orientation it receives in works such as *Gender Trouble*, the critiques of poststructuralism within the cultural Left have expressed strong skepticism toward the claim that anything politically progressive can come of its premises. In both accounts, however, poststructuralism is considered something unified, pure, and monolithic. In recent years, however, that theory, or set of theories, has migrated into gender and sexuality studies, postcolonial and race studies. It has lost the formalism of its earlier instance and acquired a new and transplanted life in the domain of cultural theory. There are continuing debates about whether my own work or the work of Homi K. Bhabha, Gayatri Chakravorty Spivak, or Slavoj Žižek belongs to cultural studies or critical theory, but perhaps such questions simply show that the strong distinction between the two enterprises has broken down. There will be theorists who claim that all of the above belong to cultural studies, and there will be cultural studies practitioners who define themselves against all manner of theory (although not, significantly, Stuart Hall, one of the founders of cultural studies in Britain). But both sides of the debate sometimes miss the point that the face of theory has changed precisely through its cultural appropriations. There is a new venue for theory, necessarily impure, where it emerges in and as the very event of cultural translation. This is not the displacement of theory by historicism, nor a simple historicization of theory that exposes the contingent limits of its more generalizable claims. It is, rather, the emergence of theory at the site where cultural horizons meet, where the demand for translation is acute and its promise of success, uncertain.

Gender Trouble is rooted in "French Theory," which is itself a curious American construction. Only in the United States are so many disparate theories joined together as if they formed some kind of unity. Although the book has been translated into several languages and has had an especially strong impact on discussions of gender and politics in Germany, it will emerge in France, if it finally does, much later than in other countries. I mention this to underscore that the apparent Francocentrism of the text is at a significant distance from France and from the life of theory in France. *Gender Trouble* tends to read together, in a syncretic vein, various French intellectuals (Lévi-Strauss, Foucault, Lacan, Kristeva, Wittig) who had few alliances with one another and whose readers in France rarely, if ever, read one another. Indeed, the intellectual promiscuity of the text marks it precisely as American and makes it foreign to a French context. So does its emphasis on the Anglo-American sociological and anthropological tradition of "gender" studies, which is distinct from the discourse of "sexual difference" derived from structuralist inquiry. If the text runs the risk of Eurocentrism in the U.S., it has threatened an "Americanization" of theory in France for those few French publishers who have considered it.[2]

Of course, "French Theory" is not the only language of this text. It emerges from a long engagement with feminist theory, with the debates on the socially constructed character of gender, with psychoanalysis and feminism, with Gayle Rubin's extraordinary work on gender, sexuality, and kinship, Esther Newton's groundbreaking work on drag, Monique Wittig's brilliant theoretical and fictional writings, and with gay and lesbian perspectives in the humanities. Whereas many feminists in the 1980s assumed that lesbianism meets feminism in lesbian-feminism, *Gender Trouble* sought to refuse the notion that lesbian practice instantiates feminist theory, and set up a more troubled relation between the two terms. Lesbianism in this text does not represent a return to what is most important about being a woman; it does not consecrate femininity or signal a gynocentric world. Lesbianism is not the erotic consummation of a set of political beliefs (sexuality and belief are related in a much more complex fashion, and very often at odds with one another). Instead, the text asks, how do non-normative sexual practices call into question the stability of gender as a category of analysis? How do certain sexual practices compel the question: what is a woman, what is a man? If gender is no longer to be understood as consolidated through normative sexuality, then is there a crisis of gender that is specific to queer contexts?

The idea that sexual practice has the power to destabilize gender emerged from my reading of Gayle Rubin's "The Traffic in Women" and sought to establish that normative sexuality fortifies normative gender. Briefly, one is a woman, according to this framework, to the extent that one functions as one within the dominant heterosexual frame and to call the frame into question is perhaps to lose something of one's sense of place in gender. I take it that this is the first formulation of "gender trouble" in this text. I sought to understand some of the terror and anxiety that some people suffer in "becoming gay," the fear of losing one's place in gender or of not knowing who one will be if one sleeps with someone of the ostensibly "same" gender. This constitutes a certain crisis in ontology experienced at the level of both sexuality and language. This issue has become more acute as we consider various new forms of gendering that have emerged in light of transgenderism and transsexuality, lesbian and gay parenting, new butch and femme identities. When and why, for instance, do some butch lesbians who become parents become "dads" and others become "moms"?

What about the notion, suggested by Kate Bornstein, that a transsexual cannot be described by the noun of "woman" or "man," but must be approached through active verbs that attest to the constant transformation which "is" the new identity or, indeed, the "in-betweenness" that puts the being of gendered identity into question? Although some lesbians argue that butches have nothing to do with "being a man," others insist that their butchness is or was only a route to a desired status as a man. These paradoxes have surely proliferated in recent years, offering evidence of a kind of gender trouble that the text itself did not anticipate.[3]

But what is the link between gender and sexuality that I sought to underscore? Certainly, I do not mean to claim that forms of sexual practice produce certain genders, but only that under conditions of normative heterosexuality, policing gender is sometimes used as a way of securing heterosexuality. Catharine MacKinnon offers a formulation of this problem that resonates with my own at the same time that there are, I believe, crucial and important differences between us. She writes:

> Stopped as an attribute of a person, sex inequality takes the form of gender; moving as a relation between people, it takes the form of sexuality. Gender emerges as the congealed form of the sexualization of inequality between men and women.[4]

In this view, sexual hierarchy produces and consolidates gender. It is not heterosexual normativity that produces and consolidates gender, but the gender hierarchy that is said to underwrite heterosexual relations. If gender hierarchy produces and consolidates gender, and if gender hierarchy presupposes an operative notion of gender, then gender is what causes gender, and the formulation culminates in tautology. It may be that MacKinnon wants merely to outline the self-reproducing mechanism of gender hierarchy, but this is not what she has said.

Is "gender hierarchy" sufficient to explain the conditions for the production of gender? To what extent does gender hierarchy serve a more or less compulsory heterosexuality, and how often are gender norms policed precisely in the service of shoring up heterosexual hegemony?

Katherine Franke, a contemporary legal theorist, makes innovative use of both feminist and queer perspectives to note that by assuming the primacy of gender hierarchy to the production of gender, MacKinnon also accepts a presumptively heterosexual model for thinking about sexuality. Franke offers an alternative model of gender discrimination to MacKinnon's, effectively arguing that sexual harassment is the paradigmatic allegory for the production of gender. Not all discrimination can be understood as harassment. The act of harassment may be one in which a person is "made" into a certain gender. But there are others [*sic*] ways of enforcing gender as well. Thus, for Franke, it is important to make a provisional distinction between gender and sexual discrimination. Gay people, for instance, may be discriminated against in positions of employment because they fail to "appear" in accordance with accepted gendered norms. And the sexual harassment of gay people may well take place not in the service of shoring up gender hierarchy, but in promoting gender normativity.

Whereas MacKinnon offers a powerful critique of sexual harassment, she institutes a regulation of another kind: to have a gender means to have entered already into a heterosexual relationship of subordination. At an analytic level, she makes an equation that resonates with some dominant forms of homophobic argument. One such view prescribes and condones the sexual ordering of gender, maintaining that men who are men will be straight, women who are women will be straight. There is another set of views, Franke's included, which offers a critique precisely of this form of gender regulation. There is thus a difference between sexist and feminist views on the relation between gender and sexuality: the sexist claims that a woman only exhibits her womanness in the act of heterosexual coitus in which her subordination becomes her pleasure (an essence emanates and is confirmed in the sexualized subordination of women); a feminist view argues that gender should be overthrown, eliminated, or rendered fatally ambiguous precisely because it is always a sign of subordination for women. The latter accepts the power of the former's orthodox description, accepts that the former's description already operates as powerful ideology, but seeks to oppose it.

I belabor this point because some queer theorists have drawn an analytic distinction between gender and sexuality, refusing a causal or structural link between them. This makes good sense from one perspective: if what is meant by this distinction is that heterosexual normativity ought *not* to order gender, and that such ordering ought to be opposed, I am firmly in favor of this view.[5] If, however, what is meant by this is that (descriptively speaking), there is no sexual regulation of gender, then I think an important, but not exclusive, dimension of how homophobia works is going unrecognized by those who are clearly most eager to combat it. It is important for me to concede, however, that the performance of gender subversion can indicate nothing about sexuality or sexual practice. Gender can be rendered ambiguous without disturbing or reorienting normative sexuality at all. Sometimes gender ambiguity can operate precisely to contain or deflect non-normative sexual practice and thereby work to keep normative sexuality intact.[6] Thus, no correlation can be drawn, for instance, between drag or transgender and sexual practice, and the distribution of hetero-, bi-, and homo-inclinations cannot be predictably mapped onto the travels of gender bending or changing.

Much of my work in recent years has been devoted to clarifying and revising the theory of performativity that is outlined in *Gender Trouble*.[7] It is difficult to say precisely what performativity is not only because my own views on what "performativity" might mean have changed over time, most often in response to excellent criticisms,[8] but because so many others have taken it up and given it their own formulations. I originally took my clue on how to read the performativity of gender from Jacques Derrida's reading of Kafka's "Before the Law." There the one who waits for the law, sits before the door of the law, attributes a certain force to the law for which one waits. The anticipation of an authoritative disclosure of meaning is the means by which that authority is attributed and installed: the anticipation conjures its object. I wondered whether we do not labor under a similar expectation concerning gender, that it operates as an interior essence that might be disclosed, an expectation that ends up producing the very phenomenon that it anticipates. In the first instance, then, the performativity of gender revolves around this metalepsis, the way in which the anticipation of a gendered essence produces that which it posits as outside itself. Secondly, performativity is not a singular act, but a repetition and ritual, which achieves its effects through its naturalization in the context of a body, understood, in part, as a culturally sustained temporal duration.[9]

Several important questions have been posed to this doctrine, and one seems especially noteworthy to mention here. The view that gender is performative sought to show that what we take to be an internal essence of gender is manufactured through a sustained set of acts, posited through the gendered stylization of the body. In this way, it showed that what we take to be an "internal" feature of ourselves is one that we anticipate and produce through certain bodily acts, at an extreme, an hallucinatory effect of naturalized gestures. Does this mean that everything that is understood as "internal" about the psyche is therefore evacuated, and that internality is a false metaphor? Although *Gender Trouble* clearly drew upon the metaphor of an internal psyche in its early discussion of gender melancholy, that emphasis was not brought forward into the thinking of performativity itself.[10] Both *The Psychic Life of Power* and several of my recent articles on psychoanalytic topics have sought to come to terms with this problem, what many have seen as a problematic break between the early and later chapters of this book. Although I would deny that all of the internal world of the psyche is but an effect of a stylized set of acts, I continue to think that it is a significant theoretical mistake to take the "internality" of the psychic world for granted. Certain features of the world, including people we know and lose, do become "internal" features to the self, but they are transformed through that interiorization, and that inner world, as the Kleinians call it, is constituted precisely as a consequence of the interiorizations that a psyche performs. This suggests that there may well be a psychic theory of performativity at work that calls for greater exploration.

Although this text does not answer the question of whether the materiality of the body is fully constructed, that has been the focus of much of my subsequent work, which I hope will prove clarifying for the reader.[11] The question of whether or not the theory of performativity can be transposed onto matters of race has been explored by several scholars.[12] I would note here not only that racial presumptions invariably underwrite the discourse on gender in ways that need to be made explicit, but that race and gender ought not to be treated as simple analogies. I would therefore suggest that the question to ask is not whether the theory of performativity is transposable onto race, but what happens to the theory when it tries to come to grips with race. Many of these debates have centered on the status of "construction," whether race is constructed in the same way as gender. My view is that no single account of construction will do, and that these categories always work as background for one another, and they often find their most powerful articulation through one another. Thus, the sexualization of racial gender norms calls to be read through multiple lenses at once, and the analysis surely illuminates the limits of gender as an exclusive category of analysis.[13]

Although I've enumerated some of the academic traditions and debates that have animated this book, it is not my purpose to offer a full apologia in these brief pages. There is one aspect of the conditions of its production that is not always understood about the text: it was produced not merely from the academy, but from convergent social movements of which I have been a part, and within the context of a lesbian and gay community on the east coast of the United States in which I lived for fourteen years prior to the writing of this book. Despite the dislocation of the subject that the text performs, there is a person here: I went to many meetings, bars, and marches and saw many kinds of genders, understood myself to be at the crossroads of some of them, and encountered sexuality at several of its cultural edges. I knew many people who were trying to find their way in the midst of a significant movement for sexual recognition and freedom, and felt the exhilaration and frustration that goes along with being a part of that movement both in its hopefulness and internal dissension. At the same time that I was ensconced in the academy, I was also living a life outside those walls, and though *Gender Trouble* is an academic book, it began, for me, with a crossing-over, sitting on Rehoboth Beach, wondering whether I could link the different sides of my life. That I can write in an autobiographical mode does not, I think, relocate this subject that I am, but perhaps it gives the reader a sense of solace that there is someone here (I will suspend for the moment the problem that this someone is given in language.)

It has been one of the most gratifying experiences for me that the text continues to move outside the academy to this day. At the same time that the book was taken up by Queer Nation, and some of its reflections on the theatricality of queer self-presentation resonated with the tactics of Act Up, it was among the materials that also helped to prompt members of the American Psychoanalytic Association and the American Psychological Association to reassess some of their current doxa on homosexuality. The questions of performative gender were appropriated in different ways in the visual arts, at Whitney exhibitions, and at the Otis School for the Arts in Los Angeles, among others. Some of its formulations on the subject of "women" and the relation between sexuality and gender also made its way into feminist jurisprudence and antidiscrimination legal scholarship in the work of Vicki Schultz, Katherine Franke, and Mary Jo Frug.

In turn, I have been compelled to revise some of my positions in *Gender Trouble* by virtue of my own political engagements. In the book, I tend to conceive of the claim of "universality" in exclusive negative and exclusionary terms. However, I came to see the term has important strategic use precisely as a non-substantial and open-ended category as I worked with an extraordinary group of activists first as a board member and then as board chair of the International Gay and Lesbian Human Rights Commission (1994–7), an organization that represents sexual minorities on a broad range of human rights issues. There I came to understand how the assertion of universality can be proleptic and performative, conjuring a reality that does not yet exist, and holding out the possibility for a convergence of cultural horizons that have not yet met. Thus, I arrived at a second view of universality in which it is defined as a future-oriented labor of cultural translation.[14] More recently, I have been compelled to relate my work to political theory and, once again, to the concept of universality in a co-authored book that I am writing with Ernesto Laclau and Slavoj Žižek on the theory of hegemony and its implications for a theoretically activist Left (to be published by Verso in 2000).

[...]

I grew up understanding something of the violence of gender norms: an uncle incarcerated for his anatomically anomalous body, deprived of family and friends, living out his days in an "institute" in the Kansas prairies; gay cousins forced to leave their homes because of their sexuality, real and imagined; my own tempestuous coming out at the age of 16; and a subsequent adult landscape of lost jobs, lovers, and homes. All of this subjected me to strong and scarring condemnation but, luckily, did not prevent me from pursuing pleasure and insisting on a legitimating recognition for my sexual life. It was difficult to bring this violence into view precisely because gender was so taken for granted at the same time that it was violently policed. It was assumed either to be a natural manifestation of sex or a cultural constant that no human agency could hope to revise. I also came to understand something of the violence of the foreclosed life, the one that does not get named as "living," the one whose incarceration implies a suspension of life, or a sustained death sentence. The dogged effort to "denaturalize" gender in this text emerges, I think, from a strong desire both to counter the normative violence implied by ideal morphologies of sex to uproot the pervasive assumptions about natural or presumptive heterosexuality that are informed by ordinary and academic discourses on sexuality. The writing of this denaturalization was not done simply out of a desire to play with language or prescribe theatrical antics in the place of "real" politics, as some critics have conjectured (as if theatre and politics are always distinct). It was done from a desire to live, to make life possible, and to rethink the possible as such. What would the world have to be like for my uncle to live in the company of family, friends, or extended kinship of some other kind? How must we rethink the ideal morphological constraints upon the human such that those who fail to approximate the norm are not condemned to a death within life?[15]

Some readers have asked whether *Gender Trouble* seeks to expand the realm of gender possibilities for a reason. They ask, for what purpose are such new configurations of gender devised, and how ought we to judge among them? The question often involves a prior premise, namely, that the text does not address the normative or prescriptive dimension of feminist thought. "Normative" clearly has at least two meanings in this critical encounter, since the word is one I use often, mainly to describe the mundane violence performed by certain kinds of gender ideals. I usually use "normative" in a way that is synonymous with "pertaining to the norms that govern gender." But the term "normative" also pertains to ethical justification, how it is established and what concrete consequences proceed therefrom. One critical question posed of *Gender Trouble* has been: how do we proceed to make judgments on how gender is to be lived on the basis of the theoretical descriptions offered here? It is not possible to oppose the "normative" forms of gender without at the same time subscribing to a certain normative view of how the gendered world ought to be. I want to suggest, however, that the positive normative vision of this text, such as it is, does not and cannot take the form of a prescription: "subvert gender in the way that I say, and life will be good."

Those who make such prescriptions or who are willing to decide between subversive and unsubversive expressions of gender, base their judgments on a description. Gender appears in this or that form, and then a normative judgment is made about those appearances and on the basis of what appears. But what conditions the domain of appearance for gender itself? We may be tempted to make the following distinction: a *descriptive* account of gender includes considerations of what makes gender intelligible, an inquiry into its conditions of possibility, whereas a *normative* account seeks to answer the question of which expressions of gender are acceptable, and which are not, supplying persuasive reasons to distinguish between such expressions in this way. The question, however, of what qualifies as "gender" is itself already a question that attests to a pervasively normative operation of power, a fugitive operation of "what will be the case" under the rubric of "what is the case." Thus, the very description of the field of gender is no sense prior to, or separable from, the question of its normative operation.

I am not interested in delivering judgments on what distinguishes the subversive from the unsubversive. Not only do I believe that such judgments cannot be made out of context, but that they cannot be made in ways that endure through time ("contexts" are themselves posited unities that undergo temporal change and expose their essential disunity). Just as metaphors lose their metaphoricity as they congeal through time into concepts, so subversive performances always run the risk of becoming deadening cliches [*sic*] through their repetition and, most importantly, rough their repetition within commodity culture where "subversion" carries market value. The effort to name the criterion for subversiveness will always fail, and ought to. So what is at stake in using the term at all?

What continues to concern me most is the following kinds of questions: what will and will not constitute an intelligible life, and how do presumptions about normative gender and sexuality determine in advance what will qualify as the "human" and the "livable"? In other words, how do normative gender presumptions work to delimit the very field of description that we have for the human? What is the means by which we come to see this delimiting power, and what are the means by which we transform it?

The discussion of drag that *Gender Trouble* offers to explain the constructed and performative dimension of gender is not precisely *an example* of subversion. It would be a mistake to take it as the paradigm of subversive action or, indeed, as a model for political agency. The point is rather different. If one thinks that one sees a man dressed as a woman or a woman dressed as a man, then one takes the first term of each of those perceptions as the "reality" of gender: the gender that is introduced through the simile lacks "reality," and is taken to constitute an illusory appearance. In such perceptions in which an ostensible reality is coupled with an unreality, we think we know what the reality is, and take the secondary appearance of gender to be mere artifice, play, falsehood, and illusion. But what is the sense of "gender reality" that founds this perception in this way? Perhaps we think we know what the anatomy of the person is (sometimes we do not, and we certainly have not appreciated the variation that exists at the level of anatomical description). Or we derive that knowledge from the clothes that the person wears, or how the clothes are worn. This is naturalized knowledge, even though it is based on a series of cultural inferences, some of which are highly erroneous. Indeed, if we shift the example from drag to transsexuality, then it is no longer possible to derive a judgment about stable anatomy from the clothes that cover and articulate the body. That body may be preoperative, transitional, or postoperative; even "seeing" the body may not answer the question: for *what are the categories through which one sees?* The moment in which one's staid and usual cultural perceptions fail, when one cannot with surely read the body that one sees, is precisely the moment when one is no longer sure whether the body encountered is that of a man or a woman. The vacillation between the categories itself constitutes the experience of the body in question.

When such categories come into question, the *reality* of gender is also put into crisis: it becomes unclear how to distinguish the real from the unreal. And this is the occasion in which we come to understand that what we take to be "real," what we invoke as the naturalized knowledge of gender is, in fact, a changeable and revisable reality. Call it subversive or call it something else. Although this insight does not in itself constitute a political revolution, no political revolution is possible without a radical shift in one's notion of the possible and the real. And sometimes this shift comes as a result of certain kinds of practices that precede their explicit theorization, and which prompt a rethinking of our basic categories: what is gender, how is it produced and reproduced, what are its possibilities? At this point, the sedimented and reified field of gender "reality" is understood as one that might be made differently and, indeed, less violently.

The point of this text is not to celebrate drag as the expression of a true and model gender (even as it is important to resist the belittling of drag that sometimes takes place), but to show that the naturalized knowledge of gender operates as a preemptive and violent circumscription of reality. To the extent the gender norms (ideal dimorphism, heterosexual complementarity of bodies, ideals and rule of proper and improper masculinity and femininity, many of which are underwritten by racial codes of purity and taboos against miscegenation) establish what will and will not be intelligibly human, what will and will not be considered to be "real," they establish the ontological field in which bodies may be given legitimate expression. If there is a positive normative task in *Gender Trouble*, it is to insist upon the extension of this legitimacy to bodies that have been regarded as false, unreal, and unintelligible. Drag is an example that is meant to establish that "reality" is not as fixed as we generally assume it to be. The purpose of the example is to expose the tenuousness of gender "reality" in order to counter the violence performed by gender norms.

In this text as elsewhere I have tried to understand what political agency might be, given that it cannot be isolated from the dynamics of power from which it is wrought. The iterability of performativity is a theory of agency, one that cannot disavow power as the condition of its own possibility. This text does not sufficiently explain performativity in terms of its social, psychic, corporeal, and temporal dimensions. In some ways, the continuing work of that clarification, in response to numerous excellent criticisms, guides most of my subsequent publications.[16]

Notes

1. Republished with permission of Taylor and Francis Group LLC Books, *Gender Trouble: Feminism and the Subversion of Identity* by Judith Butler, © 1999; permission conveyed through Copyright Clearance Center, Inc. This excerpt is from the Preface to the Second Edition.

2. At this printing, there are French publishers considering the translation of this work, but only because Didier Eribon and others have inserted the arguments of the text into current French political debates on the legal ratification of same-sex partnerships.

3. I have written two brief pieces on this issue: "Afterword" for *Butch\Femme: Inside Lesbian Gender*, ed. Sally Munt (London: Cassell, 1998), and another Afterword for "Transgender in Latin America: Persons, Practices and Meanings," a special issue of the journal *Sexualities*, Vol. 5, No. 3, 1998.

4. Catharine MacKinnon, *Feminism Unmodified: Discourses on Life and Law* (Cambridge: Harvard University Press, 1987), pp. 6–7.

5. Unfortunately, *Gender Trouble* preceded the publication of Eve Kosofsky Sedgwick's monumental *Epistemology of the Closet* (Berkeley and Los Angeles: University of California Press, 1991) by some months, and my arguments here were not able to benefit from her nuanced discussion of gender and sexuality in the first chapter of that book.

6. Jonathan Goldberg persuaded me of this point.

7. For a more or less complete bibliography of my publications and citations of my work, see the excellent work of Eddie Yeghiayan at the University of California at Irvine Library: http://sun3.lib.uci.edu/~scctr/Wellek/index.html.

8. I am especially indebted to Biddy Martin, Eve Sedgwick, Slavoj Žižek, Wendy Brown, Saidiya Hartman, Mandy Merck, Lynne Layton, Timothy Kaufmann-Osborne, Jessica Benjamin, Seyla Benhabib, Nancy Fraser, Diana Fuss, Jay Presser, Lisa Duggan, and Elizabeth Grosz for their insightful criticisms of the theory of performativity.

9. This notion of the ritual dimension of performativity is allied with the notion of the habitus in Pierre Bourdieu's work, something which I only came to realize after the fact of writing this text. For my belated effort to account for this resonance, see the final chapter of *Excitable Speech: A Politics of the Performative* (New York: Routledge, 1997).

10. Jacqueline Rose usefully pointed out to me the disjunction between the earlier and later parts of this text. The earlier parts interrogate the melancholy construction of gender, but the later seem to forget the psychoanalytic beginnings. Perhaps this accounts for some of the "mania" of the final chapter, a state defined by Freud as part of the disavowal of loss that is melancholia. *Gender Trouble* in its closing pages seems to forget or disavow the loss it has just articulated.

11. See *Bodies that Matter* (New York: Routledge, 1993) as well as an able and interesting critique that relates some of the questions raised there to contemporary science studies by Karen Barad, "Getting Real: Technoscientific Practices and the Materialization of Reality," *Differences*, Vol. 5, No. 2, pp. 87–126.

12. Saidiya Hartman, Lisa Lowe, and Dorinne Kondo are scholars whose work has influenced my own. Much of the current scholarship on "passing" has also taken up this question. My own essay on Nella Larsen's "Passing" in *Bodies That Matter* sought to address the question in a preliminary way. Of course, Homi Bhabha's work on the mimetic splitting of the postcolonial subject is close to my own in several ways: not only the appropriation of the colonial "voice" by the colonized, but the split condition of identification are crucial to a notion of performativity that emphasizes the way minority identities are produced and riven at the same time under conditions of domination.

13. The work of Kobena Mercer, Kendall Thomas, and Hortense Spillers has been extremely useful to my post-*Gender Trouble* thinking on this subject. I also hope to publish an essay on Frantz Fanon soon engaging questions of mimesis and hyperbole in his *Black Skins, White Masks.* I am grateful to Greg Thomas, who has recently completed his dissertation in rhetoric at Berkeley, on racialized sexualities in the U.S., for provoking and enriching my understanding of this crucial intersection.

14. I have offered reflections on universality in subsequent writings, most prominently in chapter 2 of *Excitable Speech.*

15. See the important publications of the Intersex Society of North America (including the publications of Cheryl Chase) which has, more than any other organization, brought to public attention the severe and violent gender policing done to infants and children born with gender anomalous bodies. For more information, contact them at http://www.isna.org.

16. I thank Wendy Brown, Joan W. Scott, Alexandra Chasin, Frances Bartkowski, Janet Halley, Michel Feher, Homi Bhabha, Drucilla Cornell, Denise Riley, Elizabeth Weed, Kaja Silverman, Ann Pellegrini, William Connolly, Gayatri Chakravorty Spivak, Ernesto Laclau, Eduardo Cadava, Florence Dore, David Kazanjian, David End, and Dina Al-kassim for their support and friendship during the Spring of 1999 when this preface was written.

22 Performing Interaction Design with Judith Butler

Ann Light

Judith Butler's work can be viewed historically as a late twentieth-century isthmus, bringing together aspects of Foucault, Derrida, and Nietzsche with the psychoanalytics of Freud and Lacan and the French feminist philosophical tradition of de Beauvoir, Irigaray, and Kristeva; then spanning forward into new destabilized conceptualizations of gender, sex, race, and even broader issues, such as what it is to be human. Her notion of performativity helped launch the performative turn in the social sciences, and queer theory is now a recognized discipline spawning methodological as well as theoretical insights in the treatment of identity. A single excerpt cannot do justice to her range of work. She has, for instance, devoted herself to reconciling the inner psyche and politics, extrapolating her understanding of how (little) we come to know about ourselves and others into a consideration of the limits of ethical responsibility. And her academic concern for a more informed base from which to consider difference is supported by public campaigning to make a world that moves away from categorization on simplistic grounds of race, gender, and nationhood.

So the excerpt here was chosen to reflect my interest in identity and personhood, how this is operationalized in the tools around us, and how embedding narrow versions of identity in our tools might be resisted. We have already met the agenda I want to apply to HCI in the naming of the book from which the excerpt is taken. *Gender Trouble* (1999) is not only a neat summary of a major theme within the book, but it also draws attention to two radical and complementary aspects: the exploration of *gender* and sexuality to ask difficult questions about identity and its construction; and the search for a means to *trouble* these taken-for-granted arrangements. Butler talks in the first person about her motivations in this extract. I intend to do likewise here, since we are both giving a personal account of what informs our activism.

I have used her work both reflectively (Light and Wright, 2009; Light, 2011b) and generatively (Light and Coles-Kemp, 2013) to study designing. Here I want to explore the meaning of performativity in designing IT systems that deal with identity, in the short term of, say, social media, and in the longer term of what may come to be a highly digitized and mediated future world. In doing so, I have brought the very nature of human-computer interaction into question, with the chance that a deepened understanding of the terms "humans" and "interaction" might profitably lead to new conceptions in computing.

This questioning comes at a time when we are creating our world again in the digital sphere, with an underlying binary of zeroes and ones feeding a new quantitative emphasis on relations between people and their institutions, and when we are contemplating a global "internet of things" joined up around us in both the materials of life and the infrastructures that will link them. Butler's work reminds us that there is always the possibility of hardwiring narrow bureaucratic regimens in code, information categorization systems, and networks (see Bowker and Star, 1999). Acknowledging that all knowledge and interpretation is political, Butler's work supports scrutiny of how we understand ourselves and others as social beings embedded in a vast ecology that is always altering. Thus, Butler has become a valuable ally, not only in thinking through aspects of control, choice, and mutability, but, further, in developing an antidote to the potentially prescriptive nature of decisions we must make now in innovating for contexts to come.

Two Notes at Outset

First, in presenting Butler's interpretation of identity and its relation to society, I am not suggesting that other readings of identity in HCI are invalid or less useful as a design prompt. I do not single out existing work in the form of a literature review, since all has its value and some challenge might be implied in mentioning others' approaches. My approach, based on Butler's insights, is introduced in contrast to readings that start from identity as an established phenomenon, to supplement them, with the same motivation as hers: to invigorate; to open opportunities for flexibility of thought and approach; and to make change in the world so that future generations can find meaningful ways of coexisting on their own terms.

Second, I make a distinction between personhood, that is, the nature of humanity and how it is understood in systems (described here as "what we are") and individual selves and characteristics (which I describe in the following pages as "who we are"). These two aspects are not identical, but I subsume them both in my use of the term "identity." Further than that, I do not wish to define identity at this point, but much of the rest of the commentary will go on to explain how Butler uses it.

Gender/Identity

> [H]ow do normative gender presumptions work to delimit the very field of description that we have for the human? What is the means by which we come to see the delimiting power, and what are the means by which we transform it?
>
> —Butler (1999, xxii)

Butler observes that the male/female binary of gender has been fundamental to social organization throughout history, but she looks beyond the previous theoretical deadlock over what women and men are or how they should relate by asking more foundational questions. Taking gender, sex, and hetero-normativity as her starting points, she asks: What is identity? How is it constructed and assigned? In other words, how do we know that a child is born "a girl" and what further assumptions might this lead to? And why have we fastened on this simple binary among others to identify the people of the world?

In Butler's work and that of those who have followed her lead, the idea of individual identity is regarded principally as an effect of how identity more generally is produced by social mechanisms. This meeting of cultural studies and critical theory argues that human identity is something fluid and performed, with no essential core, produced by the constant repetition of interactions from day to day. Gender is primordial to understanding how identity affects individuals, in that we are born into a world where gender norms are already shaping our lives. Thus, identity has little base in bodies and their functioning, such as chromosomes, but is shaped by what has become accepted about them and repeated. Identity is wide open and eludes categorization until manifested at the individual level by the norms operating in a particular milieu.

What Is Performativity?

Rejecting an essentialist view of identity, which regards characteristics such as race, sexuality, and gender as foundational, Butler takes a performative view, which sees all traits as enacted and created through this enactment, part of a discursive realm as much as a material one. The lack of an essence to identity means that "one is not simply a body, but, in some very key sense, one does one's body and, indeed, one does one's body differently from one's contemporaries and from one's embodied predecessors and successors as well" (Butler, 1990).

Identity is not a given property of a person, but inscribed on the body by others in society's constant rehearsal of behaviors. There are no biological givens as to how a human is understood; instead distinctions are the product of social forces congealed over time through repetition.

> Performativity cannot be understood outside of a process of iterability, a regularized and constrained repetition of norms. And this repetition is not performed *by* a subject; this repetition is what enables a subject and constitutes the temporal condition for the subject. This iterability

implies that "performance" is not a singular "act" or event, but a ritualized production, a ritual reiterated under and through constraint, under and through the force of prohibition and taboo, with the threat of ostracism and even death controlling and compelling the shape of the production, but not, I will insist, determining it fully in advance. (Butler, 1993, 95)

In other words, we have "to 'cite' the norm in order to qualify and remain a viable subject.... Indeed, there is no 'one' who takes on a gender norm. On the contrary, this citation of the gender norm is necessary in order to qualify as a 'one,' to become viable as a 'one,' where subject-formation is dependent on the prior operation of legitimating gender norms" (232).

Drawing on the power of language to enact, rather than merely describe, Butler argues that "the initiatory performative, 'It's a girl!' anticipates the eventual arrival of the sanction, 'I pronounce you man and wife.' Hence, also, the peculiar pleasure of the cartoon strip in which the infant is first interpellated into discourse with 'It's a lesbian!' Far from an essentialist joke, the queer appropriation of the performative mimes and exposes both the binding power of the heterosexualizing law *and its expropriability*" (232).

Her arguments have activated an identity politics that "may better be understood as promoting a non-identity—or even anti-identity—politics [... sharing only] the knowledge that identities are fictitious—that is, produced by and productive of material effects but nevertheless arbitrary, contingent and ideologically motivated" (Jagose, 1996, 130).

Performing HCI

Interaction design is ultimately a pragmatic endeavor, primed to produce functional and desirable technology, so a shift that undermines the familiar tenets of identity may appear counterproductive in a discussion of how we design. However, I would suggest that the same pragmatism allows us to embrace any approach that promotes creative thinking, and so there is a positive side to a framing that opens identity up: "[Q]ueerness constitutes not just a resistance to social norms or a negation of established values, but a positive and creative construction of different ways of life ... an identity without an essence, not a given condition, but a horizon of possibility" (Halperin, 1997, 62). In other words, recognizing the potential of relations in the world to be lived on a wholly different basis allows us to see through current incarnations of identity and consider difference and change. The rejection of essentialism is then part of a "necessary resistance to discursive norms which have congealed into givens" (Salih and Butler, 2004, 303). Further, if we are looking to counter a tendency to rigidity, then a view that humans are mutable will position researchers and designers well.

But Butler does not suggest that people choose how they understand and act upon their identity, rather the opposite. She makes the case that these aspects of identity (i.e., *who we are*) persist because of social repetition. In other words, you perform as the weight of interactions has decreed, with some potential to resist norms and choose how you behave, but no capacity to rewrite the wider relations that position you.

For me, interested in social dynamics and how they are mediated, these complementary positions produce thought-provoking implications for design. The first, that relations could be different at the inherent level of how we define ourselves and how we relate, opens up the potential for change to the interactions of society (including those mediated by digital means). The second suggests that individuals struggle to make change at a personal level, contending with the design of the structures around them. The detail of these repeated interactions, as manifestation of existing norms, produces the inscription that denies us a freer interpretation of what and who we are. Included in these designed structures is, of course, all digital technology. So can Butler's notion of subversion come into play as a means of challenging the norms that institute identity? For this, we need to pick up her idea of "queer," and the act of making trouble, or "queering," to send usual relations awry.

Trouble/Queer

How must we rethink the ideal morphological constraints upon the human such that those who fail to approximate the norm are not condemned to a death within life?

—Butler (1999, xx)

Influenced by Foucault's work on sexuality and identity (1988–1990) and developed by Butler and her successors, the term "queer" is now associated with sexuality and sexual behavior in contrast to, set apart from, or challenging unquestioned norms of behavior. Exploring queer identity online harks back to Wakeford (1997) and O'Riordan and Phillips (2007). But the idea of queering, or challenging unquestioned norms, extends more widely and has been applied to technology; for instance, Star talks about queering to consider infrastructure radically (Star, 1997). There may be inherited trouble with gender, but we have at our disposal the deliberate troubling of categories.

What this queering offers, according to Butler and her interpreters, is the means to cut through the repetition of interactions that define us to let in the hope of something new. If we can never be fully determined by norms, then this is the means to give ourselves the space for play, discovery and change. Queering has a subversive intent, but no specific form. It can be playful or rude. Its nature is never fixed, for it queers in relation to what it stands in contrast to, expropriating the mainstream. In other words, queering can only manifest in opposition to a dominant state—usually a rigid or exclusive state, such as an identity category. To continue to try to queer in the same way repeatedly runs the risk of moving from subversion to cliché. Butler uses the many moods of drag to illustrate potential for trouble: it can be provocative, either flamboyantly or subtly, or so far in keeping with acceptable behavior that it does nothing to challenge norms. Elsewhere, it has been said that the very instability and reinvention at the heart of queer theory as a discipline is particularly apt, given its subject matter. And I could argue that even presenting the ideas of queer theory to an HCI audience is a form of queering, since it introduces ideas that might decenter the domain a little.

In sum, if society is inscribing identity through its mechanisms, and those mechanisms include various forms of digital technology, queering is a method for destabilizing that relationship. By queering, we use a tactic at our disposal to avoid designs that are overtly rigid in how they let us "perform" ourselves and each other.

Why Might We Need to Queer Design?

My commentary has so far focused principally on what Butler has achieved during a period rich in both scholarship and new forms of social engagement. When she wrote *Gender Trouble*, first published in 1990, there was no Web, mobile phones belonged to the few, and most people's experience of digital technology was at work. When she wrote the updated introduction quoted here, in 1999, the industrialized world was facing the dotcom crash, and social media and Web 2.0 were yet to come. Since then, the application of digital technology to new areas of our lives promises to involve us in new social and domestic practices and has already begun to change our relations.

Digital tools are no longer confined to working and learning but prevalent through many of the more intimate activities with which we define ourselves. Increasingly we use "expressive technologies" (Tufekci, 2008)—tools principally for presenting aspects of oneself to others through connecting, discussing, and creating (e.g., social media) as distinct from those that control processes, manage tasks, and enable searches, where the primary purpose is instrumental. There are many representations of who we are, both ones we are enabled to make ourselves through using that media and those in the design of the system, which facilitate what we can say and how. Indeed, our very (inter)subjectivity becomes profit for a new breed of producers offering us tools to meet, share, and define ourselves and make content out of these relations.

Further, structures that are socially maintained at present can be hardwired into (semi)intelligent, autonomous digital systems. Here, possible examples include health monitoring, care of the elderly, voting, and delivering school curricula. By bringing technology into such intimate relations and equipping it to act on our behalf, we implicate it in helping us develop our social structures with a knock-on effect on how we understand and manage ourselves as a world. An example of how this happens is described by Finken and Mörtberg (2011) on living in a smart house and its adapted older user. Here the principal agent of representation is the machine. Light and Wright (2009) note that machines judge people based on algorithms prepared by people, embedding beliefs about what people are and of what they are capable. We see these aspects of representation meeting in the tools of inference appearing, as algorithms correlate user-generated data with other data on behavior and demography to infer demographic patterns of behavior and act on them. These trends are recognized as leading to different understandings of self, grouped under initiatives like Quantified Self (http://quantifiedself

.com), which makes a virtue out of the metrical data being accumulated through digital encounters and uses these to reveal as much information about individual personal functions as possible.

This codification of the self as a series of data points has a correlate in how information infrastructures can turn us into bureaucratic entities. The act of definition is described with detail and compassion by Bowker and Star (1999), who look at the history of medicine and apartheid through this lens and observe that definition inevitably creates exclusions, often serving to introduce new political structures. Once coded in information or wired into computation tools, descriptions of *what we are* become harder to modify; they become standard, widely used, and costly to reconfigure.

I see this in the way that interactive digital systems offer a concept of how people behave (e.g., Strengers's [2011] analysis of rational choice theory in environmental change tools), or what DiSalvo, Sengers, and Brynjarsdóttir (2010) call an "implicit theory of human action through technology" after Goodman (130). These concepts are, in effect, modeling back at users what it is to be a user of the system. If these representations stay largely in the realm of supporting actions, such as those in cars and cookers, this has little consequence. As interactions become more bound up in expression and identity, the model may be closer to an interpretation of *what people are*, rather than *what they do.*

There is critical commentary within HCI on people's relationship with tools. How far tools can (and should) anticipate the needs of users and act for them is a theme Shneiderman and Maes (1997) addressed in the 1990s as advocates for control through direct manipulation. More recently, as new tools and practices have been called into being by rapid innovation, Redström (2006) has criticized the practice of "designing the user" (127) or designing digital tools so that they make "people fit into systems, societies and strategies" (128). Redström speaks about "experience design," arguing that "if we think of this process of becoming users as being a process of inviting and accepting the things that will become the building blocks of our lifeworlds, it is ... less clear that this is a process that designers want to or should try to control, compared to when we understand use as a matter of communication of designer intent" (130).

If we are constraining people in their use of tools to be or do only what the tool allows, then we have a responsibility to think outside current restrictive norms. For instance, Kannabiran and Graves Petersen (2010) examine the constraints of entering personal details into Facebook, describing the hypothetical resistance to the design of the profile page by a transsexual woman who wishes to define her gender differently. They suggest that, having struggled to express her choice, since the site offers just male/female, she could choose to convey her gender through the "Bio" section in her profile (writing "I am a transgendered woman"). "By making an attempt to construct an identity that the system actively prohibits, she is negotiating her power relationship with the system through her interactions" (2010, 2). And Light (2011b) asks whether we should accept the cultural values of a society in which no women will be expected to use a particular interface by only testing this product with men? My argument was that designing for diversity requires us to think queerly about inheritance of norms and our role in perpetuating them.

Design Now, Live Later

Another, more obscure aspect of this shaping of individuals and the society around them is what happens in the long term. This, more than anything, is the reason that I think interaction design might need queering.

It is well recognized outside HCI that the design of interactive systems (and of the information structures supporting them) has an impact on people and their behavior together. We see this recognition across many strands of thought about the nature of society that do not agree in other ways (e.g., Bijker, 2009; Latour, 2007; MacKenzie and Wajcman, 1998). As observed above, digital technologies have the potential to inform the experience of being human as well as form our day-to-day experience by contributing to the inscription process. Indeed, it would be strange if something that mediated our relationships so pervasively had no effect. Turkle (2011) sums it up: "We make our technologies and they, in turn, shape us" (19). Thus, the mirror we see in our technology can prove significant. Society shapes tools, but in shaping tools we are also shaping society.

Much design rhetoric shies away from considering longer-term outcomes for decisions made now, even though design as an interventionist practice is, by nature, future-orientated. I've previously criticized HCI for being apolitical and ahistorical as a discipline, ignoring that life is constantly in flux and that values, priorities, contexts, and behaviors will change (2011b). Others (including some in this volume) argue that HCI might do well to consider environmental issues more holistically and with greater future orientation (e.g., DiSalvo, Sengers, and Brynjarsdóttir, 2010), and there have been calls to design for peace (Hourcade and Bullock-Rest, 2011). Shaowen Bardzell (2010) has written explicitly on the need for HCI to become more responsive to a feminist agenda, raising the concern that designers have no mandate to become social engineers and wondering how to combine political conviction with design outcomes in an ethical fashion. But, by and large, HCI as a discipline follows industrial precedents and short-term trends, and has remained concerned with the usable, not the ethical, except where these two meet. I see the wider domain taking very little account of our roles as social engineers, witting or unwitting.

Nonetheless, whether or not we have a mandate to be social engineers, any designed intervention into the fabric of society is going to make change. And our heirs, our peers in other places (such as those left behind as innovations take root elsewhere—see Light, 2011a), and the wider world we share (the geological formations altered by pursuit of minerals used in manufacture, animal, and plant life coexisting with our digital edifices) are all impacted through our interventions. We cannot predict exactly how. We can predict, though frequently it is not part of our reckoning, that taking the world in a particular direction through our innovations will affect the options for the people coming after us. Indeed, Reeves (2012) notes the effect of envisioning activities to homogenize and corral technology research work toward particular interpretations and warns of lack of diversity of vision. He observes that, from the perspective of the present, diversity has value in recognizing the inherent uncertainty of the future.

Friedman (1996) suggests that values may change or differ, describing the problem of the future in early work on designing with conscious moral values, in terms of "bias [that] typically emerges some time after a design is completed, as a result of a change in societal knowledge, user population, or cultural values" (21). She gives the following example: "Educational software developed in the United States embeds learning activities in a game environment that rewards competitive and individual playing strategies. When such software is used by students with a cultural background that eschews competition and instead promotes cooperative endeavors, such students can be placed at a disadvantage in the learning process" (21).

However, I am making a different, perhaps more scary, point. As, globally, certain versions of technology dominate, so too do the lessons they offer us about what we are. We are mutable beings by nature and queer theory helps reveal this by looking at the power of norms. Designing for the future would be simpler and less ethically fraught if personhood over time was constant, unyielding, unaffected by surrounding changes, and static over history. In that case, embedding a snapshot of current relations in the design of our technology would be simply a matter of description. However, our cultural mutability over time as a species makes us open to the possibility of versions of the future reflecting different influences (see, for instance, Henrich, Heine, and Norenzayan, 2010, who have upset beliefs about the uniformity of economic reckoning). There is no final edition of what personhood is, just as there is no single model of what an individual person may be. The Butler preface that precedes this commentary makes this poignantly and abundantly clear. If there is no description without normative definition, we need to work with the knowledge of our mutability in mind.

To make the point decisively, let me introduce a more remote example from the history of our understanding of self- and personhood. The appearance of psychology as a discipline—and with it a redefinition of mental states and processes—affected how we understand ourselves, how we behave, and prevalent social norms in Europe and the Americas. Though the appearance of the theories that informed the discipline in the late 1800s did not effect an immediate change in notions of identity, they represented a novel interpretation of human life that gradually allowed and fed a different way of thinking about behavior and, with it, different behaviors. This shift in the understanding of what it is to be a person introduced new ways of relating to others, new forms of explanation for behavior, and different remedies for people considered to be behaving outside the realms of acceptability (see Foucault, 1988). So, for instance, instead of locking people up until their demons have left them, we are more likely to think in terms of cognitive behavioral therapy, with quite different implications for the individual and the wider group. Thus, societies reinvent themselves in ways deemed more or less morally progressive by outsiders and commentators with the benefit of hindsight. If we value this process of reinvention, redefinition, and discovery—with the hope of relevant adaptation and benign evolution—our question must remain: how do we maximize conditions for inspiration and learning, rather than hardwire expected relations into a new rigid exoskeleton of computation?

So, it is not just that working with current norms might marginalize or exclude those outside the "normal" group, but that, in reinforcing cultural norms through encoding them in our interfaces and underlying systems without room for alternatives, we have also made a contribution to our future: certain paths are less obvious or less possible henceforward. And, since people learn what they are from the messages around them and become who they are through interactions in the world, human capacity to transform may be constrained by a narrow view of what and who we are at this crucial juncture of rapid technological change. My greater point, then, is that if researchers and designers remove potential, they do it for the future as well as the present.

Meta-Values and Openness

Butler's perspectives on gender and trouble have successively enabled me to argue that (1) if we wish to give our inheritors the chance to evolve different, and thus possibly better, outcomes than our own, we do not want to presume that we know best about future norms, values, and behaviors, and (2) we can promote flexibility and learning by leaving room for play in our systems. This application of queering to design allows for the overarching social value of making space for value sets to continue to evolve, leaving room for diversity in understanding personhood. I've called this avoidance of overdefinition a "meta-value," part of "a value system predicated on making space for divergent and evolving beliefs, principles, standards and morals … [and an] intention to create resistance to an orthodoxy rather than seeking to assign predefined characteristics to a design outcome" (Light, 2011b).

It could be observed that making such spaces merely allows a new, less tolerant, regime to take over. I would counter that argument by saying that this is not to advocate queering just once, but to cultivate the plural, agonistic (DiSalvo, 2012), and subversive in our designs as a necessary complement to the dominant form. This is to recall that we are ever in the process of becoming. Or, to quote Butler on democracy, "The incompletion of every ideological formulation is central to the radical democratic project's notion of political futurity. The subjection of every ideological formation to a rearticulation of these linkages constitutes the temporal order of democracy as an incalculable future, leaving open the production of new subject-positions, new political signifiers, and new linkages to become the rallying points for politicization" (Butler, 1993, 193).

Queer theory has both a theoretical and methodological role to play in this project. If designs are constructed deliberately to make an open space for novel experience and thought, they work to undermine the constraints of the field, and this is what Butler discusses here and in other contexts by looking at subversion. Queer theory suggests that identity is open and unspecified until we start to act on the world and the world acts on us. Although queer theory incorporates an understanding of human relations, it is one stressing potential for adaptation, making no claims for outcomes. Instead, it advocates resistance to stasis and using naughtiness to maintain a space of play. This clearly has potential as a method as well as a framing. Using this approach to design allows us to contemplate difference; using this approach in design promotes spaces to act that do not require definition, where the model of humanity is deliberately left open rather than made to follow a specific understanding of behavior—where underspecification is the norm, and gaps and challenges are incorporated. Queering, then, is a way of thinking about the research and design of computation and digital networks that resists the tendency to model human nature too tightly. But how might we enact this in practice?

Doing Queering

The contributors to Browne and Nash (2010) argue that "queer research" can be any form of research positioned within conceptual frameworks that highlight the instability of taken-for-granted meanings and resulting power relations, and Boellstorff (2010) considers how "the 'studies' of 'queer studies' [might] act less like a noun and more like a verb: queer studying even of things not self-evidently queer" (215), giving much scope for queer-informed approaches. Boellstorff (2010) goes on to ask, "What might queer studies look like if it sought to produce not episteme, but techne" (230), where "techne" is "human action that alters the world through crafting" (216), which takes the queer theorists into the world of designing.

In other words, Boellstorff asks theoretically what I have begun to ask practically: what is queer(ed) design? How might we, as researchers and designers, work with queering as method? I began by finding examples in existing tools (Light, 2011b): looking at forgetting, obscuring, cheating and eluding as human behaviors that can be designed into technology to destabilize the formalization of identity in social networks, entertainment, games, privacy management, and the Semantic Web. Light and Coles-Kemp (2013) used queering and the idea of performativity to develop the research design of a study of Facebook users, in order to learn how a small geographical community manages privacy online and off. Instead of asking specific questions, the authors stressed particular roles, inviting participants to attend in family groups, letting the dynamics play out, and exploring tensions relating to identity. Both these studies benefitted from analytic frameworks supported by Butler's work: the first, looking at queered design; the second, making queered design research.

We can further ask what it takes, not just to analyze or research, but to make designs queerly and/or make queered designs. Is it the preserve of radicals? I think not. Subtle attention to how identity is incorporated in the shape of tools can extend from designers working for industry giants to those in small commercial agencies, as well as people working deliberately in identity politics or challenging society more broadly.

At the subtle end, it may be as simple as giving users choices about when and what information collected from them is transmitted and to whom, rather than indiscriminately maximizing the automation of data streams. It might be designing to stress what people do in interactions rather than to suggest there are fixed aspects to their identity: for instance, do you *do* or *have* sexuality and how does that affect the design of computer games and the avatars of their players? It might be to ask what changes if you assume that *being* is molten. It does not have to be politically countercultural to queer machine culture.

But, in thinking about the design of interaction (be that of software, hardware, or networks), queering can push into more contentious territory. To show what I mean, here are more disruptive examples of queer thinking:

- Software: Folksonomies and Twitter hashtags are two examples of open, collectively generated categorization systems. Registration pages that ask for values for age and gender contrast with these by dictating a categorization, so their system is closed. In other words, if we focus on gender, we see that a gender is often requested during registration; this is presented as a binary choice—male or female; and programmed so that the field requires a value. It is not possible to register for a multitude of services without accepting this categorization. An open field asking for a personal description of identity (maybe through tagging) would avoid this. It would allow self-definition of whether to mention gender and what to say—and then the peer group, rather than the software producers, would be setting the norms for what is stated and how. Clearly this would affect the generation of demographic metrics and, consequently, business models and targeted advertising related to demographics would have to adapt.
- Hardware: The whole body is now an interface: Kinect and Wii use bodily movements to input data and then represent actions; there are applications that allow you to virtually try on clothes by modeling your form in a mirror and so on. These play back to us a version of ourselves performing activities. What happens if we bring a fairground Hall of Mirrors into the mix so that any representation of our movements is prefaced by a unique amalgam of widening, shortening, lengthening, and bulging before our more normal translation to the screen resumes? Would it help us love our actual forms more; raise the specter of body dysmorphia, or make us laugh? How long might such a distortion last and in what contexts would it be acceptable? Could it be part of a new game? The thought is not a sensible one, but the questions it generates may be.

• Networks: People can be identified not just by personal profiles, but by their links to others. These links form a distinct pattern that can be used to harness our intersubjectivity, for marketing, for tracking down associates or for aggregating data on relations. To resist this, we might create false patterns to mask and give privacy to our actual pattern of connections; some links might be hidden and some added to random strangers. If this practice were known to operate extensively, it would add complexity to tracing and interfere with surveillance practices. Hence, it would not be popular with security services in many countries. It also would interfere with some commercial activities, such as the algorithm that throws up on our homepage that our Facebook friends like sponsored commodities. Again, I do not suggest it as a practical alternative, but as a thought experiment.

In these descriptions, queering becomes both a means of asking critical questions about identity and a tool for destabilizing norms so that space for the flexible interpretation of self can be designed into products or services. It is a process that finds some expression in the training exercises of design schools, but less expression in the commercial world that follows. Yet it can help designers conceive of and search out awkward and/or unarticulated perspectives and thereby design for a less constrained way of being.

How does this differ from the "open" design already discussed in HCI? Bentley and Dourish (1995) offer a distinction between medium and mechanism, where the benefit of designing a medium is "the extent to which systems can be repurposed to support activities that they were not designed for" (135). Dix (2007), giving recommendations for design for appropriation, says, "As design can never be complete, such appropriation is regarded as an important and positive phenomenon" (1). With Stolterman (2001), Bentley and Dourish and Dix share the premise that since one cannot predict what users want, what they need, or how they will use a tool, offering flexibility in the design and the chance to adapt it to local contexts is part of the designer's job. A variant is to introduce ambiguity, where the design's meaning is underdetermined, instead of (or as well as) its use: "[Ambiguity] allows designers to engage users with issues without constraining how they respond. In addition, it allows the designer's point of view to be expressed while enabling users of different sociocultural backgrounds to find their own interpretations" (Gaver, Beaver, and Benford, 2003, 233). Such design asks how a tool might integrate into people's lives, leaving the purpose of use undefined and thus opening up the role of the user. But the writings of Gaver, Beaver, and Benford suggest that his interest in ambiguity is principally an interpretation of the technology and its place, not the self. As with other writing on openness, such as the authors just cited, the focus is on the meaning of the object, not on what the design means for user identity. Nonetheless, these ideas can be seen through the lens of queer theory as forms of queering. The distinction can be seen most clearly in the genre of critical design (and art with similar motivations).

If technology is problematized, does this throw us back on our social relations with each other and help us to see alternatives? The Huggable Atomic Mushroom Cloud cushion by Dunne and Raby, who coined the term "critical design" (Dunne, 2005), offers a good test case. I suggest this queers our relationship with nuclear energy, but not particularly with each other. It is part of a whole suite of intellectual challenges that offer a nuance to queering. But it is just one instance of queering and not one that engages especially with Butler's interests, which are to provide intrusion into the formation and inscription of identity norms.

Designing critically, in contrast with the more pragmatic goals of much HCI, throws attention back on queering as a design tool, a process providing the means of critiquing design ideas or working to understand identity issues more fully through performative styles of research engagement. And, with greater intent to provide flexibility in how people are able to define themselves, we might expect more variants, subtleties, and definitions of queered method to appear.

Conclusion

In conclusion, it can be seen that Butler's work offers more than a theoretical framework for understanding identity as it becomes more absolutely embedded in the tools that we use. It offers a way of understanding the implications of this shift—addressing a mutability which is responsive to our innovating. And it offers a means of leaving a space in systems, interfaces, and ways of conducting user research; queering accepted practices not only of thought and value, but of processes of design. If our future were assured, then perhaps Butler's work would look less interesting. However, not only are our lives not fully determined, but the world we are living through is not stable. Queered thinking may ultimately be a form of resilience as many of the givens that we hold onto, beyond gender, race, and sexuality, turn round on themselves. Butler's active appreciation of the dynamics of our experience must be an asset when the only certainty as we look ahead is that we will have to change and go on changing. Then cultivating diversity and flexibility starts to look very important indeed.

References

Bardzell, S. (2010) "Feminist HCI: Taking Stock and Outlining an Agenda for Design." *Proceedings of the SIGCHI Conference on Human Factors in Computing Systems (CHI'10)*. New York: ACM, 1301–1310.

Bentley, R., and P. Dourish. (1995) "Medium versus Mechanism: Supporting Collaboration through Customisation." *Proceedings of the Fourth European Conference on Computer-Supported Cooperative Work (ECSCW'95)*, edited by H. Mormolin, Y. Sundblad, and K. Schmidt, 133–148. Dordrecht: Springer Science and Business Media.

Bijker, W. E. (2009) "Social Construction of Technology." In *A Companion to the Philosophy of Technology*, edited by J.-K. B. Olsen, S. A. Pedersen, and V. F. Hendricks, 88–94. Oxford: Wiley-Blackwell.

Boellstorff, T. (2010) "Queer Techne: Two Theses on Methodology and Queer Studies." In *Queer Methods and Methodologies: Intersecting Queer Theories and Social Science Research*, edited by K. Browne and C. Nash, 215–230. London: Ashgate.

Bowker, G. C., and S. L. Star. (1999) *Sorting Things Out: Classification and Its Consequences*. Cambridge, MA: MIT Press.

Browne, K., and C. J. Nash, eds. (2010) *Queer Methods and Methodologies: Intersecting Queer Theories and Social Science Research*. London: Ashgate.

Butler, J. (1990) "Performative Acts and Gender Constitution: An Essay in Phenomenology and Feminist Theory." In *Performing Feminisms: Feminist Critical Theory and Theatre*, edited by S.-E. Case, 270–282. Baltimore: Johns Hopkins University Press.

Butler, J. (1993) *Bodies That Matter: On the Discursive Limits of "Sex."* New York: Routledge.

Butler, J. (1999) *Gender Trouble: Feminism and the Subversion of Identity*, 2nd ed. New York: Routledge.

DiSalvo, C. (2012) *Adversarial Design*. Cambridge, MA: MIT Press.

DiSalvo, C., P. Sengers, and H. Brynjarsdóttir, H. (2010) "Mapping the Landscape of Sustainable HCI," *Proceedings of the SIGCHI Conference on Human Factors in Computing Systems (CHI'10)*. New York: ACM, 1975–1984.

Dix, A. (2007) "Designing for Appropriation." *Proceedings of the 21st British HCI Group Annual Conference on People and Computers: HCI … But Not as We Know It*, vol. 2. Swindon, UK: ACM, 27–30.

Dunne, A. (2005) *Hertzian Tales: Electronic Products, Aesthetic Experience, and Critical Design*. Cambridge, MA: MIT Press.

Finken, S., and C. Mörtberg. (2011) "The Thinking House: Configurings of an Infrastructure of Care." *Infrastructures for Healthcare: Global Healthcare, Proceedings of the 3rd International Workshop*, edited by P. Bjorn, F. Kensing, and L. R. Christensen, 43–46. Copenhagen: IT University and University of Copenhagen.

Foucault, M. (1988) Madness and Civilization: A History of Insanity in the Age of Reason. New York: Vintage.

Foucault, M. (1988–1990) *History of Sexuality*. 3 vols. Translated by R. Hurley. New York: Vintage.

Friedman, B. (1996) "Value-Sensitive Design." *Interactions* 3 (6): 16–23.

Gaver, W. W., J. Beaver, and S. Benford. (2003) "Ambiguity as a Resource for Design." *Proceedings of the SIGCHI Conference on Human Factors in Computing Systems (CHI'03)*. New York: AMC, 233–240.

Halperin, D. M. (1997) *Saint Foucault: Towards a Gay Hagiography*. Oxford: Oxford University Press.

Henrich, J., S. J. Heine, and A. Norenzayan. (2010) "The Weirdest People in the World?" *Behavioral and Brain Sciences* 33 (2–3): 61–83.

Hourcade, J. P., and N. E. Bullock-Rest. (2011) "HCI for Peace: A Call for Constructive Action." *Proceedings of the SIGCHI Conference on Human Factors in Computing Systems (CHI'11).* New York: AMC, 443–452.

Jagose, A. (1996) *Queer Theory.* Carlton South, Victoria: Melbourne University Press.

Kannabiran, G., and M. Graves Petersen. (2010) "Politics at the Interface: A Foucauldian Power Analysis." *Proceedings of the 6th Nordic Conference on Human-Computer Interaction: Extending Boundaries (NordiCHI'10).* New York: AMC, 695–698.

Latour, B. (2007) *Reassembling the Social: An Introduction to Actor-Network-Theory.* Oxford: Oxford University Press.

Light, A. (2011a) "Digital Interdependence and How to Design for It." *Interactions* 18 (2): 34–39.

Light, A. (2011b) "HCI as Heterodoxy: Technologies of Identity and the Queering of Interaction Design." *Interacting with Computers* 23 (5): 430–438.

Light, A., and L. Coles-Kemp. (2013) "Granddaughter Beware! An Intergenerational Case Study of Managing Trust Issues in the Use of Facebook." In *Trust and Trustworthy Computing,* edited by M. Huth, N. Asokan, S. Čapkun, I. Flechais, and L. Coles-Kemp, 196–204. Berlin: Springer.

Light, A., and P. C. Wright. (2009) "The Panopticon and the Performance Arena: HCI Reaches Within." Proc. INTERACT 2009, 2009.

MacKenzie, D., and J. Wajcman, eds. (1999) *Social Shaping of Technology,* 2nd ed. Buckingham: Open University Press.

O'Riordan, K., and D. J. Phillips, eds. (2007) *Queer Online: Media Technology and Sexuality* New York: Peter Lang.

Redström, J. (2006) "Towards User Design? On the Shift from Object to User as the Subject of Design." *Design Studies* 27 (2): 123–139.

Reeves, S. (2012) "Envisioning Ubiquitous Computing." *Proceedings of the SIGCHI Conference on Human Factors in Computing Systems (CHI'12).* New York: AMC, 1573–1582.

Salih, S., and J. P. Butler. (2004) *The Judith Butler Reader.* Malden, MA: Blackwell.

Shneiderman, B., and P. Maes. (1997) "Direct Manipulation vs. Interface Agents." *Interactions* 4 (6): 42–61.

Star, S. L. (1997) "The Politics Question in Feminist Science and Technology Projects: The Queering of Infrastructure." Paper presented at the Technology and Democracy Comparative Perspectives Conference, University of Oslo, Norway; January 18.

Stolterman, E. (2001) "Creating Community in Conspiracy with the Enemy." In *Community Informatics: Shaping Computer-Mediated Social Relations,* edited by L. Keeble and B. D. Loader, 43–52. London: Routledge.

Strengers, Y. (2011) "Designing Eco-Feedback Systems for Everyday Life." *Proceedings of the SIGCHI Conference on Human Factors in Computing Systems (CHI'11).* New York: ACM, 2135–2144.

Suchman, L. A. (1997) "Do Categories Have Politics? The Language/Action Perspective Reconsidered." In *Human Values and the Design of Computer Technology*, edited by B. Friedman, 91–106. Stanford, CA: Center for the Study of Language and Information.

Tufekci, Z. (2008) "Can You See Me Now? Audience and Disclosure Management in Online Social Network Sites." *Bulletin of Science, Technology, and Society* 11 (4): 544–564.

Turkle, S. (2011) *Alone Together: Why We Expect More from Technology and Less from Each Other.* New York: Basic.

Wakeford, N. (1997) "Cyberqueer." In *Lesbian and Gay Studies: A Critical Introduction*, edited by S. R. Munt and A. Medhurst, 20–23. London: Cassell.

23 Why Has Critique Run Out of Steam? From Matters of Fact to Matters of Concern (2004)

Bruno Latour

Wars. So many wars. Wars outside and wars inside. Cultural wars, science wars, and wars against terrorism. Wars against poverty and wars against the poor. Wars against ignorance and wars out of ignorance. My question is simple: Should we be at war, too, we, the scholars, the intellectuals? Is it really our duty to add fresh ruins to fields of ruins? Is it really the task of the humanities to add deconstruction to destruction? More iconoclasm to iconoclasm? What has become of the critical spirit? Has it run out of steam?

Quite simply, my worry is that it might not be aiming at the right target. To remain in the metaphorical atmosphere of the time, military experts constantly revise their strategic doctrines, their contingency plans, the size, direction, and technology of their projectiles, their smart bombs, their missiles; I wonder why we, we alone, would be saved from those sorts of revisions. It does not seem to me that we have been as quick, in academia, to prepare ourselves for new threats, new dangers, new tasks, new targets. Are we not like those mechanical toys that endlessly make the same gesture when everything else has changed around them? Would it not be rather terrible if we were still training young kids—yes, young recruits, young cadets—for wars that are no longer possible, fighting enemies long gone, conquering territories that no longer exist, leaving them ill-equipped in the face of threats we had not anticipated, for which we are so thoroughly unprepared? Generals have always been accused of being on the ready one war late—especially French generals, especially these days. Would it be so surprising, after all, if intellectuals were also one war late, one critique late—especially French intellectuals, especially now? It has been a long time, after all, since intellectuals were in the vanguard. Indeed, it has been a long time since the very notion of the avant-garde—the proletariat, the artistic—passed away, pushed aside by other forces, moved to the rear guard, or maybe lumped with the baggage train.[1] We are still able to go through the motions of a critical avant-garde, but is not the spirit gone?

In these most depressing of times, these are some of the issues I want to press, not to depress the reader but to press ahead, to redirect our meager capacities as fast as possible. To prove my point, I have, not exactly facts, but rather tiny cues, nagging doubts, disturbing telltale signs. What has become of critique, I wonder, when an editorial in the *New York Times* contains the following quote?

> Most scientists believe that [global] warming is caused largely by man-made pollutants that require strict regulation. Mr. Luntz [a Republican strategist] seems to acknowledge as much when he says that "the scientific debate is closing against us." His advice, however, is to emphasize that the evidence is not complete.
>
> "Should the public come to believe that the scientific issues are settled," he writes, "their views about global warming will change accordingly. Therefore, you need to continue to make the *lack of scientific certainty* a primary issue."[2]

Fancy that? An artificially maintained scientific controversy to favor a "brownlash," as Paul and Anne Ehrlich would say.[3]

Do you see why I am worried? I myself have spent some time in the past trying to show "'*the lack of scientific certainty*'" inherent in the construction of facts. I too made it a "'primary issue.'" But I did not exactly aim at fooling the public by obscuring the certainty of a closed argument—or did I? After all, I have been accused of just that sin. Still, I'd like to believe that, on the contrary, I intended to *emancipate* the public from prematurely naturalized objectified facts. Was I foolishly mistaken? Have things changed so fast?

In which case the danger would no longer be coming from an excessive confidence in ideological arguments posturing as matters of fact—as we have learned to combat so efficiently in the past—but from an excessive *distrust* of good matters of fact disguised as bad ideological biases! While we spent years trying to detect the real prejudices hidden behind the appearance of objective statements, do we now have to reveal the real objective and incontrovertible facts hidden behind the *illusion* of prejudices? And yet entire Ph.D. programs are still running to make sure that good American kids are learning the hard way that facts are made up, that there is no such thing as natural, unmediated, unbiased access to truth, that we are always prisoners of language, that we always speak from a particular standpoint, and so on, while dangerous extremists are using the very same argument of social construction to destroy hard-won evidence that could save our lives. Was I wrong to participate in the invention of this field known as science studies? Is it enough to say that we did not really mean what we said? Why does it burn my tongue to say that global warming is a fact whether you like it or not? Why can't I simply say that the argument is closed for good?

Should I reassure myself by simply saying that bad guys can use any weapon at hand, naturalized facts when it suits them and social construction when it suits them? Should we apologize for having been wrong all along? Or should we rather bring the sword of criticism to criticism itself and do a bit of soul-searching here: what were we really after when we were so intent on showing the social construction of scientific facts? Nothing guarantees, after all, that we should be right all the time. There is no sure ground even for criticism.[4] Isn't this what criticism intended to say: that there is no sure ground anywhere? But what does it mean when this lack of sure ground is taken away from us by the worst possible fellows as an argument against the things we cherish?

Artificially maintained controversies are not the only worrying sign. What has critique become when a French general, no, a marshal of critique, namely, Jean Baudrillard, claims in a published book that the Twin Towers destroyed themselves under their own weight, so to speak, undermined by the utter nihilism inherent in capitalism itself—as if the terrorist planes were pulled to suicide by the powerful attraction of this black hole of nothingness?[5] What has become of critique when a book that claims that no plane ever crashed into the Pentagon can be a bestseller? I am ashamed to say that the author was French, too.[6] Remember the good old days when revisionism arrived very late, after the facts had been thoroughly established, decades after bodies of evidence had accumulated? Now we have the benefit of what can be called *instant revisionism*. The smoke of the event has not yet finished settling before dozens of conspiracy theories begin revising the official account, adding even more ruins to the ruins, adding even more smoke to the smoke. What has become of critique when my neighbor in the little Bourbonnais village where I live looks down on me as someone hopelessly naïve because I believe that the United States had been attacked by terrorists? Remember the good old days when university professors could look down on unsophisticated folks because those hillbillies naïvely believed in church, motherhood, and apple pie? Things have changed a lot, at least in my village. I am now the one who naïvely believes in some facts because I am educated, while the other guys are too *un*sophisticated to be gullible: "Where have you been? Don't you know that the Mossad and the CIA did it?" What has become of critique when someone as eminent as Stanley Fish, the "enemy of promises" as Lindsay Waters calls him, believes he defends science studies, my field, by comparing the laws of physics to the rules of baseball?[7] What has become of critique when there is a whole industry denying that the Apollo program landed on the moon? What has become of critique when DARPA uses for its Total Information Awareness project the Baconian slogan *Scientia est potentia*? Didn't I read that somewhere in Michel Foucault? Has knowledge-slash-power been co-opted of late by the National Security Agency? Has *Discipline and Punish* become the bedtime reading of Mr. Ridge (figure 23.1)?

Let me be mean for a second. What's the real difference between conspiracists and a popularized, that is a teachable version of social critique inspired by a too quick reading of, let's say, a sociologist as eminent as Pierre Bourdieu (to be polite I will stick with the French field commanders)? In both cases, you have to learn to become suspicious of everything people say because of course we all know that they live in the thralls of a complete *illusio* of their real motives. Then, after disbelief has struck and an explanation is requested for what is really going on, in both cases again it is the same appeal to powerful agents hidden in the dark acting always consistently, continuously,

Figure 23.1
Information Awareness Office seal.

relentlessly. Of course, we in the academy like to use more elevated causes—society, discourse, knowledge-slash-power, fields of forces, empires, capitalism—while conspiracists like to portray a miserable bunch of greedy people with dark intents, but I find something troublingly similar in the structure of the explanation, in the first movement of disbelief and, then, in the wheeling of causal explanations coming out of the deep dark below. What if explanations resorting automatically to power, society, discourse had outlived their usefulness and deteriorated to the point of now feeding the most gullible sort of critique?[8] Maybe I am taking conspiracy theories too seriously, but it worries me to detect, in those mad mixtures of knee-jerk disbelief, punctilious demands for proofs, and free use of powerful explanation from the social neverland many of the weapons of social critique. Of course conspiracy theories are an absurd deformation of our own arguments, but, like weapons smuggled through a fuzzy border to the wrong party, these are our weapons nonetheless. In spite of all the deformations, it is easy to recognize, still burnt in the steel, our trademark: *Made in Criticalland.*

Do you see why I am worried? Threats might have changed so much that we might still be directing all our arsenal east or west while the enemy has now moved to a very different place. After all, masses of atomic missiles are transformed into a huge pile of junk once the question becomes how to defend against militants armed with box cutters or dirty bombs. Why would it not be the same with our critical arsenal, with the neutron bombs of deconstruction, with the missiles of discourse analysis? Or maybe it is that critique has been miniaturized like computers have. I have always fancied that what took great effort, occupied huge rooms, cost a lot of sweat and money, for people like Nietzsche and Benjamin, can be had for nothing, much like the supercomputers of the 1950s, which used to fill large halls and expend a vast amount of electricity and heat, but now are accessible for a dime and no bigger than a fingernail. As the recent advertisement of a Hollywood film proclaimed, "Everything is suspect ... Everyone is for sale ... And nothing is what it seems."

What's happening to me, you may wonder? Is this a case of midlife crisis? No, alas, I passed middle age quite a long time ago. Is this a patrician spite for the popularization of critique? As if critique should be reserved for the elite and remain difficult and strenuous, like mountain climbing or yachting, and is no longer worth the trouble if everyone can do it for a nickel? What would be so bad with critique for the people? We have been complaining so much about the gullible masses, swallowing naturalized facts, it would be really unfair to now discredit the same masses for their, what should I call it, gullible criticism? Or could this be a case of radicalism gone mad, as when a revolution swallows its progeny? Or, rather, have we behaved like mad scientists who have let the virus of critique out of the confines of their laboratories and cannot do anything now to limit its deleterious effects; it mutates now, gnawing everything up, even the vessels in which it is contained? Or is it an another [*sic*] case of the famed power of capitalism for recycling everything aimed at its destruction? As Luc Boltanski and Eve Chiapello say, the new spirit of capitalism has put to good use the artistic critique that was supposed to destroy it.[9] If the dense and moralist cigar-smoking reactionary bourgeois can transform him- or herself into a free-floating agnostic bohemian, moving opinions, capital, and networks from one end of the planet to the other without attachment, why would he or she not be able to absorb the most sophisticated tools of deconstruction, social construction, discourse analysis, postmodernism, postology?

In spite of my tone, I am not trying to reverse course, to become reactionary, to regret what I have done, to swear that I will never be a constructivist any more. I simply want to do what every good military officer, at regular periods, would do: retest the linkages between the new threats he or she has to face and the equipment and training he or she should have in order to meet them—and, if necessary, to revise from scratch the whole paraphernalia. This does not mean for us any more than it does for the officer that we were wrong, but simply that history changes quickly and that there is no greater intellectual crime than to address with the equipment of an older period the challenges of the present one. Whatever the case, our critical equipment deserves as much critical scrutiny as the Pentagon budget.

My argument is that a certain form of critical spirit has sent us down the wrong path, encouraging us to fight the wrong enemies and, worst of all, to be considered as friends by the wrong sort of allies because of a little mistake in the definition of its main target. The question was never to get *away* from facts but *closer* to them, not fighting empiricism but, on the contrary, renewing empiricism.

What I am going to argue is that the critical mind, if it is to renew itself and be relevant again, is to be found in the cultivation of a *stubbornly realist attitude*—to speak like William James—but a realism dealing with what I will call *matters of concern*, not *matters of fact*. The mistake we made, the mistake I made, was to believe that there was no efficient way to criticize matters of fact except by moving *away* from them and directing one's attention *toward* the conditions that made them possible. But this meant accepting much too uncritically what matters of fact were. This was remaining too faithful to the unfortunate solution inherited from the philosophy of Immanuel Kant. Critique has not been critical enough in spite of all its sore-scratching. Reality is not defined by matters of fact. Matters of fact are not all that is given in experience. Matters of fact are only very partial and, I would argue, very polemical, very political renderings of matters of concern and only a subset of what could also be called *states of affairs*. It is this second empiricism, this return to the realist attitude, that I'd like to offer as the next task for the critically minded.

To indicate the direction of the argument, I want to show that while the Enlightenment profited largely from the disposition of a very powerful descriptive tool, that of matters of fact, which were excellent for *debunking* quite a lot of beliefs, powers, and illusions, it found itself totally disarmed once matters of fact, in turn, were eaten up by the same debunking impetus. After that, the lights of the Enlightenment were slowly turned off, and some sort of darkness appears to have fallen on campuses. My question is thus: Can we devise another powerful descriptive tool that deals this time with matters of concern and whose import then will no longer be to debunk but to protect and to care, as Donna Haraway would put it? Is it really possible to transform the critical urge in the ethos of someone who *adds* reality to matters of fact and not *subtract* reality? To put it another way, what's the difference between deconstruction and constructivism?

"So far," you could object, "the prospect doesn't look very good, and you, Monsieur Latour, seem the person the least able to deliver on this promise because you spent your life debunking what the other more polite critics had at least respected until then, namely matters of fact and science itself. You can dust your hands with flour as much as you wish, the black fur of the critical wolf will always betray you; your deconstructing teeth have been sharpened on too many of our innocent labs—I mean lambs!—for us to believe you." Well, see, that's just the problem: I have written about a dozen books to inspire respect for, some people have said to uncritically glorify, the objects of science and technology, of art, religion, and, more recently, law, showing every time in great detail the complete implausibility of their being socially explained, and yet the only noise readers hear is the snapping of the wolf's teeth. Is it really impossible to solve the question, to write not matter-of-factually but, how should I say it, in a matter-of-concern way?[10]

Martin Heidegger, as every philosopher knows, has meditated many times on the ancient etymology of the word *thing*. We are now all aware that in all the European languages, including Russian, there is a strong connection between the words for thing and a quasi-judiciary assembly. Icelanders boast of having the oldest Parliament, which they call *Althing*, and you can still visit in many Scandinavian countries assembly places that are designated by the word *Ding* or *Thing*. Now, is this not extraordinary that the banal term we use for designating what is out there, unquestionably, a thing, what lies out of any dispute, out of language, is also the oldest word we all have used to designate the oldest of the sites in which our ancestors did their dealing and tried to settle their disputes?[11] A thing is, in one sense, an object out there and, in another sense, an *issue* very much *in* there, at any rate, a *gathering*. To use the term I introduced earlier now more precisely, the same word *thing* designates matters of fact and matters of concern.

Needless to say, although he develops this etymology at length, this is not the path that Heidegger has taken. On the contrary, all his writing aims to make as sharp a distinction as possible between, on the one hand, objects, *Gegenstand*, and, on the other, the celebrated *Thing*. The handmade jug can be a thing, while the industrially made can of Coke remains an object. While the latter is abandoned to the empty mastery of science and technology, only the former, cradled in the respectful idiom of art, craftsmanship, and poetry, could deploy and gather its rich set of connections.[12] This bifurcation is marked many times but in a decisive way in his book on Kant:

> Up to this hour such questions have been open. Their questionability is concealed by the results and the progress of scientific work. One of these burning questions concerns the justification and limits of mathematical formalism in contrast to the demand for an immediate return to intuitively given nature.[13]

What has happened to those who, like Heidegger, have tried to find their ways in immediacy, in intuition, in nature would be too sad to retell—and is well known anyway. What is certain is that those pathmarks off the beaten track led indeed nowhere. And, yet, Heidegger, when he takes the jug seriously, offers a powerful vocabulary to talk also about the object he despises so much. What would happen, I wonder, if we tried to talk about the object of science and technology, the *Gegenstand*, as if it had the rich and complicated qualities of the celebrated *Thing?*

The problem with philosophers is that because their jobs are so hard they drink a lot of coffee and thus use in their arguments an inordinate quantity of pots, mugs, and jugs—to which, sometimes, they might add the occasional rock. But, as Ludwik Fleck remarked long ago, their objects are never complicated enough; more precisely, they are never simultaneously *made* through a complex history and new, real, and *interesting* participants in the universe.[14] Philosophy never deals with the sort of beings we in science studies have dealt with. And that's why the debates between realism and relativism never go anywhere. As Ian Hacking has recently shown, the engagement of a rock in philosophical talk is utterly different if you take a banal rock to make your point (usually to lapidate a passing relativist!) or if you take, for instance, dolomite, as he has done so beautifully.[15] The first can be turned into a matter of fact but not the second. Dolomite is so beautifully complex and entangled that it resists being treated as a matter of fact. It too can be described as a gathering; it too can be seen as engaging the fourfold. Why not try to portray it with the same enthusiasm, engagement, and complexity as the Heideggerian jug? Heidegger's mistake is not to have treated the jug too well, but to have traced a dichotomy between *Gegenstand* and *Thing* that was justified by nothing except the crassest of prejudices.

Several years ago another philosopher, much closer to the history of science, namely Michel Serres, also French, but this time as foreign to critique as one can get, meditated on what it would mean to take objects of science in a serious anthropological and ontological fashion. It is interesting to note that every time a philosopher gets closer to an object of science that is at once historical and interesting, his or her philosophy changes, and the specifications for a realist attitude become, at once, more stringent and completely different from the so-called realist philosophy of science concerned with routine or boring objects. I was reading his passage on the *Challenger* disaster in his book *Statues* when another shuttle, *Columbia*, in early 2003 offered me a tragic instantiation of yet another metamorphosis of an object into a thing.[16]

What else would you call this sudden transformation of a completely mastered, perfectly understood, quite forgotten by the media, taken-for-granted, matter-of-factual projectile into a sudden shower of debris falling on the United States, which thousands of people tried to salvage in the mud and rain and collect in a huge hall to serve as so many clues in a judicial scientific investigation? Here, suddenly, in a stroke, an object had become a thing, a matter of fact was considered as a matter of great concern. If a thing is a gathering, as Heidegger says, how striking to see how it can suddenly *disband*. If the "thinging of the thing" is a gathering that always connects the "united four, earth and sky, divinities and mortals, in the simple onefold of their self-unified fourfold,"[17] how could there be a better example of this making and unmaking than this catastrophe unfolding all its thousands of folds? How could we see it as a normal accident of technology when, in his eulogy for the unfortunate victims, your president said: "The crew of the shuttle Columbia did not return safely to Earth; yet we can pray that all are safely home"?[18] As if no shuttle ever moved simply in space, but also always in heaven.

This was on C-Span 1, but on C-Span 2, at the very same time, early February 2003, another extraordinary parallel event was occurring. This time a Thing—with a capital T—was assembled to try to coalesce, to gather in one decision, one object, one projection of force: a military strike against Iraq. Again, it was hard to tell whether this gathering was a tribunal, a parliament, a command-and-control war room, a rich man's club, a scientific congress, or a TV stage. But certainly it was an assembly where matters of great concern were debated and proven—except there was much puzzlement about which type of proofs should be given and how accurate they were. The difference between C-Span 1 and C-Span 2, as I watched them with bewilderment, was that while in the case of *Columbia* we had a perfectly mastered object that suddenly was transformed into a shower of burning debris that was used as so much evidence in an investigation, there, at the United Nations, we had an investigation that tried to coalesce, in one unifying, unanimous, solid, mastered object, masses of people, opinions, and might. In one case the object was metamorphosed into a thing; in the second, the thing was attempting to turn into an object. We could witness, in one case, the head, in another, the tail of the trajectory through which matters of fact emerge out of matters of concern. In both cases we were offered a unique window into the number of *things* that have to participate in the gathering of an *object*. Heidegger was not a very good anthropologist of science and technology; he had only four folds, while the smallest shuttle, the shortest war, has millions. How many gods, passions, controls, institutions, techniques, diplomacies, wits have to be folded to connect "earth and sky, divinities and mortals"—oh yes, especially mortals. (Frightening omen, to launch such a complicated war, just when such a beautifully mastered object as the shuttle disintegrated into thousands of pieces of debris raining down from the sky—but the omen was not heeded; gods nowadays are invoked for convenience only.)

My point is thus very simple: things have become Things again, objects have reentered the arena, the Thing, in which they have to be gathered first in order to exist later as what *stands apart*. The parenthesis that we can call the modern parenthesis during which we had, on the one hand, a world of objects, *Gegenstand*, out there, unconcerned by any sort of parliament, forum, agora, congress, court and, on the other, a whole set of forums, meeting places, town halls where people debated, has come to a close. What the etymology of the word *thing—chose, causa, res, aitia*—had conserved for us mysteriously as a sort of fabulous and mythical past has now become, for all to see, our most ordinary present. Things are gathered again. Was it not extraordinarily moving to see, for instance, in the lower Manhattan reconstruction project, the long crowds, the angry messages, the passionate emails, the huge agoras, the long editorials that connected so many people to so many variations of the project to replace the Twin Towers? As the architect Daniel Libeskind said a few days before the decision, building will never be the same.

I could open the newspaper and unfold the number of former objects that have become things again, from the global warming case I mentioned earlier to the hormonal treatment of menopause, to the work of Tim Lenoir, the primate studies of Linda Fedigan and Shirley Strum, or the hyenas of my friend Steven Glickman.[19]

Nor are those gatherings limited to the present period as if only recently objects had become so obviously things. Every day historians of science help us realize to what extent we have never been modern because they keep revising every single element of past matters of fact from Mario Biagioli's Galileo, Steven Shapin's Boyle, and Simon Schaffer's Newton, to the incredibly intricate linkages between Einstein and Poincaré that Peter Galison has narrated in his latest masterpiece.[20] Many others of course could be cited, but the crucial point for me now is that what allowed historians, philosophers, humanists, and critics to trace *the* difference between modern and premodern, namely, the sudden and somewhat miraculous appearance of matters of fact, is now thrown into doubt with the merging of matters of fact into highly complex, historically situated, richly diverse matters of concern. You can do one sort of thing with mugs, jugs, rocks, swans, cats, mats but not with Einstein's Patent Bureau electric coordination of clocks in Bern. Things that gather cannot be thrown at you like objects.

And, yet, I know full well that this is not enough because, no matter what we do, when we try to reconnect scientific objects with their aura, their crown, their web of associations, when we accompany them back to their gathering, we always appear to *weaken* them, not to *strengthen* their claim to reality. I know, I know, we are acting with the best intentions in the world, we want to *add* reality to scientific objects, but, inevitably, through a sort of tragic bias, we seem always to be subtracting some bit from it. Like a clumsy waiter setting plates on a slanted table, every nice dish slides down and crashes on the ground. Why can we never discover the same stubbornness, the same solid realism by bringing out the obviously webby, "thingy" qualities of matters of concern? Why can't we ever counteract the claim of realists that only a fare of matters of fact can satisfy their appetite and that matters of concern are much like nouvelle cuisine—nice to look at but not fit for voracious appetites?

One reason is of course the position objects have been given in most social sciences, a position that is so ridiculously useless that if it is employed, even in a small way, for dealing with science, technology, religion, law, or literature it will make absolutely impossible any serious consideration of objectivity—I mean of "thinginess." Why is this so? Let me try to portray the critical landscape in its ordinary and routine state.[21]

We can summarize, I estimate, 90 percent of the contemporary critical scene by the following series of diagrams that fixate the object at only two positions, what I have called the *fact* position and the *fairy* position—*fact* and *fairy* are etymologically related but I won't develop this point here. The fairy position is very well known and is used over and over again by many social scientists who associate criticism with antifetishism. The role of the critic is then to show that what the naïve believers are doing with

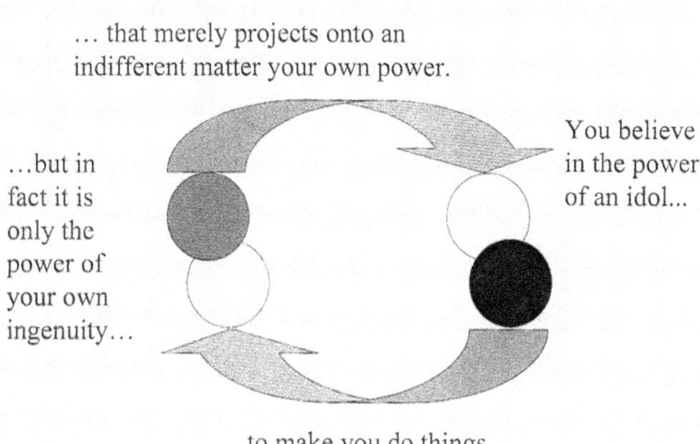
Critical Gesture: Move One
... that merely projects onto an indifferent matter your own power.
You believe in the power of an idol...
...but in fact it is only the power of your own ingenuity...
...to make you do things...

Figure 23.2

objects is simply a projection of their wishes onto a material entity that does nothing at all by itself. Here they have diverted to their petty use the prophetic fulmination against idols "they have mouths and speak not, they have ears and hear not," but they use this prophecy to decry the very objects of belief—gods, fashion, poetry, sport, desire, you name it—to which naïve believers cling with so much intensity.[22] And then the courageous critic, who alone remains aware and attentive, who never sleeps, turns those false objects into fetishes that are supposed to be nothing but mere empty white screens on which is projected the power of society, domination, whatever. The naïve believer has received a first salvo (figure 23.2).

But, wait, a second salvo is in the offing, and this time it comes from the fact pole. This time it is the poor bloke, again taken aback, whose behavior is now "explained" by the powerful effects of indisputable matters of fact: "You, ordinary fetishists, believe you are free but, in reality, you are acted on by forces you are not conscious of. Look at them, look, you blind idiot" (and here you insert whichever pet facts the social scientists fancy to work with, taking them from economic infrastructure, fields of discourse, social domination, race, class, and gender, maybe throwing in some neurobiology, evolutionary psychology, whatever, provided they act as indisputable facts whose origin, fabrication, mode of development are left unexamined) (figure 23.3).

Do you see now why it feels so good to be a critical mind? Why critique, this most ambiguous *pharmakon*, has become such a potent euphoric drug? You are always right! When naïve believers are clinging forcefully to their objects, claiming that they are made to do things because of their gods, their poetry, their cherished objects, you can

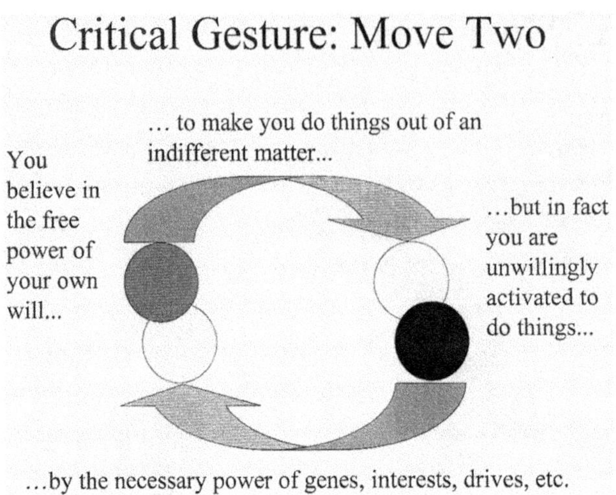
Critical Gesture: Move Two
... to make you do things out of an indifferent matter...
You believe in the free power of your own will...
...but in fact you are unwillingly activated to do things...
...by the necessary power of genes, interests, drives, etc.

Figure 23.3

turn all of those attachments into so many fetishes and humiliate all the believers by showing that it is nothing but their own projection, that you, yes you alone, can see. But as soon as naïve believers are thus inflated by some belief in their own importance, in their own projective capacity, you strike them by a second uppercut and humiliate them again, this time by showing that, whatever they think, their behavior is entirely determined by the action of powerful causalities coming from objective reality they don't see, but that you, yes you, the never sleeping critic, alone can see. Isn't this fabulous? Isn't it really worth going to graduate school to study critique? "Enter here, you poor folks. After arduous years of reading turgid prose, you will be always right, you will never be taken in any more; no one, no matter how powerful, will be able to accuse you of naïveté, that supreme sin, any longer? Better equipped than Zeus himself you rule alone, striking from above with the salvo of antifetishism in one hand and the solid causality of objectivity in the other." The only loser is the naïve believer, the great unwashed, always caught off balance (figure 23.4).

Is it so surprising, after all, that with such positions given to the object, the humanities have lost the hearts of their fellow citizens, that they had to retreat year after year, entrenching themselves always further in the narrow barracks left to them by more and more stingy deans? The Zeus of Critique rules absolutely, to be sure, but over a desert.

One thing is clear, not one of us readers would like to see *our* own most cherished objects treated in this way. We would recoil in horror at the mere suggestion of having them socially explained, whether we deal in poetry or robots, stem cells, blacks holes [*sic*], or impressionism, whether we are patriots, revolutionaries, or lawyers, whether we pray to God or put our hope in neuroscience. This is why, in my opinion, those of us

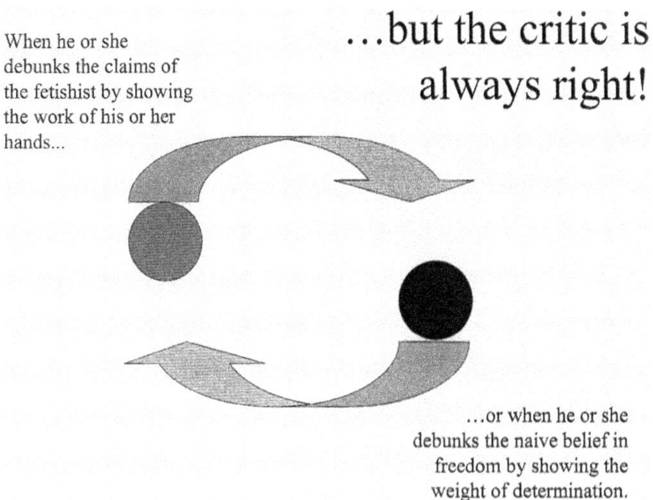
When he or she
debunks the claims of
the fetishist by showing
the work of his or her
hands...
...but the critic is
always right!
...or when he or she
debunks the naive belief in
freedom by showing the
weight of determination.

Figure 23.4

who tried to portray sciences as matters of concern so often failed to convince; readers have confused the treatment we give of the former matters of fact with the terrible fate of objects processed through the hands of sociology, cultural studies, and so on. And I can't blame our readers. What social scientists do to our favorite objects is so horrific that certainly we don't want them to come any nearer. "Please," we exclaim, "don't touch them at all! Don't try to explain them!" Or we might suggest more politely: "Why don't you go further down the corridor to this other department? *They* have bad facts to account for; why don't you explain away those ones instead of ours?" And this is the reason why, when we want respect, solidity, obstinacy, robustness, we all prefer to stick to the language of matters of fact no matter its well-known defects.

And yet this is not the only way because the cruel treatment objects undergo in the hands of what I'd like to call *critical barbarity* is rather easy to undo. If the critical barbarian appears so powerful, it is because the two mechanisms I have just sketched are never put together in one single diagram (figure 23.5). Antifetishists debunk objects they don't believe in by showing the productive and projective forces of people; then, without ever making the connection, they use objects they do believe in to resort to the causalist or mechanist explanation and debunk conscious capacities of people whose behavior they don't approve of. The whole rather poor trick that allows critique to go on, although we would never confine our own valuables to their sordid pawnshop, is that there is never any *crossover between the two lists of objects* in the fact position and the fairy position. This is why you can be at once and without even sensing any contradiction (1) an antifetishist for everything you don't believe in—for

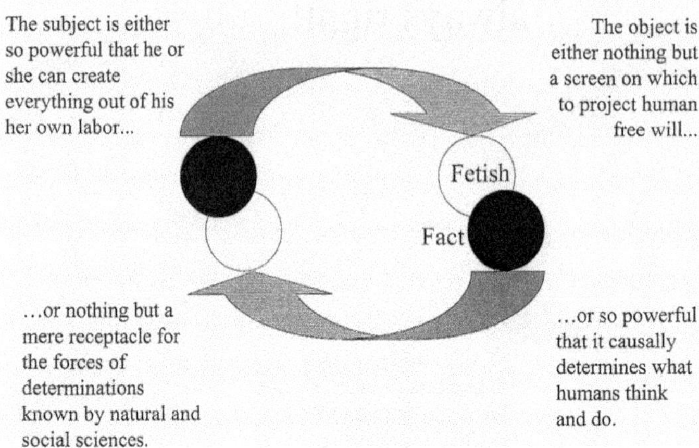
The Critical Trick: Two Objects-Two Subjects
The subject is either so powerful that he or she can create everything out of his her own labor...
The object is either nothing but a screen on which to project human free will...
Fetish
Fact
...or nothing but a mere receptacle for the forces of determinations known by natural and social sciences.
...or so powerful that it causally determines what humans think and do.

Figure 23.5

the most part religion, popular culture, art, politics, and so on; (2) an unrepentant positivist for all the sciences you believe in—sociology, economics, conspiracy theory, genetics, evolutionary psychology, semiotics, just pick your preferred field of study; and (3) a perfectly healthy sturdy realist for what you really cherish—and of course it might be criticism itself, but also painting, bird-watching, Shakespeare, baboons, proteins, and so on.

If you think I am exaggerating in my somewhat dismal portrayal of the critical landscape, it is because we have had in effect almost no occasion so far to detect the total mismatch of the three contradictory repertoires—antifetishism, positivism, realism—because we carefully manage to apply them on *different* topics. We explain the objects we don't approve of by treating them as fetishes; we account for behaviors we don't like by discipline whose makeup we don't examine; and we concentrate our passionate interest on only those things that are for us worthwhile matters of concern. But of course such a cavalier attitude with such contradictory repertoires is not possible for those of us, in science studies, who have to deal with states of affairs that fit neither in the list of plausible fetishes—because everyone, including us, does believe very strongly in them—nor in the list of undisputable facts because we are witnessing their birth, their slow construction, their fascinating emergence as matters of concern. The metaphor of the Copernican revolution, so tied to the destiny of critique, has always been for us, science students, simply moot. This is why, with more than a good dose of field chauvinism, I consider this tiny field so important; it is the little rock in the shoe that might render the routine patrol of the critical barbarians more and more painful.

The mistake would be to believe that we too have given a social explanation of scientific facts. No, even though it is true that at first we tried, like good critics trained in the good schools, to use the armaments handed to us by our betters and elders to crack open—one of their favorite expressions, meaning to destroy—religion, power, discourse, hegemony. But, fortunately (yes, fortunately!), one after the other, we witnessed that the black boxes of science remained closed and that it was rather the tools that lay in the dust of our workshop, disjointed and broken. Put simply, critique was useless against objects of some solidity. You can try the projective game on UFOs or exotic divinities, but don't try it on neurotransmitters, on gravitation, on Monte Carlo calculations. But critique is also useless when it begins to use the results of one science uncritically, be it sociology itself, or economics, or postimperialism, to account for the behavior of people. You can try to play this miserable game of explaining aggression by invoking the genetic makeup of violent people, but try to do that while dragging in, at the same time, the many controversies in genetics, including evolutionary theories in which geneticists find themselves so thoroughly embroiled.[23]

On both accounts, matters of concern never occupy the two positions left for them by critical barbarity. Objects are much too strong to be treated as fetishes and much too weak to be treated as indisputable causal explanations of some unconscious action. And this is not true of scientific states of affairs only; this is our great discovery, what made science studies commit such a felicitous mistake, such a *felix culpa*. Once you realize that scientific objects cannot be socially explained, then you realize too that the so-called weak objects, those that appear to be candidates for the accusation of antifetishism, were never mere projections on an empty screen either.[24] They too act, they too do things, they too *make you do* things. It is not only the objects of science that resist, but all the others as well, those that were supposed to have been ground to dust by the powerful teeth of automated reflex-action deconstructors. To accuse something of being a fetish is the ultimate gratuitous, disrespectful, insane, and barbarous gesture.[25]

Is it not time for some progress? To the fact position, to the fairy position, why not add a third position, a *fair* position? Is it really asking too much from our collective intellectual life to devise, at least once a century, some *new* critical tools? Should we not be thoroughly humiliated to see that military personnel are more alert, more vigilant, more innovative than we, the pride of academia, the crème de la crème, who go on ceaselessly transforming the whole rest of the world into naïve believers, into fetishists, into hapless victims of domination, while at the same time turning them into the mere superficial consequences of powerful hidden causalities coming from infrastructures whose makeup is never interrogated? All the while being intimately certain that the things really close to our hearts would in no way fit any of those roles. Are you not all tired of those "explanations"? I am, I have always been, when I know, for instance, that the God to whom I pray, the works of art I cherish, the colon cancer I have been fighting, the piece of law I am studying, the desire I feel, indeed, the very book I am writing could in no way be accounted for by fetish or fact, nor by any combination of those two absurd positions?

To retrieve a realist attitude, it is not enough to dismantle critical weapons so uncritically built up by our predecessors as we would obsolete but still dangerous atomic silos. If we had to dismantle social theory only, it would be a rather simple affair; like the Soviet empire, those big totalities have feet of clay. But the difficulty lies in the fact that they are built on top of a much older philosophy, so that whenever we try to replace matters of fact by matters of concern, we seem to lose something along the way. It is like trying to fill the mythical Danaid's barrel—no matter what we put in it, the level of realism never increases. As long as we have not sealed the leaks, the realist attitude will always be split; matters of fact take the best part, and matters of concern are limited to a rich but essentially void or irrelevant *history*. More will always seem less. Although I wish to keep this paper short, I need to take a few more pages to deal with ways to overcome this bifurcation.

Alfred North Whitehead famously said, "The recourse to metaphysics is like throwing a match into a powder magazine. It blows up the whole arena."[26] I cannot avoid getting into it because I have talked so much about weapon systems, explosions, iconoclasm, and arenas. Of all the modern philosophers who tried to overcome matters of fact, Whitehead is the only one who, instead of taking the path of critique and directing his attention *away* from facts to what makes them possible as Kant did; or adding something to their bare bones as Husserl did; or avoiding the fate of their domination, their *Gestell*, as much as possible as Heidegger did; tried to get *closer* to them or, more exactly, to see through them the reality that requested a new respectful realist attitude. No one is less a critic than Whitehead, in all the meanings of the word, and it's amusing to notice that the only pique he ever directed against someone else was against the other W., the one considered, wrongly in my view, as the greatest philosopher of the twentieth century, not W. as in Bush but W. as in Wittgenstein.

What set Whitehead completely apart and straight on our path is that he considered matters of fact to be a very poor rendering of what is given in experience and something that muddles entirely the question, What is there? with the question, How do we know it? as Isabelle Stengers has shown recently in a major book about Whitehead's philosophy.[27] Those who now mock his philosophy don't understand that they have resigned themselves to what he called the "bifurcation of nature." They have entirely forgotten what it would require if we were to take this incredible sentence seriously: "For natural philosophy everything perceived is in nature. We may not pick up and choose. For us the red glow of the sunset should be as much part of nature as are the molecules and electric waves by which men of science would explain the phenomenon" (*CN*, pp. 28–29).

All subsequent philosophies have done exactly the opposite: they have picked and chosen, and, worse, they have remained content with that limited choice. The solution to this bifurcation is not, as phenomenologists would have it, adding to the boring electric waves the rich lived world of the glowing sun. This would simply make the bifurcation greater. The solution or, rather, the adventure, according to Whitehead, is to dig much further into the realist attitude and to realize that matters of fact are totally implausible, unrealistic, unjustified definitions of what it is to deal with things:

> Thus matter represents the refusal to think away spatial and temporal characteristics and to arrive at the bare concept of an individual entity. It is this refusal which has caused the muddle *of importing the mere procedure of thought into the fact of nature*. The entity, bared of all characteristics except those of space and time, has acquired a physical status as the ultimate texture of nature; so that the course of nature is conceived as being merely the fortunes of matter in its adventure through space. [*CN*, p. 20]

It is not the case that there would exist solid matters of fact and that the next step would be for us to decide whether they will be used to explain something. It is not the case either that the other solution is to attack, criticize, expose, historicize those matters of fact, to show that they are made up, interpreted, flexible. It is not the case that we should rather flee out of them into the mind or add to them symbolic or cultural dimensions; the question is that matters of fact are a poor *proxy* of experience and of experimentation and, I would add, a confusing bundle of polemics, of epistemology, of modernist politics that can in no way claim to represent what is requested by a realist attitude.[28]

Whitehead is not an author known for keeping the reader wide awake, but I want to indicate at least the *direction* of the new critical attitude with which I wish to replace the tired routines of most social theories.

The solution lies, it seems to me, in this promising word *gathering* that Heidegger had introduced to account for the "thingness of the thing." Now, I know very well that Heidegger and Whitehead would have nothing to say to one another, and, yet, the word the latter used in *Process and Reality* to describe "actual occasions," his word for my matters of concern, is the word *societies*. It is also, by the way, the word used by Gabriel Tarde, the real founder of French sociology, to describe all sorts of entities. It is close enough to the word *association* that I have used all along to describe the objects of science and technology. Andrew Pickering would use the words "mangle of practice."[29] Whatever the words, what is presented here is an entirely different attitude than the critical one, not a flight into the conditions of possibility of a given matter of fact, not the addition of something more human that the inhumane matters of fact would have missed, but, rather, a multifarious inquiry launched with the tools of anthropology, philosophy, metaphysics, history, sociology to detect *how many participants* are gathered in a *thing* to make it exist and to maintain its existence. Objects are simply a gathering that has failed—a fact that has not been assembled according to due process.[30] The stubbornness of matters of fact in the usual scenography of the rock-kicking objector—"It is there whether you like it or not"—is much like the stubbornness of political demonstrators: "the U.S., love it or leave it," that is, a very poor substitute for any sort of vibrant, articulate, sturdy, decent, long-term existence.[31] A gathering, that is, a thing, an issue, inside a Thing, an arena, can be very sturdy, too, on the condition that the number of its participants, its ingredients, nonhumans as well as humans, not be limited in advance.[32] It is entirely wrong to divide the collective, as I call it, into the sturdy matters of fact, on the one hand, and the dispensable crowds, on the other. Archimedes spoke for a whole tradition when he exclaimed: "Give me one fixed point and I will move the Earth," but am I not speaking for another, much less prestigious but maybe as respectable tradition, if I exclaim in turn "Give me one matter of concern and I will show you the whole earth and heavens that have to be gathered to hold it firmly in place"? For me it makes no sense to reserve the realist vocabulary for the first one only. The critic is not the one who debunks, but the one who assembles. The critic is not the one who lifts the rugs from under the feet of the naïve believers, but the one who offers the participants arenas in which to gather. The critic is not the one who alternates haphazardly between antifetishism and positivism like the drunk iconoclast drawn by Goya, but the one for whom, if something is constructed, then it means it is fragile and thus in great need of care and caution. I am aware that to get at the heart of this argument one would have to renew also what it means to be a constructivist, but I have said enough to indicate the direction of critique, not *away* but *toward* the gathering, the Thing.[33] Not westward, but, so to speak, eastward.[34]

The practical problem we face, if we try to go that new route, is to associate the word *criticism* with a whole set of new positive metaphors, gestures, attitudes, knee-jerk reactions, habits of thoughts. To begin with this new habit forming, I'd like to extract another definition of critique from the most unlikely source, namely, Allan Turing's original paper on thinking machines.[35] I have a good reason for that: here is the typical paper about formalism, here is the origin of one of the icons—to use a cliché of antifetishism—of the contemporary age, namely, the computer, and yet, if you read this paper, it is so baroque, so kitsch, it assembles such an astounding number of metaphors, beings, hypotheses, allusions, that there is no chance that it would be accepted nowadays by any journal. Even *Social Text* would reject it out of hand as another hoax! "Not again," they would certainly say, "once bitten, twice shy." Who would take a paper seriously that states somewhere after having spoken of Muslim women, punishment of boys, extrasensory perception: "In attempting to construct such machines we should not be irreverently usurping [God's] power of creating souls, any more than we are in the procreation of children: rather we are, in either case, instruments of His will providing mansions for the souls that He creates" ("CM," p. 443).

Lots of gods, always in machines. Remember how Bush eulogized the crew of the *Columbia* for reaching home in heaven, if not home on earth? Here Turing too cannot avoid mentioning God's creative power when talking of this most mastered machine, the computer that he has invented. That's precisely his point. The computer is in for many surprises; you get out of it much more than you put into it. In the most dramatic way, Turing's paper demonstrates, once again, that all objects are born things, all matters of fact require, in order to exist, a bewildering variety of matters of concern.[36] The surprising result is that we don't master what we, ourselves, have fabricated, the object of this definition of critique:[37]

> Let us return for a moment to Lady Lovelace's objection, which stated that the machine can only do what we tell it to do. One could say that a man can "inject" an idea into the machine, and that it will respond to a certain extent and then drop into quiescence, like a piano string struck by a hammer. Another simile would be an atomic pile of less than critical size: an injected idea is to correspond to a neutron entering the pile from without. Each such neutron will cause a certain disturbance which eventually dies away. If, however, the size of the pile is sufficiently increased, the disturbance caused by such an incoming neutron will very likely go on and on increasing until the whole pile is destroyed. Is there a corresponding phenomenon for minds, and is there one for machines? There does seem to be one for the human mind. The majority of them seem to be "sub-critical," *i.e.* to correspond in this analogy to piles of sub-critical size. An idea presented to such a mind will on average give rise to less than one idea in reply. A smallish proportion are supercritical. An idea presented to such a mind may give rise to a whole "theory" consisting of secondary, tertiary and more remote ideas. Animals' minds seem to be very definitely sub-critical. Adhering to this analogy we ask, "Can a machine be made to be super-critical?" ["CM," p. 454]

We all know subcritical minds, that's for sure! What would critique do if it could be associated with *more*, not with *less*, with *multiplication*, not *subtraction*. Critical theory died away long ago; can we become critical again, in the sense here offered by Turing? That is, generating more ideas than we have received, inheriting from a prestigious critical tradition but not letting it die away, or "dropping into quiescence" like a piano no longer struck. This would require that all entities, including computers, cease to be objects defined simply by their inputs and outputs and become again things, mediating, assembling, gathering many more folds than the "united four." If this were possible then we could let the critics come ever closer to the matters of concern we cherish, and then at last we could tell them: "Yes, please, touch them, explain them, deploy them." Then we would have gone for good beyond iconoclasm.

Bruno Latour teaches sociology at the École des Mines in Paris.

Notes

All text in this chapter is reprinted from "Why Has Critique Run out of Steam?," *Critical Theory* 30: 2 (2004): 225–248. Reprinted with permission of the University of Chicago Press.

For Graham Harman. This text was written for the Stanford presidential lecture held at the humanities center, 7 Apr. 2003. I warmly thank Harvard history of science doctoral students for many ideas exchanged on those topics during this semester.

1. On what happened to the avant-garde and critique generally, see *Iconoclash: Beyond the Image Wars in Science, Religion, and Art,* ed. Bruno Latour and Peter Weibel (Cambridge, Mass., 2002). This article is very much an exploration of what could happen beyond the image wars.

2. "Environmental Word Games," *New York Times,* 15 Mar. 2003, p. A16. Luntz seems to have been very successful; I read later in an editorial in the *Wall Street Journal:*

> There is a better way [than passing a law that restricts business], which is to keep fighting on the merits. There is no scientific consensus that greenhouse gases cause the world's modest global warming trend, much less whether that warming will do more harm than good, or whether we can even do anything about it.
>
> Once Republicans concede that greenhouse gases must be controlled, it will only be a matter of time before they end up endorsing more economically damaging regulation. They could always stand on principle and attempt to educate the public instead. ["A Republican Kyoto," *Wall Street Journal,* 8 Apr. 2003, p. A14.]

And the same publication complains about the "pathological relation" of the "Arab street" with truth!

3. Paul R. and Anne H. Ehrlich, *Betrayal of Science and Reason: How Anti-Environmental Rhetoric Threatens Our Future* (Washington, D.C., 1997), p. 1.

4. The metaphor of shifting sand was used by neomodernists in their critique of science studies; see *A House Built on Sand: Exposing Postmodernist Myths about Science,* ed. Noretta Koertge (Oxford, 1998). The problem is that the authors of this book looked backward, attempting to reenter the solid rock castle of modernism, and not forward to what I call, for lack of a better term, nonmodernism.

5. See Jean Baudrillard, *"The Spirit of Terrorism" and "Requiem for the Twin Towers"* (New York, 2002).

6. See Thierry Meyssan, *911: The Big Lie* (London, 2002). Conspiracy theories have always existed; what is new in instant revisionism is how much scientific proof they claim to imitate.

7. See Lindsay Waters, *Enemy of Promises* (forthcoming); see also Nick Paumgarten, "Dept. of Super Slo-Mo: No Flag on the Play," *The New Yorker,* 20 Jan. 2003, p. 32.

8. Their serious as well as their popularized versions have the defect of using society as an already existing cause instead of as a possible consequence. This was the critique that Gabriel Tarde always made against Durkheim. It is probably the whole notion of *social* and *society* that is responsible for the weakening of critique. I have tried to show that in Latour, "Gabriel Tarde and the End of the Social," in *The Social in Question: New Bearings in History and the Social Sciences,* ed. Patrick Joyce (London, 2002), pp. 117–32.

9. See Luc Boltanski and Eve Chiapello, *Le Nouvel Esprit du capitalisme* (Paris, 1999).

10. This is the achievement of the great novelist Richard Powers, whose stories are a careful and, in my view, masterful enquiry into this new "realism." Especially relevant for this paper is Richard Powers, *Plowing the Dark* (New York, 2000).

11. See the erudite study by the remarkable French scholar of Roman law, Yan Thomas, "Res, chose et patrimoine (note sur le rapport sujet-objet en droit romain)," *Archives de philosophie du droit* 25 (1980): 413–26.

12. See Graham Harman, *Tool-Being: Heidegger and the Metaphysics of Objects* (Chicago, 2002).

13. Martin Heidegger, *What Is a Thing?* trans. W. B. Barton, Jr., and Vera Deutsch (Chicago, 1967), p. 95.

14. Although Fleck is the founder of science studies, the impact of his work is still very much in the future because he has been so deeply misunderstood by Thomas Kuhn; see Thomas Kuhn, foreword to Ludwik Fleck, *Genesis and Development of a Scientific Fact* (1935; Chicago, 1979), pp. vii–xi.

15. See Ian Hacking, *The Social Construction of What?* (Cambridge, Mass., 1999), in particular the last chapter.

16. See Michel Serres, *Statues: Le Second Livre des fondations* (Paris, 1987). On the reason why Serres was never critical, see Serres with Latour, *Conversations on Science, Culture, and Time*, trans. Roxanne Lapidus (Ann Arbor, Mich., 1995).

17. Heidegger, "The Thing," *Poetry, Language, Thought*, trans. Albert Hofstadter (New York, 1971), p. 178.

18. "Bush Talking More about Religion: Faith to Solve the Nation's Problems," CNN website, 18 Feb. 2003, www.cnn.com/2003/ALLPOLITICS/02/18/bush.faith/

19. Serres proposed the word *quasi-object* to cover this intermediary phase between things and objects—a philosophical question much more interesting than the tired old one of the relation between *words* and *worlds*. On the new way animals appear to scientists and the debate it triggers, see *Primate Encounters: Models of Science, Gender, and Society*, ed. Shirley Strum and Linda Fedigan (Chicago, 2000), and Vinciane Despret, *Quand le loup habitera avec l'agneau* (Paris, 2002).

20. See Peter Galison, *Einstein's Clocks, Poincaré's Maps: Empires of Time* (New York, 2003).

21. I summarize here some of the results of my already long anthropological inquiry into the iconoclastic gesture, from Latour, *We Have Never Been Modern*, trans. Catherine Porter (Cambridge, Mass., 1993) to *Pandora's Hope: Essays on the Reality of Science Studies* (Cambridge, Mass., 1999) and of course *Iconoclash*.

22. See William Pietz, "The Problem of the Fetish, I," *Res* 9 (Spring 1985): 5–17, "The Problem of the Fetish, II: The Origin of the Fetish" *Res* 13 (Spring 1987): 23–45, and "The Problem of the Fetish, IIIa: Bosman's Guinea and the Enlightenment Theory of Fetishism," *Res* 16 (Autumn 1988): 105–23.

23. For a striking example, see Jean-Jacques Kupiec and Pierre Sonigo, *Ni Dieu ni gène: Pour une autre théorie de l'hérédité* (Paris, 2000); see also Evelyn Fox-Keller, *The Century of the Gene* (Cambridge, Mass., 2000).

24. I have attempted to use this argument recently on two most difficult types of entities, Christian divinities (Latour, *Jubiler ou les tourments de la parole religieuse* [Paris, 2002]) and law (Latour, *La Fabrique du droit: Une Ethnographie du Conseil d'État* [Paris, 2002]).

25. The exhibition in Karlsruhe, Germany, *Iconoclash,* was a sort of belated ritual in order to atone for so much wanton destruction.

26. Alfred North Whitehead, *The Concept of Nature* (Cambridge, 1920), p. 29; hereafter abbreviated *CN.*

27. See Isabelle Stengers, *Penser avec Whitehead: Une Libre et sauvage création de concepts* (Paris, 2002), a book which has the great advantage of taking seriously Whitehead's science as well as his theory of God.

28. That matters of fact represent now a rather rare and complicated historical rendering of experience has been made powerfully clear by many writers; see, for telling segments of this history, Christian Licoppe, *La Formation de la pratique scientifique: Le Discours de l'expérience en France et en Angleterre (1630–1820)* (Paris, 1996); Mary Poovey, *A History of the Modern Fact: Problems of Knowledge in the Sciences of Wealth and Society* (Chicago, 1999); Lorraine Daston and Katherine Park, *Wonders and the Order of Nature, 1150–1750* (New York, 1998); and *Picturing Science, Producing Art,* ed. Caroline A. Jones, Galison, and Amy Slaton (New York, 1998).

29. See Andrew Pickering, *The Mangle of Practice: Time, Agency, and Science* (Chicago, 1995).

30. See Latour, *Politics of Nature: How to Bring the Sciences into Democracy,* trans. Porter (Cambridge, Mass., 2004).

31. See the marvelously funny rendering of the realist gesture in Malcolm Ashmore, Derek Edwards, and Jonathan Potter, "The Bottom Line: The Rhetoric of Reality Demonstrations," *Configurations* 2 (Winter 1994): 1–14.

32. This is the challenge of a new exhibition I am curating with Peter Weibel in Karlsruhe and that is supposed to take place in 2004 under the provisional title "Making Things Public." This exhibition will explore what *Iconoclash* had simply pointed at, namely, beyond the image wars.

33. This paper is a companion of another one: Latour, "The Promises of Constructivism," in *Chasing Technoscience: Matrix for Materiality,* ed. Don Ihde and Evan Selinger (Bloomington, Ind., 2003), pp. 27–46.

34. This is why, although I share all of the worries of Thomas de Zengotita, "Common Ground: Finding Our Way Back to the Enlightenment," *Harper's* 306 (Jan. 2003): 35–45, I think he is entirely mistaken in the *direction* of the move he proposes back to the future; to go back to the "natural" attitude is a sign of nostalgia.

35. See A. M. Turing, "Computing Machinery and Intelligence," *Mind* 59 (Oct. 1950): 433–60; hereafter abbreviated "CM." See also what Powers in *Galatea 2.2* (New York, 1995) did with this paper; this is critique in the most generous sense of the word. For the context of this paper, see Andrew Hodges, *Alan Turing: The Enigma* (New York, 1983).

36. A nonformalist definition of formalism has been proposed by Brian Rotman, *Ad Infinitum: The Ghost in Turing's Machine: Taking God out of Mathematics and Putting the Body Back In* (Stanford, Calif., 1993).

37. Since Turing can be taken as the first and best programmer, those who believe in defining machines by inputs and outputs should meditate his confession:

> Machines take me by surprise with great frequency. This is largely because I do not do sufficient calculation to decide what to expect them to do, or rather because, although I do a calculation, I do it in a hurried, slipshod fashion, taking risks. Perhaps I say to myself, "I suppose the voltage here ought to be the same as there: anyway let's assume it is." Naturally I am often wrong, and the result is a surprise for me for by the time the experiment is done these assumptions have been forgotten. These admissions lay me open to lectures on the subject of my vicious ways, but do not throw any doubt on my credibility when I testify to the surprises I experience. ["CM," pp. 450–51]

On this nonformalist definition of computers, see Brian Cantwell Smith, *On the Origin of Objects* (Cambridge, Mass., 1997).

24 Bruno Latour as Sociologist and Design Theorist?

Carl DiSalvo

Bruno Latour is one of those scholars whose practices and effects move between and across fields. Trained as a sociologist, he is known for his work on the sociology of science and technology, and his work is central to the field of science and technology studies. Using broadly ethnographic methods, his research is far-ranging and explores laboratory work (Latour and Wolgar, 1986), histories of scientific discovery and invention (1988), law (2010b), and failed attempts at innovation (1996). Drawing from that research, Latour's scholarship also extends into theory. He has been referred to as an "empirical metaphysician" (Restivo, 2011, 69)—a label he seems to resist but one that is nonetheless at times accurate. For instance, over the course of multiple books Latour identifies, analyzes, and ultimately discounts the presumed distinctions between nature and society. This leads to one of Latour's enduring themes and provocative claims: that if modernism is characterized by the separation of nature and society, then "we have never been modern" (1993). Rather than distinct fields that somehow keep nature and society pure, and thus too science, culture, and politics, Latour argues that our condition is one of hybrids that cannot be contained by our familiar categorical schemes and that are best described as imbroglios. If we want these imbroglios to seem a bit more tidy, we might call them networks.

Latour is also one of the originators of actor-network theory (ANT). A maligned and perhaps tragic intellectual construct, ANT works to produce a distinctive perspective on how things act in the world. One of the core aspects of ANT is that it grants symmetry to humans and nonhumans—that is, nonhumans are considered to be active agents (or "actants") in the construction of action and the maintenance of order. Agency, rather than being a quality of humans alone, is instead understood as a quality of a network of actors and actants, dynamic and changing, with authority and capacities being delegated across the components of a network. What ANT does is produce a view that takes seriously and attempts to empirically account for the role of objects, animals, equipment, regulations, databases, and all manner of nonhumans in constituting the world. Society and the social, then, are not human constructs alone but (again) hybrids composed together by humans and nonhumans alike. Although it has significant influence in

Science and Technology Studies (STS) and other fields, ANT is also widely criticized. For some the problem with ANT is epistemological (Collins and Yearley, 1992), whereas for others the problem is that ANT purportedly makes critical perspectives on power difficult to articulate (Whittle and Spicer, 2008). Regardless of one's perspective on the legitimacy of ANT, as a construct it provides a new way of understanding and analyzing action, which challenges common notions regarding the constitution of society, the social, and the presumed autonomy of humans in the making of the world.

Given Latour's commitment to understanding objects, their making, and their effects, his work has always had a connection to design. Since the 2000s, this has become explicit. In 2005 Latour and Peter Weibel curated the exhibition Making Things Public: Atmospheres of Design at the Center for Art and Media (ZKM) in Karlsruhe, Germany.[1] Arguably, this exhibition was as much a design exhibition as an art exhibition. The exhibition was accompanied by a massive book with the same title. The opening essay for the book, "From Realpolitik to Dingpolitik or How to Make Things Public" (2005), is part of a set of essays that includes "Why Has Critique Run Out of Steam? From Matters of Fact to Matters of Concern" (2004), which can be read as a (perhaps unintentional) foray by Latour into design theory. The others that comprise this constellation of design theory are "An Attempt at a Compositionist Manifesto" (2010) and "A Cautious Prometheus? A Few Steps Toward a Philosophy of Design (with Special Attention to Peter Sloterdijk)" (2008). The shared feature of all of these essays is that not only does Latour question limits of familiar humanities and social science critique throughout them, he also, implicitly and explicitly, suggests that design might take the place of or extend such familiar humanities and social science critique. Throughout these essays Latour makes a distinction between activities of revealing and activities of assembling and composing. More specifically, he argues that what is needed is a move from revealing historical or current conditions to composing new future conditions. This endeavor of composing is, I argue, an endeavor of design.

"Why Has Critique Run Out of Steam?" and a Few Other Texts of Concern

The essay "Why Has Critique Run Out of Steam?" is important to interaction design because in it Latour questions practices common to the humanities and social sciences and begins a conversation about new modes of action and scholarship. Latour challenges the idea that there is some notion of the real social setting or meaning that must be exposed and made known through traditional humanistic and social scientific inquiry. Instead, Latour asks us to attend to how issues take living form and come to be expressed as meaningful. Such exploration, which mingles inquiry with materiality and experience, could dialogically engage design in a transformative manner that gives new purpose to design and new form to the humanities and social sciences. Others before Latour have made similar claims about the possible relationships between design, the humanities, and the social sciences. Authors have discussed the notion of design as a liberal art (Buchanan, 1985) and the use of anthropological or sociological methods in design (Frascara, 2002), and have suggested that making objects might be a form of philosophical inquiry (Bogost, 2012). Latour, however, adds a twist: the critical impulse. This focus on critique and the critical is different and particularly salient. There has long been a critical component to design. However, since the 2000s, this critical component has garnered renewed and increased attention across multiple design communities. Latour's take on the critical impulse gives pause to this trend—it prompts us to consider the critical practices of design in relation to the critical impulse in the humanities and the social sciences, and to probe how these perspectives might inform each other. What is the productive purpose and form of critical inquiry through design, what are the limitations and potentials?

Latour begins "Why Has Critique Run Out of Steam?" in a reflexive mode, questioning not only the discipline he is committed to (STS / Sociology) but also his contributions to that discipline and more generally to social thought. He points out that although much of the work of STS was meant to help us understand the practices of science, perhaps even to better appreciate the practices of science, its most potent use may be the most virulent—skepticism regarding science used for political ends, for example, to question climate change. The fact that the social construction of facts is now a rhetorical commonplace employed to cast doubt and thwart action with regard to a pressing condition for which there are significant consequences, troubles Latour. He asks, "While we spent years trying to detect the real prejudices hidden behind the appearance of objective statements, do we now have to reveal the real objective and incontrovertible facts hidden behind the *illusion* of prejudices?" (227). His recourse to this situation is to question the familiar critical impulse and undertaking, and to suggest an alternative, or adjustment to the practice of critique.

For Latour, the problem is that critique is no longer enough, or perhaps even appropriate. Latour, quite critically, casts critique as a mode of inquiry concerned with revealing and debunking (e.g., the hidden operations of capitalism, patriarchy, and so forth); that is, with making that which is presumed to be invisible visible, and thereby performing intellectual appraisal and advancement. Latour's assessment of this endeavor is that it, alone, today, is a weak form of theory and action—there was a time when that was the work to be done, but doing that work and just that work today is insufficient. Part of the problem, and the solution, is captured in the second half of the essay title, "From Matters of Fact to Matters of Concern." Matters of fact are taken to be the domain of familiar critique: questioning what is a fact and how facts come to be. But attention only to matters of fact is limiting and tends to, according to Latour, focus on subtracting from reality (debunking) rather than contributing to reality (232).

What are matters of concern? Latour does little to elaborate a definition in this essay, but by drawing from other essays we can understand matters of concern as issues—contested "state of affairs." Their significance is predicated on more than veracity. Their significance is often an expression of the controversy they engender and that envelopes them. Climate change is an example of a matter of concern. Within it are facts, such as data about the change in the temperature of the ocean. But the issue of climate change is much more than these facts; it also includes a host of potential consequences and courses of action. The facts are important. But our concern should not be with the facts alone—our concern should be with the consequences and courses of action; with the question of what we are to do and how.

More interesting than the argument of why critique has run out of steam is the proposal of what is to be done now, in its place. What needs to be done, according to Latour, is to transform the role of the critic. As captured in perhaps the most often quoted lines of the essay he states, "The critic is not the one who debunks, but the one who assembles. The critic is not the one who lifts the rugs from under the feet of the naïve believers, but the one who offers the participants arenas in which to gather" (246). So, at least in this essay, it seems that Latour does not want to unequivocally dispatch the endeavor of critique, but rather to reanimate it with new purpose, to reconceptualize its practice.

Before proceeding, a few words on Latour's treatment of the critic and critique. It seems Latour dismisses the critic and critique "whole cloth." This is unfortunate because there are plenty of examples within the humanities and social sciences of critics and critiques that do not simply debunk and that do precisely the kind of assembling of spaces for gathering that Latour calls for. Such dismissal serves a rhetorical strategy—it helps makes the argument more direct—but it also misses an opportunity to engage the role of the critique and the practices of critique in a depth that might lead to useful insights about what constitutes generative criticism. In my interpretation of Latour, what I take to be the issue is not the humanities and social sciences writ large but rather a problematic stance within those disciplines that for far too long has adopted a hostile perspective to science and technology and moreover, has far too often seemed to dismiss, if not disdain, direct engagement with the practices of science and technology as a possible mode of critique.[2]

For our purposes, the essay, "Why Critique Has Run Out of Steam?" is important, but incomplete. It identifies a shortcoming in the social sciences and humanities and it makes a suggestion toward the next move, but it does not elucidate that move. Fortunately, Latour is prolific in his writing. In the essay "An Attempt at a Compositionist Manifesto" (2010), which can be read as a companion piece, he begins to outline a practice to counter those shortcomings and take scholarship in a new direction. "Compositionism," the name he gives to this practice, is an "alternative," a suggestive expression:

> Even though the word "composition" is a bit too long and windy, what is nice is that it underlines that things have to be put together (Latin *componere*) while retaining their heterogeneity. Also, it is connected with composure; it has clear roots in art, painting, music, theater, dance, and thus is associated with choreography and scenography; it is not too far from "compromise" and "compromising," retaining a certain diplomatic and prudential flavor. (473–474)

Although the practice of composition remains vague, characterized by allusion, it is differentiated from that of critique. Its vagueness may also be taken as a strength, as an aspect of this practice is, for Latour, "to move slowly, with caution and precaution" (487). And though he does not list design among the arts he alludes to, design has a role to play here.

Our direct connection to design (through Latour) is found in the transcript of his keynote lecture to the Design History Society, entitled "A Cautious Prometheus? A Few Steps Toward a Philosophy of Design (with Special Attention to Peter Sloterdijk)" (2008). Latour begins this lecture by exploring five notions of design that he considers to be advantageous qualities of its practice and that lend design to his project of being nonmodern: (1) there is a humility in design because there is nothing foundational in design; (2) design is about details not heroic narratives; (3) design is about meaning; (4) to design is always to redesign, that is, to act in response to; and (5) design necessarily involves ethics (3–7). In the final section of this lecture Latour muses that design could be a way of "drawing together," that is, of expressing matters of concern and providing a space of gathering within controversy. That is, design could be a way to do the work of the critic. So, when he states, "To put it more provocatively, I would argue that design is one of the terms that has replaced the word 'revolution'!" (2), he is not only saying that design has the capacity to transform; he is also casting design as a practice in line with his desire for a critical practice that extends common notions of critique.

What Are We to Make of This?

One way to interpret "Why Has Critique Run Out of Steam?" with regard to design is as a cautionary tale, a warning about the limits of familiar critical perspectives and practices. Such a warning might be appropriate, and certainly cautionary tales are worth hearing out. Critical design developed out of the work of Tony Dunne and Fiona Raby and is an identifiable, perhaps even established practice in design, with significant exhibitions, publications, and coverage in design journalism. Like ANT, critical design may be generally misunderstood and maligned by some, but it broadly offers alternative ways of framing the purpose of design. We can also witness an even broader practice of contemporary design that is critical, captured in exhibitions and accompanying publications such as *Forms of Inquiry* (Kyes and Owens, 2007) and *Design and the Elastic Mind* (Antonelli, 2008) and through the work of a range of individuals and collectives, notably including Natalie Jeremijenko, Bill Gaver and the Interaction Design Research Studio at Goldsmiths University of London, the Metahaven collective, and Laura Kurgan. Across the differences of form, medium, and content, the common feature of all these designers and collectives is that they treat the practices and products of design as a means to engage social issues in ways not reducible to the common, rote commodities or service instrumentalizations of design.

A similar cluster of critical work is found in human-computer interaction (HCI) research. Critical-reflective HCI is an ever-more-distinguishable corpus of work at the intersection of design, social science, computer science, and the humanities. What critical-reflective HCI purports to offer are modes of analysis and criticism informed by theories and methods from the humanities and interpretive social sciences, directed toward analyzing the practices and products of interactive systems design, including the assumptions, values, desires, and proclivities that undergird those practices and are exhibited through those products. A prime example of critical-reflective HCI is, in fact, this book. Significant contributions from critical-reflective HCI include the development of a practice of interaction criticism (J. Bardzell, 2011), critical investigations of sustainability (DiSalvo et al., 2009), and the articulation of feminism and post-colonialism with interactive systems design (S. Bardzell, 2010; Irani et al., 2010). Design plays an important role in critical-reflective HCI, both as a subject and as a medium of investigation. Although there is some overlap and exchange between these domains, they are certainly not identical—it is important to recognize that they tend to circulate through different networks of institutions and discursive formations, are informed by different histories, and contribute to different professional practices. But this expansiveness only serves to exemplify the breadth of the critical perspectives and practices in contemporary design.

What, then, is the relation between an essay admonishing the critical impulse and undertaking to these practices of interaction design (broadly construed) that take "critical" to be a defining component? First and foremost, we can read "Why Has Critique Run Out of Steam?" as a cautionary tale about the possible limits of critique, about the ways in which critique has the potential to devolve into a conservative and reductive project, its proponents' intentions notwithstanding. In addition, an important lesson to draw from reading that essay together with "An Attempt at a Compositionist Manifesto" is that critique is not the end but rather a point along a trajectory. The analysis of discourses and conditions, the identification of logics and implications, are an important part of a process of inquiry leading to the kind of gathering or assembly that Latour argues for. He might argue against them now, but he was not arguing against them in the past. And new conditions do come into being, new issues and controversies emerge that require critical analysis. So these activities should not be abandoned. But neither can they be considered sufficient in and of themselves. They need to be recognized as pursuits along a course of inquiry.

Once we realize that critique is not the end, we might ask what the ends are, or being less grandiose, at least what other points along this trajectory might be. There are two further points along this course of trajectory that are compelling for design: giving form to controversy and composing alternatives.

Giving Form to Controversy

Contemporary life, in both the public domain and in expert realms such as science and law, is filled with controversies: multiplicities of conflicting perspectives on issues, the consequences of issues, and how to act. Climate change, genetically modified organisms, fracking, reproductive technologies, big data—each of these are rife with pressing matters of concern that are debated and around which there is dissension, and through which we enact collective beliefs, desires, hopes, and values. Such controversy is central to Latour's work. Just as controversy is central to Latour, form-giving is central to design. Form, in this context, is not reducible to shape and volume, and certainly not reducible to style. Form is the experiential whole, the coherence of an artifact, interaction, environment, or system. There is an opportunity, recognized by Latour, for employing design to give form to controversy.

> In its long history, design practice has done a marvellous job of inventing the practical skills for drawing objects, from architecture drawing, mechanical blueprints, scale models, prototyping, etc. But that has always been missing from those marvellous drawings (designs in the literal sense) are an impression of the controversies and the many contradicting stake holders that are born within these. (Latour, 2008, 12)

Latour has pursued this endeavor of giving form to controversies in the Mapping Controversies on Science for Politics (MACOSPOL) project. Over the years, he has worked with designers, architects, computer scientists, and STS scholars to construct a platform for visualizing scientific and technical controversies.[3] To date this includes a collection of exemplary visualizations, case studies, and resources for producing visualizations (collections of publically available tools and data). By and large the forms of these visualizations are standard computational diagrams, but what is significant about them is the attempt to represent the varied actors and relations that comprise the controversy. Moreover, they express steps toward a new mode of inquiry, perhaps even a new mode of critique. But they don't quite get there. These visualizations are still a form of revealing—they function to show the constitution of a given controversy. They are worthwhile, but as with other forms of critique, we must move on.

Visualization might be the most obvious form of design representation, but it is not the only form of design expression.[4] It is in other modes of design that we should look to invent ways of giving form to controversy, particularly if the objective is to do more than reveal, but to assemble, to provide these spaces for gathering. Some design does this—it provides an object that functions as a space for gathering the factors of an issue and expressing them in the form of product. The products work to express the conditions of a future, or parallel, state in which the conditions of a controversy are made manifest. We might call this "critical design" or "speculative design" or "design fiction," and although the differences between those modes of design are important, equally important is the common work of communicating controversy in a compelling manner. By extending design beyond documentary or explanatory formats, we can begin to push toward a kind of engagement that should avoid the shortcomings of critique that Latour highlights.

Participatory design, a field at the outskirts of much of contemporary interaction design, also offers promise for this idea of moving beyond critique and working to draw together. New practices of participatory design are developing that extend its roots in work from the workplace into a wide range of public settings. Along with this expansion of site is an expansion of purpose. One of these is the development of the notion of "design things" (Binder et al., 2011; Ehn, 2008). This term—"design things"—refers to the construction of socio-material assemblages through methods of participatory and public design. These assemblages, then, enact controversy and may lead to the formation of publics.

The idea of design things is firmly rooted in the work of Latour. In his paper "Participation in Design Things," design scholar Pelle Ehn grounds the notion of "things" in Latour's use of the term and the history of the term: the *thing* as the historical site of public gathering to address matters of concern (Ehn, 2008). For Ehn and others committed to this idea "thinging" is a design endeavor that uses the methods and methodologies of participatory design to make matters of concern public (DiSalvo et al., 2014). Through such efforts, we can begin to move beyond representation toward enactment, beyond revealing to providing new courses of action. And through this, we can move from giving form to controversies to composing alternatives.

Composing Alternatives

Compositionism is what takes the place of critique. "Compositionism" seems to mean something like "design" for Latour, though he does not use that term. Perhaps using the term "design" would have unduly limited the range of possible action and the passage to participate in these new practices. Regardless, we can take compositionism as one possible design endeavor, as another point along a critical course of action.

Latour is vague about compositionism. One way to imagine compositionism in regards to design is as a way of experimenting with different sociotechnical configurations, in a deliberate attempt to explore the constitution of a controversy and how we might respond to controversies in new ways, for instance, with care. From the perspective of design, this requires a set of skills that go beyond those of visualization. If we can imagine a field of practice that combines interaction design and service design—when they escape the self-imposed boundaries of defining themselves in relation to a specific medium or technology—with methods from participatory design, we would be moving in the right direction. I call this practice "public design," because it is fundamentally concerned with the articulation of issues and working toward assembling—drawing together—those concerned with the consequences of an issue to experiment with new ways of living in the world, new ways of acting within controversy.

There are a range of technique and methods that design can contribute to this endeavor, including ways of prototyping hybrid systems (Kuznetsov et al., 2011), creating toolkits (Wylie et al., 2014), and infrastructuring (Le Dantec and DiSalvo, 2013). The Public Laboratory for Open Technology and Science (PLOTS) provides a relatively concise example. PLOTS provides a host of resources for what they term "civic science," which is the practice of science in the public realm, used to address public issues. These resources include technical platforms (hardware and software) for sensing, monitoring, and reporting on environmental conditions, forums for sharing techniques, and workshops that span the social and technical. As an organization PLOTS works with local advocacy groups and publishes in academic journals. In short, it exemplifies a sort of hybrid practice that, while it is critical of science, also enables participation in science and the enactment of new forms of what it means to do science, particularly in relation to matters of concern. This is a critical practice. Critique is implicit and at times explicit, but it is not limited to that. It does something more as well, not only through representational forms but also through events; even its organization draws together, making assemblies of various scales, in some cases public, that allow for both the enactment of a variety of values and desires and a reflection on the implications, consequences, possibilities of those configurations.

This idea of design as a practice that can engage with broader social issues—as an active force in the construction society—is not new. Certainly, it is not an idea discovered by Latour (nor does he claim that). What Latour provides those of us concerned with design is a new, an other, way to speak about the critical impulse in design. What these practices—of giving form to controversy and composing alternatives—do is label and provide examples of a reanimated critical impulse. Perhaps critique in the social sciences and humanities *has* run out of steam. But perhaps the issue is not with critique itself but with the engine—with the idea that critical endeavor needs be driven by the social sciences and the humanities. This is not a claim that design or the arts will do any better on their own. After all, there is a long tradition of critique from the arts and almost an equally long tradition of wringing our hands over the efficacy of that critique. No, what we see here is instead a truly hybrid critical practice between design, the humanities, and the social sciences. But it is incomplete. And we cannot deny that there are challenges, too.

Challenges

Given the discussion so far, it might seem that interaction design is doing fine and that we should just leave it alone to develop into some special hybrid practice that offers promise of a more engaged and productive form of critique. This is not entirely the case. The challenge is that, by and large, interaction design and the related field of human-computer interaction avoid controversy—these fields most often do not try to directly engage conflicting perspectives on issues or foster the kind of dissension and dissensus that characterizes controversy. And when design does engage controversy, it often reduces it from matters of concern to matters of fact. That is, it often tries to remove, or "design away," the controversial qualities of a situation, or to mitigate them in ways that render the situation less problematic. This has the effect of stifling the potential of design and this new mode of critique. And ironically, it also has the effect of reinstantiating the need for the very kind of revealing that Latour argues is no longer needed.

Sustainability provides a case in point. Since the 2000s the theme of sustainability has grown to comprise a significant field within interaction design and human-computer interaction. There are, for instance, subfields of sustainable interaction design (SID) and sustainable human-computer interaction (S-HCI) with publications, tracks at conferences, and so on. However, some scholars within critical reflective HCI (this author among them) point out that in many cases the issues of sustainability are largely removed from human-computer interaction design research and practice. The imbroglio of factors and relations, commitments, attachments, and consequences that constitute sustainability as a matter of concern are set aside. For instance, within HCI it is rare to find discussions of race, class, labor, or gender articulated with the issues of sustainability. Or, more generally, there is noticeably little discussion concerning how economic models and ideologies inform either the current conditions of sustainability or possible courses of action toward greater sustainment. And almost completely absent are perspectives that meaningful change is no longer possible. Instead, what we find is sustainability cast as a series of relatively bounded problems to be solved. Within this, mitigating resource consumption (e.g., use of water, electricity, etc.) is a common theme. Too often, then, design engagements with sustainability are reduced to information feedback devices, letting you know it would be best to turn off a light or wash your clothes at another time. In part, this series of moves, this simplification of sustainability, makes sense because it makes sustainability tractable. But at the same time, it limits the possible courses of action one might take with regard to the issue of sustainability.

Within critical reflective HCI there is a body of work that makes precisely this argument, elucidating the ways in which sustainability is construed and the limitations of that construal (Brynjarsdóttir et al., 2012). This is important work, but it also the kind of critique that troubles Latour. Here is a real tension. On the one hand, Latour is correct, revealing alone is insufficient. But revealing, or more generally the articulation and elucidation work of critique, is still necessary, precisely because there is a common move within the fields of design to transform matters of concern back into matters of fact. What is needed is the critical impulse to resist this move and to provide the means for productive action to be taken forward.

Within but also beyond sustainability we are witnessing a trend of designing for behavior change. This is another example of the abdication of the issue in favor of the (purportedly) tractable problem. Whether the situation is one of sustainability or health or governance, there is a growing body of work that suggests that we need to "nudge," "persuade," or otherwise benignly fool or coerce users into proper courses of action to address the pressing concerns of society. Behavior change has its place. There are cases where behavior change works and such initiatives and tactics may be a worthwhile component in an ecology of actions. But alone it is insufficient, and moreover, its predominance is indicative of the solutionist imperative that seems to drive too much design (Morozov, 2013) and attempts to reduce maters of concern to matters of fact. Rather than engage in the mess of relations between people, objects, organizations, and values—rather than engage controversy—the common reflex action in design is to frame the controversy as a problem at the scale of the individual, mostly rational, human actor. The repetition of this move across domains (that is, across matters of concern) signals fundamental problems with how the fields of interaction design and human-computer interaction conceptualize their own identities. Criticism of this is certainly necessary. But in taking the purpose of compositionism seriously, we also need to consider how we compose the practice design and take on the endeavor of composing new forms of design as a project itself. Perhaps the behavior that needs to be changed is the behavior of designers.

The growth and seeming resilience of critical practices in design and critical-reflective HCI provide a pluralistic and vibrant approach to critically informed and inspired design practice, research, and scholarship. Efforts should be made to develop and further this work. At the same time, the limitations of critique outlined in "Why Has Critique Run Out of Steam?" should be heeded with regard to design. If we are scholars and designers and critics committed to critique we must work to make sure that we continue to consider even our own perspective and practices open to contest. For those committed to the critical impulse in and through design, we must remember, on occasion, to turn the critical impulse back on ourselves, to question, challenge, and redirect our own efforts. Critique should be a lively endeavor, always shifting in a dialogic exchange with its subjects and context. It is the responsibility of those who practice critique to keep it animated.

Notes

1. Full disclosure: The author was included in that exhibition.

2. Thanks to Jeffrey Bardzell for his help in articulating this point.

3. See http://www.mappingcontroversies.net (accessed March 5, 2015).

4. Design scholar Pelle Ehn made a passing comment similar to this with regard to the Mapping Controversies project in a panel presentation at the 2012 European Society for the Study of Science and Technology. This is not surprising given that Ehn's work is among those that explicitly take up this challenge of giving form to controversy and do so through modes other than visualization.

References

Antonelli, P. (2008) *Design and the Elastic Mind.* New York: Museum of Modern Art Press.

Bardzell, J. (2011) "Interaction Criticism: An Introduction to the Practice." *Interacting with Computers* 23 (6): 604–621.

Bardzell. S. (2010) "Feminist HCI: Taking Stock and Outlining an Agenda for Design." *Proceedings of the SIGCHI Conference on Human Factors in Computing Systems (CHI'10).* New York: ACM, 1301–1310.

Binder, T., G. De Michelis, P. Ehn, G. Jacucci, P. Linde, and I. Wagner. (2011) *Design Things.* Cambridge, MA: MIT Press.

Bogost, I. (2012) *Alien Phenomenology, or What It's Like to Be a Thing.* Minneapolis: University of Minnesota Press.

Brynjarsdóttir, H., M. Håkansson, J. Pierce, E. Baumer, C. DiSalvo, and P. Sengers. (2012) "Sustainably Unpersuaded: How Persuasion Narrows Our Vision of Sustainability." *Proceedings of the SIGCHI Conference on Human Factors in Computing Systems (CHI'12).* New York: ACM, 947–956.

Buchanan, R. (1985) "Declaration by Design: Rhetoric, Argument, and Demonstration in Design Practice." *Design Issues* 2 (1): 4–22.

Collins, H. M., and S. Yearley. (1992) "Epistemological Chicken." In *Science as Practice and Culture,* edited by A. Pickering, 301–326. Chicago: University of Chicago Press.

DiSalvo, C., K. Boehner, N. A. Knouf, and P. Sengers. (2009) "Nourishing the Ground for Sustainable HCI: Considerations from Ecologically Engaged Art." *Proceedings of the SIGCHI Conference on Human Factors in Computing Systems (CHI'09).* New York: ACM, 385–394.

DiSalvo, C., J. Lukens, T. Lodato, T. Jenkins, and T. Kim. (2014) "Making Public Things: How HCI Design Can Express Matters of Concern." *Proceedings of the SIGCHI Conference on Human Factors in Computing Systems (CHI'14).* New York: AMC, 2397–2406.

Ehn, P. (2008) "Participation in Design Things." *Proceedings of the Tenth Anniversary Conference on Participatory Design (PDC '08)*. Indianapolis: Indiana University, 92–101.

Frascara, J., ed. (2002) *Design and the Social Sciences: Making Connections*. London: CRC Press.

Irani, L., J. Vertesi, P. Dourish, K. Philip, and R. E. Grinter. (2010) "Postcolonial Computing: A Lens on Design and Development." *Proceedings of the SIGCHI Conference on Human Factors in Computing Systems (CHI'10)*. New York: AMC, 1311–1320.

Kuznetsov, S., G. Davis, J. Cheung, and E. Paulos. (2011) "Ceci n'est pas une Pipe Bombe: Authoring Urban Landscapes with Air Quality Sensors." *Proceedings of the SIGCHI Conference on Human Factors in Computing Systems (CHI'11)*. New York: ACM, 2375–2384.

Kyes, Z., and M. Owens, eds. (2007) *Forms of Inquiry*. London: Architectural Association Press.

Latour, B. (1988) *The Pasteurization of France*. Cambridge, MA: Harvard University Press.

Latour, B. (1993) *We Have Never Been Modern*. Trans. Catherine Porter. Cambridge, MA: Harvard University Press.

Latour, B. (1996) *Aramis, or the Love of Technology*. Cambridge, MA: Harvard University Press.

Latour, B. (2004) "Why Has Critique Run Out of Steam? From Matters of Fact to Matters of Concern." *Critical Inquiry* 30 (2): 225–248.

Latour, B. (2005) "From Realpolitik to Dingpolitik: An Introduction to *Making Things Public*." In *Making Things Public: Atmospheres of Democracy*, edited by B. Latour and P. Weibel, 4–31. Cambridge, MA: MIT Press.

Latour, B. (2008) "A Cautious Prometheus? A Few Steps toward a Philosophy of Design (with Special Attention to Peter Sloterdijk)." Keynote lecture for the Networks of Design meeting of the Design History Society, Falmouth, Cornwall. *Proceedings of the 2008 Annual International Conference of the Design History Society*, edited by F. Hackne, J. Glynne, and V. Minto. Irvine, CA: Universal Publishers, 2–10. Accessed April 13, 2013. http://www.bruno-latour.fr/sites/default/files/112-DESIGN-CORNWALL-GB.pdf.

Latour, B. (2010a) "An Attempt at a 'Compositionist Manifesto.'" *New Literary History* 41 (3): 471–490.

Latour, B. (2010b) *The Making of Law: An Ethnography of the Conseil d'Etat*, translated by M. Brilman and A. Pottage. Cambridge: Polity.

Latour, B., and S. Woolgar. (1986) *Laboratory Life: The Construction of Scientific Facts*. Princeton, NJ: Princeton University Press.

Le Dantec, C. A., and C. DiSalvo. (2013) "Infrastructuring and the Formation of Publics in Participatory Design." *Social Studies of Science* 43 (2): 241–264.

Morozov, E. (2013) *To Save Everything, Click Here: The Folly of Technological Solutionism*. New York: Public Affairs.

Restivo, S. (2011) *Red, Black, and Objective: Science, Sociology, and Anarchism.* Farnham, UK: Ashgate.

Whittle, A., and A. Spicer. (2008) "Is Actor Network Theory Critique?" *Organization Studies* 29 (4): 611–629.

Wylie, S. A., K. Jalbert, S. Dosemagen, and M. Ratto. (2014) "Institutions for Civic Technoscience: How Critical Making Is Transforming Environmental Research." *Information Society* 30 (2): 116–126.

25 The Politics of Amnesia (2003)

Terry Eagleton

The golden age of cultural theory is long past. The pioneering works of Jacques Lacan, Claude Lévi-Strauss, Louis Althusser, Roland Barthes and Michel Foucault are several decades behind us. So are the path-breaking early writings of Raymond Williams, Luce Irigaray, Pierre Bourdieu, Julia Kristeva, Jacques Derrida, Hélène Cixous, Jurgen Habermas, Fredric Jameson and Edward Said. Not much that has been written since has matched the ambitiousness and originality of these founding mothers and fathers. Some of them have since been struck down. Fate pushed Roland Barthes under a Parisian laundry van, and afflicted Michel Foucault with Aids. It dispatched Lacan, Williams and Bourdieu, and banished Louis Althusser to a psychiatric hospital for the murder of his wife. It seemed that God was not a structuralist.

Many of the ideas of these thinkers remain of incomparable value. Some of them are still producing work of major importance. Those to whom the title of this book suggests that "theory" is now over, and that we can all relievedly return to an age of pre-theoretical innocence, are in for a disappointment. There can be no going back to an age when it was enough to pronounce Keats delectable or Milton a doughty spirit. It is not as though the whole project was a ghastly mistake on which some merciful soul has now blown the whistle, so that we can all return to whatever it was we were doing before Ferdinand de Saussure heaved over the horizon. If theory means a reasonably systematic reflection on our guiding assumptions, it remains as indispensable as ever. But we are living now in the aftermath of what one might call high theory, in an age which, having grown rich on the insights of thinkers like Althusser, Barthes and Derrida, has also in some ways moved beyond them.

The generation which followed after these path-breaking figures did what generations which follow after usually do. They developed the original ideas, added to them, criticized them and applied them. Those who can, think up feminism or structuralism; those who can't, apply such insights to *Moby-Dick* or *The Cat in the Hat*. But the new generation came up with no comparable body of ideas of its own. The older generation had proved a hard act to follow. No doubt the new century will in time give birth to its own clutch of gurus. For the moment, however, we are still trading on the past—and this in a world which has changed dramatically since Foucault and Lacan first settled to their typewriters. What kind of fresh thinking does the new era demand?

Before we can answer this question, we need to take stock of where we are. Structuralism, Marxism, post-structuralism and the like are no longer the sexy topics they were. What is sexy instead is sex. On the wilder shores of academia, an interest in French philosophy has given way to a fascination with French kissing. In some cultural circles, the politics of masturbation exert far more fascination than the politics of the Middle East. Socialism has lost out to sado-masochism. Among students of culture, the body is an immensely fashionable topic, but it is usually the erotic body, not the famished one. There is a keen interest in coupling bodies, but not in labouring ones. Quietly-spoken middle-class students huddle diligently in libraries, at work on sensationalist subjects like vampirism and eye-gouging, cyborgs and porno movies.

Nothing could be more understandable. To work on the literature of latex or the political implications of navel-piercing is to take literally the wise old adage that study should be fun. It is rather like writing your Master's thesis on the comparative flavour of malt whiskies, or on the phenomenology of lying in bed all day. It creates a seamless continuity between the intellect and everyday life. There are advantages in being able to write your Ph.D. thesis without stirring from in front of the TV set. In the old days, rock music was a distraction from your studies; now it may well be what you are studying. Intellectual matters are no longer an ivory-tower affair, but belong to the world of media and shopping malls, bedrooms and brothels. As such, they re-join everyday life—but only at the risk of losing their ability to subject it to critique.

Today, the old fogeys who work on classical allusions in Milton look askance on the Young Turks who are deep in incest and cyber-feminism. The bright young things who pen essays on foot fetishism or the history of the codpiece eye with suspicion the scrawny old scholars who dare to maintain that Jane Austen is greater than Jeffrey Archer. One zealous orthodoxy gives way to another. Whereas in the old days you could be drummed out of your student drinking club if you failed to spot a metonym in Robert Herrick, you might today be regarded as an unspeakable nerd for having heard of either metonyms or Herrick in the first place.

This trivialization of sexuality is especially ironic. For one of the towering achievements of cultural theory has been to establish gender and sexuality as legitimate objects of study, as well as matters of insistent political importance. It is remarkable how intellectual life for centuries was conducted on the tacit assumption that human beings had no genitals. (Intellectuals also behaved as though men and women lacked stomachs. As the philosopher Emmanuel Levinas remarked of Martin Heidegger's rather lofty concept of *Dasein*, meaning the kind of existence peculiar to human beings: "*Dasein* does not eat.") Friedrich Nietzsche once commented that whenever anybody speaks crudely of a human being as a belly with two needs and a head with one, the lover of knowledge should listen carefully. In an historic advance, sexuality is now firmly established within academic life as one of the keystones of human culture. We have come to acknowledge that human existence is at least as much about fantasy and desire as it is about truth and reason. It is just that cultural theory is at present behaving rather like a celibate middle-aged professor who has stumbled absent-mindedly upon sex and is frenetically making up for lost time.

Another historic gain of cultural theory has been to establish that popular culture is also worth studying. With some honourable exceptions, traditional scholarship has for centuries ignored the everyday life of the common people. Indeed, it was life itself it used to ignore, not just the everyday. In some traditionalist universities not long ago, you could not research on authors who were still alive. This was a great incentive to slip a knife between their ribs one foggy evening, or a remarkable test of patience if your chosen novelist was in rude health and only thirty-four. You certainly could not research on anything you saw around you every day, which was by definition not worth studying. Most things that were deemed suitable for study in the humanities were not visible, like nail-clippings or Jack Nicholson, but invisible, like Stendhal, the concept of sovereignty or the sinuous elegance of Leibniz's notion of the monad. Today it is generally recognized that everyday life is quite as intricate, unfathomable, obscure and occasionally tedious as Wagner, and thus eminently worth investigating. In the old days, the test of what was worth studying was quite often how futile, monotonous and esoteric it was. In some circles today, it is whether it is something you and your friends do in the evenings. Students once wrote uncritical, reverential essays on Flaubert, but all that has been transformed. Nowadays they write uncritical, reverential essays on *Friends*.

Even so, the advent of sexuality and popular culture as kosher subjects of study has put paid to one powerful myth. It has helped to demolish the puritan dogma that seriousness is one thing and pleasure another. The puritan mistakes pleasure for frivolity because he mistakes seriousness for solemnity. Pleasure falls outside the realm of knowledge, and thus is dangerously anarchic. On this view, to *study* pleasure would be like chemically analysing champagne rather than drinking the stuff. The puritan does not see that pleasure and seriousness are related in this sense: that finding out how life can become more pleasant for more people is a serious business. Traditionally, it is known as moral discourse. But "political" discourse would do just as well.

Yet pleasure, a buzz word for contemporary culture, has its limits too. Finding out how to make life more pleasant is not always pleasant. Like all scientific inquiry, it requires patience, self-discipline and an inexhaustible capacity to be bored. In any case, the hedonist who embraces pleasure as the ultimate reality is often just the puritan in full-throated rebellion. Both of them are usually obsessed with sex. Both of them equate truth with earnestness. Old-style puritanical capitalism forbade us to enjoy ourselves, since once we had acquired a taste for the stuff we would probably never see the inside of the workplace again. Sigmund Freud held that if it were not for what he called the reality principle, we would simply lie around the place all day in various mildly scandalous states of *jouissance*. A more canny, consumerist kind of capitalism, however, persuades us to indulge our senses and gratify ourselves as shamelessly as possible. In that way we will not only consume more goods; we will also identify our own fulfilment with the survival of the system. Anyone who fails to wallow orgasmically in sensual delight will be visited late at night by a terrifying thug known as the superego, whose penalty for such non-enjoyment is atrocious guilt. But since this ruffian also tortures us for having a good time, one might as well take the ha'pence with the kicks and enjoy oneself anyway.

So there is nothing inherently subversive about pleasure. On the contrary, as Karl Marx recognized, it is a thoroughly aristocratic creed. The traditional English gentleman was so averse to unpleasurable labour that he could not even be bothered to articulate properly. Hence the patrician slur and drawl. Aristotle believed that being human was something you had to get good at through constant practice, like learning Catalan or playing the bagpipes; whereas if the English gentleman was virtuous, as he occasionally deigned to be, his goodness was purely spontaneous. Moral effort was for merchants and clerks.

Not all students of culture are blind to the Western narcissism involved in working on the history of pubic hair while half the world's population lacks adequate sanitation and survives on less than two dollars a day. Indeed, the most flourishing sector of cultural studies today is so-called post-colonial studies, which deals with just this dire condition. Like the discourse of gender and sexuality, it has been one of the most precious achievements of cultural theory. Yet these ideas have thrived among new generations who, for no fault of their own, can remember little of world-shaking political importance. Before the advent of the so-called war on terrorism, it seemed as though there might be nothing more momentous for young Europeans to recount to their grandchildren than the advent of the euro. Over the dreary decades of post-1970s conservatism, the historical sense had grown increasingly blunted, as it suited those in power that we should be able to imagine no alternative to the present. The future would simply be the present infinitely repeated—or, as the postmodernist remarked, "the present plus more options." There are now those who piously insist on "historicizing" and who seem to believe that anything that happened before 1980 is ancient history.

To live in interesting times is not, to be sure, an unmixed blessing. It is no particular consolation to be able to recall the Holocaust, or to have lived through the Vietnam war. Innocence and amnesia have their advantages. There is no point in mourning the blissful days when you could have your skull fractured by the police every weekend in Hyde Park. To recall a world-shaking political history is also, for the political left at least, to recall what is for the most part a history of defeat. In any case, a new and ominous phase of global politics has now opened, which not even the most cloistered of academics will be able to ignore. Even so, what has proved most damaging, at least before the emergence of the anti-capitalist movement, is the absence of memories of collective, and effective, political action. It is this which has warped so many contemporary cultural ideas out of shape. There is a historical vortex at the centre of our thought which drags it out of true.

Much of the world as we know it, despite its solid, well-upholstered appearance, is of recent vintage. It was thrown up by the tidal waves of revolutionary nationalism which swept the globe in the period after the Second World War, tearing one nation after another from the grip of Western colonialism. The Allies' struggle in the Second World War was itself a successful collaborative action on a scale unprecedented in human history—one which crushed a malevolent fascism at the heart of Europe, and in doing so laid some of the foundations of the world we know today. Much of the global community we see around us was formed, fairly recently, by collective revolutionary projects—projects which were launched often enough by the weak and hungry, but which nevertheless proved successful in dislodging their predatory foreign rulers. Indeed, the Western empires which those revolutions dismantled were themselves for the most part the product of revolutions. It is just that they were those most victorious revolutions of all—the ones which we have forgotten ever took place. And that usually means the ones which produced the likes of us. Other people's revolutions are always more eye-catching than one's own.

But it is one thing to make a revolution, and another to sustain it. Indeed, for the most eminent revolutionary leader of the twentieth century, what brought some revolutions to birth in the first place was also what was responsible for their ultimate downfall. Vladimir Lenin believed that it was the very backwardness of Tsarist Russia which had helped to make the Bolshevik revolution possible. Russia was a nation poor in the kind of civic institutions which secure the loyalty of citizens to the state, and thus help to stave off political insurrection. Its power was centralized rather than diffuse, coercive rather than consensual: it was concentrated in the state machine, so that to overthrow that was to seize sovereignty at a stroke. But this very same poverty and backwardness helped to scupper the revolution once it had been made. You could not build socialism in an economic back-water, encircled by stronger, politically hostile powers, among a mass of unskilled, illiterate workers and peasants without traditions of social organization and democratic self-government. The attempt to do so called for the strong-armed measures of Stalinism, which ended up subverting the very socialism it was trying to construct.

Something of the same fate afflicted many of those nations who managed in the twentieth century to free themselves from Western colonial rule. In a tragic irony, socialism proved least possible where it was most necessary. Indeed, post-colonial theory first emerged in the wake of the failure of Third World nations to go it alone. It marked the end of the era of Third World revolutions, and the first glimmerings of what we now know as globalization. In the 1950s and 60s, a series of liberation movements, led by the nationalist middle classes, had thrown off their colonial masters in the name of political sovereignty and economic independence. By harnessing the demands of an impoverished people to these goals, the Third World elites could install themselves in power on the back of popular discontent. Once ensconced there, they would need to engage in an ungainly balancing act between radical pressures from below and global market forces from outside.

Marxism, an internationalist current to its core, lent its support to these movements, respecting their demand for political autonomy and seeing in them a grievous setback to world capitalism. But many Marxists harboured few illusions about the aspiring middle-class elites who spearheaded these nationalist currents. Unlike the more sentimental brands of post-colonialism, most Marxism did not assume that "Third World" meant good and "First World" bad. They insisted rather on a class-analysis of colonial and post-colonial politics themselves.

Isolated, poverty-stricken and poor in civic, liberal or democratic traditions, some of these regimes found themselves taking the Stalinist path into crippling isolation. Others had to acknowledge that they could not go it alone—that political sovereignty had brought with it no authentic economic self-government, and could never do so in a West-dominated world. As the world capitalist crisis deepened from the early 1970s onwards, and as a number of Third World nations sank further into stagnation and corruption, the aggressive restructurings of a Western capitalism fallen upon hard times finally put paid to illusions of national-revolutionary independence. "Third Worldism" accordingly gave way to "post-colonialism." Edward Said's magisterial *Orientalism*, published in 1978, marked this transition in intellectual terms, despite its author's understandable reservations about much of the post-colonial theory which was to follow in its wake. The book appeared at the turning-point of the fortunes of the international left.

Given the partial failure of national revolution in the so-called Third World, post-colonial theory was wary of all talk of nationhood. Theorists who were either too young or too obtuse to recall that nationalism had been in its time an astonishingly effective anti-colonial force could find in it nothing but a benighted chauvinism or ethnic supremacism. Instead, much post-colonial thought focused on the cosmopolitan dimensions of a world in which post-colonial states were being sucked inexorably into the orbit of global capital. In doing so, it reflected a genuine reality. But in rejecting the idea of nationhood, it also tended to jettison the notion of class, which had been so closely bound up with the revolutionary nation. Most of the new theorists were not only "post" colonialism, but "post" the revolutionary impetus which had given birth to the new nations in the first place. If those nation-states had partly failed, unable to get on terms with the affluent capitalist world, then to look beyond the nation seemed to mean looking beyond class as well—and this at a time when capitalism was more powerful and predatory than ever.

It is true that the revolutionary nationalists had in a sense looked beyond class themselves. By rallying the national people, they could forge a spurious unity out of conflicting class interests. The middle classes had rather more to gain from national independence than hard-pressed workers and peasants, who would simply find themselves presented with a native rather than a foreign set of exploiters. Even so, this unity was not entirely bogus. If the idea of the nation was a displacement of class conflict, it also served to give it shape. If it fostered some dangerous illusions, it also helped to turn the world upside down. Indeed, revolutionary nationalism was by far the most successful radical tide of the twentieth century. In one sense, different groups and classes in the Third World indeed faced a common Western antagonist. The nation had become the major form which the class struggle against this antagonist had assumed. It was, to be sure, a narrow, distorting form, and in the end would prove woefully inadequate. *The Communist Manifesto* observes that the class struggle first of all takes a national form, but goes well beyond this form in its content. Even so, the nation was a way of rallying different social classes—peasants, workers, students, intellectuals—against the colonial powers which stood in the way of their independence. And it had a powerful argument in its favour: success, at least to begin with.

Some of the new theory, by contrast, saw itself as shifting attention from class to colonialism—as though colonialism and post-colonialism were not themselves matters of class! In its Eurocentric way, it identified class conflict with the West alone, or saw it only in national terms. For socialists, by contrast, anti-colonial struggle was class struggle too: it represented a strike against the power of international capital, which had not been slow to respond to that challenge with sustained military violence. It was a battle between Western capital and the sweated labourers of the world. But because this class conflict had been framed in national terms, it helped to pave the way for the dwindling of the very idea of class in later post-colonial writing. This is one sense in which, as we shall see later, the highpoint of radical ideas in the mid-twentieth century was also the beginning of their downward curve.

Much post-colonial theory shifted the focus from class and nation to ethnicity. This meant among other things that the distinctive problems of post-colonial culture were often falsely assimilated to the very different question of Western "identity politics." Since ethnicity is largely a cultural affair, this shift of focus was also one from politics to culture. In some ways, this reflected real changes in the world. But it also helped to depoliticize the question of post-colonialism, and inflate the role of culture within it, in ways which chimed with the new, post-revolutionary climate in the West itself. "Liberation" was no longer in the air, and by the end of the 1970s "emancipation" had a quaintly antiquated ring to it. It seemed, then, that having drawn a blank at home, the Western left was now hunting for its stomping ground abroad. In travelling abroad, however, it brought with it in its luggage the burgeoning Western obsession with culture.

Even so, Third World revolutions had testified in their own way to the power of collective action. So in a different way did the militant actions of the Western labour movements, which in the 1970s helped to bring down a British government. So, too, did the peace and student movements of the late 1960s and early 1970s, which played a central part in ending the Vietnam war. Much recent cultural theory, however, has little recollection of all this. From its viewpoint, collective action means launching wars against weaker nations rather than bringing such adventures to a merciful end. In a world which has witnessed the rise and fall of various brutally totalitarian regimes, the whole idea of collective life comes to seem vaguely discredited.

For some postmodern thought, consensus is tyrannical and solidarity nothing but soulless uniformity.[1] But whereas liberals oppose this conformity with the individual, postmodernists, some of whom doubt the very reality of the individual, counter it instead with margins and minorities. It is what stands askew to society as a whole—the marginal, mad, deviant, perverse, transgressive—which is most politically fertile. There can be little value in mainstream social life. And this, ironically, is just the kind of elitist, monolithic viewpoint which postmodernists find most disagreeable in their conservative opponents.

In retrieving what orthodox culture has pushed to the margins, cultural studies has done vital work. Margins can be unspeakably painful places to be, and there are few more honourable tasks for students of culture than to help create a space in which the dumped and disregarded can find a tongue. It is no longer quite so easy to claim that there is nothing to ethnic art but pounding on oil drums or knocking a couple of bones together. Feminism has not only transformed the cultural landscape but, as we shall see later, has become the very model of morality for our time. Meanwhile, those white males who, unfortunately for themselves, are not quite dead have been metaphorically strung upside down from the lamp-posts, while the ill-gotten coins cascading from their pockets have been used to finance community arts projects.

What is under assault here is the *normative*. Majority social life on this view is a matter of norms and conventions, and therefore inherently oppressive. Only the marginal, perverse and aberrant can escape this dreary regimenting. Norms are oppressive because they mould uniquely different individuals to the same shape. As the poet William Blake writes, "One Law for the Lion & Ox is oppression." Liberals accept this normalizing as necessary if everyone is to be granted the same life-chances to fulfil their unique personalities. It will, in short, lead to consequences which undercut it. Libertarians, however, are less resigned to this levelling. In this, they are ironically close to conservatives. Sanguine libertarians like Oscar Wilde dream of a future society in which everyone will be free to be their incomparable selves. For them, there can be no question of weighing and measuring individuals, any more than you could compare the concept of envy with a parrot.

By contrast, pessimistic or shamefaced libertarians like Jacques Derrida and Michel Foucault see that norms are inescapable as soon as we open our mouths. The word "ketch," which as the reader will know means a two-masted fore-and-aft rigged sailing boat with a mizzen mast stepped forward of the rudder and smaller than its foremast, sounds precise enough, but it has to stretch to cover all sorts of individual crafts of this general kind, each with its own peculiarities. Language levels things down. It is normative all the way down. To say "leaf" implies that two incomparably different bits of vegetable matter are one and the same. To say "here" homogenizes all sorts of richly diverse places.

Thinkers like Foucault and Derrida chafe against these equivalences, even if they accept them as unavoidable. They would like a world made entirely out of differences. Indeed, like their great mentor Nietzsche, they think the world *is* made entirely out of differences, but that we need to fashion identities in order to get by. It is true that nobody in a world of pure differences would be able to say anything intelligible—that there could be no poetry, road signs, love letters or log sheets, as well as no statements that everything is uniquely different from everything else. But this is simply the price one would have to pay for not being constrained by the behaviour of others, like paying that little bit extra for a first-class rail ticket.

It is a mistake, however, to believe that norms are always restrictive. In fact it is a crass Romantic delusion. It is normative in our kind of society that people do not throw themselves with a hoarse cry on total strangers and amputate their legs. It is conventional that child murderers are punished, that working men and women may withdraw their labour, and that ambulances speeding to a traffic accident should not be impeded just for the hell of it. Anyone who feels oppressed by all this must be seriously oversensitive. Only an intellectual who has overdosed on abstraction could be dim enough to imagine that whatever bends a norm is politically radical.

Those who believe that normativity is always negative are also likely to hold that authority is always suspect. In this, they differ from radicals, who respect the authority of those with long experience of fighting injustice, or of laws which safeguard people's physical integrity or working conditions. Similarly, some modern-day cultural thinkers seem to believe that minorities are always more vibrant than majorities. It is not the most popular of beliefs among the disfigured victims of Basque separatism. Some fascist groups, however, may be flattered to hear it, along with UFO buffs and Seventh Day Adventists. It was majorities, not minorities, which confounded imperial power in India and brought down apartheid. Those who oppose norms, authority and majorities as such are abstract universalists, even though most of them oppose abstract universalism as well.

The postmodern prejudice against norms, unities and consensuses is a politically catastrophic one. It is also remarkably dim-witted. But it does not only spring from having precious few examples of political solidarity to remember. It also reflects a real social change. It is one result of the apparent disintegration of old-fashioned bourgeois society into a host of sub-cultures. One of the historic developments of our age has been the decline of the traditional middle class. As Perry Anderson has argued, the solid, civilized, morally upright bourgeoisie which managed to survive the Second World War has given way in our time to "starlet princesses and sleazeball presidents, beds for rent in the official residence and bribes for killer ads, disneyfication of protocols and tarantinization of practices." The "solid (bourgeois) amphitheatre," Anderson writes with colourful contempt, has yielded to "an aquarium of floating, evanescent forms—the projectors and managers, auditors and janitors, administrators and speculators of contemporary capital: functions of a monetary universe that knows no social fixities and stable identities."[2] It is this lack of stable identities which for some cultural theory today is the last word in radicalism. Instability of identity is "subversive"—a claim which it would be interesting to test out among the socially dumped and disregarded.

In this social order, then, you can no longer have bohemian rebels or revolutionary avant-gardes because they no longer have anything to blow up. Their top-hatted, frock-coated, easily outraged enemy has evaporated. Instead, the non-normative has become the norm. Nowadays, it is not just anarchists for whom anything goes, but starlets, newspaper editors, stockbrokers and corporation executives. The norm now is money; but since money has absolutely no principles or identity of its own, it is no kind of norm at all. It is utterly promiscuous, and will happily tag along with the highest bidder. It is infinitely adaptive to the most bizarre or extremist of situations, and like the Queen has no opinions of its own about anything.

It seems, then, as though we have moved from the high-minded hypocrisy of the old middle classes to the low-minded effrontery of the new ones. We have shifted from a national culture with a single set of rules to a motley assortment of sub-cultures, each one at an angle to the others. This, of course, is an exaggeration. The old regime was never as unified as that, nor the new one as fragmented. There are still some powerful collective norms at work in it. But it is true, by and large, that our new ruling elite consists increasingly of people who snort cocaine rather than people who look like Herbert Asquith or Marcel Proust.

The current of cultural experiment we know as modernism was fortunate in this respect. Rimbaud, Picasso and Bertolt Brecht still had a classical bourgeoisie to be rude about. But its offspring, postmodernism, has not. It is just that it seems not to have noticed the fact, perhaps because it is too embarrassing to acknowledge. Postmodernism seems at times to behave as though the classical bourgeoisie is alive and well, and thus finds itself living in the past. It spends much of its time assailing absolute truth, objectivity, timeless moral values, scientific inquiry and a belief in historical progress. It calls into question the autonomy of the individual, inflexible social and sexual norms, and the belief that there are firm foundations to the world. Since all of these values belong to a bourgeois world on the wane, this is rather like firing off irascible letters to the press about the horse-riding Huns or marauding Carthaginians who have taken over the Home Counties.

This is not to say that these beliefs do not still have force. In places like Ulster and Utah, they are riding high. But nobody on Wall Street and few in Fleet Street believe in absolute truth and unimpeachable foundations. A lot of scientists are fairly sceptical about science, seeing it as much more of a hit-and-miss, rule-of-thumb affair than the gullible layperson imagines. It is people in the humanities who still naïvely think that scientists consider themselves the white-coated custodians of absolute truth, and so waste a lot of time trying to discredit them. Humanists have always been sniffy about scientists. It is just that they used to despise them for snobbish reasons, and now do so for sceptical ones. Few of the people who believe in absolute moral values in theory do so in practice. They are known mainly as politicians and business executives. Conversely, some of the people who might be expected to believe in absolute values believe in nothing of the kind, like moral philosophers and clap-happy clerics. And though some genetically upbeat Americans may still have faith in progress, a huge number of constitutionally downbeat Europeans do not.

But it is not only the traditional middle class which has faded from view. It is also the traditional working class. And since the working class stood for political solidarity, it is scarcely surprising that we should now have a form of radicalism which is deeply distrustful of all that. Postmodernism does not believe in individualism, since it does not believe in individuals; but it does not pin much faith in working-class community either. Instead, it puts its trust in pluralism—in a social order which is as diverse and inclusive as possible. The problem with this as a radical case is that there is not much in it with which Prince Charles would disagree. It is true that capitalism quite often creates divisions and exclusions for its own purposes. Either that, or it draws upon ones which already exist. And these exclusions can be profoundly hurtful for a great many people. Whole masses of men and women have suffered the misery and indignity of second-class citizenship. In principle, however, capitalism is an impeccably inclusive creed: it really doesn't care who it exploits. It is admirably egalitarian in its readiness to do down just about anyone. It is prepared to rub shoulders with any old victim, however unappetizing. Most of the time, at least, it is eager to mix together as many diverse cultures as possible, so that it can peddle its commodities to them all.

In the generously humanistic spirit of the ancient poet, this system regards nothing human as alien to it. In its hunt for profit, it will travel any distance, endure any hardship, shack up with the most obnoxious of companions, suffer the most abominable humiliations, tolerate the most tasteless wallpaper and cheerfully betray its next of kin. It is capitalism which is disinterested, not dons. When it comes to consumers who wear turbans and those who do not, those who sport flamboyant crimson waistcoats and those who wear nothing but a loincloth, it is sublimely even-handed. It has the scorn for hierarchies of a truculent adolescent, and the zeal to pick and mix of an American diner. It thrives on bursting bounds and slaying sacred cows. Its desire is unslakeable and its space infinite. Its law is the flouting of all limits, which makes law indistinguishable from criminality. In its sublime ambition and extravagant transgressions, it makes its most shaggily anarchic critics look staid and suburban.

There are other, familiar problems with the idea of inclusiveness, which need not detain us too long. Who gets to decide who gets included? Who—the Groucho Marx query—would want to be included in this set-up anyway? If marginality is as fertile, subversive a place as postmodern thinkers tend to suggest, why would they want to abolish it? Anyway, what if there is no clear division between margins and majority? For a socialist, the true scandal of the present world is that almost everyone in it is banished to the margins. As far as the transnational corporations go, great masses of men and women are really neither here nor there. Whole nations are thrust to the periphery. Entire classes of people are deemed to be dysfunctional. Communities are uprooted and forced into migration.

In this world, what is central can alter overnight: nothing and nobody is permanently indispensable, least of all corporation executives. Who or what is key to the system is debatable. The destitute are obviously marginal, as so much debris and detritus thrown up by the global economy; but what of the low-paid? The low-paid are not central, but neither are they marginal. It is they whose labour keeps the system up and running. And on a global scale, the low-paid means an enormous mass of people. This, curiously, is a set-up which shuts out most of its members. And in that it is like any class-society which has ever existed. Or, for that matter, like patriarchal society, which disadvantages roughly half of its members.

As long as we think of margins as *minorities*, this extraordinary fact is conveniently obscured. Most cultural thinking these days comes from the United States, a country which houses some sizeable ethnic minorities as well as most of the world's great corporations. But because Americans are not much used to thinking in international terms, given that their governments are more interested in ruling the world than reflecting upon it, "marginal" comes to mean Mexican or African-American, rather than, in addition, the people of Bangladesh or the former coalminers and shipbuilders of the West. Coalminers don't seem all that Other, except in the eyes of a few of D. H. Lawrence's characters.

Indeed, there are times when it does not seem to matter all that much who the Other is. It is just any group who will show you up in your dismal normativity. A murky subcurrent of masochism runs beneath this exoticizing, laced with a dash of good old-fashioned American puritan guilt. If you were white and Western, it was better to be more or less anyone but yourself. The felicitous unearthing of a Manx great-grandmother or serendipitous stumbling across a Cornish second cousin might go some way towards assuaging your guilt. With an arrogance thinly masked as humility, the cult of the Other assumes that there are no major conflicts or contradictions within the social majority themselves. Or, for that matter, within the minorities. There is just Them and Us, margins and majorities. Some of the people who hold this view are also deeply suspicious of binary oppositions.

There can be no falling back on ideas of collectivity which belong to a world unravelling before our eyes. Human history is now for the most part both post-collectivist and post-individualist; and if this feels like a vacuum, it may also present an opportunity. We need to imagine new forms of belonging, which in our kind of world are bound to be multiple rather than monolithic. Some of those forms will have something of the intimacy of tribal or community relations, while others will be more abstract, mediated and indirect. There is no single ideal size of society to belong to, no Cinderella's slipper of a space. The ideal size of community used to be known as the nation-state, but even some nationalists no longer see this as the only desirable terrain.

If men and women need freedom and mobility, they also need a sense of tradition and belonging. There is nothing retrograde about roots. The postmodern cult of the migrant, which sometimes succeeds in making migrants sound even more enviable than rock stars, is a good deal too supercilious in this respect. It is a hangover from the modernist cult of the exile, the Satanic artist who scorns the suburban masses and plucks an elitist virtue out of his enforced dispossession. The problem at the moment is that the rich have mobility while the poor have locality. Or rather, the poor have locality until the rich get their hands on it. The rich are global and the poor are local—though just as poverty is a global fact, so the rich are coming to appreciate the benefits of locality. It is not hard to imagine affluent communities of the future protected by watchtowers, searchlights and machine-guns, while the poor scavenge for food in the waste lands beyond. In the meantime, rather more encouragingly, the anti-capitalist movement is seeking to sketch out new relations between globality and locality, diversity and solidarity.

Notes

1. By "postmodern," I mean, roughly speaking, the contemporary movement of thought which rejects totalities, universal values, grand historical narratives, solid foundations to human existence and the possibility of objective knowledge. Postmodernism is sceptical of truth, unity and progress, opposes what it sees as elitism in culture, tends towards cultural relativism, and celebrates pluralism, discontinuity and heterogeneity.

2. Perry Anderson, *The Origins of Postmodernity*, London, 1998, pp. 86 and 85.

26 After Critical Design

Mark Blythe

In his autobiography, *The Gatekeeper* (2001), Terry Eagleton tells a story about an Oxbridge don loudly lamenting from his bedroom window that a burglar had stolen all of his research papers. This story was popular among Oxford colleagues under pressure to publish, but a scarcity of outputs was never a problem for Eagleton, who was and remains one of the most prolific and influential contributors to literary and cultural criticism. He has written an astonishing number of books on literary theory, cultural studies, and philosophy. He has also written a novel, *Saints and Scholars* (imagining a meeting between Wittgenstein, Bakhtin, and Leopold Bloom), the script for the Derek Jarman film *Wittgenstein*, and several plays, including *Saint Oscar*, in which he achieves the feat of making new aphorisms that could pass for quotations from Wilde himself. If this were not enough to make most of us feel inadequate he also writes songs such as "the Ballad of English Literature" to be sung to the tune of "Land of Hope and Glory," which begins:

Chaucer was a class traitor
Shakespeare hated the mob
Donne sold out a bit later
Sidney was a nob
(Eagleton, 1986a)

Titles of his academic work, such as *Why Marx Was Right* (2011), give a clear indication of his intellectual stance. He has taken a consistently Marxist approach throughout his career and resisted the drift to the right (unlike comrades of his youth, such as Christopher Hitchens) through sheer "horror of the cliché" (Eagleton, 2001, 98–99).

Eagleton is a public intellectual who frequently contributes to newspapers like *The Guardian* and the *London Review of Books*, and he is unafraid of controversy. He was a colleague of the novelist Martin Amis at the University of Manchester when Amis said in an interview that Muslims should not be allowed to travel until they "set their house in order." Amis claimed his remarks were a "thought experiment" but Eagleton called it out as blatant racism. Eagleton has also been a fierce opponent of "the new atheism," comparing Richard Dawkins on theology to someone holding forth on biology whose knowledge is based exclusively on the *British Book of Birds* (Eagleton, 2006). As the author of one of the most widely used texts on the topic in the field, *Literary Theory: An Introduction* (1986b), Eagleton holds a central place in studies of critical theory. His book not only provides an accessible and witty guide to the major schools of continental theory but also offers a critical stance on each of them.

Eagleton's supervisor at Cambridge, Raymond Williams, was one of the founding figures of cultural studies. It is important to consider the wider development of cultural studies as a context for Eagleton's politically engaged literary criticism. In the 1950s and 1960s, Raymond Williams was one of the first scholars of literature to apply techniques of literary analysis to other forms of cultural text. While continental intellectuals like Barthes and Eco performed close readings of "texts" like advertisements and wrestling matches, Williams focused his attention on the cultural achievements of the working class. For Williams these took the form of great social institutions like the trade unions (Williams, 1961). This focus on the cultural life of the working class was developed by Richard Hoggart in *The Uses of Literacy.* Hoggart, who also studied English as an undergraduate, went on to found the Birmingham Centre for Cultural Studies (BCCCS) in 1964; the BCCCS had a profound impact on cultural studies around the world until its closure. The influence of the BCCCS on global cultural studies is astonishing given that the number of staff seldom rose above three or four. PhD students of the BCCCS like Paul Willis and Angela McRobbie went on to write foundational texts as influential in anthropology and sociology as they were in literary studies. Paul Willis recalls thinking about the significance of biker's badges as seriously as he had thought about the lines "Tyger Tyger, burning bright" (pers. comm.). *Learning to Labour* (1977), Willis' account of how working-class kids get working class jobs, became a totemic text and is still perhaps the best example of critical ethnography.

As cultural studies took shape throughout the 1970s and 1980s, Eagleton worked at Oxford, one of most elitist universities in the world, as a scholar of English literature. The literature studied there was seldom a working-class cultural achievement and the appreciation of it was very often a maker and marker of class distinction (Bourdieu, 1986). And yet Eagleton's work is as critical and politically engaged as any that emerged from the BCCCS. Although his subject matter might be construed as "high art," his perspective is always one of historical materialism. His readings are grounded in the historical and material contexts of production and consumption. For example it is common to attribute the rise of the novel to the invention of the Gutenberg press, but Eagleton points out that the development of the form also depended on a literate reading public able to buy and appreciate the books (Eagleton, 2003).

Literary Theory (1986b) charts the development of English literature as a field of study and introduces critical theories like structuralism, poststructuralism, deconstruction, psychoanalysis, and feminism. The language of critical theory is notoriously difficult, and Eagleton's book elucidates key concepts while holding them at a critical distance. He often achieves this distance through irony and humor, and these devices are key to Eagleton's own critical practice. Eagleton's irony allows for a serious engagement with key concepts from a range of sometimes contradictory perspectives without a final commitment to any of them. Although his own readings are broadly Marxist, he very often borrows concepts from psychoanalysis, deconstruction, and feminism.

Eclecticism is common to many of the key figures in the development of cultural studies. Eagleton offers an interesting account of the eclecticism of Stuart Hall, who ran the BCCCS. In a review of Hall's work Eagleton points out that an ungenerous account of Hall's career could portray him as modish:

> Under his aegis, the Centre for Contemporary Cultural Studies at Birmingham University moved in the Seventies from left-Leavisism to ethnomethodology, flirted half-heartedly with phenomenological sociology, emerged from a brief affair with Lévi-Straussian Structuralism into the glacial grip of Louis Althusser, moved straight through Gramsci to post-Marxism, dived into discourse theory and teetered on the brink of Post-Modernism. (Eagleton, 1996, 3)

But Eagleton rejects the ungenerous view and argues that Hall's open-endedness and suspicion of grand intellectual systems was a core strength. He speculates that Hall's perspective may have been informed by his biography: "Hall was pitched between conceptual systems as well as countries, alert to the rough edges of any single doctrinal system, as heterodox in theory as he was hybrid in culture" (Eagleton, 1996, 5). Hall emigrated from Jamaica to England, and Eagleton argues that his position as a cultural outsider gave him a clearer perspective on Britain than those who had always lived there. The taken-for-granted and the everyday can seem very odd to someone who has not been brought up with the same idea of normality. Eagleton is an outsider as well, a "class traveler" whose working-class, Irish Catholic origins are far removed from the elite English, Protestant institutions where he spent his working life. In the United Kingdom just 7 percent of British students attend private, fee-paying secondary schools, but they take around 40 percent of places at Oxbridge (Oxford and Cambridge). The UK government's own 2014 report on social mobility found elitism so stark it was "almost social engineering," with private school and Oxbridge graduates accounting for 75 percent of high court judges and 59 percent of the cabinet (Social Mobility, 2014). The British class system is only slightly more flexible than medieval feudalism, but it presents itself as a meritocracy.

This elitism is often not obvious or even plausible to those that have grown up enjoying and taking for granted its privileges, but it is rather more striking to cultural outsiders. Eagleton, like Richard Hoggart, was a grammar school boy and part of a tiny minority of working-class students attending and then teaching at Oxbridge. He has remained very aware of the contradictions between the claims and the actuality of the society he lives in. It is perhaps this frame which allows Eagleton to remain alert, like

Hall, to the rough edges of any doctrine. The title of his autobiography, *The Gatekeeper*, refers to his service as an altar boy in a Carmelite convent when he would assist with the ceremony where young girls said goodbye to their families and began their lives as nuns. Gatekeepers are between worlds, as an academic Eagleton continued to stand at the borders.

Literary Theory (1986b) introduces a wide range of sometimes contradictory theoretical perspectives, and part of its continuing success is Eagleton's ironic distance from each of them. Eagleton's irony demystifies the language of critical theory without dismissing it as jargon. It also allows him to elucidate and employ concepts from a variety of perspectives—psychoanalysis, feminism, poststructuralism, and so on, without necessarily subscribing to them.

This chapter discusses the language of critical theory and attempts an Eagletonian view of critical design.

The Language of Literary and Critical Theory

The study of English literature was not proposed until the late nineteenth century. Eagleton (1983) points out that it was originally regarded as a means of inculcating a sense of morality and ethics in response to the declining influence of religion. Victorians such as Mathew Arnold recommended a study of culture based on "the best that has been thought and said" (Arnold, [1875] 2009). I. A. Richards's *Practical Criticism* (1929) provided a "guide to the formation of taste in literature" and argued that the greats of English literature were as worthy of study as any of the classics of Ancient Greece. The inclusion of Chaucer and other Middle English texts in the curriculum would also require students to become familiar with decrepit if not dead languages so the courses would have academic rigor. The notion of "a great tradition" (Leavis, [1948] 1993) or canon became the basis for studying English literature as the subject formed. But debates over what constitute "great art" have never really gone away; canons are always contested. One man's greatest writer of the twentieth century is another woman's "queasy undergraduate scratching his pimples" as Virginia Woolf said of James Joyce (Woolf, 1980).

Over time, new authorities and new criteria have informed the notion of what a "great tradition" is or should be. Over time, the canon accordingly has come to include better representation of female writers, writers of color, colonial subjects, and so forth in an attempt to pluralize the concept of literary greatness. Some criticized this as watering down the greatness of the canon (e.g., Harold Bloom), while others criticized it as not going far enough to discredit the very notion of a canon as a politically regressive concept through and through. This issue continues to animate discussion in literary theory today. Although the canon was revised to include marginalized voices, the "great tradition" and the idea of a canon became more and more difficult to defend.

The impulse toward social, political, and philosophical theory came from continental Europe.

Critical theory translated from French or German sources appeared in a form of English that unnerved many readers. It contained a great many technical terms from linguistics and semiotics that often seemed impenetrable to those not familiar with the concepts. But there was an obscurity in much critical theory far beyond the use of unfamiliar terms. Much academic writing is like this, and in *Sense of Style* Stephen Pinker wonders why this is the case (Pinker, 2014). The popular explanation is that scholars have nothing to say and dress their opinions up in grand-sounding jargon; Pinker rejects this view but some have taken it so seriously they have attempted to prove it.

Alan Sokal famously carried out a hoax on a journal of postmodern cultural studies by submitting an article called "Transgressing the Boundaries: Towards a Hermeneutics of Quantum Gravity" (Sokal, 1996). This exercise proved that cultural studies journals are fairly easily duped, but we now know that scientific journals are also easily fooled. Recently Springer and IEEE were forced to withdraw 120 published papers after Cyril Labbé demonstrated that they had been generated by computers (Van Noorden, 2014). And as Ben Goldacre tirelessly points out, a very great deal of bad science is published not as a prank but to cynically benefit corporate sponsors (Goldacre, 2008). Regardless, Eagleton would agree that there are stylistic difficulties with the language of critical theory that go beyond the use of unfamiliar technical terms: "Not all of Derrida's writing is to everyone's taste. He had an irritating habit of overusing the rhetorical question, which lends itself easily to parody: 'What is it, to speak? How can I even speak of this? Who is this "I" who speaks of speaking?'" (Eagleton, 2012). Sokal and Bricmont (1998) go further in their book *Fashionable Nonsense* by taking the stylistics of critical theory absolutely literally. The psychoanalysts Jacques Lacan and Julia Kristeva frequently expressed their ideas using algebraic formulae. For example, a key concept in Lacan is the "big other" of the symbolic order. This is a complex notion that he sometimes represents as in algebraic formulae as "A." Sokal and Bricmont take Lacan's equations and ask if they in fact mean anything at all. They conclude Lacan has "a vague idea of the mathematics he invokes" (36), but their judgment of Julia Kristeva is much harsher. Kristeva, they say, "tries to impress the reader with technical jargon" and "does not understand the mathematics she invokes (46). They note that "Kristeva concedes that her 'theory' is only a metaphor" but clearly this is no concession, it is the main point. It would make as much sense to criticize Hegel for not knowing enough about the habits of owls when he says the one that belonged to Minerva flew at midnight. It is ludicrous to dismiss Lacan and Kristeva as frauds but it is difficult to argue that they are accessible writers.

Stephen Pinker dissects a passage by another critical theorist, Judith Butler, as an exemplar of bad writing:

> A reader of this intimidating passage can marvel at Butler's ability to juggle abstract propositions about still more abstract propositions, with no real world referent in sight. We have a move from an account of an understanding to a view with a rearticulation of a question, which reminds me of the Hollywood party in Annie Hall where a movie producer is overheard saying "Right now it's only a notion, but I think I can get money to make it into a concept and later turn it into an idea." What the reader cannot do is understand it—to see with her own eyes what Butler is seeing. (Pinker, 2014, 36)

For Pinker, metadiscourse (language about language) and metaconcepts (ideas about ideas) often involve unnecessary abstraction and bad writing. Almost by definition critical theory qualifies as bad writing because it is so often concerned precisely with metadiscourse and metaconcepts. Critical theory is easy to dismiss as pretentious; Sokal called it "fashionable nonsense," but as Eagleton points out, it is no longer fashionable. And yet (as this volume demonstrates) critical theory continues to turn up in unexpected places, not least HCI.

Sherry Turkle's groundbreaking book *Life on Screen* pointed out that some of the opaque reasoning of writers like Lacan, Derrida, and Foucault was vividly illustrated through emerging technology. The notion of sex as "an exchange of signifiers" could seem willfully obscure and abstract in the 1980s, but in the nineties it was just a mundane description of what happens in online chat rooms. "In my computer mediated worlds, the self is multiple, fluid, and constituted in interaction with machine connections; it is made and transformed by language; sexual congress is an exchange of signifiers" (Turkle, 1996, 15). It is perhaps no accident that critical theory continues to resonate strongly in HCI. Over a decade ago the field turned from usability to enjoyment. Now this scope seems ludicrously narrow. Following Snowden's revelations of computer-mediated state surveillance it is clearly naïve to consider interactive technology as a neutral tool. We have moved now from enjoyment to politics and critical theory is more relevant than ever, not least in critical design.

The Discourse of Critical Design

Dunne and Raby's notion of "critical design" was groundbreaking in HCI because it demonstrated that design need not be simply a solution to a set of requirements specified in response to a given task or set of constraints. Design might also be a critique, like a political essay or satirical sketch. Critical design seeks to challenge preconceptions about the role that designed products play in everyday life (Dunne, 1999). In *Design Noir: The Secret Life of Electronic Objects*, Dunne and Raby make a number of innovative and subversive proposals, such as head-mounted cameras that allow users to tune into different people's lives as if they were TV channels: "Proposals like these can really only exist outside the marketplace as a form of 'conceptual design'—meaning not the conceptual stage of a design project, but a design proposal intended to challenge preconceptions about how electronics shape our lives" (Dunne and Raby, 2001, 65). They suggest that such designs might be expressed as text or films and that academic designers might be best placed to explore this socially responsible role. This reframing of design is a seminal contribution that continues to broaden the scope of what design means.

The book *Design Noir* describes many ingenious examples of critical design. The Compass Table, for instance, contains twenty-five compasses, which "twitch and spin" whenever a mobile phone, laptop, or similar device is put onto it. The table may be either "sinister or charming depending on the viewer's state of mind" (Dunne and Raby, 2001, 78). Such objects are not merely things in themselves but provocations intended to cause viewers to reflect on their own preconceptions and values. In this sense, the designed objects imply a critique; they make strange or defamiliarize the everyday and the taken for granted (Dunne and Raby, 2001).

Dunne and Raby's work builds on the Italian anti-design movement and the radical design movement. Italian design had flourished in the postwar period, coming to represent style and sophistication in home, fashion, and car design. But by the end of the 1960s there was growing disillusionment with intensifying consumerism (Sparke, 1988). Radical architectural groups like Superstudio produced provocative visions of future cities such as "New-New York," where a strange grid is slotted over existing skyscrapers to create a new space "freeing the environment of its ideological content" (187).

Such conceptual architecture remains troubling because it amplifies existing trends; it forms a visual pun on the notion of the superhighway—the city is at once more accessible and more enclosed in this empty white grid. It is disturbing perhaps because of its size, and the literally "top down" approach to city planning. Similarly the Archizoom Associati imagined the "No-stop City," which Andrea Branzi describes as a "fluid metropolis" (2003) with artificial light and climate control. In a 2003 interview, Branzi declared that the no-stop city was the group's most influential work, describing the imagined place in this way: "A series of beds, tables, chairs and cupboards; the domestic and urban furniture fully coincide. To qualitative utopias, we oppose the only possible utopia: that of Quantity" (Branzi, 2003). The city is represented as connected blocks on a bleak grid; the home, the workplace, and the shopping mall are so inextricably linked that they become the same place. The links are physical rather than digital, and the grainy black-and-white images seem threatening and sinister. These provocative architectural concept designs are represented in pictures, but members of the group also made product prototypes such chairs and beds that critiqued functionalist bourgeois design (Sparke, 1988). Later such radical approaches to furniture themselves became popular. For example, the inflatable "blow" chair by Italian designer Paolo Lomazzi made of transparent PVC represented "anti-form" and was originally suggested for use in swimming pools but became a popular consumer item. There are clear parallels between the work of the Italian anti-design movement and Dunne and Raby's critical design, not only in the form of the work, provocative concepts, and prototypes, but also in some of its concerns.

The practices of critical design sometimes draw on critical theory, in particular the work of the Frankfurt school. Bardzell and Bardzell (2013) say of Dunne and Raby: "Their language 'illusion of choice,' 'passivity,' 'reinforces the status quo,' 'easy pleasure and conformist values,' and 'fuelled by the capitalist system' bear the unmistakable stamp of the Frankfurt view of ideology" (2). Members of the Frankfurt school, most notably Theodor Adorno, were deeply mistrustful of what they called the cultural industries. They saw Hollywood movies and popular music as a means to lull and distract the masses from their conditions of oppression and exploitation. This idea was later developed by Guy Debord, in the *Society of the Spectacle*, where he argues that mass media serves to distract and enchant its audiences in order to ultimately subdue them. Debord and Wolman and other "situationists" sought to disrupt the spectacle through "detournement" (1956) and defamiliarization and their influence can be seen in contemporary anti-advertisements like Adbusters.

The notion that audiences are passive receivers of cultural messages is now deeply unfashionable. Empirical studies of the ways that people consume television, for example, reveal behavior that is far from passive. When researchers like Paul Willis studied footage of people watching television, they found that their eyes were not even on the screen much of the time (Willis, 1990). Viewers talk across shows, argue with the news, and exclaim in exasperation or otherwise. Stuart Hall demonstrated the ways in which ideological messages are resisted and read with oppositional codes. Theodor Adorno and Herbert Marcuse have become unfashionable not least because they were in certain respects somewhat elitist. Adorno, for instance, hated jazz, deriding the fact that people danced to it rather than sitting in a darkened room and listening to it as he did with classical music. Though politically radical, Adorno's kind of critique can sit quite comfortably with somewhat elitist notions of taste. There is an echo of this position in Dunne and Raby's 2014 book, *Speculative Everything*.

In *Speculative Everything* Dunne and Raby provide a number of examples of critical or speculative designs from their own and other people's work. The work is appraised as either "close to" or far away from their "interests." The criteria for approval or legitimacy, then, is that expert practitioners such as themselves do or do not like it. For example: "Timothy Archibald's 'Sex Machines: Photographs and Interviews' (2005) is a wonderful example of people tinkering with the world around them to accommodate their desires. It is a shame the machines are so phallic and so mechanical but nonetheless the technical ingenuity is fascinating" (162). There is little indication as to why it is a shame that the machines are phallic; rather, there is an assumption that their readers will agree that it is a shame. Much as early literary critics constructed canons of "the best that has been thought and said," Dunne and Raby seem willing to position themselves as legislators of taste: "A pitfall with many speculative design projects is a clumsy use of parody and pastiche. To maintain links to the world as we know it, designers try too hard to reference what is already known" (182). The tone here is that of the final judgment. Whether something is clumsy is not debatable—it is presented as a property of a design rather than a subjective response. Similarly, Dunne and Raby note that humor is a very important aspect of critical or speculative design but warn that it is often misused: "Deadpan or black humour work best but a certain amount of absurdity is useful too. It helps resist streamlined thinking and instrumental logic that leads to passive acceptance; it is disruptive and appeals to the imagination" (40). The subject matter must also be carefully controlled: "Critical design might borrow heavily from art's methods and approaches but that is it. We expect art to be shocking and extreme. Critical design needs to be closer to the everyday: that's where its power to disturb lies" (43).

Dunne and Raby argue that critical design is not art, although it is sometimes perceived as such. They claim that art is more bracketed from everyday life and more shocking than design. Bardzell and Bardzell (2013) dispute both claims and argue that if critical design is not art then the distinction is made in the discourse around the object and not in the object itself.

Certainly the language of critical design and much contemporary art practice overlap: both transgress, challenge, and question social norms. Indeed, the proclivity of fine artists to claim that their work is subversive, challenging, and critical has been empirically demonstrated (Rule and Levine, 2012). Rule and Levine analyzed thirteen years' worth of art gallery press releases in order to identify the characteristics of "International Art English" (IAE). They define it as follows:

> IAE has a distinctive lexicon: aporia, radically, space, proposition, biopolitical, tension, transversal, autonomy. An artist's work inevitably interrogates, questions, encodes, transforms, subverts, imbricates, displaces—though often it doesn't do these things so much as it serves to, functions to, or seems to (or might seem to) do these things. (Rule and Levine, 2012)

The vocabulary of critical design is similarly concerned with subverting and questioning norms through détournement, defamiliarization, and estrangement (Dunne and Raby, 2013). Given these parallels it is inevitable that critical design faces the same problem of assimilation that radical art and, indeed, critical theory encountered almost as soon as it was conceived. The Marxist critic John Berger points out that however radical or disturbing a painting by Francis Bacon might be, it could not escape the fate of becoming a desirable object (Berger, 2001).

Critical and satirical work has always both challenged and confirmed existing orders. This is clear in Shakespeare's various uses of the figure of the fool. In *Troilus and Cressida*, Thersites is licensed to mock Ajax while Ajax beats him: "He beats me and I rail at him: O worthy satisfaction! Would that it were otherwise; that I could beat him whilst he railed at me" (act 2, scene 3, line 3). Power relations are affirmed rather than contested when opposition is expressed through licensed criticism. Ultimately it does not matter what Thersites says, which is why he is given the freedom to say it. In raillery he confirms the power relationship which he rails against. It is perhaps for this reason that during times of great social upheaval (the 1960s, the 1980s, and today) there is a concurrent boom in satire. Nowhere in *Speculative Everything* do the authors provide any evidence of anyone actually being disturbed by any of the work featured. This might seem like vulgar empiricism but questions of how works of art or design function in the world are central to Eagleton's perspective.

Exponents of critical design such as Freddie Yauner have attempted to broaden the audience by using film and social media to showcase the work. But an analysis of comments across social media sites like YouTube and Vimeo indicate little debate. More often there is appreciation (LOLs) or agreement (Blythe, Yauner, and Rodgers, 2015). In this sense critical design is often more didactic than disturbing. Perhaps for this reason designers like Gatehouse are beginning to draw on the radical pedagogy of Paulo Freire as a means of creating more nuanced critical design (Gatehouse, 2015). The context for critical design is usually a seminar room, a museum exhibit, or an academic publication. In such contexts, the critical and radical points made by such work are foregrounded. But there is another context for much of Dunne and Raby's work: the art house auction. The Compass Table sold at auction for £9,600. The Compass Table, in a discussion like this one, is a critical design that succeeds in provoking discussion and debate. A Compass Table in the living room of an art collector might still provoke debate and discussion but it would also be a fabulous object used to inspire admiration and envy of the owner. Like radical art, and indeed Italian anti-art, critical design is all too easily assimilated by the culture it seeks to critique.

Critical Design and the Infighting Left

The discourse and dilemmas of critical design mirror those of critical theory. At times the language of critical design comes uncomfortably close to making canons. At others it engages with the language of radicalism and makes large claims about challenging assumptions while remaining embedded in and indeed expressing existing power structures. As Eagleton points out in relation to the novel, the way that a cultural artifact is received by an audience is critical to the very existence of that artifact. Dunne and Raby's *Speculative Everything* frequently claims that the work featured will disturb those that see it and cause them to ask questions. But increasingly the questions such work raises are being directed at critical designers themselves. Prado de O. Martins and Oliveira (2014a, 2014b) argue that critical design is patronizing and elitist. The designer is placed in the position of the enlightened pedagogue and the viewer as the passive cultural dope. Critics of critical design also argue that the dystopian futures imagined by Royal College of Art graduates are often the lived realities of the people making iPhones. If there are debates today around critical and speculative design they are most often about the designers' intentions and not the designs themselves. The debates are also increasingly ferocious. Cameron Tonkinwise, former director of studies at Carnegie Mellon, presents design fictions about critical designs. The final fiction takes the form of an iPhone screen shot of a threatening message sent to a number of art and design schools practicing critical design:

> In every probable and possible future people like you—white and wealthy—will be in the minority.
>
> If you don't have a theory of change being constantly tested, we will change you without you even noticing.
>
> If it's not art, don't do it in a museum.
>
> Designers, even Speculative Critical Designers are in the Consequence Business—a business with no limited liability. (Tonkinwise, 2015, 75)

Below the image is a note explaining that some of the recipients suspect the message was written by researchers "more committed to Social Design and Participatory Design." This critique does not reference a particular design but rather the committedness or authenticity of the designers themselves.

These games of "more critical than thou," or "more radical than thou," or "more committed than thou," recall the scene in Monty Python's *Life of Brian* where a group of revolutionaries are asked if they are the Judean People's Front and their leader, Reg, replies "Fuck off! We're the People's Front of Judea!" In his political writing Eagleton points out that the Left has always been very good at self-criticism. This has often resulted in the Left being engaged in vigorous in-fighting while an ever more confident and united global Right ignores them and gets on with the business of shaping the world to suit its interests (Eagleton, 2011).

Uncritical Design

Like satire, critical and speculative design offers certain challenges and critiques, but it also and at the same time offers comfort and consolation. That is perhaps why people pay thousands of pounds to own a Compass Table or other critical design. The term "design fiction" has been adopted enthusiastically by many practitioners who might previously have used a term like "critical design" or "speculative design" to describe their practice. Some definitions center on design fiction as being "diegetic" (Bleecker, 2009; Sterling, 2013). Diegesis suggests the existence of a larger fictional world to which the design belongs and this is indeed a powerful dimension of term. If these fictions are to be useful we must develop a critical lexicon beyond the kind of expressions of taste that result in a canon. But we must also move beyond the more-radical-than-thou games of an infighting left.

There is, of course, a long tradition of literary fiction that attempts to challenge preconceptions and stimulate reflection and debate. And again there is also a long tradition of failure and disillusionment. In a recent introduction to Bertolt Brecht's *Mahogany*, the novelist Will Self is trenchantly skeptical about the notion that fiction can now, or indeed ever could, inspire political debate and engagement: "I've been a writer of fiction for twenty-five years and I started out as a satirist. And I believed in the capacity of satire to morally reform society and I don't anymore.... I don't think our society is a society that is amenable to having its moral failings brought to its attention because it has lost its moral purpose altogether" (Self, 2015). For Self, we live in too jaded and cynical an age to be disturbed or shocked by anything. It is not possible to hold to account social and political elites that subscribe to no higher ethical code than self-interest. The notion that any form of critical practice will wake us from false consciousness seems increasingly unlikely. An entirely cynical (and defeatist view) would be that the real function of critical design, and indeed critical theory, is to comfort and console those who already agree with the critique being articulated.

Terry Eagleton sees the whole of critical theory as a dialogue with Marxism, and as a Marxist he is keen to understand the historical and material conditions under which critical theory emerged. In *After Theory* he points out that critical theory arose during the age of civil rights marches, antinuclear protests, and the women's movement, a time of mass disaffection but also of vision and hope (2003, 24). He also notes that during this time there was a struggle over knowledge itself, between those who thought it should be applied to military, commercial, and administrative goals, and those who saw it as a means of social emancipation. For Eagleton much critical theory is born of political defeat:

> Western Marxism's shift to culture was born partly out of political impotence and disenchantment. Caught between capitalism and Stalinism, groups like the Frankfurt School could compensate for their political homelessness by turning to cultural and philosophical questions.... Western Marxism ended up as a somewhat gentrified version of its militant revolutionary forebears, academicist, disillusioned and politically toothless. This too, it passed on to its successors in cultural studies, for whom such thinkers as Antonio Gramsci came to mean theories of subjectivity rather than workers' revolution. (Eagleton, 2003, 31)

In this view, critical theorists compensate for their political impotence by taking on philosophical questions, and perhaps the same could be said for critical design. But this kind of bleak pessimism must also be placed in its historical context. The triumph of the radical right may seem certain now, but as Owen Jones points out it did not seem at all likely or even possible in the 1960s. Free-market fundamentalists like Friedman and Hayek were marginal figures who were not at all optimistic that their ideology would ever make any difference to practical politics (Jones, 2015). They were quite wrong to be pessimistic and perhaps so too are we.

Although academics on the left have had little to no impact on global or national politics, their influence on the study of culture has been profound. In a debate between the conservative philosopher Roger Scruton and Terry Eagleton, Scruton countered Eagleton's claim that universities had capitulated entirely to the demands of capitalism by arguing that the humanities had entirely capitulated to socialism, often under the influence of Terry Eagleton himself (Eagleton, 2012c). Scruton defended the notion of culture as a form of knowledge and wisdom against Eagleton's brand of "debunking" historical and materialist criticism. In *After Theory* (2003), Eagleton describes the arc of cultural studies in characteristically aphoristic terms. He points out that nowadays undergraduates no longer write uncritical appreciations of Jane Austen; instead, they write uncritical appreciations of *Friends*. Eagleton's concern here is less the shifting object of study and more the lack of a critical perspective.

Although literary and cultural studies is now "after theory," Eagleton insists it can never return to an innocent "before theory" state. This is in part because Eagleton himself has so consistently argued that the interpretation and indeed making of cultural artefacts is always already deeply embedded in political and social struggle:

> Any body of theory concerned with human meaning, value, language, feeling and experience will inevitably engage with broader, deeper beliefs about the nature of human individuals and societies, problems of power and sexuality, interpretations of past history, versions of the present and hopes for the future. It is not a matter of regretting that this is so—of blaming literary theory for being caught up with such questions, as opposed to some "pure" literary theory which might be absolved from them. Such "pure" literary theory is an academic myth: some of the theories we have examined in this book are nowhere more clearly ideological than in their attempts to ignore history and politics altogether. Literary theories are not to be upbraided for being political, but for being on the whole covertly or unconsciously so—for the blindness with which they offer as a supposedly "technical," "self-evident," "scientific" or "universal" truth doctrines which with a little reflection can be seen to relate to and reinforce the particular interests of particular groups of people at particular times. (Eagleton, 1983, 194–195)

It is interesting to reread the passage above substituting the topic of design for literature. The history of design is also part of the political and ideological history of the epoch. From Walter Gropius to Apple's Jony Ive, design is bound up with political beliefs and ideological values. The idea of a pure design innocent of ideological or political significance is likewise a myth. Design is always already shot through with ideological assumptions and beliefs. In this sense the term "critical design" is problematic because it implies a corollary of "uncritical" or ideologically neutral design. Unless we come to design "after theory" in Eagleton's sense, it is all too easy to imagine undergraduates writing uncritical appreciations not just of *Friends* but of Apple's latest product.

References

Arnold, M. ([1875] 2009) *Culture and Anarchy*. Oxford World Classics. Oxford: Oxford University Press.

Bardzell, J., and S. Bardzell. (2013) "What Is 'Critical' about Critical Design?" *Proceedings of the SIGCHI Conference on Human Factors in Computing Systems (CHI'13)*. New York: ACM, 3297–3306.

Berger, J. (2001) "Francis Bacon and Walt Disney." In *Selected Essays*, edited by G. Dyer, 315–319. London: Bloomsbury.

Bleecker, J. (2009) *Design Fiction: A Short Essay on Design, Science, Fact and Fiction*. Accessed December 27, 2017. http://drbfw5wfjlxon.cloudfront.net/writing/DesignFiction_WebEdition.pdf.

Blythe, M., F. Yauner, and P. Rodgers. (2015) "The Context of Critical Design: Exhibits, Social Media and Auction Houses." *Design Journal* 18 (1): 83–105.

Bourdieu, P. (1986) *Distinction: A Social Critique of the Judgement of Taste*. London: Routledge Kegan and Paul.

Branzi, A. (2003) Interview in *DesignBoom*, Feburary 21, http://www.designboom.com/interviews/andrea-branzi/.

Branzi, A. (2006) *No-Stop City*. Archizoom Associati. Orléans: Hyx.

Debord, G.-E., and G. J. Wolman. (1956) "Mode d'emploi du détournement." Biblioteque-Virtuelle. Accessed February 13, 2018. http://sami.is.free.fr/Oeuvres/debord_wolman_mode_emploi_detournement.html.

Dunne, A. (1999) *Hertzian Tales: Electronic Products, Aesthetic Experience, and Critical Design*. Cambridge, MA: MIT Press.

Dunne, A., and F. Raby. (2001) *Design Noir: The Secret Life of Electronic Objects*. Basel: Birkhauser.

Dunne, T., and F. Raby. (2013) *Speculative Everything: Design, Fiction, and Social Dreaming*. Cambridge, MA: MIT Press.

Eagleton, T. (1986a) *Against the Grain: Essays 1975–1985*. London: Verso.

Eagleton, T. (1986b) *Literary Theory: An Introduction*. Oxford: Blackwell.

Eagleton, T. (1996) "The Hippest." *London Review of Books* 18 (5–7): 3–5.

Eagleton, T. (2001) *The Gatekeeper: A Memoir*. London: Allen Lane.

Eagleton, T. (2003) *After Theory*. London: Penguin.

Eagleton, T. (2006) "Lunging, Flailing, Mispunching." Review of *The God Delusion*, by R. Dawkins. *London Review of Books* 28 (20): 32–34.

Eagleton, T. (2011) *Why Marx Was Right*. New Haven, CT: Yale University Press.

Eagleton, T. (2012) Review of *Derrida: A Biography*, by B. Peeters. *Guardian*, November 14.

Gatehouse, C. (2015) "Free as in Wifi, Public as in Network: A Practice Based Investigation of Public Space." *Proceedings of the 2nd Biennial Research through Design Conference (RTD'15).* Accessed October 11, 2017. https://s3-eu-west-1.amazonaws.com/pfigshare-u-files/1967063/RTD2015 28DAY3AMGatehouse260.pdf.

Goldacre, B. (2008) *Bad Science.* London: 4th Estate.

Jones, O. (2015) *The Establishment and How They Get Away with It.* London: Penguin.

Leavis, F. R. (1993) *The Great Tradition: George Eliot, Henry James and Joseph Conrad.* Harmondsworth, UK: Penguin.

McCarthy, J., and P. Wright. (2007) Technology as Experience. Cambridge, MA: MIT Press.

Morozov, E. (2013) *To Save Everything Click Here: Technology, Solutionism, and the Urge to Fix Problems That Don't Exist.* London: Allen Lane.

Pinker, S. (2014) *Sense of Style: The Thinking Person's Guide to Writing in the 21st Century.* London: Allen Lane.

Prado de O. Martins, L., and P. Oliveira. (2014a) "Futuristic Gizmos, Conservative Ideas: On (Speculative) Anachronistic Design." *Modes of Criticism 1.* February 11. http://modesofcriticism .org/futuristic-gizmos-conservative-ideals/.

Prado de O. Martins, L., and P. Oliveira. (2014b) "Questioning the 'Critical' in Speculative & Critical Design." *Medium.* Accessed October 11, 2017. https://medium.com/designing-the-future /5a355cac2ca4.

Richards, I. A. (1929) *Practical Criticism: A Study of Literary Judgement.* London: Routledge.

Rule, A., and D. Levine. (2012) "International Art English." Triple Canopy. Accessed October 17, 2017. http://canopycanopycanopy.com/contents/international_art_english.

Scruton, R. (2012) "Terry Eagleton in Conversation with Roger Scruton." Intelligence Squared Debate. YouTube, 1:26:58, September 19, https://www.youtube.com/watch?v=qOdMBDOj4ec.

Self, W. (2015) "Contain Yourself." Lecture originally streamed live from Royal Opera House, March 4, https://www.youtube.com/watch?v=rPqlMsyZoug.

Social Mobility and Child Poverty Commission. (2014) *Elitist Britain?* Gov.UK. Accessed October 11, 2017. https://www.gov.uk/government/publications/elitist-britain.

Sokal, A. D. (1996) "A Physicist Experiments with Cultural Studies." *Lingua Franca,* May–June. Accessed February 13. 2018. http://www.physics.nyu.edu/faculty/sokal/lingua_franca_v4/lingua _franca_v4.html.

Sokal, A. D., and J. Bricmont. (1998) *Fashionable Nonsense: Postmodern Intellectuals' Abuse of Science.* New York: Picador.

Sparke, P. (1988) *Design in Italy: 1870 to the Present.* New York: Abbeville.

Sterling, B. (2013) "Fantasy Prototypes and Real Disruption." Keynote NEXT Berlin. Accessed February 13, 2018. https://www.youtube.com/watch?v=M7KErICTSHU.

Tonkinwise, C. (2015) "Design Fictions about Critical Design." *Modes of Criticism 1*, February 11. http://modesofcriticism.org/design-fictions-about-critical-design/.

Van Noorden, R. (2014) "Publishers Withdraw More Than 120 Gibberish Papers." *Nature / News*, February 24. https://www.nature.com/news/publishers-withdraw-more-than-120-gibberish-papers-1.14763.

Willis, P. (1977) *Learning to Labour: How Working Class Kids Get Working Class Jobs.* Farnborough, UK: Saxon House.

Willis, P. (1990) *Common Culture: Symbolic Work at Play in the Everyday Cultures of the Young.* Buckingham, UK: Open University Press.

Woolf, V. (1980) *The Diary of Virginia Woolf, vol. 2, 1920–1924,* edited by A. O. Bell. New York: Harcourt Brace.

27 The Artworld (1964)

Arthur C. Danto

Hamlet: Do you see nothing there?
The Queen: Nothing at all; yet all that is I see.
—Shakespeare, *Hamlet,* Act III, Scene IV

Hamlet and Socrates, though in praise and deprecation respectively, spoke of art as a mirror held up to nature.[1] As with many disagreements in attitude, this one has a factual basis. Socrates saw mirrors as but reflecting what we can already see; so art, insofar as mirrorlike, yields idle accurate duplications of the appearances of things, and is of no cognitive benefit whatever. Hamlet, more acutely, recognized a remarkable feature of reflecting surfaces, namely that they show us what we could not otherwise perceive—our own face and form—and so art, insofar as it is mirrorlike, reveals us to ourselves, and is, even by socratic criteria, of some cognitive utility after all. As a philosopher, however, I find Socrates' discussion defective on other, perhaps less profound grounds than these. If a mirror-image of *o* is indeed an imitation of *o,* then, if art is imitation, mirror-images are art. But in fact mirroring objects no more is art than returning weapons to a madman is justice; and reference to mirrorings would be just the sly sort of counterinstance we would expect Socrates to bring forward in rebuttal of the theory he instead uses them to illustrate. If that theory requires us to class *these* as art, it thereby shows its inadequacy: "is an imitation" will not do as a sufficient condition for "is art." Yet, perhaps because artists *were* engaged in imitation, in Socrates' time and after, the insufficiency of the theory was not noticed until the invention of photography. Once rejected as a sufficient condition, mimesis was quickly discarded as even a necessary one; and since the achievement of Kandinsky, mimetic features have been relegated to the periphery of critical concern, so much so that some works survive in spite of possessing those virtues, excellence in which was once celebrated as the essence of art, narrowly escaping demotion to mere illustrations.

It is, of course, indispensable in socratic discussion that all participants be masters of the concept up for analysis, since the aim is to match a real defining expression to a term in active use, and the test for adequacy presumably consists in showing that the former analyzes and applies to all and only those things of which the latter is true. The popular disclaimer notwithstanding, then, Socrates' auditors purportedly knew what art was as well as what they liked; and a theory of art, regarded here as a real definition of "Art," is accordingly not to be of great use in helping men to recognize instances of its application. Their antecedent ability to do this is precisely what the adequacy of the theory is to be tested against, the problem being only to make explicit what they already know. It is *our* use of the term that the theory allegedly means to capture, but we are supposedly able, in the words of a recent writer, "to separate those objects which are works of art from those which are not, because ... we know how correctly to use the word 'art' and to apply the phrase 'work of art.'" Theories, on this account, are somewhat like mirror-images on Socrates' account, showing forth what we already know, wordy reflections of the actual linguistic practice we are masters in.

But telling artworks from other things is not so simple a matter, even for native speakers, and these days one might not be aware he was on artistic terrain without an artistic theory to tell him so. And part of the reason for this lies in the fact that terrain is constituted artistic in virtue of artistic theories, so that one use of theories, in addition to helping us discriminate art from the rest, consists in making art possible. Glaucon and the others could hardly have known what was art and what not: otherwise they would never have been taken in by mirror-images.

I

Suppose one thinks of the discovery of a whole new class of artworks as something analogous to the discovery of a whole new class of facts anywhere, viz., as something for theoreticians to explain. In science, as elsewhere, we often accommodate new facts to old theories via auxiliary hypotheses, a pardonable enough conservatism when the theory in question is deemed too valuable to be jettisoned all at once. Now the Imitation Theory of Art (IT) is, if one but thinks it through, an exceedingly powerful theory, explaining a great many phenomena connected with the causation and evaluation of artworks, bringing a surprising unity into a complex domain. Moreover, it is a simple matter to shore it up against many purported counterinstances by such auxiliary hypotheses as that the artist who deviates from mimeticity is perverse, inept, or mad. Ineptitude, chicanery, or folly are, in fact, testable predications. Suppose, then, tests reveal that these hypotheses fail to hold, that the theory, now beyond repair, must be replaced. And a new theory is worked out, capturing what it can of the old theory's competence, together with the heretofore recalcitrant facts. One might, thinking along these lines, represent certain episodes in the history of art as not dissimilar to certain episodes in the history of science, where a conceptual revolution is being effected and where refusal to countenance certain facts, while in part due to prejudice, inertia, and self-interest, is due also to the fact that a well-established, or at least widely credited theory is being threatened in such a way that all coherence goes.

Some such episode transpired with the advent of post-impressionist paintings. In terms of the prevailing artistic theory (IT), it was impossible to accept these as art unless inept art: otherwise they could be discounted as hoaxes, self-advertisements, or the visual counterparts of madmen's ravings. So to get them accepted *as* art, on a footing with the *Transfiguration* (not to speak of a Landseer stag), required not so much a revolution in taste as a theoretical revision of rather considerable proportions, involving not only the artistic enfranchisement of these objects, but an emphasis upon newly significant features of accepted artworks, so that quite different accounts of their status as artworks would now have to be given. As a result of the new theory's acceptance, not only were post-impressionist paintings taken up as art, but numbers of objects (masks, weapons, etc.) were transferred from anthropological museums (and heterogeneous other places) to *musées des beaux arts,* though, as we would expect from the fact that a criterion for the acceptance of a new theory is that it account for whatever the older one did, nothing had to be transferred out of the *musée des beaux arts*—even if there were internal rearrangements as between storage rooms and exhibition space. Countless native speakers hung upon suburban mantelpieces innumerable replicas of paradigm cases for teaching the expression "work of art" that would have sent their Edwardian forebears into linguistic apoplexy.

To be sure, I distort by speaking of a theory: historically, there were several, all, interestingly enough, more or less defined in terms of the IT. Art-historical complexities must yield before the exigencies of logical exposition, and I shall speak as though there were one replacing theory, partially compensating for historical falsity by choosing one which was actually enunciated. According to it, the artists in question were to be understood not as unsuccessfully imitating real forms but as successfully creating new ones, quite as real as the forms which the older art had been thought, in its best examples, to be creditably imitating. Art, after all, had long since been thought of as creative (Vasari says that God was the first artist), and the post-impressionists were to be explained as genuinely creative, aiming, in Roger Fry's words, "not at illusion but reality." This theory (RT) furnished a whole new mode of looking at painting, old and new. Indeed, one might almost interpret the crude drawing in Van Gogh and Cézanne, the dislocation of form from contour in Rouault and Dufy, the arbitrary use of color planes in Gauguin and the Fauves, as so many ways of drawing attention to the fact that these were *non-imitations,* specifically intended not to deceive. Logically, this would be roughly like printing "Not Legal Tender" across a brilliantly counterfeited dollar bill, the resulting object (counterfeit *cum* inscription) rendered incapable of deceiving anyone. It is not an illusory dollar bill, but then, just because it is nonillusory it does not automatically become a real dollar bill either. It rather occupies a freshly opened area between real objects and real facsimiles of real objects: it is a non-facsimile, if one requires a word, and a new contribution to the world. Thus, Van Gogh's *Potato Eaters,* as a consequence of certain unmistakable distortions, turns out to be a non-facsimile of real-life potato eaters; and inasmuch as these are not facsimiles of potato eaters, Van Gogh's picture, as a non-imitation, had as much right to be called a real object as did its putative subjects. By means of this theory (RT), artworks re-entered the thick of things from which socratic theory (IT) had sought to evict them: if no *more* real than what carpenters wrought, they were at least no *less* real. The Post-Impressionist won a victory in ontology.

It is in terms of RT that we must understand the artworks around us today. Thus Roy Lichtenstein paints comic-strip panels, though ten or twelve feet high. These are reasonably faithful projections onto a gigantesque scale of the homely frames from the daily tabloid, but it is precisely the scale that counts. A skilled engraver might incise *The Virgin and the Chancellor Rollin* on a pinhead, and it would be recognizable as such to the keen of sight, but an engraving of a Barnett Newman on a similar scale would be a blob, disappearing in the reduction. A *photograph* of a Lichtenstein is indiscernible from a photograph of a counterpart panel from *Steve Canyon;* but the photograph fails to capture the scale, and hence is as inaccurate a reproduction as a black-and-white engraving of Botticelli, scale being essential here as color there. Lichtensteins, then, are not imitations but *new entities,* as giant whelks would be. Jasper Johns, by contrast, paints objects with respect to which questions of scale are irrelevant. Yet his objects cannot be imitations, for they have the remarkable property that any intended copy of a member of this class of objects is automatically a member of the class itself, so that these objects are logically inimitable. Thus, a copy of a numeral just *is* that numeral: a painting of 3 is a 3 made of paint. Johns, in addition, paints targets, flags, and maps. Finally, in what I hope are not unwitting footnotes to Plato, two of our pioneers—Robert Rauschenberg and Claes Oldenburg—have made genuine beds.

Rauschenberg's bed hangs on a wall, and is streaked with some desultory housepaint. Oldenburg's bed is a rhomboid, narrower at one end than the other, with what one might speak of as a built-in perspective: ideal for small bedrooms. As beds, these sell at singularly inflated prices, but one *could* sleep in either of them: Rauschenberg has expressed the fear that someone might just climb into his bed and fall asleep. Imagine, now, a certain Testadura—a plain speaker and noted philistine—who is not aware that these are art, and who takes them to be reality simple and pure. He attributes the paintstreaks on Rauschenberg's bed to the slovenliness of the owner, and the bias in the Oldenburg bed to the ineptitude of the builder or the whimsy, perhaps, of whoever had it "custom-made." These would be mistakes, but mistakes of rather an odd kind, and not terribly different from that made by the stunned birds who pecked the sham grapes of Zeuxis. They mistook art for reality, and so has Testadura. But it was meant to *be* reality, according to RT. Can one have mistaken reality for reality? How shall we describe Testadura's error? What, after all, prevents Oldenburg's creation from being a misshapen bed? This is equivalent to asking what makes it art, and with this query we enter a domain of conceptual inquiry where native speakers are poor guides: *they* are lost themselves.

II

To mistake an artwork for a real object is no great feat when an artwork is the real object one mistakes it for. The problem is how to avoid such errors, or to remove them once they are made. The artwork is a bed, and not a bed-illusion; so there is nothing like the traumatic encounter against a flat surface that brought it home to the birds of Zeuxis that they had been duped. Except for the guard cautioning Testadura not to sleep on the artworks, he might never have discovered that this was an artwork and not a bed; and since, after all, one cannot discover that a bed is not a bed, how is Testadura to realize that he has made an error? A certain sort of explanation is required, for the error here is a curiously philosophical one, rather like, if we may assume as correct some well-known views of P. F. Strawson, mistaking a person for a material body when the truth is that a person *is* a material body in the sense that a whole class of predicates, sensibly applicable to material bodies, are sensibly, and by appeal to no different criteria, applicable to persons. So you cannot *discover* that a person is not a material body.

We begin by explaining, perhaps, that the paintstreaks are not to be explained away, that they are *part* of the object, so the object is not a mere bed with—as it happens—streaks of paint spilled over it, but a complex object fabricated out of a bed and some paintstreaks: a paint-bed. Similarly, a person is not a material body with—as it happens—some thoughts superadded, but is a complex entity made up of a body and some conscious states: a conscious-body. Persons, like artworks, must then be taken as irreducible to *parts* of themselves, and are in that sense primitive. Or, more accurately, the paintstreaks are not part of the real object—the bed—which happens to be part of the artwork, but are, *like* the bed, part of the artwork as such. And this might be generalized into a rough characterization of artworks that happen to contain real objects as parts of themselves: not every part of an artwork *A* is part of a real object *R* when *R* is part of *A* and can, moreover, be detached from *A* and seen *merely* as *R*. The mistake thus far will have been to mistake *A* for *part* of itself, namely *R*, even though it would not be incorrect to say that *A* is *R*, that the artwork is a bed. It is the "is" which requires clarification here.

There is an *is* that figures prominently in statements concerning artworks which is not the *is* of either identity or predication; nor is it the *is* of existence, of identification, or some special *is* made up to serve a philosophic end. Nevertheless, it is in common usage, and is readily mastered by children. It is the sense of *is* in accordance with which a child, shown a circle and a triangle and asked which is him and which his sister, will point to the triangle saying "That is me"; or, in response to my question, the person next to me points to the man in purple and says "That one is Lear"; or in the gallery I point, for my companion's benefit, to a spot in the painting before us and say "That white dab is Icarus." We do not mean, in these instances, that whatever is pointed to stands for, or represents, what it is said to be, for the *word* "Icarus" stands for or represents Icarus: yet I would not in the same sense of *is* point to the word and say "That is Icarus." The sentence "That *a* is *b*" is perfectly compatible with "That *a* is not *b*" when the first employs this sense of *is* and the second employs some other, though *a* and *b* are used nonambiguously throughout. Often, indeed, the truth of the first *requires* the truth of the second. The first, in fact, is incompatible with "That *a* is not *b*" only when the *is* is used nonambiguously throughout. For want of a word I shall designate this the *is of artistic identification;* in each case in which it is used, the *a* stands for some specific physical property of, or physical part of, an object; and, finally, it is a necessary condition for something to be an artwork that some part or property of it be designable by the subject of a sentence that employs this special *is*. It is an *is,* incidentally, which has near-relatives in marginal and mythical pronouncements. (Thus, one *is* Quetzalcoatl; those *are* the Pillars of Hercules.)

Let me illustrate. Two painters are asked to decorate the east and west walls of a science library with frescoes to be respectively called *Newton's First Law* and *Newton's Third Law.* These paintings, when finally unveiled, look, scale apart, as follows:

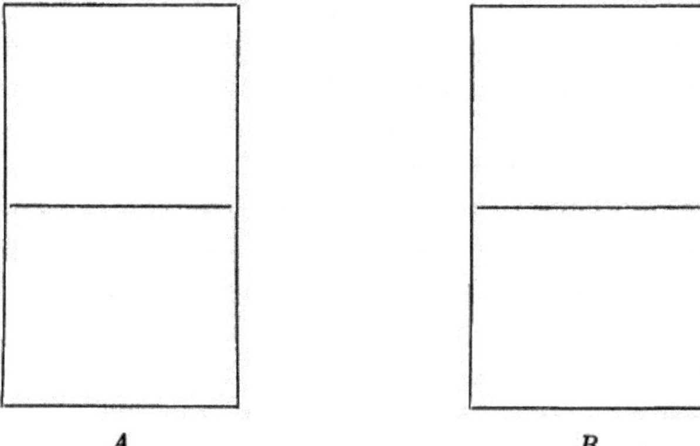

Figure 27.1

As objects I shall suppose the works to be indiscernible: a black, horizontal line on a white ground, equally large in each dimension and element. *B* explains his work as follows: a mass, pressing downward, is met by a mass pressing upward: the lower mass reacts equally and oppositely to the upper one. *A* explains his work as follows: the line through the space is the path of an isolated particle. The path goes from edge to edge, to give the sense of its *going beyond.* If it ended or began within the space, the line would be curved: and it is parallel to the top and bottom edges, for if it were closer to one than to another, there would have to be a force accounting for it, and this is inconsistent with its being the path of an *isolated* particle.

Much follows from these artistic identifications. To regard the middle line as an edge (mass meeting mass) imposes the need to identify the top and bottom half of the picture as rectangles, and as two distinct parts (not necessarily as two masses, for the line could be the edge of *one* mass jutting up—or down—into empty space). If it is an edge, we cannot thus take the entire area of the painting as a single space: it is rather composed of two forms, or one form and a non-form. We could take the entire area as a single space only by taking the middle horizontal as a *line* which is not an edge. But this almost requires a three-dimensional identification of the whole picture: the area can be a flat surface which the line is *above (Jet-flight),* or *below (Submarine-path),* or *on (Line),* or *in (Fissure),* or *through (Newton's First Law)*—though in this last case the area is not a flat surface but a transparent cross section of absolute space. We could make all these prepositional qualifications clear by imagining perpendicular cross sections to the picture plane. Then, depending upon the applicable prepositional clause, the area is (artistically) interrupted or not by the horizontal element. If we take the line as *through* space, the edges of the picture are not really the edges of the space: the space goes beyond the picture if the line itself does; and we are in the same space as the line is. As *B,* the edges of the picture can be *part* of the picture in case the masses go right to the edges, so that the edges of the picture are *their* edges. In that case, the vertices of the picture would be the vertices of the masses, except that the masses have four vertices more than the picture itself does: here four vertices would be part of the artwork which were not part of the real object. Again, the faces of the masses could be the face of the picture, and in looking at the picture, we are looking at these faces: but *space* has no face, and on the reading of *A* the work has to be read as faceless, and the face of the physical object would not be part of the artwork. Notice here how one artistic identification engenders another artistic identification, and how, consistently with a given identification, we are *required* to give others and *precluded* from still others: indeed, a given identification determines how many elements the work is to contain. These different identifications are incompatible with one another, or generally so, and each might be said to make a different artwork, even though each artwork contains the identical real object as part of itself—or at least parts of the identical real object as parts of itself. There are, of course, senseless identifications: no one could, I think, sensibly read the middle horizontal as

Love's Labour's Lost or *The Ascendency of St. Erasmus.* Finally, notice how acceptance of one identification rather than another is in effect to exchange one *world* for another. We could, indeed, enter a quiet poetic world by identifying the upper area with a clear and cloudless sky, reflected in the still surface of the water below, whiteness kept from whiteness only by the unreal boundary of the horizon.

And now Testadura, having hovered in the wings throughout this discussion, protests that *all he sees is paint:* a white painted oblong with a black line painted across it. And how right he really is: that is all he sees or that anybody can, we aesthetes included. So, if he asks us to show him what there is further to see, to demonstrate through pointing that this is an artwork *(Sea and Sky),* we cannot comply, for he has overlooked nothing (and it would be absurd to suppose he had, that there was something tiny we could point to and he, peering closely, say "So it is! A work of art after all!"). We cannot help him until he has mastered the *is of artistic identification* and so *constitutes* it a work of art. If he cannot achieve this, he will never look upon artworks: he will be like a child who sees sticks as sticks.

But what about pure abstractions, say something that looks just like *A* but is entitled No. 7? The 10th Street abstractionist blankly insists that there is nothing here but white paint and black, and none of our literary identifications need apply. What then distinguishes him from Testadura, whose philistine utterances are indiscernible from his? And how can it be an artwork for him and not for Testadura, when they agree that there is nothing that does not meet the eye? The answer, unpopular as it is likely to be to purists of every variety, lies in the fact that this artist has returned to the physicality of paint through an atmosphere compounded of artistic theories and the history of recent and remote painting, elements of which he is trying to refine out of his own work; and as a consequence of this his work belongs in this atmosphere and is part of this history. He has achieved abstraction through rejection of artistic identifications, returning to the real world from which such identifications remove us (he thinks), somewhat in the mode of Ch'ing Yuan, who wrote:

> Before I had studied Zen for thirty years, I saw mountains as mountains and waters as waters. When I arrived at a more intimate knowledge, I came to the point where I saw that mountains are not mountains, and waters are not waters. But now that I have got the very substance I am at rest. For it is just that I see mountains once again as mountains, and waters once again as waters.

His identification of what he has made is logically dependent upon the theories and history he rejects. The difference between his utterance and Testadura's "This is black paint and white paint and nothing more" lies in the fact that he is still using the *is* of artistic identification, so that his use of "That black paint is black paint" is not a tautology. Testadura is not at that stage. To see something as art requires something the eye cannot decry—an atmosphere of artistic theory, a knowledge of the history of art: an artworld.

III

Mr. Andy Warhol, the Pop artist, displays facsimiles of Brillo cartons, piled high, in neat stacks, as in the stockroom of the supermarket. They happen to be of wood, painted to look like cardboard, and why not? To paraphrase the critic of the *Times,* if one may make the facsimile of a human being out of bronze, why not the facsimile of a Brillo carton out of plywood? The cost of these boxes happens to be 2×10^3 that of their homely counterparts in real life—a differential hardly ascribable to their advantage in durability. In fact the Brillo people might, at some slight increase in cost, make their boxes out of plywood without these becoming artworks, and Warhol might make *his* out of cardboard without their ceasing to be art. So we may forget questions of intrinsic value, and ask why the Brillo people cannot manufacture art and why Warhol cannot *but* make artworks. Well, his are made by hand, to be sure. Which is like an insane reversal of Picasso's strategy in pasting the label from a bottle of Suze onto a drawing, saying as it were that the academic artist, concerned with exact imitation, must always fall short of the real thing: so why not just *use* the real thing? The Pop artist laboriously reproduces machine-made objects by hand, e.g., painting the labels on coffee cans (one can hear the familiar commendation "Entirely made by hand" falling painfully out of the guide's vocabulary when confronted by these objects). But the difference cannot consist in craft: a man who carved pebbles out of stones and carefully constructed a work called *Gravel Pile* might invoke the labor theory of value to account for the price he demands; but the question is, What makes it art? And why need Warhol *make* these things anyway? Why not just scrawl his signature across one? Or crush one up and display it as *Crushed Brillo Box* ("A protest against mechanization ...") or simply display a Brillo carton as *Uncrushed Brillo Box* ("A bold affirmation of the plastic authenticity of industrial ...")? Is this man a kind of Midas, turning whatever he touches into the gold of pure art? And the whole world consisting of latent artworks waiting, like the bread and wine of reality, to be transfigured, through some dark mystery, into the indiscernible flesh and blood of the sacrament? Never mind that the Brillo box may not be good, much less great art. The impressive thing is that it is art at all. But if it is, why are not the indiscernible Brillo boxes that are in the stockroom? Or *has* the whole distinction between art and reality broken down?

Suppose a man collects objects (ready-mades), including a Brillo carton; we praise the exhibit for variety, ingenuity, what you will. Next he exhibits nothing but Brillo cartons, and we criticize it as dull, repetitive, self-plagiarizing—or (more profoundly) claim that he is obsessed by regularity and repetition, as in *Marienbad.* Or he piles them high, leaving a narrow path; we tread our way through the smooth opaque stacks and find it an unsettling experience, and write it up as the closing in of consumer products, confining us as prisoners: or we say he is a modern pyramid builder. True, we don't say these things about the stockboy. But then a stockroom is not an art gallery, and we cannot readily separate the Brillo cartons from the gallery they are in, any more than we can separate the Rauschenberg bed from the paint upon it. Outside the gallery, they are pasteboard cartons. But then, scoured clean of paint, Rauschenberg's bed is a bed, just what it was before it was transformed into art. But then if we think this matter through, we discover that the artist has failed, really and of necessity, to produce a mere real object. He has produced an artwork, his use of real Brillo cartons being but an expansion of the resources available to artists, a contribution to *artists' materials,* as oil paint was, or *tuche.*

What in the end makes the difference between a Brillo box and a work of art consisting of a Brillo Box is a certain theory of art. It is the theory that takes it up into the world of art, and keeps it from collapsing into the real object which it is (in a sense of *is* other than that of artistic identification). Of course, without the theory, one is unlikely to see it as art, and in order to see it as part of the artworld, one must have mastered a good deal of artistic theory as well as a considerable amount of the history of recent New York painting. It could not have been art fifty years ago. But then there could not have been, everything being equal, flight insurance in the Middle Ages, or Etruscan typewriter erasers. The world has to be ready for certain things, the artworld no less than the real one. It is the role of artistic theories, these days as always, to make the artworld, and art, possible. It would, I should think, never have occurred to the painters of Lascaux that they were producing *art* on those walls. Not unless there were neolithic aestheticians.

IV

The artworld stands to the real world in something like the relationship in which the City of God stands to the Earthly City. Certain objects, like certain individuals, enjoy a double citizenship, but there remains, the RT notwithstanding, a fundamental contrast between artworks and real objects. Perhaps this was already dimly sensed by the early framers of the IT who, inchoately realizing the nonreality of art, were perhaps limited only in supposing that the sole way objects had of being other than real is to be sham, so that artworks necessarily had to be imitations of real objects. This was too narrow. So Yeats saw in writing "Once out of nature I shall never take/My bodily form from any natural thing." It is but a matter of choice: and the Brillo box of the artworld may be just the Brillo box of the real one, separated and united by the *is* of artistic identification. But I should like to say some final words about the theories that make artworks possible, and their relationship to one another. In so doing, I shall beg some of the hardest philosophical questions I know.

I shall now think of pairs of predicates related to each other as "opposites," conceding straight off the vagueness of this *démodé* term. Contradictory predicates are not opposites, since one of each of them must apply to every object in the universe, and neither of a pair of opposites need apply to some objects in the universe. An object must first be of a certain kind before either of a pair of opposites applies to it, and then at most and at least one of the opposites must apply to it. So opposites are not contraries, for contraries may both be false of some objects in the universe, but opposites cannot both be false; for of some objects, neither of a pair of opposites *sensibly* applies, unless the object is of the right sort. Then, if the object is of the required kind, the opposites behave as contradictories. If *F* and non-*F* are opposites, an object *o* must be of a certain kind *K* before either of these sensibly applies; but if *o* is a member of *K*, then *o* either is *F* or non-*F*, to the exclusion of the other. The class of pairs of opposites that sensibly apply to the *(ô) Ko* I shall designate as the class of *K-relevant predicates.* And a necessary condition for an object to be of a kind *K* is that at least one pair of *K*-relevant opposites be sensibly applicable to it. But, in fact, if an object is of kind *K,* at least and at most one of each *K*-relevant pair of opposites applies to it.

I am now interested in the *K*-relevant predicates for the class *K* of artworks. And let *F* and non-*F* be an opposite pair of such predicates. Now it might happen that, throughout an entire period of time, every artwork is non-*F*. But since nothing thus far is both an artwork and *F,* it might never occur to anyone that non-*F* is an artistically relevant predicate. The non-*F*-ness of artworks goes unmarked. By contrast, all works up to a given time might be *G,* it never occurring to anyone until that time that something might both be an artwork and non-*G*; indeed, it might have been thought that *G* was a *defining trait* of artworks when in fact something might first have to be an artwork before *G* is sensibly predicable of it—in which case non-*G* might also be predicable of artworks, and *G* itself then could not have been a defining trait of this class.

Let *G* be "is representational" and let *F* be "is expressionist." At a given time, these and their opposites are perhaps the only art-relevant predicates in critical use. Now letting "+" stand for a given predicate *P* and "–" for its opposite non-*P*, we may construct a style matrix more or less as follows:

The rows determine available styles, given the active critical vocabulary: representational expressionistic (e.g., Fauvism); representational nonexpressionistic (Ingres);

Table 27.1

F	*G*
+	+
+	–
–	+
–	–

nonrepresentational expressionistic (Abstract Expressionism); nonrepresentational nonexpressionist (hard-edge abstraction). Plainly, as we add art-relevant predicates, we increase the number of available styles at the rate of 2^n. It is, of course, not easy to see in advance which predicates are going to be added or replaced by their opposites, but suppose an artist determines that *H* shall henceforth be artistically relevant for his paintings. Then, in fact, both *H* and non-*H* become artistically relevant for *all* painting, and if his is the first and only painting that is *H,* every other painting in existence becomes non-*H,* and the entire community of paintings is enriched, together with a doubling of the available style opportunities. It is this retroactive enrichment of the entities in the artworld that makes it possible to discuss Raphael and De Kooning together, or Lichtenstein and Michelangelo. The greater the variety of artistically relevant predicates, the more complex the individual members of the artworld become; and the more one knows of the entire population of the artworld, the richer one's experience with any of its members.

In this regard, notice that, if there are *m* artistically relevant predicates, there is always a bottom row with *m* minuses. This row is apt to be occupied by purists. Having scoured their canvasses clear of what they regard as inessential, they credit themselves with having distilled out the essence of art. But this is just their fallacy: exactly as many artistically relevant predicates stand true of their square monochromes as stand true of any member of the Artworld, and they can *exist* as artworks only insofar as "impure" paintings exist. Strictly speaking, a black square by Reinhardt is artistically as rich as Titian's *Sacred and Profane Love.* This explains how less is more.

Fashion, as it happens, favors certain rows of the style matrix: museums, connoisseurs, and others are makeweights in the Artworld. To insist, or seek to, that all artists become representational, perhaps to gain entry into a specially prestigious exhibition, cuts the available style matrix in half: there are then $2^n/2$ ways of satisfying the requirement, and museums then can exhibit all these "approaches" to the topic they have set. But this is a matter of almost purely sociological interest: one row in the matrix is as legitimate as another. An artistic breakthrough consists, I suppose, in adding the possibility of a column to the matrix. Artists then, with greater or less alacrity, occupy the positions thus opened up: this is a remarkable feature of contemporary art, and for those unfamiliar with the matrix, it is hard, and perhaps impossible, to recognize certain positions as occupied by artworks. Nor would these things be artworks without the theories and the histories of the Artworld.

Brillo boxes enter the artworld with that same tonic incongruity the *commedia dell'arte* characters bring into *Ariadne auf Naxos.* Whatever is the artistically relevant predicate in virtue of which they gain their entry, the rest of the Artworld becomes that much the richer in having the opposite predicate available and applicable to its members. And, to return to the views of Hamlet with which we began this discussion,

Brillo boxes may reveal us to ourselves as well as anything might: as a mirror held up to nature, they might serve to catch the conscience of our kings.

Arthur Danto
Columbia University

Note

1. All text in this chapter is reprinted from by A. C. Danto, "The Artworld," *Journal of Philosophy* 61: 19 (1964): 571–584. Reprinted with permission from Journal of Philosophy, Inc.

28 Danto's Artworld: Art—and Design—as Inquiry

Jeffrey Bardzell

An exciting thread of design and HCI research and practice has devoted itself to the idea that it is possible to use design as a form of inquiry. That is, design processes, methods, and objects can be used as research methods whose intended outcome is knowledge as opposed to products. Many variations of this idea have been proposed, including research through design (Archer, 1995; Frayling, 1994; Gaver, 2012; Zimmerman, Forlizzi, and Evenson, 2007), critical design (Bardzell and Bardzell, 2013; Bardzell, Bardzell, and Stolterman, 2014; Dunne and Raby, 2001, 2007, 2013; Mazé and Redström, 2007), speculative design (Dunne and Raby, 2013), constructive design (Koskinen et al., 2011), design fictions (Bleecker, 2009; Blythe, 2014a, 2014b), and even expanding beyond design into, for example, critical making (Ratto, 2011). The basic idea is that by going through the design process to create and share with others the designs that challenge us, reframe our design thinking, and/or propose alternative but plausible formulations of the future, *design itself* can contribute new knowledge.

But how exactly is design supposed to do this work? What is the practice and the medium of design such that it can do work—sustaining and expressing inquiry—more intuitively ascribed to written discourses? The basic idea is as follows. All designs inscribe within them a set of assumptions, expected practices, materialized purposes, social roles, aesthetic norms, time scales of use, and so on—all of which can be rendered visible and analyzed using various forms of critique, including those explored throughout this book. Thus, it should be possible, in a way, to reverse that process—to design in a way that intentionally reworks these assumptions, projected practices, social relations, and so forth, to present alternatives. These alternatives facilitate the exploration and framing of design problems and preferred states. In this way, the design engages our attention and prompts thoughts and cognitive connections that are new to us.

In saying this, I am grouping together practices that are clearly distinct from one another, such as design fictions and research through design. I do not deny that these are important distinctions, but to acknowledge them does not mean we need to ignore their underlying similarities. Shakespearean sonnets, e. e. cummings's concrete poetry, and Japanese haikus are obviously and easily distinguished from each other, yet we still call

all of them "poetry"—and how impoverished would our understanding of any of them be if we did not have "poetry" as an underlying term, perhaps not reducible to a single all-encompassing definition, but at least as a way of pointing to family resemblances. Similarly, I find important underlying commonalties in the practices I'm grouping here (critical design, research through design, constructive design, design fictions, critical making, etc.) under the umbrella term of "design as inquiry," which I define as follows:

> Design as inquiry is the practice of fabricating objects for the purposes of inquiry, commonly qualified in the following two ways: (1) The fabrication reflects one or more mature traditions of fabrication (e.g., product design, fine art, interaction design, speculative fiction, traditional craft); and (2) beyond fabrication, the practice also entails presenting objects to peers, prospective users or stakeholders, and/or the public to engage them.

Even from this brief sketch we can begin to see what sort of knowledge we can expect from design as inquiry. It is unlikely to yield "findings" in any scientific sense or build "theory" in the sense of universally true explanations or predictions of natural or social phenomena. Rather, I design as inquiry has the potential to press up against the very edges of our thought of how we might bring change into the world, what it is possible for us to imagine, what we can realize that we need or desire, and our sense for how we could or should intervene in situations in the world.

This claim—that the practices of fabricating symbolically complex objects and making those objects available to the public contribute to inquiry—is hardly new. Notions that, for example, the arts serve a cognitive benefit have been put forward and debated since ancient times. Greek poets used tragedy "to engage in a communal process of inquiry, reflection, and feeling with respect to important civic and personal ends" (Nussbaum, 1990, 15). The Roman poet Horace famously wrote that the purpose of poetry is to delight and to instruct, and public funding of the arts two thousand years later implies that we still basically agree with him. More recent thinking, including John Dewey's notions of aesthetic experience, Nelson Goodman's aesthetic cognitivism, and Richard Shusterman's somaesthetics all continue to develop in this tradition: knowledge and understanding are at least some of the byproducts of our encounters with art.

In a similar vein, scholars of film have recently claimed that films can "do" philosophy. In a well-known analysis of the *Alien* tetralogy, philosopher Stephen Mulhall writes,

> The sophistication and self-awareness with which these films deploy and develop [the issue of the relation of human identity to embodiment] together with a number of related issues also familiar to philosophers, suggest to me that they should themselves be taken as making real contributions to these intellectual debates. In other words, I do not look to these films as handy or popular illustrations of views and arguments properly developed by philosophers; I see them rather as themselves reflecting on and evaluating such views and arguments, as thinking seriously and systematically about them in just the ways that philosophers do. Such films are not philosophy's

> raw material, not a source for its ornamentation; they are philosophical exercises, philosophy in action—film as philosophizing. (Mulhall, quoted in Goodenough, 2005, 20; Goodenough's editorial additions in brackets)

Mulhall's argument is not so different from this one by Christopher Frayling, who is often cited as a primary source of the concept of research through design in our field:

> Research where the end product is an artefact—where the thinking is, so to speak, *embodied in the artefact*, where the goal is not primarily communicable knowledge in the sense of verbal communication, but in the sense of visual or iconic or imagistic communication. I've mentioned the cognitive tradition in fine art, and that seems to me to be a tradition out of which much future research could grow: a tradition which stands outside the artefact at the same time as standing within it. (Frayling, 1994, 5, emphasis in original)

Similar to both is this description of "research-oriented design" by Daniel Fallman:

> In research-oriented design, the artifact is the primary outcome; it is regarded as the main "result" of the efforts undertaken. It is quite obvious, however, that this conduct also generates various kinds of knowledge, in terms of experience, competence, implicit knowledge, as well as, sometimes, the more general kind of knowledge that can be rather similar to that typically coming out of a research project. (Fallman, 2007, 198)

These diverse arguments assert that objects themselves can serve as a medium for thought. They seem, at first blush, reasonable and in many ways appealing. But in spite of the promise, there are also problems with design as inquiry. What are the distinctive qualities of a good research through design project? How does or should the peer community review design as inquiry research projects and papers (Zimmerman and Forlizzi, 2014)? How can we distinguish between critical design and fine art? How can we persuade the scientific members of the HCI community—whether they are embedded in academic, industry, or government funding agencies—that design as inquiry is a legitimate inquiry methodology? What is at stake in drawing boundaries between speculative, critical, research through-, constructive design? What knowledge outcomes can we expect? For example, Bill Gaver (2012) advocates for a modest role of theory in research through design, while philosopher Martha Nussbaum argues that works of art "are indispensable [*sic*] to a philosophical inquiry in the ethical sphere" (1990, 23). How could both of these positions be correct?

These questions take on a new urgency when we consider an example, Amisha Gadani's Porcupine Dress (figure 28.1). Porcupine Dress is one of a series of "defensive dresses," in which Gadani adds a defensive trait from the animal kingdom to a fashionable cocktail dress. When the wearer of the Porcupine Dress bends into a fetal position (as an instinctive response to a physical attack on her person), over thirty quills rise on the back to protect her. Similarly, with Skink Dress, parts of the dress simply fall off when an attacker grasps at it, and with Blowfish dress, the dress inflates to isolate the body when the wearer is attacked.

Figure 28.1
Porcupine Dress, by Amisha Gadani.

Is Porcupine Dress design or art? Many of us will intuitively read it as art, because it surprises and challenges us in ways that contemporary art does, and Gadani refers to herself as an artist and shows this work in art galleries. Yet it is also reasonable to read it as design, specifically as a product of avant-garde fashion design, and of course, it is possible to read it as research through design, speculative design, or critical design. (But which? All of them? Does it matter?) We might also ask: Is Porcupine Dress a critical design? No—because it is not connected with Dunne and Raby and their critical design practice, and Gadani makes no reference to that practice. Yes—because it is clearly a design that serves fairly obvious critical purposes, and it has been identified as an example of critical design in published research (Bardzell, Bardzell, and Stolterman, 2014). Is Porcupine Dress research? Clearly Gadani, in developing a series of defensive dresses, has explored a set of concepts via art and/or design, but she does not appear to have written any papers explicating what she "found." What if other researchers, such as ourselves in the aforementioned paper, were able to derive research knowledge from Porcupine Dress through their critical engagement with it? If Gadani did not see herself doing research, yet we used her work to generate research knowledge, is it still design as inquiry? What if Gadani went a step further and said that we misunderstood the design?

I make two arguments at this point. First, the questions asked in the previous three paragraphs are *theory* questions. That is, they circle about defining key vocabulary ("what is design as inquiry?"), probing distinctions ("what is the difference between critical design and speculative design, and when/why does that distinction matter?"), elucidating the epistemology of design as inquiry ("what can we learn from design as inquiry, and how do we establish confidence in its knowledge claims?"), and placing all of the above in pragmatic contexts ("what is at stake for HCI or design research and practice, for funding this research, for integrating our findings with more traditional social scientific research?"). Second, to pursue questions like these, the research community has to seriously study actual examples—designs and objects themselves as well as the methodologies, processes, and forms of documentation that attend them.

To analyze a range of difficult objects in order to construct a theoretical perspective that facilitates our ability to understand, learn from, and further the practices that generated a certain class of objects is difficult work. It is also recursive, in the sense that we must do inquiry with designs in order to develop a theory of design-as-inquiry! But this is not a new problem. In philosophy, for example, works of art are used to theorize the contributions of art to knowledge—how horror cinema (Carroll, 1990) and artistic forgeries (Goodman, 1976) serve cognitive purposes, how literature indispensably aids philosophical ethics (Nussbaum, 1990) or mounts a defense against skepticism (Cavell, 2002), how science fiction epistemically supports social activism (Freedman, 2000) or the philosophy of personhood (Mulhall, 2014).

In this commentary, I've chosen to focus on philosopher Arthur C. Danto's encounter with Andy Warhol's *Brillo Box*, first explored in his now classic 1964 article, "The Artworld," and continued through dozens of major philosophical works over the next forty years. "The Artworld" is one of the most influential, and most thoroughly impressive, criticism-as-philosophy projects ever undertaken. It takes Warhol's *Brillo Box* very seriously, interpreting it as contributing directly to philosophical theories of art, understood as we will see, in a technical sense. I see in Danto's article a model for our community, both in the ways that Danto thinks originally with and through an object—offering a superior example of what knowledge outcomes are possible with design as inquiry beyond the immediate intentions and goals of the designers—and in the answers Danto actually provides to the problems in art theory that he addresses.

Reading Danto's "The Artworld"

This section of my commentary is intended to scaffold this difficult reading, offering specific techniques for reading philosophy followed by a précis of Danto's argument, which teases out issues that are most central to the argument I want to make about the role of art and design objects in inquiry.

"The Artworld" as a Piece of Writing

For those not trained in philosophy, "The Artworld" is a difficult and possibly even very enigmatic essay. It is difficult, because in places it becomes philosophically technical, as when Danto deploys predicate logic to reason through difficult issues. It may seem enigmatic because its range of examples moves from classic paintings to absurd hypotheticals—sometimes in the space of a paragraph. Its tone is conversational and informal, almost as though Danto is talking to a friend—except when he works through formal logical analyses of concepts! At first, the article even seems to ramble—if it has a structure, it is not obvious what that structure is. But I "The Artworld" in fact does have a structure, and moreover it is both sophisticated and lean, Danto's easygoing style notwithstanding.

Another difficulty is a major philosophical issue featured prominently in the paper, though never explicitly named: the philosophical notion of "the Identity of Indiscernables," which the *Stanford Encyclopedia of Philosophy* defines as

> a principle of analytic ontology [that] states that no two distinct things exactly resemble each other. This is often referred to as "Leibniz's Law" and is typically understood to mean that no two objects have exactly the same properties. The Identity of Indiscernibles is of interest because it raises questions about the factors which individuate qualitatively identical objects.[1]

"The Artworld" can be summarized as Danto's application of this concept to two qualitatively identical objects that nonetheless are individuated: the Brillo box that appears in a supermarket (individuated as nonart) and the *Brillo Box* by Andy Warhol that is perceptually identical to its supermarket counterpart, but which is individuated as art.

Among the uptakes of Danto's argument for HCI and design is that he provides one model of what can be achieved by taking design objects seriously; his arguments suggest several ways that design directed at inquiry can be understood, internally assessed, and legitimated to others as a research methodology; and his arguments suggest some of the ways that the HCI and design research communities might build theory to strengthen the epistemic potentials of research through design.

Précis of "The Artworld"

In this section I summarize Danto's argument in some detail. I do so not merely to summarize the doctrine of "The Artworld" that Danto offers, but also to give a sense of his analytical methodology. Simply seeing the structures and textures of Danto's argument provides a powerful model of how to combine knowledge of art (in our case, design) history, a given artist's or work's theoretical and socio-historical context, close analysis of individual works, and philosophical thinking—including raising difficult (and even absurd) examples that threaten theoretical givens, as well as the logical analysis of propositions—to generate insights that help us understand the meaning and significance of works and all that implies for relevant practices (in Danto's case, art, art criticism, philosophy of art) and society at large.

Prelude: Two Senses of "Artworld"

The notion of an "artworld" can be (and historically has been) understood in at least two different ways. One is to understand "artworld" sociologically to describe a community of (art-) practice in a given sociocultural place and time, where factors of taste and social class, educational regimes, and ideological formation all come together. In such an artworld, there are artists, critics, buyers, educators—all actual people in concrete sociopolitical contexts—who heavily shape what counts as art, art practice, or "good" or even "canonically important" art, with consequences that reflect and even perpetuate sociocultural and political norms.

But Danto's work does not focus on or contribute directly to such an understanding of "artworld." Instead, Danto scopes his inquiry to a much more abstract and logical notion of artworld: he is interested in the system of concepts that that we deploy in order to perceive objects as art objects in the first place. Why is this painted wall "merely" a wall, while that painted wall belongs in a museum or is worth several million dollars? Why is this book a "trashy novel," while that one must be taught in every ninth-grade classroom? More basically, how can any person look at dabs of colorful paint and see in them a landscape or portrait in the first place? For most philosophers and theorists of art, including Danto, people's ability to make such distinctions is based on a set of theories (also variously known as predispositions, hermeneutic skills, prejudices, competencies, horizons, etc.) that they bring to the work. Danto wants to understand the logical or conceptual criteria that allow people to make such judgments at all, and he wants to intervene on these criteria. He is "doing" theory. But the theory he is primarily interested in here is not so much what professional philosophers say to each other about art in philosophy journals and conferences, but something more at the level of the set of concepts and the criteria that make possible the artworld at all.

There are important methodological implications at stake in these two ways of thinking about the artworld. Many of the sociological dimensions of the artworld can be researched empirically by observing which paintings are popular in museums, interviewing artists about a project, seeing how experts talk about films or poems, obtaining data about ticket sales (and who bought them) over time in opera houses and movie theaters, finding out why curators exhibited these works in that particular way, and so forth. Such methods can reveal what theories, practices, tastes, ideological predispositions, and so forth individuals have and use. What Danto offers in contrast is a sustained and reflective conceptual analysis that helps us see more clearly the logical consequences and implications of such aesthetic concept systems, and at his best helps us intervene on, to improve, or even to transform those concept systems to bring them into better alignment with what we aspire our art practices to be.[2]

What I hope is clear from this is that both sociological and philosophical analyses of artworld practice are important, and they offer complementary sorts of insights. Also hopefully clear is that to me, neither offers a more "correct" account of "artworld" than the other—not least because logical concept systems are deployed by actual people in sociological groups; instead, the two approaches to artworld operate at different levels of analysis and for different purposes.

So why, then, do I view Danto's logical take on artworld as especially relevant or helpful to design as inquiry (in all of its various forms, including critical design, research through design, design fictions, constructive design, etc.)? Because, and in spite of the excitement in the HCI and design communities, there is no consensus about how to establish the intellectual rigor of any of these practices, what marks their best processes, what their paradigm exemplars are, what their knowledge contributions are or should be, or even how to evaluate whether a given project has been done (or presented) successfully.

To myself and others, it is clear that we lack (among other things) a sufficiently sophisticated and stable theoretical account of design as inquiry, an equivalent of what natural and social scientists have, that art historians and literary critics have—an "artworld"-like system of concepts, methods, and practices simultaneously capable of supporting and legitimating an infinite number of individual projects while yet embracing them together as a recognizable practice. This is not a problem with a solely empirical solution (though empirical studies can certainly play a part); but I think that the relevant research and design communities also need to take on the deep tangle of epistemological and methodological issues at stake in design as inquiry at the level of theory. This commentary will not propose (or advocate for) any single solution. But I hope it will model one way of doing theory that we might, as a community, be able to try out ourselves to improve our epistemic handle on design as inquiry. And so, to Danto.

§0: Problems of Imitations and Originals

The opening of "The Artworld" recalls the oldest and most influential theory of art in the western world: art is imitation. *Mimesis*, or the imitation theory of art, states that art imitates reality, like a mirror. For Plato's Socrates, this was proof of art's inferiority to philosophy, since art only produces copies (i.e., artworks copy objects of the material world) of copies (i.e., material objects are copies of their ideal forms), whereas philosophy seeks the truth itself. Danto offers several compelling arguments against

Socrates' position that *mimesis* is an adequate definition of—and the problem with—art. Danto cites Hamlet's observation that mirrors can show us ourselves, which we can't see otherwise—a strong argument that mirrors have epistemic value. Danto also notes that much important art in our era is not representational at all—the abstract works of Kandinsky, for example.

Stepping up one level of abstraction, Danto observes that theories, and not just artworks, are also treated as mimetic. He notes that some believe that our everyday linguistic uses of words (e.g., "art" and "nonart") reflect (mimetically) what we already know (here he is implicitly referencing ordinary language philosophy). That is, theorizing art as a philosopher in this view is a matter of making explicit what we already know; it does not offer anything that's actually new.

And this leads to the challenge that Danto would spend much of the rest of his career confronting: this common view presupposes that we in fact *do* have the skill of distinguishing between artworks and nonartworks. But as readymades and pop art (e.g., Duchamp's *Fountain* and Warhol's *Brillo Box*) demonstrate, it is far from clear that we do have that skill. In short, a philosophical lexicography—that is, an attempt to render in explicit terms how ordinary people deploy ordinary vocabulary—is not sufficient to tell us what art is; it can reveal to us what those theories are, and it can demonstrate where they succeed and fail, but they cannot help us deal with the failure directly.

By extension, empirical studies of communities of art practice, such as Csikszentmihalyi and Robinson's (1991) study of more than sixty art museum curators' descriptions of aesthetic experience, also cannot directly contribute to a philosophy of art, because while such studies reveal what that group thinks and does, they do not systematically interrogate the limits of that thinking to reconstructively improve it. Such studies are akin to Socrates asking his friends what love, justice, the good, or art is, but stopping there instead of pursuing his logical and example-driven follow-up questions, which constitute the majority of Plato's *Dialogues*. Therefore, there is an opportunity for philosophy to contribute, with its critical interrogation of definitions, difficult (counter-) examples, and logical transformations of propositions that reveal hidden implications that demand a response from us.

§1. From Imitation Theory to Reality Theory of Art

Danto's first move is genealogical. He traces the historical role of the imitation theory of art (which he refers to as "IT") and the historical moment it broke down. He then explores the formulation that replaced it, which he refers to as RT (the reality theory of art). Once he's established this history, he then offers a philosophical account of some of the conundrums raised by RT.

IT functioned as a successful theory of art from Ancient Greece to the nineteenth century because it "explain[ed] a great many phenomena connected with the causation and evaluation of artworks, bringing a surprising unity to a complex domain" (Danto, 1964, 572). Danto compares this to a scientific theory, which serves the same purpose. Then he argues that just as a scientific theory can be derailed as soon as evidence is provided that seems to contradict it, so too for IT. The arrival of post-impressionist paintings (e.g., of Manet, Seurat, and Cezanne) in the 1860s created such a crisis. From the point of view of IT (uncritically embraced by established tastes at the time), "it was impossible to accept these as art unless inept art"—which most can agree now it was not (573). To deal with this required "a *theoretical revision* of rather considerable proportions, involving not only the artistic enfranchisement of these objects, but an emphasis upon newly significant features of accepted artworks" (1964, 573; emphasis added). By "theoretical revision," Danto does not mean that philosophers writing books to each other about art led this change; again, the "theory" Danto is talking about includes the concepts and criteria (i.e., the productive "language games" or "forms of life," to use Wittgenstein's terminology) of artists, critics, exhibitors, buyers, and publics at the time.

A new theory of art emerged: "the artists in question were to be understood not as unsuccessfully imitating real forms but as successfully creating new ones, quite as real as the forms which the older art had been though, in its best examples, to be credibly imitating" (1964, 573). This is the reality theory of art (RT): artworks do not imitate real objects; they *are* real objects. Danto expresses the idea using Van Gogh's *Potato Eaters*: on the one hand, it is a recognizable representation of a group of people around a table. On the other hand, its "unmistakable distortions" make it a nonfacsimile, which in turn implies that Van Gogh has introduced a new thing—the distortions taken as a whole—into the world. And the whole of those distortions is just as real as a table that any carpenter might make. He also uses the example of artists Robert Rauschenberg's bed, which is a real bed, streaked with house paint, and hung on a wall in a museum.

At this point, Danto deploys one of his outlandish speculations. He imagines a hypothetical museum visitor named Testadura (the name in Latin means "hard head"), a construct intended to represent an otherwise typical and competent individual, except that he categorically lacks any concept of art; in creating such a hypothetical individual, Danto is seeking to clarify what having a concept of art actually does by imagining an aesthetic encounter without it. So Danto places Testadura in front of Rauschenberg's bed. Testadura recognizes the bed as a bed. He also notices the paint streaks and infers from them that the bed's owner must be a little bit slovenly. Perhaps Testadura even wants to lay down on the bed and take a nap. Danto writes, "These would be mistakes, but mistakes of rather an odd kind": Testadura has mistaken art for reality. Danto continues, "But it was meant to *be* reality, according to RT. Can one have mistaken reality for reality?" (1964, 575). Ordinary language has now properly failed us, not because Testadura misunderstood the bed, but because this example has revealed that RT equivocates on the "reality" of the object around which the whole theory is based.

§2. The "*Is* of Artistic Identification" and "Artworld"

In my reading, this section is the most important in the essay. It develops and proposes what was at the time a radical new theory of art, and this theory was then able to explain why certain works of modernist art—hardly recognizable as art at all—are, in fact, art. The section concludes with one of the most famous passages in the philosophy of art, which I quote in full below.

The problem that Danto is starting with in this section is that, following RT, we all know that Testadura is wrong but can't really say why. Rauschenberg's bed is and is not a regular bed: "To mistake an artwork for a real object is no great feat when an artwork is the real object one mistakes it for" (Danto, 1964, 575). This implies that we are all Testaduras unless we can explain why Rauschenberg's bed is not a bed, even though, of course, in a very literal sense it is. This issue is not limited to Rauschenberg, either. The furor over Tracy Emin's bed continues this tradition; Emin, after spending several days in it during a suicidal depression, put the bed on display in the Tate Gallery, complete with blood-stained underwear and condoms strewn about.

Danto's strategy is to turn to logic, exploring the relations between objects and properties (e.g., personhood, bodies, and thought; and then analogously, artworks, material properties, and "what makes them art"). He argues that what's confusing us with Testadura's assertion that "Rauschenberg's bed is a bed" is that he's using the word "is" with equivocation. Equivocation refers to when we use a word that has distinctly different senses interchangeably, thus creating confusion. Danto points to three common uses of "is": the *is of identity* (that person is Sarah); the *is of predication* (Sarah is thirsty); and the *is of existence* (Sarah is real and not a figment of my imagination). And as long as "is" has only these three meanings, it's hard to resolve the puzzle Testadura poses for RT.

So Danto proposes a fourth sense of "is," which he calls "the *is* of artistic identification." This proposal is the hinge on which the whole essay turns. Danto exemplifies this sense of "is" as follows: when we point to a dab of paint on a painting and say, "that is Icarus,"[3] it cannot be that that dab represents Icarus (i.e., "the is of identification"), because the word "Icarus" also represents Icarus and no one would point to the word and say that that word "is Icarus." Stated in plain terms, Danto is saying that there is a fourth sense of "is," which is "to see as art": the daub of paint is Icarus-in-art.

The "is of artistic identification" has some very important logical consequences, which Danto illustrates using another strange example. He invites us to imagine a science library that has invited painters to represent Newton's first and third laws. (The first law is the law of inertia, while the third law is that for every action there is an equal and opposing reaction.) When the paintings are unveiled, it turns out that they look exactly alike! Both have a single, horizontal black line across the enter center of the painting, separating a white background into two fields (table 28.1).

Table 28.1
Paintings of Newton's first (a) and third (b) laws of physics.

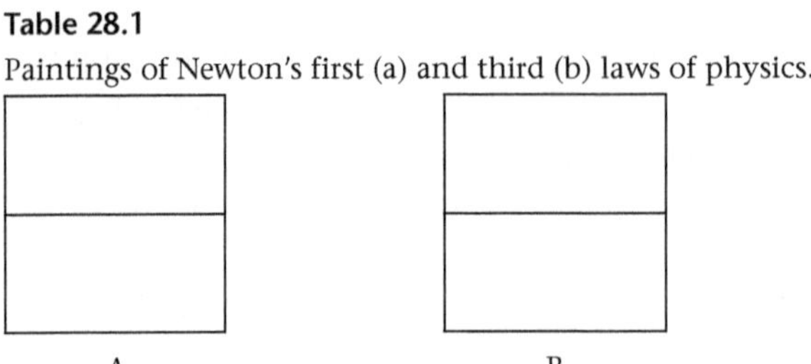

Danto explains the two paintings as follows:

> *B* [i.e., the painter of Newton's third law] explains his work as follows: a mass, pressing downward, is met by a mass pressing upward: the lower mass reacts equally and oppositely to the upper one. *A* [the painter of Newton's first law] explains his work as follows: the line through the space is the path of an isolated particle. The path goes from edge to edge, to give the sense of its *going beyond*. If it ended or began within the space, the line would be curved: and it is parallel to the top and bottom edges, for if it were closer to one than the other, there would have to be a force accounting for it .... (1964, 577, italics in original)

Danto then offers a detailed analysis of the different conventions of representation in each painting, which I won't attempt to summarize. Its upshot is crucial to his argument, however: *any single artistic identification* (e.g., once you see the horizontal line as an *edge* in *B*'s case or a *path* in *A*'s) *commits one to making several more artistic identifications*: for example, the meaning of the edges of the painting, of the location and significance of the white areas (e.g., planar bodies in B and empty void in A), of what's going on outside the edges of painting, of the direction of movement within the painting. That is, for both paintings, in order to understand them at all, one must assent to a whole *system* of art identifications: "Notice," Danto writes, "how acceptance of one identification rather than another is in effect to exchange one *world* for another" (578, emphasis in original).

Danto develops this point one more step by bringing Testadura into the library to look at the paintings. Testadura sees neither painting as having to do with physics; all he sees is paint. And he is right: all there is, is paint (i.e., the "is of existence"). Danto continues, "We cannot help him until he has mastered the *is of artistic identification* and so *constitutes* it a work of art. If he cannot achieve this, he will never look upon artworks" (579, emphases in original).

Danto's final analytic move is to bring in the point of view of a minimalist painter in the New York art scene, who claims that his work is literally nothing but paint. This artist's statement presents a conundrum, because surely this abstract artist doesn't mean "there is nothing here but paint" in the same sense that Testadura does, even though (again) in an existential sense they are both right: paint is all that is there. Danto solves this conundrum as follows: the difference between the abstractionist and Testadura is that the latter offers his materialist position because he has never understood art at all. But the abstractionist has arrived at his materialist position by first mastering the history and conventions of painting and then subsequently rejecting them, reducing (what he sees as) all of the "extraneous" conventions and meanings of painting in order to arrive at its "purest" form: "He has achieved abstraction through rejection of artistic identifications" (Danto, 1964, 579). Danto famously concludes this section as follows:

> [The abstractionist's] identification of what he has made is logically dependent upon the theories and history he rejects. The difference between his utterance and Testadura's "This is black paint and white paint and nothing more" lies in the fact that he is still using the *is* of artistic identification, so that his use of "That black paint is black paint" is not a tautology. Testadura is not at that stage. To see something as art requires something the eye cannot descry[4]—an atmosphere of artistic theory, a knowledge of the history of art: an artworld. (579–580)

Interlude: A Commentary on §2

Danto's notion of artworld, of course, was extremely influential, game-changing even. Danto's artworld helped shape philosopher George Dickie's institutional theory of art, and both remain major theories in the philosophy of art today. Beyond philosophy, both Danto's and Dickie's formulations were appropriated by sociologist Howard Becker, and the concept is foundational to major theories by Pierre Bourdieu and Bruno Latour (Van Manaan, 2009) and (it seems obvious to me) Mihaly Csikszentmihalyi's theory of social creativity, which views creativity as unfolding within a structured system of productive roles (involving communities of practice, knowledge domains, and individual talents/experience), and which has been heavily influential in HCI (e.g., Fischer et al., 2005).

I have taken some pains to lay out Danto's argument in detail, however, in order to stress that for Danto, the concept of artworld is distinct from a sociological category (that is, a social group, engaged in a specialized practice, influenced by a set of politics, etc., as exemplified by George Dickie's institutional theory of art in analytic aesthetics, Pierre Bourdieu's "distinctions" in continental theory, and Csikszentmihalyi's social creativity in psychology). Danto sees artworld as a logical and philosophical system (i.e., a system of concepts that is productive in the sense that it renders objects as art). Danto's work is not centrally about actual communities of actual people; he was not proposing an art version of "communities of practice," and much of what he did achieve is lost if he is read that way (which is not to say that Dickie's and Bourdieu's approaches lack merit).

A more accurate way of reading Danto is that "artworld" refers to (1) a coherent theory of art and (2) a compatible system of artistic identifications, and that these identifications make it possible for an object to be understood as a work of art in the first place. For Danto, this is an ontological move: what is an object in the world (say that bed) now *becomes* a work of art (that bed-as-art). The ability for any work to *be art* depends on someone (or, more typically, a group or community) to designate it as such, and that can only occur if there is a theory and system of compatible artistic identifications.

For example, we cannot recognize a traditional landscape painting without identifying that all these daubs of paint add up to a wide-view representation of land, sky, flora, and fauna. We must understand that the bounded, two-dimensional surface of the painting is like a window opening onto a three-dimensional landscape behind it; we assume that the world continues in every direction outside the painting. We also understand that often such landscapes serve artistic purposes by being both visually appealing and by offering connotatively appropriate settings for various cultural and religious themes (e.g., threatening vs. bucolic weather).

If we do not understand these themes we lack a part of the system of art identifications. For example, in Christian allegorical paintings, a lion and a lamb are frequently shown together, where the lamb symbolizes Christ (*agnus Dei*, the lamb of God) and its peaceful coexistence with the lion symbolizes the divine plenitude of God's love. Lacking this art identification (i.e., the lamb is [art-identified as] Christ), then the two animals' peaceful coexistence in the painting might undermine the whole painting: a viewer might exclaim, "That's a very stupid lamb to sit next to a lion like that!" Following this reasoning, later in this commentary I argue that design as inquiry is a mere activity or object (Testadura's bed) until a community has theories of design, theories of research, and a system of identifiers by which to recognize ways that design can be/do research. Without such a theory and system of design-as-inquiry identifiers, those engaging in design as inquiry are vulnerable to the response, "that's not really design," or, more likely, "that's not really research," and have few shared theoretical resources with which to mount a defense.

Danto has also shown that there has to be a *fit* between this theory and individual works, if they are perceived to be art. We saw that Van Gogh's *Potato Eaters* is at best "inept art" given the imitation theory of art; there is no way for it to be otherwise. To Testadura, *Potato Eaters* is nothing more than a painted object, as a painted dresser is a painted object—to him, the world behind its window doesn't exist and neither does the window. To the New York abstractionist, *Potato Eaters* is bloated and impure, introducing all sorts of unnecessary stuff (including mimetic representations and creative self-expressions) that distracts us from seeing the paint itself. In other words, *no painting is sufficient to generate a correct account of itself*: a system of artistic identifications, compatible with at least one theory of art, is needed; otherwise, the object is not art but merely an object, a painted surface.

Though Danto doesn't have much to say about them, it should be obvious to most readers of this volume that communities of practice are involved: those critics, curators, painters, and viewers who accept the imitation theory of art or abstractionism. Even Testadura represents a hypothetical community of practice, that is, a community with a fully functional perceptual and cognitive apparatus and a cogent theory of the world that is able to explain details of the work, if not see it as art; it's just that this community has presumably zero members. Thus, in Danto, the artworld defined in terms of a community of practice would consist of the set of individuals who have sufficiently mastered the theory and corresponding system of conventions to be able to recognize an object as art. This is a logical definition and sheds little light on the sociology of actual social groups; one might say that in Danto's view the existence and definition of this social group is logically derived from the existence of the artworld itself. HCI and design researchers and practitioners need not fully embrace Danto's position as a complete view of the artworld (I don't). But on a pragmatic level, I do argue that the scope of his analysis—the rigorous but a priori logical analysis of an extant conceptual theory (and its related individual identifications)—brings to light conceptual knots and suggests ways of dealing with them that are hard to perceive or engage using other theoretical stances (such as community of practice theory) or research methods (including empirical ones).

§3. What Makes *Brillo Box* Art

Now that Danto has proposed "the *is* of artistic identification" and the "artworld," he is finally in a position to take on the art work that set all of this in motion.

Warhol's *Brillo Box* (figure 28.2) is a sculpture first presented in 1964 at Stable Gallery in New York City, which had been known prior to that for featuring the work of abstract expressionist painters, such as Willem de Kooning, Robert Motherwell, and Jackson Pollack. Warhol's sculpture is a replica of the mass-produced cardboard box that Brillo pads—a common dish-scouring pad—came in at that time. Warhol's version is constructed from plywood and hand-painted by the artist, so it does differ in some ways from the cardboard version actually sold in supermarkets. That said, in photographs the two are perceptually indiscernible from one another, and that is the foundation of Danto's analysis.

Brillo Box all but demands us to ask: What makes this art? In the previous section, Danto has proposed a way into this—the "*is* of artistic identification" and his formulation of artworld—but he begins this section by excluding a number of other, more common explanations. First, he asks if perhaps there is more intrinsic value in Warhol's version: his, after all, are plywood, rather than cardboard. But Danto argues that Brillo could decide to start making their boxes out of plywood and that wouldn't make them art. Likewise, had Warhol made them out of cardboard they wouldn't be any less art. Second, he proposes the labor theory of value to account for the difference: Warhol's are hand-painted by an expert painter, while the originals are mass-produced, so the labor itself adds value. But many things are laboriously crafted yet we do not call them art, so that cannot explain it, either. Perhaps, then, the whole distinction between art and nonart has broken down altogether. But we do, in fact, treat *Brillo Box* as art: it was shown in a museum; today, "originals" sell in the millions in art auctions. Danto concludes that Warhol "has produced an artwork, his use of the real Brillo cartons being but an expansion of the resources available to artists, a contribution to *artists' materials*,

Figure 28.2
Brillo Boxes by Andy Warhol.
Source: Richard Winchell, http://www.flickr.com/photos/richardwinchell/2432660543/. Reprinted here in accordance with the Creative Commons Attribution-NoDeriv License: http://creativecommons.org/licenses/by-nd/2.0/deed.en.

as oil paint was" (Danto, 1964, 581). Supporting this reading is the fact that in 2005 artist Mike Bidlo had an exhibition called "Not Andy Warhol," featuring Brillo boxes that Bidlo had hand-painted to replicate Warhol's replicas. Danto continues,

> What in the end makes the difference between a Brillo box and a work of art consisting of a certain Brillo Box is a certain theory of art. It is the theory that takes it up into the world of art, and keeps it from collapsing into the real object which it is (in a sense of *is* other than that of artistic identification).[5] Of course, without the theory, one is unlikely to see it as art, and in order to see it as part of the artworld, one must have mastered a good deal of artistic theory as well as a considerable amount of the history of recent New York painting.... It is the role of artistic theories, these days as always, to make the artworld, and art, possible. (581)

Just as Testadura cannot see why Rauschenberg's bed is not merely a bed but is also art, so many of us struggle to see why Warhol's *Brillo Box* is not merely a Brillo box but also a sculpture, why Duchamp's *Fountain* is a sculpture and not a urinal. The concepts developed in section 2 gives us a means to explain the difference within the scope of theory, that is, the concept system that makes it possible for anyone to perceive an object-as-art. It also adds some crucial nuance to, say, the common "moral of the story" of Duchamp's *Fountain:* a work of art is whatever is put into art galleries. While there is a lot of truth to that, what makes it so is that in those galleries at that time, there is an active theory that can accommodate a urinal offered as a sculpture; no one believes a seventeenth-century art museum would have accepted such a urinal, and it would be difficult today to try that again—the institutions, and the theories of art with which they operate—have changed. In other words, Duchamp's *Fountain* points not only to a specific art-institutional moment, but also to a specific art-theoretical moment, and of course the two are intertwined (i.e., the relevant art theory is shared among actual actors in the historical institutions).

§4. "The Hardest Philosophical Questions I Know"

In the final section, Danto writes, "I shall beg some of the hardest philosophical questions I know." It features some symbolic logical analyses that may appear technical to a reader not trained in it. The argument is, however, somewhat easy to paraphrase (but remember that Danto is seeking to prove that he is right, not merely to advance a position, so I will summarize his position but not his proof).

Each theory of art implies a system of art identifications. Throughout this section Danto refers to two theories in particular: the imitation theory of art (IT), which we have seen throughout this piece, and the expressionistic theory of art (ET). The latter is the romantic notion that artworks express the deep inner emotions of artists. Art identifications connected to the imitation theory of art would include perceiving a face in a portrait, expecting the portrait to resemble the actual face, and understanding how shading and gradients are used to suggest light, shadow, and three dimensions. Art identifications connected to the expressionistic theory of art would involve understanding distortions, odd colorings, and breakdowns of painterly illusionism as reflecting the subjective attitudes, perceptions, and intentions of the painter.

With this in mind, we can agree that some works are both representational and expressionistic: Van Gogh's *Potato Eaters* is in this group, because we can see people around a table represented in a painting, but it is distorted in ways suggestive of a special subjective point of view. Other artworks are nonrepresentational but expressionistic, such as the works of Jackson Pollack and the abstract expressionists. Some are representational but not expressionistic, such as the neoclassical paintings of Jean Auguste Dominique Ingres. Finally, some are nonrepresentational and nonexpressionistic, such as the paintings of the minimalist abstractionists. In other words, we can express these theories in a matrix (table 28.2), and we can use this matrix to explain why given material objects are also art.

There are a few points that Danto develops in relation to this. As long as all art fits within a single theory (e.g., all art is representational), then it is extremely difficult to imagine art outside of that theory (e.g., nonrepresentational art). Socrates's theory

Table 28.2
A matrix of art theories.

	Expressionist	Non-Expressionist
Representational	Post-impressionists (Van Gogh)	Neo-classicists (Ingres)
Non-representational	Abstract expressionists (Pollack)	Minimalist abstractionists (Reinhardt)

of art does not accommodate abstract expressionism because it didn't exist in fifth-century BCE Greece. Once a work is offered that falls outside the theory, then more theory and more "*is* of art identifications" need to be added to the artworld for the work to be art. But once that happens, all prior art is necessarily modified as not- whatever the new "*is* of art identification" is. So, for example, Ingres is a representational painter until the romantics come along, and then he becomes a representational and also a nonexpressionistic painter thereafter; today, he is also a nonabstractionist and nonpostmodernist painter. Thus, adding a new theoretical dimension has a doubling effect: art works can feature that dimension or they can occupy the not-that-feature position. The upshot of course is that this theory of art becomes increasingly complicated over time, as art works demand an ever-increasing theoretical apparatus—a kind of matrix of has-F (artistic property) and not-has-F to understand them. Danto also notes that artworks tend to occupy very specific places within that matrix—but again, one can only perceive these as artworks if one has mastered that matrix (as Testadura has not). Additionally, Danto is able to account for minimalist "purists": they are those who occupy the not- position at every point in the matrix; so for example, hard-edge abstractionism is only possible once "impure" positions such as representationalism and expressionism are bona fide parts of the matrix, so they can be rejected—clearly a very different position than Testadura's philistine materialism.

Danto makes two further interesting claims in his conclusion. First, he acknowledges that there are fashions about which matrix positions are hot or not in the social world. But he makes his lack of interest in this very clear: "But this is a matter of almost purely sociological interest: one row in the matrix is [logically speaking] as legitimate as another" (1964, 584). He then drops the matter (though once again, I don't believe we should drop the matter in pursuing a theoretical consensus about design as inquiry).

Next, he offers a theory of artistic innovation:

> An artistic breakthrough consists, I suppose, in adding the possibility of a column to the matrix. Artists then, with greater or less alacrity, occupy positions thus opened up: this is a remarkable feature of contemporary art, and for those unfamiliar with the matrix, it is hard, perhaps impossible, to recognize certain positions as occupied by artworks. (584)

In my reading, this account gestures toward the cognitive aspect of art; one important way that art can be a form of inquiry is to add columns to the matrix, that is, generate new theories and systems of artistic identifications, which can be generative of new art practices and also new understandings of the significances and meanings of all prior art.

Interlude: A Summary of Danto's Theory of Artworld

By way of summary, I wish to bring forward several key points. The artworld for Danto is not a social group or community of practice. Rather, the artworld is a conceptual and theoretical apparatus that is logically required for a physical object both to *be* and to *be seen as* a work of art. More specifically, the artworld (as I read Danto) entails the following features:

- *One or more high-level organizing theories of art.* Danto refers to the imitation theory of art, the reality theory of art, and the expression theory of art. More such theories are logically possible.
- *Coherent clustering of a significant number of lower-level art identifications* (what Danto calls "the *is* of artistic identification"). I tend to view these as codes or conventions, such as the following: that daub of paint is a shadow, Icarus' legs, or the edge separating two masses. Accepting one such identification commits one to accepting many more, collections of which seem to add up to the high-level organizing theory of the work (i.e., an interpretation), which presumably reflects one or more of the high-level organizing theories of art.
- *A set of material objects that are also art.* Material works become art by occupying positions within these theories and by exhibiting specific clusterings of art identifications. So, for example, Rauschenberg's bed is a literal bed with paint on it (i.e., is a material work) that combines readymade objects and abstract expressionist painting techniques (i.e., is art).
- *The set of individuals who have mastered this theory sufficiently to recognize the physical works as art.* That set of individuals of course can also be seen as a social group and sociologically studied, but that is out of the scope of Danto's project. (The sociologist Howard Becker is arguably the key resource for developing that scope and understanding of artworld.)

The most basic implications of this is that an artworld, so defined, is logically necessary before an object can be (in an ontological sense) or can be seen as (in an epistemological sense) art. To understand art at all, one must have some level of mastery of this artworld. Finally, any artwork that forces a change in the theory of art not only modifies the theory and its attendant clusterings of art identifications, but also the meanings of all the artworks that have gone before it.

Design as Inquiry

Having presented Danto's arguments in some detail, I now return to the issues in the opening of this commentary. How can design inquire? What can design inquire after? How do we know if a design-based research project is successful? How do we evaluate design as inquiry knowledge claims? Why do I regard Danto's "Artworld" as exemplary—indeed, among the very best examples I've ever seen—of thinking with objects?

Brillo Box as Philosophy

A reasonable person might object at this point that although I have demonstrated that Danto's "The Artworld" is an important and fascinating piece of philosophy, I have not offered an account of why *Brillo Box* itself is philosophy. And since the idea that art (and by extension design) can do inquiry is my whole point, I've got a problem on my hands. Happily, Danto seeks to answer precisely this question—what is the philosophical structure of *Brillo Box?*—in a much later essay, called "The Philosopher as Andy Warhol." In it, he writes,

> I have felt [Warhol] to possess a philosophical intelligence of an intoxicatingly high order. He could not touch anything without at the same time touching the very boundaries of thought, at the very least thought about art.... I believe it was among Warhol's chief contributions to the history of art that he brought artistic practice to a level of philosophical self-consciousness never before attained.... I shall, in the essay that follows, endeavor to reveal some fragments of the philosophical structure of Warhol's art.... But my essay differs from the standard art-historical exercise in that I seek to identify the importance of the art I discuss not in terms of the art it influenced (or which it was influenced by) but in terms of the thought it brought to our awareness.... Warhol's art ... goes immediately to the defining boundaries of the medium and brings these boundaries to conceptual awareness. (Danto, 1999, 62–67)

I will not summarize Danto's later essay, but I want to focus on the claim he is making that Warhol's art "does" philosophy, because it can serve as one basis from which to answer how design can do inquiry.

Paraphrased, Danto's basic argument seems to be something like this:

1. In a given time and place, a set of thoughts (e.g., about what art does, about how to recognize material features as artistically significant) is active, possible, and also bounded. Now, we have seen in "The Artworld" that the primary structures that enable and constrain such thought are high-level theories, such as IT or ET. As we have also seen, the constraining effects of such theories can be very difficult to perceive, let alone overcome.
2. Anything that reveals those boundaries as a focus for thought is a philosophical contribution inasmuch as it adds a column to and/or transforms the matrix by which it is possible for art to be art.

3. Warhol's *Brillo Box* reveals the boundaries of our thinking about art simply and directly, and by doing so raises those boundaries as a focus for thought.
4. Therefore, Warhol's *Brillo Box* is philosophical.

There are a few features of this argument that I wish to stress in the context of this book.

First is that Danto is nowhere claiming that Warhol has offered a cogent metaphysical system, the way Plato, Aristotle, or Marx, for example, did. It is important to distinguish, then, "doing philosophy" from "proposing totalizing metaphysical systems"—a point obvious to most philosophers today but perhaps not as clear to those outside of that community. Doing philosophy—and we've seen this throughout Danto's paper—has more to do with exploring the boundaries of thought, of developing and evaluating concepts and concept systems that are adequate to support our engagements with the world. Danto proposed a concept, artworld, which has helped philosophers, sociologists, educators, and designers do what they do. So, the argument follows, Warhol's *Brillo Box* has made a proposal—that *Brillo Box* is art and that the perceptually indiscernible Brillo boxes are not. This prompts the thoughts that lead to Danto's "finding," which might be summarized as follows:

1. *Brillo Box* and Brillo boxes are perceptually indiscernible.
2. But we do distinguish between them.
3. Therefore, something nonperceptual distinguishes them.
4. It is a theory, including a system of art identifications, that distinguishes them.

Second, I want to stress that the philosophical contribution of *Brillo Box* is contingent on certain theories, ways of thinking, and boundaries of thought being extant at the time of its presentation. "Boundaries of thought" is not a psychological universal—Warhol didn't make our perceptual processors faster!—but rather a cultural contingent: it refers to how society understands symbolizations at a given time. In the New York art scene of the early 1960s (especially abstract expressionism), thinking about art was constrained in certain ways (e.g., art was elitist, romanticized by the myth of the genius, had pretentions of being above capitalism, saw itself in relation to prevailing cultural theories, etc.), and *Brillo Box* exposed the boundaries of such thinking.

Brillo Box remains relevant in part because that thinking is active today. Designers such as Dunne, Raby, and Gaver have been described as "elitist taste-makers" (Burdick, 2016); their work is exhibited in elite cultural institutions such as the Museum of Modern Art in New York and sold in public art auctions (the prices of which are only available to paying subscribers). Their design practices are so carefully branded that they are commonly capitalized as proper names (Critical Design, Speculative Design, Ludic Design) and even treated as inalienable from the individual designers who coined and promote them. Such practices fit with an academic (Cross, 2006) and commercial (e.g., TED, IDEO, *Fast Company*) theory of "design thinking" that celebrates designers' distinctive innovative practices, with clear echoes of romantic "genius." And like artists of the 1960s New York art scene, Dunne and Raby even claim to subvert capitalism.

Danto argues that *Brillo Box* amounts to a sophisticated conceptual response to such theories. He links *Brillo Box* to active debates in 1960s philosophy, the post-Wittgenstein ordinary language philosophy of J. L. Austin in particular. He characterizes Warhol's philosophical methodology as deploying a *"via negativa"*; that is, it operates through subtraction, not addition, which again is important if one mistakenly assumes that philosophy is only about inventing concepts (it also destroys them!). One wonders what a *via negativa* response to critical design, speculative design, and ludic design might reveal to us.

Inquiring Designs

All of the foregoing sets us up nicely to return to design as inquiry. I propose to adapt Danto's thinking and offer the following as a candidate formulation[6] of design as inquiry: Design does inquiry by operating on and revealing to us at least one boundary of the active conceptual system that makes it possible for human works and performances to be designs.

If we want to pick out what is distinctive about design as inquiry, we have two immediately obvious problems to solve. First, there are objects in the world that challenge the boundaries of our schema that are not designs—science, philosophy, and art, among others. These are inquiry (on Danto's account), but they're not design. Now, objects in the world are only recognizable as designs to the extent that they fit our schema for what constitutes a design: in Danto's idiom, we might say that we need to be able to make "'is' of design identifications" based on one or more general theories of design (e.g., that design solves problems or dis a plan or is a specification). Second, some designs do not reveal the boundaries of or extend our conceptual systems with regard to any given domain of human life or design space (in fact, most designs are in this category). These designs are not inquiry, at least not in the sense that Danto claims that *Brillo Box* and other works are inquiry.

When we put these two problems together, what we are seeking is something recognizable as a design that pushes the boundaries of what we can imagine as a design. This might seem odd, but actually it's commonsense: we especially cherish designs that reveal to us and satisfy desiderata that we didn't even know we had (Nelson and Stolterman, 2014). In Danto's idiom, we might say that design as inquiry comes up not merely with new interventions (all designs do that), but new *categories* of potential interventions, whole new "worlds." In the words of Zimmerman, Forlizzi, and Evenson (2007), such design "describe[s] a vision of a preferred state" and "reveals the framing of the problem and the balance the researchers have made between the intersecting and conflicting perspectives." (6)

Porcupine Dress as Design-Based Inquiry

I want to return to the Porcupine Dress, which I introduced at the beginning of this essay. There, I argued that the dress opened up all sorts of definitional questions about whether it was art or design, whether it was critical, whether it counted as research. Again, since I don't embrace an essentialist position, I don't offer or want a final answer to whether it is art or design. What I want instead is a set of conceptual resources that help me analyze its contributions as a design-as-inquiry project. If I have such resources, and an art critic wishes to analyze Porcupine Dress *qua* art, my project is not threatened by that; neither is it threatened if Gadani were to assert that my analysis did not capture her intentions.

I have some theoretical resources now. I begin with some basic observations. Cocktail dresses conventionally seek to meet several criteria: a cocktail dress should be fashionable, comfortable, observant of relevant fashion norms including gender and cocktail party norms, protect the body from the elements, affordable, able to perform/express the identity (in some way) of the wearer, easy to maintain, and so on. These criteria are reflected in fabric choices (which can bear prints, survive the washing machine, be produced on a mass scale, withstand rain), silhouettes and cuts (which contribute to comfort, their ability to flatter the body of the wearer, ability to communicate identity particulars), and conventional meanings (e.g., the objective features and intersubjectively understood connotations that distinguish a cocktail dress from a wedding dress, dress suit, nightgown, or female flight attendant's uniform). These features begin to suggest a design matrix that Porcupine Dress is operating within.

But what makes Porcupine Dress interesting as design-based inquiry, of course, is what distinguishes it (and Skink Dress and Blowfish Dress) from that matrix. The distinction is, of course, the qualities that make these "defensive" dresses. These distinctions spill across numerous design dimensions of the object, including formal and material qualities, analysis of the social world, desiderata, and sociocultural memes and other conventions. For the twist that makes these dresses "defensive" seems not to compromise them as dresses: overall all the dresses remain fashionable and flattering of the female figure, in conventional ways. The defensive modifications are of materials, shapes, colors, and forms that are fully compatible with the dresses otherwise everyday cocktail dress gestalt. Even the notion of clothing as protection is not radical, since clothes are already intended to protect our bodies from the elements; all Gadani is adding is protection against violence against women to another functional feature of the dress.

Additionally, all three of the dresses use biomimicry as a design tactic to defend against gender violence—the quills of a porcupine, the removable body parts of the skink (a type of lizard, which can detach its tail to get out of danger and later regrow it), the inflatability of the blowfish. The use of biomimicry here is designerly, in linking beauty and functionality seamlessly. The dresses show that the defensive additions can be made using existing fashion languages of decoration, detail, accessory, and ornament. Moreover, not only do each of these defensive mechanisms protect the body, but they do so in a way that does not hurt the body. Carrying a knife or a bottle of mace as self-defense could be turned against a woman, but it would be difficult for a woman wearing one of these dresses to be hurt by it. At the level of connotation, the use of biomimicry reminds us of our animality, proposing that our clothing can be like skin, shells, spikes, feathers, which protect us from violent predators. Extending the connotations of animality, the dress proposes that violence against women is a form of bestial predation. The matrix column that Gadani's design adds to fashion design is the use of fashionable biomimicry to protect the body from gendered violence—offering three proofs of concept to demonstrate that this can be achieved using the criteria, conventions, fabrication practices, and distribution mechanisms[7] of fashion. And that, in turn, expands the theory of fashion design to include protection from gender violence as one of its functional objectives.

Earlier I quoted Danto saying, "Notice how acceptance of one identification rather than another is in effect to exchange one *world* for another" (Danto, 1964, 578), and we can see that at work with Porcupine Dress. To comprehend the new features of the defensive dresses requires one to imagine a new world, where the meaning of fashion means something other than it used to. Porcupine Dress places the agency of protecting women against gender violence on women themselves. It reinforces in a surprising way a common media claim that women bring assault on themselves by dressing in sexually attractive ways. In literalizing that notion, the Porcupine Dress proposes that a woman can do more than dress modestly to avoid assault—she can dress defensively. This move introduces a range of practical moral and legal questions (i.e., this is Danto's "exchange [of] one *world* for another"): If one woman wears this dress and her friend does not, and the friend gets attacked, is it her friend's fault for not protecting herself? Should the quills be able to injure an attacker? If a male attacker were in fact injured by this dress, could the woman be prosecuted for assault? What if the dress accidentally injured someone who was not an attacker—who would be liable? Would it make sense for clothes to be designed for prospective sexual assaulters, to protect them from defensive mechanisms such as quills? At what age should girls start dressing defensively—and does the first time a girl dresses defensively amount to a claim that she has reached sexual maturity?

Stepping back, most of us will understand that Gadani's dresses serve a provocative purpose, that is, that she is not seriously proposing that henceforth commercial women's clothing uses biomimicry to add a measure of self-protection against sexual assault. Most of us can intuitively understand that she is critiquing gender violence and its links to fashion. But I hope my analysis here shows that the dresses do more than merely argue that gender violence is bad, or assert that fashion is implicated in gender violence—true enough, but fairly banal propositions. These dresses do more work than that. They link formal and material choices, fashion conventions, notions of beauty, tactics of self-protection, functionality, metaphor, and more in a coherent, plausible, and fully realized *design*. A protestor can make a statement about gender violence; a playwright could dramatize it; a policymaker could write law about it; a philosopher could explicate Rawlsian terms why gender violence is unethical—but none of these would be *design*. Gadani has expanded design to intervene in a problem domain in a transformative way. In exploring this problem from a design perspective, she reveals the particular entanglements of tangibles (such as fabrics, cuts, silhouettes, vulnerable areas of the human body) and intangibles (gender violence, looking feminine, dressing for success) that together compose design's role in this space. If her work falls short of design patterns in Alexander's sense, she has nonetheless made headway. In revealing this place, in opening it up for closer public debate, she is doing inquiry—doing *design* inquiry—using design as her methodology.

If we look at the sorts of claims made by those writing about the research through design, design fiction, constructive design projects—whether reporting on their own design projects or critiquing or analyzing others'—I think we see a tendency—somewhat vague but hopefully made clearer through this commentary—to claim that the process and product of design as a methodology opened up new ways of thinking about how to design in that space. Porcupine Dress does not, after all, give us new data or theory about the sociology of gender violence. Neither does it propose new critical or ethical understandings of, say, the role of capitalist ideology in the ways journalists or judges produce discourses about gender violence. Rather, it shows us how design could be appropriated to intervene in the space, and it is generative, in the sense that it invites us to think creatively within its world.

If we are looking for a set of criteria by which to evaluate the claims advanced by design as inquiry, perhaps our Danto-inspired analysis of Porcupine Dress has given us some workable ideas.

- The object in question should be recognizably based in a mature fabrication/distribution practice (e.g., product, fashion, interaction design; literary, painted, or sculpted fine art; handwork and craftsmanship), meaningfully deploying while creatively reworking its existing disciplinary tactics, skills, conventions, and techniques.
- It will have the potential to expand that practice's current conventional theory (what Danto referred to as a "matrix") to offer a new design angle or tactic (Danto: "column") that brings forth not only new objects or even products, but more importantly new ways of being, experiences, conventions, significances, practices, intentions (i.e., the sorts of things that we might follow Danto in referring to as "design identifications" that collectively "exchange … one *world* for another").
- The combination of exhibitions, deployments, documentary films, narratives, experience reports, and so forth that the design process or product generates through its

contacts with interpreting publics (including, but not limited to researchers) have the potential to render these new ways of being, experiences, conventions (etc.) clearly, visibly, and with sufficient motivation to engage the research community as contributions to design knowledge.

Although without a doubt there are important differences between the research through design practices reported in the HCI literature, the critical design practices of Dunne and Raby, or the design fictions of Julian Bleecker—my sense is that the most successful of these met all three of the above criteria, however diverse they were in the means, materials, and outcomes that got them there.

Conclusion

In 1964, Andy Warhol showed *Brillo Box* at an art gallery in New York City. Arthur Danto saw in this work a profound philosophical question about the very definition of art. It seemed to him that Warhol's work could not be accommodated by extant theories of art, even very sophisticated ones. This prompted Danto to deploy his abilities as a philosopher to work out a new theory of art. The new theory he worked out—the "is of artistic identification" and the "artworld"—had an enormous influence in philosophy and later beyond, especially in areas of sociology and social psychology, many of which have subsequently been influential in HCI.

Clearly, Danto deserves much credit for doing the intellectual labor of rearticulating Warhol's project in a conceptual vocabulary with so much utility. But just as clearly, Warhol's *Brillo Box* did much more than merely reflect exist philosophical concepts or serve as a handy example of someone else's thinking. It staged and embodied a philosophical challenge. That is, *Brillo Box* was the medium for philosophical inquiry. It did not propose a grand system, like Hegel's transcendental idealism or the Stoics' metaphysical-logical-ethical system. What *Brillo Box* did instead was reveal the very edges of thinking in its time. Once the philosopher Danto took up his challenge and explored those edges, he ended up proposing a new discursive concept and conceptual vocabulary that changed the meaning of art and gave new significances to art and related practices.

I draw two broad analogies from all this.

First, *design has the potential to do inquiry, just as art has*. To that extent, I offered the following formulation of how that might happen:

Design does inquiry by operating on and revealing to us at least one boundary of the active conceptual system.

That is, a design that is recognizable as a design but which also challenges our conceptualization of design (or one or more important parts of it) contributes to inquiry. Appropriating Danto, a design can do this by adding a new column to the matrix of theories that make it possible for an object to be a design. Or it can operate *via negativa* by rejecting positions in the schema and working towards a more "purist" position.

The second analogy I draw is that *there is a worthwhile intellectual labor in the broader HCI community taking these inquiring designs seriously, as Danto takes art objects seriously.* We should not limit our understanding of design objects to the accounts offered by these objects' designers; rather we should learn from precursors like Danto to cultivate an ability to do that labor ourselves, not least because works often have significances that their creators did not intend or anticipate (the notoriously under-articulate Warhol is a case in point).

Several features distinguish the rigor of Danto's approach. Above all, he takes objects very seriously. Epistemically, he allows them to do much more than merely exemplify existing ideas. Methodologically, he develops erudite, lengthy, and sophisticated arguments about them—not a one-paragraph blurb with a picture in a design book. He uses numerous established philosophical tools of analysis. He turns to predicate logic to deduce consequences from propositions. He contrasts our intuitive understanding of abstract concepts (such as art and nonart) with concrete examples that probe or even break such understandings. He deploys hypotheticals and thought experiments—even outlandish ones, such as Testadura before the paintings in the science library—as a disciplined strategy to resolve conundrums at the edges of thought. As with scientific theory, the output of Danto's work consists of comparatively simple theories that explain, as he describes the imitation theory of art during its era, "a great many phenomena connected with the causation and evaluation of artworks, bringing a surprising unity to a complex domain."

As we see from the example of the Porcupine Dress, Danto's analysis provides a vocabulary and set of interpretative tactics that allow us to articulate and assess what makes a design object or process become inquiry or research. I have argued that design as inquiry projects reflects the discipline, skills, techniques, and practices of one or more mature disciplines of fabrication and exhibition/deployment (design, art, craft, etc.). I have argued that they transform these from within, by adding a twist or a new feature (what Danto calls a "column" in his theory matrix), which in turn is generative of useful or interesting new ways of thinking about design materials, desiderata, forms, conventions, ways of life, practices, social structures, etc. And it is the discovery of the latter group via the transformation from within of design's underlying conceptual system that makes design as inquiry a bona fide research practice.

By this means we might attempt to answer the hardest design questions we know.

Acknowledgments

I am grateful for the critical feedback various drafts of this received, in particular from Mark Blythe, Shaowen Bardzell, and Michael Kelly. This work was supported by the Intel Science and Technology Center for Social Computing.

Notes

1. http://plato.stanford.edu/entries/identity-indiscernible/ (accessed February 7, 2014).

2. There is an important philosophical issue at stake here that I want to acknowledge without dwelling on it in this commentary: Danto took an essentialist position with regard to art; that is, he believed that it is ultimately possible to distinguish between art and nonart (i.e., that the predicate "is art" is not merely a historically contingent social construction, but rather part of a truthful ontological statement). This partly explains his emphasis on logic and his dismissiveness of the sociology of actual artworld practices. I personally disagree with Danto's essentialism, which is not at all to assert that I believe his thinking is crude or naïve (I have not attempted to do justice to his essentialist arguments in this footnote), but only to say that the technicalities of this aspect of his argument are out of the scope of the present commentary. I will merely state here my belief that it is possible to take seriously the logical and conceptual dimensions of art (or design as inquiry) theory philosophically (which is the strength of Danto's work), without committing to essentialism and thereby dismissing the benefits of a sociological understanding of relevant institutions and practices.

3. Danto is referring here to the sixteenth-century painting *Landscape with the Fall of Icarus*, long attributed to Pieter Bruegel, which depicts the moment the mythological figure of Icarus, who made wings of wax and feathers but flew too close to the sun, causing the wax to melt, and plummeted into the sea. Only Icarus' legs are visible in the painting, the rest of him has already submerged.

4. The original article actually has the word "decry" here, but Danto almost certainly intended "descry."

5. In other words, the same way that Rauschenberg's bed is a bed.

6. I say "candidate formulation" because I have no illusion that this is a satisfyingly complete definition of design as inquiry. I consider much of this commentary a thought experiment—what if I tried to replicate the reasoning of a work that contributed to art theory (i.e., Danto's "The Artworld") in a way broadly analogous to what that I think design theory needs? Other thought experiments would yield other candidate formulations, and a field of formulations critically applied to existing practices and objects would likely help contribute towards a more compelling, and more consensus-based, formulation.

7. In addition to web portfolio and museum showings, these dresses have also been shown on fashion runways.

References

Archer, B. (1995) "The Nature of Research." *Co-design, Interdisciplinary Journal of Design*, January, 6–13.

Bardzell, J., and S. Bardzell. (2013) "What Is Critical about Critical Design?" *Proceedings of the SIGCHI Conference on Human Factors in Computing Systems (CHI'13)*. New York: ACM, 3297–3306.

Bardzell, J., S. Bardzell, and E. Stolterman. (2014) "Reading Critical Designs: Supporting Reasoned Debates about Critical Designs." *Proceedings of the SIGCHI Conference on Human Factors in Computing Systems (CHI'14).* New York: ACM, 1951–1960.

Bleecker, J. (2009) "Design Fiction: A Short Essay on Design, Science, Fact and Fiction." *Near Future Laboratory* (blog). Accessed October 12, 2017. http://blog.nearfuturelaboratory.com/2009/03/17/design-fiction-a-short-essay-on-design-science-fact-and-fiction/.

Blythe, M. (2014a) "The Hitchhiker's Guide to Ubicomp: Using Techniques from Literary and Critical Theory to Reframe Scientific Agendas." *Personal and Ubiquitous Computing* 18 (4): 795–808.

Blythe, M. (2014b) "Research through Design Fiction: Narrative in Real and Imaginary Abstracts." *Proceedings of the SIGCHI Conference on Human Factors in Computing Systems (CHI'14).* New York: ACM, 703–712.

Burdick, A. (2016) "Introduction." Presentation at Alt-D: Design, Technology, and Criticality Panel Discussion. Media Design Practices, Pasadena, CA, February 11.

Carroll, N. (1990) *The Philosophy of Horror: Or, Paradoxes of the Heart.* New York: Routledge.

Cavell, S. (2002) *Must We Mean What We Say? A Book of Essays.* Updated ed. Cambridge: Cambridge University Press.

Cross, N. (2006) *Designerly Ways of Knowing.* Basel: Birkhäuser.

Csikszentmihalyi, M., and R. E. Robinson. (1991) *The Art of Seeing: An Interpretation of the Aesthetic Encounter.* Los Angeles: J. Paul Getty Museum.

Danto, A. C. (1964) "The Artworld." *Journal of Philosophy* 61 (19): 571–584.

Danto, A. C. (1999) *Philosophizing Art: Selected Essays.* Berkeley: University of California Press.

Dunne, A., and F. Raby. (2001) *Design Noir: The Secret Life of Electronic Objects.* Berlin: Birkhäuser.

Dunne, A., and F. Raby. (2007) "Critical Design FAQ." Dunne & Raby. Accessed September 1, 2012. http://www.dunneandraby.co.uk/content/bydandr/13/0.

Dunne, A., and F. Raby. (2013) *Speculative Everything.* Cambridge, MA: MIT Press.

Fallman, D. (2007) "Why Research-Oriented Design Isn't Design-Oriented Research: On the Tensions between Design and Research in an Implicit Design Discipline." *Knowledge, Technology and Policy* 20 (3): 193–200.

Fischer, G., E. Giaccardi, H. Eden, M. Sugimoto, and Y. Ye. (2005) "Beyond Binary Choices: Integrating Individual and Social Creativity." *International Journal of Human-Computer Studies* 63 (4/5): 482–512.

Frayling, C. (1994) "Research in Art and Design." *Monograph. Royal College of Art Research Papers* 1 (1): 1–5.

Freedman, C. (2000) *Critical Theory and Science Fiction.* Middleton, CT: Wesleyan University Press.

Gaver, W. (2012) "What Should We Expect from Research through Design?" *Proceedings of the SIGCHI Conference on Human Factors in Computing Systems (CHI'12).* New York: ACM, 937–946.

Goodenough, J. (2005) "Introduction I: The Philosopher Goes to the Cinema." In *Film as Philosophy: Essays on Cinema after Wittgenstein and Cavell*, edited by R. J. Read and J. Goodenough, 1–28, New York: Palgrave Macmillan.

Goodman, N. (1976) *Languages of Art: An Approach to a Theory of Symbols.* Indianapolis: Hackett.

Koskinen, I., J. Zimmerman, T. Binder, J. Redström, and S. Wensveen. (2011) *Design Research through Practice: From the Lab, Field, and Showroom.* Waltham, MA: Morgan Kaufmann.

Mazé, R., and J. Redström. (2007) "Difficult Forms: Critical Practices of Design and Research." *Proceedings of the International Association of Societies of Design Research (IASDR'07).* https://www.sd.polyu.edu.hk/iasdr/proceeding/papers/Difficult%20forms_%20Critical%20practices%20in%20design%20and%20research.pdf.

Mulhall, S. (2014) *On Film.* 2nd ed. New York: Routledge.

Nelson, H., and E. Stolterman. (2014) *The Design Way: Intentional Change in an Unpredictable World.* 2nd ed. Cambridge, MA: MIT Press.

Nussbaum, M. (1990) *Love's Knowledge: Essays on Philosophy and Literature.* Oxford: Oxford University Press.

Ratto, M. (2011) "Critical Making: Conceptual and Material Studies in Technology and Social Life." *Information Society* 27 (4): 252–260.

Van Manaan, H. (2009) *How to Study Art Worlds: On the Societal Functioning of Aesthetic Values.* Amsterdam: Amsterdam University Press.

Zimmerman, J., and J. Forlizzi. (2014) "Research through Design in HCI." In *Ways of Knowing in HCI*, edited by J. Olson and W. Kellogg, 167–190. New York: Springer.

Zimmerman, J., J. Forlizzi, and S. Evenson. (2007) "Research through Design as a Method for Interaction Design Research in HCI." *Proceedings of the SIGCHI Conference on Human Factors in Computing Systems (CHI'07).* New York: ACM, 493–502.

III

Lucidly Bewildered: Participatory and Political Design

Shaowen Bardzell

Angels of and in the fallen world, alert in perception and sympathy, lucidly bewildered, surprised by the intelligence of love
—Martha Nussbaum (paraphrasing Henry James)

The epigraph above is drawn from Nussbaum's *Love's Knowledge*. In it, she confronts the desire, common in philosophy and elsewhere, to transcend the human, to overcome human finitude and take on more godlike attributes and concerns. Seeing in such an objective a sort of narcissism that draws us away from our humanity and our relationships with others, she proposes instead a philosophy offered "as a way of being human and speaking humanly" (Nussbaum, 1990, 53). And for such a project, she argues, literature is an important guide, because it expands our experience, which in literature's absence, would be "too confined and too parochial." She continues, "Literature extends [experience], making us reflect and feel about what might otherwise be too distant for feeling. The importance of this for both morals and politics cannot be underestimated" (47).

This problem of "what might otherwise be too distant for feeling" is a social problem—the problem of understanding, forming empathy with, and even simply being able to hear an "other" as a fellow human being. Racism, sexism, xenophobia, and genocide are all symptoms of this very human failure to feel for an other.

So too are inhumane products and services. For design often entails encounters with others. It might be a person from the future—who inhabits a world where what we are designing exists. It might be a person from a different part of this world, such as someone from the Global South who is now construed as a "user" for Western technological innovators. It could be someone from our own towns—a battered woman in a shelter, an immigrant, a member of a different social class, a person with a disability—whose lived world is far enough from that of a designer, even a well-intentioned designer, that it risks becoming "too distant for feeling." Yet our ability to frame design or research questions, to meet users' and other stakeholders needs, to alleviate their suffering, to help them flourish: all are dependent on our being close enough for a kind of designerly intimacy.

How we as designers and technologists relate to others, and the understandings and moral orientations that we form from them ("love's knowledge" in Nussbaum's elegant formulation), is a key topic of all the commentators in this section. In particular, they engage a series of interrelated topics that all get at this issue of designers understanding others: how aesthetic engagement can facilitate participatory methodologies; how knowledge-production is enmeshed in systems of power—and what that does for and to us as knowers; and finally what is at stake when we represent the voices, views, needs, and desires of others.

Art, Politics, and Participation

We begin with approaches that leverage the ability of art to foster communal understandings. In their commentary on Bakhtin's *From Notes Made in 1970–1971* (chapter 29), Peter Wright and John McCarthy (chapter 30) grapple with the problem of participation in design using Mikhail Bakhtin's dialogical concepts of "creative understanding," "surplus," and "encountering the other." Specifically, Wright and McCarthy reimagine designer-user relationships and explore what it means to "know the user" in experience-centered design. They argue that a Bakhtinian perspective, as with participatory design, commits to notions of participative democracy, equality, and mutual learning of all participants. But Bakhtin adds to these a special emphasis on the aesthetic qualities of experience: aesthetic self-expression, identity formation/performance, creativity, appropriation, and playfulness—qualities that are fundamental to life.

For Wright and McCarthy, participation-oriented design methodologies should therefore take these aesthetic qualities as central to the inquiry. Bakhtin's nonreductive, dialogical understanding involves each person becoming attuned to the other as unique and particular with their own lived experiences and subjectivities, and neither the empirical observation of the other nor the empathic appreciation of them is sufficient to achieve true understanding of the other's experience. To Wright and McCarthy, both aspects of the "the ethical and aesthetical understanding" between user and designer, researcher and participant are of equal importance, and they demand a creative and interpretative relationship.

Kirsten Boehner uses Allan Kaprow's *Essays on the Blurring of Art and Life* (chapter 31) to explicate the participation-oriented design practice of the Interaction Research Studio (IRS) at Goldsmiths, University of London. In chapter 32, she uses Kaprow to illustrate what makes the flavor of participation in the IRS's work unique and reflects on the notion of participation in HCI research more generally. Boehner begins by contrasting critical design (Dunne, 1996; Dunne and Raby, 2001) and IRS's ludic design. She argues that participation in critical design is constrained by gallery settings and through media coverage, with imagined users and speculative scenarios of use. In IRS's ludic design practice, actual participants are sought out to scope and shape what the design might be.

Such a practice opens up several opportunities for participation. The pattern of participation resembles a drawn-out conversation between designers and participants over time, with rich and intensive engagement from the participants. Information shared between the participants and the designers thus never presents a complete picture of participants. Participation is also reciprocal in that both the participants and designers give and receive. Participation as conceived and practiced by IRS is "participation in a design mindset," which "shifts focus somewhat from participation in a thing more to participation in an attitude," and thereby participation in IRS design processes becomes "a concerted inquiry into life."

Boehner concludes the commentary by turning to Kaprow's notions of "artlike art" and "lifelike art" to explore whether Kaprow's criteria (e.g., revelatory, appropriate, etc.) for evaluation apply to IRS and how IRS's approach to evaluation maps to Kaprow's. To Boehner, some of Kaprow's evaluation approaches do mirror those in the IRS projects, especially how people experience in a particular context and how particularities in material and form shape inquiry and reflection. However, Boehner also points out an opportunity space in reconceptualizing the research subject's role in evaluation, informed by Kaprow's work and perspectives: participants as both the performers and audience of design inquiry.

Power, Institutions, and Critique

Critical theorists and philosophers such as Michel Foucault have argued that knowledge—social scientific knowledge in particular—is tied up in systems of power. The doctor, the pedagogue, the criminologist—all produce knowledge by means of their power relations with their subjects. To what extent is design knowledge likewise inextricable from power and subordination?

In his commentary on Foucault's "Panopticism" (chapter 33), John Bowers examines a characteristically Foucauldian research agenda for HCI (chapter 34). Bowers devotes the first half of his commentary to Foucault's analysis of Bentham's Panopticon—a design for a prison—as emblematic of an emerging system not just of institutional power, but also of knowledge production and its dependence on new forms of individualizing, observing, managing, and optimizing people. The explication of Panopticon lays the foundation for Bowers's subsequent examination of HCI as a discipline, in the Foucauldian sense, along the axis of the user and the use, paradigms and waves of HCI research. Bowers encourages us to not just apply Foucault to HCI but to treat many of HCI's characteristic concerns as further illustration of the subtle action of power/knowledge. To Bowers, differing research agendas and discourses are not just means to produce knowledge but also means for engendering different kinds of researchers who are "the subject of discourse and regulated by the disciplinary techniques of the academy," and he encourages us to consider how this plays out in HCI.

To conclude his commentary, Bowers speculates what a Foucauldian "design sensibility" for HCI might look like. He suggests five qualities for us to think with: "dark design" (where Foucault's world is dramatized and extrapolated as science fiction for critical reflection); "deviant design" (design possibilities that negate power—purposefully useless and anti-utilitarian); "design as deflection" (designs that misdirect and/or exacerbate power—artefacts that purport to be one thing but are something else); "design and porosity" (designs that work against power to create bilateral, bidirectional, and symmetrical interactions); and "design and deprofessionalization" (design artefacts, practices, and events that further perturb professional dominance). To Bowers, "we can not only explore the potentiality for Foucault as an inspiration for design but also occasion a reciprocal critical examination of his conceptions of power and resistance—their utility for us and for those others who experience the discomfort or pain of the present."

The issue of power and control is further taken up by Hrönn Brynjarsdóttir Holmer, Phoebe Sengers, and Kaiton Williams in their commentary on a chapter from James C. Scott's *Seeing Like a State*, titled "Nature and Space" (chapter 35). In *Seeing Like a State*, Scott warns against the celebratory rhetoric of technological and scientific progress. He shows how many modern, state-engineered system designs and infrastructures—while systematically comprehensive, optimizable, and manipulable—have unintended consequences that can be downright dystopian, leading to nightmarish urban environments and slavish working conditions. Design becomes an accessory to this technoscientific project and implicated in all of that project's dehumanizing implications. Using the "Nature and Space" chapter from *Seeing Like a State* leads Holmer, Sengers, and Williams (chapter 36) to initially encourage readers to consider the ways that technological design perpetuates technopolitical processes of rendering legible, calculating, and optimizing aspects of society within political regimes that function with authoritarian power.

But their essay then makes a twist, as it looks back on itself and wonders what it means to "see like *Seeing Like a State*." In other words, they reflect on the ways that seeing like a state itself simplifies and renders the complex world tractable—at the expense of recognizing its complexity. They note that seeing like *Seeing Like a State* seems to commit them to certain oversimplified distinctions and binarisms, and they try again to look outside of those binarisms. Along the way, they try out and reflect on several critical practices in an attempt to theorize the role(s) of criticism in technology research and design. Significantly, the chapter discloses and even embodies the very doubts its authors raise, as they reveal and confront the blindnesses that accompany acts of "seeing like" and the fragility of knowledge in general.

Representing Others

The next four selections focus on a specific sort of power: the power to represent others. Commenting on Edward Said's "Knowing the Oriental" (chapter 37), Beki Grinter (chapter 38) examines three topics related to the notion of power in the context of human-computer interaction for development (HCI4D) research: the relationship between knowledge production and the power it confers, how people and spaces are represented in such accounts, and the methods of knowledge production itself. Grinter observes that Said's focus on the importance of affiliation explains the underrepresentation in scholarship in HCI4D and how Euro-American institutions have come to dominate knowledge production and dissimulation about technology use in the Global South. She invites us to consider "who is representing whom, and who controls the means of representation" in HCI research. Following Said, Grinter explains that "othering" happens when people who are in control of knowledge production represent those who do not, which is especially prevalent in social media and images in print. Grinter encourages us to be careful how we write about people, places, and practices, and how we make sense of the accounts of others.

Said's writing also leads Grinter to reflect on how the use of different research methods in different cultural contexts exposes values and assumptions about the notion of participation in HCI4D. For example, the use of participatory design in developing nations is problematic in part because "our methods embed values, but we have tended to write about them as if they were value-neutral and generalizable." In Grinter's view, Said's postcolonial theory offers both critical and generative possibilities for HCI, HCI4D, and information and communication technologies and development (ICTD) scholars, in particular in issues such as power, othering, and participation.

My own commentary (chapter 40) on Seyla Benhabib's "The Generalized and the Concrete Other" from *Situating the Self: Gender, Community, and Postmodernism in Contemporary Ethics* (chapter 39), demonstrates how Benhabib's ethical philosophy can support practices aimed at ambitious social change in a robustly democratic way, applied in the context of IT design. Benhabib's normative ethics critiques and synthesizes two fundamental theories of ethics that had been characterized as in opposition to one another: the ethics of justice (associated with the masculine philosophical tradition) and the ethics of care (associated with feminism and women's ethics). In articulating this distinction, Benhabib lays out two competing positions in contemporary moral philosophy, the "generalized other" and the "concrete other." The generalized other is a generic person entitled to the same rights as all other individuals, as enshrined in many legal systems. The concrete other is an embodied being with a unique history, identity, and affective-emotional constitution who needs specific acts of care, such as those embodied in our everyday relations. Benhabib argues that we need "others" and it is a false choice to assume we can only have one or the other.

I use Benhabib's moral philosophy as a resource to analyze Intel Research's "Heterogeneous Home" (HH) as a vision of smart home of ubiquitous computing. My analysis of HH's formulation of "the resident" in the future domestic design suggests it epistemologically reflects justice ethics and Enlightenment rationality, because "the resident" is presented as a generic person lacking individuating features. I then propose a speculative alternative of "the resident" in HH through the perspective of the concrete self of care ethics. In doing so, I caution how designers' theoretical commitments might push them toward acting against their own values by tacitly legitimating the status quo while turning a blind eye to marginalized groups. I conclude the commentary by introducing Benhabib's proposal for a discourse ethics, which combines the strengths of both justice and care ethics to systematically build institutions and infrastructures and thus ensure that minority voices are heard and taken seriously. The implication for HCI is clear: Design must be an outcome of "actual dialogue" that Benhabib advocates, where the dialogue is conducted with political equality, wide access, and that it must centrally contribute to emancipatory outcomes.

Taken together, the six selections and six commentaries in this section suggest some challenges for designers and technologists as they relate to others. In particular, structural power relations seem to be simultaneously a condition of knowledge and an inhibitor of more peer-based mutual understanding. Utilitarian goals, such as optimizing and maximizing, can also become dehumanizing, as can even well-intentioned efforts to represent users and their needs. But the readings also suggest some ways forward, including the use of critique as both a reflexive intellectual strategy and as a design tactic, as well as art-based approaches that find mutual understanding through the sharing of aesthetic experiences.

References

Dunne, A. (1996) *Hertzian Tales: Electronic Products, Aesthetic Experience, and Critical Design.* Cambridge, MA: MIT Press.

Dunne, A., and F. Raby. (2001) *Design Noir: The Secret Life of Electronic Objects.* Basel: Birkhauser.

Nussbaum, M. (1990) *Love's Knowledge: Essays on Philosophy and Literature.* Oxford: Oxford University Press.

29 From Notes Made in 1970–1971

Mikhail M. Bakhtin, translated by Vern W. McGee

The false tendency toward reducing everything to a single consciousness, toward dissolving in it the other's consciousness (while being understood). The principal advantages of outsideness (spatially, temporally, and nationally). One cannot understand understanding as emotional empathy [*Einfühlung*] as the placement of the self in the other's position (loss of one's own position). This is required only for peripheral aspects of understanding. One cannot understand understanding as a translation from the other's language into one's own language.

To understand a given text as the author himself understood it. But our understanding can and should be better. Powerful and profound creativity is largely unconscious and polysemic. Through understanding it is supplemented by consciousness, and the multiplicity of its meanings is revealed. Thus, understanding supplements the text: it is active and also creative by nature. Creative understanding continues creativity, and multiplies the artistic wealth of humanity. The cocreativity of those who understand.

Understanding and evaluation. Understanding is impossible without evaluation. Understanding cannot be separated from evaluation: they are simultaneous and constitute a unified integral act. The person who understands approaches the work with his own already formed world view, from his own viewpoint, from his own position. These positions determine his evaluation to a certain degree, but they themselves do not always stay the same. They are influenced by the artwork, which always introduces something new. Only when the position is dogmatically inert is there nothing new revealed in the work (the dogmatist gains nothing; he cannot be enriched). The person who understands must not reject the possibility of changing or even abandoning his already prepared viewpoints and positions. In the act of understanding, a struggle occurs that results in mutual change and enrichment.

A meeting with a great human being,[1] as something that determines, obligates, and unites—this is the highest moment of understanding.

Meeting and communication in Karl Jaspers (*Philosophie*, 2 vols. [Berlin, 1932]).[2]

Active agreement/disagreement (if it is not dogmatically predetermined) stimulates and deepens understanding, makes the other's word more resilient and true to itself, and precludes mutual dissolution and confusion. The clear demarcation of two consciousnesses, their counterposition and their interrelations.

Understanding repeatable elements and the unrepeatable whole. Recognizing and encountering the new and unfamiliar. Both of these aspects (recognition of the repeated and discovery of the new) should merge inseparably in the living act of understanding. After all, the unrepeatability of the whole is reflected in each repeatable element that participates in the whole (it is, as it were, repeatably unrepeatable). The exclusive orientation toward recognizing, searching only for the familiar (that which has already been), does not allow the new to reveal itself (i.e., the fundamental, unrepeatable totality). Quite frequently, methods of explanation and interpretation are reduced to this kind of disclosure of the repeatable, to a recognition of the already familiar, and, if the new is grasped at all, it is only in an extremely impoverished and abstract form. Moreover, the individual personality of the creator (speaker), of course, disappears completely. Everything that is repeatable and recognizable is fully dissolved and assimilated solely by the consciousness of the person who understands: in the other's consciousness he can see and understand only his own consciousness. He is in no way enriched. In what belongs to others he recognizes only his own.

I understand the other's word (utterance, speech work) to mean any word of any other person that is spoken or written in his own (i.e., my own native) or in any other language, that is, any word that is *not mine*.[3] In this sense, all words (utterances, speech, and literary works) except my own are the other's words. I live in a world of others' words. And my entire life is an orientation in this world, a reaction to others' words (an infinitely diverse reaction), beginning with my assimilation of them (in the process of initial mastery of speech) and ending with assimilation of the wealth of human culture (expressed in the word or in other semiotic materials). The other's word sets for a person the special task of understanding this word (such a task does not exist with respect to one's own word, or it exists in an entirely different sense). Everything that is expressed in the word collapses into the miniature world of each person's own words (words sensed as his own). This and the immense, boundless world of others' words constitute a primary fact of human consciousness and human life that, like all that is primary and taken for granted, has not yet been adequately studied (consciously perceived). In any case, it has not been consciously perceived in view of its immense and essential significance. The immense significance of this for the personality, for the human *I* (in its unrepeatability). The complex interrelations with the other's word in all spheres of culture and activity fill all of man's life. But neither the word in the cross section of these interrelations nor the *I* of the speaker in that same interrelation has been studied.

All of each individual's words are divided into the categories of his own and others', but the boundaries between them can change, and a tense dialogic struggle takes place on the boundaries. But when language and various areas of ideological creativity are studied, this struggle becomes distant and abstract, for there exists an abstract *position of a third party* that is identified with the "objective position" as such, with the position of some "scientific cognition." The position of the third party is quite justified when one person can assume another's position, when a person is completely replaceable. But it is justified only in those situations, and when solving those problems, where the integral and unrepeatable individuality of the person is not required, that is, when a person, so to speak, is specialized, reflecting only a part of his individuality that is detached from the whole, when he is acting not as *I myself*, but "as an engineer," "as a physicist," and so forth. In the area of abstract scientific cognition and abstract thought, such a replacement of one person with another, that is, abstraction from the *I* and *thou*, is possible (but even here, probably, only up to a certain point). In life as the object of thought (abstract thought), man in general exists and a third party exists, but in the most vital, experienced life only *I*, *thou*, and *he* exist. And only in this life are such primary realities as *my word* and the *other's word* disclosed (exist). And in general those primary realities that have not yet been the subjects of cognition (abstract, generalizing) therefore go unnoticed by it.

The complex event of encountering and interacting with another's word has been almost completely ignored by the corresponding human sciences (and above all by literary scholarship). Sciences of the spirit; their field of inquiry is not one but two "spirits" (the studied and the person who studies, which must not be merged into one spirit). The real object of study is the interrelation and interaction of "spirits."

The attempt to understand the interaction with another's word by means of psychoanalysis and the "collective unconscious." What psychologists (mainly psychiatrists) disclose existed at one time; it was retained in the unconscious (if only the collective unconscious) and was fixed in the memories of languages, genres, and rituals; from here it penetrates into the speech and dreams (related, consciously recalled) of people (who have a particular psychic constitution and are in a particular state). The role of psychology and of the so-called psychology of culture.

The first task is to understand the work as the author himself understood it, without exceeding the limits of his understanding. This is a very difficult problem and usually requires introducing an immense amount of material.

The second task is to take advantage of one's own position of temporal and cultural outsideness. Inclusion in our (other's for the author) context.

The first stage is understanding (there are two tasks here); the second stage is scholarly study (scientific description, generalization, historical localization).

The distinction between the human and natural sciences. The rejection of the idea of an insurmountable barrier between them. The notion that they are opposed to one another (Dilthey, Rickert) was refuted by subsequent development of the human sciences.[4] The infusion of mathematical and other methods—an irreversible process, but at the same time specific methods, a general trend toward specifics (for example, the axiological approach)—is and should be developing. A strict demarcation between understanding and scientific study.

False science, based on communication that is not experienced, that is, without the initial given of the actual object. The degree of perfection of this given (of the true experience of art). At a low level, scientific analysis is inevitably superficial or even false.

The other's word should be transformed into one's own/other (or other/one's own). Distance (outsideness) and respect. In the process of dialogic communication, the object is transformed into the subject (the other's *I*).

The simultaneity of artistic experience and scientific study. They cannot be separated, but they do not always pass through their various stages and degrees at the same time.

With meaning I give *answers* to questions. Anything that does not answer a question is devoid of sense for us.

It is not only possible to understand a unique and unrepeatable individuality; there can also be individual causality.

The responsive nature of contextual meaning. Meaning always responds to particular questions. Anything that does not respond to something seems meaningless to us; it is removed from dialogue. Contextual meaning and formal definition. Formal definition is removed from dialogue, but it is deliberately and conventionally abstracted from it. It contains potential meaning.

The universalism of contextual meaning, its universality and omnitemporality.

Contextual meaning is potentially infinite, but it can only be actualized when accompanied by another (other's) meaning, if only by a question in the inner speech of the one who understands. Each time it must be accompanied by another contextual meaning in order to reveal new aspects of its own infinite nature (just as the word reveals its meanings only in context). Actual contextual meaning inheres not in one (single) meaning, but only in two meanings that meet and accompany one another. There can be no "contextual meaning in and of itself"—it exists only for another contextual meaning, that is, it exists only in conjunction with it. There cannot be a unified (single) contextual meaning. Therefore, there can be neither a first nor a last meaning; it always exists among other meanings as a link in the chain of meaning, which in its totality is the only thing that can be real. In historical life, this chain continues infinitely, and therefore each individual link in it is renewed again and again, as though it were being reborn.

The impersonal system of sciences (and knowledge in general) and the organic whole of consciousness (or the individual personality).

The problem of the speaker (of the person, the speaking subject, author of the utterance, and so forth). Linguistics knows only the system of language and the text. Yet every utterance, even a standard greeting, has a specific form of an author (and addressee).

Notes

All text in this chapter is from *Speech Genres and Other Late Essays* by M. M. Bakhtin, translated by Vern W. McGee, edited by Caryl Emerson and Michael Holquist, © 1986. By Permission of the University of Texas Press.

1. Compare the description of the "meeting" as one of the most important chronotopic motifs in literature in "Forms of Tim and Chronotope in the Novel," in *The Dialogic Imagination*, pp. 97–99, 244.

2. Karl Jaspers (1883–1969)—his basic concept is "encompassing," an essentially religious concept intended to suggest the all-embracing transcendent reality within which human existence is enclosed. Jaspers is deeply aware of the limitations of abstract science (in the human as well as the natural sciences) because they cloud perception of the specific situatedness of human being. Communication is the means by which human beings exercise freedom in their situatedness.

3. The notes on "the other's word" are associated with an article intended for *Voprosy filosofii* (Questions of Philosophy), the major journal for philosophy in the Soviet Union. In "Notes Made in 1970–71," Bakhtin gives two possible titles for the piece: "The Other's Word as the Specific Object of Investigation in the Human Sciences" and "The Problem of the Other's Word (other's Speech) in Culture and Literature: From essays on Metalingusistics." He also was considering an epigraph from *Faust*: "Was ihr den Geist der Zeiten nennt …" (What they *name* the spirit of the times …). Bakhtin was probably quoting from memory, for the correct quote is: "Was ihr den Geist der Zeiten heist …" (What they *call* the spirit of the times …).

4. Dilthey developed what he felt were the foundations for a "science of the spirit" (*Geistesvissenschaft*) as distinct from the natural sciences. The method of *Gesteswissenschaft* was to be grounded in understanding, as opposed to causal explanation in the natural sciences. Understanding coincides with our interpretation of significant experience; thus, the means for becoming aware of spirit—Dilthey's hermeneutics—coincide with attempts to understand psychology. Bakhtin discusses his differences with Dilthey in *Marxism and the Philosophy of Language* (pp. 26–28 in English ed.).

30 Bakhtin's Dialogics and the "Human" in Human-Centered Design

Peter Wright and John McCarthy

One of the liberating developments in human-computer interaction (HCI) research back in the late 1990s was a shift away from office systems, workflows, and information technologies toward a broader conception of people-technology relations, which included all manner of interactive technologies and experiences, from texting teenagers (Kasesniemi and Rautiainen, 2002) to people having fun with answering machines (Blythe et al., 2003). For us, the interesting thing about this shift in focus was that it seemed to require new ways of thinking about those people referred to as "users" and "designers" in HCI. But it is often quite hard to critically rethink foundational concepts like "users" from within a discipline. Sometimes it requires a viewpoint from outside in order to see clearly the kind of assumptions, presumptions, and "taken-for-granteds" that populate the discipline.

So it was in 2000, when we wanted to develop a perspective on user experience that would challenge ourselves and the HCI community to move beyond a functional conception of "users" and "designers." We sought a perspective on human experience that was some distance from our own methodologically and epistemologically (we were both trained as cognitive psychologists), and we found the writings of John Dewey and Mikhail Bakhtin particularly valuable in this regard. Reading Dewey and Bakhtin revealed new worlds and provided new conceptual tools that helped us to develop our account of technology as experience (McCarthy and Wright, 2004). The ideas of Dewey and Bakhtin have inspired many disciplines, but their writing is not always approachable and for us the experience of reading their work, Bakhtin's especially, was sometimes as much a journey of poetic imagination and inspiration as it was critical analysis. Thankfully, there is much scholarship around the works of these two inspirational thinkers that can provide help and guidance for those not trained in philosophy or literary criticism (see for example Morson and Emerson, 1990). This was valuable to us as it provided entry points and routes through their complex texts that helped us find the relevance of their ideas for our own discipline of HCI.

For the current volume, we struggled to choose a single text from the rich abundance of writings of Dewey and Bakhtin. But eventually we chose this somewhat unusual text from Bakhtin. It is a collection of notes rather than a completed essay. The collection includes notes on understanding in the world of others' words, utterances, and speech work in which we live; notes on the worlds created when people encounter and interact with each other; notes on the potential and innovation created by interacting voices. This is a lot and yet it is a small fragment of even those parts of Bakhtin's work that we found useful in developing our approach to HCI. We chose the extract in part because its freewheeling fragmentary style creates many opportunities for us to jump off and make connections to other parts of his work and from there to resonances with issues that we find relevant for understanding user experience in HCI. We also chose it because it illustrates the often complex character of Bakhtin's writings, as well as its poetry, the liveliness of Bakhtin's voice, and the open-ended way in which he articulates his aesthetics of experience, all of which inspired us in the early 2000s to look for those resonances between Bakhtin's world of words and HCI.

In the commentary that follows, we draw out from Bakhtin's notes the dialogical concept of "creative understanding" and some associated ideas that exemplify how Bakhtin's thinking scaffolded the construction of our particularly aesthetic account of technology as experience. We explain how our reading of his conceptual development of "dialogue" and "dialogic," and associated concepts such as "surplus" and "encountering the other," provided us with a different way of looking at the creative potential of relationships between "designer" and "user," and a critical language for understanding experience. In his notes, Bakhtin (1986) states "anything that does not answer a question is devoid of sense for us" (145). Bakhtin's understanding of utterances and accounts as responsive, always in some sense answering questions, whether those questions have been asked or implied or heard in a previous utterance, suggests a dialogical approach to exploring experience and the meanings people make of it that informs our work with participants in experience-centered design. In the following sections, we hope to give a taste of how reading Bakhtin has helped us to answer some of our, at the time, inchoate questions about experience and potential in HCI and in designer-user relationships, and to formulate afresh a question that has driven much of our thinking since 2004, namely, what does it mean to "know the user" in the world of experience-centered design?

Dialogical Understanding

A recurring theme in Bakhtin's notes is resistance to reductive accounts of understanding, which he saw as objectifying experience, relationships, and knowledge. Such reduction has a tendency to feature not only in academic understanding but also in our everyday understanding. It's what we refer to as the "this X is just a Y" game. Bakhtin describes this as "the false tendency to reduce everything to a single consciousness, toward dissolving in it the other's consciousness (while being understood)" (Bakhtin,

1986, 141). It is an exclusive, monological understanding in which other voices are displaced and not heard or recognized. In the following extract he notes that reductive understanding tends toward interpretation in terms of concepts and language that is already well known and away from anything new. "Quite frequently, methods of explanation and interpretation are reduced to this kind of disclosure of the repeatable, to a recognition of the already familiar, and, if the new is grasped at all, it is only in an extremely impoverished and abstract form" (Bakhtin, 1986, 142–143).

Bakhtin's resistance to reductive accounts arises from his commitment to the concept of dialogue as not only the method of enquiry but also as the fundamental character of human understanding. This dialogical approach takes as its premise that understanding is an encounter between two or more consciousnesses. It is clear from Bakhtin's earlier work, *Toward a Philosophy of the Act* (1993), that when he writes about consciousness, he is referring to individuated selves—distinct and particular people aware of themselves as experiencing, speaking, evaluating, and feeling. Against this background, dialogical understanding is achieved in encounters between particular people participating with each other in lived experiences to which they are responsively committed.

Bakhtin's dialogical understanding occurs in particularly intoned situations in which self and other are mutually and reciprocally constituted through their emotional-volitional responsive relationship with each other (McCarthy and Wright, 2004; Wright, 2011). As Hicks (2000) puts it, "Dialogue entails a type of responsivity that is ethically particular and answerable to uniquely felt and known others" (229). This ethical and aesthetic particularity of dialogue suggests that human understanding involves each person becoming attuned to the other as a unique and particular person who is also trying to make their and others' experiences meaningful in their responsively committed words and actions.

Bakhtin's interest in literature led him to exemplify dialogical understanding in terms of the relations between author and hero, author and reader, reader and novel, and ethnographer and a foreign culture. The kinds of question he asked were: what does it mean for the author to understand his hero (character or protagonist), how is it that a character can surprise his/her author (Morson and Emerson, 1990)? What does it mean for a reader to understand a work? Does it mean that the reader needs to understand the author's intentions? What does it mean to understand another person? Does it mean that we have to "become" the other person for a while; to walk in their shoes; to see the world only though their eyes; to "fuse" with them as Bakhtin would say? Or is it sufficient to observe them from a distance without affecting what is observed; to analyze objectively and scientifically; to classify and to measure?

For Bakhtin, neither the objective observation of the other nor an empathic "fusing" with them is sufficient to achieve a deep understanding of the experience of the other. He argues that the objective stance has a tendency to reduce understanding to a process of recognizing in the other what we already know, reducing unfamiliar categories to familiar ones. This is what we referred to above as the "this X is just a Y" game. This form of understanding is not conducive to innovation or imagination. But Bakhtin also argues that an attempt to lose ourselves empathically in the subjectivity of the other is equally unhelpful to a deep understanding of the other, because if our only available response is to disregard our own experience and to lose ourselves in the other's experience, then we are equally unable to innovate, because we cannot add anything to their situation. Morson and Emerson (1990, 99–100) sum this argument up very well:

> How, then, does one deal creatively and responsibly with otherness? One cannot become a mere duplicate of the other through total empathy or "fusing" of horizons; that could add nothing truly new. Nor should one "modernize or distort" the other by turning the other into a version of oneself. Both these alternatives, which are often seen as the only possible ones, reduce two voices and two perspectives to one. But true responsibility and creative understanding are dialogic, and dialogue gives rising to *unexpected* questions. "If an answer does not give rise to a new question from itself, it falls out of dialogue and enters systemic cognition, which is essentially impersonal." (Morson and Emerson quoting from Bakhtin, 1986, 168)

As the above excerpt makes clear, dialogical thinking often begins by trying to dissolve the mutually exclusive logic with "it's either X or Y" distinctions, in favor of an inclusive "it's both X and Y" thinking, because where the former limits relational thinking, the latter requires it. Dialogical thinking requires us to find intermediary concepts in order to make it possible for "both X and Y" to be imaginable as coexistent. In that spirit, Bakhtin developed the concepts of creative understanding and surplus, which reframe what it means to understand the other.

Creative Understanding

Bakhtin's concept of creative understanding is defined earlier in the book *Speech Genres and Other Late Essays* than the extract we have chosen, but it is a concept that permeates many of his texts and it suggests a context for appreciating the relevance of the text we are commenting on for innovation in HCI. Bakhtin's concept of creative understanding seeks to dissolve the distinction between subjective and objective understanding by introducing the concept of potential. Creative understanding is achieved by combining an empathic engagement with the other, seeing the other and the situation (including oneself) from the other's position, while at the same time remembering one's own unique position. Through seeing the mutual difference in perspectives on the situation, both parties can read into each other and the situation the meanings and possibilities that each alone could not see. This relational approach is captured in the following definition of creative understanding:

> *Creative understanding* does not renounce itself, its own place in time, its own culture; and it forgets nothing. In order to understand, it is immensely important for the person who understands to be *located outside* the object of his or her creative understanding—in time, in space, in culture. For

> one cannot even really see one's own exterior and comprehend it as a whole, and no mirrors or photographs can help; our real exterior can be seen and understood only by other people, because they are located outside us in space and because they are *others*. (Bakhtin, 1986, 7)

For Bakhtin any "other" has potential, which they themselves cannot see. Only by coming into dialogue with another who is different or outside can such potential be revealed. This seems to be in line with Seyla Benhabib's notion of discourse ethics in that we strive to systematically develop mechanisms to make visible the voice of others (see S. Bardzell's commentary in chapter 40). To both Bakhtin and Benhabib, this outside position is not the objective and reductive stance of scientific observation. It is not simply a matter of looking for the familiar, for the sameness between our own situation and the other's—it requires an openness to the new and unexpected in the other, and an ability to reconfigure the self in response to this surprise. In Bakhtin's dialogical world, creative understanding works both ways; both the culture studied and the analyst studying can recognize the surplus in the other.

For us, creative understanding is a useful concept when talking about a number of recent HCI projects we have been involved in with colleagues in Culture Lab, in the UK. In these projects designers and users have worked together to imagine new ways of doing things and designing interactive technologies to support that imaginary (for examples, see McCarthy and Wright, 2015; Wright and McCarthy, 2010). A particularly relevant example is the work of Jon Hook who, in the course of his PhD research, worked with video-jockeys (VJs) to understand their practices and to design forms of interactive technology that would take their practice in new directions (Hook et al., 2013).

VJs create and perform video, film, and graphics effects to accompany live musical performances. Jon's approach to understanding the practices of the VJs he designed with focused on finding ways in which he and the VJs could engage with and respond to what is new and different in each other's practice. In the first of two studies, Jon and his team produced a film documentary about the VJs' practices. This enabled Jon and his team to express their observations of VJing as a personal interpretation, which in turn created for VJs the experience of seeing their own practices from another's point of view. Then, Jon invited the VJs to edit the film in response to discussions that allowed them to reflect on—and respond to—both the familiar and the unexpected in what they had seen and heard about their practices.

In the second long-term study (Hook et al., 2013), Jon took a more idiographic approach by focusing on the experiences of a single VJ. He worked with one of the VJs, Andrew, on the iterative design of Waves, a system for Andrew's practice. Andrew was invited to experiment with and contribute to the iteration of Waves. While developing a series of prototypes together, both Jon and Andrew refined their understandings of Andrew's experience of VJing and of both of their experiences of live performance. Andrew and Jon brought different experience, skills, and interests to their encounter, and by engaging responsively with each other created opportunities for change for each other. The real design skill here was in imagining ways in which different perspectives could be encouraged to encounter and creatively understand each other.

The VJing project illustrates two important points about creative understanding. First, the project's opening assumption is that there is equality in difference among participants. Designers (e.g., Jon and his team) and users (e.g., the VJs) are both assumed to bring to the encounter a certain outsideness. But both parties are respected as their own experts with something of relevance to contribute. The user is "the expert" in his or her own culture and practices, as is the designer. Second, the aim of an encounter between designer and user is to create a new understanding of the activity (e.g., VJing), not to simply replicate the user's understandings or the designer's. Both designer and user have unique positions with respect to that activity, which is more than just their formal knowledge of their respective domains or the training they have received—it is also their lived history of experiences of their activity and practices in the web of other experiences that is their life. Thus designer and user have a surplus of meaning relative to each other and a common interest or situation, which are the prerequisites for a dialogue involving creative understanding.

Bakhtin's creative understanding and his articulation of the idea of surplus lead to a nuanced account of dialogue in which both designer and user have something that Morson and Emerson (1990) refer to as "addressive surplus." This is an attitude toward each other that allows them to ask the kinds of questions that provide the stimulus for new ways of looking. It requires mutual and genuine curiosity about the other that involves a willingness to be surprised by the new and not simply to be looking for a confirmation that X is just another Y:

> The addressive surplus is the surplus of the good listener, one capable of "live entering" (vzhivanie). It requires "an active (not a duplicating) understanding, a willingness to listen" (TRDB p. 299). Without trying to finalise the other or define him once and for all, one uses one's "outsideness" and experience to ask the right sort of questions. Recognising the other's capacity for change, one provokes or invites him to reveal and outgrow himself. (Morson and Emerson, 1990, 242)

This is how we understand Bakhtin's notes when he writes:

> To understand a given text as the author himself understood it. But our understanding of it can and should be better.... Through understanding it is supplemented by consciousness, and the multiplicity of its meanings revealed. Thus understanding supplements the text. It is active and also creative by nature. Creative understanding continues creativity, and multiplies the artistic wealth of humanity. The co-creativity of those who understand. (Bakhtin, 1986, 141–142).

If a designer simply understands the world the way the user understands it, then nothing is gained. The designer's understanding should add something interpretively that the user alone could not see. Bakhtin sees evaluation as a significant feature of what is added and gained. "Understanding is impossible without evaluation. Understanding cannot be separated from evaluation: they are simultaneous and constitute a unified integral act" (1986, 142) Bakhtin saw the uniqueness of human experience "as being rooted in how individuals 'shade' or intone acts of living with evaluative response" (Hicks, 2000, 230). In this context, evaluation is seen in those lived moments in which an individual engages with another in an answerable response—answerable in the sense that he or she "owns" this response, and intones it with both his or her own meanings and those compelled by the other" (2000, 230). In these lived moments, in which people encounter each other openly and answerably, and in which words are spoken and acted out in an emotionally and evaluatively intoned way, something new—new meaning, understanding, feelings, values—is created. For example: Words acquire expressiveness in their live use in concrete utterances; relationships develop as people attune to each other's evaluative, answerable expression; understandings accompany this aesthetic seeing that characterizes mutually responsive encounter and dialogue.

Designers have to make their knowledge relevant to the user's situation. In this sense the designer's understanding is evaluative because it is a committed response—owned by the designer who intones it as something for which he or she is answerable—and is always making a judgment of difference and making sense of that difference. Lest we forget, of course, in dialogical relationship (characterized by equality in difference), what is true for the designer is also true for the user. The user's understanding of the designer's situation is always different from the designer's, and, when expressed as their particular understanding, creatively adds something to it.

But while partners in a dialogical relationship approach a situation from a position of their own experience, they are at the same time adding to that experience through the encounter and in so doing must also be open to having that position or point of view changed. In his notes Bakhtin says, "The person who understands must not reject the possibility of changing or even abandoning his already prepared viewpoints and positions. In the act of understanding a struggle occurs that results in mutual change and enrichment" (Bakhtin, 1986, 142). In inviting someone to outgrow themselves, we must also be prepared to outgrow ourselves. In Jon Hook's study, the Waves system introduced into Andrew's practice the potential of a semitransparent touchscreen surface, which allowed Andrew to reconfigure the relationship between himself and the audience. He could now stand and perform in front of the audience and the audience could see for themselves the relationship between his actions and the multimedia content. The project enriched the designer's understanding of live performance and pushed him to develop novel methods for creatively engaging with the practices and cultures of VJs in the first instance, and others beyond too.

Rethinking the Principle of "Knowing the User"

Elsewhere (Wright and McCarthy, 2005), we have argued that the sensibilities that Bakhtin captures in his idea of creative understanding offer a way to critically position the contribution of different approaches to involving people in design. This can be usefully summed up by the question, what does it mean to know the user? The answer to this question is different for each of the various approaches.

In an engineering approach to user-centered design, the designer is configured to stand above the activity of users. Engineers observe and talk about users and represent the users' activities in ways that will be useful for other designers to work with. Here users are subjects of analysis, not participants. There is no reflexive component to this way of seeing; rather, designers seek to take an objective stance and create an accurate record of what it is that users do through the classification and categorization of observables. This sort of approach is exemplified in the following quote: "The user experience development process is all about ensuring that no aspect of the user's experience with your site happens without your conscious, explicit intent. This means taking into account every possibility of every action the user is likely to take and understanding the user's expectations at every step of the way through that process" (Garrett, 2002, 21). As the quote makes clear, the aim is to eliminate any possibility of surprise and any possibility of learning, which are the very features that Bakhtin argues are at the heart of what it means to creatively understand the other.

Contextual design (Beyer and Holtzblatt, 1998) is another approach to involving users, but one which is differently positioned with respect to what it means to know the user. Beyer and Holtzblatt suggest that designers should adopt the role of an "apprentice" when interviewing users (Beyer and Holtzblatt, 1995). The apprenticeship relationship moves the designer from a "superior" position of knowing to an "inferior" position of learning, hence inverting the hierarchical assumptions of the engineering approach. Using this approach Beyer and Holtzblatt document the genuine surprise and astonishment that designers and developers experience when they take up the role of apprentice, appreciating—in some cases for the first time—how complex a users' practice is and how ill-suited their technology is for supporting it. But the apprenticeship relationship is also rather one-sided from the point of view of dialogical understanding. While it disrupts the traditional hierarchy, it replaces it with a quasi-inverted one rather than removing it entirely. While moving toward seeing the world like the user does is important, users must also come toward seeing the world like the designer; only in this way can the potential of each be used to develop a real shared understanding of possible design futures. For us this is what is distinctive about a dialogical approach to user-centered design. We can see in Bakhtin's notes why this dialogical conception of understanding leads him to argue that disagreement is a sign of a nonreductive encounter that "stimulates and deepens understanding, makes the other's word more true to itself, and precludes mutual dissolution and confusion" (Bakhtin, 1986, 42).

For many (ourselves included), Simonsen and Robertson's (2012) conception of participatory design (PD), because of its attempt to challenge hierarchical relationships between designers and users and to give users a real voice in design, is much closer to a dialogical approach than either the engineering approach or contextual design.

Both PD and the dialogical approach that we are discussing here are committed to the participation of users in design and, as a result, draw attention to issues of ownership, authorship, and voice in design practice. It is also clear that many contributors to Simonsen and Robertson (2012) are committed not only to a more participative approach to design and appropriation but also to opening up the design process in a way that fosters the cocreation of digital and social futures.

These are commitments and values that echo much of what you will find in Bakhtin. They can be read as commitments to creative understanding and to the cocreativity of understanding as dialogue. However, as we have seen above, for Bakhtin, dialogue is ontologically aesthetic and ethical, self-expressive as well as informative, affective as well as communicative. This understanding of dialogue provides different challenges and opportunities for understanding participatory projects and participative experience, in which ownership, authorship, and voice are aesthetic as well as ethical qualities of practice, a difference which has made quite a difference to our practice.

We have argued elsewhere (McCarthy and Wright, 2015) that the nature of the invitation to participate in a project is seminal in terms of the engagement and interaction that follows, more specifically in terms of how ownership, authorship, and voice play out in the prosaic work of shaping and sustaining participant subjectivity in a project. As Dave Beech (2008), an artist and critic, puts it, "Participation always involves a specific invitation and a specific formation of the participant's subjectivity, even when the artist asks them simply to be themselves" (3). At a minimum, creative understanding requires that difference is not diminished in participation. It is only when affective, aesthetic, ethical, and expressive differences are appreciated and provoke genuine curiosity that creative understanding is possible. Sometimes the invitation to participate in a project itself neutralizes difference and dampens participants' powers to subvert, a high cost for outsiders to pay (Beech, 2008).

According to Bakhtin, Beech, and others, we cannot know the other—know the user—without listening and responding to the ways in which they intone their experience in their own particular embodied voice. As articulated by Shaowen Bardzell in her commentary on Benhabib (chapter 40), Benhabib argues that it is through the voices of others, especially how they intone their experience, that we come to know them as concrete others with particular identities and sensibilities: "Neither the concreteness nor the otherness of the 'concrete other' can be known in the absence of the *voice* of the other. The viewpoint of the concrete other emerges as a distinct one only as a result of self-definition. It is the other who makes us aware both of her concreteness and her otherness" (Benhabib, 1992, 168). Voice is something richly aesthetic and ethical in Benhabib's and Bakhtin's formulations, a process of self-construction and expression that suggests a lived experience and subjectivity, which perhaps entails an invitation to be known. Knowing the other—the user—entails creatively responding to this invitation. As Beech, Benhabib, and Bakhtin suggest, any approach that neutralizes the heterogeneity of users' voices and that underestimates the cost to them of their participation loses the richness of their experience and voice.

In some strongly experience-centered approaches to involving users, designers seek to spend extended periods of time living with and learning from individuals and communities, and strive to keep the experience alive as a resource for design. Rachel Clarke (Clarke et al., 2013), another of our colleagues in Culture Lab, in her experience-centered design research in a women's center, spent over two years first as a volunteer and then as a participatory artist and designer working with black and Asian women who had experienced domestic abuse. Rachel worked closely with a number of the women, including Zahrah and Aseeda, helping them to create digital portraits before designing a digital system that responded to some of the experiences the women had shared. Likewise Jayne Wallace (Wallace et al., 2013) worked with Gillian, a person suffering from (at the beginning of the project) early stage dementia, and with Gillian's husband and carer, John, over a period of years developing digital pieces with them that responded to their shared experiences and celebrated their lives together.

These projects seem to us to embody a Bakhtinain sensibility toward creative understanding because they are attentive and answerably responsive to the particular named people and they focus on relationships. The projects are not about dementia or violence. They are about Gillian, John, and Jayne, and Rachel, Zahrah, and Aseeda. The projects are about each participant (including the designers and researchers) responding to the other's stories, hopes, and voices, and about design as geared toward making those voices heard. In these extended encounters with the other, the aim is to keep experience alive throughout the design process. In those projects, designers come to know participants as concrete others, with their own lived experiences and subjectivities, by responding creatively to the ways in which participants intone their experience in their own particular, embodied voices. Jayne gets to know Gillian and John, and vice versa, by building relationships with them in which each is so attuned and responsive to the intoned words of the other that they trust that their own responses will also be felt and received as efforts after meaning in the project that they are involved in together.

While an extended three-year project working with a single user or a single community provides remarkably profound understandings of the experience of domestic violence or dementia, for many situations it is not a practical or desirable approach. The value of attending to these projects here is in the way in which they throw into relief questions of what the relationship between designer and user is, what it could be, and what it should be in any given circumstance. What is lost and what is gained when your research participant becomes your friend? It also throws into relief assumptions about how different approaches configure the user, what is means to know the user, and how that knowledge relates to design.

Looking at how Bakhtin grapples with what it means to understand the other helped us to understand the complexity of issues around the HCI principle of "knowing the user." It highlighted first of all, that there is more than one way of knowing (Belenky et al., 1986) and that, as well as personal disposition and experience, how you choose to approach knowing depends very much on what you want to know and what you want to do with that knowledge. Our reading of Bakhtin made evident to us that what is at issue here is a different conception of what it means to be human, and by implication, what it means to be the persons we refer to as designers, engineers, researchers, and users in our everyday discourses.

In Bakhtin's notes there are a number of allusions to the distinction between natural and human sciences and between science and art that resonate with tensions in design research between scientific, engineering, and artistic movements. Appreciating these resonances may help frame a dialogical understanding of relationships between designer, materials, and practices. At one point, Bakhtin makes a similar distinction to Belenky et al. (1986) between separated and connected knowing. He emphasizes the uniqueness of each person when making this distinction, and therefore the need to engage responsively with particular others: "There exists an abstract position of a third party that is identified with the 'objective position' as such with the position of 'scientific cognition.' The position of the third party is quite justified when one person can assume another's position, when a person is completely replaceable" (Bakhtin, 1986, 143). This extract crystallizes a key ontological commitment of the experience-centered projects of Hook, Clarke, and Wallace discussed above, namely that the individual as a unique person is integral and irreplaceable. In other fragments, Bakhtin captures something of the relationships that characterize creative understanding in those projects. For example: "The other's word should be transformed into one's own/other (or other/one's own). Distance (outsideness) and respect. In the process of dialogic communication, the object is transformed into the subject (the other's *I*)" (Bakhtin, 1986, 145). With Bakhtin's perspective comes a deep commitment to recognizing the other as a living, feeling, unique, named, and particular person. For Bakhtin, the responsivity of recognition is both ethical and aesthetic, as ethical sensitivity to an other is intimately linked to the creative understanding and the responsibilities that come with being responsive to the other which manifests itself in addressive surplus and the concern to see the other outgrow themselves. In so doing we take part in a shared responsibility for creating a new way of being for the other, what Bakhtin describes as authoring the self in other.

Building on Bakhtin's perspective, in each of the design examples we have given above we see the designers (Jon Hook, Rachel Clarke, and Jayne Wallace) and the other participants (Andrew, Zahrah, and Aseeda, and Gillian and John) as different yet equal participants in a negotiation of meaning that increases the repertoire of responses available in the communities in which the projects are situated. In these projects, designers and other participants become authors, together ethically and aesthetically creating the potential for reconfiguring self and other. For example, because they are responsive and responsible to each other in the participatory projects they create together, Jon and Andrew, Rachel, Zahrah, and Aseeda, Jayne, Gillian, and John enable each other to experience the potential for creative change in their encounters with each other.

With this dialogical sensibility, the aesthetics and ethics of the relation between user and designer, researcher and participant, become of paramount importance. Rather than being something added on as a procedural checklist and a signed consent form, our relationship emerges from a genuine concern and connection to particular others. This ethical and aesthetical understanding becomes a space in which the creative relationship evolves.

In Conclusion

When we first encountered Bakhtin's philosophy, we were trying to find a way of thinking and writing about people's experiences with technology as creative, fun, connective, and prosaic. Thinking about mobile phones and music players as information technologies did not allow us to capture the feelings that people had about them or the ways in which they seemed to express the identities of their owners. Nor did it capture the creative ways in which people appropriated them, which often seemed to go far beyond anything intended by the designers of the technologies. Reading Bakhtin's treatment of how characters in novels live in the imaginations of writers and readers opened up for us a journey of the imagination that has been both poetic and critical. Realizing the potential of digital media to inhabit people's lived experience led us to construct a world in which technology could share some of the imaginative potential of characters in a novel and design could be like the dialogue between writers (and readers) and the characters that take them on journeys of imagination.

Realizing how our own engagement with Bakhtin's writing had expanded our own appreciation of lived experience more generally also led us to think of design in terms of the construction of dialogical spaces in which designers and users encounter one another. In these responsive encounters, designers and users already have a voice, and in recognizing this fact they are able to reconfigure each other and the situation from which their encounter springs. The meaning of "user" and "designer" can never be particular and specific enough, in Bakhtin's world. In this world, the encounter is between real people—Jon and Andrew, Rachel and Zahrah and Aseeda, Jayne and Gillian—imagining together potential futures and new ways of making meaning. In this world, design is inspired by the lived experience of others even though such experience is often inchoate and has to be kept alive in the imagination. Dialogical space does not make itself. Like novelists, experience-centered designers imagine and create ways of bringing different perspectives together to creatively understand each and to creatively understand the potential for transforming the situation and each other.

References

Bakhtin, M. M. (1986) *Speech Genres and Other Late Essays,* edited by C. Emerson and M. Holquist, translated by V. W. McGee. Austin: University of Texas Press.

Bakhtin, M. M. (1993) *Toward a Philosophy of the Act,* edited by M. Holquist, translated by V. Liapunov. Austin: University of Texas Press.

Beech, D. (2008) "Include Me Out!" *Art Monthly* 8 (4): 1–4.

Belenky, M. F., B. McVicar Clinchy, N. R. Goldberger, and J. M. Tarkle. (1986) *Women's Ways of Knowing: The Development of Self, Voice and Mind.* New York: Basic Books.

Benhabib, S. (1992) *Situating the Self: Gender, Community and Postmodernism in Contemporary Ethics.* Cambridge: Polity.

Beyer, H., and K. Holtzblatt. (1995) "Apprenticing with the Customer." *Communications of the ACM* 38 (5): 45–52.

Beyer, H., and K. Holtzblatt. (1998) *Contextual Design: Defining Customer-Centered Systems.* San Francisco: Morgan Kaufman.

Blythe, M. A., A. F. Monk, K. Overbeeke, and P. C. Wright. (2003) *Funology: From Usability to Enjoyment.* Amsterdam: Kluwer.

Clarke, R., P. Wright, M. Balaam, and J. McCarthy. (2013) "Digital Portraits: Photo-Sharing after Domestic Violence." In *Proceedings of the SIGCHI Conference on Human Factors in Computing Systems (CHI'13).* New York: ACM, 2517–2526.

Garrett, J. J. (2002) *The Elements of User Experience: User-Centered Design for the Web and Beyond.* Indianapolis: New Riders.

Hicks, D. (2000) "Self and Other in Bakhtin's Early Philosophical Essays: Prelude to a Theory of Prose Consciousness." *Mind, Culture, and Activity* 7 (3): 227–242.

Hook, J., J. McCarthy, P. Wright, and P. Olivier. (2013) "Waves: Exploring Idiographic Design for Live Performance." *Proceedings of the SIGCHI Conference on Human Factors in Computing Systems (CHI'13).* New York: ACM, 2969–2978.

Kasesniemi, E.-L., and P. Rautiainen. (2002) "Mobile Culture of Children and Teenagers in Finland." In *Perpetual Contact: Mobile Communication, Private Talk, Public Performance,* edited by J. E. Katz and M. A. Aakhus, 170–192. Cambridge: Cambridge University Press.

McCarthy, J., and P. Wright. (2004) *Technology as Experience.* Cambridge, MA: MIT Press.

McCarthy, J., and P. Wright. (2015) *Taking [A]part: The Politics and Aesthetics of Participation in Experience-Centered Design.* Cambridge, MA: MIT Press.

Morson, G. S., and C. Emerson. (1990) *Mikhail Bakhtin: Creation of a Prosaics.* Stanford, CA: Stanford University Press.

Simonsen, J., and T. Robertson. (2012) *Routledge International Handbook of Participatory Design.* Routledge.

Wallace, J., P. Wright, J. McCarthy, D. Green, J. Thomas, and P. Olivier. (2013) "A Design-Led Inquiry into Personhood in Dementia." *Proceedings of ACM CHI'13.* New York: ACM, 2617–2626.

Wright, P. (2011) "Reconsidering the H, the C, and the I: Some Thoughts on Reading Suchman's Human-Machine Reconfigurations." *Interactions* 18 (5): 28–31.

Wright, P. C., and J. McCarthy. (2005) "The Value of the Novel in Designing for Experience." In *Future Interaction Design,* edited by A. Pirhonen, H. Isomäki, C. Roast, and P. Saariluoma, 9–30. London: Springer.

Wright, P. C., and J. McCarthy. (2010) *Experience-Centered Design: Designers, Users, and Communities in Dialogue.* New York: Morgan Claypool.

31 Nontheatrical Performance (1993)

Allan Kaprow

Traditional theater: an empty room except for those who've come to watch. The lights dim. End of performance. Audience leaves.

West Berlin, 1973. Wolf Vostell arranged a Happening called *Berlin Fever.* It involved close to a hundred participants. Driving from various parts of the city, they converged on a vast empty field near the wall dividing Berlin's western and eastern sectors. Above the wall in a tower were armed border guards. At one edge of the field were small flower and vegetable gardens tended by local residents. The field itself had been cleared of the ruins of buildings bombed in the last war. It was a warm, sunny September weekend. The plan given to the participants read:

(A) Come with your car to Osdorfer Street in Berlin Lichterfeld (dead end), last stretch of the street on the right side.
(B) Take up a position with your car in rows of ten each, as thickly as possible, with the cars next to and behind one another.
(C) At a signal start all the cars and try to drive as slowly as possible. Try to remain as tightly grouped as you started.
(D) If you have a companion in the car, he should write down how many times you shift gears, clutch and step on the gas. If you're alone, try to be conscious of every smallest action. Add up all these activities in your brain as psycho-esthetic productions.
(E) After 30 minutes of this extremely slow driving, get out of the car (turn off motor) and go to the trunk of your vehicle. There open and close the trunk lid 750 times; and put a white plate inside and take it out 375 times. This ritual should be accomplished as fast as possible, without interruption, and without dramatization.
(F) When this event is completed, lay strips of cloth on the ground in front of the columns of cars; then place the white plate which is in your car trunk onto the cloth.
(G) Take a handful of salt out of a bag beneath the biggest nearby tree. Pour it onto the plate which you've previously placed on the cloth.
(H) After this, the auto columns begin to move again at the slowest possible speed. All cars pass over the cloths, the plates and the salt.

(I) During the whole passage, lick the hand you previously held the salt in.
(J) Now the motors are turned off again. Everyone sews up his over-ridden plate or its remains into the strips of cloth. A derrick arrives along with supplies of wire for hanging purposes.
(K) Everyone now goes with their cloth to the tree where the bag of salt lies. Each one decides where in the tree their cloth (with sewed-up plate) should hang. With the derrick's help the cloths and their contents are fastened to the branches.
(L) The notebook with records of clutching, shifting, stepping on the gas, etc. should be fastened with Scotch tape to the inside of the trunk.
(M) When you next have a fever, take the notebook out of the trunk and tear it up.
(N) 3 days after the Happening, Berlin Fever, meet with Vostell for a talk. Note your dreams for these 3 days and bring the notes to the discussion.

Vostell's Happenings have always been grandly scaled. Their images are consistently charged with impact: border guards, banners in trees, lanes of slow-moving cars ... Spectacle and apocalypse re-echo in whatever he conceives. Yet they are only for the participants to experience. The guards in the tower watched curiously and strollers in the gardens beyond gazed for a few moments before going their way. Such casual observation is accidental, without information or expectations. The participants, however, were voluntary initiates in a quasi-ritual, for which the ongoing world, undisturbed and hardly caring, was the context. This, for me, was part of the piece's poignancy.

Like any experimental work, the Happening's language was strange. Only gradually, while going through it, did the participants begin to sense its pervasive political reference: West Berlin's ideological and economic isolation in Communist East Germany; its reduction to an artificial island confined by a wall and three foreign military encampments; the piped-in, superficial affluence in the midst of surrounding austerity and a disadvantaged Turkish working force; an island whose population is dwindling and whose industry is leaving; an island whose artistic culture is imported or pumped up by political machinery, mainly in Bonn and Washington; this island's "fevered" self-consciousness; and saddest of all, its present garrison-town identity compared with the impressive city it once was. The symbolism was personal, but it was based on so many other Vostell works over the years that such a reading could be intuited at the time.

I have spoken of the casual passerby. But not even intentional watchers could have *experienced* this drama or these references without literally opening and closing a car trunk 750 times (hearing the drumming thumps of other cars), without tasting the salt on their own hands, without actually feeling and hearing the plates crushed under their own cars, without sewing up the broken pieces into white shrouds to be lofted by a derrick to hang in a giant tree. The internalization would escape such an observer. But that is what Vostell was seeking, not esthetic detachment.

Vostell built into the Happening an aftermath—a telling of dreams three days later and the task of remembering at a next fever to tear up the account of gear shiftings, starts, and stops, along with all the sensations felt during a particular thirty minutes of *Berlin Fever.* On the one hand, he was curious about its possible effect upon near-future fantasy, and, on the other, he wanted to keep the past alive by binding a person to a symbolic pact: associating a personal fever with Berlin's.

Although Vostell was a participant too, he viewed his piece as a consciousness-raising device, as teaching, as behavior changing. This goal was, I recall, hard to measure, but it is crucial to take into account his hope to see *Berlin Fever* extend into the real lives of all the participants.

By way of contrast, a much cooler effect comes across from the text or "program" of an Activity of mine. Its printed language is sparse, its repeated *-ing* verb endings convey a continuous present, its images are low-key and perhaps a little funny, and its context is the home environment of the participants.

Called *7 Kinds of Sympathy,* it uses a modular participational unit of two persons (A and B), who carry out a given program of moves. The program was discussed beforehand with five other couples, who then separated to perform the piece and reconvened the next day to exchange experiences. As usual, I was one of the participants. *7 Kinds of Sympathy,* whose text follows, took place this year in Vienna.

A, writing
occasionally blowing nose
B, watching
copying A blowing nose
continuing
(later) B, reading A's writing
occasionally scratching groin, armpit
A, watching
copying B scratching
continuing
(later) A, examining something
occasionally feeling for something in pocket
B, watching
copying A feeling for something
continuing
(later) B, examining A's object
occasionally coughing
A, watching
clearing throat in reply
continuing
(later) A and B, close together
B, holding tissue to A's nose
A, occasionally blowing into it
B, clearing throat in reply
continuing

(later) B and A, close together
B, describing and pointing to itching
in groin and armpit
A, scratching where B itches
occasionally coughing
B, continuing description
instructing A until relieved
A, occasionally coughing
(later) A, feeding silent B
copying B's mouth movements
saying: open chew swallow
continuing

The notes accompanying the program intentionally pointed out guidelines to interpretation. It is worthwhile mentioning this aspect of the preparation for participating. An unfamiliar genre like this one does not speak for itself. Explaining, reading, thinking, doing, feeling, reviewing, and thinking again are commingled. Thus the following comments accompanied the main text:

There is the well-known story of a little boy who was being loudly chastised by his mother for misbehaving. The mother ranted and raved while the boy stared curiously at her, seeming not to listen. Exasperated, she demanded to know if he had heard her. He answered that it was funny the way her mouth moved when she was angry. The boy had ignored one set of messages and focused on another.

In *7 Kinds of Sympathy* primary and secondary messages are similarly contrasted. A person "sympathizes" with a partner by copying secondary, normally unconscious, ones (blowing the nose) while disregarding the primary ones (writing). The observer/observed roles are then reversed and the original primary message is attended to while a secondary message (scratching an itch) is sent out and copied.

The exchange continues, with coughs and throat clearings added, next developing into a virtual repertory of such moves. The partners come much closer together, one helping the other to blow the nose, scratch an itch, and finally to eat. Primary and secondary become thoroughly mixed up, as do observer and observed. And unlike ordinary behavior, both partners are aware from the start of all these factors as they perform the program; hence the socially acceptable and personally private are also mixed up.

But the partners will naturally tell about themselves in other ways, sending perhaps tertiary messages; these may be picked up quite consciously, thereby provoking quarternary ones, and so on ...

What occurred in the doing was, on the surface, a vaudeville routine in seven simple parts, requiring neither special skills nor anyone's loss of identity. From a briefing and the notes, the partners expected that there would be more to it than the schematic plan suggested.

They understood, for instance, that since durations were unspecified except by the words *continuing* and *later*, they could stretch on and on or be quite short. They understood that prolongation of mimicry could become caricature and that too much brevity might prevent attentiveness. But since the Activity used mutual scrutiny as the partners' means of finding out about each other, they had a protective formula in the very absurdity of their moves: absurdity allowed them to drop their normal constraints and go with the program as long as it seemed appropriate.

As always, there was a range of responses to a commonly shared plan. There was, to begin, a certain self-conscious indifference and some laughter. Then there were loaded silences, subtle aggressions, artful manipulations, and dodges of the uncontrollable messages going back and forth between individuals. There were also feelings of closeness (perhaps born of the absurdity of what each participant was doing), intimations of ceremonials, sensations of vulnerability (each one wondered what the other "saw"). And of course there was a feigned disregard and simultaneous acknowledgment of the sexual connotations of scratching a partner's itch "until relieved." Finally, at the end there was that vague feeling that "sympathy" implies carrying the burden of another's foolishness. It is important to record here that my own prior knowledge of the concept did nothing to jade me to these experiences; if anything, it sensitized me.

The texts of George Brecht's *Events* of 1959–62 are even more neutral than mine, but unlike mine were not likely to stimulate interpersonal action. If anything, they were finely attenuated thought, rather philosophical in their inclination, though never ponderous. Printed on small cards, they appeared to be a sort of shorthand, or chapter notes without the chapters. Their language, like their scale, was minimal, uninflected, and apparently as small in scope of operation as in implication. The impression was that you couldn't do much with them, but they were very impressive and very elegant.

Some pieces were in fact performed in the United States, Europe, and Japan, in Fluxus festivals and related performance presentations, using conventional theater formats and audiences. Others were carried out privately and were never documented or reported to the art press. Many were performed in the head.

But in any case, most of the cards were ambiguous about how they were to be used. It was clear to some of us then that this was their point: to be applicable to various requirements. Those wishing to conventionalize the brief scores (as Brecht called them) into a neo-Dada theater could and did do so. Those who wanted to project their tiny forms into daily activity, or into contemplation, were also free to follow that route. [Box 31.1 offers] one example that does specify a site.

Ten or twelve of us went late one afternoon to the station and were quickly lost to our own devices in the rush-hour crowd. Each interpreted freely the bare indications. For instance, sounds of any kind were to be made by chance selection of departure and arrival times listed in a train schedule. We were also to remain visible to each other. But

Box 31.1
TIME-TABLE MUSIC

For performance in a railway station.

The performers enter a railway station and obtain time-tables.

They stand or seat themselves so as to be visible to each other and, when ready, start their stop watches simultaneously.

Each performer interprets the tabled time indications in terms of minutes and seconds (e.g., 7:16=7 minutes and 16 seconds). He selects one time by chance to determine the total duration of his performing. This done, he selects one row or column and makes a sound at all points where tabled times within that row or column fall within the total duration of his performance.

George Brecht

Summer, 1959

Box 31.2
TWO ELIMINATION EVENTS

- **empty vessel**
- **empty vessel**

Summer, 1961

the masses of commuters swallowed us and our sounds, and we became aware of what was, in the final analysis, a group of private performances.

In a version of 1961, that outcome was accounted for as the most logical result, so the group action and specification for making sounds were left out. The participant was given the responsibility of determining or discovering, in some fashion, what would happen.

In the following pieces [see Box 31.2], however, the absence of instruction leaves no doubt about their appeal to ambiguous use.

If *Two Elimination Events* is judged a performance score, one or more persons in any environment(s) can interpret the repeated word *empty* as a verb or an adjective; the two identical phrases can refer to two empty containers that should be accounted for somehow or can be taken as instructions that two containers be emptied.

As a Conceptual piece, the work invites participants to consider that these possibilities may be simply thought about. The title's key word, *elimination*, suggests a reductive attitude that can be assumed toward them—a getting rid of something undesired or unneeded. This could lead to the physical act of performance as such, and it could allude to the "empty" (but full) state of Zen.

Brecht's indirect call to the reader to share in the making of a piece is playfully revealed in [Box 31.3] which prompts one, after a while, to ask where the third window event is. One answer is that the question is the third event; another is looking out the window; another is the thought that there are countless possibilities. Naturally, a performer can actually do what is described on the card and then add the missing component.

Three Aqueous Events, however, does explain itself exactly in three words, the solid, liquid, and vaporous forms of the universal solvent [Box 31.4]:

It tends to rest at that point as a Conceptual piece because the words are most easily read as nouns. But they can be felt as promptings, if not commands: I once made a delicious iced tea on the stimulation of the piece and thought about it while drinking.

This fifth example, *Two Exercises*, depends on being read more than anything else [Box 31.5].

Nevertheless, if it were put into physical practice, it would quickly become apparent that the piece is written as a verbal smoke screen. Suppose there were two baskets of apples, one called object, and one called other. By substituting for the word *object* in the first exercise the word *basket*, and for the word *other* the same word *basket* and, further, by substituting for the next use of the word *object* the word *apple*—you will have a simple recipe. Rewritten, it would read: EXERCISE: Add to the basket of apples, from the other basket, another apple, to form a new (or bigger) basket and a new quantity of

Box 31.3
THREE WINDOW EVENTS

opening a closed window

closing an open window

Box 31.4
THREE AQUEOUS EVENTS

- **ice**
- **water**
- **steam**

Summer, 1961

Box 31.5
TWO EXERCISES

Consider an object. Call what is not the object "other."

EXERCISE: Add to the object, from the "other," another object, to form a new object and a new "other."

Repeat until there is no more "other."

EXERCISE: Take a part from the object and add it to the "other," to form a new object and a new "other."

Repeat until there is no more object.

Fall, 1961

apples. Repeat until there are no more apples in the other basket. The second exercise simply reverses the process and you end up where you began.

What Brecht does here, with some wit, is confuse the ear with repetitions and different applications of the words *object, other,* and *another.* Consequently, the mind performs and mystifies itself. It is a species of conundrum.

Ordinarily, a performance is some kind of play, dance, or concert presented to an audience—even in the avant-garde. But actually there are two types of performance currently being made by artists: a predominant theatrical one, and a less recognized nontheatrical one. They correspond, interestingly, to the two meanings the word *performance* has in English: one refers to artistry, as in performing on the violin; the other has to do with carrying out a job or function, as in carrying out a task, service, or duty—viz. a "high-performance engine."

Theatrical performance, in the broadest sense, takes not only the form of plays but also marriage ceremonies, stock-car races, football games, aerial stunts, parades, TV shows, classroom teaching, and political rallies. Something occurs in a certain place, someone comes to attend it in an adjacent place, and it begins and ends after a usually conventional time has elapsed. These characteristics have been as unchanging as the seasons.

Thus it would still be theater if spectators gathered to watch an artist on a television monitor watching herself on a different monitor in another room. From time to time she would come into the spectators' space to do the same thing. In this way the piece would build its layers of real and reproduced realities. Such a piece typifies a kind of sophisticated performance seen in galleries and art lofts but is structurally similar to others that might appear more conservative in content. Take away the video, take away what the artist is doing, and she could replace these with Shakespeare or gymnastics.

Nontheatrical performance does not begin with an envelope containing an act (the fantasy) and an audience (those affected by the fantasy). By the early sixties the more experimental Happenings and Fluxus events had eliminated not only actors, roles, plots, rehearsals, and repeats but also audiences, the single staging area, and the customary time block of an hour or so. These are the stock-in-trade of any theater, past or present. (Plays such as Robert Wilson's, along with certain Chinese performances and the operas of Richard Wagner, extend duration but in all other respects hold to theatrical conditions.)

Since those first efforts, Activities, Landworks, Concept pieces, Information pieces, and Bodyworks have added to the idea of a performance that isn't theater. Besides my own work and the examples of Vostell and Brecht, already described, it is not difficult to see the performance aspects of a telephone conversation, digging a trench in the desert, distributing religious tracts on a street corner, gathering and arranging population statistics, and treating one's body to alternating hot and cold immersions. But it *is* difficult not to conventionalize them. What tends to happen is that the performances are referred to by photos and texts presented as art shows in galleries; or whole situations are brought intact into galleries, like Duchamp's urinal; or art audiences are taken to the performances as theater. The transformed "artification" is the focus; the "cooked" version of nonart, set into a cultural framework, is preferred to its "raw" primary state.

For the majority of artists, art agents, and their publics, it probably could not be otherwise. Most could not sustain enough interest and personal motivation to dispense with the historical forms of legitimation. The framework tells you what it is: a cow in a concert hall is a musician; a cow in a barn is a cow. A man watching the musician-cow is an audience; a man in a cow barn is a farmer. Right?

But the experimental minority apparently does not need these settings, though the reason they do not has nothing to do with daring or heroic indifference. Instead (as I've written in "The Happenings Are Dead: Long Live the Happenings!"), it has to do with artists themselves, who today are so trained to accept anything as annexable to art that they have a ready-made "art frame" in their heads that can be set down anywhere, at any time. They do not require the traditional signs, rooms, arrangements, and rites of performance because performance is an attitude about involvement on some plane in something going on. It does not have to be onstage, and it really does not have to be announced.

To understand nontheatrical performance as an idea, it might be worthwhile to consider the current state of the art profession in the West. All artists have at their fingertips a body of information about what has been done and what is being done. There are certain options. Making performances of some sort is one of them. Making nonart into art is another. Nonart art, when applied to performing, means making a performance that doesn't resemble what's been called art performance. Art performance is that range of doing things called theater. An artist choosing to make nonart performances simply has to know what theatrical performances are and avoid doing them, quite consciously, at least in the beginning. The value in listing one's options is to make things as conscious as possible; experimenters can experiment more when they know what's what. Accordingly, here is the ball game I perceive: an artist can

(1) work within recognizable art modes and present the work in recognizable art contexts
e.g., paintings in galleries
poetry in poetry books
music in concert halls, etc.
(2) work in unrecognizable, i.e., nonart, modes but present the work in recognizable art contexts
e.g., a pizza parlor in a gallery
a telephone book sold as poetry, etc.
(3) work in recognizable art modes but present the work in nonart contexts
e.g., a "Rembrandt as an ironing board"
a fugue in an air-conditioning duct
a sonnet as a want ad, etc.
(4) work in nonart modes but present the work as art in nonart contexts
e.g., perception tests in a psychology lab
anti-erosion terracing in the hills
typewriter repairing
garbage collecting, etc. (with the proviso that the art world knows about it)
(5) work in nonart modes and nonart contexts but cease to call the work art, retaining instead the private consciousness that sometimes it may be art, too
e.g., systems analysis
social work in a ghetto
hitchhiking
thinking, etc.

All artists can locate themselves among these five options. Most belong to the first, very few occupy the fourth, and so far, I know of no one who fits the fifth who hasn't simply dropped out of art entirely. (One runs into such postgraduates from time to time, but their easy testimonials to the good life lack the dense ironies of doublethink that would result from simultaneous daily participation in art and, say, finance.)

Performance in the nontheatrical sense that I am discussing hovers very close to this fifth possibility, yet the intellectual discipline it implies and the indifference to validation by the art world it requires suggest that the person engaged in it would view art less as a profession than as a metaphor. At present such performance is generally nonart activity conducted in nonart contexts but offered as quasi-art to art-mined people. That is, to those not interested in whether it is or isn't art, who may, however, be interested for other reasons, it need not be justified as an artwork. Thus in a performance of 1968 that involved documenting the circumstances of many tire changes at gas stations in New Jersey, curious station attendants were frequent told it was a sociological study (which it was, in a way), while those in the cars knew it was also art.

Suppose, in the spirit of things nonartistic, that having a stance of some sort was important for making experimental performances. A stance includes not just a feeling tone but also a rough idea of the human and professional values you are dealing with. A stance gives a shape and an explanation to an unfamiliar course of action. It may be valuable to bring up this issue here because new art tends to generate new stances, even though while this happens old notions are carried over that are incompatible with the new situation. For instance, an Existentialist stance was helpful to action painting because it could explain, and therefore justify, personal isolation and crisis better than the Marxism of the thirties. At present, a formalist stance would be inadequate for a performance genre that intentionally blurs categories and mixes with everyday life.

My own stance has evolved, somewhat pragmatically, in actual working conditions. I describe it here as an example rather than as a prescription for others. With that caveat in mind, suppose that performance artists were to adopt the emphasis of universities and think tanks on basic research. Performance would be conceived as inquiry. It would reflect the word's everyday meaning of performing a job or service and would relieve the artist of inspirational metaphors, such as creativity, that are tacitly associated with making art, and therefore theater art.

The intent of this shift is not to do away with feeling or even inspiration—these belong to scholars and scientists as well as to artists. It is to identify the inquisitive and procedural approach of researchers to their work so that the artist adopting it would be free to feel without being beholden to the look and feeling of prior art. But most of all, the artist as researcher can begin to consider and act upon substantive questions about consciousness, communication, and culture without giving up membership in the profession of art.

When you attempt to interact with animal and plant life, and with wind and stones, you may also be a naturalist or highway engineer, but you and the elements are performers–and this can be basic research.

Basic research is inquiry into whole situations—for example, why humans fight—even if, like art, they are elusive and constantly changing. What is basic research at one moment becomes detail work or something trivial at another; and seeking what is worth researching at a particular moment is where the guesswork comes in. My hunch about art is that a field that has changed in appearance as fast as it has must also have changed in meaning and function, perhaps to the extent that its role is qualitative (offering a way of perceiving things) rather than quantitative (producing physical objects or specific actions).

When you use the postal system to send mail around the globe to persons known or unknown and when you similarly use the telephone, telegraph, or newspaper—these message carriers are performers and this communication can be basic research.

Who is interested in performance by artists? The art world, obviously. It is an art world that is trained in the visual contemplation of objects made by visual artists. It has next to no experience in theater, yet because of this naïveté it is free to innovate. Its boundless enthusiasm has led to astonishing works one wouldn't find in professional theater, yet it applauds the rankest amateurism along with what is genuine. When faced with nontheatrical performance, the art world cannot recognize what is happening because it responds to art as art. It believes in studios, galleries, collectors, museums, and reverential and meditative ways to look at art. A gallery performance or its equivalent is framed like a painting by its shrinelike setting; an Activity out in the real world, if announced, is beyond the pale.

When you experiment with brain waves and related biofeedback processes in order to communicate with yourself, with others, and with the nonhuman world—these performances can be basic research.

Who sponsors performances by artists? Promotion of both the theatrical and nontheatrical kinds rests mainly with dealers and museum officials (universities, which were once supportive, are now economically crippled; they continue their interest indirectly by hiring performance artists to teach in their art departments). This encouragement praiseworthy and is acknowledged by the press. But because it is so uninformed, it is almost disastrous.

The first American Happenings, Fluxus events, and parallel works in Japan, Europe, and South America were presented as distinct modes of art. Today their progeny have become part of the public relations of influential galleries and arts institutions, which offer them as front-office attractions to the sale or display of other artists' tangibles in the showrooms.

When you view a normal routine in your life as a performance and carefully chart for a month how you greet someone each day, what you say with your body, your pauses, and your clothing; and when you carefully chart the responses you get—this can be basic research.

Artists who might prefer to devote all or most of their time to performance are pressured to make documentary prints and objects on the theme of the performance—as a guarantee against financial loss by the sponsor. Among such salables are bits and pieces of paraphernalia left over from the event, signed and numbered, and dressed up as tokens of the live experience. They are offered and sometimes collected like pieces of the True Cross, or a sock worn by a deceased matinee idol. I do not want to ignore the quasi-magical import of relics and tokens; but these are now preferred to the performance. And I am not decrying commerce here; but an artist rarely receives a fee for a performance alone, because it is used as a come-on.

With ignorance of what is at stake so widespread, sponsors tend to have a negative influence on the actual performances. Without intending harm, they urge that they be given conveniently in their own galleries or museums when a laboratory, subway, bedroom, or a combination of these might be better. From habit, they and the public expect the duration of the pieces to be a comfortable hour or so, when ten seconds, ten days, or discontinuous time might make more sense.

When you attend to how your performance affects your real life and the real life of your co-performers; and when you attend to how it may have altered the social and natural surroundings—this follow-up is also performance, and it can be basic research.

Because strong visual imagery is always suitable for advertising flyers and pamphlets, and because all artists are supposed to be visually oriented, performances with such imagery are most welcomed. Those that might involve darkness, tactility, or Conceptual matters are discouraged with the eager reminder that the media people will have nothing to see.

Similarly, with recording technology, particularly videotape, artists are regularly solicited to gear their performances to what will look good and fit easily on a standard cassette. The performance, via the document, reverts to an object that can be merchandised in replica like a print. In many cases the once-only nature of a performance precludes having anything at all left over.

Ironically, some of these objections could be dropped if everyone were clear about the issues. There is nothing wrong with strong visual images being used to promote a work, if the artist is in charge and wants it. There is nothing wrong with making editions of documents and relics, if the artist is in charge and wants it. (A performance could be conceived around the subject of documentation per se.) There is nothing wrong with a performance that only lasts a convenient hour, if the artist is in charge and wants it. And there is nothing wrong with being a front-office attraction to an art gallery, if the artist makes it very clear that she or he is to be paid for public relations work. PR is performance ... The artist's role is not merely to make performances. It is to guide agents and the public to their appropriate use.

When you collaborate in scholarly, socio-political, and educational work; and when you direct your performance to some definite utility—this can be basic research. Being purposive, it is neither Ready-made art nor just playing at real life, since its value is measured by its practical yield.

Note

32 Kaprow and HCI: Reflections on "Participation" in Research through Design

Kirsten Boehner

In this essay, I use Allan Kaprow's work to reflect on the participatory style of practice emerging from Interaction Research Studio (IRS) at Goldsmiths, University of London. I propel this investigation first through a broad survey of participatory approaches before taking a closer look at some of IRS's on-the-ground practices. Kaprow's writing provides a reference for articulating subtle but critical aspects of participation and for anticipating rich areas for further exploration and discussion in the studio's work.

Background Motivation and Objective

To some extent, a simple observational moment provided the inspiration for this exploration into participation. During a recent tenure with IRS as a research fellow,[1] I interviewed several of the studio's study participants about their experiences with a set of indoor weather stations, described in detail later in this chapter. In one exchange, a participant referred to his involvement on the project as "like being part of a deranged club that had no meaning." At face value, such a quote may seem like an indictment, but in this particular context I understood him to be expressing an affinity for the experience. This single articulation echoed several other comments from participants and suggested, to me, a prominent characteristic of IRS's work. There was something compelling about the way in which the studio conceptualized and invited participation—something that differentiated it from what one might expect from other contemporary practices of user-led, participatory, or critical design.

To argue that IRS has a particular approach to participation is perhaps unremarkable. Any particular research group or design studio will develop its own perspective on participation. This observation resonated for me as a topic for further inquiry, however, for several reasons. Participation as a concept has become increasingly called on in popular culture as well as across fields of study. Through the rise of the internet, tools for creative expression, and social media, new outlets and forms of participation in modern society have appeared. In theory, this "participatory culture" (Jenkins et al., 2005) enables more active producers as opposed to passive consumers of things like government policy and laws, news and public opinion, education and knowledge, entertainment and arts, products and services. Diverse movements such as citizen science, participatory art, the maker movement, and participatory design, to name but a few, all hinge at some level on how participation is defined and supported. Within my field of study, human-computer interaction (HCI), participation is a key dimension for segmenting different approaches such as user-centered, user-experience, participatory design, and codesign (Koskinen et al., 2011; Sanders and Stappers, 2008). Across branches of HCI, participation means something different according to who is classified as participant, the level of agency in the participation, the value of participation, and so on.

Participation presents an interesting subject then for its topicality as well as for its influence on shaping different practices. My next step was to consider how to follow this thread in relation to the work at IRS. This involved looking across the portfolio of IRS work, talking with people inside the studio as well as other close observers of their work, and reading historical accounts of IRS's process and practice. Some of this analysis is alluded to here, but for the purpose of this chapter I focus on using the humanities as a resource for analysis, namely the work of Allan Kaprow.

The choice to look at Kaprow was twofold: one personal and one contextual reason. I first came across the work of Kaprow and his contemporaries in a course on performance studies during early graduate work almost twenty years ago. At that time, at least to my knowledge, a wide gulf separated performance art and digital technology research. One could see interesting parallels with performance and computer design (e.g., Bruckman, 1998; Laurel, 1991; Suchman, 1987; Turkle, 1984) but the trajectories were easy to keep separate. In fact, many hallmarks of performance art, such as defying conventions and destabilizing expectations, would be considered anathema to HCI's then-primary focus on usability and transparency.

The performance art pieces I found most disorienting from the perspective of technology design were pieces that seemed to almost rely on, or at least benefit from, the stupefied viewer. For example, in the early 1990s, artists Coco Fusco and Guillermo Gómez-Peña presented themselves for display in various public locations as caged aboriginal inhabitants from an undiscovered island in the Gulf of Mexico.[2] The piece was meant to take on, among other things, notions of colonialism, domination, and authenticity. The artists had not imagined that so many viewers—they estimated half—would miss the parody and take the exhibit literally, resulting in reactions ranging from shock, sympathy, and solidarity, to ambivalence and acceptance, and even to actively adding to their humiliation as objects in a cage. By getting it wrong, the audience unwittingly became participants in the spectacle. This made the piece even more powerful, yet I couldn't help feeling that those in the know got the message and could assert themselves over those who missed it, whereas those not in the know left with a further affirmation of their cultural assumptions.

In contrast, the performance work of Kaprow did not suggest to me such divisions between an in-group versed in a particular agenda and an out-group left to struggle with an unfamiliar code. Kaprow's happenings could be described as nonsensical or random at times, but they toed a playful line of surprise or defamiliarization more than shock and alienation. It is perhaps this early exposure to and personal affinity for the work of Kaprow that biased me toward certain approaches of drawing on arts inspiration in technology design later on in my graduate career.

After a period of professional practice, I returned to graduate studies in 2001 to find a rich ground of study in technology design crossing boundaries between the arts and the sciences. Looking to performance studies for inspiration was no longer a marginal approach. One practice in particular that stood out was the work of current IRS members who were at that time with the Computer Related Design (CRD) department at the Royal College of Art (RCA) in London. One of their most noted examples, cultural probes, is an arts-inspired methodology for design (e.g., Gaver and Dunne, 1999; Gaver, Dunne, and Pacenti, 1999; Gaver, Hooker, and Dunne, 2001) that sparked an immense amount of interest in the HCI community (Boehner et al., 2007). Cultural probes were created explicitly in opposition to traditional modes of requirements-gathering and research relationships. Instead of straightforward questionnaires or researcher-driven observations, cultural probes present exercises in expression, reflection, and conversation that engage participants in unexpected ways—for example, asking people to take a picture of the spiritual center of their home or providing people with a "dream recorder" to capture ten seconds of recounting a dream on waking. Several of the probe activities could be read as an instruction set from Kaprow himself. This is perhaps not surprising, as Kaprow's work is cited by IRS as the inspiration for what they call "ludic design" (Gaver et al., 2004), an approach that uses technology to engage and explore the curiosity, playfulness, and improvisational nature of people.

This declared identification and resonance between the playful spirit of Kaprow and the work of IRS suggests that a close reading of Kaprow could elicit further insights into participation in IRS projects. My objective was to use Kaprow's work as a comparison point for characterizing what makes the flavor of participation in IRS's work unique and how this participation might evolve. In looking at these two sympathetic bodies of work, I reflect on more general questions of participation in HCI. Finally, in the spirit of this collection of work, I aim to demonstrate how drawing from the humanities is a useful and viable approach for HCI researchers and practitioners.

Participation, HCI, and the Interaction Research Studio

Participation is at best defined provisionally because its meaning shifts depending on usage and context. It is beyond the scope of this chapter to delve further into the varied histories of participation, so I only note here that the concept is both rich in theory and amorphous in reality. Yet this does not diminish the value of trying to articulate how participation differs broadly and across certain dimensions. In this section, I use an early taxonomy outlining different design practices based on participation as a starting point for describing broad outlines of IRS's approach. In order to fill in this outline with more details, I then describe several IRS projects, ending with a more textured overview of the studio's take on participation. In the subsequent section, I turn to Kaprow as a resource for illuminating and pushing on what participation means, or could mean, for IRS.

Observations across Practices

In the introduction, I reference taxonomies of participation that identify different practices in HCI. As one example, in figure 32.1, Sanders and Stappers (2008) use participation type, from user-as-subject to user-as-designer, as one axis identifying a landscape of design approaches. Although there are several taxonomies of design landscapes, I found this one instructive for thinking about IRS for two reasons. The first observation revolves around the identification of critical design, and the bundling of probes, as a self-contained unit. Bardzell et al. (2012) seek to unpack this neatly circumscribed bubble, demonstrating the complexities of the critical design space, in particular arguing how the practice of critical design (e.g., Dunne, 1999) developing from the RCA is but one approach to designing from a critical tradition.

The fact that the ludic design approach merging from IRS is often equated with critical design is partly due to the historical collaboration between Tony Dunne from

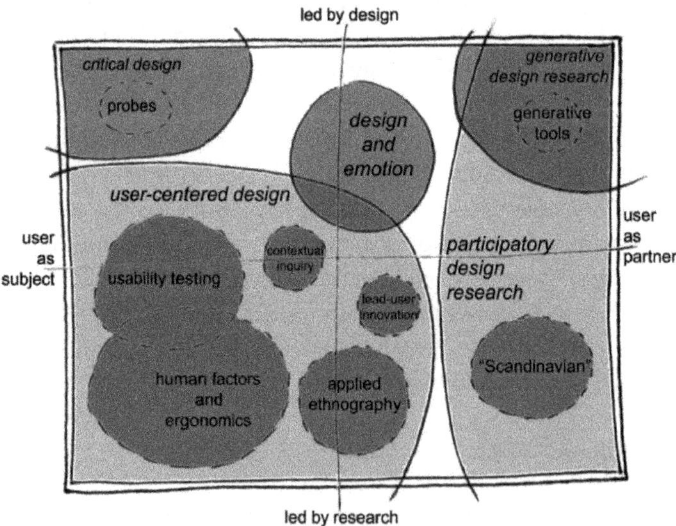

Figure 32.1
Design landscape by Sanders and Stappers (2008).

the RCA and Bill Gaver from IRS. These practices share many similarities, such as drawing on avant-garde work and using technology design as a vehicle for questioning and exploring values in design. Yet, although one could argue that both practices fall under an umbrella of critical approaches to design, several nuances distinguish them (Swan and Boehner, 2013). This is the value and the drawback of any kind of abstract taxonomy—each drawing of boundaries isolates some variables for consideration at the expense of others. For my purpose, the reason this taxonomy is interesting is because what is lost is partly what it proposes to draw out: the nature of participation.

The critical design approach, as generally practiced by Dunne and colleagues at the RCA, assumes what appears to be a different flavor of participation than the ludic design approach of IRS. Classic examples of critical design projects include Dunne and Raby's Faraday Chair,[3] a speculative piece of furniture that encases the sitter in a tank-like structure promising sanctuary from electro-magnetic fields, and Auger and Loizeau's AfterLife,[4] a project that explores harvesting energy from a deceased loved one into a battery for powering flashlights, toothbrushes, or even remote-controlled airplanes. In both of these examples, participation by people other than the designers is largely constrained by the exhibition format that was once the primary mode of presentation for critical design. Participants are drawn on in the early design process largely as an imagined other and rarely are actual participants involved in scoping or shaping what the design might be.[5]

Actual participation with critical design pieces usually occurs in a gallery-like space or through media coverage[6] and takes shape primarily through thought and dialogue around near-future applications. Many of the pieces exist as speculative concepts—such as seeking protection from invisible currents—where engagement consists of imagining scenarios of use. Critical designs skate the fine line between reality and fiction, creating a tension about whether something is an actual prototype and how one might use it if it did indeed exist. Does the AfterLife, for example, violate or celebrate the somberness of life and death? The potential increases, therefore, for appealing to an in-group conditioned to reading art and criticism and alienating an out-group who lack footholds into the work. This mix of possible outcomes is not meant to be sorted out.

Ludic design pieces also work with near-future and speculative concepts exploring alternative applications and values, but ludic design seeks out a different level of engagement from participants. Participants are involved in stages throughout the design process, communicating not just with other participants but also directly with the design team. Perhaps more importantly, whereas alienation is not incompatible with success for a critical design piece, lack of engagement by participants in a ludic design project due to confusion, disinterest, or cryptic codes would be considered signs of failure.

Whereas figure 32.1 and related overviews of technology research and design might overplay similarities between the RCA's critical design and IRS's ludic design, such characterizations also tend to underplay the similarity between ludic design and approaches that highlight participant involvement such as participatory design, user-led design, or codesign. To be sure, the IRS team is quick to acknowledge that they do not engage is such practices as they are conventionally defined. Participation in ludic design is less a matter of collaboration toward an agreed-on brief or joint end and more aptly described as a kind of conversation of give and take, with each party owner and expert of their own skills and experiences, and each party to the conversation possibly walking away with a slightly different view of what transpired and the value of it. Furthermore, time horizons for ludic design projects tend more toward the speculative and less toward here-and-now applications for solving seemingly definable problems, such as designing "better" photocopy machines (Suchman, 1987). In these ways, ludic design differs dramatically from the types of projects that tend to be labeled participatory.

Yet there remain interesting synergies between ludic design and the ideals of approaches that call on participation. Again, as with the difficulty in pinning down critical design and its myriad of incarnations, it is impossible to capture the complexity of something as vast as participatory design, to take but one broad example. Within the HCI community, however, one of the oft-cited foundational references regarding the importance of user participation is the work of Pelle Ehn (1988) in detailing the theoretical mindset and accompanying practices for involving the eventual users of—and indeed an entire range of stakeholders for—computer systems in the design process. Users participate iteratively as codesigners, giving voice to the scope and form of the final product. There is a notion of shared responsibility or accountability for making the work relevant and useable. Transparency of the design process is valued and projects are evaluated not only in terms of success metrics for the final product but the process as well.

Work from IRS, although not described in these terms, also concerns itself with the political stance of the designer and the process of design, recognizing and honoring the expertise and authority of participants and ultimately leaving the value of a system in the hands of participants. Whereas in critical design, the eventual summation from participants is not tracked, in ludic design, there is a sense that how participants use the prototypes completes the process. The designs are considered open-ended in the sense that although design choices will constrain possibilities, the eventual use and meaning associated with the design lies with the participants and not the designers. Although participants in ludic design are not considered codesigners in the sense that many participatory design and user-led projects espouse, the participation is more active than the Sanders and Stappers's landscape would suggest.

The point in using the Sanders and Stappers taxonomy is not as a ready straw man to dismantle but, on the one hand, to identify some general points of comparison regarding participation for IRS and, on the other hand, to demonstrate the difficulty in trying to encapsulate the work of a movement or practice around a concept that is fluid and contextual. In drawing ludic design away from critical design and toward practices deemed participatory, I am not simply suggesting a reworking of the framework or a replacement of ludic design. Instead, I find it illuminating to think of the ways in which ludic design—and I imagine many of the other practices as well—may morph through this landscape. The language around this particular taxonomy also seems to suggest implicitly that "more" participation in a design process is better—for example, more stakeholders involved in more parts of the design process. I am not arguing against this ideal but suggesting that there are other interesting avenues and qualities to explore with participation as well. To this end, let's look at some specific IRS projects for further insights into possible shapes of participation.

Observations across Studio Examples

A quick look at three examples of ludic design will sketch out some of the common attributes as well as variation in participation for IRS's work. My goal in this section is to leave external comparisons and taxonomies aside and focus instead on internal comparisons, in order to draw out, from the ground up, the qualities of participation indicative of the studio's approach. For this exercise, I chose three examples—the Drift Table, the Prayer Companion, and the Indoor Weather Stations—because they suggest both core practices and values but with interesting twists.

The Drift Table (Gaver et al., 2004) came out of a larger, EU-funded project, Equator, for studying ludic design in domestic spaces, in particular, designing technology for playful experiences such as daydreaming and exploring, as opposed to productivity-focused systems. Participants were invited to engage in the Equator project through a minimally descriptive newspaper advert and they began their participation through an open-ended, interpretive Probe study and several, but not all, had ethnographic home visits. From this initial contact with participants and from independent research and exploration, several design treatments were eventually reduced to three prototype designs exploring different digital surfaces in the home.

One of these designs was the Drift Table: a large coffee table fitted with loadbearing sensors and a video portal on its top surface and a computer database tucked inside (figure 32.2). Peering through the portal, one can see moving aerial footage of the English countryside. Drifting across this landscape is controlled by placing different amounts of weight for speed and height around different parts of the table for direction. Three households lived with the system for a period of months. The research team had contact with all three households during their turn with the Drift Table. One household, however, was visited several times by an ethnographer and by an independent documentary filmmaker in the capacity of a cultural commentator (Gaver, 2007), a practice of using professional practitioners outside of academia and outside the project to present different takes on the systems and their use.

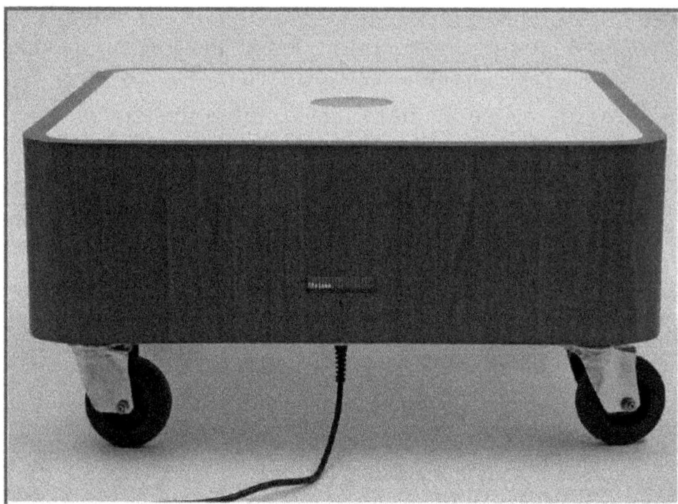

Figure 32.2
The Drift Table, © Interaction Research Studio. Used with permission of Bill Gaver.

A second example, the Prayer Companion (Gaver et al., 2010), differs markedly from the Drift Table in terms of participation (see chapter 2 for more analysis of the Prayer Companion). This project started as part of a larger research effort to understand technology and the elderly and to challenge stereotypes of both. One member of the research team met the relative of a nun who lived in cloister in the north of England, and on his advice contacted them to see if they'd be interested in participating in a design research effort. The nuns did not engage in a Probe study prior to the design work and ethnographic observations and encounters were limited given the nature of the nuns' community. During most the design phase, meetings were held in the monastery's visiting room, which is constructed so that the sisters can remain in an enclosure while talking with people outside the enclosure. While most of the team only met for a few short sessions, a local team member made numerous visits that culminated in his being invited into the enclosure to take photographs that could contextualize some of the initial design work. During the short sessions with one of the sisters and the mother superior, the team presented a workbook of sketches and concepts imagining possible designs and soliciting feedback from the sisters.

Although not necessarily a practice of iterative participatory design, this particular project garnered more feedback on design directions than any other studio project. The final design (figure 32.3) was a digital resource for prayer that scraped headlines from numerous news sources as well as posts from the social media site "I feel fine." The Prayer Companion took on a material form that resembled the Tau cross, with a

Figure 32.3
The Prayer Companion, © Interaction Research Studio. Used with permission of Bill Gaver.

scrolling display of the "prayer requests" on the top of the cross. It was situated on a table in a high-traffic hallway and the sisters lived with it for over a year. The sisters documented their own use of the device as well as gave feedback to the design research team through interviews.

Finally, the Indoor Weather Stations (IWS) (Gaver et al., 2013) differ from both the Drift Table and the Prayer Companion in terms of several factors of participation. The IWS project is also part of a larger research effort to apply a ludic design approach for exploring issues of the environment, technology and sustainability. The most notable difference with this project compared to others is its scale of deployment. Whereas the previous projects all had a single device, the weather stations were a set of three devices, each set deployed up to twenty households. An initial group of participants worked with a storybook Probe to explore the home as "an environment." This narrative of imagined views helped inform the three eventual designs of a wind tunnel that measured and depicted microgusts, a light collector that measured and displayed changes in the quality of light, and a temperature tape that measured and displayed the gradient changes in temperature across a space of five meters (figure 32.4). We recruited a new set of participants to use these devices primarily through local blogs and posters in community areas such as coffee shops and parks. Participant households lived with

Figure 32.4
An Indoor Weather Station, © Interaction Research Studio. Used with permission of Bill Gaver.

the devices for a varying length of time depending on the deployment schedule; most had them for at least three months and some continued to use them for a year or more. We asked participants to self-report on their experiences through prompts on a website that collated data views and through self-report forms. We conducted ethnographic visits to several households and we hosted a final feedback session for participants to share their experiences.

As the examples above demonstrate, ludic design projects vary on a number of factors regarding participation. Participants typically, although not always, engage in initial efforts to imagine design possibilities and to flesh out a possible design space. The process is not as straightforward as a user requirements gathering workshop, for example, but instead involves more oblique methods such as the Probes. The research team never directly asks people what problem they are trying to solve or what solutions they are looking for but instead seek inspiration from people's everyday lives and experiences. Some participants engage in multiple stages of design, from sparking new design ideas or experimenting with prototypes to engaging in different forms of ethnographic evaluations, whereas a number of participants may participate in early design activities but never actually receive a final prototype to try out. Many IRS designs are social in experience, as participants make sense of them through sharing them with family and friends. The IRS research team also engages with participants throughout their experience of use, starting with the initial call for participation, to informal visits for troubleshooting devices, to more formal observations and interviews, to occasionally coming together as a group to share experiences about the design space and use of the designs.

(Some) Characteristics of Participation for IRS

From the comparisons across these three projects, there are several differences in terms of evidencing "more or less" participation. In some of the projects, participants engage in more aspects of the design cycle than in others. In some of the projects, the designers have more touch points with participants than in others. In some of the projects there are more participants than in others. These variables give a sense of the range of participation opportunities. However, these need to be supplemented by illuminating the texture of participation across the projects. One marked characteristic in these projects is a kind of temporal patterning: an alternating between moments of close contact and communication to periods of no contact at all. During the many months of working with participants, there will be periods of close engagement interspersed with periods of almost no engagement. Although many practices will have this ebb of engagement, IRS work tends to have longer time horizons and a particular kind of intensity during the periods of contact. The pattern of IRS participation resembles, as I described earlier, more of a conversation stretched out over time.

The nature of this conversation, its intensity, tends toward rich exchanges as opposed to small talk. More often than not, people participate in IRS projects in a highly personal, intimate way, sharing evocative and meaningful details and profound insight into their lives. People have shared secrets, lies, fantasies, and poignant memories. People have sent pictures of their bedrooms, sacred spaces, and even body parts.[7] They have reflected on the presence of God in their work and the role of enigma in living one's life. If conversation provides the analogy for participation in IRS work, then it is a conversation between intimate strangers.

At the same time, the studio takes great care to see this conversation as incomplete and open ended. An important tenet in the studio's work is the assumption that information shared will never present a complete picture of participants. This belief is disclosed in probe packet instructions, for example, which encourage participants to share as much as they want, to withhold information if they desire, and even to play with deception if so inclined. Participants' ideal or imagined lives are perceived as just as interesting and inspirational as their actual lives.

Through this approach, studio members become close to participants while maintaining a sense of distance. The relationship is not elevated to a special kind of friendship, as this would require mutual sharing of intimate details. Instead this kind of arm's-length intimacy protects participants' privacy and authority while generating a murky space of knowing an "other." Misunderstanding can, at times, lead to surprising new directions that challenge assumptions. Again, in the conversation analogy, the studio does not aim to create a shared point of view between participants and studio members but assumes that each party in the conversation may come away with very different ideas and perspectives of what sense to make of the encounters.

This idea of give and take suggests the notion of reciprocity in participation: that all parties both give and receive. I've described a bit already in terms of what the studio receives from participants. Design imaginings are enriched and grounded through participants' willingness to share their ideas, hopes, dreams, and life experiences generously. Critically, IRS systems wouldn't work without participant engagement, and research efforts would stall if participants didn't thoughtfully reflect on how they used the devices and what this might mean to them. On the flip side, participants receive the opportunity to engage in something different and exploratory. They can play with some hopefully interesting experimental activities and devices, and share this experience with others. In the Indoor Weather Stations project described above, one of our participants described himself as "a participant in life"—someone who seeks out new situations and experiences. This led us to start thinking about participation in the studio work as being part of the participation-in-a-design mindset—where participants are not collaborating with us on a joint system design but like us engaging in discovery and exploration work into the home, spirituality, age, technology, intimacy, politics, play, and so on. This idea of participation in a design mindset shifts focus somewhat from participation in a thing toward participation in an attitude. What, we wondered, are the implications of this?

Participation and Kaprow

At this point in the essay, Kaprow has faded far into the background from initial my starting point. This was a purposeful move in an attempt to demonstrate how my work in HCI has intersected intermittently with the arts and humanities, and how in this particular turn I'm leaning into Kaprow. The chronological narrative is somewhat misleading as it suggests a kind of linear thinking and a search for specific answers. Instead, I want to suggest that one valuable benefit of intersecting with the arts and humanities in HCI is as a source for inspiration and reflection. I am not seeking answers so much as I am exploring different ways of thinking about participation.

As it is, Kaprow's approach to participation resonates closely with the studio's in that he pursues playful experimentation with everyday experiences. For Kaprow, participation is essentially about a concerted inquiry into life. He notes, "Playing with everyday life is just paying attention to what is conventionally hidden" (Kaprow, 2003, 250). Identifying conventions and either upending them or delving deep into them is the material of Kaprow's work. Throughout his writings, he plays with the language of collapsing life and art, enjoying the tensions this creates. On the one hand, Kaprow follows Dewey's framing of experience as bounded events with beginnings and ends (Dewey, 1980)—for Kaprow these might be the heightened moments of attention to details and conventions of living. So in this sense, there is an act of separation in Kaprow's art, a heightening of attention to certain details, such as negotiating the coordinated movement of two people through an entryway in the happening *Maneuvers*, performed in 1976 (Kaprow, 2003). He recognizes that an intensity of focus cannot be maintained for everything, that one moves in and out of focus. This idea of separateness can be taken too far, resulting in what Kaprow calls "artlike art" that exaggerates distinction, specialness, and objects with recognizable borders (Kaprow, 2003, 204). It results in thinking "I'm performing a bit of theater as I walk through this door" as opposed to intently focusing on walking through the door. On the other hand, to say that everything is art is exactly the point Kaprow wants to make: everything has this potential for heightened engagement. Art, as a kind of focused inquiry, depends on what we choose to attend to and so much of our daily lives simply goes unnoticed. The act of noticing is what Kaprow refers to as "lifelike art": an engagement that emphasizes "connectedness," "wide-angle awareness," and "a process of events with no definite outline" (Kaprow, 2003, 204). Artlike art for Kaprow is epitomized by a painting in a gallery that transports one away from the everyday, whereas lifelike art is more akin to elevating a routine moment in one's life to a heightened sense of engagement.

Throughout the trajectory of Kaprow's work, he illustrates this difference between artlike art and lifelike art. His 1976 essay "Nontheatrical Performance" (2003, 163–180) is not Kaprow's most recognized or referenced work, but it provides a nice illustration of how his thinking about this distinction between artlike and lifelike art evolved. In the beginning of the essay, he describes the spectacle of a happening (not one of his own constructions) and toward the end of the essay shifts to smaller, more intimate instructions for what became known as Activities. Kaprow's initial development of happenings, and what he called "Environments" before that, spawned from his training in action painting and from his desire to upend all existing genres by literally surrounding someone within the art. He wanted to break the frame, but what he found was that the frame just reappeared in a different form. In moving the spectacle from the art gallery to an abandoned loft space or to a field, he merely changed the setting. In asking his audience to participate by moving around and speaking on cue in an orchestrated fashion, he ended up using people as "ingredients of the performance" as opposed to actual participants (Kaprow, 2003, 194). Ultimately, he declared the happenings simply another form of vanguard theater (Kaprow, 2003, xxix).

To distance himself from this re-creation of existing art, Kaprow had to continue finding and confronting conventions, such as "belief in objects that can be possessed; belief in eternity; belief in control and skill; belief in creativity; belief in publicity and fame; belief in marketability" (Kaprow, 2003, xxviii). Gradually he worked to eliminate each of these in turn, but "the biggest problem ... was the presence of audiences at happenings. Audiences have been the standard requirements of theatre and music, popular and highbrow, since the remote past ..." (Kaprow, 2003, xxix). It is on this question of audience, and thus participation, that Kaprow's work turns. In *Participation Performance* (2003), written in 1977, he comments that "without either audience or a formally designated stage or clearing, the performer becomes simultaneously agent and watcher. She or he takes on the task of 'framing' the transaction internally, by paying attention in motion" (Kaprow, 2003, 188). In this way, the audience is eliminated not necessarily by creating more performers but by suggesting that the performer is his or her own audience.

Supporting this shift to focusing on participants as both performers and audience required some changes in the form and enactment of the events from the original happenings. It became more important, for example, to consider who was involved and their level of willingness and commitment to participate (Kostelanetz, 1970). Although participants in the happenings had chosen to be there, they had little choice but to follow the articulated script once they were there. The activities were still guided by a script, although perhaps simplified, but the role of invitation and orientation increased. Kaprow explained: "You invite people to play a game, in which the rules are explained and the expressive nature is clear. If they want to play, they will respond. Once they've made the commitment, you can play your game to your heart's content" (Kostelanetz, 1970, 111).

The forms or instruction sets became less elaborate, simpler, and sparse. The idea was to keep people in the moment as opposed to searching for symbolism or references to other artist's or cultural works. Keeping the forms minimal allowed for more openness in what people could take away from the experience. Kaprow reacted against work that appeared to be too didactic: "It's exactly the opposite of what I seem to find most useful, and that is to leave things open and not determine anything except the very clear form. The form is always very simple and clear. What is experienced is uncertain and unforeseeable, which is why I do it, and its point is never clear to me, even after I've done it" (Morgan, 1991). In an interview regarding Kaprow's work, the interviewer speculated that one of Kaprow's activities, in which he cleaned a friend's floor with a Q-tip and his own spit, was reminiscent of Andres Serrano's *Piss Christ* because both drew on the use of bodily fluids. Kaprow accepted that in theory there could be a slight nod to this, but he went on to explain the range of influences in how he arrives at activity sets and the difficulty in pulling out any one connection or linear linking. He purposefully tries to avoid pieces that are in direct reference to an arts discourse or require this kind of awareness to engage. Furthermore, in something like *Piss Christ*, Kaprow suggests there is a definite message, and an intention to shock. Once the message is out, there isn't much else to say. Kaprow's objective, in contrast, is to keep the conversation going.

Another move along the trajectory from happenings to activities was to root the activities in more familiar, everyday routines. In the happening example in "Nontheatrical Performance" (2003, 163–180), the overall spectacle and conditions are much more fantastical than the everyday; whereas the activity described later in the essay is more focused on everyday expressions of sympathy. Over time, Kaprow's activities became even more intimate and mundane, exploring things such as the act of breathing, shaking hands, carrying heavy objects, or brushing one's teeth. The activities still contained a bit of whimsy—for example, Kaprow describes a game of follow the leader wherein the follower must step on the leader's shadow until roles are ceremoniously shifted and the game starts again. Kaprow found that without this familiar frame of a habitual routine—what he called "a grounding in ordinary experience" (Kaprow, 2003, 186)—the tendency was to try to insert a more theatrical frame of performance and audience.

Although not uniformly, activities tend to involve a smaller number of people as participants. Kaprow describes activities he proposes for individuals or for small groups to perform in private or public. The choice of setting, and whether an inadvertent audience is desired or not, is left up to the reader. An audience in this respect is more of a bystander—just as someone might watch a nontheatrical event transpire on the street. Bystanders are interesting to Kaprow as part of the life scene as well as possible second-order participants. Someone who watches an activity unfold has not experienced it but recreates it in the retelling—what Kaprow refers to as a kind of gossip mongering, to be encouraged. The scale of the actual activities, in terms of numbers, did not concern Kaprow as he saw personal transformation on the same plane as a social one (Kaprow, 2003).

From the "Nontheatrical Performance" essay, and from a larger look at a broader collection of Kaprow's essays, the move from happenings to activities outlines essential perspectives and methods that persist as well as important attributes that evolve. These consistencies and changes give us a sense of how Kaprow evaluated and reshaped his interventions in the world. In terms of more formal evaluations, as pieces from the world of art (lifelike though they are), these formal assessments are left to the critics.

Kaprow's essays do not end as many HCI studies might, with a formal evaluation of a piece.[8] At most, he refers to informal sessions with participants talking through what people experienced. In one interview, however, Kaprow responds to the question of why certain pieces work where others fall flat (Kostelanetz, 1970). His first response is recognition that this is in fact the case—some worked better than others. It was not a matter of subjective opinion to draw out some pieces working beautifully and some simply failing. He suggests that the clues are not necessarily in the instructions—what might be considered the "objects" or "devices" of his work. Some of the instructions read well but when activated, fail, whereas some read less well and end up creating very interesting experiences. Other times, the piece both reads and enacts favorably.

Kaprow suggests that it is easier for him, after the fact, to deduce why a piece may have gone wrong—citing, for example, issues of practicality or attempts to be too symbolic—whereas he refuses to generalize on what might make something succeed. This again tends to be in contrast to a typical HCI approach that performs evaluation and draws out successful or less successful practices in order to inform future projects. Short of identifying essential ingredients to predict or guarantee success, Kaprow offers interesting (but not exclusive or expounded on) criteria for valuing a piece of work, whether it is revelatory, appropriate, and realized. These criteria serve as reflection points but Kaprow resists inflating them into a formal guide for evaluation.

What persists throughout Kaprow's body of work even as his methods may change is the attitude or stance he advocates. In the reading selected for this volume, Kaprow refers to this as an approach to performance as inquiry where art becomes a kind of basic research into questions of "consciousness, communication, and culture" (Kaprow, 2003, 177). He compares the arts with other disciplines as a way of perceiving things as opposed to merely producing things. But it is not just a stance motivated to inquiry, it is a stance conditioned by a kind of attitude toward the world that Kaprow characterizes as "perhaps more permissive, a little bit more humorous, more gently ironical, more accepting" (Morgan, 1991). He acknowledges that his playful stance may be a privileged one and one doubted in the face of serious issues. Yet he maintains that this playful attitude, one that takes the world as it is and attends to it as opposed to trying to control it, is at the root of compassion. Perhaps most critical, for our purposes here, is to understand this stance not just for Kaprow the artist but a stance assumed by his participants as well.

Reflections on Participation

The idea of Kaprow's participants as both performers and audience resonates with the notion of the studio's participants as engaging in a kind of design mindset. With this perspective, participants are intervening in everyday experiences in new ways. This alignment with Kaprow suggests ways for thinking through issues about participation in studio projects past, present, and future. I'll touch on only some of these ideas here, under the headings of accessibility and accountability, two important criteria for HCI audiences. Although these terms have a variety of meanings, I use "accessibility" mainly to mean participants being able to gain footholds in an IRS project and "accountability" as process evaluation, including the use of designed systems and experiences.

Accessibility

One of our ongoing questions at the studio is how to frame projects for participants. If the intention is for participants to draw their own conclusions about a device and to accommodate or appropriate it in ways of their own choosing, we try not to bias them with too much back story about the design intention. Handing over the Weather Stations by saying "these are meant to complicate the way we think about the environment and our impact on it" feels a bit like cheating. It preempts participants forming their own perspectives and feels more like an exercise in speculative design or even marketing, where what we say about the project counts more than what people actually make of it. Because of this caution with framing, in past projects the studio has tried saying virtually nothing about the devices during the handover (Gaver et al., 2009), only to find this absence of communication actually spoke louder than giving a simple explanation. We still, however, try to err on the side of saying less rather than more, to describe what a system does but not necessarily what it is for or what it means. This is similar to Kaprow's strategy of simple instructions or forms that clearly outline activities for people to do without specifying how or why.

Reflecting on Kaprow, however, expands the notion of framing. Framing is not simply at the moment of hand-off, but it begins the moment the invitations are extended to participate and each touch point, from the probes to informal visits, from the initial deployment to subsequent visits, from self-assessment to assessing the evaluation artifacts we use—all of these act as frames for bounding the experience and for conditioning how participants, and ourselves, approach it. When written like this, it is obvious that the invitation is a frame, and given the time we spend on wording, placement, and forms of invitations it is not something we have taken lightly. Yet in some ways we could consider the invitation almost as a kind of probe, with which one may choose to engage or not, and likewise the probes stand as a kind of precursor to the eventual device, all the way through to the evaluation artifacts standing as another probe or framing device. All of these touch points and artifacts are frames for thinking and reflecting in new ways. Thinking about framing more broadly is aligned with the move Wilkie (2013) advances when he discusses prototyping as an event, where it is not solely the material object, but all the activities that happen around these objects that concern us.

Kaprow recognized that framing cannot be escaped but is instead replaced. In trying to escape frames of conventional art, he needed to replace these with the conventional frames of everyday routines. In the early days of the studio's work, one of the frames challenged was the conventional view of technology as a tool for productivity and efficiency. IRS disrupted this frame by creating alternate systems for daydreaming, spirituality, intimacy, and other aspects of life that do not require us, necessarily, to be faster and better.[9] Inserting novel or curious technology into people's lives highlights how new routines develop as well as how existing routines might change (or not). Today's environment, however, is much more accustomed to playful technologies—ironic avatars, data drifting, digital mashups, poetic status updates, all make the landscape for curious technology a more familiar and well-trodden terrain. Future work in the studio can take advantage of this by exploring, and perhaps disrupting, the new conventions developing around playful experiences with technology.

Finally, the issue of framing points to what we mean by "openness" in our projects. One sense of openness is the idea of simple systems or forms that can be interpreted in many different ways. However, the argument could be made that all forms are to some degree open. I could put a flowerpot on my head and say it is a hat, but we do not normally think of flowerpots as open systems. Furthermore, one could argue that many of the studio's projects are less open than advertised. The Drift Table supported drifting and the Prayer Companion resourced prayer, for example. The language surrounding much of the studio's work suggests it is about play and not work, yet the Prayer Companion is certainly about resourcing the work of the nuns. To some extent then, the studio's work is open in the sense that the areas of focus, such as daydreaming, spirituality, and intimacy, are more open and amorphous than areas amenable to more goal-oriented objectives often defined by improving efficiency or productivity. However, the studio systems are also open in a different sense. In the same manner as Kaprow, our interventions are designed not just to be open to interpretation but open *for* interpretation, for the act of interpretation. The studio designs objects and activities for facilitating participants' attentiveness, inquiry, and meaning-making about their day-to-day lives and surrounding culture.

Accountability

Finally, Kaprow's work contributes to our current thinking about accountability[10] with regards to participation. In particular, I want to end by discussing what it means to evaluate our systems. For Kaprow, evaluation is an informal process that takes place on different levels. On one level, there is feedback from the participants about what they experience—how they attend to their maneuvers, what thoughts occur to them, what they feel. As Kaprow is a participant himself in many of these activities, he adds his own reflections to this dialogue. On another level, Kaprow considers how effective a particular activity is in stimulating or facilitating inquiry. Did he choose an interesting situation? Were the instructions practical but the experience revelatory? Finally, on a third level, Kaprow talks about how attentiveness in the context of a framed activity may then rub off on different aspects of participants' lives. Although certainly something he can account for in terms of himself, tracking the long-term effects of an activity is not something Kaprow sets out to capture or measure, only something that he remarks on as a possible outcome.

Some of these levels of evaluation mirror those in the IRS projects. At the first level is the question of how people experienced and inquired into a particular context, such as the home or conditions of a particular place or rhythms of certain relationships. At the next level is the question of how the device or intervention facilitated, prompted, or perhaps changed this inquiry. How did the particular form, features, and instantiation of the Drift Table, for example, prompt reflections around drifting and daydreaming as an activity in the home? How did it lend to conversations around the nature of the home and/or technology? Evaluation of IRS projects has tended not to extend to the third level, in terms of the carry-on effects of an intervention, just as Kaprow remarks on the potential for this but does not take up the challenge. I'll take each of these three levels of evaluation to reflect on how Kaprow's work and perspectives might inform how we think about accountability and evaluation in the studio.

For many in HCI, accountability largely revolves around being accountable to methods and objectives. Did you do what you set out to do? Did you learn something surprising or confirm a hypothesis? And did you go about your work in a recognized, valid, and repeatable way? These questions refer to a specific kind of accountability to our professional community—and to our funders. There is also the sense of accountability to our participants in terms of creating systems that people want and that they can use, and by respecting their rights as individuals. If our intention in the studio is to engage participants in a kind of design mindset, in an inquiry into particular situations, how do we measure whether this happens, the role of the device and its attributes, and whether it has some kind of generalizing or carry-over effect?

I will take up this last question first because it seems on the face of it the most mismatched with our current approach to evaluation. The studio did not articulate as a criterion of success that the Drift Table, for example, should have some lingering effect on how participants viewed the interplay of their home and technology. Likewise, the studio did not presume that the nuns' approach to prayer would be forever redefined from their use of the Prayer Companion. Although we could imagine these devices having some carry- on effects, we are careful not to elevate the role of the device, and of that particular moment in time, past its relevance. At the same time, it is interesting to consider what residual effects engagement in the project as a whole has for participants. How might they draw on this experience as a resource, just as any other, informing future inquiries? This is not an argument for increasing the lifespan of particular devices but opening the possibility that returning to past participants may afford insights about designing for inquiry. How does the context of inquiry and the tools we use for it change? I am wary that such a suggestion falls into the familiar move of advocating for "more" in terms of participation—in this case, a longer window of engagement. What I find interesting here, though, is not using a further time horizon as a way to look back and say "ah ha … now we can see what really happened," but recognizing how the experience of the past becomes one point of many in reflecting on the present moment. It also reflects back to the comment that propelled my line of research into participation—the comment about becoming a "member of a deranged club with no meaning." This club of increasing members might afford us insights not just about curious technology or the curious home but curious people.

For the second level of evaluation, concerning the instruction sets in Kaprow's work or the built systems in the IRS context, Kaprow provides hints as opposed to explicit guides. For Kaprow, reflections on why a particular instruction set works or not are part of his process of noticing in the moment. He is not embarking on an iterative design of a particular happening set up or rewriting instructions for an activity do-over. He makes note of certain attributes that tend to lead to failure of engagement—for instance, when the instructions are too heavy handed or rife with symbolism. But other than identifying some of the criteria by which he judges the experience—whether it is revelatory, appropriate, and realized—he stops short of identifying attributes that lead to success. Furthermore, he leaves open the possibility that his criteria will change over time. For Kaprow, the evaluation of the instruction set is another opportunity to reflect and focus his attention on particular details and combinations of circumstances. But he never pretends to have noticed everything; there is a constant awareness that his attention is a matter of choice and the variable of time will always create new experiences. This approach to evaluation would not sit well with many in HCI. If we design tools, we want more than a subjective assessment determining whether the tools we have designed are any good, and ideally we want to inform the development of new tools based on our systematic research. Perhaps all we can take from Kaprow is his list of criteria and explore how these might apply to the work of the studio in particular and HCI more generally.

However, Kaprow's evaluation of his tool sets as another instance of reflecting and inquiring into the situation at hand suggests other possible synergies with the IRS work. As it is, our current methods for evaluation such as ethnographic field studies and cultural commentators do not attempt to create a complete authoritative picture of what happened, but they do focus on creating a static account to facilitate our own thinking about what has transpired. Participants become "subjects" in a sense, and those trained in codes of evaluation create accounts of what has happened. This realization was partly behind our move to ask participants in the Indoor Weather Stations project to conduct their own evaluations based on whatever language and codes made the most sense to them. Granted, interviews, observations, and filming from our field work and cultural commentators also prompt reflection on the part of participants as the act of being observed and questioned produces a level of self-awareness. However, these interventions do not have the same open-ended feel as the methods we use on the front end of the design process. In instructions for our Probe activities, for example, we ask participants to have fun with the activities—to fill out what they want; to leave other places blank; to tell truths, half-truths, or outright lies. In one Probe exercise the instructions read: "Each of the pages may suggest new ways to explore your home, and you can use them to tell us about what you find.... There are no rules for how to do this.... You can introduce new materials, cover the pictures or change the words, even tear it up and make your own. This is an experiment; it's not science." Yet, when we move into the evaluation phase of our project, we explicitly ask participants to tell us the truth—to not lie to us in an effort, for example, to spare our feelings if they had a less than favorable opinion. Our methods shift to become, if not hard science, more recognized as social science.

At the point of evaluation, then, we seem to move away from the playful inquiry we seek to prompt during the exploratory stages of design and for engaging with the designed devices themselves. Why is there this marked shift from the tone of the Probes, for example, and the tone of the evaluation stage of the project? In the opening of this essay, I discuss the analogy of a conversation and the sense that our participants will walk away with some shared perspectives as well as one of their own making. Could we provide prompts and cues that make the reflective stage as playful as the exploratory one? This is not an argument away from our use of ethnographic reports or use of other cultural commentators, but these interventions seem primarily for us. Instead, this reflection suggests experimenting with Probe-like interventions for the evaluation as well. Such interventions may produce things we only see glimpses of—if we see anything at all—and such interventions could make a messy entanglement of design, deployment, and evaluation artifacts. This entanglement bleeds together the different levels of evaluation identified in Kaprow's work into the first level—reflecting on the situation at hand, turning our gaze slightly from the specific tool that mediates intimacy or spirituality or curiosity and instead noticing intimate, spiritual, and curious acts. In this way, even in the evaluation stage, participants act as both the performers and audience of design inquiry.

Conclusion

Through this chapter, I examine the nature of participation in the Interaction Research Studio's practice. I began with an overview of broad comparisons against related areas in the field of HCI before turning to an internal analysis across a range of studio projects. This exercise highlights characteristics such as the particular temporal patterning, the level of intensity, and the recognized incompleteness in our encounters and interpretations. A prominent mark of the studio's work is how participation involves joining in an exploration of values and practices through designed systems. The participation is in a design mindset more than in collaboratively working toward a jointly defined and negotiated end. To explore this idea of participation in a kind of attitude, I turned to the work of Kaprow and examined how the notion of participation evolved in his practice using art, or lifelike art, as a means for exploring and connecting with others and cultural conventions.

Through this reading of Kaprow, I returned to ongoing questions in the studio. Kaprow opens the frame of when participation begins and ends, from the initial invitations through the evaluation. Kaprow stimulates questions such as how participation in ludic design changes when the landscape of what is considered "play" continues to shift, or how participants sympathetic to a design mindset are sought out and how potentially unsympathetic participants are drawn in (or whether they even should be), or how do we extend participation in a design mindset from the start of a project through to well after its conclusion. These are but some questions that a reading of Kaprow provoked in my review of IRS's work.

Although the evolution of our thoughts about participation in studio work is not dependent on Kaprow alone, the discussion here outlines how his practice both resonates and can challenge the way we situate our work in an HCI context. Kaprow's activities, and other arts-based practices, redirect our attention in HCI. They present different ways of thinking about and questioning humanity, questions articulated by Kaprow around consciousness, communication, and culture. Every discipline creates a practice around understanding, and in some cases changing, aspects of the world. Every discipline cuts the world up in certain ways to aid this understanding. Within these disciplines are a myriad of nuances in approach that largely rest on the values informing where we direct our attention. Looking outside one's practice and discipline is almost like a Kaprow activity, directing attention by making the familiar strange through comparison. For Kaprow this is always an ongoing, playful activity, as what we can pay attention to is limitless and always changing. "You'd go crazy paying attention to everything. One becomes more attentive to the things that might engage one thereafter. So many things we don't pay attention to just go on. As such, both you and the world are better for it" (Kaprow, cited in Kostelanetz, 1970, 132).

Acknowledgments

This essay is a personal take on existing reflective research we are doing in the studio regarding our approach to participation. As such, the ideas are very much informed by conversations with Bill Gaver, John Bowers, Tobie Kerridge, Andy Boucher, Sarah Pennington, Nadine Jarvis, David Cameron, Mark Hauenstein, Alex Wilkie, Liliana Ovalle, and Matthew Plummer Fernandez.

Notes

1. In this essay, I at times switch between the third person and first person when referring to the work of IRS. For the Weather Station project, of which I was part of the team, and for speculation on future directions based on discussions with IRS colleagues, I use first person. For historical work and overviews of IRS in general, I use the third person.

2. http://bombsite.com/issues/42/articles/1599.

3. http://collections.vam.ac.uk/item/O63805/faraday-chair-chair-dunne-raby/.

4. http://www.auger-loizeau.com/index.php?id=9.

5. There are notable exceptions, such as Biojewellery, which involves participants in the design phase as well as conducts roundtable discussions about issues around bioengineering. See https://research.gold.ac.uk/2317/2/biojewellery-booklet.pdf.

6. The Placebo Project is an exception, as several prototype systems were placed in the homes of participants and participants were interviewed about their experiences in a manner more familiar to HCI.

7. Some of these are prompted directly from the Probes, such as "tell us a secret" or "take a picture of a sacred spot in your home." The body parts information was unsolicited. Given that the IRS work is set in the home, a setting that by nature is personal and intimate, perhaps it is unremarkable that personal details are shared, as simply inviting strangers into one's space indicates a degree of willingness to share private details. Yet the tone of interaction IRS takes care to set lends participants a kind of license to play with their disclosures. Participants are explicitly encouraged to engage only in exercises that compel them, to reorient or modify the materials we give them, even to lie to us and present us with imagined others. This suggests a very different take on participation than perhaps a market research approach in the home where the goal is to understand routines as input for designing or improving products.

8. The inclusion of formal evaluation in HCI has been challenged by various voices (e.g., Dourish, 2006), but the historical and arguably most recognizable practice in HCI is to build, implement, and test or evaluate a system.

9. IRS is not alone in this approach but part of a much larger movement to complicate and enrich the agenda for design in HCI.

10. The term "accountability" has a very specific meaning within ethnomethodology. I am using it much more generally here in terms of evaluation—what sense do both participants and the research team make of the design process, systems and experiences.

References

Bardzell, S., J. Bardzell, J. Forlizzi, J. Zimmerman, and J. Antanitis. (2012) "Critical Design and Critical Theory: The Challenge of Designing for Provocation." *Proceedings of the Designing Interactive Systems Conference (DIS'12)*. New York: ACM, 288–297.

Boehner, K., J. Vertesi, P. Sengers, and P. Dourish. (2007) "How HCI Interprets the Probes." *Proceedings of the SIGCHI Conference on Human Factors in Computing Systems (CHI'07)*. New York: ACM, 1077–1086.

Bruckman, A. (1998) "Community Support for Constructionist Learning." *Computer Supported Cooperative Work* 7 (1–2): 47–86.

Dewey, J. (1980) *Art as Experience*. New York: Perigee.

Dourish, P. (2006) "Implications for Design." *Proceedings of the SIGCHI Conference on Human Factors in Computing Systems (CHI'06)*. New York: ACM, 541–550.

Dunne, A. (1999) *Hertzian Tales: Electronic Products, Aesthetic Experience and Critical Design.* London: RCA Computer Related Design Research.

Ehn, P. (1988) *Work-Oriented Design of Computer Artifacts.* Stockholm: Arbetslivcentrum.

Gaver, W. (2007) "Cultural Commentators: Non-native Interpretations as Resources for Polyphonic Assessment." *International Journal of Human-Computer Studies* 65 (4): 292–305.

Gaver, W., J. Bowers, K. Boehner, A. Boucher, D. Cameron, M. Hauenstein, N. Jarvis, and S. Pennington. (2013) "Indoor Weather Stations: Investigating a Ludic Approach to Environmental HCI through Batch Prototyping." In *Proceedings of the SIGCHI Conference on Human Factors in Computing Systems (CHI '13).* New York: ACM, 3451–3460. DOI:10.1145/2470654.2466474.

Gaver, W., J. Bowers, A. Boucher, H. Gellerson, S. Pennington, A. Schmidt, A. Steed, N. Villars, and B. Walker. (2004) "The Drift Table: Designing for Ludic Engagement." *Extended Abstracts on Human Factors in Computing Systems (CHI EA'04).* New York: ACM, 885–900.

Gaver, W., J. Bowers, T. Kerridge, A. Boucher, and N. Jarvis. (2009) "Anatomy of a Failure: How We Knew When Our Design Went Wrong, and What We Learned from It." *Proceedings of the SIGCHI Conference on Human Factors in Computing Systems (CHI'09).* New York: ACM, 2213–2222.

Gaver, W., M. Blythe, A. Boucher, N. Jarvis, J. Bowers, and P. Wright. (2010) "The Prayer Companion: Openness and Specificity, Materiality and Spirituality." *Proceedings of the SIGCHI Conference on Human Factors in Computing Systems (CHI'10).* New York: ACM, 2055–2064.

Gaver, W., and A. Dunne. (1999) "Projected Realities: Conceptual Design for Cultural Effect." *Proceedings of the SIGCHI Conference on Human Factors in Computing Systems (CHI'99).* New York: ACM, 600–607.

Gaver, W., A. Dunne, and E. Pacenti. (1999) "Design: Cultural Probes." *Interactions* 6 (1): 21–29.

Gaver, W., B. Hooker, and A. Dunne. (2001) *The Presence Project.* London: Royal College of Art.

Jenkins, H., R. Purushotma, K. Clinton, M. Weigel, and A. J. Robison. (2005) "Confronting the Challenges of Participatory Culture: Media Education for the 21st Century." New Media Literacies white paper. Accessed April 28, 2013. http://www.newmedialiteracies.org/wp-content/uploads/pdfs/NMLWhitePaper.pdf.

Kaprow, A. (2003) *Essays on the Blurring of Art and Life,* edited by J. Kelley. Berkeley: University of California Press.

Koskinen, I., J. Zimmerman, T. Binder, J. Redström, and S. Wensveen. (2011) *Design Research through Practice: From the Lab, Field, and Showroom.* New York: Morgan Kaufmann.

Kostelanetz, R. (1970) *The Theatre of Mixed Means: An Introduction to happenings, Kinetic Environments, and Other Mixed-Means Performances.* London: Pitman.

Laurel, B. (1991) *Computers as Theatre.* Reading, MA: Addison-Wesley.

Morgan, R. C. (1991) Interview of Allan Kaprow. *Journal of Contemporary Art* 4 (2): 56–69. http://www.google.com/url?sa=t&rct=j&q=&esrc=s&source=web&cd=2&ved=0ahUKEwj57Lfd9

_XWAhXI8YMKHc4OCeIQFgguMAE&url=http%3A%2F%2Fwww.sussex.ac.uk%2Fesw%2Fcircy%2Fdocuments%2Fallan-kaprow-journal-of-contemporary-art.docx&usg=AOvVaw0u08jHHp-KqcXw-p9KVdAg.

Sanders, E., and P. J. Stappers. (2008) "Co-creation and the New Landscapes of Design." *CoDesign* 4 (1): 5–18.

Suchman, L. (1987) *Plans and Situated Actions: The Problem of Human-Machine Communication.* Cambridge: Cambridge University Press.

Swan, L., and K. Boehner. (2013) "Design Research: Observing Critical Design." In *The Sage Handbook of Digital Technology Research,* edited by S. Price, C. Jewitt, and B. Brown, 286–301. New York: Sage.

Turkle, S. (1984) *The Second Self: Computers and the Human Spirit.* New York: Simon and Schuster.

Wilkie, A. (2013) "Prototyping as Event: Designing the Future of Obesity." *Journal of Cultural Economy* 7 (4): 476–492. http://dx.doi.org/10.1080/17530350.2013.859631.

33 Panopticism (1975)

Michel Foucault, translated by Alan Sheridan

The following, according to an order published at the end of the seventeenth century, were the measures to be taken when the plague appeared in a town.[1] First, a strict spatial partitioning: the closing of the town and its outlying districts, a prohibition to leave the town on pain of death, the killing of all stray animals; the division of the town into distinct quarters, each governed by an intendant. Each street is placed under the authority of a syndic, who keeps it under surveillance; if he leaves the street, he will be condemned to death. On the appointed day, everyone is ordered to stay indoors: it is forbidden to leave on pain of death. The syndic himself comes to lock the door of each house from the outside; he takes the key with him and hands it over to the intendant of the quarter; the intendant keeps it until the end of the quarantine. Each family will have made its own provisions; but, for bread and wine, small wooden canals are set up between the street and the interior of the houses, thus allowing each person to receive his ration without communicating with the suppliers and other residents; meat, fish and herbs will be hoisted up into the houses with pulleys and baskets. If it is absolutely necessary to leave the house, it will be done in turn, avoiding any meeting. Only the intendants, syndics and guards will move about the streets and also, between the infected houses, from one corpse to another, the "crows," who can be left to die: these are "people of little substance who carry the sick, bury the dead, clean and do many vile and abject offices." It is a segmented, immobile, frozen space. Each individual is fixed in his place. And, if he moves, he does so at the risk of his life, contagion or punishment.

Inspection functions ceaselessly. The gaze is alert everywhere: "A considerable body of militia, commanded by good officers and men of substance," guards at the gates, at the town hall and in every quarter to ensure the prompt obedience of the people and the most absolute authority of the magistrates, "as also to observe all disorder, theft and extortion." At each of the town gates there will be an observation post; at the end of each street sentinels. Every day, the intendant visits the quarter in his charge, inquires whether the syndics have carried out their tasks, whether the inhabitants have anything to complain of; they "observe their actions." Every day, too, the syndic goes into the street for which he is responsible; stops before each house: gets all the inhabitants to appear at the windows (those who live overlooking the courtyard will be allocated a window looking onto the street at which no one but they may show themselves); he calls each of them by name; informs himself as to the state of each and every one of them—"in which respect the inhabitants will be compelled to speak the truth under pain of death"; if someone does not appear at the window, the syndic must ask why: "In this way he will find out easily enough whether dead or sick are being concealed." Everyone locked up in his cage, everyone at his window, answering to his name and showing himself when asked—it is the great review of the living and the dead.

This surveillance is based on a system of permanent registration: reports from the syndics to the intendants, from the intendants to the magistrates or mayor. At the beginning of the "lock up," the role of each of the inhabitants present in the town is laid down, one by one; this document bears "the name, age, sex of everyone, notwithstanding his condition": a copy is sent to the intendant of the quarter, another to the office of the town hall, another to enable the syndic to make his daily roll call. Everything that may be observed during the course of the visits—deaths, illnesses, complaints, irregularities—is noted down and transmitted to the intendants and magistrates. The magistrates have complete control over medical treatment; they have appointed a physician in charge; no other practitioner may treat, no apothecary prepare medicine, no confessor visit a sick person without having received from him a written note "to prevent anyone from concealing and dealing with those sick of the contagion, unknown to the magistrates." The registration of the pathological must be constantly centralized. The relation of each individual to his disease and to his death passes through the representatives of power, the registration they make of it, the decisions they take on it.

Five or six days after the beginning of the quarantine, the process of purifying the houses one by one is begun. All the inhabitants are made to leave; in each room "the furniture and goods" are raised from the ground or suspended from the air; perfume is poured around the room; after carefully sealing the windows, doors and even the keyholes with wax, the perfume is set alight. Finally, the entire house is closed while the perfume is consumed; those who have carried out the work are searched, as they were on entry, "in the presence of the residents of the house, to see that they did not have something on their persons as they left that they did not have on entering." Four hours later, the residents are allowed to re-enter their homes.

This enclosed, segmented space, observed at every point, in which the individuals are inserted in a fixed place, in which the slightest movements are supervised, in which all events are recorded, in which an uninterrupted work of writing links the centre and periphery, in which power is exercised without division, according to a continuous hierarchical figure, in which each individual is constantly located, examined and distributed among the living beings, the sick and the dead—all this constitutes a compact model of the disciplinary mechanism. The plague is met by order; its function is to sort out every possible confusion: that of the disease, which is transmitted when bodies are mixed together; that of the evil, which is increased when fear and death overcome prohibitions. It lays down for each individual his place, his body, his disease and his death, his well-being, by means of an omnipresent and omniscient power that subdivides itself in a regular, uninterrupted way even to the ultimate determination of the individual, of what characterizes him, of what belongs to him, of what happens to him. Against the plague, which is a mixture, discipline brings into play its power, which is one of analysis. A whole literary fiction of the festival grew up around the plague: suspended laws, lifted prohibitions, the frenzy of passing time, bodies mingling together without respect, individuals unmasked, abandoning their statutory identity and the figure under which they had been recognized, allowing a quite different truth to appear. But there was also a political dream of the plague, which was exactly its reverse: not the collective festival, but strict divisions; not laws transgressed, but the penetration of regulation into even the smallest details of everyday life through the mediation of the complete hierarchy that assured the capillary functioning of power; not masks that were put on and taken off, but the assignment to each individual of his "true" name, his "true" place, his "true" body, his "true" disease. The plague as a form, at once real and imaginary, of disorder had as its medical and political correlative discipline. Behind the disciplinary mechanisms can be read the haunting memory of "contagions," of the plague, of rebellions, crimes, vagabondage, desertions, people who appear and disappear, live and die in disorder.

If it is true that the leper gave rise to rituals of exclusion, which to a certain extent provided the model for and general form of the great Confinement, then the plague gave rise to disciplinary projects. Rather than the massive, binary division between one set of people and another, it called for multiple separations, individualizing distributions, an organization in depth of surveillance and control, an intensification and a ramification of power. The leper was caught up in a practice of rejection, of exile-enclosure; he was left to his doom in a mass among which it was useless to differentiate; those sick of the plague were caught up in a meticulous tactical partitioning in which individual differentiations were the constricting effects of a power that multiplied, articulated and subdivided itself; the great confinement on the one hand; the correct training on the other. The leper and his separation; the plague and its segmentations. The first is marked; the second analysed and distributed. The exile of the leper and the arrest of the plague do not bring with them the same political dream. The first is that of a pure community, the second that of a disciplined society. Two ways of exercising power over men, of controlling their relations, of separating out their dangerous mixtures. The plague-stricken town, traversed throughout with hierarchy, surveillance, observation, writing; the town immobilized by the functioning of an extensive power that bears in a distinct way over all individual bodies—this is the utopia of the perfectly governed city. The plague (envisaged as a possibility at least) is the trial in the course of which one may define ideally the exercise of disciplinary power. In order to make rights and laws function according to pure theory, the jurists place themselves in imagination in the state of nature; in order to see perfect disciplines functioning, rulers dreamt of the state of plague. Underlying disciplinary projects the image of the plague stands for all forms of confusion and disorder; just as the image of the leper, cut off from all human contact, underlies projects of exclusion.

They are different projects, then, but not incompatible ones. We see them coming slowly together, and it is the peculiarity of the nineteenth century that it applied to the space of exclusion of which the leper was the symbolic inhabitant (beggars, vagabonds, madmen and the disorderly formed the real population) the technique of power proper to disciplinary partitioning. Treat "lepers" as "plague victims," project the subtle segmentations of discipline onto the confused space of internment, combine it with the methods of analytical distribution proper to power, individualize the excluded, but use procedures of individualization to mark exclusion—this is what was operated regularly by disciplinary power from the beginning of the nineteenth century in the psychiatric asylum, the penitentiary, the reformatory, the approved school and, to some extent, the hospital. Generally speaking, all the authorities exercising individual control function according to a double mode; that of binary division and branding (mad/sane; dangerous/harmless; normal/abnormal); and that of coercive assignment, of differential distribution (who he is; where he must be; how he is to be characterized; how he is to be recognized; how a constant surveillance is to be exercised over him in an individual way, etc.). On the one hand, the lepers are treated as plague victims; the tactics of individualizing disciplines are imposed on the excluded; and, on the other hand, the universality of disciplinary controls makes it possible to brand the "leper" and to bring into play against him the dualistic mechanisms of exclusion. The constant division between the normal and the abnormal, to which every individual is subjected, brings us back to our own time, by applying the binary branding and exile of the leper to quite different objects; the existence of a whole set of techniques and institutions for measuring, supervising and correcting the abnormal brings into play the disciplinary mechanisms to which the fear of the plague gave rise. All the mechanisms of power which, even today, are disposed around the abnormal individual, to brand him and to alter him, are composed of those two forms from which they distantly derive.

Bentham's Panopticon is the architectural figure of this composition. We know the principle on which it was based: at the periphery, an annular building; at the centre, a tower; this tower is pierced with wide windows that open onto the inner side of the ring; the peripheric building is divided into cells, each of which extends the whole width of the building; they have two windows, one on the inside, corresponding to the windows of the tower; the other, on the outside, allows the light to cross the cell from one end to the other. All that is needed, then, is to place a supervisor in a central tower and to shut up in each cell a madman, a patient, a condemned man, a worker or a schoolboy. By the effect of backlighting, one can observe from the tower, standing out precisely against the light, the small captive shadows in the cells of the periphery. They are like so many cages, so many small theatres, in which each actor is alone, perfectly individualized and constantly visible. The panoptic mechanism arranges spatial unities that make it possible to see constantly and to recognize immediately. In short, it reverses the principle of the dungeon; or rather of its three functions—to enclose, to deprive of light and to hide—it preserves only the first and eliminates the other two. Full lighting and the eye of a supervisor capture better than darkness, which ultimately protected. Visibility is a trap.

To begin with, this made it possible—as a negative effect—to avoid those compact, swarming, howling masses that were to be found in places of confinement, those painted by Goya or described by Howard. Each individual, in his place, is securely confined to a cell from which he is seen from the front by the supervisor; but the side walls prevent him from coming into contract with his companions. He is seen, but he does not see; he is the object of information, never a subject in communication. The arrangement of his room, opposite the central tower, imposes on him an axial visibility; but the divisions of the ring, those separated cells, imply a lateral invisibility. And this invisibility is a guarantee of order. If the inmates are convicts, there is no danger of a plot, an attempt at collective escape, the planning of new crimes for the future, bad reciprocal influences; if they are patients, there is no danger of contagion; if they are madmen there is no risk of their committing violence upon one another; if they are schoolchildren, there is no copying, no noise, no chatter, no waste of time; if they are workers, there are no disorders, no theft, no coalitions, none of those distractions that slow down the rate of work, make it less perfect or cause accidents. The crowed, a compact mass, a locus of multiple exchanges, individualities merging together, a collective effect, is abolished and replaced by a collection of separated individualities. From the point of view of the guardian, it is replaced by a multiplicity that can be numbered and supervised; from the point of view of the inmates, by a sequestered and observed solitude (Bentham, 60–64).

Hence the major effect of the Panopticon: to induce in the inmate a state of conscious and permanent visibility that assures the automatic functioning of power. So to arrange things that the surveillance is permanent in its effects, even if it is discontinuous in its action; that the perfection of power should tend to render its actual exercise unnecessary; that this architectural apparatus should be a machine for creating and sustaining a power relation independent of the person who exercises it; in short, that the inmates should be caught up in a power situation of which they are themselves the bearers. To achieve this, it is at once too much and too little that the prisoner should be constantly observed by an inspector: too little, for what matters is that he knows himself to be observed; too much, because he has no need in fact of being so. In view of this, Bentham laid down the principle that power should be visible and unverifiable. Visible: the inmate will constantly have before his eyes the tall outline of the central tower from which he is spied upon. Unverifiable: the inmate must never know whether he is being looked at at any one moment; but he must be sure that he may always be so. In order to make the presence or absence of the inspector unverifiable, so that the prisoners, in their cells, cannot even see a shadow, Bentham envisaged not only venetian blinds on the windows of the central observation hall, but, on the inside, partitions that intersected the hall at right angles and, in order to pass from one quarter to the other, not doors but zig-zag openings; for the slightest noise, a gleam of light, a brightness in a half-opened door would betray the presence of the guardian.[2] The Panopticon is a machine for dissociating the see/being seen dyad: in the peripheric ring, one is totally seen, without ever seeing; in the central tower, one sees everything without ever being seen.[3]

It is an important mechanism, for it automatizes and disindividualizes power. Power has its principle not so much in a person as in a certain concerted distribution of bodies, surfaces, lights, gazes; in an arrangement whose internal mechanisms produce the relation in which individuals are caught up. The ceremonies, the rituals, the marks by which the sovereign's surplus power was manifested are useless. There is a machinery that assures dissymmetry, disequilibrium, difference. Consequently, it does not matter who exercises power. Any individual, taken almost at random, can operate the machine: in the absence of the director, his family, his friends, his visitors, even his servants (Bentham, 45). Similarly, it does not matter what motive animates him: the curiosity of the indiscreet, the malice of a child, the thirst for knowledge of a philosopher who wishes to visit this museum of human nature, or the perversity of those who take pleasure in spying and punishing. The more numerous those anonymous and temporary observers are, the greater the risk for the inmate of being surprised and the greater his anxious awareness of being observed. The Panopticon is a marvellous machine which, whatever use one may wish to put it to, produces homogeneous effects of power.

A real subjection is born mechanically from a fictitious relation. So it is not necessary to use force to constrain the convict to good behaviour, the madman to calm, the worker to work, the schoolboy to application, the patient to the observation of the regulations. Bentham was surprised that panoptic institutions could be so light: there were no more bars, no more chains, no more heavy locks; all that was needed was that the separations should be clear and the openings well arranged. The heaviness of the old "houses of security," with their fortress-like architecture, could be replaced by the simple, economic geometry of a "house of certainty." The efficiency of power, its constraining force have, in a sense, passed over to the other side—to the side of its surface of application. He who is subjected to a field of visibility, and who knows it, assumes responsibility for the constraints of power; he makes them play spontaneously upon himself; he inscribes in himself the power relation in which he simultaneously plays both roles; he becomes the principle of his own subjection. By this very fact, the external power may throw off its physical weight; it tends to the non-corporal; and, the more it approaches this limit, the more constant, profound and permanent are its effects: it is a perpetual victory that avoids any physical confrontation and which is always decided in advance.

Bentham does not say whether he was inspired, in his project, by Le Vaux's menagerie at Versailles: the first menagerie in which the different elements are not, as they traditionally were, distributed in a park (Loisel, 104–7). At the centre was an octagonal pavilion which, on the first floor, consisted of only a single room, the king's *salon*; on every side large windows looked out onto seven cages (the eighth side was reserved for the entrance), containing different species of animals. By Bentham's time, this menagerie had disappeared. But one finds in the programme of the Panopticon a similar concern with individualizing observation, with characterization and classification, with the analytical arrangement of space. The Panopticon is a royal menagerie; the animal is replaced by man, individual distribution by specific grouping and the king by the machinery of a furtive power. With this exception, the Panopticon also does the work of a naturalist. It makes it possible to draw up differences: among patients, to observe the symptoms of each individual, without the proximity of beds, the circulation of miasmas, the effects of contagion confusing the clinical tables; among school-children, it makes it possible to observe performances (without there being any imitation or copying), to map aptitudes, to assess characters, to draw up rigorous classifications and, in relation to normal development, to distinguish "laziness and stubbornness" from "incurable imbecility"; among workers, it makes it possible to note the aptitudes of each worker, compare the time he takes to perform a task, and if they are paid by the day, to calculate their wages (Bentham, 60–64).

So much for the question of observation. But the Panopticon was also a laboratory; it could be used as a machine to carry out experiments, to alter behaviour, to train or correct individuals. To experiment with medicines and monitor their effects. To try out different punishments on prisoners, according to their crimes and character, and to seek the most effective ones. To teach different techniques simultaneously to the workers, to decide which is the best. To try out pedagogical experiments—and in particular to take up once again the well-debated problem of secluded education, by using orphans. One would see what would happen when, in their sixteenth or eighteenth year, they were presented with other boys or girls; one could verify whether, as Helvetius thought, anyone could learn anything; one would follow "the genealogy of every observable idea"; one could bring up different children according to different systems of thought, making certain children believe that two and two do not make four or that the moon is a cheese, then put them together when they are twenty or twenty-five years old; one would then have discussions that would be worth a great deal more than the sermons or lectures on which so much money is spent; one would have at least an opportunity of making discoveries in the domain of metaphysics. The Panopticon is a privileged place for experiments on men, and for analysing with complete certainty the transformations that may be obtained from them. The Panopticon may even provide an apparatus for supervising its own mechanisms. In this central tower, the director may spy on all the employees that he has under his orders: nurses, doctors, foremen, teachers, warders; he will be able to judge them continuously, alter their behaviour, impose upon them the methods he thinks best; and it will even be possible to observe the director himself. An inspector arriving unexpectedly at the centre of the Panopticon will be able to judge at a glance, without anything being concealed from him, how the entire establishment is functioning. And, in any case, enclosed as he is in the middle of this architectural mechanism, is not the director's own fate entirely bound up with it? The incompetent physician who has allowed contagion to spread, the incompetent prison governor or workshop manager will be the first victims of an epidemic or a revolt. "'By every tie I could devise,' said the master of the Panopticon, 'my own fate had been bound up by me with theirs'" (Bentham, 177). The Panopticon functions as a kind of laboratory of power. Thanks to its mechanisms of observation, it gains in efficiency and in the ability to penetrate into men's behaviour; knowledge follows the advances of power, discovering new objects of knowledge over all the surfaces on which power is exercised.

The plague-stricken town, the panoptic establishment—the differences are important. They mark, at a distance of a century and a half, the transformations of the disciplinary programme. In the first case, there is an exceptional situation: against an extraordinary evil, power is mobilized; it makes itself everywhere present and visible; it invents new mechanisms; it separates, it immobilizes, it partitions; it constructs for a time what is both a counter-city and the perfect society; it imposes an ideal functioning, but one that is reduced, in the final analysis, like the evil that it combats, to a simple dualism of life and death: that which moves brings death, and one kills that which moves. The Panopticon, on the other hand, must be understood as a generalizable model of functioning; a way of defining power relations in terms of the everyday life of men. No doubt Bentham presents it as a particular institution, closed in upon itself. Utopias, perfectly closed in upon themselves, are common enough. As opposed to the ruined prisons, littered with mechanisms of torture, to be seen in Piranese's engravings, the Panopticon presents a cruel, ingenious cage. The fact that it should have given rise, even in our own time, to so many variations, projected or realized, is evidence of the imaginary intensity that it has possessed for almost two hundred years. But the Panopticon must not be understood as a dream building: it is the diagram of a mechanism of power reduced to its ideal form; its functioning, abstracted from any obstacle, resistance or friction, must be represented as a pure architectural and optical system: it is in fact a figure of political technology that may and must be detached from any specific use.

It is polyvalent in its applications; it serves to reform prisoners, but also to treat patients, to instruct schoolchildren, to confine the insane, to supervise workers, to put beggars and idlers to work. It is a type of location of bodies in space, of distribution of individuals in relation to one another, of hierarchical organization, of disposition of centres and channels of power, of definition of the instruments and modes of intervention of power, which can be implemented in hospitals, workshops, schools, prisons. Whenever one is dealing with a multiplicity of individuals on whom a task or a particular form of behaviour must be imposed, the panoptic schema may be used. It is—necessary modifications apart—applicable "to all establishments whatsoever, in which, within a space not too large to be covered or commanded by buildings, a number of persons are meant to be kept under inspection" (Bentham, 40; although Bentham takes the penitentiary house as his prime example, it is because it has many different functions to fulfil—safe custody, confinement, solitude, forced labour and instruction).

In each of its applications, it makes it possible to perfect the exercise of power. It does this in several ways: because it can reduce the number of those who exercise it, while increasing the number of those on whom it is exercised. Because it is possible to intervene at any moment and because the constant pressure acts even before the offences, mistakes or crimes have been committed. Because, in these conditions, its strength is that it never intervenes, it is exercised spontaneously and without noise, it constitutes a mechanism whose effects follow from one another. Because, without any physical instrument other than architecture and geometry, it acts directly on individuals; it gives "power of mind over mind." The panoptic schema makes any apparatus of power more intense: it assures its economy (in material, in personnel, in time); it assures its efficacity by its preventative character, its continuous functioning and its automatic mechanisms. It is a way of obtaining from power "in hitherto unexampled quantity," "a great and new instrument of government ...; its great excellence consists in the great strength it is capable of giving to any institution it may be though proper to apply it to" (Bentham, 66).

It's a case of "it's easy once you've thought of it" in the political sphere. It can in fact be integrated into any function (education, medical treatment, production, punishment); it can increase the effect of this function, by being linked closely with it; it can constitute a mixed mechanism in which relations of power (and of knowledge) may be precisely adjusted, in the smallest detail, to the processes that are to be supervised; it can establish a direct proportion between "surplus power" and "surplus production." In short, it arranges things in such a way that the exercise of power is not added on from the outside, like a rigid, heavy constraint, to the functions it invests, but is so subtly present in them as to increase their efficiency by itself increasing its own points of contact. The panoptic mechanism is not simply a hinge, a point of exchange between a mechanism of power and a function; it is a way of making power relations function in a function, and of making a function function through these power relations. Bentham's Preface to *Panopticon* opens with a list of the benefits to be obtained from his "inspection-house": *"Morals reformed—health preserved—industry invigorated—instruction diffused—public burthens lightened*—Economy seated, as it were, upon a rock—the gordian knot of the Poor-Laws not cut, but untied—all by a simple idea in architecture!" (Bentham, 39).

Furthermore, the arrangement of this machine is such that its enclosed nature does not preclude a permanent presence from the outside: we have seen that anyone may come and exercise in the central tower the functions of surveillance, and that, this being the case, he can gain a clear idea of the way in which the surveillance is practised. In fact, any panoptic institution, even if it is as rigorously closed as a penitentiary, may without difficulty be subjected to such irregular and constant inspections: and not only by the appointed inspectors, but also by the public; any member of society will have the right to come and see with his own eyes how the schools, hospitals, factories, prisons function. There is no risk, therefore, that the increase of power created by the panoptic machine may degenerate into tyranny; the disciplinary mechanism will be democratically controlled, since it will be constantly accessible "to the great tribunal committee of the world."[4] This Panopticon, subtly arranged so that an observer may observe, at a glance, so many different individuals, also enables everyone to come and observe any of the observers. The seeing machine was once a sort of dark room into which individuals spied; it has become a transparent building in which the exercise of power may be supervised by society as a whole.

The panoptic schema, without disappearing as such or losing any of its properties, was destined to spread throughout the social body; its vocation was to become a generalized function. The plague-stricken town provided an exceptional disciplinary model: perfect, but absolutely violent; to the disease that brought death, power opposed its perpetual threat of death; life inside it was reduced to its simplest expression; it was, against the power of death, the meticulous exercise of the right of the sword. The Panopticon, on the other band, has a role of amplification; although it arranges power, although it is intended to make it more economic and more effective, it does so not for power itself, nor for the immediate salvation of a threatened society: its aim is to strengthen the social forces—to increase production, to develop the economy, spread education, raise the level of public morality; to increase and multiply.

How is power to be strengthened in such a way that, far from impeding progress, far from weighing upon it with its rules and regulations, it actually facilitates such progress? What intensification of power will be able at the same time to be a multiplicator of production? How will power, by increasing its forces, be able to increase those of society instead of confiscating them or impeding them? The Panopticon's solution to this problem is that the productive increase of power can be assured only if, on the one hand, it can be exercised continuously in the very foundations of society, in the subtlest possible way, and if, on the other hand, it functions outside these sudden, violent, discontinuous forms that are bound up with the exercise of sovereignty. The body of the king, with its strange material and physical presence, with the force that he himself deploys or transmits to some few others, is at the opposite extreme of this new physics of power represented by panopticism; the domain of panopticism is, on the contrary, that whole lower region, that region of irregular bodies, with their details, their multiple movements, their heterogeneous forces, their spatial relations; what are required are mechanisms that analyse distributions, gaps, series, combinations, and which use instruments that render visible, record, differentiate and compare: a physics of a relational and multiple power, which has its maximum intensity not in the person of the king, but in the bodies that can be individualized by these relations. At the theoretical level, Bentham defines another way of analysing the social body and the power relations that traverse it; in terms of practice, he defines a procedure of subordination of bodies and forces that must increase the utility of power while practising the economy of the prince. Panopticism is the general principle of a new "political anatomy" whose object and end are not the relations of sovereignty but the relations of discipline.

The celebrated, transparent, circular cage, with its high tower, powerful and knowing, may have been for Bentham a project of a perfect disciplinary institution; but he also set out to show how one may "unlock" the disciplines and get them to function in a diffused, multiple, polyvalent way throughout the whole society body. These disciplines, which the classical age had elaborated in specific, relatively enclosed places—barracks, schools, workshops—and whose total implementation had been imagined only at the limited and temporary scale of a plague-stricken town, Bentham dreamt of transforming into a network of mechanisms that would be everywhere and always alert, running through society without interruption in space or in time. The panoptic arrangement provides the formula for this generalization. It programmes, at the level of an elementary and easily transferable mechanism, the basic functioning of a society penetrated through and through with disciplinary mechanisms.

There are two images, then, of discipline. At one extreme, the discipline-blockade, the enclosed institution, established on the edges of society, turned inwards towards negative functions: arresting evil, breaking communications, suspending time. At the other extreme, with panopticism, is the discipline-mechanism: a functional mechanism that must improve the exercise of power by making it lighter, more rapid, more effective, a design of subtle coercion for a society to come. The movement from one project to the other, from a schema of exceptional discipline to one of generalized surveillance, rests on a historical transformation: the gradual extension of the mechanisms of discipline throughout the seventeenth and eighteenth centuries, their spread throughout the whole social body, the formation of what might be called in general the disciplinary society.

A whole disciplinary generalization—the Benthamite physics of power represents an acknowledgement of this—had operated throughout the classical age. The spread of disciplinary institutions, whose network was beginning to cover an ever larger surface and occupying above all a less and less marginal position, testifies to this: what was an islet, a privileged place, a circumstantial measure, or a singular model, became a general formula; the regulations characteristic of the Protestant and pious armies of William of Orange or of Gustavus Adolphus were transformed into regulations for all the armies of Europe; the model colleges of the Jesuits, or the schools of Batencour or Demia, following the example set by Sturm, provided the outlines for the general forms of educational discipline; the ordering of the naval and military hospitals provided the model for the entire reorganization of hospitals in the eighteenth century.

But this extension of the disciplinary institutions was no doubt only the most visible aspect of various, more profound processes.

1. *The functional inversion of the disciplines.* At first, they were expected to neutralize dangers, to fix useless or disturbed populations, to avoid the inconveniences of over-large assemblies; now they were being asked to play a positive role, for they were becoming able to do so, to increase the possible utility of individuals. Military discipline is no longer a mere means of preventing looting, desertion or failure to obey orders among the troops; it has become a basic technique to enable the army to exist, not as an assembled crowd, but as a unity that derives from this very unity an increase in its forces; discipline increases the skill of each individual, coordinates these skills, accelerates movements, increases fire power, broadens the fronts of attack without reducing their vigour, increases the capacity for resistance, etc. The discipline of the workshop, while remaining a way of enforcing respect for the regulations and authorities, of preventing thefts or losses, tends to increase aptitudes, speeds, output and therefore profits; it still exerts a moral influence over behaviour, but more and more it treats actions in terms of their results, introduces bodies into a machinery, forces into an economy. When, in the seventeenth century, the provincial schools or the Christian elementary schools were founded, the justifications given for them were above all negative: those poor who were unable to bring up their children left them "in ignorance of their obligations: given the difficulties they have in earning a living, and themselves having been badly brought up, they are unable to communicate a sound upbringing that they themselves never had"; this involves three major inconveniences: ignorance of God, idleness (with its consequent drunkenness, impurity, larceny, brigandage); and the formation of those gangs of beggars, always ready to stir up public disorder and "virtually to exhaust the funds of the Hôtel-Deiu" (Demia, 60–61). Now, at the beginning of the Revolution, the end laid down for primary education was to be, among other things, to "fortify," to "develop the body," to prepare the child "for a future in some mechanical work," to give him "an observant eye, a sure hand and prompt habits" (Talleyrand's Report to the Constituent Assembly, 10 September 1791, quoted by Léon, 106). The disciplines function increasingly as techniques for making useful individuals. Hence their emergence from a marginal position on the confines of society, and detachment from the forms of exclusion or expiation, confinement or retreat. Hence the slow loosening of

their kinship with religious regularities and enclosures. Hence also their rooting in the most important, most central and most productive sectors of society. They become attached to some of the great essential functions: factory production, the transmission of knowledge, the diffusion of aptitudes and skills, the war-machine. Hence, too, the double tendency one sees developing throughout the eighteenth century to increase the number of disciplinary institutions and to discipline the existing apparatuses.
2. *The swarming of disciplinary mechanisms*. While, on the one hand, the disciplinary establishments increase, their mechanisms have a certain tendency to become "de-institutionalized," to emerge from the closed fortresses in which they once functioned and to circulate in a "free" state; the massive, compact disciplines are broken down into flexible methods of control, which may be transferred and adapted. Sometimes the closed apparatuses add to their internal and specific function a role of external surveillance, developing around themselves a whole margin of lateral controls. Thus the Christian School must not simply train docile children; it must also make it possible to supervise the parents, to gain information as to their way of life, their resources, their piety, their morals. The school tends to constitute minute social observatories that penetrate even to the adults and exercise regular supervision over them; the bad behaviour of the child, or his absence, is a legitimate pretext, according to Demia, for one to go and question the neighbours, especially if there is any reason to believe that family will not tell the truth; one can then go and question the parents themselves, to find out whether they know their catechism and the prayers, whether they are determined to root out the vices of their children, how many beds there are in the house and what the sleeping arrangements are; the visit may end with the giving of alms, the present of a religious picture, or the provision of additional beds (Demia, 39–40). Similarly, the hospital is increasingly conceived of as a base for the medical observation of the population outside; after the burning down of the Hôtel-Dieu in 1772, there were several demands that the large buildings, so heavy and so disordered, should be replaced by a series of smaller hospitals; their function would be to take in the sick of the quarter, but also to gather information, to be alert to any endemic or epidemic phenomena, to open dispensaries, to give advice to the inhabitants and to keep the authorities informed of the sanitary state of the region.[5]

One also sees the spread of disciplinary procedures, not in the form of enclosed institutions, but as centres of observation disseminated throughout society. Religious groups and charity organizations had long played this role of "disciplining" the population. From the Counter-Reformation to the philanthropy of the July monarchy, initiatives of this type continued to increase; their aims were religious (conversion and moralization), economic (aid and encouragement to work) or political (the struggle against discontent or agitation). One has only to cite by way of example the regulations for the charity associations in the Paris parishes. The territory to be covered was divided into quarters and cantons and the members of the associations divided themselves up along the same lines. These members had to visit their respective areas regularly. "They will strive to eradicate places of ill-repute, tobacco shops, life-classes, gaming house, public scandals, blasphemy, impiety, and any other disorders that may come to their knowledge." They will also have to make individual visits to the poor; and the information to be obtained is laid down in regulations: the stability of the lodging, knowledge of prayers, attendance at the sacraments, knowledge of a trade, morality (and "whether they have not fallen into poverty through their own fault"); lastly, "one must learn by skilful questioning in what way they behave at home. Whether there is peace between them and their neighbours, whether they are cartful to bring up their children in the fear of God ... whether they do not have their older children of different sexes sleeping together and with them, whether they do not allow licentiousness and cajolery in their families, especially in their older daughters. If one has any doubts as to whether they are married, one must ask to see their marriage certificate."[6]

3. *The state-control of the mechanisms of discipline.* In England, it was private religious groups that carried out, for a long time, the functions of social discipline (cf. Radzinovitz, 203–14); in France, although a part of this role remained in the hands of parish guilds or charity associations, another—and no doubt the most important part—was very soon taken over by the police apparatus.

The organization of a centralized police had long been regarded, even by contemporaries, as the most direct expression of royal absolutism; the sovereign had wished to have "his own magistrate to whom he might directly entrust his orders, his commissions, intentions, and who was entrusted with the execution of orders and orders under the King's private seal" (a note by Duval, first secretary at the police magistrature, quoted in Funck-Brentano, 1). In effect, in taking over a number of pre-existing functions—the search for criminals, urban surveillance, economic and political supervision—the police magistratures and the magistrature-general that presided over them in Paris transposed them into a single, strict, administrative machine: "All the radiations of force and information that spread from the circumference culminate in the magistrate-general.... It is he who operates all the wheels that together produce order and harmony. The effects of his administration cannot be better compared than to the movement of the celestial bodies' (Des Essarts, 344 and 528).

But, although the police as an institution were certainly organized in the form of a state apparatus, and although this was certainly linked directly to the centre of political sovereignty, the type of power that it exercises, the mechanisms it operates and the elements to which it applies them are specific. It is an apparatus that must be coextensive with the entire social body and not only by the extreme limits that it embraces, but by the minuteness of the details it is concerned with. Police power must bear "over everything": it is not however the totality of the state nor of the kingdom as visible and invisible body of the monarch; it is the dust of events, actions, behaviour, opinions—"everything that happens";[7] the police are concerned with "those things of every moment," those "unimportant things," of which Catherine II spoke in her Great Instruction (Supplement to the *Instruction for the drawing up of a new code*, 1769, article 535). With the police, one is in the indefinite world of a supervision that seeks ideally to reach the most elementary particle, the most passing phenomenon of the social body: "The ministry of the magistrates and police officers is of the greatest importance; the objects that it embraces are in a sense definite, one may perceive them only by a sufficiently detailed examination" (Delamare, unnumbered Preface): the infinitely small of political power.

And, in order to be exercised, this power had to be given the instrument of permanent, exhaustive, omnipresent surveillance, capable of making all visible, as long as it could itself remain invisible. It had to be like a faceless gaze that transformed the whole social body into a field of perception: thousands of eyes posted everywhere, mobile attentions ever on the alert, a long, hierarchized network which, according to Le Maire, comprised for Paris the forty-eight *commissaires*, the twenty *inspecteurs*, then the "observers," who were paid regularly, the *"basses mouches,"* or secret agents, who were paid by the day, then the informers, paid according to the job done, and finally the prostitutes. And this unceasing observation had to be accumulated in a series of reports and registers; throughout the eighteenth century, an immense police text increasingly covered society by means of a complex documentary organization (on the police registers in the eighteenth century, cf. Chassaigne). And, unlike the methods of judicial or administrative writing, what was registered in this way were forms of behaviour, attitudes, possibilities, suspicions—a permanent account of individuals' behaviour.

Now, it should be noted that, although this police supervision was entirely "in the hands of the king," it did not function in a single direction. It was in fact a double-entry system: it had to correspond, by manipulating the machinery of justice, to the immediate wishes of the king, but it was also capable of responding to solicitations from below; the celebrated *lettres de cachet*, or orders under the king's private seal, which were long the symbol of arbitrary royal rule and which brought detention into disrepute on political grounds, were in fact demanded by families, masters, local notables, neighbours, parish priests; and their function was to punish by confinement a whole infra-penality, that of disorder, agitation, disobedience, bad conduct; those things that Ledoux wanted to exclude from his architecturally perfect city and which he called "offences of non-surveillance." In short, the eighteenth-century police added a disciplinary function to its role as the auxiliary of justice in the pursuit of criminals and as an instrument of the political supervision of plots, opposition movements or revolts. It was a complex function since it linked the absolute power of the monarch to the lowest levels of power disseminated in society; since, between these different, enclosed institutions of discipline (workshops, armies, schools), it extended an intermediary network, acting where they could not intervene, disciplining the non-disciplinary spaces; but it filled in the gaps, linked them together, guaranteed with its armed force an interstitial discipline and a meta-discipline. "By means of a wise police, the sovereign accustoms the people to order and obedience" (Vattel, 162).

The organization of the police apparatus in the eighteenth century sanctioned a generalization of the disciplines that became co-extensive with the state itself. Although it was linked in the most explicit way with everything in the royal power that exceeded the exercise of regular justice, it is understandable why the police offered such slight resistance to the rearrangement of the judicial power; and why it has not ceased to impose its prerogatives upon it, with ever-increasing weight, right up to the present day; this is no doubt because it is the secular arm of the judiciary; but it is also because, to a far greater degree than the judicial institution, it is identified, by reason of its extent and mechanisms, with a society of the disciplinary type. Yet it would be wrong to believe that the disciplinary functions were confiscated and absorbed once and for all by a state apparatus.

"Discipline" may be identified neither with an institution nor with an apparatus; it is a type of power, a modality for its exercise, comprising a whole set of instruments, techniques, procedures, levels of application, targets; it is a "physics" or an "anatomy" of power, a technology. And it may be taken over either by "specialized" institutions (the penitentiaries or "houses of correction" of tile nineteenth century), or by institutions that use it as an essential instrument for particular end (schools, hospitals), or by pre-existing authorities that find in it a means of reinforcing or reorganizing their internal mechanisms of power (one day we should show how intra-familial relations, essentially in the parents-children cell, have become "disciplined," absorbing since the classical age external schemata, first educational and military, then medical, psychiatric, psychological, which have made the family the privileged locus of emergence for the disciplinary question of the normal and the abnormal); or by apparatuses that have made discipline their principle of internal functioning (the disciplinarization of the administrative apparatus, from the Napoleonic period), or finally by state apparatuses whose major, if not exclusive, function is to assure that discipline reigns over society as a whole (the police).

On the whole, therefore, one can speak of the formation of a disciplinary society in this movement that stretches from the enclosed disciplines, a sort of social "quarantine," to an indefinitely generalizable mechanism of "panopticism." Not because the disciplinary modality of power has replaced all the others; but because it has infiltrated the others, sometimes undermining them, but serving as an intermediary between them, linking them together, extending them and above all making it possible to bring the effects of power to the most minute and distant elements. It assures an infinitesimal distribution of the power relations.

A few years after Bentham, Julius gave this society its birth certificate (Julius, 384–6). Speaking of the panoptic principle, he said that there was much more there than architectural ingenuity: it was an event in the "history of the human mind." In appearance, it is merely the solution of a technical problem; but, through it, a whole type of society emerges. Antiquity had been a civilization of spectacle. "To render accessible to a multitude of men the inspection of a small number of objects": this was the problem to which the architecture of temples, theatres and circuses responded. With spectacle, there was a predominance of public life, the intensity of festivals, sensual proximity. In these rituals in which blood flowed, society found new vigour and formed for a moment a single great body. The modern age poses the opposite problem: "To procure for a small number, or even for a single individual, the instantaneous view of a great multitude." In a society in which the principal elements are no longer the community and public life, but, on the one hand, private individuals and, on the other, the state, relations can be regulated only in a form that is the exact reverse of the spectacle: "It was to the modern age, to the ever-growing influence of the state, to its ever more profound intervention in all the details and all the relations of social life, that was reserved the task of increasing and perfecting its guarantees, by using and directing towards that great aim the building and distribution of buildings intended to observe a great multitude of men at the same time."

Julius saw as a fulfilled historical process that which Bentham had described as a technical programme. Our society is one not of spectacle, but of surveillance; under the surface of images, one invests bodies in depth; behind the great abstraction of exchange, there continues the meticulous, concrete training of useful forces; the circuits of communication are the supports of an accumulation and a centralization of knowledge; the play of signs defines the anchorages of power; it is not that the beautiful totality of the individual is amputated, repressed, altered by our social order, it is rather that the individual is carefully fabricated in it, according to a whole technique of forces and bodies. We are much less Greeks than we believe. We are neither in the amphitheatre, nor on the stage, but in the panoptic machine, invested by its effects of power, which we bring to ourselves since we are part of its mechanism. The importance, in historical mythology, of the Napoleonic character probably derives from the fact that it is at the point of junction of the monarchical, ritual exercise of sovereignty and the hierarchical, permanent exercise of indefinite discipline. He is the individual who looms over everything with a single gaze which no detail, however minute, can escape: "You may consider that no part of the Empire is without surveillance, no crime, no offence, no contravention that remains unpunished, and that the eye of the genius who can enlighten all embraces the whole of this vast machine, without, however, the slightest detail escaping his attention" (Treilhard, 14). At the moment of its full blossoming, the disciplinary society still assumes with the Emperor the old aspect of the power of spectacle. As a monarch who is at one and the same time a usurper of the ancient throne and the organizer of the new state, he combined into a single symbolic, ultimate figure the whole of the long process by which the pomp of sovereignty, the necessarily spectacular manifestations of power, were extinguished one by one in the daily exercise of surveillance, in a panopticism in which the vigilance of intersecting gazes was soon to render useless both the eagle and the sun.

The formation of the disciplinary society is connected with a number of broad historical processes—economic, juridico-political and, lastly, scientific—of which it forms part.

1. Generally speaking, it might be said that the disciplines are techniques for assuring the ordering of human multiplicities. It is true that there is nothing exceptional or even characteristic in this; every system of power is presented with the same problem. But the peculiarity of the disciplines is that they try to define in relation to the multiplicities a tactics of power that fulfils three criteria: firstly, to obtain the exercise of power at the lowest possible cost (economically, by the low expenditure it involves; politically, by its discretion, its low exteriorization, its relative invisibility, the little resistance it arouses); secondly, to bring the effects of this social power to their maximum intensity and to extend them as far as possible, without either failure or interval; thirdly, to link this "economic" growth of power with the output of the apparatuses (educational, military, industrial or medical) within which it is exercised; in short, to increase both the docility and the utility of all the elements of the system. This triple objective of the disciplines corresponds to a well-known historical conjuncture. One aspect of this conjuncture was the large demographic thrust of the eighteenth century; an increase in the floating population (one of the primary objects of discipline is to fix; it is an anti-nomadic technique); a change of quantitative scale in the groups to be supervised or manipulated (from the beginning of the seventeenth century to the eve of the French Revolution, the school population had been increasing rapidly, as had no doubt the hospital population; by the end of the eighteenth century, the peace-time army exceeded 200,000 men). The other aspect of the conjuncture was the growth in the apparatus of production, which was becoming more and more extended and complex; it was also becoming more costly and its profitability had to be increased. The development of the disciplinary methods corresponded to these two processes, or rather, no doubt, to the new need to adjust their correlation. Neither the residual forms of feudal power nor the structures of the administrative monarchy, nor the local mechanisms of supervision, nor the unstable, tangled mass they all formed together could carry out this role: they were hindered from doing so by the irregular and inadequate extension of their network, by their often conflicting functioning, but above all by the "costly" nature of the power that was exercised in them. It was costly in several senses: because directly it cost a great deal to the Treasury; because the system of corrupt offices and

farmed-out taxes weighed indirectly, but very heavily, on the population; because the resistance it encountered forced it into a cycle of perpetual reinforcement; because it proceeded essentially by levying (levying on money or products by royal, seigniorial, ecclesiastical taxation; levying on men or time by *corvées* of press-ganging, by locking up or banishing vagabonds). The development of the disciplines marks the appearance of elementary techniques belonging to a quite different economy: mechanisms of power which, instead of proceeding by deduction, are integrated into the productive efficiency of the apparatuses from within, into the growth of this efficiency and into the use of what it produces. For the old principle of "levying-violence," which governed the economy of power, the disciplines substitute the principle of "mildness-production-profit." These are the techniques that make it possible to adjust the multiplicity of men and the multiplication of the apparatuses of production (and this means not only "production" in the strict sense, but also the production of knowledge and skills in the school, the production of health in the hospitals, the production of destructive force in the army).

In this task of adjustment, discipline had to solve a number of problems for which the old economy of power was not sufficiently equipped. It could reduce the inefficiency of mass phenomena: reduce what, in a multiplicity, makes it much less manageable than a unity; reduce what is opposed to the use of each of its elements and of their sum; reduce everything that may counter the advantages of number. That is why discipline fixes; it arrests or regulates movements; it clears up confusion; it dissipates compact groupings of individuals wandering about the country in unpredictable ways; it establishes calculated distributions. It must also master all the forces that are formed from the very constitution of an organized multiplicity; it must neutralize the effects of counter-power that spring from them and which form a resistance to the power that wishes to dominate it: agitations, revolts, spontaneous organizations, coalitions—anything that may establish horizontal conjunctions. Hence the fact that the disciplines use procedures of partitioning and verticality, that they introduce, between the different elements at the same level, as solid separations as possible, that they define compact hierarchical networks, in short, that they oppose to the intrinsic, adverse force of multiplicity the technique of the continuous, individualizing pyramid. They must also increase the particular utility of each element of the multiplicity, but by means that are the most rapid and the least costly, that is to say, by using the multiplicity itself as an instrument of this growth. Hence, in order to extract from bodies the maximum time and force, the use of those overall methods known as time-tables, collective training, exercises, total and detailed surveillance. Furthermore, the disciplines must increase the effect of utility proper to the multiplicities, so that each is made more useful than the simple sum of its elements: it is in order to increase the utilizable effects of the multiple that the disciplines define tactics of distribution, reciprocal adjustment of bodies, gestures and rhythms, differentiation of capacities, reciprocal coordination in relation to apparatuses or tasks. Lastly, the disciplines have to bring into play the power relations, not above but inside the very texture of the multiplicity, as discreetly as possible, as well articulated on the other functions of these multiplicities and also in the least expensive way possible: to this correspond anonymous instruments of power, coextensive with the multiplicity that they regiment, such as hierarchical surveillance, continuous registration, perpetual assessment and classification, In short, to substitute for a power that is manifested through the brilliance of those who exercise it, a power that insidiously objectifies those on whom it is applied; to form a body of knowledge about these individuals, rather than to deploy the ostentatious signs of sovereignty. In a word, the disciplines are the ensemble of minute technical inventions that made it possible to increase the useful size of multiplicities by decreasing the inconveniences of the power which, in order to make them useful, must control them, A multiplicity, whether in a workshop or a nation, an army or a school, reaches the threshold of a discipline when the relation of the one to the other becomes favourable.

If the economic take-off of the West began with the techniques that made possible the accumulation of capital, it might perhaps be said that the methods for administering the accumulation of men made possible a political take-off in relation to the traditional, ritual, costly, violent forms of power, which soon fell into disuse and were superseded by a subtle, calculated technology of subjection. In fact, the two processes—the accumulation of men and the accumulation of capital—cannot be separated; it would not have been possible to solve the problem of the accumulation of men without the growth of an apparatus of production capable of both sustaining them and using them; conversely, the techniques that made the cumulative multiplicity of men useful accelerated the accumulation of capital. At a less general level, the technological mutations of the apparatus of production, the division of labour and the elaboration of the disciplinary techniques sustained an ensemble of very close relations (cf. Marx, *Capital*, vol. 1, chapter XIII and the very interesting analysis in Guerry and Deleule). Each makes the other possible and necessary; each provides a model for the other. The disciplinary pyramid constituted the small cell of power within which the separation, coordination and supervision of tasks was imposed and made efficient; and analytical partitioning of time, gestures and bodily forces constituted an operational schema that could easily be transferred from the groups to be subjected to the mechanisms of production; the massive projection of military methods onto industrial organization was an example of this modelling of the division of labour following the model laid down by the schemata of power. But, on the other hand, the technical analysis of the process of production, its "mechanical" breaking-down, were projected onto the labour force whose task it was to implement it: the constitution of those disciplinary machines in which the individual forces that they bring together are composed into a whole and therefore increased is the effect of this projection. Let us say that discipline is the unitary technique by which the body is reduced as a "political" force at the least cost and maximized as a useful force. The growth of a capitalist economy gave rise to the specific modality of disciplinary power, whose general formulas, techniques of submitting forces and bodies, in short, "political anatomy," could be operated in the most diverse political régimes, apparatuses or institutions.

2. The panoptic modality of power—at the elementary, technical, merely physical level at which it is situated—is not under the immediate dependence or a direct extension of the great juridico-political structures of a society; it is nonetheless not absolutely independent. Historically, the process by which the bourgeoisie became in the course of the eighteenth century the politically dominant class was masked by the establishment of an explicit, coded and formally egalitarian juridical framework, made possible by the organization of a parliamentary, representative régime. But the development and generalization of disciplinary mechanisms constituted the other, dark side of these processes. The general juridical form that guaranteed a system of rights that were egalitarian in principle was supported by these tiny, everyday, physical mechanisms, by all those systems of micro-power that are essentially non-egalitarian and asymmetrical that we call the disciplines. And although, in a formal way, the representative régime makes it possible, directly or indirectly, with or without relays, for the will of all to form the fundamental authority of sovereignty, the disciplines provide, at the base, a guarantee of the submission of forces and bodies. The real, corporal disciplines constituted the foundation of the formal, juridical liberties. The contract may have been regarded as the ideal foundation of law and political power; panopticism constituted the technique, universally widespread, of coercion. It continued to work in depth on the juridical structures of society, in order to make the effective mechanisms of power function in opposition to the formal framework that it had acquired. The "Enlightenment," which discovered the liberties, also invented the disciplines.

In appearance, the disciplines constitute nothing more than an infra-law. They seem to extend the general forms defined by law to the infinitesimal level of individual lives; or they appear as methods of training that enable individuals to become integrated into these general demands. They seem to constitute the same type of law on a different scale, thereby making it more meticulous and more indulgent. The disciplines should be regarded as a sort of counter-law. They have the precise role of introducing insuperable asymmetries and excluding reciprocities. First, because discipline creates between individuals a "private" link, which is a relation of constraints entirely different from contractual obligation; the acceptance of a discipline may be underwritten by contract; the way in which it is imposed, the mechanisms it brings into play, the non-reversible subordination of one group of people by another, the "surplus" power that is always fixed on the same side, the inequality of position of the different "partners" in relation to the common regulation, all these distinguish the disciplinary link from the contractual link, and make it possible to distort the contractual link systematically from the moment it has as its content a mechanism of discipline. We know, for example, how many real procedures undermine the legal fiction of the work contract: workshop discipline is not the least important. Moreover, whereas the juridical systems define juridical subjects according to universal norms, the disciplines characterize, classify, specialize; they distribute along a scale, around a norm, hierarchize individuals in relation to one another and, if necessary, disqualify and invalidate. In any case, in the space and during the time in which they exercise their control and bring into play the asymmetries of their power, they effect a suspension of the law that is never total, but is never annulled either. Regular and institutional as it may be, the discipline, in its mechanism, is a "counter-law." And, although the universal juridicism of modem society seems to fix limits on the exercise of power, its universally widespread panopticism enables it to operate, on the underside of the law, a machinery that is both immense and minute, which supports, reinforces, multiplies the asymmetry of power and undermines the limits that are traced around the law. The minute disciplines, the panopticisms of every day may well be below the level of emergence of the great apparatuses and the great political struggles. But, in the genealogy of modern society, they have been, with the class domination that traverses it, the political counterpart of the juridical norms according to which power was redistributed. Hence, no doubt, the importance that has been given for so long to the small techniques of discipline, to those apparently insignificant tricks that it has invented, and even to those "sciences" that give it a respectable face; hence the fear of abandoning them if one cannot find any substitute; hence the affirmation that they are at the very foundation of society, and an element in its equilibrium, whereas they are a series of mechanisms for unbalancing power relations definitively and everywhere; hence the persistence in regarding them as the humble, but concrete form of every morality, whereas they are a set of physico-political techniques.

To return to the problem of legal punishments, the prison with all the corrective technology at its disposal is to be resituated at the point where the codified power to punish turns into a disciplinary power to observe; at the point where the universal punishments of the law are applied selectively to certain individuals and always the same ones; at the point where the redefinition of the juridical subject by the penalty becomes a useful training of the criminal; at the point where the law is inverted and passes outside itself, and where the counter-law becomes the effective and institutionalized content of the juridical forms. What generalizes the power to punish, then, is not the universal consciousness of the law in each juridical subject; it is the regular extension, the infinitely minute web of panoptic techniques.

3. Taken one by one, most of these techniques have a long history behind them. But what was new, in the eighteenth century, was that, by being combined and generalized, they attained a level at which the formation of knowledge and the increase of

power regularly reinforce one another in a circular process. At this point, the disciplines crossed the "technological" threshold. First the hospital, then the school, then, later, the workshop were not simply "reordered" by the disciplines; they became, thanks to them, apparatuses such that any mechanism of objectification could be used in them as an instrument of subjection, and any growth of power could give rise in them to possible branches of knowledge; it was this link, proper to the technological systems, that made possible within the disciplinary element the formation of clinical medicine, psychiatry, child psychology, educational psychology, the rationalization of labour. It is a double process, then: an epistemological "thaw" through a refinement of power relations; a multiplication of the effects of power through the formation and accumulation of new forms of knowledge.

The extension of the disciplinary methods is inscribed in a broad historical process: the development at about the same time of many other technologies—agronomical, industrial, economic. But it must be recognized that, compared with the mining industries, the emerging chemical industries or methods of national accountancy, compared with the blast furnaces or the steam engine, panopticism has received little attention. It is regarded as not much more than a bizarre little utopia, a perverse dream—rather as though Bentham had been the Fourier of a police society, and the Phalanstery had taken on the form of the Panopticon. And yet this represented the abstract formula of a very real technology, that of individuals. There were many reasons why it received little praise; the most obvious is that the discourses to which it gave rise rarely acquired, except in the academic classifications, the status of sciences; but real reason is no doubt that the power that it operates and which it augments is a direct, physical power that men exercise upon one another. An inglorious culmination had an origin that could be only grudgingly acknowledged. But it would be unjust to compare the disciplinary techniques with such inventions as the steam engine or Amici's microscope. They are much less; and yet, in a way, they are much more. If a historical equivalent or at least a point of comparison had to be found for them, it would be rather in the "inquisitorial" technique.

The eighteenth century invented the techniques of discipline and the examination, rather as the Middle Ages invented the judicial investigation. But it did so by quite different means. The investigation procedure, an old fiscal and administrative technique, had developed above all with the reorganization of the Church and the increase of the princely states in the twelfth and thirteenth centuries. At this time it permeated to a very large degree the jurisprudence first of the ecclesiastical courts, then of the lay courts. The investigation as an authoritarian search for a truth observed or attested was thus opposed to the old procedures of the oath, the ordeal, the judicial duel, the judgement of God or even of the transaction between private individuals. The investigation was the sovereign power arrogating to itself the right to establish the truth by a number of regulated techniques. Now, although the investigation has since then been an integral part of western justice (even up to our own day), one must not forget either its political origin, its link with the birth of the states and of monarchical sovereignty, or its later extension and its role in the formation of knowledge. In fact, the investigation has been the no doubt crude, but fundamental element in the constitution of the empirical sciences; it has been the juridico-political matrix of this experimental knowledge, which, as we know, was very rapidly released at the end of the Middle Ages. It is perhaps true to say that, in Greece, mathematics were born from techniques of measurement; the sciences of nature, in any case, were born, to some extent, at the end of the Middle Ages, from the practices of investigation. The great empirical knowledge that covered the things of the world and transcribed them into the ordering of an indefinite discourse that observes, describes and establishes the "facts" (at a time when the western world was beginning the economic and political conquest of this same world) had its operating model no doubt in the Inquisition—that immense invention that our recent mildness has placed in the dark recesses of our memory. But what this politico-juridical, administrative and criminal, religious and lay, investigation was to the sciences of nature, disciplinary analysis has been to the sciences of man. These sciences, which have so delighted our "humanity" for over a century, have their technical matrix in the petty, malicious minutiae of the disciplines and their investigations. These investigations are perhaps to psychology, psychiatry, pedagogy, criminology, and so many other strange sciences, what the terrible power of investigation was to the calm knowledge of the animals, the plants or the earth. Another power, another knowledge. On the threshold of the classical age, Bacon, lawyer and statesman, tried to develop a methodology of investigation for the empirical sciences. What Great Observer will produce the methodology of examination for the human sciences? Unless, of course, such a thing is not possible. For, although it is true that, in becoming a technique for the empirical sciences, the investigation has detached itself from the inquisitorial procedure, in which it was historically rooted, the examination has remained extremely close to the disciplinary power that shaped it. It has always been and still is an intrinsic element of the disciplines. Of course it seems to have undergone a speculative purification by integrating itself with such sciences as psychology and psychiatry. And, in effect, its appearance in the form of tests, interviews, interrogations and consultations is apparently in order to rectify the mechanisms of discipline: educational psychology is supposed to correct the rigours of the school, just as the medical or psychiatric interview is supposed to rectify the effects of the discipline of work. But we must not be misled; these techniques merely refer individuals from one disciplinary authority to another, and they reproduce, in a concentrated or formalized form, the schema of power-knowledge proper to each discipline (on this subject, cf. Tort). The great investigation that gave rise to the sciences of nature has become detached from its politico-juridical model; the examination, on the other hand, is still caught up in disciplinary technology.

In the Middle Ages, the procedure of investigation gradually superseded the old accusatory justice, by a process initiated from above; the disciplinary technique, on the other hand, insidiously and as if from below, has invaded a penal justice that is still, in principle, inquisitorial. All the great movements of extension that characterize modern penality—the problematization of the criminal behind his crime, the concern with a punishment that is a correction, a therapy, a normalization, the division of the act of judgement between various authorities that are supposed to measure, assess, diagnose, cure, transform individuals—all this betrays the penetration of the disciplinary examination into the judicial inquisition.

What is now imposed on penal justice as its point of application, its "useful" object, will no longer be the body of the guilty man set up against the body of the king; nor will it be the juridical subject of an ideal contract; it will be the disciplinary individual. The extreme point of penal justice under the Ancien Régime was the infinite segmentation of the body of the regicide: a manifestation of the strongest power over the body of the greatest criminal, whose total destruction made the crime explode into its truth. The ideal point of penality today would be an indefinite discipline: an interrogation without end, an investigation that would be extended without limit to a meticulous and ever more analytical observation, a judgement that would at the same time be the constitution of a file that was never closed, the calculated leniency of a penalty that would be interlaced with the ruthless curiosity of an examination, a procedure that would be at the same time the permanent measure of a gap in relation to an inaccessible norm and the asymptotic movement that strives to meet in infinity. The public execution was the logical culmination of a procedure governed by the Inquisition. The practice of placing individuals under "observation" is a natural extension of a justice imbued with disciplinary methods and examination procedures. Is it surprising that the cellular prison, with its regular chronologies, forced labour, its authorities of surveillance and registration, its experts in normality, who continue and multiply the functions of the judge, should have become the modern instrument of penality? Is it surprising that prisons resemble factories, schools, barracks, hospitals, which all resemble prisons?

Notes

1. Archives militaires de Vincennes, A 1,1516 91 sc. Pièce. This regulation is broadly similar to a whole series of others that date from the same period and earlier.

2. In the *Postscript to the Panopticon*, 1791, Bentham adds dark inspection galleries painted in black around the inspector's lodge, each making it possible to observe two storeys of cells.

3. In his first version of the *Panopticon*, Bentham had also imagined an acoustic surveillance, operated by means of pipes leading from the cells to the central tower. In the *Postscript*, he abandoned the idea, perhaps because he could not introduce into it the principle of dissymmetry and prevent the prisoners from hearing the inspector as well as the inspector hearing them. Julius tried to develop a system of dissymmetrical listening (Julius, 18).

4. Imagining this continuous flow of visitors entering the central tower by an underground passage and then observing the circular landscape of the Panopticon, was Bentham aware of the Panoramas that Barker was constructing at exactly the same period (the first seems to have dated from 1787) and in which the visitors, occupying the central place, saw unfolding around them a landscape, a city or a battle. The visitors occupied exactly the place of the sovereign gaze.

5. In the second half of the eighteenth century, it was often suggested that the army should be used for the surveillance and general partitioning of the population. The army, as yet to undergo discipline in the seventeenth century, was regarded as a force capable of instilling it. Cf., for example, Servan, *Le Soldat citoyen*, 1780.

6. Arsenal, MS. 2565. Under this number, one also finds regulations for charity associations of the seventeenth and eighteenth centuries.

7. Le Maire in a memorandum written at the request of Sartine, in answer to sixteen questions posed by Joseph II on the Parisian police. This memorandum was published by Gazier in 1879.

34 Michel Foucault on the Panopticon: A Commentary

John Bowers

Michel Foucault (1926–1984) is widely held to be the most influential social theorist of the latter half of the twentieth century. In 1970, appointed to a new professorship at the Collège de France, he characterized himself as a historian of systems of thought. His work, however, goes beyond the history of ideas as conventionally studied, to encompass an appreciation of the reciprocal relationship between knowledge and the production of different social formations, their institutions, and the identities of those who are their subjects. For Foucault, social formations and the forms of power they manifest depend not merely on material relations but also on how discourses—broadly, authoritative ways of speaking and writing—operate to create, mobilize, identify, and distinguish different subject-forms: the mad and the sane, the criminal and the citizen, the well and the sick, the deviant and the sexually healthy, and so forth. These discourses include those of legislature and religion, as social theorists would readily recognize, but also those of the varied professions and bodies of specialized knowledge, including the human sciences themselves—medicine, psychology, criminology, economics, and the rest—which come to be seen as intimately bound up with the functioning of institutions and forms of discipline and control, influencing ever more intimate aspects of thought and embodiment.

From his first major book, *Madness and Civilization* (1965) to *The History of Sexuality*, volumes 1, 2, and 3 (1979–1986), Foucault explored the history of the human sciences in a manner that sought to resist "totalizing" stories of progress and the accumulation of knowledge—accounts which typically serve to rationalize or excuse how things happen to be at the present time. Rather, Foucault sought to write a "history of the present" that makes plain how current preoccupations have emerged from earlier systems of thought, which had their own methods of reasoning and effectivity. In many ways, Foucault is an iconoclast, smashing the icons of the Enlightenment and ideas of progress and teleology, and putting so-called rational thought and received ideas of legitimacy into harsh relief. Behind democracy and much reformist politics and humanitarian wishful thinking, Foucault skeptically sees the operation of power in ever more fine-grained ways. Through this, Foucault anticipates the emergence of new political strategies that might create alternative forms of truth in opposition to the forms of control and domination that subtly characterize modernity.

Many textbooks systematically go through Foucault's entire corpus, typically characterizing early ("archeological") texts and later ("genealogical") ones (e.g., Dreyfus and Rabinow, 1982; Guting, 1994). Some critical studies relate Foucault to other currents of critical thinking and to specifically postwar contexts of French thought. Then there are those that seek rapprochements between Foucault and other tendencies: Foucault and deconstruction, Foucault and Marxism, Foucault and psychoanalysis, Foucault and phenomenology. Other writers apply his thinking to many domains, from experimental psychology to the history of medicine, from museology to landscape gardening, from musicology to fashion. I am not going to review such work. Rather, I am going to try and unfold many Foucauldian preoccupations from a single source—his chapter on the panopticon from *Discipline and Punish* (1979)—though I will have recourse to a number of other pieces from around the same period (his writings on sexuality and theorizations of power/knowledge and the status of intellectuals).

My broad concern, other than giving an exposition of some Foucauldian concepts, is to explore how we might work with Foucault in HCI, what a Foucauldian HCI might look like. I devote the first half of this commentary to these concerns, focusing on Foucault's celebrated analysis of Bentham's panopticon—a design for a prison—as emblematic of an emerging system not just of institutional power but also of knowledge production and its dependence on new forms of individualizing, observing (via systems of surveillance), and managing and optimizing people, including prisoners, students, hospital patients, and citizens. At the end of this commentary, I return to the idea of a design practice that draws, in one way or another, but hopefully with both eyes open, on Foucault's writings. Specifically, I examine HCI as a "discipline" in the Foucauldian sense, reflect on the limits of Foucault's thinking for HCI, and imagine what some of the qualities of a Foucauldian "design sensibility" for HCI might look like.

Michel Foucault and Me

But now a personal note. I first read Foucault as an experimental psychology Ph.D. student in the early 1980s. Although Foucault wrote very little about the Anglo-American intellectual traditions I was working in, his studies of the psychological being confined to quite devastating examinations of psychoanalysis, he offered ways of making sense of the discomfort I was experiencing in that discipline with its methods and concerns which I did not quite identify with. I was uncomfortable having my curiosity professionalized and constrained. I was specifically warned away from studying literary criticism, structuralism, and Russian formalism, even though they were concerned with topics that seemed to have an affinity with some aspects of my research, in particular theories of narrative, reading, and textuality. I was fascinated by the history of psychology but was warned against looking too hard at it, lest I became disenchanted with the present. I found in Foucault a writer who made sense of how the multiple senses of discipline work together: discipline as a body of knowledge, as a way of keeping its practitioners in line, as a way of legitimating the exercise of power over others. I also found in Foucault and those who drew from him a way of doing historical research that did not end up as a covert celebration of the present, but which brought to light aspects of significant figures in the history of the human sciences I was unaware of. These figures were out of place with narratives of scientific progress, which connected up the very logic of some of the statistical methods I was trained in with the history of eugenics, which made me see that it was no accident that the institution I was working at was founded during the Second World War.

Foucault gave me a kind of comfort. I was not (entirely) mad to be discontent and ill-disciplined. I was also not alone. After (eventually) finishing my Ph.D., I became involved with the Changing the Subject collective, a group of British psychologists exploring Foucault-inspired strategies for the Anglo-American research context I was now finding jobs in. I cofounded a series of workshop-seminars based in Manchester, England, which I called Psychology-Politics-Resistance. I published a number of pieces myself along Foucauldian lines, looking for critical insight into the status of cognitivism, HCI, and CSCW as "knowledge producing practices," some of which I am still reasonably happy with, some much less so. I tried and failed to connect Foucault with my more Marxist-derived activism, something which perhaps can be done, but which I made a particularly bad attempt at in a number of unpublished conference papers and seminars to political groups.

I felt and still feel his allure. I am attracted to the sceptical iconoclasm and a certain discernable dystopian thrill and near sadomasochistic eroticism I find in the writing. I feel it salutary how his account of the emergence of the modern human sciences implicates academic researchers and intellectuals in political processes they might think, loftily, that they are above or beyond, and so might deepen their responsibilities for what is done in the name of the professions or science or engineering or art or design. But I am cautious about taking him as a "grand theoretician" with new insights which are just so. I am queasy about his broad, vague historical periodizations, his tendency to read off from a few historical sources emblems for whole eras and whole bodies of thought, never mind some palpable differences within them. As my work in the late 1980s and 1990s migrated to topics in the social sciences, HCI, and CSCW, I looked elsewhere for insights and methods for the empirical study of "practice." But in the twenty-first century, I, like many academics, feel again uneasy about our situation, its connection to contemporary politics, to the ongoing crises in late capitalism, to institutions that are moving to postwelfare identities, to intellectual imperatives that are less about curiosity and more about impact.

So maybe it is time for me to look at Foucault again, to navigate my ambivalence about him, and to try to find something productive, if not comforting, in his histories of the present.

Discipline and Punish

My commentary takes as its specific focus a single chapter in Foucault's *Discipline and Punish: The Birth of the Prison*, first published in France in 1975, and in English in 1979 (the translation used here). It is one of Foucault's most famous texts, a tour de force examining the proposals of the English philosopher and reformer Jeremy Bentham for a new penitentiary design: the panopticon. The book's general business is to argue against a received view of the emergence of the prison as a form of punishment motivated and justified by humanitarian concerns. Rather, the prison is connected to a panoply of disciplinary practices that can be also found in schools, hospitals, and military barracks, which in varied ways target the human body, subject its capabilities to increasing surveillance, and maximize its usefulness and productive effectiveness.

The book starts with the juxtaposition of two dramatically different examples of penalty: the first, the violent public torture and dismemberment of Robert-François Damiens, who attempted to assassinate King Louis XV in 1757; the second, the regimented daily schedules of the prisoners at Mettray Penal Colony, less than a hundred years later. Foucault asks why this shift from horrific public punishment to private discipline occurred, and why so rapidly. To do this, he explicates the rationality of torture and public punishment, less to castigate it as an inhuman form of penalty than to show it as systematically tied to forms of social organization and power where, among other things, law-breaking was construed as an act of violence performed on the sovereign's body. However, public torture and execution was found to have undesired side effects. While such demonstrations should show the violent recompense the sovereign can extract, and instruct the populace accordingly, they can also be occasions for the convict's body to become an object of sympathy and admiration, or for riotous opposition to the sovereign, or uncontrollable mirth-making. Torture and public execution became politically untenable and such spectacles were first replaced by more focused and controlled public displays of punishment and then by more developed, generalized, and efficient "technologies" for the criminal body, ultimately in the form of the prison.

The Panopticon

The prison which emerged in the late eighteenth century is, for Foucault, a disciplinary technology that combines a method of containment and segregation of the criminal from those who are innocent with opportunities for the surveillance of the inmates in new ways—ways which come to have application throughout the "social body." Foucault takes as emblematic of this shift in punishment the proposals of Jeremy Bentham (1748–1832) for a specific design, the panopticon. Before his exposition of the panopticon, Foucault details some contrasting practices for surveillance that are characteristic of earlier historical periods. During a plague epidemic, for example, an infected village might be required to subject itself to a routine of confinement and daily inspection. Villagers would not be allowed to come and go. Household members would be forced to stay in their homes. An inspection would require the living to show themselves at their windows so that the numbers in a particular house could be compared with previous records. By methods of confinement, separation, inspection, reporting, and recording, the progress of the disease could be traced and, perhaps, itself confined and halted.

These responses to the plague represent, for Foucault, a model of discipline based around order and hierarchy, which could be imposed throughout an entire settlement or infected region. As techniques of confinement and surveillance, they contrast with methods for dealing with lepers, which emphasize rejection, exclusion, and banishment. This response to the plague is starkly different from a medieval life organized around festivity, yearly rhythms, and free intermingling among people. The surveillance methods of the plague contain the beginnings of a model of discipline that could, if need be, be applied throughout society.

This model finds a refined expression in the panopticon. In Bentham's plans, the panopticon features a set of cells arranged in a ring around a central observation tower. Each cell is to be occupied by just one prisoner. The cells are arranged in relation to the central tower so that any prisoner can be observed at any time, but the prisoners cannot see each other. The curvature of the building, the size of the apertures in the cells through which observation can take place, and the position of the central tower create a thorough visual asymmetry. This is reinforced by brightly illuminating the cells. The central tower has openings in it which allow for continuous, unconstrained observation of the prisoners but allow the prisoners only glimpses of the back-lit shadows of the observers. Panoptical prisons were in fact built and several exist to this day, Presidio Modelo in Cuba being the most striking example. Importantly though, elements of panoptical thinking, if not Bentham's complete design, can be found ubiquitously in institutional architecture wherever some form of surveillance is called for.

For Foucault, the panoptical arrangement marks a new "physics of power" different from the exclusion of the leper or the confinement of the plague sufferers but building on both. As such, the panopticon is an emblem of modern power. Foucault deduces with fastidious care several features of the panopticon which characterize this form of power.

The panopticon is a subtly organized architecture. It is quite different from earlier prisons and dungeons. The cells have a meticulous arrangement in relation to each other and in relation to the central tower. They give an institution architectural form. Or rather, better, they enable a new sense for "institution" to emerge, one intimately related to characteristic architectures.

The panopticon individualizes. In each cell appears just one prisoner, who is separated from others and who can be studied, now, as an individual, not so much as a constituent of a "mass" or a mob or a crowd. In principle, different regimes of exercise, work, and food can be specified at this level, per inmate, in response to individual crimes or changes in behavior.

The panopticon prioritizes observation. Its architecture, lighting, asymmetries of vision all work together to create a compact machinery of observation, where prisoners can be viewed at any time. As such it contrasts with the daily rounds of the inspectors of the plague village or other forms of discipline through interrogation and periodic examination. In the panopticon, the inmates are always available to the gaze.

The panopticon engenders discipline. Because the prisoners may be viewed at any time, they may come to act as if they are continually inspected. The gaze from the central tower is of itself a disciplinary technique, and a potentially more effective one than corporal punishment or other forms of forceful coercion. Out of the observational asymmetry of the panopticon, there might arise the self-discipline, and hence potential reform, of the criminal.

The panopticon is a model of efficiency. A single prison can concentrate hundreds without overcrowding. Those hundreds can be kept under surveillance by a single guard. The efficiency of the panopticon does not merely arise from the strength of its bricks and mortar, nor from how a kind of individualized discipline can be created within, but from all of its features working together. As Foucault emphasizes, this efficiency is important to the growth of industrial capitalism, its managerial techniques, and its concern for extracting maximum surplus value from all workers.

The panopticon is impersonal. It is not necessary for particular persons or particular identities to be mobilized to make panoptical power work. This contrasts with the magistrate, the prison-keeper of earlier arrangements, the king or those who operate in his name, the priesthood, the precious skills of the torturer or executioner, and so forth. Observation becomes anonymous. Who inhabits the fleeting shadows in the central tower is of little consequence, at least to create the rudiments of the panopticon's "physics."

The panopticon is a laboratory. New methods of exercise, diet, medication, education, and punishment can be tried out on the prisoners and their responses observed, recorded, and tabulated, and conclusions drawn. Different kinds of prisoners, categorized by crime or character, can be identified and different treatments investigated to see which is the most effective for each category.

The panopticon is polyvalent. It can take many forms and its play of power can permeate throughout the social body. It finds ubiquitous application in some degree or another in schools, hospitals, and factories. It can be used to educate, to punish, to cure, to set the beggars to work. Foucault refers to the panopticon as a "diagram," a specification of relationships, flows, visibilities, arrangements which are omni-applicable. Not all applications will present such a closed wall to the outside as the penitentiary does, but its techniques of individualization, observation, concentration, and efficiency exemplify much of what we might identify as modernity.

This painstaking exegesis of the panopticon lays the way for Foucault to make a number of audacious remarks with a quite disarming straightforwardness. First, he understands the panoptical diagram as bringing about an "inversion of the disciplines." The disciplines turn from being devoted to the neutralization of dangers, the protection from extreme circumstance, or the "fixing" of threatening populations into something positive, productive, and devoted to promoting the utility of individuals. Military discipline is no longer a matter of preventing looting or desertion but becomes the means by which effective military action is possible. The workshop or factory is no longer disciplined to prevent thefts or vandalism but to promote production and profitability. Schools change from being sites where potential delinquency is combated by the fear of God into the means for cultivating the aptitudes, bodily fitness, and self-control of effective future workers. What Foucault means by "the disciplines" in this is left deliberately open, but several remarks in *Discipline and Punish* make it clear that this can include the human sciences, always Foucault's fascination and a consistent object of his historical interrogation. Medicine, psychology, the social sciences, and so forth all come into existence in recognizably modern forms with a concern for observation, individualization, experimentation, and impersonal methodical operation to positively promote the productivity, health, and well-being of the social body.

Second, Foucault notes the "swarming of disciplinary mechanisms." We have already noted the broad utility of the panoptical diagram making it possible for otherwise dissimilar institutions to be organized on similar lines. But these mechanisms are not confined to large-scale architectures like prisons or large factories. They can be found in small neighborhood schools which serve as "minute laboratories" in which to create not only docile and skilled students but also responsible parents who take their disciplining role seriously and carry on the school's work outside of classroom hours by promoting good conduct, hard work, and exercise. Hospitals, similarly, are not just places where the sick might be segregated from the healthy but sites for research into the health of the population at large. In the late eighteenth and into the nineteenth century, many charities and religious and philanthropic organizations come into existence. For Foucault, these can be understood against the background of disciplinary mechanisms "swarming" and permeating the social body ever more finely. Whether they offer aid or promote faith, diligence, and hygiene, they come along with disciplinary and surveillance practices, as, for example, only the observably good are to benefit.

Third, Foucault notes the emergence of the modern state in an overall role of controlling disciplinary practices, particularly through the agency of the police as an organized judicial force. The police and the judiciary are no longer, and certainly not in the republic of France, a means for enforcing the absolute rule of the monarch. Policing becomes all-pervasive and highly organized. The police and magistrates have a local presence, not just for the dispensing of justice and punishment in the event of wrongdoing, but as an ever-present disciplinary force. Even in countries that retain a sovereign, the social body is no longer organized by means of the exercise of sovereign power. Crimes are no longer conceived of as violence perpetrated against the body of the king, so the tortures and executions so vividly described by Foucault in the opening pages of *Discipline and Punish* no longer have a use (see the opening pages of chapter 36. Discipline is a "type of power, a modality for its exercise, comprising a whole set of instruments, techniques, procedures, levels of application, targets; it is a 'physics' or 'anatomy' of power, a technology" (215). The formation of disciplinary society, then, is a manifold of power effects with institutions practicing a kind of "social quarantine" (e.g., the prison) at one extreme through a generalizable panopticism to an everyday self-policing we might all practice at the other.

Foucault presents us with a stark image. Power is ubiquitous. Our society is a disciplinary one in which all our institutions have some resemblance to a prison. A form of discipline involving individualization, observation, and efficiency is all-pervasive. The human sciences are underlaborers in the creation of disciplinary formations, their objects of study, their methods and their values emerging as techniques for "ordering human multiplicities ... to increase both the utility and the docility of all elements of the system" (218). Discipline operates as an "infra-law." It is not subject to the logic of a contract or allied legal arrangement. It is the dark side of democracy and the liberalism of reformers such as Bentham. "The 'Enlightenment,' which discovered the liberties, also invented the disciplines" (222).

While I am confining my commentary to *Discipline and Punish*, and in particular the chapter on panopticism, it is important to note how some of the arguments I have just presented are further developed in Foucault's monumental *The History of Sexuality*, three volumes of which were published before his death (Foucault 1979, 1985, 1986), and in essays at around the same time. We have seen how Foucault argues that the human sciences and disciplinary techniques and institutions have a reciprocal relationship. The panopticon is not only a new design for a penitentiary, it is a laboratory. Furthermore, the panopticon marks the emergence, and helps create, the very subject of the human sciences in their modern form: the observable, measurable, analyzable, calculable individual. Foucault came to denote this close tie between the human sciences and techniques of discipline using the couplet "power/knowledge" (Foucault, 1977b). More fine-grained and detailed knowledge facilitates the operation of power, just as more pervasive observation and control of what people do enable knowledge of them.

The operation of power/knowledge is further elaborated in the first volume of *The History of Sexuality*, published in France in 1976, the year following *Discipline and Punish* (the English version, used here, was published in 1979). Here Foucault provocatively inverts many very commonly held views about sexuality. In particular, he queries the widely held belief that discourse about sexuality was repressed during the seventeenth to early twentieth century, with only the late twentieth century marking the beginnings of "sexual liberation" (Foucaut, 1979). On the contrary, Foucault emphasizes a steadily increasing impetus to talk and write about sex, from the conduct of the Catholic confessional through religious and governmental edicts defining and promoting the sexual health of the population, to the identification in the eighteenth and nineteenth centuries of a "world of perversion" inhabited by different kinds of sexual subjects. Far from being subject to, and only recently released from, any kind of repression of sexuality and its expression, sexuality has been persistently and variably formulated. In the nineteenth century, what Foucault calls the "scientia sexualis" emerges, founded on confession and scientific enquiry.

These arguments underline the ubiquity of the operation of power/knowledge and deepen and complement the emphases we have seen in *Discipline and Punish*. Power/knowledge operates in the most intimate of realms of human life, indeed over human life itself, in what Foucault calls "biopower" (Foucault, 1979). The panopticon expresses one mode of biopower: the disciplining of the body, the optimization of its capabilities, the increase of its usefulness, productivity, and docility. In contrast to this mechanization of the body, biopower can also emphasize biological processes, the reproductive fecundity of the body, birth and mortality, life expectancy, and health and well-being. In both cases, power/knowledge is insinuating itself into life itself. "Power is everywhere ... because it comes from everywhere" (Foucault, 1979, 63). Our acts of disclosure and confession, when we seem to be releasing ourselves from repression and speaking in our own name, are not separate from the operation of power but a deep and ubiquitous constituent of it.

Foucault into HCI

Foucault's work has proven enormously influential in the human sciences and there certainly is not enough space to review all of that here. My intention is rather to examine the prospects for a characteristically Foucauldian research agenda for HCI. What would Foucauldian HCI look like? What might some of its topics, emphasis, and methods be? Here again, I acknowledge that there is already much work in HCI under the influence of Foucault. However, the current chapter is an opportunity for a specific approach, one in which we do not just "apply" Foucault to HCI but see many of HCI's characteristic concerns as, perhaps unwittingly, further demonstrating the subtle capillary action of power/knowledge.

I have characterized Foucault's image of the operation of power as "stark." I want to take this starkness into a discussion of some of HCI's foundational commitments.

User, Use, Usability, and Usefulness: The Very Ideas

HCI discourses very characteristically speak of "the user," and of "use," "usability," and "usefulness." After an encounter with Foucault, it is hard to employ these concepts innocently. As cognate terms, they all orbit around the forms of utility and efficiency identified in *Discipline and Punish* as being born with the panopticon. With Geoff Cooper many years ago (Cooper and Bowers, 1995), I presented a detailed analysis of the early chapters of Card, Moran, and Newell's (1983) *The Psychology of Human-Computer Interaction* from a Foucauldian perspective. For us, Card et al. served the role of Bentham. In their book, Card et al. do much to characterize the foundational concepts of what we called first-wave HCI, marking out its distinctive concern for the user as opposed to ergonomics' characteristic concern for the operator. For Card et al., computing technologies require the identification of the user as a new subject for research. A new configuration of disciplines and methods is required in order for us to know the user, most especially the techniques and theories of experimental cognitive psychology, rather than the engineering-oriented methods of computer science or ergonomics. The methods advocated by Card et al. and the analysis techniques they formulate could scarcely better exemplify the individualization, measurement, tabulation, and calculation that Foucault sees as being born with the panopticon and the techniques of power/knowledge that proliferated through the eighteenth and nineteenth centuries. From a Foucauldian perspective, the HCI of the late 1970s and early 1980s brought the mechanized mode of biopower to the interface.

Experimental cognitive psychology, at least as practiced during this period, was well suited to HCI, which had a technological focus on interactive applications running on workstations engaged with by individual users. HCI papers and textbooks dating from these times are replete with diagrams showing a kind of symmetry either side of a line, the interface. The user and the application make a kind of dual mechanism, both, in their ways, processing information or transforming representations. The computational metaphor for mind eases the match, as like connects with like, or at least it might with good design. While various aspects of cognitivism in HCI have been roundly critiqued, just as cognitivism itself has, it is somewhat rarer to see this as a Foucauldian "diagram"—as a set of relationships that can be ubiquitously applied to further the capillary action of power/knowledge. Once we conceive of an individual in this fashion and give the name "user," we permit new questions to be asked about the goodness of fit either side of the line, of the software we should make to be usable, but also of the kinds of capabilities to inculcate, refine, or exploit both in those who engage with the software and in those who design it. Diagrams of users in dialogue with applications can be seen as depictions of a microphysics of power.

It is trivial, but nonetheless important, to connect the diagrams of first-wave HCI to the development of the new senses of productive efficiency that have been relevant to computing at least since the 1970s. From a Foucauldian perspective, it is straightforward to argue that, just as the creation of architectures of observation and calculation like the panopticon provided a model for the factory during industrial capitalism, so do the scenarios of first-wave HCI give us a glimpse of the bureaucratic "factories" of late capitalism—the offices where words are processed and spreadsheets manipulated. Proposals for the organization of menu systems, the design of onscreen icons and pointing devices, and so forth and so on, are classically assessed in terms of the speed with which tasks are completed and the errors that are made along the way, such matters typically being made the subject of laboratory experimentation. In this sense, first-wave HCI furthers the disciplinary regimes documented in *Discipline and Punish* with their concern for the maximization of productive capability.

This kind of discipline, too, operates as an "infra-law." While of course there is legislature governing computers and their use (of course there is), the kind of disciplining a Foucauldian might have in mind operates in a more intimate way, as soon as the body aligns itself with the screen, as soon as the hand reaches for the mouse or strokes the touchpad, as soon as the eye sees separate items in the display, as soon as a gesture is targeted toward them. We have become, in the same sense as a mechanism might be, "engaged." We have become users, already positioned in an anatomy of power, the affordances of our artefacts an infra-law of discipline.

Wave upon Wave

It is commonplace to distinguish the concerns for HCI research that Card, Moran, and Newell write about from other "waves." During the 1980s, first-wave HCI was criticized for not capturing the social identity of the user, the social organization of the user's activities, and the social context of computing technology. Geoff and I wrote about second-wave HCI to capture this turn to the social and political, and we cited the growth of computer-supported cooperative work (CSCW) as emblematic of these concerns—Liam Bannon served as another Bentham for us with his tellingly entitled "From Human Factors to Human Actors" (Bannon, 1991). Since the turn of the century, a number of authors have sought to add a third wave to this historical and conceptual picture. For Bødker (2006) and Bardzell and Bardzell (2011), the third wave is characterized by nonwork settings and topics such as lived experience, intimacy, pleasure, and embodiment. It is commonplace to break computing development into three waves too: from the mainframe, through the era of the personal computer, to a time of ubiquitous computing (Harrison, Tatar, and Sengers, 2007; Rogers, 2012).

From a Foucauldian perspective, these further waves do not so much annul earlier HCI research as add to the proliferation of discourses on the subject. We can conceive of not merely users, but workers, citizens, consumers, activists—all potential subjects of HCI research. We can be concerned not merely with applications and workstations, but distributed computing and networks, social media and the cloud, virtual reality and augmented reality, ubiquitous computing and embedded computing, from the internet of things to implants under the skin, and so on. Our domain of concern is ubiquitous, from the office to workplaces of all sorts, from work settings to leisure activities, from life to death, from this world to those others of religion and spirituality. There are professional knowledges, methods and prototype designs for all aspects of life and beyond. Just as the *scientia sexualis* has grown into an all-encompassing biopower, so HCI has infiltrated all of our relationships with machines, making it now facile to speak of us as cyborgs.

A first glance, this might seem liberating, both for those who practice research and for those who are its subjects and in whose name the research is often done, but Foucault would urge a kind of dark caution. If knowledge and power have the reciprocal relationship that he argues, then the proliferation of knowledge is also a "swarming of disciplinary mechanisms." If first-wave HCI gave a relatively small number of ways of knowing, dominated by those from cognitive psychology, then the later waves give us many: sociological, anthropological, artistic, experiential, designerly, political, spiritual, and more. If a form of knowledge is also a form of entrapment (if not in a penitentiary, at least in the terms of its discourse), then we may now be multiply entrapped. Our identities may now be fixed in an overdetermined fashion, through ever-multiplying professional discourses, each claiming to know, and each with its techniques of discipline, its way of moving from an *is* to an *ought.*

Consider social media—consider Facebook. I am invited to report on my "status." Over the lifetime of Facebook, the hint given in the status field has varied. As I write this, I am being prompted, "What is on your mind?" In Foucauldian terms, I am being incited to a confessional. I have the opportunity to reveal all, or at least "my mind." Of course, I, like many accomplished Facebook-keepers, confess only the most interesting, only the most witty, only the most insightful, only the most intriguing, only the most (literally) status-enhancing things that might be on my mind or encountered by me. Sometimes, of course, equally obviously, I ironically play with those expectations and say something utterly mundane or even mildly offensive. Other times, I may counterpose things that satisfy intellectual or high cultural expectations people (my "friends") might have of me with something low-brow, stupid, eccentric, or tawdry. Yet other times, I may send occult messages, in the guise of a broadcast to all, yet intended for a secret lover. And on yet other occasions, I may subtly issue something barbed, something hurtful, a small act of vengeance. Most revealing, perhaps, is when I do not go on Facebook for days, because, frankly, too much is on my mind. I may do any or none of these things. But whatever I am doing, I am fashioning a presentation of myself. Facebook's iron-clad "infra-law" is operating on me just as strongly as if a priest had urged me to tell of my sins or an observer had, from their central tower, noted down my latest nervous tick. For Foucault, it would be fruitless to argue over whether I am telling the truth of myself or not, or whether I have done this voluntarily. I have a will-to-truth, the truth of myself, a compulsion to reveal, to entertain, to celebrate. What I do voluntarily, what my will might be or become, is being shaped in all this—by me, by my friends, by Facebook. Of course, all the time specifically tailored adverts appear which perhaps might offer products or services that would appeal to just this kind of self, just my kind of self, adverts selected by mechanisms as carefully researched as those that work out which of my friends are most newsworthy to me and whose activities I am regularly exposed to.

The use and usability of technologies in HCI is bound up with the utility of individuals. While I have made this point in relationship to early HCI, where it is an easy point to make, we can now see more and more ways in which individuals can be useful or make themselves into useful selves. I am useful in my avowal of an identity, or in the revelation of its traces, which can be the subject of marketing. I am useful as a searcher for information as my queries to Google reveal what I, and those like me, desire. The latest waves of HCI research are not exempt from a logic of efficiency, productivity, and the utility of individuals. On the contrary, HCI works in a context of such logics insinuating themselves ever more deeply in our lives. Or so a Foucauldian might say.

Surveillance

It may be a surprise that I have held back from, perhaps, the most obvious connection *Discipline and Punish* might make with questions of concern in HCI: surveillance. Surely, the panopticon is all about surveillance and surveillance technologies are ever proliferating in the "interneted" world, raising important issues of rights and liberties. Of course, that is true but it is how those technologies are bound up with the changing shape of the disciplines (in both scholarly and power-exercising senses) that I have wanted to emphasize first. Surveillance is, for Foucault, not something that those with power do to those without. That would be a remnant of the sovereign concept of power that Foucault is at pains to argue against. If we were to say that, we would not, in our understanding, have fully "cut off the head of the King" to use Foucault's memorable phrase (Foucault, 1979, 89). We would have just relocated the sovereign to one end of a piece of surveillance apparatus. Besides, for Foucault, power is ubiquitous and relational. It is not a substance that some have and others do not have. Power is in circulation. It is ascribed to anatomies, physics, diagrams, and sets of relationships—impersonally and anonymously.

If we still think of surveillance as an expression of a kind of sovereign power, then, from a Foucauldian perspective, we will miss many key aspects of its operation. We will see surveillance in only the most obvious of places: in CCTV technology or in the activities of governments snooping on the populace to pursue pedophiles or terrorists. We may miss the surveillance relationships that exist in medical technologies and patient monitoring, in smart homes for the wealthy or the vulnerable, in the use of computer control systems in cars, in apps that count our caloric intake and number of steps taken, in every point-of-sale shopping transaction, in every online registration form, in every internet sale, or, as I emphasize in the previous section, in every status message, search query, or photograph posted and tagged or in every tweet, in which we voluntarily give ourselves over to inspection by the whole world in up to 140 characters at a time.

Ubiquitous computing is, in this view, ubiquitous surveillance. Our conduct is anonymously analyzed by a carefully crafted algorithm, which then dispenses whatever is deemed appropriate to us. Reciprocally, our conduct has to be just so for the sensors to be appropriately responsive. We or our actions have to be within range, detectable, identifiable, and consequential. If you doubt the disciplining effects of sensor technology, you only have to try to change channel on a gesture-driven or voice-operated TV set: move just so, speak just so. When we speak of "data capture" in regard to sensor systems we are letting slip their dual character. We are giving ("data," Latin for "things that are given") but we are being entrapped ("capture," a hunting or imprisonment metaphor). Or so a Foucauldian like Mark Poster, who sees panoptical surveillance in every computer database, might say.

Foucault's emphasis on the noncontractual, infra-legal status of surveillance should make us realize the limits of campaigns based around legal or related judicial concepts. As long as our politics is one of freedoms, rights, and obligations, which we think might be enforced by law, we will not notice the underbelly of democracy, the relationships of power and discipline that were equally a product of the Enlightenment. We may campaign for privacy on the internet or for limits on the use of personal data by the state or commercial agencies but, in so doing, we may not realize the sheer ubiquity of how we give things off (data) and how those things are taken (captured) and put to use. At the time of writing, many researchers in HCI are becoming interested in political activism and supporting political participation in some form or another. Reading Foucault would encourage a wide agenda for such political thinking, one not confined to a reassertion of Enlightenment values of liberty and privacy and security for the individual, especially as that very being, the very subject of liberal democracy, the individual, has been in part produced by those same disciplinary mechanisms we may feel queasy about. We must do more than reassert Enlightenment values. We must do more than just cut off the head of the king.

The Professions, the Disciplines, and Intellectuals

Foucault can make for uncomfortable reading for a professional intellectual—an academic, a researcher, someone like myself. The human sciences which throughout my adult life I have variably worked in, first philosophy and psychology, then the empirically inclined social sciences, then the social scientifically inclined wings of CSCW and HCI, then various artistic and design-oriented fields, are all implicated in power/knowledge. The academic world is not a place of escape from the mechanisms by which the social body is constituted and disciplined. There are no ivory towers.

Universities with their various specialisms exist in the circulation of power alongside the prison, the hospital, the school, the factory. While some universities have a history reaching back to the higher education of monks or priests or politicians or diplomats with church or royal patronage, most of those founded in the nineteenth century appear in the cities of commerce, often through the charity of local entrepreneurs or philanthropists. In the twentieth century, many universities became, or new ones were created as, state institutions. This is exactly the trajectory Foucault documents in *Discipline and Punish* and in *The History of Sexuality*, volume 1. And now, as the prison, the hospital, the school, the factory (or for that matter, the museum, the zoological gardens) are all in their various ways being reconstituted or neglected, so there appear research challenges to fashion them anew or to limit or displace the damage. There are no ivory towers.

Consider the following.

1982–1988 None.
1989 Wings for the mind.
1990 Empowering people.
1991 Reaching through technology.
1992 Striking a balance.
1993 Bridge between worlds.
1994 Celebrating independence.
1995 Mosaic of creativity.
1996 Common ground.
1997 Looking to the future.
1998 Making the impossible possible.
1999 The CHI is the limit.
2000 The future is here.
2001 Anyone. Anywhere.
2002 Changing the world, changing ourselves.
2003 New horizons.
2004 Connect.
2005 Technology, safety, community.
2006 Interact. Inform. Inspire.
2007 Reach beyond: look how far we have come, imagine how far we can go.
2008 Art.Science.Balance.
2009 Digital life, new world.
2010 We are HCI.
2011 Connecting.
2012 It's the experience.
2013 Changing perspective.
2014 One of a CHInd.
2015 Crossings.
2016 Chi4good.

These are the straplines (or subtitles) for the Association of Computing Machinery's CHI conferences from their inception in 1982 through 2016. Complex work is being done here (at least since 1989, prior to which no further words beyond a formal institutional attachment to the ACM and an allegiance to human factors seemed necessary). Each strapline can be regarded as a condensation of professional sentiment, concrete enough to be idiomatic for HCI, abstract enough to be inclusive of a variety of work. As such, they express changing professional moods, sometimes celebratory, sometimes aspirational or, from time to time, a little anxious. I will leave space for you to do the (not very hard) full Foucauldian discourse analysis on them but let me offer just two observations.

First, many of these identities for HCI are oriented toward the future and its challenges or the instability or provisionality of the present. In 1997, we were looking to the future. In 2000, the future was here. In 2002, we needed to change the world and change ourselves in time, a year later (2003), to meet new horizons. In 2007, we were urged to reach beyond and look how far we have come, while imagining how far we can go into, presumably, the digital life and new world of two years later (2009). In 2013, we felt that perspectives were changing or, perhaps, needed to be changed. In all this, though, we keep our individuality (2014) while relating to others (2015, 2016). These would be facetious points were it not for the fact that technological and social change are persistently evoked as creating challenges and responsibilities for the HCI researcher. A standard first paragraph in an HCI paper presents a changing technological context, typically as a matter of progress, increase, or proliferation, to which one needs to, indeed one must, respond. Geoff Cooper and I found numerous examples of such "progressivist rhetoric" in Card, Moran, and Newell's book. The emerging problems at the interface were too important to be left in the hands of software engineers.

Second, many of these straplines are, effectively, characterizations of optimal relationships between different forms of knowledge. Many assert relatedness and consensus (1992, 1993, 1996, 2004, 2007 again, 2008, 2011, 2015), sometimes a kind of unity through difference (1995, 2014), or a balance between different elements (1992, 2008, or 2005's post-9/11 trio of technology, safety, and community). Occasionally, one is enjoined to go beyond narrow or fixed (2013) perspectives, for example, to reach beyond technology alone (1991). 1994 celebrated independence, presumably from the ignorant software engineers demonized by Card et al. Again, I risk being facetious but, out of this, I want to try a stronger Foucauldian claim.

It is in these subtle ways that professional identities and obligations get created. The disciplines do not merely mobilize techniques for observing and regulating their subjects. They act equally on those who practice them. The identities which these straplines hint at are not merely identities for HCI but injunctions or compact formalisms of good professional practice or expressions of consensual or taken-for-granted value. In short, discipline is multilateral. The observer and the observed are equally positioned either side of the surveillance apparatus or architecture. The discourses of HCI that we encounter are not just means for producing and analysing different subjects, they are means for engendering different kinds of researchers. The cognitive ergonomist, the social-science-inclined CSCW researcher, the ludic or critical designer of third-wave HCI are all, in their various ways, the subject of discourse and regulated by the disciplinary techniques of the academy.

In experiencing these incitements and regulatory techniques, the intellectual, according to an interview Foucault gave in 1977, experiences something of the condition of the proletariat and the masses.

> Intellectuals have got used to working, not in the modality of "the universal," or "the exemplary," or the "just-and-true-for-all," but within specific sectors, at the precise point where their own conditions of life or work situate them (housing, the hospital, the asylum, the laboratory, the university, family and sexual relations). This has given them a much more immediate and concrete awareness of struggles. And they have met here with problems which are specific, "non-universal," and often different from those of the proletariat or the masses. And yet I believe intellectuals have actually been drawn closer to the proletariat and the masses, for two reasons. Firstly, because it has been a question of real, material, everyday struggles, and secondly because they have often been confronted, albeit in a different form, by the same adversary as the proletariat, namely the multinational corporations, the judicial and police apparatuses, the property speculators, etc. This is what I would call the "specific" intellectual as opposed to the "universal" intellectual. (Foucault, 1977c, 126)

It is precisely because there are no ivory towers that specific intellectuals emerge with their concrete awareness of struggles, their own confrontations with common adversaries, and, one might add, their self-awareness of their own role in the reproduction of discipline. For Foucault, "the university and the academic emerge, if not as principal elements, at least as 'exchangers,' privileged points of intersection" (127). He conjectures that it is with Oppenheimer and the Manhattan Project that we see the point of transition between the universal intellectual, the writer, the one who speaks in the name of others and represents universal truths and sentiments, and the specific intellectual, "the savant or expert" (128), whose knowledge can be a political threat if not appropriately harnessed. While the specific intellectual risks being manipulated or marginalized, Foucault believes that this figure should be reexamined, rather than abandoned. And certainly we should not return nostalgically to new universal philosophies or worldviews, nor unquestioningly join in with the "monotonous, lyrical little chants" (130) which make sense only within self-regarding intellectual groups—chants made up of expressions of professional self-interest or over-believed straplines that read like advertising slogans.

The possibility that HCI researchers and professional academics might work as specific intellectuals and, through that identification, reform their research and design practices is, for me, one of the most promising ways of working out a Foucauldian HCI—more interesting and challenging than simply applying Foucauldian concepts to HCI problems. I will sketch some possibilities for this shortly. But first …

Turning Critical

I have several problems with Foucault, even though he has been an influence on many of my critical writings in cognitive science, HCI, and CSCW. There have been junctures in the above exposition where my nerve has failed and I have written "or so a Foucauldian would have us believe" or some similar distancing technique. This chapter is not the place for a thoroughgoing critique of Foucault, just as it has not the place for a full exposition of him. Just as I have pointed to possibilities for a Foucauldian HCI, taking the discussion of the panopticon in *Discipline and Punish* as my point of departure, and left it to the reader to evaluate or enact those prospects, I shall offer here at best a sketch of criticism, equally focusing on Foucault's discussion of panopticism and with HCI in mind.

The Details, the Details

Much of my work in HCI and CSCW, and the designerly and artistic orientations to research problems that I currently pursue, has been informed by ethnographic research. The status of ethnography is itself a matter of dispute and, naturally, there are many ways of doing research with an ethnographic accent. But one thing ethnography has given me is a sensitivity to the details of everyday practice, exactly how things are done, in real time, on a moment-by-moment basis, a concern for the mundane, the ordinary, as something achieved against a background of contingency. At first glance, Foucault might seem to be a fellow traveler but we do not see in his account of panopticism, for example, any studies of exactly how observation takes place in institutions such as prisons, hospitals, and factories. We are told that the architectural arrangements of the panoptical penitentiary create the conditions of a laboratory and enable the detailed observation of a new subject, the individual with its potential for utility and productivity. But we do not see this analyzed in depth. We do not encounter in Foucault accounts of actual surveillance practices. We do not see records of scientists or other agents of discipline actually making the connections between observation, institutional arrangements, and knowledge which Foucault claims are there. We do not read about exemplary cases of prisoners experiencing the potential of omnipresent gaze and, through this, reforming themselves. And so forth. There is an empirical gap in Foucault, a postulation of the capillary operation of power but little documentation of it in action, in all its contingent detail.

Apriorism

Rather Foucault has a strategy for reading historical documents which I will characterize as a kind of apriorism. The power effects of the panopticon are "read-off" Bentham's texts and diagrams. The meticulous reading that I have given an exposition of has a remorseless logic to it. First one thing, then another. It makes for a thrillingly stark (as

I have characterized it a number of times) picture of modernity. But its accumulation of impact is accomplished by a quasi-deductive reading of Bentham and a few other sources. From the design of the panopticon, Foucault deduces a disciplinary operation of power characteristic of modernity. Again, the contingent details of how plans such as Bentham's might be put into operation are not so visible. Things just seem to work. This can give Foucault's writing a deterministic feel, and the more he emphasizes the ubiquity of power and its ever fine-grained operation, the more this is reinforced.

Overgeneralizing Surveillance

I am not disputing Foucault's characterization of the panopticon as an observational and disciplinary technology. I am rather requesting evidence of the details of its operation in a more determined fashion than Foucault provides. Indeed, from this most empirical of critical theorists, I am requesting more empiricism. In its absence, I feel that followers of Foucault have tended to overgeneralize surveillance and panopticism. It has become routine to characterize society as panoptical. In the United Kingdom, with the contemporary proliferation of CCTV in public spaces, this almost seems like a given. I mention above Mark Poster's reading of panopticism into every database. This would have us believe Foucauldian discipline is in operation every time we open a spreadsheet or process a file of comma-separated values. But without having the connections traced between those activities (deploying and viewing CCTV cameras, creating databases, and visualizing their contents) and their consequences, we really do not know what kind of discipline is being enacted or even whether that is the right concept to apply. Bruno Latour characterizes what goes on at control centers (and other "centres of calculation") not as panopticism but as oligopticism, as making visible not a totality of elements taken from *everywhere* (*pan*-opticism) but a *few* highly selective visibilities (*olig*-opticism, *oligoi*, ancient Greek, "the few"), which are made consequential through the interworking of multiple actors. I do not have space here to examine Latour's concept (and I would also ask him for the details and urge him to resist aprioristic readings of the evidence he uses) but I cite him as an antidote to overzealous panpanopticism (*sic*, seeing panopticism everywhere).

The Trouble with Theory

While etymologically *theoria* is "a way of seeing," we often require something beyond a way of seeing. We often want some kind of generalizability, explanatory value, and, in the natural sciences at least and in the HCI which aspires to their condition, some kind of predictive power. Theories are often taken to be abstractions semidetached from the phenomena they describe, perhaps capturing "underlying realities." While this picture of theory is something that Foucault would take issue with (for one thing, it characterizes the standard mode of practice of the universal intellectual Foucault thinks has had its day), many followers of Foucault seek to apply his concepts to new phenomena rather than seek a more critical relationship between theory and instance. Throughout the 1980s and 1990s, there grew a Foucault "cottage industry" that found Foucauldian things to say about psychology, sociology, medicine, media studies, literature, information systems, what have you. We see panopticism everywhere (panpanopticism). Everything becomes a matter of power relations. Power and knowledge and subjectivity are inexorably tied because Foucault says so.

This erection of Foucault as a new theoretical king (or at the very least, prince) is objectionable for a number of reasons. For one thing, we have little room for phenomena to speak, for new instances to matter, for empiricism to have a proper motivation. Prima facie exceptions can get ignored or automatically recast or redescribed into being phenomena that are in fact consistent with the theory after all. For example, Foucault makes much of how panopticism is a very different form of discipline than the exercise of absolutist sovereign power. But this should not imply that we ignore or underplay contemporary possibilities for a kind of absolutist power. The way in which many so-called democratic states respond to terrorism and other threats can, arguably, be described as absolutist and a kind of exercise of sovereignty even if no king is involved. Georgio Agamben (2005) writes of "the state of exception" that exists when typically democratic states suspend democratic arrangements to act either outside the law or through hastily created legislatures or other authoritarian means, sometimes enforced by military might—Guantanamo Bay and the practice of extraordinary rendition being conspicuous examples. To appreciate fully the state's continued capacity for absolutism, one must, I suggest, augment the Foucauldian picture of the development of the state and understand such exceptions and their increasing normalcy as, perhaps, the absolutism of a headless king. Equally, it would be wrong to think of HCI as just another way of assembling power/knowledge or fashioning new subjectivities without documenting exactly how this takes place or considering critically whether and when those are the right terms to articulate HCI's subject matter.

The Omnipresence of Resistance and Contingency

While Foucault's concept of power and its operation seems stark and inescapable, he did claim that power always operates against resistance. Power and resistance form another couplet.

> There are no relations of power without resistances; the latter are all the more real and effective because they are formed right at the point where relations of power are exercised; resistance to power does not have to come from elsewhere to be real, nor is it inexorably frustrated through being the compatriot of power. It exists all the more by being in the same place as power; hence, like power, resistance is multiple and can be integrated in global strategies. (Foucault, 1979, 142)

While power and resistance in part mutually constitute each other, it has to be noted that Foucault's histories are not from the side of resistance. He documents the panopticon, the inspection of the plague village, the asylum, the dominant discourses of sexuality formulated in religious, legal, or scientific terms, and so forth. He does not chronicle the acts of popular resistance or insurrection. We see few accounts of prison revolts, political movements, industrial sabotage, joyous perversion, or lawlessness, except in so far as they prompt more refined technologies of power in response.

In some ways, this is Foucault cautiously avoiding recreating himself as a universal intellectual who could speak in the name of the subjectified, the dominated, or the oppressed. Foucault may facilitate political action through informing us of power's operation in ways that might be more effective than the crude use of the traditional leftist concepts of ideology, class, class-interest, and revolution (and it is easy to detect the French Communist Party of the 1970s as an unnamed opponent in much of his writing, and a little harder to detect, equally unnamed, Louis Althusser). But his caution makes it hard to see positively how the resistances he insists on (but does not explicate) could be mobilized or in any way linked up politically (Gordon, 1977). However, I think there is more here than political reticence. Insisting on the reciprocal relationship between power and resistance hides an analytic neglect for the detailed examination of how prisons, hospitals, factories, schools, and so forth—the institutions—operate in their everyday, mundane practice. Similarly, Foucault analytically neglects the everyday working practices of the professions, the scientists, the intellectuals, and so forth, whose knowledge has a partial dependence on such institutions and helps reproduce them. Equally, he is not concerned with documenting the everyday lives of those who are positioned in such relations of power/knowledge—the prisoner, the patient, the worker, the student—their biographies are off the page.

At this juncture, I am tempted to make the perhaps surprising assertion that the Foucauldian can learn from just those parts of HCI and CSCW that concern themselves with such affairs: the studies of work practice, reflective accounts of design research, studies of information systems in actual, empirical organizational contexts, examinations of the detailed organization of computer mediated communication, research into spirituality, sexuality, and play as lived, embodied phenomena, and the rest. If one appreciates the organization of the work of the professions, their creation and mobilization of knowledge, and their contribution to the reproduction of institutions as accomplishments against a background of contingency, as much of this corpus of research does, then a less stark picture of the organization of the social body emerges—one in which the marginalia, sketch-marks, and annotations on any "diagram" become as visible as its straight lines and architectonic forms—though one may find oneself, as I am these days, less motivated to immediately reach for big critical theoretical categories like power, discipline, surveillance, and resistance to articulate what one finds. Or at least, less motivated than a Foucauldian would be.

A Foucauldian Design Sensibility (In Fact Five Such)

Let me take stock of the argument I have been working out here. To be sure, you can "apply" Foucault to HCI and look at questions of surveillance, discipline, and the constitution of power/knowledge in HCI, with *Discipline and Punish* clasped to your breast. You could fill out the picture I sketched of how HCI research is equally implicated in the swarming of disciplinary mechanisms. You could—but I would urge some caution if it were at the cost of an appreciation of the specificity of what you have before you. It is at best redundant and at worst misleading to find yet another place in which Foucault speaks the truth. However, if you are benefitting from Foucault's suspicion of quasi-liberal, superficially humanitarian, Enlightenment promises, his insistence on the infra-legal operation of discipline, on the dark shadow of democracy, his naggings about observation and subjectification and the complicit role of research itself—if any of that opens out new topics, concerns, or methods for you, then go ahead, be a Foucauldian. With care.

But there are other options. To set the stage for this, I want to return to some of Foucault's remarks about the situation of intellectuals, and in particular, the possibilities for "specific intellectuals."

> The intellectual has a three-fold specificity: that of his class position (whether as petty-bourgeois in the service of capitalism or "organic" intellectual of the proletariat); that of his conditions of life and work, linked to his condition as an intellectual (his field of research, his place in a laboratory, the political and economic demands to which he submits or against which he rebels, in the university, the hospital, etc.); lastly, the specificity of the politics of truth in our societies. And it's with this last factor that his position can take on a general significance and that his local, specific struggle can have effects and implications which are not simply professional or sectoral. The intellectual can operate and struggle at the general level of that régime of truth which is so essential to the structure and functioning of our society. There is a battle "for truth," or at least "around truth." …
>
> The essential political problem for the intellectual is not to criticize the ideological contents supposedly linked to science, or to ensure that his own scientific practice is accompanied by a correct ideology, but that of ascertaining the possibility of constituting a new politics of truth. The problem is not changing people's consciousnesses—or what's in their heads—but the political, economic, institutional régime of the production of truth.
>
> It's not a matter of emancipating truth from every system of power (which would be a chimera, for truth is already power) but of detaching the power of truth from the forms of hegemony, social, economic and cultural, within which it operates at the present time. (132–133)

Foucault here is raising a challenge to work out a way in which intellectuals can reflect on their own position and practices—existing as they do as "exchangers" in "privileged points of intersection"—and connect that lived experience with the struggles of others as they, similarly, bump up against dominant regimes of truth. We do that not by having recourse to any higher ground of correctness but by seeing a (partial) affinity of "operation and struggle" and, through that, creating "a new politics of truth"—truth being a "thing of this world" and not something that exists as "the reward of free spirits, the child of protracted solitude, nor the privilege of those who have succeeded in liberating themselves" (131).

As always, Foucault does not say exactly how this could take place. His caution is in place again. But I am going to risk a little more, perhaps only a little, and very tentatively. To me, Foucault sketches something which could form the basis of a *design strategy*, a way of working with others, and creating not just new things but new practices that could serve, for a Foucauldian, as a "new politics of truth" or, in other terms, embody new kinds of value or commitment, ones that "intersect" our specific practices and struggles with those of the others we work with. Let me offer five ways in which this could be unpacked, five sensibilities for Foucauldian design if you will. You may recognize existing work in HCI and allied fields that has some consistency with these sensibilities. I do not have space here to offer a full review, so I make only a few illustrative connections with existing work. Rather my concern is to show how these five sensibilities could flow from a critical sympathy with Foucault. But I must warn you: I am on insecure ground here.

Dark Design

I mentioned at the outset that Foucault's characterization of the machineries of power has an iconoclastic allure for me. It is quite possible, for design purposes, to play along with this and withhold the nuanced criticism one might wish to have on social scientific, philosophical, or historical grounds. That is, we can linger a little longer with Foucault in all the starkness of his account of the operation of modern power, stay with his metaphors of capillary action, of power having an anatomy or a physics, keep with the dark erotics that are in the very notion of biopower, with (even) the seemingly inescapable ubiquitous operation of techniques of discipline, itself a sadomasochistically charged image. We can dare to work with all that, affirm it even, in the creation of a dystopia that can form the object of critical reflection. We can dramatize Foucault's world, perhaps extrapolate it as a kind of science fiction or elaborate it as a kind of imaginative historical work, to create artefacts for critical design and practices to support, with those we are working with, an exploratory discourse. Foucault, in this conception, could inform design futures or living laboratories or other participatory exercises in which we work with those with whom we have some kind of intersection of practice or struggle. Put another way, dark Foucauldian design mechanizes the diagrams of power but knowingly, as an object of critical discourse. Let us build an even better prison. Let us create even more insidious techniques for the regulation of sexuality. Let us industrialize the production of knowledge even more efficiently. Not so much as a matter of ironic humor but to create objects for critical reflection.

Deviant Design

My second Foucauldian strategy is exactly the opposite of the first. Let us examine design possibilities that negate the operation of power, that jam it somehow, that attempt to sever power relationships by separating the subject-objects implicated in the relationship, if necessary by force. This is better explored territory. I have in mind the creation of technologies of so-called sousveillance (observation not from above, sur-, but from below, sous-), practices such as video recording the police as they video record a political demonstration, and more mocking works such as webcasting a camera trained on Jeremy Bentham's stuffed and preserved body on show at University College London. We can also include projects such as Lady Ada's microwave blockers, which create a mobile-phone-network-free zone or TV-B-Gone, a universal remote control capable of switching off all televisions within range. Some of Chris Csikszentmihályi and his colleagues' design work can also be thought of as an attempt to negate the operation of state power through various methods of deviation or obstruction (Csikszentmihályi, 2017). I would like to propose a project called "Keeping Mum" which somehow obstructs our tendencies toward confessional disclosure (I do not yet know how, though perhaps an implant will electrostimulate the face to keep a stiff upper lip). Under this theme I would also like to allow space for forms of willful anarchistic insurrection, sabotage, and other possibilities that become perspicuous from a Foucauldian problematic with varying degrees of "liberal-democratic" acceptability. From the design of the intentionally useless and anti-utilitarian (an aim which motivates much of the design of Bill Gaver and his colleagues, including me from time to time) to design for criminality, outright. Let us disconnect the diagram.

Design as Deflection

Here I have in mind a sensitivity that is more subtle than either (strategically) affirming Foucault's dark image of the operation of power or (equally strategically) negating and blocking it. While it is easy to concretize my dark and deviant design themes by reference to their different footings with respect to elements in Foucault's writings, here I cannot be so exact. I have in mind not so much the dramatization of Foucauldian relationships of power but their misdirection (or conjuring). This might involve creating illusory or partially ill-conceived subjects for the exercise of power, knowingly false personas perhaps, and designing for them. Or perhaps we can imagine projects that purport to be one thing but are also, or are more faithfully, something else. Maybe we can proliferate traces for ourselves in the internet that systematically confuse Google's or Facebook's algorithms. Maybe we already do. But let's really do it. Perhaps we can identify the turbulences or reverse salients or side effects (choose your metaphor) in the physics of power, the vestigial organs (or choose another) in its anatomy, and design for them. Perhaps we can identify, working with others with whom we intersect, the contingencies of power's operation and not manage or calm them but exacerbate them. Let us blur the diagram.

Design and Porosity

In 1968, Foucault cofounded the Prison Information Group. It was a relatively short-lived project but it manifested a variety of forms of activism specifically targeted at prisons and their operation. Some of these strategies can be regarded as forms of counterveillance. The group persistently held prison administrators to account for their actions in a reversal of the manner in which prisoners might be held to account for their conduct. One of the group's publications, for example, drew attention to the high rate of suicide in prisons, holding the prison system to account for these deaths. The group engaged in a variety of activities aimed at making the otherwise rigid boundaries between those confined and those at liberty more porous. For example, they shouted news reports by megaphone outside prisons so that the inmates could be informed of current events, even when denied access to newspapers. Reciprocally, the group published letters from prisoners describing their conditions and everyday routines. A similar project, Between the Bars, supports the U.S. prison population in blogging, circumventing the ban on internet access through tools that allow handwritten letters to be easily scanned and published. In each of these examples, a technology of power that creates a division or an exclusion is worked against to make surveillance bilateral, the communication flows bidirectional, or the borders porous. Let us imagine symmetrical diagrams.

Design and Deprofessionalization

The members of the Prison Information Group did not deny their situation as intellectuals, but their activism was of a very different sort than that of those who speak in the name of the oppressed or excluded. They served rather as a channel for information or a relay making connections where otherwise none would exist. They offered their resources to prisoners, including such services as photocopying and distributing pamphlets written by the inmates. In an important sense, I would argue that this activism involves the deprofessionalization of the intellectuals who made up the group. They were not acting on the basis of their professional practice or in the terms of their professional discourses. In fact, their lack of decorum might seem most unprofessional. Through withholding a traditional recourse to "universal" intellectual practices and the "official" knowledge associated with them, they allowed the local, minority knowledge of the prisoners to find a voice and an audience, at least in principle. In many respects, it mattered more to Foucault's activism in the group that he had a megaphone and a photocopier than that he was a scholar of the history of prisons and asylums. French philosopher Gilles Deleuze contrasts such local knowledge in all its "nomadicity" with the "Royal Road of Science," which he sees as ultimately in the service of the state and "territorialization." Strategic deprofessionalization allows the byways off the Royal Road to be explored. Let us imagine the design of artefacts, practices, events, pranks, and so forth, to further perturb professional dominance, from exploiting the resources that accrue to "the exchangers who inhabit the privileged points of intersection" to subjecting the conceits of the professions to ridicule, perhaps tongue-in-cheek, perhaps more venomous. Let us imagine more diagrams, no matter how artfully drawn. Let us imagine cartoons and graffiti too.

It is through seeing Foucault as an inspiration for design that I am able to navigate my ambivalence toward him. I find him a problematic social theorist. He opens out new perspectives on the relationship between the human sciences and the constitution of the social body, but I find many of his historiographic methods suspect. I am uneasy with his invocation and ubiquitous application of grand theoretical terms such as knowledge and power. I am uncomfortable with those who merely apply his perspectives as yet further demonstrations of the truth of his work. While Foucault is often celebrated for his attention to detail, I find him and those who follow him neglectful of the details of the everyday practice of those who work in the institutions he characterizes, or who create the knowledge he is concerned with, or the form of the everyday lives of those who are "subjected" by them. I do not believe the life of a prisoner in Mettray Penal Colony can be just read off from a rota or an operational manual, no more than can the practices of imprisonment and observation be read off from an architectural design.

And yet I find Foucault valuable in urging a skepticism oversimplistic views of progress, Enlightenment, liberal democracy, humanism, or of the rhetoric of "empowerment" of well-meaning intellectuals. I find a vividness in his accounts, no matter how problematic they may be as social theory—a vividness which we can put to work in design and in intellectual self-reflection. I find in Foucault's writings about the "specific intellectual" possibilities for strategies for intervention—and in HCI specifically, for design—which might enable the creation of artefacts as objects for critical discourse and the exploration of alternative ways of being. Through this, perhaps, we can not only explore the potential for Foucault as an inspiration for design but also occasion a reciprocal critical examination of his conceptions of power and resistance—their utility for us and for those others who experience the discomfort or pain of the present.

References

Agamben, G. (2005) *State of Exception.* Chicago: University of Chicago Press.

Bannon, L. (1991) "From Human Factors to Human Actors: The Role of Psychology and Human-Computer Interaction Studies in System Design." In *Design at Work: Cooperative Design of Computer Systems,* edited by J. Greenbaum and M. Kyng, 25–44. Hillsdale, NJ: Erlbaum.

Bardzell, J., and S. Bardzell. (2011) "Pleasure Is Your Birthright: Digitally Enabled Designer Sex Toys as a Case of Third-Wave HCI." *Proceedings of the SIGCHI Conference on Human Factors in Computing Systems (CHI'11).* New York: ACM, 257–266.

Between the Bars: Human Stories from Prison. Accessed October 24, 2017. https://betweenthebars.org.

Bødker, S. (2006) "When Second Wave HCI Meets Third Wave Challenges." *Proceedings of the 4th Nordic Conference on Human-Computer Interaction: Changing Roles (NordiCHI'06).* New York: AMC, 1–8. DOI: 1182475.1182476.

Card, S., T. Moran, and A. Newell. (1983) *The Psychology of Human-Computer Interaction.* Hillsdale, NJ: Lawrence Erlbaum.

Cooper, G., and J. Bowers. (1995) "Representing the User: Notes on the Disciplinary Rhetoric of Human-Computer Interaction." In *The Social and Interactional Dimensions of Human-Computer Interfaces,* edited by P. Thomas, 48–66. Cambridge: Cambridge University Press.

Csikszentmihályi, C. (2017) "Critical Technical Practice Lab, M-ITI." *Interactions* 24 (3): 16–19.

Dreyfus, H., and P. Rabinow. (1982) *Michel Foucault: Beyond Structuralism and Hermeneutics.* Chicago: University of Chicago Press.

Foucault, M. (1965) *Madness and Civilization: A History of Insanity in the Age of Reason,* translated by R. Howard. New York: Pantheon.

Foucault, M. (1977a) *Discipline and Punish: The Birth of the Prison,* translated by A. Sheridan. New York: Vintage.

Foucault, M. (1977b) "Power and Strategies." In *Power/Knowledge: Selected Interviews and Other Writings 1972–1977,* by M. Foucault, edited by C. Gordon, 134–145. New York: Pantheon.

Foucault, M. (1977c) "Truth and Power." In *Power/Knowledge: Selected Interviews and Other Writings 1972–1977,* by M. Foucault, edited by C. Gordon, 109–133. New York: Pantheon Books.

Foucault, M. (1979) *The History of Sexuality,* vol. 1, *An Introduction.* Translated by R. Hurley. London: Allen Lane.

Foucault, M. (1985) *The History of Sexuality,* vol. 2, *The Use of Pleasure.* Translated by R. Hurley. London: Penguin.

Foucault, M. (1986) *The History of Sexuality,* vol. 3, *The Care of the Self.* Translated by R. Hurley. London: Penguin.

Gordon, C. (1977) "Afterword." In *Power/Knowledge: Selected Interviews and Other Writings 1972–1977 by Michel Foucault,* edited by C. Gordon, 229–260. New York: Pantheon.

Guting, G., ed. (1994) *The Cambridge Companion to Foucault.* Cambridge: Cambridge University Press.

Harrison, S., D. Tatar, and P. Sengers. (2007) "The Three Paradigms of HCI." *Proceedings of the SIGCHI Conference on Human Factors in Computing Systems (AltCHI'07).* New York: ACM, 1–18.

Rogers, Y. (2012) *HCI Theory: Classical, Modern, and Contemporary.* Synthesis Lectures on Human-Centered Informatics. London: Morgan and Claypool. https://doi.org/10.2200/S00418ED1V01Y201205HCI014.

35 Nature and Space (1998)

James C. Scott

Would it not be a great satisfaction to the king to know at a designated moment every year the number of his subjects, in total and by region, with all the resources, wealth & poverty of each place; [the number] of his nobility and ecclesiastics of all kinds, of men of the robe, of Catholics and of those of the other religion, all separated according to the place of their residence? ... [Would it not be] a useful and necessary pleasure for him to be able, in his own office, to review in an hour's time the present and past condition of a great realm of which he is the head, and be able himself to know with certitude in what consists his grandeur, his wealth, and his strengths?

—Marquis de Vauban, proposing an annual census to Louis XIV in 1686

Certain forms of knowledge and control require a narrowing of vision. The great advantage of such tunnel vision is that it brings into sharp focus certain limited aspects of an otherwise far more complex and unwieldy reality. This very simplification, in turn, makes the phenomenon at the center of the field of vision more legible and hence more susceptible to careful measurement and calculation. Combined with similar observations, an overall, aggregate, synoptic view of a selective reality is achieved, making possible a high degree of schematic knowledge, control, and manipulation.

The invention of scientific forestry in late eighteenth-century Prussia and Saxony serves as something of a model of this process.[1] Although the history of scientific forestry is important in its own right, it is used here as a metaphor for the forms of knowledge and manipulation characteristic of powerful institutions with sharply defined interests, of which state bureaucracies and large commercial firms are perhaps the outstanding examples. Once we have seen how simplification, legibility, and manipulation operate in forest management, we can then explore how the modern state applies a similar lens to urban planning, rural settlement, land administration, and agriculture.

The State and Scientific Forestry: A Parable

I [Gilgamesh] would conquer in the Cedar Forest.... I will set my hand to it and will chop down the Cedar.
—*Epic of Gilgamesh*

The early modern European state, even before the development of scientific forestry, viewed its forests primarily through the fiscal lens of revenue needs. To be sure, other concerns—such as timber for shipbuilding, state construction, and fuel for the economic security of its subjects—were not entirely absent from official management. These concerns also had heavy implications for state revenue and security.[2] Exaggerating only slightly, one might say that the crown's interest in forests was resolved through its fiscal lens into a single number: the revenue yield of the timber that might be extracted annually.

The best way to appreciate how heroic was this constriction of vision is to notice what fell outside its field of vision. Lurking behind the number indicating revenue yield were not so much forests as commercial wood, representing so many thousands of board feet of saleable timber and so many cords of firewood fetching a certain price. Missing, of course, were all those trees, bushes, and plants holding little or no potential for state revenue. Missing as well were all those parts of trees, even revenue-bearing trees, which might have been useful to the population but whose value could not be converted into fiscal receipts. Here I have in mind foliage and its uses as fodder and thatch; fruits, as food for people and domestic animals; twigs and branches, as bedding, fencing, hop poles, and kindling; bark and roots, for making medicines and for tanning; sap, for making resins; and so forth. Each species of tree—indeed, each part or growth stage of each species—had its unique properties and uses. A fragment of the entry under "elm" in a popular seventeenth-century encyclopedia on aboriculture conveys something of the vast range of practical uses to which the tree could be put.

Elm is a timber of most singular use, especially whereby it may be continually dry, or wet, in extremes; therefore proper for water works, mills, the ladles and soles of the wheel, pumps, aqueducts, ship planks below the water line, ... also for wheelwrights, handles for the single handsaw, rails and gates. Elm is not so apt to rive [split] ... and is used for chopping blocks, blocks for the hat maker, trunks and boxes to be covered with leather, coffins and dressers and shovelboard tables of great length; also for the carver and those curious workers of fruitage, foliage, shields, statues and most of the ornaments appertaining to the orders of architecture.... And finally ... the use of the very leaves of this tree, especially the female, is not to be despised, ... for they will prove of great relief to cattle in the winter and scorching summers when hay and fodder is dear.... The green leaf of the elms contused heals a green wound or cut, and boiled with the bark, consolidates bone fractures.[3]

In state "fiscal forestry," however, the actual tree with its vast number of possible uses was replaced by an abstract tree representing a volume of lumber or firewood. If the princely conception of the forest was still utilitarian, it was surely a utilitarianism confined to the direct needs of the state.

From a naturalist's perspective, nearly everything was missing from the state's narrow frame of reference. Gone was the vast majority of flora: grasses, flowers, lichens, ferns, mosses, shrubs, and vines. Gone, too, were reptiles, birds, amphibians, and innumerable species of insects. Gone were most species of fauna, except those that interested the crown's gamekeepers.

From an anthropologist's perspective, nearly everything touching on human interaction with the forest was also missing from the state's tunnel vision. The state did pay attention to poaching, which impinged on its claim to revenue in wood or its claim to royal game, but otherwise it typically ignored the vast, complex, and negotiated social uses of the forest for hunting and gathering, pasturage, fishing, charcoal making, trapping, and collecting food and valuable minerals as well as the forest's significance for magic, worship, refuge, and so on.[4]

If the utilitarian state could not see the real, existing forest for the (commercial) trees, if its view of its forests was abstract and partial, it was hardly unique in this respect. Some level of abstraction is necessary for virtually all forms of analysis, and it is not at all surprising that the abstractions of state officials should have reflected the paramount fiscal interests of their employer. The entry under "forest" in Diderot's *Encyclopédie* is almost exclusively concerned with the *utilité publique* of forest products and the taxes, revenues, and profits that they can be made to yield. The forest as a habitat disappears and is replaced by the forest as an economic resource to be managed efficiently and profitably.[5] Here, fiscal and commercial logics coincide; they are both resolutely fixed on the bottom line.

The vocabulary used to organize nature typically betrays the overriding interests of its human users. In fact, utilitarian discourse replaces the term "nature" with the term "natural resources," focusing on those aspects of nature that can be appropriated for human use. A comparable logic extracts from a more generalized natural world those flora or fauna that are of utilitarian value (usually marketable commodities) and, in turn, reclassifies those species that compete with, prey on, or otherwise diminish the yields of the valued species. Thus, plants that are valued become "crops," the species that compete with them are stigmatized as "weeds," and the insects that ingest them are stigmatized as "pests." Thus, trees that are valued become "timber," while species that compete with them become "trash" trees or "underbrush." The same logic applies to fauna. Highly valued animals become "game" or "livestock," while those animals that compete with or prey upon them become "predators" or "varmints."

The kind of abstracting, utilitarian logic that the state, through its officials, applied to the forest is thus not entirely distinctive. What is distinctive about this logic, however, is the narrowness of its field of vision, the degree of elaboration to which it can be subjected, and above all, as we shall see, the degree to which it allowed the state to impose that logic on the very reality that was observed.[6]

Scientific forestry was originally developed from about 1765 to 1800, largely in Prussia and Saxony. Eventually, it would become the basis of forest management techniques in France, England, and the United States and throughout the Third World. Its emergence cannot be understood outside the larger context of the centralized state-making initiatives of the period. In fact, the new forestry science was a subdiscipline of what was called cameral science, an effort to reduce the fiscal management of a kingdom to scientific principles that would allow systematic planning.[7] Traditional domainal forestry had hitherto simply divided the forest into roughly equal plots, with the number of plots coinciding with the number of years in the assumed growth cycle.[8] One plot was cut each year on the assumption of equal yields (and value) from plots of equal size. Because of poor maps, the uneven distribution of the most valuable large trees (*Hochwald*), and very approximate cordwood (*Bruststaerke*) measures, the results were unsatisfactory for fiscal planning.

Careful exploitation of domainal forests was all the more imperative in the late eighteenth century, when fiscal officials became aware of a growing shortage of wood. Many of the old-growth forests of oak, beech, hornbeam, and linden had been severely degraded by planned and unplanned felling, while the regrowth was not as robust as hoped. The prospect of declining yields was alarming, not merely because it threatened revenue flows but also because it might provoke massive poaching by a peasantry in search of firewood. One sign of this concern were the numerous state-sponsored competitions for designs of more efficient woodstoves.

The first attempt at more precise measurements of forests was made by Johann Gottlieb Beckmann on a carefully surveyed sample plot. Walking abreast, several assistants carried compartmentalized boxes with color-coded nails corresponding to five categories of tree sizes, which they had been trained to identify. Each tree was tagged with the appropriate nail until the sample plot had been covered. Because each assistant had begun with a certain number of nails, it was a simple matter to subtract the remaining nails from the initial total and arrive at an inventory of trees by class for the entire plot. The sample plot had been carefully chosen for its representativeness, allowing the foresters to then calculate the timber and, given certain price assumptions, the revenue yield of the whole forest. For the forest scientists (*Forstwissenschaftler*) the goal was always to "deliver the greatest possible *constant* volume of wood."[9]

The effort at precision was pushed further as mathematicians worked from the cone-volume principle to specify the volume of saleable wood contained by a standardized tree (*Normalbaum*) of a given size-class. Their calculations were checked empirically against the actual volume of wood in sample trees.[10] The final result of such calculations was the development of elaborate tables with data organized by tree size and age under specified conditions of normal growth and maturation. By radically narrowing his vision to commercial wood, the state forester had, with his tables, paradoxically achieved a synoptic view of the entire forest.[11] This restriction of focus reflected in the tables was in fact the only way in which the whole forest could be taken in by a single optic. Reference to these tables coupled with field tests allowed the forester to estimate closely the inventory, growth, and yield of a given forest. In the regulated, abstract forest of the forstwissenschaftler, calculation and measurement prevailed, and the three watchwords, in modern parlance, were "minimum diversity," the "balance sheet," and "sustained yield." The logic of the state-managed forest science was virtually identical with the logic of commercial exploitation.[12]

The achievement of German forestry science in standardizing techniques for calculating the sustainable yield of commercial timber and hence revenue was impressive enough. What is decisive for our purposes, however, was the next logical step in forest management. That step was to attempt to create, through careful seeding, planting, and cutting, a forest that was easier for state foresters to count, manipulate, measure, and assess. The fact is that forest science and geometry, backed by state power, had the capacity to transform the real, diverse, and chaotic old-growth forest into a new, more uniform forest that closely resembled the administrative grid of its techniques. To this end, the underbrush was cleared, the number of species was reduced (often to monoculture), and plantings were done simultaneously and in straight rows on large tracts. These management practices, as Henry Lowood observes, "produced the monocultural, even-age forests that eventually transformed the Normalbaum from abstraction to reality. The German forest became the archetype for imposing on disorderly nature the neatly arranged constructs of science. Practical goals had encouraged mathematical utilitarianism, which seemed, in turn, to promote geometric perfection as the outward sign of the well-managed forest; in turn the rationally ordered arrangements of trees offered new possibilities for controlling nature."[13]

The tendency was toward regimentation, in the strict sense of the word. The forest trees were drawn up into serried, uniform ranks, as it were, to be measured, counted off, felled, and replaced by a new rank and file of lookalike conscripts. As an army, it was also designed hierarchically from above to fulfill a unique purpose and to be at the disposition of a single commander. At the limit, the forest itself would not even have to be seen; it could be "read" accurately from the tables and maps in the forester's office.

How much easier it was to manage the new, stripped-down forest. With stands of same-age trees arranged in linear alleys, clearing the underbrush, felling, extraction, and new planting became a far more routine process. Increasing order in the forest made it possible for forest workers to use written training protocols that could be widely applied. A relatively unskilled and inexperienced labor crew could adequately carry out its tasks by following a few standard rules in the new forest environment. Harvesting logs of relatively uniform width and length not only made it possible to forecast yields successfully but also to market homogeneous product units to logging contractors and timber merchants.[14] Commercial logic and bureaucratic logic were, in this instance, synonymous; it was a system that promised to maximize the return of a single commodity over the long haul and at the same time lent itself to a centralized scheme of management.

The new legible forest was also easier to manipulate experimentally. Now that the more complex old-growth forest had been replaced by a forest in which many variables were held constant, it was a far simpler matter to examine the effects of such variables

Figure 35.1
Mixed temperate forest, part managed, part natural regeneration.

as fertilizer applications, rainfall, and weeding, on same-age, single-species stands. It was the closest thing to a forest laboratory one could imagine at the time.[15] The very simplicity of the forest made it possible, for the first time, to assess novel regimens of forest management under nearly experimental conditions.

Although the geometric, uniform forest was intended to facilitate management and extraction, it quickly became a powerful aesthetic as well. The visual sign of the well-managed forest, in Germany and in the many settings where German scientific forestry took hold, came to be the regularity and neatness of its appearance. Forests might be

Figure 35.2
One aisle of a managed popular forest in Tuscany.

inspected in much the same way as a commanding officer might review his troops on parade, and woe to the forest guard whose "beat" was not sufficiently trim or "dressed." This aboveground order required that underbrush be removed and that fallen trees and branches be gathered and hauled off. Unauthorized disturbances—whether by fire or by local populations—were seen as implicit threats to management routines. The more uniform the forest, the greater the possibilities for centralized management; the routines that could be applied minimized the need for the discretion necessary in the management of diverse old-growth forests.

The controlled environment of the redesigned, scientific forest promised many striking advantages.[16] It could be synoptically surveyed by the chief forester; it could be more easily supervised and harvested according to centralized, long-range plans; it provided a steady, uniform commodity, thereby eliminating one major source of revenue fluctuation; and it created a legible natural terrain that facilitated manipulation and experimentation.

This utopian dream of scientific forestry was, of course, only the *immanent* logic of its techniques. It was not and could not ever be realized in practice. Both nature and the human factor intervened. The existing topography of the landscape and the vagaries of fire, storms, blights, climatic changes, insect populations, and disease conspired to thwart foresters and to shape the actual forest. Also, given the insurmountable difficulties of policing large forests, people living nearby typically continued to graze animals, poach firewood and kindling, make charcoal, and use the forest in other ways that prevented the foresters' management plan from being fully realized.[17] Although, like all utopian schemes, it fell well short of attaining its goal, the critical fact is that it did partly succeed in stamping the actual forest with the imprint of its designs.

The principles of scientific forestry were applied as rigorously as was practicable to most large German forests throughout much of the nineteenth century. The Norway spruce, known for its hardiness, rapid growth, and valuable wood, became the bread-and-butter tree of commercial forestry. Originally, the Norway spruce was seen as a restoration crop that might revive overexploited mixed forests, but the commercial profits from the first rotation were so stunning that there was little effort to return to mixed forests. The monocropped forest was a disaster for peasants who were now deprived of all the grazing, food, raw materials, and medicines that the earlier forest ecology had afforded. Diverse old-growth forests, about three-fourths of which were broadleaf (deciduous) species, were replaced by largely coniferous forests in which Norway spruce or Scotch pine were the dominant or often only species.

In the short run, this experiment in the radical simplification of the forest to a single commodity was a resounding success. It was a rather long short run, in the sense that a single crop rotation of trees might take eighty years to mature. The productivity of the new forests reversed the decline in the domestic wood supply, provided more uniform stands and more usable wood fiber, raised the economic return of forest land, and appreciably shortened rotation times (the time it took to harvest a stand and plant another).[18] Like row crops in a field, the new softwood forests were prodigious producers of a single commodity. Little wonder that the German model of intensive commercial forestry became standard throughout the world.[19] Gifford Pinchot, the second chief forester of the United States, was trained at the French forestry school at Nancy, which followed a German-style curriculum, as did most U.S. and European forestry schools.[20] The first forester hired by the British to assess and manage the great forest resources of India and Burma was Dietrich Brandes, a German.[21] By the end of the nineteenth century, German forestry science was hegemonic.

The great simplification of the forest into a "one-commodity machine" was precisely the step that allowed German forestry science to become a rigorous technical and commercial discipline that could be codified and taught. A condition of its rigor was that it severely bracketed, or assumed to be constant, all variables except those bearing directly on the yield of the selected species and on the cost of growing and extracting them. As we shall see with urban planning, revolutionary theory, collectivization, and rural resettlement, a whole world lying "outside the brackets" returned to haunt this technical vision.

In the German case, the negative biological and ultimately commercial consequences of the stripped-down forest became painfully obvious only after the *second* rotation of conifers had been planted. "It took about one century for them [the negative consequences] to show up clearly. Many of the pure stands grew excellently in the first generation but already showed an amazing retrogression in the second generation. The reason for this is a very complex one and only a simplified explanation can be given.... Then the whole nutrient cycle got out of order and eventually was nearly stopped.... Anyway, the drop of one or two site classes [used for grading the quality of timber] during two or three generations of pure spruce is a well known and frequently observed fact. This represents a production loss of 20 to 30 percent."[22]

A new term, *Waldsterben* (forest death), entered the German vocabulary to describe the worst cases. An exceptionally complex process involving soil building, nutrient uptake, and symbiotic relations among fungi, insects, mammals, and flora—which were, and still are, not entirely understood—was apparently disrupted, with serious consequences. Most of these consequences can be traced to the radical simplicity of the scientific forest.

Only an elaborate treatise in ecology could do justice to the subject of what went wrong, but mentioning a few of the major effects of simplification will illustrate how vital many of the factors bracketed by scientific forestry turned out to be. German forestry's attention to formal order and ease of access for management and extraction led to the clearing of underbrush, deadfalls, and snags (standing dead trees), greatly reducing the diversity of insect, mammal, and bird populations so essential to soil-building processes.[23] The absence of litter and woody biomass on the new forest floor is now seen as a major factor leading to thinner and less nutritious soils.[24] Same-age, same-species forests not only created a far less diverse habitat but were also more vulnerable to massive storm-felling. The very uniformity of species and age among, say, Norway spruce also provided a favorable habitat to all the "pests" which were specialized to that species. Populations of these pests built up to epidemic proportions, inflicting losses in yields and large outlays for fertilizers, insecticides, fungicides, or rodenticides.[25] Apparently the first rotation of Norway spruce had grown exceptionally well in large part because it was living off (or mining) the long-accumulated soil capital of the diverse old-growth forest that it had replaced. Once that capital was depleted, the steep decline in growth rates began.

As pioneers in scientific forestry, the Germans also became pioneers in recognizing and attempting to remedy many of its undesirable consequences. To this end, they invented the science of what they called "forest hygiene." In place of hollow trees that had been home to woodpeckers, owls, and other tree-nesting birds, the foresters provided specially designed boxes. Ant colonies were artificially raised and implanted in the forest, their nests tended by local schoolchildren. Several species of spiders, which had disappeared from the monocropped forest, were reintroduced.[26] What is striking about these endeavors is that they are attempts to work around an impoverished habitat still planted with a single species of conifers for production purposes.[27] In this case, "restoration forestry" attempted with mixed results to create a *virtual* ecology, while denying its chief sustaining condition: diversity.

The metaphorical value of this brief account of scientific production forestry is that it illustrates the dangers of dismembering an exceptionally complex and poorly understood set of relations and processes in order to isolate a single element of instrumental value. The instrument, the knife, that carved out the new, rudimentary forest was the razor-sharp interest in the production of a single commodity. Everything that interfered with the efficient production of the key commodity was implacably eliminated. Everything that seemed unrelated to efficient production was ignored. Having come to see the forest as a commodity, scientific forestry set about refashioning it as a commodity machine.[28] Utilitarian simplification in the forest was an effective way of maximizing wood production in the short and intermediate term. Ultimately, however, its emphasis on yield and paper profits, its relatively short time horizon, and, above all, the vast array of consequences it had resolutely bracketed came back to haunt it.[29]

Even in the realm of greatest interest—namely, the production of wood fiber—the consequences of not seeing the forest for the trees sooner or later became glaring. Many were directly traceable to the basic simplification imposed in the interest of ease of management and economic return: monoculture. Monocultures are, as a rule, more fragile and hence more vulnerable to the stress of disease and weather than polycultures are. As Richard Plochmann expresses it, "One further drawback, which is typical of all pure plantations, is that the ecology of the natural plant associations became unbalanced. Outside of the natural habitat, and when planted in pure stands, the physical condition of the single tree weakens and resistance against enemies decreases."[30] Any unmanaged forest may experience stress from storms, disease, drought, fragile soil, or severe cold. A diverse, complex forest, however, with its many species of trees, its full complement of birds, insects, and mammals, is far more resilient—far more able to withstand and recover from such injuries—than pure stands. Its very diversity and complexity help to inoculate it against devastation: a windstorm that fells large, old trees of one species will typically spare large trees of other species as well as small trees of the same species; a blight or insect attack that threatens, say, oaks may leave lindens and hornbeams unscathed. Just as a merchant who, not knowing what conditions her ships will face at sea, sends out scores of vessels with different designs, weights, sails, and navigational aids stands a better chance of having much of her fleet make it to port, while a merchant who stakes everything on a single ship design and size runs a higher risk of losing everything, forest biodiversity acts like an insurance policy. Like the enterprise run by the second merchant, the simplified forest is a more vulnerable system, especially over the long haul, as its effects on soil, water, and "pest" populations become manifest. Such dangers can only partly be checked by the use of artificial fertilizers, insecticides, and fungicides. Given the fragility of the simplified production forest, the massive outside intervention that was required to establish it—we might call it the administrators' forest—is increasingly necessary in order to sustain it as well.[31]

Notes

1. Henry E. Lowood, "The Calculating Forester: Quantification, Cameral Science, and the Emergence of Scientific Forestry Management in Germany," in Tore Frangsmyr, J. L. Heilbron, and Robin E. Rider, eds., *The Quantifying Spirit in the Eighteenth Century* (Berkeley: University of California Press, 1991), pp. 315–342. The following account is largely drawn from Lowood's fine analysis.

2. The most striking exception was the royal attention to the supply of "noble game" (e.g., deer, boars, foxes) for the hunt and hence to the protection of its habitat. Lest one imagine this to be a quaint premodern affectation, it is worth recalling the enormous social importance of the hunt to such recent "monarchs" as Erich Honeker, Nicolae Ceauşescu, Georgy Zhuvkov, Władysław Gomutka, and Marshal Tito.

3. John Evelyn, *Sylva, or A Discourse of Forest Trees* (London, 1664, 1679), p. 118, cited in John Brinckerhoff Jackson, *A Sense of Place, a Sense of Time* (New Haven: Yale University Press, 1994), pp. 97–98.

4. Ramachandra Guha reminds me that the verb "ignore" is inadequate here, for the state typically sought to control, regulate, and extinguish those practices that interfered with its own management policies. For much of my (admittedly limited) early education in the history of forestry, I am grateful to Ramachandra Guha and his two books, *The Unquiet Woods: Ecological Change and Peasant Resistance in the Himalaya* (Berkeley: University of California Press, 1989), and, with Madhav Gadgil, *This Fissured Land: An Ecological History of India* (Delhi: Oxford University Press, 1992). For an evocative and wide-ranging exploration of the changing cultural meaning

of the forest in the West, see Robert Pogue Harrison, *Forests: The Shadow of Civilization* (Chicago: University of Chicago Press, 1992).

5. Harrison, *Forests*, p. 121.

6. This last is a kind of twist on the Heisenberg Principle. Instead of altering the phenomenon observed through the act of observation, so that the pre-observation state of the phenomenon is unknowable in principle, the effect of (interested) observation in this case is to alter the phenomenon in question over time so that it, in fact, more closely resembles the stripped down, abstract image the lens had revealed.

7. See Keith Tribe, *Governing Economy: The Reformation of German Economic Discourse, 1750–1840* (Cambridge: Cambridge University Press, 1988). The more general process of codifying the principles of state administration in seventeenth- and eighteenth-century Europe is examined by Michel Foucault under the (misleading) headline of "police state" (from *Polizeiwissenschaft*) in his lectures on "governmentality," delivered at the Collège de France. See Graham Burchell, Colin Gordon, and Peter Miller, eds., *The Foucault Effect: Studies in Governmentality* (London: Harvester Wheatsheaf, 1991), especially chap. 4.

8. In the late seventeenth century, Jean-Baptiste Colbert had extensive plans to "rationalize" forest administration in order both to prevent poaching and to generate a more reliable revenue yield. To this end, Etienne Dralet's *Traité du régime forestier* proposed regulated plots (*tire-aire*) "so that the growth is regular and easy to guard." Despite these initiatives, nothing much came of it in France until 1820, when the new German techniques were imported. See Peter Sahlins, *Forest Rites: The Ware of the Demoiselles in Nineteenth-Century France*, Harvard Historical Studies no. 115 (Cambridge: Harvard University Press, 1994).

9. Lowood, "The Calculating Forester," p. 338.

10. Various techniques were tried, including cutting an actual tree into bits and then compressing them to find the volume of the tree, and putting wood in a barrel of known volume and adding measured amounts of water to calculate the volume of the barrel *not* occupied by the wood (ibid., p. 328).

11. The utilitarian framework could, in principle, have been used to emphasize some other calculable "end" of the forest—e.g., game populations, mast-quality timber, or grazing acreage. Where several agencies superintending the forest have conflicting utilitarian agendas, the result can be incoherence and room for the local population to maneuver. See the fine study by K. Sivaramakrishnan, "Forests, Politics, and Governance in Bengal, 1794–1994" (Ph.D. diss., Department of Anthropology, Yale University, 1996).

12. I was tempted to add that, with regard to the use of forests, the view of the state might be longer and broader than that of private firms, which can, and have, plundered old-growth forests and then sold their acreage or surrendered it for back taxes (e.g., the "cutover" in the Upper Midwest of the United States at the turn of the century). The difficulty is that in cases of war or a fiscal crisis, the state often takes an equally shortsighted view.

13. Lowood, "The Calculating Forester," p. 341. See also Harrison, *Forrests*, pp. 122–23.

14. The recent cloning of tree stock to produce genetically uniform members of a given species is a yet more dramatic step in the direction of uniformity and control.

15. One of the innovations such experimentation gave rise to was "financial rotation." Close attention to annual rates of growth over the life of a pure stand and the surer knowledge about timber yields enabled foresters to calculate precisely the point at which the added value of another year of growth was exceed by the added value (minus the amortized cost of earlier felling and replanting) of new growth. The precision was, of course, predicated on the comparisons made possible by the assumption of homogenous units of timber and market prices.

16. The term "redesigned" is adopted from Chris Maser's valuable book, *The Redesigned Forest* (San Pedro: R. and E. Miles, 1988). Much of his argument can be inferred from the oppositions he emphasizes in the headings of the early sections: "Nature designed a forest as an experiment in unpredictability.... We are trying to design a regulated forest"; "Nature designed a forest of long-term trends.... We are trying to design a forest of short-term absolutes"; "Nature designed a forest with diversity.... We are designing a forest with simplistic uniformity"; "Nature designed a forest with interrelated processes.... We are trying to design a forest based on isolated products" (p. vii).

17. See, for example, Honoré de Balzac's *Les paysans* (Paris: Pleiades, 1949); E. P. Thompson, *Whigs and Hunters: The Origin of the Black Act* (New York: Pantheon, 1975); Douglas Hay, "Poaching on Cannock Chase," in Douglas Hay et al., eds., *Albion's Fatal Tree* (New York: Pantheon, 1975); and Steven Hahn, "Hunting, Fishing, and Foraging: Common Rights and Class Relations in the Postbellum South," *Radical History Review* 26 (1982): 37–64. For an apposite German case, see one of Karl Marx's first published articles linking the theft of wood to the business cycle and unemployment in the Rhineland: reported in Peter Linebaugh, "Karl Marx, the Theft of Wood, and Working-Class Composition: A Contribution to the Current Debate," *Crime and Social Justice*, Fall-Winter 1976, pp. 5–16.

18. The results of three rotations might require as much as two hundred years, or the working lives of perhaps six foresters, to observe. Compare this with, say, the results of three rotations of maize, which would require only three years. For most contemporary forests, the results of the third rotation are not yet in. In forest experimentation, the experimental period easily stretches well beyond a single lifetime. See Maser, *The Redesigned Forest.*

19. There was within Germany a debate between the utilitarian outlook I have described and an anti-utilitarian, anti-Manchester School stream of thought represented by, among others, Karl Geyer, an exponent of the *Mischwald* and natural regeneration. But the short-run success of the utilitarians ensured that their view became the hegemonic "export model" of German scientific forestry. I am grateful to Arvid Nelson for this information and for sharing his deep knowledge about the history of forest policy in Germany. In 1868, Deitrich Brandes, the German chief of colonial India's forests, proposed a plan that would have encouraged community forests as well as state production forests, but the first part of his plan was vetoed by British administrators. The interests of state officials, it appears, tended to select out of the mixed heritage of German forestry those elements most favorable to legibility, management, and revenue.

20. Pinchot toured Prussian and Swiss forests after his studies in Nancy. Carl Schenk, the founder of the first forestry school in the United States, was a German immigrant trained in German universities, and Bernhard Fernow, the chief of the federal government's forestry division from 1886 to 1898 (before Pinchot), was a graduate of the Prussian Forest Academy at Meunden. I am grateful to Carl Jacoby for this information.

21. For a detailed and analytically searching account of colonial forest policy in India, see Sivaramakrishnan, "Forests, Politics, and Governance in Bengal." In chap. 6 he shows how three principles of scientific forestry—that pure stands of commercial timber did better than mixed stands, that fire was a destructive factor to be avoided, and that grazing or firewood collecting could only threaten the forest management program—were overthrown by accumulating evidence in India.

22. Richard Plochmann, *Forestry in the Federal Republic of Germany*, Hill Family Foundation Series (Corvallis: Oregon State University School of Forestry, 1968), pp. 24–25; quoted in Maser, *The Redesigned Forest*, pp. 197–98. The elided sentences, for those interested in the specific interactions, continue: "A spruce stand may serve as an example. Our spruce roots are normally very shallow. Planted on former hardwood soil, the spruce roots could follow the deep root channels of the former hardwoods in the first generation. But in the second generation the root systems turned shallow on account of progressive soil compaction. As a result, the available nutrient supply for the trees became smaller. The spruce stand could profit from the mild humus accumulated in the first generation by the hardwoods, but it was not able to produce a mild humus itself. Spruce litter rots much more slowly than broadleaf litter and is much more difficult for the fauna and flora of the upper soil layer to decompose. Therefore a raw humus developed in most cases. Its humic acids started to leach the soil under our humid climate and impoverished the soil fauna and flora. This caused an even poorer decomposition and a faster development of raw humus." Plochmann points out that the process in pine plantations is roughly similar. I have confirmed this pattern with David Smith of Yale's School of Forestry and Environmental Studies, author of *The Practice of Silviculture*, an important reference on modern forestry techniques. For a similar account of how the techniques of scientific forestry, particularly its aversion to fire and its preference for monoculture, negatively affected forest health and production, see Nancy Langston, *Forest Dreams, Forest Nightmares: The Paradox of Old Growth in the Inland West* (Seattle: University of Washington Press, 1995).

23. "When snags are removed from short-rotation stands, 10% of the wildlife species (excluding birds) will be eliminated; 29% of the wildlife species will be eliminated when both snags and fallen trees (logs) are removed from intensively managed young growth forests. As pieces are continually removed from the forest with the notion of the simplistic uniformity that is termed 'intensive timber management,' we come closer to the ultimate simplistic view of modern forestry—the plantation or 'Christmas tree farm"' (Maser, *The Redesigned Forest*, p. 19).

24. The key step in this process seems to be the below-ground, symbiotic fungus-root structures (mycorrhizal association) studied closely by Sir Albert Howard. See chapter 7.

25. Some of the pests in question included the "pine looper moth, pine beauty, pine moth, Nun moth, saw flies, bark beetles, pine needle cast fungus, pine bluster rust, honey fungus, red rot" (Maser, *The Redesigned Forest*, p. 78).

26. For a brief description of these practices, see Rachel Carson, *Silent Spring* (Boston: Houghton Mifflin, 1962, 1987). Carson praised these advances because they seemed to herald the use of biological controls rather than pesticides.

27. The untoward consequences of engineering a forest in order to maximize the production of a single commodity is by now a worldwide experience. After World War II, Japan adopted a policy of replacing many of the forests that had been plundered for fuelwood and building materials with a single species: the Japanese cedar, selected for its rapid growth and commercial value. Now it is clear that the miles of tall, slender, uniform cedars have caused heavy soil erosion and landslides, have reduced the water table, and are easily felled by storms. They allow little sunlight to filter through to the forest floor and provide little protection or food for fauna. For urban Japanese, the chief short-term inconvenience of the cedars is their seasonal massive release of pollen, which triggers severe allergic responses. But allergies are just the most manifest symptom of the deeper consequences of such radical simplification. See James Sterngold, "Japan's Cedar Forests Are a Man-Made Disaster," *New York Times*, January 17, 1995, pp. Cl, C10.

28. Maser, *The Redesigned Forest*, pp. 54–55. The "commodity" in question in a great many contemporary forests is not wood per se but pulp for making paper. This has led, in turn, to the genetic engineering of species and cloned stock that will produce the ideal quality and quantity of pulp.

29. In the context of welfare economics, the practice of scientific forestry was able to externalize a large number of costs to the community at large which did not appear on its own balance sheet: e.g., soil depletion, loss of water retention capacity and water quality, reduction of game, and loss of biodiversity.

30. Plochmann, *Forestry in the Federal Republic of Germany*, p. 25. There are, of course, naturally occurring pure stands of timber, usually in constrained ecological conditions, including, diagnostically, those found on severely degraded sites. For a range of views on this issue, see Matthew J. Kelty, Bruce C. Larson, and Chadwick D. Oliver, eds., *The Ecology and Silviculture of Mixed-Species Forests: A Festschrift for David W. Smith* (Dordrecht and Boston: Kluwer Academic Publishing, 1992).

31. Nancy Langston has a more global assessment: "Everyone who has ever tried to fix the forests has ended up making them worse" (*Forest Dreams, Forest Nightmares*, p. 2).

36 Seeing Like *Seeing Like a State*

Hrönn Brynjarsdóttir Holmer, Phoebe Sengers, and Kaiton Williams

There is no sure ground even for criticism.
—Latour, "Why Has Critique Run Out of Steam?" 2004, 227

I

Writing this chapter was going to be easy.

The world of *Seeing Like a State* (Scott, 1998) is full of grand, top-down schemes by ambitious designers and statesmen, schemes that draw on scientific insight to revolutionize how society functions by making everyday activities legible, manipulable, improvable, and optimizable. The book's examples range across the reshaping of forests into linear and legible monoculture plantations (see chapter 35), to the creation of a new national capital sectioned and optimized for home, business, and governmental activities, and the reorganization of informal peasant agriculture into vast industrial farms with clear divisions of labor. To revolutionize society's functions, each of these schemes draws on scientific insights to make everyday activities newly legible and thus manipulable, improvable, and optimizable. This is a world which we too inhabit in our professional roles as researchers in technology design, and in our free time as inhabitants of early twenty-first-century modernity. It is a world in which relationships have become social networks, knowledge has become information, and the village square has become Amazon (and by that we don't mean the rainforest).

While these shifts are commonly celebrated in technological discourses, Scott warns us of their dangers. He does so by recounting how technocratic accounting systems run roughshod over the complexities of everyday practice and leave cultural (and literal) dead zones in their wake. Scott demonstrates how these systems are eventually disfigured by their own limitations but not before the human and ecological damage is done: forests full of dying, monocultured trees (see chapter 35), cities without the warmth and interaction of street life, and giant industrialized farms with meager crops and deadened laborers. These are dangers that we too readily recognize in the technological world around us: emotional surveillance mechanisms that constrain the richness of human experience into a few, flat emotional states (Boehner et al., 2007); health tracking systems that substitute social and medical authority for an individual's own embodied experience (Purpura et al., 2011); and "green" technologies that erase politics and materiality to frame sustainability as an optimization of consumption (Brynjarsdóttir et al., 2012). Explain what *Seeing Like a State* means for technology design? Piece of cake.

That's what we thought.

Some people say that it is the job of criticism to make things that are simple, complicated. Those who are not themselves aficionados of criticism say—sometimes dismissively, sometimes aggressively, frequently *nervously*, given the notorious abilities of critics to, well, criticize back—that the problem with criticism is that it just feeds on itself: criticism on criticism on criticism on criticism—turtles, all the way down. At some point, they say, you have to stop talking and *get things done*. The problem, we realized, with the way we had quickly—and lovingly—begun to deploy the critical lens provided by *Seeing Like a State* is that we had stopped short and gotten things done a little too soon. Impressed by the power of its argument, we had taken *Seeing Like a State* at its word, applied it to technology design, and been appropriately horrified by the consequences it revealed. But the more we sat with *Seeing Like a State*, the less secure we felt with the lessons we had taken from its central story.

And so, a few turtles in, we found ourselves embodying our caricatures and poking holes in the very argument that we had only just been so satisfied to apply. As we worked through Scott's examples in "Nature and Space" (chapter 35) and across his entire book, we accumulated more and more stories of technical knowledge and surveillance conquering by local practices. The places changed, as did the times, but the results hardly wavered. His argument began to feel as if it were constituted through the same central mechanism that he critiqued. It was a movement that was simultaneously brilliant, ambitious, and all-encompassing, yet inflexible and unresponsive to the vagaries of local practice.

But to stop there, to be just as satisfied with the deconstruction of what we had originally tried to build, to negate the insights that we originally thought *Seeing Like a State* would bring to technology design and to find ourselves back to the status quo, would again be stopping too soon. Grappling with *Seeing Like a State* had raised now unshakeable questions about the nature of our critical project in technology design. Was our goal simply to *apply* critical theories to technology design? Was it then to criticize those applications, and then to criticize those, and so on, adding turtles as we went?

Or was there another way for us to think about what criticism in technology design could do? Was there a way to hold on to what was good about *Seeing Like a State* and use it to illuminate issues in technology design, while still questioning its role as an outside authority? Could we build on it without being limited by it? Could we build on it by interrogating it? Could we take the disciplines of technology design, not just as sites to apply theory, but as places where the ongoing work of theory happens? What would this look like in practice?

And that's how writing this chapter became hard.

II

To the reader.

In this chapter we offer a personal account of our journey with this excerpt of *Seeing Like a State* and the ideas that branch out from it. What we hope to provide, within the context of a volume intended to open pathways into critical theory for other scholars, is not a definitive accounting of the analytical possibilities the book provides. Instead, we offer an account of our time with it that is scaled to resonate with your own journey. In doing so we have elaborated our outcomes as well as our breakdowns along the way: the blind alleys we stumbled into, and the mistakes we made and then hopefully recovered from.

Some of these stumbles may correspond to concerns about critical work that as readers you might bring to the table; the idea that critique may dismiss too quickly or block useful progress comes to mind readily but there are many others to be sure. We refer to our own work to show how these concerns might manifest in a particular project and to give a sense of how they can be overcome. Where we identify these problems, we critique ourselves, not the entire project of criticism. We don't claim that all critics have stumbled as we have, and we are thankful that the efforts of others are available to help us back to our feet.

Our approach is rooted in a variety of critical traditions, geographical locations, and commitments to action. Jointly, being 'critical' has largely meant identifying unstated assumptions and values related to technology design, bringing them to conscious awareness, and making room for consideration of what might otherwise be relegated to the margin or periphery. Technology design in the context of our work does not refer specifically to design practices coming from arts and design traditions, but to a broader cultural project of creating technologies, including, centrally, the work of engineers, computer scientists, and marketers. This orientation to critical work in technology design has roots in three main areas. First, as demonstrated by, for example, Bardzell (2010), Blythe (2014), Irani et al. (2010), and Kannabiran, Bardzell, and Bardzell (2012), we draw a political and activist stance toward uncovering unarticulated meanings from cultural studies, notably the Birmingham and Frankfurt Schools (e.g., Althusser, 1971; Hall, 1980; Horkheimer, [1937] 1976; Lukács, 1971; Williams, 1958) and feminist theory (e.g., Barad, 2007; Butler, 1990; Haraway, 1988). Second, as demonstrated in DiSalvo et al. (2014), Jackson and Kang (2014), and Williams and Irani (2010), we follow critical work in social sciences of technology (e.g., Gillespie, 2007; Morozov, 2014; Zuboff, 1988) to understand empirically the cultural aspirations and consequences of technology. Third, as seen in work such as Irani and Silberman (2013), Kuznetsov et al. (2011), and Pierce and Paulos (2014), we draw from critical making traditions, including the situationists (Ball, 1987), tactical media (Thompson et al., 2004), critical, interrogative, and speculative design (Dunne and Raby, 2001; Michael, 2012; Wodiczko; 1999), and critical technical practice (Agre, 1997) to embed critical insights in designed objects and processes.

This, however, is by no means the only way to understand what critical work in technology design is or could be about. For example, Bardzell and Bardzell (2013) lay out a key role in critical approaches to technology design for metacriticism, based in the aesthetic traditions in the humanities, and both Bertelsen and Pold (2004) and Greenberg and Buxton (2008) highlight the importance of criticism as a mode within design practice that finds its heritage in the traditions of product design. We trust the rest of this volume will help to lay out the full contours of what is possible in this space.

III

A return to the beginning.

In the excerpt in chapter 35, Scott (1998) analyzes the development of scientific forestry in late eighteenth-century Germany. The goal of scientific forestry was to maximize the forest's saleable wood by measuring, analyzing, and ultimately seeing forests solely in terms of that wood's possible yield. Forests were then reconstructed to maximize this measure. Species of wood that were not saleable were replaced by ones that were, while other plants, people, and practices were removed or ignored. In the short term, this drastically improved production but the improvement in the predictability and short-term yield of the forest caused significant damage to its long-term prospects.

The forest became difficult to sustain beyond a single generation. Soil quality suffered with the loss of underbrush and animal species. Monocultured trees were joined together in a shared fate of blowdowns and blights. And peasants, deprived of their subsistence practices, worked against their restrictions to undermine foresters' goals.

Scott uses this example to illustrate a core conceptual issue with modernist, top-down, engineering solutions to complex problems. As Scott puts it, "The metaphorical value of this brief account of scientific production forestry is that it illustrates the dangers of dismembering an exceptionally complex and poorly understood set of relations and processes in order to isolate a single element of instrumental value" (Scott, 1998, 21). In his terms, modernist solutions work because they are ultimately based on a "narrowing of vision" (11) which brings into sharp focus the particular aspects of a reality that the viewer cares about, presumably at the expense of other features deemed trivial. What we get from this simplification, he contends, is that the "phenomenon at the center of the field of vision [becomes] more legible and hence more susceptible to careful measurement and calculation" (Scott, 1998, 11). Repeated, narrow views combine to constitute what he refers to as an aggregate or synoptic view of "a selective reality" that makes possible a "high degree of schematic knowledge, control, and manipulation" (11). But as the scientific forestry example demonstrates, while this narrowing of vision simplifies the world and makes it amenable to technocratic solutions, those solutions have to contend within a complex reality which includes the factors bracketed from view:

> Utilitarian simplification in the forest was an effective way of maximizing wood production in the short and intermediate term. Ultimately, however, its emphasis on yield and paper profits, its relatively short time horizon, and, above all, the vast array of consequences it had resolutely bracketed came back to haunt it. (Scott, 1998, 21)

The features that appear to guarantee the design's early success become the limitations that eventually lead to its downfall.

Scott's argument starts in the forest, but in the chapters that follow, he telescopes out to a broad range of state-engineered social projects that include Brasilia's design as a city iconic of a modern Brazil, and the development of large-scale industrial farms in the Russian countryside. The goal of these projects is to rationalize and improve society through the application of top-down scientific design, and these examples display, in more detail than in the forest example, what happens when people and their activities are directly considered for optimization. As the subtitle of the book—*How Certain Schemes to Improve the Human Condition Have Failed*—lays bare, the result of these well-intentioned and often highly subsidized projects is a series of disasters: forests that fail to thrive, city streets devoid of human contact, and people turned essentially into slaves.

Through these examples, Scott outlines four essential elements that need to be present in order for such large-scale state-initiated social engineering to fail so spectacularly. First, there needs to be an effort to make society legible (countable, measurable) to the state for the purpose of governance. The standardization of weights and measurements, population surveys, and city planning are all parts of these efforts, and these lay the groundwork for defining and tracking improvement. The second element is ideological: an unquestioning belief in scientific and technical progress as the means for ordering nature and society.

Taken at face value, these two elements only seem naïve, at worst, or maybe just optimistic. But it is when they are coupled with a third element, a powerful oppressive state, that we see the potential for a shift from the state's imagined utopia to the actualized but dystopic reality for its citizens. This potential is realized when Scott's fourth element is in place: a society that—whether through war, revolution, depression, or a struggle for national liberation—has become powerless to resist those transformational efforts.

Scott is a political scientist and anthropologist, concerned with political economy, class relations, and how societies are governed or resist governance. Yet his argument about the historical consequences of modernist design deeply resonate with considerations that matter to scholars engaged in the design and analysis of technological systems, particularly those who are concerned about their potential unintended consequences for the everyday qualities of human life. Looking at *Seeing Like a State*, we start to understand that reliance on expert knowledge and mechanisms of control place both state schemes and technologies in a position of authority over users' lives. We come to see this control as authoritarian: imposed through a centralized scheme based on the conceiver's frame of reference, and pitched to solve a problem only to the degree that it achieves compliance with its model. We come to see this control as tenuous: built only on those aspects of reality that are within view. And we come to recognize the role that imbalances of power play in determining whether the results are simply shortcomings or full-fledged disasters.

IV

In which we, as critics, see like *Seeing Like a State*.

One of your authors is a photographer and finds—even with shelves filled with lenses, cameras, and other ephemera (all, tellingly, in various states of repair and disuse)—that there's something distinctly wonderful about a new acquisition. It represents another way to make an image, and another way to understand or see the world. But it's also a curio, an object worthy of collection in its own right, worthy for the way in which it illuminates what we already have and pushes us toward what we might need next. Might we acquire theories in much the same way? As new ways to look at and understand the world? In that light, what does *Seeing Like a State* bring to our collection and to our understanding of technology's design?

One perspective is provided by Dourish (2007), whose investigation of the field of ubiquitous and mobile computing explored how the primary thesis of *Seeing Like a State* could be used to critically examine the design of technology. At the time, mobile computing was becoming a constant feature in the landscape of daily life, and a significant and fast-growing field of inquiry for HCI. Dourish recognized that this soon-to-be routine embedding of digital devices begged for radically different tools in order to examine and understand that new relationship.

Dourish puts *Seeing Like a State*'s powerful notions of legibility to work through his central question: "How do computer systems help us read the world?" Where previously in HCI legibility would have been understood as a question for Human Factors—an issue of usability—through *Seeing Like a State* it becomes one of human factors—of agents and rationality. That is, as social and cultural realities are instantiated and performed as part of everyday technology usage, how do our technological systems shape the way we all see the world? This represented a dramatic, and for us exciting, departure from common approaches in the field.

The similarities between the modernist grid of *Seeing Like a State* and the practices in information systems design are laid out in Dourish's descriptions. Given the ideal vantage point, the software development practices Dourish describes align with the practice of rationalism and high modernity as revealed by Scott. Both contain abstractions, representations, and computationally manipulable variables. In both cases the troubles begin when the abstractions are no longer seen for what they are, and are instead seen as real—when the territory is seen as identical to its map.

Dourish's work demonstrates the ready applicability of *Seeing Like a State* to technology criticism. We continued this application in our own examination of the use of persuasive computing approaches, specifically techniques used in the design of systems intended to promote sustainability (Brynjarsdóttir et al., 2012). These systems generally aim to encourage sustainability by tracking and reporting metrics of consumer resource use. Our work built on other critical pieces in HCI (DiSalvo, Sengers, and Brynjarsdóttir, 2010; Pierce et al., 2011; Purpura et al., 2011; Strengers, 2011) that analyzed approaches to human-computer interaction that were in turn tackling hard, socially relevant problems (e.g., energy and water conservation or personal health issues). Solutions to these issues had the potential to have significant effects not just on individual lives but on a wider social order.

In that look at the nexus of persuasive techniques and sustainable initiatives, we saw the catastrophic scenarios of *Seeing Like a State* mapped onto the problems we had identified with persuasive technology design. We outlined how the design and implementation of persuasive sustainability systems reflected several modernist attributes identified by Scott: calculability, efficiency, and synoptic control. We argued that these modernist attributes were reflected not just in the systems' designs but in the field's very orientation. While we recognized the value that the simplification of perhaps too complex sustainability issues gave to persuasive design approaches, we pointed back to Scott's recounting of the dangers of narrowed vision to argue that, by focusing on the calculability of certain aspects of everyday practices, the field might be missing the complexity of the forest for the trees: the complicated political and sociocultural complexities inherent in the kinds of everyday life where sustainability mattered the most. The consequences seemed terrifying, but the discovery of a toolkit for describing them was exhilarating.

We, as critics, were triumphant.

V

The signs niggled.

Even while submitting "Sustainably Unpersuaded" we wondered if its story was too slick, and if we had really done justice to the practices we were critiquing. Why weren't the exceptions we had found as much a part of the story as the practices that fit Scott's argument? A conversation in a conference hallway with a respected—and annoyed—designer went like this: "You just don't know the work it takes to actually make these systems work." Our answer that we had in fact built lots of systems felt weak. But it wasn't until we sat down with *Seeing Like a State* again and studied it all the way through that we began to see beyond the way we had first approached it.

If the problem with modernist schemes is that they narrow our vision of the worlds we seek to understand and improve, then it is only fair to ask what falls outside the vision of Scott's own theory. The problem, we came to realize, was that Scott's theory relies on a series of oppositions: the state vs. the nonstate, scientific knowledge vs. traditional knowledge, and technical schemes vs. everyday practices. Each pole is positioned as if to wholly conquer its opposite. In this view, states attempt to domesticate populations that would otherwise not be under control, scientific knowledge trumps and does away with traditional or local knowledge, and technical schemes corral, simplify, and impoverish everyday practice. Seeing like *Seeing Like a State* provides a clear view of how these categories collide, but, as other critics have noted, it might hide from us the blurry, messy ways in which they hybridize and dissolve (Coronil, 2001; Li, 2005; Ferguson, 2005).

Scott was right about a lot, and *Seeing Like a State* is and remains an inspiring, insightful, and brilliant argument. There *are* rationalizing projects of legibility all around us, they *do* often have negative effects in our world, and they *do* erase local contingencies, memories, and knowledge. But that's not *all* they do. They also produce new forms of knowledge—both synoptic and local—and their simplifications, despite themselves, still yield complex techno-social arrangements (Coronil, 2001; Li, 2005).

When we see technology design like *Seeing Like a State*, we see agents ranging from corporations to the NSA and public health NGOs rendering populations legible and optimizable by collecting and processing vast amounts of data on everyday life. We see technologies of sense-making replacing everyday intuition and meaning-making. And we see authoritarian technologies surveying and simplifying the world of everyday practice. These things are all true and important. But what we *don't* see is how various persons, organizations, and groups draw on similar data practices to engage in political contestation. We don't see how technologies of sense-making are themselves made accountable and meaningful. And we don't see how everyday practices proliferate around and reframe what authoritarian technologies intend.

Seeing Like a State is about consequences, intended and otherwise, and one consequence of seeing like *Seeing Like a State* is a tendency to take modernist schemes at their word. We see the world in modernists' terms, where these schemes are separate from and imposed on everyday practices, as are those who design and implement them. What we're left with are outcomes of success or failure that are too narrowly construed. In doing all this, we risk reenacting and reinforcing the very patterns that *Seeing Like a State* critiques.

While *Seeing Like a State* aims to deconstruct the logic of high modernist schemes, its own logic remains paradoxically modern. We mean this in the sense described by

Latour (1993), who argues that the essence of modernity is its move to purify and separate, among other things, nature from society, modern from traditional, science from law, and technology from culture. What this way of knowing fails to grasp, or, more precisely, systematically represses, is the hybrid forms that appear between such poles. In the case of *Seeing Like a State*, this includes the ways in which technical schemes can only ever be implemented and sustained through everyday practices.

This perspective risks blinding us to important yet variegated arrangements of power and politics, and to the ways in which the act of seeing like *Seeing Like a State* might itself induce similarly polemic distinctions in the technological movements we survey. We risk purifying these movements (and the resistance to them) of their rough edges and internal tensions, and risk lending them an unearned consistency and power. This mode of seeing discovers solid blocs of a rigidly composed entity and makes of it an "ideological artifact" with "unity, morality, and independence" when it is at times "disunited, amoral and dependent" (Li, 2005, 385).

As Li (2005, 384) notes, in our haste to see like *Seeing Like a State*, what we might otherwise have seen as contested, or as a complex and tenuous set of claims, we instead make cogent and factual, and we miss the subtleties of power in practice: all the groups that inform power structures and their varying agendas. We miss that everyday practices and knowledge, which *Seeing Like a State* positions as opposite to the state's synoptic pole, are often not wholly opposed to that power but "imbricated with it." We miss that that those we consider subjects are often willing partners in development schemes, and we gain little purchase on how state-powered oppression and coercion give way to equally powerful notions and degrees of improvements.

The ease with which we can see like *Seeing Like a State* can blind us to more dialogic or performative alternatives. Its power can seduce us into romanticizing resistance and into handily making villains of those with whom we disagree. If the processes of legibility Scott describes seek to create maps from the territories they survey, do we, by applying *Seeing Like a State* inaptly, risk producing territories from critical maps? How might we move past this point and come to view our role in producing the worlds that we critique?

VI

"The critic is always right."

Latour (2004, 240) was joking but, in all seriousness, here it seems more like the critic is always wrong. We relied on *Seeing Like a State* to question the directions of technology design, and then found ourselves questioning *Seeing Like a State* and dismantling our own tools. Had we simply been mistaken? Are things just as they are, no more, no less?

When clandestine monitoring tools report the emotional states of unproductive workers, perhaps we should see it not as surveillance but simply as a moment when manager and worker achieve emotional communication. When fitness tracking tools tell their bearers they haven't exercised enough, this might not be technology asserting authority over users' wills but simply one tool among others informing a newly empowered user. When smart meters suggest that unplugging appliances after use may save money, these designs may not be skirting complex natural resource issues to narrowly focus on incremental and perhaps inconsequential changes, but providing the individual with a deeper understanding of the total impact of discrete actions in daily life.

Is our deconstruction of a deconstruction a return to the status quo? Is this, then, the ignoble end of our critical project? Should we quit critiquing and go back to doing the hard work of building systems?

Yes.

Well, no.

The critical project in technology design we staked out for ourselves in section II is not over, but it doesn't look like what we tried to do either. In the words of Latour:

> The critic is not the one who debunks, but the one who assembles. The critic is not the one who lifts the rugs from under the feet of the naïve believers, but the one who offers the participants arenas in which to gather. The critic is not the one who alternates haphazardly between antifetishism and positivism like the drunk iconoclast drawn by Goya, but the one for whom, if something is constructed, then it means it is fragile and thus in great need of care and caution. (Latour, 2004, 246)

The critical methods we have employed so far are based loosely in what Ricœur (1970) terms "the hermeneutics of suspicion." By "hermeneutics," he means a method or philosophy of interpretation; a hermeneutics of suspicion is, then, an orientation to interpretation that distrusts surface appearances and seeks to uncover the darker truths underneath. Classic examples include Marxism and psychoanalysis, each of which in their original form posit that the human world is a chimera under which lurk forces—economic realities, or the workings of the unconscious—of which we are only dimly aware.

The role of the critic in such a mode is in some ways similar to that of the relationship between a magician and an audience—the critic can pull away the superficial trappings to reveal an unexpected reality underneath. Such a hermeneutics leads to great joys for the critic and the audience, as whole new worlds emerge from under what appeared to be a mundane reality. Unfortunately, it also leads to great despair, as each such new world can be reinterpreted as another chimera overlaying yet another secret dark reality. All the while, our beleaguered critic, ever newly revealing, also tumbles down a deepening rabbit hole of fleeting realities at breakneck speed, never able to bring the trick to an end.

This disorienting dynamic may sound a world away from the too-clear certainties and distinctions of both high modernism and Scott's critique of it, but it is driven by a similar underlying logic. While the hermeneutics of suspicion have been deployed to trouble the appearance of rationality in many facets of human life, they are still paradoxically grounded in the idea that there is a stable human world about which we aim to achieve knowledge, and that it is the job of experts to reveal the truth of this world. In this sense, our joy in Scott is a joy that *Seeing Like a State* reveals new dimensions of the truth of technology, while our despair is born from the realization that *Seeing Like a State* is also not a final description of the world and that it too constructs the world it purports to find. But this is only a problem as long as we continue our search for magic, and for experts and theories that can reveal to us the final truth. Giving this up suggests new options.

Ours is not a singular realization. Others have faced this issue. For example, Bardzell (2011) places the role of critical readings as providing suggestive views, rather than uncovering truths. Bertelsen and Pold (2004) emphasize interpretations drawing on specific, detailed theories of aesthetics rather than attempting to develop more grand truths. And Irani and Silberman (2013) tie critical commitments to a call to develop concrete interventions that situate themselves within the complexity and contestability of their results.

Our way out begins with Leahu's (2012) analysis and reformulation of the critical project in HCI and computer-supported cooperative work (CSCW). A key insight of this work is that stepping back from making particular critical interventions allows us to view the complex dance being executed jointly in these disciplines by the actions and reactions of sociologically informed critical and technical researchers. The classic articulation of the central problem of CSCW is as a "sociotechnical gap," which Ackerman (2000) describes as "the divide between what we know we must support socially and what we can support technically" (179). While Ackerman suggests that the goal of CSCW should be "understanding and, hopefully, ameliorating" (179) the gap, Leahu paints a picture in which every time some technical work is done to better address human practices and thereby close the gap, some sociological work is done to open it back up again and demonstrate how the technical work still misses the true complexity of what people do. Leahu argues that the gap is not a revealed artifact of how the world works, but one that is continually enacted and reenacted through the discourse of moves and countermoves by both sociological and technical researchers.

We see the potential for similar movements in our own work on a larger scale. These are movements that would be productive for research churn but perhaps less so for deepening our understanding of technology, its design, and its implications. With the advent of substantial critical discourses within technology design generally, and HCI specifically (of which this volume is one sign), what role is critical work playing in the discourses to which we speak? As Busse et al.'s (2013) call for a discussion of the potentially paralyzing fallout from critique of sustainable technology design suggests, the consequences are not clear. In an ideal world, critique would deepen and strengthen technology design projects and discourses, but in a world where technological discourses are frequently rushing toward the shiny new, perhaps critique becomes a convenient excuse to jettison the old and race more speedily onward: ideas are disposable, so critique and toss them. We need to recognize that this may happen irrespective of the intentions of the critics, or the quality of critique.

As critics we wield words with alacrity, power, and effect, and if we are leaving what we consider to be problematic approaches broken apart in our wake, we are accumulating more fads and fields at our bow. Are these crises that are created for our benefit when none have truly yet begun? Does our "defence of marginality presuppos[e] the existence of a totalitarian centre" (Latour, 1993, 124)? As Latour goes on to note, "Protecting human beings from the domination of machines and technocrats is a laudable enterprise, but if the machines are full of human beings who find their salvation there, such a protection is merely absurd" (124). Our taste for recognizing and rescuing those at the margins of practice may make us similar in all but sign with the rationalizing forces we critique.

Our way out might involve—following Leahu's (2012) building on Barad (2007)—recognizing this dynamic in our work, and then finding a way to hold on to our theoretical apparatus while remaining attuned to how it shapes what we can see and what Taylor refers to as "our own roles in the processes of configuring 'out there'" (Taylor, 2011). This is perhaps easier said than done. How might we actually move past the point of what we now see as risky dualisms and come to view our role in producing the world that we critique?

We can start by recognizing, following Latour (1993), that there has never been a separation between high-modernist designs and the complexities of everyday lifeworlds, or between the practices of technology design and the work of its critics. We produce these arrangements; we do not just discover them already at work in pure forms in our fields. These distinctions, and those between state and nonstate, between scientific and local knowledge, and between technical schemes and everyday practices, are indeed useful and do not need to be abandoned. Instead, their relationship can be reframed. Following Latour (1993) again, rather than purifying them as clean distinctions and enacting these categories as hardened differences, we can hold onto the categories while paying attention to how their boundaries dissolve.

VII

Reading this essay was going to be easy.

The task assigned to us by this volume's editors was to provide accessible ways into *Seeing Like a State* for an audience within technology design warming up to the project of critique. We imagined a helpful set of lessons that drew straightforwardly from the text to help the reader grapple with design questions. What it became—though you can't say we didn't warn you—was a *Seeing Like a State*-inspired meditation on the nature of our critical project in technology design. We challenged ourselves—and you—to see whether we could rethink that project and center it as a place to both apply and produce theory.

In a manner, we did fulfill our ostensible purpose. We grounded the excerpt in the overall work and gave you a taste of how its key concepts can and have been put to use. But there is more work to be done, especially for those who are new to critique and are just beginning to accumulate theory. Our larger goal is to clarify that *Seeing Like a State* is just one of many ways to understand the world and that its application entails strategic choices by the interpreter. By sharing our struggles with it, we hope we have given you an inside view into the difficulties of the critical project, and the doubts and problems we faced along the way. We hope this lends credence, and a practical reality, to our claim that truths are not just found but constructed.

Section V, in which we highlight how a tool we had relied on to understand the world in some ways hindered our understanding of that world and of our role in it, is the most emblematic of our struggle. After this, we put the brakes on deconstruction and highlight instead the constructive role of the critic and the need for care and caution in our work. Section VI addresses how to get to work while recognizing all the moving parts in the work of our criticism. We want to pay attention as we move forward to our performance and its consequences.

Along the way we've created a multipart challenge for ourselves that we now need to resolve by demonstrating through practice: the practice of technology design and production, of technology use and appropriation, and of critique. We need to show you how to make use of a theory like *Seeing Like a State* without being used by it, and to demonstrate how to make use of the distinctions and boundaries that theories like this produce while keeping an eye on how those forms hybridize. This means looking with, not seeing like or through, *Seeing Like a State.*

Seen through *Seeing Like a State*'s point of view, current mobile and ubiquitous computing efforts reveal attempts by contemporary technological regimes to sense, represent, and actively manage social life. Our view on mobile platforms through *Seeing Like a State* might highlight the apparent core structuration of these technologies around harvesting consumer data and shaping consumption behavior. As a lens, we recognize that *Seeing Like a State* highlights and frames particular keywords associated with such technologies. The language of "revolution," for instance, used prodigiously in the discourse around this "big data" behavior, takes on a sinister cast when *Seeing Like a State* reminds us of the disastrous consequences of revolution for Soviet peasants. *Seeing Like a State* raises red flags about the potential catastrophes structurally related to such approaches—catastrophes both in the sense of their potential to channel human activity and drain it of meaning, and in terms of how the noble aims of these approaches are limited by how they can sense, represent, and act.

At the same time, we must remember that Scott's argument is not that high modernist approaches of the type we may recognize in ubiquitous computing necessarily lead to catastrophes but that they do so when coupled with the power and violence of an authoritarian power that civil society lacks the power to resist. This combination allows an escalation into full-scale disaster. This suggests that, beyond the logic of the design itself, we should pay as much attention to evaluating the power of those deploying the technologies and to identifying the practices and institutions that can resist that power. In a reflection on the work of ICT and HCI efforts to aid international development (e.g., in ICT4D or HCI4D) at the global margins, Irani et al. (2010) note that many of the individually focused strategies therein are part of an effort to build a market of consumers as a means of empowerment, yet this very action could be disempowering, making uneven relations possible by "bringing resources and people in line with the interests of powerful capital and commercial actors" (5). But they note this is rarely analyzed within that literature. This is also a problem closer to the putative center, where this attention poses disciplinary challenges for our field. In the worlds of HCI and CSCW, analyzing the corporate or economic structure of technology change or proposing a new institutional frame for technology deployment or activism would not be considered part of what we do. Yet it might make a huge difference to what the technology ends up doing.

Seeing with *Seeing Like a State* means paying attention, too, to the limits of its logic. Scott himself points out that a focus on the authoritarianism and hubris of high modernist projects fails to do full justice to the significant societal benefits brought about by planners, scientists, and engineers. One conclusion from *Seeing Like a State* is that the aim to do good in the end does not absolve us of the need to carefully choose the means. Nevertheless, it does not necessarily follow that a high modernist approach must lead to disaster, nor that there can be no middle ground where such approaches can be applied usefully. While one somewhat fair reading of Scott would be as a social conservative (intervene at your peril!), recognizing the limitations and fraught political stakes of historical attempts by experts to shape social improvements does not absolve us of a responsibility to improve. Grappling with *Seeing Like a State* leaves us with a better sense of the immense challenges involved in figuring out how to do so.

Seeing Like a State makes a key distinction between high modernist, technocratic design and everyday practices, which these designs are seen as systematically corralling, simplifying, erasing, or ignoring. This distinction highlights inherent limitations in how well technical systems can address the complexities of everyday life. As we discussed earlier, this was a distinction we drew on to argue that persuasive sustainability systems face inherent challenges when integrating into everyday life (Brynjarsdóttir et al., 2012). If, following the second part of our challenge, we can hold onto this distinction while examining how its poles interact, this may turn our attention away from an inherent gap between the logic of persuasive calculability and the practices of everyday life, and toward tracing the meanings and contradictions of how that logic is taken up in everyday practice. Our goal would be to pursue a fuller understanding of that logic as it is enacted on the ground (e.g., Broms et al., 2010) not to reveal an aha moment that shows why it fails to work.

The entanglement of technocratic systems with everyday practices opens up new approaches to thinking about the present and future of systems design (Leahu, 2012). When analyzing personal fitness tracking devices, for example, if we focus on distinguishing representations and practices, we might find ourselves spending attention on aspects of health and fitness that are not captured by these devices, the limited notion of fitness they promote, and the possibility that such devices—while promising to tell users more about their fitness—may actually reduce the user's sense of health and fitness by replacing it with the machine's more authoritative representations. But when we keep in mind how representations and practices are entangled, we can focus critical and design attention on how devices and users co-construct dynamic understandings of health and fitness, and what role that dynamic plays in the local and global politics of health.

Attention to the hybridization of formal representations and everyday practice is relevant not only to understanding the activities of users but also to critically analyzing the work of researchers and designers. From this perspective, we note that the artifacts on which critical projects within technology design are frequently based are only a narrow representation of the practices involved. That is, we tend to critique technical practice and discourse primarily as represented in research papers, but this narrows our vision to those aspects of practice that are explicitly documented within a research discourse (for alternatives see Bardzell and Bardzell, 2011 and Goodman, Stolterman, and Wakkary, 2011, which analyze design practice through ethnographic methods). Recognizing that even the most high-modernist plan can only be accomplished through the contingencies of everyday practice suggests a need for more attention in critical work to just those everyday practices through which technology design is enacted, both in research and in production (e.g., Woolgar, 1991). While a top-down, synoptic view may highlight the authoritarian and closed nature of the logic of persuasive sustainability, a grounded view of the contingencies of design practice may reveal richer potential than that logic would appear to allow. Said more generally, the logic of research and design is not necessarily the logic of production and deployment, and the latter needs critical attention as well (compare Schüll, 2013; Irani and Silberman, 2013).

Stepping back from these specific technology examples and insights, what we have tried to do here is not only to describe but also to perform what it means to work out critical projects within technology design. We have tried to do this in a manner that does not depend on turtles-on-turtles, that not only purifies but also uncovers hybrids, and that recognizes that while there is no sure ground in criticism, there are still concrete places to stand and useful vantage points from which to look. While we have discussed some shortcomings of Scott's approach, the goal of this chapter is not to refute *Seeing Like a State*. Rather, we wish to trace its shape. This means laying out not only what it cannot do, but what it can, and how it goes about doing so. Every theory has its contours, and when we import theory those contours shape our work as well. If, as is common in HCI, we borrow theories from others who have borrowed them in turn, we must work to retain both our sensitivity for how those nested contours shape our projects and our imagination for other ways in which to deploy them.

Finally, it is important to recognize that *Seeing Like a State* is, indeed, about the state. The "state" for Scott is about an administrative gaze that views, orders, and manipulates, and that is capable of marshaling violence to achieve its aims. We have been careful in this chapter—though we have not said so explicitly—not to frame the state narrowly as a governmental institution. As Dourish (2007) points out, these institutions are an important part of the history of computing generally, and the work of HCI specifically. But when viewed from the world of contemporary technology design and deployment, the state moves beyond the narrowly governmental and encompasses the practices of corporations and markets as technocratic formations. A key conclusion from our story then is the need to attend to how HCI and other disciplines of technology research and design participate in particular networks of power and influence, particularly when allied with market, industrial, corporate, or governmental interests. This is important for technology design (including critics) because, as we noted previously, we tend to focus on the designs themselves and not on the institutional arrangements of power that complete the picture.

This is broadly about arrangements of power: the power of representation, and the power to represent. Considerations of the will to improve social order and any potential unintended consequences challenge those engaged with technology design to reflect on whether new social orders are made in or through design, or whether changes to the social order are decided elsewhere—by the market, by science, by corporations, by states—and if our only role is to implement them. When we view the public goal or the ends of design as being settled outside of our purview, we fail to account for our own role as part of the institutional arrangements of power.

The question, then, is how we all compose the public good and what role HCI, generally, and critics of it specifically, should play in that composition. As hybrid actors, we cannot absolve ourselves from being involved in the calculations of the plans that we execute in our designs, nor can we as critics limit our roles to just talking about technology or producing theory just for HCI. In this sense, we move from a hermeneutics of suspicion to a hermeneutics of accountability, in which we recognize and carefully wield the power of our position within a larger technosocial dynamic, whether this dynamic is between design and use, critic and design, or subject and state.

Acknowledgments

This work was funded in part by the Intel Science and Technology Center for Social Computing and by NSF Grant IIS-1217685; all opinions are those of the authors. Thanks to Shaowen Bardzell, Mark Blythe, and Erik Stolterman for very helpful criticisms and suggestions.

References

Ackerman, M. S. (2000) "The Intellectual Challenge of CSCW: The Gap between Social Requirements and Technical Feasibility." *Human-Computer Interaction* 15 (2): 179–203.

Agre, P. E. (1997) *Computation and Human Experience.* Cambridge: Cambridge University Press.

Althusser, L. (1971) *Lenin and Philosophy, and Other Essays.* Translated by B. Brewster. New York: Monthly Review Press.

Ball, E. (1987) "The Great Sideshow of the Situationist International." "Everyday Life." Special issue, *Yale French Studies* 73: 21–37.

Barad, K. M. (2007) *Meeting the Universe Halfway: Quantum Physics and the Entanglement of Matter and Meaning.* Durham, NC: Duke University Press.

Bardzell, J. (2011). "Interaction Criticism: An Introduction to the Practice." *Interacting with Computers* 23 (6): 604–621.

Bardzell, J., and S. Bardzell. (2011) "Pleasure Is Your Birthright: Digitally Enabled Designer Sex Toys as a Case of Third-Wave HCI." *Proceedings of the SIGCHI Conference on Human Factors in Computing Systems (CHI'11).* New York: ACM, 257–266.

Bardzell, J., and S. Bardzell. (2013) "What is 'Critical' About Critical Design?" *Proceedings of the SIGCHI Conference on Human Factors in Computing Systems (CHI'13).* New York: ACM, 3297–3306.

Bardzell, S. (2010). "Feminist HCI: Taking Stock and Outlining an Agenda for Design." *Proceedings of the SIGCHI Conference on Human Factors in Computing Systems (CHI'10).* New York: ACM, 1301–1310.

Bertelsen, O. W., and S. Pold. (2004) "Criticism as an Approach to Interface Aesthetics." *Proceedings of the Third Nordic Conference on Human-Computer Interaction (NodriCHI'04).* New York: ACM, 23–32.

Blythe, M. (2014) "The Hitchhiker's Guide to Ubicomp: Using Techniques from Literary and Critical Theory to Reframe Scientific Agendas." *Personal and Ubiquitous Computing* 18 (4): 795–808.

Boehner, K., R. DePaula, P. Dourish, and P. Sengers. (2007) "How Emotion Is Made and Measured." *International Journal of Human-Computer Studies* 65 (4): 275–291.

Broms, L., C. Katzeff, M. Bång, A. Nyblom, S. I. Hjelm, and K. Ehrnberger. (2010) "Coffee Maker Patterns and the Design of Energy Feedback Artefacts." *Proceedings of the 8th ACM Conference on Designing Interactive Systems (DIS'10).* New York: ACM, 93–102.

Brynjarsdóttir, H., M. Håkansson, J. Pierce, E. Baumer, C. DiSalvo, and P. Sengers. (2012) "Sustainably Unpersuaded: How Persuasion Narrows Our Vision of Sustainability." *Proceedings of the SIGCHI Conference on Human Factors in Computing Systems (CHI'12)*. New York: ACM, 947–956.

Busse, D. K., S. Mann, L. Nathan, and C. Preist. (2013) "Changing Perspectives on Sustainability: Healthy Debate or Divisive Factions?" *Extended Abstracts on Human Factors in Computing Systems*. New York: ACM, 2505–2508.

Butler, J. (1990) *Gender Trouble: Feminism and the Subversion of Identity*. New York: Routledge.

Coronil, F. (2001) "Smelling Like a Market." *American Historical Review* 106 (1): 119–129.

DiSalvo, C., J. Lukens, T. Lodato, T. Jenkins, and T. Kim. (2014) "Making Public Things: How HCI Design Can Express Matters of Concern." *Proceedings of the SIGCHI Conference on Human Factors in Computing Systems (CHI'14)*. New York: ACM, 2397–2406.

DiSalvo, C., P. Sengers, and H. Brynjarsdóttir. (2010) "Mapping the Landscape of Sustainable HCI." *Proceedings of the SIGCHI Conference on Human Factors in Computing Systems (CHI'10)*. New York: ACM, 1975–1984.

Dourish, P. (2007) "Seeing Like an Interface." *Proceedings of the 19th Australasian Conference on Computer-Human Interaction: Entertaining User Interfaces (OZCHI'07)*. New York: AMC, 1–8.

Dunne, A., and F. Raby. (2001) *Design Noir: The Secret Life of Electronic Objects*. Basel: Birkhäuser.

Ferguson, J. (2005) "Seeing Like an Oil Company: Space, Security, and Global Capital in Neoliberal Africa." *American Anthropologist* 107 (3): 377–382.

Gillespie, T. (2007) *Wired Shut: Copyright and the Shape of Digital Culture*. Cambridge, MA: MIT Press.

Goodman, E., E. Stolterman, and R. Wakkary. (2011) "Understanding Interaction Design Practices." *Proceedings of the SIGCHI Conference on Human Factors in Computing System (CHI'11)*. New York: ACM, 1061–1070.

Greenberg, S., and B. Buxton. (2008) "Usability Evaluation Considered Harmful (Some of the Time)." *Proceedings of the SIGCHI Conference on Human Factors in Computing System (CHI'08)*. New York: ACM, 111–120.

Hall, S. (1980) "Cultural Studies: Two Paradigms." *Media, Culture and Society* 2 (1): 57–72.

Haraway, D. (1988) "Situated Knowledges: The Science Question in Feminism and the Privilege of Partial Perspective." *Feminist Studies* 14 (3): 575–599.

Horkheimer, M. ([1937] 1976) "Traditional and Critical Theory." In *Critical Sociology: Selected Readings*, edited by Paul Connerton, 206–225. Harmondsworth, UK: Penguin.

Irani, L., J. Vertesi, P. Dourish, K. Philip, and R. E. Grinter. (2010) "Postcolonial Computing: A Lens on Design and Development." *Proceedings of the SIGCHI Conference on Human Factors in Computing Systems (CHI'10)*. New York: AMC, 1311–1320.

Irani, L. C., and M. S. Silberman. (2013) "Turkopticon: Interrupting Worker Invisibility in Amazon Mechanical Turk." *Proceedings of the SIGCHI Conference on Human Factors in Computing Systems (CHI'13)*. New York: ACM, 611–620.

Jackson, S. J., and L. Kang. (2014) "Breakdown, Obsolescence and Reuse: HCI and the Art of Repair." *Proceedings of the SIGCHI Conference on Human Factors in Computing Systems (CHI'14)*. New York: ACM, 449–458.

Kannabiran, G., S. Bardzell, and J. Bardzell. (2012) "Designing (for) Desire: A Critical Study of Technosexuality in HCI." *Proceedings of the 7th Nordic Conference on Human-Computer Interaction (NordCHI'12)*. New York: ACM, 655–664.

Kuznetsov, S., G. N. Davis, E. Paulos, M. D. Gross, and J. C. Cheung. (2011) "Red Balloon, Green Balloon, Sensors in the Sky." *Proceedings of the 13th International Conference on Ubiquitous Computing (Ubicomp'11)*. New York: ACM, 237–246.

Latour, B. (1993) *We Have Never Been Modern*. Cambridge, MA: Harvard University Press.

Latour, B. (2004) "Why Has Critique Run Out of Steam? From Matters of Fact to Matters of Concern." *Critical Inquiry* 30 (2): 225–248.

Leahu, L. (2012) "Representation without Representationalism." PhD diss., Cornell University.

Li, T. M. (2005) "Beyond 'the State' and Failed Schemes." *American Anthropologist* 107 (3): 383–394.

Lukács, G. (1971) *History and Class Consciousness: Studies in Marxist Dialectics*. Cambridge, MA: MIT Press.

Michael, M. (2012) "'What Are We Busy Doing?': Engaging the Idiot." *Science, Technology and Human Values* 37 (5): 528–554.

Morozov, E. (2014) *To Save Everything, Click Here: The Folly of Technological Solutionism*. New York: PublicAffairs.

Pierce, J., H. Brynjarsdóttir, P. Sengers, and Y. Strengers. (2011) "Everyday Practice and Sustainable HCI: Understanding and Learning from Cultures of (Un)Sustainability." *Extended Abstracts on Human Factors in Computing Systems (CHI EA'11)* New York: ACM, 9–12.

Pierce, J., and E. Paulos. (2014) "Counterfunctional Things: Exploring Possibilities in Designing Digital Limitations." *Proceedings of the 2014 conference on Designing interactive systems (DIS'14)*. New York: ACM, 375–384.

Purpura, S., V. Schwanda, K. Williams, W. Stubler, and P. Sengers. (2011) "Fit4life: The Design of a Persuasive Technology Promoting Healthy Behavior and Ideal Weight." *Proceedings of the SIGCHI Conference on Human Factors in Computing Systems (CHI'11)*. New York: AMC, 423–432.

Ricœur, P. (1970) *Freud and Philosophy: An Essay on Interpretation*. New Haven, CT: Yale University Press.

Schüll, N. D. (2013) "The Folly of Technological Solutionism: An Interview with Evgeny Morozov." Public Books, September 9, http://www.publicbooks.org/interviews/the-folly-of-technological-solutionism-an-interview-with-evgeny-morozov.

Scott, J. C. (1998) *Seeing Like a State: How Certain Schemes to Improve the Human Condition Have Failed.* New Haven, CT: Yale University Press.

Strengers, Y. (2011) "Designing Eco-Feedback Systems for Everyday Life." *Proceedings of the SIGCHI Conference on Human Factors in Computing Systems (CHI'11).* New York: ACM, 2135–2144.

Taylor, A. S. (2011) "Out There." *Proceedings of the SIGCHI Conference on Human Factors in Computing Systems (CHI'11).* New York: AMC, 685–694.

Thompson, N., G. Sholette, J. Thompson, N. Mirzoeff, C. O. Chavoya, and A. Noordeman. (2004) *The Interventionists: Users' Manual for the Creative Disruption of Everyday Life.* North Adams, MA: MASS MoCA.

Williams, A. M., and L. Irani. (2010) "There's Methodology in the Madness: Toward Critical HCI Ethnography." *Extended Abstracts on Human Factors in Computing Systems (CHIEA'10).* New York: AMC, 2725–2734.

Williams, R. (1958) *Culture and Society, 1780–1950.* New York: Columbia University Press.

Wodiczko, K. (1999) *Critical Vehicles: Writings, Projects, Interviews.* Cambridge, MA: MIT Press.

Woolgar, S. (1991) "Configuring the User: The Case of Usability Trials." In *A Sociology of Monsters: Essays on Power, Technology and Domination,* edited by John Law, 58–97. London: Routledge.

Zuboff, S. (1988) *In the Age of the Smart Machine: The Future of Work and Power.* New York: Basic Books.

37 Knowing the Oriental (1978)

Edward W. Said

On June 13, 1910, Arthur James Balfour lectured the House of Commons on "the problems with which we have to deal in Egypt." These, he said, "belong to a wholly different category" than those "affecting the Isle of Wight or the West Riding of Yorkshire." He spoke with the authority of a long-time member of Parliament, former private secretary to Lord Salisbury, former chief secretary for Ireland, former secretary for Scotland, former prime minister, and veteran of numerous overseas crises, achievements, and changes. During his involvement in imperial affairs Balfour served a monarch who in 1876 had been declared Empress of India; he had been especially well placed in positions of uncommon influence to follow the Afghan and Zulu wars, the British occupation of Egypt in 1882, the death of General Gordon in the Sudan, the Fashoda Incident, the battle of Omdurman, the Boer War, the Russo-Japanese War. In addition his remarkable social eminence, the breadth of his learning and wit—he could write on such varied subjects as Bergson, Handel, theism, and golf—his education at Eton and Trinity College, Cambridge, and his apparent command over imperial affairs all gave considerable authority to what he told the Commons in June 1910. But there was still more to Balfour's speech, or at least to his need for giving it so didactically and moralistically. Some members were questioning the necessity for "England in Egypt," the subject of Alfred Milner's enthusiastic book of 1892, but here designating a once-profitable occupation that had become a source of trouble now that Egyptian nationalism was on the rise and the continuing British presence in Egypt no longer so easy to defend. Balfour, then, to inform and explain.

Recalling the challenge of J. M. Robertson, the member of Tyneside, Balfour himself put Robertson's question again: "What right have you to take up these airs of superiority with regard to people whom you choose to call Oriental?" The choice of "Oriental" was canonical; it had been employed by Chaucer and Mandeville, by Shakespeare, Dryden, Pope, and Byron. It designated Asia or the East, geographically, morally, culturally. One could speak in Europe of an Oriental personality, an Oriental atmosphere, an Oriental tale, Oriental despotism, or an Oriental mode of production, and be understood. Marx had used the word, and now Balfour was using it; his choice was understandable and called for no comment whatever.

> I take up no attitude of superiority. But I ask [Robertson and anyone else] ... who has even the most superficial knowledge of history, if they will look in the face the facts with which a British statesman has to deal when he is put in a position of supremacy over great races like the inhabitants of Egypt and countries in the East. We know the civilization of Egypt better than we know the civilization of any other country. We know it further back; we know it more intimately; we know more about it. It goes far beyond the petty span of the history of our race, which is lost in the prehistoric period at a time when the Egyptian civilisation had already passed its prime. Look at all the Oriental countries. Do not talk about superiority or inferiority.

Two great themes dominate his remarks here and in what will follow: knowledge and power, the Baconian themes. As Balfour justifies the necessity for British occupation of Egypt, supremacy his mind is associated with "our" knowledge of Egypt and not principally with military or economic power. Knowledge to Balfour means surveying a civilization from its origins to its prime to its decline—and of course, it means *being able to do that.* Knowledge means rising above immediacy, beyond self, into the foreign and distant. The object of such knowledge is inherently vulnerable to scrutiny; this object is a "fact" which, if it develops, changes, or otherwise transforms itself in the way that civilizations frequently do, nevertheless is fundamentally, even ontologically stable. To have such knowledge of such a thing is to dominate it, to have authority over it. And authority here means for "us" to deny autonomy to "it"—the Oriental country—since we know it and it exists, in a sense, *as* we know it. British knowledge of Egypt *is* Egypt for Balfour, and the burdens of knowledge make such questions as inferiority and superiority seem petty ones. Balfour nowhere denies British superiority and Egyptian inferiority; he takes them for granted as he describes the consequences of knowledge.

> First of all, look at the facts of the case. Western nations as soon as they emerge into history show the beginnings of those capacities for self-government ... having merits of their own.... You may look through the whole history of the Orientals in what is called, broadly speaking, the East, and you never find traces of self-government. All their great centuries—and they have been very great—have been passed under despotisms, under absolute government. All their great contributions to civilisation—and they have been great—have been made under that form of government. Conqueror has succeeded conqueror; one domination has followed another; but never in all the revolutions of fate and fortune have you seen one of those nations of its own motion establish what we, from a Western point of view, call self-government. That is the fact. It is not a question of superiority and inferiority. I suppose a true Eastern sage would say that the working government which we have taken upon ourselves in Egypt and elsewhere is not a work worthy of a philosopher—that it is the dirty work, the inferior work, of carrying on the necessary labour.

Since these facts are facts, Balfour must then go on to the next part of his argument.

> Is it a good thing for these great nations—I admit their greatness—that this absolute government should be exercised by us? I think it is a good thing. I think that experience shows that they have got under it far better government than in the whole history of the world they ever had before, and which not only is a benefit to them, but is undoubtedly a benefit to the whole of the civilised West.... We are in Egypt not merely for the sake of the Egyptians, though we are there for their sake; we are there also for the sake of Europe at large.

Balfour produces no evidence that Egyptians and "the races with whom we deal" appreciate or even understand the good that is being done them by colonial occupation. It does not occur to Balfour, however, to let the Egyptian speak for himself, since presumably any Egyptian who would speak out is more likely to be "the agitator [who] wishes to raise difficulties" than the good native who overlooks the "difficulties" of foreign domination. And so, having settled the ethical problems, Balfour turns at last to the practical ones. "If it is our business to govern, with or without gratitude, with or without the real and genuine memory of all the loss of which we have relieved the population [Balfour by no means implies, as part of that loss, the loss or at least the indefinite postponement of Egyptian independence] and no vivid imagination of all the benefits which we have given to them; if that is our duty, how is it to be performed?" England exports "our very best to these countries." These selfless administrators do their work "amidst tens of thousands of persons belonging to a different creed, a different race, a different discipline, different conditions of life." What makes their work of governing possible is their sense of being supported at home by a government that endorses what they do. Yet

> directly the native populations have that instinctive feeling that those with whom they have got to deal have not behind them the might, the authority, the sympathy, the full and ungrudging support of the country which sent them there, those populations lose all that sense of order which is the very basis of their civilisation, just as our officers lose all that sense of power and authority, which is the very basis of everything they can do for the benefit of those among whom they have been sent.

Balfour's logic here is interesting, not least for being completely consistent with the premises of his entire speech. England knows Egypt; Egypt is what England knows; England knows that Egypt cannot have self-government; England confirms that by occupying Egypt; for the Egyptians, Egypt is what England has occupied and now governs; foreign occupation therefore becomes "the very basis" of contemporary Egyptian civilization; Egypt requires, indeed insists upon, British occupation. But if the special intimacy between governor and governed in Egypt is disturbed by Parliament's doubts at home, then "the authority of what ... is the dominant race—and as I think ought to remain the dominant race—has been undermined." Not only does English prestige suffer; "it is vain for a handful of British officials—endow them how you like, give them all the qualities of character and genius you can imagine—it is impossible for them to carry out the great task which in Egypt, not we only, but the civilised world have imposed upon them."[1]

As a rhetorical performance Balfour's speech is significant for the way in which he plays the part of, and represents, a variety of characters. There are of course "the English," for whom the pronoun "we" is used with the full weight of a distinguished, powerful man who feels himself to be representative of all that is best in his nation's history. Balfour can also speak for the civilized world, the West, and the relatively small corps of colonial officials in Egypt. If he does not speak directly for the Orientals, it is because they after all speak another language; yet he knows how they feel since he knows their history, their reliance upon such as he, and their expectations. Still, he does speak for them in the sense that what they might have to say, were they to be asked and might they be able to answer, would somewhat uselessly confirm what is already evident: that they are a subject race, dominated by a race that knows them and what is good for them better than they could possibly know themselves. Their great moments were in the past; they are useful in the modern world only because the powerful and up-to-date empires have effectively brought them out of the wretchedness of their decline and turned them into rehabilitated residents of productive colonies.

Egypt in particular was an excellent case in point, and Balfour was perfectly aware of how much right he had to speak as a member of his country's parliament on behalf of England, the West, Western civilization, about modem Egypt. For Egypt was not just another colony: it was the vindication of Western imperialism; it was, until its annexation by England, an almost academic example of Oriental backwardness; it was to become the triumph of English knowledge and power. Between 1882, the year in which England occupied Egypt and put an end to the nationalist rebellion of Colonel Arabi, and 1907, England's representative in Egypt, Egypt's master, was Evelyn Baring (also known as "Over-baring"), Lord Cromer. On July 30, 1907, it was Balfour in the Commons who had supported the project to give Cromer a retirement prize of fifty thousand pounds as a reward for what he had done in Egypt. Cromer *made* Egypt, said Balfour:

> Everything he has touched he has succeeded in.... Lord Cromer's services during the past quarter of a century have raised Egypt from the lowest pitch of social and economic degradation until it now stands among Oriental nations, I believe, absolutely alone in its prosperity, financial and moral.[2]

How Egypt's moral prosperity was measured, Balfour did not venture to say. British exports to Egypt equaled those to the whole of Africa; that certainly indicated a sort of financial prosperity, for Egypt and England (somewhat unevenly) together. But what really mattered was the unbroken, all-embracing Western tutelage of an Oriental country, from the scholars, missionaries, businessmen, soldiers, and teachers who prepared and then implemented the occupation to the high functionaries like Cromer and

Balfour who saw themselves as providing for, directing, and sometimes even forcing Egypt's rise from Oriental neglect to its present lonely eminence.

If British success in Egypt was as exceptional as Balfour said, it was by no means an inexplicable or irrational success. Egyptian affairs had been controlled according to a general theory expressed both by Balfour in his notions about Oriental civilization and by Cromer in his management of everyday business in Egypt. The most important thing about the theory during the first decade of the twentieth century was that it worked, and worked staggeringly well. The argument, when reduced to its simplest form, was clear, it was precise, it was easy to grasp. There are Westerners, and there are Orientals. The former dominate; the latter must be dominated, which usually means having their land occupied, their internal affairs rigidly controlled, their blood and treasure put at the disposal of one or another Western power. That Balfour and Cromer, as we shall soon see, could strip humanity down to such ruthless cultural and racial essences was not at all an indication of their particular viciousness. Rather it was an indication of how streamlined a general doctrine had become by the time they put it to use—how streamlined and effective.

Unlike Balfour, whose theses on Orientals pretended to objective universality, Cromer spoke about Orientals specifically as what he had ruled or had to deal with, first in India, then for the twenty-five years in Egypt during which he emerged as the paramount consul-general in England's empire. Balfour's "Orientals" are Cromer's "subject races," which he made the topic of a long essay published in the *Edinburgh Review* in January 1908. Once again, knowledge of subject races or Orientals is what makes their management easy and profitable; knowledge gives power, more power requires more knowledge, and so on in an increasingly profitable dialectic of information and control. Cromer's notion is that England's empire will not dissolve if such things as militarism and commercial egotism at home and "free institutions" in the colony (as opposed to British government "according to the Code of Christian morality") are kept in check. For if, according to Cromer, logic is something "the existence of which the Oriental is disposed altogether to ignore," the proper method of ruling is not to impose ultrascientific measures upon him or to force him bodily to accept logic. It is rather to understand his limitations and "endeavor to find, in the contentment of the subject race, a more worthy and, it may be hoped, a stronger bond of union between the rulers and the ruled." Lurking everywhere behind the pacification of the subject race is imperial might, more effective for its refined understanding and infrequent use than for its soldiers, brutal tax gatherers, and incontinent force. In a word, the Empire must be wise; it must temper its cupidity with selflessness, and its impatience with flexible discipline.

To be more explicit, what is meant when it is said that the commercial spirit should be under some control is this—that in dealing with Indians or Egyptians, or Shilluks, or Zulus, the first question is to consider what these people, who are all, nationally speaking, more or less *in statu pupillari*, themselves think is best in their own interests, although this is a point which deserves serious consideration. But it is essential that each special issue should be decided mainly with reference to what, by the light of Western knowledge and experience tempered by local considerations, we conscientiously think is best for the subject race, without reference to any real or supposed advantage which may accrue to England as a nation, or—as is more frequently the case—to the special interests represented by some one or more influential classes of Englishmen. If the British nation as a whole persistently bears this principle in mind, and insists sternly on its application, though we can never create a patriotism akin to that based on affinity of race or community of language, we may perhaps foster some sort of cosmopolitan allegiance grounded on the respect always accorded to superior talents and unselfish conduct, and on the gratitude derived both from favours conferred and from those to come. There may then at all events be some hope that the Egyptian will hesitate before he throws in his lot with any future Arabi.... Even the Central African savage may eventually learn to chant a hymn in honour of Astraea Redux, as represented by the British official who denies him gin but gives him justice. More than this, commerce will gain.[3]

How much "serious consideration" the ruler ought to give proposals from the subject race was illustrated in Cromer's total opposition to Egyptian nationalism. Free native institutions, the absence of foreign occupation, a self-sustaining national sovereignty: these unsurprising demands were consistently rejected by Cromer, who asserted unambiguously that "the real future of Egypt ... lies not in the direction of a narrow nationalism, which will only embrace native Egyptians ... but rather in that of an enlarged cosmopolitanism."[4] Subject races did not have it in them to know what was good for them. Most of them were Orientals, of whose characteristics Cromer was very knowledgeable since he had had experience with them both in India and Egypt. One of the convenient things about Orientals for Cromer was that managing them, although circumstances might differ slightly here and there, was almost everywhere nearly the same.[5] This was, of course, because Orientals were almost everywhere nearly the same.

Now at last we approach the long-developing core of essential knowledge, knowledge both academic and practical, which Cromer and Balfour inherited from a century of modern Western Orientalism: knowledge about and knowledge of Orientals, their race, character, culture, history, traditions, society, and possibilities. This knowledge was effective: Cromer believed he had put it to use in governing Egypt. Moreover, it was tested and unchanging knowledge, since "Orientals" for all practical purposes were a Platonic essence, which any Orientalist (or ruler of Orientals) might examine, understand, and expose. Thus in the thirty-fourth chapter of his two-volume work *Modern Egypt*, the magisterial record of his experience and achievement, Cromer puts down a sort of personal canon of Orientalist wisdom:

Sir Alfred Lyall once said to me: "Accuracy is abhorrent to the Oriental mind. Every Anglo-Indian should always remember that maxim." Want of accuracy, which easily degenerates into untruthfulness, is in fact the main characteristic of the Oriental mind.

The European is a close reasoner; his statements of fact are devoid of any ambiguity; he is a natural logician, albeit he may not have studied logic; he is by nature sceptical and requires proof before he can accept the truth of any proposition; his trained intelligence works like a piece of mechanism. The mind of the Oriental, on the other hand, like his picturesque streets, is eminently wanting in symmetry. His reasoning is of the most slipshod description. Although the ancient Arabs acquired in a somewhat higher degree the science of dialectics, their descendants are singularly deficient in the logical faculty. They are often incapable of drawing the most obvious conclusions from any simple premises of which they may admit the truth. Endeavor to elicit a plain statement of facts from any ordinary Egyptian. His explanation will generally be lengthy, and wanting in lucidity. He will probably contradict himself half-a-dozen times before he has finished his story. He will often break down under the mildest process of cross-examination.

Orientals or Arabs are thereafter shown to be gullible, "devoid of energy and initiative," much given to "fulsome flattery," intrigue, cunning, and unkindness to animals; Orientals cannot walk on either a road or a pavement (their disordered minds fail to understand what the clever European grasps immediately, that roads and pavements are made for walking); Orientals are inveterate liars, they are "lethargic and suspicious," and in everything oppose the clarity, directness, and nobility of the Anglo-Saxon race.[6]

Cromer makes no effort to conceal that Orientals for him were always and only the human material he governed in British colonies. "As I am only a diplomatist and an administrator, whose proper study is also man, but from the point of view of governing him," Cromer says, "… I content myself with noting the fact that somehow or other the Oriental generally acts, speaks, and thinks in a manner exactly opposite to the European."[7] Cromer's descriptions are of course based partly on direct observation, yet here and there he refers to orthodox Orientalist authorities (in particular Ernest Renan and Constantin de Volney) to support his views. To these authorities he also defers when it comes to explaining why Orientals are the way they are. He has no doubt that *any* knowledge of the Oriental will confirm his views, which, to judge from his description of the Egyptian breaking under cross-examination, find the Oriental to be guilty. The crime was that the Oriental was an Oriental, and it is an accurate sign of how commonly acceptable such a tautology was that it could be written without even an appeal to European logic or symmetry of mind. Thus any deviation from what were considered the norms of Oriental behavior was believed to be unnatural; Cromer's last annual report from Egypt consequently proclaimed Egyptian nationalism to be an "entirely novel idea" and "a plant of exotic rather than of indigenous growth."[8]

Notes

1. This and the preceding quotations from Arthur James Balfour's speech to the House of Commons are from Great Britain, *Parliamentary Debates* (Commons), 5th ser., 17 (1910): 1140–46.

See also A. P. Thornton, *The Imperial Idea and Its Enemies: A Study in British Power* (London: MacMillan & Co., 1959), pp. 357–60. Balfour's speech was a defense of Eldon Gorst's policy in Egypt; for a discussion of that see Peter John Dreyfus Mellini, "Sir Eldon Gorst and British Imperial Policy in Egypt," unpublished Ph.D. dissertation, Stanford University, 1971.

2. Denis Judd, *Balfour and the British Empire: A Study in Imperial Evolution, 1874–1932* (London: MacMillan & Co., 1968), p. 286. See also p. 292: as late as 1926 Balfour spoke—without irony—of Egypt as an "independent nation."

3. Evelyn Baring, Lord Cromer, *Political and Literary Essays, 1908–1913* (1913; reprint ed., Freeport, N.Y.: Books for Libraries Press, 1969), pp. 40, 53, 12–14.

4. Ibid., p. 171.

5. Roger Owen, "The Influence of Lord Cromer's Indian Experience on British Policy in Egypt 1883–1907," in *Middle Eastern Affairs, Number Four: St. Antony's Papers Number 17*, ed. Albert Hourani (London: Oxford University Press, 1965), pp. 109–39.

6. Evelyn Baring, Lord Cromer, *Modern Egypt* (New York: Macmillan Co., 1908), 2: 146–67. For a British view of British policy in Egypt that runs totally counter to Cromer's, see Wilfrid Scawen Blunt, *Secret History of the English Occupation of Egypt: Being a Personal Narrative of Events* (New York: Alfred A. Knopf, 1922). There is a valuable discussion of Egyptian opposition to British rule in Mounah A. Khouri, *Poetry and the Making of Modern Egypt, 1882–1922* (Leiden: E. J. Brill, 1971).

7. Cromer, *Modern Egypt*, 2: 164.

8. Cited in John Marlowe, *Cromer in Egypt* (London: Elek Books, 1970), p. 271.

38 Representing Others: HCI and Postcolonialism

Beki Grinter

Introducing Edward Said and *Orientalism*

Edward Said (1935–2003) is considered to be one of the founders of the field of postcolonial studies—a field of research that examines the cultural legacies of colonialism (Ashcroft and Ahluwalia, 2001). In *Orientalism,* Said focuses on how colonial powers used texts (e.g., essays, speeches) to assert their control over the colonized (rather than a sole focus on force). Said argues that texts should be read in the context surrounding their creation in order to really understand their import. In Chapter 1 of *Orientalism,* "Knowing the Oriental" (see chapter 37 of this text), he demonstrates how the British authored texts that supported their control over Egypt. Specifically, Said describes member of Parliament Arthur Balfour's lecture in the House of Commons on "the problems with which we have to deal in Egypt" and Evelyn Baring's (Lord Cromer) writings based on his time as consul-general in Egypt. Said uses these to illustrate how the British represented the Orient in texts and in so doing legitimated British control over Egypt.

In this chapter, I take up three themes, all focused on the power of texts. First, I examine the power conferred on people who control the production of knowledge. Second, I discuss how people and places are represented in accounts. Third, and finally, I focus on the methods of knowledge production. I reflect on each of these themes by putting Said into conversation with human-computer interaction for development (HCI4D) research. HCI4D, an emerging area of importance within the field of HCI, focuses on the human-centered design of technologies for marginalized people in the Global South (Irani and Silberman, 2013; Toyama, 2010).

In addition to HCI4D and HCI literature, I draw on literature from the information and communications technologies and development (ICTD) field. ICTD researchers focus on understanding the role of technology in development [46]. It is important to separate ICTD from the way that international organizations (e.g., the United Nations), governments, and nongovernmental organizations (NGOs) engage in development, which is often described in terms of economic progress and resource transfer. In contrast, ICTD research takes development as an open question—what is it, what ought it to be? Development remains open to a variety of interpretations, including those influenced by critical theory (e.g., Unwin, 2009). The difference between development as practiced by governments and so forth and development as a focus of research has not always been made clear in HCI accounts of ICTD, potentially marginalizing the role that ICTD scholarship plays within the field of HCI. As I hope to demonstrate, there is much to learn from ICTD, and we share many exciting commonalities (Toyama, 2010).

In the rest of this chapter, I use HCI4D and ICTD as the context for exploring the themes as follows. First, in considering the power conferred through knowledge production, I focus on the importance of institutional affiliation. Second, in discussing representation, I explore possibilities for research into the uses of technologies that give voice to others, and provide a cautionary tale about whose accounts we use. Third, I raise questions about methods used in HCI research and the assumptions embedded within them through an examination of the problems encountered with their export to HCI4D problems. Finally, I conclude by arguing that while Said's ideas are perhaps easiest to engage within the context of HCI4D research, their impact has significance for the entire field of HCI.

Knowledge as Power and the Importance of Institutional Affiliation

> As Balfour justifies the necessity for the British occupation of Egypt, supremacy in his mind is associated with "our" knowledge of Egypt and not principally with military of economic power. Knowledge to Balfour means surveying a civilization from its origins to its prime and then to its decline—and of course, it means *being able to do that.*
>
> —Said, 1993, 32; italics in original

Said introduces us to the relationship between knowledge production and the power it confers through a critical examination of Balfour's speech. He highlights how Balfour's argument was based on the idea that a British-produced knowledge of Egypt was the power by which occupation was achieved and maintained. Reflecting on how a postcolonialism in general, and Said in particular, applies to HCI (and HCI4D) leads us to two related questions about representation through authorship. First, who is representing whom? Second, who controls the means of representation?

In asking these questions of HCI4D it is not difficult to see that the research subjects are marginalized people in the Global South. By contrast, it is tempting to suggest that the researchers often come from countries that were either colonial powers (e.g., the United Kingdom) or are in a position of contemporary global power (e.g., the United States). But that draws us into a taxonomic view of culture by assigning researchers a national identity that explains their motivation. Postcolonial scholars warn us about the problems of taking a taxonomic approach to the researched (e.g., Kam et al., 2006), but it is equally as complicated in applying it to the researchers. Surely, it is possible that the HCI4D community includes scholars who embrace multiple cultural identities, including ones that they share with the places and people who are the focus of their research. Indeed, I see no reason why some HCI4D researchers may not be motivated in the same way that Said's complex cultural identity (as both an American citizen academic and an exiled Palestinian Christian) influenced both his research and his desire to be a public intellectual—to be a voice for the unvoiced people with whom he shared an identify (Ashcroft and Ahluwalia, 2001).

Said invites us to focus on institutional affiliation [4]. Research organizations encourage and support the production of knowledge, and they provide access to resources (e.g., American universities have access to the National Science Foundation). But not all research organizations are the same, and the difference in the practices and resources has not gone unnoticed in the ICTD community. In their paper, Gitau, Plantinga, and Diga (2010) examined the institutional affiliation of ICTD researchers. They found that the continent of Africa—especially sub-Saharan Africa—was a very significant site of research, but researchers affiliated with African institutions produced very little of that scholarship. Analyzing the last twenty years of conference and journal publications, they found that scholars affiliated with African institutions wrote just 9 percent of articles (150 out of 1,633). Of that 150, 30 of them (20 percent of those affiliated with African institutions) had non-African coauthors and 56 (37 percent) came from the Republic of South Africa.

Gitau, Plantinga, and Diga are not alone in their concern about this underrepresentation in scholarship. Other scholars have argued that the lack of African academic input leads ill-formed policies and puts Africans into situations where they are the passive consumers of Western knowledge rather than active, innovative, producers (Elovaara, Igira, and Mörtberg, 2006; Grinter and Eldridge, 2001; Merritt and Stolterman, 2012). Gitau, Plantinga, and Diga (2010) further identify how institutional affiliation shapes differential practices that affect the production of African ICTD scholarship. For example, they suggest that Euro-American universities emphasize research over teaching, whereas African institutions balance these equally. They also cite access challenges such as bandwidth and the high cost of databases of publications. These arguments may appear somewhat taxonomically, especially when made briefly. For example, research institutions in any country likely do not have the same equal access to resources. However, their findings do invite reflection on the importance of institutional affiliation for the production of knowledge, and how differences in affiliation influence the body of knowledge that comes to define a field including HCI.

To Gitau, Plantinga, and Diga's list I would add two other barriers. First is the high cost of HCI conferences. Others have argued that these costs limit participation by humanities scholars, but we lose more than just disciplinary voices—people who cannot afford to attend are shut out of the conversations by which we produce knowledge.

Second, many conferences are held in venues that present significant and differential immigration barriers. Immigration systems reflect power arrangements between countries, such as the relative ease of traveling to the United States or the European Union if one is a national of either, in comparison with the barriers presented if one is not. At ICTD 2012, we held a session to discuss conference location, in which our African colleagues shared many of their lengthy, costly, and difficult immigration experiences.

Said's focus on the importance of affiliation can be used to explain how Euro-American institutions came to dominate the production of knowledge about technology use in African countries. ICTD researchers have begun to ask questions about what the implications of this imbalance are for policy and practice. Turning to HCI4D and HCI, the same questions are relevant: how does institutional affiliation exert control over research and what are the implications for the body of knowledge produced?[1] Gitau, Plantinga, and Diga's (2010) analysis includes the CHI conference from 2007–2009, during which 616 papers appeared in the conference proceedings. In 2007 and 2009 there were no papers from researchers affiliated with African institutions; in 2008 there were four papers, three of which came from a single institution.

In focusing on the relationship between the ability to produce knowledge and power, Said invites us to consider the importance of institutional affiliation. Focusing on the different affiliations of researchers invites conversation about who is producing the body of knowledge. This has been made visible in HCI and ICT4D as part of questioning who is writing about whom. Next we turn to the accounts being created.

Representation: Giving Voice and Accounting for Accounts

> To have such knowledge of such a thing is to dominate it, to have authority over it. And authority here means for "us" to deny autonomy to "it"—the Oriental country—since we know it and it exists, in a sense, *as* we know it. British knowledge of Egypt *is* Egypt for Balfour.
>
> —Said, 1978, 32; italics in original

Othering happens when the people who control knowledge production represent those who do not. Othering is central to Balfour's speech; he gives legitimacy to the continued British presence by asserting the English knowledge of the Egyptians as *all* knowledge about Egypt. The Egyptians subject to British colonial rule had no voice; what they thought is not represented. Again, turning to HCI we can ask how given the dominance of Euro-American scholarship, how we give voice to others in our accounts.

Relatively little has been said about othering. However, Winschiers-Theophilus and Bidwell (2013) do highlight examples that they have encountered. For example, the use of the phrase "throughout Africa" can collapse the diversity that exists across the continent. One area where we can see othering, and a resistance to it, is through social media.

Recently, the *Washington Post* reported how Kenyans with access to Twitter used the system to critique American (CNN) and French (France 24) media reports that—from their perspective—overemphasized the potential for violence and disorganization at the polls during the Kenyan presidential election (Dewey, 2013). This wasn't the first time that they had responded to foreign accounts, and even today reading the *#SomeoneTellCNN* tweet stream is to observe Kenyans critiquing those representations of Kenya and offering alternative accounts. I am reminded of Miller and Slater's (2000) critique of research that decouples identity and geography from online activities; instead, they argue that the internet is always used "somewhere in particular" (1). Understanding how some Kenyans use Twitter is an opportunity to see how they assert their voices about how Kenya is portrayed by the global media. In Said's terminology, we can witness attempts by Kenyans to reclaim their autonomy. Importantly, while people have critiqued others' representation of them for a long time, social media makes it more visible (e.g., the media attention around the *#SomeoneTellCNN* tweet stream in the American press).

Images can also other. In *Reading National Geographic*, Lutz and Collins (1993) illustrate how the images of non-Western people used by the magazine create strong impressions about others in its Euro-American readership. For example, the authors showed readers images of groups of people where some wore native dress and other Western-style clothing. In response, readers spoke of how those pictures provided evidence of the arrival of civilization and modernity! Again, social media offers similar opportunities. For example, Walton (2010) compares pictures taken of Guguletu, a township in Cape Town, posted on Flickr (a popular photo-sharing website) versus those on the Grid (a South African mobile platform that supports image sharing). Guguletu was established during apartheid; today it is a popular "township tour" destination for tourists (although this is not without controversy). Comparing the two collections, Walton finds that Flickr images are tourist accounts documenting the poverty. By contrast the Grid's pictures tell stories about friends, with many being self-portraits taken by residents. Comparing Flickr's volume of pictures and its global accessibility, she argues that Guguletu is being seen by the majority as a poor urban township that people visit, which is in stark contrast to the way that people who live there document the township.

Social media offers us an opportunity to examine questions of representation. First, it suggests value in social media research that is grounded "somewhere in particular" in contrast to accounts that present information about what happens online, divorced from people's locations and experiences. For example, to understand who is producing the images of Guguletu is to understand what gets produced. Second, social media offers researchers an opportunity to hear the voices of those who are speaking out about how they are represented by others. While I do not wish to suggest that the Internet gives equity to those voices, in research we can understand how the network is implicated in challenging control over representation. Beyond understanding, HCI4D (and HCI more generally) should embrace an agenda in the design of emancipatory social media systems that give a voice to the unvoiced (or raise the volume of those who have some presence but not the same ability to promote their representations).

Fortunately this has begun. Irani and Silberman's (2013) Turkopticon system empowers Amazon Mechanical Turk's crowdworkers by helping them share information about good and exploitative employers. Dimond et al.'s (2013) Hollaback! system encourages women to share their experiences of street harassment and through doing so find their individual and collective voices to fight against it. Both of these studies use feminist theory and methodology—and draw on work that explains its value to HCI (Bardzell, 2010; Bardzell and Bardzell, 2011)—and I highlight them here because feminism and postcolonialism share a commitment to empowering people by giving them voice (Said, 1978).

Questions of representation also surface in quantitative accounts. In their postcolonial criticism of ubiquitous computing, Dourish and Mainwaring (2012) describe how institutions such as Kew Gardens and the knowledge it produced (including quantified accounts), supported British colonial occupation. In HCI we embrace both qualitative and quantitative knowledge. However, irrespective of the methods we use in our own research, we can and do rely on quantified accounts to justify research projects. For example, my colleagues and I have used quantified data to explain the importance of religion in American life (Wyche et al., 2006) and illustrate the increase in the use of the Short Message Service (SMS) among teens (Grinter and Eldridge, 2001). But quantified knowledge is also subject to debate and now that discussion is also visible online. For example, consider the Kibera slum in Nairobi, Kenya. In 2010, Kenya's national census found it was smaller than previously reported by the United Nations (which had been used to depict Kibera internationally as the "largest slum in Africa") (Karanja, 2010)—a cautionary tale about whose statistics we cite as support for our own research.

A central contribution of Said was to examine how texts represent people (othering). Over the years, the HCI community has produced a large corpus of knowledge about people and places. I have contributed to it, and so have many of the people reading this chapter. Said encourages us to ask how we write about people and places, how we interpret the accounts of others. He invites important reflection on how the corpus of knowledge represents people and places as we know them (and in our future related work). Social media provides a research opportunity in this regard, not just to expand and enrich our understanding, but also to see and hear from people who want to and are fighting to control how they are represented. We have much to learn.

Participation: Exposing Values and Assumptions in Methods via Failures of Export

Unlike Balfour, whose theses on Orientals pretended to objective universality, Cromer spoke about Orientals specifically as what he had ruled or had to deal with, first in Indian, then for the twenty-five years in Egypt.
—Said, 1993, 36

"But it is essential that each special issue should be decided mainly with reference to what, by the light of Western knowledge and experience tempered by local considerations, we conscientiously think is best for the subject race."
—Said, 1993, 37 (quoting Cromer)

A pervasive theme in Said's critique of Lord Cromer's (British Consul-General in Egypt) accounts of the "management of everyday business" (Said, 1993, 36) is the lack of engagement with Egyptians. Cromer, and others, created their own accounts that did not involve any Egyptian representation, and then used those texts to manage Egypt and legitimize British colonial occupation.

By contrast with Lord Cromer specifically, and British colonists more generally, HCI has had since its inception an emphasis on participation. Beginning with user-centered design, HCI has been centrally concerned with developing methods that involve user participation. However, the turn to HCI4D sheds light on the values and assumptions about participation embedded in our methods.

Assumptions about participation have been made particularly visible when HCI methods have broken down, or failed to work (e.g., Anokwa et al., 2009; Dewey, 2013; Gitau, Plantinga, and Diga, 2010; Henrich, Heine, and Norenzayan, 2010b; Irani and Silberman, 2013; Lutz and Collins, 1993; Winschiers-Theophilus and Bidwell, 2013; Winschiers-Theophilus et al., 2010, 50). For example, researchers have found that users were unwilling to criticize prototypes during sessions intended to elicit problems with designs (Dearden and Rizvi, 2008; Kam et al., 2006). Marsden, Maunder, and Parker (2008) attribute this reluctance to the power relationship between potential end-users and the expert designer. Reflecting on how to facilitate participation, Puri et al. (2004) compared projects in different countries and found that in South Africa the principle of *ubuntu*—collective personhood and morality—drove participation, while in India respecting the hierarchy was key, and by contrast in Mozambique they leveraged support from mediating organizations such as academics to spur engagement. Finally, a number of studies report challenges in supporting women's participation due to societal gender inequity (Wyche, Forte, and Schoenebeck 2013) and norms about whether women can be alone in the presence of male researchers (Anokwa et al., 2009). Researchers responding to these difficulties report showing a woman's husband a prototype before inviting the wife to comment [45] and in a study of sexual harassment having women researchers collect data that the male colleagues did not have access to (Ahmed et al., 2014).

Less has been written about the participation of the researcher, but it too highlights challenges. Blake and Tucker (2006) report on the difficulty of using critical action research because the method requires software designers to bridge cultural and linguistic gulfs, which proved hard in practice. Dearden and Rizvi's (2008) survey offers insight into why this gulf between rationality and reality may occur, citing problems with researchers overemphasizing techniques used and underemphasizing the need to build relationships with participants—the lack of which inhibits discussion of the effects of power relationships on the process. Finally, women researchers describe how their gender, age, race, and socioeconomic status influence their ability to conduct ethnographic and experimental research because of how their participants respond to them (Lutz and Collins, 1993).

Reading the HCI4D literature is to be repeatedly confronted with questions about participation framed as a relationship between the researcher and the researched (Dewey, 2013; Gitau, Plantinga, and Diga, 2010; Henrich, Heine, and Norenzayan, 2010a; Irani and Silberman, 2013; Winschiers-Theophilus and Bidwell, 2013; Winschiers-Theophilus et al., 2010). Reflecting on the difficulties of using participatory design (PD) in developing nations, Merritt and Stolterman (2012) offer a historical explanation for why PD might not export well, citing the origins of this method as being "in a society with a lively ideological public discourse inside an unusually homogenous culture" (73). Indeed, as Kensing and Blomberg (1998) point out, the movement of PD from Scandinavia to the United States was not without value shifts that caused changes in practice.

The history of PD reveals the root of the issue: exporting methods exposes the values people hold about participation. What I am suggesting is that the difficulties that HCI4D researchers report stem from the fact that the methods they have tried to use were designed with very different values about how to facilitate participation. The use of these methods in different cultural contexts exposes those assumptions about participation. For example, we assume women can participate equally, consent on their own (as adults, without permission of their spouses), and work in rooms where they may be alone with a male researcher. Also, we assume that people with less technological knowledge and who may not have a PhD feel comfortable or believe it is appropriate to critique our designs. But, these values are not universally shared.

Our methods embed values, but we have tended to write about them as if they were value-neutral and generalizable. We are not alone. In a survey of behavioral science journal papers, Henrich, Heine, and Norenzayan (2010a, 2010b) argue that results about human psychology and behavior have been based on studies that sampled Western, educated, industrialized, rich, and democratic (WEIRD) populations. They argue that the lack of consideration of whether these subject pools are globally representative has produced broad claims that may not actually be generalizable to all people. Closer to home, Bidwell and Winschiers-Theophilus (2010) have written eloquently about the challenges of using HCI textbooks in their classes, finding that what we may consider value-neutral texts contain assumptions that collide with those held by their students.

Said (1993) shows how Lord Cromer's methods of managing Egypt took no account of Egyptians because they were subjects of and subject to British colonial occupation. That is not a choice for HCI. However we approach human-computer interaction, participation by the researched is, and has always been, required. And in HCI4D that has meant adapting and innovating methods that facilitate more meaningful participation (Anokwa et al., 2009; Irani and Silberman, 2013; Lutz and Collins, 1993; Putnam et al., 2009; Winschiers-Theophilus and Bidwell, 2013; Winschiers-Theophilus et al., 2010). As a result, we have methods that are customized to work with particular people, places, and problems.

This in turn begs the question of what it means if our methods do not work everywhere. One solution might be to strive to maintain a separation of HCI and HCI4D, but we should resist that. Separating HCI4D out runs the risk that it becomes a collection of settings where traditional HCI methods do not work, and allowing us to preserve, dare I say it, a false sense of their generalizability where those breakdowns do not occur. I say this as an advocate for HCI4D, but also as someone one who ultimately wants to see it as a part of a vision of HCI that is about supporting human-computer interaction for anyone, anywhere. This is especially important as our agenda expands to explicitly account for differences within countries that have long been in focus for HCI (e.g., focus on race and class in the United States [2, 14, 15, 40]). As HCI4D is currently defined, work within the United States and Europe would not be included, but these settings may also require reflection on our methods [33].

There is a body of knowledge to build about the assumptions and values embedded in our methods, a contribution to understanding of the third paradigm of HCI proposed by Harrison, Sengers, and Tatar (2011), who describe a science that is socially, culturally, politically, and historically situated. This body of knowledge also asks the HCI community to be more careful about the presentation of its methods. That does not make the methods wrong, it just gives them focus and makes their assumptions available so that we can decide when and with whom to use them, while building a broader base of alternatives that work well and allow us to continue to build useful and usable technologies for different people in different places. The HCI community has the opportunity to be a leader in how we handle that diversity and how we manage our methods and make appropriately scoped claims.

Concluding Thoughts

In this chapter I focused on HCI4D because it offers a starting point that echoes *Orientalism*'s focus on relations between Western producers of knowledge and non-Western "others" studied, and because the ICTD research community offers valuable reflections on issues that Said addresses. But I do not believe that HCI is somehow exempt from these questions, particularly as we embark—and I include myself in this—on agendas with the underserved and underrepresented. But it runs deeper than that. Said's writings confront us with something we've always told others and ourselves—that HCI is the discipline of not designing for ourselves but for others. We have always been focused on the other, the reason we evolved our methods, theories, and practices. Said invites us to take up the question of the other. What is the role of the researcher-author in the creation of texts (such as papers, personas, measurements, slides)? What are the power relationships between the authors and those represented within the texts? What does it mean to export our methods and what would it mean to design indigenous responses? In this chapter I surface some possible responses and offer some suggestions for possible directions for HCI, but this just scratches the surface. There is far more to discover.

Finally, Said was an advocate for the intellectual in public life. He was passionate about using his understanding of the problems of Orientalism not just to further scholarship but also in political action (Bardzell, 2010; Bidwell and Winschiers-Theophilus, 2010). In his Reith lectures (1993) he argues that this should be achieved through clarity of writing, not by using "approved jargon of a group of insiders." I agree: in communicating the value of postcolonial arguments to HCI's research and practitioner community, we will need to be clear, forsaking the use of overly specialized and obscure terminology. I hope I have achieved that here. Said's commitment to using scholarship to engage in policy reminds me of HCI4D and ICTD. Scholars in those fields have often decided that despite the difficulties of development doing something is better than just criticizing the status quo (Le Dantec and Fox, 2015). I hope that this chapter encourages people to go forward with these theories rather than feeling trapped in a type of criticism that deconstructs but provides very little help with what next. It is in the "what next" that HCI will be moved forward, and postcolonialism offers exciting possibilities.

Acknowledgments

I would like to thank Susan Wyche, Jonathan Grudin, Ellen Zegura, and the anonymous reviewers for their advice, feedback, and suggestions. I thank Shaowen Bardzell, Jeffrey Bardzell, and Mark Blythe for taking a chance on me. Lilly Irani introduced me to postcolonialism and her research continues to be a source of inspiration. Finally, I dedicate this to Gary Marsden, who made a difference. I hope that in a small way I have continued to encourage reflection on and advocacy for a more inclusive, change-based HCI.

Note

1. One area of HCI where people are raising the question of advantage associated with institutional affiliation is in "big data" research. Specifically, given that many of the largest data sets are owned by commercial corporations, it is recognized that there is an advantage to being associated

with those corporations, and that university researchers may have a harder time in this research space (boyd and Crawford, 2012).

References

Ahmed, S. I., S. J. Jackson, N. Ahmed, H. S. Ferdous, M. R. Rifat, A. S. M. Rizvi, S. Ahmed, and R. S. Mansur. (2014) "*Protibadi:* A Platform for Fighting Sexual Harassment in Urban Bangladesh." *Proceedings of the SIGCHI Conference on Human Factors in Computing Systems (CHI'14).* New York: ACM, 2695–2704.

Ames, M., J. Go, J. J. Kaye, and M. Spasojevic. (2011) "Understanding Technology Choices and Values through Social Class." *Proceedings of the ACM 2011 Conference on Computer-Supported Cooperative Work (CSCW'11).* New York: ACM, 55–64.

Anokwa, Y., T. N. Smyth, D. Ramachandran, J. Sherwani, Y. Schwartzman, R. Luk, M. Ho, N. Moraveji, and B. DeRenzi. (2009) "Stories from the Field: Reflections on HCI4D Experiences." *Information Technologies and International Development* 5 (4): 101–116.

Ashcroft, B., and P. Ahluwalia. (2001) *Edward Said.* New York: Routledge.

Bardzell, S. (2010) "Feminist HCI: Taking Stock and Outlining an Agenda for Design." *Proceedings of the SIGCHI Conference on Human Factors in Computing Systems (CHI'10).* New York: ACM, 1301–1310.

Bardzell, S., and Bardzell, J. (2011) "Towards a Feminist HCI Methodology: Social Science, Feminism, and HCI." *Proceedings of the SIGCHI Conference on Human Factors in Computing Systems (CHI'11).* New York: AMC, 675–684.

Bidwell, N. J., and H. Winschiers-Theophilus. (2010) "UNDER DEVELOPMENT: Beyond the Benjamins: Toward an African Interaction Design." *Interactions* 17 (1): 32–35.

Blake, E. H., and W. D. Tucker. (2006) "User Interfaces for Communication Bridges across the Digital Divide." *AI and Society* 20 (2): 232–242.

boyd, d., and K. Crawford. (2012) "Critical Questions for Big Data: Provocations for a Cultural, Technological, and Scholarly Phenomenon." *Information, Communication and Society* 15 (5): 662–679.

Chetty, M., W. Tucker, and E. Blake. (2004) "Developing Locally Relevant Software Applications for Rural Areas: A South African Example." *Proceedings of the 2004 Annual Research Conference of the South African Institute of Computer Scientists and Information Technologists on IT Research in Developing Countries (SAICSIT'04).* South Africa: SAICSIT, 239–243.

Dearden, A., and H. Rizvi. (2008) "Participatory IT Design and Participatory Development: A Comparative Review." *Proceedings of the Tenth Anniversary Conference on Participatory Design (PDC'08).* New York: AMC, 81–91.

Dewey, C. (2013) "Kenyans Mock Foreign Media Coverage on Twitter." *Washington Post,* March 4. http://www.washingtonpost.com/blogs/worldviews/wp/2013/03/04/kenyans-mock-foreign-media-coverage-on-twitter/.

Dillahunt, T. R. (2014) "Fostering Social Capital in Economically Distressed Communities." *Proceedings of the SIGCHI Conference on Human Factors in Computing Systems.* New York: ACM, 531–540.

Dillahunt, T. R., J. Mankoff, E. Paulos, and S. Fussell. (2009) "It's Not All About 'Green': Energy Use in Low-Income Communities." *Proceedings of the 11th International Conference on Ubiquitous Computing (UbiComp'09).* New York: ACM, 255–264.

Dimond, J. P., M. Dye, D. Larose, and A. S. Bruckman. (2013) "Hollaback!: The Role of Storytelling Online in a Social Movement Organization." *Proceedings of the 2013 Conference on Computer-Supported Cooperative Work (CSCW'13).* New York: ACM, 477–490.

Dourish, P., and S. D. Mainwaring. (2012) "Ubicomp's Colonial Impulse." *Proceedings of the 2012 ACM Conference on Ubiquitous Computing.* New York: ACM, 133–142.

Dray, S. M., D. A. Siegel, and P. Kotzé. (2003) "Indra's Net: HCI in the Developing World." *Interactions* 10 (2): 28–37.

Elovaara, P., F. T. Igira, and C. Mörtberg. (2006) "Whose Participation? Whose Knowledge? Exploring PD in Tanzania-Zanzibar and Sweden." *Proceedings of the Ninth Conference on Participatory Design: Expanding Boundaries in Design (PDC'06),* vol. 1. New York: ACM, 105–114.

Gitau, S., P. Plantinga, and K. Diga. (2010) "ICTD Research by Africans: Origins, Interests, and Impact." *Proceedings of Information and Communication Technologies and Development (ICTD'10).* London: IEEE Press.

Grinter, R. E., and M. Eldridge. (2001) "y do tngrs luv 2 txt msg?" *Proceedings of the Seventh European Conference on Computer-Supported Cooperative Work (ECSCW'01).* Dordrecht: Kluwer Academic, 219–238.

Harrison, S., P. Sengers, and D. Tatar. (2011) "Making Epistemological Trouble: Third-Paradigm HCI as Successor Science." *Interacting with Computers* 23 (5): 385–292.

Heeks, R. (1999) "The Tyranny of Participation in Information Systems: Learning from Development Projects." Working Paper. Institute for Development Policy and Management, University of Manchester, Manchester, UK. Accessed October 20, 2017. http://www.participatorymethods.org/resource/tyranny-participation-information-systems-learning-development-projects.

Henrich, J., S. J. Heine, and A. Norenzayan. (2010a) "Most People Are Not WEIRD." *Nature* 466 (29): doi:10.1038/466029a.

Henrich, J., S. J. Heine, and A. Norenzayan. (2010b) "The Weirdest People in the World?" *Behavioral and Brain Sciences* 33 (2–3): 61–83.

Ho, M. R., T. N. Smyth, M. Kam, and A. Dearden. (2009) "Human-Computer Interaction for Development: The Past, Present, and Future." *Information Technologies and International Development* 5 (4): 1–18.

Irani, L. C., and M. S. Silberman. (2013) "Turkopticon: Interrupting Work Invisibility in Amazon Mechanical Turk." *Proceedings of the SIGCHI Conference on Human Factors in Computing Systems (CHI'13).* New York: ACM, 611–620.

Irani, L. C., J. Vertesi, P. Dourish, K. Philip, and R. E. Grinter. (2010) "Postcolonial Computing: A Lens on Design and Development." *Proceedings of the SIGCHI Conference on Human Factors in Computing Systems (CHI'10).* New York: ACM, 1311–1320.

Kam, M., D. Ramachandran, A. Raghavan, J. Chiu, U. Sahni, and J. Canny. (2006) "Practical Considerations for Participatory Design with Rural School Children in Underdeveloped Regions: Early Reflections from the Field." *Proceedings of the 2006 Conference on Interaction Design and Children.* New York: AMC, 25–32.

Karanja, M. (2010) "Myth Shattered: Kibera Numbers Fail to Add Up." *Daily Nation,* September 3, http://www.nation.co.ke/News/Kibera-numbers-fail-to-add-up/-/1056/1003404/-/2lmrpq/-/index.html.

Kensing, F., and J. Blomberg. (1998) "Participatory Design: Issues and Concerns." *Computer-Supported Cooperative Work* 7 (3–4): 167–185.

Kleine, D. (2013) *Technologies of Choice? ICTs, Development, and the Capabilities Approach.* Cambridge, MA: MIT Press.

Le Dantec, C. A., and S. Fox. (2015) "Strangers at the Gate: Gaining Access, Building Rapport, and Co-Constructing Community-Based Research." *Proceedings of the 18th ACM Conference on Computer Supported Cooperative Work & Social Computing (CSCW'15).* New York: ACM, 1348–1358.

Light, A., N. Sambasivan, S. Gitau, I. Ladeira, N. J. Bidwell, J. Roberson, and N. Rangaswamy. (2010) "Gender Matters: Female Perspectives in ICT4D Research." *Proceedings of the 4th IEEE/AMC Conference on Information and Communication Technologies and International Development (ICTD'10).* N.p.: IEEE Press.

Lutz, C.A., and J. L. Collins. (1993) *Reading National Geographic.* Chicago: University of Chicago Press.

Marsden, G., A. Maunder, and M. Parker. (2008) "People Are People, but Technology Is Not Technology." *Philosophical Transactions of the Royal Society A* 366 (1881): 3795–3804.

Mbarika, V., and P. Meso. (2008) "Information Systems Research for Africa: A Renewed Focus." *African Journal of Information Systems* 1 (1): i–iv.

Merritt, S., and E. Stolterman. (2012) "Cultural Hybridity in Participatory Design." *Proceedings of the 12th Participatory Design Conference: Exploratory Papers, Workshop Descriptions, Industry Cases,* vol. 2. New York: ACM, 73–76.

Miller, D., and D. Slater. (2000) *The Internet: An Ethnographic Approach.* Oxford: Berg.

Parker, A. G., V. Kantroo, H. R. Lee, M. Osornio, M. Sharma, and R. E. Grinter. (2012) "Health Promotion as Activism: Building Community Capacity to Effect Social Change." *Proceedings of the SIGCHI Conference on Human Factors in Computing Systems (CHI'12).* New York: ACM, 99–108.

Puri, S. K., E. Byrne, J. L. Nhampossa, and Z. B. Quraishi. (2004) "Contextuality of Participation in IS Design: A Developing Country Perspective." *Proceedings of the Eighth Conference on Participatory*

Design: Artful Integration: Interweaving Media, Materials and Practices (PDC'04), vol. 1. New York: ACM, 42–52.

Putnam, C., E. Rose, E. J. Johnson, and B. Kolko. (2009) "Adapting User-Centered Design Methods to Design for Diverse Populations." *Information Technologies and International Development* 5 (4): 51–74.

Quayson, A. (2000) *Postcolonialism: Theory, Practice or Process?* Cambridge: Polity Press.

Said, E. (1978) *Orientalism*. New York: Random House.

Said, E. (1993) "Edward Said: Representation of the Intellectual: 1993." *The Reith Lectures*. BBC Radio 4. http://www.bbc.co.uk/programmes/p00gmx4c.

Shroff, G., and M. Kam. (2011) "Towards a Design Model for Women's Empowerment in the Developing World." *Proceedings of the SIGCHI Conference on Human Factors in Computing Systems (CHI'11)*. New York: ACM, 2867–2876.

Toyama, K. (2010) "Human-Computer Interaction and Global Development." *Foundations and Trends in Human-Computer Interaction* 4 (1): 1–79.

Unwin, T., ed. (2009) *ICT4D: Information and Communication Technology for Development*. Cambridge: Cambridge University Press.

Walton, M. (2010) "Social Distance, Mobility and Place: Global and Intimate Genres in Geo-Tagged Photographs of Guguletu, South Africa." *Proceedings of the 8th ACM Conference on Designing Interactive Systems (DIS'10)*. New York: ACM, 35–38.

Winschiers-Theophilus, H., and N. J. Bidwell. (2013) "Toward an AfroCentric Indigenous HCI Paradigm." *International Journal of Human-Computer Interaction* 29 (4): 243–255.

Winschiers-Theophilus, H., S. Chivuno-Kuria, G. K. Kapuire, N. J. Bidwell, and E. Blake. (2010) "Being Participated: A Community Approach." *Proceedings of the 11th Biennial Participatory Design Conference (PDC'10)*. New York: ACM, 1–10.

Wyche, S. P., A. Forte, and S. Y. Schoenebeck. (2013) "Hustling Online: Understanding Consolidated Facebook Use in an Informal Settlement in Nairobi." *Proceedings of the SIGCHI Conference on Human Factors in Computing Systems (CHI'13)*.New York: ACM, 2823–2832.

Wyche, S. P., G. R. Hayes, L. D. Harvel, and R. E. Grinter. (2006) "Technology in Spiritual Formation: An Exploratory Study of Computer Mediated Religious Communication." *Proceedings of the ACM Conference on Computer-Supported Cooperative Work (CSCW'06)*. New York: ACM, 199–208.

39 The Generalized and the Concrete Other (1992)

Seyla Benhabib

What concerns me in this chapter is the question: what can feminist theory contribute to this debate? Since Kohlberg himself regards an interaction between normative philosophy and the empirical study of moral development as essential to his theory, the insights of contemporary feminist theory and philosophy can be brought to bear upon some aspects of his theory.[1] I want to define two premises as constituents of feminist theorizing. First, for feminist theory the gender-sex system is not a contingent but an essential way in which social reality is organized, symbolically divided and lived through experientially. By the "gender-sex" system I understand the social-historical, symbolic constitution, and interpretation of the anatomical differences of the sexes. The gender-sex system is the grid through which the self develops an *embodied* identity, a certain mode of being in one's body and of living the body. The self becomes an I in that it appropriates from the human community a mode of psychically, socially and symbolically experiencing its bodily identity. The gender-sex system is the grid through which societies and cultures reproduce embodied individuals.[2]

Second, the historically known gender-sex systems have contributed to the oppression and exploitation of women. The task of feminist critical theory is to uncover this fact, and to develop a theory that is emancipatory and reflective, and which can aid women in their struggles to overcome oppression and exploitation. Feminist theory can contribute to this task in two ways: by developing an *explanatory-diagnostic analysis* of women's oppression across history, culture and societies, and by articulating an *anticipatory-utopian critique* of the norms and values of our current society and culture, such as to project new modes of togetherness, of relating to ourselves and to nature in the future. Whereas the first aspect of feminist theory requires critical, social-scientific research, the second is primarily normative and philosophical: it involves the clarification of moral and political principles, both at the meta-ethical level with respect to their logic of justification and at the substantive, normative level with reference to their concrete content.[3]

In this chapter I shall be concerned with articulating such an anticipatory-utopian critique of universalistic moral theories from a feminist perspective. I want to argue that the definition of the moral domain, as well as the ideal of moral autonomy, not only in Kohlberg's theory but in universalistic, contractarian theories from Hobbes to Rawls, lead to a *privatization* of women's experience and to the exclusion of its consideration from a moral point of view (part 1). In this tradition, the moral self is viewed as a *disembedded* and *disembodied* being. This conception of the self reflects aspects of male experience; the "relevant other" in this theory is never the sister but always the brother. This vision of the self, I want to claim, is incompatible with the very criteria of reversibility and universalizability advocated by defenders of universalism. A universalistic moral theory restricted to the standpoint of the "generalized other" falls into epistemic incoherencies that jeopardize its claim to adequately fulfill reversibility and universalizability (part 2).

Universalistic moral theories in the Western tradition from Hobbes to Rawls are substitutionalist, in the sense that the universalism they defend is defined surreptitiously by identifying the experiences of a specific group of subjects as the paradigmatic case of the human as such. These subjects are invariably white, male adults who are propertied or at least professional. I want to distinguish *substitutionalist* from *interactive* universalism. Interactive universalism acknowledges the plurality of modes of being human, and differences among humans, without endorsing all these pluralities and differences as morally and politically valid. While agreeing that normative disputes can be settled rationally, and that fairness, reciprocity and some procedure of universalizability are constituents, that is, necessary conditions of the moral standpoint, interactive universalism regards difference as a starting point for reflection and action. In this sense, "universality" is a regulative ideal that does not deny our embodied and embedded identity, but aims at developing moral attitudes and encouraging political transformations that can yield a point of view acceptable to all. Universality is not the ideal consensus of fictitiously defined selves, but the concrete process in politics and morals of the struggle of concrete, embodied selves, striving for autonomy.

1 Justice and the Autonomous Self in Social Contract Theories

Kohlberg defines the privileged object domain of moral philosophy and psychology as follows:

> We say that *moral* judgments or principles have the central function of resolving interpersonal or social conflicts, that is, conflicts of claims or rights.... Thus moral judgments and principles imply a notion of equilibrium, or reversibility of claims. In this sense they ultimately involve some reference to justice, at least insofar as they define "hard" structural stages. ("Synopses," p. 216)

Kohlberg's conception of the moral domain is based upon a strong differentiation between justice and the good life.[4] This is also one of the cornerstones of his critique of Gilligan. Although acknowledging that Gilligan's elucidation of a care-and-responsibility orientation "usefully enlarges the moral domain" ("Synopses," p. 340), Kohlberg defines the domain of *special relationships of obligation* to which care and responsibility are oriented as follows: "the spheres of kinship, love, friendship, and sex that elicit considerations of care are usually understood to be spheres of personal decision-making, as are, for instance, the problems of marriage and divorce" (pp. 229–30). The care orientation is said thus to concern domains that are more "personal" than "moral in the sense of the formal point of view" (p. 360). Questions of the good life, pertaining to the nature of our relationships of kinship, love, friendship and sex, on the one hand, are included in the moral domain but, on the other hand, are named "personal" as opposed to "moral" issues.

Kohlberg proceeds from a definition of morality that begins with Hobbes, in the wake of the dissolution of the Aristotelian-Christian world-view. Ancient and medieval moral systems, by contrast, show the following structure: a definition of man-as-he-ought-to-be, a definition of man-as-he-is, and the articulation of a set of rules or precepts that can lead man as he is into what he ought to be.[5] In such moral systems, the rules which govern just relations among the human community are embedded in a more encompassing conception of the good life. This good life, the telos of man, is defined ontologically with reference to man's place in the cosmos.

The destruction of the ancient and medieval teleological conception of nature through the attack of medieval nominalism and modern science, the emergence of capitalist exchange relations and the subsequent division of the social structure into the economy, the polity, civil associations and the domestic-intimate sphere, radically alter moral theory. Modern theorists claim that the ultimate purposes of nature are unknown. Morality is thus emancipated from cosmology and from an all-encompassing worldview that normatively limits man's relation to nature. The distinction between justice and the good life, as it is formulated by early contract theorists, aims at defending this privacy and autonomy of the self, first in the religious sphere and then in the scientific and philosophical spheres of "free thought" as well.

Justice alone becomes the center of moral theory when bourgeois individuals in a disenchanted universe face the task of creating the legitimate basis of the social order for themselves. What "ought" to be is now defined as what all would have rationally to agree to in order to ensure civil peace and prosperity (Hobbes, Locke), or the "ought" is derived from the rational form of the moral law alone (Rousseau, Kant). As long as the social bases of cooperation and the rights claims of individuals are respected, the autonomous bourgeois subject can define the good life as his mind and conscience dictate.

The transition to modernity does not only privatize the self's relation to the cosmos and to ultimate questions of religion and being. First with western modernity the conception of privacy is so enlarged that an intimate domestic-familial sphere is subsumed under it. Relations of "kinship, friendship, love, and sex," indeed, as Kohlberg takes them to be, come to be viewed as spheres of "personal decision-making." At the beginning of modern moral and political theory, however, the "personal" nature of the spheres does not mean the recognition of equal, female autonomy, but rather the removal of gender relations from the sphere of justice. While the bourgeois male celebrates his transition from conventional to post-conventional morality, from socially accepted rules of justice to their generation in light of the principles of a social contract, the domestic sphere remains at the conventional level. The sphere of justice from Hobbes through Locke and Kant is regarded as the domain where independent, male heads of household transact with one another, while the domestic-intimate sphere is put beyond the pale of justice and restricted to the reproductive and affective needs of the bourgeois paterfamilias. Agnes Heller has named this domain the "household of the emotions."[6] An entire domain of human activity, namely, nurture, reproduction, love and care, which becomes the woman's lot in the course of the development of modern, bourgeois society, is excluded from moral and political considerations, and relegated to the realm of "nature."

Through a brief historical genealogy of social contract theories, I want to examine the distinction between justice and the good life as it is translated into the split between the public and the domestic. This analysis will also allow us to see the implicit ideal of autonomy cherished by this tradition.

At the beginning of modern moral and political philosophy stands a powerful metaphor: the "state of nature." This metaphor is at times said to be fact. Thus, in his *Second Treatise of Civil Government*, John Locke reminds us of "the two men in the desert island, mentioned by Garcilasso de la Vega ... or a Swiss and an Indian, in the woods of America."[7] At other times it is acknowledges [*sic*] as fiction. Thus, Kant dismisses the colorful reveries of his predecessors and transforms the "state of nature" from an empirical fact into a transcendental concept. The state of nature comes to represent the idea of *Privatrecht*, under which are subsumed the right of property and "thinglike rights of a personal nature" ("auf dingliche Natur persönliche Rechte"), which the male head of a household exercises over his wife, children and servants.[8] Only Thomas Hobbes compounds fact and fiction, and against those who consider it strange "that Nature should thus dissociate, and render men apt to invade, and destroy one another,"[9] he asks each man who does not trust "this Inference, made from the passions," to reflect why "when taking a journey, he arms himself, and seeks to go well accompanied; when going to sleep, he lockes his dores; when even in his house he lockes his chests.... Does he not there as much accuse mankind by his actions, as I do by my words?" (*Leviathan*, p. 187). The state of nature is the looking glass of these early bourgeois thinkers in which they and their societies are magnified, purified and reflected in their original, naked verity. The state of nature is both nightmare (Hobbes) and utopia (Rousseau). In it the bourgeois male recognizes his flaws, fears and anxieties, as well as dreams.

The varying content of this metaphor is less significant than its simple and profound message: in the beginning man was alone. Again it is Hobbes who gives this thought its clearest formulation. "Let us consider men ... as if but even now sprung out of the earth, and suddenly, like mushrooms, come to full maturity, without all kind of engagement to each other."[10] This vision of men as mushrooms is an ultimate picture of autonomy. The female, the mother of whom every individual is born, is now replaced by the earth. The denial of being born of woman frees the male ego from the most natural and basic bond of dependence. Nor is the picture very different for Rousseau's noble savage who, wandering wantonly through the woods, occasionally mates with a female and then seeks rest.[11]

The state-of-nature metaphor provides a vision of the autonomous self: this is a narcissist who sees the world in his own image; who has no awareness of the limits of his own desires and passions; and who cannot see himself through the eyes of another. The narcissism of this sovereign self is destroyed by the presence of the other. As Hegel expresses it: "Self-consciousness is faced by another self-consciousness; it has come *out of itself*. This has a twofold significance: first, it has *lost* itself, for it finds itself as an *other* being; secondly, in doing so it has superseded the other, for it does not see the other as an essential being, but in the other sees its own self."[12] The story of the autonomous male ego is the saga of this initial sense of *loss* in confrontation with the other, and the gradual recovery from this original narcissistic wound through the sobering experience of war, fear, domination, anxiety and death. The last installment in this drama is the social contract: the establishment of the law to govern all. Having been thrust out of their narcissistic universe into a world of insecurity by their sibling brothers, these individuals have to reestablish the authority of the father in the image of the law. The early bourgeois individual not only has no mother but no father as well; rather, he strives to reconstitute the father in his own self-image. What is usually celebrated in the annals of modern moral and political theory as the dawn of liberty is precisely this destruction of political patriarchy in bourgeois society.

The constitution of political authority civilizes sibling rivalry by turning their attention from war to property, from vanity to science, from conquest to luxury. The original narcissism is not transformed; only now ego boundaries are clearly defined. The law reduces insecurity, the fear of being engulfed by the other, by defining mine and thine. Jealousy is not eliminated but tamed; as long as each can keep what is his and attain more by fair rules of the game, he is entitled to it. Competition is domesticized and channeled towards acquisition. The law contains anxiety by defining rigidly the boundaries between self and other, but the law does not cure anxiety. The anxiety that the other is always on the lookout to interfere in your space and appropriate what is yours; the anxiety that you will be subordinated to his will; the anxiety that a group of brothers will usurp the law in the name of the "will of all" and destroy "the general will," the will of the absent father, remains. The law teaches how to repress anxiety and to sober narcissism, but the constitution of the self is not altered. The establishment of private rights and duties does not overcome the inner wounds of the self; it only forces them to become less destructive.

This imaginary device of early moral and political theory has had an amazing hold upon the modern consciousness. From Freud to Piaget, the relationship to the brother is viewed as the humanizing experience that teaches us to become social, responsible adults.[13] As a result of the hold of this metaphor upon our imagination, we have also come to inherit a number of philosophical prejudices. For Rawls and Kohlberg, as well, the autonomous self is disembedded and disembodied; moral impartiality is learning to recognize the claims of the other who is just like oneself; fairness is public justice; a public system of rights and duties is the best way to arbitrate conflict, to distribute rewards and to establish claims.

Yet this is a strange world; it is one in which individuals are grown up before they have been born; in which boys are men before they have been children; a world where neither mother, nor sister, nor wife exist. The question is not what Hobbes says about men and women, or what Rousseau sees the role of Sophie to be in Emile's education. The point is that in this universe the experience of the early modern female has no place. Woman is simply what man is not; namely they are not autonomous, independent, but by the same token, nonaggressive but nurturant, not competitive but giving, not public but private. The world of the female is constituted by a series of negations. She is simply what he happens not to be. Her identity becomes defined by a lack—the lack of autonomy, the lack of independence, the lack of the phallus. The narcissistic male takes her to be just like himself, only his opposite.

It is not the misogynist prejudices of early modern moral and political theory alone that lead to women's exclusion. It is the very constitution of a sphere of discourse which bans the female from history to the realm of nature, from the light of the public to the interior of the household, from the civilizing effect of culture to the repetitious burden of nurture and reproduction. The public sphere, the sphere of justice, moves into historicity, whereas the private sphere, the sphere of care and intimacy, is unchanging and timeless. It pulls us toward the earth even when we, as Hobbesian mushrooms, strive to pull away from it. The dehistoricization of the private realm signifies that, as the male ego celebrates his passage from nature to culture, from conflict to consensus, women remain in a timeless universe, condemned to repeat the cycles of life.

This split between the public sphere of justice, in which history is made, and the atemporal realm of the household, in which life is reproduced, is internalized by the male ego. The dichotomies are not only without but within. He himself is divided into the public person and the private individual. Within his chest clash the law of reason and the inclination of nature, the brilliance of cognition and the obscurity of emotion. Caught between the moral law and the starry heaven above and the earthly body below,[14] the autonomous self strives for unity. But the antagonism—between autonomy and nurturance, independence and bonding, sovereignty of the self and relations to others—remains. In the discourse of modem moral and political theory, these dichotomies are reified as being essential to the constitution of the self. While men humanize outer nature through labor, inner nature remains ahistorical, dark and obscure. I want to suggest that contemporary universalist moral theory has inherited this dichotomy between autonomy and nurturance, independence and bonding, the sphere of justice and the domestic, personal realm. This becomes most visible in its attempt to restrict the moral point of view to the perspective of the "generalized other."

2 The Generalized versus the Concrete Other

Let me describe two conceptions of self–other relations that delineate both moral perspectives and interactional structures. I shall name the first the standpoint of the "generalized"[15] and the second that of the "concrete" other. In contemporary moral theory these conceptions are viewed as incompatible, even as antagonistic. These two perspectives reflect the dichotomies and splits of early modem moral and political theory between autonomy and nurturance, independence and bonding, the public and the domestic, and more broadly, between justice and the good life. The content of the generalized as well as the concrete other is shaped by this dichotomous characterization, which we have inherited from the modern tradition.

The standpoint of the generalized other requires us to view each and every individual as a rational being entitled to the same rights and duties we would want to ascribe to ourselves. In assuming the standpoint, we abstract from the individuality and concrete identity of the other. We assume that the other, like ourselves, is a being who has concrete needs, desires and affects, but that what constitutes his or her moral dignity is not what differentiates us from each other, but rather what we, as speaking and acting rational agents, have in common. Our relation to the other is governed by the norms of *formal equality* and *reciprocity:* each is entitled to expect and to assume from us what we can expect and assume from him or her. The norms of our interactions are primarily public and institutional ones. If I have a right to X, then you have the duty not to hinder me from enjoying X and conversely. In treating you in accordance with these norms, I confirm in your person the rights of humanity and I have a legitimate claim to expect that you will do the same in relation to me. The moral categories that accompany such interactions are those of right, obligation and entitlement, and the corresponding moral feelings are those of respect, duty, worthiness and dignity.

The standpoint of the concrete other, by contrast, requires us to view each and every rational being as an individual with a concrete history, identity and affective-emotional constitution. In assuming this standpoint, we abstract from what constitutes our commonality, and focus on individuality. We seek to comprehend the needs of the other, his or her motivations, what she searches for, and what s/he desires. Our relation to the other is governed by the norms of *equity* and *complementary reciprocity:* each is entitled to expect and to assume from the other forms of behavior through which the other feels recognized and confirmed as a concrete, individual being with specific needs, talents and capacities. Our differences in this case complement rather than exclude one another. The norms of our interaction are usually, although not exclusively private, non-institutional ones. They are norms of friendship, love and care. These norms require in various ways that I exhibit more than the simple assertion of my rights and duties in the face of your needs. In treating you in accordance with the norms of friendship, love and care, I confirm not only your *humanity* but your human *individuality.* The moral categories that accompany such interactions are those of responsibility, bonding and sharing. The corresponding moral feelings are those of love, care and sympathy and solidarity.

In contemporary universalist moral psychology and moral theory, it is the viewpoint of the "generalized other" that predominates. In his article on "Justice as Reversibility: The Claim to Moral Adequacy of a Highest Stage of Moral Development," for example, Kohlberg argues that:

> moral judgments involve role-taking, taking the viewpoint of the others conceived as *subjects* and coordinating these viewpoints.... Second, equilibriated moral judgments involve principles of justice of fairness. A moral situation in disequilibrium is one in which there are unresolved, conflicting claims. A resolution of the situation is one in which each is "given his due" according to some principle of justice that can be recognized as fair by all the conflicting parties involved.[16]

Kohlberg regards Rawl's concept of "reflective equilibrium" as a parallel formulation of the basic ideas of reciprocity, equality and fairness intrinsic to all moral judgments. The Rawlsian "veil of ignorance," in Kohlberg's judgment, not only exemplifies the formalist idea of universalizability but that of perfect *reversibility* as well.[17] The idea behind the veil of ignorance is described as follows: "The decider is to initially decide from a point of view *that ignores his identity* (veil of ignorance) under the assumption that decisions are governed by maximizing values from a viewpoint of rational egoism in considering each party's interest" ("Justice as Reversibility," p. 200; my emphasis).

What I would like to question is the assumption that "taking the viewpoint of others" is truly compatible with this notion of fairness as reasoning behind a "veil of ignorance."[18] The problem is that the defensible kernel of the ideas of reciprocity and fairness are thereby identified with the perspective of the disembedded and disembodied generalized other. Now since Kohlberg presents his research subjects with hypothetically constructed moral dilemmas, it may be thought that his conception of "taking the standpoint of the other" is not subject to the epistemic restrictions that apply to the Rawlsian original position. Subjects in Kohlbergian interviews do not stand behind a veil of ignorance. However, the very language in which Kohlbergian dilemmas are presented incorporates these epistemic restrictions. For example, in the famous Heinz dilemma, as in others, the motivations of the druggist as a concrete individual, as well as the history of the individuals involved, are excluded as irrelevant to the definition of the moral problem at hand. In these dilemmas, individuals and their moral positions are represented by abstracting from the narrative history of the self and its motivations. Gilligan also notes that the implicit moral epistemology of Kohlbergian dilemmas frustrates women, who want to phrase these hypothetical dilemmas in a more contextual voice, attuned to the standpoint of the concrete other. The result is that

> though several of the women in the abortion study clearly articulate a postconventional metaethical position, none of them are considered principled in their normative moral judgments of Kohlberg's hypothetical dilemmas. Instead, the women's judgments point toward an identification of the violence inherent in the dilemma itself, which is seen to compromise the justice of any of its possible resolutions. (Gilligan, *In a Different Voice*, p. 101)

Through an immanent critique of the theories of Kohlberg and Rawls, I want to show that ignoring the standpoint of the concrete other leads to epistemic incoherence in universalistic moral theories. The problem can be stated as follows: according to Kohlberg and Rawls, moral reciprocity involves the capacity to take the standpoint of the other, to put oneself imaginatively in the place of the other, but under conditions of the "veil of ignorance" the *other as different from the self* disappears. Unlike in previous contract theories, in this case the other is not constituted through projection, but as a consequence of total abstraction from his or her identity. Differences are not denied; they become irrelevant. The Rawlsian self does not know

> his place in society, his class position or status; nor does he know his fortune in the distribution of natural assets and abilities, his intelligence and strength, and the like. Nor, again, does anyone know his conception of the good, the particulars of his rational plan of life, or even the special features of his psychology such as his aversion to risk or liability to optimism or pessimism.[19]

Let us ignore for a moment whether such selves who also do not know "the particular circumstances of their own society" can know anything at all that is relevant to the human condition, and ask instead, are these individuals *human selves* at all? In his attempt to do justice to Kant's conception of noumenal agency, Rawls recapitulates a basic problem with the Kantian conception of the self, namely, that noumenal selves cannot be *individuated.* If all that belongs to them as embodied, affective, suffering creatures, their memory and history, their ties and relations to others, are to be subsumed under the phenomenal realm, then what we are left with is an empty mask that is everyone and no one. Michael Sandel points out that the difficulty in Rawls's conception derives from his attempt to be consistent with the Kantian concept of the autonomous self, as a being freely choosing his or her own ends in life.[20] However, this moral and political concept of autonomy slips into a metaphysics according to which it is meaningful to define a self independently of *all* the ends it may choose and all and any conceptions of the good it may hold.[21] At this point we must ask whether the identity of any human self can be defined with reference to its capacity for agency alone. Identity does not refer to my potential for choice alone, but to the actuality of my choices, namely to how I, as a finite, concrete, embodied individual, shape and fashion the circumstances of my birth and family, linguistic, cultural and gender identity into a coherent narrative that stands as my life's story. Indeed, if we recall that every autonomous being is one born of others and not, as Rawls, following Hobbes, assumes, a being "not bound by prior moral ties to another,"[22] the question becomes: how does this finite, embodied creature constitute into a coherent narrative those episodes of choice and limitation, agency and suffering, initiative and dependence? The self is not a thing, a substrate, but the protagonist of a life's tale. The conception of selves who can be individuated prior to their moral ends is incoherent. We could not know if such a being was a human self, an angel, or the Holy Spirit.

If this concept of the self as mushroom, behind a veil of ignorance, is incoherent, then it follows that there is no real plurality of perspectives in the Rawlsian original position, but only a definitional identity. For Rawls, as Sandel observes, "our individuating characteristics are given empirically, by the distinctive concatenation of wants and desires, aims and attributes, purposes and ends that come to characterize human beings in their particularity."[23] But how are we supposed to know what these wants and desires are independently of knowing something about the person who holds these wants, desires, aims and attributes? Is there perhaps an "essence" of anger that is the same for each angry individual; an essence of ambition that is distinct from ambitious selves? I fail to see how individuating characteristics can be ascribed to a transcendental self who can have any and none of these, who can be all or none of them.

If selves who are epistemologically and metaphysically prior to their individuating characteristics, as Rawls takes them to be, cannot be human selves at all; if, therefore, there is no human *plurality* behind the veil of ignorance but only *definitional identity*, then this has consequences for criteria of reversibility and universalizability said to be constituents of the moral point of view. Definitional identity leads to *incomplete reversibility*, for the primary requisite of reversibility, namely, a coherent distinction between me and you, the self and the other, cannot be sustained under these circumstances. Under conditions of the veil of ignorance, the other disappears.

It is no longer plausible to maintain that such a standpoint can universalize adequately. Kohlberg views the veil of ignorance not only as exemplifying reversibility but universalizability as well. This is the idea that "we must be willing to live with our judgment or decision when we trade places with others in the situation being judged."[24] But the question is, *which* situation? Can moral situations be individuated independently of our knowledge of the agents involved in these situations, of their histories, attitudes, characters and desires? Can I describe a situation as one of arrogance or hurt pride without knowing something about you as a concrete other? Can I know how to distinguish between a breach of confidence and a harmless slip of the tongue, without knowing your history and your character? Moral situations, like moral emotions and attitudes, can only be individuated if they are evaluated in light of our knowledge of the history of the agents involved in them.

While every procedure of universalizability presupposes that "like cases ought to be treated alike" or that I should act in such a way that I should also be willing that all others in a like situation act like me, the most difficult aspect of any such procedure is to know what constitutes a "like" situation or what it would mean for another to be exactly in a situation like mine. Such a process of reasoning, to be at all viable, must involve the viewpoint of the concrete other, for situations, to paraphrase Stanley Cavell, do not come like "envelopes and golden finches" ready for definition and description, "nor like apples ripe for grading."[25] When we morally disagree, for example, we do not only disagree about the principles involved; very often we disagree because what I see as a lack of generosity on your part you construe as your legitimate right not to do something; we disagree because what you see as jealousy on my part I view as my desire to have more of your attention. Universalistic moral theory neglects such everyday, interactional morality and assumes that the public standpoint of justice, and our quasi-public personalities as right-bearing individuals, are the center of moral theory.[26]

Kohlberg emphasizes the dimension of ideal role-taking or taking the viewpoint of the other in moral judgment. Because he defines the other as the generalized other, however, he perpetuates one of the fundamental errors of Kantian moral theory. Kant's error was to assume that I, as a pure rational agent reasoning for myself, could reach a conclusion that would be acceptable for all at all times and places.[27] In Kantian moral theory, moral agents are like geometricians in different rooms who, reasoning alone for themselves, all arrive at the same solution to a problem. Following Habermas, I want to name this the "monological" model of moral reasoning. Insofar as he interprets ideal role-taking in the light of Rawls's concept of a "veil of ignorance," Kohlberg as well sees the silent thought process of a single self who imaginatively puts himself in the position of the other as the most adequate form of moral judgment.

I conclude that a definition of the self that is restricted to the standpoint of the generalized other becomes incoherent and cannot individuate among selves. Without assuming the standpoint of the concrete other, no coherent universalizability test can be carried out, for we lack the necessary epistemic information to judge my moral situation to be "like" or "unlike" yours.

Notes

1. For background context on the Kohlberg-Gilligan debate that sets up this chapter, see chapter 40.

2. Let me explain the status of this premise. I would characterize it as a "second-order research hypothesis" that both guides concrete research in the social sciences and can, in turn, be falsified by them. It is not a statement of faith about the way the world is: the cross-cultural and transhistorical universality of the sex-gender system is an empirical fact. It is also most definitely not a normative proposition about the way the world *ought* to be. To the contrary, feminism radically challenges the validity of the sex-gender system in organizing societies and cultures, and advocates the emancipation of men and women from the unexamined and oppressive grids of this framework.

3. For further clarification of these two aspects of critical theory, see part 2, "The Transformation of Critique," in my *Critique, Norm, and Utopia: A Study of the Foundations of Critical Theory* (Columbia University Press, New York, 1986).

4. Although frequently invoked by Kohlberg, Nunner-Winkler and also Habermas, it is still unclear *how* this distinction is drawn and how it is justified. For example, does the justice/good life distinction correspond to the sociological definitions of the public versus the private? If so, what is meant by the "private"? Is women-battering a "private" or a "public" matter? As I have argued in chapter 3 above, the relevant sociological definitions of the private and the public are shifting in our societies, as they have shifted historically.

5. Alasdair MacIntyre, *After Virtue* (University of Notre Dame Press, Notre Dame, 1981), pp. 50–1.

6. Agnes Heller, *A Theory of Feelings* (Van Gorcum, Holland, 1979), pp. 184ff.

7. John Locke, "The Second Treatise of Civil Government," in *Two Treatises of Government*, ed. and introd. Thomas I. Cook (Haffner, New York, 1947), p. 128.

8. Immanuel Kant, *The Metaphysical Elements of Justice*, trans. John Ladd (Liberal Arts Press, New York, 1965), p. 55.

9. Thomas Hobbes, *Leviathan* (1651), ed. and introd. C. B. Macpherson (Penguin, Harmondsworth, 1980), p. 186. All future citations in the text are to this edition.

10. Thomas Hobbes, "Philosophical Rudiments Concerning Government and Society," in *The English Works of Thomas Hobbes*, ed. W. Molesworth (Wissenschaftliche Buchgesellschaft, Darmstadt, 1966), vol. 2, p. 109.

11. J. J. Rousseau, "On the Origin and Foundations of Inequality Among Men," in Rousseau, *The First and Second Discourse*, ed. R. D. Masters, trans. Roger D. Masters and Judith R. Masters (St. Martin's, New York, 1964), p. 116.

12. G. W. F. Hegel, *Phänomenologie des Geistes*, 6th edn, ed. Johannes Hoffmeister (Felix Meiner, Hamburg, 1952), Philosophische Bibliothek 114, p. 141; translation used here *Phenomenology of Spirit*, trans. A. V. Miller (Clarendon, Oxford, 1977), p. 111.

13. Sigmund Freud, *Moses and Monthesim*, trans. Katharine Jones (Random House, New York, 1967), pp. 103ff.; Jean Piaget, *The Moral Judgment of the Child*, trans. Majorie Gabain (Free Press, New York, 1965), pp. 65ff., cf. the following comment on boys' and girls' games: "The most

superficial observation is sufficient to show that in the main the legal sense is far less developed in little girls than in boys. We did not succeed in finding a single collective game played by girls in which there were as many rules and, above all, as fine and consistent an organization and codification of these rules as in the game of marbles examined above" (p. 77).

14. Kant, "Critique of Practical Reason" in *Critique of Practical Reason and Other Writings in Moral Philosophy*, trans., ed. and introd. Louis White Beck (University of Chicago Press, Chicago, 1949), p. 258.

15. Although the term "generalized other" is borrowed from George Herbert Mead, my definition of it differs from his. Mead defines the "generalized other" as follows: "The organized community or social group which gives the individual his unity of self may be called the 'generalized other.' The attitude of the generalized other is the attitude of the whole community." George Herbert Mead, *Mind, Self and Society. From the Standpoint of a Social Behaviorist*, ed. and introd. Charles W. Morris (University of Chicago Press, Chicago, 1955), p. 154. Among such communities Mead includes a ball team as well as political clubs, corporations and other more abstract social classes or subgroups such as the class of debtors or the class of creditors (p. 157). Mead himself does not limit the concept of the "generalized other" to what is described in the text. In identifying the "generalized other" with the abstractly defined, legal and juridical subject, contract theorists and Kohlberg depart from Mead. Mead criticizes the social contract tradition precisely for distorting the psychosocial genesis of the individual subject, cf. ibid., p. 233.

16. Kohlberg, "Justice as Reversibility: The Claim to Moral Adequacy of a Highest Stage of Moral Judgment," in *Essays on Moral Development* (Harper and Row, San Francisco, 1981), vol. 1: *The Philosophy of Moral Development*, p. 194.

17. Whereas all forms of reciprocity involve some conceptions of reversibility these vary in degree: reciprocity can be restricted to the reversibility of actions but not of moral perspectives, to behavioral role models but not to the principles which underlie the generation of such behavioral expectations. For Kohlberg, the "veil of ignorance" is a model of perfect reversibility, for it elaborates the procedure of "ideal role-taking" or "moral musical chairs" where the decider "is to successively put himself imaginatively in the place of each other actor and consider the claims each would make from his point of view" (Kohlberg, "Justice as Reversibility," p. 199). My question is: are there any real "others" behind the "veil of ignorance" or are they indistinguishable from the self?

18. I find Kohlberg's general claim that the moral point of view entails reciprocity, equality and fairness unproblematic. Reciprocity is not only a fundamental *moral* principle, but defines, as Alvin Gouldner has argued, a fundamental *social norm*, perhaps in fact the very concept of a social norm: "The Norm of Reciprocity: A Preliminary Statement," *American Sociological Review*, 25 (April 1960), pp. 161–78. The existence of ongoing social relations in a human community entails some definition of reciprocity in the actions, expectations and claims of the group. The fulfillment of such reciprocity, according to whatever interpretation is given to it, would then be considered fairness by members of the group. Likewise, members of a group bound by relations of reciprocity and fairness are considered equal. What changes through history and culture are not these formal structures implicit in the very logic of social relations (we can even call

them social universals), but the criteria of inclusion and exclusion. Who constitutes the relevant human groups: Masters versus slaves, men versus women, Gentiles versus Jews? Similarly, which aspects of human behavior and objects of the world are to be regulated by norms of reciprocity: in the societies studied by Levi-Strauss, some tribes exchange sea shells for women. Finally, in terms of what is the equality among members of a group established: would this be gender, race, merit, virtue, or entitlement? Clearly Kohlberg presupposes a *universalist-egalitarian* interpretation of reciprocity, fairness and equality, according to which all humans, in virtue of their mere humanity, are to be considered beings entitled to reciprocal rights and duties.

19. John Rawls, *A Theory of Justice*, 2nd edn. (Harvard University Press, Cambridge Mass., 1971), p. 137

20. Michael J. Sandel, *Liberalism and the Limits of Justice* (Harvard University Press, Cambridge, Mass., 1982), p. 9.

21. Ibid., pp. 47ff.

22. Rawls, *A Theory of Justice*, p. 128.

23. Sandel, *Liberalism and the Limits of Justice*, p. 51.

24. Kohlberg: "Justice as Reversibility," p. 197.

25. Stanley Cavell, *The Claims of Reason* (Oxford University Press, Oxford, 1982), p. 265.

26. A most suggestive critique of Kohlberg's neglect of interpersonal morality has been developed by Norma Haan in "Two Moralities in Action Contexts," pp. 286–305. Haan reports that "formulation of formal morality appears to apply best to special kinds of hypothetical, rule-governed dilemmas, the paradigmatic situation in the minds of philosophers over the centuries" (p. 302). Interpersonal reasoning, by contrast, "arises within the context of moral dialogues between agents who strive to achieve balanced agreement, based on compromises they reach or on their joint discovery of interest they hold in common" (p. 303). For a more extensive statement, see also Norma Haan, "An Interactional Morality of Everyday Life," in *Social Science as Moral Inquiry*, pp. 218–51.

27. Cf. E. Tugendhat, "Zur Entwicklung von moralischen Begründungsstrukturen in modernen Recht," *Archiv für Recht of Sozialphilosophie*, vol. 69 (1980), pp. 1–20.

40 Through the "Cracks and Fissures" in the Smart Home to Ubiquitous Utopia

Shaowen Bardzell

Interaction designers seeking to bring about social change in an ethical way, such as those in domains like the developing world, poverty, sustainability, health, social justice, democratization of technology, gender, and so forth, face daunting practical challenges that go far beyond issues of traditional usability. Designers are responsible not just for interfaces, but for complicity in social configurations, norms, roles, and access; they reinforce, undermine, or transform power relations; designers inscribe social values that shape the experiences of users, stakeholders, and society itself; they assert claims about "the good" and through their designs propose actions, practices, and methods of realizing it. The sociopolitical consequences of design are more obvious in some areas of HCI than others: in ubiquitous computing, for example, researchers are designing for "smart cities"—but what makes a city "smart"? Who decides which IT infrastructural initiatives, which information needs, and which areas of the city are served first? How should the following be prioritized in smart cities: attracting new business, improving the overall IT infrastructure for everyone, alleviating the suffering of the city's poorest inhabitants, attracting tourists?

To what extent designers act on or distribute the moral and political agency is variable. Many design methodologies deploy structural mechanisms to help diffuse this power and give voice and agency to users and stakeholders, including user-centered design (UCD) (e.g., Gould and Lewis, 1985; popularized in books like Kuniavsky, 2003) and in a more systemic way, participatory design (PD) (e.g., Nygaard, 1990; Simonsen and Robertson, 2013). But even with such methodologies, it is by no means clear how to design in an ethical or democratic way for robustly networked digital cities fifteen years from now (which is a common framing in ubicomp), for improving the quality of life while respecting existing ways of life for those living in developing areas of the world (which is a common framing in HCI4D), or for designing technologies to accommodate the collapse of cities and perhaps civilization itself as a consequence of climate change (Tomlinson et al., 2012). Interaction design in these contexts is almost a form of civilization design. We may not want to take these challenges on, but we have no choice. Because of the extraordinary ethical burdens that designers collectively face, it seems reasonable to argue that we need to develop theory and methodologies to support us in these roles.

One resource for relevant theories, concept systems, and methodologies is the realm of philosophical ethics. Focusing on questions of how to develop social structures that are truly democratic, how to live the good life, how to decide which actions are best or most just, philosophical ethics would seem to provide a trove of conceptual and methodological resources that could be appropriated within design fields that are—willingly or not—actors in massive-scale social change.

The work of feminist philosopher Seyla Benhabib has resonated with me personally, and I hope to use this commentary to explain why. Simply, I argue that Benhabib's ethical philosophy suggests practical approaches to achieving ambitious social change in a robustly democratic way, and I believe that interaction design can and should participate in such a program. Indeed, Benhabib's work can be characterized as *utopian*, though unlike much utopian thinking hers is solidly democratic and pragmatic in its orientation.

In this chapter, I outline the overall project of Benhabib's (1992) book *Situating the Self: Gender, Community and Postmodernism in Contemporary Ethics* to set the background context for the reading I've included in this volume, which is the fifth chapter of Benhabib's book, "The Generalized and the Concrete Other" (see chapter 39). Broadly speaking, in this chapter Benhabib expresses concern that postmodern attacks on Enlightenment rationality have swung too hard in the opposite direction, threatening to flatten all normative thinking into relativism. For example, common postmodern arguments critique Western science and philosophy's claims to "truth" as serving and perpetuating dominant ideologies and social classes and/or resting on rotten foundations and being internally incoherent. (Similar positions are also vogue in HCI and are well represented in this book, such as the commentaries on Judith Butler [chapter 22], Michel Foucault [chapter 34], and James C. Scott [chapter 36]; philosopher Jacques Derrida's deconstruction is another major theory in this tradition.)

Postmodernism is problematic for Benhabib and other thinkers (see, e.g., Latour's and Eagleton's articles, chapters 23 and 25), because its relativism threatens to deny any basis to say that one way of life is significantly better than another. The challenge that Benhabib takes up, then, is to develop a philosophical ethics that is both substantively responsive to postmodern critiques of rationalism, social engineering, and traditional (authoritarian) utopias, and that nonetheless leaves moral, intellectual, and practical space for a more democratic utopian social imaginary. As a way both to introduce and also to demonstrate the usefulness of Benhabib's thinking, I work through her arguments with an example from ubiquitous computing: the vision of "Heterogeneous Home" developed by Intel Research (Aipperspach, Hooker, and Woodruff, 2007, 2008). I argue that the reasoning behind "Heterogeneous Home" bears many of the epistemological hallmarks of traditional Enlightenment rationalism. I next explore an alternative framing from feminism (i.e., care ethics), then follow Benhabib to argue why both, their virtues notwithstanding, are limited but also lay the groundwork for a framing that is more promising. To conclude the commentary, I return to the question of the utopian in HCI and specifically which aspects of thinkers like Benhabib can best serve as resources for our own utopianism.

Selves and Others: Benhabib's Feminist Universalism

Much feminist thought is skeptical about universal claims, arguing that such claims have a tendency to naturalize, legitimize, and thereby crucially support dominant social groups, in particular men over women as well as colonizers over indigenous peoples, whites over nonwhites, rich over poor, straight over LGBT, and so on. So to characterize Benhabib in terms of "feminist universalism" might seem to be surprising, even oxymoronic. Let's begin describing her project by taking each half of the phrase separately.

Benhabib's feminism: Benhabib, a contemporary Turkish-American philosopher and political science scholar, explicitly calls her project "feminist" throughout her book and states in several places what she understands the core of feminism in her thought to be. The key idea of her formulation of feminism is confronting the gender-sex system. Like most feminists, Benhabib distinguishes between gender and sex: whereas the latter refers to biological differences, the former is a socially constructed interpretation of what those biological differences mean. That is, "gender" is what it *means* to be female or male, what is understood to be feminine vs. masculine, and what sorts of things can be predicated of men vs. women (e.g., "… is an alpha male," "… is a bitch," "… is a woman doctor," "… must be on the rag"). Anatomical difference in the gender-sex system is used to naturalize and enforce the formation of different social roles, what it means to be a girl or a boy, a man or a woman, and what agencies, constraints, behavioral norms, and so forth are appropriate for each. Feminists take the further step and say that even though different cultures across place and time have had different gender-sex systems, the known ones have all oppressed and exploited women. In Benhabib's words:

> For feminist theory the gender-sex system is not a contingent but an essential way in which social reality is organized, symbolically divided, and lived through experientially. By the "gender-sex" system I understand the social-historical, symbolic constitution, and interpretation of the anatomical differences of the sexes. The gender-sex system is the grid through which the self develops an *embodied* identity, a certain mode of being in one's body and of living the body ….. The gender-sex system is the grid through which societies and cultures reproduce embodied individuals.… The historically known gender-sex systems have contributed to the oppression and exploitation of women. The task of feminist critical theory is to uncover this fact, and to develop a theory that is emancipatory and reflective, and which can aid women in their struggles to overcome oppression and exploitation. (1992, 152; emphasis in original)

What makes Benhabib's project specifically feminist, then, is her commitment to the position that any social vision of a better future that does not take the gender-sex system into account—for example by remaining "blind" to gender—is defective.

Benhabib's universalism: Understanding Benhabib's universalism requires a bit more context than does her feminism. My reading is that her universalism is partly reactive—that she is reacting to an increasingly dominant and mainstream critique of universalism which, even though she is sympathetic to many of that critique's main arguments, seems to throw out the proverbial baby with the bathwater. The following is drastically simplified but should serve the purpose of sketching out the needed background.

Much of twentieth-century thought—in philosophy, feminism, critical theory, postmodernism, and so on—expresses a strong skepticism against Enlightenment rationalism, including Jean-François Lyotard, Michel Foucault, Jacques Derrida, and Judith Butler. The Enlightenment tradition (typified in the West by thinkers such as Descartes, Kant, and Rousseau) sought to overthrow tradition and religion and replace them with rational intellectual methods, rational states/societies, rational (rather than conventional) ethics, and so forth. Part of the project was to downplay an embodied individual's own concrete situation in rational thought: all of us are equal in our rationality, and we have the same rationality, and each of us can appeal to it in the same ways. "All men are created equal" is perhaps the most celebrated clause of the *Declaration of Independence*, written during and reflecting the values of the Enlightenment (although its slaveholder authors failed to fully implement these values). Twentieth-century postmodernists challenged Enlightenment rationalism's attempts to obtain a universal point of view and its aspirations to universal and totalizing solutions. For thinkers like Lyotard, these projects (from the emancipation of the masses via Marxist revolution to the triumph of science itself) were little more than "illusory 'metanarratives' created by the West to aggrandize its own view of things" (How, 2003, 162). Lyotard countered by championing *petit récits*, which are local micro-narratives that capture the specificities of individual events.

One alternative political view that emerged alongside this critique, multiculturalism, seeks to respect the diversity of all cultural groups rather than viewing nondominant groups as "deviants" of dominant groups or "primitive" in relation to their "civilized" or "advanced" counterparts. Such a view has the important benefit of denaturalizing and de-universalizing the claims of dominant groups of how society should be. Additionally, by relegitimating nondominant groups' ways of life, sociocultural activists and reformers have a broadened set of ways of life to draw from in imagining a better society. However, without modification, the multiculturalist view introduces another problem: if all communities' ways of being are to be respected, how is anyone to judge among them? Which community offers better models for the social reformer? To take this logic to an extreme, imagine a community that democratically embraces cannibalism, pedophilia, or genocide. On what basis can one say that such communities are not as valid as other democratic communities?

Benhabib is not arguing that multiculturalists side with genocide and pedophiles. Her point is that ruling such communities out requires an appeal to the sorts of universals that feminists and postmodernists have attacked. Some universals (e.g., that genocide is wrong) need to be maintained. Benhabib states her position as follows, while listing several of the universals she seeks to protect:

> Among the legacies of modernity which today need reconstructing but not wholesale dismantling are moral and political universalism, committed to the now seemingly "old-fashioned" and suspect ideals of universal respect for each person in virtue of their humanity; the moral autonomy of the individual; economic and social justice and equality; democratic participation; the most extensive civil and political liberties compatible with principles of justice; and the formation of solidaristic human associations.... This book is an attempt to defend the tradition of universalism in the face of this triple-pronged critique by engaging with the claims of feminism, communitarianism and postmodernism and by learning from them. (1992, 2)

She is saying here that Enlightenment rationalism has put forward a set of ideals, including universal respect for each person, moral autonomy of the individual, democratic participation, civil liberties, and so on. She is also acknowledging that feminist, communitarian, and postmodern critiques of these values, which have rendered them into "suspect ideals," have some validity. But she is arguing that while these ideals need reconstructing in the face of such criticisms, they should not be dismantled.

She summarizes the overall goal of her project as follows:

> A post-Enlightenment defense of universalism, without metaphysical props and historical conceits, is still viable. Such universalism would be interactive not legislative, cognizant of gender difference and not gender blind, contextually sensitive and not situation indifferent.... I intend to soften the boundaries which have often been drawn around universalist theories and feminist positions, communitarian aspirations and postmodernist skepticism.... I hope to illuminate the contradictory potentials of the present moment in our intellectual lives. It is my hope to create cracks and fissures in the edifice of discursive traditions large enough so that a new ray of reason which still reflects the dignity of justice [i.e., Enlightenment moral theory] along with the promise of happiness may shine through them. (3–4)

In this passage, Benhabib clarifies which parts of Enlightenment rationality are the proverbial baby and which the bathwater. In the bathwater category are "metaphysical props and historical conceits": she is referring here to the disembodied knower of Western metaphysics and the hypothetical narrative that philosophers use of an originary founding of society based on rational principles (e.g., in social contract theory). Yet she still intends to champion certain universal ideals, including democratic participation and moral autonomy of the individual. Her intellectual burden here is to construct a new moral philosophy that can defend and champion these universal ideals, without making recourse to the disembodied knower or the hypothetical narrative of social contract theory.

The Generalized and the Concrete Other

I am summarizing Benhabib's broader project as a way of contextualizing the dense and difficult chapter I have chosen to include in this volume. This chapter in particular takes as its subject two competing moral theories, the *ethics of justice* versus the *ethics of care*. The former reflects recent moral theory in traditional philosophy, while the latter reflects a significant feminist contribution to moral theory in recent decades. The debate is important because the moral commitments we make have deep implications for the design of future society.

The two theories came into confrontation during what is known as the Kohlberg-Gilligan controversy, with which Benhabib begins the chapter. Briefly, Lawrence Kohlberg was a psychologist known for his theory of stages of moral development. Empirical work he and his colleagues conducted using his model showed that women scored lower than their male peers, implying that women were less morally developed than men. This led Carol Gilligan, who was one of Kohlberg's colleagues on these studies, to argue that Kohlberg's theory made assumptions about "higher" versus "lower" ethical decisions based on gendered assumptions that privileged male perspectives. Specifically, Gilligan argued that women were socialized into an ethical orientation grounded in concrete relationships and narratives (i.e., care ethics), rather than abstract principles, which reflects the ethical stance into which men are socialized (i.e., justice ethics). Kohlberg and Gilligan debated each other for several years, and philosophically analyzing this debate forms a significant portion of Benhabib's chapter.

One might expect, given Benhabib's feminism, that she would champion care ethics over justice ethics, and indeed she offers in this chapter a deep and lengthy critique of justice ethics. But rather than defending care ethics in its place, she instead argues that it is a false choice, and she seeks to offer a view that combines and preserves the strengths of each. This solution is consistent with Benhabib's feminist universalist position. Before exploring Benhabib's proposed position, let me quickly summarize justice versus care ethics.

Much of Benhabib's chapter is devoted to linking Kohlberg's theory to the history of moral philosophy. She offers a genealogy of moral and political philosophy to establish the affinity of Kohlberg's theory with thinking in this tradition: John Locke, Immanuel Kant, Thomas Hobbes, G. W. F. Hegel and through to Freud, Piaget, and most recently John Rawls. This tradition provides for us justice ethics and its foundational subject, the "generalized other":

> The standpoint of the generalized other requires us to view each and every individual as a rational being entitled to the same rights and duties we would want to ascribe to ourselves. In assuming the

> standpoint, we abstract from the individuality and concrete identity of the other.... Our relation to the other is governed by the norms of *formal equality* and *reciprocity*.... In treating you in accordance with these norms, I confirm in your person the rights of humanity and I have a legitimate right to expect that you will do the same in relation to me. The moral categories that accompany such interactions are those of right, obligation, and entitlement; the corresponding moral feelings are those of respect, duty, worthiness, and dignity. (Benhabib, 1992, 158–159; emphasis in original)

Key to this ethic is a hypothetical narrative of "the original position," which is characterized by "the veil of ignorance." In the "original position" narrative, the moral actor suspends all characteristics that individuate the self in society (e.g., gender, social class, age), applies a "veil of ignorance" to the self to think *as if* they don't actually know what societal position they will occupy when the veil is lifted, and then rationally devises an ethical system from this position as a means of identifying the most just possible solution. So, to take an example, anyone participating in this thought experiment can derive that slavery is wrong, because when the veil is lifted, one might be in the slave position, and no one wants to be in that position, and therefore slavery is not a moral social relation. The "generalized other" is called that because individuating details of our human existence are abstracted out of this model: what is moral applies to everyone or to no one in virtue of their general humanity (e.g., no one should be a slave or a slave owner, regardless of individuating characteristics like race).

The alternative that Gilligan and other feminists develop in response to justice ethics, again significantly motivated by Kohlberg's study and its findings, is care ethics, with its foundational subject, the "concrete self." This view

> requires us to view each and every rational being as an individual with a concrete history, identity and affective-emotional constitution.... We seek to comprehend the needs of the other, his or her motivations, what she searches for, and what s/he desires. Our relation to the other is governed by norms of *equity* and *complementary reciprocity*.... Our differences in this case complement rather than exclude one another. The norms of our interaction are usually, although not exclusively, private, non-institutional ones. They are the norms of friendship, love and care.... I confirm not only your *humanity* but your human *individuality*. The moral categories that accompany such interactions are those of responsibility, bonding and sharing. The corresponding moral feelings are those of love, care and sympathy and solidarity. (159; emphases in original)

The key to care ethics is the notion of "complementary reciprocity." That is, instead of a reciprocity of undifferentiated subjects (e.g., I will respect your property if you respect mine), complementary reciprocity is based on difference: if you have a need that I can fulfill, I am obligated to do so, and I expect the same of you. Thus, a parent cares for an infant who cannot reciprocate, because the parent recognizes that the child has a need that the parent is in a position to provide for. Later in life, of course, the situations might be reversed, but the obligation remains.

Table 40.1 summarizes the two ethical orientations relative to each other. The generalized other connects to justice ethics, to traditional moral philosophy, to male

Table 40.1
Summary of the generalized other vs. the concrete other.

	Generalized Other	Concrete Other
Individual is	A rational being entitled to the same rights as all other individuals, *qua* rational beings entitled to those rights	A rational being with a unique history, identity, affective-emotional constitution
Nature of relations between individuals	Based on similarity: all of us are indifferentiable under the law	Based on a recognition of and a response to the needs of the other
Relationship governance	Norms of formal equality and reciprocity	Norms of equity and complementary reciprocity
Our differences	Exclude one another: what is my property is not yours, and vice-versa	Complement one another: I have special abilities that you lack and need
Norms that guide moral transactions are	Institutional, legal, contractual	Friendship, love, care
Moral treatment of the other constitutes	A recognition of their humanity	A recognition of their individuality (beyond humanity)
Moral categories	Right, obligation and entitlement, worthiness, dignity	Responsibility, bonding, sharing

socialization, and to Kohlberg's tacit assumptions; the concrete other connects to care ethics, to feminist theory, to female socialization, and to Gilligan's critique of Kohlberg's assumptions.

As I alluded earlier, according to Benhabib's analysis, each of these has serious shortcomings, and she offers a detailed and technical argument about the problems of the generalized other in particular. Briefly, she identifies what she believes to be a fundamental logical confound at the heart of the generalized other theory that dooms it: the veil of ignorance requires the moral legislator both (1) to suspend all individuality in order to access a sufficiently disinterested state required for rational thinking, and (2) to take into account individuality, because that is what creates different social positions in the first place. The logical confound is that in one and the same act, the moral legislator simultaneously has to abstract from and take into account individual difference: if one suspends one's own individuality, one cannot be individuated from anyone else, and so social conflict and the need for morality evaporates with it: "Selves who do not have knowledge of their distinct interests can also not have adequate information about the interests of relevant others" (166). Thus the whole thought experiment results in "epistemic incoherence" (161). From this, Benhabib concludes that concrete otherness logically must be taken into any moral account.

Oddly, Benhabib does not, in this chapter, offer a detailed parallel critique of the ethic of care, even though she is explicit in not accepting it. However, based on what she says in the chapter and elsewhere in the book, I infer what the problem of care ethics is: it fails the criterion of universality. That is, the care ethics focus on concrete relations and individual narratives offers no way to get back up to the level of the universal. That is, if it focuses on the micro narratives of this particular individual needing care and that particular individual able to provide it, and moral situations are based solely in the concrete, there is no need to hold them up against abstractions (such as "universal respect for each person in virtue of their humanity"), since no abstractions are relevant to the situation. "It may be asked," Benhabib writes, "whether, without the standpoint of the generalized other, it would be possible to identify a moral point of view at all.... [W]ould a moral theory restricted to the standpoint of the concrete other not be a racist, sexist, cultural relativist and discriminatory one" (164)? In short, care ethics fails to account for what is owed universally to all humans, some of which I quoted above, including "universal respect for each person in virtue of their humanity; the moral autonomy of the individual; economic and social justice and equality; democratic participation; the most extensive civil and political liberties compatible with principles of justice"—all of which justice ethics, in contrast to care ethics, provides for.

I return later to Benhabib's own contribution to this debate, the gist of which is to develop a position from which it is possible to see the universal humanity through engagement with concrete others. But now I think it's high time to explore what HCI's stakes in debates like this might be.

The "Heterogeneous Home" as a Normative Ethical Vision

I claim in the introduction that HCI is increasingly in the vision business, concerned as we are nearly as much about the good life, sustainability, and economic justice as we are about supporting cognition, collaboration, and task completion. But HCI does not engage in "mere utopianism," the fantasy project of imagining an ideal society, but rather in the elaboration of social futures that are both sufficiently desirable and actionable to motivate working toward them. To unpack what I mean by this, and of course to explore how Benhabib's moral philosophy can serve as a resource, I turn now to the heterogeneous home (HH), a vision of the future home, partly an elaboration of and partly a critique of the "smart home" of ubiquitous computing. This work was published in a highly influential white paper and separate academic paper in 2007–2008 by Ryan Aipperspach, Ben Hooker, and Allison Woodruff of Intel Research Berkeley (Aipperspach, Hooker, and Woodruff, 2007, 2008).

The Heterogeneous Home Project Overview

The central argument of the HH project is that modern homes have transitioned from heterogeneity toward homogeneity, that this is an undesirable trend, and that digital technologies are making it worse. In a traditional home, the house is heterogeneous in that it physically demarcates boundaries between different modes of life. The home, as a physical space, is a refuge from outside work, the elements, and the social world. Within the home, rooms have purposes, such as bedrooms, bathrooms, living rooms, and kitchens. At different times of the year, we use these spaces differently; for example, the hearth is the center of the home in the winter but not in the summer, where the porch might become more central.

In contemporary suburbia, the authors note, many of these distinctions are becoming effaced. Central heating and air conditioning eliminates the seasonal connotations of the interior (what happens to the hearth when one has centralized heat?). Great rooms comprising kitchens, dining areas, and living areas blur food preparation, dining, leisure, and homework functions together. Suburban houses all look the same, inside and out. A television can be found in every room. The problem is heightening with digital technologies. Wireless networks make it possible to access the internet anywhere, anytime. We check work emails in bed, log into virtual worlds even as we sit beside family members, and watch news videos in the woods. Human experience is becoming homogenized, but the state of affairs that is emerging—one in which we are all on all the time—is anxiety inducing.

The authors explain this anxiety using information processing theory: when an environment fails to support people's information-seeking needs, it depletes their attention resource, causing anxiety. According to this theory, the homogeneous home is not a restorative environment, because all of our life practices (work, leisure, care, sleep, intimacy, rest, etc.) are equally possible and clamoring for our attention all at once everywhere we go. This greatly increases the psychological costs of managing information, leading to experiences of anxiety.

The solution is the "heterogeneous home" of the title: the design of the home to make it once again a restorative environment by reasserting distinctions among diverse life practices and reassigning them to differential locations within the home. Added to this, of course, is designing information technologies that fit within and contribute to this heterogeneous home. As a very simple example of the sort of thinking the authors have in mind, one might imagine designing the master bedroom as a private sanctuary, and thereby not allow internet, email, television, radio, and other signals into it.

The authors offer dozens of design concepts as a way of envisioning what this semi-smart home ("semi-" because a fully smart home would tend toward homogeneity) as restorative environment would look like. Concepts include indoor lighting that mimics outdoor light, small displays in potted plants, videoconferencing screens in closeable cabinets, a wall-hanging printer just inside the front door, a live video feed of a nearby park, virtual attics for storing less important information that you don't want to throw away, and a bright LED "Weekend" light that comes on only during the weekend. Typically, each design concept allows the residents access to information that is scoped in relevance to their specific location and its associated life practices, while providing an effective but limited connection to the outside world, including nature and the diurnal cycle, immediate neighbors, and the broader physical and social networks residents are embedded in.

With that summary of the HH behind us, let us turn to a Benhabib-supported analysis. I argue that HH is not merely proposing a technology agenda—that is, the sorts of domestic systems and infrastructures that the IT community should invest in—but is also explicitly advocating a normative vision of good (domestic) living, an applied ethics. And while HH is more explicit, and more honest, about its applied ethics agenda than much of HCI work, the fact is that every technology project or initiative has, perhaps tacitly, an applied ethics behind it that renders it comprehensible and desirable in the first place.

I want to stress at the outset that the following analysis of "Heterogeneous Home" includes both positive and negative interpretative statements about the design thinking as it is presented via these two publications. My purpose in doing so is in no way to impeach the politics of the researchers, who appear to share the emancipatory ideals that I do (e.g., Woodruff, 2008). Rather, my purpose is to offer an epistemological analysis, to critically interrogate the concept systems by which the researchers produce the design knowledge that they present. In doing so, I attempt to analyze the strengths and blind spots of those concept systems, some of which, I argue, have hidden political implications. In explicating these concept systems and their hidden implications, I hope to contribute to the design research community's existing efforts to be accountable to its own sociocultural power—as a fellow traveler.

The "Heterogeneous Home" as an Enlightenment Project

I begin by reading "Heterogeneous Home" in light of justice ethics. At the center of justice ethics is the generalized other, that is, a generic human being understood as participating in a set of identical rights and obligations as every other individual *qua* human being. The generalized other lacks any features that distinguish it from every other human being. Analogously, at the center of the HH is the "resident," a generic human being understood as relating to an external environment—the home—in a way identical to how every other individual *qua* resident relates to the home.

More fundamentally, both subjects (the generalized other and the resident) can be understood as structural positions inside of a broader abstract system. In Western philosophy, that abstract system includes a theory of the universal structures, capabilities, and limitations of human rationality (e.g., Kant's *Critique of Pure Reason*) set in relation to social contract theory, the hypothetical scenario in which each individual (so-constituted) enters into a contract in order to join society as a full-fledged member. Because the individual is understood in universal terms, its differences from other individuals become abstracted away, so it's no wonder that social relationships are accordingly understood in terms of formal equality and an ethics of reciprocity, rights, obligations, entitlements, and so forth.

In "Heterogeneous Home," the abstract system that contains the "resident" is information-processing theory. According to this theory, the mind is like a computer that manages flows of information through inputs and outputs (e.g., perception, motor behavior). We see this theory at work in the introduction to "Heterogeneous Home," where Aipperspach et al. cite the work of cognitive psychologists Kaplan and Kaplan (1989) on "restorative environments" as shaping their own distinction between homogeneous and heterogeneous homes. Aipperspach et al. summarize Kaplan and Kaplan as follows:

> Restorative environments are environments that help to reduce the mental fatigue resulting from situations that deplete people's limited attention. Studies have shown that restorative environments increase the capacity for directed attention, or the ability to be selective in thought and attention, that is depleted during stressful activities or intense thought. Kaplan and Kaplan frame environments in terms of their ability to either help or hinder people in dealing with the psychological costs of managing information. In particular, they frame restorative environments in terms of their ability to support the needs of understanding and exploring information. People have a desire to understand the environment around them, and a lack of understanding can result in stress. However, people also want to explore environments and uncover new information and ideas. (2007, 6–7)

Whether an environment, such as a home, is appealing or stressful is here framed very explicitly in terms of information management. The key to a restorative environment is to reduce *mental fatigue*, which is avoided when people have sufficient *understandings* of their environment. Such understandings are acquired through *attention to information* in environments. But attention is a limited resource that can be *depleted* due to the "psychological *costs* of *managing information*." (I italicize key words here to emphasize the driving role of information processing theory in producing a normative vision of a good home.)

This resident is characterized as a "knower," almost entirely abstracted from her or his body—a seeker of information whose information processing is supported or strained by features of its information environment. In the homogeneous home, the environment provides too much information, depleting (or costing too much to) attention resources. In a heterogeneous setting, information is neatly compartmentalized and the resident *qua* information processor is limited to a relatively small number of coherent tasks; that is, the physical diversity of the setting performs a sort of cognitive offloading; that is, some basic functions of attention management are performed by the environment, rather than the resident as knower. In a homogeneous setting, lacking physical diversity and its offloading of certain categories of information, the resident's mind-as-processor is confronted with a bewildering amount of information to process (including decisions about how many resources to allocate to which forms of processing). Since all residents are indiscernibly domestic information processors with the same capabilities and limitations, all residents are identically subject to the same domestic needs and requirements: the collocation of everyday practices, domestic arrangements, and information I/O systems.

With this theory of the resident as domestic information processor established, the next step for the authors is to flesh out the constitution of the home-as-information-domain. The authors are systematic in constructing a model. They have already established the general principle that a heterogeneous home is better than a homogeneous one, because of the information processing requirements (low vs. high) and experiential consequences (calm vs. anxiety) attendant on each. The next step is to identify different dimensions of the domestic environment, and they identify seven: the house vs. the home; domestic labor as merely instrumental vs. as "living process"; domestic technologies as seamless vs. seamful; domestic temporality as uniform vs. varied; the outside of the home as cordoned off vs. integrated with its physical surroundings; the home as self-enclosed vs. open to the social world; and the spatiality of the home as having low vs. high spatial complexity (what they refer to as the "fractal coefficient" of the space). As my paraphrase of these seven dimensions suggests, each dimension can be described as inhabiting a spectrum from a homogeneous variant (the first half of all the oppositional pairings above) to a heterogeneous variant (the second half of the above pairings). Again, the heterogeneous is viewed as superior to homogeneous in all seven cases, and particular ways that predigital homes can be one or the other are elaborated (as in the example of the hearth vs. central heating). Next, the authors propose design concepts for digital technologies that would integrate well in the heterogeneous half of each of the seven dimensions.

What I am trying to show here is that both the resident and the home have been rendered as practical resources for design thinking through a rearticulation in terms of information processing theory. This rearticulation in turn legitimates and inspires the development of certain kinds of domestic design concepts—which are then provided. I will critique this view in a moment, but before I do I want to note several positive consequences of this view. It tightly aligns design norms with universal human needs, which is obviously a desirable outcome. It also subordinates technology to human needs, which mitigates in favor of being human-centered rather than technology-centered. Finally, it establishes a framework by which as yet unimagined design concepts and products can be evaluated vis-à-vis their contributions toward domestic well-being. So, for example, the research, published in 2007, emphasizes virtual worlds like Second Life much more than we would today and does not anticipate the proliferation of tablets in domestic life. Yet it is easy to see how these technologies relate to the norms that the authors are proposing: in the case of tablets, it is easy to see how they push the home toward even more homogeneity, and this theory explains why so many people express anxiety about their use.

If the preceding analysis suggests ways that "Heterogeneous Home" epistemologically reflects justice ethics and Enlightenment rationality, it follows that imagining a home that reflects care ethics should also be possible. It is well out of the scope of this commentary to attempt such a project in earnest, but I can at least sketch some preliminaries, primarily by developing a feminist critique of HH to problematize the domestic IT design norms it offers and to suggest some alternative norms instead.

Cracks and Fissures: A Feminist Critique of "Heterogeneous Home"

In the previous section, I read "Heterogeneous Home" from the perspective of justice ethics and its key concept, the generalized other. Now I pivot to a critique of it based on how I would expect a feminist or politically minded critical theorist to read this project, especially one who emphasizes the concrete self of care ethics. This analysis proposes a more negative view of "Heterogeneous Home," but it should be read as an opportunity to make and explore the merits of a particular kind of analytical argument and not as my considered position. I remind readers that Benhabib, while taking this kind of analysis seriously, does not give it the final word, and neither do I.

A political critique informed by care ethics would reject the HH formulation of "the resident" because it excludes personally identifying differences, including demographic categories (gender, age, ethnicity, race, social class, etc.) and the ways that these are socialized into common performance types in domestic settings (e.g., the mother as cook in Western homes, or the live-in daughter-in-law in traditional Chinese homes); the unique history, identity, and affective-emotional constitution of individual residents; and their needs and capabilities to provide care, which are required to render visible to analysis the care ethics norm of complementary reciprocity. Without these individually differentiating features, several aspects important to domestic life as many of us experience it become difficult to take into analytic account. Table 40.2 shows the sorts of household questions that Aipperspach, Hooker, and Woodruff raise (left column) compared to questions that could be asked if they took a more care-centered perspective (right column).

The questions in the right-hand column of table 40.2 foreground the care ethics notion of complementary reciprocity, where the asker is in a position to care for someone with a need. Each question gets at individual identifying characteristics of residents and their relationships, as well as their desires, conflicts, and needs. Because the questions on the right are grounded in individual specificity, they are difficult to imagine from the perspective of minimizing the psychological costs of information

Table 40.2
Two types of everyday domestic question.

Questions Derived from Aipperspach, Hooker, and Woodruff (2007)	Questions Relevant to Care Ethics
• Are my online friends logged in? • Where are those planes outside my window flying? • What are the ingredients for potato salad? • How can I augment this beautiful sunset? • How can our family turn this huge folder of digital photos into a meaningful album? • Where should I sit to read my novel? • Which of my neighbors is out tonight? • Which of my friends should I invite over to dinner virtually tonight?	• Does Dad look more lethargic recently? How can I keep a better eye on him? • My partner has had a long day at work and I want to prepare a special dinner for her. Should I clear the kids' stuff off the dining room table and serve it there, or should I set a more intimate meal by the fireplace? • My oldest son needs to study for the SAT: how can I give him space but also help him understand that I'm here if he needs me? • Did my husband go out with his friends after work tonight? He gets violent with me and the kids when he's drunk. • My daughter moved back in with her boyfriend. At night I can hear them fighting. When will they move back out? • Can we make love without waking up the kids?

management for generic humans in an environment; certainly, the authors of " Heterogeneous Home" don't raise cases like these. Even in their diction and framing—to "go out with the boys," to "make love," to "keep an eye on," "when will they move back out?"—the questions at the right all suggest specific, rather than generalized, relationships between family members. These are the sorts of issues that are raised in ethnographic studies of domestic settings (e.g., Bell, Blythe, and Sengers, 2005; Wakkary and Maestri, 2007; Woodruff, Hasbrouck, and Augustin, 2007). Yet it's easy to see that these are important everyday domestic questions, and it seems hard to argue—as an ethical subject or as a technology designer—that the questions in the left-hand column should be central to how the field understands smart homes, while the questions in the right-hand column are not important or should only be relegated to specialists.

Indeed, these two sets of questions throw into relief how privileged this HH is, a home where family interpretations of vacation photos and curiosity about overflying planes' final destinations are important preoccupations; a home where not being troubled by work is a matter of not allowing certain devices to operate in some parts of the house; a home where better connections to nature, the neighborhood, and one's family can be actually achieved with better designs. When sociological issues are filtered out by the universalism of information processing theory, it can be easy to overlook such questions. One epistemological counter is, then, to imagine concrete particulars of poor urban families, nonwhite families, single-parent families, and other marginalized populations' domestic environments. Augmenting a view of one's former neighbor's burnt-out slum is less appealing than live video feeds of a nearby park, and inviting a virtual guest to have dinner with you makes sense in a home with one to three residents, but not in the crowded multigenerational households common in many Asian cultures. HH, a home whose design is based on universals concerning the relationships between human cognition and the physical and information environments in which it takes place, is suspiciously like the white, middle-class home portrayed in *Leave It to Beaver*, future-fitted with electronic devices. We can see here some merit to the critical theorist's and feminist's critique that what is presented as "universally good" all too often only really applies to dominant social groups, is often used to justify and normalize their way ways of life over others', and is structurally blinded to the real problems experienced by marginalized groups.

Critical theorists would further note that HH supports the status quo in several other ways as well. Domestic labor, one of the most gendered aspects of the home, is often in mainstream society not recognized as "real" labor at all, leading feminists to argue that women's labor is unacknowledged and uncompensated and therefore a form of exploitation. The HH has an entire section devoted to domestic labor, called "Hybrid Homemaking." It's worth quoting to capture not only its argument but also its tone.

> Although there has been extensive discussion of problems around issues such as division-of-labor in the home, the physical labor of housekeeping such as cleaning and cooking can sometimes be pleasurable because it involves visibly and viscerally making the home a better place.... Some have even lamented the introduction of "labor saving" domestic technologies because they can make housework less rewarding.... Key to the enjoyment of domestic work is the idea of living processes, actions that are enjoyable in and of themselves, as opposed to actions that are enjoyable only because of the end they achieve.... We propose that it is important to support management and maintenance activities in the design of domestic technologies, incorporating the physical and social activities that can make traditional homemaking rewarding. (Aipperspach, Hooker, and Woodruff, 2007, 15)

This section's acknowledgement and dismissal of the problems of gendered division of labor happens so fast that it requires less than half a sentence, and the second half of that same sentence elaborates on how pleasurable domestic labor can be! The effect of this line of reasoning is not merely to propose design strategies to support domestic labor, but also to deny that it is really "labor" at all. In effect, the HH in its gender blindness tacitly reinforces a patriarchal norm that exploits women.

Human residents are not the only embodied entities in HH. This is a house filled to the brim with devices:

> Tourist objects [a design concept proposed in HH as a norm for domestic devices] are single-purposed, portable electronic devices that take on many heterogeneous forms such as books,

robots, or portable PDA-like pads and tabs. The devices have homes or "parking places" where they naturally return (for example to charge their batteries), creating a flow of devices around the home, such as objects that occasionally visit an otherwise technology-free bedroom. (2007, 19)

A critical theorist would likely also note how much Intel would economically benefit from a scenario where every home was filled with single-purpose devices, each with an Intel chip powering it. But, beyond reducing the psychological costs of information management, what would be the consequences of this vision, if implemented in our material world? American consumerism, with its endless buying and disposal cycles, is certainly left intact in this vision. Americans replace their smart phones every two years, and here we have a house filled with hundreds of single-purpose devices. So would each home produce dozens or even hundreds of e-waste products every year—which we know (albeit not from HH, which is silent on the issue of disposal) end up in e-waste villages in developing regions of the world, often dismantled by child labor, while poisoning villages' water supplies with mercury (Puckett and Smith, 2002; Walsh, 2009)?

In short, the HH normalizes North American white middle class suburban domesticity; it presents domestic labor as "pleasurable" and "rewarding" recreation, while offering no reason to believe that this work will not be done disproportionately by women in five to ten years, as it is today; and it perpetuates a consumerist model that benefits multinationals while materially harming some of the most vulnerable populations in the world. A critical theorist could mount a credible case that HH fails to support emancipatory values.

More fundamentally, a critical theorist might ask, is there any evidence that anyone wants this home? No evidence is offered that actual individuals *qua* residents—besides the authors and their colleagues—had significant input into or reviewed this vision. The designers of HH, therefore, are in an epistemologically comparable position to the traditional legislator of ethics operating behind the veil of ignorance: suspending their own individual preferences (i.e., their own preferred domestic arrangements), appealing to a universal rational system (i.e., the psychology of restorative environments), the designers here legislate rules for domestic living for all of us (i.e., design concepts for the seven heterogeneous dimensions of HH).

Again, it is not my view that Aipperspach, Hooker, and Woodruff embrace the view that they are legislators of how people should live. Rather, my argument is that the sort of analysis that feminist critical theory can provide helps reveal how the designers' theoretical commitments push them toward such a position. Once this has happened, they inherit the problem that Benhabib identifies with the justice ethics veil of ignorance: "Selves who do not have knowledge of their distinct interests can also not have adequate information about the interests of relevant others" (Benhabib, 1992, 166). The consequence is predictable, given how feminists like Benhabib have shown time and again that pronouncements from disembedded and disembodied thinkers in the name of universal rationality serve and legitimate the dominating status quo while turning a blind eye to marginalized groups.

Reimagining Smart Homes with Norms of Care

A critique committed to feminist critical theory proposes a link between the epistemological commitments of Aipperspach, Hooker, and Woodruff's smart home design thinking (i.e., deducing design concepts from the generic "resident" as a domestic information processor) and its regressive sociological consequences (i.e., solving problems for the privileged while remaining blind to domestic issues of the underprivileged; legitimating the exploitation of women's labor; reinforcing consumerism at the expense of sustainability; and producing wealth for industry while physically harming the bodies of villagers in developing parts of the world).

The question becomes, how will epistemological commitments to care ethics in smart home design thinking connect to sociological consequences? Two substantial barriers prevent me from doing justice to this question. First, short of undertaking Aipperspach, Hooker, and Woodruff's original project—which involved a substantial amount of research and design by any measure—it is practically impossible to offer an apple-to-apples comparison. Second, a commitment to care ethics is among other things a commitment to hearing the voices of concrete others, which would entail a substantial empirical study well outside of the scope of this commentary (though readily available in ethnographic and participatory design approaches to domestic computing, including Bell, Blythe, and Sengers, 2005; Wakkary and Maestri, 2007; Woodruff, Hasbrouck, and Augustin, 2007). What I can do is map a strategy of how such a project might proceed and speculate where it might go, but this leads to yet another compromise: this activity puts me in a position not all that different from the Enlightenment legislator of the "original position," because I am deriving ethical rules (i.e., norms of domesticity) from a rational system (i.e., care ethics). Even with these substantial barriers in place, the thought experiment is worthwhile, I believe, because it nonetheless suggests a different vision of the smart home, one that is potentially generative of design concepts, and I invite readers to imagine for themselves how such a vision could be developed with real scientific and design resources behind it.

I'll begin in the same technology-driven opportunity space that Aipperspach, Hooker, and Woodruff do, updated a few years to reflect the present. This includes a present in which 70 percent of U.S. households have broadband access in the home[1] and about half of U.S. households have a tablet.[2] Google's 2014 acquisition of Nest for $3.2 billion reflects expectations that the home will soon feature a hardware network, in which lighting, thermostats, home security, home entertainment, and so forth are interlinked and app-controllable. It can be exciting to imagine how these technologies can change our domestic lives.

But a commitment to care ethics is a commitment to individuals understood in the concreteness of their physical settings and life histories, as opposed to abstracted into universal models, which I argue entails a shift from focusing on their information processing needs toward their socioeconomic needs. In that spirit, we should note the same decade that has given rise to tablets, WiFi, and networked domestic appliances has also witnessed other domestic trends. In the UK, about 30 percent of young adults now live with their parents, up 25 percent in the past decade.[3] In the United States, the post-2007 economy sent nearly 200,000 Californians between fifty and sixty-four years of age back to live with their long-retired parents.[4] Retirees are increasingly moving in with their children. In sum, recent decades have seen a 33 percent increase in Americans living in multigenerational households.[5]

It is possible, of course, to frame these developments in information-processing terms—for example, by noting that additional people in the household produce additional cognitive demands, which is surely true—but such a formulation seems to miss the point, which is that homes are becoming more crowded and this is happening by economic necessity not by choice. Multigenerational households are only one sociological trend that we might consider when thinking about designing for the future home. Single-parent and divorced households is another. We might also take into account households with chronic underemployment, domestic abuse and violence, parents working multiple jobs, latchkey children, dangerous neighborhoods, home depreciation, racially segregated neighborhoods, and so forth.

A care ethics-based, emancipatory view of domestic technology design would not set such issues aside because they are merely contingent on some households, unlike the universal needs of all residents for restorative environments. That is, rather than using the opportunity of potentially transformative new technologies as an opportunity to revisit the design of middle class homes (as HH does), let us instead ask how these new technologies could potentially transform the most experientially important domestic problems that actual people experience.

Let us imagine, as an example, a single working mother who holds down two part-time jobs to provide for herself and her teenaged child. It is easy to imagine her fear that her unsupervised teen, instead of studying to improve chances of college admission, could be out getting hurt or experimenting with sex or drugs. This mother probably feels frustrated and guilty that she can't do more. What would domestic ubicomp look like if this were a canonical example? It appears to raise issues of communication, affect, and trust, all of which have seen significant advances in recent computation and HCI. But it is also easy to imagine ways a design intervention in this space could be misused and even become abusive. In short, it seems like a challenging and interesting problem for design.

There are two general points I want to make about this simple thought experiment, one positive and one critical. Positively, this thought experiment brings forward the experiential grit of everyday domestic life, and it is only able to do so by means of taking seriously the individuating features (age, gender, relationship, economic class, understood not as biological givens but as socially prescribed performance types), of the residents involved. For example, we might imagine the concrete ways that teenaged girls explore and act out their identity and emerging relationship with their mothers in diverse racial and socioeconomic contexts, such as African-American girls in the industrial Midwest, Chinese-American girls raised in urban ethnic enclaves, or rural white girls. It also couples the design problem framing more tightly with the concrete experiences of particular and embodied individuals, rather than an idealized suburban middle class home, newly improved with wireless. It also situates interaction design itself in a care relation with concrete individuals, as opposed to situating design in a logical relation with a theory.

I have suggested that Benhabib would not endorse a vision of domestic computing based solely on care ethics, either. Taken to a theoretical and methodological extreme, one where universal concepts such as "domestic computing" and "resident" are categorically rejected in favor of concrete particulars, another problem comes into view, which Benhabib's analysis anticipates. Recall that Benhabib's criticism of care ethics is that lacking any appeal to the universal, it can't ever transcend out of micro-situations, or be able to ethically distinguish between two micro-situations to say one is better than the other. Benhabib writes, "It may be asked whether, without the standpoint of the generalized other, it would be possible to identify a moral point of view at all.... Would a moral theory restricted to the standpoint of the concrete other not be a racist, sexist, cultural relativist and discriminatory one" (164)?

Applying this thought experiment—and again, we are working here with an extreme version of the care ethics epistemological stance—back to the domain of ubiquitous homes, it may be asked whether it would be possible to pursue domestic computing at all, without the concept of the generic resident, someone who inhabits and adapts to a concrete environment and is capable of feeling satisfaction or anxiety. Indeed, the very concept of "domestic computing" becomes suspect, at best an empty abstraction and at worst a tactic of hegemonic social domination. Such a scenario would be disastrous for research: it would inhibit theory-building, researchers' ability to communicate across different domestic computing problems and domains, and even our ability to judge among different domestic design proposals; indeed, it would fail in all the ways that HH presently succeeds.

Benhabib's "Discourse Ethics" and Normative Design Visions

I have summarized Benhabib's analysis of justice vs. care ethics, and I've shown how that analysis can apply broadly to any social vision, developing my own analysis of the ubicomp vision of the heterogeneous home as an example. As Benhabib showed that both justice and care ethics on their own have appealing qualities but are also deeply flawed, I have shown that the "Heterogeneous Home" can be read as both appealing in some ways and flawed in others, as is a speculative alternative to HH that I presented based on care ethics. The view that Benhabib develops solves many of the problems raised and is, I believe, applicable beyond the immediate issues with which she concerns herself.

Benhabib's own view turns on a feminist rereading of John Rawls, a preeminent philosopher of ethics in the late twentieth century. While it is possible to read Rawls as continuing the justice ethics of traditional philosophy, feminists have read him with more nuance, and in that nuance Benhabib sees a way forward. The key concept is not the ability to rationally substitute oneself for another based on an abstractly shared humanity (as in justice ethics), nor on the ability to perceive a need in the other that one can provide for (as in care ethics), but rather on what Benhabib calls "enlarged mentality" building on a concept from Hannah Arendt (Benhabib, 1992, 164). An "enlarged mentality" allows a moral self to acknowledge universal humanity and universal human rights while accounting for the specificities of the other. Along these lines, Benhabib paraphrases how this works in Rawls's ethics:

> Rawls then asks us to imagine what distribution of material goods it would be most rational and reasonable to choose under the circumstances if we did not know who we were, what our talents and abilities, class, gender and race, etc., would be [i.e., the traditional original position and veil of ignorance]. Instead of thinking from the standpoint of all involved, that is instead of reversing perspectives and asking ourselves, "what would it really be like to reason from the standpoint of a black welfare mother?" we are simply asked to think what distribution of material goods would be most rational and reasonable to adopt, if we did know in a general way that our society is such that one may be a black welfare mother of three children out of wedlock living in a rapidly decaying urban neighborhood. (166–167)

For Benhabib, this formulation is an improvement over traditional justice ethics, because it does acknowledge individuating differences among people and factors them explicitly into political thought. In doing so, it sidesteps the epistemological incoherence of the traditional formulation of the original position and veil of ignorance.

But Rawls's improved justice ethics still has a serious defect for Benhabib. The thought experiment still depends on one's ability to acknowledge that in our society there is such-and-such an other, in such-and-such a circumstance, that needs accounting for. In Rawls's example, he asks us to imagine the circumstance of "a black welfare mother of three children out of wedlock living in a rapidly decaying urban neighborhood"—presumably selected as exemplifying one of the most marginalized subject positions in contemporary U.S. society. But Rawls's approach, Benhabib critiques, provides little epistemological mechanism to ensure that one really understands this "other." Does a Rawlsian thinker really understand a black welfare mother of three children out of wedlock living in a rapidly decaying urban neighborhood—well enough to decide on her behalf what is just?

> There is no injunction in the original position to face the "otherness of the other," one might even say to face their "alterity," their irreducible distinctness and difference from the self. I do

not doubt that respect for the other and their individuality is a central guiding concern for the Rawlsian theory; but the problem is that the Kantian presuppositions also guiding the Rawlsian theory are so weighty that the equivalence of all selves qua rational agents dominates and stifles any serious acknowledgment of difference, alterity and of the standpoint of the "concrete other." (167)

Benhabib is suggesting that Rawls has only partly addressed the underlying problem of traditional justice ethics. It is this issue of alterity—otherness—that is key for Benhabib's understanding of enlarged mentality: "Neither the concreteness nor the otherness of the 'concrete other' can be known in the absence of the *voice* of the other" (168). Without the voice of the other, "we tend to constitute the otherness of the other by projection and fantasy or ignore it in indifference" (168). Even empathy is insufficient to provide this enlarged mentality, because empathy blurs the boundaries between self and other, again preventing one from confronting the otherness of the other. Benhabib calls for "principles, institutions and procedures to enable articulation of the voice of 'others'" (168), and in so doing appeals back to universals (e.g., principles) in their traditional social framework (e.g., institutions and procedures), as a means to bring into view precisely what these frameworks in the past had aspired to be blind to: individual differences.

Building on all of this, Benhabib proposes a "discourse ethics," which combines the strengths of both justice and care ethics:

According to discourse ethics, the moral standpoint is not to be construed primarily as a *hypothetical* thought process, carried out singly by the moral agent or moral philosopher [i.e., like the original position with the veil of ignorance], but rather as an *actual* dialogue situation in which moral agents communicate with one another. Second, in the discourse model no epistemic restrictions are placed on moral reasoning and moral disputation [e.g., pretend that you don't know your own race, gender, and social class], for the more knowledge is available to moral agents about each other, their history, the particulars of their society, its structure and future, the more rational will be the outcome of their deliberations.... Third, if there are no knowledge restrictions to be placed upon such an argumentative situation, then it also follows that there is no privileged subject matter of moral disputation [e.g., we should be talking about rights and entitlements, but to raise issues of gender, race, or social class is just class warfare and has no business here].... Finally, in such moral discourse agents can also change levels of reflexivity, that is they can introduce metaconsiderations about the very conditions and constraints under which such dialogue takes place and they can evaluate their fairness. (169)

In the spirit of care ethics, Benhabib is rejecting hypothetical people (the disembodied "knower") in hypothetical situations (the original position with the veil of ignorance, consenting to the social contract) determining universal outcomes to be applied to (or imposed on) all actual people. In insisting on actual dialogue with actual people, she also greatly increases the scope of what the moral debate can encompass, not merely expanding beyond a narrow set of privileged concepts (i.e., rights, responsibilities, entitlements), but adding a meta-communicative layer where disputants can challenge the very rules of the discourse, both of which benefits are difficult to achieve in traditional justice ethics. In the spirit of justice ethics, the debate itself must adhere to certain universals (i.e., "respect for each person in virtue of their humanity; the moral autonomy of the individual; economic and social justice and equality; democratic participation; the most extensive civil and political liberties compatible with principles of justice; and the formation of solidaristic human associations"). And these universals are to be protected with institutions, such as the legal system and democratic governance.

Translated into HCI and design for domestic computing, this implies a central epistemic role for empirical research (in which the "voice" of the other can he heard) and participatory approaches. In such scenarios, designers cannot unilaterally legislate designs based on concept systems such as information processing theory, no matter how good they are. Instead, design must be an outcome of this "actual dialogue" that Benhabib refers to. I understand "dialogue" here to mean multiple voices—and so empirical social science, such as those used in user-centered design and ethnographic user research, as well as participatory design approaches, meet this criterion. I understand "*actual* dialogue" to raise the ante, to mean that the dialogue should be conducted with political equality (i.e., no group can unilaterally control, establish the terms of, or assert the outcomes of the dialogue), wide access (i.e., any stakeholder can participate as a full-fledged conversant) and that it must centrally, not incidentally, contribute to outcomes—partly by contributing toward the "enlarged mentality" that Benhabib describes. It seems doubtful that most user-centered design meets these criteria (because the researcher unilaterally sets the agenda and interprets the results), but ethnographic research and participatory design seem well positioned to do so (whether or not they actually do, of course, is a question of implementation).

All of this leads me to a puzzle, with regard to "Heterogeneous Home." I stated earlier that I focused my analysis on the presentation of the authors' design thinking in the form of two papers, because the publications are what is publicly available. I trust my quotations were sufficient to demonstrate that these papers really did frame the project in terms of information processing theory and the "resident" as an undifferentiated universal, a domestic information processor. Yet if one looks at the career and publications of some of its participants—Allison Woodruff in particular—it strains belief that this project was literally uninformed by the voice of the other, that is, of concrete individuals, given the authors' own records of empirical research, much of it in domestic settings and/or involving marginalized groups, or their connection to Intel's People and Practices Research Lab. That said, the design concepts as presented offer little evidence that they were informed by any such dialogue. All of this leads me to infer a gap between the stated design process in the reports and all of the theories and methods that actually shaped that process, although I still cannot easily explain why the design concepts selected for publication were so vulnerable to a political critique.

The reason for this gap is also unclear. Is it a mere failure of reporting, or was it ideologically motivated either by their institutional positioning in industry (e.g., the need to be legible to engineers or to be perceived as valuable to marketing and management?) or by the (perceived?) bias toward information processing theory in the HCI research community? At any rate, if I am right that there's more to HH than reported, then it seems likely that the project did in fact benefit from some form of "dialogue," though it is more doubtful that it was an "actual dialogue" according to the high standards that Benhabib attaches to that term.

The upshot of all of this for envisioning the future of domestic life in the age of ubiquitous computing can be summarized as follows. As the authors of "Heterogeneous Home" are correct to bring forward, the design of the home of the future is not merely a collection of otherwise unrelated technical problems in need of solving; it entails a normative vision of what a good smart home is. While I here offer some critiques of their vision, I appreciate that they explicitly proposed their normative vision and offered justifications for it and developing out its consequences. But because such normative visions once implemented have serious sociocultural consequences, they should be subjected to scrutiny and to debate, not merely the judgment of the marketplace. All stakeholders of this vision—which in this case appears to be most of society—should in principle be empowered to participate in the debate, as a way to support, challenge, or reprioritize the universals implied in any such vision. It is not clear that, beyond voting with their wallets, most stakeholders today in fact have this ability. Further, different participants will differentially participate. That is, the psychological expertise of researchers like Aipperspach, Hooker, and Woodruff is not equally shared by all stakeholders, and these researchers should not be forced to abandon their hard-won perspective. Likewise, Rawls's hypothetical black welfare mother of three may bring to the table a privileged perspective about her own experiences and their implications for domestic technology. But for the articulated perspective of this mother to have impact, she must be heard. That is, researchers, designers, industry product strategists, and others in privileged positions of power should not merely be experts in domain or technology but must also have enlarged mentalities—the discipline to confront the otherness of the other and to change and grow as a result of it.

The content of any discourse on what the future of the home ought to be should also reflect more than what one group (e.g., industry researchers) decide is the most relevant model (e.g., psychological theories of information management and restorative environments). That is, the terms of the debate should be part of the debate: if a constituency feels that its perspective (i.e., its alterity in relation to others) is unrepresented, it can debate the very structures that (may) have led to this outcome. In that spirit, historically, geographically, and culturally contingent sociological issues should not be abstracted out in the name of a one-size-fits-all model of the ideal home (which HH comes across as). At the same time, universals should not be rejected in the name of respecting alterity. Universals do have a role to play, be they Benhabib's short list of moral universals ("respect for each person in virtue of their humanity," etc.), psychological universals about how the human mind processes information in different environments, normative folk theories of what the home is or should be, or normative or descriptive academic theories of domestic computing. Finally, the universal value of emancipation, rather than merely furthering the status quo, should function as a guiding force of the discourse.

Whose responsibility is it to ensure that this democratic approach to envisioning the future of domestic life unfolds along these lines? I want to argue that part of the responsibility is ours—the HCI and design community's. Just as we have research ethics about the treatment of research subjects, I believe we need to adopt the ethics of imagining and implementing normative social visions, such as that of the good home. As a field, we have some processes, such as participatory design (Nygaard, 1990; Simonsen and Robertson, 2013), that seek to achieve these goals. However, traditional participatory design has been about the design of professional systems that had a relatively well defined and limited set of stakeholders, though more recent ethnography and participatory design has been seeking to broaden that, with research in developing contexts, the homeless in Western cities, and older people. In the case of ubicomp in the home, stakeholders arguably could include the majority of living individuals today and in the foreseeable future. It has become a norm that key decisions influencing the everyday lives of millions are made behind closed doors at global corporations, often with government complicity (e.g., DMCA, net neutrality laws, corporate mergers), and this is a norm that the HCI community has, if not the power to unilaterally eradicate, some agency to resist. The HCI and design communities are already asking how we can leverage our intellectual and political resources to make the normative envisioning of future life more democratic (e.g., Bardzell and Bardzell, 2014; Dourish, 2013; Light, 2011; Winschiers-Theophilus and Bidwell, 2013); I believe that Benhabib provides resources that support this rising agenda.

And Finally … Designing Ubiquitous Utopias

At the beginning of this commentary, I argue that many IT design projects today are of sufficient scale to have substantial sociocultural consequences, including issues of sustainability, social justice, privacy, and more subtly shaping everyday forms of life via smart cities, smart homes, and more. My analysis of "Heterogeneous Home" shows some of the ways that IT research agendas entail the construction and inscription of normative social visions into technologies. Now we are not in the business of traditional utopianism, that is, the unilateral development of a comprehensive vision of the ideal society, all its institutions, laws, social positions, and so forth. Rather, the normative social visions we work with must meet high criteria of technological and economic plausibility, and so there are practical constraints on our social visioning. Whether we embrace it or not, we are in certain limited senses applied moral philosophers.

What a moral philosopher like Benhabib provides is a set of tactics that we can use to support the democratization of normative sociotechnical visioning. One is that Benhabib proposes a two-stage methodology, which involves

> developing an *explanatory-diagnostic analysis* of women's oppression across history, culture and societies, and by articulating an *anticipatory-utopian critique* of the norms and values of our current society and culture, such as to project new modes of togetherness, of relating to ourselves, and to nature in the future. Whereas the first aspect of feminist theory requires critical, social-scientific research, the second is primarily normative and philosophical: it involves the clarification of moral and political principles, both at the meta-ethical level with respect to their logic of justification and at the substantive, normative level with reference to their concrete content. (152; emphasis in original).

Applied in the context of smart homes, we can see that critical social science has already provided much of the relevant explanatory-diagnostic analysis, such as critiques of the exploitation of women vis-à-vis the denial that domestic labor counts as labor and postcolonial critiques of well-meaning yet still imperial Western design efforts in the Global South, and so on. Ethnography has been one of the primary ways that feminists have conducted explanatory-diagnostic. Benhabib's work can be seen as offering resources that support emancipatory ethnography. What is now becoming clearer is that HCI and design are deeply implicated in the anticipatory-utopian critique of the norms and values of current society. There is no question that HH clarifies moral and political principles, even if it doesn't use that vocabulary explicitly. To reveal the manifest ways, as HH does, in which mass-scale architectural, interior, media, and IT design have, however inadvertently, colluded to create environments hostile to our most basic psychological abilities and needs is a clarification of the moral and political principles at stake in design. To demand of multiple industries and academic fields sweeping theoretical and material changes, as HH does, is a political act: if pursued in earnest, it would affect project teams and structures, industrial priorities, and design education curricula, among other things. Indeed, HH is normative and philosophical in the sense that Benhabib describes. Benhabib writes that the second aspect of feminist theory—its anticipatory-utopian critique—"involves the clarification of moral and political principles, both at the meta-ethical level with respect to their logic of justification and at the substantive, normative level with reference to their concrete content." HH offers both normative principles (the homogeneous-heterogeneous home distinction and its operationalization along seven dimensions) and normative concrete content (in the form of their design work).

I offered a critique of HH and offered a counterfactual sketch of how their reasoning might have looked had it been realigned with a different ethical framework—a sketch

I myself critiqued for introducing one set of new problems while solving a set of old ones. And this raises the issue that I want to close with: two competing views of the home have been advanced and critiqued in this chapter. Alternative research views can be found throughout the academic literature on ubiquitous computing. How can one judge among them? Who is empowered to judge among them? The market, of course, offers one answer: the winner in the marketplace is presumably among the better views (if not necessarily the best). However, the market structurally lacks any commitment to emancipation. Sometimes we buy into systems in spite of ambivalences and misgivings (as many HCI and design researchers today express about their own use of Apple products).

Even as the construction of a given normative view, such as domestic ubicomp, should be democratic, so should the choice among competing normative views be democratic. Here again Benhabib's thought offers guidance. By way of background: a mainstay of both philosophical and folk ethics is what Kant calls the "categorical imperative," which is similar to the "golden rule" of Christian thought: "act in such a way that the maxim of your actions can always be a universal law of nature" (136). That is, treat others as you yourself wish to be treated. It should be easy to anticipate Benhabib's critique of this: its substitutionalism treats all individuals as identical and abstracts out their individual differences; it actively prevents one from confronting the otherness of the other. Instead, building on Hannah Arendt, Benhabib reformulates as follows: "Act in such a way that the maxim of your actions takes into account the perspective of everyone else in such a way that you would be in a position to 'woo their consent'" (136). That is, individual acts, if construed as universal maxims, should have the ability to woo the consent of others to accept them; in our context, particular designs would presumably serve as these acts.

But to woo consent, stakeholders must be in a meaningful position to consent, which is clearly not the case today, the advances of user-centered design and especially participatory design notwithstanding. It concerns me that as a professional community we have not yet achieved more critical mass when it comes to empowering our stakeholders to participate in and eventually achieve consensus about the normative social visions that our design substantively and concretely embody. I hope that engaging with thinkers like Seyla Benhabib will provide those of us in the community already seeking to change this state of affairs with some conceptual and tactical resources to help us act in accordance with emancipatory values that I know many in HCI and design embrace.

The labor of normative sociotechnical visioning, of utopia, turns out not to be fantasizing in one's own mind what an ideal end-state would look like. It rather involves a disciplined analysis of the present set in relation to universal emancipatory values, including a genealogy of how we got here, that diagnoses oppressions. From there, it's a matter of anticipating a future that more adequately reflects those universal values by means of concrete proposals for change—which for us means design concepts, design research agendas, and normative sociotechnical visions—and of wooing others to join the labor of bringing this future into the present.

Acknowledgments

I wish to thank Mark Blythe and Jeffrey Bardzell for their editorial guidance and thoughtful feedback.

Notes

1. "Internet/Broadband Fact Sheet," Pew Research Center, last modified January 12, 2017, http://www.pewinternet.org/fact-sheets/broadband-technology-fact-sheet/.

2. "Almost Half of US Households Own a Tablet," Marketing Charts, May 6, 2014, http://www.marketingcharts.com/wp/online/almost-half-of-us-households-own-a-tablet-42441/.

3. H. Osborne, "Record Levels of Young Adults Living at Home, Says ONS," *Guardian*, January 21, 2014, http://www.theguardian.com/money/2014/jan/21/record-levels-young-adults-living-home-ons.

4. Source: W. Hamilton. "Moving in with Parents Becomes More Common for the Middle-Aged," *Los Angeles Times*, April 20, 2014, http://www.latimes.com/business/la-fi-adults-in-parents-home-20140421-story.html.

5. S. Epperson and C. Murphey, "Together Again: More Retirees Moving in with Children, *Today*, December 22, 2010, http://www.today.com/id/40772471/ns/today-money/t/together-again-more-retirees-moving-children/#.U9krL4BdWF8.

References

Aipperspach, R., B. Hooker, and A. Woodruff. (2007) "The Heterogeneous Home (Design Sketchbook)." Accessed June 30, 2014. http://www.benhooker.com/heterogeneoushome/. Site no longer available.

Aipperspach, R., B. Hooker, and A. Woodruff (2008) "The Heterogeneous Home." *Proceedings of the 10th International conference on Ubiquitous Computing (UbiComp'08)*. New York: ACM, 222–231.

Bardzell, J., and S. Bardzell, S. (2014) "'A Great and Troubling Beauty': Cognitive Speculation and Ubiquitous Computing." *Personal and Ubiquitous Computing* 18 (4): 779–794.

Bell, G., M. Blythe, and P. Sengers. (2005) "Making by Making Strange: Defamiliarization and the Design of Domestic Technologies." *Transactions on Computer-Human Interaction* 12 (2): 149–173.

Benhabib, S. (1992) *Situating the Self: Gender, Community, and Postmodernism in Contemporary Ethics*. New York: Routledge.

Dourish, P. (2013) "HCI and Environmental Sustainability: The Politics of Design and the Design of Politics." In *Proceedings of the 8th ACM Conference on Designing Interactive Systems (DIS'10)*. New York: ACM, 1–10.

Gould, J., and C. Lewis. (1985) "Designing for Usability: Key Principles and What Designers Think." *Communications of the ACM* 28 (3): 300–311.

How, A. (2003) *Critical Theory*. Basingstoke, UK: Palgrave.

Kaplan, R., and S. Kaplan. (1989) *The Experience of Nature: A Psychological Perspective*. Cambridge: Cambridge University Press.

Kuniavsky, M. (2003) *Observing the User Experience: A Practioner's Guide for User Research*. San Francisco: Morgan Kaufmann.

Light, A. (2011) "The Politics of Representing Cultures in Ubiquitous Media: Challenging National Cultural Norms by Studying a Map with Indian and British Users." *Personal and Ubiquitous Computing* 15 (6): 585–596.

Nygaard, K. (1990) "The Origins of the Scandinavian School, Why and How?" *Participatory Design Conference 1990 Transcript*. Computer Professionals for Social Responsibility.

Puckett, J., and T. Smith, eds. (2002) *Exporting Harm: The High-Tech Trashing of Asia*. Seattle: Basel Action Network. Accessed June 24, 2015. http://www.ban.org/E-waste/technotrashfinalcomp.pdf.

Simonsen, J., and T. Robertson. (2013) *Routledge International Handbook of Participatory Design*. New York: Routledge.

Tomlinson, B., M. S. Silberman, D. Patterson, Y. Pan, and E. Blevis. (2012) "Collapse Informatics: Augmenting the Sustainability and ICT4D Discourse in HCI." *Proceedings of the SIGCHI Conference on Human Factors in Computing Systems (CHI'12)*. New York: ACM, 655–664.

Wakkary, R., and L. Maestri. (2007) "The Resourcefulness of Everyday Design." *Proceedings of the 6th ACM SIGCHI Conference on Creativity and Cognition 2007*. New York: ACM, 163–172.

Walsh, B. (2009). "E-Waste Not." *Time*. http://content.time.com/time/magazine/article/0,9171,1870485,00.html.

Winschiers-Theophilus, H., and N. J. Bidwell. (2013) "Toward an AfroCentric Indigenous HCI Paradigm." *International Journal of Human-Computer Interaction* 29 (4): 243–255.

Woodruff, A. (2008). "You Can Go Home Again: Revisiting a Study of Domestic Computing." In *HCI Remix*, edited by T. Erickson and D. W. McDonald, 141–145. Cambridge, MA: MIT Press.

Woodruff, A., J. Hasbrouck, and S. Augustin. (2007) "A Bright Green Perspective on Sustainable Choices." *Proceedings of the SIGCHI Conference on Human Factors in Computing Systems (CHI'07)*. New York: ACM, 313–322.

Contributors

Louis Althusser (1918–1990) was a French Marxist theorist and professor of philosophy at École Normale Supérieure in Paris.

Aristotle (384–322 BCE) was an ancient Greek philosopher and student of Plato.

Mikhail M. Bakhtin (1895–1975) was a Russian philosopher and literary critic, whose writing spans a variety of subjects including anthropology, humor, and religion.

Jeffrey Bardzell is a professor of informatics and director of the HCI/Design program at the School of Informatics, Computing, and Engineering at Indiana University, Bloomington.

Shaowen Bardzell is a professor of informatics in the School of Informatics, Computing, and Engineering and an affiliated faculty of the Kinsey Institute at Indiana University, Bloomington.

Roland Barthes (1915–1980) was a French philosopher and semiotician, noted for his influence across a variety of fields including design theory, anthropology, and poststructuralism.

Seyla Benhabib is the Eugene Meyer Professor of Political Science and Philosophy in the Department of Political Science at Yale University.

Walter Benjamin (1892–1940) was a German-Jewish philosopher and essayist who was affiliated with the Frankfurt School and is known for his writings on aesthetics, Marxism, and German idealism.

Olav W. Bertelsen is an associate professor in the Department of Computer Science at Aarhus University.

Alan F. Blackwell is a professor at the Computer Laboratory at the University of Cambridge.

Mark Blythe is a professor of interdisciplinary design at Northumbria University in Newcastle.

Kirsten Boehner is a visiting scholar at the Georgia Institute of Technology.

John Bowers is a professor of creative digital practice in the School of Arts and Cultures at Newcastle University.

Judith Butler is the Maxine Elliot Professor in the Department of Comparative Literature and the Program of Critical Theory at the University of California, Berkeley. She is also the Hannah Arendt Chair at the European Graduate School.

Elizabeth F. Churchill is Director of User Experience at Google in Mountain View, California; executive vice president of the Association of Computing Machinery's Special Interest Group on Human Computer Interaction (ACM SigCHI); and an ACM Distinguished Scientist.

Gilbert Cockton is the head of Visual Communications Academic Community of Practice and a professor of design theory in the School of Design at Northumbria in Newcastle.

Arthur C. Danto (1924–2013) was an American art critic and theorist, and the Johnsonian Professor Emeritus of Philosophy at Columbia University.

Carl DiSalvo is an associate professor in the School of Literature, Media, and Communication at the Georgia Institute of Technology.

Paul Dourish is the Chancellor's Professor of Informatics and an associate dean for research in the Donald Bren School of Information and Computer Sciences at the University of California, Irvine.

Terry Eagleton is a distinguished professor of English literature at Lancaster University.

Umberto Eco (1932–2016) was an Italian novelist and philosopher. He was also the founder of the Department of Media Studies at the University of the Republic of San Marino, and the president of the Graduate School for the Study of the Humanities at the University of Bologna, a member of the Accademia dei Lencie, and an honorary fellow of Kellogg College, Oxford.

Melanie Feinberg is an associate professor in the School of Library and Information Science at the University of North Carolina at Chapel Hill.

Michel Foucault (1926–1984) was a French philosopher and historian best known for his critiques of modernity, which are often associated with poststructuralism and postmodernism.

Stuart Hall (1932–2014) was a cultural theorist and political activist, founder of the *New Left Review*, and director of the Center for Contemporary Cultural Studies at Birmingham University.

Hrönn Brynjarsdóttir Holmer is a PhD candidate in the Information Science department at Cornell University.

Beki Grinter is a professor of interactive computing in the College of Computing and the Scheller College of Business at the Georgia Institute of Technology.

Wolfgang Iser (1926–2007) was a German literary theorist and emeritus professor of comparative literature at the University of Konstanze (1967–1991) and University of California, Irvine (1978–2005).

Allan Kaprow (1927–2006) was an American artist, known for coining the term "happening" in the 1950s and for his association with the Fluxus art movement.

Jofish Kaye is a principal research scientist at Mozilla.

Søren Kierkegaard (1813–1855) was a Danish philosopher known for his contributions to theology, aesthetics, and existentialism.

Bruno Latour is a French philosopher and anthropologist. He recently retired from his position as vice president of research at Sciences Po Paris.

Ann Light is a professor of design and creative technology at the University of Sussex.

Herbert Marcuse (1898–1979) was a German-American philosopher, political theorist, and prominent member of the Frankfurt School of Critical Theory.

John McCarthy is the head of school in the Department of Applied Psychology at University College, Cork.

Søren Bro Pold is an associate professor in the School of Communication and Culture at Aarhus University.

Edward W. Said (1935–2003) was a professor of literature at Columbia University, best known as a founder of postcolonial studies and his analysis of "Orientalism."

James C. Scott is the Sterling Professor of Political Science and the director of the Agrarian Studies Program at Yale University.

Phoebe Sengers is an associate professor of information sciences and science and technology studies at Cornell University.

Erik Stolterman is a professor of informatics in the School of Informatics, Computing, and Engineering at Indiana University, Bloomington.

Kaiton Williams is a PhD candidate in the Information Sciences program at Cornell University.

Peter Wright is a professor of social computing at Newcastle University.

Slavoj Žižek is a philosopher and cultural critic. He is a senior researcher in the Department of Philosophy at the University of Ljubljana, a Global Distinguished Professor of German at New York University, and the international director of the Birkbeck Institute for the Humanities at the University of London. He is the author of more than thirty books.

Index

Note: Figures and tables are indicated by "f" and "t" respectively, following page numbers.

Aaron, Sam, 180
Abrams, M. H., 12
Absolute truth, 494–495
Absolutist power, 670
Abstract expressionism, 545–546
Abstraction, 504, 540–541, 681
  artistic identification rejection and, 522
  from I and thou, 567
Abstractionism, 542, 545
Accessibility, 614–616
Accidental engagement, 89
Accountability, 621n10
  participation and, 616–619
Accusatory justice, 649
Action
  collective, 492
  critical, 730
  interruption of, 328
  production and, 273–274
  reason and, 272
  reflection on, 301, 303
  situated, 18
  user, 263, 264
Action painting, 595, 611
Active reading, 267
Activism, 323, 675
  political, 173–174
  social, 533
Activities, 593, 611
Activity theory, 86
Actor-network theory (ANT), 471–472, 475
Act Up, 423
Addressive surplus, 576
Adolphus, Gustavus, 636
Adorno, Theodor, 313, 409, 414, 506
Adversarial design, 367
Aesthetic cognitivism, 530
Aesthetic experience, 249, 266, 530
Aesthetic information, quantitative information and, 164
Aesthetic meaning, 166n20
Aesthetic philosophers, 317
Aesthetics
  analytic, 541
  contemporary, 178
  material, 332, 333
  media, 332
  quantitative, 175
  somaesthetics, 530
  superstructure of, 333
Aesthetic sustainability, 90
African academics, 725–726
AfterLife, 603
After Theory (Eagleton), 4, 12, 510
Agamben, Georgio, 670

Agency
  ANT and, 471
  nonhuman, 312
  reader, 264–265
Agre, Phil, 414
Agriculture, water use by, 141
Aipperspach, Ryan, 759, 762, 764, 765, 768, 774
Alibi, 105, 108
Alien associations, 243, 244
Alienated labor, 392
Alienation, 351, 392
Alien tetralogy, 530
Allegorical paintings, 542
Allen, Woody, 32, 56
Alterity, 772
Althusser, Louis, 4, 6, 10, 11, 202, 312–315, 407–408, 413, 415, 485, 671
  on ideology, 388–404
Alvarado, Laurance, 53
Amazon, 335
Amazon Mechanical Turk, 728
Ambiguity, 245–246
  gender, 421
  of myth, 105
  of term for information, 167
American consumerism, 767
American Psychoanalytic Association, 423
Amis, Martin, 499
Analytic aesthetics, 541
Analytic philosophy, 316–317
Ancient world, 7
Anderson, Perry, 494
Android smartphones, 173, 336, 337, 341
Annie Hall (film), 32
Annotation, in Spyn, 254, 262
Ant colonies, 688
Anthropology, 500, 681
Anti-capitalist movement, 489
Anti-design movement, 505–506
Antifetishism, 456, 458, 459, 460, 464, 704
Aporiai, 303–305
Apple, 314, 335, 341, 414, 511
  platform access control by, 332, 337
Apprenticeship, 387, 578
Appropriation, 86, 87–88, 707
  designing for, 441
App Store, 314, 332, 337
Apriorism, 668–669
Arbitrariness, 74–75
  communities of practice, 537
Archer, Jeffrey, 486
Archizoom Associati, 505
Arendt, Hannah, 771, 777
Aristophanes, 64
Aristotle, 7, 15, 33–34, 271, 287, 288, 290–292, 294, 302, 488
  on art, 274, 291
  puzzles used by, 303–305
  on science, 273–275
Arnold, Matthew, 5, 502
Art, 515
  Aristotle on, 274, 291
  artlike, 561, 611
  cognitive benefit, 530
  expressionistic theory of, 545, 547
  framing and, 615
  imitation theory of, 516–518, 536–537, 542, 545, 547
  institutional theory of, 541
  knowledge and, 530
  lifelike, 561, 611
  novelty in, 156
  philosophical inquiry and, 531
  philosophy of, 317
  politics, participation, and, 560–561
  reality theory of, 517–519, 537–538, 547
  theories of, 545–546, 546t
  understanding and, 530
Art education, 317
Articulated language, 110
Artificial controversies, 448–449
Artificial intelligence, 169
Artificial myth, 112, 113
Artistic creativity, 366

Artistic identification, 554
abstraction through rejection of, 522
artworld and, 541
clustering of lower-level, 547
"is" of, 520–522, 524, 539–541, 543
systems of, 540, 545
theories of art and, 545
Artistic innovation, 546
Artistic theory, 522
Artlike art, 561, 611
Art performance, 593
Artwork
defining traits of, 525
objects and, 519
style matrix for, 525–526, 525t
Artworld, 554
conceptual analysis of, 535–536
"is" of, 539–541
logical analysis of, 535–536
philosophical understanding of, 535–536
readings of, 541
real world relationship to, 524
sociological understanding of, 535
theory of, 547
Asquith, Herbert, 494
Assessment, 644
Assimilation, 566
Association for Computing Machinery, 666
Associative meaning, 192
Attention, 762
Auden, W. H., 311–312
Audience research, 190
Austen, Jane, 486, 511
Austin, J. L., 550
Authenticity, 600
Authorial personas, 257
Authoritarianism, 708
Authoritarian power, 708
Authoritarian technologies, 702
Authors
implied, 247, 257
production and, 322–325, 327, 333–335
Autocorrelation, of textual signs, 238
Automation, of power, 630
Autonomous self, 738–743, 745
state of nature metaphor and, 741–742
striving for unity, 742–743
Autonomy
men as mushrooms, 741, 742
moral, 738, 755, 773
women lacking, 742
Avant-garde, 115, 122, 169, 172–174

Bacon, Francis, 507
Bakhtin, Mikhail, 4, 19, 84, 499, 560, 571–582
Balázs, Bodó, 338
Balfour, Arthur James, 715, 716, 723, 724, 726
Bannon, Liam, 661
Bardzell, Jeffrey, 1, 20, 317
Bardzell, Shaowen, 1, 14, 20, 579
Baring, Evelyn. *See* Cromer, Lord
Barthes, Roland, 11, 29–30, 131–133, 138, 141, 202, 485
Base, 331, 375–376, 409. *See also* Infrastructure
IT reconfiguring superstructure relation to, 339
Basic principle, 64
Basic research, 595
Baudrillard, Jean, 449
Baumgarten, Alexander, 8
Bayes theorem, 175
BBC, 53, 723
Beauty, 45–46
Becker, Howard, 541, 547
Beckmann, Johann Gottlieb, 682
Beech, Dave, 579
Behavior change, designing for, 481
Behaviorism, 352, 354
Benhabib, Seyla, 10, 563–564, 575, 579, 752, 760–778, 767
on feminist theory, 776
feminist universalism of, 753–756
generalized and concrete other, 756–759
Benjamin, Walter, 10, 311, 313–314, 332–334, 338–340

Bentham, Jeremy, 561, 628–635, 647, 649–650, 654–655, 658, 669
Berger, John, 507
Bergson, Henri, 39–40
Berlin Fever (Happening), 585–587
Bertelsen, Olav, 28–29
Best, Michael, 140
Between the Bars, 675
Bhabha, Homi K., 418
Biagioli, Mario, 456
Bias, facts hidden by, 448
Bidlo, Mike, 544
Big Data, 30, 136, 707, 732n1
Binary division and branding, 628
BinCam, 3
Biomass, 687
Biomimicry, 551–552
Biopower, 659, 662
Birmingham Centre for Cultural Studies (BCCCS), 500, 501
Birmingham School, 697
Birtwistle, Harrison, 175
Bits, 147, 167
Blackwell, Alan, 30–31
Blake, William, 492
Bleecker, Julian, 554
Blogging, 675
Bloom, Harold, 9, 12, 312
Bloom, Leopold, 499
Bloomberg, Michael, 258
Blowfish Dress, 531
Blythe, Mark, 1, 2, 20, 28, 316
Body dysmorphia, 440
Bodyworks, 593
Boehner, Kirsten, 560–561
Bohr, Niels, 57
Bolshevik revolution, 489
Boltanski, Luc, 451
Bolter, J. D., 332
Boltzmann, Ludwig, 148
Bonding, 744
Boredom, 64–65, 67–69, 82, 83
Bornstein, Kate, 419
Boswell, Samuel, 4
Boundaries of thought, 549
Bourdieu, Pierre, 46–47, 449, 485, 541
Bourgeois ex-nomination, 116, 120, 121
Bourgeois ideology, 115, 125, 396
Bourgeoisie, 129n17
  as joint-stock company, 114–117
  juridical frameworks and, 645
  myth of, 121–122
Bourgeois morality, 125
Bowers, John, 6, 561–562
Branch systems, 148, 149
Brand, Russell, 216f, 217
Brandes, Dietrich, 687, 691n19
Branzi, Andrea, 505
Brasilia, Brazil, 699
Bratton, Benjamin, 3
Brecht, Bertolt, 323–324, 326–328, 334, 336–337, 494, 510
Brecht, George, 589, 591–593
Bridgman, P. W., 352
Brightest Flashlight Free app, 336
Brillo Box (sculpture), 523–524, 526, 533–534, 543–545, 544f, 554
  as philosophy, 548–550
British class system, 501
Broadband access, 768
Broadcasting
  as ideological apparatus, 207
  institutional structures of, 188, 189
  perspective produced by, 206
  source-receiver asymmetry in, 190
Brownlash, 448
Bruno, Giordano, 305
Bullet theory of communication, 203–204
Butler, Judith, 10, 184n8, 311, 315, 429, 433, 438, 503–504
  Enlightenment skepticism, 754
Byzantine mosaic, 158–159

Cage, John, 172, 182
Calculation, 660, 661
Cambridge Analytica, 32

Cameron, James, 59
Cancogni, Anna, 168
Capital (Marx), 187–188, 372, 388
Capital, accumulation of, 644
Capitalism, 83, 114, 129n15, 511, 550, 661
  consumerist, 488
  Ideological State Apparatus under, 386
  inclusiveness of, 495–496
  margins and, 496
  monopoly, 340
  puritanical, 487
  restructurings of, 490
Capitalist education, 374
Capitalists, 372, 373
Capitalist social formations, 386, 387
Care, 757
  considerations of, 738–739
  reimagining smart homes with norms of, 768–770
Care ethics, 563–564, 753, 756–759, 764–765, 765t
  commitment to, 768–769
  epistemological commitments to, 768
Caring, 744
Carroll, Noël, 13, 317
Categorical imperative, 777
Categorization, 440
Catherine II, 639
Cavell, Stanley, 14, 747
CCTV, 663
Censorship, 378
Centralized police, 638
Centre for Contemporary Cultural Studies, 414, 501
Changing the Subject collective, 653
Character, 302
Chesterton, G. K., 28, 43, 57
  on modernism, 58
Chiapello, Eve, 451
CHI conferences, 666
Childhood-as-Poet myth, 122
Children
  boredom and, 65
  judgement of, 748n13
  latchkey, 769
Chomsky, Noam, 6
Christian allegorical paintings, 542
Christianity, Žižek and, 57
Christian religious ideology, 399–401
Chronic underemployment, 769
Churchill, Elizabeth, 31–32
Circuit of culture framework, 217–219, 218f
  cultural artifact interpretation and, 220–221
Circulation, 206, 210
Circumspective looking, 304
Cities, smart, 751
Civic science, 479
Cixous, Hélène, 485
Clarke, Rachel, 580, 581
Class conflict, revolutionary nationalism and, 491
Class distinctions, equalization of, 349
Classification, 644
Class interests, 319
Class nature, 403
Class positions, 389
Class ritual, 116
Class societies, 403
Class struggle, 319, 385, 398
  anti-colonial struggle as, 491
  ISAs and, 404, 405n11
Class systems, British, 501
Class travelers, 501
Clausius, Rudolf, 147
Closed gestalt, 240, 241
Cockton, Gilbert, 33–34
Code, 149, 150, 154
  connotative, 193
  dominant, 195, 206
  of encoding and decoding, 189
  hegemonic, 206
  ideology and, 205
  language as, 172–173
  naturalization of, 191, 204
  negotiated, 196–197, 211, 214
  oppositional, 197

Code (cont.)
power and, 173–174, 205
professional, 195, 207
reference, 210
semantic, 192
Codesign, 600
Codification, of self, 435
Coercive assignment, 628
Cognitive behavioral therapy (CBT), 56
Cognitive ergonomics, 667
Cognitive psychology, 660
Cognitivism, 530, 660
Coherence, good continuation principle of, 241
Colbert, Jean-Baptiste, 690n8
Collective action, 492
Collective cultural meaning-making, 215
Collective unconscious, 567
Collectivization, 321
Collision (Wilson), 52
Colonialism, 100, 117, 133, 136, 489, 491, 600
Colonial occupation, 717
Commune (journal), 329
Communication, 145, 772–773
bullet theory of, 203–204
critical analysis as, 162
Hall four-stage theory of, 206
mass, 168–169
media, 204
meeting and, 565
painting as, 162–163
perfectly transparent, 195
process of, 187
Shannon-Weaver model of, 202–203, 203f
systematically distorted, 195
transmission conception of, 202–203
Communicative events, 188
Communicative process, television, 188–191
Communist Institute for the Study of Fascism, 333
Communist Manifesto, 376, 388, 390, 491
Communities of art practice, 537, 541
Communities of practice, 542–543
arbitrariness, 537
Community forests, 691n19
Compass Table, 505, 508
Competition, 741
Complementary reciprocity, 744, 757
Compositionism, 474, 478–479
Comprehension, 242
consistency-building and, 245
Computer games, as cultural artifacts, 132
Computer-generated papers, 503
Computer Related Design (CRD), 601
Computers
as instrumental medium, 333
universal, 335
"Computers as Theatre" (Laurel), 33
Computer-supported cooperative work (CSCW), 18, 19, 87, 200, 653, 661, 667, 705, 708
Computing
mobile, 700, 708
ubiquitous, 664, 700, 707, 708, 751–778
Concept, 100–104
Concept pieces, 593
Conceptual architecture, 505
Concordat, 385
Concrete music, 158
Concrete other, 563, 579, 743–747
generalized other vs., 758t
smart home and, 756–759
Concrete self, 757
Concrete subject, 397
Conditions of existence, ideology as representation of relationship to, 391–396
Configurative meaning, 247
Confinement, 627, 629
Conflict, in cultural formations, 201
Connotation, 191–192, 205
Connotative codes, 193
Connoted meaning, 205
Consciousness, 402
false, 351
familiar and, 566
recognition and, 397

reducing to single, 565, 572
self, 586, 741
of servitude, 348
understanding and, 565
Consensus, 492
Consent
ideology and, 314
social order and, 202
wooing, 777–778
Considerations of care, 738–739
Consistency-building, 237–243
comprehension and, 245
Consistent interpretation, 237
Conspiracists, 449–450
Constructive design, 529
Constructivism, 255, 452
Consumer data, 707
Consumerism, 505, 767
Consumerist capitalism, 488
Consumer resource use, 701
Consumption
in circuit of culture, 217–220
design process and, 219
in Hall four-stage theory, 206
meaning and, 219–220
technology shaped through, 220
Containment, 354
Contemporary aesthetics, 178
Contemporary feminist theory, 737
Context, 200
social, 320, 661
Contextual design, 578
Contextual meaning, 568
Contextual research, 302
Contingency, 86, 670–671
Controlled environments, 686
Controversy, 480–481
Cooper, Geoff, 660, 666
Copernican revolution metaphor, 460
Coppede, Adolfo, 37
Cosmopolitanism, 720
Counter-law, 645–646
Counter-power, 643
Counter-Reformation, 637
Courage, 290
Cox, Geoff, 335–336
Coyne, Richard, 17
CreateSpace Kindle Direct Publishing, 335
Creation, customization and reconfiguring, 179–182
Creative practice, innovation and, 410, 413
Creative understanding, 572, 574–577, 579
Creativity
artistic, 366
social, 541
Critical action research, 730
Critical analysis, 162
Critical barbarity, 459, 461
Critical design, 367, 442, 475, 478, 529, 532, 549, 550, 667, 698
discourse of, 504–508
humor in, 507
language of, 508
participation in, 560–561, 602–603, 604
Critical design practice, 413–414
Critical essays, 1
Critical gesture, 457f, 458f, 459f
Critical making, 529, 698
Critical readings, role of, 705
Critical-reflective HCI, 476, 480
Critical technical practice, 414, 698
Critical theory, 58, 418, 431, 465, 669
defining, 6–7
Frankfurt School, 7
history of, 7–14
interaction design and, 14–20
for IT reconfiguring of base-superstructure relations, 339
language of, 500–504
Marxism and, 510
of media, 409
multiculturalist, 312
philosophy, reason, and, 361
reading, 2–6
technology design and, 697
on YouTube, 41

Critical thinking, 222, 652
Critical trick, 460f
Critique, 457–458, 473–474, 479
artifacts of, 709
building and, 704
constructive role of, 707
Copernican revolution metaphor and, 460
limitations of, 461
popularization of, 449–451
power, institutions, and, 561–562
technology design and, 705–707
Critique of Pure Reason (Kant), 761
Cromer, Lord, 718–721, 729, 731
Crop rotation, 29, 69, 82–84, 86–88, 691n18
in design and use of IT, 85–89
Crowdworkers, 728
Csikszentmihalyi, Chris, 674
Csikszentmihalyi, Mihaly, 541
Cultural artifacts, 29, 44
analysis of, 217
circuit of culture and interpretation of, 220–221
computer games as, 132
critical design and, 508
design of, 219
Cultural commentary, 618
Cultural criticism, 132
design practice as, 413–414
Cultural divides, 730
Cultural expectations, 662
Cultural formations, conflict in, 201
Cultural identity, 725
Cultural intermediaries, designers as, 219
Cultural meanings, 219
Cultural probes, 88, 601
Cultural studies, 199, 418, 431, 500, 511, 697
Hall shaping, 200–202
margins and, 492
postmodern, 503
theory in, 58
Cultural theory, 487, 488
Cultural translation, 417, 424
Culture
circuit of culture framework, 217–221, 218f
educational software and, 437
mass, 30
monocultures, 686, 688, 695
organizational, 219
popular, 487
psychology of, 567
semantic codes of, 192
social nature of, 201
subcultures, 202, 220, 494
superstructure of, 333
supportive, 302
Culture industry, 414
Culture Lab, 575, 580
Currie, Gregory, 13
Customization, 179–182
Cybernetics, 149

Dadaism, 325
Dali, Salvador, 46
Damiens, Robert-François, 654
Danto, Arthur, 13, 311, 313, 317, 533, 534–550, 552–555, 556n2
Dark design, 562, 673
DARPA, 449
Data capture, 664
Dawkins, Richard, 52, 57, 500
Daydreaming, 615, 616
Debord, Guy, 506
Debunking, 452, 459, 511, 704
Declaration of Independence, 754
Decoding, 188
in chunks, 229
codes of, 189
encoding and, 195
Hall on, 210–214
naturalized codes and, 191
reading positions and, 195–197, 210–212
social practices and, 189
Deconstruction, 452, 500–501, 704, 707
Foucault and, 652

Dedalus, Stephen, 33
Defensive dresses, 531
Definitional identity, 746
Deformation, 104
Deinstitutionalization, 637
de la Vega, Garcilasso, 740
Deleuze, Gilles, 675
Deliberation, 278–279, 292
DeLillo, Don, 51–52
Dementia, 580
Democracy, 438, 670
  normative envisioning and, 775
  of normative view, 777
Denmark, 65–66
Denotation, 191–193, 205, 228–229
Depoliticized speech, 117–119
Deprofessionalization, 562, 675–676
Derrida, Jacques, 11, 315, 421, 485, 493
  Enlightenment skepticism, 754
Descriptive account of gender, 425
Descriptive theory, of State, 377–378
Design. *See also* Interaction design; Participatory design
  as deflection, 562, 674
  deprofessionalization and, 562, 675–676
  ethics and, 475
  family interaction and, 765–766
  as inquiry, 529, 530, 531, 533
  as outcome of dialogue, 773
  porosity and, 562, 675
  queering, 434–436
  research through, 529, 531
Design as inquiry, 529, 530, 548–554
  HCI and, 531, 536, 555
  theory questions, 533
Designers
  as apprentices, 578
  as cultural intermediaries, 219
  evaluative understanding and, 577
Designer-user relationships, 560
Design fiction, 478, 509–511, 529
Design identification, 550
Design imaginings, 610
Designing Information Technology in the Postmodern Age (Coyne), 17
Design knowledge, 288
Design landscapes, 602, 602f
Design Noir: The Secret Life of Electronic Objects (Dunne and Raby), 504–505
Design outcomes, 299
Design practice, 300, 301
  as cultural criticism, 413–414
  ethics and, 304
  innovation and, 413
  user visibility in, 412–413
Design problem, scientific models and, 86, 87
Design purposes, 299, 300
Design research, 306
  intellectual excellences and, 297
  intellectual virtues practice implications for, 292–294
  primary, 295
  project scope and, 302
  subjective factors in, 303
  ultimate particular and, 300
Design sensibility, 562
  Foucauldian, 672–676
Design strategies, 673
Design theory, 313
Design things, 478
Design thinking, 287–288, 313, 550
Design truths, 300
Design-use relations, 413
Design work, intellectual virtues in, 294–298
Deviant design, 562, 674
Dewey, John, 84, 248, 249, 530, 571
Dialogical understanding, 572–574, 578
Dialogue, design and, 773
"Diapsalmata" (Kierkegaard), 85
DiCaprio, Leonardo, 59
Dickie, George, 541
Diegesis, 509
Digital artifacts, experience of, 262
Digital economy, 336

Digital media, 182, 410
 subjectivity and, 412
 subject positions and, 412
Digital Planet (radio program), 53
Digital representation, 410, 411
Digitizing Race: Visual Cultures of the Internet (Nakamura), 16
Dignity, 743
DiSalvo, Carl, 316, 413
Disavowed knowledge, 50
Discernment, 240
Disciplinary generalization, 635, 640
Disciplinary institutions, 636
Disciplinary mechanisms, 626–627
 democratic control of, 634
 state control of, 638, 657–658
 swarming of, 637, 657, 662
Disciplinary power, 627–628
 individualization and exclusion by, 628
Disciplinary pyramid, 644
Disciplinary society, 640, 642, 658
Discipline, 627, 656
 as counter-law, 645–646
 development of, 642–643
 in education, 636, 640
 functional inversion of, 636–637
 HCI as, 652
 human sciences and, 657
 individualizing, 628
 as infra-law, 645, 658, 661
 inversion of, 657
 knowledge and, 644
 mass phenomena efficiency and, 643
 military, 636
 multilateral, 666
 multiplicity and, 643
 objectives of, 642
 production and, 644
 professions and intellectuals and, 664–667
 social, 638
 technological threshold crossed by, 647
Discipline and Punish (Foucault), 652, 654, 657, 658, 660, 661, 663, 668, 672
Discipline-blockade, 635
Discipline-mechanism, 635
Discourse
 of critical design, 504–508
 historical events and, 188
 literature as, 98
 meta, 504
 moral, 487
 political, 487
 syntagmatic chain of, 187–188, 204
Discourse ethics, 564, 575, 770–775
Discovery, 566
Discursive knowledge, 190
Discursive production, 187
Disembodied knower, 772
Disindividualization, of power, 630
Distortion
 of communication, systematic, 195
 of meaning, 104
Diversity, respecting, 754
Division of labor, 644, 766
 social, 350
 technical, 403
Divorced households, 769
DJs, 178
Dobbins, Michael, 3
Doctorow, Cory, 335, 336
Domestic abuse, 769
Domestic computing, 770, 773
Domestic environment dimensions, 763
Domestic information processors, 762–763, 773
Domestic labor, 763, 766
Domestic questions, 764–765, 765t
Domestic technologies, 763, 766
Domestic temporality, 763
Domestic violence, 580
Dominance
 through ideology, 412
 structures of, 207, 214, 223
Dominant code, 195, 206
Dominant cultural order, 193, 205
Dominant definitions, 196
Dominant-hegemonic messages, 214

Dominant-hegemonic position, 195, 210, 214
Dominant meanings, 193, 194
Domination, 600
 liberty as instrument of, 349
Dourish, Paul, 314–315, 700
Drag, 425–426, 433
Dream recorder, 601
Dreyfus, Hubert, 17
Drift Table, 605, 606f, 616, 617
Drouet, Minou, 95, 122
Duchamp, Marcel, 317, 537, 544–545, 593
Dunne, Anthony, 311, 313, 475, 504, 506, 507, 508, 532, 550, 602, 603
Duty, 743
Dynabook, 87

Eagleton, Terry, 4, 10, 12, 312, 313, 316, 499–504, 508, 510–511
Eames, Charles, 300
Eco, Umberto, 11, 12, 30–31, 167, 242
Economic freedom, 347
Economic self-government, 490
Education, 5, 8
 art, 317
 capitalist, 374
 discipline in, 636, 640
 live coding for, 183
 as privilege, 330
 secluded, 631
Educational apparatus, 380, 382, 384–386, 404
Educational psychology, 648
Educational software, 437
Egotism, 719
Egypt, 715–721, 724
Ehn, Pelle, 478, 482n4, 604
Ehrlich, Anne, 448
Ehrlich, Paul, 448
Either/Or (Kierkegaard), 81, 85, 90
Electronic music, 158
Elitism, 501
Elliott, Philip, 189
Emancipation, 775
 HH failing to support, 767
Emancipatory social media systems, 728
Embodied identity, 737
Emin, Tracy, 539
Emotional communication, 703–704
Empathy, 772
Empirical knowledge, 648
Empiricism, 352, 669, 670
 HCI and, 365
 one-dimensionality and, 365
Empowerment, 708
Empson, William, 175
Encoding, 188
 codes of, 189
 decoding and, 195
 Hall on, 206–210
 process of, 207
Encompassing, 569n2
ender research of, 756
Engagement, 617–618
Engineering psychology, cognitivist approach to, 86
England, 715, 717, 718, 719
Enlarged mentality, 771, 772, 773
Enlightenment, 8, 452, 658, 664, 755
 HH as project of, 761–764
 skepticism of, 754
Eno, Brian, 175
Entitlement, 743
Entropy, 147–153, 171
 information in proportion to, 154–155
Enzensberger, Hans Magnus, 340
Epic theater, 328, 336
Episteme, 287, 290, 293–295, 302, 303, 305
Epistemic incoherence, 758
Epistemological breaks, 408
Equality, 744
 formal, 743, 757
 social relationships and, 762
Equator project, 605
Equity, 744, 757
E-readers, 335
Ergonomics, 660, 667
Eschaton, 298–299

Essays on the Blurring of Art and Life (Kaprow), 560
Essence of emotion, 746
Essentialism, 556n2
 rejection of, 432
Ethics, 128n7, 304. *See also* Justice ethics; *Nicomachean Ethics*
 care, 563–564, 753, 756–759, 764–765, 765t, 768–769
 design and, 475
 discourse, 564, 575, 770–775
 gender and, 756
 history and, 389
 interaction design and, 752
 justice, 756
 literature study and, 502
 myth and, 128n7
 normative, 563, 759–764
 of normative social visions, 775
 philosophical, 752
Ethnicity, post-colonial theory and, 491
Ethnic minorities, 496
Ethnographic field studies, 618
Ethnographic research, 413, 668, 730
Ethnomethodology, 18
 accountability in, 621n10
Etymology, 453, 455
Euclid, 46
Evaluation
 accountability as, 621n10
 of morality, 746–747
 participation and, 617–619
 understanding and, 565, 576–577
Events
 consistency building and text as, 237–243
 text as, 243–250
Events (Brecht, G.), 589
E-waste products, 767
Examination, 647, 648
Exclusion, 655
 individualization and, 628
 rituals of, 627
Exclusionary gender norms, 417
Existence
 ideology as representation of relationship to conditions of, 391–396
 "is" of, 539
 material, of ideology, 393–395
 spiritual, of ideology, 393
Existentialism, 595
Ex-nomination
 bourgeois, 116, 120, 121
 revolutionary, 120
Expectations
 cultural, 662
 memory and, 237
 reading and, 127, 230–231, 245
Experience
 aesthetic, 249, 266, 530
 of digital artifacts, 262
 familiarity and, 248
 interaction, 258–259
 of interactive artifacts, 256
 involvement as condition of, 245–250
 literature extending, 559
 privatization of, 738
 reading and, 248
 restructuring, 248
 structure of, 249
 technology, 86
 of text, 248
 user, 571, 578
Experience-centered design, 572, 580
Experience design, 435
Experience-oriented interaction, 87
Experimental myth, 113
Expert subject, 302
Exploitation, 387
 legitimizing, 768
 relations of, 383
 of women, 737, 753, 768, 776
Expressionistic theory of art, 545, 547
Expressiveness of language, 110
Expressive technologies, 434

Extraordinary rendition, 670
Eye-voice span, 229

Facebook, 32, 214, 215, 257–258, 332, 335, 340, 414, 674
advertising on, 415
infra-law and, 662
personal details in, 435
Fact
ideological arguments posing as, 448
naturalized, 448
philosophy and matters of, 462
reality and matters of, 452
scientific, 461
social construction of, 448, 556n2
statement of, 125
Fact position, 456, 459, 461
Faculties, 271–273
builder's, 274
formed, 273
prudence as formed, 274–275
Failure, insights from, 142
Fairness, 744
Fair position, 461
Fairy position, 456, 459, 461
Fake news, 32
Fallman, Daniel, 531
False consciousness, 351
False needs, 347, 360
False science, 568
Familiarity, 248, 566
Faraday Chair, 603
Fashion, 526
defensive dresses changing meaning of, 552
power of, 363
sub-codes of, 192
Faulkner, William, 232
Fear of Flying (Jong), 38
Fedigan, Linda, 456
Feinberg, Melanie, 32–33
Female autonomy, recognition of, 740
Feminism, 10, 313, 367, 417, 492, 500–501, 728
enlarged mentality related to, 771
ethics of care and, 756
HCI responsiveness to, 436
Feminist theory, 419, 737, 748n2
designers influenced by, 767
gender-sex system, 753–756
HH critique and, 764–768
Feminist universalism, 753–756
Fernandez, Ramón, 319
Fernow, Bernhard, 692n20
Fetishism, 457
Fetishistic disavowal, 50, 52
Fetishistic techno-utopianism, 140
Fictionality
in HCI, 267–268
reader awareness of, 266–267
Fielding, Henry, 264, 268
Filter bubbles, 214
Financial meltdown of 2008, 52–53
Financial rotation, 691n15
Finlay, Janet, 19
Finnegan's Wake (Joyce), 27
Fiscal forestry, 680–681
Fish, Stanley, 449
Fitness, 709
Fitness tracking tools, 704, 709
Fleck, Ludwik, 454
Flickr, 727
Fluxus events, 589, 593, 596
Focusing, 108
Folksonomies, 440
Forced migration, 496
Forest death, 687
Forest hygiene, 688
Forestry
fiscal, 680–681
restoration, 688
scientific, 679, 680–689, 698–699
Forgetting, 69, 70–71

Form, 100–103
  language as, 113
  meaning and, 101, 105
  message, 188
  mode of presence, 104
  openness and, 161–164
  rhetorical, of myth, 122–125
  subjunctive, 129n13
Formal definition, 568
Formal equality, 743, 757
Formalism, 97, 249, 464, 652
Foucauldian design sensibilities, 672–676
Foucault, Michel, 11, 13, 29, 202, 315, 433, 485, 493, 561–562, 651–676
  Enlightenment skepticism, 754
Fountain (sculpture), 537, 544–545
Fractal coefficient, of space, 763
Framing, 615
Franke, Katherine, 420, 421, 423
Frankfurt School, 7, 10, 313, 314, 316, 359, 409, 506, 697
Frayling, Christopher, 531
Free choice, 349
Freedom, 345, 347, 353
Freedom of enterprise, 346
Free/Libre Open Source Software (FLOSS), 174
Free-market fundamentalism, 510
Free software, 341
Free Software Foundation, 173
Freire, Paulo, 508
French Revolution, 385, 642
French Theory, 418–419
Freud, Sigmund, 487
Freudian theory, 44
  as semiological system, 98, 102
Friendship, 71–73, 88, 744
"From Human Factors to Human Actors" (Bannon), 661
From Notes Made in 1970–1971 (Bakhtin), 560
Frug, Mary Jo, 423
Fry, Roger, 517
Frye, Northrop, 8
Fusco, Coco, 600
Gadamer, Hans-Georg, 12, 261
Gadani, Amisha, 531–533, 532f, 551–553
Galileo Galilei, 305
Galison, Peter, 456
Game consoles, 335
Gamergate, 217
Gatehouse, 508
Gatherings, objects and, 463–464
Gaver, Bill, 53, 476, 531, 603
Gegenstand, 453–455
Gender, 417
  ambiguity in, 421
  denaturalizing, 424
  descriptive account of, 425
  identity and, 431
  meaning, 753
  naturalized knowledge of, 426
  normative account of, 424–425
  performativity of, 421–422
  sexuality and, 420, 421
  subordination and, 420–421
  subversive and unsubversive expressions of, 425
  tool constraints and, 435
Gender hierarchy, 420
Gender norms
  exclusionary, 417
  violence of, 424
Gender relations, justice and, 740
Gender research, 756
Gender-sex system, 737, 753–756
Gender studies, 418–419
Gender violence, 551–553
Generalization
  disciplinary, 635, 640
  of natural world, 681
"Generalized and the Concrete Other, The" (Benhabib), 563
Generalized other, 563, 743–747, 749n15
  concrete other vs., 758t
  resident and, 761
  smart home and, 756–759
Generalized self, 743–747

Generic human being, 761
Geography
  of myth, 122
  online activities decoupled from, 727
German Ideology, The (Marx), 388, 389–390
Gestalt, 237
  closed, 240, 241
  consistency from grouping, 242
  groupings and, 238, 242
  linguistic signs and, 239
  open, 240
  process of forming, 245–246
Gestalten
  literary devices and forming, 247
  of memory, 242
Gesture, 163
Geyer, Karl, 691n19
Gilligan, Carol, 739, 745
  gender research of, 756
Glickman, Steven, 456
Global-contrary position, 197, 211–212, 214
Globalization, 489
Global margins, 708
Global South, 338, 559, 563, 723, 724
God Is Not Great (Hitchens), 52
"God Save the Queen" (Sex Pistols), 174
Goldacre, Ben, 503
Golden ratio, 45–46
Golden rule, 777
Gómez-Peña, Guillermo, 600
Good continuation principle of coherence, 241
Good life, 739
  justice distinguished from, 740
Goodman, Nelson, 530
Google, 167, 171–174, 178–179, 183n1, 183n2, 335, 340–341, 663, 674, 768
Gottman, John, 56
Governance
  cultural studies engaging with, 201
  society and, 699
  statistical reasoning and, 411
Governmentality, 109
Gramsci, Antonio, 199, 202, 380, 405n7
Grand Theft Auto (game series), 132
Grand theory, 9–13, 315
Grass-root movements, 367–368
Great Firewall, 311
Greenspan, Alan, 53
Greenwald, Glenn, 338
Grid, the, 727
Grinter, Beki, 563
Gropius, Walter, 511
Grouping
  consistency from, 242
  gestalt, 239, 242
  meaning and, 237
Gründel, Günter, 327
Grundrisse (Marx), 187
Grusin, Richard, 332
Guantanamo Bay, 670
Guaranteed Minimum Wage, 373
Guardian (newspaper), 337
Guguletu township, 727

Habermas, Jurgen, 485, 747
Habitus, 46–47
Hacking, Ian, 454
Hailing, 398
Hall, Stuart, 10, 31–32, 199, 418, 501–502, 506
  cultural studies shaped by, 200–202
  on decoding, 210–214
  on encoding, 206–210
  four-stage theory of communication, 206
  HCI and, 221–223
  state apparatuses and, 409–410
Happenings, 585–586, 593, 596, 601, 611, 612
Haraway, Donna, 138, 452
"Has Critique Run Out of Steam" (Latour), 12
Hashtags, 440
HCI4D, 139, 563, 708, 723–725, 731, 751
Health, 709
Heartfield, John, 325
Heat, 147
Hegel, G. W. F., 359, 756
  self-consciousness, 741
Hegemonic code, 206

Hegemonic definitions, 196–197
Heidegger, Martin, 359, 453–454, 455, 462, 463, 486
Heinz dilemma, 744–745
Heisenberg Principle, 690n6
Heller, Agnes, 740
Hermeneutic interpretation, 391
Hermeneutics of suspicion, 704–705
Heterogeneous Home (HH), 564, 752–753
  domestic questions, 764–765, 765t
  as Enlightenment Project, 761–764
  feminist critique of, 764–768
  moral and political issues of, 776
  as normative ethical vision, 759
  overview, 760–761
  smart home and, 759–764, 774
Heterosexism, 417
Heterosexuality, 420
Hierarchical surveillance, 644
Historical criticism, 97
Historical events, discourse and, 188
Historical materialism, 500
History
  of critical theory, 7–14
  ethics and, 389
  ideology and, 389–391
  of myth, 122
  mythology and, 126
  privation of, 123
History of Sexuality, The (Foucault), 651, 658
Hitchens, Christopher, 52, 57, 499
Hoax papers, 503
Hobbes, Thomas, 738, 756
  men as mushrooms, 741, 742
  on morality, 739
  state of nature, 740–741
Hoggart, Richard, 199, 500, 501
Holmer, Hrönn Brynjarsdóttir, 562
Home
  division of labor in, 766
  human centered vs. technology centered, 762–763
  integrated outside and inside, 763
Home-as-information domain, 763
Home depreciation, 769
Homogenous home, 760
Homophobia, 417, 421
Hook, Jon, 575, 577, 581
Hooker, Ben, 759, 764, 768, 774
Horace, 530
Horkheimer, Max, 313, 409
Household of emotions, 740
House vs. home, 763
Housework, 766
Huggable Atomic Mushroom Cloud cushion, 442
Human body, as interface, 440
Human-centered design paradigm, 295–296
Human-centered home, 762–763
Human-computer interaction (HCI), 4, 407, 751
  accountability and, 617
  conference costs, 725
  controversy and, 480–481
  critical project in, 705
  critical-reflective, 476, 480
  critical theory and, 14–20
  critical turn in, 200
  design as inquiry and, 531, 536, 555
  as design-centered discipline, 413
  as discipline, 652
  early, 17–18
  empiricism and, 365
  environmental issues and, 436
  feminism and, 436
  fictionality in, 267–268
  first wave, 200, 660–661
  Foucauldian analysis of, 562
  Foucauldian sensibilities in, 672–676
  Foucault and, 659–667
  Hall and, 221–223
  HH and, 759–768
  identity and, 430
  ideology and, 315, 316, 362
  imaginary enacted in, 268
  innovation and practice of, 413–415

institutional affiliation and, 732n1
intersubjective comprehensibility in, 262–264
legibility in, 700
metaphor in, 176
myth in, 139–141, 142
open design in, 441
participation and, 601–610, 729
performing, 432–433
psychology and, 55–58
research purposes and motives, 357
second wave, 200, 661
social creativity theory and, 541
surveillance and, 663–664
sustainable, 139, 140–141, 480
third wave, 15, 19, 20, 200, 661, 667
user agency and interpretation process in, 265–266
Human factors, 200, 700
Human identity, 746
Humanity, 744, 757, 773
respecting, 775
universal, 759
Human perspective, 774
Human rights, 423–424
Humans, treatment of others, 777
Human sciences, 567, 581, 651, 664
discipline and, 657
examination and, 648
Humor, 507
Humphrys, John, 2–3
Hunting, 689n2
Husserl, 359, 462
Hybrid Homemaking, 766
Hypertext, 262

Iconic signs, 191
Iconographic meaning, 166n20
ICT4D, 139, 140, 708
Identification, 123
artistic, 520–522, 524, 539–541, 543, 545, 547, 554
design, 550
meaning change by, 552
with society, 351
Identity, 201, 217, 219, 429
cultural, 725
definitional, 746
embodied, 737
formalization in social networks, 439
formalization of, 439
gender and, 431
HCI and, 430
of indiscernibles, 534
instability of, 494
"is" of, 539
online activities decoupled from, 727
performativity and, 431–432
social mechanisms and, 431
Identity politics, 432, 491
Identity production, 215
Ideological apparatuses, 379–382
Ideological arguments, 448
Ideological artifact, 703
Ideological assumptions, interactive systems and, 411
Ideological edifice, 37
Ideological recognition, 397
Ideological reproduction, 196
Ideological State Apparatuses (ISAs), 379–386, 393, 395, 402, 403, 409, 410, 412, 414
class struggle in, 404, 405n11
Ideological structures, 314
Ideologism, 127
Ideology, 408
absorption into reality of, 351
agents of production and, 374
Althusser on, 388–404
bourgeois, 115, 125, 396
broadcasting as apparatus of, 207
Christian religious, 399–401
class nature of, 403
class positions and, 389
code and, 205
consent and, 314
democracy and, 438

Ideology (cont.)
  design-use relations and, 413
  dominance through, 412
  duplicate mirror-structure of, 401
  HCI and, 315, 316, 362
  history and, 389–391
  ideology of, 394
  as imaginary relationship of individuals to reality, 391–393
  individuals interpellated by, as subjects, 396–399
  industrial society and, 351
  interpretations of, 391
  material existence of, 393–395
  material externality and, 37–38
  as representation of relationship to conditions of existence, 391–396
  ruling, 384
  of ruling class, 382
  subject and, 396, 412
  subjecthood and, 315
  technology design and, 362
  utility and, 38
Idleness, 67
Ignorance, veil of, 744–746, 757–758, 767
Image sharing, 727
Imaginary
  HCI and enacting, 268
  meaning and, 257
  reality relationship with, 391–393
  social media streams invoking, 257–258
Imagination, 366
Imitation Theory of Art (IT), 516–518, 536–537, 542, 547
Immigration barriers, 726
Impenetrable objectivity, 241
Imperative mode, 110
Imperialism, 718
Implied author, 247, 257
Imprisonment, 654
Improbability, 153
Inclusiveness, of capitalism, 495–496
Incomplete reversibility, 746
India, 729
Indicative mode, 110
Indices of effectivity, 375–376
Indiscernibles, identity of, 534
Individualism, 495
Individuality, 744, 757
  one-dimensionality and, 364
  suspending, 758
Individualization, 629, 656, 660
  exclusion and, 628
Individualizing discipline, 628
Individual needs, 349
Individuals
  ideology interpellating, as subjects, 396–399
  as subjects, 399
  utility of, 663
Individuation, 745
Indoctrinating power, 349
Indoor Weather Stations (IWS), 607–608, 608f, 610, 615, 618
Industrialism, 359
Industrial society
  disruption in, 363
  freedom and, 345, 347, 361
  identification and, 351
  ideology and, 351
  needs and, 349
  progress and, 354
  rational character of irrationality of, 350
  totalitarian tendency of, 346, 360
Infinite, 77n20
Information
  as additive quantity, 146
  aesthetic, 164
  ambiguity of term, 167
  engineering definitions of, 170
  entropy in proportion to, 154–155
  meaning difference from, 151–152, 156
  measuring, 170–172
  measuring changes in, 147–148
  openness and, 156–161
  in poetic message, 152–154
  quantification of, 145–147

quantitative, 164
transmission of, 154–156
Wiener and, 149
Information and communications technologies and development (ICTD), 723–724, 732
institutional affiliation in, 725, 726
Information Awareness Office, 450f
Information management, restorative homes and, 762
Information overload, 210
Information pieces, 593
Information-processing theory
HH and, 762–763
multigenerational households and, 769
Information-seeking needs, environment to support, 760–761
Information theory, 145–149, 155, 167, 170, 203
Infrastructure, 375–376, 402
Ingres, Jean Auguste Dominique, 545
Ink blots, 159
Inklings, 5
Innovation
artistic, 546
creative practice and, 410, 413
design practice and, 413
HCI practice and, 413–415
user-driven, 88
Inquiry, 278
design as, 529, 530
playful, 619
Inquisition, 648, 649
Instability of identities, 494
Instant revisionism, 449
Institute for Social Research, 359
Institutional affiliation, 724–726, 732n1
Institutional theory of art, 541
Institutions, 561–562
Instrumental medium, 333
Intel, 767, 773
Intellectual freedom, 347
Intellectual labor, 555
Intellectual virtues
design research and practice implications, 292–294
in design work, 294–298
in *Nicomachean Ethics*, 289–292
Intelligence, Aristotle on, 280
Intel Research, 564
Intensive timber management, 692n23
Intentional sentence correlates, 229–230
Interaction
experience, 258–259
experience-oriented, 87
poetics of, 174–177
Interaction criticism, 20
Interaction design
critical theory and, 14–20
as empirically trapped, 365
ideology and, 362
as individualistic enterprise, 364–365
queering, 436, 440–441
smart homes, 751–778
sustainable, 480
Interaction Design Research Studio, 476
Interaction Research Studio (IRS), 560–561, 599, 601–610, 617
participation characteristics for, 609–610
projects, 605–609
Interactive artifacts, 254, 256, 267
Interactive mimesis, 87
Interactive systems
behavioral impact of, 436
codification of self in, 435
ideological assumptions and, 411
Interactive universalism, 738
Interface criticism, 20
Interfaces
body as, 440
openness in, 87
user-friendly, 335–336
Internality, 422
International Art English (IAE), 507
International development, 708

International Gay and Lesbian Human Rights Commission, 423
Internet of things, 430
Internet studies, 15–17
Interpellation, 4, 314, 401, 402, 408, 411
  ideology and, 412
  of individuals, by ideology, 396–399
Interpretation
  complex, 259
  consistent, 237
  of cultural artifacts, 220–221
  HCI and process of, 265–266
  hermeneutic, 391
  of ideology, 391
  as integration of perspectives, 261
  mechanistic, 391
  openness of, 87
  reader agency and, 264–265
  of social media, 259
  textual, 254–260
  types of, 391
  user agency and, 265–266
Interpretations
  of ideology, 391
  of Prayer Companion, 53–54
Interpretive Probe studies, 605
Interrogative design, 698
Interruption, 328
Intersubjective comprehensibility, 261
  in HCI, 262–264
Introjection, 350
Intuitive wisdom, 297
Investigation, 647–649
iOS platform, 341
iPhone, 332, 340, 509
IPSOS Mori, 214
Irigaray, Luce, 485
Irony, 236, 246
Irreversibility, principle of, 148
Iser, Wolfgang, 12, 32–33, 253, 260
  on intersubjective comprehensibility, 261, 263
Italian anti-design movement, 505–506
IT appliances, 335, 336, 337
IT design
  base and superstructure in, 331
  political role of, 332
IT design projects, HH and, 775
Ive, Jony, 511
Iyer, Lars, 2

Jackson, Michael, 37, 58
James, Henry, 244
James, William, 452
Jameson, Fredric, 16, 43, 485
  vanishing mediator and, 49
Jarman, Derek, 499
Jaspers, Karl, 565, 569n2
Jealousy, 741
Jeremijenko, Natalie, 476
Johns, Jasper, 518
Johnson, Alan, 43
Johnson, Steven, 16
Joint-stock companies, 114–117
Jones, Owen, 510
Jong, Erica, 38
Joyce, James, 27, 168, 232, 246, 247, 311, 502
Judgment, 280–281, 292
Judicial power, 640
Judiciary, 658
July monarchy, 637
Juridical frameworks, 645
Juridical investigation, 647
Juridical norms, 646
Juridical systems, 646
Jurisprudence, 647
Justice, 658, 738–743
  accusatory, 649
  good life and, 739, 748n4
  good life distinguished from, 740
  misogyny and, 742
  penal, 649
  as reversibility, 744
  split of public and private sphere, 742–743
"Justice as Reversibility: The Claim to Moral Adequacy of a Highest State of Moral Development" (Kohlberg), 744

Justice ethics, 563–564, 757–758, 767, 771–772
moral theory and, 756
normative ethical vision and, 759–764

Kant, Immanuel, 452, 462, 756, 761
categorical imperative, 777
justice, 740
moral theory of, 747
state of nature of, 740
Kaprow, Allan, 560–561, 599–601, 610–620
Kästner, Erich, 326
Kay, Alan, 176
Kaye, Jofish, 29–30
Kelty, Christopher, 341
Kenya, 727, 728
Kew Gardens, 728
Keynote, 414
Keystroke-level model, 86
Kierkegaard, Søren, 28–29, 81
Kindle, 340
Kinect, 440
Kleiner, Dmitry, 334
Knower, resident as, 762–763
"Knowing the Oriental" (Said), 563
Knowing the user, 577–582
Knowledge
art and, 530
Balfour on, 716
design, 288
disavowed, 50
discipline and, 644
discursive, 190
empirical, 648
as entrapment, 662
formation of, 648
industrialization of production of, 673
narrowing of vision and, 679
naturalized, 426
power and, 658–659, 672, 703, 724–726
science and, 287
scientific, 290, 702
situated, 138
of social structures, 193
tacit, 297
theoretical, 294–295
traditional, 702
universal, 303
Knowledge producing practices, 653
Kohlberg, Lawrence, 737, 756
autonomous self, 742
on justice, 744
on moral domain, 738
on morality, 739, 750n26
moral theory and, 747
personal decision-making, 740
special relationships of obligation, 739
Kohlberg-Gilligan controversy, 756–758
Kolkhoz (collective farm), 321
de Kooning, Willem, 543
K-relevant predicates, 525
Kristeva, Julia, 485, 503
Krysa, Joasia, 335–336
Kuhn, Thomas, 3–4
Kundera, Milan, 32
Kurgan, Laura, 476

Labbé, Cyril, 503
Labor. *See also* Division of labor
alienated, 392
domestic, 763, 766
gender blindness of, 766
intellectual, 555
Labor movements, 492
Labor power, reproduction of, 372–375
Labor saving technology, 766
Labor theory of value, 543
Lacan, Jacques, 16, 43, 50, 485, 503
Lady Ada, 674
Landworks, 593
Language, 95. *See also* Metalanguage
articulated, 110
as code, 172–173
of critical design, 508
of critical theory, 500–504
defining, 96

Language (cont.)
  expressiveness of, 110
  as form, 113
  of literary criticism, 502–504
  mathematical, 111
  meaning at level of, 238
  myth as stolen, 110–114
  mythical, 96
  normative, 493
  of oppressed, 121
  of oppressor, 121
  redundancy of, 151
  revolutionary, 120, 707
  second-order, 119
  semiotics and engineering of, 168–170
  signifier-signified ratio in, 103
  understanding, 566
Language object, 99, 105, 118
  metalanguage distinction from, 119
Language of New Media, The (Manovich), 16
Latchkey children, 769
Latour, Bruno, 12, 312, 315, 471–477, 479, 541, 669, 695, 704, 706
Laurel, Brenda, 15–16, 33, 87, 313
Lavatory, 38–39, 41
Law, social contract and, 741–742
Lawrence, D. H., 311, 496
Leavis, F. R., 8, 12
Left-wing myth, 120
Legibility, 700, 702
Lehrer, Tom, 170
Lenin, Vladimir, 489
Lenoir, Tim, 456
Lepers, 627, 628, 655
Lesbianism, 419
Levinas, Emmanuel, 486
Lévi-Strauss, Claude, 38, 39, 44, 202, 485
Lewis, C. S., 5
Liberal humanism, 8–9
Liberation movements, 489–490
Libertarianism, 172, 492–493
Liberties, 345–346
Liberty, 658
  destruction of political patriarchy and, 741
  as instrument of domination, 349
Libeskind, Daniel, 455
Lichtenstein, Roy, 518
Lifelike art, 561, 611
Life on the Screen (Turkle), 16, 504
Light, Ann, 184n8, 315, 413
Limited IT appliances, 335, 336
Linguistic divides, 730
Linguistic redundancy, 151
Linguistic signs, 239
Linguistic system, 99, 101
  poetry and, 153
Linguistic theory, 191
Linux, 181, 414
Literary criticism, 8, 313, 652
  political tendency and, 320
Literary fiction, 510
Literary object, 229
Literary quality, 320
Literary reading, 267
Literary realism, 113
Literary studies, 312, 511
Literary text
  denotation and, 228–229
  flow of, 231–232
  reader position in, 230, 233
Literary theory, language of, 502–504
Literature
  Bakhtin interest in, 573
  as discourse, 98
  ethics and study of, 502
  experience extended by, 559
  linear flow of, 262
  as mythical system, 112–113
  as signification, 112
  software and access to, 338–339
  study of, 502
  tendency and quality in, 319–321
Live coding, 178–179, 180, 182
Live transmission, 242

Locke, John, 756
justice, 740
state of nature metaphor, 740
Logocracy, 323
Lomazzi, Paolo, 505
Lopate, Phillip, 1
Louis XIV (King), 679
Louis XV (King), 654
Love, 744, 757
Love's Knowledge (Nussbaum), 559
Lowood, Henry, 683
Ludic design, 549, 550, 560–561, 601, 619, 667
critical design and, 602–603
participation in, 604
studio examples, 605–609
Lyall, Alfred, 720
Lyotar, Jean-François, Enlightenment skepticism, 754

McCarthy, John, 19, 560
MacKinnon, Catharine, 420
McLuhan, Marshall, 32, 332, 415
Mac OS, 173
McRobbie, Angela, 500
Madness and Civilization (Foucault), 651
Man and the Echo, The (Yeats), 32
Mandiargues, André Pieyre de, 161–162
Maneuvers (Happening), 611
Mann, Heinrich, 323
Manovich, Lev, 16, 262, 332
Mapping, 193
Mapping Controversies on Science for Politics (MACOSPOL), 477, 482n4
Maps of meaning, 219, 223
Marcuse, Herbert, 10, 311, 313–314, 357–360, 363, 506
Marginalized people, 724
Margins, 492, 496
global, 708
Marriage, 72, 73, 88
Marx, Karl, 202, 341n1, 354, 359, 371, 372, 375, 389, 392, 405n11, 408, 409, 488
Marxism, 316, 486, 490, 704
critical theory and, 510
Foucault and, 652
Marxism Today, 199
Marxist theory, 4, 10, 227, 312–315
base and superstructure in, 331, 375–376
media and aesthetics theories and, 332
media theory and, 332
state ideological apparatus, 379–382
State in, 376–377, 378–379
topography, 375–376
Mass communication technology, 168–169
Mass culture, 30
Massively open online courses (MOOCs), 30, 136
Mass media
class distinctions and, 349
one-dimensional thought and, 353
Mass phenomena, discipline reducing inefficiency of, 643
Material aesthetics, 332, 333
Material alienation, 392
Material existence, of ideology, 393–395
Material externality, ideology and, 37–38
Materialism, 393
historical, 500
Materialist analysis, 320
media theory and, 332
Materialist dialectics, 338
Material rituals, 397
Mathematical language, 111
Maublanc, Réne, 329, 330
Max/MSP, 179
Meaning
aesthetic, 166n20
associative, 192
collective cultural making of, 215
configurative, 247
connoted, 205
consumption and, 219–220
contextual, 568
cultural, 219
decoded, 189

Meaning (cont.)
denoted, 205
dialogical approach to making, 259–260
discourse and, 187–188
distortion of, 104
dominant, 193, 194
form and, 101, 105
grouping and, 237
iconographic, 166n20
identification changing, 552
imaginary and, 257
information difference from, 151–152, 156
at language level, 238
maps of, 219, 223
media communication and, 204
of pictures, 100
in poetic message, 152–154
preferred, 193
receiver participating in making of, 205–206
second-order, 102
utility as, 38
Mechanical performance, 178, 179
Mechanistic interpretation, 391
Mechanization, 345, 346
Media. *See also* Social media; Television
critical theories of, 409
digital, 182, 410, 412
economic base and, 409
indoctrinating power of, 349
Kenya portrayal in, 727
representation and, 727
tactical, 698
Media aesthetics, 332
Media communication, meaning and, 204
Mediascape, 414
Media studies, 15–17
Media theory, 170
Marxist thinking in, 332
Medical surveillance, 637, 663
Meeting, communication and, 565
Memory
expectations and, 237
gestalten of, 242
in reading process, 230–231, 234, 235
wandering viewpoint and, 234, 235
Memory-oriented systems, 256
Men
autonomous male ego, 741
denying being born of woman, 741
gender-sex system, 753
morality transition of, 740
as mushrooms, 741, 742
narcissistic, 741, 742
Menageries, 631
Mental fatigue, restorative environment reducing, 762
Mercury poisoning, 767
Message
decoding, 189, 210
discursive form of, 188
dominant-hegemonic, 214
encoded, 189
encoding process, 207
information quantity in, 145–147
models of sending and receiving, 202–203, 203f
production of television, 188–189, 206–207
reception of television, 189
Message form, 188
Metaconcepts, 504
Metacriticism, 698
Metadata, in Spyn, 254, 256, 258
Metadiscourse, 504
Metahaven collective, 476
Metalanguage, 99, 105, 118
language object distinction from, 119
mythology and, 126
Metaphor, 176
Copernican revolution, 460
spatial, 375–376
state of nature, 740–742
Metaphysical systems, 549
Meta-values, 438–439
Mettray Penal Colony, 654, 676
Microsoft Word, 414
Microwave blockers, 674

Middle Ages, 647–649
MIDI, 178
Militarism, 719
Military discipline, 636
Miller, Alain, 52
Milner, Alfred, 715
Mimesis, 351, 536–537
Mind, as computer, 762
Minecraft, 30, 180–182
Minimum wage, 373
Minix, 181
Mirrors, 515, 537
Misrecognition, 397
Mission of the Young Generation (Gründel), 327
Misunderstandings, 194, 195, 197, 215, 610
Mobile computing, 700, 707
Modernism, 494, 704, 708
  Chesterton on, 58
Modernity, 701–703
  transition to, 738–739
Moles, Abraham, 175
Molleindustria, 311, 332, 337
Monk, Andrew, 19, 56
Monocropped forests, 686
Monocultures, 686, 688, 695
Monological model of moral reasoning, 747
Monopoly capitalism, 340
Moods, control of, 74
Moore's law, 167
Moral autonomy, 738, 755, 773
Moral disagreements, 747
Moral discourse, 487
Moral domain, 738
Moral impartiality, 742
Morality, 739, 750n26
  bourgeois, 125
  design and, 751
  evaluating, 746–747
  literature study and, 502
Moral judgements, 738
Moral philosophy, 756
Moral reasoning, monological model of, 747
Moral self, 737–738
Moral theory
  ethics of justice and, 756
  of Kant, 747
  point of view and, 759
  universalistic, 737–738, 747, 756
Moral universals, 775
Moral virtue, 272, 282, 283, 289, 290
Morozov, Evgeny, 3
Morphology of the Folktale (Propp), 4
Mortimore, Roger, 214
Mosaics, 158–159
Motherwell, Robert, 543
Motivation
  myth and, 106–107
  of signification, 106–107
Mozambique, 729
Mulhall, Stephen, 530–531
Multiculturalism, 754–755
Multiculturalist critical theory, 312
Multigenerational households, 766, 769
Multiplicities, 642–644, 658
Mulvey, Laura, 313
Mundane objects, 131–132
Music, 157, 172, 175
  concrete, 158
  electronic, 158
  live coding, 178–179
  performance of, 177
  reproduction of, 325–326
  tonal system in, 150
Music for Airports (album), 175
Myth, 135
  ambiguity of, 105
  artificial, 112, 113
  bourgeoisie, 121–122
  as depoliticized speech, 117–119
  as double system, 104–105
  ethics and, 128n7
  experimental, 113
  form and concept of, 100–103
  in HCI, 139–141, 142
  history and geography of, 122
  history transformed into nature by, 109

Myth (cont.)
instability in concepts, 103
on left, 119–121
left-wing, 120
literature as system of, 112–113
manifestation and, 104
meaning distorted by concept in, 104
motivation and, 106–107
as negative criticism, 141
petite bourgeoisie, 121
poetry and, 112
reading and deciphering, 108–110
rhetorical forms of, 122–125
on right, 121–126
as semiological system, 96–100, 104–105
signification of, 103–107
signifier of, 100
as speech stolen and restored, 106
Stalin, 120–121
as stolen language, 110–114
tridimensional pattern in, 98–99
as type of speech, 95–96
as value, 105
voluntary acceptance of, 112
Mythology
history and, 126
metalanguage and, 126
necessity and limits of, 126–128

Nakamura, Lisa, 16
Nake, Frieder, 333
Name of the Rose, The (Eco), 30, 169
Narcissism, 559
state-of-nature metaphor and, 741–742
Western, 488
Nationalism, 720
revolutionary, 489–492
National Science Foundation, 725
National Security Agency (NSA), 332, 337, 449, 702
National Socialism, 316
Naturalism, 190
Naturalization, 136
of codes, 191, 204
Naturalized facts, 448
Naturalized knowledge, 426
Natural regeneration, 691n19
Natural resources, 681, 704
Natural sciences, 567, 581
Natural sign, 191
Natural virtue, 283
Nature
class, 403
history transformed into, by myth, 109
organizing, 681
social, of culture, 201
state of, 740–742
"Nature and Space" (Scott), 562
Nazism, 333, 386
Needs, 347–349, 360
Negotiated code position, 196–197, 211, 214
Neighborhoods, dangerous, 769
Neither/Norism, 124
Nelson, Ted, 176
Neo-Dada theater, 589
Neologism, 103, 109
Neo-Marxism, 408
Nest, 768
Netflix, 3
New atheism, 499
New Left, 199, 359
New Left Review, 199
Newman, Barnett, 518
New Man ideal, 37–38
New Matter-of-Factness, 323–326, 330
Newspapers, 322, 334
Newsstand app store, 337
Newton, Esther, 419
Nicomachean Ethics (Aristotle), 33, 288, 293–294, 298–304
intellectual excellences in, 289–292
Nietzsche, Friedrich, 486, 493
Noble game, 689n2
Noise, 150, 158, 170–172
Nonart performance, 594–595

Nongovernmental organizations (NGOs), 723
Nonhuman agency, 312
Nontheatrical performance, 593, 594, 596, 611, 613
Normative account of gender, 424–425
Normative design
  discourse ethics and, 770–775
  smart home and, 774
Normative ethics, 563
  smart home and, 759–764
Normative sexuality, 419, 421
Normative sociotechnical vision of utopia, 775–778
Normativity, 492–493
Norms, 492–493
  juridical systems and, 646
North American white middle class, HH normalizing, 767
Notch, 181
Noumenal agency, 745
Nous, 287, 293, 294, 302, 303, 305
Novelty, 156
Nussbaum, Martha, 531, 559
Nutrient cycle, 687

Objective position, 567, 581
Objectivity, 456, 458
  ideology and, 44
  impenetrable, 241
Objects
  artwork and, 519
  critical barbarity and, 459
  gatherings and, 463–464
  literary, 229
  mundane, 131–132
  perceptual, 229
  in philosophy, 454
  scientific, 456
  of social world, 411
  solidity of, 461
  things and, 454–456
  virtual, 411
  weak, 461
Obligation, 743
Observation, 656, 661
Obviousness, 396
Official posts, 73
Oldenburg, Claes, 518
Old-growth forests, 686
Oligopticism, 669
One-dimensionality, 360–363
  breaking, 366
  empiricism and, 365
  individuality and, 364
One-dimensional man, 358
One-dimensional thought, 352, 353, 358
One Laptop Per Child, 140
Online commerce, 176
Online content delivery, 415
Open design, 441
Open gestalt, 240
Openness, 145, 438–439
  form and, 161–164
  information and, 156–161
  in interfaces, 87
  of interpretation, 87
  participation and, 616
  as political commitment, 173–174
  sandbox games and, 180
Open source software, 173–174
Open text, 30
Open work, in visual arts, 156–164
"Open Work, The" (Eco), 12, 168–170
Open world video games, 180, 184n9
Opera, 327
Operating systems, 173
Operationalism, 352, 354, 365
Oppositional code, 197
Oppressed, 671
  language of, 121
  speech of, 121
  world made by, 121
Oppression, of women, 737, 753
Oppressor
  language of, 121
  world conserved by, 121

Organizational culture, 219
Orientalism (Said), 490, 723–724, 731
"Original position," 757
Other. *See also* Concrete other; Generalized other
  representing, 563–564
  self relationship with, 573
Othering, 726
Otherness, 78n31, 496
Otherness of the other, 771–772, 777
Overspecialization, 88
Overtone, 179

PageRank, 167, 171, 179, 183n2
Painting, 161, 177, 518, 539–541
  Action, 595, 611
  allegorical, 542
  as communication, 162–163
Panopticism, 635, 640, 643, 645–647, 658, 668–670
"Panopticism" (Foucault), 561
Panoptic modality of power, 645
Panopticon, 561, 628–635, 654–659
Pantheism, 68, 82
Papanek, Victor, 313
Paradox, Prayer Companion and, 57–58
Parallax views, 54–55
Parody social media profiles, 258
Participation, 579, 599–600, 729–731
  accessibility and, 614–616
  accountability and, 616–619
  assumptions about, 729
  characteristics for IRS, 609–610
  in critical design, 560–561, 602–603, 604
  evaluation and, 617–619
  framing and, 615
  HCI and, 601–610, 729
  HCI approach segmentation and, 600
  Kaprow and, 610–614
  in ludic design, 604
  observations across practices, 602–605
  observations across studio examples, 605–609
  of researchers, 730
  as subjects, 618
  taxonomies of, 600, 602
"Participation in Design Things" (Ehn), 478
Participation-oriented design, 560
Participation Performance (Kaprow), 612
Participatory design (PD), 88, 331–332, 339, 478–479, 578–579, 600, 604, 773, 775
  in developing nations, 730
  iterative, 606
Partitioning, 643
  disciplinary, 628
  tactical, 627
Pasta sauce, 29–30
Pater, Walter, 243
Pedagogical experiments, 631
Peer-reviewed journals, 137–138
Peirce, Charles Sanders, 132
Penal justice, 649
People and Practices Research Lab, Intel, 773
People-technology relations, 571
Perception, 84
  selective, 194–195
Perceptual *noema*, 239
Perceptual objects, 229
Perfectly transparent communication, 195
Performance, 177–179, 184n8
  art, 593
  customization and reconfiguring, 179–182
  as inquiry, 614
  mechanical, 178, 179
  nonart, 594–595
  nontheatrical, 593, 594, 596, 611, 613
  sponsorship of, 596–597
  theatrical, 592
Performance art, 600
Performative rules, 193
Performativity, 184n8, 429, 439
  of gender, 421–422
  identity and, 431–432
  race and, 422
PERMA theory, 54, 56
Personal decision-making, 740

Personhood, 429, 430, 437
Perspective, honoring, 774, 777
Persuasive sustainability, 701, 708
Persuasive technology design, 701
Petite bourgeoisie, 116
  identification, 123
  myth of, 121
Petit récits, 754
Petrarch, 153
Phantasmagoria, 341n1
Phenomenology, 17, 18, 257, 359, 463
  Foucault and, 652
Philosophical ethics, 752, 772
Philosophy
  aesthetic, 317
  analytic, 316–317
  of art, 317
  art and inquiry in, 531
  artworld understanding with, 535–536
  Brillo Box as, 548–550
  critical theory and, 361
  matters of fact and, 462
  objects in, 454
Phone Story, 332, 337
Photography, 325, 326
Phronesis, 291–298, 300–301, 303, 304
Pickering, Andrew, 463
Pictures, 96, 99
  meaning of, 100
Pinchot, Gifford, 686, 692n20
Pinker, Stephen, 503
Pirate shadow libraries, 339
Piss Christ, 612
Plague, 625–628, 632, 634, 655
Platforms, control of access to, 332
Plato, 7, 289, 311, 319, 536, 537
Playful inquiry, 619
Playful technologies, 615
Pleasure, 487
Plochmann, Richard, 688, 692n22
Pluralism, 193
Poesis, 293
Poetic recollection, 84, 87–89
Poetics (Aristotle), 15, 304
Poetics, of interaction, 174–177
Poetry, 129n10, 530
  meaning and information in message of, 152–154
  metaphor in, 176
  myth and, 112
  as semiological system, 111–112
Poets, 319
"Point of View for My Work as an Author, The" (Kierkegaard), 85
Pold, Søren, 314
Police
  centralized, 638, 657–658
  generalization of discipline and, 640
  political pressure on, 639
  power of, 638–639
  surveillance and power of, 639
Political activism, 173–174
Political discourse, 487
Political freedom, 347, 360
Political power, 346
Political sovereignty, 490
  police and, 638
Political tendency, 319–320, 327, 338
Political wisdom, 291
Politics
  art, participation, and, 560–561
  Foucault and, 671
  of health, 709
  identity, 432, 491
  IT design role in, 332
  one-dimensional thought and, 353
Pollack, Jackson, 543, 545
Polling, 214
Pollock, Jackson, 163
Polysemy, 193
Pop art, 523
Popular culture, as subject of study, 487
Porcupine Dress, 531–533, 532f, 551–554, 555
Portrait of the Artist as a Young Man (Joyce), 27

Position of third party, 567
Positive psychology, 56
Positivism, 460, 464, 704
Postcolonial analysis, 10, 367
Postcolonialism, 490, 491, 724, 728
Postcolonial studies, 488
Poster, Mark, 664, 669
Post-Frankfurt School, 409
Post-impressionists, 517, 538
Postmodern cultural studies, 503
Postmodernism, 16, 488, 494, 497n1, 752
  consensus and, 492
  individualism and, 495
  norms and, 493
Poststructuralism, 10, 11, 13, 417–418, 486, 500
Potato Eaters (painting), 518, 538, 542, 545
Power, 202, 561–562, 651, 658
  absolutist, 670
  arrangements of, 710
  authoritarian, 708
  automation of, 630
  bio, 659, 662
  code and, 173–174, 205
  costs of, 642–643
  counter, 643
  cultural studies and, 201
  disciplinary, 627–628
  disindividuation of, 630
  everyday practices and knowledge and, 703
  exercise of, 633
  of fashion industry, 363
  indoctrinating, 349
  intensification of, 634
  judicial, 640
  knowledge and, 658–659, 672, 703, 724–726
  panoptic modality of, 645
  Panopticon as laboratory of, 631–632
  physics of, 635, 655
  plague and, 634
  police, 638–639
  political, 346
  of representation, 710
  reproduction of labor, 372–375
  resistance and, 670–671
  rituals of, 630
  social, 642
  State, 378, 380, 385, 412
  surveillance and, 663
  visibility and, 629–630
Power relations, 644
Practical Criticism (Richards), 502
Practical rituals, 397
Practical wisdom, 291, 292
  in design work, 294–298
Praxis, 293, 294, 300–301, 304
Prayer Companion, 28, 46f, 48f, 51, 59, 616, 617
  accounts of, 45–47
  interpretations of, 53–54
  media reception of, 47–49
  as paradoxical device, 57–58
  parallax views and, 54–55
  participation and, 606–607, 607f
Preconditioning, 349
Predicate logic, 524–526, 534
Predication, "is" of, 539
Preferred meanings, 193
Prejudice, illusory, 448
Presidio Modelo, 655
Primary education, 636
Primary generator, 299, 301
Prison Information Group, 675
Prisons, 654, 675, 676. *See also* Panopticon
Privacy, 664, 741
  western modernity and, 739–740
  women and, 742
Private institutions, 380–381
Private space, technology and invasion of, 350
Privatrect, 740
Probability, 146, 150, 153
  in music systems, 157
Probe studies, 605–607, 619, 621n7
Production, 643
  action and, 273–274
  authors and, 322–325, 327, 333–335

in circuit of culture, 217–219
discipline and, 644
discursive, 187
in Hall four-stage theory, 206–207
identity, 215
intellectual means of, 322, 325, 327, 330
newspapers and means of, 322
reproduction of conditions of, 371–375
reproduction of means of, 372
reproduction of relations of, 383–388, 403
social conditions and, 320
of television message, 188–189, 206–207
by users, 339
Productivity, 346
ProdUsers, 339, 340
Professional code, 195, 207
Progress, 354
Proletariat, 114, 115, 330
Propp, Vladimir, 4
Protensions, 230, 231
Protestant work ethic, 49, 83
Proust, Marcel, 494
Prudence, 274–277, 282–284, 291
Psyche, 290
Psychoanalysis, 104, 314, 422, 500–501, 567, 704
Foucault and, 652
HCI and, 55–58
Psychoanalytic approach, 10
Psychology
cognitive, 660
of culture, 567
educational, 648
engineering, 86
HCI and, 55–58
Psychology-Politics-Resistance, 653
Public design, 479
Public execution, 654
Public good, 710
Public health NGOs, 702
Public Laboratory for Open Technology and Science (PLOTS), 479
Public shaming, 217
Publishing
as production, 322, 333
software and access to, 338–339
Punk rock, 174, 181
Purely material sincerity, 39–40
Pythagoras, 45

Qualitative change, 355
Quality
literary, 320
quantification of, 124
tendency and, 319–321
Quantification
of information in messages, 145–147
of quality, 124
Quantified Self, 434
Quantitative aesthetics, 175
Quantitative information, aesthetic information and, 164
Quarantine, 625–626
social, 640
Queered design, 439–440
Queering, 433, 438, 439–442
of design, 434–436
Queer Nation, 423
Queer studies, 439
Queer theory, 420, 421, 429, 439

Raby, Fiona, 311, 313, 475, 504–508, 532, 550, 603
Race, performativity and, 422
Races, subject, 718
Racially segregated neighborhoods, 769
Racism, 499
Radical architecture groups, 505
Radical design movement, 505
Radicalism, 494, 508
Radway, Janice, 313
Rationalism, 17, 353, 701
Rationality
limitations of, 761–762
technological, 346
Rationalization, 325–326

Rationalizing projects, 702
Rational Self, 290
Rauschenberg, Robert, 518, 524
Rawls, John, 738, 756, 771, 774
  autonomous self, 742
  reflective equilibrium, 744
  self concept, 745
  veil of ignorance, 747
Read, Herbert, 160
Reader
  agency of, 264–265
  fictionality and, 266–267
  position in text, 230, 233
  presence in text, 237
  text interplay with, 227–228
  wandering viewpoint of, 228–237
Reading
  active, 267
  of artworld, 541
  critical, 705
  critical theory, 2–6
  expectations and, 127, 230–231, 245
  experience and, 248
  of interactive artifacts, 255, 256
  literary, 267
  memory and, 230–231, 234, 235
  myth, 108–110
  process of, 229–236, 255
  selection and, 243
  textual strategies manipulating, 244
Reading positions, 195–197, 210–212, 214
Realism, 113, 190, 460, 462
Reality
  of ideology, 351
  imaginary relationship with, 391–393
  matters of fact and, 452
Reality principle, 488
Reality Theory of Art (RT), 517–519, 537–538, 547
Reason, 353–354
  action and, 272
  critical theory and, 361
  imposition of, 348
  technological social control and, 350
Reception
  meaning-making and, 205–206
  of television message, 189
Reciprocity, 743, 744, 749n17, 749n18, 757. *See also* Complementary reciprocity
Recognition
  of familiar, 566
  of female autonomy, 740
  ideological, 397
  of repeated elements, 566
Recollecting, 69, 70, 71, 84, 87, 89
Recording technology, 597
Redundancy, 150–151
Reference code, 210
Reflective equilibrium, 744
Reformation, 384
Regimentation, 683
Registration, 626, 644
Regressive semiological systems, 111
Regulation, 217, 220
  of armies, 636
Reichenbach, Hans, 148
Relationships, 72–73
Relations of exploitation, 383
Relations of production, 383–388, 403
Religious ideology, Christian, 399–401
Repeatable elements, 566
Representation, 217, 219, 724, 726
  digital, 410, 411
  media and, 727
  power of, 710
  social media and, 727–728
Representational media, software as, 410
Representing others, 563–564
Repression
  State and, 376–377
  State Apparatus and, 380–381, 383, 402, 409
Repressive needs, 348
Reproduction, 206
  of conditions of production, 371–375
  ideological, 196

of labor-power, 372–375
of means of production, 372
of music, 325–326
of relations of production, 383–388, 403
Reputation, 215
Requirements gathering, 601
Research. *See also* Design research
audience, 190
basic, 595
contextual, 302
critical action, 730
through design, 529, 531
ethnographic, 413, 668, 730
gender, 756
HCI waves and, 660–662
purpose and motives for, 357
Researcher participation, 730
Research Excellence Framework (REF), 2
Research methods, universality of, 140
Research organizations, 725
Research-oriented design, 531
Resident, of home, 761
care of ethics critique, 764
domestic computing and, 770
as domestic information processor, 762–763, 773
reimagining smart homes with norms of care and, 768–770
Resiliency, 70
Resistance, 670–671
Respect, 743, 754, 759, 773, 775
Responsibility, 744
Restoration, 385
Restoration forestry, 688
Restorative environments, 762
Retelling, 613
Retirees, 769
Reversibility, 744
incomplete, 746
Revisionism, 449
Revolutionary ex-nomination, 120
Revolutionary language, 120, 707
Revolutionary nationalism, 489–492
Rhetorical forms, of myth, 122–125
Richards, I. A., 8, 502
Rights, 345, 743
Ritchie, B., 245
Rituals
class, 116
of exclusion, 627
material, 397
of power, 630
practical, 397
Robertson, J. M., 715
Ronson, Jon, 31
Root causes, 357
Rosner, Daniela, 254, 262, 266
Rotten, Johnny, 174, 175, 181
Row crops, 686
Royal College of Art (RCA), 601–603
RSS feeds, 45
Rubin, Gayle, 419
Ruling class, 382
Ruling ideology, 384
Russian Formalism, 11
Ryokai, Kimiko, 254, 262, 266

Sacco, Justine, 31, 217
Said, Edward, 10, 485, 490, 563, 723–727, 729, 731–732
Saint Francis, 47
Sandbox games, 180
Sandel, Michael, 745
Sapir-Whorf hypothesis, 131
Satchell, Christine, 412
Satire, 508
de Saussure, Ferdinand, 11, 96, 98, 103, 132, 202
Schaffer, Simon, 456
Schenk, Carl, 692n20
Schmidt, Eric, 167, 183n1
Scholasticism, 169, 174, 287
Schön, Donald, 313
Schönberg, Arnold, 175

School of Resentment, 12
Schools
  discipline in, 636
  surveillance and, 637
Schramm, Wilbur, 203
Schultz, Vicki, 423
Science, 137, 138
  Aristotle on, 273, 274, 275
  civic, 479
  distinction between human and natural, 567, 581
  false, 568
  historians of, 456
  knowledge and, 287
  virtues and, 273
Science and technology studies (STS), 17, 472, 473
Scientific certainty, 448
Scientific cognition, 567, 581
Scientific facts, 461
Scientific forestry, 679, 680–689, 698–699
Scientific knowledge, 290, 702
Scientific objects, 456
Scientific Revolution, 287, 305
Scientific talks, 3
Scientific theory, 538, 555
Scientific wisdom, 295
Scope, 302
Scott, James, 10, 562, 695–710
Scruton, Roger, 511
Secondhand selling, software platforms and, 340
Second law of thermodynamics, 147
Second Life, 180, 764
Second-order language, 119
Second-order meaning, 102
Second-order semiological systems, 98–99
Second Treatise of Civil Government (Locke), 740
Seeing Like a State (Scott), 562, 695–710
"Seismographic Art, A" (Read), 160
Selection
  consistency-building and, 243
  reading and, 243
Selective perception, 194–195
Self
  codification of, 435
  defined, 747
  generalized, 743–747
  knowledge of others, 767
  moral, 771
  as mushroom, 746
  other relationship with, 573
  as protagonist of life, 746
  sovereign, 741
Self, Will, 510
Self-awareness, 530, 618
Self-consciousness, 586, 741
Self-criticism, 509
Self-defense, 551–552
Self-definition, 579
Self-governance, 201
Self-government, 717
Self-other relations, 743–747
Self-variation, 84
Seligman, Martin, 54, 56
Semantic codes, 192
Semantic pointers, 230
Semantics, 135
Semantic units, 229
Semantic Web, 169, 439
Semiological systems
  complex, 104
  Freudian theory as, 98, 102
  myth as, 96–100, 104–105
  poetry as, 111–112
  regressive, 111
Semiology, 96–97
Semiotic engineering, 169
Semiotics, 30, 86, 132–134, 202
  language and, 168–170
Semiotic triangle, 38, 39
Semi-smart home, 760–761
Sengers, Phoebe, 562

Sense-making technologies, 702
Sense of Style (Pinker), 503
Sentences, 229–233
September 11, 2001 terrorist attacks, 449
Serfdom, 384
Serrano, Andres, 612
Serres, Michel, 454
Servitude, consciousness of, 348
7 Kinds of Sympathy, 587–588
Sex, gender differentiated from, 753–756
Sex Pistols, 174, 181, 182
Sexual difference fundamentalism, 417–418
Sexual harassment, 420
Sexuality
  academia and, 486–487
  Foucault on, 659
  gender and, 420, 421
  normative, 419, 421
  trivialization of, 486
Sexual practice, 421
Shakespeare, 515
Shannon-Weaver model of communication, 202–203, 203f
Shapin, Steven, 456
Sharing, 744
Short Message Service (SMS), 728
Shusterman, Richard, 530
Sibling rivalry, 741
Signal, 170–172
  textual perspectives differentiated by, 233
Signification, 134, 135
  literature as, 112
  motivation of, 106–107
  of myth, 103–107
Signified, 97–98, 100, 102, 132–135, 137
  rationalization of, 109
  signifier ratio to, 103
Signifier, 97–99, 132–137
  distortion and, 104
  empty, 104, 108
  focusing on, 108
  full, 108
  multiple, 102
  of myth, 100
  signified ratio to, 103
  ubiquity in myth of, 105
Signs, 97–98, 133–134, 163, 204–205
  autocorrelation of, 238
  iconic, 191
  linguistic, 239
  natural, 191
  televisual, 190, 193
  textual, 235–236, 238
  visual, 192
Silver, Nate, 214
Simians, Cyborgs and Women (Haraway), 138
Simon, Herbert, 313
Single-parent households, 769
Situated action, 18
Situated knowledges, 138
Situating the Self: Gender, Community, and Postmodernism in Contemporary Ethics (Benhabib), 752
Situationists, 506, 698
Skink Dress, 531
Smart cities, 751
Smart home
  designing ubiquitous utopia and, 775–778
  as Enlightenment project, 761–764
  exploitation of women and, 776
  feminist critique of HH, 764–768
  feminist universalism and, 753–756
  generalized and concrete other, 756–759
  heterogeneous home as normative ethical vision, 759–764
  HH and, 759–764, 774
  normative design vision and discourse ethics, 770–775
  reimagining, 768
Smart homes, interaction design, 751–778
Smart meters, 704
Smartphones, 335, 767. *See also* Android smartphones; iPhone
  platform access control and, 332, 337
Smith, Geoffrey, 214
Snowden, Edward, 337, 504

Social activism, 533
Social class, 114, 116
Social construction, 556n2
  of fact, 448
Social context, 320, 661
Social contract theory, 741, 755
  justice and autonomous self, 738–743
Social control, 349, 350
Social creativity, 541
Social discipline, 638
Social division of labor, 350
Social engineering, 699
Social formations, 651
Social geography, of myth, 122
Social groups, 201
Socialism, 323, 324, 334, 489, 511
Social life, 89
  crop rotation and, 83, 84
Social media, 430, 434, 662
  comments on, 508
  complex interpretation of, 259
  emancipatory, 728
  imaginary invoked via, 257–258
  representation and, 727–728
Social needs, 349
Social networks, 217
  control of access to, 332
  identity formalization in, 439
  user empowerment on, 337
Social norms, 437
Social order, consent and, 202
Social power, 642
Social practices
  decoding and, 189
  discourse translated into, 187
Social quarantine, 640
Social relationships, 762
Social structures, 312
  knowledge of, 193
Social sustainability, 90
Social theory, 201
Social whole, 375
Social world, objects of, 411
Societal conditions, 364
Societal structures and processes
  control by, 358
  one-dimensionality and, 364
Society. *See also* Industrial society
  disciplinary, 640, 642, 658
  governance and, 699
  identification with, 351
  spectacle and, 641
  of surveillance, 641
Society of the Spectacle (Debord), 506
Sociology, 463, 471, 500
  artworld understanding with, 535
Sociotechnical gap, 705
Socrates, 283, 515–516, 536–537, 545
Software
  educational, 437
  FLOSS, 174
  free, 341
  literature and publishing access and, 338–339
  open source, 173–174
  as representational medium, 410
Soil-building, 687
Sokal, Alan, 503, 504
Solidaristic human associations, 755, 773
Solidarity, 492, 744, 757
Solutionism, 3, 340
Somaesthetics, 530
Sontag, Susan, 311
Sony Walkman, 217–218
Sophia, 287, 290, 291, 293, 294–298, 302, 305
Soul, parts of, 271
South Africa, 729
South Park, 31
de Souza, Clarisse Sieckenius, 169
Sovereign self, narcissism and, 741
Soviet Union
  New Man ideal, 37–38
  public buildings in, 37
Space shuttles, 454–455
Spatiality of home, 763
Spatial metaphors, 375–376

Spatial partitioning, 625
Spectacle, 641
Speculative design, 367, 478, 529, 532, 549, 550, 698
  humor in, 507
Speculative Everything (Dunne and Raby), 506, 508
Speech
  defining, 96
  depoliticized, 117–119
  as message, 96
  myth as type of, 95–96
  of oppressed, 121
  stolen and restored, myth as, 106
Speech-act theory, 18
Speech Genres and Other Late Essays (Bakhtin), 574
Spiritual existence, of ideology, 393
Spivak, Gayatri Chakravorty, 418
Spyn, 33, 266, 267
  intersubjective comprehensibility and, 262–264
  textual interpretation and, 254–260
Stalinism, 37, 316, 489
Stalin myth, 120–121
Stallman, Richard, 173, 181, 341
Standardization, 346
Standardized tree (*Normalbaum*), 682, 683
State, 376–382, 710
  disciplinary mechanisms controlled by, 638
  scientific forestry and, 680–689
  utilitarian, 681
State Apparatus, 377, 378, 379, 380, 383–386, 402, 403, 409–410
State-engineered social projects, 699
State ideological apparatuses, 379–382, 393, 395, 402
Statement of fact, 125
State of nature metaphor, 741–742
  bourgeois thinkers and, 740
State power, 378, 380, 412
  transfer of, 385
State production forests, 691n19
Statesmanship, 276, 277
Statistical reasoning, governance and, 411
Status messages, 86
Status quo, 312, 313
Stengers, Isabelle, 462
Sterne, Laurence, 227–228
Stolterman, Erik, 314
Storybook Probe, 607
Strawson, P. F., 519
Stress, restorative environments for, 762
Structuralism, 11, 168, 169, 174, 202, 314, 408, 485, 486, 500, 652
Structured prefigurement, 227
Structure of Scientific Revolutions (Kuhn), 3
Structures of dominance, 207, 214, 223
Strum, Shirley, 456
Student movements, 367
Style, 129n12
Sub-codes
  of fashion, 192
  romantic, 193
Subcultures, 202, 220, 494
Subject
  concrete, 397
  consciousness of, 394
  digital media and positions of, 412
  ideology and, 396, 412
  individual interpellated as, 396–399
  individuals as, 399
Subjecthood, ideology and, 315
Subjection, 644, 647
Subjective capacity, 194
Subjectivism, 85
Subjectivity, digital media and, 412
Subject races, 718
"Subject supposed to know," 52
Subjunctive form, 129n13
Subjunctive mode, 110
Subordination, gender and, 420–421
Substitutionalist universalism, 738
Subversion, 433, 439
  identity instability and, 494
SuperCollider, 179

Superstructure, 312, 331, 375–376, 402, 409
of aesthetics and culture, 333
IT reconfiguring base relation to, 339
Superstudio, 505
Supportive cultures, 302
Surplus, 560, 572, 574–576
Surveillance, 625–629, 634, 655
of emotional states, 703
HCI and, 663–664
hierarchical, 644
medical, 637, 663
overgeneralizing, 669
police power and, 639
power and, 663
schools and, 637
society of, 641
ubiquitous computing and, 664
Sustainability, 480–481, 701, 708
Sustainable HCI, 480
Sustainable human-computer interaction (S-HCI), 139, 140–141, 480
Sustainable interaction design (SID), 480
Swarming, of disciplinary mechanisms, 637, 657
Symbolic vehicles, 187
Sympathy, 744, 757
Systematically distorted communication, 195
Systems design, 709
Systems of thought, 651

Tablets, 768, 769
platform access control and, 332
Tachisme, 160–161
Tacit knowledge, 297
Tactical media, 698
Tanenbaum, Andrew, 181
Tarde, Gabriel, 463, 466n8
Tautology, 123–124
Techne, 293, 294, 295, 301, 304
Technical division of labor, 403
Technocratic design, 708, 709
Technological determinism, 332
Technological rationality, 346
Technology
assumptions about, 139–140
authoritarian, 702
circuit of culture framework and, 217–221
consumption shaping, 220
domestic, 763, 766
expressive, 434
freedom and, 345
labor saving, 766
mass communication, 168–169
playful, 615
private space and, 350
problematized, 442
recording, 597
sense-making, 702
social context of, 661
social control and, 350
social nature of engagement with, 200
transparency and, 339
universality of, 139–140
use of, 707
Technology-as-experience, 86
Technology-centered home, 762–763
Technology design, 696
critical theory and, 697
critique and, 705–707
ideology and, 362
persuasive, 701
practice of, 707
Techno-utopianism, 140
TED talks, 3
Telecommunications, 203
Telegraphic style, 151
Telephony, 203
Television
communicative process, 188–191
live transmissions, 242
news broadcasts, 206, 207
production of message, 188–189, 206–207
reception of message, 189
Televisual sign, 190
denotative level of, 193

Temperance, 275
Testadura, 518–519, 522, 538–541, 542, 555
Text
  consistency-building and involvement in, as event, 237–243
  denotation and, 228–229
  as event, 243–250
  experience of, 248
  flow of, 231–232
  hypertext, 262
  open, 30
  presence of, 247
  reader interplay with, 227–228
  reader position in, 230, 233
  reader presence in, 237
Textual interpretation, Spyn and, 254–260
Textual perspectives, 232–234, 236
Textual signs, 235–236, 238
Textual strategies, reading process manipulated by, 244
Texturology, 162
Thatcherism, 199
Theater, 327–328, 336
Theatrical performance, 592
Theoretical knowledge, design work and, 294–295
Theorizing, 366, 367
Thermodynamics, 147–148
Things, 453–456
  design, 478
Third Worldism, 490
Thomas Aquinas, 168
Thompson, Bill, 50
Thompson, E. P., 199
Three Aqueous Events, 591, 591f
Tibetan prayer wheels, 51
Time
  inner consciousness of, 230
  wandering viewpoint and, 261
Time-management tools, 364
Time-Table Music, 590f
Titanic (film), 59
Tolkien, J. R. R., 5
Tonal grammars, 157
Tonal system, 150
Tonkinwise, Cameron, 509
Tools, people's relationship with, 435
Topography, 375–376
Torture, 654
Torvalds, Linus, 181
"To Save Everything Click Here" (Morozov), 3
Total Information Awareness, 449
Totalitarianism, 346, 353, 360, 492
Tourists, 766–767
Toward a Philosophy of the Act (Bakhtin), 573
Traditional knowledge, 702
"Traffic in Women, The" (Rubin), 419
Tragedies, 327
Transmission of information, 154–156
Transparency, 600
  of communication, 195
  of design process, 604
  technology and, 339
Transsexuality, 419, 426, 435
Tretiakov, Sergei, 321–322
Tristram Shandy (Sterne), 227
True needs, 347, 360
Truth, absolute, 494–495
Tunnel vision, 679
Turing, Alan, 464–465, 469n37
Turkle, Sherry, 16, 504
Turkopticon system, 728
TV-B-Gone, 674
Twitter, 31, 214, 254, 257–258, 267, 335, 727
  hashtags, 440
Two Elimination Events, 590, 591f
Two Exercises, 591, 592f

Ubiquitous computing (ubicomp), 664, 700, 707, 708, 751–778
  democratic, 777
Ubiquitous utopia, 759
  designing, 775–778
Ultimate particular, 298–301
Ulysses (Joyce), 242, 246
Uncritical design, 509–511

Understanding, 292, 302
art and, 530
of artworld, 535–536
consciousness and, 565
creative, 572, 574–577, 579
dialogical, 572–574, 578
evaluation and, 565, 576–577
language, 566
misunderstandings, 194, 195, 197, 215, 610
philosophical, 535–536
repeatable elements and unrepeatable whole, 566
sociological, 535
of words of others, 567
Universal computers, 335
Universal humanity, 759
Universalism
of Benhabib, 753–756
feminist, 753–756
interactive, 738
post-Enlightenment defense of, 755
substitutionalist, 738
Universalistic moral theories, 737–738, 747, 756
Universality, 423–424, 493, 719, 738
of contextual meaning, 568
ethic of care and, 759
of research methods, 140
Universalizability, 744, 747
Universal juridicism, 646
Universal knowledge, subjective factors and, 303
Universal respect, 759
Universals, 773, 774
moral, 775
Unreliable narrator, 247
Unrepeatable whole, 566
Urban planning, 3
Usability, 600, 660
utility of individuals and, 663
Use, 660
utility of individuals and, 663
Usefulness, 660
User actions
intersubjective comprehensibility and, 264
wandering viewpoint and, 263
User agency, interpretation in HCI and, 265–266
User-centered design (UCD), 49, 314, 407, 412, 600, 751, 773
engineering approach to, 578
User-driven innovation, 88
User experience, 571
development process, 578
User experience design, 600
User-friendly interfaces, 335–336
User research, 295
Users, 339, 660
as codesigners, 604
designer relationships to, 560
design practice and visibility of, 412–413
distant from designers, 559
evaluative understanding and, 577
experience-centered design and, 580
knowing, 577–582, 580–581
Uses of Literacy, The (Hoggart), 500
Utilitarianism, 690n11, 691n19
Utilitarian simplification, 688, 699
Utilitarian state, 681
Utility
ideology and, 38
as meaning, 38
natural world and, 681
use and usability and, 663
Utopianism, 82, 686

Van Gogh, Vincent, 517–518, 538, 542, 545–546
Vanishing mediator, 48–50
Vauban, Marquis de, 679
Veil of ignorance, 744, 745, 767
definitional identity and, 746
more legislator requirement, 758
original position and, 757
Verticality, 643

Video games, 180–182
Video-jockeys (VJs), 575–576
Viewpoint, 744–745, 746
  role-taking in, 747
Vimeo, comments on, 508
da Vinci, Leonardo, 46
Violence
  domestic, 580
  gender, 551–553
  of gender norms, 424
Virtual ecology, 688
Virtual objects, 411
Virtual possibilities, 243–244
Virtual worlds, 763–764
Virtues, 387
  classes of, 271
  intellectual, 289–298
  moral, 272, 282, 283, 289, 290
  natural, 283
  science and, 273
Visibility
  power and, 629–630
  as trap, 629
Visual arts, open work in, 156–164
Visual imagery, 597
Visualization, 477
Visual sign, 192
Vitality, 161
Vocabulary, nature organized through, 681
Voice, 579
  of other, 772, 773
Vostell, Wolf, 585–587, 593

Wages, 373
Wagner, Richard, 593
Wallace, Jayne, 580, 581
Wandering viewpoint, 228–237, 261–262
  correlatives produced by, 237–250
  user actions and, 263
War, 447
Warhol, Andy, 317, 523, 533, 534, 537, 543–544, 544f, 548–550, 554
Water consumption, 141
Waters, Lindsay, 449
Waves, 575, 577
Weak objects, 461
Weaver, Warren, 155, 172
Web 2.0, 334, 335, 336, 434
Web series, 415
Weibel, Peter, 472
Weimar Republic, 386
WEIRD populations, 730
Westphaler, Gert, 71
Whitehead, Alfred North, 462–463
White noise, 158
White Noise (DeLillo), 51–52
"Why Only an Atheist Can Believe" (Žižek), 51
Wiener, Norbert, 149–151, 152
WiFi, 769
Wii, 440
Wilde, Oscar, 492
Wildlife, 687, 688
William of Orange, 636
Williams, Charles, 5
Williams, Kaiton, 562
Williams, Raymond, 199, 332, 485, 500
Willis, Paul, 500, 506
Wilson, Douglas, 52
Wilson, Robert, 593
Windows, 173
Winslet, Kate, 59
Wisdom, 276–277, 281–282, 284
  intuitive, 297
  political, 291
  practical, 291, 292, 294–298
  scientific, 295
Wittgenstein, Ludwig, 462, 499
Wittgenstein Jr. (Iyer), 2
Wittig, Monique, 419
Women
  early modern, 742
  exploitation of, 737, 753, 768, 776
  gender research and, 756
  gender-sex system, 753
  on Kohlberg dilemmas, 745

Women (cont.)
Kohlberg research on, 756
lack of autonomy, 742
marginalized labor of, 766
negation of, 742
oppression of, 737, 753
privacy and, 742
privatization of experience, 738
single-parent households, 769
Woodruff, Allison, 759, 764, 768, 773, 774
Wooing consent, 777–778
Woolf, Virginia, 232, 502
Work, 67, 147
crowdworking, 728
CSCW, 18, 19, 87, 200, 653, 661, 667, 705, 708
design, 294–298
housework, 766
open, 156–164
World Wide Web, 171, 173
Worthiness, 743
Wright, Peter, 19, 560

Xerox PARC, 336

Yauner, Freddie, 508
Yeats, W. B., 32
YouTube, 335
comments on, 508
critical theory on, 41
user comments on, 42
Žižek and, 41–44
Yuan, Ch'ing, 522

Žižek, Slavoj, 6, 10, 27, 28, 41–45, 42f, 418
atheism and, 57
Christianity and, 57
critics of, 59
on fetishistic disavowal, 50, 52
film criticism by, 59
on parallax views, 54–55
psychology and, 56
vanishing mediator and, 49
Zuckerberg, Mark, 215